Lecture Notes in Computer Science

Lecture Notes in Artificial Intelligence 16618

Founding Editor

Jörg Siekmann

The series Lecture Notes in Artificial Intelligence (LNAI) was established in 1988 as a topical subseries of LNCS devoted to artificial intelligence.

The series publishes state-of-the-art research results at a high level. As with the LNCS mother series, the mission of the series is to serve the international R & D community by providing an invaluable service, mainly focused on the publication of conference and workshop proceedings and postproceedings.

Raymond Chi-Wing Wong · Hanghang Tong ·
Hua Lu · James Kwok · Flora Salim ·
Yuanfeng Song · Man Lung Yiu
Editors

Data Science: Foundations and Applications

30th Pacific-Asia Conference
on Knowledge Discovery and Data Mining, PAKDD 2026
Hong Kong, China, June 9–12, 2026
Proceedings, Part II

Springer

Editors
Raymond Chi-Wing Wong
Hong Kong University of Science and Technology
Hong Kong, China

Hua Lu
Aalborg University
Copenhagen, Denmark

Flora Salim
University of New South Wales
Sydney, NSW, Australia

Man Lung Yiu
Hong Kong Polytechnic University
Hong Kong, China

Hanghang Tong
University of Illinois Urbana-Champaign
Urbana, IL, USA

James Kwok
Hong Kong University of Science and Technology
Hong Kong, China

Yuanfeng Song
ByteDance
Shanghai, China

ISSN 0302-9743 ISSN 1611-3349 (electronic)
Lecture Notes in Artificial Intelligence
ISBN 978-981-92-1946-9 ISBN 978-981-92-1947-6 (eBook)
https://doi.org/10.1007/978-981-92-1947-6

LNCS Sublibrary: SL7 – Artificial Intelligence

This Springer imprint is published by the registered company Springer Nature Singapore Pte Ltd.
The registered company address is: 152 Beach Road, #21-01/04 Gateway East, Singapore 189721, Singapore

Foreword

On behalf of the Organizing Committee, we are delighted to welcome all participants to the 30th Pacific-Asia Conference on Knowledge Discovery and Data Mining (PAKDD 2026). Since the first PAKDD conference in 1997, PAKDD has established itself as one of the leading international conferences on data mining and knowledge discovery. PAKDD provides an international forum for researchers and industry practitioners to share their new ideas, original research results, and practical development experiences across all areas of data mining. This year, after its previous edition in Hong Kong (2001), PAKDD was held for the second time in the fascinating city of Hong Kong, during June 9–12, 2026.

We extend our sincere gratitude to the researchers who submitted their research work to the PAKDD 2026 conference. The main conference of PAKDD 2026 had three tracks, namely Main Track, Survey Track, and Special Track on LLMs for Data Science. Following the initial practice of PAKDD 2025, this year, we organized a Special Session on Data Science Foundations and Applications (DSFA). The conference program was further enriched with an AI forum (involving 11 invited speakers), ten high-quality tutorials, six workshops on cutting-edge topics, and a doctoral consortium. We would like to express our sincere thanks to all authors for their efforts in research, as well as in preparing high-quality presentations. We also express our appreciation to all the collaborators and sponsors for their support, trust, and cooperation. We were honored to have five distinguished keynote speakers joining the conference: Zhi-Hua Zhou (Nanjing University), Geoff Webb (Monash University), Xin Luna Dong (Meta Reality Labs), Xia "Ben" Hu (Shanghai AI Laboratory), and Qingsong Wen (Squirrel AI Learning), each with high reputations in their respective areas. Moreover, we had three award talks, namely (1) PAKDD Distinguished Research Contributions Award Talk (by Jian Pei (Duke University)), (2) PAKDD Most Influential Paper Award Talk (by Truyen Tran (Deakin University)), and (3) PAKDD Early Career Research Award Talk (by Guansong Pang (Singapore Management University)). We enjoyed their participation and talks, which made the conference one of the best academic platforms for knowledge discovery and data mining. We also included a panel session, moderated by Flora Salim (University of New South Wales), involving the following panelists: Geoff Webb (Monash University), Jian Pei (Duke University), Cyrus Shahabi (University of Southern California), and Xia "Ben" Hu (Shanghai AI Laboratory).

We would like to express our sincere gratitude for the contributions of the members and reviewers in the Senior Program Committee and the Program Committee, led by program chairs Raymond Wong, Hanghang Tong, and Hua Lu, and the track chairs including Elena Baralis and Guandong Xu on the Survey Track, and Carl Yang and Xiang Li on the Special Track on LLMs for Data Science. It is through their untiring efforts that the conference had an excellent technical program. We are also thankful to the other Organizing Committee members: including the Chairs of the DSFA Special Session: Guansong Pang, Xuyun Zhang, and Xin Wang; Workshop Chairs Cheng Long,

Jieming Shi, and Yuxuan Liang; Tutorial Chairs Jianliang Xu, Gao Cong, and Sinno Jialin Pan; Doctoral Consortium Chairs Xiao Huang and Byron Choi; Publicity Chairs Chen Ma, Yixiang Fang, and Huiping Cao; Industrial Chairs Xiaoli Li, Jason Zhang, and James Cheng; Proceedings Chairs Yuanfeng Song and Man Lung Yiu; Finance Chair Xin Huang and Yuchen Li; Web and Content Chairs Wenqi Fan and Chenhao Ma; Registration Chairs Haibo Hu and Harry Chan; and Sponsorship Chairs Yangqiu Song, Amelia Jing Li, Wei Bi, Mi-Yen Yeh, and Lu Hou. We would like to particularly thank the Local Arrangement Team, Hong Va Leong and Sibo Wang. The conference would not have been successful without their dedication, commitment, and efforts. We are also grateful to the PAKDD Steering Committee for their guidance, the hosting organizations, and all our sponsors for continuously providing institutional and financial support to PAKDD 2026.

Finally, we hope that you found our program interesting and thought-provoking and will preserve a cherished memory of the conference and Hong Kong. Once again, our warmest welcome to you all!

June 2026

James Kwok
Flora Salim

Preface

It is our great pleasure to present the 30th Pacific-Asia Conference on Knowledge Discovery and Data Mining (PAKDD 2026) as Program Committee Chairs. PAKDD is one of the longest-established and leading international conferences in the areas of data mining and knowledge discovery. It provides an international peer-reviewed forum for presenting and sharing new ideas, original research results, and practical development experiences from all data science areas, including data mining, data warehousing, machine learning, artificial intelligence, databases, statistics, knowledge engineering, visualization, decision-making systems, and emerging applications.

The PAKDD 2026 technical program featured three tracks, the Main Track, the Survey Track, and a Special Track on Large Language Models in Data Science. The Main Track continued its tradition of being the premier forum for the presentation of research results and experience reports on knowledge discovery, data science, and machine learning. The Survey Track was introduced in 2025 for the first time, to promote the dissemination of insightful survey papers: survey papers are intended to provide a structured synthesis of a particular topic in the area of data mining, including but not limited to theoretical foundations of mining, inference, and learning, big data technologies, as well as security, privacy, and integrity, for the perusal of junior researchers and of experts from other research fields. As the rapid advancements in Large Language Models (LLMs) have opened new avenues for innovation and research across various domains, particularly in the field of data science, we introduced the Special Track on LLMs, which aimed to explore the transformative potential of LLMs for data science, bringing together researchers, practitioners, and industry experts to discuss the latest developments, challenges, and opportunities in this rapidly growing area.

This year's conference was highly competitive. The three tracks received 728 submissions with 552 to the Main Track, 39 to the Survey Track, and 137 to the Special Track on LLMs. The selection process was competitive, rigorous, and thorough, involving 532 PC and 206 Senior PC (SPC) members. Each submission was double-blindly reviewed by at least 3 reviewers with many receiving 4 or more reviews, followed by a discussion, and then further evaluated by a designated SPC member, the Track chairs, and the PC program co-chairs. The final selection considered multiple factors such as novelty, technical depth, experimental validation, and relevance to the conference. We accepted 139 papers in the Main Track, 12 in the Survey Track, and 33 in the LLM Track, thus having an acceptance rate of approximately 25% for the main conference. Following the practice of PAKDD 2025, in PAKDD 2026, considering the high quality of some of the rejected submissions, we decided to have a Special Session on Data Science – Foundations and Applications (DSFA), to which we recommended 125 of the original submissions. 281 of all submissions accepted to the main conference program and to the DSFA Special Session were presented orally during the conference. We would like to thank the Chairs of the Survey Track (Elena Baralis and Guandong Xu) and the Chairs of the LLM Track (Carl Yang and Xiang Li), the SPC members, PC members, and external reviewers, together with the Chairs of the DSFA special session (Guansong Pang, Xuyun Zhang, and Xin Wang), for their invaluable efforts in ensuring a timely, fair, and highly effective paper review and selection procedure. We formed the PAKDD 2026 Best Paper Selection Committee, involving all PC co-chairs, all chairs of the Survey Track and the LLM Track and two new members, namely De-Nian Yang and Xintao Wu, for selecting the best paper award, the best student paper award, and the best survey paper award. Their diligence, dedication, and expertise helped produce the high-quality program for PAKDD 2026.

In addition to the exciting technical presentations, our program also featured five outstanding keynotes, a panel session, three award talks, the AI forum, ten high-quality tutorials, six workshops, and a doctoral consortium. We hope our PAKDD 2026 program provided a wonderful journey for researchers, users, practitioners, and developers.

June 2026

Raymond Chi-Wing Wong
Hanghang Tong
Hua Lu

Organization

Organizing Committee

General Chairs

James Kwok	Hong Kong University of Science and Technology, China
Flora Salim	University of New South Wales, Australia

Program Committee Chairs

Raymond Wong	Hong Kong University of Science and Technology, China
Hanghang Tong	University of Illinois Urbana-Champaign, USA
Hua Lu	Aalborg University, Denmark

Sponsorship Chairs

Yangqiu Song	Hong Kong University of Science and Technology, China
Amelia Jing Li	Hong Kong Polytechnic University, China
Wei Bi	Tencent AI Lab, China
Mi-Yen Yeh	Academia Sinica, Taiwan
Lu Hou	Huawei, China

Best Paper Selection Committee

Raymond Wong	Hong Kong University of Science and Technology, China
Hanghang Tong	University of Illinois Urbana-Champaign, USA
Hua Lu	Aalborg University, Denmark
Elena Baralis	Politecnico di Torino, Italy
Guandong Xu	Education University of Hong Kong, China
Carl Yang	Emory University, USA
Xiang Li	East China Normal University, China
De-Nian Yang	Institute of Information Science, Academia Sinica, Taiwan
Xintao Wu	University of Arkansas, USA

Local Arrangement Chairs

Hong Va Leong	Hong Kong Polytechnic University, China
Sibo Wang	Chinese University of Hong Kong, China

Industrial Track Chairs

Xiaoli Li	Agency for Science, Technology and Research, Singapore
Jason Zhang	Hong Kong Polytechnic University, China
James Cheng	Chinese University of Hong Kong, China

Survey/Vision Track Chairs

Elena Baralis	Politecnico di Torino, Italy
Guandong Xu	Education University of Hong Kong, China

Special Track on Large Language Models in Data Science Chairs

Carl Yang	Emory University, USA
Xiang Li	East China Normal University, China

Special Session on Data Science: Foundations and Applications (DSFA) Chairs

Guansong Pang	Singapore Management University, Singapore
Xuyun Zhang	Macquarie University, Australia
Xin Wang	University of Calgary, Canada

Tutorial Chairs

Jianliang Xu	Hong Kong Baptist University, China
Gao Cong	Nanyang Technological University, Singapore
Sinno Jialin Pan	Chinese University of Hong Kong, China

Workshop Chairs

Cheng Long	Nanyang Technological University, Singapore
Jieming Shi	Hong Kong Polytechnic University, China
Yuxuan Liang	Hong Kong University of Science and Technology (Guangzhou), China

Doctoral Consortium Chairs

Xiao Huang	Hong Kong Polytechnic University, China
Byron Choi	Hong Kong Baptist University, China

Publicity Chairs

Chen Ma	City University of Hong Kong, China
Yixiang Fang	Chinese University of Hong Kong (Shenzhen), China
Huiping Cao	New Mexico State University, USA

Financial Chairs

Xin Huang	Hong Kong Baptist University, China
Yuchen Li	Singapore Management University, Singapore

Proceedings Chairs

Yuanfeng Song	ByteDance, China
Man Lung Yiu	Hong Kong Polytechnic University, China

Web Masters

Wenqi Fan	Hong Kong Polytechnic University, China
Chenhao Ma	Chinese University of Hong Kong (Shenzhen), China

Registration Chairs

Haibo Hu	Hong Kong Polytechnic University, China
Harry Chan	University of Sheffield, UK

PAKDD Steering Committee

Chair

Longbing Cao	University of Technology Sydney, Australia

Vice Chair

Gill Dobbie	University of Auckland, New Zealand

Treasurer

Longbing Cao	University of Technology Sydney, Australia

Working Group

Longbing Cao (Chair)	University of Technology Sydney, Australia
Ming-Syan Chen (Senior Award Chair)	National Taiwan University, Taiwan
Gill Dobbie (Vice Chair and Treasurer)	University of Auckland, New Zealand
Hady W. Lauw (Diversity, Equity, and Inclusion Chair)	Singapore Management University, Singapore
Jaideep Srivastava (Strategy Chair)	University of Minnesota, USA
Raymond Chi-Wing Wong (Junior Award Chair)	Hong Kong University of Science and Technology, China
Min-Ling Zhang (Engagement Chair)	Southeast University, China

Members

Ramesh Agrawal	Jawaharlal Nehru University, India
Gill Dobbie	University of Auckland, New Zealand
Joao Gama	University of Porto, Portugal
Zhiguo Gong	University of Macau, China
Hisashi Kashima	Kyoto University, Japan
Hady W. Lauw	Singapore Management University, Singapore
Jae-Gil Lee	Korea Advanced Institute of Science & Technology, South Korea
Dinh Phung	Monash University, Australia
Kyuseok Shim	Seoul National University, South Korea
Geoff Webb	Monash University, Australia
Raymond Chi-Wing Wong	Hong Kong University of Science and Technology, China
De-Nian Yang	Institute of Information Science, Academia Sinica, Taiwan
Xintao Wu	University of Arkansas, USA

Life Members

Longbing Cao	University of Technology Sydney, Australia
Ming-Syan Chen	National Taiwan University, Taiwan
David Cheung	University of Hong Kong, China
Joshua Z. Huang	Shenzhen Institutes of Advanced Technology, Chinese Academy of Sciences, China
Masaru Kitsuregawa	Tokyo University, Japan
Rao Kotagiri	University of Melbourne, Australia
Ee-Peng Lim	Singapore Management University, Singapore
Huan Liu	Arizona State University, USA
Hiroshi Motoda	AFOSR/AOARD and Osaka University, Japan
Jian Pei	Simon Fraser University, Canada
P. Krishna Reddy	International Institute of Information Technology, Hyderabad, India
Jaideep Srivastava	University of Minnesota, USA
Thanaruk Theeramunkong	Thammasat University, Thailand
Tu-Bao Ho	Japan Advanced Institute of Science and Technology, Japan
Vincent S. Tseng	National Yang Ming Chiao Tung University, Taiwan
Takashi Washio	Osaka University, Japan
Kyu-Young Whang	Korea Advanced Institute of Science & Technology, South Korea
Graham Williams	Australian National University, Australia
Chengqi Zhang	University of Technology Sydney, Australia
Ning Zhong	Maebashi Institute of Technology, Japan
Zhi-Hua Zhou	Nanjing University, China

Past Members

Arbee L. P. Chen	Asia University, Taiwan
Hongjun Lu	Hong Kong University of Science and Technology, China
Takao Terano	Tokyo Institute of Technology, Japan

Senior Program Committee

Albert Bifet	Université Paris-Saclay, France
Amparo Alonso-Betanzos	University of A Coruña-CITIC, Spain
Anirban Dasgupta	IIT Gandhinagar, India

Arianna Dagliati	University of Pavia, Italy
Aris Anagnostopoulos	Sapienza University of Rome, Italy
Binbin Hu	Ant Group, China
Bo Han	Hong Kong Baptist University, China/RIKEN, Japan
Bo Yuan	University of Queensland, Australia
Branislav Kveton	Adobe Research, USA
Byung Suk Lee	University of Vermont, USA
Chang Tang	China University of Geosciences, Wuhan, China
Chang-Tien Lu	Virginia Tech, USA
Chao Chen	RMIT University, Australia
Chao Huang	University of Hong Kong, China
Chao Lan	University of Oklahoma, USA
Chen Gong	Nanjing University of Science and Technology, China
Chen Wang	Huazhong University of Science and Technology, China
Chen Zhao	Baylor University, USA
Cheng Wang	Amazon, USA
Chenhao Ma	Chinese University of Hong Kong (Shenzhen), China
Christan Grant	University of Florida, USA
Chuxu Zhang	University of Connecticut, USA
Da Yan	Indiana University Bloomington, USA
De-Nian Yang	Academia Sinica, Taiwan
Depeng Xu	University of North Carolina at Charlotte, USA
Di Jin	Tianjin University, China
Dongjin Song	University of Connecticut, USA
Dongxiao He	Tianjin University, China
Dongxiao Yu	Shandong University, China
Eirini Ntoutsi	University of the Bundeswehr Munich, Germany
Elio Masciari	University of Naples, Italy
Elisa Bertino	Purdue University, USA
Fabrizio Marozzo	Università della Calabria, Italy
Feiping Nie	Northwestern Polytechnical University, China
Feng Chen	University of Texas at Dallas, USA
Feng Xia	RMIT University, Australia
Fenglong Ma	Pennsylvania State University, USA
Fu-lai Chung	Hong Kong Polytechnic University, China
Gan Sun	South China University of Technology, China
Gang Li	Deakin Univeristy, Australia
Giancarlo Sperlì	University of Naples Federico II, Italy

Gianlorenzo D'Angelo	Gran Sasso Science Institute, Italy
Giovanni Montana	University of Warwick, UK
Grigorios Loukides	King's College London, UK
Guanfeng Liu	Macquarie University, Australia
Guansong Pang	Singapore Management University, Singapore
Guodong Long	University of Technology Sydney, Australia
Guo-Sen Xie	Nanjing University of Science and Technology, China
Hady W. Lauw	Singapore Management University, Singapore
Hai Lan	University of Queensland, Australia
Haipeng Dai	Nanjing University, China
Hamid Bouchachia	Bournemouth University, UK
Hao Liao	Shenzhen University, China
Hao Wang	Sichuan University, China
Hao Wang	Xidian University, China
Heitor M. Gomes	Victoria University of Wellington, New Zealand
Hengshu Zhu	Computer Network Information Center, Chinese Academy of Sciences, China
Hisashi Kashima	Kyoto University, Japan
Hongkai Xiong	Shanghai Jiao Tong University, China
Hongsheng Hu	University of Newcastle, Australia
Hongyan Liu	Tsinghua University, China
Hongzhi Yin	University of Queensland, Australia
Hua Wei	Arizona State University, USA
Huaming Du	Southwestern University of Finance and Economics, China
Huawen Liu	Shaoxing University, China
Hung-Yu Kao	National Cheng Kung University, Taiwan
Ioanna Miliou	Stockholm University, Sweden
Jae-Gil Lee	KAIST, South Korea
James Jianqiao Yu	Harbin Institute of Technology, China
Jeffrey Chan	RMIT University, Australia
Jerry Chun-Wei Lin	Silesian University of Technology, Poland
Jian Kang	Mohamed bin Zayed University of Artificial Intelligence, United Arab Emirates
Jiangchao Yao	Shanghai Jiao Tong University, China
Jianxin Li	Beihang University, China
Jiapu Wang	Hefei University of Technology, China
Jiaying Lu	Emory Univesity, USA
Jicong Fan	Chinese University of Hong Kong (Shenzhen), China
Jie Shao	University of Electronic Science and Technology of China, China

Jie Wen	Harbin Institute of Technology, China
Jie Yin	University of Sydney, Australia
Jing Jiang	University of Technology Sydney, Australia
Jingrui He	University of Illinois Urbana-Champaign, USA
Jinyu Tian	Macau University of Science and Technology, China
Johannes Fürnkranz	Johannes Kepler University Linz, Austria
Jose Machado	University of Minho, Portugal
Jose M. Alvarez	NVIDIA, USA
Jun Wang	Shandong University, China
Junbo Zhang	JD Intelligent Cities Research, China
Junchi Yan	Shanghai Jiao Tong University, China
Jundong Li	University of Virginia, USA
Kai Shu	Emory University, USA
Kaiqi Zhao	Harbin Institute of Technology (Shenzhen), China
Kamalakar Karlapalem	IIIT Hyderabad, India
Ke Liang	National University of Defense Technology, China
P. Krishna Reddy	IIIT Hyderabad, India
Kui Yu	Hefei University of Technology, China
Kunpeng Liu	Portland State University, USA
Laizhong Cui	Shenzhen University, China
Lan-Zhe Guo	Nanjing University, China
Leandro Minku	University of Birmingham, UK
Lei Zou	Peking University, China
Leopoldo Bertossi	Carleton University, Canada
Lianhua Chi	La Trobe University, Australia
Lianyong Qi	China University of Petroleum (East China), China
Lili Su	Northeastern University, USA
Lin Li	Wuhan University of Technology, China
Lina Yao	University of New South Wales, Australia
Lisi Chen	University of Electronic Science and Technology of China, China
Longbing Cao	Macquarie University, Australia
Luca Romeo	University of Macerata, Italy
Ludovico Boratto	University of Cagliari, Italy
Mahardhika Pratama	University of South Australia, Australia
Masashi Sugiyama	RIKEN/University of Tokyo, Japan
Meikang Qiu	Augusta University, USA
Meng Jiang	University of Notre Dame, USA
Miao Xu	University of Queensland, Australia

Ming Li	Nanjing University, China
Mingbo Zhao	Donghua University, China
Mingming Gong	University of Melbourne, Australia
Min-Ling Zhang	Southeast University, China
Mirco Nanni	CNR-ISTI Pisa, Italy
Mi-Yen Yeh	Academia Sinica, Taiwan
Muhammad Aamir Cheema	Monash University, Australia
Nan Ye	University of Queensland, Australia
Neil Shah	Snap Inc., USA
Nizar Bouguila	Concordia University, Canada
Noseong Park	KAIST, South Korea
Panagiotis Papapetrou	Stockholm University, Sweden
Pang-Ning Tan	Michigan State University, USA
Paul Honeine	University of Rouen Normandy, France
Paulo Cortez	University of Minho, Portugal
Pengpeng Zhao	Soochow University, China
Qi Yu	Rochester Institute of Technology, USA
Qiang Cheng	University of Kentucky, USA
Qinghua Hu	Tianjin University, China
Quanming Yao	Tsinghua, China
Rajeev Raman	University of Leicester, UK
Rajiv Khanna	Purdue University, USA
Ranga Raju Vatsavai	North Carolina State University, USA
Ricardo J. G. B. Campello	University of Southern Denmark, Denmark
Riccardo Guidotti	University of Pisa, Italy
Sang-Wook Kim	Hanyang University, South Korea
Sen Wang	University of Queensland, Australia
Shirui Pan	Griffith University, Australia
Shui Yu	University of Technology Sydney, Australia
Shuo Wang	Shanghai Jiao Tong University, China
Siyu Huang	Clemson University, USA
Slawomir Nowaczyk	Halmstad University, Sweden
Suhang Wang	Pennsylvania State University, USA
Sung-Bae Cho	Yonsei University, South Korea
Tingting Wang	RMIT University, Australia
Tong Chen	University of Queensland, Australia
Tru Hoang Cao	UTHealth, USA
Tsuyoshi Ide	IBM Research, T. J. Watson Research Center, USA
Tzung-Pei Hong	National University of Kaohsiung, Taiwan
Uday Kiran Rage	University of Aizu, Japan
Wei Fan	University of Oxford, UK

Wei Ju	Sichuan University, China
Wei Emma Zhang	University of Adelaide, Australia
Weiqing Wang	Monash University, Australia
Wei-Shinn Ku	Auburn University, USA
Wenbin Zhang	Florida International University, USA
Wenqi Fan	Hong Kong Polytechnic University, China
Wenqing Lin	Tencent, China
Xia Ning	Ohio State University, USA
Xiang Deng	Harbin Institute of Technology (Shenzhen), China
Xiangyu Zhao	City University of Hong Kong, China
Xiao Huang	Hong Kong Polytechnic University, China
Xiaoning Liu	RMIT University, Australia
Xiaowei Jia	University of Pittsburgh, USA
Xin Cao	University of New South Wales, Australia
Xindong Wu	Hefei University of Technology, China
Xintao Wu	University of Arkansas, USA
Xun Zhou	Harbin Institute of Technology (Shenzhen), China
Xuyun Zhang	Macquarie University, Australia
Yanchang Zhao	CSIRO, Australia
Yanchao Tan	Fuzhou University, China
Yang Cao	Institute of Science Tokyo, Japan
Yibing Zhan	JD Explore Academy, China
Yinbin Miao	Xidian University, China
Ying Li	AwanTunai, Indonesia
Yingxia Shao	Beijing University of Posts and Telecommunications, China
Yipeng Zhou	Macquarie University, Australia
Yiqun Xie	University of Maryland, USA
Yongkai Wu	Clemson University, USA
Yu Zhang	Southern University of Science and Technology, China
Yuan Luo	Northwestern University, USA
Yue Xu	Queensland University of Technology, Australia
Yufei Han	Inria, France
Yu-Feng Li	Nanjing University, China
Yunjun Gao	Zhejiang University, China
Yunlong Yu	Zhejiang University, China
Yunyun Wang	Nanjing University of Posts and Telecommunications, China
Yuxuan Liang	Hong Kong University of Science and Technology (Guangzhou), China

Zhao Kang	University of Electronic Science and Technology of China, China
Zheng Wang	University of Leeds, UK
Zhengming Ding	Tulane University, USA
Zhengzhang Chen	NEC Laboratories America, USA
Zhong Ji	Tianjin University, China
Zhongfei Zhang	Binghamton University, USA
Zimu Zhou	City University of Hong Kong, China
Ziwei Zhu	George Mason University, USA
Ziyu Jia	Chinese Academy of Sciences, China

Program Committee

Abdur Rehman Khan	Queensland University of Technology, Australia
Abheek Dhingra	University of the Bundeswehr Munich, Germany
Akhlaque Ahmad	Indiana University Bloomington, USA
Akihiro Yamaguchi	Toshiba Corporation; Kyushu University, Japan
Akira Sakai	Fujitsu Laboratories Ltd., Japan
Alex Memory	Johns Hopkins University Applied Physics Laboratory, USA
Alfredo Cuzzocrea	University of Calabria, Italy
Amir Gandomi	University of Technology, Sydney, Australia
Andrzej Skowron	University of Warsaw, Poland
Ankit Sharma	University of Minnesota, USA
Anne Denton	North Dakota State University, USA
Antonela Tommasel	ISISTAN, CONICET-UNICEN, Argentina
Anushka Vidanage	Australian National University, Australia
Arindam Pal	TechSoftX, Australia
Aris Gkoulalas-Divanis	Merative, USA
Arnab Sharma	Paderborn University, Germany
Aryya Gangopadhyay	University of Maryland, Baltimore County, USA
Ashwin Viswanathan Kannan	Amazon, USA
Ashwini Kodipalli	RV University, India
Atsuhiro Takasu	National Institute of Informatics, Japan
Augusto A. Santos	Instituto de Telecomunicações, Portugal
Bang An	University of Akron, USA
Baodi Liu	China University of Petroleum (East China), China
Beibei Li	Chongqing University, China
Bijay Prasad Jaysawal	University of Southampton, UK
Bijaya Adhikari	University of Iowa, USA

Dai Hai Nguyen	Hokkaido University, Japan
Dalin Zhang	Hangzhou Dianzi University, China
Dan Simovici	University of Massachusetts Boston, USA
Daokun Zhang	Monash University, Australia
De-Chuan Zhan	Nanjing University, China
Deguang Kong	Yahoo Research, USA
Delvin Ce Zhang	Singapore Management University, Singapore
Derui Lyu	University of Science and Technology of China, China
Dharmalingam Muthusamy	Bharathiar University, India
Dong Li	Baylor University, USA
Dong-Dong Wu	University of Tokyo, Japan
Dongqi Fu	Meta, USA
Dongyuan Li	Tokyo Institute of Technology, Japan
Dugang Liu	Shenzhen University, China
Edouard Fouché	Karlsruhe Institute of Technology, Germany
Eduardo Ogasawara	Federal Center for Technological Education of Rio de Janeiro, Brazil
Ekta Gujral	University of California, Riverside, USA
Eliana Pastor	Politecnico di Torino, Italy
Enea Vincenzo Napolitano	University of Naples Federico II, Italy
Erhu He	University of Pittsburgh, USA
Esra Akbas	Georgia State University, USA
Fali Wang	Penn State University, USA
Fan Wu	Central South University, China
Fanglan Chen	Virginia Tech, USA
Fei Zhao	University of Alabama at Birmingham, USA
Felipe R. Azúa	University of Edinburgh, UK
Feng Xiao	Chinese University of Hong Kong (Shenzhen), China
Fengxin Li	Renmin University of China
Florent Masseglia	Inria, France
Francesco Marcelloni	University of Pisa, Italy
Francesco Spinnato	University of Pisa, Italy
Fuqiang Yu	Qilu University of Technology, China
Fuyuan Cao	Shanxi University, China
Giovanna Nicora	University of Pavia, Italy
Giuseppe Albi	University of Pavia, Italy
Guangyan Huang	Deakin University, Australia
Guimu Guo	Rowan University, USA
Guixian Zhang	China University of Mining and Technology, China

Guodu Xiang	Hefei University of Technology, China
Guoyin Wang	Chongqing University of Posts and Telecommunications, China
Guozhong Li	King Abdullah University of Science and Technology, Saudi Arabia
Hadi Talal Jaafar	University of Birmingham, UK
Haidong Kang	Northeastern University, China
Haifang Li	Baidu Inc., China
Hailiang Zhao	Zhejiang Univerisity, China
Haiquan Chen	California State University, Sacramento, USA
Hanchen Wang	University of New South Wales, Australia
Hang Yu	Shanghai University, China
Hao Xue	University of New South Wales, Australia
Hao Zhen	University of Georgia, USA
Hao Zheng	Central South University, China
Haomin Yu	Aalborg University, Denmark
Haoran Duan	Wuhan University, China
Haoran Luo	Nanyang Technological University, Singapore
He Kong	Jilin University, China
He Li	Xidian University, China
Heitor M. Gomes	Victoria University of Wellington, New Zealand
Hezhe Qiao	Singapore Managment University, Singapore
Hoang H. Nguyen	University of Tennessee at Chattanooga, USA
Hongchao Qin	Beijing Institute of Technology, China
Hongliang Zhang	Nanjing University of Science and Technology, China
Hongtao Wang	North China Electric Power University, China
Hongzu Su	University of Electronic Science and Technology of China, China
Huaiyuan Yao	Arizona State University, USA
Huan Li	Zhejiang University, China
Huan Wang	University of Wollongong, Australia
Huan Zhang	Zhengzhou University, China
Huaxiang Zhang	Shandong Normal University, China
Hui Fang	Shanghai University of Finance and Economics, China
Huifang Ma	Northwest Normal University, China
Huiping Cao	New Mexico State University, USA
Huizhong Wang	Chinese University of Hong Kong (Shenzhen), China
Ickjai Lee	James Cook University, Australia, Australia
Jae Oh Woo	Samsung SDS America, USA

Jahnavi A. Kachhia	meta, USA
Ja-Hwung Su	National University of Kaohsiung, Taiwan
Jean Paul Barddal	Pontifical Catholic University of Paraná, Brazil
Jean-Paul Calbimonte	University of Applied Sciences and Arts of Western Switzerland HES-SO, Switzerland
Jeongwhan Choi	KAIST, South Korea
Jeremiah D. Deng	University of Otago, New Zealand
Jia Chen	University of California, Riverside, USA
Jiahao Li	Guangdong University of Technology, China
Jialiang Li	Roskilde University, Denmark
Jiancheng Lv	Sichuan University, China
Jianfei Zhang	Université de Sherbrooke, Canada
Jiangneng Li	Nanyang Technological University, Singapore
Jianwu Wang	University of Maryland, Baltimore County, USA
Jianxin Li	Beihang University, China
Jian-Yun Nie	Université de Montréal, Canada
Jianzhong Qi	University of Melbourne, Australia
Jiaqi Zhao	China University of Mining and Technology, China
Jiatan Huang	University of Connecticut, USA
Jiaxin Jiang	National University of Singapore, Singapore
Jiaxing Xu	National University of Singapore, Singapore
Jiayan Guo	Peking University, China
Jiazheng Li	University of Connecticut, USA
Jie Li	RMIT University, Australia
Jie Wang	Southwest Jiaotong University, China
Jie Yang	University of Technology Sydney, Australia
Jierong Li	Yunnan University, China
Jilin Hu	Aalborg University, Denmark
Jimmy Xiangji Huang	York University, Canada
Jin Liu	Shanghai Maritime University, China
Jin Lu	University of Georgia, USA
Jinbin Huang	Shenzhen University, China
Jinghui Yuan	Northwestern Polytechnical University, China
Jinhua Guo	Southern University of Science and Technology, China
Jin-Hui Wu	Nanjing University, China
Jinjun Chen	Swinburne University of Technology, Australia
Jinpeng Chen	Beijing University of Posts and Telecommunications, China
Jinyi Liu	Tianjin University, China

Jipeng Guo	Beijing University of Chemical Technology, China
Jiuding Duan	Allianz Global Investors, Japan Co., Japan
Jonathan A Zhu	Carnegie Mellon University, USA
Jože Rožanec	Jožef Stefan Institute, Slovenia
Jun Huang	Anhui University of Technology, China
Jun Wang	National University of Defense Technology, China
Jun Wu	Michigan State University, USA
Jungeun Kim	Inha University, South Korea
Junjie Yao	East China Normal University, China
Jun-Ki Min	Korea University of Technology and Education, South Korea
Junlin Wu	Washington University in St. Louis, USA
Jun-Zhao Du	Xidian University, China
K. Selcuk Candan	Arizona State University, USA
Kai Guo	Sichuan University, China
Kai Zhao	Aalborg University, Denmark
Kaiqiang Yu	Nanjing University, China
Kaiqun Fu	South Dakota State University, USA
Kaixin Wang	Beijing University of Technology, China
Kang Xu	Nanjing University of Posts and Telecommunications, China
Karim Tabia	CRIL, Artois University, France
Keith Burghardt	University of North Carolina at Charlotte, USA
Kejia Chen	Nanjing University of Posts and Telecommunications, China
Kewen Liao	Deakin University, Australia
Ki Yong Lee	Sookmyung Women's University, South Korea
Kia Teymourian	University of Texas at Austin, USA
Ki-Hoon Lee	Kwangwoon University, South Korea
Kijung Shin	KAIST, South Korea
Kishlay Jha	University of Iowa, USA
Kohei Hatano	Kyushu University/RIKEN AIP, Japan
Koji Maruhashi	Fujitsu Research, Fujitsu Limited, Japan
Kok-Leong Ong	RMIT University, Australia
Krishnamoorthy Sivakumar	Washington State University, USA
Krisztian Buza	Budapest University of Economics and Business, Hungary
Kuan-Ting Lai	National Taipei University of Technology, Taiwan
Kun Fang	Hong Kong Polytechnic University, China
Kunpeng Liu	Portland State University, USA

Kunpeng Xu	University of Sherbrooke, Canada
Kun-Ta Chuang	National Cheng Kung University, Taiwan
Kun-Yang Yu	Nanjing University, China
Lam Ngo	RMIT University, Australia
Lecheng Zheng	Virginia Tech, USA
Lei Chen	Tsinghua University, China
Lei Duan	Sichuan University, China
Lei Gu	Nanjing University of Posts and Telecommunications, China
Lei Li	Hong Kong University of Science and Technology (Guangzhou), China
Lei Zhang	Nanjing Normal University, China
Li Hu	Hong Kong Polytechnic University, China
Li Tang	Yunnan University, China
Liang Hong	Wuhan University, China
Liang Li	National University of Defense Technology, China
Liang Qu	Edith Cowan University, Australia
Libin Wang	Northwestern Polytechnical University, China
Lihui Liu	Wayne State University, USA
Lijing Wang	New Jersey Institute of Technology, USA
Likang Wu	University of Science and Technology of China, China
Lin Zhang	IDEA.EDU, USA
Ling Ding	Tianjin University, China
Ling Zheng	Fujian Provincial Maternity and Children's Hospital, China
Lingwei Chen	Rochester Institute of Technology, USA
Lingyang Chu	McMaster University, Canada
Liu Xichao	Yunnan University, China
Liwei Deng	Aalborg University, Denmark
Lizhong Ding	Beijing Institute of Technology, China
Lo Pang-Yun Ting	National Cheng Kung University, Taiwan
Longxu Sun	Hong Kong Baptist University, China
Lu Jiang	Dalian Maritime University, China
Luca Cagliero	Politecnico di Torino, Italy
Lujun Li	Hong Kong University of Science and Technology, China
Lulwah AlKulaib	Kuwait University, Kuwait
Luyuan Yang	University of Oklahoma, USA
Luzhi Wang	Dalian Maritime University, China
Lyu Xu	Nanyang Technological University, Singapore

Lyuheng Yuan	Indiana University Bloomington, USA
Maciej Grzenda	Warsaw University of Technology, Poland
Mandar Chaudhary	eBay, USA
Man-Sheng Chen	Sun Yat-sen University, China
Maolin Wang	City University of Hong Kong, China
Marc Plantevit	EPITA, France
Marcellin M Atemkeng Teufack	Rhodes University, China
Maria Luisa Sapino	Università di Torino, Italy
Marzena Kryszkiewicz	Warsaw University of Technology, Poland
Masahiro Nakano	NTT Communication Science Laboratories, Japan
Matej Mihelčić	University of Zagreb, Croatia
Matjaž Gams	Jožef Stefan Institute, Slovenia
Melike Yildiz Aktas	Virginia Tech, USA
Meng Wang	Tongji University, China
Mengdi Huai	Iowa Sate University, USA
Menghan Wang	eBay, USA
Miao Hu	University of Southampton, UK
Miguel Rodriguez	Google, USA
Milos Radovanovic	University of Novi Sad, Serbia
Milos Savic	University of Novi Sad, Serbia
Min Gao	Chongqing University, China
Ming Yang	Nanjing University, China
Minglai Shao	Tianjin University, China
Minglong Lei	Beijing University of Technology, China
Mingyu Yang	Hong Kong University of Science and Technology (Guangzhou), China
Mingyue Cheng	University of Science and Technology of China, China
Mingzhong Wang	University of the Sunshine Coast, China
Minh-Hao Van	University of Arkansas, USA
Minhua Lin	Pennsylvania State University, USA
Min-Te Sun	National Central University, Taiwan
Mohamad El-Hajj	MacEwan University, Canada
Mohammad M. Masud	United Arab Emirates University, United Arab Emirates
Morteza Saberi	University of Technology Sydney, Australia
Moshe Eliasof	University of Cambridge, UK
Mrinal Das	IIT Palakkad, India
Muhammad Abulaish	South Asian University, India
Muhammad Daffa Robani	AwanTunai, Indonesia
Nannan Wu	Tianjin University, China
Nassim Belmecheri	Simula Research Laboratory, Norway

Nathan S. Gavenski	King's College London, UK
Nian Liu	National University of Singapore, Singapore
Ning Liu	Shandong University, China
Ou Wu	Tianjin University, China
P. Radha Krishna	National Institute of Technology, Warangal, India
Panagiotis Liakos	Athens University of Economics and Business, Greece
Paolo Garza	Politecnico di Torino, Italy
Pedro G. Ferreira	University of Porto, Portugal
Peer Kröger	Christian Albrechts University Kiel, Germany
Peiliang Zhang	Wuhan University of Technology, China
Peng Li	Dalian University of Technology, China
Peng Qian	Zhejiang University, China
Pengfei He	University of Washington, USA
Pengpeng Zhao	Soochow University, China
Pengyang Wang	University of Macau, China
Pinhan Fu	Shanxi University, China
Pranjal Shankhdhar	Meta Platforms, USA
Praveen Kumar Donta	Stockholm University, Sweden
Primoz Kocbek	University of Maribor, Slovenia
Purushottam Panta	University of Kentucky, USA
Qian Li	Curtin University, Australia
Qian Sun	Hong Kong University of Science and Technology, China
Qiang Gao	Southwestern University of Finance and Economics, China
Qiang Tang	Luxembourg Institute of Science and Technology, Luxembourg
Qiange Wang	National University of Singapore, Singapore
Qianying Ren	University of Connecticut, USA
Qiao Xue	Nanjing University of Aeronautics and Astronautics, China
Qiheng Sun	Hong Kong Polytechnic University, China
Qing Liao	Harbin Institute of Technology (Shenzhen), Singapore
Qing Liu	Zhejiang University, China
Qing Tian	Nanjing University of Information Science and Technology, Singapore
Qingxiang Liu	Chinese Academy of Sciences, China
Qiqi Wang	Nankai University, China
Qisen Cheng	Samsung Display America Lab, USA
Qixu Gong	New Mexico State University, USA
Qizhou Wang	Monash University, Australia

Quangui Zhang	Liaoning Technical University, China
Qun Liu	Louisiana State University, USA
Rajatsubhra Chakraborty	University of North Carolina at Charlotte, USA
Ravi Chhabra	Nvidia, USA
Renchi Yang	Hong Kong Baptist University, China
Renqiang Luo	Jilin University, China
Robert J. Churchill	Georgetown University, USA
Rong Du	Taiyuan University of Technology, China
Rosalba Giugno	University of Verona, Italy
Ru Wang	Shandong Normal University, China
Ruiqi Zheng	University of Queensland, Australia
Ruliang Xiao	Fujian Normal University, China
Rundong Zuo	Hong Kong Baptist University, China
Runlong Yu	University of Alabama, USA
Sadok Ben Yahia	Southern Denmark University, Denmark
Senzhang Wang	Central South University, China
Shafiq Alam	Massey University Auckland, New Zealand
Shangqing Zhao	University of Oklahoma, Oklahoma
Shao-Yuan Li	Nanjing University of Aeronautics and Astronautics, China
Shengchao Chen	University of Technology Sydney, Australia
Shengda Zhuo	Jinan University, China
Shengkun Wang	Virginia Tech, USA
Shen-Shyang Ho	Rowan University, USA
Shichao Zhang	Central South University, China
Shifei Ding	China University of Mining and Technology, China
Shiyu Yang	Guangzhou University, China
Shi-Yu Tian	Nanjing University, China
Shridhar B Devamane	Amrita Vishwa Vidyapeetham, India
Shu Wang	Chinese University of Hong Kong (Shenzhen), China
Shuai Li	University of Cambridge, UK
Shubham Jain	Visa Research, USA
Shuichi Miyazawa	Graduate University for Advanced Studies, Japan
Shuo Li	Guangxi University, China
Shuo Yu	Dalian University of Technology, China
Siddhartha Bhattacharyya	University of Illinois Chicago, USA
Simone Monaco	Politecnico di Torino, Italy
Siqi Liang	Amazon, USA
Siqing Li	Unversity of New South Wales, Australia

Siru Zhong	Hong Kong University of Science and Technology (Guangzhou), China
Siyang Liu	Nanjing University, China
Song Wu	Aalborg University, Denmark
Sungsu Lim	Chungnam National University, South Korea
Tadashi Nomoto	National Institute of Japanese Literature, Japan
Tai Le Quy	University of Koblenz, Germany
Tao Chen	China University of Geosciences, Wuhan, China
Tao Meng	Central South University of Forestry and Technology, China
Tao Wang	University of Chinese Academy of Sciences, China
Tetsuya Yoshida	Nara Women's University, Japan
Thi Huyen Nguyen	L3S Research Center, Germany
Thilina N Ranbaduge	Australian National University, Australia
Tianrui Li	Southwest Jiaotong University, China
Tiantian Liu	Aalborg University, Denmark
Tianyi Li	Aalborg University, Denmark
Tiejin Chen	Arizona State University, USA
Tim Oates	University of Maryland, Baltimore County, USA
Tong Chen	University of Queensland, Australia
Trung-Hoang Le	Nanyang Technological University, Singapore
Tsunenori Mine	Kyushu University, Japan
Tuan Le	New Mexico State University, USA
Tung Kieu	Aalborg University, Denmark
Vahid Taslimitehrani	PhysioSigns Inc., USA
Vana Kalogeraki	Athens University of Economics and Business, Greece
Wanfu Gao	Jilin University, China
Wang Lizhen	Yunnan University, China
Waqas Jamil	Bournemouth University, UK
Wei Chen	Beihang University, China
Wei Wang	Fudan University, China
Wei Ye	Tongji University, China
Wei Emma Zhang	University of Adelaide, Australia
Weifeng Liu	China University of Petroleum, China
Weiwei Jiang	Beijing University of Posts and Telecommunications, China
Wenbo Shang	Hong Kong Baptist University, China
Wen-Chao Hu	Nanjing University, China
Wenda Zhang	Walmart Inc., USA
Wengen Li	Tongji University, China

Wenjian Xu	Zhejiang University of Science and Technology, China
Wenjie Xi	George Mason University, USA
Wenke Du	Cornell University, USA
Wenlu Wang	Texas A&M University-Corpus Christi, USA
Wensheng Luo	Hunan University, China
Wensheng Wu	University of Southern California, USA
Wentao Fan	Nanjing University, China
Wentao Li	University of Leicester, UK
William Hsu	Kansas State University, USA
Xi Chen	Soochow University, China
Xiang Lian	Kent State University, USA
Xiangmin Zhou	RMIT University, Australia
Xiangyang Gou	University of New South Wales, Australia
Xiao Cheng	University of New South Wales, Australia
Xiaobo Zhang	Southwest Jiaotong University, China
Xiaocao Ouyang	Southwestern University of Finance and Economics, China
Xiaoguang Guo	University of Connecticut, USA
Xiaohui Chen	Baylor University, USA
Xiaojuan Cheng	Deakin University, Australia
Xiaoou Liu	Arizona State University, USA
Xiaoping Zhou	Beijing University of Civil Engineering and Architecture, China
Xiaoshan Yu	Anhui University, China
Xiaoyang Li	Adelaide University, Australia
Xiaoyang Wang	University of New South Wales, Australia
Xiaoyu Ding	University of Technology Sydney, Australia
Xin Li	Macquarie University, Australia
Xin Luo	Shandong University, China
Xin Peng	National University of Defense Technology, China
Xin Sun	City University of Macau, China
Xin Wang	University of Calgary, Canada
Xin Zheng	RMIT University, Australia
Xing Xing	Tongji University, China
Xingbo Fu	University of Virginia, USA
Xinghao Yang	China University of Petroleum (East China), China
Xinguo Feng	University of Queensland, Australia
Xingyu Zhao	Nanjing University of Aeronautics and Astronautics, China

Xinyu Su	University of Melbourne, Australia
Xinyu Wu	Baylor University, USA
Xinyue Sun	Harbin Institute of Technology, China
Xiuling Wang	Stevens Institute of Technology, USA
Xiwen Chen	Clemson University, USA
Xu Zhang	Macquarie University, Australia
Xuliang Zhu	Shanghai Jiao Tong University, China
Xuyun Zhang	Macquarie University, Australia
Yan Cao	University of Texas at Dallas, USA
Yan Ru Pei	NVIDIA, USA
Yanchao Liu	Communication University of China, China
Yanchao Tan	Fuzhou University, China
Yang Cao	Great Bay University/Tsinghua University, China
Yang-Sae Moon	Kangwon National University, South Korea
Yanhao Wang	East China Normal University, China
Yanwei Yu	Ocean University of China, China
Yaqian Zhang	University of Waikato, New Zealand
Yi Zhang	University of Queensland, Australia
Yibing Zhan	JD Explore Academy, China
Yifan Wang	University of Hawaii, USA
Yifeng Gao	University of Texas Rio Grande Valley, USA
Yi-Hui Chen	Chang Gung University, Taiwan
Yijun Lin	University of Minnesota, USA
Yimin Wen	Wuyi University, China
Yiming Tang	Hefei University of Technology, China
Yin Xian	Hong Kong Baptist University, China
Yingjie Wang	Nanyang Technological University, Singapore
Yingli Zhou	Chinese University of Hong Kong (Shenzhen), China
Yiran Li	University of Toronto, Canada
Yi-Shin Chen	National Tsing Hua University, Taiwan
Yixin Liu	Monash University, Australia
Yongcan Huang	University of Georgia, USA
Yongjie Wang	Nanyang Technological University, Singapore
Yongjing Hao	Suzhou University of Science and Technology, China
Yongmin Yoo	Macquarie University, Australia
Yongpan Sheng	Southwest University, China
Yongyu Wang	Michigan Technological University, USA
Yu Li	Hangzhou Dianzi University, China
Yu Liu	Beijing Jiaotong University, China
Yuanbo Xu	Jilin University, China

Yuanyuan Xu	University of New South Wales, Australia
Yuanyuan Zhu	Wuhan University, China
Yuchen Fang	University of Electronic Science and Technology of China, China
Yucong Dai	Clemson University, USA
Yudong Zhang	University of Science and Technology of China, China
Yue Deng	Michigan State University, USA
Yue Kou	Northeastern University, China
Yue Pang	Hong Kong University of Science and Technology, China
Yue Zhang	Chinese University of Hong Kong (Shenzhen), China
Yuefeng Li	Queensland University of Technology, Australia
Yue-Shi Lee	Ming Chuan University, Taiwan
Yuexuan An	Hohai University, China
Yufei Han	Inria, France
Yujie Wang	Hefei University of Technology, China
Yukun Yuan	University of Tennessee at Chattanooga, USA
Yulong Gu	Bytedance, China
Yun Li	Nanjing University of Posts and Telecommunications, China
Yuncheng Hua	University of New South Wales, Australia
Yunjun Gao	Zhejiang University, China
Yuping Wang	Xidian University, China
Yuqing Sun	Shandong University, China
Yuqing Zhou	George Mason University, USA
Yushan Jiang	University of Connecticut, USA
Yutong Feng	Hong Kong University of Science and Technology (Guangzhou), China
Yuwen Liu	China University of Petroleum (East China), China
Yuxiang Wang	Hangzhou Dianzi University, China
Yuyang Luo	Emory University, USA
Zee Hen Tang	Academia Sinica, Taiwan
Zeyu Wang	Zhejiang University of Technology, China
Zhanke Zhou	Hong Kong Baptist University, China
Zhaohong Deng	Jiangnan University, China
Zhen Wu	Nanjing University, China
Zhenfeng He	National University of Singapore, Singapore
Zheng Liu	Nanjing University of Posts and Telecommunications, China
Zhichao Huang	JD Intelligent Cities Research, China

Zhichun Guo	University of Washington, USA
Zhiguo Gong	University of Macau, China
Zhiwei Liu	University of Illinois Chicago, USA
Zhiwei Zhang	Pennsylvania State University, USA
Zhiwen Xiao	Southwest Jiaotong University, China
Zhiyu Chen	Chinese University of Hong Kong (Shenzhen), China
Zhong Chen	Southern Illinois University, USA
Zhongkui Ma	University of Queensland, Australia
Zhun Zhou	MobiusVision, USA
Zhuo Huang	University of Sydney, Australia
Zichong Li	Rensselaer Polytechnic Institute, USA
Zihan Feng	Hong Kong Baptist University, China
Zi-Jian Cheng	Nanjing University, China
Zijie Pan	University of Connecticut, USA
Ziming Li	University of Connecticut, USA
Ziwen Wang	Anhui University, China
Ziyan Wang	Georgia Institute of Technology, USA
Ziye Zhu	Nanjing University of Posts and Telecommunications, China
Ziyue Li	University of Cologne, Germany
Zong Ke	National University of Singapore, Singapore
Zongqian Wu	University of Electronic Science and Technology of China, China

External Reviewers

Abdul Wahid	IIIT Dharwad, India
Adam Pazdor	University of Manitoba, Canada
Akhlaque Ahmad	Indiana University Bloomington, USA
Alessio Cascione	University of Pisa, Italy
Baha Rababah	University of Manitoba, Canada
Baobao Song	University of Technology Sydney, Australia
Binhao Wang	City Univerisity of Hong Kong, China
Blaise Delattre	Institute of Science Tokyo, Japan
Boris Sedlak	Universitat Pompeu Fabra, Spain
Cássio Prazeres	Federal University of Bahia (UFBA), Brazil
Chao Yan	Vanderbilt University Medical Center, USA
Chaudhary Muhammad Shaheer Yasir	Rowan University, USA
Chunyang Li	Xidian University, China

Congning Ni	Vanderbilt University Medical Center, USA
Cristiano Mesquita Garcia	Instituto Federal de Santa Catarina, Brazil
Dazhi Fu	Chinese University of Hong Kong (Shenzhen), China
Enea Vincenzo Napolitano	University of Naples Federico II, Italy
Eric Inae	University of Notre Dame, USA
Fangwei Ye	Nanjing University of Aeronautics and Astronautics, China
Feng Xiao	Chinese University of Hong Kong (Shenzhen), China
Fuhong Song	Guizhou University of Finance and Economics, China
Gözde Tataroglu Özbulak	University of Lausanne, Switzerland
Hadi Al-Kadhimi	University of Birmingham, UK
Hao Yuan	Northeastern University, China
Hoang Hai Nguyen	University of Manitoba, Canada
Huan Wang	University of Wollongong, Australia
Huy-Son Nguyen	TU Delft, Netherlands
Hy Dang	University of Notre Dame, USA
Ichsan Budiman	University of Birmingham, UK
Jaime Hieu Do	Singapore Management University, Singapore
Jianzhe Li	East China Normal University, China
Jiaqi Zhao	China University of Mining and Technology, China
Kan Guo	Beijing University of Technology, China
Kexin Meng	Zhengzhou University, China
Liqun Deng	China University of Petroleum (East China), China
Lorenzo Peracchio	University of Pavia, Italy
Lorenzo Corso	University of Pavia, Italy
Ludovico Ferreri	University of Pavia, Italy
Lyuheng Yuan	Indiana University Bloomington, USA
Manuel Tognon	Verona University, Italy
Marco De Luca	Politecnico di Torino, Italy
Matteo Berta	Politecnico di Torino, Italy
Miguel Rodriguez	Google, USA
Mong Yuan Sim	Adelaide University, Australia
Moshe Eliasof	University of Cambridge, UK
Nan Zhang	East China Normal University, China
Padipat Sitkrongwong	National Institute of Informatics, Japan
Paolo Garza	Politecnico di Torino, Italy
Peiliang Zhang	Wuhan University of Technology, China

Sponsors

Exclusive Diamond Sponsor

王寬誠教育基金會
K. C. WONG EDUCATION FOUNDATION

Gold Sponsors

香港科技大學
THE HONG KONG UNIVERSITY OF SCIENCE AND TECHNOLOGY

AsianArk

Silver Sponsor

THE HONG KONG POLYTECHNIC UNIVERSITY
香港理工大學

Bronze Sponsors

香港浸會大學
HONG KONG BAPTIST UNIVERSITY

香港教育大學
The Education University of Hong Kong

香港中文大學(深圳)
The Chinese University of Hong Kong, Shenzhen

Publication

Springer

Contents

Main and LLM Track

Main and LLM Track

PathoLLM: Accurate Endometrial Cancer Subtyping Using Clinically-Aligned Language Models

Yifan Lu[1], Qian Wang[2], Qinpei Zhao[1(✉)], Xiaojun Chen[2], Weijie Wang[1], and Weixiong Rao[1]

[1] School of Software Engineering, Tongji University, Shanghai, China
qinpeizhao@tongji.edu.cn

[2] Shanghai Tenth People's Hospital of Tongji University, Shanghai, China

Abstract. The utility of Large Language Models (LLMs) in high-stakes clinical reasoning is often hindered by a lack of deep domain knowledge and the ambiguity of real-world data. Taking Endometrial Cancer FIGO staging as a challenging exemplar, general models struggle with evolving guidelines and extreme class imbalance. To address this, we propose PathoLLM, a specialized framework featuring a systematic two-stage fine-tuning strategy: (1) Domain Knowledge Injection from expert literature, followed by (2) a novel Logic-aware Human-in-the-Loop (HIL) Refinement process. Crucially, this HIL strategy employs a 3-tiered feedback mechanism to rectify not only the model's final output but also its underlying reasoning pathways, constructing a high-fidelity, logic-enriched dataset for task adaptation. This process is further enhanced by iterative prompt optimization. Validated on a hold-out test set, PathoLLM achieves an Overall Accuracy of 0.961 and a Macro-F1 of 0.8192. Notably, despite using only 32B parameters, it demonstrates performance competitive with massive state-of-the-art general models, establishing a superior balance between accuracy and computational efficiency for complex clinical decision support, offering a solution for logic-dependent tasks in resource-constrained environments.

Keywords: Large language model · Human-In-The-Loop · Endometrial cancer · Clinical decision support

1 Introduction

The advent of Large Language Models (*LLMs*), like GPT [1] and Gemini [2], has ushered in a transformative era for AI, demonstrating unprecedented capabilities in language understanding, generation, and complex reasoning across diverse domains. However, effectively translating this immense power to highly specialized and accuracy-critical fields, such as clinical medicine, presents challenges. The medical domain is characterized by intricate information, esoteric terminology, rapid knowledge evolution, and severe implications of diagnostic errors.

R. C.-W. Wong et al. (Eds.): PAKDD 2026, LNAI 16618, pp. 3–14, 2027.
https://doi.org/10.1007/978-981-92-1947-6_1

Particularly in oncology, accurate clinical staging is the cornerstone for tailoring individualized treatment plans and assessing patient prognosis.

Endometrial cancer (*EC*) serves as a highly representative example, whose incidence has been rising globally. The 2023 FIGO staging system, through the integration of anatomical extent, pathology, degree of invasion, lymph node status, and molecular classification, not only enables more accurate prognostic prediction but also directly guides surgical planning, adjuvant therapeutic strategies, and precision treatment decisions [3]. It transforms the management of EC from previous "anatomy-based staging" to "biological plus anatomical dual-dimension staging", thereby truly realizing individualized clinical management and serving as an irreplaceable foundation for clinical practice and research [4]. Clinicians determine FIGO staging on the basis of postoperative pathological reports [5]. However, the reports are typically narrative, unstructured documents, and their expressions are not uniform across different pathologists or institutions. Manual staging requires extracting and synthesizing these complex, multi-dimensional features—ranging from tumor grade to lymph node metastasis status—while strictly adhering to evolving logical rules. Consequently, the process is vulnerable to variations in clinician experience, fatigue, and interpretation of guidelines, leading to staging errors. Using LLMs for FIGO staging auto-generation not only enables accurate and efficient assessments but also improves the standardization of pathological text interpretation. In resource-limited settings, such automated systems have the potential to substantially optimize clinical workflows and enhance the quality of diagnostic and therapeutic care, thereby providing essential support for precision oncology and intelligent clinical decision-making.

Addressing these complex demands requires sophisticated computational capabilities, which have been well advanced by recent breakthroughs in NLP. Strategies such as Chain-of-Thought (*COT*) reasoning [6] have significantly improved models' ability to handle multi-step logic, while Parameter-Efficient Fine-Tuning (*PEFT*) methods like LoRA [7] enable efficient adaptation to downstream tasks. Furthermore, Human-in-the-Loop (*HIL*) mechanisms [8] have proven effective in aligning models with human intent. However, even directly applying domain-adapted medical LLMs (e.g., Baichuan-m1 [9]/m2 [10], Med-PaLM 2 [11], Lingshu [12]) to high-stakes tasks like FIGO staging remains insufficient. Clinical diagnosis mandates evidence traceability—the capacity to verify reasoning—which generic models often lack due to their 'black box' nature and hallucination risks. Furthermore, the intrinsic long-tail distribution of medical data predisposes these models to shortcut learning [13]. They tend to memorize high-frequency labels rather than internalizing multi-step diagnostic logic, leading to poor generalization on critical rare subtypes. This necessitates a unified framework that synergizes advanced techniques, ensuring not only accurate predictions but also the transparent, traceable reasoning essential for clinical practice.

To bridge these gaps, we propose PathoLLM, a specialized framework for EC clinical decision support. Validated on a hold-out test set, it achieves an

Accuracy of 0.961 and Macro-F1 of 0.8192. Notably, our lightweight 32B model outperforms massive generalist models, demonstrating that internalizing domain logic via fine-tuning is crucial to overcome the limitations of prompting alone. While demonstrated on endometrial cancer, this framework establishes a replicable paradigm for solving complex, rule-heavy extraction tasks in high-stakes domains characterized by extreme data imbalance.

2 The *PathoLLM* Framework

2.1 Overall Framework

As illustrated in Fig. 1, the PathoLLM framework orchestrates a progressive learning trajectory designed to instill deep clinical reasoning into a generalist model. The process commences with Domain Knowledge Injection, where the foundation model is aligned with medical terminology using Q&A pairs derived from authoritative literature. Subsequently, we implement a core Logic-aware Human-in-the-Loop (*HIL*) Refinement strategy. Here, experts employ a 3-tiered feedback mechanism to rectify not merely the final outputs but specifically the underlying reasoning pathways of preliminary predictions. This process generates a high-fidelity, logic-enriched dataset, which facilitates the second stage of Task Adaptation. Through fine-tuning on this refined data and coupled with iterative prompt optimization, the model achieves precise information extraction and logical synthesis for final FIGO staging.

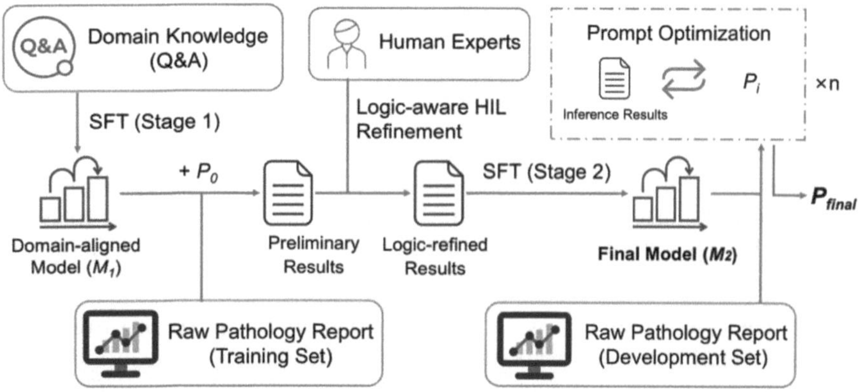

Fig. 1. The architecture and workflow of the *PathoLLM* framework. The pipeline first employs Logic-aware HIL Refinement to generate Logic-refined Results for training the Final Model ($\mathcal{M}_2$). Subsequently, the Initial Prompt (P_0) evolves into the Final Optimized Prompt (P_{final}) through n rounds of iteration guided by the Development Set.

2.2 Fine-Tuning

We designed a two-stage fine-tuning strategy, aimed at enhancing the LLM's capabilities. This strategy sequentially transforms a foundational model (denoted as $\mathcal{M}_0$) first into a domain-aligned model ($\mathcal{M}_1$) via knowledge injection, and subsequently into a task-specific model ($\mathcal{M}_2$) through HIL-refined task adaptation, addressing the inherent challenges of data annotation in the medical domain.

Stage 1: Domain Knowledge Injection. This stage's target is to preliminarily align the general-purpose LLM with the terminology and task format of endometrial cancer staging. While generic LLMs possess robust language capabilities, their depth and accuracy in specialized medical domains can be limited, often leading to "hallucinations" [14] or misinterpretations of professional jargon. Through this initial fine-tuning, we aim to mitigate knowledge biases in the model for subsequent tasks, thereby aligning its behavior more closely with domain's expected terminology.

For this stage, a suitable foundational LLM, $\mathcal{M}_0$, was selected (detailed in Sect. 3.1). The dataset employed for this stage of fine-tuning comprises a set of 235 high-quality Question-Answering ($Q\&A$) pairs, denoted as $\mathcal{D}_{Q\&A} = \{(Q_i, A_i)\}_{i=1}^{N_{Q\&A}}$, meticulously extracted and curated from authoritative medical textbooks, the latest FIGO clinical guidelines, and relevant academic literature. These Q&A pairs encompass core medical knowledge pertaining to endometrial cancer pathological features, FIGO staging definitions, critical judgment criteria, and molecular subtyping.

Supervised Fine-tuning (SFT) was performed on $\mathcal{M}_0$ to derive $\mathcal{M}_1$ by minimizing the standard cross-entropy loss over the $\mathcal{D}_{Q\&A}$ dataset:

$$\mathcal{M}_1 = \arg\min_{\theta_1} \sum_{(Q_i, A_i) \in \mathcal{D}_{Q\&A}} \mathcal{L}_{SFT1}(\mathcal{M}_0(Q_i; \theta_1), A_i) \tag{1}$$

where θ_1 +parameters of the model. The specific training parameters are elaborated in Sect. 3.1. This stage is fundamental to knowledge discovery, as the model learns structured concepts and rules from unstructured knowledge sources. This process establishes a knowledge base for the model to subsequently "mine" pertinent judgment criteria from pathological reports.

Stage 2: Task Adaptation with Human-in-the-Loop Refinement. This stage aims to enable $\mathcal{M}_1$ to accurately and efficiently apply its acquired medical knowledge to real-world, unstructured pathological reports for the FIGO staging task. Crucially, we integrate a logic-aware, 3-tiered Human-in-the-Loop (HIL) feedback mechanism, moving beyond simple label correction.

First, $\mathcal{M}_1$ was used to generate preliminary predictions (S_j^{pred}) for the unannotated reports ($\mathcal{D}_{raw\_train}$).

$$S_j^{pred} = \mathcal{M}_1(R_j, P_0) \tag{2}$$

A team of human experts (3 clinicians) completed the refinement within 5 days, evaluating both the reasoning pathways and final results, categorized as follows:

- **Case 1: Correct Reasoning and Correct Result.** The expert only corrected non-compliant output formatting. This operation reinforced adherence to the task's structured output without disturbing model's correct logic.
- **Case 2: Correct Reasoning but Incorrect Result.** The expert preserved the model's valid reasoning steps but corrected the erroneous key judgments and the final stage. This provided a "surgical" error signal, targeting the model's logical conclusion.
- **Case 3: Incorrect Reasoning and Incorrect Result.** The expert rewrote the entire reasoning process and final answer, adhering to the prescribed output format. This operation generated a "gold-standard" demonstration (S_j^{gold}) for the most complex cases.

This tiered feedback mechanism efficiently transformed the raw training set into a high-quality, high-reliability dataset, $\mathcal{D}_{HIL\_train}$. The value of this dataset lies in its enrichment with expert-validated reasoning pathways, not just final labels.

Finally, we performed a second round of SFT on $\mathcal{M}_1$ using the refined $\mathcal{D}_{HIL\_train}$ to derive $\mathcal{M}_2$. This stage aims to teach the model to accurately identify FIGO-relevant information and replicate the expert-level reasoning logic embedded in the dataset, achieved by minimizing the same cross-entropy loss objective:

$$\mathcal{M}_2 = \arg\min_{\theta_2} \sum_{(R_j, S_j^{gold}) \in \mathcal{D}_{HIL\_train}} \mathcal{L}_{SFT2}(\mathcal{M}_1(R_j, P_0; \theta_2), S_j^{gold}) \quad (3)$$

The resulting model from this stage is designated as Fine-tuned Model Version.2.

2.3 Prompt Engineering

Prompt Engineering plays a pivotal role in harnessing the full potential of Fine-tuned Model Version.2, $\mathcal{M}_2$, for precise FIGO staging [15]. While fine-tuning injects knowledge and adapts the model to the task, the prompt serves as a critical interface for guiding $\mathcal{M}_2$'s reasoning process, ensuring adherence to clinical guidelines, and refining its ability to extract and synthesize information from complex pathological reports.

Our approach involves a systematic, iterative optimization process, leveraging insights from model performance on the development set. Initially, a preliminary prompt (P_0) was designed, primarily instructing the model on its role (e.g., medical expert) and the overarching task (FIGO staging). Starting from P_0, we established a systematic feedback loop that was executed over n rounds of iterative optimization. In each iteration i (where $1 \leq i \leq n$), the prompt was refined based on the following pipeline:

1. **Development-Set Driven Analysis:** The performance of $\mathcal{M}_2$ with prompt version was evaluated on the development set $\mathcal{D}_{dev} = \{(R_k, S_k^{gold})\}_{k=1}^{N_{val}}$.
2. **Error Pattern Identification:** Experts meticulously analyzed error patterns and inconsistencies in $\mathcal{M}_2$'s predictions. This involved identifying common pitfalls such as misinterpretation of specific pathological features, incorrect application of staging rules, or failure to synthesize information.

3. **Targeted Prompt Refinement:** Based on the identified error patterns, the prompt was progressively modified to clarify ambiguous terms, emphasize critical diagnostic features, embed specific FIGO rules, and address common erroneous assumptions. For instance, observing the model's instability in distinguishing between Stage IC and IIC, we added an explicit instruction to strictly check for the presence of 'cervical stromal invasion'.

This iterative process culminated in our final refined prompt, P_{final}, as shown in Fig. 2 which incorporates several key components developed during refinement to facilitate accurate and clinically aligned reasoning:

```
You are a medical expert system specializing in gynecologic oncology staging and pathological analysis. This system stages patients based on FIGO guidelines and provides a reasonable FIGO stage according to the provided pathology report.You must strictly follow the steps and criteria below for judgment, paying special attention to the key points I have outlined at each step.
------------------------------------------------------------
# Step 1: Preliminary FIGO Staging Assessment
## Features required for this step (in order of ascending priority)
...
## Description of Features:
...
## Rules (in order of ascending priority)
...
## Special Attention!!!
...
------------------------------------------------------------
# Step 2: Molecular Subtype Decision-Making
## Features required for this step (in order of ascending priority)
...
## Rules (in order of ascending priority)
...
## Special Attention!!!
...
------------------------------------------------------------
# Below are examples of endometrial cancer staging judgments:
... (Several high-quality and typical patient cases for model reference.)
------------------------------------------------------------
Below is a patient's pathology report. Please perform a diagnosis based on this report and determine the correct FIGO stage:
```

Fig. 2. The template of the final prompt, P_{final}.

Role Assignment and Global Task Definition: The prompt begins with a clear directive, assigning the LLM the persona of a "medical expert specializing in gynecologic oncology staging and pathological analysis." This sets the context and defines the overarching task: to stage patients based on FIGO guidelines, emphasizing strict adherence to outlined steps.

Structured Chain-of-Thought (CoT) Reasoning: To decompose the complex staging process, the prompt explicitly delineates a multi-step CoT reasoning pathway. This structured approach guides the model to systematically evaluate critical information. Specifically, it includes:

– **Step 1: Preliminary FIGO Staging Assessment** This sub-section instructs the model to identify "Features required for this step" and apply

"Rules (in order of ascending priority)" based on the FIGO guidelines, with "Special Attention" notes to avoid common pitfalls.

- **Step 2: Molecular Subtype Decision-Making** Following the initial FIGO staging, the model is guided to make decisions regarding molecular subtypes, again driven by "Features required" and "Rules (in order of ascending priority)," alongside specific "Special Attention" points.

Few-Shot Example Integration: The prompt includes "examples of endometrial cancer staging judgments," providing "several high-quality and typical patient cases for model reference." These few-shot examples serve as crucial in-context learning demonstrations, enabling the model to internalize complex patterns, nuanced interpretations, and the desired output format [16].

Final Task Instruction: The prompt concludes with an instruction to perform the diagnosis based on a provided pathology report. This structured decomposition of the task, where the model's prediction for each case R_k involves a sequence of sub-judgments $J_{k,1}, J_{k,2}, \ldots, J_{k,m}$ leading to S_k^{pred}, can be formalized as:

$$S_k^{pred} = \mathrm{CoT}(\mathcal{M}_2(R_k, P_{final})) \tag{4}$$

where CoT represents the explicit multi-step reasoning pathway instructed in the prompt. This systematic approach ensures robust and clinically aligned predictions, representing a key aspect of knowledge engineering within our framework. P_{final} is then used for the ultimate evaluation on the unseen test set.

3 Experiments

3.1 Setting up

Hardware: All experiments were conducted on a server equipped with two NVIDIA A800 (80GB) GPUs, using bf16 precision for training.

Model Selection: We selected DeepSeek-R1-32B [17] as our foundational model ($\mathcal{M}_0$). This decision was based on its strong open-source support, superior language comprehension required for our dataset, and a manageable size for fine-tuning on our available hardware.

Fine-Tuning: All fine-tuning was optimized with LoRA. For both SFT stages, we used an AdamW optimizer, a cosine learning rate scheduler, a learning rate of 5e-5, and 5.0 training epochs. LoRA was configured with a rank of 8, alpha of 16, dropout of 0.0, and targeted 'all' linear layers.

3.2 Data

Our dataset was curated from 4,152 endometrial cancer (EC) patient records from January 2015 to March 2024, resulting in a final cohort of 2,410 cases after exclusions. All data was de-identified following ethical guidelines. Key inclusion criteria required postoperative pathological confirmation of EC following procedures such as total hysterectomy. Cases were excluded if they lacked essential information for staging.

The dataset consists of unstructured postoperative pathological reports. These reports contain all critical features required for 2023 FIGO staging, including histological type, grade, depth of myometrial invasion, lymphovascular space invasion (LVSI), involvement of adjacent structures (e.g., cervical stroma, adnexa, lymph nodes), and molecular classification.

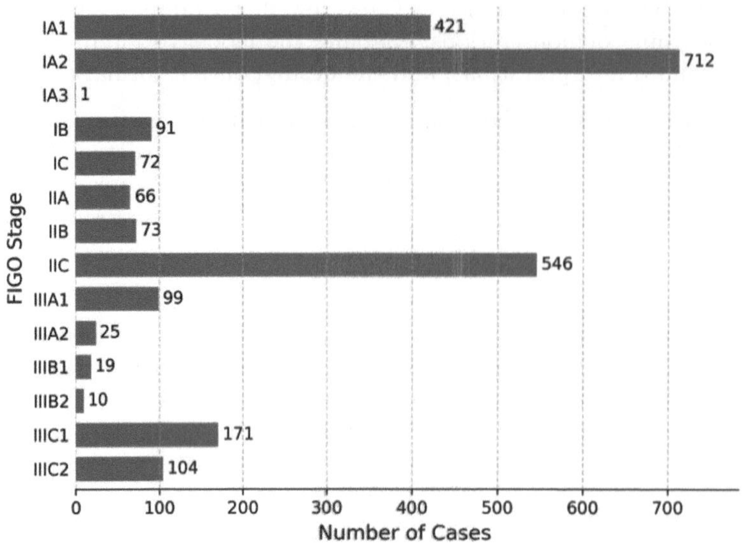

Fig. 3. Distribution of cases by FIGO stage. The dataset comprises a total of 2,410 cases, with subtype prevalence exhibiting extreme imbalance, ranging from 0.04% for IA3 to 29.5% for IA2.

As shown in Fig. 3, the data exhibits a highly imbalanced distribution of FIGO stages, mirroring real-world clinical prevalence. Specifically, the dataset contains a total of 2,410 cases, with class frequencies ranging drastically from dominant subtypes (e.g., IA2 with 712 cases, accounting for 29.5%) to extremely rare substages (e.g., IA3 with only 1 case, representing 0.04%). This distinct long-tail distribution presents a significant challenge for classification models. To ensure robust evaluation and prevent overfitting, the 2,410 cases were partitioned into three non-overlapping sets: a training set (1,600 cases) for SFT Stage 2, a development set (400 cases) for iterative prompt optimization, and a hold-out test set (410 cases) for final evaluation.

3.3 Results

In this section, we present a comprehensive evaluation of the PathoLLM framework. We first conduct a comparison of our final model against a suite of general-purpose and medical-domain LLMs. We then analyze the universal challenges of the task revealed by the metrics. Finally, we present a stepwise ablation study to quantify the contribution of each component in our framework.

3.3.1 Performance Benchmark Against Other Models

To evaluate the effectiveness of our specialized fine-tuning framework, we benchmarked PathoLLM against a diverse set of strong baselines in a prompt-only setting using the optimized prompt P_{final}, including leading general-purpose models (e.g., GPT-5, Gemini-2.5 Pro, Claude-4.5 sonnet, DeepSeek-R1-671B) and specialized medical LLMs (e.g., Baichuan-m1/m2, Med-PaLM 2, Lingshu).

Table 1 presents the performance comparison on the hold-out test set. Our Fine-tuned Model demonstrates strong performance on this highly specialized task, achieving the highest scores on all three primary metrics when benchmarked against leading general-purpose and medical LLMs used in a prompt-only setting: Overall Accuracy (0.961), Macro-F1 (0.8192), and Weighted-F1 (0.9496).

Table 1. Performance comparison of different LLMs on the FIGO staging task.

Models		Accuracy (w/o P_{final})	Accuracy (+ P_{final})	Macro-Precision	Macro-Recall	Macro-F1	Weighted-F1
General-purpose LLMs	GPT-5	**0.7561**	0.9317	0.7594	0.8560	0.8003	0.9048
	Gemini-2.5 pro	0.6537	0.9512	0.7838	**0.8679**	0.8061	0.9327
	Claude-4.5 sonnet	0.6732	0.9024	0.6755	0.7743	0.7176	0.8642
	DeepSeek-R1-671B	0.6927	0.9122	0.6884	0.7621	0.7204	0.8784
Medical LLMs	Baichuan-m1-14B	0.3244	0.8585	0.6278	0.8011	0.6895	0.8160
	Baichuan-m2-32B	0.3780	0.9390	0.7386	0.8395	0.7802	0.9181
	Med-PaLM 2	0.2317	0.7122	0.3897	0.5144	0.4385	0.6688
	Lingshu-32B	0.2804	0.8585	0.5654	0.6885	0.6130	0.8138
Fine-tuned Model (Ours)		0.3805	**0.9610**	**0.7900**	0.8565	**0.8192**	**0.9496**

We observe several key findings:

1. **The Value of Specialization:** PathoLLM consistently outperforms all prompt-only baselines. This validates that for highly complex, domain-specific reasoning tasks, a specialized, fine-tuning framework is crucial for achieving

the required accuracy, proving more effective than relying on the zero-shot or few-shot capabilities of even the most powerful general-purpose models.

2. **General-purpose vs. Medical LLMs:** Contrary to initial expectations, robust general-purpose models generally outperformed the evaluated medical-domain LLMs. We attribute this to two factors: first, the superior parameter scale and reasoning capabilities of state-of-the-art general models allow them to better follow complex prompt instructions; second, current medical LLMs are primarily aligned with broad biomedical knowledge rather than the specific, intricate logic required for FIGO staging. This finding reinforces that 'general medical pre-training' is insufficient for specialized clinical decision support. Notably, our PathoLLM, despite using a smaller 32B model, significantly outperforms these massive generalist models, proving that targeted logic alignment is more critical than sheer parameter scale for this task.
3. **Efficiency and Performance:** While comparing a fine-tuned model against prompt-only generalist LLMs presents a methodological asymmetry, it addresses a critical clinical reality: massive models (e.g., >600B) and cloud-based APIs are often precluded by strict privacy regulations and hardware constraints. PathoLLM demonstrates that specialized fine-tuning enables a lightweight (32B) model to surpass these giants, offering a privacy-compliant, high-performance solution viable for local hospital deployment.

3.3.2 Analysis of Task-Specific Metric Patterns

A deeper analysis of Table 1 reveals two universal patterns present across all models, highlighting the inherent challenges of the FIGO staging task:

1. **Extreme Class Imbalance (Weighted-F1 $\gg$ Macro-F1):** For every model, the Weighted-F1 score is significantly higher than its Macro-F1 score. This is not a model-specific flaw but a direct consequence of the dataset's extreme class imbalance (see Fig. 3). The high Weighted-F1 scores indicate strong performance on common, majority classes (e.g., IA2, IIC), whereas the lower Macro-F1 scores expose the shared difficulty all models face in correctly identifying rare, minority substages.
2. **High Inter-class Confusion (Low Macro-Precision):** Similarly, Macro-Precision scores are universally moderate (sub-0.8) for all top-performing models. This is attributed to the high inter-class confusion inherent in the task, where subtle distinctions in pathological reports (e.g., minute differences in invasion depth) lead to a high rate of False Positives (FP).

These systemic challenges, which even powerful models cannot overcome with prompting alone, validate the necessity of domain-adaptive fine-tuning approach.

3.3.3 Ablation Study

To deconstruct the effectiveness of our framework, we conducted a stepwise ablation study (Table 2), quantifying the cumulative impact of each component.

1. **Necessity of Domain Knowledge ($\mathcal{M}_0 \rightarrow M_1$):** The foundational model yields poor performance. While Domain Knowledge Injection (Stage 1) aligns

terminology and doubles the Macro-F1 (0.2564), the model still lacks the capability to handle complex staging logic, confirming that abstract knowledge alone is insufficient for clinical application.

2. **Impact of Prompt Engineering($\mathcal{M}_1$ + P_{final}):** Introducing the optimized prompt triggers a significant performance leap (Accuracy: 0.9049). This underscores the critical role of structured CoT guidance in activating the model's reasoning capabilities.
3. **Standard SFT vs. Logic-aware HIL Refinement:**To validate the necessity of our HIL strategy, we trained a contrastive model using Standard SFT, fine-tuning it directly on raw reports. While this approach improved Overall Accuracy to 0.9268, the Macro-F1 (0.6729) showed limited improvement compared to the prompt-only setting. Critically, we observed a "shortcut learning" phenomenon where the model, despite being explicitly prompted to perform step-by-step reasoning, frequently bypassed the intermediate logical generation to output the final FIGO stage directly. This indicates that without expert-refined guidance, the model tends to overfit to final labels rather than internalizing the diagnostic logic, resulting in a "black box" system that lacks the evidence traceability essential for clinical practice.
4. **Completing the Loop with HIL ($\mathcal{M}_2$ + P_{final}):**The final HIL-refined model achieves the best performance across all metrics (Macro-F1: 0.8192). By training on expert-corrected reasoning pathways, $\mathcal{M}_2$ overcomes the issue of Standard SFT. It successfully internalizes the logic dictated by the prompt, achieving a unity of accurate prediction and transparent reasoning.

This study confirms that PathoLLM's success relies on a holistic approach: SFT Stage 1 provides the knowledge, Prompt Engineering constructs the logic frame, and SFT Stage 2 with HIL Refinement ensures the model adheres to this frame without taking shortcuts.

Table 2. The result of ablation study

Model Configuration	Accuracy	Macro-Precision	Macro-Recall	Macro-F1	Weighted-F1
Baseline ($\mathcal{M}_0$)	0.3804	0.0908	0.1672	0.1163	0.2834
+ SFT Stage 1 ($\mathcal{M}_1$)	0.3902	0.2467	0.2697	0.2564	0.3799
+ Prompt Engineering ($\mathcal{M}_1$ + P_{final})	0.9049	0.6261	0.7194	0.6668	0.8677
+ Standard SFT ($\mathcal{M}_1$+D_{raw_train}+P_{final})	0.9268	0.6312	0.7300	0.6729	0.8985
+ SFT Stage 2 ($\mathcal{M}_2$ + P_{final})	**0.9610**	**0.7900**	**0.8565**	**0.8192**	**0.9496**

4 Conclusion

In this paper, we proposed PathoLLM, a specialized framework enabling an efficient 32B model to accurately perform automated FIGO staging for endometrial cancer (Macro-F1 0.8192). Our method synergistically combines domain knowledge injection, systematic prompt engineering, and a novel Logic-aware

HIL Refinement strategy. This approach allows the model to adhere to complex clinical rules and handle the ambiguity of unstructured pathological reports.

Our analysis highlights the challenge of extreme class imbalance and inter-class confusion in clinical text. PathoLLM demonstrates that aligning model logic via expert-guided fine-tuning effectively addresses these complexities. While currently validated only on endometrial cancer, this approach offers a promising foundation for logic-heavy clinical tasks. Future work will prioritize multi-center validation and targeted learning strategies for rare, long-tailed substages.

References

1. Wang, S., Hu, M., Li, Q., Safari, M., Yang, X.: Capabilities of GPT-5 on multimodal medical reasoning. arXiv preprint arXiv:2508.08224 (2025)
2. Comanici, G., Bieber, E., Schaekermann, M., Pasupat, et al.: Gemini 2.5: pushing the frontier with advanced reasoning, multimodality, long context, and next generation agentic capabilities. arXiv preprint arXiv:2507.06261 (2025)
3. Matsuo, K., et al.: Prognostic performance of the 2023 FIGO staging schema for endometrial cancer. Gynecol. Oncol. **187**, 37–45 (2024)
4. Koskas, M., et al.: Cancer of the corpus uteri: a 2025 update. Int. J. Gynecol. Obstet. **171**, 60–77 (2025)
5. Zhao, X., et al.: The past, present, and future of FIGO staging of endometrial cancer. J. Gynecol. Oncol. **36**(4), e105 (2025)
6. Miao, J., et al.: Chain of thought utilization in large language models and application in nephrology. Medicina **60**(1), 148 (2024)
7. Hu, E.J., et al.: Lora: low-rank adaptation of large language models. ICLR **1**(2), 3 (2022)
8. Mosqueira-Rey, E., et al.: Human-in-the-loop machine learning: a state of the art. Artif. Intell. Rev. **56**(4), 3005–3054 (2023)
9. Wang, B., et al.: Baichuan-m1: pushing the medical capability of large language models. arXiv preprint arXiv:2502.12671 (2025)
10. Dou, C., Liu, C., et al.: Baichuan-m2: scaling medical capability with large verifier system. arXiv preprint arXiv:2509.02208 (2025)
11. Chowdhery, A., et al.: Palm: scaling language modeling with pathways. J. Mach. Learn. Res. **24**(240), 1–113 (2023)
12. Xu, W., et al.: Lingshu: a generalist foundation model for unified multimodal medical understanding and reasoning. arXiv preprint arXiv:2506.07044 (2025)
13. Brown, A., et al.: Detecting shortcut learning for fair medical ai using shortcut testing. Nat. Commun. **14**(1), 4314 (2023)
14. Perković, G., et al.: Hallucinations in LLMs: understanding and addressing challenges. In: 47th MIPRO ICT and Electronics Convention, pp. 2084–2088 (2024)
15. Meskó, B.: Prompt engineering as an important emerging skill for medical professionals: tutorial. J. Med. Internet Res. **25**, e50638 (2023)
16. Song, Y., Wang, T., Cai, P., Mondal, S.K., Sahoo, J.P.: A comprehensive survey of few-shot learning: evolution, applications, challenges, and opportunities. ACM Comput. Surv. **55**(13s), 1–40 (2023)
17. DeepSeek-AI: Deepseek-r1: incentivizing reasoning capability in LLMs via reinforcement learning. arXiv:2501.12948 (2025)

Efficient Choice-Based Facility Location: A Hybrid AHP/DEA-Greedy Approach

Zhantu Zhao and Xiangqian Sun(✉)

Xi'an Jiaotong-Liverpool University, Suzhou, China
Zhantu.Zhao23@student.xjtlu.edu.cn, Xiangqian.Sun@xjtlu.edu.cn

Abstract. The Choice-Based Facility Location (CBFL) problem aims to optimize facility placement by modeling realistic customer choice, but its inherent NP-hard nature presents significant computational challenges, especially for large-scale applications. To overcome this limitation, we introduce an innovative AHP/DEA-Greedy hybrid framework. This two-stage approach pioneers the use of an Analytic Hierarchy Process/Data Envelopment Analysis (AHP/DEA) model to perform an initial, efficient screening of candidate facilities based on multiple criteria. By intelligently reducing the solution space, the subsequent greedy selection process becomes highly efficient, drastically cutting down on expensive marginal-utility calculations. Our empirical evaluation shows that this hybrid strategy not only maintains near-optimal solution quality, on par with Greedy and Simulated Annealing, but also dramatically reduces computation time. Critically, its performance surpasses traditional methods like Generalized Benders Decomposition (GBD) in large-scale scenarios, highlighting its robustness and scalability for real-world facility location planning.

Keywords: Facility Location Selection · Spatial Feature Modeling · Multi-Criteria Decision-Making

1 Introduction

Facility location selection is a critical strategic decision in sectors such as retail, logistics, healthcare, and urban planning, involving site choices that maximize accessibility while considering cost, competition, and customer demand [2,3]. In retail, location directly affects market coverage and competitiveness [4,6]. For example, when two major shops expand in the same city, one may choose a central district with many people passing by but intense competition, while the other selects a suburban area with fewer customers but lower competition, illustrating the trade-off between demand and competitive pressure [10,11]. Figure 1 shows a simple example of this contrast.

Traditional models often focus mainly on being close to customers but pay less attention to competition and differences in customer preferences. The *choice-based facility location* (CBFL) framework addresses this by modeling how customers choose among competing facilities based on perceived utility, offering a

R. C.-W. Wong et al. (Eds.): PAKDD 2026, LNAI 16618, pp. 15–26, 2027.
https://doi.org/10.1007/978-981-92-1947-6_2

realistic and scalable basis for complex spatial decisions [9,11,12]. As markets grow more dynamic, CBFL allows planners to incorporate customer preferences and competitive interactions [9].

Building on this foundation, modern studies increasingly integrate behavioral mechanisms into facility location optimization. Early approaches such as the p-median and competitive location models relied on static rules and could not capture diverse customer preferences [3]. Recent CBFL formulations employ simulation-based and submodular models to represent complex behavior [8], recognizing that customers form "consideration sets" of non-dominated facilities based on attractiveness and proximity [9,12]. This underscores the need for models that capture spatial and competitive interactions while remaining tractable. Traditional mixed-integer formulations may involve millions of variables; Fischetti et al. [3] mitigate this using a redesigned Benders decomposition with compact continuous representations. However, large-scale CBFL problems still require methods balancing solution quality and computational efficiency. Although scalable decomposition improves tractability, it often overlooks multi-criteria trade-offs and realistic behavioral factors. Recent work integrates multiple choice models into unified frameworks combining deterministic and probabilistic behavior with spatial and competitive features [3,11], but reconciling Multi-Criteria Decision Making (MCDM) considerations with behavioral realism remains challenging.

To address this, we introduce a framework for evaluating CBFL models across diverse instance scales [3,11]. At its core is a hybrid AHP/DEA-greedy method that screens candidates using multi-criteria priorities, then iteratively refines selection via a greedy search, enhancing scalability while maintaining near-optimal solutions. We benchmark it against exhaustive enumeration, standard greedy heuristics, simulated annealing, and generalized Benders decomposition. Results highlight trade-offs between accuracy and runtime across market complexities, demonstrating the hybrid method's consistent efficiency and performance.

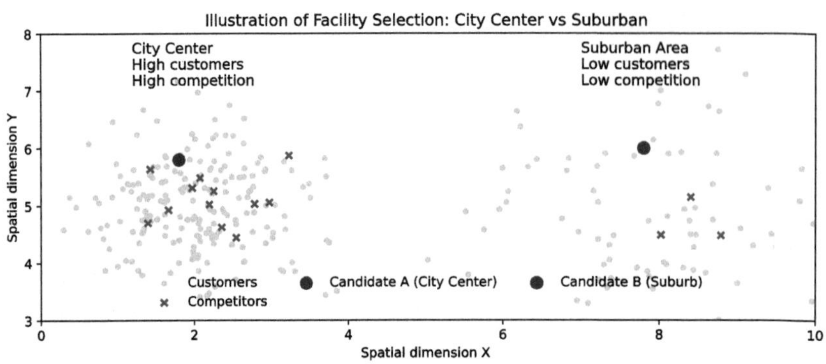

Fig. 1. Illustration of Customer Choice and Competition

2 Related Work

Facility location problems (FLPs) remain a central topic in operations research due to their wide applications in logistics, manufacturing, and service systems. In this section, we position our contributions by briefly reviewing relevant studies on single-company CBFL models and their solution approaches. Recent work extends classical distance and coverage based formulations by introducing methodological enhancements, such as spatial diagnostics, explicit choice modeling, clustering-based reduction, and competitive interaction. However, most existing studies do not simultaneously address multi-criteria evaluation and scalable behavioral modeling, motivating the development of our hybrid framework.

Building on classical and CBFL models, recent studies increasingly incorporate behavioral realism into facility location decisions. Modern CBFL frameworks address this by modeling consideration sets and spatial competition, often through simulation-based or submodular formulations [8,12]. Related advances in facility layout and manufacturing demonstrate the broader value of simulation-based optimization for high-dimensional spatial decisions. Ruiz Zúñiga et al. [13], for example, integrate discrete-event simulation with optimization to evaluate layout alternatives under realistic process constraints, illustrating how hybrid procedures enhance scalability and decision quality. Within CBFL, decomposition and dimensionality-reduction techniques [11,15] help mitigate computational growth but may overlook multi-criteria trade-offs or reduce behavioral fidelity, motivating the development of hybrid algorithms that balance realistic choice modeling with scalable optimization.

Given multi-criteria nature of facility location decisions, methods such as the Analytic Hierarchy Process (AHP) and Data Envelopment Analysis (DEA) are widely used. AHP captures qualitative preferences via pairwise comparisons but is sensitive to subjective judgments, whereas DEA evaluates efficiency objectively using input-output data but may fail to discriminate among equally efficient alternatives or reflect qualitative priorities [5,16]. Hybrid AHP-DEA frameworks combine these strengths: for instance, Gao et al. [5] used DEA-derived efficiency ratios to construct AHP matrices and reduce subjectivity, while Cheng and Wei [1] integrated AHP weights into DEA for bike-sharing location planning.

While existing studies offer diverse models and algorithms, assumptions on customer behavior and operational realism often limit applicability. This motivates integrated frameworks combining consideration set choice modeling with scale-aware algorithms to enhance computational efficiency and decision quality.

3 Methodology

This section presents the methodology for solving the CBFL problem. We first establish a utility-based demand model that characterizes how customers evaluate and choose among competing facilities, incorporating attractiveness, distance, and competitive interactions. Building on this behavioral foundation, a set of scalable optimization strategies is then introduced to search for high-quality facility configurations under different problem sizes. The subsequent subsections present the model formulation, variable definitions, and solution procedures.

3.1 Background of the Problems

Consider a firm that plans to open p new facilities from a set of candidate locations $\mathcal{N} = \{1, \ldots, J\}$. The market already contains a set of existing competitors $\mathcal{C} = \{1, \ldots, K\}$, whose facilities serve as alternative options for customers and therefore influence the attractiveness of any newly opened sites. Customer demand is represented by a set $\mathcal{M} = \{1, \ldots, I\}$, where each customer $i \in \mathcal{M}$ has an associated demand weight and preference structure. Customers evaluate all available facilities, including both chosen candidates and competitors, using perceived utilities derived from intrinsic and spatial factors. The firm's objective is to select a subset $\mathcal{S} \subseteq \mathcal{N}$ with $|\mathcal{S}| = p$ that maximizes the total customer utility generated by the resulting system of facilities.

3.2 Spatial Features and Customer Dynamics

Facility competitiveness depends on spatial attributes that link location characteristics to market performance. In our model, each candidate facility j is characterized by three key factors: the resident population P_j within its service radius, which reflects potential demand; the density of nearby competitive facilities C_j, which represents market pressure; and the number of accessible public transit stations T_j, which captures how easily customers can reach the site. These components are combined into an overall attractiveness measure ϕ_j that incorporates both positive and negative spatial influences:

$$\phi_j = \frac{P_j \cdot T_j}{C_j}. \tag{1}$$

This formulation follows the intuition that facility attractiveness should increase with local demand potential and accessibility while diminishing under competitive crowding, reflecting how these spatial factors jointly influence perceived utility [4].

3.3 Customer Consideration Set Formation: Dominance and Decision Boundaries

Customers do not evaluate every facility; instead, they form a consideration set comprising facilities relevant to their choice [10]. For customer i, facility j is dominated by k (denoted $k \succ j$) if

$$\phi_k \geq \phi_j \quad \text{and} \quad \psi_{ik} \geq \psi_{ij}, \tag{2}$$

where $\psi_{ij} = 1/d_{ij}^{\alpha}$, with d_{ij} the Euclidean distance between customer i and facility j and $\alpha \geq 1$ controlling distance sensitivity. The consideration set for customer i therefore consists of all facilities that are not dominated by any other available option:

$$Q_i = \{j \in T = \mathcal{S} \cup \mathcal{C} \mid \nexists k \in T \text{ such that } k \succ j\}. \quad (3)$$

This filtering ensures that only non-dominated facilities, those with at least one advantage in attractiveness or distance which affect customer choice, reflecting realistic decision behavior (Fig. 2).

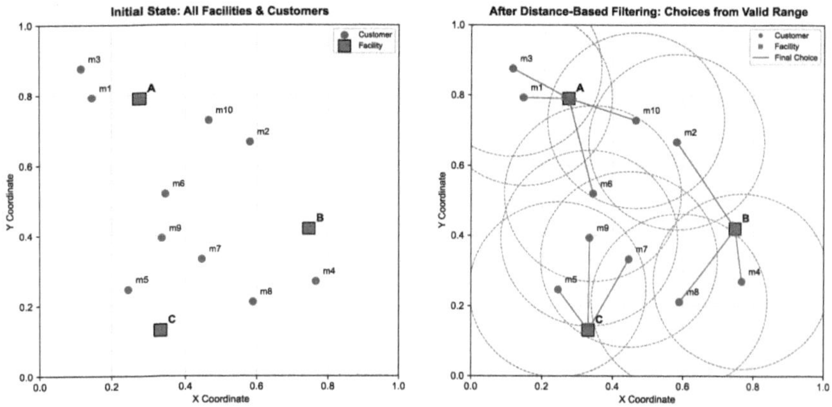

Fig. 2. Customer Consideration Sets: Before and After Distance filtering

Utility Quantification. To evaluate a selected facility set $\mathcal{S}$, we adopt a utility model linking facility attributes to customer demand. Following classic spatial interaction formulations [7], the utility of facility j for customer i is

$$u_{ij} = \phi_j \cdot \psi_{ij}, \quad (4)$$

where ϕ_j captures intrinsic attractiveness and $\psi_{ij} = 1/d_{ij}^{\alpha}$ represents distance decay with α. Let $\mathcal{C}$ denote existing competitors, and define the reachable set

$$\text{Reach}_i(\mathcal{S}) = \{\, j \in \mathcal{S} \cup \mathcal{C} : d_{ij} \le R_i \,\}, \quad (5)$$

where R_i is the search radius. The consideration set is

$$Q_i = \{\, j \in \text{Reach}_i(\mathcal{S}) : \nexists k \in \text{Reach}_i(\mathcal{S}) \text{ with } k \succ j \,\}. \quad (6)$$

The captured share of customer i from a facility set $\mathcal{S}$ is defined as

$$p_i(\mathcal{S}) = \begin{cases} \dfrac{\sum_{j \in \mathcal{S} \cap Q_i} u_{ij}}{\sum_{j \in Q_i} u_{ij}}, & Q_i \neq \varnothing, \\ 0, & Q_i = \varnothing, \end{cases} \quad (7)$$

The total utility of the facility set $\mathcal{S}$ is then computed by aggregating over all customers:

$$U(\mathcal{S}) = \sum_{i=1}^{I} p_i(\mathcal{S}). \tag{8}$$

The corresponding facility location problem is to select a subset $\mathcal{S} \subseteq \mathcal{N}$ of size p that maximizes total utility:

$$\max_{\mathcal{S} \subseteq \mathcal{N}} U(\mathcal{S}) \quad \text{subject to} \quad |\mathcal{S}| = p. \tag{9}$$

4 Hybrid AHP/DEA-Greedy Approach

The proposed hybrid algorithm integrates multi-criteria AHP/DEA pre-screening with a marginal-gain greedy selection. Its goal is to efficiently identify high-quality facility sets while reducing unnecessary utility computations. The procedure consists of two phases: Phase I performs multi-criteria evaluation to narrow the candidate set, and Phase II iteratively selects facilities based on marginal utility. For clarity, the hybrid Greedy-AHP/DEA algorithm is summarized in Algorithm 1.

4.1 Phase I: Multi-criteria Pre-screening via AHP/DEA

Each candidate facility is characterized by multiple attributes, including spatial and operational factors. Let x_{ij} denote the j-th attribute of facility i. To make these attributes comparable across criteria, they are first normalized:

$$x'_{ij} = \begin{cases} \dfrac{x_{ij}}{\max_k x_{kj}}, & \text{benefit criterion,} \\ \dfrac{\max_k x_{kj} - x_{ij}}{\max_k x_{kj} - \min_k x_{kj}}, & \text{cost criterion.} \end{cases} \tag{10}$$

This normalization ensures that all criteria are on a common scale, allowing the subsequent DEA and AHP steps to fairly evaluate and rank the candidate facilities. DEA is then applied to measure the relative efficiency of each candidate. Let y_{ir} $(r = 1, \ldots, p)$ and x_{is} $(s = 1, \ldots, q)$ be the normalized benefit and cost criteria of facility i, respectively. For facility i, the efficiency with respect to facility j is defined as [5]:

$$\max_{\mathbf{u},\mathbf{v}} \quad h_{ij} = \sum_{r=1}^{p} u_r y_{ir} + \sum_{s=1}^{q} v_s x_{is} \tag{11}$$

$$\text{s.t.} \quad \sum_{r=1}^{p} u_r y_{jr} + \sum_{s=1}^{q} v_s x_{js} \leq 1, \quad u_r, v_s \geq 0 \ \forall r, s, \tag{12}$$

and the aggregated efficiency score for facility i is computed as [5]:

$$\theta_i = \frac{1}{|\mathcal{N}|} \sum_{j \in \mathcal{N}} h_{ij}.$$

The aggregated DEA scores θ_i are then used to construct a pairwise comparison matrix for AHP:

$$a_{jk} = \frac{\theta_j}{\theta_k}, \quad \forall j, k \in \mathcal{N}. \tag{13}$$

Solving the normalized principal eigenvector of this matrix yields the AHP weights:

$$\mathbf{A}\mathbf{w} = \lambda_{\max}\mathbf{w}, \qquad w_j^{\mathrm{AHP}} = \frac{w_j}{\sum_k w_k}. \tag{14}$$

These weights reflect each facility's overall performance across multiple criteria, integrating the DEA-based efficiency assessments into a single priority score. Consequently, selecting the top K facilities according to w_j^{AHP} identifies those candidates that are most promising for contributing high utility in the subsequent greedy iteration [14]. The initial solution set $\mathcal{S}_1$ is then initialized with the facility in this top K subset that has the largest standalone utility $U(\{j\})$.

4.2 Phase II: Greedy Marginal-Gain Iteration

Starting from $\mathcal{S}_1$, the algorithm iteratively adds facilities that maximize the marginal increase in total utility. At each iteration k, the marginal utility of a candidate j is

$$\Delta U(j \mid \mathcal{S}_k) = U(\mathcal{S}_k \cup \{j\} \cup \mathcal{C}) - U(\mathcal{S}_k \cup \mathcal{C}), \quad j \in \text{top } K \setminus \mathcal{S}_k. \tag{15}$$

The facility j^* with the largest ΔU is selected and added:

$$\mathcal{S}_{k+1} = \mathcal{S}_k \cup \{j^*\}. \tag{16}$$

The selected facility j^* is also added to the competitive set $\mathcal{C}$ for the next iteration. This ensures that subsequent marginal utility calculations reflect updated competitive interactions. The process repeats until $|\mathcal{S}_{k+1}| = p$.

4.3 Remarks

This hybrid approach leverages AHP/DEA pre-screening to reduce the number of candidate facilities considered in each greedy iteration. By fixing the top K candidates and updating the competitive set with each selected facility, the algorithm captures both multi-criteria attractiveness and realistic competitive effects while achieving high-quality solutions efficiently.

5 Experiments and Results

This section reports the experimental evaluation of the proposed algorithms. Since the methodology section has already detailed the models and optimization procedures, we focus here on the empirical behavior of the methods under increasing combinatorial complexity. The experiments vary only the number of candidate facilities and the number of facilities to be opened (P), while all other factors remain fixed. This design isolates the effect of search-space growth and enables a clear assessment of the comparative performance, especially the advantage of the proposed Hybrid method in balancing efficiency and solution quality.

Algorithm 1 Hybrid Greedy-AHP/DEA Algorithm

Input: Candidate set $\mathcal{N}$, competitor set $\mathcal{C}$, customers $\mathcal{M}$, target p, top K
Output: Selected set $\mathcal{S}_p$
Normalize attributes $x_{ij} \to x'_{ij}$
Compute DEA efficiency θ_i for $i \in \mathcal{N}$
Build AHP matrix $a_{jk} = \theta_j / \theta_k$
Compute weights w_j^{AHP} (principal eigenvector)
$\mathcal{N}_{\text{top}} \leftarrow$ top K candidates by w_j^{AHP}
$j_1 = \arg\max_{j \in \mathcal{N}_{\text{top}}} U(\{j\})$, $\mathcal{S}_1 \leftarrow \{j_1\}$
$k \leftarrow 1$
while $|\mathcal{S}_k| < p$ **do**
  for $j \in \mathcal{N}_{\text{top}} \setminus \mathcal{S}_k$ **do**
    $\Delta U(j \mid \mathcal{S}_k) = U(\mathcal{S}_k \cup \{j\}) - U(\mathcal{S}_k)$
  end for
  $j^* = \arg\max_j \Delta U(j \mid \mathcal{S}_k)$
  $\mathcal{S}_{k+1} \leftarrow \mathcal{S}_k \cup \{j^*\}$
  $\mathcal{C} \leftarrow \mathcal{C} \cup \{j^*\}$
  $k \leftarrow k + 1$
end while
Return $\mathcal{S}_p$

5.1 Experimental Design

To ensure reliable and comparable results, all non-essential factors are fixed while problem scale is varied. This design isolates the impact of combinatorial growth on algorithmic performance. All experiments were conducted on a 64-bit Windows 11 laptop with a multi-core CPU and 16 GB of RAM, using Python 3.11.4. DEA subproblems were solved via CVXPY and the Gurobi optimizer. The full code is available in an anonymized repository: https://github.com/TU1717/A-Hybrid-AHP-DEA-Greedy-Approach.

Spatial Scene and Data Generation. All experiments are conducted in a 100×100 grid environment representing an abstract urban area. We uniformly generate 500 demand points to represent customers, place 15 competitive facilities to model the existing market, and include 15 public transport stations to capture accessibility effects. These spatial elements define the utility landscape for candidate evaluation. To guarantee comparability across methods, all spatial data are generated once using a fixed random seed and remain unchanged for all experiments. Candidate facilities are introduced in varying numbers, with coordinates uniformly sampled from the grid. This controlled setup enables a clear assessment of algorithmic performance and scalability.

Experimental Focus and Evaluation Logic. The experiments are designed to answer two key questions:

1. How does the global optimality of exhaustive enumeration trade off against its rapidly increasing computational burden as the problem size grows?

2. To what extent can alternative methods deliver near-optimal solutions while significantly reducing runtime?

Algorithm performance is assessed using two metrics. *Runtime* captures computational efficiency and scalability across different instance sizes. *Solution quality* is measured by the total utility defined in Sect. 3, and is further benchmarked against the optimal solution through the relative gap:

$$rg\% = \frac{|U_{\text{algorithm}} - U_{\text{optimum}}|}{U_{\text{optimum}}} \times 100\%. \tag{17}$$

This measure provides a standardized quantification of how closely each algorithm approaches the optimal solution.

5.2 Experimental Results

We illustrate the computational performance of the five algorithms in Fig. 3, where panel **(a)** shows runtime distributions on a log scale, and panel **(b)** presents performance profiles indicating the fraction of instances solved within a given time budget. Combined with Table 1, these results reveal clear trade-offs between efficiency and optimality across problem scales.

Exhaustive evaluation consistently attains the global optimum, but its runtime grows rapidly with problem size, making it infeasible for large-scale problems. SA substantially reduces computation time and often approximates the benchmark on medium-sized instances, though its stochastic nature can yield occasional suboptimal outcomes and slightly higher variability than greedy methods. The greedy algorithm offers a strong balance between speed and solution quality while the hybrid achieves comparable utility with further runtime savings through candidate pre-screening, though with minor losses when high-utility options are inadvertently filtered out. GBD is the fastest among all approaches, completing most instances within tens of seconds even for large-scale problems. Nevertheless, its solution quality is less stable, while it achieves optimal or near-optimal results for small instances, regret can rise significantly for larger instances.

5.3 Transition to Larger-Scale Evaluations

Small-scale experiments indicate that the greedy algorithm and the Greedy–AHP/DEA Hybrid achieve nearly identical performance, while simulated annealing delivers comparable utility at moderately higher runtimes. This suggests that with a limited candidate set, the search space is manageable and algorithmic differences are minor. However, real-world facility location problems typically involve selecting from much larger candidate pools, where combinatorial growth makes exhaustive enumeration impractical.

To assess algorithmic robustness under such realistic conditions, we extend the experiments to larger p and N. In this context, the greedy algorithm serves

Table 1. Computational Comparison Across Solution Strategies.

Candidate	Exhaustive		Greedy		SA		Hybrid		GBD	
	Time (s)	rg(%)	Time (s)	rg(%)	Time (s)	rg(%)	Time (s)	rg(%)	Time (s)	rg(%)
Case 1: Fixed $p = 2$										
10	4.09	0.00	2.33	0.53	27.93	0.00	1.67	0.00	7.46	0
30	43.44	0.00	7.36	0.00	45.16	0.00	5.90	1.31	15.06	0
50	127.30	0.00	13.59	0.00	76.66	0.00	11.05	0.00	17.04	2.62
80	357.01	0.00	23.22	0.00	79.34	2.76	20.20	0.00	20.77	17.67
100	578.25	0.00	31.91	0.00	120.06	0.62	31.49	0.00	21.67	7.77
Case 2: Fixed $p = 3$										
10	10.89	0.00	3.50	0.00	26.65	0.00	3.10	0.00	13.86	0
30	410.02	0.00	11.78	0.00	54.68	0.00	10.16	0.00	17.43	0.95
50	2164.44	0.00	20.28	0.00	73.82	0.00	15.38	0.00	17.63	13.38
80	10294.16	0.00	37.06	0.00	102.50	2.88	33.33	1.31	21.19	20.00
100	20725.10	0.00	52.72	0.00	123.70	2.57	48.18	0.00	23.68	9.67

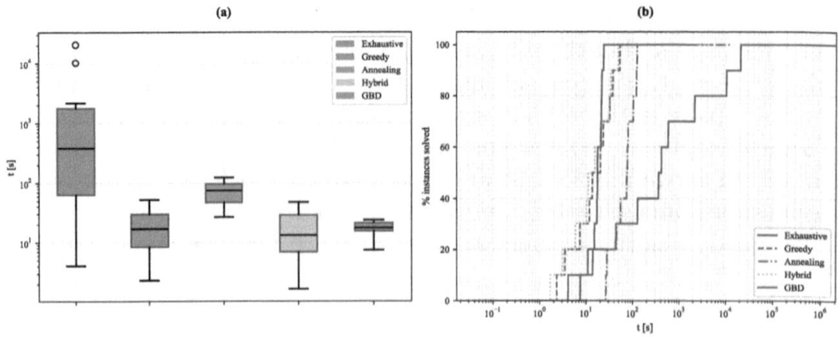

Fig. 3. Run time (a) and performance profile (b).

as a baseline for solution quality, as Exhaustive algorithm cannot be applied. For the hybrid algorithm, two pre-screening levels are tested to assess how candidate reduction affects solution quality and runtime, highlighting the method's scalability advantages. This design evaluates whether small-scale performance patterns hold in larger search spaces and which algorithms remain stable and efficient. The results are summarized in Table 2.

From a computational perspective, GBD is consistently fastest, while Hybrid reduces runtime relative to Greedy via candidate pre-screening. SA has moderate runtime but becomes more variable as instance size increases. In terms of solution quality, Hybrid with $k = N/2$ is the most reliable, consistently producing near-optimal outcomes. SA exhibits occasional deviations, and the Hybrid with $k = N/4$ shows minor quality loss at smaller scales from exclusion of high-utility candidates. GBD exhibits the largest relative gaps, likely from looseness in the

Table 2. Comparison of Greedy, Annealing, Hybrid and GBD Algorithms

Candidate	Greedy		SA		Hybrid(N/2)		Hybrid (N/4)		GBD	
	Time (s)	rg (%)	Time (s)	rg (%)	Time (s)	rg (%)	Time (s)	rg (%)	Time (s)	rg (%)
Case 1: Fixed $p = 5$										
100	62.55	0.00	300.76	0.38	52.13	0.00	40.41	4.74	22.29	10.20
200	255.06	0.00	556.32	0.07	212.10	1.39	129.21	9.94	55.26	12.54
300	997.70	0.00	877.01	0.96	634.01	0.00	382.05	1.28	72.04	9.75
400	2718.82	0.00	1619.27	3.41	1847.42	0.00	951.03	0.00	129.14	21.56
500	5157.06	0.00	2285.38	0.48	3405.33	0.00	1720.88	0.00	180.95	17.11

relaxation and limited cut generation in the masterâĂŞsubproblem decomposition, reducing its effectiveness in densely combinatorial settings. Overall, The Hybrid method balances runtime and solution quality, with the pre-screening parameter k providing flexible control over this trade-off.

6 Conclusion and Future Research

This study develops a hybrid framework for CBFL problems, combining behavioral modeling, multi-criteria evaluation, and scale-adaptive solution strategies. The AHP/DEA-greedy algorithm screens candidates via multi-criteria priorities and iteratively refines selections through a greedy search, achieving high solution quality with reduced computation. Computational experiments show the hybrid method consistently attains near-optimal utility across various scales, striking a favorable balance between efficiency and quality, especially for large instances where exhaustive or decomposition-based methods are impractical. The framework provides a practical, scalable approach for facility selection under realistic customer behavior and competition. Future work could consider dynamic demand, social influence or multiperiod planning to enhance applicability.

Acknowledgements. The authors thank anonymous reviewers for their constructive comments. This work was partially supported by XJTLU SURF project (SURF-2025-0146).

References

1. Cheng, M., Wei, W.: An AHP-DEA approach of the bike-sharing spots selection problem in the free-floating bike-sharing system. Discrete Dyn. Nat. Soc. **2020**(15) (2020). https://doi.org/10.1155/2020/7823971
2. Chung, Y.C., Su, I.F., Lee, C.: K-most suitable locations selection. GeoInformatica **22**(4), 661–692 (2018). https://doi.org/10.1007/s10707-018-0318-5
3. Fischetti, M., Ljubić, I., Sinnl, M.: Redesigning benders decomposition for large-scale facility location. Manage. Sci. **63**(7), 2146–2162 (2017). https://doi.org/10.1287/mnsc.2016.2461

4. G.-Tóth, B.: Customer selection rules in competitive facility location. Ann. Mathematicae et Informaticae **60**, 54–63 (2024). https://doi.org/10.33039/ami.2024.02.003
5. Gao, Z., Yoshimoto, K., Ohmori, S.: Application of AHP/DEA to facility layout selection. In: 2010 Third International Joint Conference on Computational Science and Optimization, vol. 2, pp. 252–254 (2010). https://doi.org/10.1109/CSO.2010.237
6. González, B., Rossit, D., Frutos, M., Méndez, M.: Modeling and solving an integrated periodic vehicle routing and capacitated facility location problem in the context of solid waste collection. Ann. Oper. Res. **350**(1), 979–1015 (2025). https://doi.org/10.1007/s10479-025-06626-4
7. Huff, D.L.: Defining and estimating a trading area. J. Mark. **28**(3), 34–38 (1964). https://doi.org/10.2307/1249154
8. Legault, R., Frejinger, E.: A model-free approach for solving choice-based competitive facility location problems using simulation and submodularity. Preprint/working paper. arXiv:2203.11329 (2022)
9. Legault, R., Frejinger, E.: A model-free approach for solving choice-based competitive facility location problems using simulation and submodularity. INFORMS J. Comput. **37**(3), 603–622 (2025). https://doi.org/10.1287/ijoc.2023.0280
10. Lin, Y.H., Tian, Q.: Branch-and-cut approach based on generalized benders decomposition for facility location with limited choice rule. Eur. J. Oper. Res. **293**(1), 109–119 (2021). https://doi.org/10.1016/j.ejor.2020.12.017
11. Lin, Y.H., Tian, Q., Zhao, Y.: Unified framework for choice-based facility location problem. INFORMS J. Comput. **36**(6), 1436–1458 (2024). https://doi.org/10.1287/ijoc.2022.0366
12. Ma, H., Guan, X., Wang, L.: A single-facility competitive location problem in the plane based on customer choice rules. J. Data Inf. Manage. **2**(4), 323–336 (2020). https://doi.org/10.1007/s42488-020-00036-w
13. Ruiz Zúñiga, E., Urenda Moris, M., Syberfeldt, A., Fathi, M., Rubio-Romero, J.C.: A simulation-based optimization methodology for facility layout design in manufacturing. IEEE Access **8**, 163818–163832 (2020). https://doi.org/10.1109/ACCESS.2020.3021753
14. Saaty, T.L.: Decision making – the analytic hierarchy and network processes (AHP/ANP). J. Syst. Sci. Syst. Eng. **13**(1), 1–35 (2004). https://doi.org/10.1007/s11518-006-0151-5
15. Sharma, A., Sharma, A., Jalal, A.S.: Clustering based hybrid approach for facility location problem. Manage. Sci. Lett. **7**, 577–584 (2017). https://doi.org/10.5267/j.msl.2017.8.007
16. Zhou, E., Murray, A.T.: Facility layout and spatial configuration efficiency assessment. Netw. Spat. Econ. (2024). https://doi.org/10.1007/s11067-024-09637-z

Fourier Neural Operator on Implicit Points for PDE Surrogate Modeling

Jiyan Qiu[1,2](✉), PengCheng Shi[1,2], Yuan Wu[1,2], Jian Zhang[1,2], and Xuebin Chi[1,2]

[1] Computer Network Information Center, Chinese Academy of Sciences, Beijing, China
{qiujiyan,chi}@cnic.cn, {yuanwu,zhangjian}@sccas.cn
[2] University of Chinese Academy of Sciences, Beijing, China

Abstract. Recent advances in Fourier Neural Operators (FNOs) have shown strong potential for efficiently approximating solutions of partial differential equations (PDEs). Yet existing FNO architectures are inherently constrained to regularly sampled, structured grids, limiting their applicability in the majority of real-world scenarios that involve irregular meshes and complex geometries. We introduce the Fourier Neural Operator on Implicit Points (IP-FNO), a new framework that lifts these restrictions and enables FNO-style spectral learning on arbitrary geometric domains and irregular discretizations. The core innovation is an Implicit Point (IP) mechanism that establishes a bidirectional mapping between physical fields of arbitrary order or length and a fixed, ordered sequence of implicit points. All spectral (Fourier) operations are performed solely in this implicit point space, decoupling computation from the original mesh topology while retaining rich physical fidelity. Inspired by cross-attention, the IP mechanism constructs fixed-order latent representations that preserve multi-scale field information with linear complexity in the number of input samples. Extensive experiments across solid and fluid mechanics validate the flexibility, expressiveness, and scalability of IP-FNO. In predicting pressure distributions over a complex automotive surface with 400,000 mesh elements, IP-FNO attains a relative L_2 loss of 0.1041, demonstrating robust accuracy and practical viability for large-scale engineering PDE surrogates.

Keywords: Fourier neural operator · Implicit points · Spectral mixing · irregular meshes · PDE solver

1 Introduction

Solving Partial Differential Equations (PDEs) is crucial across numerous engineering and scientific domains, including weather forecasting, seismic analysis, and aerodynamic optimization. Traditional numerical methods often incur massive computational resources and time, making them impractical for high-throughput, repetitive solving. Recently, deep learning approaches have emerged as highly efficient alternatives for rapid PDE solution.

R. C.-W. Wong et al. (Eds.): PAKDD 2026, LNAI 16618, pp. 27–38, 2027.
https://doi.org/10.1007/978-981-92-1947-6_3

Among these, the Fourier Neural Operator (FNO) [11] is widely recognized as one of the most effective methods, achieving significant success in solving PDEs on regular grids due to its superior spectral mixing capabilities. However, FNO is inherently limited to regular grid data, while the repetitive solving on large, irregular meshes remains a dominant source of computational cost in real-world applications.

To address this challenge, existing extensions like Geo-FNO [9] and GINO [10] have introduced geometric mapping mechanisms. Yet, these methods often rely on dense auxiliary point designs or interpolation operations between mismatched manifolds, potentially leading to error accumulation and increased memory overhead. Furthermore, recent studies such as Transolver [9] and IPOT [6] utilize physics-aware attention or inducing points to compress representations and reduce computational complexity, but they still perform expensive attention operations directly on the latent states. This prompts our question: Can we fully leverage FNO's spectral advantage by introducing implicit points to efficiently process physical sequences within the Fourier space ?

Based on this foundation, we propose the Implicit Point-based Fourier Neural Operator (IP-FNO), an efficient and generalized new paradigm for partial differential equation (PDE) solving, as detailed in Fig. 2. IP-FNO learns a small, fixed set of Implicit Points along with an aggregation/inverse aggregation function to map arbitrary, unordered input features (including irregular meshes, point clouds, or geometric descriptors) into a fixed-length, ordered one-dimensional implicit sequence. Subsequently, a lightweight one-dimensional FNO layer performs efficient spectral mixing on this sequence. The inverse aggregation process finally distributes the updated features back to the original points.

Our framework is validated across diverse tasks, including elasticity, plasticity, Darcy flow, and a complex automotive mesh comprising approximately 400,000 points. Results demonstrate that IP-FNO not only enables effective processing of irregular geometries but also significantly surpasses state-of-the-art methods in both prediction accuracy and training speed.

Our contributions can be summarized as follows:

1. Implicit Ordering for FNO: We introduce an implicit point aggregation mechanism that, for the first time, allows the highly efficient spectral operator FNO to learn on unordered and irregular geometric structures.
2. Unified One-dimensional Latent Spectral Space: We propose to unify the function spaces of one-dimensional and high-dimensional (or irregular) inputs by mapping them to a shared one-dimensional implicit sequence, enabling highly efficient Fourier spectral mixing.
3. Scalability and Accuracy Improvement: IP-FNO achieves superior results in multiple complex engineering and physics tasks, demonstrating its outstanding scalability and higher prediction accuracy when dealing with large-scale irregular meshes. Our Contributions

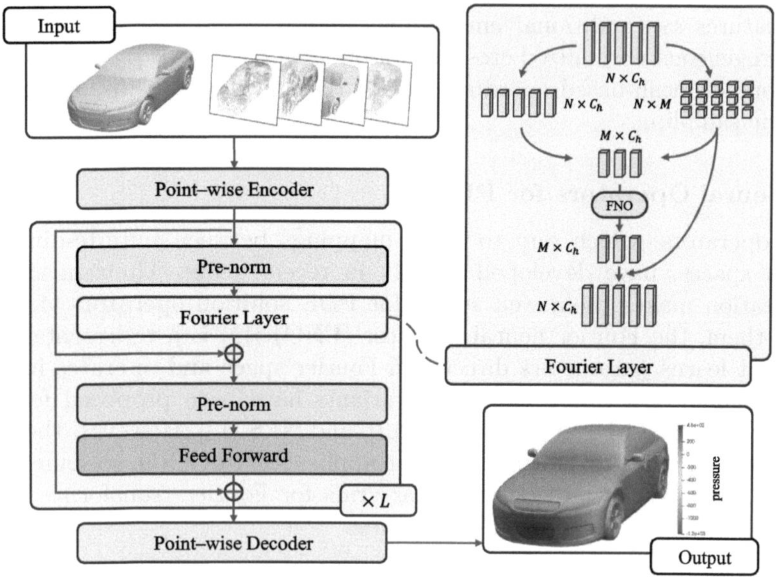

Fig. 1. Overview of the IP-FNO framework. **Left:** Overall structure of the network. The input point representation is encoded into the hidden space, after which the point embedding is sequentially processed through L same submodules. Each submodule consists of a Fourier block and a FFN block. Finally, the point-wise decoder maps the point embedding to the output space. **Right:** Detailed illustration of the Fourier block. First, the inputs are mapped into two matrices: a feature representation (like value vector in Transformer) and a mapping score (similar to attention score in Transformer). Here, we do not explicitly construct query and key vectors, but instead directly compute the learned score. The FNO is applied to the implicit point embeddings. The learned score is also used to reconstruct original point representation from implicit points.

2 Related Work

2.1 Attention-Based Solver

Transformer architectures, due to their strong capability in modeling highly nonlinear problems and handling arbitrary geometric input formats, have been widely used for solving PDEs [6–8,18]. However, standard dot-product attention is computationally expensive on large grids, and even linear-complexity variants [3,17] still face efficiency challenges.

Transolver [23] proposes Physics-Attention to learn physical interactions on a set of learned slices and applies attention to physics-aware tokens. FactFormer [8] and IFactFormer [24] adopt factorized attention for multidimensional physical decomposition and time-dependent systems, respectively. IPOT [6] performs attention on inducing points in a latent space instead of dense input discretizations, achieving more efficient computation.

OFormer [7] and its variants decouple arbitrary input functions from query points. GNOT [2] extends OFormer to multiple input functions by encoding input features as conditional embeddings and relating them to query points via heterogeneous normalized cross-attention layers. CORAL [16] overcomes the limitations of mesh-based coordinate networks and flexibly supports arbitrary geometric sampling.

2.2 Neural Operators for PDEs

Neural operators, which aim to learn mappings between infinite-dimensional function spaces, have developed rapidly in recent years. Their invariance to discretization makes them well suited for PDE solution operators [4,9,15,20]. Among them, the Fourier neural operator (FNO) [11] is a representative approach that learns parameters directly in Fourier space and operates in the frequency domain. On this basis, many variants have been proposed for diverse PDEs, such as FNO-DEQ [14], GINO [12], and NFS [13]. However, the requirement of regular-grid transforms limits the applicability of FNO, so some methods project irregular-grid data onto regular grids for Fourier transforms and then map the solutions back to irregular meshes.

3 Preliminaries

Consider that the governing equation is defined on the Euclidean space $\Omega \subset \mathbb{R}^d$, where d is the spatial dimension. The input function space over Ω may has multiple types, including geometric coordinates, condition parameters and so on. Assuming that the continuous spatial domain Ω is discretized into N points, each point could be represented as $a_i \in \mathbb{R}^{C_{in}}$. The inputs can be expressed in matrix form $A \in \mathbb{R}^{N \times C_{in}}$. C_{in} is the input channel. The output function space $B \subset \mathbb{R}^{C_{out}}$ over Ω contains physical variables of interest, like pressure, velocity. It should be noted that discretization of input domain may has various forms, for instance, regular grid for Darcy flow and irregular mesh such as flow around airfoil and pipes. In addition, for irregular meshes, the number of mesh points may vary between different cases.

The objective is to update the learned parameters in the model to learn the operator $g(a) = b$ over Ω. The goal is achieved through minimizing the error between the model output $\hat{B} \in \mathbb{R}^{N \times C_{out}}$ and the ground truth $B \in \mathbb{R}^{N \times C_{out}}$. B is obtained by numerical simulation or observation. The parameters in the neural network are updated according to the gradients of loss to parameters. For time-dependent system, the inputs $A \in \mathbb{R}^{N \times C_{in}}$ and outputs $B \in \mathbb{R}^{N \times C_{out}}$ are respectively initial physical state and physical state after a fixed time step.

The data-driven model only learns the relationship from the inputs feature A and outputs B. It does not need to know the specific form of the equation. The model trains on large-scale data and can rapidly infer in the unseen case.

4 Methodology

We follow the encoder-processor-decoder structure as the backbone to design our model. Following we present our model in detail.

4.1 Overview Structure

The IP-FNO framework, as shown in Fig. 1, consists of three main components: a point-wise encoder, L stacked processing blocks, and a point-wise decoder. The input features (e.g., mesh coordinates, physical fields) are first embedded by the encoder MLP into a hidden space $E : \mathbb{R}^{C_{in}} \rightarrow \mathbb{R}^{C_h}$.

Each processing block contains a pre-normalization layer, a Fourier layer, and a feed-forward layer, with residual connections after each sub-layer. The update rule for the i-th layer is:

$$\begin{aligned} l'_i &= l_i + \text{FNO}(\text{Norm}(l_i)) \\ l_{i+1} &= l'_i + \text{FFN}(\text{Norm}(l'_i)) \end{aligned} \tag{1}$$

In the Fourier layer, input features $N \times C$ are mapped to M implicit points ($M \ll N$) using a learnable mapping, then processed by FNO in the frequency domain ($M \times G$), and remapped back to the original points. This enables the model to extract global frequency information even for irregular meshes. The mapping and remapping operations correspond to the arrows and blocks in the right part of the figure.

The decoder MLP projects the final hidden representations to the output space $D : \mathbb{R}^{C_h} \rightarrow \mathbb{R}^{C_{out}}$, producing predictions such as pressure or velocity. The overall structure supports flexible input geometries and efficient learning of complex physical relationships, with all key symbols and operations matching those in the diagram.

4.2 Mapping Stage

Inspired by scaled dot-product attention [21] and cross-attention [5], we aggregate input features $\{x_i\}_{i=1}^N$, $x_i \in \mathbb{R}^{C_h}$, to M implicit points ($M \ll N$) via learnable mappings. Value vectors $f(x) \in \mathbb{R}^{C_h}$ and mapping scores $g(x) \in \mathbb{R}^M$ are computed by linear transformations. The implicit point representation is:

$$Mapping(X) = \text{Softmax}(g(X)^T) \times f(X) \tag{2}$$

Here, $s_{i,j}$ denotes the importance of the j-th input to the i-th implicit point. The mapping is independent of input order, and the output is a weighted sum of value vectors, enriching the implicit points.

4.3 Fourier Layer

We apply a 1D Fourier neural operator (FNO) to the implicit points $P \in \mathbb{R}^{M \times C_h}$, regardless of whether the original space Ω is 2D or 3D. The FNO extracts main frequency components:

$$v_{l+1}(p) = F^{-1}(P(F)v_l)(p) + Qv_l(p) \tag{3}$$

where F and F^{-1} are Fourier and inverse Fourier transforms, P is a linear transform in frequency domain, and Q is a bias in spatial domain. FNO [11] is well supported and connects frequency and spatial domains via trainable parameters.

Remark (Why FNO on implicit points). *Implicit points possess frequency modes, and their representation in the frequency domain can be unified as:*

$$c_i^{IP} = \int_S \int_\Omega W(u, x, t) u(x, t) \phi_i^{IP}(s) \, d\Omega \, dS \tag{4}$$

where $u(x, t)$ is the input feature, W is the mapping weight, and ϕ_i^{IP} is the i-th mode on implicit points. This shows that the Fourier coefficients on implicit points are a learnable mapping of the original coefficients, enabling FNO to operate on implicit points.

4.4 Remapping Stage

The remapping stage uses the mapping score s from Sect. 4.2 to reconstruct the original space Ω from implicit points $P \in \mathbb{R}^{M \times C}$ and mapping score $S \in \mathbb{R}^{N \times M}$, via a linear weighted sum.

4.5 Multi-subspace Learning

To enhance expressiveness, the hidden dimension C_h is split into k subspaces ($C_h = kC_k$). Each subspace learns its own mapping score s_i and value v_i in parallel. The outputs are concatenated and fed to the Fourier layer:

$$\text{MultiSubspace}(V, S) = \text{Concat}(s_1^T v_1, \ldots, s_k^T v_k) \tag{5}$$

Softmax is applied independently in each subspace. This multi-subspace approach, similar to multi-head attention [21], improves model capacity and reduces loss.

The encoder and decoder are both implemented as multilayer perceptrons (MLPs), acting independently on each point. The encoder projects low-dimensional input features to a higher-dimensional hidden space, while the decoder maps hidden representations to the output space. Formally, the encoder can be written as:

$$l_0 = F(x, W_E) \tag{6}$$

where $x \in \mathbb{R}^{C_{in}}$, $l_0 \in \mathbb{R}^{C_h}$, F is the MLP, and W_E are learnable parameters. The output is $L_0 \in \mathbb{R}^{N \times C_h}$.

The decoder is similarly defined:

$$y = G(l_L, W_D) \tag{7}$$

where l_L is the output of the last block, G is the MLP, and W_D are decoder parameters. The output shape is $N \times C_{out}$, and C_{out} is task-dependent.

The network is trained to minimize the loss between predicted output Y' and ground truth Y:

$$\mathcal{L} = \text{Loss}(Y', Y) \tag{8}$$

where $Y' = N \times C_{out}$.

Normalization is crucial for stable training. RMSNorm is efficient for standard benchmarks, while LayerNorm is preferred for large-scale tasks. Residual connections after each sub-layer help gradients propagate and mitigate vanishing gradients, which is essential for deep networks.

A key design choice is mapping all input points, regardless of their spatial arrangement or dimension, to a fixed set of M implicit points. This enables the FNO layer to operate in the frequency domain, even when the input mesh is irregular or non-uniform. The mapping is learnable and independent for each input point, ensuring flexibility and generalization across different domains.

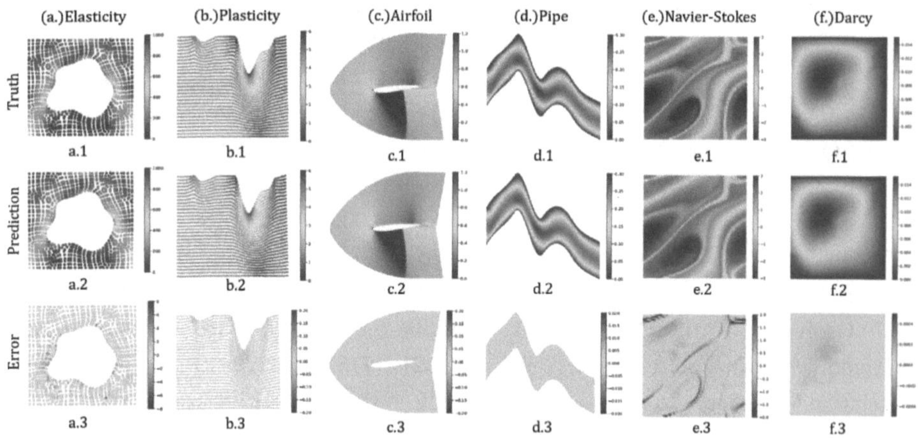

Fig. 2. Visualization of IP-FNO prediction. The first line is the ground truth. The middle line indicates the model's output. The bottle line is the error between the two.

5 Experiments

In this section, we present extensive experiments to validate the effectiveness of our method across several benchmarks. In addition, we also validate it on the prediction of car surface pressure.

5.1 Experiment Setting and Evaluation Metrics

All experiments are conducted on a single Nvidia A100 GPU with 80GB of memory. Our protocol is implemented using PyTorch 2.4.0, alongside CUDA 12.2 and Python 3.9.19. For optimization, we use AdamW optimizer with OneCycleLR learning rate scheduler. We train 500 epochs for standard benchmarks, 200 epochs for car dataset.

We use the relative L_2 error as the evaluation metric, which is defined as:

$$Relative\ L_2 = \frac{1}{D}\sum_{i=1}^{D}\frac{\| u_i - \hat{u}_i \|}{\| u_i \|} \tag{9}$$

where u_i represents the truth physical field, and $\hat{u}_i$ is the predicted field from the model. D is the scale of dataset. The objective of model optimization is to minimize the relative L_2.

Table 1. Comparison of Relative L2 error on standard benchmarks. We evaluate the performance of our model separately on solid and fluid mechanics tasks. The dimensions of the input data are indicated below the dataset name. Parentheses indicate that the input is on a regular grid, otherwise it is irregular. The lower the relative l2 error indicates better performance.

Model	Solid		Fluid			
	Elasticity	Plasticity	Airfoil	Pipe	Navier-Stokes	Darcy
	972	(101,31)	(221, 51)	(129,129)	(64,64)	(85,85)
GEO-FNO	0.0229	0.0074	0.0138	0.0067	0.1556	0.0108
F-FNO	0.0263	0.0047	0.0078	0.0070	0.2322	0.0077
LSM	0.0218	0.0025	0.0059	0.0050	0.1535	0.0065
Galerkin	0.0240	0.0120	0.0118	0.0098	0.1401	0.0084
GNOT	0.0086	0.0336	0.0076	0.0047	0.1380	0.0105
Transolver	0.0064	0.0012	0.0053	**0.0033**	0.0900	**0.0057**
IFNOsolver	**0.0054**	**0.0006**	**0.0050**	0.0050	**0.0739**	0.0065
Trainable Params	3091777	5222596	5171521	17487425	4272449	4270145
Relative Variation	−16.9%	−50%	−5.6%	51.5%	−17.8%	14.0%

5.2 Dataset Description

To demonstrate the accuracy and scalability of our method, we choose several datasets spanning various branches of mechanics, including elasticity, plasticity, aerodynamics and so on. The dataset encompass a diverse range of geometries, such as point clouds, structured meshes, and unstructured meshes.

In addition to standard benchmarks, we also conduct experiments for the prediction of car surface pressure. We adjust the shape of the car based on the public high-fidelity car shape using modeling tool Blender. Each car has about 400k meshes. Then we use the OpenFOAM for numerical simulation. We totally generate 500 car surface pressure, 450 for training and 50 for testing.

5.3 Baselines

We compare IP-FNO with a range of representative baselines, including operator-based models (Geo-FNO [9], F-FNO [19], LSM [22]) and transformer-based models (Galerkin [1], GNOT [2], Transolver [23]). These baselines cover various approaches such as mapping irregular domains, factorized Fourier transforms, neural spectral blocks, efficient attention mechanisms, and physics-aware attention.

5.4 The Results on the Benchmarks

The main results are presented in Table 1. Bolded scores in the table highlight best performance for each dataset. We also provide the number of trainable parameters and relative variation. The relative variation is calculated as: Relative variation = (Our score − Best score in baselines)/Best score in baselines.

The results of the previous method are originated from Transolver [23]. The result shows that IP-FNO outperforms the previous methods on several standard benchmarks, while achieving near state-of-the-art performance in others.

In the field of solid mechanics, our method exhibits superior accuracy, particularly on the Plasticity dataset, where it reduces error by nearly 50% compared to the best baseline score. Additionally, our approach decreases the prediction error by approximately 5.6% on the Airfoil dataset and 17.8% on the Navier-Stokes dataset. However, on the Pipe and Darcy benchmarks, IP-FNO does not achieve the highest performance.

These results have demonstrated the scalability and of our model. We also visualize the predicted results alongside the ground truth and highlight the differences in Fig. 2. Extensive experiments indicate that our method serves as an effective framework for surrogate modeling. Moreover, they demonstrate that the implicit points generated by our approach successfully capture the key complex information within the input functions.

5.5 The Results on the Car Dataset

Beyond the standard benchmarks, we further validate our model on a large-scale dataset of 3D cars. We generate 500 high-fidelity 3D cars by modifying the appearance of open-source car models and perform numerical simulations using the OpenFOAM tool. The objective of this experiment is to predict surface pressure based on the car's geometry. Each car model consists of approximately 400,000 mesh points.

Table 2. Comparison of test loss using Transolver and IP-FNO trained on high-fidelity cars.

Model	Test loss	training time	Params
Transolver	0.0969	33.9h	3885377
IP-FNO	0.1041	22.7h	3340993

We compare IP-FNO with Transolver in terms of test loss, training speed, and the number of trainable parameters, as detailed in Table 2. For the experiments, we randomly select 450 samples for training and 50 for testing. The test loss is measured using the relative L2 loss, as defined in Eq. 9.

Both models are trained for 200 epochs, using the same optimizer, learning rate scheduler, and initial learning rate to ensure consistency. Transolver is equipped with the hidden dimension of 256, while IP-FNO with 128. As shown in Table 2, IP-FNO achieves a relative l2 error of 0.1041, which is 0.0072 higher than Transolver. The test error between the two models is quite close. IP-FNO completes the training stage in 22.7 h, making it 1.49 times faster than Transolver, while also requiring fewer trainable parameters. IP-FNO performs a better cost-accuracy trade-off in the car surface pressure task.

5.6 Ablation Experiments

We also conducted ablation studies to analyze the influence of both the number of implicit points and the remaining modes in the FNO on the model's performance. We conduct experiments on Darcy dataset. Parameters are primarily governed by the hidden dimension, with minimal dependence on the number of implicit points.

Table 3. Comparison of test loss in different number of implicit points and remaining modes on Darcy.

# of IP	# of modes	# of params	test loss
256	32	5205057	0.0083
128	32	5187649	0.0070
128	18	4270145	**0.0065**
64	18	4261441	0.0076
64	10	3737153	0.0072

For consistency, we maintain the hidden size of 128, with 8 layers, 8 subspaces across all experiments. As illustrated in Table 3, increasing the number of implicit points does not necessarily result in lower loss. The findings suggest that the number of modes should not be large. It needs several experiments to find the optimal hyperparameters.

6 Conclusion

In this paper, we propose the IP-FNO framework, a novel and efficient method based on Fourier transform. Inspired by cross-attention mechanism, our method directly learn the mapping score between implicit points and input points. We construct the implicit point representation from value vectors and learned score in a way similar to cross-attention. The implicit points only have representation in hidden high-dimensional space and have no corresponding points in Euclidean space. In addition, IP-FNO is flexible with form of inputs and the order of input meshes. Any input order will result in the same representation of a set of implicit points.

The implicit points have quantity far less than the input scale, which control the computational complexity. We adopt the FNO on the implicit point embedding to extract the main modal information in frequency domain. To improve the generalization and representation ability of the model, implicit point embedding is a concatenation of multiple subspace expression. Extensive experiments has demonstrate that IP-FNO has excellent performance on standard benchmarks and car dataset. **Limitation:** During our experiment, we find that IP-FNO is not very stable. There is fluctuation in the loss decrease during the early stages of training. In the future, we will continue to explore in the direction of IP-FNO.

Acknowledgments. This work was supported by the National Key Research & Development Program of China (No. 2023YFB3001900).

References

1. Cao, S.: Choose a transformer: fourier or galerkin. In: Advances in Neural Information Processing Systems, vol. 34, pp. 24924–24940 (2021)
2. Hao, Z., et al.: GNOT: a general neural operator transformer for operator learning. In: ICML (2023)
3. Kitaev, N., Kaiser, L., Levskaya, A.: Reformer: the efficient transformer. In: ICLR (2020)
4. Kovachki, N., et al.: Neural operator: learning maps between function spaces with applications to PDEs. J. Mach. Learn. Res. **24**(89), 1–97 (2023)
5. Lee, K.H., Chen, X., Hua, G., Hu, H., He, X.: Stacked cross attention for image-text matching. In: Proceedings of the European Conference on Computer Vision (ECCV), pp. 201–216 (2018)
6. Lee, S., Oh, T.: Inducing point operator transformer: a flexible and scalable architecture for solving PDEs. In: Proceedings of the AAAI Conference on Artificial Intelligence, vol. 38, pp. 153–161 (2024)
7. Li, Z., Meidani, K., Farimani, A.B.: Transformer for partial differential equations' operator learning. Trans. Mach. Learn. Res. (2023). https://openreview.net/forum?id=EPPqt3uERT
8. Li, Z., Shu, D., Barati Farimani, A.: Scalable transformer for PDE surrogate modeling. In: Advances in Neural Information Processing Systems, vol. 36 (2024)
9. Li, Z., Huang, D.Z., Liu, B., Anandkumar, A.: Fourier neural operator with learned deformations for PDEs on general geometries. J. Mach. Learn. Res. **24**(388), 1–26 (2023)
10. Li, Z., et al.: Geometry-informed neural operator for large-scale 3D PDEs. In: Advances in Neural Information Processing Systems, vol. 36 (2024)
11. Li, Z., et al.: Fourier neural operator for parametric partial differential equations. In: International Conference on Learning Representations (2020)
12. Li, Z., et al.: Geometry-informed neural operator for large-scale 3D PDEs. arXiv preprint arXiv:2309.00583 (2023)
13. Lin, H., et al.: Non-equispaced fourier neural solvers for PDEs. In: ICLR 2023 Workshop on Physics for Machine Learning (2023)
14. Marwah, T., Pokle, A., Kolter, J.Z., Lipton, Z.C., Lu, J., Risteski, A.: Deep equilibrium based neural operators for steady-state PDEs. In: Thirty-seventh Conference on Neural Information Processing Systems (2023)

15. Rahman, M.A., Ross, Z.E., Azizzadenesheli, K.: U-no: U-shaped neural operators. In: TMLR (2023)
16. Serrano, L., et al.: Operator learning with neural fields: tackling PDEs on general geometries. In: Advances in Neural Information Processing Systems, vol. 36 (2024)
17. Shen, Z., Zhang, M., Zhao, H., Yi, S., Li, H.: Efficient attention: attention with linear complexities. In: Proceedings of the IEEE/CVF Winter Conference on Applications of Computer Vision, pp. 3531–3539 (2021)
18. Takamoto, M., Alesiani, F., Niepert, M.: Learning neural PDE solvers with parameter-guided channel attention. In: International Conference on Machine Learning, pp. 33448–33467. PMLR (2023)
19. Tran, A., Mathews, A., Xie, L., Ong, C.S.: Factorized fourier neural operators. In: The Eleventh International Conference on Learning Representations (2021)
20. Tripura, T., Chakraborty, S.: Wavelet neural operator for solving parametric partial differential equations in computational mechanics problems. Comput. Methods Appl. Mech. Eng. **404**, 115783 (2023)
21. Vaswani, A.: Attention is all you need. In: Advances in Neural Information Processing Systems (2017)
22. Wu, H., Hu, T., Luo, H., Wang, J., Long, M.: Solving high-dimensional PDEs with latent spectral models. In: Proceedings of the 40th International Conference on Machine Learning, pp. 37417–37438 (2023)
23. Wu, H., Luo, H., Wang, H., Wang, J., Long, M.: Transolver: a fast transformer solver for PDEs on general geometries. In: International Conference on Machine Learning (2024)
24. Yang, H., Li, Z., Wang, X., Wang, J.: An implicit factorized transformer with applications to fast prediction of three-dimensional turbulence. Theor. Appl. Mech. Lett. 100527 (2024)

Bridging Statistical Seasonality and Diffusion-Based Deep Learning for Multivariate Time Series Forecasting

Sarinna Maplook(✉) and Koji Eguchi

Graduate School of Advanced Science and Engineering, Hiroshima University, Higashihiroshima, Japan
d230510@hiroshima-u.ac.jp, eguchi@acm.org

Abstract. Forecasting multivariate time series with strong seasonal patterns and nonlinear dependencies is challenging for both statistical and deep learning models. Classical approaches like SARIMA decompose periodic structure in an interpretable way but cannot handle complex nonlinear interactions, whereas neural architectures often treat seasonality implicitly and may struggle with phase alignment. We propose SAD-X, a hybrid framework that combines explicit seasonal extraction via SARIMA with nonlinear residual modeling using xLSTM, enhanced by Future Mixup augmentation and diffusion-based refinement. The framework separates seasonal structure from nonlinear dynamics, then combines predictions through validation-optimized adaptive weights. SARIMA isolates interpretable 24-hour and weekly cycles; xLSTM captures residual nonlinear patterns; and diffusion refinement improves forecast consistency through multi-source conditioning. Experiments on 43,848 hourly observations from Chiang Mai show that SAD-X achieves consistent improvements over the considered baselines, including TimeDiff, transformer architectures, and standalone statistical models. Ablation results show that explicit seasonal decomposition and adaptive fusion substantially reduce forecast errors, especially at longer horizons. These findings indicate the benefit of combining classical statistical modeling with modern deep learning for complex time series forecasting.

Keywords: Time series forecasting · SARIMA · xLSTM · Diffusion models · Hybrid modeling · Seasonal decomposition

1 Introduction

Accurate forecasting of environmental time series like hourly $PM_{2.5}$ concentrations is critical for public health and environmental management. These series show a mix of strong, predictable seasonal patterns—for example, daily and weekly cycles—and nonlinear dependencies on external factors like weather [3, 7]. This combination of structured seasonality and nonlinear dynamics makes it hard for any single modeling approach to work well in all situations.

R. C.-W. Wong et al. (Eds.): PAKDD 2026, LNAI 16618, pp. 39–51, 2027.
https://doi.org/10.1007/978-981-92-1947-6_4

Classical statistical models like SARIMA are good at decomposing and modeling periodic structure, and they provide interpretable insight into seasonality. However, their linear form limits their ability to capture nonlinear interactions between variables, which often drive the system [3,4]. Modern deep learning architectures, including Transformers [13,22,26] and diffusion-based models [14,16], can learn complex nonlinear patterns, but they typically treat seasonality as something to discover implicitly rather than model explicitly. As a result, dominant periodic signals may not be fully used, and interpretability suffers. Even recent advances like xLSTM [2], which improve long-range dependency modeling, do not directly address explicit seasonal decomposition.

Our view is that forcing a single model to handle both deterministic seasonality and stochastic nonlinearity is unnecessarily limiting. Instead, we use a hybrid decomposition strategy that lets different components focus on what they do best. The proposed framework, which we call SAD-X (Seasonal–Adaptive Diffusion with xLSTM), first uses SARIMA to explicitly isolate and forecast interpretable seasonal components. The residual series, with dominant periodic patterns removed, is then modeled by an xLSTM network. To improve robustness under distributional shift, we incorporate Future Mixup and an adaptive fusion mechanism with validation-optimized mixing weights. Finally, a diffusion-based model refines the fused forecast through a denoising stage, using all component outputs as conditioning information.

Contributions. This work introduces SAD-X, a hybrid seasonal–residual forecasting framework that unifies classical decomposition with modern deep sequence modeling and diffusion-based refinement. Our main contributions are:

1. **A structured decomposition–refinement architecture.** We design SAD-X as a six-stage pipeline for multivariate time series where SARIMA extracts interpretable daily and weekly components, AR processes capture short-term linear persistence, and xLSTM models nonlinear residual dynamics. This explicit functional decomposition goes beyond ad hoc combinations of statistical and neural forecasts.
2. **Adaptive multi-source fusion with validation-optimized weights.** We introduce an adaptive mixing mechanism that balances the contributions of SARIMA, AR, persistence, Future Mixup, and xLSTM components. The mixing weights, selected via Bayesian optimization on the validation set, provide data-driven balancing across seasonal, linear, and nonlinear signals, rather than relying on fixed or rule-based fusion strategies.
3. **Diffusion-based refinement conditioned on multi-component forecasts.** We design a conditioning scheme that feeds the fused prediction together with individual component outputs into a diffusion denoiser, which performs structured refinement rather than simple averaging. This improves long-horizon stability and reduces accumulated phase errors.
4. **Consistent empirical improvements with statistical significance.** On 43,848 h of meteorological data, SAD-X achieves 12.2–19.0% MAE reduction over strong baselines including TimeDiff, Autoformer, Transformers,

and standalone statistical models. Wilcoxon signed-rank tests confirm that improvements are significant at $p < 0.001$.

5. **Practical insight into when hybrid decomposition is beneficial.** Through ablation and error-correlation analyses, we show that (i) seasonal extraction stabilizes long-horizon forecasts, (ii) SARIMA and xLSTM errors are negatively correlated, and (iii) diffusion refinement is particularly effective under distributional shift. These findings provide empirical insight into scenarios where hybrids like SAD-X may be advantageous compared with purely neural architectures.

Summary of Novelty. Compared with many existing hybrid approaches, SAD-X integrates functional decomposition, adaptive integration, and diffusion-based refinement within a unified pipeline. This results in a more structured hybrid design compared with simple combinations of statistical and neural components.

2 Related Work

Statistical Time Series Models. SARIMA extends ARIMA with multiplicative seasonal components, providing interpretable decomposition [3,7]. These models work well for univariate series with clear periodicity, but struggle with nonlinear multivariate relationships.

Deep Learning for Time Series. LSTM networks [6] capture temporal dependencies through gated recurrence, but can suffer from vanishing gradients. xLSTM [2] extends LSTMs with exponential gating and matrix memory, improving training stability and long-range modeling.

Transformer architectures [20] use self-attention for global temporal context. PatchTST [13], Informer [26], and Autoformer [22] apply attention mechanisms efficiently for time series. Despite these advances, seasonality is typically handled implicitly without explicit decomposition.

Diffusion Models. Denoising diffusion probabilistic models [5,17] learn to reverse a noising process. TimeDiff [16] and TimeGrad [14] apply diffusion to time series forecasting. CSDI [18] uses conditional score-based diffusion for imputation tasks. While powerful, these models lack explicit seasonal decomposition.

Hybrid and Augmentation Approaches. Hybrid methods combining statistical and machine learning models have a long history [9,15,25]. Future Mixup [16] adapts Mixup [24] to time series by interpolating model predictions with ground truth during training:

$$\begin{aligned} \mathbf{f}_{\text{cond}} &= \mathcal{F}(\mathbf{X}_{\text{look}}) \in \mathbb{R}^{F\times D}, \\ \mathbf{Z}_{\text{mixup}} &= \mathbf{m}_k \odot \mathbf{f}_{\text{cond}} + (1 - \mathbf{m}_k) \odot \mathbf{Y}_{\text{target}}, \end{aligned} \tag{1}$$

where $\odot$ denotes the Hadamard (element-wise) product; $\mathbf{m}_k \in \mathbb{R}^{F\times D}$ is an element-wise mixing matrix with entries drawn independently from the uniform distribution on $[0, 1)$, providing continuous interpolation weights matching the dimensions of $\mathbf{f}_{\text{cond}}$ and $\mathbf{Y}_{\text{target}}$. Here F denotes the forecast horizon and D the number of variables, defined formally in Sect. 4. Other augmentation techniques such as CutMix [23] have also been explored for regularization in computer vision, though their application to time series remains limited.

Relation to SAD-X. SAD-X differs from prior hybrids through explicit functional decomposition (SARIMA for seasonality, xLSTM for nonlinear residuals), adaptive fusion with validation-optimized weights, and diffusion refinement with multi-component conditioning.

3 Background

SARIMA. Let B denote the backshift operator ($By_t = y_{t-1}$) and s the seasonal period. A SARIMA model for a univariate time series $\{y_t\}$ can be written as

$$\phi(B)\,\Phi(B^s)\,(1-B)^d\,(1-B^s)^{D'}\,y_t = \theta(B)\,\Theta(B^s)\,\epsilon_t, \tag{2}$$

where $\phi(\cdot)$ and $\Phi(\cdot)$ are non-seasonal and seasonal autoregressive polynomials, $\theta(\cdot)$ and $\Theta(\cdot)$ are moving-average polynomials, d and D' are differencing orders, $\epsilon_t \sim \mathcal{N}(0, \sigma^2)$ is white noise, and $s \in \{24, 168\}$ captures hourly and weekly cycles [3].

xLSTM. xLSTM [2] enhances standard LSTM [6] through exponential input gating and matrix memory. For input $\boldsymbol{x}_t \in \mathbb{R}^D$ with D the input dimension, hidden state $\boldsymbol{h}_t \in \mathbb{R}^H$, and cell state $\mathbf{C}_t \in \mathbb{R}^H$ with H the hidden dimension:

$$\begin{aligned}
\boldsymbol{i}_t &= \exp(\mathbf{W}_i[\boldsymbol{h}_{t-1}, \boldsymbol{x}_t] + \boldsymbol{b}_i),\\
\boldsymbol{f}_t &= \sigma(\mathbf{W}_f[\boldsymbol{h}_{t-1}, \boldsymbol{x}_t] + \boldsymbol{b}_f),\\
\boldsymbol{o}_t &= \sigma(\mathbf{W}_o[\boldsymbol{h}_{t-1}, \boldsymbol{x}_t] + \boldsymbol{b}_o),\\
\tilde{\mathbf{C}}_t &= \tanh(\mathbf{W}_C[\boldsymbol{h}_{t-1}, \boldsymbol{x}_t] + \boldsymbol{b}_C),\\
\mathbf{C}_t &= \boldsymbol{f}_t \odot \mathbf{C}_{t-1} + \boldsymbol{i}_t \odot \tilde{\mathbf{C}}_t,\\
\boldsymbol{h}_t &= \boldsymbol{o}_t \odot \tanh(\mathbf{C}_t),
\end{aligned} \tag{3}$$

where exponential input gating improves gradient flow and numerical stability.

Diffusion Models. Following Ho et al. [5], the forward process gradually adds Gaussian noise,

$$q(\boldsymbol{x}_t \mid \boldsymbol{x}_{t-1}) = \mathcal{N}\big(\sqrt{\alpha_t}\boldsymbol{x}_{t-1}, (1-\alpha_t)\mathbf{I}\big), \tag{4}$$

and the reverse process learns to denoise via

$$p_\theta(\boldsymbol{x}_{t-1} \mid \boldsymbol{x}_t) = \mathcal{N}\big(\boldsymbol{\mu}_\theta(\boldsymbol{x}_t, t), \boldsymbol{\Sigma}_\theta\big), \tag{5}$$

where $\alpha_t \in (0, 1]$ is the noise-schedule parameter at step t that controls the signal-to-noise ratio; larger t corresponds to a smaller α_t and hence more added noise. The specific schedule (e.g., cosine) is defined when the model is instantiated (see Stage 6 in Sect. 4). $\boldsymbol{\mu}_\theta$ is predicted by a neural network trained to estimate the noise component.

Future Mixup. Mixup [24] performs data augmentation by interpolating between training samples. Future Mixup [16] adapts this to time series forecasting by mixing model predictions with ground truth targets as described above, which exposes the model to a continuum of intermediate trajectories and improves robustness.

4 Methodology

Problem Formulation. Given a multivariate time series $\mathbf{X} \in \mathbb{R}^{T \times D}$ with T timesteps and D variables, the task is to predict $\hat{\mathbf{Y}} \in \mathbb{R}^{F \times D}$ over forecast horizon F using a lookback window $\mathbf{X}_{\text{look}} \in \mathbb{R}^{L \times D}$ of length L.

4.1 Architecture Overview

Design Rationale. SAD-X separates deterministic seasonal structure from nonlinear dynamics and refines the resulting forecasts in a probabilistic way. Rather than asking a single model to learn all aspects of the signal, we use functional decomposition where:

- **SARIMA** explicitly models linear seasonal components at hourly and weekly frequencies, yielding interpretable seasonal forecasts and residuals with reduced periodic structure.
- **xLSTM** operates on the residual dynamics and the multivariate lookback window to capture nonlinear temporal dependencies and cross-variable interactions.
- **AR** captures very short-term linear persistence (1–3 lags), complementing SARIMA's focus on seasonal cycles ($s \in \{24, 168\}$). While SARIMA models periodic structure, AR emphasizes immediate temporal continuity at recent observations.
- **Adaptive fusion** combines these components via validation-optimized mixing weights, which lets the model emphasize different signals under varying conditions.
- **Diffusion-based refinement** takes the fused forecast and component outputs as conditioning information and performs a final denoising step.

This produces a hierarchical pipeline: seasonal extraction, nonlinear residual modeling, adaptive integration, and refinement.

Six-Stage Pipeline. The overall SAD-X framework consists of six stages.

Stage 1: Data Preparation. We apply adaptive imputation following standard practice [10]: linear interpolation for short gaps (up to two hours), cubic splines for intermediate gaps, and seasonal means for longer gaps. Outliers detected by the interquartile range criterion are replaced with median values. All continuous variables are standardized component-wise via

$$x_t^{(i)} = \frac{x_{\text{raw},t}^{(i)} - \mu^{(i)}}{\sigma^{(i)}}, \quad i = 1, \dots, D, \tag{6}$$

where $x_{\text{raw},t}^{(i)}$ is the raw value of variable i at time t, and $\mu^{(i)}, \sigma^{(i)}$ are the training-set mean and standard deviation of variable i.

Stage 2: SARIMA Seasonal Extraction. For each variable $j \in \{1, \ldots, D\}$, we select SARIMA orders $(p, d, q) \times (P, D', Q')_s$ using AIC minimization [1] over a small grid of candidate orders and seasonal periods $s \in \{24, 168\}$. We estimate models by maximum likelihood and check residuals using the Ljung–Box test [11]. The resulting seasonal forecasts form $\mathbf{Z}_{\text{SARIMA}} \in \mathbb{R}^{F \times D}$, which capture interpretable daily and weekly structure.

Stage 3: Autoregressive Baseline. To capture very short-term linear structure, we fit a separate AR(p) model for each variable:

$$y_t^{(j)} = c^{(j)} + \sum_{i=1}^{p} \phi_i^{(j)} y_{t-i}^{(j)} + \epsilon_t^{(j)}, \quad j = 1, \ldots, D, \tag{7}$$

with p chosen by AIC on the training set. This produces $\mathbf{Z}_{\text{AR}} \in \mathbb{R}^{F \times D}$, which emphasizes recent temporal persistence.

Stage 4: xLSTM Nonlinear Processing. We process the lookback window with a two-layer xLSTM with hidden dimension $H = 256$:

$$\mathbf{H}_{\text{xLSTM}} = \text{xLSTM}(\mathbf{X}_{\text{look}}) \in \mathbb{R}^{L \times H}. \tag{8}$$

We extract the final hidden state $\boldsymbol{h}_{\text{final}} = \mathbf{H}_{\text{xLSTM}}[L, :]$ and project it into the forecast space using a two-layer MLP:

$$\mathcal{G}(\mathbf{H}_{\text{xLSTM}}) = \mathbf{W}_2 \, \text{ReLU}(\mathbf{W}_1 \boldsymbol{h}_{\text{final}} + \boldsymbol{b}_1) + \boldsymbol{b}_2, \tag{9}$$

with $\mathbf{W}_1 \in \mathbb{R}^{512 \times H}$, $\boldsymbol{b}_1 \in \mathbb{R}^{512}$, $\mathbf{W}_2 \in \mathbb{R}^{(F \cdot D) \times 512}$, and $\boldsymbol{b}_2 \in \mathbb{R}^{F \cdot D}$. We reshape the output to $\mathbb{R}^{F \times D}$, which serves as the nonlinear forecast component.

Stage 5: Future Mixup and Adaptive Fusion. Future Mixup augmentation. During training, a conditioning network $\mathcal{F}(\cdot)$ (implemented as a two-layer MLP) produces

$$\mathbf{f}_{\text{cond}} = \mathcal{F}(\mathbf{X}_{\text{look}}) \in \mathbb{R}^{F \times D}, \tag{10}$$

which is mixed with ground truth via

$$\mathbf{Z}_{\text{mixup}} = \mathbf{m}_k \odot \mathbf{f}_{\text{cond}} + (\mathbf{1} - \mathbf{m}_k) \odot \mathbf{Y}_{\text{target}}, \tag{11}$$

where $\mathbf{m}_k \in \mathbb{R}^{F \times D}$ is an element-wise mixing matrix whose entries are independently sampled from Uniform$[0, 1)$, providing continuous interpolation weights that match the dimensions of $\mathbf{f}_{\text{cond}}$ and $\mathbf{Y}_{\text{target}}$.

Intuition. This interpolation exposes the model to intermediate trajectories between the conditioning signal and the ground truth. It improves robustness under distributional shift without altering the underlying statistical structure of the forecast sequence. *Persistence baseline.* We define a simple persistence baseline by exponentially decaying the last observation:

$$\mathbf{X}_{\text{recent}}[t,:] = \boldsymbol{x}_{\text{last}} \exp(-\lambda t), \tag{12}$$

for $t = 1, \ldots, F$, where $\boldsymbol{x}_{\text{last}} \in \mathbb{R}^D$ is the final lookback vector and $\lambda = 0.01$ is a fixed decay parameter.

Adaptive Fusion. We combine component forecasts using Bayesian-optimized weights:

$$\begin{aligned}\mathbf{Z}_{\text{mix}} = \alpha \mathbf{Z}_{\text{mixup}} + \beta \mathcal{G}(\mathbf{H}_{\text{xLSTM}}) + \gamma \mathbf{X}_{\text{recent}} \\ + \delta \mathbf{Z}_{\text{AR}} + \zeta \mathbf{Z}_{\text{SARIMA}},\end{aligned} \tag{13}$$

where $(\alpha, \beta, \gamma, \delta, \zeta) = \text{softmax}(w_\alpha, \ldots, w_\zeta)$ and the mixing weights are selected via Bayesian optimization on the validation set; $\text{softmax}(\cdot)$ denotes the standard softmax function.

For diffusion conditioning, we concatenate the fused and component forecasts:

$$\mathbf{Z}_{\text{combined}} = [\mathbf{Z}_{\text{mix}}; \mathbf{Z}_{\text{SARIMA}}; \mathbf{Z}_{\text{AR}}; \mathcal{G}(\mathbf{H}_{\text{xLSTM}})] \in \mathbb{R}^{F \times 4D}. \tag{14}$$

Stage 6: Diffusion-Based Refinement. We employ a U-Net denoiser $\boldsymbol{\epsilon}_\theta$ with cosine noise schedule [12] and $T = 1000$ diffusion steps during training. Let $\boldsymbol{y} = \text{Flatten}(\mathbf{Y}) \in \mathbb{R}^{FD}$ denote the flattened ground truth, where $\text{Flatten}(\cdot)$ stacks all entries of its matrix argument into a single vector. The forward process is

$$\boldsymbol{x}_k = \sqrt{\bar{\alpha}_k}\, \boldsymbol{y} + \sqrt{1 - \bar{\alpha}_k}\, \boldsymbol{\epsilon}, \quad \boldsymbol{\epsilon} \sim \mathcal{N}(\mathbf{0}, \mathbf{I}_{FD}), \tag{15}$$

where $\bar{\alpha}_k = \prod_{t=1}^{k} \alpha_t$, $\{\alpha_t\}_{t=1}^{T}$ denotes the cosine noise schedule, and $\mathbf{I}_{FD}$ is the $FD \times FD$ identity matrix. The reverse process is

$$\begin{aligned} p_\theta(\boldsymbol{x}_{k-1} \mid \boldsymbol{x}_k) = \mathcal{N}\Bigg(& \frac{1}{\sqrt{\alpha_k}} \Bigg[\boldsymbol{x}_k - \frac{1 - \alpha_k}{\sqrt{1 - \bar{\alpha}_k}} \\ & \times \boldsymbol{\epsilon}_\theta(\boldsymbol{x}_k, k, \mathbf{Z}_{\text{combined}}) \Bigg], \sigma_k^2 \mathbf{I}_{FD} \Bigg), \end{aligned} \tag{16}$$

where σ_k is the step-specific standard deviation determined by the same noise schedule. We use DDIM sampling [17] with 50 inference steps. The final vector $\boldsymbol{x}_0$ is reshaped to obtain $\hat{\mathbf{Y}} \in \mathbb{R}^{F \times D}$.

Effect of Diffusion Refinement. Conditioning on $\mathbf{Z}_{\text{combined}}$ enables the denoiser to exploit seasonal forecasts (SARIMA), short-term trends (AR), and nonlinear structure (xLSTM) simultaneously. Across multiple denoising steps, inconsistent component signals are gradually reconciled, reducing phase errors and yielding smoother long-horizon forecasts.

4.2 Training Objective

The training objective combines a diffusion loss with supervision on component predictions:

$$\mathcal{L} = \mathcal{L}_{\text{diff}} + \lambda_1 \mathcal{L}_{\text{pred}} + \lambda_2 \mathcal{L}_{\text{SARIMA}} + \lambda_3 \mathcal{L}_{\text{AR}} + \lambda_4 \mathcal{L}_{\text{reg}}, \tag{17}$$

where

$$\begin{aligned}
\mathcal{L}_{\text{diff}} &= \mathbb{E}_{k,\epsilon}\left[\|\boldsymbol{\epsilon} - \boldsymbol{\epsilon}_\theta(\sqrt{\bar{\alpha}_k}\boldsymbol{y} + \sqrt{1-\bar{\alpha}_k}\boldsymbol{\epsilon}, k, \mathbf{Z}_{\text{combined}})\|_2^2\right],\\
\mathcal{L}_{\text{pred}} &= \|\mathbf{Z}_{\text{mix}} - \mathbf{Y}_{\text{target}}\|_F^2, \quad \mathcal{L}_{\text{SARIMA}} = \|\mathbf{Z}_{\text{SARIMA}} - \mathbf{Y}_{\text{target}}\|_F^2,\\
\mathcal{L}_{\text{AR}} &= \|\mathbf{Z}_{\text{AR}} - \mathbf{Y}_{\text{target}}\|_F^2, \quad \mathcal{L}_{\text{reg}} = \|\mathbf{W}_1\|_F^2 + \|\mathbf{W}_2\|_F^2 + \|\boldsymbol{\theta}_{\text{xLSTM}}\|_2^2,
\end{aligned}$$

with $\lambda_1 = 1.0$, $\lambda_2 = 0.1$, $\lambda_3 = 0.1$, and $\lambda_4 = 10^{-4}$. Here $\|\cdot\|_F$ denotes the Frobenius norm, and $\boldsymbol{\theta}_{\text{xLSTM}}$ collects all trainable parameters of the xLSTM module. Note that the fusion weights $(\alpha, \beta, \gamma, \delta, \zeta)$ are not optimized as part of $\mathcal{L}$; they are fixed hyperparameters selected via Bayesian optimization on the validation set prior to training.

5 Experimental Setup

Dataset. We use meteorological data from Chiang Mai (January 2020–December 2024), comprising 43,848 hourly observations of $PM_{2.5}$ (target), PM_{10}, average/minimum/maximum temperature, relative humidity, atmospheric pressure, and rainfall. We split the data into 60%/20%/20% train/validation/test. The lookback window length is $L = 72$ hours and the forecast horizon is $F = 24$ hours.

We applied Teräsvirta neural network linearity tests [19] to SARIMA residuals for all $D = 8$ variables. The test strongly rejects linearity ($p < 0.001$), indicating substantial nonlinear structure remains after seasonal extraction, which justifies the xLSTM component. Test statistic values ranged from 12.4 to 28.7.

Baselines. We compare against SARIMA, AR, LSTM [6], xLSTM-only, TimeDiff [16], Transformer [20], and Autoformer [22]. We tune all baselines on the validation set.

Training. We train models with the Adam optimizer [8]. We select learning rates from $\{10^{-4}, 5 \times 10^{-4}, 10^{-3}\}$, batch sizes from $\{32, 64, 128\}$, and dropout rates from $\{0.1, 0.2, 0.3\}$. We apply early stopping based on validation MAE with patience of 20 epochs. The adaptive fusion weights $(\alpha, \beta, \gamma, \delta, \zeta)$ were selected via Bayesian optimization over the validation set.

Metrics and Significance Testing. We report root mean squared error (RMSE), mean absolute error (MAE), and mean absolute percentage error (MAPE). We assess statistical significance using the Wilcoxon signed-rank test [21] on per-timestep absolute errors across all test windows, with significance level $\alpha = 0.001$.

6 Results

Table 1 summarizes the main results for 24-hour $PM_{2.5}$ forecasting. SAD-X achieves RMSE of 0.378, MAE of 0.221, and MAPE of 4.12%, showing improvements across all considered baselines. Removing SARIMA increases MAE by 12.2%, which shows that explicit seasonal modeling provides substantial value. Relative to TimeDiff, the error reduction is 19.0% in MAE, and compared with Transformer-based models, the improvement reaches 41.4% over the standard Transformer and 33.8% over Autoformer.

Table 1. Overall comparison on 24-hour $PM_{2.5}$ forecasting.

Model	RMSE	MAE	MAPE (%)
SAD-X (Full)	**0.378**	**0.221**	**4.12**
w/o SARIMA	0.477	0.248	4.89
TimeDiff	0.497	0.273	5.34
xLSTM-only	0.514	0.295	5.67
Autoformer	0.587	0.334	6.43
Transformer	0.621	0.377	7.21
LSTM	0.733	0.483	8.94
SARIMA-only	0.765	0.506	9.47
AR-only	0.843	0.619	11.23

6.1 Component Interaction Analysis

Ablation Study. Table 2 reports ablation results. Removing SARIMA, diffusion, adaptive fusion, or AR uniformly degrades performance. In particular, omitting diffusion leads to a 20.8% increase in MAE, and using fixed (non-adaptive) weights for fusion increases MAE by 30.8%. These results suggest that the overall architecture benefits from both explicit decomposition and the optimized integration of components.

Bayesian-Optimized Weight Distribution. The Bayesian-optimized mixing weights are $\alpha \approx 0.42$, $\beta \approx 0.18$, $\gamma \approx 0.15$, $\delta \approx 0.10$, and $\zeta \approx 0.15$. The model assigns the largest weight to the Future Mixup component, followed by SARIMA and xLSTM, while still retaining meaningful contributions from the persistence and AR baselines. This differs substantially from equal weighting and aligns with the ablation results: components with higher optimized weights are those whose removal degrades performance most.

Table 2. Ablation study.

Configuration	MAE	RMSE
Full model (SAD-X)	**0.221**	**0.378**
w/o SARIMA	0.248 (+12.2%)	0.477 (+26.2%)
w/o Diffusion	0.267 (+20.8%)	0.512 (+35.4%)
w/o Adaptive Fusion	0.289 (+30.8%)	0.534 (+41.3%)
w/o AR	0.243 (+10.0%)	0.461 (+22.0%)
xLSTM-only	0.295 (+33.5%)	0.514 (+36.0%)
SARIMA-only	0.506 (+128.9%)	0.765 (+102.4%)
Simple ensemble	0.265 (+19.9%)	0.489 (+29.4%)

Error Complementarity and Significance. Correlation analysis of per-timestep errors shows negative correlation between SARIMA and xLSTM errors (approximately $\rho = -0.34$), which suggests that the two components tend to make errors in different situations. This complementarity helps explain why SAD-X tends to perform better than either component alone. Table 3 reports Wilcoxon signed-rank tests between SAD-X and several key baselines. All comparisons yield $p < 0.001$ for both MAE and RMSE, supporting that the improvements are statistically significant.

Table 3. Statistical significance testing using Wilcoxon signed-rank test on per-timestep absolute errors across all test windows.

	p-value	
Comparison	MAE	RMSE
SAD-X vs. w/o SARIMA	< 0.001	< 0.001
SAD-X vs. TimeDiff	< 0.001	< 0.001
SAD-X vs. Autoformer	< 0.001	< 0.001
SAD-X vs. Transformer	< 0.001	< 0.001
SAD-X vs. xLSTM-only	< 0.001	< 0.001

Horizon-Wise Behavior. Table 4 summarizes MAE across forecast horizons. The relative benefit of the hybrid architecture increases with horizon length: compared with the variant without SARIMA, the MAE reduction is 14.4% at 6 h and grows further at 24 h. This pattern is consistent with the interpretation that explicit seasonal modeling helps reduce phase errors that accumulate over longer horizons.

Table 4. MAE across forecast horizons for $PM_{2.5}$.

Model	6h	12h	18h	24h
SAD-X	0,143	0,178	0,203	0,221
w/o SARIMA	0,167	0,201	0,228	0,248
TimeDiff	0,181	0,219	0,249	0,273
xLSTM	0,194	0,235	0,268	0,295
Transformer	0,245	0,298	0,341	0,377
SARIMA	0,329	0,401	0,461	0,506

7 Conclusion

The empirical results suggest that explicit architectural decomposition can be beneficial for multivariate time series with strong seasonality and nonlinear dynamics. By combining SARIMA-based seasonal extraction, xLSTM-based nonlinear modeling, adaptive fusion, and diffusion-based refinement, SAD-X achieves 12.2–19.0% reductions in MAE under the experimental setting considered. Ablation studies and weight analyses suggest that the gains come from complementary error patterns, Bayesian-optimized fusion weights, and reduced accumulation of phase errors over long horizons.

Hybrid decomposition is particularly useful under the following conditions: (i) pronounced seasonal autocorrelation, (ii) evidence of nonlinear residual structure after seasonal removal, (iii) sufficient data to estimate statistical and neural components reliably, and (iv) tolerance for additional computational cost. Under such conditions, SAD-X is applicable beyond air quality forecasting to energy demand, traffic, and related domains.

7.1 Limitations and Future Work

This study is limited to a single urban region with strong seasonal structure; evaluating generalization to other locations, domains, and datasets with weaker seasonality is important future work. Our baseline comparison focuses on established architectures; recent methods such as D3VAE, DLinear, and FEDformer were not included. Additionally, we report point forecast metrics but do not evaluate probabilistic metrics such as CRPS, which would more directly assess uncertainty quantification. The choice of xLSTM was not exhaustively compared against alternatives such as Temporal Convolutional Networks or Mamba. Future directions include extending the framework with spatial modeling via graph neural networks, making fusion weights time-varying, and systematic comparison of backbone architectures.

Acknowledgments. The first author is supported by a Royal Thai Government Scholarship in Science and Technology.

Disclosure of Interests. The authors have no competing interests to declare that are relevant to the content of this article.

References

1. Akaike, H.: A new look at the statistical model identification. IEEE Trans. Autom. Control **19**(6), 716–723 (1974)
2. Beck, Met al.: xLSTM: extended long short-term memory. arXiv preprint arXiv:2405.04517 (2024)
3. Box, G.E.P., Jenkins, G.M., Reinsel, G.C., Ljung, G.M.: Time Series Analysis: Forecasting and Control, 5th edn. Wiley, Hoboken, NJ (2015)
4. Brockwell, P.J., Davis, R.A.: Introduction to Time Series and Forecasting, 3rd edn. Springer (2016). https://doi.org/10.1007/0-387-21657-X_8
5. Ho, J., Jain, A., Abbeel, P.: Denoising diffusion probabilistic models. In: NeurIPS, vol. 33, pp. 6840–6851 (2020)
6. Hochreiter, S., Schmidhuber, J.: Long short-term memory. Neural Comput. **9**(8), 1735–1780 (1997)
7. Hyndman, R.J., Athanasopoulos, G.: Forecasting: Principles and Practice, 2nd edn. OTexts (2018)
8. Kingma, D.P., Ba, J.: Adam: a method for stochastic optimization. In: ICLR (2015)
9. Lai, G., Chang, W.C., Yang, Y., Liu, H.: Modeling long- and short-term temporal patterns. In: SIGIR, pp. 95–104 (2018)
10. Little, R.J.A., Rubin, D.B.: Statistical Analysis with Missing Data, 3rd edn. Wiley (2019)
11. Ljung, G.M., Box, G.E.P.: On a measure of lack of fit in time series models. Biometrika **65**(2), 297–303 (1978)
12. Nichol, A.Q., Dhariwal, P.: Improved denoising diffusion probabilistic models. In: ICML, pp. 8162–8171 (2021)
13. Nie, Y., Nguyen, N.H., Sinthong, P., Kalagnanam, J.: A time series is worth 64 words. In: ICLR (2023)
14. Rasul, K., Seward, C., Schuster, I., Vollgraf, R.: Autoregressive denoising diffusion models. In: ICML, pp. 8857–8868 (2021)
15. Seyedan, M., Mafakheri, F., Wang, C.: A hybrid deep learning approach for time series demand forecasting. J. Intell. Manuf. **35**(4), 1941–1958 (2024)
16. Shen, L., Kwok, J.T.: Non-autoregressive conditional diffusion models. In: ICML, pp. 31442–31459 (2023)
17. Song, J., Meng, C., Ermon, S.: Denoising diffusion implicit models. In: ICLR (2021)
18. Tashiro, Y., Song, J., Song, Y., Ermon, S.: CSDI: conditional score-based diffusion models. In: NeurIPS, vol. 34, pp. 24804–24816 (2021)
19. Teräsvirta, T., Lin, C.F., Granger, C.W.J.: Power of the neural network linearity test. J. Time Series Anal. **14**(2), 209–220 (1993)
20. Vaswani, A., et al.: Attention is all you need. In: NeurIPS, vol. 30, pp. 5998–6008 (2017)
21. Wilcoxon, F.: Individual comparisons by ranking methods. Biometrics Bull. **1**(6), 80–83 (1945)
22. Wu, H., Xu, J., Wang, J., Long, M.: Autoformer: decomposition transformers with auto-correlation for long-term series forecasting. In: NeurIPS, vol. 34 (2021)
23. Yun, S., et al.: CutMix: regularization strategy. In: ICCV, pp. 6023–6032 (2019)

24. Zhang, H., Cisse, M., Dauphin, Y.N., Lopez-Paz, D.: Mixup: beyond empirical risk minimization. In: ICLR (2018)
25. Zhang, G.P.: Time series forecasting using a hybrid ARIMA and neural network model. Neurocomputing **50**, 159–175 (2003)
26. Zhou, H., et al.: Informer: beyond efficient transformer. In: AAAI, vol. 35, pp. 11106–11115 (2021)

DeSAM: Extracting MITRE Techniques from Cyber Threat Intelligence with Description-Semantic Attention Mechanism

Jingxian Zhou[1] and Yuxin Xue[2(✉)]

[1] Institute of Science, Technology and Innovation, Civil Aviation University of China, Tianjin 300300, China
jxzhou@cauc.edu.cn

[2] College of Safety Science and Engineering, Civil Aviation University of China, Tianjin 300300, China
snowyy01@163.com

Abstract. Effective extraction of attack knowledge from Cyber Threat Intelligence (CTI) can improve the efficiency and risk identification capabilities of CTI systems, providing robust security monitoring support for increasingly complex network environments. To address the limited semantic understanding of existing models for extracting attack techniques, this paper proposes DeSAM, a data-driven BERT model with a descriptive semantic attention mechanism. Specifically, we first design an embedded semantic fusion mechanism to effectively integrate redundant descriptions of technical sub-labels and generate vector representations that comprehensively cover their semantic information. Secondly, we introduce a semantic association attention mechanism to enhance the model's bidirectional semantic understanding of the relationship between intelligence text and technique descriptions. Finally, compared with large language models and domain-specific deep learning methods, DeSAM performs exceptionally well in identifying attack techniques. Experimental results demonstrate that DeSAM achieves superior performance, with Micro-F1 of 86.45% and Macro-F1 of 85.89%. Notably, it surpasses its backbone model, SciBERT, by 6.02% and 10.19%, respectively, verifying the significant impact of the proposed semantic mechanisms.

Keywords: Cybersecurity · Cyber threat intelligence · MITRE ATT&CK · Large language model

1 Introduction

In recent years, the severity of cybersecurity threats has increased, and complex attacks such as Advanced Persistent Threats (APTs) pose significant risks to the critical infrastructure of both enterprises and nations [19]. In this context,

R. C.-W. Wong et al. (Eds.): PAKDD 2026, LNAI 16618, pp. 52–63, 2027.
https://doi.org/10.1007/978-981-92-1947-6_5

Cyber Threat Intelligence (CTI) has become fundamental to modern defense systems. The MITRE ATT&CK framework [2], serving as the authoritative knowledge base in the field of CTI, provides a standardized lexicon to systematically describe, attribute, and mitigate attack behaviors through tactics, techniques, and procedures (TTPs) [11]. Accurately and efficiently extracting TTPs from unstructured CTI reports is essential to build dynamic threat graphs and accelerate incident response [17].

However, descriptions of attack techniques often take complex forms in the natural language. Its *verbosity* and *complexity* make traditional rule-based methods generally insufficient for generalization ability [16]. In recent years, although natural language processing (NLP) technologies, represented by Large Language Models (LLMs), have made significant progress, the performance of general LLMs and vertical domain models in TTP recognition tasks remains an open question that needs to be evaluated. Furthermore, as an intuitive approach, fine-tuning professional data can improve LLM performance, but the extent to which supervised training can further enhance performance remains to be explored. Finally, compared to traditional data fine-tuning, we can utilize the information from the task itself to guide the model closer to expert cognition.

To address the above issues, the main contributions of this article are as follows: Firstly, based on the technical description of MITRE ATT&CK, a data-driven BERT model with a descriptive semantic attention mechanism, DeSAM, is designed. Specifically, to address semantic redundancy in sub-label descriptions, an embedded semantic fusion mechanism has been developed to effectively capture a subset of the semantic information in the described semantic vector. In addition, this article proposes a semantic attention mechanism to further refine the model-generated embedding vectors and establish an association between the target sentence and its corresponding technical description in the embedding space. The experimental results show that, compared to various baseline models, including LLMs and deep learning (DL) models, DeSAM can significantly improve the recognition performance of attack techniques.

The structure of our work is as follows: Sect. 2 will review the relevant work; Sect. 3 introduces the details of the proposed method; The experimental results and analysis are presented in Sects. 4 and 5 summarizes the entire text and looks forward to future research.

2 Related Works

2.1 Machine Learning Processing

Machine learning (ML) models convert text into specific sequence information through feature engineering or other methods and use data-driven methods to predict categories. For example, [9] is based on word frequency as the main data feature, but this processing method can lead to low-frequency keywords being ignored; [14] uses a Latent Dirichlet Allocation (LDA) topic model to extract topic words, taking semantic similarity between documents and threatening behaviors as features, and using multiple machine learning algorithms to extract technical labels. [8] introduces the strategy of the threat action ontology, which focuses the TTPs extraction task on the entity relationship level. [7] introduces a DL strategy that constructs multiple inference paths based on ontology and combines the superior computational performance to vote on the task itself. However, in the face of hundreds of highly fine-grained technical labels in the ATT&CK, the problem of class imbalance is particularly prominent in ML.

2.2 Language Model Processing

With the development of LLMs, research on the extraction of CTI attack technology has undergone significant changes. [4] designed multiple pipelines around Threat Report ATT&CK Mapping (TRAM) and SciBERT [3] to verify the impact of data class imbalance on LLM performance, and also explored the performance of methods including AttackG [10] in document-level TTP extraction tasks. [1] has fine-tuned RoBerta [12] using professional terminology and text in the field of cybersecurity to achieve the SecureBERT. It has validated the feasibility of solving industry problems using standard NLP testing procedures. Besides, [18] introduced TTP in malware analysis to describe the different stages of the attack life-cycle, [15] focused on named entity recognition (NER) tasks and extracting threats from security warnings and reports, and some models focused their work on areas such as malicious code detection [5,6,13].

However, most existing work focuses either on the direct application of model architectures or on domain-adaptation pre-training. Research on how to effectively guide the model toward expert cognition during fine-tuning is limited, and the model's ability to extract attack techniques still needs improvement. Based on this, we evaluate the extraction capabilities of large models in the general and vertical-domain and fine-tune a new approach that introduces the "technical description" as a professional background constraint to achieve more accurate and robust technical recognition.

3 Methodology

3.1 Overview of Workflow

The workflow of DeSAM is illustrated in Fig. 1, where sentences from CTI reports and descriptions of various attack techniques together form the model's input. Specifically, assuming that each batch contains N sentences, the sentence input can be represented as $\mathbf{s} = \{s_1, s_2, ..., s_N\}$, and the model's goal is to predict the technique label $\hat{T}_i$ for s_i. s_i is processed by a pre-trained tokenizer to obtain a token ID sequence $\mathbf{t}_i^s = [t_1, t_2, ..., t_L]$, where L is the output length. The technique descriptions originate from MITRE ATT&CK, which describes each parent label (e.g., T1059, T1012) and its sub-labels (e.g., T1059.001, T1059.002), forming a description set $\mathbf{d} = \{d_1, d_2, ..., d_M\}$. In our study, $\mathbf{d}$ contains descriptions of 188 labels ($M = 188$). Similarly to $\mathbf{s}$, each description sentence is tokenized to obtain a sequence $\mathbf{t}_j^d$.

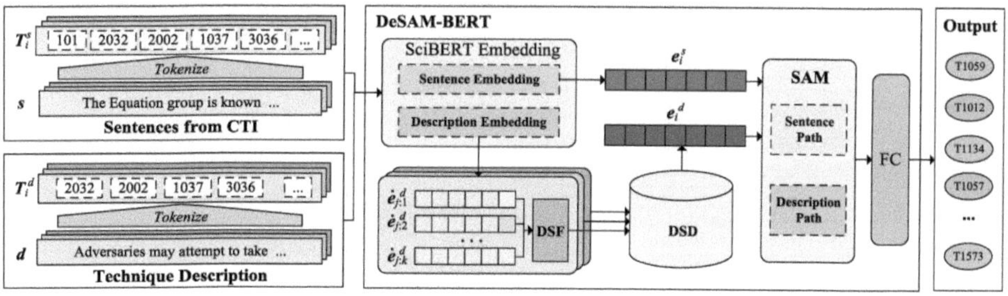

Fig. 1. Framework of DeSAM.

We use pre-trained SciBERT as the base model to embed the input sequences, obtaining sentence embedding vectors $\mathbf{e}_i^s$ and description embedding vectors $\mathbf{e}_j^d$, respectively. For the same parent label, it may contain definitions of multiple sub-labels. To enhance the model's understanding of parent labels, we design a Semantic Embedding Fusion (SEF) mechanism, which stores $\mathbf{e}_j^d$ in a Descriptive Semantic Dictionary (DSD) for model reference, $j = 1, 2, ..., N_T$, and N_T is the number of techniques' classes.

During training, for a sentence with the label $\hat{T}_i$, DeSAM searches the DSD for the corresponding description vector $\mathbf{e}_j^d$ of $\hat{T}_i$, then performs semantic understanding enhancement between the sentence and the description based on the Semantic Association Model (SAM), obtaining a mapping vector z. After processing by a fully connected layer, it is mapped to $\hat{T}_i$. The prediction process can be represented as Eq. 1.

$$\hat{T}_i = DeSAM(s_i|DSD) \tag{1}$$

3.2 Description Semantic Dictionary

The description semantic dictionary (DSD) is a key bridge between DeSAM's attack techniques and descriptive text. It maps discrete sub-label descriptions to the vector space of the parent label via embedding computation and fusion mechanisms, enabling the parent label's embedding to integrate the features of the sub-label set. Specifically, taking the label T1595 as an example, as shown in Fig. 2, SciBERT processes the descriptions to obtain an embedded vector $\dot{e}_{j:k}^d$, where $k = 0, 1, ..., K_j$, and K_j is the number of descriptions for T1595, which is 3. To aggregate semantic information described by multiple sub-labels under the same parent label, we design a Semantic Embedding Fusion (SEF) mechanism. By performing an average pooling operation on all sub-label embeddings, a parent label level fusion embedding vector is generated, as shown in Eq. 2.

$$e_j^d = \frac{1}{K_j} \sum_{k=1}^{K_j} \dot{e}_{j:k}^d \tag{2}$$

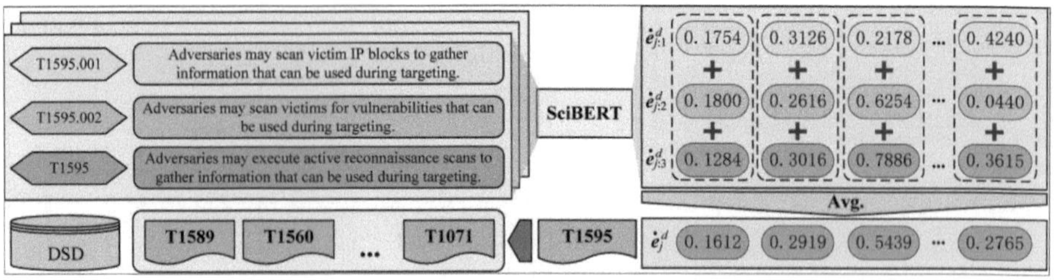

Fig. 2. Construction process of DSD.

Finally, the fused embedding vectors of all parent labels are organized into a Description Semantic Dictionary (DSD), formally defined as a set of key-value pairs $DSD = \{(T_j : e_j^d)|j = 1, 2, .., K_j\}$.

This dictionary serves as a retrievable semantic knowledge base during training and inference, providing corresponding label description embeddings for each input sentence and supporting interactive calculations in subsequent semantic association modules.

3.3 Semantic Attention Mechanism

To enhance interaction modeling between sentence semantics and label descriptions, we designed SAM based on multi-head attention (MHA). SAM achieves semantic alignment between sentence embedding and description embedding through a two-stage attention mechanism, thereby enhancing the model's ability to recognize attack technology concepts in CTI text. Specifically, as shown in Fig. 3, e^s and e^d are both in hidden size H. Based on MHA, they are divided into $\lceil H/N_H \rceil$ pieces, each piece of e^s and e^d is represented as $\tilde{e}_h^s$ and $\tilde{e}_h^d$, respectively, $h = 1, 2, .., N_H$.

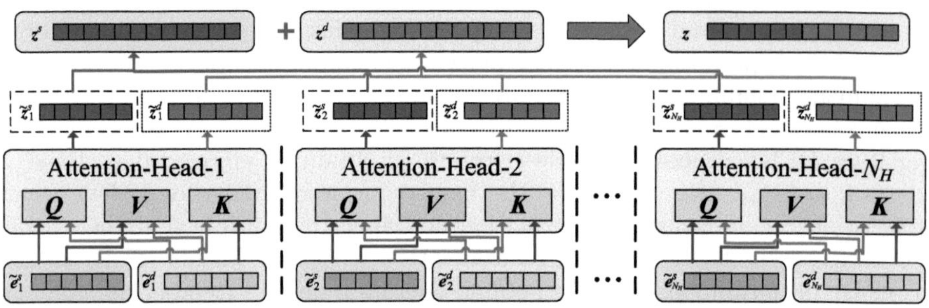

Fig. 3. Calculation process of SAM.

There are two calculation stages for each SAM head. Taking the sentence semantic piece calculation process $\tilde{z}_h^s$ as an example, in the first stage, $\tilde{e}_h^s$ is used as query (Q) and value (V), and the key (K) is represented by $\tilde{e}_h^d$. The calculation of $\tilde{z}_h^s$ can be expressed by Eq. 3.

$$\tilde{z}_h^s = \text{softmax}\left(\frac{\tilde{e}_h^s(\tilde{e}_h^d)^\top}{\sqrt{H}}\right)\tilde{e}_h^s \tag{3}$$

After all calculations are completed, concatenate the results to obtain the semantic vector under the sentence path z^s. In the second stage of computation, e_h^d takes on the roles of Q and V, while e_h^s participates as K to obtain the description path z^d. The SAM calculation path is shown in Eq. 4.

$$\begin{aligned} z^s &= \text{SAM}(\mathbf{Q} = e^s, \mathbf{K} = e^d, \mathbf{V} = e^s) \\ z^d &= \text{SAM}(\mathbf{Q} = e^d, \mathbf{K} = e^s, \mathbf{V} = e^d) \end{aligned} \tag{4}$$

SAM integrates the computational paths of the multi-head attention and cross-attention mechanisms and bidirectionally associates the embedding vectors of sentence semantics and descriptive semantics. Combine the z^s and z^d features to obtain the predicted vector $z = [z^s; z^d] \in \mathbb{R}^{2H}$.

Finally, the concatenated joint representation is mapped to the label space through a fully connected layer. Let the set of sentences of batch B be S and its corresponding attack technique label be T. After the DeSAM-BERT process, the classification vector logits $l \in \mathbb{R}^C$ are obtained, where C is the number of categories. The l is converted to a probability distribution $\mathbf{p} = [p_1, p_2, \ldots, p_C]$ by *softmax*, and the difference between the predicted probability and the one-hot encoding of the true label y_i is calculated based on the cross entropy loss function shown as Eq. 5, which optimizes the model parameters through the gradient descent algorithm to improve the classification accuracy.

$$\mathcal{L} = -\sum_{j=1}^{C} y_j \log(p_j) \tag{5}$$

4 Results and Analysis

4.1 Experiment Settings and Design

To systematically verify the effectiveness and advancement of DeSAM-BERT in the extraction task of CTI techniques, we used a public threat intelligence dataset [4] for experimental validation. This dataset consists of 9,811 intelligence sentences and their corresponding technique labels, with data augmentation strategies previously implemented using GPT-3.5 to effectively mitigate the class imbalance issue caused by long-tail distribution, thereby providing a solid data foundation for model training.

Regarding baseline model selection, to construct a comprehensive evaluation framework, we incorporated not only the general pre-trained model BERT-Large but also domain-specific models, including SecureBERT, SecBERT, and SciBERT. Furthermore, referencing the experimental paradigm of [4], we introduce

LSTM as a representative of traditional deep learning methods for the comparative study. For the specific semantic enhancement mechanism of DeSAM-BERT, we utilized the standard description set provided by [7] as the external knowledge source.

The experiments were conducted entirely in a hardware environment equipped with an RTX 3090 GPU, and the model was fine-tuned using the AdamW optimizer [20]. To ensure fairness in comparison and eliminate potential interference from hyperparameter discrepancies in performance evaluation, key hyperparameter settings, such as training epochs and learning rates, for all models in this experiment were kept strictly consistent with those in [4].

Additionally, the scale of training parameters for each model is presented in Table 1. It can be observed that, with the exception of BERT-Large, which is a large-scale model, the parameter scales of the remaining comparative models are of the same order of magnitude (approximately 110 million parameters). Notably, since DeSAM-BERT is built on the SciBERT architecture and has improved upon it, its parameter count is slightly higher than that of the SciBERT backbone due to the introduction of specific structures; however, the overall scale remains smaller than that of SecureBERT. This indicates that the model maintains competitive computational complexity and resource efficiency while significantly improving performance.

Table 1. Comparison of model parameter scale. (M:Million)

Model	BERT-Large	SciBERT	SecBERT	SecureBERT	DeSAM-BERT	LSTM
Parameters	333.63M	109.96M	83.49M	124.68M	112.40M	15.28M

4.2 Evaluation and Comparison

As presented in Table 2, a comprehensive comparative evaluation was conducted between the proposed DeSAM-BERT and other prominent baseline models. Experimental results indicate that DeSAM-BERT achieves superior performance in all evaluation metrics.

Specifically, DeSAM-BERT attains a superior Micro F1 score of 86.45%, while delivering exceptional performance in the Macro dimensions—registering 85.89% for F1, 85.27% for Recall and 86.90% for Precision, thus establishing its dominance in the current task. Of particular significance is the substantial performance leap DeSAM-BERT achieves over its foundational architecture, SciBERT. Notably, our model improves the Macro F1 score by over 10% points, indicating that the model's capabilities in semantic understanding and feature extraction have been profoundly enhanced.

Furthermore, DeSAM-BERT maintains a significant advantage over the general large-scale BERT-Large and domain-specific variants such as SecBERT and SecureBERT. For instance, it shows a significant improvement over SecureBERT

Table 2. Performance comparison of different methods.

Methods	Micro	Macro		
	F1	Recall	Precision	F1
DeSAM-BERT	**86.45%**	**85.27%**	**86.90%**	**85.89%**
BERT-Large	81.25%	77.01%	81.54%	77.73%
SecBERT	79.36%	74.74%	78.63%	74.26%
SecureBERT	47.68%	32.71%	29.84%	28.53%
SciBERT	80.43%	76.38%	80.95%	75.70%
LSTM	74.01%	72.09%	75.31%	72.33%

and clearly surpasses the traditional LSTM approach. These findings further corroborate that DeSAM-BERT has superior robustness and generalization capabilities, enabling it to address complex classification challenges with greater precision.

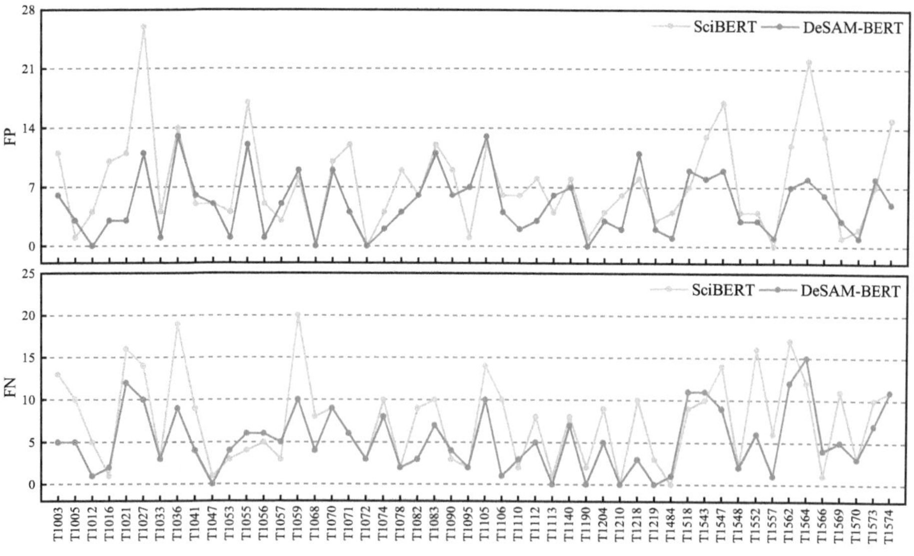

Fig. 4. False Positive and False Negative values of SciBERT and DeSAM-BERT.

To provide a granular analysis of the model's performance in fine-grained classification tasks, we conducted an in-depth comparative evaluation of the False Positive (FP) and False Negative (FN) distributions across test-set categories, as illustrated in Fig. 4. Overall, compared to the baseline SciBERT model, DeSAM-BERT exhibits significantly lower error rates in the vast majority of categories. This trend is visually characterized by the notably lower peak values and smoother fluctuations of the DeSAM-BERT curve relative to that of SciBERT, providing robust evidence of the stability of the proposed model when processing complex samples.

Specifically, with regard to false positive mitigation, DeSAM-BERT demonstrates superior noise suppression capabilities and discriminative precision. In challenging categories prone to confounds, such as T1027, T1564, and T1574, SciBERT yielded exceptionally high false alarm rates (with FP values reaching 26, 22, and 15, respectively). In contrast, DeSAM-BERT, leveraging its optimized attention mechanism, substantially reduced these misclassifications to 10, 7, and 5, respectively, thereby markedly enhancing classification accuracy.

Simultaneously, the model's advantage in the false negative dimension is equally pronounced, reflecting its acute sensitivity to target features. Empirical data indicate that in critical categories such as T1059, T1552, and T1003, SciBERT exhibited severe omission rates, with FN values peaking at 20. Conversely, DeSAM-BERT effectively addressed these recognition blind spots, constraining missed detections to minimal levels (e.g., reducing misses in T1003 to merely 5), which translates to a substantial improvement in recall.

4.3 Analysis of Prediction

As shown in Fig. 5, to comprehensively evaluate the decision boundaries and prediction consistency of various models in multi-class classification tasks, we visualized the confusion matrices of six comparative methods across 50 TTP categories. Through a comparative analysis, DeSAM-BERT demonstrates significant structural advantages in feature representation and classification robustness. Its most prominent characteristic is the perfect continuity and integrity of the main diagonal, which is devoid of any missing entries. This phenomenon indicates that the model successfully achieved effective coverage of all 50 target categories without any instance of total recognition failure, thereby reflecting exceptional stability in category recall.

In sharp contrast, the baseline models (Fig. 5(b)–(e)) exhibit visibly distinct discontinuities or gaps along their main diagonals. Specifically, BERT-Large, SciBERT, SecBERT, and SecureBERT all display significant gaps at the T1569 category, while SecBERT additionally shows a breakpoint at T1068. These observations reveal severe "blind spots" in the feature representation of these baseline models for specific categories, leading to a complete loss of predictive capability. The underlying cause is that the T1569 category contains only 69 samples in the fine-tuning dataset, accounting for merely 0.7% of the total data. Although class imbalance handling was applied prior to the experiment, the baseline models failed to effectively extract the sparse features of this category, whereas DeSAM-BERT demonstrated superior feature extraction and generalization capabilities in this extreme few-shot scenario. Furthermore, the matrix structure of SecureBERT appears highly discretized and lacks clear diagonal features, confirming its poor generalization performance in multi-class tasks.

In the analysis of off-diagonal regions, DeSAM-BERT exhibits the sparsest and lightest confusion distribution, indicating a minimal number of misclassi-

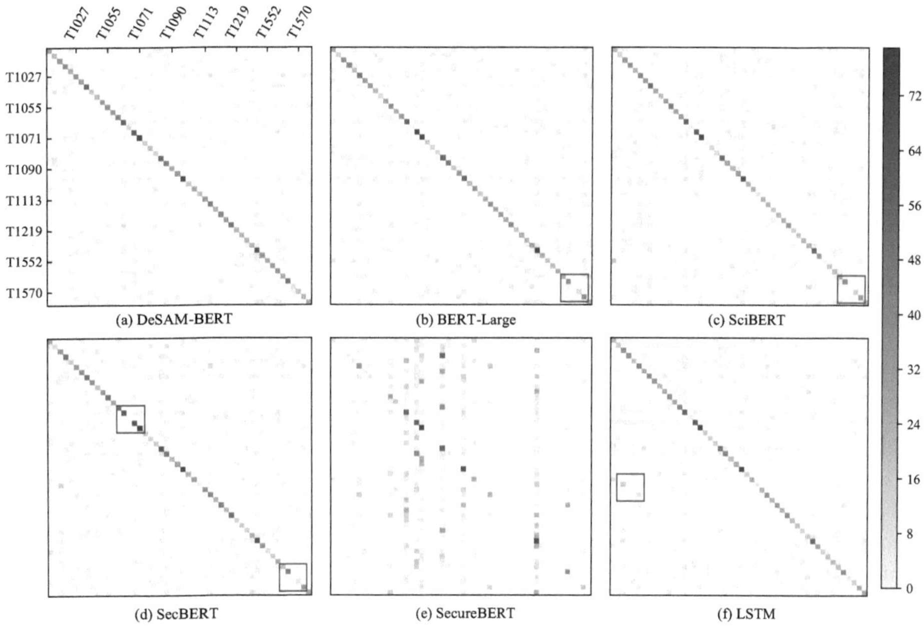

Fig. 5. Confusion Matrix Comparison for TTPs Extraction (The horizontal and vertical axes of each subplot represent 50 categories of TTPs (sorted in ascending order), with only eight labels shown in (a)).

fied samples and demonstrating strong resistance to interference alongside high discriminative power. Conversely, the other comparative models display non-diagonal regions populated with high-density, dark-toned noise patterns, which map to severe confusion and misattribution between different categories.

This is particularly evident in the LSTM model, where the lower triangular region not only contains dense noise, but also distinct dark clusters, reflecting systematic feature entanglement when processing locally related categories. Experimental observations indicate that LSTM systematically misclassified an average of 14 samples from the T1112 (Modify Registry) category as T1012 (Web Service). Taking the sample "Access to specific areas of the Registry depends on account permissions, some requiring administrator-level access" as an instance, its ground truth is T1112, yet it was misclassified. Although deep neural networks possess a "black box" nature, this misclassification can be mechanistically attributed to LSTM's limitations in capturing long-distance dependencies. The sentence is saturated with high-frequency terms common in the cybersecurity domain, such as "Access", "account permissions", and "administrator-level", which are also prevalent in descriptions of Web Services. Due to the lack of a Self-Attention mechanism similar to that in Transformers for dynamic weight assignment, the LSTM failed to focus its attention on the most discriminative entity noun, "Registry". Instead, it was misled by the dominant context of permission control, resulting in an erroneous semantic mapping in the latent feature space and leading to systematic classification errors.

5 Conclusion and Prospects

In this paper, we address the insufficient semantic understanding in CTI extraction by proposing DeSAM, a BERT-based framework enhanced with descriptive semantic attention. Leveraging a constructed dataset based on MITRE ATT&CK, we introduced an embedded semantic fusion mechanism to integrate component semantics and a semantic association attention mechanism to establish a deep, bidirectional alignment between intelligence text and technical descriptions. By incorporating professional domain constraints into an end-to-end training process, we significantly enhanced the model's capability to identify specific attack techniques. Experimental results validate the model's superiority, achieving a Micro-F1 of 86.45% and a Macro-F1 of 85.89%. DeSAM not only outperforms the strongest general baseline, BERT-Large, by 5.20% and 8.16% respectively, but also surpasses its backbone model, SciBERT, by significant margins of 6.02% and 10.19%, demonstrating exceptional robustness in handling long-tail distributions and complex semantic scenarios.

In future work, we plan to extend our research to fine-grained Entity-Relation Extraction (RE) to capture specific interactions among threat actors, malware, and infrastructure. Building upon this, we aim to construct a comprehensive CTI Knowledge Graph (KG) that integrates these extracted entities with attack techniques. This graph-based approach will facilitate automated reasoning and multi-hop analysis, enabling security analysts to gain a holistic view of attack campaigns for more proactive defense strategies.

Acknowledgments. This study was funded by Science and Technology Projects of Xizang Autonomous Region, China (grant number XZ202502ZY0062).

Disclosure of Interests. The authors have no competing interests to declare that are relevant to the content of this article.

References

1. Aghaei, E., Niu, X., Shadid, W., Al-Shaer, E.: SecureBERT: a domain-specific language model for cybersecurity. In: International Conference on Security and Privacy in Communication Systems, pp. 39–56. Springer, Cham (2022). https://doi.org/10.1007/978-3-031-25538-0_3
2. Al-Sada, B., Sadighian, A., Oligeri, G.: Mitre att&ck: state of the art and way forward. ACM Comput. Surv. **57**(1), 1–37 (2024)
3. Beltagy, I., Lo, K., Cohan, A.: SciBERT: a pretrained language model for scientific text. arXiv preprint arXiv:1903.10676 (2019)
4. Cuong Nguyen, H., Tariq, S., Baruwal Chhetri, M., Quoc Vo, B.: Towards effective identification of attack techniques in cyber threat intelligence reports using large language models. In: Companion Proceedings of the ACM on Web Conference 2025, pp. 942–946 (2025)

5. Feng, Z., et al.: CodeBERT: a pre-trained model for programming and natural languages. arXiv preprint arXiv:2002.08155 (2020)
6. Hanif, H., Maffeis, S.: VulBERTa: simplified source code pre-training for vulnerability detection. In: 2022 International Joint Conference on Neural Networks (IJCNN), pp. 1–8. IEEE (2022)
7. Huang, Y.T., et al.: Mitretrieval: retrieving mitre techniques from unstructured threat reports by fusion of deep learning and ontology. IEEE Trans. Netw. Serv. Manage. **21**(4), 4871–4887 (2024)
8. Husari, G., Al-Shaer, E., Ahmed, M., Chu, B., Niu, X.: TTPDrill: automatic and accurate extraction of threat actions from unstructured text of CTI sources. In: Proceedings of the 33rd Annual Computer Security Applications Conference, pp. 103–115 (2017)
9. Legoy, V., Caselli, M., Seifert, C., Peter, A.: Automated retrieval of att&ck tactics and techniques for cyber threat reports. arXiv preprint arXiv:2004.14322 (2020)
10. Li, Z., Zeng, J., Chen, Y., Liang, Z.: AttacKG: constructing technique knowledge graph from cyber threat intelligence reports. In: European Symposium on Research in Computer Security, pp. 589–609. Springer, Cham (2022). https://doi.org/10.1007/978-3-031-17140-6_29
11. Liu, C., Wang, J., Chen, X.: Threat intelligence att&ck extraction based on the attention transformer hierarchical recurrent neural network. Appl. Soft Comput. **122**, 108826 (2022)
12. Liu, Y., et al.: RoBERTa: a robustly optimized BERT pretraining approach. arXiv preprint arXiv:1907.11692 (2019)
13. Paul, S., Saha, S.: CyberBERT: BERT for cyberbullying identification: BERT for cyberbullying identification. Multimedia Syst. **28**(6), 1897–1904 (2022)
14. Peng, S., Zhou, A., Liao, S., Liu, L.: A threat actions extraction method based on the conditional co-occurrence degree. In: 2020 7th International Conference on Information Science and Control Engineering (ICISCE), pp. 1633–1637. IEEE (2020)
15. Ranade, P., Piplai, A., Joshi, A., Finin, T.: CyBERT: contextualized embeddings for the cybersecurity domain. In: 2021 IEEE International Conference on Big Data (Big Data), pp. 3334–3342. IEEE (2021)
16. Satvat, K., Gjomemo, R., Venkatakrishnan, V.: Extractor: extracting attack behavior from threat reports. In: 2021 IEEE European Symposium on Security and Privacy (EuroS&P), pp. 598–615. IEEE (2021)
17. You, Y., et al.: TIM: threat context-enhanced TTP intelligence mining on unstructured threat data. Cybersecurity **5**(1), 3 (2022)
18. Zhang, Y., et al.: Tactics, techniques, and procedures (TTPs) in interpreted malware: a zero-shot generation with large language models. arXiv preprint arXiv:2407.08532 (2024)
19. Zhou, J., Li, Q., Cheng, Z.: A quality assessment method for cyber threat intelligence based on multi-source heterogeneous data. J. Civ. Aviat. Univ. China **42**(04), 29–36 (2024)
20. Zhou, P., Xie, X., Lin, Z., Yan, S.: Towards understanding convergence and generalization of AdamW. IEEE Trans. Pattern Anal. Mach. Intell. **46**(9), 6486–6493 (2024)

SOAR: Selective Oversampling Using Anomaly-Based Decile Refinement for Multiclass Imbalanced Problems

Supanigarn Munkhong[1], Krung Sinapiromsaran[1](✉), and Natthawut Kertkeidkachorn[2]

[1] Chulalongkorn University, Bangkok, Thailand
6670138823@student.chula.ac.th, Krung.S@chula.ac.th

[2] Japan Advanced Institute of Science and Technology, Nomi, Ishikawa, Japan
natt@jaist.ac.jp

Abstract. Highly imbalanced scenarios remain a persistent and critical challenge in supervised learning, as standard classifiers tend to be biased toward the majority class, leading to poor recognition of minority instances. Traditional oversampling methods, such as the Synthetic Minority Oversampling Technique (SMOTE), attempt to mitigate this issue by generating synthetic instances, but SMOTE often degrades model performance because it fails to distinguish core, boundary, and noisy instances, resulting in the synthesis of uninformative regions. To address this limitation, this paper introduces Selective Oversampling Using Anomaly-based Decile Refinement (SOAR), a novel technique that strategically identifies critical minority instances for synthesis. SOAR employs the parameter-free Mass-Ratio-Variance Outlier Factor (MOF) to assign anomaly scores to minority instances and refines them through a decile-based selection strategy. Instances in the third to ninth deciles (D_3–D_9) are selected for oversampling, effectively filtering out anomalous minority instances and redundant minority instances, ensuring that oversampling focuses on the critical informative regions. Extensive experiments on seventeen UCI benchmark datasets across ten classifiers demonstrate that SOAR consistently outperforms baseline and state-of-the-art oversampling techniques in terms of F1-score. These findings indicate that anomaly-guided selection of informative minority instances provides a robust and effective strategy for improving classification performance on highly imbalanced datasets.

Keywords: Imbalanced Learning · Oversampling · Mass-Ratio-Variance Outlier Factor · Decile-based Selection

1 Introduction

Classification is one of the fundamental tasks in machine learning, assign instances to predefined classes based on their features. In real-world applications,

R. C.-W. Wong et al. (Eds.): PAKDD 2026, LNAI 16618, pp. 64–76, 2027.
https://doi.org/10.1007/978-981-92-1947-6_6

such as fraud detection and medical diagnosis [1], datasets are often imbalanced with the minority class contains significantly fewer instances than the majority class. This imbalance causes standard classifiers to be biased toward the majority class, resulting in poor recognition and high misclassification rates for minority instances. This critical challenge has motivated the development of various approaches to handle imbalanced classification [2], which are categorized into three main strategies: data-level strategy. Which adjusts class distributions to become balance; algorithm-level strategy, which adapts existing algorithms to effectively handle class imbalance; and cost-sensitive strategy, which assigns misclassification costs to improve minority class performance [3].

This paper focuses on oversampling, specifically the widely used SMOTE [4], as a foundation for developing improved oversampling methods. SMOTE synthesizes minority instances by interpolating between each minority instance and its k-nearest neighbors. Despite its effectiveness, SMOTE generates synthetic instances without considering whether minority instances are informative or noisy. Consequently, these synthetic instances may be created in overlapping regions, potentially degrading classifier performance rather than improving it.

To address these limitations, the proposed approach introduces a new oversampling technique, SOAR, a classifier-agnostic technique applicable to any standard classifier. SOAR integrates SMOTE with anomaly scoring using the Mass-Ratio-Variance Outlier Factor (MOF) [5], which assigns an anomaly score to each minority instance based on its local density. Synthetic instance generation is then focused on critical instances by excluding highly anomalous or overly common instances. Consequently, this approach improves classifier performance while significantly reducing the risk of introducing noise and avoiding redundant sampling in overly dense regions. Experimental results demonstrate that SOAR consistently achieves the best average rank based on F1-score among the baseline and state-of-the-art oversampling techniques. Its superiority is further confirmed across multiple evaluation metrics, including Precision, Recall, and F1-score.

The details of this paper are as follows: Sect. 2 reviews related oversampling and anomaly detection techniques, with particular emphasis on MOF. Section 3 introduces the proposed method. Section 4 presents the experimental results conducted on 17 UCI benchmark datasets [6] using 10 classifiers, with performance evaluated across multiple metrics. This section also includes Wilcoxon signed-rank tests to confirm the significant improvement achieved by SOAR. Finally, Sect. 5 concludes the research by summarizing the findings, discussing limitations, and outlining directions for future work.

2 Literature Reviews

2.1 Existing Oversampling Techniques

To handle class imbalance, several data-level approaches have been developed to modify the class distribution. These include Random Oversampling (ROS), and oversampling techniques such as SMOTE and its variants, including Safe-Level-SMOTE (SL-SMOTE) and Borderline-SMOTE (BD-SMOTE).

ROS [7] is a simple approach that increases the number of minority instances by randomly duplicating minority instances until a desired balance is achieved; however, this approach increases the presence of the minority class without introducing novel information.

SMOTE generates synthetic minority instances by interpolating between a minority instance and one of its k-nearest minority neighbors. This process creates new instances along the line segments connecting existing minority instances, thereby introducing essential variability and enabling classifiers to generalize more effectively.

SL-SMOTE [8] computes a safe-level score for each minority instance based on its local neighborhood structure. This safe-level score guides the interpolation process, selecting instances for synthesis from safer regions while avoiding synthesis in risk regions that are near majority instances. This reduces the likelihood of generating harmful synthetic instances and improves robustness over the standard SMOTE.

BD-SMOTE [9] targets minority instances close to the decision boundary between classes, on the hypothesis that these are the instances most critical for classification performance. To improve this, BD-SMOTE generates synthetic instances specifically for borderline instances, aiming to enhance recall for the minority class. This helps to enhance minority class coverage while minimizing noise generation.

2.2 Existing Anomaly Detection Technique

Anomaly detection techniques [10] provide an alternative approach by identifying instances based on their deviation from normal patterns rather than relying solely on class distribution. These methods assign a score to each instance to quantify their anomalous degree. Popular techniques, such as Local Outlier Factor (LOF) [11], compute anomaly scores by comparing the local density of each instance with its neighbors; instances with low local density receive high scores, indicating potential outliers. However, LOF requires careful global parameter tuning, the number of neighbors, which can affect performance. Another alternative parameter-free method is MOF, which is described below.

MOF represents a significant advancement in unsupervised, parameter-free outlier scoring. Unlike traditional methods that rely on manually defined parameters, MOF eliminates such parameters by leveraging the concept of density-ratio distribution over all instances. It computes the variance of the mass-ratio distribution between a given instance and all other instances, where the mass-ratio distribution of instances q with respect to instances p ($massR_p(q)$) is defined in Eq. 1.

$$massR_p(q) = \frac{|N_p(q)|}{|N_q(p)|} \tag{1}$$

where $N_p(q)$ denotes the number of neighborhoods within a ball centered at q with radius $d(q,p)$, where $d(q,p)$ is the Euclidean distance between q and p, and $N_q(p)$ denotes the number of neighborhoods within a ball centered at p with radius $d(p, q)$. Since both radiuses are the same, this ratio is the same as the density ratio. MOF of p is then assigned as the variance of $massR_p(\cdot)$ distribution.

The key idea is that outlier instances located far from dense regions exhibit a high variance in their mass-ratio distribution, as their local density differs substantially from the rest of the data. In contrast, normal instances surrounded by similar instances produce a low variance. Therefore, the MOF score effectively quantifies how much an instance deviates from the overall density distribution, providing a robust, parameter-free approach for identifying anomalous instances, offering advantages over other parameter-based anomaly detection techniques.

3 Proposed Method: SOAR

This section presents a novel oversampling technique called SOAR. The method aims to enhance the representativeness of synthetic minority instances by strategically selecting appropriate minority instances for generation. SOAR integrates the anomaly score, MOF, with a decile-based refinement strategy to identify the most informative regions for oversampling, thereby avoiding both highly noisy and overly redundant instances.

3.1 Motivation

Traditional oversampling techniques, such as SMOTE, often generate synthetic instances between minority instances and their nearest neighbors without considering whether those instances are appropriate for synthesis. Consequently, oversampling may occur on anomalous or uninformative instances, leading to the performance degradation. To address this limitation, SOAR is developed as an improvement over SMOTE by incorporating an anomaly-guided selection to avoid oversampling on highly anomalous and overly core instances, and instead focus the synthesis on critical regions.

3.2 Overview of SOAR Framework

The proposed SOAR framework consists of four main sequential steps as follows:

1. **Compute Anomaly Scores using the MOF.** Each minority instance x_{min} is first assigned the MOF score, which quantifies how anomalous x_{min} is relative to its local neighborhood distribution. The MOF is computed based on the variance of the mass-ratio values, capturing the deviation of x_{min} from typical density patterns in the dataset.
The mean of the mass-ratio for a minority instance x_{min}, denoted as $\mu_{x_{min}}$, is computed as shown in Eq. 2:

$$\mu_{x_{min}} = \frac{1}{n-1} \sum_{i=1,\ x_i \neq x_{min}}^{n} massR_{x_{min}}(x_i) \tag{2}$$

The MOF score for a minority instance x_{min}, denoted as $MOF(x_{min})$, is defined as the variance of the mass-ratios, as shown in Eq. 3:

$$MOF(x_{min}) = \frac{1}{n-1} \sum_{i=1,\ x_i \neq x_{min}}^{n} (massR_{x_{min}}(x_i) - \mu_{x_{min}})^2 \quad (3)$$

where n is the total number of minority instances, x_i is the i-th minority instances, and $massR_{x_{min}}(x_i)$ is the mass-ratio of instances x_i with respect to instances x_{min}.
The high MOF score exhibits high variance among mass-ratio distribution, suggesting x_{min} is an outlier. Conversely, the low MOF score suggests that instance exhibits common density with surrounding instances.

2. **Refine Scores using Decile Segmentation.** The computed MOF scores are sorted in ascending order and divided into ten equal deciles (D_1–D_{10}). Consequently, D_1 represent the lowest 10% anomalous instances, while D_{10} represent top-ten percent of anomalous instances. This step serves to normalize the selection process by ranking instances according to their anomaly scores.
3. **Select Optimal Decile Range.** Instances within the specific decile range are selected as the most informative subset for synthesis. Based on the empirical analysis detailed in Subsect. 4.3 (Determining the Optimal Decile Range for SOAR), the range D_3–D_9 is identified as the optimal range. This range effectively excludes highly anomalous noise (above D_9) and overly redundant instances (below D_3), ensuring that the synthesis process focuses exclusively on critical instances.
4. **Generate Synthetic Instances.** Using a SMOTE-like interpolation process, synthetic minority instances (x_{syn}) are generated exclusively from the selected decile range (D_3–D_9) to enhance diversity and maintain representativeness. The generation process follows the rule defined in Eq. 4:

$$x_{syn} = x_{min} + \lambda(x_{nb} - x_{min}) \quad (4)$$

where x_{min} is a selected minority instance from the range D_3–D_9, x_{nb} is one of its nearest neighbors also selected within the same decile range, and λ is a uniform random number in $[0, 1]$.

3.3 Algorithm Description

The full SOAR procedure is detailed in Algorithm 1.

Algorithm 1 : SOAR

```
Input: Imbalanced Dataset (X_imb, y_imb) and k = 5
Output: Oversampled Dataset (X_sampled, y_sampled)
Let X_min be the minority instances
Compute MOF(X_min) for each X_min ∈ (X_imb, y_imb)
Determine the minimum target size for the minority class: N_target = ⌈(N_Maj + N_Min) / 2⌉
Calculate the required number of synthetic instances: N_syn = N_target − N_min
For each minority class, sort its instances by MOF and divide into deciles (D_1–D_10)
For D_selected from D_3-D_9
    N_selected = |D_selected|
    Calculate the synthetic rate per selected instance: N_point = ⌈N_syn / (7·N_selected)⌉
    For each instance X_min ∈ D_selected:
        Define S = Set of all k nearest neighbor of X_min
        For p = 1 to N_point:
            Select X_nb from S
            Generate X_syn = X_min + λ(X_nb − X_min),   λ ~ U(0,1)
X_sampled = X_min ∪ X_syn
return (X_sampled, y_sampled)
```

SOAR addresses the class imbalance problem by generating synthetic minority instances in informative and representative regions. The algorithm begins by computing the MOF score for each minority instance to quantify its anomalous degree. The target size (N_{target}) is determined as the average of the majority and minority classes, serving as the minimum threshold for oversampling. This demonstrates that fully balancing minority class to the majority class is unnecessary; sampling up to the average is sufficient for effective performance. For each dataset, minority instances are then sorted by MOF scores and divided into deciles. Only instances located between the third and ninth deciles (D_3–D_9) are selected for oversampling to avoid highly anomalous or overly redundant instances. Consequently, the number of selected deciles is 7, which is used in the computation of N_{point}.

Within the selected deciles, each instance is assigned an equal opportunity to generate synthetic instances. This design ensures that deciles containing fewer instances receive a higher density of generated instances, thereby maintaining balanced representation across informative regions. Consequently, the final minority class size becomes slightly greater than the target size N_{target}. This strategy effectively reduces noise, enhances representativeness, and improves overall classification performance.

4 Experiments and Results

4.1 Experimental Datasets

A comprehensive set of seventeen multiclass imbalanced datasets from the UCI Repository was experimented. For each dataset, one class was designated as the minority class, while the remaining classes were collectively grouped as the majority class [12]. Table 1 summarizes the dataset characteristics, including the number of instances and features, selected minority class, class distribution (#Maj. and #Min.), and the Imbalanced Ratio (Imb. ratio), which ranges from 71.0172 to 1.1701. Datasets with Imb. ratio greater than 10 are considered highly imbalanced, whereas those below 10 represent moderate imbalance. This diversity ensures that the experiments cover both moderate and highly imbalanced scenarios.

Table 1. Description of the Experimental Datasets

Datasets	Instances	Features	Minority class	#Maj.	#Min.	Imb. ratio
Abalone	4177	8	17	4119	58	71.0172
Yeast	1484	8	ME2	1433	51	28.0980
Car Evaluation	1728	6	good	1659	69	24.0435
Letter Recognition	20000	16	D	19195	805	23.8447
Page Blocks Classification	5473	10	Horizontal line	5144	329	15.6353
Statlog (Landsat Satellite)	6435	36	damp grey soil	5809	626	9.2796
Pen-Based Recognition	10992	16	7	9850	1142	8.6252
Ecoli	336	7	imU	301	35	8.6
Dermatology	366	34	pityriasis rosea	317	49	6.4694
Glass Identification	214	9	headlamps	185	29	6.3793
Image Segmentation	2310	19	SKY	1980	330	6
Contraceptive Method	1473	9	Long-term	1140	333	3.4234
User Knowledge Modeling	403	5	High	301	102	2.9510
Statlog (Vehicle Silhouettes)	845	18	BUS	628	217	2.8940
Vertebral Column	310	6	Normal	210	100	2.1
Lymphography	148	18	malign lymph	87	61	1.4262
Balance Scale	625	4	R	337	288	1.1701

4.2 Experimental Setup

The experiments were designed to evaluate the effectiveness of SOAR in comparison with both baseline imbalanced dataset (Original) and standard oversampling techniques, including ROS, SMOTE, SL-SMOTE, and BD-SMOTE. A five-fold stratified cross-validation with ten random seeds was conducted to ensure robustness and unbiased evaluation.

To assess generalization performance, ten classifiers with default parameters were used: AdaBoost (AdaB), Decision Tree (DT), Gradient Boosting (GB), Histogram-based Gradient Boosting (HistGB), k-Nearest Neighbors (KNN), Logistic Regression (LR), Multi-layer Perceptron (MLP), Perceptron, Random Forest (RF), and Support Vector Classifier (SVC).

Performance was evaluated using Precision, Recall, and F1-score. The F1-score was selected as the primary performance measure due to its sensitivity to class imbalance. Rankings and average rankings were computed based on the F1-score to compare the effectiveness of the oversampling methods. The statistical significance of performance differences was assessed using the Wilcoxon signed-rank test at a significance level of $p < 0.05$. Paired comparisons were conducted between SOAR and other oversampling techniques.

4.3 Determining the Optimal Decile Range for SOAR

In the decile-based selection, minority instances were ranked according to their MOF scores and divided into ten deciles. These deciles were grouped into various ranges, including D_9, D_8–D_9, ..., and D_1–D_9, to identify the range yielding the highest average F1-score across all datasets. Preliminary experiments using the AdaBoost classifier, chosen for its robustness and sensitivity to class boundaries in imbalanced datasets, indicated that the average F1-score increased steadily up to D_3–D_9 and decreased for D_2–D_9, resulting in D_3–D_9 being selected as the optimal decile range for SOAR (Table 2).

Table 2. Average F1-scores of Various Decile Ranges Evaluated Using AdaBoost

D_9	D_8–D_9	D_7–D_9	D_6–D_9	D_5–D_9	D_4–D_9	D_3–D_9	D_2–D_9	D_1–D_9
0.827199	0.829897	0.832061	0.832617	0.832716	0.833279	**0.834694**	0.834503	0.834738

In addition, the t-SNE plots of the various decile ranges using the Yeast dataset are shown in Fig. 1, where blue points represent majority instances, red points represent minority instances, and green points represent synthetic instances.

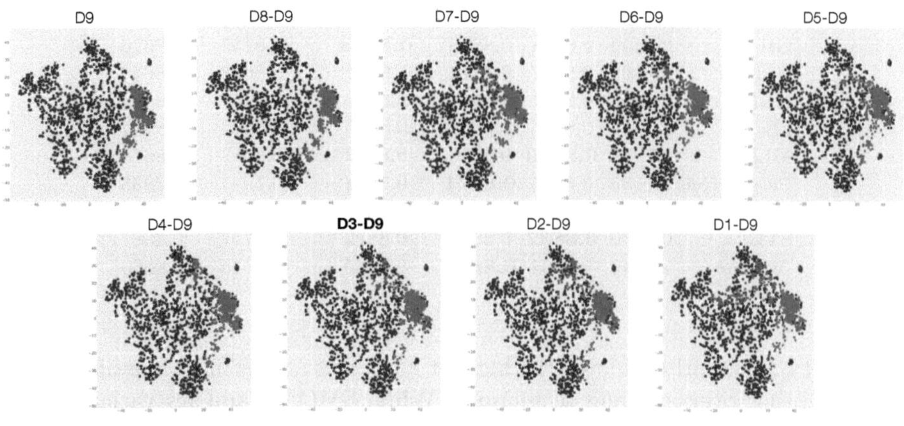

Fig. 1. t-SNE visualization of Yeast dataset across various decile ranges.

4.4 Comparative Results

This subsection reports the comprehensive performance of SOAR against Original, ROS, SMOTE, SL-SMOTE, and BD-SMOTE, using key metrics: Precision (Table 3), Recall (Table 4), and F1-score (Table 5). The evaluation also includes F1-score rankings (Table 6) and the results of the Wilcoxon signed-rank test (Table 7).

Table 3. Precision Results

Classifiers	Original	ROS	SMOTE	SL-SMOTE	BD-SMOTE	SOAR
AdaB	**0.8245**	0.8005	0.8064	0.8021	0.7984	0.8231
DT	0.8328	**0.8357**	0.8195	0.8154	0.8214	0.8246
GB	**0.8715**	0.8359	0.8349	0.8351	0.8342	0.8571
HistGB	**0.8776**	0.8642	0.8576	0.8536	0.8566	0.8690
KNN	**0.8469**	0.7897	0.7879	0.7837	0.7900	0.8012
LR	**0.7937**	0.7690	0.7725	0.7674	0.7663	0.7874
MLP	**0.8280**	0.8199	0.8231	0.8065	0.8201	0.8268
Perceptron	0.7273	0.7248	0.7324	0.7249	0.7252	**0.7443**
RF	**0.8855**	0.8728	0.8627	0.8611	0.8610	0.8722
SVC	0.7467	0.7773	0.7815	0.7714	0.7805	**0.7834**
Average	**0.8234**	0.8090	0.8079	0.8021	0.8054	0.8189

Table 4. Recall Results

Classifiers	Original	ROS	SMOTE	SL-SMOTE	BD-SMOTE	SOAR
AdaB	0.7963	0.8898	**0.8909**	0.8906	0.8782	0.8683
DT	0.8322	0.8297	0.8392	**0.8429**	0.8322	0.8362
GB	0.8400	0.8788	0.8825	**0.8848**	0.8759	0.8626
HistGB	0.8503	0.8657	0.8719	**0.8758**	0.8673	0.8640
KNN	0.8056	0.8561	**0.8715**	0.8540	0.8647	0.8676
LR	0.7614	0.8635	**0.8638**	0.8625	0.8578	0.8494
MLP	0.7988	**0.8820**	0.8766	0.8792	0.8687	0.8678
Perceptron	0.7180	0.8035	**0.8071**	0.7943	0.7941	0.7935
RF	0.8344	0.8509	0.8695	**0.8697**	0.8599	0.8523
SVC	0.7030	**0.8837**	0.8829	0.8812	0.8757	0.8387
Average	0.7940	0.8604	**0.8656**	0.8635	0.8574	0.8500

SOAR consistently achieves the highest F1-scores across most classifiers compared to other oversampling techniques. While SMOTE and its variants often boost Recall, this improvement is frequently offset by a drop in Precision due to oversampling near noisy regions. Conversely, SOAR balances these two metrics by concentrating on representative minority regions, leading to superior F1-scores. While SOAR may not maximize individual Precision or Recall, it keeps both reasonably stable. This approach allows the method to retain a high rate of

Table 5. F1-score Results

Classifiers	Original	ROS	SMOTE	SL-SMOTE	BD-SMOTE	SOAR
AdaB	0.8024	0.8141	0.8203	0.8163	0.8119	**0.8347**
DT	0.8300	**0.8302**	0.8242	0.8232	0.8231	0.8267
GB	0.8498	0.8472	0.8473	0.8470	0.8457	**0.8562**
HistGB	0.8579	0.8619	0.8618	0.8606	0.8589	**0.8640**
KNN	0.8143	0.8080	0.8061	0.7986	0.8081	**0.8190**
LR	0.7626	0.7717	0.7761	0.7707	0.7693	**0.7983**
MLP	0.7970	0.8209	0.8227	0.8080	0.8221	**0.8315**
Perceptron	0.6930	0.6914	0.7040	0.6870	0.6983	**0.7161**
RF	0.8498	0.8566	**0.8633**	0.8622	0.8578	0.8583
SVC	0.6983	0.7871	**0.7919**	0.7815	0.7898	**0.7919**
Average	0.7955	0.8089	0.8118	0.8055	0.8085	**0.8197**

correctly predicted positive cases (Precision) while simultaneously capturing a significant fraction of actual minority instances (Recall) [13]. This simultaneous strength in both metrics is what drives SOAR's robust F1 performance, unlike other techniques that typically focus on only one.

Table 6. Algorithm Rankings Based on F1-Score

Classifiers	Original	ROS	SMOTE	SL-SMOTE	BD-SMOTE	SOAR
AdaB	6	4	2	3	5	**1**
DT	2	**1**	4	5	6	3
GB	2	4	3	5	6	**1**
HistGB	6	2	3	4	5	**1**
KNN	2	4	5	6	3	**1**
LR	6	3	2	4	5	**1**
MLP	6	4	2	5	3	**1**
Perceptron	4	5	2	6	3	**1**
RF	6	5	**1**	2	4	3
SVC	6	4	2	5	3	**1**
Average	4.6	3.6	2.6	4.5	4.3	**1.4**

Based on the average F1-score rankings shown in Table 6, SOAR consistently achieves the highest performance, with an overall mean rank of 1.4, across most classifiers, including AdaBoost, Gradient Boosting, Histogram-based Gradient Boosting, k-Nearest Neighbors, Logistic Regression, Multi-Layer Perceptron, Perceptron, and Support Vector Classification.

The Wilcoxon signed-rank test results in Table 7 indicate that SOAR yields statistically significant improvements ($p < 0.05$) over most competing methods, particularly with ensemble and neural classifiers such as AdaBoost, GB, HistGB, LR, MLP, Perceptron, and SVC. These results confirm that the performance gain of SOAR is not due to random variation but to the algorithm's ability to identify informative synthetic instances in relevant regions of the feature space.

Table 7. Wilcoxon Signed-Rank Test on F1-Score Comparisons Between SOAR and Other Oversampling Techniques

Classifiers	Original	ROS	SMOTE	SL-SMOTE	BD-SMOTE
AdaB	**0**	**0**	**0**	**0**	**0**
DT	0.3748	**0.0070**	0.8426	**0.0081**	0.1168
GB	**0**	**0**	**0**	**0**	**0**
HistGB	**0**	**0.0021**	**0.0051**	**0**	**0**
KNN	0.9651	**0**	**0**	**0**	**0**
LR	**0**	**0**	**0**	**0**	**0**
MLP	**0**	**0**	**0**	**0**	**0**
Perceptron	**0.0021**	**0**	**0.0059**	**0**	**0**
RF	**0**	0.8248	**0**	**0.0070**	0.2792
SVC	**0**	**0**	**0**	**0**	**0**

Overall, SOAR demonstrates consistent superiority in balanced performance and statistical significance across classifiers. While SOAR may not achieve absolute highest Recall or Precision, it attains the highest overall F1-score. This result confirms its ability to effectively balance these two critical metrics. By integrating anomaly detection via MOF with decile-based selection, SOAR minimizes noise and focuses the generation of synthetic instances exclusively on the most informative borderline regions.

5 Conclusion

This study proposed SOAR, a novel oversampling technique that effectively handles class imbalance by generating synthetic minority instances exclusively in the most informative borderline regions, utilizing the MOF and a decile-based selection within the range D_3 to D_9. Extensive experiments on seventeen UCI benchmark datasets across ten classifiers demonstrated that SOAR consistently achieves superior F1-scores compared to baseline and existing oversampling techniques. Crucially, while SOAR may not maximize minority class recall or precision individually, it consistently achieves the most robust trade-off between these two metrics, with the resulting performance gains confirmed as statistically significant by the Wilcoxon signed-rank test.

The superior performance of SOAR is a direct result of integrating anomaly detection with decile-based refinement, as this approach successfully minimizes the presence of highly anomalous and redundant core instances during the synthesis process. This ensures that instances within the most informative deciles receive a proportionally higher density of synthetic instances, which in turn minimizes sampling bias and significantly enhances classifier generalizability and robustness across various datasets and imbalance scenarios.

In addition to its superior performance, SOAR provides a clear foundation for future research. Future work should focus on extending SOAR into a hybrid sampling framework by combining it with informed undersampling strategies. Specifically, majority instances with high MOF scores, which are likely to be outliers, would be removed, while SOAR continues to generate synthetic minority instances in the most informative regions. This integrated approach is expected to further improve classifier performance, particularly in highly imbalanced datasets, providing a robust and generalizable framework applicable to a wide range of real-world classification problems.

References

1. Li, Y., Yang, Y., Song, P., Duan, L., Ren, R.: An improved SMOTE algorithm for enhanced imbalanced data classification by expanding sample generation space. Sci. Rep. **15**, 23521 (2025). https://doi.org/10.1038/s41598-025-09506-w
2. Gosain, A., Sardana, S.: Handling class imbalance problem using oversampling techniques: a review. In: 2017 International Conference on Advances in Computing, Communications and Informatics (ICACCI), pp. 79–85 (2017). https://doi.org/10.1109/ICACCI.2017.8125820
3. Galar, M., Fernandez, A., Barrenechea, E., Sola, H., Herrera, F.: A review on ensembles for the class imbalance problem: bagging-, boosting-, and hybrid-based approaches. IEEE Trans. Appl. Rev. **42**, 463–484 (2012). https://doi.org/10.1109/TSMCC.2011.2161285
4. Chawla, N.V., Bowyer, K.W., Hall, L.O., Kegelmeyer, W.P.: SMOTE: synthetic minority over-sampling technique. J. Artif. Intell. Res. **16**, 321–357 (2002). https://doi.org/10.1613/jair.953
5. Changsakul, P., Boonsiri, S., Sinapiromsaran, K.: Mass-ratio-variance based outlier factor. In: 2021 18th International Joint Conference on Computer Science and Software Engineering (JCSSE), pp. 1–5 (2021). https://doi.org/10.1109/JCSSE53117.2021.9493811
6. Markelle, K., Rachel, L., Kolby, N.: The UCI Machine Learning Repository. https://archive.ics.uci.edu
7. Batista, G.E.A.P.A., Prati, R.C., Monard, M.C.: A study of the behavior of several methods for balancing machine learning training data. ACM SIGKDD Explor. Newsl. **6**(1), 20–29 (2004). https://doi.org/10.1145/1007730.1007735
8. Bunkhumpornpat, C., Sinapiromsaran, K., Lursinsap, C.: Safe-level-SMOTE: safe-level-synthetic minority over-sampling TEchnique for handling the class imbalanced problem. In: Theeramunkong, T., Kijsirikul, B., Cercone, N., Ho, T.-B. (eds.) PAKDD 2009. LNCS (LNAI), vol. 5476, pp. 475–482. Springer, Heidelberg (2009). https://doi.org/10.1007/978-3-642-01307-2_43
9. Han, H., Wang, W.-Y., Mao, B.-H.: Borderline-SMOTE: a new over-sampling method in imbalanced data sets learning. In: Huang, D.-S., Zhang, X.-P., Huang, G.-B. (eds.) ICIC 2005. LNCS, vol. 3644, pp. 878–887. Springer, Heidelberg (2005). https://doi.org/10.1007/11538059_91
10. Toshniwal, A., Mahesh, K., Jayashree, R.: Overview of anomaly detection techniques in machine learning. In: 2020 Fourth International Conference on I-SMAC, pp. 808–815. IEEE (2020). https://doi.org/10.1109/I-SMAC49090.2020.9243329
11. Breunig, M.M., Kriegel, H.-P., Ng, R.T., Sander, J.: LOF: identifying density-based local outliers. SIGMOD Rec. **29**(2), 93–104 (2000). https://doi.org/10.1145/335191.335388

12. Bunkhumpornpat, C., Boonchieng, E., Chouvatut, V., Lipsky, D.: FLEX-SMOTE: synthetic over-sampling technique that flexibly adjusts to different minority class distributions. Patterns **5**(11), 101073 (2024). https://doi.org/10.1016/j.patter.2024.101073
13. Erickson, B.J., Kitamura, F.: Magician's corner: 9. performance metrics for machine learning models. Radiol. Soc. North America **3**(3), e200126 (2021). https://doi.org/10.1148/ryai.2021200126

MedGLM: Unifying Graph Neural Networks and Large Language Models for Knowledge Graph-Grounded Healthcare Prediction

Tri Khang Ho[1(✉)], Linhao Luo[2], Zihang Liu[3], Haishuai Wang[3], and Ling Chen[1]

[1] University of Technology Sydney, Ultimo, NSW 2007, Australia
trikhang.ho@student.uts.edu.au
[2] Monash University, Clayton, Melbourne, VIC 3800, Australia
[3] Zhejiang University, Hangzhou, China

Abstract. The use of Electronic Health Records (EHRs) for healthcare prediction has gained significant attention in clinical decision-support systems. While integrating Large Language Models (LLMs) into healthcare prediction offers new possibilities for clinical reasoning and decision support, these models have limited access to domain-specific medical knowledge and can generate hallucinated responses, undermining reliable medical reasoning. Medical knowledge graphs (KGs), which store extensive medical concepts, have been used to inject knowledge into LLMs. However, KGs are often large and complex, making it difficult for current KG+LLM methods to retrieve the most relevant information for specific patients to ensure accurate predictions. To address these challenges, we present MedGLM, an innovative framework that combines graph neural networks (GNNs) with LLMs for KG-grounded healthcare prediction. MedGLM first uses a GNN to predict potential candidates by reasoning over a large-scale medical KG. Based on these candidates, we extract and rank patient-specific evidence paths by leveraging community structures within the KG. Using these paths, MedGLM performs fine-grained LLM reasoning to generate reliable predictions along with interpretable rationales. Experiments on two publicly available clinical datasets show that MedGLM outperforms state-of-the-art methods, delivering superior performance and interpretability in tasks such as diagnostic prediction and drug recommendation.

Keywords: Large Language Models · Knowledge Graphs · Graph Neural Networks

1 Introduction

Healthcare prediction using Electronic Health Records (EHRs) has become increasingly vital in modern clinical decision-support systems. EHRs contain

R. C.-W. Wong et al. (Eds.): PAKDD 2026, LNAI 16618, pp. 77–89, 2027.
https://doi.org/10.1007/978-981-92-1947-6_7

rich medical data such as diagnoses, medications, and procedures, which can inform predictive models for tasks like disease diagnosis [33], drug recommendation [20], and mortality prediction [20]. However, achieving accurate predictions from EHR data remains challenging due to the complex and interdependent relationships among medical concepts, necessitating the use of advanced modeling techniques.

Traditional machine learning (ML) methods have been widely applied to EHR-based prediction, showing strong performance thanks to their ability to learn historical patterns [5,8,24]. However, these models often lack interpretability and fail to incorporate domain-specific medical knowledge, which limits their generalizability. Recently, Large Language Models (LLMs) have been explored for healthcare predictions [6] due to their strong natural language processing capabilities. Nevertheless, their lack of specialized medical knowledge and tendency to generate hallucinated responses make them unreliable for critical tasks in healthcare [11,21].

Integrating medical Knowledge Graphs (KGs) via Retrieval-Augmented Generation (RAG) offers a promising direction to enhance the factual reliability and reasoning performance of LLMs [12,14,34]. However, existing methods often rely on ad-hoc retrieval or simple embeddings that fail to capture the complex, multi-relational nature of KGs, limiting their ability to model dependencies between medical concepts like disease progression [31]. While Graph Neural Networks (GNNs) have emerged as a powerful solution for encoding these graph structures and patient-specific contexts [9,13,22], current approaches integrating GNNs with LLMs remain under-explored. They either solely rely on GNNs for direct prediction or overwhelming LLMs with noisy and irrelevant information from KGs, highlighting the urgent need for a more effective synergy between GNN-based structural reasoning and LLM-based generation.

To address this gap, we propose MedGLM, a novel framework that integrates GNNs and LLMs for KG-grounded healthcare prediction. Specifically, we use a query-dependent GNN to first extract task-specific candidate entities from a medical KG. The predicted candidates are then used to retrieve patient-specific reasoning paths from the KG. To ensure the reliability and relevance of the extracted paths, we exploit the KG's community structure to group concepts by medical theme, then extract paths within these communities. Following, we leverage both the GNN and LLM to rank the reasoning paths. These paths capture structured relationships among medical concepts, providing rich evidence for LLM reasoning. Finally, we prompt the LLM to reason over the ranked paths to generate accurate predictions along with interpretable rationales. Experimental results on two public EHR datasets show that MedGLM achieves state-of-the-art performance on two healthcare tasks: diagnostic prediction and drug recommendation tasks, while also providing high interpretability through faithful and high-quality rationales. Our contribution can be summarized as follows:

- We introduce MedGLM, a unified KG-grounded framework that tightly couples query-conditioned GNN candidate extraction with evidence-guided LLM

reasoning, grounding predictions in structured medical knowledge and reducing LLM hallucination.
- We design a community-aware evidence retrieval pipeline with hybrid ranking modules powered by GNNs and LLMs to extract high-quality reasoning paths.
- We demonstrate that MedGLM achieves state-of-the-art results on diagnostic prediction and drug recommendation and produces faithful, human-readable rationales, improving both accuracy and interpretability.

2 Related Work

Machine Learning-Based Healthcare Prediction. Machine learning models like CNN [4], RNN [19], Transformer [5], have been widely used to learn statistical patterns from patient EHR records and support data-driven decision making. Although these methods can achieve high predictive accuracy, they often suffer from limited interpretability and generalizability due to their black-box nature.

LLM-Based Healthcare Prediction. LLMs have recently been leveraged for healthcare prediction tasks, benefiting from the extensive knowledge encoded during the pretraining [25]. These models have strong contextual understanding and reasoning capabilities, enabling them to overcome some shortcomings of ML approaches. Several studies have directly employed LLMs to make clinical predictions and to generate interpretable explanations for their decisions [6,18, 26]. However, these approaches still face notable limitations, as relying solely on the inherent knowledge within LLMs can lead to hallucinations and unreliable outputs, particularly in complex medical tasks [17,21].

KG-Enhanced LLM Healthcare Prediction. Medical KGs [1,3] provide a promising solution to mitigate LLM hallucinations by supplying structured and reliable domain knowledge during inference. Early studies typically rely on cosine similarity between concept embeddings [12,33] to extract relevant concepts and relationships from KGs, or leverage LLMs to construct and retrieve data from KG communities [14,32]. However, such methods often struggle to effectively capture complex relationships among medical entities in KGs and can be computationally inefficient, requiring multiple inference steps to retrieve appropriate knowledge. This motivates us to leverage GNNs, which are well-suited for graph-structured data and can effectively model intricate dependencies among medical entities within patient information.

GNN-Based KG Reasoning. Recent studies have explored integrating GNNs with LLMs for general KG question answering [22,23], yet their application to healthcare prediction remains under-explored. Some pioneering frameworks employ GNNs for healthcare tasks. For example, GraphCare [13] proposes a bi-attention augmented GNN for direct prediction but does not incorporate LLMs for deeper reasoning and interpretability. Dr. KNOWS [9] combines a stacked graph isomorphism network with an attention-based path ranker to support LLM-based diagnosis prediction. However, its path retrieval relies mainly on cosine similarity and patient context, often introducing noisy or weakly relevant paths. These limitations highlight the need for more effective GNN–LLM integration to improve both accuracy and interpretability in healthcare prediction.

3 Methodology

3.1 Preliminary

Medical KGs $\mathcal{G} = (\mathcal{E}, \mathcal{R})$ store extensive medical concepts entities $\mathcal{E}$ and their relationships $\mathcal{R}$, providing a structured representation of domain-specific knowledge, such as (`CKD`, `may cause`, `anemia`) or (`hemodialysis`,`treats`, `CKD`). In healthcare prediction tasks, patients' Electronic Health Records (EHRs) are represented as a set of medical concepts $X = (D, P, M)$, including diagnosed conditions $D \subseteq \mathbb{D}$, procedures $P \subseteq \mathbb{P}$, and medications $M \subseteq \mathbb{M}$, which can be linked to corresponding entities $\mathcal{E}$ in the KG. We focus on two key healthcare prediction tasks: *diagnosis prediction*, which aims to predict future conditions $\hat{D}$ based on current patient status X, and *drug recommendation*, which predicts medications $\hat{M}$ given the patient's current conditions D and procedures P.

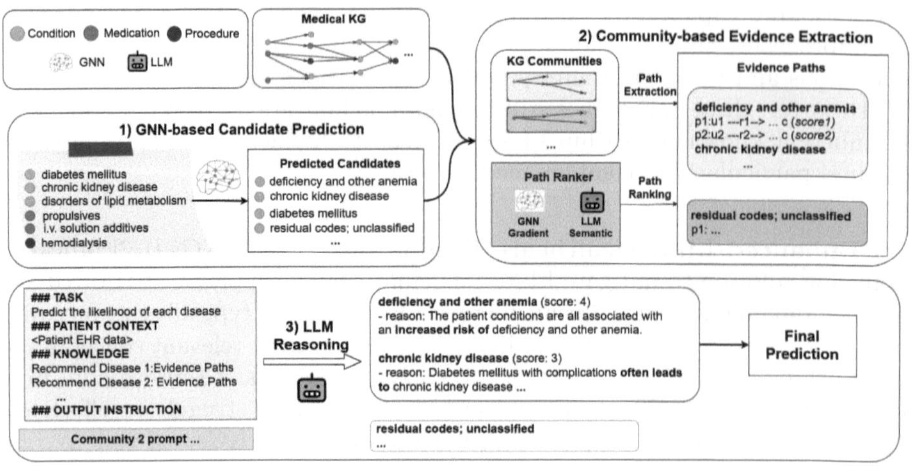

Fig. 1. MedGLM Framework Overview: MedGLM leverages a medical KG and patient EHR records through a multi-step process: 1) it employs a GNN to identify relevant candidates, 2) extracts and ranks reasoning paths based on the predicted candidates and the KG community structure, and 3) utilizes an LLM to reason over extracted paths, generating both predictions and rationales.

Figure 1 provides an overview of the MedGLM framework. MedGLM follows a three-stage pipeline that synergizes structured graph reasoning with language-based semantic reasoning. First, a query-conditioned GNN encodes patient EHR context and the KG to identify task-specific candidate entities. Second, we extract patient-specific reasoning paths by partitioning the KG into communities and retrieving paths that connect patient concepts to the predicted candidates within relevant communities. These paths are then ranked using a hybrid scheme that combines GNN-derived structural importance with LLM-assessed semantic relevance. Finally, an LLM performs evidence-guided reasoning over the top-ranked paths to produce final predictions and concise, human-readable rationales. This design reduces noisy retrieval, grounds LLM outputs in structured medical knowledge, and yields accurate, interpretable clinical recommendations.

3.2 GNN Candidate Prediction

MedGLM utilizes the powerful graph reasoning capability of GNNs to reason over the medical KG $\mathcal{G}$ to extract task-specific candidates for downstream healthcare prediction tasks. For a patient $X = (D, P, M)$ and a downstream task ρ (either diagnosis or drug recommendation), we define a text query template $q = f_{\text{EHR}}(X, \rho)$ to encode both the patient context and task-specific information for context-aware GNN reasoning.

Given the query q and the medical KG $\mathcal{G}$, we employ a query-dependent GNN [22] to predict a score s_e for each candidate relevant to the task ρ:

$$s_e = f^L_{\text{GNN}}(e \mid \mathcal{G}, H^0, q), \quad \forall e \in \mathcal{E}, \quad H^0 = \begin{cases} \mathbf{q}, & e \in X, \\ \mathbf{0}, & \text{otherwise}, \end{cases} \tag{1}$$

where $\mathbf{q}$ denotes the text embedding of the query q. For all the nodes mentioned in patient context X, we initialize their embedding with $\mathbf{q}$, while keeping others as zero vector. The query-dependent GNN will perform message passing to propagate patient-specific information over the KG. After L-layer message passing, we can obtain the final node embedding to compute the relevance score s_e to the query q. Finally, the top-k entities with the highest scores are selected as the candidate set C:

$$C = \text{Top-k}\{(s_e | e \in \mathcal{T}_\rho)\} \tag{2}$$

where $\mathcal{T}_\rho$ denotes the target candidates of each task, i.e., $\mathbb{D}$ for the disease diagnosis and $\mathbb{M}$ for drug recommendation.

3.3 Patient-Specific Reasoning Path Extraction

While the candidate set C predicted by the GNN provides relevant entities for the downstream task, they fail to capture the structured relationships among medical concepts necessary for reliable reasoning. To address this, we extract patient-specific reasoning paths from the KG that connect patient context nodes X to the predicted candidates C. These paths serve as structured evidence to guide LLM reasoning.

KG Community Construction and Community Retrieval. Early studies directly connect all candidate entities to patient concepts to form reasoning paths [9,23]. However, this often results in an overwhelming number of paths, many of which may be irrelevant or noisy, hindering effective LLM reasoning. To mitigate this, we leverage the inherent community structure within the KG to group related concepts under shared medical themes, enabling more focused and relevant path extraction within the community. Specifically, we first apply the Leiden algorithm [28] to partition the KG into K communities: $\mathcal{G} = \{\mathcal{G}_1, \mathcal{G}_2, \ldots, \mathcal{G}_K\}$. We then perform community retrieval to select the minimum set of communities whose nodes collectively cover all the predicted candidates in C, formulated as:

$$\mathcal{G}^* = \arg\min_{\mathcal{S} \subseteq \mathcal{G}} |\mathcal{S}| \quad \text{s.t.} \quad \bigcup_{\mathcal{G}_i \in \mathcal{S}} \mathcal{E}_i = C, \tag{3}$$

where $\mathcal{E}_i$ represents the set of entities in community $\mathcal{G}_i$, and $\mathcal{S}$ is the selected subset of communities. In this way, we could find the smallest subset of communities whose union of entities covers all the candidate entities in C.

Reasoning Path Generation. For each retrieved community $\mathcal{G}_i \in \mathcal{G}^*$ and a candidate covered by such community $c \in C_i$, we extract a set of patient-specific evidence paths that connect community-specific patient concepts $x \in X_i$ to c. Path extraction is constrained to ensure clinical relevance: (i) paths must match task-specific metapaths $\mathcal{M}_\rho$ (e.g. `medication` $\rightarrow$ `diagnosis`), and (ii) all nodes on a path must belong to the same community $\mathcal{G}_i$. This can be formulated as:

$$\mathcal{P}_i(c) = \bigcup\nolimits_{x \in X_i} \left\{ p = (x \rightarrow e_1 \rightarrow \ldots \rightarrow c) \,\middle|\, p \text{ respects } \mathcal{M}_\rho,\ p \subseteq \mathcal{G}_i \right\}. \tag{4}$$

The resulting paths $\mathcal{P}_i(c)$ capture structured relationships among medical concepts, e.g., causal relation between past diagnoses to future conditions or drug-disease treatment chains, providing rich evidence for LLM reasoning.

Reasoning Path Ranking. To ensure the quality and relevance of the extracted reasoning paths, we implement a hybrid ranking mechanism that combines both GNN-based structural importance and LLM-based semantic relevance to rank the extracted paths.

The GNN-score $s_{\text{GNN}}(p)$ quantifies how much each path contributes to the GNN's prediction of candidate c, which can be quantified by the partial derivative of the prediction score with respect to the triplets at each hop:

$$s_{\text{GNN}}(p) = \sum_{j=1}^{L} \left\| \frac{\partial s_c}{\partial t_j} \right\|, \tag{5}$$

where t_j denotes the triplet at hop j in path p, and s_c is the GNN prediction score for candidate c.

The LLM-score $s_{\text{LLM}}(p)$ evaluates the semantic relevance of each path to the downstream task ρ. We prompt the LLM to assess the relevance of each triplet in the path and extract the maximum relevance score among all triplets:

$$s_{\text{LLM}}(p) = \max_{j=1,\dots,L} \phi_{\text{LLM}}(t_j, \rho). \tag{6}$$

The final hybrid score for ranking paths combines both GNN and LLM scores, adjusted by a length penalty to favor concise paths:

$$\text{score}(p) = \frac{\alpha \cdot s_{\text{GNN}}(p) + (1-\alpha) \cdot s_{\text{LLM}}(p)}{|p|^{\beta}}, \tag{7}$$

where $|p|$ is the path length, and $\beta > 0$ penalizes longer paths. $\alpha \in [0, 1]$ balances the GNN predictive relevance and LLM semantic relevance.

We then select the top-m paths with the highest scores, forming the final evidence paths for each candidate $c \in C_i$

$$\mathcal{P}_i^*(c) = \text{Top-m}\{score(p) | p \in \mathcal{P}_i\} \tag{8}$$

3.4 Evidence-Based LLM Prediction

After extracting reasoning paths, we use the LLM to score and justify candidates using the community-level evidence. For each community $\mathcal{G}_i$, the LLM returns a community-level score $s_i(c)$ and a short rationale $\gamma_i(c)$ for every candidate:

$$s_i(c), \gamma_i(c) = f_{\text{LLM}}(C_i, \mathcal{P}_i^*, X), c \in C_i \tag{9}$$

where $\mathcal{P}_i^*$ is the set of selected evidence paths and X is the patient concepts. Then we aggregate all the community-level scores to obtain the final score $s(c)$ for each candidate c. The final rationale $\gamma(c)$ is defined as the rationale from the community that yields the highest community-level score for candidate c. The final predicted set is selected by threshold τ:

$$\hat{C} = \{c \mid s(c) \geq \tau\}, \tag{10}$$

where $\hat{C}$ can be either predicted diseases or medications depending on the task.

4 Experimental Results

4.1 Experimental Setups

Datasets. Experiments are conducted on two publicly available datasets, MIMIC-III (v1.4) [15] and MIMIC-IV (v2.0) [16]. For each dataset, we construct two task-specific sets, one for diagnostic prediction and one for drug recommendation, following the approach in [14]. The statistics are summarized in Table 1.

Medical KG. Following [14], we construct a medical KG from reliable sources [1,2], and prune it to include only entities related to diseases, procedures, and medications. The final graph has 700 nodes and 42,482 edges, capturing key medical concepts and their relationships.

Table 1. Summary Statistics for MIMIC-III and MIMIC-IV datasets. #D-P-M denotes the mean numbers of conditions, medications and procedures per sample.

Dataset/Split	MIMIC-III				MIMIC-IV			
	Diagnosis		Drugrec		Diagnosis		Drugrec	
	#Sample	#D-P-M	#Sample	#D-P-M	#Sample	#D-P-M	#Sample	#D-P-M
Train	7,814	16.5 - 37.1 - 5.1	35,578	12.4 - 29.9 - 4.4	8,056	17.9 - 35.0 - 4.3	31,907	15.7 - 28.8 - 4.0
Val	896	15.1 - 34.9 - 4.8	4,346	12.1 - 29.9 - 4.3	934	18.3 - 34.7 - 4.5	4,025	15.5 - 28.9 - 3.9
Test	983	15.5 - 37.4 - 4.9	1,000	10.8 - 29.1 - 4.6	1,000	17.9 - 35.5 - 4.4	1,000	16.0 - 29.0 - 4.0

Metrics. We evaluate the performance of the proposed method on two primary metrics: F1 score and Jaccard index, which respectively capture the balance between precision and recall, and the overlap between predicted and ground-truth label sets. For the diagnosis task, we define an additional metric called novel-F1 that evaluates the model's ability to predict new diseases that are not part of the existing conditions.

Baselines. We compare MedGLM with four categories of baseline methods: (1) ML methods: GRU [19], Transformer [29], RETAIN [5], and StageNet [8]; (2) LLM-only method: We prompt the LLM to directly predict candidate diseases, using different LLM families: Qwen3 [27], GPT [25], Llama3 [10] and DeepSeek [7]; (3) KG + LLM methods: KARE [14], MedRAG [33], MKGRank [20], MedReason [31] and MedIKAL [12]; and (4) ML + KG + LLM methods: EMERGE [34], RetCare [30], and GraphCare [13]—a GNN-based approach.

Implementation Details. For candidate prediction, we adapt the query dependent GNN from `GFM-RAG` [22] and train it on MIMIC-III and MIMIC-IV to predict candidate diseases and drugs. Queries are embedded using *neutrl/pubmedbert-base*, and the GNN consists of six message-passing layers with hidden dimension 512, `sum` aggregation, and `DistMult` operator. The model is trained for 20 epochs with AdamW (learning rate 5×10^{-4}), using a top-k threshold of 25.

For community detection, we run the Leiden algorithm 200 times with different random seeds to construct KG communities for each task. This process yields 8,167 communities for disease prediction (average size of 17 nodes) and 3,343 communities for drug recommendation (average size of 42 nodes). For the path-ranking component, we set the parameters to $\alpha = 0.5$, $\beta = 0.5$, and $m = 5$.

For final LLM-based prediction, we use GPT-4o-mini as the primary backbone and additionally evaluate Qwen3-8B. The selection threshold τ and aggregation strategy are searched within the range of 1–4 and using mean or max, respectively, to optimize F1 score for both diagnosis and drug recommendation.

Table 2. Performance comparison on MIMIC-III and MIMIC-IV for diagnostic prediction and drug recommendation. **Bold:** Best. <u>Underline:</u> Second best. **nF1** denotes novel prediction F1.

Category	Method	Diagnostic Prediction						Drug Recommendation			
		MIMIC-III			MIMIC-IV			MIMIC-III		MIMIC-IV	
		F1	Jac.	nF1	F1	Jac.	nF1	F1	Jac.	F1	Jac.
ML	GRU	0.340	0.222	0.075	0.334	0.220	0.051	0.606	0.457	0.538	0.391
	Transformer	0.349	0.229	0.047	0.338	0.226	0.023	0.575	0.426	0.498	0.352
	RETAIN	<u>0.393</u>	<u>0.264</u>	0.075	<u>0.392</u>	<u>0.267</u>	0.039	0.601	0.452	0.531	0.384
	StageNet	0.350	0.232	0.039	0.344	0.231	0.021	<u>0.630</u>	<u>0.482</u>	<u>0.572</u>	<u>0.418</u>
LLM	Qwen3-8B	0.156	0.091	0.086	0.104	0.060	0.050	0.158	0.089	0.184	0.105
	Qwen3-32B	0.294	0.182	0.086	0.243	0.148	0.060	0.194	0.112	0.200	0.115
	Qwen3-235B	0.350	0.223	0.116	0.285	0.179	0.066	0.224	0.131	0.216	0.126
	Qwen3-235B-Think	0.094	0.055	0.056	0.055	0.032	0.029	0.105	0.060	0.114	0.066
	Llama3-70B	0.244	0.147	0.079	0.188	0.111	0.048	0.167	0.094	0.177	0.100
	DeepSeek-R1-14B	0.126	0.075	0.045	0.085	0.005	0.027	0.112	0.062	0.130	0.074
	DeepSeek-R1-32B	0.165	0.097	0.063	0.124	0.072	0.040	0.130	0.073	0.144	0.082
	GPT-4o-mini	0.283	0.174	0.073	0.235	0.142	0.047	0.141	0.078	0.145	0.081
	GPT-oss-120B	0.220	0.130	0.120	0.137	0.079	0.068	0.250	0.148	0.258	0.153
KG+LLM	KARE										
	- Qwen3-8B	0.318	0.200	0.100	0.285	0.178	0.097	0.335	0.207	0.304	0.185
	- Qwen3-8B (FT)	0.240	0.139	0.134	0.223	0.130	0.117	0.474	0.322	0.379	0.243
	- DeepSeek-V3	0.280	0.170	0.113	0.248	0.151	0.098	0.348	0.215	0.313	0.191
	MedRAG	0.352	0.222	<u>0.152</u>	0.320	0.200	<u>0.130</u>	0.297	0.178	0.278	0.165
	MKGRank	0.340	0.212	-	0.303	0.186	-	0.365	0.237	0.343	0.220
	MedReason	0.278	0.167	0.125	0.258	0.155	0.112	0.306	0.186	0.291	0.176
	MedIKAL	0.233	0.137	0.130	0.187	0.111	0.098	0.417	0.272	0.389	0.248
ML+KG+LLM	GraphCare	0.282	0.178	-	0.255	0.161	-	0.625	0.474	0.513	0.364
	EMERGE	0.301	0.183	-	0.266	0.161	-	0.460	0.310	0.375	0.239
	RetCare	0.295	0.178	-	0.301	0.168	-	0.393	0.276	0.378	0.237
	MedGLM (Ours)										
	- GPT-4o-mini	**0.444**	**0.298**	**0.190**	**0.433**	**0.294**	**0.177**	**0.659**	**0.507**	**0.581**	**0.424**
	- Qwen3-8B	**0.430**	**0.287**	**0.195**	**0.412**	**0.277**	**0.178**	**0.662**	**0.511**	**0.587**	**0.430**

4.2 Main Results

Table 2 summarizes diagnostic and drug recommendation results on MIMIC-III and MIMIC-IV. Traditional ML models outperform LLMs in predictive accuracy but lack interpretable rationales. Adding medical KGs provides LLMs with extra knowledge, though noisy and ad-hoc KG retrieval limits improvements. Hybrid ML+KG+LLM approaches show promise but still struggle to effectively utilize KGs. Our MedGLM excels through GNN-based candidate extraction, community-aware path retrieval and path ranking, achieving significant F1 gains compared to the best baseline methods (e.g., +13.0% on MIMIC-III and +10.5% on MIMIC-IV). Moreover, the highest performance on **novel diagnosis** indicates that MedGLM can analyze complex medical relationships to predict new diseases, rather than merely repeating historical conditions, a common limitation of LLM-based methods.

4.3 Interpretability

Interpretability is essential for trustworthy clinical decision-making. We evaluate it by comparing the generated rationales for predictions in 150 random samples from the MIMIC-III dataset between our method and each baseline approach. For each sample, we randomly select 20 predictions shared by both our method and the baseline. For each shared prediction, we gather the rationale generated by our method and the corresponding rationale from the baseline, and then prompt GPT-4o-mini to judge which rationale is superior based on four criteria: Factuality (grounding in KG knowledge), Granularity (level of detail), Consistency (alignment with patient records), and Readability (clarity and fluency). For each criterion, if our rationale is judged better, it receives a score of +1; otherwise, the baseline receives +1. We then sum these scores across all predictions to obtain a final comparison between our method and the baseline.

Figure 2 shows that MedGLM outperforms MedRAG, KARE, and MedReason, and matches MediKAL in all metrics. Notably, MedGLM achieves remarkable win rates of 90%/40.1%/91.5%/89.1% for Factuality and 97.5%/45.4%/97.5 %/96.7% for Granularity. This highlights the effectiveness of GNN-based candidate extraction, community-based path retrieval, and subsequent path ranking in enhancing LLM interpretability.

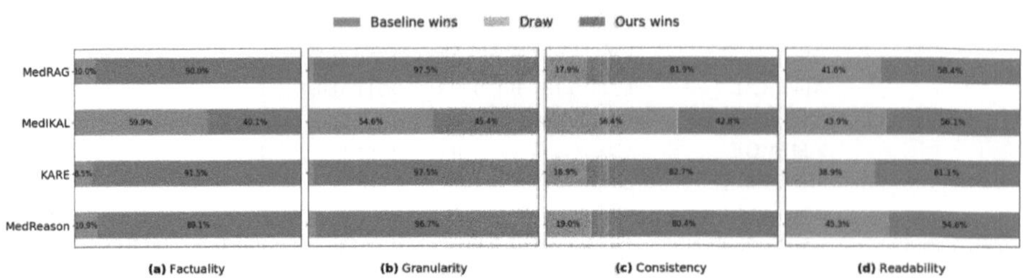

Fig. 2. Interpretability comparison on MIMIC-III diagnosis.

Table 3. Ablation study on the MIMIC-III dataset.

Variants	Diagnostic Prediction				Drug Recommendation			
	F1 (Δ%)	Prec.	Rec.	#AvgP	F1 (Δ%)	Prec.	Rec.	#AvgP
Full	**0.444**	**0.449**	**0.489**	<u>142.6</u>	**0.659**	0.734	**0.629**	<u>170.2</u>
w/o Comm	0.401 (−4.3)	0.419	0.426	**64.4**	0.483 (−17.6)	0.760	0.392	**93.3**
w/o Rank	0.432 (−1.2)	0.430	0.484	431.5	0.611 (−4.8)	0.745	0.547	183.3
w/o Comm+Rank	0.385 (−5.9)	0.413	0.400	896.8	0.481 (17.8)	0.760	0.390	200.0
w/o GNN	0.156 (−28.8)	0.176	0.157	-	0.158 (−50.1)	0.323	0.111	-

4.4 Ablation Study

We assess each component's contribution through ablation studies with the following settings: *w/o Comm* (treat all concepts as one community), *w/o Rank* (remove the path ranker), *w/o Comm+Rank* (remove both community-based evidence extraction and the path ranker), and *w/o GNN* (direct prediction without GNN-generated candidates). As shown in Table 3, retaining all components yields the best performance while keeping the number of reasoning paths manageable. Removing either the community module or the path ranker results in a slight performance drop, as both work together to produce relevant evidence that facilitates fine-grained and precise LLM reasoning. Meanwhile, removing GNN candidates causes a substantial decline, since these candidates are essential for identifying plausible paths and guiding evidence extraction.

4.5 Case Study

Figure 3 illustrates a case study about how we leverage community-guided evidence to perform reasoning. Based on the per-candidate evidence paths, the LLM assigns scores of 4 and 3 to *deficiency and other anemia* and *chronic kidney disease* respectively. These diseases are selected due to the presence of strong evidence relationships, such as *often develops* (scored 0.9/1.0) and *often leads to* (scored 1.0/1.0) linking them to the patient's context. In contrast, the candidate *residual codes; unclassified* shows only a moderate relationship with the patient's context, resulting in a final score of 2, which leads to its rejection.

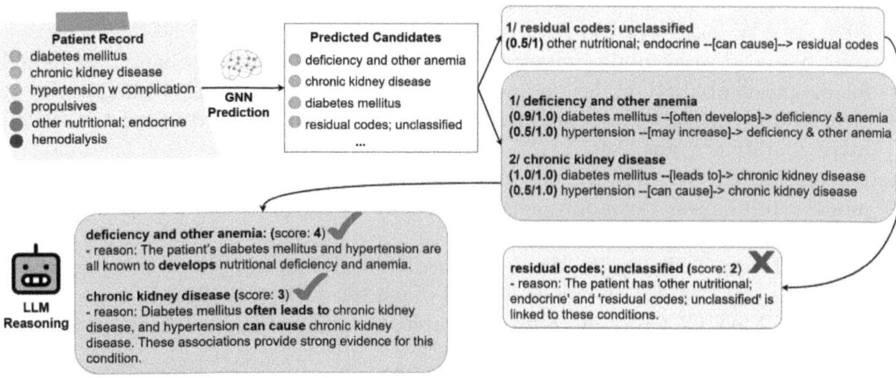

Fig. 3. A case study for disease prediction. A tick indicates the diseases selected, while an X represents those that are rejected.

5 Conclusion

In this study, we present MedGLM, a novel approach that combines GNNs and LLMs to extract trustworthy KG-grounded reasoning paths to enhance healthcare predictions. Experiments on the MIMIC-III and MIMIC-IV datasets demonstrate MedGLM's superiority over state-of-the-art methods in both disease prediction and drug recommendation tasks. Future work will focus on scaling MedGLM to tackle more complex medical reasoning tasks, as well as exploring advanced techniques for community construction and evidence extraction to further improve performance and mitigate hallucinations in LLMs.

References

1. Bodenreider, O.: The unified medical language system (UMLs): integrating biomedical terminology. Nucleic Acids Res. **32**(suppl_1), D267–D270 (2004)
2. Canese, K., Weis, S.: PubMed: the bibliographic database. In: The NCBI Handbook. National Center for Biotechnology Information (NCBI) (2013)
3. Chandak, P., Huang, K., Zitnik, M.: Building a knowledge graph to enable precision medicine. Nat. Sci. Data (2023)
4. Chen, J., Yin, C., Wang, Y., Zhang, P.: Predictive modeling with temporal graphical representation on electronic health records (2024)
5. Choi, E., Bahadori, M.T., et al.: RETAIN: an interpretable predictive model for healthcare using reverse time attention mechanism (2017)
6. Cui, H., Shen, Z., Zhang, J., Shao, H.: LLMs-based few-shot disease predictions using EHR: a novel approach combining predictive agent reasoning and critical agent instruction (2024)
7. DeepSeek-AI: DeepSeek-R1: incentivizing reasoning capability in LLMs via reinforcement learning (2025)
8. Gao, J., Xiao, C., Wang, Y., Tang, W., Glass, L.M., Sun, J.: StageNet: stage-aware neural networks for health risk prediction. In: Proceedings of The Web Conference 2020, WWW 2020, pp. 530–540. ACM, April 2020
9. Gao, Y., et al.: Leveraging medical knowledge graphs into large language models for diagnosis prediction: design and application study. JMIR AI **4** (2025)
10. Grattafiori, A., Dubey, A., Jauhri, A., et al.: The llama 3 herd of models (2024). https://arxiv.org/abs/2407.21783
11. Huang, L., Yu, W., Ma, W., et al.: A survey on hallucination in large language models: principles, taxonomy, challenges, and open questions. ACM Trans. Inf. Syst. **43**(2), 1–55 (2025)
12. Jia, M., Duan, J., Song, Y., Wang, J.: mediKAL: integrating knowledge graphs as assistants of LLMs for enhanced clinical diagnosis on EMRs (2025)
13. Jiang, P., Xiao, C., Cross, A., Sun, J.: GraphCare: enhancing healthcare predictions with personalized knowledge graphs (2024)
14. Jiang, P., Xiao, C., et al.: Reasoning-enhanced healthcare predictions with knowledge graph community retrieval. arXiv preprint arXiv:2410.04585 (2024)
15. Johnson, A.E.W., et al.: MIMIC-III, a freely accessible critical care database. Sci. Data **3**, 160035 (2016)
16. Johnson, A.E.W., et al.: MIMIC-IV, a freely accessible electronic health record dataset. Sci. Data **10**(1), 1–9 (2022)
17. Kim, Y., Jeong, H., Chen, S., et al.: Medical hallucinations in foundation models and their impact on healthcare (2025)
18. Kwon, T., et al.: Large language models are clinical reasoners: reasoning-aware diagnosis framework with prompt-generated rationales (2024)

19. Cho, K., van Merrienboer, B., Gulcehre, C., et al.: Learning phrase representations using RNN encoder-decoder for statistical machine translation (2014)
20. Li, F., Chen, Y., Liu, H., et al.: MKG-Rank: enhancing large language models with knowledge graph for multilingual medical question answering (2025)
21. Liu, L., et al.: A survey on medical large language models: technology, application, trustworthiness, and future directions (2024)
22. Luo, L., Zhao, Z., Haffari, G., Phung, D., Gong, C., Pan, S.: GFM-RAG: graph foundation model for retrieval augmented generation. In: NeurIPS 2025 (2025)
23. Mavromatis, C., Karypis, G.: GNN-RAG: graph neural retrieval for large language model reasoning (2024)
24. Nguyen, P., Tran, T., Wickramasinghe, N., Venkatesh, S.: Deepr: a convolutional net for medical records (2016)
25. OpenAI: GPT-4 technical report (2024)
26. Shoham, O.B., Rappoport, N.: CPLLM: clinical prediction with large language models (2024)
27. Qwen Team: Qwen3 technical report (2025)
28. Traag, V.A., Waltman, L., van Eck, N.J.: From Louvain to Leiden: guaranteeing well-connected communities. Sci. Rep. **9**(1) (2019)
29. Vaswani, A., et al.: Attention is all you need (2023)
30. Wang, Z., et al.: RetCare: towards interpretable clinical decision making through LLM-driven medical knowledge retrieval. In: Proceedings of the KDD-AIDSH (2024)
31. Wu, J., Deng, W., Li, X., et al.: MedReason: eliciting factual medical reasoning steps in LLMs via knowledge graphs (2025)
32. Wu, J., Zhu, J., Qi, Y., et al.: Medical graph rag: towards safe medical large language model via graph retrieval-augmented generation (2024)
33. Zhao, X., Liu, S., Yang, S.Y., Miao, C.: MedRAG: enhancing retrieval-augmented generation with knowledge graph-elicited reasoning for healthcare copilot (2025)
34. Zhu, Y., et al.: EMERGE: enhancing multimodal electronic health records predictive modeling with retrieval-augmented generation. In: Proceedings of the CIKM (2024)

CadST: Correlation-aware Alignment and Disentanglement in Multi-modal Spatio-Temporal Traffic Prediction

Limei Liu[1], Peibo Duan[1], Zhenliang Ma[2], Leizhen Wang[1], Yibo Wang[1], and Jia Rong[1](✉)

[1] Monash University, Melbourne, Australia
{limei.liu,peibo.duan,leizhen.wang,yibo.wang}@monash.edu, jiarong@acm.org
[2] KTH Royal Institute of Technology, Stockholm, Sweden
zhema@kth.se

Abstract. Accurate traffic prediction is crucial for intelligent transportation systems (ITS). Multi-modal data including sensor readings, textual incident reports, and environmental indicators, jointly shape traffic dynamics. Although there is research in multi-modal traffic prediction, they fused the heterogeneous modalities without considering the noise and confounding factors, and usually ignored the domain shift across events. To address these challenges, we propose a Correlation-aware Alignment and Disentanglement Spatio-Temporal (*CadST*) framework for multi-modal traffic prediction. *CadST* consists of two main components: (1) a correlation-aware feature filtering and alignment module for efficient cross-modal fusion, and (2) a channel-wise regularized disentanglement module to generalize to different traffic situations. Experiments on the real-world BjTT dataset demonstrate that *CadST* achieves higher prediction accuracy compared to the baselines, demonstrating its effectiveness and efficiency.

Keywords: Multi-modal · Feature Alignment · Feature Disentanglement

1 Introduction

Traffic prediction is a basic task of intelligent transportation systems (ITS), enabling proactive traffic management and improving urban mobility. Traditional approaches focus on numerical sensor streams (e.g., traffic volume and speed) and thus fail to capture the contextual semantics that drive traffic dynamics [1–4], which are especially salient during holidays and special events. To bridge this gap, text-attributed multi-modal traffic prediction has emerged as a promising paradigm that integrates structured spatio-temporal traffic signals with unstructured textual information, such as event reports, weather descriptions, or social media posts [6,7]. These text attributes provide complementary cues (e.g., incidents, roadworks, public events) that influence traffic speed and

R. C.-W. Wong et al. (Eds.): PAKDD 2026, LNAI 16618, pp. 90–101, 2027.
https://doi.org/10.1007/978-981-92-1947-6_8

volume but are not directly observable in numerical data. By fusing heterogeneous modalities, models can form richer and more interpretable representations of the latent factors underlying real-world traffic variations.

Recent multi-modal traffic prediction studies integrate spatio-temporal numerical signals from road segments with contextual text from diverse events. While cross-modal alignment and fusion can enrich representations and improve pattern learning, most methods do not explicitly filter noise or confounding factors in textual inputs, which can introduce spurious correlations and degrade both accuracy and interpretability. Moreover, coping with domain shift induced by non-stationary exogenous factors (e.g., weather, planned events, or holidays) remains critical for robust and practically deployable ITS.

To address the above two challenges in this work, we propose *CadST* framework for multi-modal traffic prediction. It includes two modules: (1) a Correlation-aware Feature Filtering and Alignment (CFFA) module for efficient cross-modal fusion, and (2) a novel Channel-wise Regularized Disentanglement (CRD) module for domain generalization. CFFA filters out noise and spurious associations to improve the accuracy of feature representation. CRD decouples domain-invariant representations from domain-specific, spurious information, thus ensuring reliable performance in non-stationary environments.

The main contributions of this work can be highlighted as follows:

- CFFA filters text embeddings via nonlinear dependence estimation prior to cross-attention-based multimodal fusion. By identifing and retaining textual features that exhibit strong statistical dependence with graph-structural representations, CFFA suppresses task-irrelevant semantic components and reduces feature noise in the fusion process, yielding cleaner and more task-relevant multimodal representations.
- CRD enforces statistical independence between domain-invariant and domain-specific latent representations by minimizing the statistical dependence across feature channels, thereby mitigating the impact of spurious correlations across heterogeneous traffic scenarios and improving generalization under domain shift.
- Extensive experiments on the real-world BjTT dataset demonstrate that the proposed *CadST* framework achieves state-of-the-art (SOTA) performance across multiple spatio-temporal prediction tasks. Specifically, *CadST* reduces MAE by 14.81%, 3.16%, and 3.07% on three prediction horizons with the STGCN [2] backbone, respectively.

2 Related Work

Traditional traffic prediction models, relying on DCRNN, Graph Neural Networks (GNNs) like STGCN and Graph WaveNet [1,2,4], mainly encode numerical features (e.g., speed, volume) and spatio-temporal dependencies. While effective for recurrent patterns, these numerical approaches inherently fail to model non-recurrent congestion caused by exogenous factors like accidents, events, or severe weather due to the domain shift in unseen traffic situations. Consequently, research has shifted toward multi-modal traffic prediction, integrating modalities, such as visual [11], meteorological [6], and textual information [7,10]. Textual information from incident reports or social media provides semantic priors that are essential for interpretable and contextually informed prediction of unexpected traffic situations.

Although text-attributed multi-modal prediction is prevalent in ITS due to data availability, existing fusion techniques often lack robust integration. Zhou et al. [10,12] integrate multiple modalities for real-time traffic speed prediction, however, their concatenation-based or shallow fusion designs may introduce noise and spurious correlations. More advanced approaches have been explored outside the traffic domain. TAPE [14] employs LLMs to generate text-attributed graphs and reports strong performance, but evaluation is largely limited to non-traffic benchmarks (e.g., Cora and PubMed). LLMEnhCausalMechanism [15] improves information transfer via self-attention yet focuses on synthetic and benchmark graph datasets. E2-CSTP [13] uses cross-modal attention and gating for efficient fusion with competitive results on general graph data. Despite this progress, two core challenges remain: explicitly mitigating spurious information and achieving generalization under domain shift.

Moreover, multi-task learning (MTL) is a parallel strategy that helps enhance model robustness by jointly optimizing multiple factors or in multiple cities (e.g., speed, volume, and congestion level) [16–18]. MTL leverages shared representations to improve generalization and prevent overfitting across related prediction tasks. Although few studies successfully integrate rich textual semantics within a unified multi-task, graph-based traffic prediction framework. Most of them either treat the textual feature as mere auxiliary input or fail to achieve robust alignment between linguistic and numerical modalities, and result in sub-optimal fusion strategies that do not fully leverage the synergistic potential of MTL [8,9].

In summary, while considerable progress has been made in multi-modal traffic prediction, a crucial limitation remains: the explicit failure to mitigate spurious correlations and ensure generalization against real-world domain shift.

3 CadST

The proposed *CadST* framework aims to achieve both high prediction accuracy and domain generalization by seamlessly integrating multi-modal spatio-temporal representations with statistical dependence modeling. As illustrated in Fig. 1, the framework comprises two key modules: (1) *CFFA*, which filters textual embeddings by suppressing potentially confounding information prior to cross-modal fusion, yielding cleaner and more task-aligned representations; and (2) *CRD*, which decouples domain-invariant and domain-specific feature variables via independence regularization, encouraging representations that remain stable under distribution shift across heterogeneous traffic scenarios.

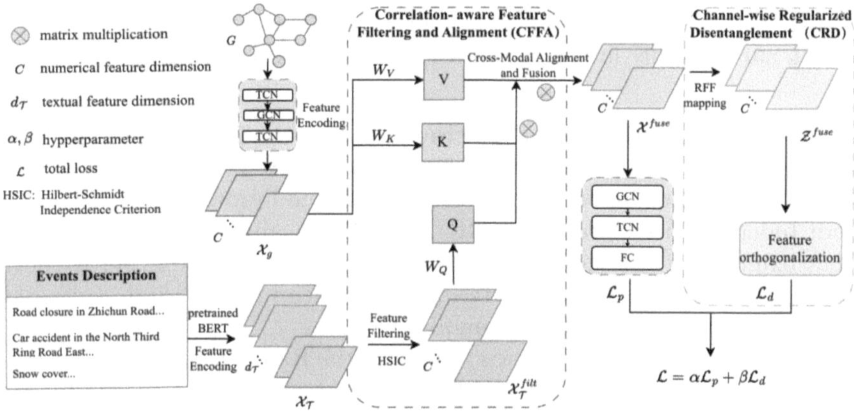

Fig. 1. Overview of the *CadST* framework. CFFA suppresses task-irrelevant and confounding components in textual embedding, CRD decouples domain-invariant and domain-specific representations to mitigate distribution shift between different events.

3.1 Correlation-Aware Feature Filtering and Alignment Module

This module performs two key steps: (1) the filtering of the text embeddings to remove confounding features, and (2) the cross-attention alignment and fusion of textual and numerical data. The filtering step ensures only the clean and correlated variables in the feature alignment and fusion, mitigating the intervention of spurious correlations.

Feature Encoding. In spatio-temporal encoding of numerical data, the traffic graph is defined as $G = (V, E)$, where V represents the set of N road segments (nodes) with $N = |V|$ and E denotes the edges that capture the spatial connectivity. The raw numerical traffic data are denoted by $\mathbf{X}_g \in \mathbb{R}^{N\times T\times F}$, where T is the observed time steps and F is the feature dimension (e.g., speed, volume). The numerical embedding $\mathcal{X}_g \in \mathbb{R}^{N\times T\times C}$ is obtained from two sequential Temporal Convolutional Network (TCN) layers sandwiching one Graph Convolutional Network (GCN) layer, with C the dimension of the hidden layer, $\mathbf{A}$ the adjacent matrix of G, Θ and $\mathbf{W}$ the weights of TCN and GCN in Eq. (1).

$$\begin{aligned}
\mathbf{H}_g &= \mathrm{ReLU}\left(\Theta_1 \star_{\mathcal{T}} \mathbf{X}_g\right) \\
\mathbf{Z}_g &= \sigma\left(\tilde{\mathbf{D}}^{-\frac{1}{2}}\tilde{\mathbf{A}}\tilde{\mathbf{D}}^{-\frac{1}{2}}\mathbf{H}_g\mathbf{W}\right) \\
\mathcal{X}_g &= \mathrm{ReLU}\left(\Theta_2 \star_{\mathcal{T}} \mathbf{Z}_g\right)
\end{aligned} \tag{1}$$

Textual descriptions $\mathcal{T} = \{\mathcal{T}_t\}_{t=1}^{T}$ are encoded via a pre-trained BERT model [19], producing contextual embeddings $\mathcal{X}_{\mathcal{T}} \in \mathbb{R}^{T\times d_{\mathcal{T}}}$ ($d_{\mathcal{T}} = 768$) that capture semantic information across incidents, roadworks, weather conditions, and special events. BERT is preferred over generative LLMs given the short and domain-specific nature of traffic texts, offering efficient and stable representations with substantially lower computational overhead [12,14,27].

Correlation-Aware Feature Filtering via HSIC. To mitigate the impact of noise and confounding components inherent in textual embeddings $\mathcal{X}_\mathcal{T}$, we propose a dependence-based feature selection method grounded in the Hilbert-Schmidt Independence Criterion (HSIC) [21]. Specifically, we identify features in $\mathcal{X}_\mathcal{T}$ that exhibit the strongest statistical dependence with the graph-structural traffic embeddings $\mathcal{X}_g$, thereby filtering out task-irrelevant and confounding semantic components prior to cross-modal fusion.

To capture complex relationships, we adopt the Radial Basis Function (RBF) kernel [20] to construct the kernel matrix $\mathbf{K}$ between feature sets $\mathbf{X}$ and $\mathbf{Y}$:

$$K_{ij} = \exp\left(-\frac{\|\mathbf{x}_i - \mathbf{y}_j\|^2}{2\eta^2}\right) \tag{2}$$

where η denotes the bandwidth parameter, determined adaptively via the median heuristic over the pairwise squared distance matrix:

$$\eta = \sqrt{\frac{\text{median}(\|\mathbf{x}_i - \mathbf{y}_j\|^2)}{2}} \tag{3}$$

In the proposed method, HSIC quantifies the statistical dependence between $\mathcal{X}_\mathcal{T}$ and $\mathcal{X}_g$. The empirical estimation of HSIC is given by:

$$\text{HSIC}(\mathcal{X}_\mathcal{T}, \mathcal{X}_g) = \frac{1}{(S-1)^2}\,\text{tr}(\mathbf{KHLH}) \tag{4}$$

where S is the number of samples, $\mathbf{K}, \mathbf{L} \in \mathbb{R}^{S\times S}$ are the kernel matrices for $\mathcal{X}_\mathcal{T}$ and $\mathcal{X}_g$, and $\mathbf{H} = \mathbf{I}_{S\times S} - \frac{1}{S}\mathbf{1}_{S\times S}$ is the centering matrix.

In feature filtering, the numerical features $\mathcal{X}_g \in \mathbb{R}^{S\times T\times N\times C}$ is reshaped and averaged across the N dimension to align with text embedding is $\mathcal{X}_\mathcal{T} \in \mathbb{R}^{S\times T\times d_\mathcal{T}}$:

$$\mathcal{X}'_\mathcal{T} \in \mathbb{R}^{(ST)\times d_\mathcal{T}}, \qquad \mathcal{X}'_g = \frac{1}{N}\sum_{n=1}^{N} \mathcal{X}_{g,:,n} \in \mathbb{R}^{(ST)\times C} \tag{5}$$

For each channel of $\mathcal{X}'_\mathcal{T}$, we compute its HSIC score with the pooled numerical data $\mathcal{X}'_g$:

$$s_i = \widehat{\text{HSIC}}(\mathcal{X}'_{\mathcal{T}:,i}, \mathcal{X}'_g), \quad i = 1, \ldots, d_\mathcal{T} \tag{6}$$

The top-k most informative features are selected with $k = C$. The filtered text embeddings are then extracted: $\mathbf{X}_\mathcal{T}^{filt} = \mathcal{X}'_{\mathcal{T}:,\mathcal{I}}$, where $\mathcal{I}$ is the set of selected feature indices. This process ensures that only the most relevant semantic information is retained for traffic dynamics and avoids interference from confusing factors and noise.

Cross-Modal Alignment and Fusion. Finally, the filtered text embedding $\mathcal{X}_T^{filt}$ and the numerical embedding $\mathcal{X}_g$ are aligned and fused using a cross-attention mechanism [25] to project both modalities into a shared latent space $\mathcal{X}^{fuse}$. In Eq. (7), the query is obtained from $\mathcal{X}_{T,t}^{filt}$, the key and value are from $\mathcal{X}_{g,t}$. The fused representation $\mathcal{X}^{fuse} \in \mathbb{R}^{N \times T \times C}$ is then passed to the downstream CRD module for domain generalization.

$$\begin{gathered} \mathbf{Q}_t = \mathbf{W}_q \mathcal{X}_{T,t}^{filt}, \quad \mathbf{K}_t = \mathbf{W}_k \mathcal{X}_{g,t}, \quad \mathbf{V}_t = \mathbf{W}_v \mathcal{X}_{g,t} \\ \mathcal{X}_t^{fuse} = \text{Softmax}\left(\frac{\mathbf{Q}_t \mathbf{K}_t^\top}{\sqrt{d_k}}\right) \mathbf{V}_t \end{gathered} \tag{7}$$

3.2 Channel-Wise Regularized Disentanglement Module

This module is designed to mitigate domain shift in multi-modal traffic prediction by decoupling domain-invariant and domain-specific representations within the fused feature embedding $\mathcal{X}^{fuse}$. To promote domain generalization, we introduce an orthogonalization constraint on $\mathcal{X}^{fuse}$, encouraging its feature channels to capture statistically independent and non-redundant components. Specifically, we impose an orthogonalization regularization loss to minimize statistical dependence among the channels of $\mathcal{X}^{fuse}$. By reducing inter-channel overlap, the model is encouraged to learn more disentangled representations, where domain-invariant factors are better separated from domain-specific variations, thereby improving generalization across heterogeneous traffic scenarios.

To measure this non-linear independence efficiently, we leverage the Random Fourier Features (RFF) kernel [22] to map $\mathcal{X}^{fuse}$ to $\mathcal{Z}$:

$$\mathcal{Z} = \phi(\mathcal{X}^{fuse}) = \sqrt{\frac{2}{N_{RFF}}} \left[\cos(\mathcal{X}^{fuse}\mathbf{W}_r + \mathbf{b}), \sin(\mathcal{X}^{fuse}\mathbf{W}_r + \mathbf{b})\right] \tag{8}$$

where $\mathbf{W}_r \in \mathbb{R}^{C \times N_{RFF}}$ and $\mathbf{b} \in \mathbb{R}^{N_{RFF}}$ are fixed, randomly sampled weights and biases. N_{RFF} is the number of random features. Next, we calculate the centered empirical covariance matrix $\mathbf{\Sigma}$ of $\mathcal{Z}$, with μ the mean of $\mathcal{Z}$ in Eq.(9).

$$\mathbf{\Sigma} = \frac{1}{S \cdot T \cdot N - 1}(\mathcal{Z} - \mu)^\top (\mathcal{Z} - \mu) \tag{9}$$

The orthogonalization loss is defined as the Frobenius norm of the off-diagonal elements of $\mathbf{\Sigma}$, minimizing the statistical dependency between the feature dimensions:

$$\mathcal{L}_d = \|\mathbf{\Sigma} - \text{diag}(\mathbf{\Sigma})\|_F^2 \tag{10}$$

The overall training objective is the multi-task loss function $\mathcal{L}$ combining the standard prediction loss $\mathcal{L}_p$ and the regularization loss $\mathcal{L}_d$:

$$\mathcal{L} = \sum_{k \in \{\text{cong, v}\}} \alpha_k \mathcal{L}_p(Y_k, \hat{Y}_k) + \beta \mathcal{L}_d \tag{11}$$

where, *cong* and v mean congestion level and speed prediction task; α_k is the task-specific weight; and β is a hyperparameter balancing the trade-off between prediction accuracy and feature independence.

4 Experiments and Results

A set of experiments validate the effectiveness and robustness of the proposed *CadST* framework. It handles noise and spurious features in textual data, and the domain shift between training and test data by CFFA and CRD modules.

4.1 Datasets and Evaluation Metrics

We evaluated *CadST* on the Beijing Traffic and Text (BjTT) dataset [8], which comprises 32,400 synchronized records (sampled every 4 min, January–March 2022) containing spatio-temporal traffic observations (e.g., speed and congestion level) alongside textual event descriptions (e.g., accidents, road closures, and weather reports). The dataset is split into training, validation, and test sets following a 6:2:2 ratio, with partitions designed to be non-overlapping in both weather and event distributions. Specifically, the test set contains domain-distinct scenarios (e.g., sandstorms, Paralympics) relative to the training contexts (e.g., Winter Olympics, snowstorms), thereby rigorously simulating out-of-distribution (OOD) conditions that reflect the challenges of deploying pre-trained traffic models in unfamiliar real-world environments.

The performance metrics of the model are the mean absolute error (MAE), the root mean square error (RMSE), and the weighted mean absolute percentage error (WMAPE) [8,23]. WMAPE $= \frac{\sum_{i=1}^{S}|Y_i - \hat{Y}_i|}{\sum_{i=1}^{S} Y_i} \times 100\%$ (with S the number of samples) mitigates the disproportionate penalty of standard MAPE on data points with near-zero actual values in this work [26].

4.2 Baselines and Experimental Settings

We compared the proposed framework against several representative models spanning spatio-temporal traffic prediction:

- **DCRNN** [1]: Utilize diffusion convolution based on random walks and a Recurrent Neural Network (RNN) for powerful temporal sequence modeling.
- **STGCN** [2]: Integrate GCNs for spatial dependency modeling with 1D temporal convolutions for time series prediction efficiently.
- **STGAT** [5]: Address the limitation of fixed adjacency matrices by utilizing the graph attention mechanism, allowing the model to adapt to time-variant spatial relationships.
- **GWaveNet** [4]: Graph WaveNet combines a learned adaptive adjacency matrix for flexible spatial modeling with dilated causal TCNs to capture long-range temporal dependencies without complex recurrent structures.

We implemented the framework on a NVIDIA L40S. The historical and prediction horizons are 15 (60 min). In CFFA, top-C channels of $\mathcal{X}_\mathcal{T}$ are chosen. The RFF dimensionality N_{RFF} in CRD is set to 1. The optimization process uses the Adam optimizer with a learning rate of 10^{-3}, and the total loss is balanced using the hyperparameters $\alpha_{cong} = 0.5, \alpha_v = 1.0$, and $\beta = 7e5$ for $\mathcal{L}_d$. The code is available at https://github.com/Chloe-Liu33/CadST.

4.3 Effectiveness of *CadST*

Comparison Experiments. This section compares CadST with DCRNN, STGCN, GWaveNet, and ST-GAT to evaluate the effectiveness. Table 1 shows that STGCN, GWaveNet, and ST-GAT outperform DCRNN, likely because TCN-based backbones capture long-range temporal dependencies via dilated convolutions, and ST-GAT models dynamic non-local interactions through attention. Across all metrics, CadST consistently improves performance, with the largest gains when paired with ST-GAT. Specifically, CadST(STGCN) reduces MAE for congestion, speed, and travel time by 14.81%, 3.16%, and 3.07%, respectively. CadST(GWaveNet) reduces MAE by 5.05%, 1.79%, and 1.86%, and CadST(ST-GAT) reduces MAE by 2.12%, 1.54%, and 1.39% across the three tasks. These results indicate that filtering and disentanglement improve robustness under domain shift in multi-modal traffic prediction.

Table 1. Comparative traffic prediction results (60-min).

Model	Congestion Level			Speed			Travel Time(s)		
	MAE	RMSE	WMAPE (%)	MAE	RMSE	WMAPE (%)	MAE	RMSE	WMAPE (%)
DCRNN	0.0746	0.3961	0.0694	3.2887	4.6328	0.0475	2.6313	3.9646	0.0499
STGCN	0.0729	0.2650	0.0679	2.538	3.4831	0.0366	1.9326	2.6132	0.0367
GWaveNet	0.0555	0.2915	0.0517	2.4855	3.4911	0.0359	1.887	2.622	0.0358
ST-GAT	0.0520	0.2718	0.0484	2.4410	3.4352	0.0352	1.8508	2.5747	0.0351
CadST(STGCN)	0.0621	**0.2436**	0.0578	2.4578	**3.3915**	0.0355	1.8733	2.5509	0.0355
CadST(GWaveNet)	0.0527	0.2761	0.049	2.4410	3.4357	0.0352	1.8561	2.5761	0.0352
CadST(ST-GAT)	**0.0509**	0.2661	**0.0474**	**2.4034**	3.4031	**0.0347**	**1.825**	**2.5506**	**0.0346**

Note: best performance in **bold** and second best is underlined.

Computational Efficiency of *CadST* To assess the computational overhead of CadST, we benchmark total parameters, throughput (samples/s), total training time, training time per epoch, and inference time against all baselines on a single NVIDIA L40S, as reported in Table 2. While the training time per epoch of CadST(STGCN) increases modestly relative to the STGCN baseline (201.64 s $\rightarrow$ 278.24 s), attributable to the dependence-based filtering in CFFA and the RFF-based orthogonalization loss in CRD, the inference time (5.14 ms) and throughput (194.56 samples/s) remain competitive. These results indicate that the overhead of additional complexity introduced by CFFA and CRD is acceptable during the forward pass, confirming that CadST achieves a good trade-off between prediction accuracy and computational efficiency for real-world deployment.

Table 2. Computational efficiency analysis.

Model	Parameters	Throughput	Training time(s)	Training time(s)/ epoch	Inference time (ms)
STGCN	833,474	223.79	10485.38	201.64	4.47
DCRNN	224,386	142.22	30603.09	373.21	7.04
GWaveNet	325,330	100.88	29335.09	564.14	9.92
ST-GAT	1,229,406	14.58	143778.10	2764.96	68.58
CadST(STGCN)	895,876	194.56	14468.27	278.24	5.14
CadST(GWaveNet)	369,140	91.93	37425.92	719.73	10.88
CadST(ST-GAT)	1,291,808	13.33	162539.75	3125.76	75.05

4.4 Efficacy of *CFFA* and *CRD* Modules

This section presents an ablation study to quantify the contributions of the CFFA and the CRD modules to the overall efficacy of the framework.

Table 3. Ablation Study of CFFA and CRD modules (60-min).

Model	Congestion Level			Speed			Travel Time(s)		
	MAE	RMSE	WMAPE (%)	MAE	RMSE	WMAPE (%)	MAE	RMSE	WMAPE (%)
Base Model	0.0729	0.2650	0.0679	2.538	3.4831	0.0366	1.9326	2.6132	0.0367
+CFFA	0.0651	0.2452	0.0606	2.4862	3.4129	0.0359	1.8946	2.5549	0.0359
+CFFA&CRD	**0.0621**	**0.2436**	**0.0578**	**2.4578**	**3.3915**	**0.0355**	**1.8733**	**2.5509**	**0.0355**

Ablation Study of CFFA and CRD. We choose STGCN as the backbone for ablation due to its computational efficiency. We compare three configurations: **Base Model** (STGCN), **+CFFA** (STGCN with CFFA), and **+CFFA&CRD** (STGCN with both modules).

Table 3 shows consistent gains from each component. Adding CFFA reduces MAE by 10.70%, 2.04%, and 1.97% for congestion level, speed, and travel time, respectively, indicating that dependence-aware filtering removes spurious textual cues and aligns informative features. Adding CRD on top of CFFA yields further MAE reductions of 4.61%, 1.14%, and 1.12%, confirming that disentangling invariant and domain-specific factors improves robustness across domains.

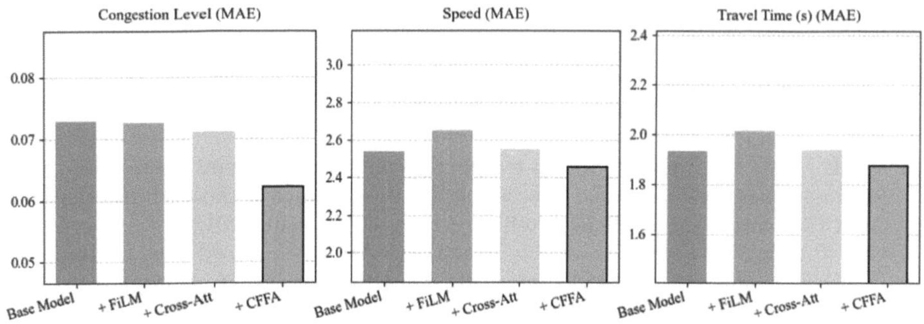

Fig. 2. Experimental results of different data fusion methods (60-min).

Comparison of CFFA, FiLM and Cross-Att. Figure 2 provides a rigorous justification of CFFA module by comparing against two widely adopted feature fusion methods: Feature-wise Linear Modulation (FiLM) [24] and the Cross-Attention (Cross-Att) [25]. The results validate the superiority of CFFA module over the other fusion approaches. A critical observation is that FiLM and Cross-Att degrade prediction performance, especially FiLM in speed and travel time prediction. This phenomenon highlights the challenge posed by spurious correlations and noise inherent in text data and the integrating of multi-modal data. Unlike pre-existing methods, CFFA is designed to filter out uninformative signals and enforce the alignment of true correlated features. The proposed module minimizes the negative impact of spurious information, ensuring feature robustness and leading to the observed high performance gains in prediction accuracy.

5 Conclusion

In this work, we propose the *CadST* framework for multi-modal and multi-task traffic prediction, which aims at reducing spurious correlations within heterogeneous textual data and domain shift in unseen scenarios. The CFFA module in *CadST* eliminates confounders and noise in textual embeddings prior to cross-modal fusion. *CRD* disentangles the invariant representation from unstable domain-specific components to reduce domain shift. Extensive experiments on BjTT dataset demonstrate that *CadST* significantly gets SOTA results across speed, congestion level, and travel time prediction tasks. For future work, we plan to explore the impact of different events on traffic patterns via LLMs to improve the interpretibility of prediction model.

References

1. Li, Y., Yu, R., Shahabi, C., Liu, Y.: Diffusion convolutional recurrent neural network: data-driven traffic forecasting. In: International Conference on Learning Representations (2018)
2. Yu, B., Yin, H., Zhu, Z.: Spatio-temporal graph convolutional networks: a deep learning framework for traffic forecasting. In: Proceedings of the 27th International Joint Conference on Artificial Intelligence, pp. 3634–3640. (2018)
3. Guo, S., Lin, Y., Feng, N., Lu, C., Zhang, D.: Attention Based Spatial-Temporal Graph Convolutional Networks for Traffic Flow Forecasting. In: Proceedings of the AAAI Conference on Artificial Intelligence, pp. 922–929. (2019)
4. Wu, Z.: Graph WaveNet for deep spatial-temporal graph modeling. In: Proceedings of the 27th International Joint Conference on Artificial Intelligence, (2019)
5. Song, J., Son, J., Seo, D., Han, K., Kim. N., Kim. S.: St-gat: a spatio-temporal graph attention network for accurate traffic speed prediction. In: Proceedings of the 31st ACM International Conference on Information & Knowledge Management, pp. 4500–4504 (2022)
6. Zhong, H., Wang, J., Chen, C., Wang, J., Li, D., Guo, K.: Weather interaction-aware spatio-temporal attention networks for urban traffic flow prediction. Buildings **14**(3), 647 (2024)
7. Huang, X.: Enhancing traffic prediction with textual data using large language models, (2024). arXiv:2405.06719 arXiv preprint
8. Zhang, C., et al.: BjTT: a large-scale multimodal dataset for traffic prediction. IEEE Trans. Intell. Transp. Syst. **25**(11), 18992–19003 (2024)
9. Zhao, Y., Shi, S., Ravi, R., Wang, Z., Lam, E. Y., Zhao, J.: H4M: Heterogeneous, multi-source, multi-modal, multi-view and multi-distributional dataset for socioeconomic analytics in the case of Beijing. In: International Conference on Data Science and Advanced Analytics, pp. 1–10, IEEE (2022)
10. Zhou, B., Liu, J., Cui, S., Zhao, Y.: A large-scale spatio-temporal multimodal fusion framework for traffic prediction. Big Data Mining Anal. **7**(3), 621–636 (2024)
11. Qin, X.: Traffic flow prediction based on two-channel multi-modal fusion of MCB and attention. IEEE Access **11**, 58745–58753 (2023)
12. Zhou, B., Liu, J., Cui, S., Zhao, Y.: Large-scale traffic congestion prediction based on multimodal fusion and representation mapping. In: International Conference on Data Science and Advanced Analytics, pp. 1–9. IEEE (2022)
13. Huang, Y., Fang, Z., Zeng, Z., Chen, L., Gao, Y.: Causal Spatio-temporal prediction: an effective and efficient multi-modal approach. In: Conference on Neural Information Processing Systems, (2025)
14. He, X., Bresson, X., Laurent, T., Perold, A., LeCun, Y., Hooi, B.: Harnessing explanations: LLM-to-LM interpreter for enhanced text-attributed graph representation learning. In: International Conference on Learning Representations (2024)
15. Gao, H., Huang, W., Wu, F., Zhao, J., Zheng, C., Liu, H.: LLM enhancers for GNNs: an analysis from the perspective of causal mechanism identification. In: International Conference on Machine Learning, pp. 18585–18611. PMLR (2025)
16. Zhao, L., Sun, Q., Ye, J., Chen, F., Lu, C.T., Ramakrishnan, N.: Multi-task learning for spatio-temporal event forecasting. In: Proceedings of the 21th ACM SIGKDD International Conference on Knowledge Discovery and Data Mining, pp. 1503–1512. (2015)
17. Marrimanu, C.T., Pogaku, A.C.: A novel multi-task learning framework for predicting traffic congestion. In: International Conference on Big Data Analytics, pp. 200–216. (2024)

18. Wang, F., Xu, J., Liu, C., Zhou, R., Zhao, P.: On prediction of traffic flows in smart cities: a multitask deep learning based approach. World Wide Web **24**(3), 805–823 (2021). https://doi.org/10.1007/s11280-021-00877-4
19. Devlin, J., Chang, M.W., Lee, K., Toutanova, K.: Bert: pre-training of deep bidirectional transformers for language understanding. In: Proceedings of the 2019 Conference of the North American Chapter of the Association for Computational Linguistics: Human Language Technologies, vol. 1, pp. 4171–4186. (2019)
20. Bishop, C. M., Nasrabadi, N. M.: Pattern Recognition and Machine Learning. ISS, Springer, New York (2006). https://doi.org/10.1007/978-0-387-45528-0_9
21. Gretton, A., Fukumizu, K., Teo, C., Song, L., Schölkopf, B., Smola, A.: A kernel statistical test of independence. In: Advances in Neural Information Processing Systems, vol. 20, (2007)
22. Zhang, Q., Filippi, S., Gretton, A., Sejdinovic, D.: Large-scale kernel methods for independence testing. Stat. Comput. **28**(1), 113–130 (2018)
23. Zhou, Z.H.: Machine learning, Springer nature (2021)
24. Perez, E., Strub, F., De Vries, H., Dumoulin, V., Courville, A.: Film: Visual reasoning with a general conditioning layer. In: Proceedings of the AAAI Conference on Artificial Intelligence **32**(1) (2018)
25. Wei, X., Zhang, T., Li, Y., Zhang, Y., Wu, F.: Multi-modality cross attention network for image and sentence matching. In: Proceedings of the IEEE/CVF Conference on Computer Vision and Pattern Recognition, pp. 10941–10950 (2020)
26. Hyndman, R.J., Athanasopoulos, G.: Forecasting: principles and practice. OTexts , (2018)
27. Zhang, C., et al.: ChatTraffic: Text-to-traffic generation via diffusion model. IEEE Trans. Intell. Transport. Syst. **26**(2), 2656–2668 (2024)

EPLKG: Efficient Prompt Learning with Knowledge Graph

Yongtaek Lim[1], Suho Kang[2], Yewon Kim[3], Dokyuung Yoon[4], Jiyoung Jung[4], and Kyungwoo Song[2](✉)

[1] Datumo Inc., Seoul, Republic of Korea
yongtaek.lim@selectstar.ai
[2] Yonsei University, Seoul, Republic of Korea
{suhokang91,kyungwoo.song}@gmail.com
[3] ADD, Daejeon, Republic of Korea
[4] University of Seoul, Seoul, Republic of Korea
jyjung@uos.ac.kr

Abstract. Large-scale pre-trained models such as CLIP excel in transferability and robust generalization across diverse datasets. However, adapting these models to new datasets or domains is computationally costly, especially in low-resource or few-shot settings, and existing prompt-learning methods often lack interpretability. We introduce Efficient Prompt Learning with Knowledge Graph (EPLKG), which uses a knowledge graph to curate diverse, interpretable prompts and, where KG coverage is limited, augments this bank with LLM-generated human-readable visual descriptions. EPLKG operates entirely on cached CLIP image and text embeddings and employs a lightweight Gumbel-Softmax module to select a single prompt per imageâĂŞclass pair, enabling low-memory, fast training. Across 11 benchmarks, EPLKG reduces per-image training time by up to 45% and peak GPU memory by around 30–40% compared to strong prompt-learning baselines, while keeping the average base–new harmonic-mean accuracy within 2% points, thereby improving the efficiency of model adaptation without sacrificing competitive performance or interpretability. Our code is available at https://github.com/MLAI-Yonsei/RPLKG.

Keywords: Multimodal learning · Prompt learning · Knowledge graph

1 Introduction

Large-scale pre-trained models have become essential for various tasks, showcasing remarkable transferability and competitive performance across diverse downstream applications, even with limited datasets. Their success has ignited extensive research in computer vision [4,8] and natural language processing [1,7]. Recently, there has been a surge in efforts to expand large-scale pre-trained models into the realm of multimodal learning, capable of handling heterogeneous

R. C.-W. Wong et al. (Eds.): PAKDD 2026, LNAI 16618, pp. 102–114, 2027.
https://doi.org/10.1007/978-981-92-1947-6_9

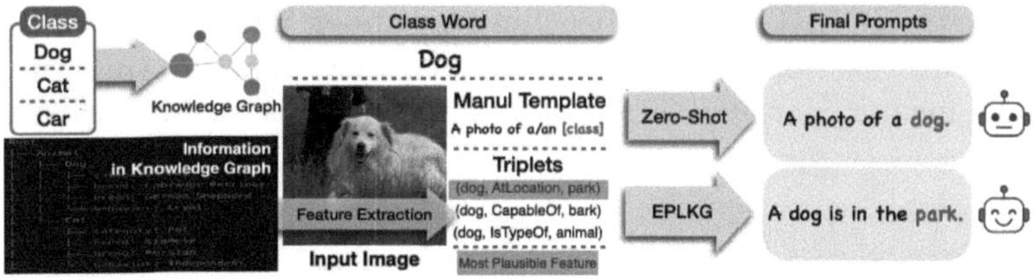

Fig. 1. The motivation behind EPLKG is to leverage a knowledge graph to extract semantically relevant information for each class, forming triplets that capture plausible attributes of class labels and generating interpretable prompts from these structured relations. The resulting prompt enhances both the model's classification performance and interpretability, surpassing that of conventional zero-shot prompts.

datasets encompassing both images and text. A notable multimodal model, Contrastive Language-Image Pre-training (CLIP) [20], has shown significant performance improvements in various multimodal tasks, including retrieval [23] and caption generation [19]. CLIP stands out for its high transferability, excelling in zero-shot image classification by utilizing the text embedding module instead of a traditional classifier. This design allows CLIP to not only perform effective zero-shot classification but also to demonstrate competitive results in few-shot learning scenarios. However, adapting CLIP to new datasets by fine-tuning its parameters incurs high computational and memory costs. To mitigate this, several methods focus on training only a small subset of parameters, and prompt learning has emerged as a promising approach that introduces learnable parameters into the input layer to guide model behavior [28,29]. This paper introduces EPLKG an efficient method for enhancing few-shot learning in large-scale pretrained models. EPLKG uses a knowledge graph (KG) to generate text prompts, automatically selecting the optimal prompt for specific images. This approach addresses the challenge of creating large-scale prompt texts, which presents a combinatorial problem, through a Gumbel-Softmax-based prompt selection module [10,15]. EPLKG introduces three key enhancements over prior prompt learning approaches. First, it is computationally efficient, adding only 0.79M trainable parameters (about 0.5% of CLIP) and avoiding backpropagation through the CLIP encoders. Second, it leverages human knowledge by converting KG triples into plain-text prompts, and third, it preserves interpretability by keeping prompts in natural language rather than continuous embeddings. As illustrated in Fig. 1, EPLKG extracts semantically relevant triples from the KG and aligns them with class labels to construct informative prompts.

The contributions of this work are summarized as follows:

- We propose an optimal prompt selection mechanism that combines attention with Gumbel-Softmax on cached CLIP embeddings, adding only 0.79M parameters (about 0.5% of CLIP).
- We design a simple framework to build interpretable plain-text prompts from a knowledge graph and augment them with LLM-generated visual descriptions when KG coverage is limited.

- We validate EPLKG on 11 benchmarks under few-shot, base–new, and domain generalization settings, reducing per-image training time (up to 45%) and peak memory (around 30–40%) while maintaining competitive accuracy.

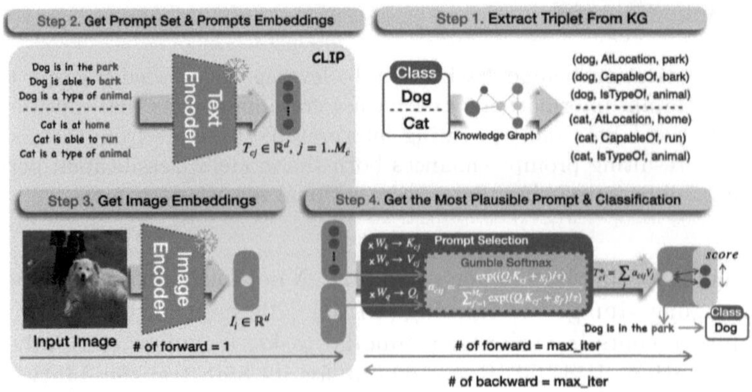

Fig. 2. Overview of EPLKG. For each class, KG triplets are converted into textual prompts and embedded with a frozen text encoder, while the input image is encoded with a frozen image encoder. EPLKG applies Gumbel-Softmax over CLIP imageâĂŞ-text cosine similarities to select a compatible prompt for classification. Only the selection module is trained on cached embeddings, without backpropagation through the CLIP encoders, resulting in lower memory and compute cost and faster training.

2 Related Work

2.1 Multimodal Learning

Recent research has sought to bridge NLP and computer vision by jointly leveraging image and text data to improve vision–language models (VLMs). Early efforts improved multimodal alignment using bidirectional neural networks [25] and attention mechanisms [13], while tasks such as visual question answering (VQA) further emphasized the importance of multimodal learning [6]. Large-scale pre-trained models such as VirTex [5] and CLIP [20] have since shown broad applicability and strong performance. However, their zero-shot and few-shot capabilities remain imperfect [24], motivating extensive work on improving vision–language alignment, particularly through prompt learning [9,26,28,29]. Recent approaches further use LLM-generated descriptions that explicitly capture discriminative features among visually similar classes, improving both performance and interpretability [11].

2.2 Prompt Learning

Prompt learning has become a powerful way to leverage pre-trained knowledge, first in NLP and later in vision–language models (VLMs). In NLP, model performance is highly sensitive to prompt templates, motivating automated prompt construction methods such as AutoPrompt [22] and, more recently, soft prompts that learn continuous prompt embeddings end-to-end [12, 14]. This paradigm has since been extended to VLMs, where prompt learning substantially improves few-shot recognition and generalization. CoOp [29] and CoCoOp [28] introduced continuous prompts for pre-trained VLMs, while PLOT [2] used multiple prompts aligned with local image features for fine-grained tasks. KgCoOp [26] further improved open-domain generalization via knowledge-guided prompting, but the interpretability of learned prompts remains underexplored. Recent studies address this by using GPT-3/4-generated visual descriptions to produce interpretable prompts and improve transfer to novel categories [16, 18]. In contrast, EPLKG retrieves class- and attribute-level prompts from a knowledge-graph–conditioned repository at inference time, providing human-interpretable prompts without fine-tuning the VLM and offering a lightweight alternative.

2.3 Knowledge Graph

KG has been widely used to inject structured prior knowledge into neural models. More recently, several works have explored using KG to guide prompt construction for large language models. vspace [3] extracts paths from a KG via reinforcement learning and turns them into prompts to enhance black-box LLMs such as GPT-3.5 [1]. While effective, this design may introduce some hyperparameter sensitivity and additional compute. while KG-Prompt [27] presents an enhanced approach that leverages structured KG without requiring any modification to the architecture of LLMs. In contrast, EPLKG uses KGs in a visionâĂŞlanguage setting with CLIP [20]. We convert KG triples associated with each class into natural-language prompts and learn only a lightweight prompt-selection module on top of frozen CLIP embeddings, rather than backprop through the CLIP encoders. This design keeps the KG-induced prompts interpretable while enabling efficient adaptation with minimal additional parameters.

3 Methodology

3.1 Cached Embeddings

To efficiently adapt large-scale pre-trained models, we decouple prompt learning from repeated forward–backward passes through CLIP. As shown in Fig. 2, EPLKG uses cached embeddings by precomputing KG-derived text embeddings and training image embeddings with frozen CLIP encoders. During training, only a lightweight Gumbel-Softmax–based prompt selector and classification head are updated. This avoids backpropagation through CLIP, reduces the number of trainable parameters, and substantially lowers training time and peak memory usage. Further analysis is provided in Sect. 4.2.

3.2 Prompt with Knowledge Graph

We leverage ConceptNet to enable simple, scalable prompt design and the incorporation of human knowledge. ConceptNet provides structured entity–relation information for prompt construction. Given a label $entity_i$, we query ConceptNet to obtain a triplet $(entity_i, relation_{ij}, entity_j)$, e.g., (*headphone*, *UsedFor*, *listening to music*), and convert it into a natural-language sentence such as "A headphone is used for listening to music." Here, $entity_j$ denotes a concept semantically associated with $entity_i$, and $relation_{ij}$ is mapped to a relation-specific phrase (e.g., "is used for," "is capable of," "is typically found in") describing their relationship. While ConceptNet is effective for generating semantically rich prompts on general-purpose datasets, it is less effective for fine-grained or domain-specific labels (e.g., FGVC-Aircraft, Stanford Cars). When a class is missing from ConceptNet or our prompt bank, we perform a one-time GPT-4.1 captioning pass on the few-shot training images. By prompting the LLM to extract visual attributes rather than abstract descriptions, we encourage the model to focus on discriminative cues during inference. This compensates for the limitations of symbolic resources in specialized domains while improving prompt interpretability and effectiveness.

3.3 Optimal Prompt Selection

$$Q_i = I_i W_q, \quad K_{cj} = T_{cj} W_k, \quad V_{cj} = T_{cj} W_v, \tag{1}$$

$$u_j \sim \text{Uniform}(0,1) \tag{2}$$

$$g_j = -\log(-\log(u_j)) \tag{3}$$

$$\alpha_{cij} = \frac{\exp((Q_i K_{cj} + g_j)/\tau)}{\sum_{j'=1}^{M_c} \exp((Q_i K_{cj'} + g_{j'})/\tau)} \tag{4}$$

$$T^*_{ci} = \sum_j \alpha_{cij} V_{cj} \tag{5}$$

$$\widehat{c} = \text{argmax}_{c'} I_i \cdot T^*_{ci} \tag{6}$$

In this section, we present our prompt optimization technique, which focuses on selecting the optimal prompt for each instance from a diverse set of interpretable text prompts. Traditional methods face a combinatorial challenge, with time complexity denoted as M_c^{NC}, where N is the number of data instances, C the number of classes, and M_c the number of prompts for each class c. This approach is impractical for large-scale datasets due to its exponential time complexity. To address this, we propose a Gumbel-Softmax-based method, EPLKG, which uses cached embeddings for images (I) and prompts (T) to optimize prompt selection efficiently. For each i-th image embedding I_i, we apply a linear transformation using weights W_q. Similarly, for each j-th prompt embedding of class c, T_{cj}, we apply transformations with W_k and W_v. We then calculate the similarity between transformed image queries Q_i and key vectors K_{cj} for all prompts $j = 1, ..., M_c$, applying Gumbel-Softmax to normalize the similarity scores, as opposed to traditional Softmax, to select a single, optimal prompt. This choice is due to Gumbel-Softmax's ability to produce sparse output vectors, allowing for selecting a singular optimal prompt,

Table 1. Comparison of accuracy and training time for prompt-based learning methods. EPLKG improves training speed while maintaining competitive accuracy; red text indicates the accuracy gap to the best baseline, and blue text indicates our relative training-time reduction (%) compared to that baseline.

Methods	Prompts	Accuracy			Training-time
		Base	New	H	
CLIP	hand-crafted	69.34	74.22	71.70	-
CoOp	textual	**82.63**	67.99	74.60	6ms/image
ProGrad	textual	82.48	70.75	76.16	22ms/image
CoCoOp	textual+visual	80.47	71.69	75.83	160ms/image
KgCoOp	textual	80.73	**73.60**	**77.00**	6ms/image
EPLKG	textual	81.18 (-1.75%)	71.37 (-3.03%)	75.96 (-1.35%)	**3.3ms/image (-45%)**

Table 2. We compare the peak memory (MB) of CoOp, CoCoOp, KgCoOp, and our model, EPLKG at training time. EPLKG shows the lowest peak memory usage across all batch sizes on both DTD and Oxford Pets datasets.

(a) Peak memory on DTD.

Model	Batch Size			
	1	4	32	64
CoOp	988	988	1,005	1,025
CoCoOp	988	3,101	22,943	45,615
KgCoOp	1,038	1,040	1,056	1,075
EPLKG	**625 (-36.74%)**	**625 (-36.74%)**	**632 (-37.11%)**	**651 (-36.49%)**

(b) Peak memory on Oxford Pets.

Model	Batch Size			
	1	4	32	64
CoOp	988	988	1,005	1,025
CoCoOp	988	3,101	22,943	45,615
KgCoOp	913	915	924	929
EPLKG	**625 (-31.54%)**	**625 (-31.69%)**	**632 (-31.60%)**	**651 (-29.92%)**

which is both performance-enhancing and more interpretable. To implement the Gumbel-Softmax, we sample the random variable from the Gumbel (0,1) distribution by using inverse transformation, as shown in Eqs. 2-3. With the Gumbel random variable, we compute the softmax function by following [10,15], as shown in Eq. 4. Upon selecting the optimal prompt T_{ci} for the i-th image and c-th class, we compute the similarity between I_i and T_{ci} for all classes $c = 1, ..., C$, choosing the class $\widehat{c}$ that maximizes this similarity. The model's parameters, Wq, W_k, W_v, are optimized using cross-entropy loss between the ground-truth label c^* and the predicted $\widehat{c}$. EPLKG's approach is characterized by its computational efficiency, requiring fewer resources than traditional prompt learning approaches.

4 Results

4.1 Experimental Settings

For few-shot classification, following prior work [11,17,21], we use ViT-B/16 and evaluate 11 datasets with 1, 2, 4, 8, and 16 shots per class. For domain generalization, we train ViT-B/16 and ViT-B/32 on ImageNet with 16 shots per class and evaluate on multiple ImageNet variants. For base-to-new generalization, following [28,29], we train CoOp, CoCoOp, KgCoOp, and EPLKG on base classes with 16 shots and test on all classes. We search over $\alpha \in \{0.1, 0.3, 0.5, 0.7, 1.0\}$, weight decay $\in$ {3e-3, 1e-2, 5e-2, 0.1}, Gumbel-Softmax temperature $\in \{0.001, 0.01, 0.1\}$, and dropout $\in \{0.1, 0.3, 0.5, 0.7\}$, and use the prompt template "A photo of [CLASS]" for zero-shot CLIP.

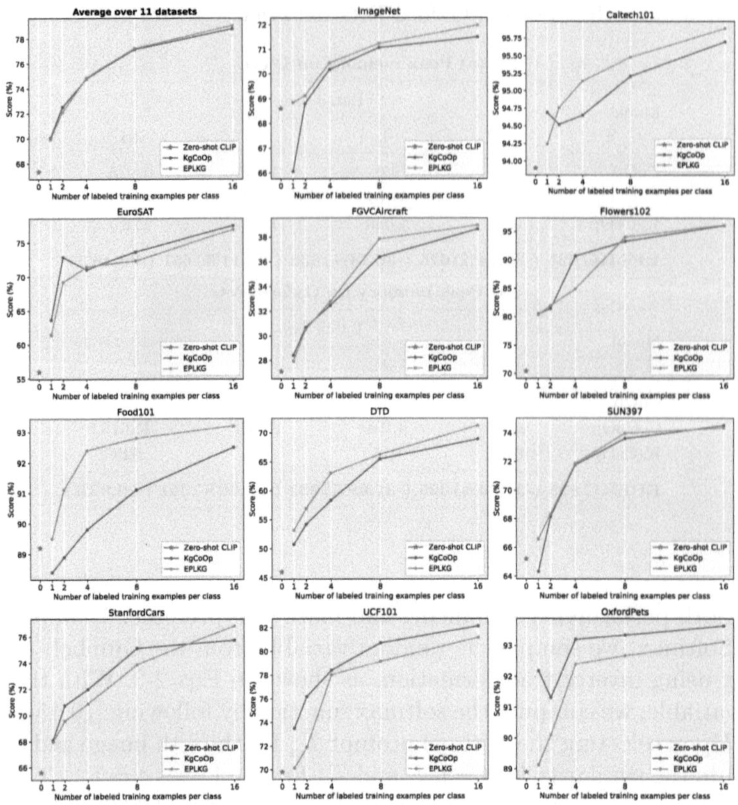

Fig. 3. The first subplot shows the average performance over 11 datasets; the others show EPLKG and baseline performance per dataset for $k \in \{1, 2, 4, 8, 16\}$ shots.

4.2 Time and Memory Efficiency

We compare the peak memory usage and training time of EPLKG with CoOp, CoCoOp, and KgCoOp on DTD and Oxford Pets under a 16-shot setting (batch size 64). The training times of all methods are reported in Table 1. EPLKG achieves competitive accuracy while reducing training time by ∼45% compared to the strong baseline KgCoOp, with less than 4% performance drop. Tables 2(a) and 2(b) further show that EPLKG consistently requires less memory than the baselines across different batch sizes. Overall, EPLKG achieves performance comparable to existing prompt learning methods with substantially lower time and memory costs.

4.3 Few-Shot Classification

We conduct few-shot classification experiments on 11 datasets with k in 1, 2, 4, 8, 16-shots. As shown in Fig. 3, our model, EPLKG is compared against Zero-shot CLIP and a strong baseline, KgCoOp. The results clearly demonstrate that EPLKG outperforms or matches on most datasets both baselines across almost all datasets and shot counts. Notably, the performance gap is significant even with a single training example (1-shot), and this advantage is maintained as the number of shots increases, highlighting our method's effectiveness and scalability in few-shot learning scenarios.

4.4 New Class Generalization

Table 3 presents the results for the base-to-new generalization setting, which evaluates how well models generalize to new classes after being trained on base classes. Despite using significantly less peak memory and requiring shorter training times than CoOp, CoCoOp, and KgCoOp, our model, EPLKG consistently achieves competitive performance across all 11 datasets. Notably, EPLKG attains a competitive overall harmonic mean, indicating strong generalization. These results show that EPLKG is efficient and scalable while matching or surpassing more resource-intensive baselines. The strong generalization capability of EPLKG is attributed to its robust prompt selection mechanism. Unlike CoOp and CoCoOp, which optimize continuous prompt vectors from scratch, EPLKG first generates a diverse set of candidate prompts derived from triplets in a structured knowledge base. It then leverages a few training examples to select the optimal prompt, which in turn enhances its generalization performance without the need for resource-intensive, end-to-end parameter optimization.

4.5 Domain Generalization

We conducted domain generalization experiments to evaluate robustness under distribution shifts. Following the protocol of [29] on the datasets in Table 4, EPLKG consistently outperforms Zeroshot-CLIP across all ImageNet variants and backbone architectures. Moreover, unlike Linear Probe CLIP, which

Table 3. Base-to-new performance on 11 datasets. Following Zhou et al. [28], we train CoOp, CoCoOp, KgCoOp, and EPLKG on base classes with 16 shots and test on all classes. Despite its lower training-time and memory footprint, EPLKG attains the second-best average base–new harmonic mean across all 11 datasets, competitive with the strongest baseline. Best and second-best results are shown in **bold** and underlined, respectively; H denotes the harmonic mean.

(a) average of 11 datasets.

	Base	New	H
CLIP	69.34	**74.22**	71.70
CoOp	**82.69**	63.22	71.66
CoCoOp	80.47	71.69	75.83
KgCoOp	80.73	73.60	**77.00**
EPLKG	81.18	71.37	75.96

(b) ImageNet

	Base	New	H
CLIP	72.43	68.14	70.22
CoOp	**76.47**	67.88	71.92
CoCoOp	75.98	**70.43**	**73.10**
KgCoOp	75.83	69.96	72.78
EPLKG	76.30	66.47	71.05

(c) Caltech101.

	Base	New	H
CLIP	96.84	94.00	95.40
CoOp	98.00	89.81	93.73
CoCoOp	97.96	93.81	95.84
KgCoOp	97.72	**94.39**	**96.03**
EPLKG	**98.04**	93.56	95.75

(d) OxfordPets.

	Base	New	H
CLIP	91.17	97.26	94.12
CoOp	93.67	95.29	94.47
CoCoOp	**95.20**	97.69	**96.43**
KgCoOp	94.65	**97.76**	96.18
EPLKG	93.83	96.33	95.06

(e) StanfordCars.

	Base	New	H
CLIP	63.37	74.89	68.65
CoOp	**78.12**	60.40	68.13
CoCoOp	70.49	73.59	72.01
KgCoOp	71.76	**75.04**	**73.36**
EPLKG	73.67	71.58	72.61

(f) Flowers102.

	Base	New	H
CLIP	72.08	**77.80**	74.83
CoOp	**97.60**	59.67	74.06
CoCoOp	94.87	71.75	81.71
KgCoOp	95.00	74.73	**83.65**
EPLKG	96.52	70.04	81.18

(g) Food101.

	Base	New	H
CLIP	90.10	91.22	90.66
CoOp	88.33	82.26	85.19
CoCoOp	**90.70**	91.29	90.99
KgCoOp	90.50	**91.70**	**91.09**
EPLKG	89.68	88.54	89.10

(h) FGVCAircraft.

	Base	New	H
CLIP	27.19	**36.29**	31.09
CoOp	**40.44**	22.30	28.75
CoCoOp	33.41	23.71	27.74
KgCoOp	36.21	33.55	**34.83**
EPLKG	35.55	31.07	33.16

(i) SUN397.

	Base	New	H
CLIP	69.36	75.35	72.23
CoOp	80.60	65.89	72.51
CoCoOp	79.74	**76.86**	78.27
KgCoOp	80.29	76.53	**78.36**
EPLKG	**80.86**	74.26	77.42

(j) DTD.

	Base	New	H
CLIP	53.24	**59.90**	56.37
CoOp	79.44	41.18	54.24
CoCoOp	77.01	56.00	64.85
KgCoOp	77.55	54.99	64.35
EPLKG	**81.13**	54.95	**65.52**

(k) EuroSAT.

	Base	New	H
CLIP	56.48	64.05	60.03
CoOp	**92.19**	54.74	68.69
CoCoOp	87.49	60.04	71.21
KgCoOp	85.64	64.34	73.48
EPLKG	84.18	**65.30**	**73.55**

(l) UCF101.

	Base	New	H
CLIP	70.53	**77.50**	73.85
CoOp	**84.69**	56.05	67.46
CoCoOp	82.33	73.45	77.64
KgCoOp	82.89	76.67	**79.65**
EPLKG	83.25	72.99	77.78

is trained only on the source domain and degrades substantially under shift, EPLKG maintains stable performance. These results suggest that incorporating external semantic knowledge from a KG into prompt learning provides useful inductive biases, improving robustness by promoting more invariant representations and better semantic consistency across domains. Overall, our findings indicate that EPLKG is effective not only for few-shot classification but also for domain-agnostic transfer.

Table 4. Domain generalization performance on ImageNet variants. Models are trained on ImageNet and evaluated in a zero-shot setting on multiple ImageNet variants. EPLKG consistently outperforms the baselines across all datasets and backbone networks.

	Source	Target			
Method	ImageNet	-V2	-Sketch	-A	-R
ViT-B/32					
Zeroshot-CLIP	62.06	54.76	40.83	29.83	65.93
Linear Probe CLIP	59.58	49.73	28.06	19.67	47.20
CLIP + EPLKG	**66.11**	**57.07**	**41.11**	**30.19**	**66.19**
ViT-B/16					
Zeroshot-CLIP	66.73	60.85	46.16	47.80	73.99
Linear Probe CLIP	65.85	56.26	34.77	35.68	58.43
CLIP + EPLKG	**71.74**	**64.01**	**46.67**	**48.49**	**74.94**

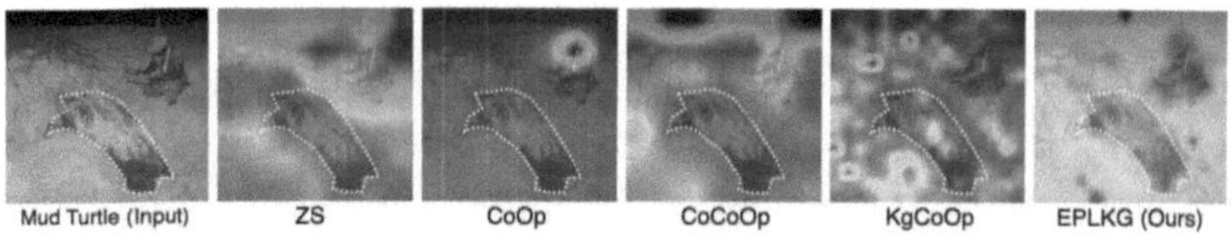

(a) ImageNet – Mud Turtle. Chosen Prompt: "A mud turtle has a low, rounded shell."

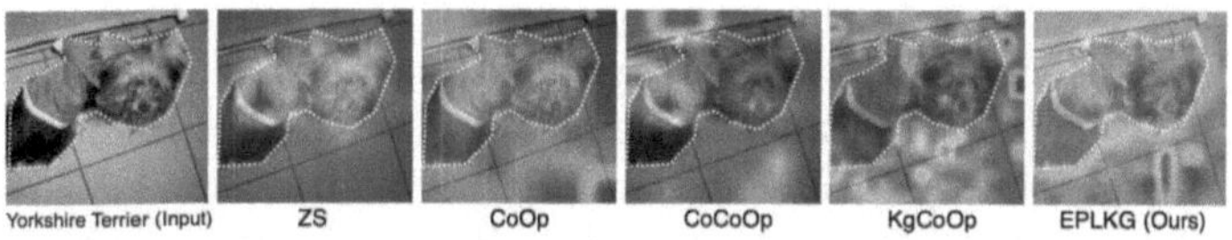

(b) Oxford Pets – Yorkshire Terrier. Chosen Prompt: "A Yorkshire Terrier has long, silky hair."

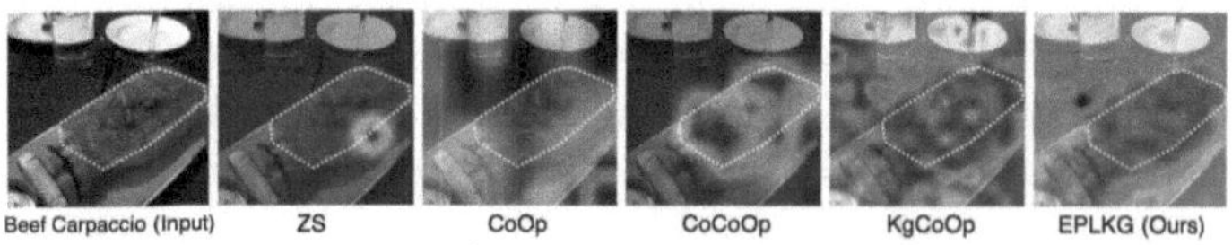

(c) Food-101 – Beef Carpaccio. Chosen Prompt: "Beef carpaccio shows thin slices of raw red meat."

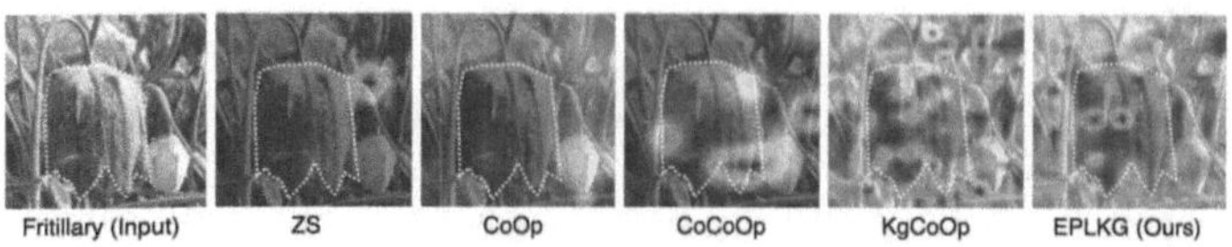

(d) Flowers-102 – Fritillary. Chosen Prompt: "A fritillary has a drooping, bell-shaped flower."

Fig. 4. Each row presents Grad-CAM visualizations for zero-shot (ZS), CoOp, CoCoOp, KgCoOp and EPLKG (ours). Red regions indicate higher Grad-CAM relevance scores for the target class. In cases where the baseline models fail to make correct predictions, EPLKG succeeds by selecting an optimal prompt from the KG. (Color figure online)

4.6 Grad-CAM Analysis

As illustrated in Fig. 4, baseline methods such as ZS, CoOp, CoCoOp and KGCoOp frequently fail to capture the correct semantics or attend to task-relevant visual regions. In contrast, our proposed method, EPLKG exhibits more semantically grounded and interpretable attention patterns. Across various dataset examples, EPLKG consistently selects prompts that closely align with the target class attributes. For instance, in the case of the *Mud Turtle*, while other methods tend to focus on irrelevant background regions or overly broad areas surrounding the fish, EPLKG precisely attends to the fish itself. The Grad-CAM reveals that it focuses on discriminative features in a more concentrated and human-aligned manner. These results provide compelling evidence of EPLKG's superior interpretability and robustness in prompt-based learning.

5 Conclusion

We presented EPLKG, an efficient prompt learning framework that builds interpretable KG- and LLM-derived prompts and selects them with a lightweight Gumbel-Softmax module on cached CLIP embeddings. Across 11 datasets and few-shot, base–new, and domain generalization settings, EPLKG achieves competitive accuracy while reducing training time by up to 45% and peak memory by 30–40%, and keeping the base–new harmonic mean within a few percentage points of the best baseline; Grad-CAM analyses show that it focuses on semantically meaningful regions. While effective in our experiments, EPLKG may be sensitive to KG coverage and quality and to the stochastic nature of Gumbel-Softmax, especially in domains with sparse or noisy knowledge. Future work includes leveraging domain-specific KGs, designing stable or uncertainty-aware selection, and applying EPLKG to continual, online, and federated learning scenarios where parameter-efficient, interpretable adaptation is crucial.

References

1. Brown, T., et al.: Language models are few-shot learners. Adv. Neural. Inf. Process. Syst. **33**, 1877–1901 (2020)
2. Chen, G., Yao, W., Song, X., Li, X., Rao, Y., Zhang, K.: Prompt learning with optimal transport for vision-language models (2022). https://openreview.net/forum?id=b9APFSTylGT
3. Chen, L., Liu, J., Duan, Y., Wang, R.: Kg-prompt: Interpretable knowledge graph prompt for pre-trained language models. Knowl.-Based Syst. **311**, 113118 (2025). https://doi.org/10.1016/j.knosys.2025.113118, https://www.sciencedirect.com/science/article/pii/S0950705125001650
4. Chen, T., Kornblith, S., Norouzi, M., Hinton, G.: A simple framework for contrastive learning of visual representations. In: International Conference on Machine Learning, pp. 1597–1607. PMLR (2020)
5. Desai, K., Johnson, J.: Virtex: Learning visual representations from textual annotations. In: Proceedings of the IEEE/CVF Conference on Computer Vision and Pattern Recognition, pp. 11162–11173 (2021)

6. Desta, M.T., Chen, L., Kornuta, T.: Object-based reasoning in VQA. In: 2018 IEEE Winter Conference on Applications of Computer Vision (WACV), pp. 1814–1823. IEEE (2018)
7. Devlin, J., Chang, M.W., Lee, K., Toutanova, K.: Bert: Pre-training of deep bidirectional transformers for language understanding. arXiv preprint arXiv:1810.04805 (2018)
8. Grill, J.B., et al.: Bootstrap your own latent-a new approach to self-supervised learning. Adv. Neural. Inf. Process. Syst. **33**, 21271–21284 (2020)
9. Gu, Y., Han, X., Liu, Z., Huang, M.: Ppt: Pre-trained prompt tuning for few-shot learning. arXiv preprint arXiv:2109.04332 (2021)
10. Jang, E., Gu, S., Poole, B.: Categorical reparametrization with gumble-softmax. In: International Conference on Learning Representations (ICLR 2017). OpenReview.net (2017)
11. Lee, H., Seo, G., Choi, W., Jung, G., Song, K., Jung, J.: Enhancing visual classification using comparative descriptors. In: 2025 IEEE/CVF Winter Conference on Applications of Computer Vision (WACV), pp. 5274–5283. IEEE (2025)
12. Lester, B., Al-Rfou, R., Constant, N.: The power of scale for parameter-efficient prompt tuning. arXiv preprint arXiv:2104.08691 (2021)
13. Li, L., Tang, S., Zhang, Y., Deng, L., Tian, Q.: GLA: Global-local attention for image description. IEEE Trans. Multimedia **20**(3), 726–737 (2017)
14. Li, X.L., Liang, P.: Prefix-tuning: Optimizing continuous prompts for generation (2021)
15. Maddison, C., Mnih, A., Teh, Y.: The concrete distribution: A continuous relaxation of discrete random variables. In: Proceedings of the International Conference on Learning Representations (2017)
16. Maniparambil, M., Vorster, C., Molloy, D., Murphy, N., McGuinness, K., O'Connor, N.E.: Enhancing clip with GPT-4: Harnessing visual descriptions as prompts (2023). https://arxiv.org/abs/2307.11661
17. Menon, S., Vondrick, C.: Visual classification via description from large language models. arXiv preprint arXiv:2210.07183 (2022)
18. Menon, S., Vondrick, C.: Visual classification via description from large language models. In: The Eleventh International Conference on Learning Representations (2023). https://openreview.net/forum?id=jlAjNL8z5cs
19. Mokady, R., Hertz, A., Bermano, A.H.: Clipcap: Clip prefix for image captioning. arXiv preprint arXiv:2111.09734 (2021)
20. Radford, A., et al.: Learning transferable visual models from natural language supervision. In: International Conference on Machine Learning, pp. 8748–8763. PMLR (2021)
21. Roth, K., Kim, J.M., Koepke, A., Vinyals, O., Schmid, C., Akata, Z.: Waffling around for performance: Visual classification with random words and broad concepts. In: Proceedings of the IEEE/CVF International Conference on Computer Vision, pp. 15746–15757 (2023)
22. Shin, T., Razeghi, Y., IV, R.L.L., Wallace, E., Singh, S.: AutoPrompt: Eliciting knowledge from language models with automatically generated prompts. In: Empirical Methods in Natural Language Processing (EMNLP) (2020)
23. So, J., Oh, C., Lim, Y., Byun, H., Shin, M., Song, K.: Geodesic multi-modal mixup for robust fine-tuning. arXiv preprint arXiv:2203.03897 (2022)
24. Wang, C., Jia, R., Liu, X., Song, D.: Benchmarking zero-shot robustness of multimodal foundation models: A pilot study (2024). https://arxiv.org/abs/2403.10499
25. Wu, J., Hu, H.: Cascade recurrent neural network for image caption generation. Electron. Lett. **53**(25), 1642–1643 (2017)

26. Yao, H., Zhang, R., Xu, C.: Visual-language prompt tuning with knowledge-guided context optimization (2023). https://arxiv.org/abs/2303.13283
27. Zhang, Q., Dong, J., Chen, H., Zha, D., Yu, Z., Huang, X.: Knowgpt: Knowledge graph based prompting for large language models (2024). https://arxiv.org/abs/2312.06185
28. Zhou, K., Yang, J., Loy, C.C., Liu, Z.: Conditional prompt learning for vision-language models. In: Proceedings of the IEEE/CVF Conference on Computer Vision and Pattern Recognition, pp. 16816–16825 (2022)
29. Zhou, K., Yang, J., Loy, C.C., Liu, Z.: Learning to prompt for vision-language models. Int. J. Comput. Vision **130**(9), 2337–2348 (2022)

Logits-Aware Rank-and-Reason: Enhancing LLM Reasoning via Preliminary Option Ranking and Cognitive-Specific Demonstrations

Song Qin, Jianxin Xue(✉), Feifan Hao, Sen Niu, and Xi Chang

Shanghai Polytechnic University, Shanghai, China
jxxue@sspu.edu.cn

Abstract. Large Language Models often struggle with plausible distractors in mathematical multiple-choice reasoning tasks, leading to cognitive overload and erroneous outputs. In this paper, we propose a novel framework named Logits-aware Rank-and-Reason, abbreviated as LRR, to mitigate this distraction effect. Unlike dynamic retrieval methods that incur high computational costs during inference, LRR introduces a data-efficient offline mechanism to construct cognitive-specific demonstration libraries. By utilizing a lightweight Scout model to extract statistical fingerprints from logit distributions, we objectively segregate candidate questions into confusion-dominant and uncertainty-dominant patterns. This facilitates a stage-adaptive inference process consisting of two sequential phases. The first is Preliminary Option Ranking, which utilizes confusion-resolution demonstrations to filter noise and prioritize plausible candidates. The second is Rank-Aware Reasoning, which employs general-reasoning demonstrations alongside a hint-first strategy to guide the model through complex solution paths. Extensive experiments on benchmarks such as MMLU, AQuA, and GSM8K demonstrate that LRR significantly outperforms standard prompting baselines and achieves highly competitive performance using a GPT-3.5-turbo backbone, comparable to the zero-shot performance of GPT-4 on specific algebraic reasoning tasks.

Keywords: Mathematical Multiple-Choice Questions · Large Language Models · Chain-of-Thought · In-Context Learning

1 Introduction

Large Language Models have demonstrated remarkable capabilities in complex reasoning tasks, particularly when empowered by prompting strategies [2,6,16, 23,25,26]. Despite these advancements, applying these models to mathematical multiple-choice questions presents unique challenges [10,19,22,29]. A primary

R. C.-W. Wong et al. (Eds.): PAKDD 2026, LNAI 16618, pp. 115–126, 2027.
https://doi.org/10.1007/978-981-92-1947-6_10

obstacle is the distraction effect caused by plausible but incorrect options. Standard prompting methods typically force the model to evaluate all options simultaneously with equal initial attention [19,21]. Specifically, when options exhibit high similarity, a common occurrence in arithmetic problems, the model often struggles to discriminate the correct answer from plausible distractors [10,21]. This interference disperses the attention of the model across multiple competing candidates, thereby increasing the likelihood of erroneous selection.

To mitigate such issues, recent research has diverged into two main streams: refining generic instructions and optimizing in-context demonstration selection. Generic instruction methods, such as Plan-and-Solve [24] or Zero-shot CoT [11], aim to regulate the reasoning process by enforcing explicit planning or step-by-step deduction. However, relying solely on generic instructions often fails to prevent the model from falling into cognitive traps set by adversarial distractors. Conversely, Few-Shot Learning strategies seek to guide the model through specific examples. Approaches like AutoCoT [27] and SCoT [12] utilize clustering or structural constraints to select demonstrations. Yet, these methods predominantly rely on semantic similarity or structural diversity, which do not necessarily equate to reasoning affinity. Two problems may share similar topics but present vastly different cognitive hurdles, such as confusion between specific options versus a lack of reasoning path. Existing retrieval methods often overlook these internal decision boundaries, leading to suboptimal guidance.

To address these limitations, we propose a novel framework named Logits-aware Rank-and-Reason, abbreviated as LRR. Our approach mimics the structured human decision-making process through a two-stage mechanism supported by a logits-driven demonstration library. Unlike methods that perform computationally expensive retrieval during inference, we introduce an offline Demonstration Library Construction module. We employ a lightweight Scout model to compute statistical fingerprints of candidate questions based on their logit distributions. These fingerprints allow us to objectively segregate questions into two specialized pools: a Confusion-Resolution Pool for questions inducing high inter-option conflict, and a General-Reasoning Pool for questions causing high overall uncertainty. During the inference phase, the framework operates in two sequential stages. In the first stage, termed Preliminary Option Ranking, the model utilizes demonstrations from the Confusion-Resolution Pool to evaluate and re-order the options based on plausibility. In the second stage, Rank-Aware Reasoning, the model utilizes demonstrations from the General-Reasoning Pool to derive the final answer. To prevent the model from losing focus after the ranking step, we integrate the Plan-and-Solve strategy [24], requiring the model to generate a high-level solution hint before executing the detailed calculation.

In summary, this work proposes a generic two-stage reasoning framework that integrates preliminary option ranking with hint-guided reasoning to effectively mitigate the distraction effect in mathematical multiple-choice tasks. A core innovation of our approach is the data-efficient construction of cognitive-specific demonstration libraries using statistical fingerprints derived from a lightweight Scout model, which ensures stage-adaptive guidance without the overhead of real-time retrieval. Extensive experiments on mathematical benchmarks including MMLU [8], AQuA [14], and GSM8K [5] demonstrate that our method significantly outperforms standard Chain-of-Thought [25] and existing prompting strategies, achieving highly competitive performance with a GPT-3.5-turbo backbone that is comparable to GPT-4 benchmarks in specific algebraic tasks.

2 Related Works

2.1 Enhancing Reasoning via Generic Instructions

The introduction of Chain-of-Thought prompting [25] has fundamentally shifted the paradigm of large language model reasoning by encouraging the generation of intermediate steps. Early iterations such as Zero-Shot CoT demonstrated that generic triggers like "Let's think step by step" could elicit latent reasoning capabilities without task-specific fine-tuning. Building on this, more structured approaches have emerged to regulate the reasoning process. Plan-and-Solve prompting [24] decomposes complex problems into a planning phase followed by execution, effectively reducing calculation errors in multi-step arithmetic tasks. Similarly, methods like Least-to-Most prompting [31] breaks down intricate queries into manageable sub-questions to maintain logical coherence. Other works such as Progressive-Hint Prompting [28] leverage previously generated answers as auxiliary hints to guide the model toward convergence. Despite these advancements, generic instruction-based methods primarily rely on the inherent capability of the model to self-correct. In the context of multiple-choice questions where distractors are designed to be adversarial, generic instructions often fail to prevent the model from falling into cognitive traps. Our framework addresses this by integrating a specific ranking stage to filter noise before employing a hint-based planning strategy, thereby grounding the reasoning process in a cleaner context.

2.2 In-Context Demonstration Selection

The performance of few-shot learning is heavily contingent on the quality and relevance of the provided demonstrations. To automate this, AutoCoT [27] utilizes clustering techniques to sample diverse questions as provisional exemplars. Other works focus on the structural quality of examples; for instance, SCoT [12] emphasizes pivotal structures within examples to constrain code generation, while MoT [13] enhances effectiveness by pre-thinking high-confidence thoughts as memory. While these methods improve upon random selection, they primarily rely on semantic similarity or structural diversity. However, semantic proximity does not necessarily equate to reasoning affinity. Existing retrieval methods often overlook internal decision boundaries, such as confusion between specific options. In contrast, our LRR framework introduces a logits-driven selection mechanism that characterizes questions through statistical fingerprints derived from a Scout model, ensuring demonstrations match the specific cognitive state rather than just topical content.

3 Methodology

In this section, we formally introduce the Logits-aware Rank-and-Reason framework. As illustrated in Fig. 1, LRR decouples demonstration selection from inference to align with the cognitive state of the model. The framework comprises an offline Demonstration Library Construction module, which segregates questions into cognitive-specific pools using statistical fingerprints, and an online two-stage inference pipeline. During inference, the Preliminary Option Ranking stage uses confusion-resolution shots to filter distractors, followed by the Rank-Aware Reasoning stage, which employs general-reasoning shots to derive the final answer.

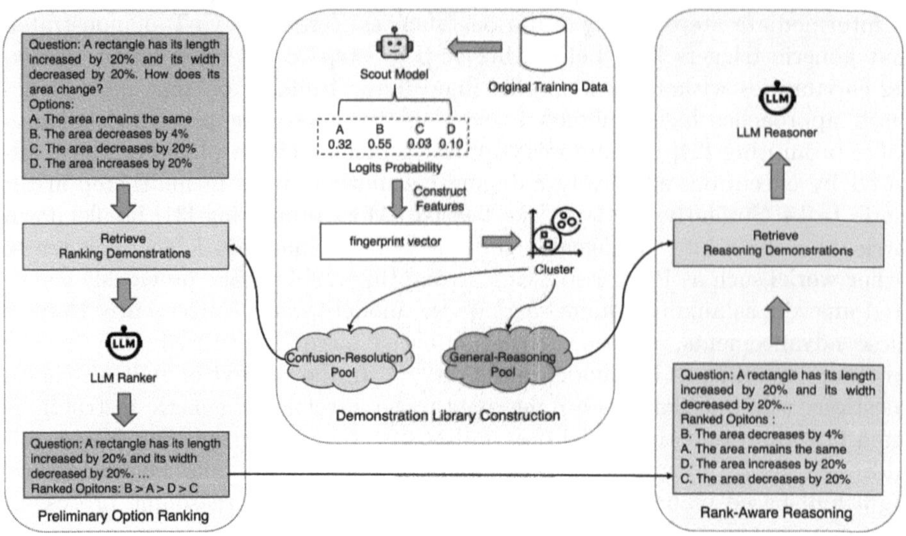

Fig. 1. Overview of the Logits-aware Rank-and-Reason framework. The process begins with the offline construction of cognitive-specific demonstration pools using a Scout Model (Center). During inference, the framework proceeds through Preliminary Option Ranking to organize the search space (Left), followed by Rank-Aware Reasoning to derive the solution (Right).

3.1 Demonstration Library Construction

To effectively guide the Large Language Model through complex reasoning paths, we propose to select the most appropriate category of demonstrations based on the internal uncertainty of the model rather than semantic similarity. This is an offline process involving a collaborative architecture where a lightweight Scout model based on BERT [6] computes the probability distribution over the options.

The utilization of a lightweight model to approximate the cognitive states of larger models is grounded in recent advancements in model alignment and proxy tuning. Specifically, we employ a fine-tuned BERT model to act as a Scout. This model is trained on logit patterns distilled from robust reasoning models, specifically Qwen2.5-3B [20] and Llama-3.2-3B [7], using datasets such as AQuA [14] and MATHQA [1].

The theoretical validity of using a smaller Scout model to guide a larger model relies on the principle of weak-to-strong generalization. As demonstrated by Burns et al. [3], weaker models can effectively elicit capabilities in stronger models because the latent knowledge describing problem difficulty is often correlated across model scales. Furthermore, Liu et al. [15] introduced the concept of tuning language models by proxy, suggesting that the distributional characteristics of smaller proxy models can successfully guide the decoding process of larger black-box models. Additionally, research on the transferability of adversarial examples [17] indicates that decision boundaries for confusing distractors are frequently shared across different architectures; thus, a question that induces high "confusion" in the Scout model is statistically likely to present similar cognitive hurdles for the main inference model. Finally, employing a lightweight Scout model aligns with the FrugalGPT paradigm [4], ensuring that the high computational cost of the main model is reserved strictly for inference rather than retrieval tasks.

To construct the demonstration library, we aggregate training samples from these datasets into a unified candidate pool. For each question Q in this pool, let $\mathcal{O} = \{o_1, o_2, \ldots, o_m\}$ be the set of options, where m denotes the number of options. The Scout model outputs a logit vector which is normalized via the Softmax function to obtain a probability distribution $P = \{p_1, p_2, \ldots, p_m\}$. Since the number of options m varies across datasets, direct usage of logit vectors results in mismatched dimensions. To address this, we construct a statistical fingerprint vector $\mathbf{f}$ that captures the shape of the distribution independent of the option count. We define the key metrics as follows:

$$H(P) = -\sum_{i=1}^{m} p_i \log p_i, \quad C(P) = \max_i p_i \tag{1}$$

$$M(P) = p_{(1)} - p_{(2)} \tag{2}$$

Here, $H(P)$ represents the Entropy quantifying overall uncertainty, $C(P)$ denotes the Confidence, and $M(P)$ is the Margin between the top-1 probability $p_{(1)}$ and the top-2 probability $p_{(2)}$. Additionally, we include the Standard Deviation σ, Skewness $\mathcal{S}$, and Kurtosis $\mathcal{K}$ to describe the morphological characteristics of the distribution. The final fingerprint is represented as:

$$\mathbf{f} = [H, C, M, \sigma, \mathcal{S}, \mathcal{K}] \tag{3}$$

Based on these fingerprints, we segregate the candidate questions from the unified pool into two specialized libraries. The Confusion-Resolution Pool contains questions with a low Margin M, representing scenarios where the model is confused by strong distractors. We manually craft reasoning paths for these samples that focus on distinguishing subtle differences between options. Conversely, the General-Reasoning Pool contains questions with high Entropy H and low Standard Deviation σ, indicating dispersed probability mass and a lack of clear direction. The demonstrations for these samples emphasize constructing a robust problem-solving plan from scratch.

3.2 Preliminary Option Ranking

Standard prompting methods often force the model to process the correct answer and multiple plausible distractors simultaneously, imposing a heavy cognitive load. To address this, the first stage in our pipeline focuses on organizing the option space using demonstrations from the Confusion-Resolution Pool.

Formally, given a test question Q and the option set $\mathcal{O}$, we retrieve the Top-K shots from the Confusion-Resolution Pool based on fingerprint similarity, where K is set to 4 in our implementation. The model is instructed not to solve the problem immediately but to evaluate the plausibility of each option and sort them. Let $\mathcal{M}$ denote the model function and p_{rank} denote the ranking prompt. The ranking process is formulated as:

$$\mathcal{O}' = \mathcal{M}(Q, \mathcal{O}; p_{rank}) \tag{4}$$

where $\mathcal{O}'$ is the re-ordered list of options sorted by descending plausibility. This process functions as a soft filter, establishing a plausibility hierarchy that shifts the attention mechanism of the model towards the head of the list while naturally suppressing the noise from the tail options.

3.3 Rank-Aware Reasoning

In the final stage, the framework performs the deductive reasoning required to reach the solution. This stage utilizes demonstrations from the General-Reasoning Pool which are tailored for high-uncertainty scenarios.

The input to the model comprises the original question Q, the sorted option list $\mathcal{O}'$, and the Top-K selected general-reasoning shots set $\mathcal{D}_{reason}$, and we set K as 4. Since the options are now ordered, the cognitive hurdle shifts from distinguishing distractors to deriving the solution. Crucially, we instruct the model to generate a *Hint* or plan before deriving the final solution. Let p_{reason} denote the reasoning prompt. This intermediate step is essential because the explicit ranking process in the previous stage might subtly alter the focus of the model. By enforcing a planning phase, we ensure the model realigns its reasoning logic with the structured context, ultimately leading to the final answer prediction A:

$$A = \mathcal{M}(Q, \mathcal{O}', \mathcal{D}_{reason}; p_{reason}) \tag{5}$$

4 Experiments

4.1 Experimental Setup

Datasets. We evaluate our framework on five mathematical reasoning benchmarks categorized by difficulty and domain. MMLU [8] is used for comprehensive knowledge evaluation, specifically utilizing its College Math, High School Math, Elementary Math, and Abstract Algebra subsets. We also include AQuA [14] and SAT-Math [30] to represent standard multiple-choice datasets focusing on algebraic reasoning. For the GSM8K [5] and AddSub [9] datasets, which were originally open-ended arithmetic reasoning tasks, we adapted them to the multiple-choice format required for our experimentation. Specifically, we employed GPT-3.5-Turbo to generate three plausible distractors for each question, combining them with the ground truth to form 4-option multiple-choice questions.

Model Configuration. To ensure a fair comparison, all baseline methods and our proposed LRR framework utilize GPT-3.5-Turbo as the main Large Language Model for both the ranking and reasoning stages. We additionally include results from GPT-4 solely as a reference to gauge the performance gap between our method and a state-of-the-art large model. The GPT-4 reference is evaluated under a standard zero-shot setting without specific prompt engineering to represent the model's native capability. For the internal Demonstration Library Construction module, we employ the fine-tuned BERT model described in the methodology as the Scout.

Baseline Methods. We compare our method against five representative strategies. These include 0-prompting which is the standard zero-shot inference, 0-shot CoT which uses the "Let's think step by step" trigger [11], Random-shot representing standard In-Context Learning with randomly selected examples from the training set, and Cot-PS denoting the Plan-and-Solve strategy [24].

4.2 Main Results

Table 1 presents the comparative performance. We explicitly analyze the impact of different reasoning strategies within our LRR framework. Specifically, we report Rank+CoT, where standard Chain-of-Thought is applied after ranking, and Rank+Hint, where the Plan-and-Solve strategy is integrated in the second stage.

Overall Performance. As illustrated in Table 1, our proposed LRR framework consistently outperforms standard prompting baselines across the majority of datasets. The Rank+Hint variant yields the most robust performance. On the challenging AQuA dataset, LRR achieves 61.81% accuracy, significantly surpassing both the Cot-PS baseline at 59.06% and the GPT-4 zero-shot reference at 46.06%. Similarly, in MMLU Elementary Mathematics, it reaches 87.30%,

Table 1. Accuracy comparison on benchmark datasets. All methods except the GPT-4 reference utilize GPT-3.5-Turbo as the main backbone. Note that GPT-4 results are reported under a standard zero-shot setting to serve as a reference for the unguided capability of larger models. The Rank+Hint variant (Ours) demonstrates that structured guidance enables smaller models to achieve performance competitive with unoptimized larger baselines.

Method	MMLU				AQuA	SatMath	GSM8K	addSub
	College	High	Elem.	Algebra				
0-prompting	32.00	37.04	54.49	27.00	44.88	66.36	50.34	45.82
0-shot CoT	38.00	**60.37**	80.16	47.00	56.30	75.91	81.50	78.73
Random-shot	37.00	55.92	81.75	42.00	54.33	75.45	83.32	89.87
Cot-PS	37.00	51.85	78.84	31.00	59.06	**79.55**	81.20	81.77
LRR Variants (Ours)								
Rank+CoT	45.00	55.56	77.51	42.00	55.91	75.45	80.74	78.48
Rank+Hint	**48.00**	59.63	**87.30**	**51.00**	**61.81**	77.27	**84.23**	**91.39**
Reference								
GPT-4 (0-shot)	49.00	52.59	75.93	52.00	46.06	65.00	88.02	95.70

demonstrating a substantial improvement over 0-shot CoT which scored 80.16%. These results validate that incorporating a preliminary ranking phase combined with cognitive-specific demonstration selection effectively empowers a smaller model like GPT-3.5-Turbo to solve complex reasoning tasks.

Analysis of Reasoning Strategies. We observe an interesting phenomenon when comparing the two variants of our framework. The Rank+CoT method, which simply appends standard Chain-of-Thought after ranking, sometimes underperforms compared to standalone CoT methods or Random-shot baselines. We hypothesize that the explicit ranking process may introduce a shift in the focus of the model, causing it to lose track of the primary solving objective when immediately asked to reason. In contrast, the Rank+Hint variant addresses this by requiring the model to first generate a high-level plan or hint based on the sorted options. This step effectively realigns the attention of the model with the problem-solving goal, leveraging the organized context from the ranking stage to produce more accurate deductions. Consequently, Rank+Hint consistently achieves superior performance, confirming the necessity of structured guidance in multi-stage reasoning frameworks.

4.3 Visualization of Cognitive Patterns

To empirically validate our strategy of constructing two distinct demonstration pools, we performed an unsupervised analysis on the comprehensive demonstration library. We extracted the statistical fingerprint vector **f** for a random subset

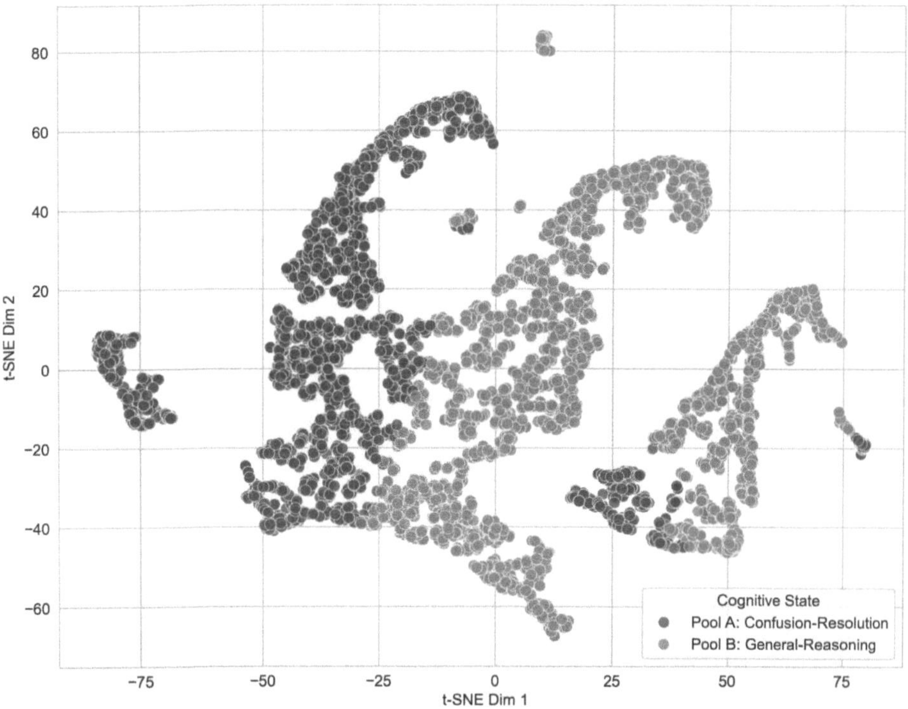

Fig. 2. t-SNE visualization of statistical fingerprints from the unified demonstration library. The clear separation between the Confusion-Resolution pool (Blue) and General-Reasoning pool (Orange) validates the intrinsic cognitive duality across mathematical tasks. (Color figure online)

of samples processed by the Scout model and applied K-Means clustering with $k = 2$. The resulting t-SNE projection [18], visualized in Fig. 2, reveals a compelling phenomenon: the candidate questions spontaneously organize into two highly separable clusters with minimal overlap.

A quantitative analysis of the cluster centroids confirms the physical meaning of this separation. The Blue Cluster is characterized by a significantly lower Margin, representing "Confusion-Dominant" scenarios where the model struggles to discriminate between the top options. Conversely, the Orange Cluster exhibits high Entropy, representing "Uncertainty-Dominant" scenarios where the probability mass is dispersed. This unsupervised discovery provides empirical grounding for our framework design, confirming that the division into Confusion-Resolution and General-Reasoning pools aligns with the intrinsic probability landscapes captured by the Scout model across diverse mathematical domains.

5 Conclusion

In this paper, we proposed Logits-aware Rank-and-Reason, a framework that enhances Large Language Model reasoning in mathematical multiple-choice tasks by addressing distractor interference. By decoupling demonstration selection from inference, we utilized a lightweight Scout model to construct cognitive-specific demonstration libraries offline based on statistical fingerprints, efficiently distinguishing between confusion and uncertainty patterns. This supports a two-stage inference process where Preliminary Option Ranking filters noise and Rank-Aware Reasoning with a hint-first strategy derives solutions. Extensive experiments on benchmarks like AQuA and GSM8K demonstrate that LRR achieves highly competitive performance with a GPT-3.5-turbo backbone, demonstrating capability comparable to the zero-shot performance of GPT-4 on specific algebraic tasks, while unsupervised visualization confirms the validity of our cognitive-pattern-based design.

References

1. Amini, A., Gabriel, S., Lin, S., Koncel-Kedziorski, R., Choi, Y., Hajishirzi, H.: MathQA: towards interpretable math word problem solving with operation-based formalisms. In: Proceedings of the 2019 Conference of the North American Chapter of the Association for Computational Linguistics: Human Language Technologies, Volume 1 (Long and Short Papers), pp. 2357–2367 (2019)
2. Brown, T., et al.: Language models are few-shot learners. In: Advances in Neural Information Processing Systems, vol. 33, pp. 1877–1901 (2020)
3. Burns, C., et al.: Weak-to-strong generalization: eliciting strong capabilities with weak supervision. In: Proceedings of the 41st International Conference on Machine Learning (2024)
4. Chen, L., Zaharia, M., Zou, J.: FrugalGPT: how to use large language models while reducing cost and improving performance. Transactions on Machine Learning Research (2024)
5. Cobbe, K., et al.: Training verifiers to solve math word problems. arXiv preprint arXiv:2110.14168 (2021)
6. Devlin, J., Chang, M.W., Lee, K., Toutanova, K.: BERT: Pre-training of deep bidirectional transformers for language understanding. In: Proceedings of the 2019 Conference of the North American Chapter of the Association for Computational Linguistics: Human Language Technologies, Volume 1 (Long and Short Papers), pp. 4171–4186 (2019)
7. Dubey, A., et al.: The Llama 3 herd of models. arXiv preprint arXiv:2407.21783 (2024)
8. Hendrycks, D., et al.: Measuring massive multitask language understanding. In: International Conference on Learning Representations (2021)
9. Hosseini, M.J., Hajishirzi, H., Etzioni, O., Kushman, N.: Learning to solve arithmetic word problems with verb categorization. In: Proceedings of the 2014 Conference on Empirical Methods in Natural Language Processing (EMNLP), pp. 523–533 (2014)
10. Khatun, A., Brown, D.G.: A study on large language models' limitations in multiple-choice question answering. arXiv preprint arXiv:2401.07955 (2024)

11. Kojima, T., Gu, S.S., Reid, M., Matsuo, Y., Iwasawa, Y.: Large language models are zero-shot reasoners. In: Advances in Neural Information Processing Systems vol. 35, pp. 22199–22213 (2022)
12. Li, J., Li, G., Li, Y., Jin, Z.: Structured chain-of-thought prompting for code generation. ACM Trans. Softw. Eng. Methodol. (2023)
13. Li, X., Qiu, X.: MoT: Pre-thinking and recalling enable ChatGPT to self-improve with memory-of-thoughts. arXiv preprint arXiv:2305.05181 (2023)
14. Ling, W., Yogatama, D., Dyer, C., Blunsom, P.: Program induction by rationale generation: Learning to solve and explain algebraic word problems. In: Proceedings of the 55th Annual Meeting of the Association for Computational Linguistics (Volume 1: Long Papers), pp. 158–167 (2017)
15. Liu, A., Han, X., Wang, Y., Tsvetkov, Y., Choi, Y., Smith, N.A.: Tuning language models by proxy. arXiv preprint arXiv:2401.08565 (2024)
16. Liu, H., Sferrazza, C., Abbeel, P.: Chain of hindsight aligns language models with feedback. In: The Twelfth International Conference on Learning Representations (2024)
17. Liu, Y., Chen, X., Liu, C., Song, D.: Delving into transferable adversarial examples and black-box attacks. In: International Conference on Learning Representations (2017)
18. Maaten, L.v.d., Hinton, G.: Visualizing data using t-SNE. J. Mach. Learn. Res. **9**(Nov), 2579–2605 (2008)
19. Pezeshkpour, P., Hruschka, E.: Large language models sensitivity to the order of options in multiple-choice questions. In: Findings of the Association for Computational Linguistics: NAACL 2024, pp. 2006–2017 (2024)
20. Qwen Team, et al.: Qwen2 technical report. arXiv preprint arXiv:2407.10671 (2024)
21. Robinson, J., Rytting, C., Wingate, D.: Leveraging large language models for multiple choice question answering. arXiv preprint arXiv:2210.12353 (2022)
22. Savelka, J., Agarwal, A., Bogart, C., Sakr, M.: Large language models (GPT) struggle to answer multiple-choice questions about code. arXiv preprint arXiv:2303.08033 (2023)
23. Vaswani, A., et al.: Attention is all you need. In: Advances in Neural Information Processing Systems, vol. 30 (2017)
24. Wang, L., et al.: Plan-and-solve prompting: Improving zero-shot chain-of-thought reasoning by large language models. In: Proceedings of the 61st Annual Meeting of the Association for Computational Linguistics (Volume 1: Long Papers), pp. 2609–2634 (2023)
25. Wei, J., et al.: Chain-of-thought prompting elicits reasoning in large language models. In: Advances in Neural Information Processing Systems, vol. 35, pp. 24824–24837 (2022)
26. Yang, C., et al.: Large language models as optimizers. In: The Twelfth International Conference on Learning Representations (2024)
27. Zhang, Z., Zhang, A., Li, M., Smola, A.: Automatic chain of thought prompting in large language models. In: The Eleventh International Conference on Learning Representations (2023)
28. Zheng, C., Liu, Z., Xie, E., Li, Z., Li, Y.: Progressive-hint prompting improves reasoning in large language models. arXiv preprint arXiv:2304.09797 (2023)
29. Zheng, C., Zhou, H., Meng, F., Zhou, J., Huang, M.: Large language models are not robust multiple choice selectors. In: The Twelfth International Conference on Learning Representations (2024)

30. Zhong, W., et al.: AGIEval: A human-centric benchmark for evaluating foundation models. In: Findings of the Association for Computational Linguistics: NAACL 2024 (2024)
31. Zhou, D., et al.: Least-to-most prompting enables complex reasoning in large language models. In: The Eleventh International Conference on Learning Representations (2023)

RGS: Relation-Guided Graph State Network for Multimodal Emotion Recognition in Conversations

Juntao Wang(✉) and Tsunenori Mine

Kyushu University, Fukuoka, Japan
juntao.wang26@gmail.com, mine@ait.kyushu-u.ac.jp

Abstract. Emotion Recognition in Conversations (ERC) aims to identify the emotions expressed by speakers in each utterance of a dialogue. ERC is essential for developing empathetic dialogue systems in human–computer interaction. Despite its importance, ERC performance relies heavily on complex contextual information, including emotional states that shift over time and across conversational turns. Accurately detecting such emotion shifts, however, remains a major challenge. To tackle this challenge and improve emotion recognition performance, we propose a Relation-Guided Graph State Network (RGS). Our model first constructs a dual-channel relational Graph Attention Network (GAT) module that captures discourse structure in text as well as acoustic cues reflecting emotion shifts. Building upon this, we introduce a relation-guided recursive state space model (SSM) for cross-modal information fusion, enabling the dynamic aggregation of semantic content and signals of emotional change. By interleaving relational GAT and relation-guided SSM layers, RGS more effectively models the inherent semantics and emotional dynamics of dialogues, ultimately enhancing ERC performance. Experiments on two benchmarks demonstrate the effectiveness of our approach.

Keywords: Emotion Recognition in Conversations · Multimodal Learning · Emotional Dynamics Modeling

1 Introduction

Emotion Recognition in Conversations (ERC) addresses the problem of predicting the emotional state expressed in each utterance of a dialogue. As an essential component of empathetic human–computer interaction, ERC has attracted increasing attention in recent years, particularly in applications such as customer service and psychological support.

However, ERC remains highly challenging because the emotion of an utterance is context-dependent and evolves continuously as the conversation unfolds. Prior studies [6,12] show that modeling emotional dynamics can significantly improve recognition performance. Yet most existing approaches rely solely on

R. C.-W. Wong et al. (Eds.): PAKDD 2026, LNAI 16618, pp. 127–138, 2027.
https://doi.org/10.1007/978-981-92-1947-6_11

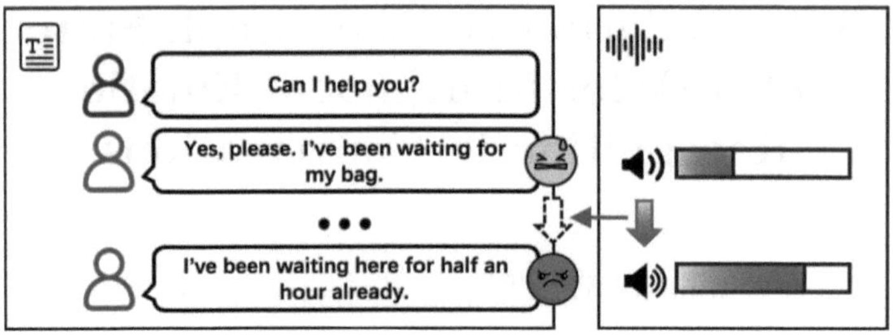

Fig. 1. A sample dialogue between a customer and an agent, demonstrating the limitation of text-only analysis. Although the utterance "I've been waiting here for half an hour already" appears neutral or mildly impatient in text, acoustic features such as rising loudness indicate emotional escalation.

textual content, making it difficult to capture how emotions change over time based on text alone. In addition, while multimodal ERC methods introduce speech or visual information, they mainly emphasize modality fusion and do not explicitly model temporal emotional transitions. Relation-based models likewise focus on structural dependencies but overlook acoustic patterns that reflect emotional dynamics. As a result, current ERC approaches seldom exploit speech cues that explicitly reflect changes in emotional intensity, leaving emotional dynamics insufficiently modeled.

Figure 1 illustrates this limitation with a short dialogue between a customer and a service agent. Although the statement "I've been waiting here for half an hour already" may sound impatient, it remains unclear from the text alone whether the speaker is calmly stating a fact or experiencing escalating frustration. In contrast, acoustic cues—such as rising loudness—provide clear evidence of increasing emotional agitation, revealing dynamic trends that are not directly encoded in the text.

These observations suggest that incorporating audio-based change patterns can more effectively model emotional dynamics and thus improve ERC accuracy. To capture the correlation between emotional shifts and acoustic variation, and to better exploit such cues alongside semantic structure, we propose a Relation-Guided Graph State Network (RGS) that encodes audio change trends as relation types and jointly models semantic and acoustic relational structures. In our approach, we construct two relational graphs. The first is a semantic relation graph, derived from discourse parsing, where edge types encode functional and semantic dependencies between utterances. The second is an emotional dynamics graph, built from loudness trends across utterances, capturing dynamic acoustic signals that correlate with changes in emotional intensity. These two relational structures guide information aggregation in the graph network, enabling effective modeling at both the semantic and emotional dynamics levels. Beyond relational graph encoding, we further introduce a relation-guided recursive state space model (SSM) that propagates along the dialogue timeline. By injecting semantic and acoustic cues as control signals, the SSM dynamically integrates the two relational streams, capturing evolving emotional states throughout the conversation.

Our main contributions are summarized as follows:

1. We construct two relational conversation graphs: a semantic relation graph derived from discourse parsing and an emotional dynamics graph built from speech loudness trends, enabling explicit modeling of structural and emotional dependencies across utterances.
2. We propose a relation-guided recursive SSM that dynamically integrates semantic and acoustic cues along the conversational timeline, providing effective state updates for modeling emotional dynamics.
3. We conduct extensive experiments on two multimodal ERC benchmarks. The results show that RGS achieves state-of-the-art performance on IEMOCAP and exhibits strong competitiveness on MELD.

2 Related Work

Prior work models emotional dynamics using various strategies, such as DialogueRNN [12], which tracks speaker states via recurrent propagation. ESD-ERC [6] employs multi-task learning to model emotion shifts explicitly. However, text alone is insufficient, as emotional changes are often conveyed through prosody, speech rate, and facial expressions. Recent multimodal ERC methods focus on cross-modal fusion rather than explicitly modeling emotional dynamics. For instance, MGLRA [13] emphasizes modality alignment, while MM-DFN [9] primarily performs multimodal fusion rather than capturing intrinsic emotional change trends. Recent work such as GS-MCC [2] further explores multimodal ERC from a graph spectral perspective. To address these limitations, we leverage speech signals and propose a relation-guided multimodal approach to model emotional dynamics. Relation modeling has also become an effective strategy in recent ERC research. DualGATs [16] leverage syntactic structures to capture semantic dependencies across utterances via Graph Attention Networks (GAT). In multimodal settings, DER-GCN [1] constructs a multi-relation graph to jointly model speaker-level and event-level dependencies, achieving more fine-grained cross-modal context reasoning. These studies demonstrate that relational structures help models capture complex dependencies in dialogue. Building on this insight, our work explicitly encodes both semantic and acoustic relationships to guide the model in understanding how emotions shift and propagate throughout a conversation.

3 Methodology

The overall structure of RGS is illustrated in Fig. 2 and consists of three components: graph construction, feature extraction, and model architecture. Graph construction builds both the semantic relation graph and the emotional dynamics graph. Feature extraction processes and fuses textual and acoustic modality

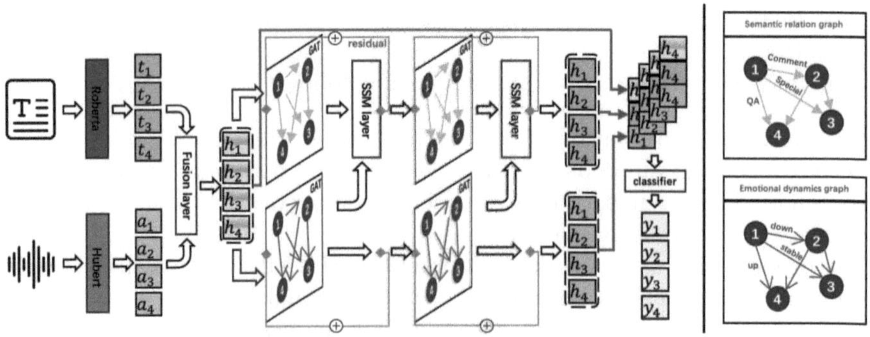

Fig. 2. The overall architecture of RGS.

Table 1. Relation encoding rules for semantic relation graph and emotional dynamics graph.

(a) Semantic relation graph

$r_{\mathbf{t}}(e)$	Condition
$r(e)$	$e \in E_{\text{dis}}$
18	$e \in E_{\text{spk}} \setminus E_{\text{dis}}$

(b) Emotional dynamics graph

$r_{\mathbf{a}}(e)$	Condition
$1 + t(e)$	$e \in E_{\text{dis}} \cap E_{\text{spk}}$
$4 + t(e)$	$e \in E_{\text{spk}} \setminus E_{\text{dis}}$
$7 + t(e)$	$e \in E_{\text{dis}} \setminus E_{\text{spk}}$
10	$e \in \{(u_i, u_j) \mid i = j\}$

features. The model architecture consists of stacks of relational GAT layers and relation-guided recursive SSM layers. Details of these components are presented in Sects. 3.2–3.5.

3.1 Task Definition

ERC is defined as the task of predicting the emotion of each utterance in a dialogue. Given a dialogue $\mathcal{C} = \{(u_1, s_1), (u_2, s_2), \ldots, (u_N, s_N)\}$, where u_i denotes the i-th utterance and s_i its speaker, the goal of ERC is to predict the corresponding emotion label y_i for each utterance u_i.

3.2 Relational Graph Construction

We model each dialogue as a graph (V, E). Given a dialogue with N utterances, we define the node set $V = \{u_1, u_2, \ldots, u_N\}$, where each u_i denotes an utterance. Each edge is denoted as $e = (u_i, u_j) \in E$, representing a directed link equipped with a relation label. Based on this shared node set, we construct two relational graphs to capture textual semantic structure and acoustic emotional dynamics.

Discourse-Based and Speaker-Based Edges. To obtain structural connections among utterances, we derive a discourse-based edge set $E_{\text{dis}} \subseteq V \times V$

using a discourse parser trained on the STAC [3] corpus under the SDDP [5] framework. The parser predicts directed discourse links between utterances and assigns each link one of the 17 discourse relations in R_{dis}.[1] In addition, we define a same-speaker edge set $E_{\text{spk}} = \{(u_i, u_j) \mid s_i = s_j\}$, capturing within-speaker contextual continuity. The final edge set is $E = E_{\text{dis}} \cup E_{\text{spk}}$.

Semantic Relation Graph. The semantic relation graph is defined over the node set V and edge set E. Each edge $e \in E$ is assigned a semantic relation ID $r_{\text{t}}(e)$. For each discourse edge $e \in E_{\text{dis}}$, we let $r(e)$ denote the discourse relation ID assigned by R_{dis}. Edges between same-speaker utterances without a discourse relation are assigned a separate speaker-continuity type. Since discourse parsers do not produce self-loops, we assign self-loops to the Special category of R_{dis}, where Special serves as a general fallback relation type for cases not belonging to the standard discourse labels. The encoding rules are summarized in Table 1(a). This yields 18 semantic relation types in total, covering both discourse-level semantic links and same-speaker contextual continuity.

Emotional Dynamics Graph. The emotional dynamics graph is constructed over the same node set V and structural edge set E. For each utterance u_i, we obtain a normalized loudness score z_i based on its mean intensity. Loudness variation provides a simple acoustic cue for capturing emotional changes. Concretely, we first compute the average intensity in dB over the utterance as its raw loudness q_i, using Parselmouth with a 10 ms frame step. We then perform per-dialogue z-score normalization, i.e., $z_i = (q_i - \mu_d)/\sigma_d$, where μ_d and σ_d are the mean and standard deviation of q_k over all utterances in the same dialogue.

For each edge $e = (u_i, u_j) \in E$, we compute the loudness difference $\Delta_{ij} = z_j - z_i$ and categorize the acoustic trend using an empirical threshold τ: an upward trend if $\Delta_{ij} > \tau$, a downward trend if $\Delta_{ij} < -\tau$, and a stable trend otherwise. These three categories form the acoustic relation indicator $t(e) \in \{0, 1, 2\}$. To capture how loudness changes interact with the underlying semantic or speaker-based structure, each edge is assigned an acoustic relation ID $r_{\text{a}}(e)$ according to both its structural category and its loudness trend. This design reflects our intuition that emotional change patterns may differ depending on whether the utterances are semantically connected or produced by the same speaker. Unlike the semantic graph, the emotional dynamics graph explicitly includes self-loops. Since self-loops do not correspond to any structural category or loudness-trend combination used in the emotional dynamics graph, we treat each self-loop as a distinct acoustic relation type. The complete set of acoustic relation types is summarized in Table 1(b). This yields 10 acoustic relation types in total, capturing how semantic structure and speaker identity interact with loudness-based emotional dynamics.

[1] The 17 discourse relation types include: Continuation, Question–Answer, Contrast, Question–Elaboration, Explanation, Comment, Background, Result, Correction, Parallel, Alternation, Conditional, Clarification Question, Acknowledgement, Elaboration, Narration, and Special.

3.3 Feature Extraction and Fusion

For each utterance u_i, we extract its textual embedding $\mathbf{t}_i$ using a RoBERTa-large encoder [11] fine-tuned on the ERC dataset for utterance-level emotion classification. Its acoustic embedding $\mathbf{a}_i$ is obtained from a pretrained HuBERT model [8] without additional fine-tuning. Both modalities are projected into a shared d-dimensional space via modality-specific linear layers. The resulting features are then fused through:

$$\mathbf{h}_i^{(0)} = \sigma\big(W_f\big[\sigma(W_t\mathbf{t}_i);\ \sigma(W_a\mathbf{a}_i)\big]\big),$$

where W_t and W_a are modality-specific linear projections, W_f is a fusion projection, $\sigma(\cdot)$ denotes a non-linear activation, and $[\cdot;\cdot]$ is concatenation. The fused vectors $\mathbf{h}_i^{(0)} \in \mathbb{R}^d$ serve as the initial node states for subsequent graph reasoning.

3.4 Relational Graph Attention Network

Inspired by DualGATs [16], which augments GAT with discrete relation-type encoding, we similarly integrate our relational graphs into a relation-aware graph attention mechanism. For each edge e, the semantic graph provides a relation ID $r_{\mathrm{t}}(e)$, and the emotional graph provides $r_{\mathrm{a}}(e)$. These discrete relation IDs are mapped to trainable embeddings by two lookup tables:

$$\mathbf{o}^{\mathrm{t}} = \mathrm{Embed}_{\mathrm{t}}(r_{\mathrm{t}}(e)) \in \mathbb{R}^{d_r}, \qquad \mathbf{o}^{\mathrm{a}} = \mathrm{Embed}_{\mathrm{a}}(r_{\mathrm{a}}(e)) \in \mathbb{R}^{d_r},$$

where $\mathrm{Embed}_{\mathrm{t}}$ and $\mathrm{Embed}_{\mathrm{a}}$ denote trainable embedding layers, and both embeddings lie in $\mathbb{R}^{d_r}$, with d_r denoting the relation embedding dimension.

In both the semantic graph and the emotional graph, node representations are updated through relation-aware message passing. The fused representation $\mathbf{h}_i^{(0)}$ serves as the initial node state for each graph. Given the input node features $\mathbf{h}_i^{*,(\ell)}$ at layer ℓ, where $* \in \{t, a\}$ indexes the semantic and emotional graphs, the attention coefficient for an edge (u_i, u_j) in graph $*$ is computed as

$$\alpha_{ij}^{*} = \mathrm{softmax}\Big(\mathrm{LeakyReLU}\big(\mathbf{a}^{\top}[\,W_h\mathbf{h}_i^{*,(\ell)}\ ;\ W_h\mathbf{h}_j^{*,(\ell)}\ ;\ \mathbf{o}_{ij}^{*}\,]\big)\Big),$$

where $W_h \in \mathbb{R}^{d\times d}$ is a learnable projection, $\mathbf{a}$ is a trainable attention vector, and $\mathbf{o}_{ij}^{*}$ is the relation embedding for edge (i, j). The semantic and emotional graphs are parameterized independently, allowing each graph to learn its own relational patterns without interference.

The neighbor aggregation is performed as

$$\tilde{\mathbf{h}}_i^{*,(\ell)} = \sigma\left(\sum_{j:(i,j)\in E} \alpha_{ij}^{*}\, W_h\, \mathbf{h}_j^{*,(\ell)}\right),$$

where $\sigma(\cdot)$ is a non-linear activation. Applying this aggregation to both graphs yields the semantic and acoustic intermediate features $\tilde{\mathbf{h}}_i^{t,(\ell)}$ and $\tilde{\mathbf{h}}_i^{a,(\ell)}$.

3.5 Relation-Guided Recursive State Space Model

SSMs provide a stable mechanism for modeling long-range temporal dependencies through latent states. Recent advances, such as Mamba [7] reformulate SSM computation to enable highly parallel execution and substantial efficiency gains on modern hardware. In contrast to these parallel formulations, we focus on leveraging the dynamics of the latent state to perform controlled updates along the conversational timeline. To propagate structural cues from the semantic graph and incorporate complementary acoustic signals, we design a relation-guided recursive SSM.

To explicitly inject discourse structure into the temporal dynamics, we encode semantic relations as typed edges and allow each relation type to exert a learnable influence on state propagation. We represent semantic relations in matrix form using the adjacency matrix $A^{(\mathrm{t})} \in \{0, \ldots, 18\}^{N \times N}$, where 0 indicates the absence of an edge and values in 1–18 denote the semantic relation types listed in Table 1(a):

$$A_{ij}^{(\mathrm{t})} = \begin{cases} r_{\mathrm{t}}(e), & \text{if } e = (u_i, u_j) \in E, \\ 0, & \text{otherwise.} \end{cases}$$

Each semantic relation ID $k \in \{1, \ldots, 18\}$ is assigned a learnable diffusion parameter w_k, which is mapped to a non-negative weight via $\omega_k = \mathrm{softplus}(w_k)$. Using these weights, we define the continuous diffusion operator

$$\hat{A}_{ij} = \begin{cases} \omega_{A_{ij}^{(\mathrm{t})}}, & A_{ij}^{(\mathrm{t})} \neq 0, \\ 0, & \text{otherwise.} \end{cases}$$

which allows different relation types to modulate the propagation strength over the dialogue structure.

We adopt a state space formulation. Let $\mathbf{x}_t \in \mathbb{R}^d$ denote the latent state of the model at timestep t, summarizing all past contextual information, and let $\mathbf{y}_t^{(\ell)} \in \mathbb{R}^d$ denote the SSM output at layer ℓ. The initial latent state is set to zero, allowing the SSM to be fully driven by the graph-enhanced semantic and acoustic inputs. The latent state evolves according to

$$\mathbf{x}_{t+1} = \alpha\, \mathbf{x}_t + \beta\, (\hat{A}\mathbf{x}_t) + B_u\, \tilde{\mathbf{h}}_t^{t,(\ell)} + B_a\, \tilde{\mathbf{h}}_t^{a,(\ell)},$$

where α and β regulate the temporal transition dynamics. The matrices $B_u, B_a \in \mathbb{R}^{d \times d}$ project the semantic and acoustic representations into the latent state space.

The SSM output is computed as

$$\mathbf{y}_t^{(\ell)} = C\, \mathbf{x}_t + D_u\, \tilde{\mathbf{h}}_t^{t,(\ell)} + D_a\, \tilde{\mathbf{h}}_t^{a,(\ell)},$$

where $C, D_u, D_a \in \mathbb{R}^{d \times d}$ are output projection matrices that map the latent state and modality-specific signals into a unified representation. All parameters in the SSM module are learned jointly during training. The resulting $\mathbf{y}_t^{(\ell)}$ serves as the SSM-refined semantic representation at layer ℓ.

We then apply residual connections and layer normalization to obtain the final layer outputs:

$$\mathbf{h}_i^{t,(\ell+1)} = \mathrm{LN}_t\left(\mathbf{h}_i^{t,(\ell)} + \mathbf{y}_i^{(\ell)}\right), \qquad \mathbf{h}_i^{a,(\ell+1)} = \mathrm{LN}_a\left(\mathbf{h}_i^{a,(\ell)} + \tilde{\mathbf{h}}_i^{a,(\ell)}\right).$$

Here LN_t and LN_a denote layer normalization for the semantic and acoustic streams, respectively. After several layers of GAT–SSM integration, each utterance node obtains its final semantic and acoustic representations, denoted as $\mathbf{h}_i^{t,\mathrm{final}}$ and $\mathbf{h}_i^{a,\mathrm{final}}$.

3.6 Emotion Prediction

For each utterance u_i, we obtain three representations: the initial fused representation $\mathbf{h}_i^{(0)}$, the final semantic representation $\mathbf{h}_i^{t,\mathrm{final}}$, and the final acoustic representation $\mathbf{h}_i^{a,\mathrm{final}}$. These representations are concatenated to form the final utterance feature, which is then fed into a linear classifier:

$$\mathbf{p}_i = \mathrm{softmax}\left(W_c\,[\mathbf{h}_i^{(0)}; \mathbf{h}_i^{t,\mathrm{final}}; \mathbf{h}_i^{a,\mathrm{final}}] + b_c\right),$$

where $W_c \in \mathbb{R}^{|\mathcal{Y}|\times 3d}$ and $b_c \in \mathbb{R}^{|\mathcal{Y}|}$ are trainable parameters, and $|\mathcal{Y}|$ denotes the number of emotion categories.

4 Experiments

4.1 Datasets

We evaluate RGS on two multimodal ERC datasets. IEMOCAP [4] is a dyadic multimodal dialogue dataset recorded in a controlled environment, containing aligned speech, video, motion-capture data, and transcripts. It includes six emotions: neutral, excited, happy, sad, angry, and frustrated. MELD [14] is a multi-speaker dataset from the TV series Friends, providing aligned audio, video, and text for each utterance, with seven emotions: neutral, anger, joy, disgust, surprise, sadness, and fear.

4.2 Implementation Details

We used the same fixed random seed for both datasets and manually tuned the hyperparameters based on the performance of each validation set. For both the IEMOCAP and MELD datasets, the learning rate was 5e-5, and training was performed using the Adam optimizer. Batch sizes were set to 64 and 8, respectively, and the hidden layer dimension was set to 300 for both models. The number of GAT–SSM layers was 2, and the loss functions chosen were cross-entropy loss for IEMOCAP and FocalLoss for MELD. All experiments were performed on a single NVIDIA Quadro RTX 8000 GPU with 48 GB of memory.

4.3 Baseline Models

We compare RGS against several strong ERC baselines. Text-based baselines include DualGATs [16] and DualRAN [10]. Multimodal baselines include MM-DFN [9], ConxGNN [15], DER-GCN [1], and MGLRA [13].

Following previous studies, we adopt weighted-average F1 and accuracy as the evaluation metrics.

5 Results and Analysis

5.1 Main Result

Table 2. Performance comparison on IEMOCAP and MELD using Weighted F1 and Accuracy. t, a, and v represent information in the three modalities of text, audio, and video, respectively. **Bold** indicates the best result, and underline indicates the second-best.

Model	modal	IEMOCAP		MELD	
		w-F1	Acc	w-F1	Acc
DualGATs [16]	t	67.68	-	**66.90**	-
DualRAN [10]	t	69.73	69.62	66.24	**67.70**
MM-DFN [9]	t+a+v	68.18	68.21	-	-
ConxGNN [15]	t+a+v	68.64	68.52	65.69	66.28
DER-GCN [1]	t+a+v	69.40	69.70	66.10	66.80
MGLRA [13]	t+a+v	<u>70.10</u>	<u>71.30</u>	64.90	66.40
RGS	t+a	**71.82**	**71.66**	<u>66.36</u>	<u>67.01</u>

The overall experimental results are presented in Table 2. Our model achieves strong performance on both weighted F1 and accuracy metrics. On the IEMOCAP dataset, RGS obtains the best results among all baseline methods. Its weighted F1 score exceeds that of the state-of-the-art MGLRA model by 1.72, while relying only on bimodal inputs (text and speech), unlike other multimodal baselines. On the MELD dataset, the highest weighted F1 score is achieved by the text-specialized model DualGATs, and the best accuracy is likewise obtained by the text-based DualRAN. We attribute the stronger performance of text-only models to the nature of MELD itself. Since the dataset originates from scripted sitcom dialogues, the audio tracks often contain background noise and soundtrack elements, meaning that emotions are expressed primarily through linguistic content rather than acoustic signals. Consequently, text-specialized models perform more effectively in this setting. In contrast, the dialogues in IEMOCAP are recorded in controlled, simulated real-life interactions where vocal expressions more faithfully reflect emotional changes. This makes the audio modality more informative and better aligned with emotional dynamics, thereby providing greater benefit to RGS. Nevertheless, RGS still achieves a competitive second-place performance on both metrics in MELD, demonstrating robustness to noisy conditions and strong capability in extracting and aggregating multimodal emotional cues. The consistently strong results on both multimodal datasets highlight the generalization ability of our model.

5.2 Ablation and Fusion Strategy Analysis

Table 3. Ablation study results, Δ indicates the degree of decrease.

Model	All		ES	
	w-F1	Δ	w-F1	Δ
RGS	71.82	-	54.89	-
-*Rel*	70.38	↓1.44	54.32	↓0.57
-*SSM*	69.43	↓2.39	54.31	↓0.58
-*Rel* -*SSM*	69.26	↓2.56	53.70	↓1.19

Table 4. Results of fusion strategy comparison.

Fusion type	w-F1	Δ
SSM	71.82	-
Linear	69.61	↓2.21
Gated	68.93	↓2.89
Cross-Attn	68.52	↓3.30

We conducted ablation studies on the IEMOCAP dataset to evaluate the contributions of the proposed relational graph and the relation-guided SSM, and the results are presented in Table 3. Weighted F1 scores were used as the evaluation metric. Removing relation types from Relational GAT, removing the SSM module, or removing both components simultaneously all led to substantial performance degradation, demonstrating that each module in RGS plays an essential role in improving ERC performance.

In addition to evaluating the full dataset, we further isolated samples exhibiting Emotion Shift (ES). An ES sample is defined as an utterance in which the speaker's current emotion label differs from that of their immediately preceding utterance within the same dialogue. The IEMOCAP dataset contains 410 such ES samples. Consistently, removing either module resulted in decreased performance on these samples as well. This further indicates that our relation modeling and interaction mechanisms effectively capture dynamic emotional transitions, thereby improving performance even on the more challenging ES cases.

To evaluate whether our proposed relation-guided recursive SSM module provides more effective feature fusion than conventional approaches, we conduct fusion comparison experiments on the IEMOCAP dataset and compare it with several widely used baselines, including Linear Fusion, Gated Fusion, and Cross-Attention. All fusion methods are assessed using weighted F1 scores. Linear Fusion concatenates $\tilde{\mathbf{h}}_i^{t,(\ell)}$ and $\tilde{\mathbf{h}}_i^{a,(\ell)}$ and feeds the merged representation into a linear projection; Gated Fusion introduces a learnable gate to adaptively balance the contributions of the two modalities; and Cross-Attention treats $\tilde{\mathbf{h}}_i^{t,(\ell)}$ as the query while using $\tilde{\mathbf{h}}_i^{a,(\ell)}$ as the key and value, allowing semantic features to retrieve complementary emotional cues. The results in Table 4 show that all traditional fusion strategies underperform our SSM-based fusion. Interestingly, the more sophisticated gating and attention mechanisms yield larger performance drops than the simple linear baseline, indicating that increased architectural complexity does not necessarily lead to better multimodal fusion in this setting. In contrast, our relation-guided recursive SSM integrates semantic structure and emotional dynamics through controlled state transitions, enabling more effective fusion and resulting in significantly improved representations.

6 Conclusion

In this study, we propose a method to capture emotional change cues that are difficult to infer from text alone by leveraging speech information. We model emotional dependencies using graph structures and introduce a relation-guided SSM interaction mechanism to facilitate information exchange across graph modules. Experiments on IEMOCAP and MELD show that RGS outperforms existing baselines on IEMOCAP and achieves competitive performance on MELD, demonstrating its effectiveness in modeling emotional transitions and integrating semantic and acoustic information.

Acknowledgment. This work was supported by JST SPRING, Grant Number JPMJSP2136.

References

1. Ai, W., Shou, Y., Meng, T., Li, K.: DER-GCN: dialog and event relation-aware graph convolutional neural network for multimodal dialog emotion recognition. IEEE Trans. Neural Netw. Learn. Syst. **36**(3), 4908–4921 (2025). https://doi.org/10.1109/TNNLS.2024.3367940
2. Ai, W., Zhang, F., Shou, Y., Meng, T., Chen, H., Li, K.: Revisiting multimodal emotion recognition in conversation from the perspective of graph spectrum. In: Proceedings of the AAAI Conference on Artificial Intelligence, vol. 39, pp. 11418–11426 (2025)
3. Asher, N., Hunter, J., Morey, M., Farah, B., Afantenos, S.: Discourse structure and dialogue acts in multiparty dialogue: the STAC corpus. In: Calzolari, N., et al., (eds.) Proceedings of the Tenth International Conference on Language Resources and Evaluation (LREC'16), pp. 2721–2727. European Language Resources Association (ELRA), Portorož, Slovenia (May 2016), https://aclanthology.org/L16-1432/
4. Busso, C., et al.: Iemocap: interactive emotional dyadic motion capture database. Lang. Resour. Eval. **42**(4), 335–359 (2008)
5. Chi, T.C., Rudnicky, A.: Structured dialogue discourse parsing. In: Lemon, O., et al., (eds.) Proceedings of the 23rd Annual Meeting of the Special Interest Group on Discourse and Dialogue, pp. 325–335. Association for Computational Linguistics, Edinburgh, UK (Sep 2022). https://doi.org/10.18653/v1/2022.sigdial-1.32, https://aclanthology.org/2022.sigdial-1.32/

6. Gao, Q.: Emotion recognition in conversations with emotion shift detection based on multi-task learning. Knowl.-Based Syst. **248**, 108861 (2022)
7. Gu, A., Dao, T.: Mamba: Linear-time sequence modeling with selective state spaces. In: First Conference on Language Modeling (2024)
8. Hsu, W.N., Bolte, B., Tsai, Y.H.H., Lakhotia, K., Salakhutdinov, R., Mohamed, A.: Hubert: Self-supervised speech representation learning by masked prediction of hidden units. IEEE/ACM Trans. Audio, Speech, Lang. Process. **29**, 3451–3460 (2021). https://doi.org/10.1109/TASLP.2021.3122291
9. Hu, D., Hou, X., Wei, L., Jiang, L., Mo, Y.: MM-DFN: multimodal dynamic fusion network for emotion recognition in conversations. In: ICASSP 2022-2022 IEEE International Conference on Acoustics, Speech and Signal Processing (ICASSP), pp. 7037–7041. IEEE (2022)
10. Li, J., Wang, X., Zeng, Z.: A dual-stream recurrence-attention network with global-local awareness for emotion recognition in textual dialog. Eng. Appl. Artif. Intell. **128**, 107530 (2024)
11. Liu, Y., et al.: Roberta: A robustly optimized bert pretraining approach (2019). arXiv:1907.11692 arXiv preprint
12. Majumder, N., Poria, S., Hazarika, D., Mihalcea, R., Gelbukh, A., Cambria, E.: DialogueRNN: an attentive RNN for emotion detection in conversations. In: Proceedings of the AAAI Conference on Artificial Intelligence, vol. 33, pp. 6818–6825 (2019)
13. Meng, T., Zhang, F., Shou, Y., Shao, H., Ai, W., Li, K.: Masked Graph Learning with Recurrent Alignment for Multimodal Emotion Recognition in Conversation. Speech, and Language Processing, IEEE/ACM Transactions on Audio (2024)
14. Poria, S., Hazarika, D., Majumder, N., Naik, G., Cambria, E., Mihalcea, R.: MELD: A multimodal multi-party dataset for emotion recognition in conversations. In: Korhonen, A., Traum, D., Màrquez, L. (eds.) Proceedings of the 57th Annual Meeting of the Association for Computational Linguistics, pp. 527–536. Association for Computational Linguistics, Florence, Italy (Jul 2019) https://doi.org/10.18653/v1/P19-1050, https://aclanthology.org/P19-1050/
15. Van, C.T., Tran, T.V.T., Nguyen, V., Hy, T.S.: Effective context modeling framework for emotion recognition in conversations. In: ICASSP 2025 - 2025 IEEE International Conference on Acoustics, Speech and Signal Processing (ICASSP), pp. 1–5 (2025). https://doi.org/10.1109/ICASSP49660.2025.10888112
16. Zhang, D., Chen, F., Chen, X.: DualGATs: dual graph attention networks for emotion recognition in conversations. In: Rogers, A., Boyd-Graber, J., Okazaki, N. (eds.) Proceedings of the 61st Annual Meeting of the Association for Computational Linguistics (Volume 1: Long Papers), pp. 7395–7408. Association for Computational Linguistics, Toronto, Canada (Jul 2023). https://doi.org/10.18653/v1/2023.acl-long.408, https://aclanthology.org/2023.acl-long.408/

Table-Aware Group Relative Policy Optimization: Reward Design for Large Vision–Language Models

Jiyoon Lee[1], Hwangseon Park[2], and Hayoung Oh[1](✉)

[1] Department of Applied Artificial Intelligence, Sungkyunkwan University, Seoul, Republic of Korea
lkjyoon@g.skku.edu, hyoh79@skku.edu

[2] Department of Immersive Media Engineering, Sungkyunkwan University, Seoul, Republic of Korea
zkdtjs11@skku.edu

Abstract. Recent advances in large-scale vision-language models (LVLMs) have improved performance on multimodal tasks. While Chain-of-Thought (CoT) supervision is used to enhance reasoning, it relies on manual annotations and has scalability limits. As an alternative, Group Relative Policy Optimization (GRPO) introduced in DeepSeek R1 has shown promising reinforcement-learning gains. However, vanilla GRPO mainly rewards final-answer correctness, making it insufficient for Table-Based Visual Question Answering (Table VQA), which requires structured data understanding and intermediate reasoning. We propose Table-Aware Group Relative Policy Optimization (TAG), a reinforcement-learning framework that injects table-structure awareness into the reward. TAG provides structure-aware intermediate rewards that check whether the model correctly uses column headers, row headers, and cell values, encouraging explicit use of table structure instead of shallow pattern matching. Built on the Qwen3-VL-4B-Instruct model, TAG employs a reward function combining answer accuracy, output-format validity, and table-keyword agreement. Experiments on seven benchmarks, including TableVQA, TableBench, Wild, and ChartQAPro, show that TAG outperforms vanilla GRPO and, despite its 4B scale, matches or surpasses several SOTA 32B+ models and closed-source systems such as GPT-4.1. This demonstrates that structure-aware rewards can boost Table VQA performance in LVLMs. All code, datasets, models, and evaluation scripts will be released at https://github.com/Emilia0608/TAG

Keywords: Table vqa · GRPO · LVLM reasoning

1 Introduction

Table-based Visual Question Answering (Table VQA) is a multimodal reasoning task that requires interpreting visually presented tables and answering high-level

J. Lee and H. Park—Equal contribution.

R. C.-W. Wong et al. (Eds.): PAKDD 2026, LNAI 16618, pp. 139–150, 2027.
https://doi.org/10.1007/978-981-92-1947-6_12

queries grounded in their structured content [22]. As it involves multiple intermediate reasoning steps—such as multi-condition filtering, numerical computation, and logical comparison [30]—structured and compositional multimodal reasoning is essential.

Early Table VQA approaches serialized tables into text and fed them into language models [7,27]. While effective for simple tasks, they rely heavily on OCR and fail to capture visual layout and complex structures. With the emergence of Large Vision-Language Models (LVLMs) [12,28], models like Table-LLaVA process table images directly [31], yet still struggle with structural understanding and multi-step reasoning [32].

To improve reasoning, Chain-of-Thought (CoT) supervision has been widely studied [18,25], but requires costly large-scale annotations and lacks generalizability [29]. Reinforcement learning (RL) has emerged as an alternative, encouraging diverse reasoning via answer-based rewards [20]. In particular, GRPO from DeepSeek R1 [6,14] optimizes reasoning paths using relative rewards across sampled outputs.

Recent extensions combining GRPO with RLVR [21] and LVLM-oriented variants such as VLM-R1 and VLAA-Thinking [5,15] have also been applied to Table VQA. However, limitations remain, including difficulty with non-linear table layouts, unstable reasoning due to weak structural understanding [8,9], limited reproducibility, and reward designs overly focused on final answers rather than intermediate reasoning quality [4].

Question:
What is the accuracy of the deep learning solution at Thr(2) when the Damkohler number is 2.6*10^-10?

De	Thr(2)	Thr(1)	Thr(0.5)
2.6*10-5	73.38%	66.39%	61.45%
2.6*10-7	84.29%	82.48%	76.21%
2.6*10-10	89.29%	87.78%	82.27%
2.6*10-12	88.57%	86.54%	82.12%
2.6*10-15	81.33%	75.91%	70.67%

TAG

<think>To find the accuracy of the deep learning solution at Thr(2) when the Damkohler number (De) is 2.6*10^-10.. In this row, the value under the "Thr(2)" column is 89.29%.</think>
<answer>89.29%</answer> ✓

GRPO

<think>The accuracy of the deep learning solution at Thr(2) when the Damkohler number is 2.6*10^-10 is 88.57%.</think>
<answer>88.57%</answer> ✗

Fig. 1. Example of GRPO's limitation in table recognition.

As shown in Fig. 1, vanilla GRPO rewards correct final answers even when intermediate reasoning is inconsistent or structurally incorrect. Although LVLMs can extract basic cell values, they remain weak in tasks requiring conditional filtering, aggregation, and multi-step reasoning over table structures [32]. This gap arises from insufficient learning of relationships among row headers, column headers, and cell values.

To address this, we propose Table-Aware Group Relative Policy Optimization (TAG), a novel RL framework that incorporates table-structure recognition into the reward function. TAG extends GRPO with a Table Recognition Reward that evaluates the correctness of column headers, row headers, and cell references in intermediate reasoning. This encourages structurally grounded reasoning rather than superficial pattern matching, improving generalization in domains involving structured visual data such as tables and charts.

Our contributions include the following:

- We explore GRPO for Table VQA and demonstrate the effectiveness of RL-based structured visual reasoning.
- We propose TAG, integrating table-structure understanding into reward design for quantitative evaluation of intermediate reasoning.
- We conduct extensive experiments on seven benchmarks, including TableVQA [10], TableBench [22], MMSci [24], TABMWP [11], ComTQA [30], Wild-Table, and ChartQA Pro [13], showing consistent improvements over GRPO and CoT baselines.

Experiments show that TAG, built on a 4B model, achieves competitive or superior performance compared to 32B LVLMs and some closed-source models across benchmarks. It also shows strong gains on ChartQA Pro, highlighting the effectiveness of incorporating table-structure awareness into RL reward design for improving LVLM reasoning.

2 Method

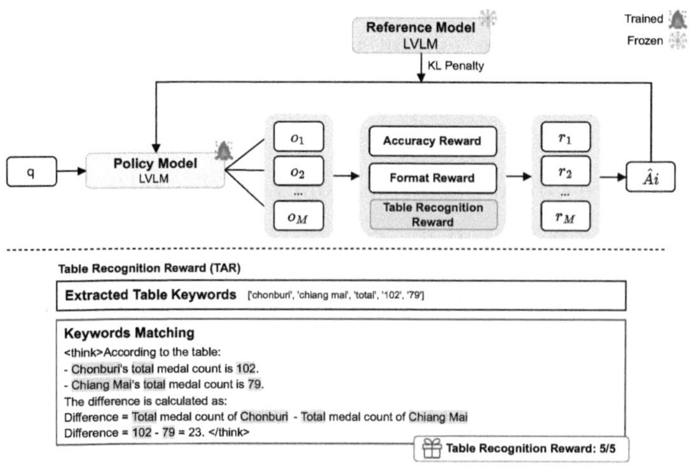

Fig. 2. The overall pipeline of Table-Aware Group Relative Policy Optimization.

2.1 Preliminaries

In this work, we perform table-based question answering (Table VQA) using a pretrained Large Vision-Language Model (LVLM). For a given question, we generate multiple reasoning trajectories from a policy π_θ and apply RLVR (Reinforcement Learning with Verifiable Rewards)-based Group Relative Policy Optimization (GRPO) to compare and normalize rewards across trajectories, thereby selecting the optimal trajectory. Unlike the original GRPO, which uses only the total reward over textual and visual information, this paper additionally introduces a Table Recognition Reward so that the model is encouraged to explicitly refer to row and column headers as well as cell values.

We consider two types of questions: short-answer and multiple choice (MCQ). A short-answer question q consists of the question text and an image, while a multiple-choice question consists of the question text, answer choices, and an image. For each question Q, the policy π_θ generates M trajectories $\{o_i\}_{i=1}^{M}$ per group. Each trajectory o_i is a string of the form

<think>...</think> <answer>...</answer>

where the reasoning process is contained inside <think> and the final answer is contained inside <answer>. The group size M denotes the number of candidate trajectories compared in a single update.

For each trajectory o_i, we compute a total reward r_i, which combines three components: accuracy, format compliance, and table recognition. The group-relative advantage $\hat{A}_i$ represents the relative superiority within the same group, and the loss function $L(\theta)$ serves as the objective for updating the policy parameters θ. Here, π_θ denotes the current trainable policy, π_{ref} denotes the frozen reference policy just before the update, and β is the weight of the KL divergence term that controls the magnitude of policy updates.

2.2 Table-Aware Group Relative Policy Optimization

Table-**A**ware **G**roup Relative Policy Optimization (TAG) is an online reinforcement learning framework which, as shown in Fig. 2, introduces a table recognition reward so that the model explicitly refers to key information in the table and thereby performs more accurate and consistent reasoning.

Reward Composition. In TAG, for each trajectory o_i, we compute three types of rewards—Accuracy, Format, and Table Recognition—and sum them to obtain the final reward r_i.

Accuracy Reward. The accuracy reward r_i^{acc} is defined differently depending on the question type. For multiple-choice questions, we assign 1.0 if the option selected by the model matches the correct answer, and 0.0 otherwise. For short-answer questions in numeric or formula form, we first perform symbolic equivalence checking; if the two expressions are equivalent, we assign 1.0, and if they are not equivalent, we assign a value between 0.0 and 1.0 depending on the numerical error. For short-answer questions in string form, we use a similarity score between 0.0 and 1.0 based on the Levenshtein distance, i.e., the edit distance from the ground-truth text, as the reward.

Format Reward. The format reward r_i^{fmt} is given by checking whether the output satisfies a predefined format. If the reasoning process is clearly contained inside the <think> tag and the final answer is clearly contained inside the <answer> tag, we assign 1.0; otherwise, we assign 0.0.

Table Recognition Reward. The table recognition reward r_i^{tar} measures how extensively the reasoning process refers to essential table keywords such as row and column headers and cell values. To this end, we first construct a keyword set $K = \{k_1, k_2, \ldots, k_N\}$, then convert the text inside the <think> tag generated by the model to lowercase and compute the keyword matching ratio as

$$r_i^{\mathrm{tar}} = \frac{|\{\, k_j \in K \mid k_j \subseteq \mathrm{think\_text}_i \,\}|}{N}, \tag{1}$$

where $\mathrm{think\_text}_i$ denotes the text inside the <think> tag of the i-th trajectory.

The total reward r_i, obtained by summing the three rewards, is given by

$$r_i = r_i^{\mathrm{acc}} + r_i^{\mathrm{fmt}} + r_i^{\mathrm{tar}}. \tag{2}$$

Group Relative Advantage. TAG computes a group-relative advantage $\hat{A}_i$ by normalizing the rewards at the group level over the M trajectories $\{o_i\}_{i=1}^{M}$ generated per question. Using the group mean reward μ and standard deviation σ, we define

$$\hat{A}_i = \frac{r_i - \mu}{\sigma + \epsilon}, \quad \mu = \frac{1}{M}\sum_{j=1}^{M} r_j, \quad \sigma = \sqrt{\frac{1}{M}\sum_{j=1}^{M}(r_j - \mu)^2}, \tag{3}$$

where ϵ is a small constant for numerical stability.

Group Relative Policy Optimization Loss. GRPO updates the policy using the group-relative advantage $\hat{A}_i$ defined above. To this end, we use a PPO (Proximal Policy Optimization)-style loss function, and the model parameters θ are updated to minimize the following loss $L(\theta)$:

$$L(\theta) = -\frac{1}{M}\sum_{i=1}^{M} \hat{A}_i \log \pi_\theta(o_i \mid q) + \beta D_{\mathrm{KL}}\big(\pi_\theta \,\|\, \pi_{\mathrm{ref}}\big). \tag{4}$$

The first term is the policy gradient loss weighted by the relative advantage, and the second term is the KL divergence between the current policy and the reference policy. Here, β is a hyperparameter that controls the stability of the updates.

3 Experiments

3.1 Experimental Setup

Datasets. In this work, we construct a training set for TAG based on TableInstruct [22]. TableInstruct consists of challenging queries that require complex table understanding and step-by-step reasoning, making it well suited for table-based GRPO training. For each query, we additionally define a set of table keywords that must be referenced in the process of deriving the correct answer; this set is composed of row headers, column headers, and relevant cell values in the table. Although the keyword extraction method is related to the reward design of TAG, the algorithm itself is not tied to a specific extraction scheme, and comparisons of different extraction strategies are discussed in a separate section.

For evaluation, we use six table benchmarks (TableVQA [10], TableBench [22], MMSci [24], TABMWP [11], ComTQA [30], Wild[1]) and one chart benchmark (ChartQA Pro [13]). These benchmarks include various types of tasks such as short-answer numerical problems, complex table-structure interpretation, challenging queries that combine explanations and metadata, real-world unstructured table images, and charts that require table-like structured reasoning, thereby enabling a comprehensive assessment of the model'[s generalized table understanding ability.

For datasets that provide tables in text form, we convert them into image inputs using the dataframe image library. For MMSci, we use only the QA tasks (TFV, TQA), excluding the generative T2T task. For ComTQA, we randomly sample 1,000 instances from the full dataset and use them for evaluation.

Baselines. For performance comparison, we consider six categories of baseline models. (1) Open-source LVLMs: Llama-3.2-11B-Vision [1], Gemma3-4B/12B/27B [16], InternVL3.5-4B/8B/38B [19], Qwen3-VL-4B/8B/32B-Instruct [17]. (2) Closed-source LVLMs: Gemini 2.5 Flash (Dynamic Thinking)[2], Gemini 2 Flash, GPT-5[3], GPT-4.1. (3) Table-domain models: Table-LLaVA 7B/13B [31]. (4) Reasoning SFT: LLaVA-CoT [23], Mulberry-LLaVA-8B [25]. (5) Reasoning RL: R1-VL-7B/2B [26], VLAA-Thinker-3B [2], VLM-R1-3B [15]. (6) Ours: vanilla GRPO and Table-Aware GRPO (TAG).

Implementation Details. TAG uses Qwen3-VL-4B as the base model, and all GRPO training runs are fixed to 600 steps. Training is conducted on a single NVIDIA H100 80GB GPU, with a per-device batch size of 4 and gradient accumulation steps of 2, resulting in an effective batch size of 8.

Before GRPO, we perform supervised fine-tuning with 1,000 samples on the same base model to warm up the initial policy. In the reinforcement learning

[1] https://huggingface.co/datasets/TableGRPO/WildDataset.
[2] https://modelcards.withgoogle.com/model-cards.
[3] https://platform.openai.com/docs/models/gpt-5.

stage, we generate $M = 4$ rollouts per question, and fix the KL coefficient β to 0.04. The maximum output length is set to 2,048 tokens. For parameter-efficient fine-tuning, we apply LoRA with rank 64 and LoRA alpha 128.

At inference time, we set the temperature to its default value for response consistency and use the default prompt template provided by each model. For TAG, we set max new token to 2,048, while for other reasoning models we use the max new token recommended by each model. For general LVLMs and table-specific models, we append the phrase "Generate only the answer." to suppress unnecessary narration, and limit max new tokens to 50.

All Table VQA benchmarks are evaluated with accuracy. For numerical answers, to mitigate discrepancies due to decimal formatting, we accept predictions as correct if their relative error with respect to the ground-truth answer is within ±5%.

3.2 Main Results

Table 1. Accuracy (%) of baselines and TAG on TableVQA benchmarks.

Category	Models	Params	Table VQA	Table Bench	MMSci	TAB MWP	ComTQA	Wild	ChartQA Pro
Closed-Source	Gemini 2.5 Flash	–	**0.771**	**0.876**	0.787	0.943	**0.695**	**0.944**	**0.550**
	Gemini 2.0 Flash	–	0.713	0.667	0.697	0.804	0.687	0.916	0.430
	GPT-5	–	0.770	0.856	**0.806**	**0.986**	0.666	0.811	0.504
	GPT-4.1	–	0.713	0.604	0.776	0.852	0.58	0.878	0.380
LVLMs	Llama-3.2-11B-Vision	11B	0.443	0.170	0.210	0.341	0.35	0.572	0.183
	Gemma3-27B	27B	0.581	0.417	0.598	0.738	0.56	0.798	0.262
	Gemma3-12B	12B	0.513	0.356	0.575	0.637	0.528	0.641	0.235
	Gemma3-4B	4B	0.407	0.291	0.493	0.500	0.441	0.541	0.182
	InternVL3.5-38B	38B	0.647	0.506	0.649	0.812	**0.665**	**0.879**	0.395
	InternVL3.5-8B	8B	0.615	0.476	0.660	0.774	0.65	0.871	0.366
	InternVL3.5-4B	4B	0.615	0.431	0.632	0.736	0.625	0.848	0.354
	Qwen3-VL-32B-Instruct	32B	0.700	0.526	0.665	0.782	0.537	0.842	0.384
	Qwen3-VL-8B-Instruct	8B	0.608	0.458	0.616	0.691	0.506	0.862	0.312
	Qwen3-VL-4B-Instruct	4B	0.584	0.430	0.570	0.652	0.427	0.826	0.291
Table Domains	Table-LLaVA	13B	0.233	0.175	0.323	0.377	0.126	0.537	0.2
	Table-LLaVA	7B	0.233	0.126	0.189	0.355	0.125	0.616	0.214
Reasoning SFT	LLaVA-CoT	11B	0.529	0.446	0.584	0.736	0.498	0.832	0.271
	Mulberry-LLaVA-8B	8B	0.486	0.335	0.502	0.763	0.495	0.673	0.255
Reasoning RL	R1-VL-7B	7B	0.552	0.453	0.465	0.808	0.506	0.770	0.326
	R1-VL-2B	2B	0.462	0.328	0.277	0.666	0.437	0.621	0.249
	VLAA-Thinker-3B	3B	0.606	0.488	0.615	0.791	0.449	0.794	0.280
	VLM-R1-3B	3B	0.588	0.426	0.592	0.679	0.41	0.716	0.279
Ours	Qwen3-VL-4B-Instruct+GRPO	4B	0.746	0.725	0.629	0.832	0.506	0.871	0.41
	Qwen3-VL-4B-Instruct+TAG	4B	**0.761**	**0.756**	**0.726**	**0.836**	0.524	**0.879**	**0.430**

As shown in Table 1, TAG, despite having only 4B parameters, achieves performance comparable to or better than many larger LVLMs and closed-source models. For example, on TableVQA, TAG attains 0.761, surpassing both InternVL3.5-38B (0.647) and Qwen3-VL-32B (0.700), and on Wild it records 0.879, matching the 38B-parameter InternVL3.5-38B. On ChartQA Pro, TAG also achieves 0.430, outperforming all open-source LVLMs including InternVL3.5-38B (0.395) and Qwen3-VL-32B (0.384), thereby demonstrating high parameter efficiency in domains where structural information such as tables and charts is crucial.

Examining the effect of GRPO-based reinforcement learning, we observe that applying vanilla GRPO to the baseline Qwen3-VL-4B-Instruct already improves performance on most benchmarks, and further adding the Table Recognition Reward in TAG provides additional gains under the same 4B architecture (TableVQA: 0.746→0.761, TableBench: 0.725→0.756, etc.). In particular, the improvement of +0.097 points over GRPO on MMSci is more than twice the performance gap of (+0.046) between Qwen3-VL-4B and Qwen3-VL-8B on the same benchmark, suggesting that an effect comparable to simple parameter scaling can be achieved purely through reward design.

Meanwhile, table-specialized models such as Table-LLaVA (7B/13B) show lower accuracy than general LVLMs and reasoning models on most benchmarks, revealing limitations in step-by-step reasoning that leverages complex table structures. This supports the view that simple table recognition is not sufficient, and that structural understanding which carefully aligns cells, headers, and keywords, together with reasoning on top of it, is essential.

Finally, TAG also achieves the best performance among all compared models on ChartQA Pro with a score of 0.430. Since chart QA, like table QA, requires accurate interpretation of visual elements followed by numerical computation and logical reasoning, this result indicates that the keyword- and structure-recognition capabilities learned through the Table Recognition Reward naturally transfer to the chart domain.

3.3 Ablation Study

Table 2. Ablation study of TAG on Qwen3-VL-4B-Instruct. Numbers denote accuracy (relative change Δ w.r.t. TAG in parentheses).

Method	TableBench	ComTQA	WILD	ChartQA Pro
TAG (full)	0.756	0.524	0.879	0.430
w/o TAG	0.725 (–0.031)	0.506 (–0.018)	0.871 (–0.008)	0.410 (–0.020)
w/o Warm-up	0.730 (–0.026)	0.516 (–0.008)	0.877 (–0.002)	0.404 (–0.026)

Table 2 shows the ablation results of TAG based on Qwen3-VL-4B-Instruct. TAG achieves the highest accuracy on all four benchmarks. When the table recognition reward is removed, w/o TAG (i.e., applying only accuracy reward and format reward) shows performance degradation compared to TAG, with especially large drops on TableBench and ComTQA. This indicates that explicit rewards on table-structure-related keywords contribute to improving structure-based reasoning performance.

w/o Warm-up is the setting where GRPO+TAG is applied directly without prior supervised warm-up, and it consistently underperforms TAG. Because TAG computes rewards from the reasoning text inside the < *think* > tags, a small-scale SFT warm-up phase is crucial to stabilize early trajectories and reward signals and to fully realize the performance gains of combining GRPO with the table recognition reward in TAG(full).

3.4 Case Study: Keyword Extraction Strategies

Table 3. Comparison of keyword extraction strategies.

Strategy	Cost	TableBench	ComTQA	Wild	ChartQA Pro
CoMCTS	medium	0.756	0.524	0.879	0.430
Reconcile	high	0.709	0.503	0.879	0.407
Direct	low	0.754	0.516	0.875	0.412

Table 3 compares the cost and performance of three table keyword extraction strategies used in TAG. CoMCTS applies Collective Monte Carlo Tree Search [25] to multiple LLMs to generate diverse reasoning paths and extracts as keywords the row, column, and cell information that repeatedly appears in this process. Reconcile [3] is a multi-agent approach in which different LLM agents reach agreement on keywords through multi-round discussion and confidence-weighted voting. Direct is a simple prompt-based method that feeds the original QA pair and the table into a single LLM and extracts keywords in a single call.

CoMCTS achieves the most stable performance across the four benchmarks at a moderate cost, and in particular records the best accuracy on both TableBench and ChartQA Pro. Although Reconcile incurs the highest cost, it does not provide substantial additional gains over CoMCTS, while Direct, despite being the cheapest, shows some performance degradation on ChartQA Pro even though it is competitive on ComTQA. These results indicate that TAG is not structurally dependent on any specific keyword extraction method, but that CoMCTS-based keyword extraction is the most balanced choice when considering actual table/chart structure understanding and cost–performance trade-offs.

3.5 Effect of TAG on Other Model

Table 4 shows the performance changes when applying TAG to Gemma3-4B and Qwen3-4B. Both backbones exhibit consistent performance improvements across all benchmarks—TableBench, ComTQA, Wild, and ChartQA Pro—and, in particular, all metrics are significantly improved for Qwen3-4B. This suggests that the Table Recognition Reward in TAG is not a technique specialized for a specific backbone, but rather a general reinforcement learning framework that reliably enhances table and chart understanding performance across different architectures.

Table 4. Effect of TAG on Gemma3-4B and Qwen3-4B.

Model	TableBench	ComTQA	Wild	ChartQA Pro
Gemma3-4B	0.291	0.441	0.541	0.182
Gemma3-4B + TAG	0.404	0.4561	0.696	0.253
Qwen3-4B	0.430	0.427	0.826	0.291
Qwen3-4B + TAG	0.756	0.524	0.879	0.430

4 Conclusion

In this work, we proposed Table-Aware Group-Relative Policy Optimization (TAG), which uses Qwen3-VL-4B-Instruct as the base model and introduces a reward based on table keywords (rows, columns, cells) in addition to conventional accuracy and format rewards. By quantitatively incorporating table-structure information into the reasoning process, the proposed method achieves performance comparable to or better than 32B-scale state-of-the-art models and closed-source models such as GPT-4.1 on diverse table VQA benchmarks including TableVQA and TableBench, as well as on ChartQA Pro, despite having only 4B parameters.

For future work, we plan to explore methods for automatically extracting structural keywords required for the table recognition reward. Furthermore, since the proposed reward demonstrates strong performance even on unstructured image-based benchmarks such as Wild and ChartQA Pro, we confirm its potential for domain extension and aim to expand it to a variety of tasks including NL2SQL, text-based TableQA, and ChartQA. Beyond TableVQA-specialized models, we also expect that the reward function proposed in this study can contribute to overall performance improvements in general-domain model training by jointly leveraging rewards from both TableVQA and other datasets.

Acknowledgments. This research was supported by the following funding sources: (1) The Ministry of Science and ICT (MSIT), Korea, under theÂă-Graduate School ofÂăVirtual ConvergenceÂăsupport program (IITP-2026-RS-2023-00254129)Âăsupervised by the IITP(Institute for Information & Communications Technology Planning & Evaluation). (2) The Ministry of Science and ICT (MSIT), Korea, under the Global Scholars Invitation Program (grant number: RS-2024-00459638), also supervised by the IITP. (3) The Sports and Tourism R&D Program through the Korea Creative Content Agency (KOCCA), funded by the Ministry of Culture, Sports and Tourism in 2024, under the project titled "Development of game-based digital therapeutics technology for adolescent mental health (psychological and behavioral control) management" (grant number: RS-2024-00344893). (4) Institute of Information & Communications Technology Planning & Evaluation(IITP) grant funded by the Korea government(MSIT) (No. RS-2025-25442569, AI Star Fellowship Support Program(SungkyunkwanUniv.)). (5) Institute of Information & communications Technology Planning & Evaluation (IITP) grant funded by the Korea government(MSIT) (No.RS-2025-25443884, Development of Human-Oriented Next-Generation Artificial General Intelligence(AGI) Technology based on EmbodiedVisionary AI Multi-Agents).

(6) "Regional Innovation System & Education (RISE)" through the Seoul RISE Center, funded by the Ministry of Education (MOE) and the Seoul Metropolitan Government (2025-RISE-01-018-04) (7) This work was supported by KOITA grant funded by MSIT (No.S-2025-1855-000). (8) Industry collaboration with Emotionwave (https://emotionwave.com) (09) "Regional Innovation System & Education (RISE)" through the Seoul RISE Center, funded by the Ministry of Education (MOE) and the Seoul Metropolitan Government (2025-RISE-01-018-05).

Disclosure of Interests. The authors have no competing interests to declare that are relevant to the content of this article.

References

1. AI, M.: Llama 3.2 model card and prompt formats. https://www.llama.com/docs/model-cards-and-prompt-formats/llama3_2/ (2024). Accessed 22 Mar 2025
2. Chen, H., et al.: Sft or rl? an early investigation into training r1-like reasoning large vision-language models. arXiv preprint arXiv:2504.11468 (2025)
3. Chen, J., Saha, S., Bansal, M.: Reconcile: round-table conference improves reasoning via consensus among diverse llms. In: Proceedings of the 62nd Annual Meeting of the Association for Computational Linguistics (Volume 1: Long Papers), pp. 7066–7085 (2024)
4. Chen, M., Chen, G., Wang, W., Yang, Y.: Seed-grpo: semantic entropy enhanced grpo for uncertainty-aware policy optimization. arXiv preprint arXiv:2505.12346 (2025)
5. Chen, Y., Li, L., Xi, T., Zeng, L., Wang, J.: Perception before reasoning: two-stage reinforcement learning for visual reasoning in vision-language models. arXiv preprint arXiv:2509.13031 (2025)
6. Guo, D., et al.: Deepseek-r1: incentivizing reasoning capability in llms via reinforcement learning. arXiv preprint arXiv:2501.12948 (2025)
7. Herzig, J., Nowak, P.K., Müller, T., Piccinno, F., Eisenschlos, J.M.: Tapas: weakly supervised table parsing via pre-training. arXiv preprint arXiv:2004.02349 (2020)
8. Jin, R., et al.: Table-r1: self-supervised and reinforcement learning for program-based table reasoning in small language models. arXiv preprint arXiv:2506.06137 (2025)
9. Kang, X., et al.: Can grpo boost complex multimodal table understanding? In: Proceedings of the 2025 Conference on Empirical Methods in Natural Language Processing, pp. 12642–12655 (2025)
10. Kim, Y., Yim, M., Song, K.Y.: Tablevqa-bench: a visual question answering benchmark on multiple table domains. arXiv preprint arXiv:2404.19205 (2024)
11. Lu, P., et al.: Dynamic prompt learning via policy gradient for semi-structured mathematical reasoning. arXiv preprint arXiv:2209.14610 (2022)
12. Lu, Y., Yao, Y., Tu, J., Shao, J., Ma, Y., Zhu, X.: Can lvlms obtain a driver's license? a benchmark towards reliable agi for autonomous driving. In: Proceedings of the AAAI Conference on Artificial Intelligence, vol. 39, pp. 5838–5846 (2025)
13. Masry, A., et al.: Chartqapro: a more diverse and challenging benchmark for chart question answering. arXiv preprint arXiv:2504.05506 (2025)
14. Shao, Z., et al.: Deepseekmath: pushing the limits of mathematical reasoning in open language models. arXiv preprint arXiv:2402.03300 (2024)

15. Shen, H., et al.: Vlm-r1: a stable and generalizable r1-style large vision-language model. arXiv preprint arXiv:2504.07615 (2025)
16. Team, G., et al.: Gemma 3 technical report. arXiv preprint arXiv:2503.19786 (2025)
17. Team, Q.: Qwen3 technical report (2025). https://arxiv.org/abs/2505.09388
18. Thawakar, O., et al.: Llamav-o1: rethinking step-by-step visual reasoning in llms. arXiv preprint arXiv:2501.06186 (2025)
19. Wang, W., et al.: Internvl3. 5: advancing open-source multimodal models in versatility, reasoning, and efficiency. arXiv preprint arXiv:2508.18265 (2025)
20. Wang, Y., et al.: Reinforcement learning for reasoning in large language models with one training example. arXiv preprint arXiv:2504.20571 (2025)
21. Wen, X., et al.: Reinforcement learning with verifiable rewards implicitly incentivizes correct reasoning in base llms. arXiv preprint arXiv:2506.14245 (2025)
22. Wu, X., et al.: Tablebench: a comprehensive and complex benchmark for table question answering. In: Proceedings of the AAAI Conference on Artificial Intelligence, vol. 39, pp. 25497–25506 (2025)
23. Xu, G., Jin, P., Hao, L., Song, Y., Sun, L., Yuan, L.: Llava-o1: let vision language models reason step-by-step. arXiv preprint arXiv:2411.10440 (2024)
24. Yang, B., Zhang, Y., Liu, D., Freitas, A., Lin, C.: Does table source matter? benchmarking and improving multimodal scientific table understanding and reasoning. arXiv preprint arXiv:2501.13042 (2025)
25. Yao, H., et al.: Mulberry: empowering mllm with o1-like reasoning and reflection via collective monte carlo tree search. arXiv preprint arXiv:2412.18319 (2024)
26. Zhang, J., et al.: R1-vl: learning to reason with multimodal large language models via step-wise group relative policy optimization. arXiv preprint arXiv:2503.12937 (2025)
27. Zhang, T., Yue, X., Li, Y., Sun, H.: Tablellama: towards open large generalist models for tables. arXiv preprint arXiv:2311.09206 (2023)
28. Zhang, Y., et al.: Unveiling the tapestry of consistency in large vision-language models. Adv. Neural. Inf. Process. Syst. **37**, 118632–118653 (2024)
29. Zhao, Q., et al.: Cot-vla: visual chain-of-thought reasoning for vision-language-action models. arXiv preprint arXiv:2503.22020 (2025)
30. Zhao, W., et al.: Tabpedia: towards comprehensive visual table understanding with concept synergy. Adv. Neural. Inf. Process. Syst. **37**, 7185–7212 (2024)
31. Zheng, M., et al.: Multimodal table understanding. arXiv preprint arXiv:2406.08100 (2024)
32. Zhou, W., Mesgar, M., Adel, H., Friedrich, A.: Freb-tqa: a fine-grained robustness evaluation benchmark for table question answering. arXiv preprint arXiv:2404.18585 (2024)

How Much Can We Forget? On Boosting Removal Capacity in Machine Unlearning

Xiangni Lu[1], Lin Li[1(✉)], Dong Zhang[1], Kaize Shi[2], and Xiaohui Tao[2]

[1] Wuhan University of Technology, Wuhan, China
{xiangni0905,cathyllin,346728}@whut.edu.cn
[2] University of Southern Queensland, Toowoomba, QLD, Australia
{Kaize.Shi,Xiaohui.Tao}@unisq.edu.au

Abstract. Certified removal aims to ensure that a model cannot be distinguished from retraining without removed data, offering strong theoretical guarantees for machine unlearning. However, current unlearning methods often overlook the compound risks posed by hard-to-forget samples, such as boundary, poisoned, or high-loss instances. These hard-to-forget samples often leave significant residual gradients, which not only reduce robustness under adversarial removals, but also compromise privacy guarantees and substantially increase the cost of machine unlearning. To address these challenges, we introduce the Removal Capacity centric framework, a unified evaluation protocol spanning three dimensions: *robustness*, *certified guarantee*, and *efficiency*. Building upon this framework, we propose RCE, a certified unlearning method that combines Huber-style robust loss with Newton updates and Gaussian differential privacy noise. RCE achieves: (i) *Robustness*: RCE achieves performance closest to retraining under adversarial removal requests, effectively suppressing residual influence from hard-to-forget samples. (ii) *Certified Guarantee*: RCE achieves membership inference accuracy closest to random guessing among all baselines including retraining, while supporting 10–100× more certified removals than previous certified methods. (iii) *Efficiency*: RCE delivers 10–100× speedup compared to retraining. Our results establish RCE as the first approach to jointly advance all three dimensions, offering a unified and practical solution for certified machine unlearning.

Keywords: Machine Unlearning · Differential Privacy · Hard-to-Forget Samples · Efficient Removal

1 Introduction

As machine learning models become more widely used, the ability to remove specific training data is crucial for compliance, user control, and error correction. While deleting raw data from storage is easy, removing its influence on trained models is far more complex [?], as models embed data implicitly in parameters.

R. C.-W. Wong et al. (Eds.): PAKDD 2026, LNAI 16618, pp. 151–163, 2027.
https://doi.org/10.1007/978-981-92-1947-6_13

This difficulty has motivated growing interest in machine unlearning, which aims to make models behave as if the removed data had never been used.

Recent research has introduced unlearning methods, including exact unlearning, which retrains to achieve distributional equivalence [4,5,13], and certified unlearning, which uses differential privacy for secure data removal [11,27][?].

Despite progress in machine unlearning, recent studies reveal an overlooked issue: data near decision boundaries or poisoned samples can leave significant gradient residues that conventional unlearning cannot fully remove [6,19]. Even with retraining or certified methods, adversarial removal requests or poisoning attacks can degrade performance by destabilizing decision boundaries, leaking privacy, and increasing update costs [8,25]. However, there is currently no unified framework that can simultaneously characterize and optimize all three dimensions in machine unlearning: robustness, certified guarantee, and efficiency.

To address this, we propose a **Removal Capacity** centric framework that unifies the three key dimensions of machine unlearning(*Robustness*, *Certified Guarantee* and *Efficiency*) into a common evaluation foundation. Building on this, we present **RCE**, a certified unlearning method that combines a Huber-style robust loss to mitigate the influence of hard-to-forget samples, with Newton updates and differential privacy to yield tighter certified bounds.

We systematically evaluate the above three Removal Capacity dimensions on four benchmark datasets using a range of assessment protocols, including poisoning attacks and membership inference attacks [6,25]. Experimental results demonstrate that RCE consistently outperforms existing methods in both robustness and certified guarantee, while achieving 10–100× greater efficiency compared to retraining. Notably, within the certified unlearning paradigm, RCE supports 10–100× more certified removals than prior approaches. **In summary, our main contributions are:** (1) We introduce the Removal Capacity framework, which for the first time provides a unified evaluation protocol for robustness, certified guarantee, and efficiency in machine unlearning; (2) We propose the RCE unlearning method, which effectively mitigates the residual influence of hard-to-forget samples, achieving simultaneous improvements in robustness, certified guarantee, and efficiency. (3) Through experiments on four benchmarks, we show that RCE outperforms both exact and certified unlearning baselines, especially with hard-to-forget samples.

2 Related Work

Exact Unlearning. Exact unlearning aims to match the parameters of a retrained-from-scratch model without the target data [7,10,13]. Early work formalized this "complete forgetting" via retraining on simple models [5]. Later methods improved efficiency through incremental or sharded training [4,9]. While achieving perfect removal, these methods often incur high computational cost or impose architectural constraints, limiting scalability to large networks.

Certified Unlearning. Certified unlearning approximates retraining by offering formal guarantees—typically via differential privacy—that the unlearned model remains statistically close. Most methods target linear or convex models and employ second-order updates such as Newton or influence functions [11,21]. While some extend to Bayesian or graph neural networks [23,24], applying certified unlearning to deep networks remains difficult, often requiring strong convexity or high computational cost [20,27][?].

3 The Definition of Removal Capacity

3.1 Hard-to-Forget Samples

Hard-to-forget samples pose a challenge for unlearning method: removing such samples (e.g., boundary, poisoned, or high-loss instances) can induce disproportionately large model updates [6,19]. This effect is captured by the influence function under convexity and smoothness assumptions [14]:

$$\Delta w = -\frac{1}{n} H^{-1} \nabla \ell(w^*; x, y), \tag{1}$$

where w^* is the optimal model and H the Hessian at w^*. In certified unlearning, high-influence samples are hard to forget, as their removal may violate guarantees and require costly retraining [11,19]. Hard-to-forget samples expose key limitations, underscoring the need for a unified unlearning evaluation framework.

3.2 Removal Capacity

We define *Removal Capacity* through three key dimensions: **Robustness**, **Certified Guarantee**, and **Efficiency**.

Robustness measures model stability after unlearning and the extent to which removed (hard-to-forget) data is erased. For model f and unlearning set $D_u \subseteq D$, we define:

$$\mathcal{R}(f, D_u) = \sup_{\mathcal{A}} \left\{ \Pr[\mathcal{A}(f(D)) = 1] - \Pr[\mathcal{A}(f(D \setminus D_u)) = 1] \right\}, \tag{2}$$

where $\mathcal{A}$ is any adversary and $\Pr[\cdot]$ denotes probability over model randomness. Smaller $\mathcal{R}$ indicates higher stability and less residual information.

Certified Guarantee denoted as $\mathcal{G}(f, D_u)$, requiring the post-unlearning model to be statistically indistinguishable from one never trained on D_u [3,23]:

$$\mathcal{G}(f, D_u) = |\Pr[\mathcal{A}(f(D)) = 1] - \Pr[\mathcal{A}(f(D \setminus D_u)) = 1]| \leq \xi, \tag{3}$$

where ξ bounds the adversary's advantage. This is often formalized using differential privacy [1]:

$$\begin{aligned} \Pr[\mathcal{M}(D) \in \mathcal{S}] &\leq e^{\epsilon} \Pr[\mathcal{M}(D \setminus D_u) \in \mathcal{S}] + \delta, \\ \Pr[\mathcal{M}(D \setminus D_u) \in \mathcal{S}] &\leq e^{\epsilon} \Pr[\mathcal{M}(D) \in \mathcal{S}] + \delta, \end{aligned} \tag{4}$$

where (ϵ, δ) quantify divergence between output distributions.

Efficiency reflects the computational benefit of unlearning over retraining. We define:

$$C_{\text{unlearn}}(D, D_u) \ll C_{\text{train}}(D \setminus D_u), \tag{5}$$

where C_{unlearn} and C_{train} denote the costs of unlearning and retraining, respectively. Lower ratios imply better scalability.

Based on the above, we conceptually represent the **Removal Capacity** of a model with respect to D_u as the tuple:

$$\text{Removal Capacity} \sim \left\langle \mathcal{R}(f, D_u),\ \mathcal{G}(f, D_u),\ \frac{C_{\text{unlearn}}(D, D_u)}{C_{\text{train}}(D \setminus D_u)} \right\rangle, \tag{6}$$

which provides a structured view of the trade-offs between *Robustness*, *Certified Guarantee*, and *Efficiency*.

4 Methodology

4.1 RCE Framework

As shown in Fig. 1, RCE brings three key benefits: (i) *Robustness*: RCE limits hard-to-forget samples, improving stability and reducing residuals. (ii) *Certified Guarantee*: RCE ensures consistency, offering tighter bounds and more certified removals. (iii) *Efficiency*: RCE updates only the final linear head, enabling fast unlearning with $O(d^3)$ complexity, cheaper than retraining.

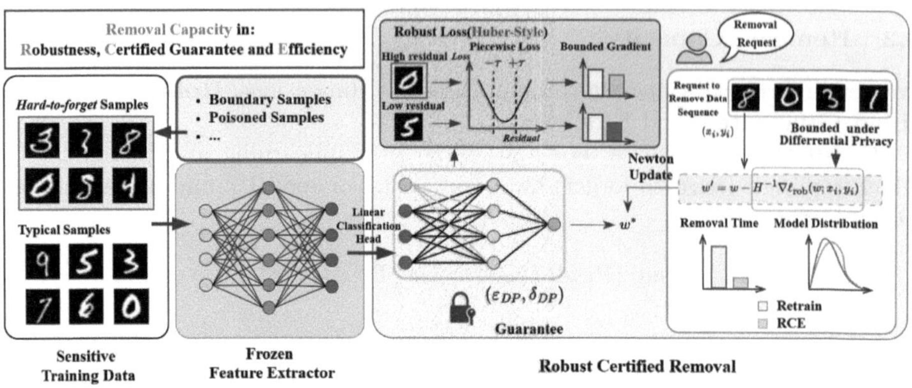

Fig. 1. Overview of RCE. In the removal stage, the feature extractor is frozen, and only the linear head is updated. A robust Huber-style loss suppresses hard-to-forget samples (e.g., boundary or poisoned), while Newton updates under differential privacy ensure certified removal.

To connect the RCE framework with the theory, we clarify its cores: (i) **Robust Loss**: A Huber-style loss suppresses hard-to-forget samples and stabilizes updates by bounding gradients. (ii) **Removal Update**: Unlearning updates the linear head with a Newton-style step, bounded by sensitivity, supported by worst-case and adaptive analyses. (iii) **Certified Guarantee**: Gaussian noise is added to achieve (ϵ, δ)-privacy and limit leakage from gradients.

4.2 Robust Loss for Stable Removal

We use a Huber-style loss to suppress hard-to-forget samples while preserving convexity. For (x, y) with $\|x\| \leq 1$, the margin residual is $r = 1 - y\langle w, x\rangle$:

$$\ell_{\text{rob}}(r; \tau) = \begin{cases} \dfrac{r^2}{2\tau}, & 0 \leq r \leq \tau, \\ r - \dfrac{\tau}{2}, & r > \tau, \\ 0, & r < 0, \end{cases} \tag{7}$$

whose gradient and Hessian satisfy

$$\|\nabla_w \ell_{\text{rob}}(w; x, y)\| \leq 1 \quad \text{and} \quad \|\nabla_w^2 \ell_{\text{rob}}(w; x, y)\| \leq 1/\tau. \tag{8}$$

4.3 Removal Update and Sensitivity Bound

Let $\mathcal{D} = \{(x_i, y_i)\}_{i=1}^n$ be a training dataset, and let $w \in \mathcal{H}$ denote the model parameter. The pre-removal model is thus $w^* = \arg\min_{w \in \mathcal{H}} \mathcal{L}(w, \mathcal{D})$.

Newton Update. Suppose we removal (x_k, y_k) from $\mathcal{D} = \{(x_i, y_i)\}_{i=1}^n$. Define $\nabla L_{\text{rob}}^-(w^*) = -\frac{1}{n-1} \nabla \ell_{\text{rob}}(w^*; x_k, y_k)$, by direct calculation, we have

$$\Delta w = \frac{1}{n-1} H_{\text{rob}}^{-1} \nabla \ell_{\text{rob}}(w^*; x_k, y_k). \tag{9}$$

Taking norms in Eq. (9) and applying the bounds from Eq. (8), we obtain $\|\Delta w\|_2 \leq \frac{1}{(n-1)\lambda_{\min}}$, where $\lambda_{\min}$ is the minimum eigenvalue of H_{rob}.

Gradient Residual Bound. We bound $\nabla L_{\text{rob}}^-(w')$ for $w' = w^* + \Delta w$. A second-order expansion and γ-smoothness implies

$$\|\nabla L_{\text{rob}}^-(w')\|_2 \leq \gamma \|\Delta w\|_2 \|H_{w^*}^{-1}\|_2 \|\nabla \ell_{\text{rob}}(w^*; x_k, y_k)\|_2. \tag{10}$$

Substituting Eq. (9) and Eq. (8), we obtain

$$\|\nabla L_{\text{rob}}^-(w')\|_2 \leq \frac{\gamma}{(n-1)\lambda_{\min}^2}. \tag{11}$$

This bound depends on the robust loss smoothness $\gamma = 1/\tau$.

Sample-Adaptive Bound. To obtain a sharper estimate, we derive a sample-adaptive bound that incorporates local curvature. Let $G(w) := \nabla L_{\text{rob}}^-(w)$, and note that by the mean-value theorem, $G(w') = G(w^*) + H_{w_\eta} \Delta w$ for some w_η between w^* and w', with Δw from (9). The leading term simplifies to $G(w') \approx (H_{w_\eta} - H_{w^*}) H_{w^*}^{-1} \nabla \ell_{\text{rob}}(w^*; x_k, y_k)$. If the Hessian is γ-Lipschitz, then $\|H_{w_\eta} - H_{w^*}\|_2 \leq \gamma \|\Delta w\|_2$, we have

$$\|\nabla L_{\text{rob}}^-(w')\|_2 \leq \frac{\gamma}{(n-1)^2} \|X^-\|_2 \|\Delta\|_2 \|X^- \Delta\|_2, \tag{12}$$

where all terms are computable at removal. This adaptive bound is often much tighter than the worst-case bound in Eq. (11).

4.4 Certified Guarantee Under Robust Loss

Merely reducing the gradient residual after removal does not ensure certified privacy, as the gradient direction may still leak information. Following [2], we add a random linear term to the loss to ensure certified removal:

$$L_b(w; \mathcal{D}) = \sum_{i=1}^{n} \ell_{\text{rob}}(w^\top x_i, y_i) + \frac{\lambda n}{2} \|w\|_2^2 + b^\top w, \tag{13}$$

where $b \sim \mathcal{N}(0, \sigma^2 I_d)$ is Gaussian noise calibrated for differential privacy, making the model indistinguishable from retraining [18].

Single Removal Guarantee. Let Δw be the Newton update for removing (x_k, y_k), with ℓ_2-sensitivity $S := \|\Delta w\|_2 \leq \frac{1}{(n-1)\lambda_{\min}}$ under robust loss. To certify removal, we calibrate Gaussian noise as

$$\sigma = \frac{S}{\epsilon} \sqrt{2 \ln \frac{1.25}{\delta}} \tag{14}$$

ensuring the post-removal model is (ϵ, δ)-indistinguishable from retraining.

Cumulative Guarantee and Budget. For m sequential removals, the privacy budget accumulates over all Newton updates with Gaussian noise:

$$\Delta w_i + b, \quad b \sim \mathcal{N}(0, \sigma^2 I_d), \quad i = 1, \ldots, m,$$

where cumulative sensitivity is $R_m = \sum_{i=1}^{m} S_i$. The global (ϵ, δ)-privacy guarantee holds as long as

$$R_m \leq \frac{\sigma \epsilon}{\sqrt{2 \ln(1.25/\delta)}}. \tag{15}$$

Intuitively, R_m serves as a removal capacity budget: as long as the total ℓ_2-sensitivity remains below this threshold, certified privacy is maintained.

5 Experiments

5.1 Experimental Setup

Datasets. We evaluate on four widely used benchmarks spanning vision and language tasks, including MNIST [16], SVHN [22], CIFAR-10 [17], Stanford Sentiment Treebank (SST-2) [26]. The full training set is D. A subset $D_u \subset D$ is randomly selected as the *unlearned set* to be removed. The *retained set* is $D_r = D \setminus D_u$, and the held-out evaluation set is denoted D_t.

Backbones. We use standard architectures: a 2-layer MLP with 256 units for MNIST, a 3-layer CNN with two FC layers for SVHN, ResNet18 [12] for CIFAR-10, and a BiLSTM with 64 hidden units and 128-d embeddings for SST-2. All models are trained from scratch.

Table 1. Micro F1-score (%) on (D_u), (D_r), and (D_t). The closer F1 on D_r and D_t are to **Retrain**, and the more F1 on D_u matches that on D_t, the better.

Method	MNIST & MLP			SVHN & CNN			CIFAR-10 & ResNet18			SST-2 & BiLSTM		
	F1 on D_u	F1 on D_r	F1 on D_t	F1 on D_u	F1 on D_r	F1 on D_t	F1 on D_u	F1 on D_r	F1 on D_t	F1 on D_u	F1 on D_r	F1 on D_t
Retrain	96.59	99.37	96.52	94.76	95.31	94.95	88.38	96.25	88.38	83.67	98.55	83.61
NEG	99.31	**99.41**	96.99	97.53	97.48	94.05	97.63	97.66	86.01	98.82	99.80	81.14
Fine Tune	98.37	99.07	96.86	97.07	97.16	93.87	95.76	**96.45**	85.05	98.52	99.68	**83.48**
Fisher	98.53	98.71	96.78	96.87	96.77	93.01	90.67	90.39	84.66	98.25	99.38	81.62
CR	85.30	96.93	86.92	91.37	91.76	86.02	90.12	90.77	77.38	81.76	85.30	79.55
SCRUB	99.64	99.60	97.19	97.86	97.83	**94.82**	91.91	91.98	86.22	98.12	99.77	82.87
CUD	96.71	97.01	95.24	92.59	92.28	89.44	97.94	98.11	**86.44**	97.68	**98.91**	82.66
RCE	**97.13**	98.54	**96.47**	**94.19**	**94.84**	94.09	**92.12**	96.68	85.54	**93.52**	96.43	84.37

Baseline Methods. We compare with a range of unlearning baselines, including retraining, exact unlearning, and certified methods. **Retrain**: Retraining the model from scratch on D_r after removing D_u, serving as the perfect exact unlearning oracle. **Fine Tune** [10]: Fine-tuning the trained model on D_r for one epoch to mitigate the influence of D_u. **NEG** [10]: Performing gradient ascent on D_u for one epoch to negate its contribution. **Fisher** [10]: Applying a Newton update where the Hessian is approximated by the Fisher information matrix. **CR** [11]: Linear certified removal via DP feature extractor and Newton update. **SCRUB** [15]: Deep unlearning via a student–teacher framework. **CUD** [27]: Certified deep unlearning using approximate Newton updates. All methods use the same backbone, training setup, and unlearn/retain splits for fair comparison.

Evaluation Metrics. We report micro F1-score (%) on D_u, D_r and D_t. High F1 on D_r and D_t indicates preserved utility and generalization. Forgetting is achieved when D_u's F1 closely matches D_t's, indicating the model treats removed data as unseen, not misclassified. To assess unlearning under Gaussian poisoning, we report TPR@FPR=0.01 [25]. We compute the normalized inner product I_z, set a threshold for 0.01 FPR on independent noise, and report TPR on poisoned data. Lower values (ideally ≈ 0.01) indicate stronger unlearning. Following [6], we assess privacy via membership inference attack (MIA) accuracy and AUC, using a black-box adversary trained on model posteriors. Both metrics approach 0.5 under ideal unlearning, indicating indistinguishability.

5.2 Removal Capacity

Overall Utility. Table 1 reports micro F1-scores on D_u, D_r, and D_t across four benchmarks. High F1 on D_r and D_t reflects preserved utility and generalization, and D_r should remain close to D_t, as an ideal unlearning process should not distort the retained data. Retraining meets this criterion with aligned F1 on D_u and D_t. Most baselines (NEG, Fine-Tune) yield higher D_u than D_t, suggesting incomplete forgetting. Fisher and SCRUB lessen this gap but slightly reduce D_r.

Table 2. Test Accuracy and TRP@FPR=0.01 under Gaussian Poisoning after unlearning. **The closer to Retrain is the better.**

Method	MNIST & MLP		SVHN & CNN		CIFAR-10 & ResNet18		SST-2 & BiLSTM	
	Test Acc.	TRP @FPR=0.01	Test Acc.	TRP @FPR=0.01	Test Acc.	TRP @FPR=0.01	Test Acc.	TRP @FPR=0.01
Retrain	96.54	0.0109	94.96	0.0097	88.48	0.0104	83.71	0.0101
NEG	90.68	0.0192	88.01	0.0162	78.66	0.0219	82.22	0.0214
Fine Tune	96.97	0.0281	93.20	0.0187	85.10	0.0224	83.18	0.0191
Fisher	95.56	0.0230	93.11	0.0189	84.03	0.0209	82.91	0.0218
CR	87.34	0.0183	84.97	0.0215	77.32	0.0176	78.33	0.0133
SCRUB	97.23	0.0271	**94.78**	0.0260	84.11	0.0252	78.99	0.0164
CUD	96.01	0.0208	91.78	0.0255	86.46	0.0217	82.78	0.0171
RCE	**96.44**	**0.0146**	93.41	**0.0161**	**85.51**	**0.0151**	**84.01**	**0.0129**

Table 3. Attack accuracy and AUC for distinguishing removed from non-member samples; lower values indicate better privacy.

Method	MNIST & MLP		SVHN & CNN		CIFAR-10 & ResNet18		SST-2 & BiLSTM	
	MIA Acc.	MIA AUC	MIA Acc.	MIA AUC	MIA Acc.	MIA AUC	MIA Acc.	MIA AUC
Retrain	94.51	96.59	93.23	96.36	88.91	93.39	50.00	77.02
NEG	95.53	98.21	95.44	97.50	91.32	94.45	50.00	83.04
Fine Tune	94.45	96.64	93.82	96.40	90.21	92.09	50.00	72.81
Fisher	95.07	97.01	94.45	96.65	82.52	95.97	50.00	80.80
CR	49.87	49.36	49.89	50.76	50.04	**52.87**	50.00	**69.92**
SCRUB	95.33	96.53	94.20	96.71	92.62	95.72	50.00	81.12
CUD	93.43	95.73	90.68	95.09	91.16	94.36	50.00	75.67
RCE	**49.22**	**49.22**	**49.77**	**49.72**	**50.02**	53.77	**50.00**	71.80

Certified approaches (CR, CUD, RCE) narrow the D_u–D_t gap further, though CR often harms D_r. **RCE** offers the best trade-off, keeping D_u and D_r close to D_t across datasets.

Robustness. To assess robustness under data poisoning, we use the TRP@FPR =0.01 metric [25]. TRP measures how strongly the model gradients still align with the injected Gaussian perturbations after unlearning. A lower TRP therefore indicates weaker dependence on the poisoned data and more complete removal. Following prior work, we inject Gaussian noise with variance $\sigma^2 = 0.32$ into 10% of the data to construct D_u.

Retraining from scratch remains the gold standard, achieving strong test accuracy and the lowest TRP (Table 2). Approximate unlearning methods (NEG, Fine-Tune, Fisher, SCRUB, CUD) recover accuracy but yield noticeably higher TRP, revealing residual influence from the poisoned samples. Certified methods reduce TRP more reliably; among them, **RCE** achieves both high accuracy and lower leakage, though a small gap to full retraining persists, underscoring the difficulty of entirely removing adversarial contamination without retraining.

Certified Guarantee. A key goal of machine unlearning is to make removed samples indistinguishable from non-members. Following prior work [6], we evaluate this via membership inference attacks (MIA) using a shadow-model setup, reporting Accuracy and AUC (ideal: 0.5). We split data evenly for shadow and target models, remove 5% as D_u, and train a logistic-regression attacker.

Table 3 shows that retraining and approximate unlearning methods (NEG, Fine-Tune, Fisher, SCRUB, CUD) generally yield high AUC, indicating that removed samples remain distinguishable. Certified approaches reduce both metrics, with **RCE** producing values closest to 0.5 across all benchmarks. We also note that on SST-2, Accuracy often stays near 0.5 while AUC remains higher. This behavior is typical in NLP tasks, where posterior scores are highly skewed, making threshold-based Accuracy unstable even when the overall ranking (reflected by AUC) remains separable.

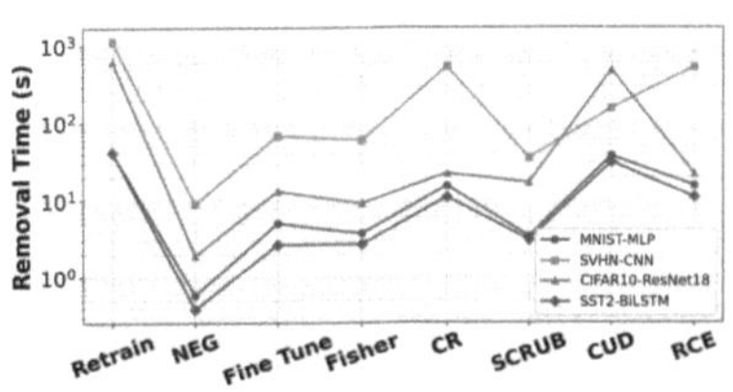

Fig. 2. Removal time across datasets (log-scale, seconds). RCE is the fastest certified method, offering strong guarantees with up to 100× speedup over retraining.

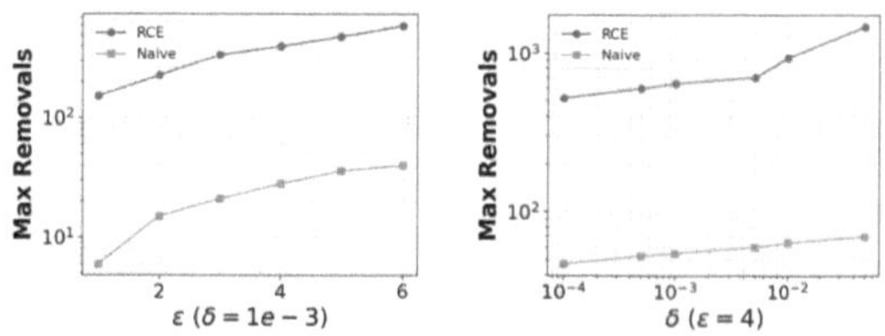

(a) $m_{\max}$ - ϵ (fixed δ) (b) $m_{\max}$ - δ (fixed ϵ)

Fig. 3. Comparison of the maximum number of certified removals supported by the robust loss method and the naive baseline under different privacy budgets. RCE consistently supports more removals than Naive.

Efficiency. Figure 2 shows that exact unlearning methods (e.g., NEG, Fine-Tune) are faster but lack formal guarantees. Among certified approaches, **RCE** achieves the best efficiency, offering strong removal guarantees with 10–100× speedup over retraining. This highlights RCE's favorable trade-off between unlearning quality and computational cost.

5.3 Ablation Study

Maximum Certified Removals. To assess the impact of robust loss, we compare our method with a naive baseline adapted from [11], applying Guo's data-dependent bound to the baseline and our sample-adaptive bound to RCE, with all other settings identical. Figure 3 shows that our method enables 1–2 orders of magnitude more certified removals under the same privacy budget, achieved by tighter control of gradient residuals. Robust loss reduces sensitivity to outliers and boundary points, allowing our method to sustain stable growth under stricter privacy (e.g., small ϵ or δ), while the baseline quickly saturates due to spiking sensitivities.

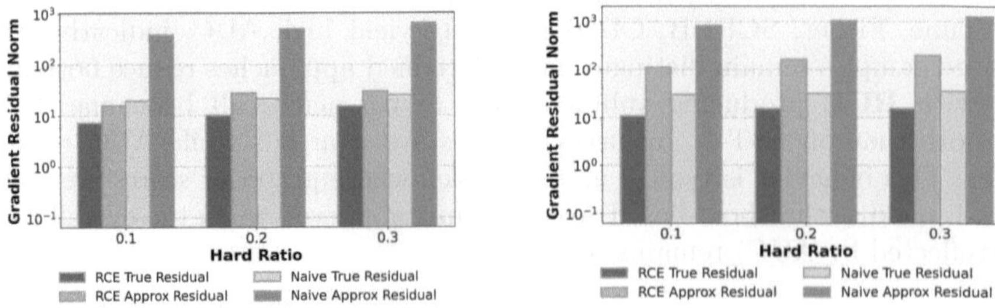

(a) SST-2 (BiLSTM) (b) SVHN (CNN)

Fig. 4. Comparison of gradient residuals under hard-to-forget removal.

Table 4. Test accuracy and retrain test accuracy (%) under different hard ratios for SVHN-CNN and SST-2-BiLSTM.

(a) SVHN-CNN

Method	Hard Ratio	Test Acc	Retrain Acc
RCE	0.1	95.88	94.26
	0.2	95.84	94.78
	0.3	95.89	95.01
Naive	0.1	93.19	94.26
	0.2	93.20	94.78
	0.3	93.19	95.01

(b) SST-2-BiLSTM

Method	Hard Ratio	Test Acc	Retrain Acc
RCE	0.1	86.88	83.76
	0.2	86.84	83.01
	0.3	86.89	83.86
Naive	0.1	83.19	83.76
	0.2	83.20	83.01
	0.3	83.19	83.86

The Effect of Hard to Forget Samples. We define the hard ratio as the fraction of high-influence(loss change under removal) samples in D_u, estimated via the naive baseline. Top 10% most influential samples are considered hard-to-forget. For each ratio, we randomly select hard samples into D_u and evaluate both methods on the same set. As shown in Fig. 4, our method yields gradient residual bounds 1–2 orders of magnitude tighter than the naive baseline, and closely tracks empirical residuals even on hard samples. This tight alignment enables accurate estimation of safe removal capacity under adversarial conditions. In contrast, the naive bound is sensitive to outliers and leads to overly conservative estimates. Table 4 shows that across all hard ratios, our method consistently preserves higher retained accuracy, demonstrating both stronger certified guarantees and better utility under challenging unlearning scenarios.

5.4 Parameter Study

Effect of Privacy Budget ϵ, Noise Magnitude σ, and Regularization λ Fig. 5 shows how certified removal capacity is affected by ϵ, σ, and λ. Increasing ϵ or σ improves capacity by relaxing privacy constraints, though large σ may degrade accuracy. Decreasing λ (lighter curves) also increases capacity but can reduce test accuracy, especially under high removal counts. These results highlight a trade-off: tuning ϵ, σ, and λ boosts capacity, but overly small λ may harm generalization.

Effect of Robustness Threshold τ and Regularization λ. Figure 5(c) shows that increasing the robustness threshold τ significantly improves certified removal capacity at a given λ, while maintaining nearly flat test accuracy curves. In contrast, decreasing λ also boosts capacity but often degrades accuracy, especially under high removal counts. These results suggest that tuning τ is a more effective and reliable strategy for scaling certified unlearning without sacrificing utility. However, overly large τ can cause gradient instability, reflected by missing points in Fig. 5 (c). We therefore recommend prioritizing τ over λ when tuning for certified removal in practice.

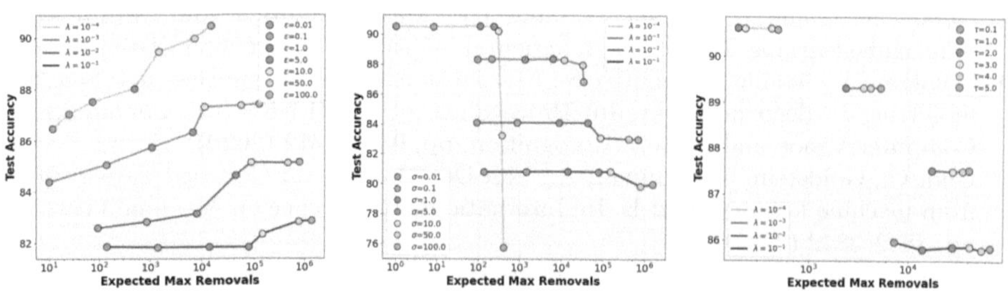

(a) ϵ-λ (b) σ-λ (c) τ-λ

Fig. 5. Removal capacity comparison under different hyperparameters.

6 Conclusions and Future Work

This work focuses on the problem of **removal capacity** in certified machine unlearning, focusing on robustness, certified guarantees, and efficiency. Extensive experiments demonstrate that our method maintains high model utility and strong guarantees, especially in the presence of hard-to-forget samples. While leveraging pretrained feature representations, further sensitivity analysis on representation quality could enhance practical applicability.

References

1. Abadi, M., Chu, A., Goodfellow, I., McMahan, H.B., Mironov, K., Zhang, L.: Deep learning with differential privacy. In: Proceedings of the 2016 ACM SIGSAC Conference on Computer and Communications Security, pp. 308–318 (2016)
2. Balle, B., Wang, Y.X.: Improving the gaussian mechanism for differential privacy: Analytical calibration and optimal denoising. In: International Conference on Machine Learning, pp. 394–403 (2018)
3. Basu, S., Pope, P., Feizi, S.: Influence functions in deep learning are fragile. In: International Conference on Learning Representations (2021)
4. Bourtoule, L., et al.: 2021 IEEE symposium on security and privacy (SP), pp. 141–159. IEEE (2021). Machine unlearning
5. Cao, Y., Yang, J.: Towards making systems forget with machine unlearning. In: 2015 IEEE Symposium on Security and Privacy, pp. 463–480. (2015)
6. Chen, M., Zhang, Z., Wang, T., Backes, M.: Humbert: when machine unlearning jeopardizes privacy. In: Proceedings of the 2021 ACM SIGSAC Conference on Computer and Communications Security (CCS), pp. 893–910. ACM (2021)
7. Chen, M., Zhang, Z., Wang, T., Backes, M., Humbert, M., Zhang, Y.: Graph unlearning. In: Proceedings of the 2022 ACM SIGSAC Conference on Computer and Communications Security, pp. 499–513 (2022)
8. Cinà, A.E., Grosse, K., Demontis, A., Vascon, S., Zellinger, W., Moser, B.A.: Oprea: Wild patterns reloaded: a survey of machine learning security against training data poisoning. ACM Comput. Surv. , 1–39 (2023)
9. Ginart, A., Guan, M., Valiant, G., Zou, J.Y.: Making ai forget you: Data deletion in machine learning. In: Advances in neural information processing systems (2019)
10. Golatkar, A., Achille, A., Soatto, S.: Eternal sunshine of the spotless net: Selective forgetting in deep networks. In: Proceedings of the IEEE/CVF Conference on Computer Vision and Pattern Recognition, pp. 9304–9312 (2020)
11. Guo, C., Goldstein, T., Hannun, A., Van Der Maaten, L.: Certified data removal from machine learning models. In: International Conference on Machine Learning, pp. 3832–3842 (2020)
12. He, K., Zhang, X., Ren, S., Sun, J.: Deep residual learning for image recognition. In: Proceedings of the IEEE Conference on Computer Vision and Pattern Recognition, pp. 770–778. (2016)
13. Kim, J., Woo, S.S.: Efficient two-stage model retraining for machine unlearning. In: Proceedings of the IEEE/CVF Conference on Computer Vision and Pattern Recognition, pp. 4361–4369 (2022)
14. Koh, P.W., Liang, P.: Understanding black-box predictions via influence functions. In: International Conference on Machine Learning, pp. 1885–1894 (2017)
15. Kurmanji, M., Triantafillou, P., Hayes, J.: Towards unbounded machine unlearning. In: Advances in neural information processing systems pp, pp. 1957–1987 (2023)
16. LeCun, Y., Bottou, L., Bengio, Y., Haffner, P.: Gradient-based learning applied to document recognition. Proc. IEEE **86**(11), 2278–2324 (1998)
17. LeCun, Y., Huang, F.J., Bottou, L.: Learning multiple layers of features from tiny images (2005)

18. Liu, Z., Wang, T., Huai, M., Miao, C.: Backdoor attacks via machine unlearning. In: AAAI, pp. 14115–14123. AAAI Press (2024)
19. Marchant, N.G., Rubinstein, B.I., Alfeld, S.: Hard to forget: Poisoning attacks on certified machine unlearning. In: Proceedings of the AAAI Conference on Artificial Intelligence, vol. 36, pp. 7691–7700 (2022)
20. Mehta, R., Pal, S., Singh, V., Ravi, S.N.: Deep unlearning via randomized conditionally independent hessians. In: Proceedings of the IEEE/CVF Conference on Computer Vision and Pattern Recognition, pp. 10422–10431 (2022)
21. Neel, S., Roth, A., Sharifi-Malvajerdi, S.: Descent-to-delete: Gradient-based methods for machine unlearning. In: Algorithmic Learning Theory, pp. 931–962 (2021)
22. Netzer, Y., Wang, T., Coates, A., Bissacco, A., Wu, B., Ng, A.Y., et al.: Reading digits in natural images with unsupervised feature learning **2011**(2), 4 (2011)
23. Nguyen, Q.P., Low, B.K.H., Jaillet, P.: Variational bayesian unlearning. Adv. Neural. Inf. Process. Syst. **33**, 16025–16036 (2020)
24. Pan, C., Chien, E., Milenkovic, O.: Unlearning graph classifiers with limited data resources. In: Proceedings of the ACM Web Conference 2023, pp. 716–726 (2023)
25. Pawelczyk, M., Di, J.Z., Lu, Y., Kamath, G., Sekhari, A., Neel, S.: Machine unlearning fails to remove data poisoning attacks. The Thirteenth ICLR (2025)
26. Socher, R., Perelygin, A., Wu, J.: Chuang: Recursive deep models for semantic compositionality over a sentiment treebank. In: Proceedings of the 2013 conference on empirical methods in natural language processing, pp. 1631–1642 (2013)
27. Zhang, B., Dong, Y., Wang, T., Li, J.: Towards certified unlearning for deep neural networks. In: ICML. Proceedings of Machine Learning Research, vol. 235, pp. 58800–58818 (2024)

Reducing Disparity in Aleatoric Uncertainty for Age Estimation from Facial Images

Ruhani Rahman[1], Zhe Fu[2], Depeng Xu[1], and Xi Niu[1](✉)

[1] University of North Carolina at Charlotte, Charlotte, NC, USA
{rrahman3,dxu7,xniu2}@charlotte.edu
[2] Renmin University of China, Beijing, China
zhefu@ruc.edu.cn

Abstract. Age estimation from facial images is a challenging task but has diverse applications in real world. Variations in image quality, facial orientation, occlusion, and lighting introduce aleatoric uncertainty (AU), the inherent randomness in data that affects machine learning performance. While previous studies have explored techniques to quantify and mitigate AU, little attention has been given to the disparity in AU across different identity groups, which can introduce biases and exacerbate social inequities. In this work, we investigate AU discrepancies in age estimation models and propose *AUFairGAN*, a generative AI model based on the generative adversarial network (GAN), to mitigate these disparities. Compared to conventional GANs, we introduce an additional AU-specific discriminator to enforce unbiased AU levels for different identity groups. We also add a penalty term in the generator's loss function to explicitly penalize large AU discrepancies at the mini-batch level during the model training. This novel architecture ensures that the model generates faithful facial images that reduce aleatoric uncertainty gap across identity groups. We evaluate *AUFairGAN* on three publicly available facial image datasets and demonstrate that our model successfully mitigates AU discrepancy, leading to improved model trustworthiness while improving the age estimation performance and maintaining the image quality.

Keywords: aleatoric uncertainty · facial images · age estimation · GAN

1 Introduction

Age estimation of a person from a facial image is a highly challenging yet crucial task. The task has wide real-world applications, including identity verification, forensic analysis, biometric health assessment, fraud detection, age-appropriate content recommendation and child protection, etc. One challenge is due to significant variability of image qualities, angles, rotations, and positions of the face, as

R. C.-W. Wong et al. (Eds.): PAKDD 2026, LNAI 16618, pp. 164–176, 2027.
https://doi.org/10.1007/978-981-92-1947-6_14

well as partial or complete facial occlusion. Such variability will raise uncertainty in machine learning performance, specifically aleatoric uncertainty (AU).

In the machine learning community, there are two inherently different sources of uncertainty, which are often referred to as aleatoric and epistemic uncertainty [8]. Aleatoric uncertainty (AU) refers to the notion of inherent noise and randomness, which may cause variability in the outcome of a machine learning model. On the other hand, epistemic uncertainty (EU) refers to a model's lack of knowledge, usually caused by insufficient training data. AU is especially important in image analysis because AU is more salient in the image data. There are many studies to quantify AU in images (e.g., [12]) or to reduce aleatoric uncertainty for images (e.g., [27]). However, in this study, we find that machine learning models tend to be aleatorically uncertain in a disparate way for different identity groups. We develop an approach to mitigate such disparity, to ensure fair and reliable model performance, especially if the model's decision affects people's lives, such as in hiring, financial decisions, criminal justice, or healthcare.

Studies find that uncertainty increases stress (e.g., [16]). Uncertainty disparity or unfairly higher uncertainty levels will further plague the underprivileged, and will amplify the existing inequities that are already harmful to the underprivileged populations. Facing higher uncertainties, banks tend to deny a legitimate loan application or approve a risky loan. Physicians have a tendency to prescribe excessive amounts of diagnostic tests [10] and are more reluctant to disclose their uncertainties to their patients when making decisions [11].

In this work, we will address the problem of mitigating different identity groups' discrepancy of AU in machine learning models. The result is a deep learning framework, named *AUFairGAN*, based on the generative adversarial network (GAN) structure [5]. GAN is chosen as the base structure due to its adversarial mechanism between a data generator and a discriminator to generate faithful synthetic training data, and therefore can 1) potentially augment the original images for the underprivileged groups to reduce aleatoric uncertainty, and more importantly can 2) potentially reduce the AU gap between different identity groups during the image generation process.

Compared to the conventional GAN structure, we add an additional discriminator as the constraint to restrict the generator to generate AU-unbiased higher-quality images for different identity groups. Thus, during the training process of *AUFairGAN*, the generator plays two adversarial games with two discriminators. In addition, we also add a penalty term to the generator's loss function to intentionally penalize the large AU discrepancies at the mini-batch level during the training. After the training, *AUFairGAN* is expected to be capable of generating both AU-unbiased and faithful image data, which can then be safely used for age estimation.

2 Related Work

This research connects the studies on facial age estimation, GAN for fair machine learning, and uncertainty quantification. We briefly review them as follows.

2.1 Facial Age Estimation

With the advent of deep learning, Convolutional Neural Networks (CNNs) have become the dominant approach in age estimation. Levi et al. [14] were the first to use CNNs to estimate age on the Adience dataset. Other notable works include Deep Expectation of Apparent Age (DEX) [19], which employed a pre-trained VGG-16 network fine-tuned on the IMDB-WIKI dataset. Other studies have explored ResNet (e.g., [20]), and vision Transformers (e.g., [13]) architectures to enhance facial feature extraction capabilities. Recent studies have also leveraged multi-task learning, where age estimation is jointly trained with related tasks such as gender or facial expression recognition (e.g., [26]).

These studies have collectively demonstrated the challenges of age estimation. They also inform us with the state-of-the-art machine learning models to estimate age. Built on those studies, we will further quantify AU and AU gap in different identity groups.

2.2 GAN for Fair Machine Learning

Generative Adversarial Networks (GANs) have emerged as a promising tool for mitigating bias and improving fairness in machine learning models. One of the key applications is fair data generation (e.g., [22]), allowing models to make more equitable predictions. Another approach involves data augmentation using GANs to counteract biases present in datasets (e.g., [3]). This method is particularly useful in facial images, where variability of image quality leads to disparity in outcomes. Studies have also shown that GANs can generate diverse and realistic images, improving model fairness by ensuring a more representative training set (e.g., [2]). Adversarial training methods using GANs have also been explored to improve fairness. In these approaches, a discriminator is trained to identify biased decisions while the generator learns to minimize bias (e.g., [25]). Such models enforce fairness by penalizing disparities in classification outcomes across different demographic groups.

These studies have spoken of GANs as a powerful tool for removing disparity and promoting fairness. We will leverage and modify GAN to ensure parity in AU for different identity groups.

3 Disparity Discovery in Aleatoric Uncertainty (AU)

Gal's well-known BNN (Bayesian Neural Network) approach in quantifying uncertainty [12] has offered this study a computational approach to estimating AU on top of a deep learning model for estimating age from facial images. In the Gal's approach, the aleatoric uncertainty (AU) is modeled as heteroscedastic, meaning it is input sample-specific. For a prediction task, AU is captured by the variance of different versions of outputs perturbed by noise. The structure is designed with two output heads: one for the primary prediction task, i.e., age estimation, and another to capture input-dependent AU.

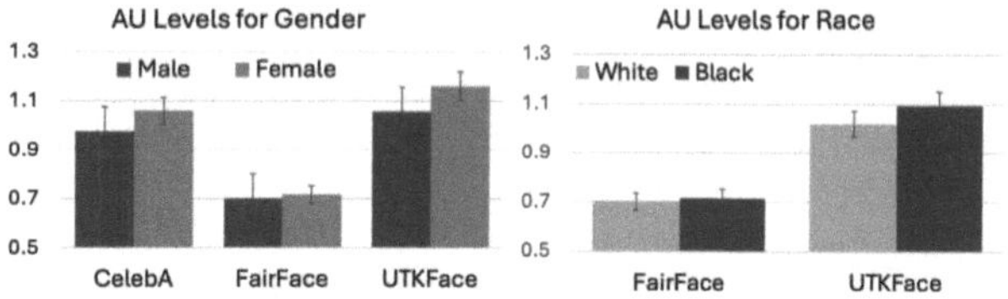

Fig. 1. Aleatoric uncertainty for different identity groups.

We trained a ResNet-18 model [6] with Gal's BNN approach [12] on three training datasets respectively. They are three publicly available facial image datasets: CelebA [15], FairFace [9], and UTKFace [19]. We will introduce them more in the experiment section (Sect. 6). During the training, we performed $T = 100$ MC simulations. The trained model is named *ResNet-BNN-AU*. It is then applied to the three testing sets of the three facial image datasets respectively, obtaining AU levels for different identity groups.

Our result, as in Fig. 1, shows that for the age estimation task, females have higher AU than males for all three datasets. The reason could be that female facial images often have greater variation in makeup, hairstyles, accessories (e.g., glasses, hats), more frequent occlusions (e.g., long hair or scarf covering parts of the face), and broader stylistic expressions. These factors add noise and complexity, making the model more aleatorically uncertain when making predictions.

Our result also shows that African Americans suffer from higher aleatoric uncertainty compared to White people. There is substantial evidence supporting that photography and imaging technologies have historically struggled to accurately capture darker skin tones due to biases built into film, lighting, digital sensors, as well as post-processing algorithms, leading to lower image quality for African American people [17]. Such aleatoric uncertainty discrepancy indicates a bias, which will lead to suboptimal model performance.

4 AUFairGAN: Mitigating AU Bias Through GAN

We propose a GAN-based deep learning model, *AUFairGAN*, to mitigate AU discrepancy in different identity groups. The architecture of *AUFairGAN* is presented in Fig. 2. The base model is Enhanced Super-Resolution Generative Adversarial Network (ESRGAN) [23], an advanced super-resolution model that enhances image details and texture realism. ESRGAN consists of a generator G and a discriminator D. G transforms a low-resolution image (LR) into a higher-resolution image (SR). On top of ESRGAN, we add another discriminator, which takes the aleatoric uncertainty score (the output of *ResNet-BNN-AU*) as the input, and predicts the sensitive attribute. It plays an additional adversarial game with the generator, in order for the generator to generate an image whose aleatoric uncertainty is independent of the sensitive attribute.

Therefore, *AUFairGAN* has one generator G and two discriminators: D, D^A, as shown in Fig. 2. The generator G takes a low-resolution (LR) image x_{LR} and generates a realistic super-resolution (SR) image $x_{SR} = G(x_{LR})$. The first (original) discriminator D is a relativistic discriminator as in ESRGAN, which guides the generator G to generate SR images that are as realistic as the high-resolution (HR) images x_{HR} through adversarial training. The purpose of the second (added) discriminator D^A is to play another adversarial game with the generator G to guide the generation of aleatorically unbiased images where aleatoric uncertainty σ_i^2 estimated by *ResNet-BNN-AU* is independent of the protected attribute S (gender, race, and others). *ResNet-BNN-AU* is pretrained in Sect. 3 to serve as a "black-box" calculation for the aleatoric uncertainty $\sigma_i^2(x_{SR})$ for each SR image. Its parameters are not updated during *AUFairGAN*'s training. The updating components are G, D, and D^A. The design above is to mitigate the discrepancy in aleatoric uncertainty for different identity groups. Since D^A is the added structure on top of ESRGAN, we will talk about it in more detail.

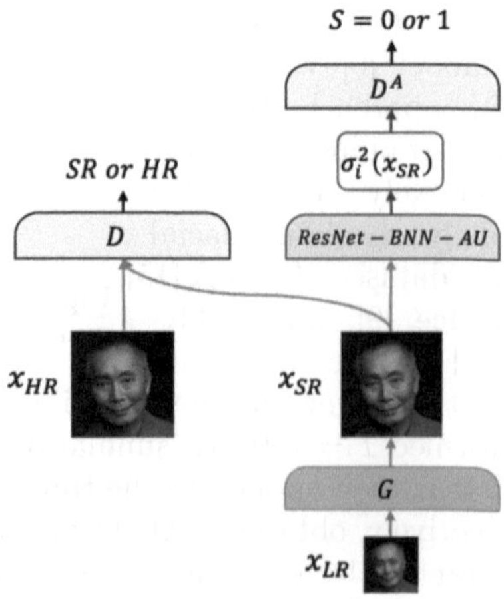

Fig. 2. The structure of *AUFairGAN*.

4.1 The Added Discriminator D^A

The added discriminator D^A serves as an unbiased constraint to restrict the generator G to generate unbiased higher-quality images for different identity groups. Its input is $\sigma_i^2(x_i)$ from *ResNet-BNN-AU*. D^A is trained to predict values of the protected attribute S from the aleatoric uncertainty σ_i^2. Let us assume S is a binary variable. The approach could be extended to other non-binary variables. D^A's loss function is defined as:

$$L_{D^A} = -\mathbb{E}_{x_{SR}|s=1}\left[\log\left(D^A(\sigma_i^2(x_{SR}))\right)\right] - \mathbb{E}_{x_{SR}|s=0}\left[\log\left(1 - D^A(\sigma_i^2(x_{SR}))\right)\right], \tag{1}$$

where $\mathbb{E}_{x_{SR}|s=1}[.]$ averages for all the samples in the mini-batch whose sensitive attribute value is 1. $\mathbb{E}_{x_{SR}|s=0}[.]$ is the same operation for the samples whose sensitive attribute value is 0. This equation is essentially a binary cross-entropy loss, where the goal for the discriminator D^A is to correctly classify the sensitive attribute S's value from the generator and ResNet-BNN-AU's output.

4.2 The Modified Generator G Loss Function

Since we add a discriminator D^A to play an adversarial game with G, the loss function of G should reflect such an additional adversarial game. Therefore, on top of the original ESRGAN's generator's loss function, we add this adversarial loss term:

$$L_G^{D_A} = -\mathbb{E}_{x_{SR}|s=1}\left[\log\left(1 - D^A(\sigma_i^2(x_{SR}))\right)\right] - \mathbb{E}_{x_{SR}|s=0}\left[\log\left(D^A(\sigma_i^2(x_{SR}))\right)\right]. \tag{2}$$

This loss is used to train the generator in such a way that it fools D^A. Opposite to D^A which tries to predict S's value, the generator G is trying to confuse it. The $L_G^{D_A}$ term in the generator G's loss function is a natural result from the added discriminator D^A.

In addition to the natural result, we propose to strengthen the unbiased generating process by adding another more explicit penalty term to G's loss function:

$$L_{penalty} = |\mathbb{E}_{x_{SR}|s=1} \sum \sigma_i^2(x_{SR}) - \mathbb{E}_{x_{SR}|s=0} \sum \sigma_i^2(x_{SR})|. \tag{3}$$

This penalty term explicitly penalizes the large AU gap in different identity groups in the same mini-batch. Combining those two added terms, the generator G's final loss function is:

$$L_G = L_G^{ESRGAN} + \alpha L_G^{D_A} + \beta L_{penalty}, \tag{4}$$

where L_G^{ESRGAN} is the original loss function of ESRGAN's generator, taking care of the image quality aspect of the image generating process. α and β are hyper-parameters, controlling the trade-off between the AU gap reduction requirement and the image quality. We experiment with different values of α and β, including setting each of them zero, which is equivalent to an ablation study. The result is shown in Sect. 6.2.

5 Experiments

5.1 Datasets and Prediction Tasks

To evaluate the effectiveness of our proposed *AUFairGAN* model, we used three publicly available datasets: CelebA [15], FairFace [9], and UTKFace [19]. CelebA comprises 202,599 celebrity images with 40 annotated attributes, where age estimation is formulated as a binary classification task (young vs. not young) and gender is considered the sensitive attribute. FairFace contains 108,652 images labeled with race, gender, and age, and we perform age group classification across nine categories while treating both gender and race as protected attributes. UTKFace includes 24,104 images with age, gender, and race annotations, and we categorize age into three groups (youths, adults, and seniors) while also adopting gender and race as sensitive attributes.

5.2 Evaluation Metrics

To evaluate *AUFairGAN*, we would like to consider three aspects: AU disparity, model performance, and generated image faithfulness. The former one is the focus of this study. The latter two relate to the model and data "utility" we need to sacrifice (if any) to accommodate the AU gap reduction requirement. For AU disparity, we report the difference of the AU values aggregated by identity groups obtained from *ResNet-BNN-AU*. To evaluate *AUFairGAN*'s performance, we use the classification accuracy. To evaluate the quality of the generated images from *AUFairGAN*, we adopt the Peak Signal-to-Noise Ratio (PSNR) [4] score and the Structural Similarity Index Measure (SSIM) [24] score. Both PSNR and SSIM quantify image faithfulness to the original image: the similarity between the SR and LR images. A higher PSNR value ($>$ 40 dB) indicates a highly faithful image. A value close to 1 for SSIM suggests that the SR and LR images are nearly identical.

5.3 Baseline Models

To compare the performance of *AUFairGAN* with the state-of-the-art, we select the following two groups of representative baseline models.

The first group consists of three models with fairness consideration:

- **FairBatch** [18]: it is a batch selection model that dynamically adjusts the composition of training batches to improve fairness in machine learning models. It is a plug-and-play approach that can be used with standard optimization pipelines like SGD.
- **FLAC** [21]: it aims to learn fair feature representations without access to protected attribute labels (a bias label–unaware approach). The model leverages a bias-capturing classifier and a sampling strategy to amplify underrepresented groups, ensuring disentangled and fair feature representations.
- **BC+BB** (**B**ias-**C**ontrastive and **B**ias-**B**alanced Learning) [7]: BB adapts contrastive learning to debias when bias labels are available. BB adds a regression-based term to push the model toward a balanced target-bias distribution, counteracting over-represented patterns.

The second group consists of the two variations of *AUFairGAN*, serving for the purpose of ablation study:

- **ResNet-BNN-AU**: it is the original model that is mentioned in Sect. 3. It is a ResNet-18 model with the BNN AU quantification approach [12]. **ResNet-BNN-AU** is applied to quantify AU as well as estimate age.
- **Fine-Tuned ESRGAN**: it is the model that removed the added discriminator D^A in *AUFairGAN*. The super-resolution (SR) images generated by the fine-tuned ESRGAN serve as the input to the *ResNet-BNN-AU* model for AU quantification and age estimation.

5.4 Implementation Details

Our proposed *AUFairGAN* leverages the pretrained ESRGAN [23] generator trained on the DIV2K dataset [1]. We fine-tuned the ESRGAN model on our three image datasets (CelebA, FairFace, and UTKFace respectively) before integrating it into *AUFairGAN*. The discriminator D is a CNN-based model that distinguishes between super-resolution (SR) and high-resolution (HR) images. The added discriminator D^A is a multi-layer feed-forward network that predicts the sensitive attribute based on the AU score of the generated SR images. For optimization, we use a learning rate of 1×10^{-4}, 5×10^{-4}, and 1×10^{-3} for G, D, and D^A respectively. Hyperparameters α and β are experimented with different values. A detailed hyperparameter sensitivity analysis is presented in the results section (Sect. 6.2). To make LR and HR images, we apply the down-sampling and up-sampling techniques on the original images to make the LR images to a resolution of $(64, 64, 3)$, and HR images to a resolution of $(128, 128, 3)$.

Table 1. The performance comparison of different models. The best (lowest) AU gap values across models are bolded. Within each sensitive attribute group, the lowest AU and the highest classification accuracy across models are bolded.

Dataset	Sensitive Attribute		FairBatch			FLAC			BC+BB			AUFairGAN		
			AU	Diff.	Accuracy	AU	Diff.	Accuracy	AU	Diff.	Accuracy	AU	Diff.	Accuracy
CelebA	Gender	Male	1.078	0.070	0.517	1.070	0.184	0.524	1.086	0.071	0.512	**0.969**	**0.066**	**0.834**
		Female	1.148		0.516	1.254		0.523	1.157		0.503	**1.035**		**0.911**
FairFace	Gender	Male	0.900	0.031	0.504	0.912	0.020	0.515	0.914	0.021	0.506	**0.698**	**0.003**	0.529
		Female	0.931		0.471	0.932		0.492	0.935		0.478	**0.701**		**0.531**
	Race	White	0.948	0.001	0.483	0.946	0.006	0.514	0.974	0.044	0.497	**0.700**	**0.000**	**0.538**
		Black	0.949		0.484	0.952		0.490	1.018		0.470	**0.700**		**0.534**
UTKFace	Gender	Male	1.050	0.018	0.457	1.098	0.076	0.467	1.175	0.041	0.480	**1.045**	**0.012**	**0.770**
		Female	1.068		0.625	1.174		0.608	1.216		0.592	**1.057**		**0.772**
	Race	White	1.069	0.046	0.453	1.069	0.047	0.467	1.095	0.035	0.488	**0.966**	**0.010**	**0.771**
		Black	1.115		0.592	1.116		0.575	1.130		0.600	**0.976**		**0.769**

6 Results

6.1 Disparity Reduction

As shown in Table 1, for all three datasets and sensitive attributes (gender and race), *AUFairGAN* consistently achieves the lowest AU differences, demonstrating its effectiveness in reducing aleatoric uncertainty gap compared to the other two state-of-the-art fairness-aware models. The reason is that during the image super-resolution augmentation process, *AUFairGAN* not only removes noises, blur, inconsistent lighting, or low contrast that cause higher AU, but also explicitly forces the generator to remove uncertainty cues that correlate with sensitive attributes.

In terms of classifier performance, *AUFairGAN* achieves better accuracy most of the time on all three datasets. Although reducing the aleatoric uncertainty gap between identity groups could potentially harm predictive performance by suppressing subtle distinctions used by the model, our empirical result, however, shows that *AUFairGAN* actually improves accuracy, probably due to the noise removing process.

We also tested the time efficiency of *AUFairGAN* and observed that the additional adversarial optimization introduces only a minor increase ($\sim 7.29\%$) in training time while the inference time remains comparable. For example, during training time, *AUFairGAN* takes 0.86 s to train a batch of 32 samples from CelebA while *Fine-Tuned ESRGAN* takes 0.74 s. For the inference time, *AUFairGAN* generates 150.2 images per second for FairFace while *Fine-Tuned ESRGAN* generates 153.2 images per second.

Table 2. Aleatoric Uncertainty (AU) levels, model performance (classification accuracy), and image quality (PSNR and SSIM) across models and sensitive attributes. The best (lowest) AU gap values across models are bolded. Within each sensitive attribute group, the lowest AU and the highest classification accuracy, PSNR, and SSIM across models are bolded.

Dataset	Sensitive Attribute		ResNet-BNN-AU			Fine-Tuned ESRGAN					AUFairGAN				
			AU	Diff.	Accuracy	AU	Diff.	Accuracy	PSNR	SSIM	AU	Diff.	Accuracy	PSNR	SSIM
CelebA	Gender	Male	0.976	0.084	0.822	0.997	0.086	0.827	**36.425**	**0.974**	**0.969**	**0.066**	**0.834**	33.558	0.963
		Female	1.060		0.901	1.083		0.904	**37.102**	**0.975**	**1.035**		**0.911**	34.258	0.966
FairFace	Gender	Male	0.700	0.004	**0.531**	0.699	0.005	0.527	**41.996**	**0.989**	**0.698**	**0.003**	0.529	39.798	0.984
		Female	0.704		0.514	0.704		0.528	**41.890**	**0.988**	**0.701**		**0.531**	39.512	0.981
	Race	White	0.700	0.002	0.511	**0.699**	0.002	0.537	**42.247**	**0.989**	0.700	**0.000**	**0.538**	39.792	0.982
		Black	0.702		0.499	0.701		**0.534**	**42.402**	**0.990**	**0.700**		**0.534**	40.322	0.986
UTKFace	Gender	Male	1.058	0.102	0.751	**1.010**	0.127	0.768	28.235	0.938	1.045	**0.012**	**0.770**	**30.671**	**0.951**
		Female	1.160		0.758	1.137		0.771	27.767	0.924	**1.057**		**0.772**	**30.172**	**0.943**
	Race	White	1.019	0.076	0.757	0.975	0.055	**0.771**	**29.686**	**0.924**	**0.966**	**0.010**	**0.771**	29.296	0.907
		Black	1.095		0.764	1.030		**0.770**	29.552	**0.938**	**0.976**		0.769	**29.929**	0.917

6.2 Ablation Studies

Without Adversarial Training or the Additional Discriminator. As shown in Table 2, we compare the AU difference, model performance, and image quality between ResNet-BNN-AU (without adversarial training), Fine-Tuned ESRGAN (without the additional discriminator), and our model *AUFairGAN*. Across all of the three datasets, *AUFairGAN* has the lowest AU disparity between sensitive attribute groups. Most of the time, *AUFairGAN* has a better classification accuracy, showing that reducing AU bias does not harm performance and can even improve it. *AUFairGAN* has slightly lower PSNR and SSIM scores than *Fine-Tuned ESRGAN*, but these scores are still strong, showing that fairness improvements do not substantially degrade visual fidelity.

Hyperparameter Sensitivity Analysis. We investigate the impact of hyperparameters α and β on *AUFairGAN* to determine their optimal values for mitigating aleatoric uncertainty disparity. A higher α strengthens the AU-specific adversarial loss, while a higher β increases the penalty for a larger AU gap. If

α is zero, *AUFairGAN* becomes a Fine-Tuned ESRGAN with the penalty term. If β is zero, it becomes an *AUFairGAN* variant without the penalty. If both α and β are zero, it is the Fine-Tuned ESRGAN.

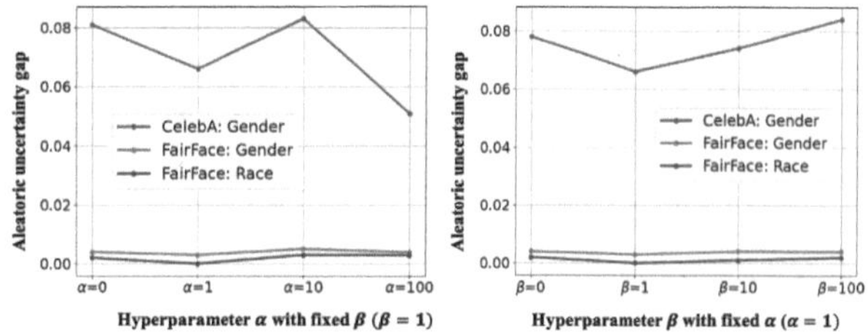

Fig. 3. Hyperparameter sensitivity analysis.

As shown in Fig. 3, neither α nor β being zero is optimal for the AU gap reduction. We observed α and β work together to mitigate the AU gap. The best combination is different for each dataset. For the gender attribute in CelebA, the best combination is $\alpha = 100$ and $\beta = 1$. For the gender and race attributes in FairFace, the best combination is $\alpha = 1$ and $\beta = 1$.

6.3 Case Studies

Figure 4 presents some cases demonstrating the pixel-level changes *AUFairGAN* has made on images, in order to reduce the AU gap. We intentionally select cases from the underprivileged groups in the CelebA and FairFace datasets, i.e., the female group in CelebA and African Americans in FairFace, because the underprivileged groups exhibited higher AU in the original images. We observe that in order to reduce the AU gap in gender, *AUFairGAN* tends to change the pixel values more around eyes, noses, and lips. These areas often include makeups, eyeglasses, or facial accessories. By enhancing clarity in these facial zones, *AUFairGAN* helps reduce the uncertainty gap for these individuals. In contrast, in order to reduce the AU gap in race, the changes are more diffuse

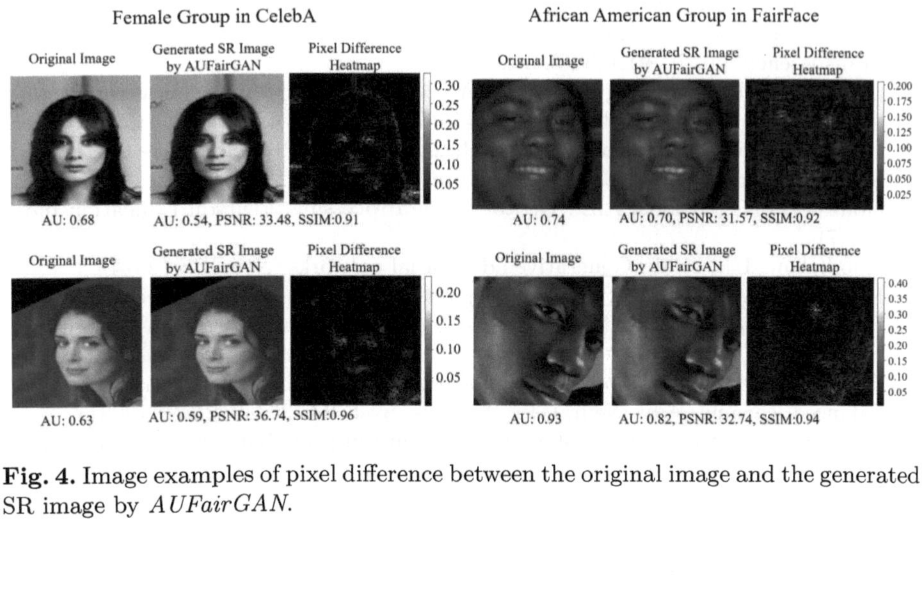

Fig. 4. Image examples of pixel difference between the original image and the generated SR image by *AUFairGAN*.

across the entire face, which makes sense for skin tones. *AUFairGAN* seems to smooth or enhance overall facial detail, improving how the face is represented and reducing the AU gap relative to White people. These pixel-level transformations demonstrate *AUFairGAN*'s sensitivity to context. Rather than uniformly applying generic super-resolution techniques, the model learns to strategically adjust image features that contribute most to AU gap, depending on the identity group.

7 Conclusion

This study addresses a critical yet underexplored issue in machine learning: disparities in aleatoric uncertainty (AU) across identity groups in facial age estimation. Our investigation reveals that underprivileged groups—specifically females and African Americans—experience disproportionately higher aleatoric uncertainty in age prediction tasks. We developed *AUFairGAN*, a novel generative adversarial network with an added discriminator and a penalty term in the generator's loss function. Evaluations on three widely used facial image datasets demonstrate that *AUFairGAN* effectively reduces aleatoric uncertainty gaps between gender and racial groups, while improving the age estimation task performance and maintaining the image utility. This study opens promising avenues for future research into more equitable AI systems that deliver not just accurate, but also fair and trustworthy decisions.

References

1. Agustsson, E., Timofte, R.: Ntire 2017 challenge on single image super-resolution: dataset and study. In: Proceedings of the IEEE Conference on Computer Vision and Pattern Recognition Workshops, pp. 126–135 (2017)
2. Buolamwini, J., Gebru, T.: Gender shades: intersectional accuracy disparities in commercial gender classification. In: Conference on Fairness, Accountability and Transparency, pp. 77–91 (2018)
3. Chen, C.H., Li, Y., Gong, B., Yang, Y.: Improved techniques for training gans to counteract bias in facial recognition. In: Proceedings of the IEEE/CVF Conference on Computer Vision and Pattern Recognition (CVPR), pp. 1317–1325 (2018). https://doi.org/10.1109/CVPR.2018.00146
4. Gonzalez, R.C., Woods, R.E.: Digital Image Processing. Pearson Education India (2007)
5. Goodfellow, I.J., et al.: Generative adversarial networks. NeurIPS (2014)
6. He, K., Zhang, X., Ren, S., Sun, J.: Deep residual learning for image recognition. In: Proceedings of the IEEE Conference on Computer Vision and Pattern Recognition, pp. 770–778 (2016)
7. Hong, Y., Yang, E.: Unbiased classification through bias-contrastive and bias-balanced learning. Adv. Neural. Inf. Process. Syst. **34**, 26449–26461 (2021)
8. Hora, S.C.: Aleatory and epistemic uncertainty in probability elicitation with an example from hazardous waste management. Reliabil. Eng. Syst. Saf. **54**(2–3), 217–223 (1996)

9. Karkkainen, K., Joo, J.: Fairface: face attribute dataset for balanced race, gender, and age for bias measurement and mitigation. In: Proceedings of the IEEE/CVF Winter Conference on Applications of Computer Vision, pp. 1548–1558 (2021)
10. Kassirer, J.P., Kopelman, R.I.: Tolerating uncertainty. Hosp. Pract. **22**(4), 21–28 (1987)
11. Katz, J.: Why doctors don't disclose uncertainty. Hastings Center Report, pp. 35–44 (1984)
12. Kendall, A., Gal, Y.: What uncertainties do we need in bayesian deep learning for computer vision? In: Advances in Neural Information Processing Systems, p. 30 (2017)
13. Kuprashevich, M., Tolstykh, I.: Mivolo: multi-input transformer for age and gender estimation. In: International Conference on Analysis of Images, Social Networks and Texts, pp. 212–226. Springer (2023)
14. Levi, G., Hassner, T.: Age and gender classification using convolutional neural networks. In: Proceedings of the IEEE Conference on Computer Vision and Pattern Recognition Workshops, pp. 34–42 (2015)
15. Liu, Z., Luo, P., Wang, X., Tang, X.: Deep learning face attributes in the wild. In: Proceedings of International Conference on Computer Vision (ICCV) (2015)
16. McCulloch, P., Kaul, A., Wagstaff, G., Wheatcroft, J.: Tolerance of uncertainty, extroversion, neuroticism and attitudes to randomized controlled trials among surgeons and physicians. J. Br. Surgery **92**(10), 1293–1297 (2005)
17. Osinubi, A.: The inherent color bias of image capturing technology: Colorism in photography (2018). https://medium.com/africana-feminisms/the-inherent-color-bias-of-image-capturing-technology-colorism-in-photography-3e1dff554548. Accessed 10 Apr 2025
18. Roh, Y., Lee, K., Whang, S.E., Suh, C.: Fairbatch: batch selection for model fairness. In: International Conference on Learning Representations (2021)
19. Rothe, R., Timofte, R., Gool, L.V.: Deep expectation of real and apparent age from a single image without facial landmarks. Int. J. Comput. Vision **126**(2–4), 144–157 (2018)
20. Rothe, R., Timofte, R., Van Gool, L.: Dex: deep expectation of apparent age from a single image. In: IEEE International Conference on Computer Vision Workshops (ICCVW), pp. 10–15. IEEE (2015). https://arxiv.org/abs/1506.05083
21. Sarridis, I., Koutlis, C., Papadopoulos, S., Diou, C.: Flac: fairness-aware representation learning by suppressing attribute-class associations. IEEE Trans. Pattern Anal. Mach. Intell. (2024)
22. Sattigeri, P., Hoffman, S.C., Chenthamarakshan, V., Varshney, K.R.: Fairness gan: generating datasets with fairness properties using generative adversarial networks. IBM J. Res. Dev. **63**(4/5), 3:1–3:10 (2019)
23. Wang, X., et al.: Esrgan: enhanced super-resolution generative adversarial networks. In: The European Conference on Computer Vision Workshops (ECCVW) (2018)
24. Wang, Z., Bovik, A.C., Sheikh, H.R., Simoncelli, E.P.: Image quality assessment: from error visibility to structural similarity. IEEE Trans. Image Process. **13**(4), 600–612 (2004)
25. Xu, D., Yuan, S., Zhang, L., Wu, X.: Fairgan: Fairness-aware generative adversarial networks. In: 2018 IEEE International Conference on Big Data (Big Data), pp. 570–575. IEEE (2018)

26. Yang, Z., Yu, X., Xu, D.: Joint age and gender estimation from face images using convolutional neural networks. In: Proceedings of the IEEE International Conference on Computer Vision (ICCV), pp. 1–9 (2015). https://doi.org/10.1109/ICCV.2015.33
27. Zhang, Q., Jiang, Z., Zhou, Y., Yuille, A.: Taming aleatoric uncertainty in medical image segmentation with super-resolution. In: Proceedings of the IEEE/CVF International Conference on Computer Vision (ICCV), pp. 6840–6850 (2021)

Perspective-Insensitive Observation Representation and Role Assignment for MARL

Wei Xiong[1,2], Tingrui Yang[1,2], Yong Heng[3], Jiebo Chen[3], Qian Gao[3], Shengze Shi[1,2], and Tao Ren[1,2](✉)

[1] State Key Laboratory of Intelligent Game, Institute of Software, Chinese Academy of Sciences, Beijing, China
{xiongwei2023,yangtingrui2023,shishengze2023,rentao22}@iscas.ac.cn
[2] University of Chinese Academy of Sciences, Beijing, China
[3] Beijing Institute of Electronic System Engineering, Beijing, China

Abstract. Sharing policy or value networks improves scalability in multi-agent reinforcement learning (MARL) but often induces behavioral homogeneity that impedes role specialization. To alleviate homogeneity among agents' behaviors, the concept of role assignment is introduced, earlier studies on which typically adopt predefined roles relying on prior domain knowledge. Most recent works are increasingly assigning roles dynamically according to the similarity of agents' local observations. However, most of them overlook the individual perspective differences on observed entity positions and quantities, that could lead to seemingly-dissimilar observations among context-similar agents. Thus, we propose a Perspective-insensitive observation representation and role assignment (*Pinnet*) framework that mitigates this issue by (i) producing entity embeddings invariant to relative positions and varying counts, and (ii) deriving attention-based, intention-aware motivations that drive dynamic role allocation. Pinnet further enforces diversity and temporal stability in assignments via two lightweight regularizers, and decodes role embeddings into role-specific policy parameters to enable distinct but shareable behaviors. Empirical results on the SMAC and Google Research Football benchmarks show that Pinnet consistently outperforms strong baselines, demonstrating more coherent and adaptive role coordination.

Keywords: Multi-Agent Reinforcement Learning · Observation Representation · Role Assignment and Coordination

1 Introduction

Cooperative multi-agent reinforcement learning (MARL) has emerged as a critical paradigm for addressing complex real-world coordination tasks, such as autonomous driving [4], swarm robotics [10], and game AI [1,20,24]. The primary objective in cooperative MARL is to train a team of agents to optimize a global

R. C.-W. Wong et al. (Eds.): PAKDD 2026, LNAI 16618, pp. 177–189, 2027.
https://doi.org/10.1007/978-981-92-1947-6_15

reward. However, this pursuit faces significant challenges. From an individual agent's perspective, the environment is non-stationary due to the concurrently evolving policies of other agents. Furthermore, the joint action-observation space expands exponentially with the number of agents, posing a severe scalability challenge [3,22].

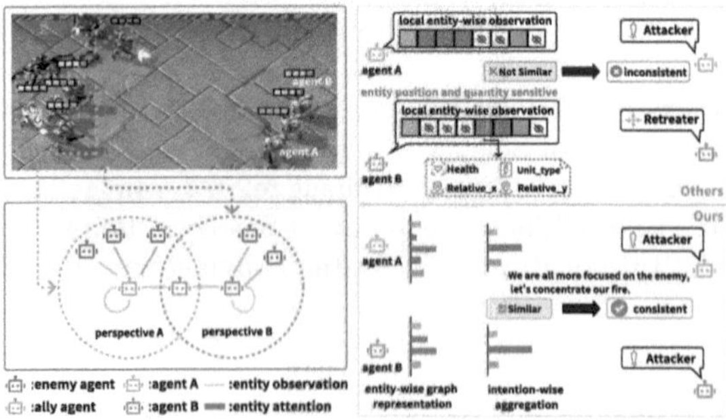

Fig. 1. A motivation example indicating the impacts of local observation perspectives on assigning behavioral roles.

A prevalent approach to mitigate these challenges is parameter sharing, where agents utilize a common policy or value network [7,8,15,23]. While enhancing scalability, this technique often enforces behavioral homogeneity, hindering performance in tasks that demand functional specialization among agents [5]. To this end, role-based methods have been proposed to foster behavioral diversity. Early works relied on pre-defined roles, limiting adaptability [6,14]. Consequently, recent research has shifted towards dynamic role assignment, where roles are allocated based on the similarity of agents' local observations, under the assumption that similar observations warrant similar roles and behaviors [9,16,17,25–27].

However, most existing dynamic role-assigning approaches in MARL tend to ***overlook the perspective differences among agents*** that could lead to seemingly non-similar local observations for actually behavior-similar agents. Taking the case in the top half of Fig. 1 as an example, due to slight differences in the relative positions and quantities of observed entities, agent A and B receive entirely different local observations (denoted by the positions and quantities of orange, blue, white and green squares in each local observation embedding) in similar scenarios (e.g., similar positions and quantities of enemies and allies). Based on the similarity of local observations, existing role-assigning approaches may designate A and B with inconsistent roles (e.g., one for Attacker and the other for Retreater), making them behave inconsistently in similar scenarios. Actually, facing with similar scenarios, agent A and B should behave consistently.

To address the issue, we propose a Perspective-insensitive observation representation and role assignment (***Pinnet***) framework for MARL, mitigating perspective-differences among scenario-similar agents through position-insensitive representation and quantity-insensitive aggregation and leveraging intrinsic behavioral motivations for dynamic role assignment. As illustrated in the bottom half of Fig. 1, Pinnet models each agent's local entity-wise observation as a graph and aggregates observed entities into three intention-related categories using graph attention, yielding type-wise attention weights that more consistently reflect behavioral motivations. Based on these motivations, each agent is assigned a role through a role selector, while a role encoder learns personalized role representations. To encourage diversity and ensure temporal stability in role assignment, two regularization terms are introduced. A role decoder further transforms role representations into role-specific policy parameters, enabling distinct role strategies while preserving shared behavior among agents with the same role. We evaluate Pinnet on the challenging SMAC benchmark, where it consistently improves performance over strong baselines, especially on *Hard* and *Super Hard* scenarios, demonstrating the effectiveness of perspective-insensitive role assignment.

2 Background

2.1 Partially Observable Markov Game

Cooperative MARL problem is often formulated as a decentralized partially observable Markov decision process [19], defined by a tuple $<\mathcal{N}, S, A, O, P, R>$, where $\mathcal{N} = \{1, 2, \ldots, N\}$ is the set of agents, S denotes the global state space, and $A = \prod_{i \in \mathcal{N}} A^i$ represents the joint action space. At each time step t, each agent i receives a local observation o_t^i drawn from the current global state $s_t \in S$ through an observation function $o_t^i = O(s_t, i)$. Besides, o_t^i is defined in an entity-wise manner as $o_t^i = \{o_t^{i,0}, o_t^{i,1}, o_t^{i,2}, \ldots, o_t^{i,M}\}$, where M is the maximum number of entities in the MARL environment, $o_t^{i,0}$ denotes the information of itself, and $o_t^{i,j}$ represents the information of the j-th entity. According to o_t^i, each agent i selects an action $a_t^i \in A^i$, and all agents' actions form a joint action $a_t \in A$. Given the current global state s_t and the joint action a_t, the global state will transit to the next one s_{t+1} according to the transition probability function $P : S \times A \times S \rightarrow [0, 1]$. Besides, during the transition, all agents receive a global reward $r_t = R(s_t, a_t)$ according to the reward function R. The goal of MARL is to obtain action-selection policies for all agents that can maximize the expected long-term rewards $\sum \gamma^{t-1} r_t$, where $\gamma \in [0, 1)$ is a discounted factor of future reward.

3 Method

This section details Pinnet, including Observation Representation and Role Assignment as shown in Fig. 2, and also describes the diversity-encouraging and fluctuation-weakening regularization objectives w.r.t. Role Assignment.

3.1 Observation Representation

Since the local entity-wise observation of each agent is inherently sensitive to the positions and quantities of entities, we adopt a graph to model each agent's entity-wise observation that achieves a position-insensitive representation of entities, and further leverage graph attention-based computation to get an intention-wise representation of each agent' observation that is quantity-insensitive.

1) Entity-Wise Graph Representation. We define the graph G_t^i for each agent i at time t as $G_t^i = (V_t^i, E_t^i)$, where the node set is $V_t^i = \{e_t^{i,0}, e_t^{i,1}, e_t^{i,2}, \dots, e_t^{i,m}\}$ with each node $e_t^{i,j}$ meaning the information of the observed entity j by agent i at time t, and the edge set is $E_t^i = \{\omega_t^{i,0}, \omega_t^{i,1}, \dots, \omega_t^{i,m}\}$ with each edge $\omega_t^{i,j}$ denoting the degree of attention agent i pays on entity j at time t.

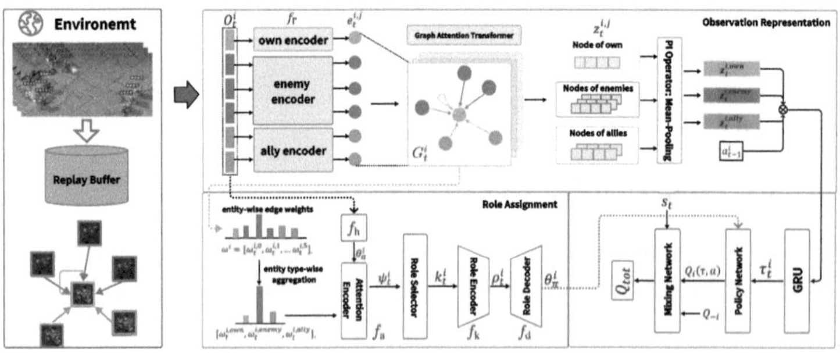

Fig. 2. The framework of Pinnet for perspective-insensitive MARL, mainly consisting of two components: Observation Representation and Role Assignment.

Node Feature Extraction: Owing to the existence of three entity types, i.e., {own, enemy, ally}, the data dimension of each entity $o_t^{i,j}$ could be different. Hence, we employ three different encoders $f_\Gamma(\cdot;\theta_\Gamma)$ to extract node features from each entity $o_t^{i,j}$ into a dimension-uniform embedding $e_t^{i,j}$ as follows:

$$e_t^{i,j} = f_\Gamma(o_t^{i,j}), \quad \Gamma \in \{\text{own}, \text{enemy}, \text{ally}\}, \tag{1}$$

where $e_t^{i,j} \in \mathbb{R}^d$ represents the node feature embedding, and f_Γ is implemented using multi-layer perceptrons. Importantly, this tripartite entity grouping is inherited from the standard observation interface of SMAC rather than injected by our method. Pinnet only treats entity types as feature groups for message aggregation; therefore, the mechanism introduces no additional domain priors and naturally generalizes to any environment with arbitrary or learned entity-type abstractions.

Edge Weight Computation: Similar to GATv2 [2], we employ graph attention Transformer as the scoring function $f_s(\cdot;\theta_s)$ to assign a weight to each edge in the graph, reflecting the importance of the feature embedding $e_t^{i,j}$ of entity j on the agent i. The scoring function is defined as follows:

$$f_{\mathrm{s}}(e_t^{i,0}, e_t^{i,j}) = \mathrm{LeakyReLU}(\alpha^T \cdot [e_t^{i,0} || e_t^{i,j}]), \tag{2}$$

where $\alpha \in \mathbb{R}^{2d}$ is a learnable vector. The entity-wise edge weight is further computed as:

$$\omega_t^{i,j} = \mathrm{Softmax}(f_s(e_t^{i,0}, e_t^{i,j})) = \frac{\exp(f_s(e_t^{i,0}, e_t^{i,j}))}{\sum_{k=0}^{m} \exp(f_s(e_t^{i,0}, e_t^{i,k}))}, \tag{3}$$

2) Intention-Wise Graph Aggregation. Different types of entities could imply different intentions on role-assigning and decision-making for each agent, so we employ graph computation to aggregate intention information from its node features, yielding the quantity-insensitive node representations:

$$z_t^{i,j} = \omega_t^{i,j} e_t^{i,j}. \tag{4}$$

Subsequently, we employ a mean pooling operation to aggregate representations of nodes of the same type, thereby obtaining the intention-wise graph representations for each agent i, denoted as $z_t^i = \{z_t^{i,\mathrm{own}}, z_t^{i,\mathrm{enemy}}, z_t^{i,\mathrm{ally}}\}$.

Last, we concatenate z_t^i with the agent's previous action a_{t-1}^i, and employ a GRU network to generate the intention-aware trajectory representation τ_t^i for agent i at time t.

3.2 Role Assignment

The edge weights $\omega_t^{i,j}$ of each agent i implicitly suggest its behavioral motivations, providing a basis for the assignment of its role. Intuitively, if an agent is more focused on enemy-type entities, it tends to be attacker-like roles; if the agent focuses on own-type entities, it tends to be retreater-like roles. Therefore, we introduce an attention encoder $f_{\mathrm{a}}(\cdot;\theta_{\mathrm{a}})$ to generate the behavioral motivation of each agent i from its graph edge weights as follows:

$$\psi_t^i = f_{\mathrm{a}}(\omega_t^{i,\mathrm{own}}, \omega_t^{i,\mathrm{enemy}}, \omega_t^{i,\mathrm{ally}}), \tag{5}$$

where $\omega_t^{i,\mathrm{own}}, \omega_t^{i,\mathrm{enemy}}, \omega_t^{i,\mathrm{ally}}$ are the type-wise edge weights aggregated from entity-wise edge weights $\omega_t^{i,j}$ that satisfy quantity-insensitive property. Here, considering the impact of different observations on the edge weights, we use a hypernetwork $f_{\mathrm{h}}(\cdot;\theta_{\mathrm{h}})$ to generate the parameters of the attention encoder f_{a}, that is, $\theta_{\mathrm{a}} = f_{\mathrm{h}}(o_t^i)$.

Subsequently, we use the Gumbel-Softmax [11] technique with categorical reparameterization to assign a role k_t^i to the agent i based on its behavioral motivation ψ_t^i:

$$k_t^i \sim \mathrm{Gumbel\text{-}Softmax}(\mathrm{MLP}(\psi_t^i)), \tag{6}$$

where $k_t^i \in \mathbb{R}^{\mathcal{K}}$ is a one-hot vector with $\mathcal{K}$ dimensions, and $\mathcal{K}$ is a role-granularity hyperparameter influenced by the complexity of tasks. **In this way, agents with similar behavioral motivations could be assigned with same roles.**

For each timestep, each agent is dynamically assigned a role to facilitate collaborative division of labor. However, abrupt role reassignments for agents across consecutive timesteps could destabilize training. Considering the period each agent's role could hold in practice in case of disorganized behavioral collaboration, we introduce a regularization term that penalizes drastic shifts in agents' attention patterns toward entities between adjacent timesteps. Formally, we impose a smoothness constraint on the aggregated type-wise edge weights:

$$\mathcal{L}_{\omega}(\theta_{\mathrm{s}}) = \mathbb{E}_{\mathcal{D}}\Big[-\sum_{t=0}\|\omega_t^i - \omega_{t+1}^i\|_2\Big], \tag{7}$$

where ω_t^i and ω_{t+1}^i are the entity-wise edge weights of agent i at time t and $t+1$, respectively.

3.3 Role-specific Role Policy

After assigning distinct roles to agents based on their behavioral motivations, we propose to learn specialized role representations for different agent categories. **This dynamic representation learning mechanism enables enhanced adaptability in environments characterized by significant uncertainties, as it allows agents to continuously refine their role-specific policies through interactive adaptation.**

Specifically, we utilize a role encoder $f_{\mathrm{k}}(\cdot;\theta_{\mathrm{k}})$ to learn the role representation. The role encoder maps the one-hot vector with $\mathcal{K}$ dimensions of k_t^i to an $\mathbb{R}^p$-dimensional representation space.

$$\rho_t^i = f_{\mathrm{k}}(k_t^i). \tag{8}$$

where f_{k} consists of a two-layer fully connected network with a tanh activation function. The role representation learning continues throughout the training process, which can automatically adapt to the dynamic changes in the environment. The overall optimization objective of the role encoder will be introduced in the next subsection.

To personalize the role representations among roles, we introduce a regularizer aimed at increasing the L_2 distance between representations of different roles as follows:

$$\mathcal{L}_{\rho}(\theta_{\mathrm{k}}) = \mathbb{E}_{\mathcal{D}}\Big[-\sum_{k\neq k'}\|f_{\mathrm{k}}(k) - f_{\mathrm{k}}(k')\|_2\Big], \tag{9}$$

where $\mathcal{D}$ is the replay buffer and k, k' are different roles.

Inspired by the natural division of responsibilities among roles, we learn specialized behavioral policies conditioned on role representations. Agents sharing the same role use identical policy parameters, while different roles maintain distinct parameter sets. To achieve this, a role decoder $f_d(\cdot;\theta_d)$ takes the role embedding ρ_i^t as input and generates the corresponding policy parameters θ_i^{π}. By leveraging discriminative role representations, the decoder produces diverse role-specific policies, effectively mitigating behavioral homogeneity and enabling complementary cooperation among agents.

3.4 Overall Training and Evaluation

Our framework is trained end-to-end following the Centralized Training with Decentralized Execution (CTDE) [12,18] paradigm. We adopt a value function factorization approach, where a mixing network aggregates individual agent utilities Q_i into a global action-value Q_{tot}. Similar to QMIX, the mixing network's parameters are generated by a hypernetwork conditioned on the global state s_t.

The entire model, denoted by parameters θ, is optimized by minimizing a composite loss function. The primary component is the standard temporal difference (TD) loss:

$$\mathcal{L}_{\text{TD}} = \mathbb{E}_{\mathcal{D}}\left[\left(r + \gamma \max_{a'} Q_{\text{tot}}(\tau', a'; \theta^-) - Q_{\text{tot}}(\tau, a; \theta)\right)^2\right] \tag{10}$$

where θ^- represents the parameters of the target network, which are periodically copied from θ. To enable specialized roles, we augment the TD loss with our proposed objectives for role assignment and representation learning. The final learning objective for our method, Pinnet, is:

$$\mathcal{L}(\theta) = \mathcal{L}_{\text{TD}}(\theta) + \lambda_\rho \mathcal{L}_\rho(\theta_{\text{k}}) + \lambda_\omega \mathcal{L}_\omega(\theta_{\text{s}}), \tag{11}$$

where $\theta = (\theta_\Gamma, \theta_{\text{s}}, \theta_{\text{h}}, \theta_{\text{k}}, \theta_{\text{d}}, \theta_{\text{m}})$, and λ_ρ, λ_ω are hyperparameter coefficients for the regularization terms.

4 Experiments

In this section, we conduct experiments to address the following research questions: (1) RQ1: Does Pinnet outperform baseline methods in performance? (2) RQ2: What is the impact of the two proposed regularizers and the number of roles $\mathcal{K}$ on model performance? (3) RQ3: What is the contribution of the role assignment module? (4) RQ4: Does Pinnet effectively learn dynamic role assignments and form coherent agent groups?

4.1 Experimental Setup

Environments: We evaluated Pinnet on the SMAC benchmark [22], a challenging multi-agent cooperative environment based on the real-time strategy game StarCraft II, whose objective is to maximize the test win rate for each battle scenario.

Baselines: We selected QMIX [21], Qatten [28], ROMA [25], LDSA [27] and ACORM [9] as our baselines. All of the baselines and Pinnet belong to value function factorization methods and use the QMIX-style mixing network for a fair comparison. QMIX is a natural baseline in which all agents share the individual Q-value network. ROMA, LDSA and ACORM are recent works that focus on role assignment and task decomposition, respectively. We implemented all baselines using their open-source code within the PyMARL [22] framework, ensuring consistent hyperparameter settings across all experiments.

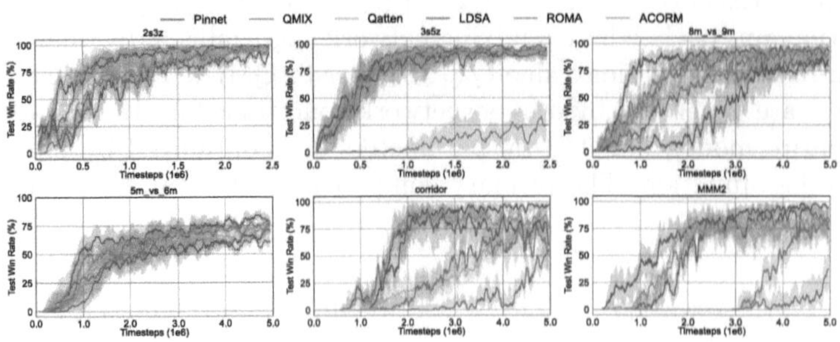

Fig. 3. Comparison of our method against baselines on six representative scenarios. The solid line shows the median test win rate across 5 seeds and the shaded areas correspond to the 25–75% percentiles.

4.2 Main Results

The scenarios in SMAC are categorized into three difficulty levels: Easy, Hard, and Super Hard, where the harder the scenario, the more efficient collaboration is required. To answer RQ1, we select two scenarios for each difficulty-level: Easy (*2s3z, 3s5z*), Hard (*5m_vs_6m, 8m_vs_9m*), and Super Hard (*corridor, MMM2*). Figure 3 illustrates the performances of Pinnet and baselines across these scenarios. Pinnet outperforms all the baselines on all Hard and Super Hard scenarios with faster convergence. On the Easy scenarios, Pinnet shows similar performance as QMIX, which indicates that our method may not improve the learning performance on simple tasks not requiring role assignment. Notably, LDSA, ROMA and ACORM, with dedicated design of role assignment or task decomposition, significantly outperform QMIX on the Hard and Super Hard scenarios, which need a much higher degree of behavioral collaboration. It is particularly noteworthy that Pinnet achieves the best performance on most of the LDSA, ROMA and ACORM, possibly benefiting from the perspective-insensitive observation representation and role assignment that more uniformly capture behavioral motivations among agents.

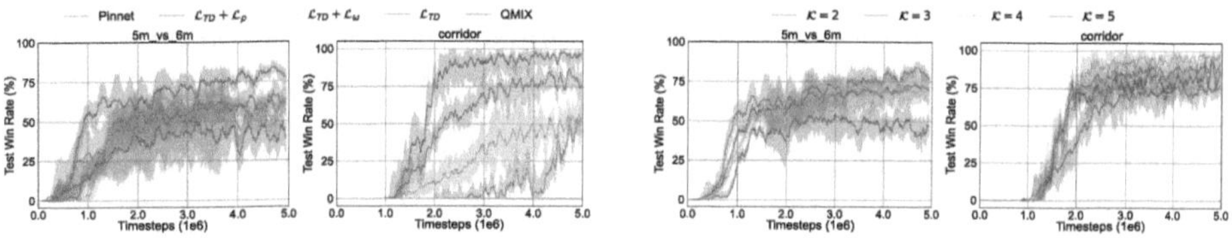

(a) Regularizer Ablation (b) Number of Roles

Fig. 4. Ablation studies w.r.t. the number of roles and the role assignment.

4.3 Ablation Studies

To answer RQ2 and RQ3, we conduct ablation studies on two scenarios: *5m_vs_6m* and *corridor*, to evaluate (1) the impact of the two regularizers, (2) the influence of the number of roles $\mathcal{K}$, and (3) the contribution of the role assignment module. Figure 4 (a) presents the performance of Pinnet when each or both of the regularizers are removed. It can be observed that removing either $\mathcal{L}_\rho$ or $\mathcal{L}_\omega$ leads to a drop in performance; notably, when both are excluded (leaving only $\mathcal{L}_{TD}$) the performance on the *5m_vs_6m* map is even worse than QMIX. Moreover, we can conclude that $\mathcal{L}_\rho$ plays a more critical role in enhancing performance compared to $\mathcal{L}_\omega$, while $\mathcal{L}_\omega$ contributes significantly to training stability. The observations indicate that personalized role representations can enhance the efficiency of role division and cooperation, while smoother role transitions contribute to a more stable training process.

To study the impact of the number of roles $\mathcal{K}$, Fig. 4 (b) illustrates the performance of Pinnet in SMAC scenarios with various values of $\mathcal{K} = 2, 3, 4, 5$. It can be observed that on the *5m_vs_6m* map, Pinnet achieves its best performance when $\mathcal{K} = 3$, while exhibiting a marked deterioration when $\mathcal{K} = 5$. This decline could be attributed to the fact that only five agents are available, and excessively divergent policies may hinder effective team coordination. Moreover, in the *corridor* and maps, the best performance is achieved when $\mathcal{K} = 4$. It demonstrates that the optimal number of roles should be adapted based on the complexity of the task and the number of agents involved.

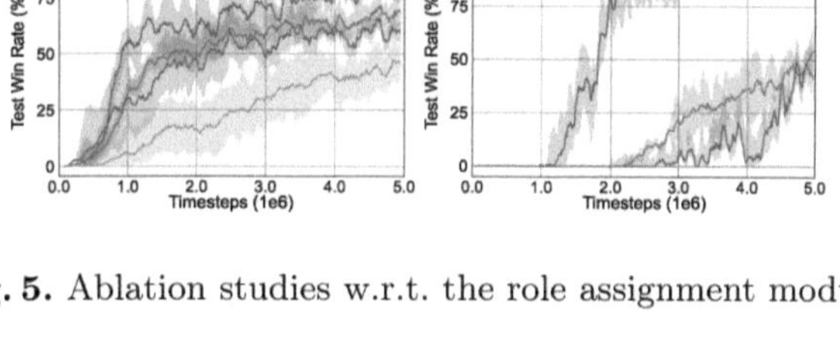

Fig. 5. Ablation studies w.r.t. the role assignment module.

To test the contribution of the role assignment module, we compare Pinnet with the following ablation settings: i) *Pinnet_ w/o_ RA*, which removes the role assignment module; ii) *Pinnet_ w_ RanRA*, wherein roles are randomly assigned to agents at each timestep; iii) *QMIX*, which excludes all additional modules. Figure 5 illustrates the ablation results on the *5 m_ vs_ 6m* and *corridor* maps. When the role assignment module is removed, Pinnet obtains decreased performance, yet it still outperforms QMIX. It demonstrates that both the observation representation module and the role assignment module contribute to performance improvements, with the role assignment module having a particularly significant impact. Moreover, the performance of Pinnet with random role assignment is substantially lower than that of Pinnet and even falls below QMIX, further verifying the effectiveness of the behavior-motivation-based role assignment in handling complex tasks.

4.4 Visualization Analysis

To answer RQ4, we provide a snapshot-based analysis on the SMAC map *8 m_ vs_ 9m*. As illustrated in Fig. 6, the upper row shows representative combat frames, while the lower row visualizes the corresponding type-wise attention weights that determine each agent's behavioral motivation. At the beginning of the episode, agents with higher attention on enemy entities are consistently assigned attacker-like roles, whereas those focusing on ally states act as protectors. During mid-battle, agents dynamically adjust their roles according to changing health conditions—low-health agents temporarily withdraw, and nearby teammates shift to protection roles by drawing enemy fire. Toward the end of the engagement, the model maintains coherent coordination: healthier agents concentrate on supporting allies or advancing the attack, while weaker agents retreat. Overall, these visualizations demonstrate that Pinnet adaptively assigns roles in response to situational changes and learns coherent division-of-labor patterns.

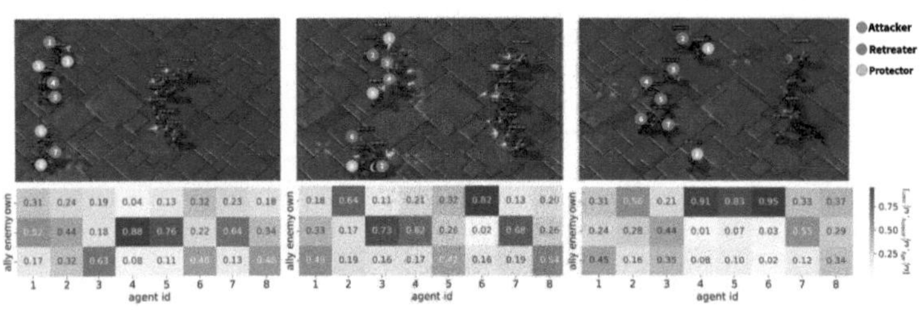

Fig. 6. Snapshots of the *8 m_ vs_ 9m* scenario (upper row) and the corresponding heatmaps (lower row) of role assignments by visualizing entity-wise edge weights.

4.5 Performance on Google Research Football

To validate Pinnet's broad applicability, we further evaluate our method on two challenging Google Research Football academy scenarios [13]: *3_vs_1_with_keeper* and *academy_counterattack_hard*. Achieving success in these tasks requires dynamic coordination, effective role differentiation, and cooperative offensive strategies. As illustrated in Fig. 7, Pinnet consistently outperforms all the baselines across all scenarios, which can be attributed to Pinnet effectively organizing agents to achieve efficient role assignment and collaboration in dynamic and complicated environments. It demonstrates the effectiveness of Pinnet on various multi-agent tasks.

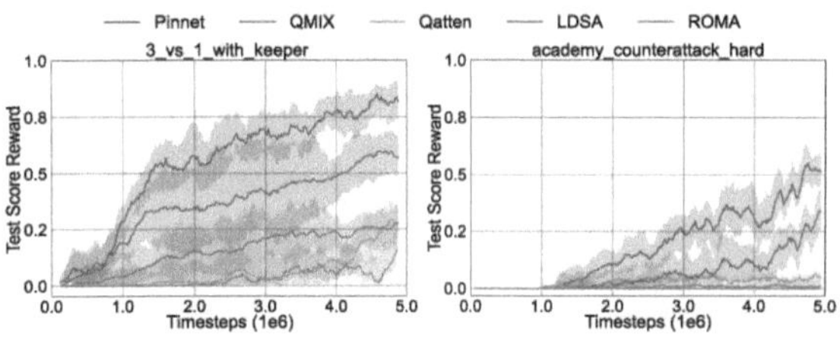

Fig. 7. The performance on Google Research Football.

5 Conclusion

This paper presented Pinnet, a perspective-insensitive MARL framework that enables dynamic role assignment and specialization in cooperative tasks. Pinnet reduces perceptual discrepancies among agents through position-invariant entity representations and quantity-invariant intention aggregation, and infers behavior-motivation-based roles via attention-derived motivations. Extensive experiments on SMAC and GRF benchmarks demonstrate that Pinnet achieves superior performance through more coherent and adaptive role coordination. Future work includes extending Pinnet to settings involving explicit communication or heterogeneous agent architectures.

References

1. Berner, C., et al.: Dota 2 with large scale deep reinforcement learning. arXiv preprint arXiv:1912.06680 (2019)
2. Brody, S., Alon, U., Yahav, E.: How attentive are graph attention networks? arXiv preprint arXiv:2105.14491 (2021)
3. Busoniu, L., Babuska, R., De Schutter, B.: A comprehensive survey of multiagent reinforcement learning. IEEE Trans. Syst. Man Cybern. Part C Appl. Rev. **38**(2), 156–172 (2008)

4. Cao, Y., Yu, W., Ren, W., Chen, G.: An overview of recent progress in the study of distributed multi-agent coordination. IEEE Trans. Industr. Inf. **9**(1), 427–438 (2012)
5. Christianos, F., Papoudakis, G., Rahman, M.A., Albrecht, S.V.: Scaling multi-agent reinforcement learning with selective parameter sharing. In: International Conference on Machine Learning, pp. 1989–1998. PMLR (2021)
6. Dastani, M., Dignum, V., Dignum, F.: Role-assignment in open agent societies. In: Proceedings of the Second International Joint Conference on Autonomous Agents and Multiagent Systems, pp. 489–496 (2003)
7. Fu, W., Yu, C., Xu, Z., Yang, J., Wu, Y.: Revisiting some common practices in cooperative multi-agent reinforcement learning. arXiv preprint arXiv:2206.07505 (2022)
8. Gupta, J.K., Egorov, M., Kochenderfer, M.: Cooperative multi-agent control using deep reinforcement learning. In: Autonomous Agents and Multiagent Systems: AAMAS 2017 Workshops, Best Papers, São Paulo, Brazil, 8–12 May 2017, Revised Selected Papers 16, pp. 66–83. Springer (2017)
9. Hu, Z., Zhang, Z., Li, H., Chen, C., Ding, H., Wang, Z.: Attention-guided contrastive role representations for multi-agent reinforcement learning. arXiv preprint arXiv:2312.04819 (2023)
10. Hüttenrauch, M., Šošić, A., Neumann, G.: Guided deep reinforcement learning for swarm systems. arXiv preprint arXiv:1709.06011 (2017)
11. Jang, E., Gu, S., Poole, B.: Categorical reparameterization with gumbel-softmax. arXiv preprint arXiv:1611.01144 (2016)
12. Kim, W., Sung, Y.: An adaptive entropy-regularization framework for multi-agent reinforcement learning. In: International Conference on Machine Learning, pp. 16829–16852. PMLR (2023)
13. Kurach, K., et al.: Google research football: a novel reinforcement learning environment **34**(04), 4501–4510 (2020)
14. Lhaksmana, K.M., Murakami, Y., Ishida, T.: Role-based modeling for designing agent behavior in self-organizing multi-agent systems. Int. J. Software Eng. Knowl. Eng. **28**(01), 79–96 (2018)
15. Li, C., Wang, T., Wu, C., Zhao, Q., Yang, J., Zhang, C.: Celebrating diversity in shared multi-agent reinforcement learning. Adv. Neural. Inf. Process. Syst. **34**, 3991–4002 (2021)
16. Liu, B., Liu, Q., Stone, P., Garg, A., Zhu, Y., Anandkumar, A.: Coach-player multi-agent reinforcement learning for dynamic team composition. In: International Conference on Machine Learning, pp. 6860–6870. PMLR (2021)
17. Liu, Y., Li, Y., Xu, X., Dou, Y., Liu, D.: Heterogeneous skill learning for multi-agent tasks. Adv. Neural. Inf. Process. Syst. **35**, 37011–37023 (2022)
18. Lowe, R., Wu, Y.I., Tamar, A., Harb, J., Pieter Abbeel, O., Mordatch, I.: Multi-agent actor-critic for mixed cooperative-competitive environments. In: Advances in Neural Information Processing Systems, p. 30 (2017)
19. Oliehoek, F.A., Amato, C.: A Concise Introduction to Decentralized POMDPs, vol. 1, Springer (2016)
20. Qu, Y., et al.: Hokoff: real game dataset from honor of kings and its offline reinforcement learning benchmarks. Adv. Neural. Inf. Process. Syst. **36**, 22166–22190 (2023)
21. Rashid, T., Samvelyan, M., De Witt, C.S., Farquhar, G., Foerster, J., Whiteson, S.: Monotonic value function factorisation for deep multi-agent reinforcement learning. J. Mach. Learn. Res. **21**(178), 1–51 (2020)

22. Samvelyan, M., et al.: The starcraft multi-agent challenge. arXiv preprint arXiv:1902.04043 (2019)
23. Terry, J.K., Grammel, N., Hari, A., Santos, L., Black, B., Manocha, D.: Parameter sharing is surprisingly useful for multi-agent deep reinforcement learning. arXiv preprint arXiv:2005.13625. p. 30 (2020)
24. Vinyals, O., et al.: Grandmaster level in starcraft ii using multi-agent reinforcement learning. Nature **575**(7782), 350–354 (2019)
25. Wang, T., Dong, H., Lesser, V., Zhang, C.: Roma: multi-agent reinforcement learning with emergent roles. arXiv preprint arXiv:2003.08039 (2020)
26. Wang, T., Gupta, T., Mahajan, A., Peng, B., Whiteson, S., Zhang, C.: Rode: learning roles to decompose multi-agent tasks. arXiv preprint arXiv:2010.01523 (2020)
27. Yang, M., Zhao, J., Hu, X., Zhou, W., Zhu, J., Li, H.: Ldsa: learning dynamic subtask assignment in cooperative multi-agent reinforcement learning. Adv. Neural. Inf. Process. Syst. **35**, 1698–1710 (2022)
28. Yang, Y., et al.: Qatten: a general framework for cooperative multiagent reinforcement learning. arXiv preprint arXiv:2002.03939 (2020)

FairFinGAN: Fairness-Aware Synthetic Financial Data Generation

Tai Le Quy[1(✉)], Dung Nguyen Tuan[2], Trung Nguyen Thanh[2], Duy Tran Cong[2], Huyen Giang Thi Thu[3], and Frank Hopfgartner[1,4]

[1] University of Koblenz, Koblenz, Germany
{tailequy,hopfgartner}@uni-koblenz.de
[2] Hanoi University of Science and Technology, Hanoi, Vietnam
[3] Banking Academy of Vietnam, Hanoi, Vietnam
huyengtt@hvnh.edu.vn
[4] University of Sheffield, Sheffield, UK

Abstract. Financial datasets often suffer from bias that can lead to unfair decision-making in automated systems. In this work, we propose FairFinGAN, a WGAN-based framework designed to generate synthetic financial data while mitigating bias with respect to the protected attribute. Our approach incorporates fairness constraints directly into the training process through a classifier, ensuring that the synthetic data is both fair and preserves utility for downstream predictive tasks. We evaluate our proposed model on five real-world financial datasets and compare it with existing GAN-based data generation methods. Experimental results show that our approach achieves superior fairness metrics without significant loss in data utility, demonstrating its potential as a tool for bias-aware data generation in financial applications.

Keywords: bias · fairness · financial data · GAN · synthetic data

1 Introduction

Data play a crucial role in automated decision-making systems within financial organizations. However, accessing and sharing financial data remain difficult and challenging due to privacy concerns. Hence, synthetic data generation offers an efficient solution for the research community [2], because such generative models provide scalable, privacy-protecting substitutes for datasets that cannot be shared because of sensitivity or ownership constraints [16]. In addition, machine learning (ML) models used in critical domains such as finance often exhibit bias toward individuals or demographic groups defined by protected attributes, such as gender, race, or age [8,11]. These biases may come from multiple sources, such as historical discrimination, data collection processes, and algorithmic shortcomings [12]. More importantly, concerns have emerged that synthetic data may reproduce or even amplify the underlying biases present in the original data [16].

To this end, we aim to address fairness at the data level in the finance domain, i.e., generating fair synthetic data, focusing on tabular data which is the most

R. C.-W. Wong et al. (Eds.): PAKDD 2026, LNAI 16618, pp. 190–202, 2027.
https://doi.org/10.1007/978-981-92-1947-6_16

widely used type in real-world settings. In general, fair data are defined as data that achieve statistical parity with respect to a known protected attribute and the target variable [9,15]. In addition, since classifiers trained on fairness-aware generated data are expected to produce fair outcomes [5], we further evaluate the fairness of classifiers trained on the generated data.

In this paper, we propose a framework for generating fair synthetic financial data using GAN, namely FairFinGAN. Our contributions are as follows: (i) we introduce FairFinGAN, a WGAN-based framework for fairness-aware synthetic financial data generation; (ii) we propose a training strategy that incorporates fairness constraints, specifically statistical parity and equalized odds, into the GAN objective based on a multi-layer perceptron classifier on generated samples, to mitigate bias at the dataset level; (iii) we conduct extensive experiments on five real-world financial datasets, showing that FairFinGAN improves fairness while preserving utility compared to baseline methods.

The rest of our paper is structured as follows. Section 2 gives an overview of the related work. The technical description of the proposed FairFinGAN model is presented in Sect. 3. Section 4 describes the details of our experiments on various datasets. Finally, the conclusion and outlook are summarized in Sect. 5.

2 Related Work

Earlier methods for generating tabular data relied on statistical models to preserve the joint distribution of mixed-type data [2,20]. Then, the creation of deep-generative models, such as generative adversarial networks (GANs) [7], represents a significant acceleration of the field. For example, MedGAN [4] used auto-encoders and GANs for the synthesis of high-dimensional binary medical records, while Table-GAN [13] used convolutional architectures to generate tabular data. CTGAN [20] incorporated mode-specific normalization as well as a conditional generator to handle mixed-type data, imbalanced categorical columns, and multi-modal continuous distributions.

In responding to the perpetuation of bias in synthetic data, efforts shifted progressively towards table generation of tabular data with fairness. Such generators work towards generations of realistic data and fairness constraint information, e.g., demographic parity, equalized odds. FairGAN [18] was one of the pioneering GAN-based frameworks to generate fair information. Using an auxiliary discriminator to ensure the independence from protected information, FairGAN was able to suppress disparate impact in the resulting synthetic data. Later, FairGAN+ [19] achieves both fair data generation and classification by jointly training the generative model and the classifier through adversarial games involving multiple discriminators. Subsequently, TabFairGAN [15] was introduced as an extension of the Wasserstein GAN (WGAN) [1] for tabular data, incorporating a fairness penalty in generator loss. TabFairGAN demonstrated improved stability and performance compared to previous GAN-based tabular data generators, and outperformed pre-processing techniques such as reweighting and disparate impact removal on multiple benchmark datasets. More recent methods include information-theoretic and representation-learning approaches, such as information-minimizing GANs [3], which minimize mutual information between protected attributes, generated data, and classifier outputs, while simultaneously maximizing both utility and fairness.

Beyond GAN-based approaches, DECAF [17] incorporates structural causal information and applies inference-time debiasing by constraining unbiased edges during data generation. This approach highlights the need to study both the data generation process and the ways in which end-users consume generated data in fairness-aware learning. In addition, PreFair [14] and FLAI library [6] employ causal Bayesian networks to generate fair synthetic data through structural and conditional probability modifications of the causal model. They can simultaneously mitigate multiple biases by defining clear, interpretable fairness mechanisms and supporting counterfactual reasoning.

3 Proposed Method

In this section, we present *FairFinGAN*, a WGAN-based fairness-aware synthetic financial data generator, inspired by the TabFairGAN [15] approach. The main idea is to employ a second training phase to penalize the discrimination score in the generated data. We use a Multi-Layer Perceptron (MLP) classifier trained on the original dataset to calculate fairness scores on generated samples as a loss component. The network is then iteratively updated based on this loss to improve its fairness performance. We define two versions, namely *FairFinGAN-SP* that uses statistical parity (SP) to score the fairness of the MLP classifier, and *FairFinGAN-EOd*, which scores with the equalized odds (EOd).

We denote $\mathcal{D} = (\mathcal{X}, \mathcal{Y}, \mathcal{S})$ as a dataset with a set of attributes $\mathcal{X}$, a class labels set $\mathcal{Y} = \{0, 1\}$ and protected attributes $\mathcal{S} = \{0, 1\}$, i.e., each data point $d^{(i)} = (x, y, s)$. The dataset contains N_{num} numerical and N_{cat} categorical attributes.

The Training Process. The FairFinGAN model training process consists of two phases, as visualized in Fig. 1. In phase 1, both the generator (G) and the critic (C) participate in the adversarial process, aiming to generate samples as realistically as possible. The generator and critic parameters, denoted by w_G and w_C, are updated by the backpropagation method, and the backward propagation is demonstrated by red flows in Fig. 1. Then, in phase 2, an MLP classifier, denoted by $\mathcal{H}$ with parameters $w_{\mathcal{H}}$, trained on real data $\mathcal{D}$, is used to evaluate the fairness of the classification on the new data generated by the generator after the first phase. The fairness metrics SP and EOd (denoted as $f(I, Y', S')$) are then considered as part of the loss function, with a parameter $\lambda_{fair} > 0$.

In particular, each noise vector z is sampled from the normal distribution P_z. Let $G(z) = (x', y', s')$ denote one synthetic sample generated by the generator G, where x' is the set of attributes, s' is the protected attribute, and y' is the class label. A batch of generated samples is denoted as (X', Y', S'), then will be criticized by the critic part of the network. In addition, we use $I = \mathcal{H}(X', S')$ to denote the predicted soft label (differentiable) obtained via Gumbel-Softmax on the synthetic data. The formal description of the training process is illustrated in

Algorithm 1. Two versions employing different fairness measures (SP and EOd) are depicted in lines 21 and 22, respectively.

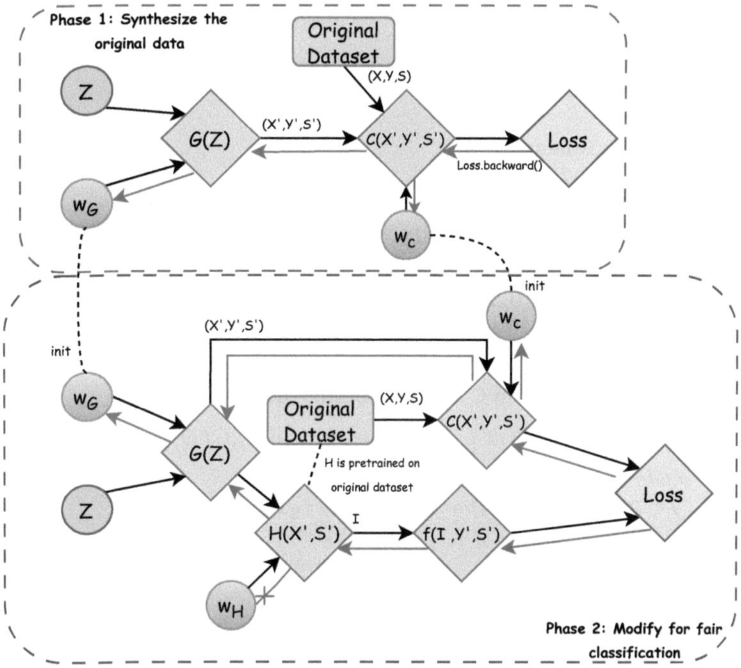

Fig. 1. Overview of the FairFinGAN model.

Neural Network Architecture. The architecture of the generator G is defined as follows:

$$\begin{cases} h_0 = z \\ h_1 = \text{ReLu}(FC_{N_{dim} \to N_{dim}}(h_0)) \\ h_2 = \text{ReLu}(FC_{N_{dim} \to N_{num}}(h_1)) \bigoplus \text{gumbel}_{0.2}(FC_{N_{dim} \to N_1}(h_1)) \bigoplus \\ \text{gumbel}_{0.2}(FC_{N_{dim} \to N_2}(h_1)) \bigoplus \ldots \bigoplus \text{gumbel}_{0.2}(FC_{N_{dim} \to N_{cat}}(h_1)) \end{cases}$$

In which, z denotes a latent vector; $FC_{a \to b}$ denotes a fully connected layer with input size a and output size b; ReLu(v) is the `ReLu` activation applied to the vector input v; gumbel$_\tau(v)$ denotes applying `Gumbel` softmax with parameter τ on a vector v (in our case $\tau = 0.2$); $\bigoplus$ denotes the concatenation of vectors; N_{dim} is the dimension of a transformed data instance, and N_i with $i = 1 \ldots N_{cat}$ is the dimension of the one-hot encoding vector of the i-th discrete attribute. In addition, the critic C is constructed as follows, where the `negative_slope` parameter of the `LeakyReLU` function is set to its default value of 0.01.

$$\begin{cases} h_0 = v \\ h_1 = \text{LeakyReLu}(FC_{N_{dim} \to N_{dim}}(h_0)) \\ h_2 = \text{LeakyReLu}(FC_{N_{dim} \to N_{dim}}(h_1)) \end{cases}$$

Algorithm 1: Training process of the FairFinGAN model

Input: Training data $\mathcal{D}$, $total\_epochs$, $fair\_epochs$, λ_{fair}, λ_{pen}, n_{critic}
Output: Generator G, critic C

Train a classifier $\mathcal{H}$ on $\mathcal{D}$
for $epoch \leftarrow 1$ **to** $total\_epochs$ **do**
  if $epoch \leq total\_epochs - fair\_epochs$ **then**
    mode $\leftarrow$ `accuracy`
  else
    mode $\leftarrow$ `fairness`
  foreach *batch in* $\mathcal{D}$ **do**
    for $k \leftarrow 1$ **to** n_{critic} **do**
      Sample batch m real data $D = (X, Y, S) = \{d^{(1)}, \ldots, d^{(m)}\}$
      Sample m noises $Z = \{z^{(1)}, \ldots, z^{(m)}\} \sim P(z)$
      Sample $\varepsilon \sim \mathcal{U}(0, 1)$
      Generate $D' = (X', Y', S') \leftarrow \{G(z^{(1)}), \ldots, G(z^{(m)})\}$
      Compute $\hat{D} = (\hat{X}, \hat{Y}, \hat{S}) \leftarrow \varepsilon(D) + (1 - \varepsilon)(D')$
      Update the critic C by descending the gradient:
      $\frac{1}{m} \nabla_{w_C} \sum_{i=1}^{m} C(D') - C(D) + \lambda_{pen} \left(\left\| \nabla_{\hat{D}} C(\hat{D}) \right\|_2 - 1 \right)^2$
    if *mode* = *accuracy* **then**
      `/* Phase 1. Synthesize the original data */`
      Sample m noises $Z = \{z^{(1)}, \ldots, z^{(m)}\} \sim P(z)$
      Update the generator G: $\frac{1}{m} \nabla_{w_G} \sum_{i=1}^{m} -(C(G(z^{(i)})))$
    else
      `/* Phase 2. Modify for fair classification */`
      Generate $D' = (X', Y', S') \leftarrow \{G(z^{(1)}), \ldots, G(z^{(m)})\}$
      $I = \{I^{(1)}, \ldots, I^{(m)}\} \leftarrow \{\mathcal{H}(G(z^{(1)})), \ldots, \mathcal{H}(G(z^{(m)}))\}$
      Update the generator G (`FairFinGAN-SP`):
      $\frac{1}{m} \nabla_{w_G} \sum_{i=1}^{m} -C(D') + \lambda_{fair} \left| \frac{\sum_{i:s'_i=0} I^{(i)}}{\sum_{i:s'_i=0} 1} - \frac{\sum_{i:s'_i=1} I^{(i)}}{\sum_{i:s'_i=1} 1} \right|$
      Or, update the generator G (`FairFinGAN-EOd`):
      $\frac{1}{m} \nabla_{w_G} \sum_{i=1}^{m} -C(D') +$
      $\lambda_{fair} \sum_{y \in \{0,1\}} \left| \frac{\sum_{i:s'_i=0,\, y'_i=y} I^{(i)}}{\sum_{i:s'_i=0,\, y'_i=y} 1} - \frac{\sum_{i:s'_i=1,\, y'_i=y} I^{(i)}}{\sum_{i:s'_i=1,\, y'_i=y} 1} \right|$
return G, C;

The classifier $\mathcal{H}$ (MLP) is implemented with two hidden layers and its architecture is defined as follows, where v is an input vector.

$$\begin{cases} h_0 = v \\ h_1 = \text{ReLU}(FC_{N_{dim} \to 128}(h_0)) \\ h_2 = \text{ReLU}(FC_{128 \to 64}(h_1)) \\ h_3 = FC_{64, \to 2}(h_2) \end{cases}$$

4 Evaluation

In this section, we evaluate our proposed method on five real-world datasets and two state-of-the-art GAN-based data generators. The source code is available at https://github.com/tailequy/FairFinGAN

4.1 Experimental Setups

We evaluate our generative methods on five commonly used datasets in the finance and fairness-aware ML domains. All datasets are imbalanced, which is indicated by the imbalance ratio (IR) in Table 1. Gaussian normalization is applied to the continuous attributes, whereas categorical attributes are encoded using one-hot encoding. The protected attribute "Age" in the Credit card and Credit scoring datasets is binarized into $\{25\text{–}65, < 25 \text{ or } 65\}$ following [11].

Table 1. An overview of financial datasets

Datasets	#Instances	#Instances (cleaned)	#Attributes	Protected attribute(s)	Class label (positive)	IR (+:-)
Adult	48,842	45,222	15	Gender, Race	$> 50K$	1:3.03
Credit card	30,000	30,000	24	Sex, Age	Default (1)	1:3.52
Credit scoring	8,755	8,755	17	Sex, Age	Good credit (1)	11.58:1
Dutch census	60,420	60,420	12	Sex	Occupation (1)	1:1.10
German credit	1,000	1,000	21	Sex	Good credit (1)	2.33:1

We generate a synthetic dataset containing the same number of records as the real-world dataset. To quantify the quality of the synthetic data, we employ four traditional classifiers, including Logistic Regression (LR), Decision Tree (DT), k-nearest neighbors (kNN), and MLP. We use these models because fairness-aware predictive models may make evaluation difficult, as they can self-adjust to produce fairer prediction results. Predictive models are evaluated with the 5-fold cross-validation strategy and average results are reported. The default hyperparameters of these predictive models are used as implemented in the scikit-learn library. Then, we compare our proposed method with the following state-of-the-art GAN-based models: CTGAN [20] and TabFairGAN [15]. We use the default hyperparameters of these models as reported in the original papers. The hyperparameters in our proposed models are set as follows: learning rate = 0.0002 (for the generator and critic), learning rate = 0.0001 (for the fairness-aware generator in the second phase), total epochs = 200, fair epochs = 50, batch size = 256,

$\lambda_{fair} = 0.5$, $\lambda_{pen} = 10$ and $n_{critic} = 4$. The generative models were executed in the Kaggle environment (https://www.kaggle.com/) equipped with a P100 GPU, 16 GB of RAM and 200 GB of storage.

4.2 Experimental Results

At the dataset level, we computed the SP values to assess the fairness of the original and synthetic datasets. The best values are in **bold**, and the second-best values are in *italic*. Our models achieve the best or second-best values in most datasets with various protected attributes (Table 2).

Table 2. The statistical parity on original and synthetic datasets

Dataset-Prot. attr.	Original	CTGAN	TabFairGan	FairFinGAN-SP	FairFinGAN-EOd
Adult-Gender	0.1989	0.1474	**0.0273**	*0.1371*	0.1989
Adult-Race	0.1040	*0.0668*	−0.7533	−0.6534	**0.0043**
Credit card-Sex	*0.0339*	−0.0347	0.0344	**0.0164**	0.0407
Credit card-Age	−0.0557	*0.0494*	−0.0966	**−0.0081**	−0.1679
German credit-Sex	0.0748	0.0235	−0.0577	**0.0118**	*0.0172*
Credit scoring-Sex	*0.0304*	0.0854	0.0597	−0.0506	**0.0017**
Credit scoring-Age	0.0752	*0.0641*	0.1019	**0.0338**	0.0850
Dutch census-Sex	0.2985	**0.2407**	*0.2708*	0.2919	0.2873

Then, we report the performance of four classifiers w.r.t. Accuracy (Acc), Balance accuracy (BA), and seven well-known fairness measures [10], including SP, equal opportunity (EO), EOd, predictive parity (PP), predictive equality (PE), treatment equality (TE) and Absolute Between-ROC Area (ABROCA). TE can be unbounded because the number of false positives can be zero [10]. In the Adult dataset (protected attribute "Gender"), FairFinGAN achieves a reasonable trade-off between fairness and accuracy. Both variants obtain Acc and BA values slightly lower than CTGAN but higher than TabFairGAN (Table 3). The fairness (SP, ABROCA) is generally better than that of CTGAN, though not as extreme as TabFairGAN which shows a good fairness but poor predictive performance. Among them, FairFinGAN-SP achieves slightly better fairness in the LR classifier, while FairFinGAN-EOd shows a comparative result in the kNN model. For the protected attribute "Race" (Table 4), although both FairFinGAN variants show mixed results, some fairness measures (SP, EO, EOd, PP) are improved with FairFinGAN-EOd (kNN and DT), but our models are better than TabFairGAN in terms of the trade-off between fairness and accuracy.

As demonstrated in Table 5 (Credit card dataset, protected attribute "Sex"), FairFinGAN-SP achieves the highest accuracy in most predictive models, while FairFinGAN-EOd often attains the best or second-best values for fairness metrics such as EO and EOd, particularly for classifiers DT and LR. TabFairGan has

Table 3. Adult: performance of predictive models. Protected attribute: Gender

Classifier	Method	Acc	BA	SP	EO	EOd	PP	PE	TE	ABROCA
MLP	Original	*0.7742*	**0.5571**	0.0242	0.0221	0.0262	**0.0808**	0.0041	-37.0920	0.0147
	CTGAN	**0.8123**	*0.5104*	0.0047	*0.0105*	*0.0107*	0.2799	*0.0003*	−**25.5417**	0.0131
	TabFairGan	0.7193	0.5	**0.0**	**0.0**	**0.0**	nan	**0.0**	nan	**0.0001**
	FairFinGAN-SP	0.7492	0.5071	−0.0042	0.0180	0.0211	0.2662	0.0032	−107.4718	*0.0084*
kNN	Original	*0.7718*	**0.6228**	0.0689	*0.0147*	*0.0369*	0.2504	0.0222	*−2.0808*	*0.0159*
	CTGAN	**0.8127**	*0.5832*	0.0343	0.0415	0.0496	0.2751	*0.0081*	−3.2464	0.0234
	TabFairGan	0.6855	0.5438	0.0157	**0.0125**	**0.0265**	**0.0195**	0.0140	**−0.0382**	**0.0140**
	FairFinGAN-SP	0.7213	0.5454	*−0.0091*	0.0781	0.0869	*0.1171*	0.0088	−2.2987	0.0583
	FairFinGAN-EOd	0.7146	0.5635	**0.0077**	0.0749	0.0818	0.2185	**0.0069**	−2.4996	0.0398
DT	Original	*0.8094*	**0.7491**	0.1989	0.0974	0.2034	0.114	0.1060	*−0.0552*	0.0433
	CTGAN	**0.8180**	0.7123	0.1438	0.1390	0.2144	0.1627	*0.0754*	−0.0596	0.0503
	TabFairGan	0.7561	0.6983	**0.0265**	**0.0172**	**0.0389**	**0.0158**	**0.0217**	**−0.004**	**0.0149**
	FairFinGAN-SP	0.7710	0.6978	*0.1321*	*0.0514*	*0.1381*	*0.0697*	0.0867	−0.0570	*0.0313*
	FairFinGAN-EOd	0.7774	*0.7139*	0.1898	0.0874	0.2021	0.1155	0.1147	-0.1062	0.0372
LR	Original	*0.7878*	**0.6194**	0.0609	**0.0195**	*0.0341*	0.2295	0.0146	*−3.7596*	*0.0270*
	CTGAN	**0.8191**	0.5603	0.0242	*0.0222*	**0.0278**	0.2214	*0.0057*	−7.1932	**0.0189**
	TabFairGan	0.7314	0.5592	0.0348	0.0446	0.0713	*0.0798*	0.0267	5.0814	0.0461
	FairFinGAN-SP	0.7483	0.5701	**0.0010**	0.1164	0.1242	**0.0577**	0.0078	**-2.8856**	0.0884
	FairFinGAN-EOd	0.7447	*0.5718*	*0.0130*	0.0946	0.0997	0.1802	**0.0051**	−4.8309	0.0584

Table 4. Adult: performance of predictive models. Protected attribute: Race

Classifier	Method	Acc	BA	SP	EO	EOd	PP	PE	TE	ABROCA
MLP	Original	*0.7864*	**0.5986**	0.0267	0.0149	0.0212	**0.0774**	0.0063	*-2.5285*	0.0085
	CTGAN	**0.8126**	*0.5114*	0.0022	0.0067	0.0075	0.1444	0.0009	−19.7778	0.0104
	TabFairGan	0.7298	0.5001	**0.0001**	**0.0002**	**0.0003**	nan	**0.0**	nan	**0.0018**
	FairFinGAN-SP	0.7523	0.5055	−0.0723	0.0713	0.1101	0.2013	0.0388	−32.0556	0.018
kNN	Original	*0.7718*	**0.6228**	0.0414	*0.0303*	*0.0462*	*0.1255*	0.0159	*−0.898*	**0.0185**
	CTGAN	**0.8127**	*0.5832*	0.0159	0.0567	0.0612	0.1729	**0.0045**	−1.6905	0.0372
	TabFairGan	0.7043	0.5556	*−0.137*	0.0614	0.1792	0.6318	0.1206	nan	0.1714
	FairFinGAN-SP	0.7283	0.5503	−0.4425	0.4022	0.7826	0.5512	0.3804	3.5177	0.2073
	FairFinGAN-EOd	0.7191	0.5623	**0.0016**	**0.0257**	**0.0350**	**0.0416**	*0.0092*	**0.0571**	*0.0340*
DT	Original	*0.8099*	**0.7498**	0.0877	*0.0324*	*0.0692*	*0.0905*	0.0368	-0.1993	*0.0203*
	CTGAN	**0.8170**	0.7127	*0.0504*	0.1214	0.1280	0.1665	**0.0065**	−0.159	0.0592
	TabFairGan	0.7730	*0.7130*	−0.7518	0.4816	1.3313	0.485	0.8433	*−0.1034*	0.1809
	FairFinGAN-SP	0.7668	0.6901	−0.5776	0.3270	0.7277	0.4058	0.4007	1.9027	0.1203
	FairFinGAN-EOd	0.7710	0.7001	**0.0087**	**0.0235**	**0.0344**	**0.0126**	*0.0109*	**0.0382**	**0.0153**
LR	Original	*0.7878*	**0.6194**	*0.0155*	*0.0452*	*0.0561*	*0.1467*	*0.0109*	−2.9489	**0.0367**
	CTGAN	**0.8191**	*0.5603*	**0.0018**	**0.0344**	**0.0443**	0.2392	**0.0098**	−7.3517	*0.0451*
	TabFairGan	0.7265	0.5498	−0.1174	0.0485	0.1044	0.5678	0.0656	nan	0.1982
	FairFinGAN-SP	0.7584	0.5544	−0.6167	0.5800	1.0027	0.4223	0.4227	*−0.9967*	0.2218
	FairFinGAN-EOd	0.7455	0.5431	−0.0243	0.0699	0.0826	**0.0767**	0.0127	**0.0387**	0.0485

good results in the case of MLP classifier but suffers from missing value in TE. For the protected attribute "Age" (Table 6), FairFinGAN-EOd achieves the best or second-best fairness measures (EO, EOd, PP, and ABROCA) with the MLP and LR classifier, while the baseline TabFairGan shows strong performance in accuracy for MLP and DT, as well as moderate quality w.r.t. fairness.

Table 5. Credit card: performance of predictive models. Protected attribute: Sex

Classifier	Method	Acc	BA	SP	EO	EOd	PP	PE	TE	ABROCA
MLP	Original	*0.7786*	0.5	0.0002	*0.0008*	0.0011	*0.2500*	0.0003	*72.0834*	0.0014
	CTGAN	0.7727	*0.5005*	–0.0003	0.003	0.0041	0.4833	0.0011	**–34.8333**	0.0027
	TabFairGan	0.7708	0.5003	**–0.0001**	**0.0004**	**0.0004**	**0.0**	**0.0**	nan	**0.0009**
	FairFinGAN-SP	**0.7829**	**0.5009**	0.0002	0.0014	0.0019	0.4667	0.0005	nan	*0.0011*
kNN	Original	0.7560	0.5506	*0.0140*	*0.0163*	*0.0251*	0.0465	**0.0088**	–0.2803	**0.0101**
	CTGAN	0.7453	0.5589	**–0.0109**	**0.0091**	**0.0205**	*0.0244*	*0.0114*	*0.2514*	0.0124
	TabFairGan	*0.8054*	**0.6683**	0.0869	0.1226	0.1835	0.0613	0.0608	1.7007	0.0177
	FairFinGAN-SP	**0.8095**	*0.6547*	0.0199	0.0264	0.0423	**0.0229**	0.0159	0.3308	0.0234
DT	Original	0.7246	0.613	0.0377	0.0478	0.0774	0.0343	0.0297	**–0.0132**	*0.0199*
	CTGAN	0.7559	0.6599	**–0.0227**	*0.0443*	*0.0534*	0.0686	**0.0091**	0.0908	0.0213
	TabFairGan	**0.8006**	**0.7204**	0.0637	0.0607	0.1055	*0.0228*	0.0448	0.2708	0.0247
	FairFinGAN-SP	*0.7951*	*0.704*	0.0371	0.0678	0.0877	**0.0186**	0.0199	0.1847	0.0263
	FairFinGAN-EOd	0.7673	0.6717	*0.0330*	**0.0334**	**0.0500**	0.0508	*0.0166*	*-0.0637*	**0.0128**
LR	Original	0.7788	0.5001	**–0.0001**	**0.0005**	**0.0007**	1.0	**0.0002**	nan	*0.0185*
	CTGAN	0.7773	0.5368	-0.0142	0.0288	0.0354	0.0609	0.0067	**–1.3176**	0.0222
	TabFairGan	*0.8085*	*0.6148*	0.0572	0.1121	0.1421	0.0858	0.0300	9.6583	**0.0164**
	FairFinGAN-SP	**0.8236**	**0.6394**	0.0332	0.0941	0.1051	**0.0242**	0.0109	*1.7570*	0.0607
	FairFinGAN-EOd	0.8064	0.5963	*0.0094*	*0.0158*	*0.0187*	*0.0516*	*0.0029*	–1.9989	0.0198

In the Credit scoring dataset (protected attribute "Sex"), FairFinGAN-EOd achieves the best or second-best fairness results (SP, EO, EOd, PP, and TE) while maintaining competitive accuracy (Table 7) across all predictive models. Moreover, FairFinGAN-SP shows balanced performance with high accuracy and improved fairness (SP, protected attribute "Age") in several classifiers (MLP and LR). FairFinGAN-EOd achieves competitive fairness in some models but with a minor trade-off in accuracy. TabFairGan performs well in accuracy, but tends to exhibit weaker fairness across most fairness measures (Table 8).

Table 9 presents the results on the Dutch census dataset. Across all classifiers, FairFinGAN-EOd achieves the highest accuracy while maintaining good fairness performance (EO, EOd, PP). In contrast, FairFinGAN-SP reduces accuracy, but yields the smallest deviations on fairness measures, especially SP across all classifiers. CTGAN and TabFairGAN often introduce notable drops in accuracy. In the German credit dataset (Table 10), FairFinGAN-SP produces good results in terms of fairness (SP, EO, EOd, and ABROCA), especially for LR and DT classifiers, although sometimes with reduced accuracy. FairFinGAN-EOd improves fairness in the MLP and DT classifiers. Interestingly, CTGAN often yields the highest accuracy and fairness (EO, EOd) across all classifiers.

Table 6. Credit card: performance of predictive models. Protected attribute: Age

Classifier	Method	Acc	BA	SP	EO	EOd	PP	PE	TE	ABROCA
MLP	Original	0.7787	0.5001	0.0004	0.0005	0.0008	nan	*0.0003*	nan	*0.0019*
	CTGAN	0.7727	**0.5009**	0.0008	0.0034	0.0045	0.4318	0.0011	−122.2619	0.0140
	TabFairGan	**0.7837**	0.5	*0.0003*	*0.0003*	*0.0006*	nan	**0.0002**	nan	**0.0007**
	FairFinGAN-SP	0.7797	0.5	**0.0002**	*0.0003*	**0.0005**	nan	**0.0002**	nan	0.0042
kNN	Original	0.7560	0.5506	−0.0582	0.0683	0.1153	*0.0524*	0.0469	*−0.6795*	*0.0349*
	CTGAN	0.7453	0.5589	**0.0086**	0.0462	**0.0555**	0.1244	**0.0093**	**−0.6202**	0.0411
	TabFairGan	*0.7771*	*0.5918*	*−0.0306*	*0.0413*	*0.0681*	**0.0516**	*0.0268*	0.8689	0.0617
	FairFinGAN-SP	0.7565	0.5619	−0.0401	**0.0380**	0.0901	0.1081	0.0520	−0.9165	0.0598
	FairFinGAN-EOd	**0.7786**	**0.5934**	−0.0809	0.0881	0.1172	0.1896	0.0291	1.3108	**0.0183**
DT	Original	0.7238	0.612	−0.0730	**0.0398**	0.1084	*0.0333*	0.0685	**−0.0720**	**0.0252**
	CTGAN	0.7554	0.6606	**0.0285**	0.0690	**0.0950**	0.0690	**0.0261**	−0.1515	*0.0320*
	TabFairGan	**0.7801**	**0.6811**	−0.0783	*0.0401*	*0.1049*	**0.0330**	0.0647	*0.1508*	0.0412
	FairFinGAN-SP	*0.7647*	*0.6664*	*−0.0667*	0.0997	0.1534	0.0372	*0.0536*	−0.3464	0.0348
	FairFinGAN-EOd	0.7588	0.6583	−0.1396	0.1134	0.1862	0.1646	0.0728	0.2177	0.0345
LR	Original	0.7788	0.5001	**0.0001**	**0.0003**	**0.0004**	nan	**0.0001**	nan	*0.0269*
	CTGAN	0.7773	0.5368	0.0206	0.0470	0.0596	*0.1265*	*0.0126*	7.5732	0.0427
	TabFairGan	**0.8078**	**0.6075**	*−0.0002*	*0.0466*	0.0631	0.1456	0.0165	11.7463	0.1055
	FairFinGAN-SP	*0.7987*	*0.5791*	−0.0706	0.1286	0.1810	0.1390	0.0525	*−7.2820*	0.0426
	FairFinGAN-EOd	0.7915	0.5604	−0.0394	0.0337	*0.0467*	**0.1135**	0.0129	**4.1103**	**0.0244**

Table 7. Credit scoring: performance of predictive models. Protected attribute: Sex

Classifier	Method	Acc	BA	SP	EO	EOd	PP	PE	TE	ABROCA
MLP	Original	**0.9980**	**0.9891**	*0.0305*	**0.0006**	**0.0218**	**0.0007**	**0.0212**	**0.0**	**0.0095**
	CTGAN	0.9011	*0.8597*	0.1358	0.0650	0.1918	0.0074	0.1269	1.3611	*0.0332*
	TabFairGan	*0.9179*	0.6419	0.0477	0.0237	0.1692	0.0368	0.1455	0.1660	0.0784
	FairFinGAN-SP	0.9064	0.5430	−0.0394	0.0280	0.1429	0.0398	0.1150	−0.2089	0.0351
kNN	Original	**0.9809**	**0.9108**	0.0324	*0.0061*	**0.0626**	**0.0044**	*0.0566*	0.3963	**0.0200**
	CTGAN	0.8103	0.5890	0.0667	0.0543	0.0963	0.0753	**0.0420**	0.1817	0.0453
	TabFairGan	*0.9212*	*0.6140*	0.0384	0.0158	0.1866	0.0385	0.1708	0.1076	0.0731
	FairFinGAN-SP	0.9124	0.5436	*−0.0252*	0.0132	0.1158	0.0395	0.1027	*−0.0601*	0.0726
	FairFinGAN-EOd	0.9162	0.5826	**0.0019**	**0.0057**	*0.0631*	*0.0067*	0.0574	**0.0465**	*0.0433*
DT	Original	**0.9983**	**0.9899**	*0.0303*	**0.0002**	**0.0151**	**0.0**	**0.0149**	**0.0**	**0.0076**
	CTGAN	0.8702	*0.7965*	0.0804	0.0268	0.0730	0.0320	0.0462	−0.1304	0.0230
	TabFairGan	*0.8778*	0.6398	0.0639	0.0416	0.1814	0.0370	0.1398	−0.0896	0.0619
	FairFinGAN-SP	0.8512	0.5617	−0.0530	0.0448	0.1194	0.0421	0.0746	0.0912	0.0248
	FairFinGAN-EOd	0.8660	0.6148	**−0.0008**	*0.0088*	*0.0534*	*0.0069*	*0.0446*	*−0.0459*	*0.0191*
LR	Original	**0.9959**	**0.9893**	0.0313	**0.0014**	**0.0183**	**0.0002**	**0.0169**	**0.0**	**0.0080**
	CTGAN	0.8973	*0.8083*	0.0935	0.0390	0.0919	0.0320	*0.0529*	0.2784	*0.0356*
	TabFairGan	*0.9309*	0.6403	0.0420	0.0146	0.2118	0.0341	0.1971	0.1680	0.0451
	FairFinGAN-SP	0.9189	0.5435	*−0.0244*	0.0111	0.1252	0.0385	0.1141	−0.0865	0.0364
	FairFinGAN-EOd	0.9247	0.6186	**0.0045**	*0.0080*	*0.0745*	*0.0053*	0.0664	*0.0724*	0.0546

Table 8. Credit scoring: performance of predictive models. Protected attribute: Age

Classifier	Method	Acc	BA	SP	EO	EOd	PP	PE	TE	ABROCA
MLP	Original	**0.9979**	**0.9898**	0.0814	**0.0035**	**0.0291**	**0.0080**	**0.0256**	**0.0**	**0.0087**
	CTGAN	0.8917	*0.7734*	*0.0581*	0.0199	0.1016	*0.0257*	0.0818	0.2029	*0.0328*
	TabFairGan	0.9285	0.6398	0.1069	0.0580	0.2591	0.0547	0.2011	0.3632	0.0750
	FairFinGAN-SP	*0.9349*	0.5112	**0.0124**	*0.0126*	*0.0391*	0.0336	*0.0265*	*0.0945*	0.0751
kNN	Original	**0.9809**	**0.9108**	0.0817	**0.0068**	0.0861	**0.0155**	0.0793	*0.0548*	**0.0267**
	CTGAN	0.8103	0.5890	*0.0240*	0.0209	*0.0823*	0.0539	*0.0615*	-0.0785	0.0507
	TabFairGan	0.9310	*0.6204*	0.0682	0.0245	0.1822	0.0623	0.1577	0.0550	0.0564
	FairFinGAN-SP	*0.9342*	0.5097	**0.0069**	*0.0082*	**0.0237**	*0.0337*	**0.0154**	**0.0139**	*0.0292*
	FairFinGAN-EOd	0.9029	0.5874	0.0471	0.0412	0.1106	0.0765	0.0694	0.1130	0.0479
DT	Original	**0.9982**	**0.9892**	*0.0792*	**0.0001**	**0.0276**	**0.0081**	**0.0275**	**0.0**	**0.0138**
	CTGAN	0.8717	*0.7988*	0.0796	*0.0387*	*0.1062*	*0.0202*	*0.0675*	0.2560	0.0368
	TabFairGan	*0.8866*	0.6229	0.0951	0.0583	0.2334	0.0646	0.1751	-0.1897	0.0733
	FairFinGAN-SP	0.8834	0.5425	**0.0599**	0.0565	0.1557	0.0296	0.0992	0.3557	0.0379
	FairFinGAN-EOd	0.8660	0.6370	0.0943	0.0725	0.1422	0.0626	0.0697	*0.0523*	*0.0337*
LR	Original	**0.9959**	**0.9893**	0.0809	*0.0049*	*0.0321*	**0.0081**	*0.0272*	**0.0**	**0.0135**
	CTGAN	0.8973	*0.8083*	0.0708	0.0175	0.0992	*0.0185*	0.0817	0.1921	*0.0355*
	TabFairGan	0.9399	0.6338	0.0806	0.0242	0.2503	0.0502	0.2261	0.1731	0.0451
	FairFinGAN-SP	*0.9400*	0.5040	**0.0038**	**0.0033**	**0.0176**	0.0326	**0.0143**	*0.0221*	0.0448
	FairFinGAN-EOd	0.9172	0.6040	*0.0629*	0.0345	0.1614	0.0594	0.1269	0.2132	0.0657

Table 9. Dutch census: performance of predictive models. Protected attribute: Sex

Classifier	Method	Acc	BA	SP	EO	EOd	PP	PE	TE	ABROCA
MLP	Original	*0.8021*	*0.8036*	0.3565	0.0945	0.3732	0.0382	0.2788	0.2509	*0.0307*
	CTGAN	0.8017	0.7919	*0.2750*	0.1467	0.2874	0.0556	**0.1407**	0.7251	**0.0186**
	TabFairGan	0.7682	0.7657	0.3599	0.2106	0.4634	*0.0312*	0.2528	1.2062	0.0407
	FairFinGAN-SP	0.6145	0.6231	**0.1805**	*0.0608*	**0.2330**	0.1948	*0.1722*	**0.1398**	0.1004
	FairFinGAN-EOd	**0.8513**	**0.8522**	0.3340	**0.0445**	*0.2773*	**0.0234**	0.2328	*0.2323*	0.0476
kNN	Original	*0.8236*	*0.8226*	0.3250	0.0759	0.2834	**0.0131**	0.2076	0.4582	0.0475
	CTGAN	0.8145	0.8074	*0.2361*	0.0695	0.1797	0.0715	*0.1103*	*-0.0291*	*0.0217*
	TabFairGan	0.7901	0.7896	0.3048	0.1154	0.3142	0.0592	0.1987	0.3170	0.0401
	FairFinGAN-SP	0.4934	0.4934	**-0.0016**	**0.0081**	**0.0176**	0.2856	**0.0094**	-0.8618	**0.0041**
	FairFinGAN-EOd	**0.8659**	**0.8657**	0.2882	*0.0342*	*0.1648*	*0.0333*	0.1306	**0.0072**	0.0379
DT	Original	*0.8152*	*0.8139*	0.3359	0.0959	0.3189	**0.0106**	0.2229	0.6652	0.0593
	CTGAN	0.8008	0.7922	*0.2446*	*0.0832*	*0.2124*	0.0624	**0.1291**	**0.0966**	*0.0364*
	TabFairGan	0.7906	0.7890	0.2887	0.1093	0.2815	0.0618	0.1722	0.2654	**0.0390**
	FairFinGAN-SP	0.6535	0.6537	**0.1381**	0.0638	0.2877	0.1720	0.2239	-0.7600	0.1019
	FairFinGAN-EOd	**0.8609**	**0.8604**	0.2962	**0.0461**	**0.1889**	*0.0236*	*0.1429*	*0.1775*	0.0465
LR	Original	*0.8160*	*0.8148*	0.3271	0.0908	0.2986	**0.0194**	0.2078	0.4886	*0.0302*
	CTGAN	0.8159	0.8065	*0.2155*	*0.0641*	*0.1489*	0.0846	*0.0848*	**-0.2971**	**0.0205**
	TabFairGan	0.7325	0.7306	0.2574	0.1097	0.2821	0.1183	0.1725	*-0.1608*	0.0330
	FairFinGAN-SP	0.7574	0.7562	**0.1204**	0.1518	0.2297	0.1198	**0.0779**	-1.6286	0.1241
	FairFinGAN-EOd	**0.8415**	**0.8400**	0.2483	**0.0288**	**0.1381**	*0.0470*	0.1094	-0.5412	0.0536

Table 10. German credit: performance of predictive models. Protected attribute: Sex

Classifier	Method	Acc	BA	SP	EO	EOd	PP	PE	TE	ABROCA
MLP	Original	0.4830	0.4974	*-0.0200*	0.0215	0.0456	0.1651	0.0241	-1.9444	0.0867
	CTGAN	**0.7784**	0.5017	0.0194	**0.0199**	*0.0370*	*0.0240*	*0.0172*	**0.0858**	**0.0216**
	TabFairGan	*0.7300*	**0.5143**	-0.0270	0.0281	0.0559	0.0704	0.0278	*-0.1697*	0.0533
	FairFinGAN-SP	0.5774	0.5072	0.0413	0.0449	0.0758	**0.0218**	0.0309	0.5652	*0.0285*
kNN	Original	0.6660	*0.5376*	**0.0004**	0.0161	0.0312	0.0766	0.0151	-0.1756	0.0786
	CTGAN	**0.7851**	0.5022	0.0102	**0.0122**	**0.0201**	*0.0252*	**0.0079**	0.0238	**0.0184**
	TabFairGan	*0.7150*	**0.5412**	-0.0116	0.0245	0.1302	0.0553	0.1058	0.1195	0.0930
	FairFinGAN-SP	0.6761	0.4976	*-0.0018*	*0.0130*	*0.0279*	**0.0173**	*0.0149*	*-0.0197*	*0.0209*
DT	Original	**0.6870**	**0.6307**	0.0224	0.0626	0.1565	0.0576	0.0939	-0.3367	0.0776
	CTGAN	*0.6824*	*0.5148*	0.0270	*0.0269*	*0.0572*	*0.0235*	*0.0303*	**0.0007**	*0.0110*
	TabFairGan	0.6010	0.5011	-0.0524	0.0972	0.1782	0.0758	0.0810	0.1844	0.0666
	FairFinGAN-SP	0.6025	0.5041	*0.0112*	**0.0160**	**0.0323**	**0.0162**	**0.0164**	*0.0052*	**0.0040**
	FairFinGAN-EOd	0.5720	0.5147	**0.0002**	0.0583	0.1825	0.0815	0.1242	-0.0229	0.0721
LR	Original	0.7210	**0.6017**	0.0453	0.0345	0.1831	0.0585	0.1486	-0.0999	0.0857
	CTGAN	**0.8125**	0.5	**0.0**	**0.0**	**0.0**	*0.0234*	**0.0**	**0.0**	**0.0298**
	TabFairGan	*0.7420*	0.5013	*0.0013*	*0.0022*	*0.0147*	0.0725	*0.0125*	*-0.0050*	0.0907
	FairFinGAN-SP	0.7346	0.5	**0.0**	**0.0**	**0.0**	**0.0165**	**0.0**	**0.0**	*0.0350*
	FairFinGAN-EOd	0.6700	*0.5106*	0.0083	0.0319	0.0900	0.0637	0.0581	0.0529	0.0965

In summary, the variation in fairness gains between predictive models suggests that the effectiveness of the proposed synthetic data approach depends on the underlying learning mechanism, underscoring the need for model-specific evaluation. In financial applications such as lending or credit scoring, fairness-aware data generation can help reduce historical bias, promote more equitable risk assessment, and better align automated decisions with regulatory requirements while preserving predictive performance.

5 Conclusions and Outlook

In this paper, we proposed FairFinGAN, a fairness-aware WGAN-based framework for generating synthetic financial datasets. By integrating a fairness score with a classifier into the GAN training process, our approach can address bias at the dataset level rather than at the classification level. Experimental results on five real-world financial datasets demonstrated that FairFinGAN effectively mitigates bias while maintaining data utility, outperforming existing GAN-based data generation methods. In the future, we plan to extend FairFinGAN to handle multiple protected attributes simultaneously and explore its application to other domains such as healthcare and education. Additionally, investigating more advanced fairness metrics and incorporating differential privacy could further enhance the reliability and applicability of the generated data.

References

1. Arjovsky, M., Chintala, S., Bottou, L.: Wasserstein generative adversarial networks. In: ICML 2017, pp. 214–223. PMLR (2017)
2. Assefa, S.A., Dervovic, D., Mahfouz, M., Tillman, R.E., Reddy, P., Veloso, M.: Generating synthetic data in finance: opportunities, challenges and pitfalls. In: ICAIF 2020, pp. 1–8 (2020)
3. Chen, Q., Ye, A., Zhang, Y., Chen, J., Huang, C.: Information-minimizing generative adversarial network for fair generation and classification. Neural Process. Lett. **56**(1), 36 (2024)
4. Choi, E., Biswal, S., Malin, B., Duke, J., Stewart, W.F., Sun, J.: Generating multi-label discrete patient records using generative adversarial networks. In: Machine learning for healthcare conference, pp. 286–305. PMLR (2017)
5. Duong, M.K., Conrad, S.: Trusting fair data: leveraging quality in fairness-driven data removal techniques. In: DaWaK 2024, pp. 375–380. Springer (2024)
6. González-Sendino, R., Serrano, E., Bajo, J.: Mitigating bias in artificial intelligence: fair data generation via causal models for transparent and explainable decision-making. Future Gener. Comput. Syst. **155**, 384–401 (2024)
7. Goodfellow, I., et al.: Generative adversarial networks. Commun. ACM **63**(11), 139–144 (2020)
8. Kozodoi, N., Jacob, J., Lessmann, S.: Fairness in credit scoring: Assessment, implementation and profit implications. Eur. J. Oper. Res. **297**(3), 1083–1094 (2022)
9. Krchova, I., Platzer, M., Tiwald, P.: Strong statistical parity through fair synthetic data. In: SyntheticData4ML Workshop@NeurIPS, p. 2023 (2023)
10. Quy, L., Nguyen, T., Friege, T.H., Ntoutsi, G., E.: Evaluation of group fairness measures in student performance prediction problems. In: SoGood Workshop@ECML PKDD 2022, pp. 119–136. Springer (2022)
11. Le Quy, T., Roy, A., Iosifidis, V., Zhang, W., Ntoutsi, E.: A survey on datasets for fairness-aware machine learning. WIREs DMKD **12**(3), e1452 (2022)
12. Mehrabi, N., Morstatter, F., Saxena, N., Lerman, K., Galstyan, A.: A survey on bias and fairness in machine learning. ACM Comput. Surv. **54**(6), 1–35 (2021)
13. Park, N., Mohammadi, M., Gorde, K., Jajodia, S., Park, H., Kim, Y.: Data synthesis based on generative adversarial networks. Proc. VLDB Endowment **11**(10), 1071–1083 (2018)
14. Pujol, D., Gilad, A., Machanavajjhala, A.: Prefair: privately generating justifiably fair synthetic data. Proc. VLDB Endowment **16**(6), 1573–1586 (2023)
15. Rajabi, A., Garibay, O.O.: TabFairGAN: fair tabular data generation with generative adversarial networks. Mach. Learn. Knowl. Extr. **4**(2), 488–501 (2022)
16. Sanchez Jr, D., Kotal, A.: Condfairgen a fair conditional generator for tabular data via adaptive sampling. In: CIKM 2025, pp. 5196–5201 (2025)
17. Van Breugel, B., Kyono, T., Berrevoets, J., Van der Schaar, M.: DECAF: generating fair synthetic data using causally-aware generative networks. NeurIPS **34**, 22221–22233 (2021)
18. Xu, D., Yuan, S., Zhang, L., Wu, X.: FairGAN: fairness-aware generative adversarial networks. In: Big Data, pp. 570–575. IEEE (2018)
19. Xu, D., Yuan, S., Zhang, L., Wu, X.: FairGAN+: achieving fair data generation and classification through generative adversarial nets. In: Big Data 2019, pp. 1401–1406. IEEE (2019)
20. Xu, L., Skoularidou, M., Cuesta-Infante, A., Veeramachaneni, K.: Modeling tabular data using conditional gan. In: NeurIPS, vol. 32 (2019)

Semantic-Driven Object Placement via Multi-modal Large Language Models

Xuzheng Chen[1], Gang Shen[2], Rundong Cao[2], and Guojie Song[3(✉)]

[1] School of Intelligence Science and Technology, Peking University, Beijing, China
cxz1022@stu.pku.edu.cn
[2] Innovation Center, China Tower Corporation Limited, Beijing, China
[3] National Key Lab of General AI, School of Intelligence Science and Technology, Peking University, Beijing, China
gjsong@pku.edu.cn

Abstract. The task of object placement involves integrating a foreground object into a background while ensuring appropriate position and size. Traditional methods rely on manually designed rules and deep learning models predict position and size based on learned foreground and background features. However, these methods often fail to ensure the plausibility of position and size semantically. In this paper, we propose a novel semantic-driven approach that leverages Multi-modal Large Language Models (MLLMs) to extract and represent the semantic relationships of background through a Semantic Tree structure. Thus, we can utilize the common-sense knowledge embedded in MLLMs to explore the tree, thereby selecting semantically appropriate placement position and size for the foreground. Furthermore, we design an MLLM-based scoring mechanism that scores different placement positions. In general, our approach provides a training-free, semantic-driven solution to object placement. Extensive experiments on the OPA dataset demonstrate its superiority over existing methods in terms of plausibility and diversity.

Keywords: Semantic-Driven Object Placement · Scene Understanding · Multi-modal Large Language Models

1 Introduction

Object placement [21], the process of integrating foreground objects into a background while ensuring appropriate positioning, size, and shape, is a fundamental task in computer vision and graphics. It plays a crucial role in applications such as image composition [17,21,25] where it involves strategically positioning objects within a given space to achieve functional, aesthetic, or operational goals.

Existing methods for object placement can be broadly categorized into traditional methods and deep learning-based methods. Traditional object placement methods [7,8,24] primarily relied on heuristic rules and geometric constraints, while recent advances in deep learning have enabled more context-aware

R. C.-W. Wong et al. (Eds.): PAKDD 2026, LNAI 16618, pp. 203–214, 2027.
https://doi.org/10.1007/978-981-92-1947-6_17

and semantically coherent placements. Traditional approaches typically employ rule-based systems, handcrafted features, and optimization techniques, such as Markov Random Fields (MRFs), to ensure objects are arranged in visually plausible configurations [11]. While these methods are interpretable and effective for constrained environments, they often struggle with complex, diverse scenes due to their reliance on predefined heuristics.

In contrast, deep learning-based methods [17,22,29,30,32] leverage large-scale data and neural network architectures to learn object relationships and spatial arrangements directly from images. Convolutional Neural Networks (CNNs) have been widely used for spatial prediction tasks, while Generative Adversarial Networks (GANs) [9], Variational Autoencoders (VAEs) [13], and diffusion models [10] have shown impressive results in generating realistic object placements. Transformer-based models [6] have further improved semantic understanding by capturing long-range dependencies, enhancing the contextual coherence of object placements. These advances enable automated, high-quality placement of objects across diverse and complex scenes.

However, these methods face several issues currently, including (1)unreasonable position, and (2)unreasonable size as shown in Fig. 1.

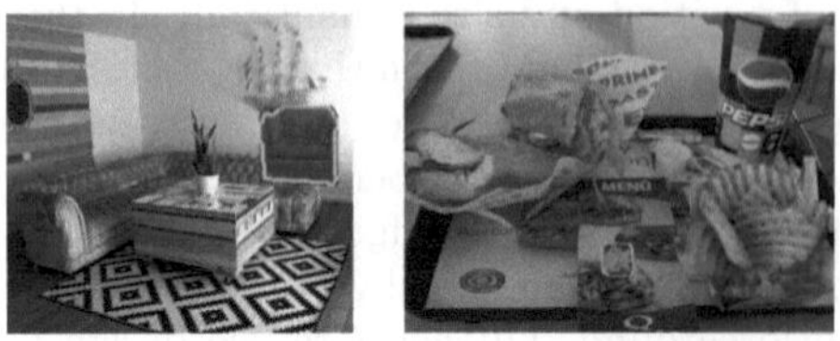

Fig. 1. Examples of current issues with object placement. The left example displayed an unreasonable position, with the sofa hanging in the air; the right example displayed an unreasonable size, the bowl appears too small compared to objects such as potato chips next to it. The inserted foreground object is marked with a green outline. (Color figure online)

These problems arise because previous methods did not formally incorporate semantics into the placement process, and the positions and sizes of foreground objects within the background were not determined based on real semantic considerations.

In fact, semantics plays a crucial role in object placement. It ensures that objects are placed in a manner that aligns with real-world physical laws and contextual norms. For example, a sofa should be placed on the floor rather than suspended in mid-air. Furthermore, leveraging semantic knowledge can help address challenges such as object-scene compatibility and spatial relationships between objects, thereby enhancing the realism and coherence of the placement. Therefore, how to introduce semantics in object placement is essential for improving the overall quality and applicability of the results.

In this work, we propose a semantic-driven framework for object placement that leverages the reasoning capabilities of Multimodal Large Language Models (MLLMs). Unlike purely data-driven approaches, our method explicitly models the semantic structure of the background. We construct a hierarchical Semantic Tree to represent scene entities and their relationships, guiding the placement process based on logical context rather than mere statistical correlation. Furthermore, we introduce a novel Scoring Mechanism that enables the MLLM to evaluate and select the optimal spatial configuration.

Our contributions are summarized as follows:

1. We propose a training-free, open-vocabulary object placement framework that harnesses MLLMs to bridge the gap between visual synthesis and semantic reasoning.
2. We introduce a Semantic Tree construction method that hierarchically organizes background semantics, ensuring logical consistency between the foreground object and the scene.
3. We design a scoring-based mechanism where the MLLM evaluates potential placement candidates within the Semantic Tree to determine the optimal bounding box (x, y, w, h).

2 Related Work

Object Placement. Object placement, defined as the seamless integration of foreground objects into backgrounds with consistent pose and scale, is pivotal in image composition [17,21,25]. Methodologies have evolved from handcrafted rules to deep learning and, recently, Large Language Model (LLM) integration. Traditional approaches rely on geometric constraints, utilizing edge detection [24,27], depth estimation [7,8], and perspective alignment [11], often refined by optimization techniques like Markov Random Fields [3]. Deep learning revolutionized this domain: CNNs extract spatial features [5], GANs generate realistic composites [14,17,29], and Transformers capture long-range dependencies [22,33]. Contemporary research emphasizes semantic coherence; for instance, GracoNet formulates placement as graph completion [32], while CA-GAN employs coalescing attention to unify foreground-background relations [22].

Large Language Models. The advent of the Transformer architecture [26] precipitated significant strides in LLMs, evolving from BERT [4] to advanced generative models like GPT-4 [1]. Consequently, Multi-modal LLMs (MLLMs) have emerged to bridge visual and textual modalities. Models such as CLIP [23] and BLIP [15,16] leverage semantic understanding for cross-modal alignment, while the GPT-4o series [12] demonstrates robust multi-modal processing. In the context of object placement, MLLMs offer distinct advantages. By interpreting complex visual scenes and semantic contexts, these models facilitate informed decision-making regarding spatial positioning, thereby enhancing the structural and semantic coherence of composite imagery.

3 Method

We propose a framework for semantic-driven object placement comprising three stages: semantic extraction, hierarchical tree construction, and MLLM-guided placement. This approach leverages a Multi-modal Large Language Model (MLLM) to ensure that the inserted object maintains semantic consistency, logical positioning, and appropriate scaling relative to the scene context (see Fig. 2).

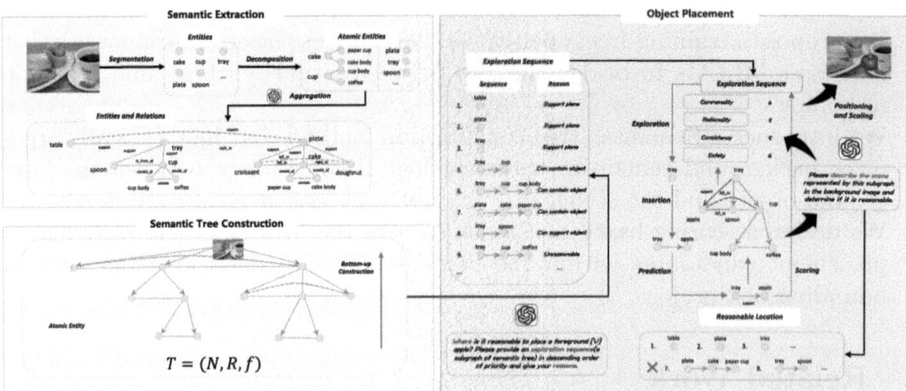

Fig. 2. Overview of our framework. (a) **Semantic Extraction**: The MLLM decomposes the background into atomic entities (F_1) and re-aggregates them (F_2) to build a hierarchy. (b) **Tree Construction**: A Semantic Tree is constructed with relationships identified via F_3. (c) **Placement**: We insert the foreground node, evaluate plausibility, and refine spatial parameters.

3.1 Step 1: Semantic Extraction

We employ an MLLM to extract semantic entities and their inter-relationships from the background image I_B. To structure this process, we design three specific prompt functions—Decomposition (F_1), Aggregation (F_2), and Relationship Identification (F_3)—to guide the MLLM's reasoning.

1. Atomic Decomposition (F_1)**.** We first extract a set of base entities $S(I_B) = \{e_i\}$ using a segmentation model. To achieve fine-grained granularity, we employ the decomposition function $F_1(e_i, I_B)$. This function instructs the MLLM to break down an entity e_i into its smallest semantic constituents (atomic entities), such that:

$$F_1(e_i) = \{e_{ij} \mid \bigcup_j e_{ij} = e_i\}$$

These atomic units serve as the leaf nodes for subsequent aggregation.

2. Recursive Aggregation (F_2). We reconstruct the scene's semantic structure by recursively aggregating atomic units into meaningful higher-level entities. The aggregation function $F_2(\{e_{ij}\}, I_B)$ evaluates a subset of entities to determine if they form a coherent semantic whole.

- **Input:** A subset of entities.
- **Output:** The name of the aggregated entity if semantically valid; otherwise `False`.

This process is formalized in Algorithm 1, which iteratively builds the entity set $\mathcal{N}$ from fine-to-coarse granularity.

Algorithm 1 Recursive Entity Aggregation

Input: Atomic entities $\mathcal{S} = \{e_{ij}\}$
Output: Aggregated entities $\mathcal{N}$
$\mathcal{N} \leftarrow \mathcal{S}, \mathcal{T} \leftarrow \mathcal{S}$
while Aggregation possible in $\mathcal{T}$ **do**
    for subset $\{e_1, \ldots, e_n\} \subseteq \mathcal{T}$ **do**
        $res \leftarrow F_2(e_1, \ldots, e_n)$
        if $res \neq$ **`False`** **then**
            $\mathcal{N} \leftarrow \mathcal{N} \cup \{res\}$
            $\mathcal{T} \leftarrow (\mathcal{T} \setminus \{e_1, \ldots, e_n\}) \cup \{res\}$
        end if
    end for
end while

3. Relationship Identification (F_3). Finally, we identify the semantic connections between the extracted entities using the relationship function $F_3(e_i, e_j, I_B)$. This function predicts the specific interaction type between two entities based on visual context, defining the edges $R_{e_i,e_j} = F_3(e_i, e_j)$ for the semantic tree.

3.2 Step 2: Semantic Tree Construction

To structure the extracted information, we construct a Semantic Tree $T = (\mathcal{N}, \mathcal{R}, f)$. Here, $\mathcal{N}$ represents the set of nodes (entities), $\mathcal{R}$ denotes the edges (relationships from F_3), and I_B serves as the root.

The semantic function $f(V)$ assigns meaning to each node $V \in \mathcal{N}$ recursively:

$$f(V) = \begin{cases} \bigcup_{v \in \text{Children}(V)} f(v) & \text{if } V \text{ is non-leaf} \\ \text{Atomic}(V) & \text{otherwise} \end{cases} \tag{1}$$

Leaf nodes correspond to atomic entities decomposed by F_1, while non-leaf nodes represent the semantic union of their children verified by F_2.

3.3 Step 3: Object Placement via MLLMs

We formulate object placement as inserting a new node V_F into T. The optimal placement minimizes semantic disruption and maximizes contextual coherence.

Exploration and Insertion. We rank potential insertion points using the MLLM to prioritize semantically compatible locations. Upon inserting V_F, we update the tree's semantics via an upward aggregation process (Algorithm 2). This algorithm utilizes F_3 to dynamically update relationships between the inserted object and its new neighbors.

Algorithm 2 Semantic Upward Aggregation

Require: Inserted node V_F, Tree T

```
1: S ← V_F, P ← Parent(V_F)
2: while S ≠ Root(T) do
3:    for v ∈ (Children(P) \ {S}) do
4:       Update relations R_{v,S} ← F_3(v, S)
5:    end for
6:    Update semantics f(P) ← f(Children(P) \ {S}) ∪ f(S)
7:    S ← P, P ← Parent(S)
8: end while
```

Spatial Localization. To determine the coordinates (x_F, y_F), we calculate offsets relative to sibling nodes $\mathcal{C} = \{c_i\}_{i=1}^{k}$. The MLLM predicts spatial relationships and assigns a relevance weight $W_{c_i} \in [0, 1]$ to each sibling. The weighted offsets $(\Delta x_i, \Delta y_i)$ are derived from the scene's spatial extent:

$$\Delta x_i = \frac{W_{c_i}}{\sum W_{c_j}} \max_{j,k} |x_j - x_k|, \quad \Delta y_i = \frac{W_{c_i}}{\sum W_{c_j}} \max_{j,k} |y_j - y_k| \tag{2}$$

The final center is the average of these adjusted references:

$$(x_F, y_F) = \frac{1}{k} \sum_{i=1}^{k} (x_{c_i} + \Delta x_i, y_{c_i} + \Delta y_i) \tag{3}$$

Scale Refinement. We estimate the target size S'_F by comparing the foreground's real-world area S_F with that of reference siblings. Let S_{r_i} be the typical real-world area of sibling c_i (retrieved via MLLM knowledge) and S_{c_i} be its bounding box area. We adjust for perspective distance:

$$S'_F = \frac{S_F}{k} \sum_{i=1}^{k} \left(\frac{S_{c_i}}{S_{r_i}} \right) \sqrt{(x_{c_i} - x_F)^2 + (y_{c_i} - y_F)^2} \tag{4}$$

The final dimensions (w_F, h_F) are scaled proportionally to maintain the aspect ratio based on $\sqrt{S'_F / S_F}$.

4 Experiments

4.1 Dataset and Implementation Details

Dataset. We evaluate our method on the OPA dataset [19], a benchmark for object placement in composite image generation. It contains 62,074 training images and 11,396 test images, covering 1,389 background scenes and 4,137 foreground objects across 47 categories. Each image is composed of a background, a foreground object, and its placement bounding box, and is annotated with a binary label indicating placement reasonableness. All images are sourced from COCO [18] with human-annotated validity labels.

Implementation Details. For the method we mentioned above, we uses **EOVSeg** [20] for open-vocabulary segmentation in Step 1 when we obtain the entities from background, **GPT-4o** API where we use MLLMs and**Yolo-World** [2] for open-vocabulary object detection in Step 3 when we localize the position of siblings. Our method is implemented based on PyTorch and run on one RTX A4090 GPU.

4.2 Evaluation Metrics

We evaluate the quality of composite images using the following metrics:

- **User Study**: Following [32], we conduct a user study with 10 participants, where each participant selects the most reasonable image among six candidates generated by different methods. The score of each method is computed as the average selection rate over all object–background pairs.
- **FID**: Fréchet Inception Distance measures the distributional discrepancy between generated and real images using features extracted from a pre-trained Inception network. Lower values indicate higher visual fidelity.
- **ACC**: Following [32], we adopt SimOPA as a classifier to evaluate placement reasonableness. ACC is defined as the proportion of generated images classified as reasonable.
- **LPIPS**: Learned Perceptual Image Patch Similarity evaluates perceptual differences between images based on deep feature representations. Lower scores indicate higher perceptual similarity, while higher scores imply greater diversity.

The first three metrics assess the plausibility of object placements, while LPIPS evaluates diversity.

4.3 Results

We compare the mentioned method with 5 existing methods. TERSE [25] adopts a rule-based approach to ensure the semantic coherence of object placements by leveraging predefined spatial constraints. PlaceNet [31] utilizes a deep learning framework to predict optimal object placements by learning spatial and contextual relationships from large-scale datasets. GracoNet [32] employs a graph-based method to infer and complete semantic relationships among objects, enhancing scene understanding for object placement. CA-GAN [28] integrates conditional adversarial learning to generate realistic object placements by refining spatial alignment and visual consistency. IOPRE [30] incorporates reinforcement learning to enable interactive object placement, allowing dynamic adjustments based on contextual feedback. The experimental results are shown in Table 1.

Table 1. Quantitative results for different methods on OPA dataset. Best results are blue and second best are orange. We compared our method with five existing methods on four indicators(User Study, FID, Accuracy and LPIPS). The experimental results demonstrate the effectiveness of our method.

Method	Plausibility			Diversity
	User Study↑	FID↓	ACC↑	LPIPS↑
TERSE [25]	0.059	46.94	0.679	0
PlaceNet [31]	0.086	36.69	0.683	0.160
GracoNet [32]	0.130	27.75	0.847	0.206
CA-GAN [28]	0.152	23.21	0.792	0.258
IOPRE [30]	0.155	21.59	0.895	0.214
TopNet [33]	0.174	20.84	0.871	0.251
Ours	**0.244**	**17.76**	**0.904**	**0.273**

The results demonstrate that our method outperforms the compared methods on both plausibility and diversity. Our method achieves superior performance across all plausibility metrics, including User Study, FID, and Accuracy, outperforming all baseline methods. The significant improvement in User Study scores indicates that human evaluators find our placements more reasonable. The lowest FID score demonstrates that our generated images are more visually similar to real images, and the highest Accuracy confirms that our placements align well with ground truth annotations. Our method did not improve significantly on Accuracy, possibly because we found that multiple placement positions were quite reasonable during the exploration process, so we may choose diverse positions for placement, but this is different from ground truth. For diversity, our approach achieves the highest LPIPS score, surpassing CA-GAN and IOPRE, suggesting that our method generates more varied object placements. Notably, TERSE exhibits no diversity due to its deterministic placement strategy (Fig. 3).

4.4 Ablation Study

To evaluate the effectiveness of the Semantic Tree and Scoring Mechanism, we conduct an ablation study on the OPA dataset. Given the extracted entities

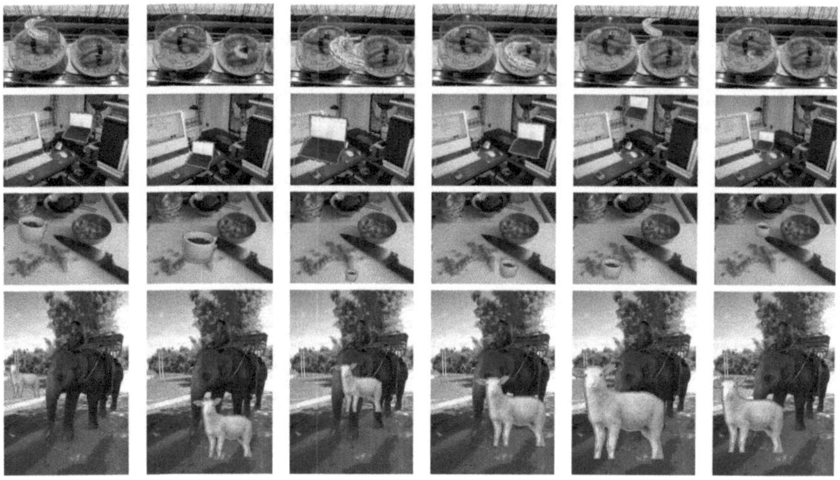

Fig. 3. The qualitative results for different methods on OPA dataset where we have set the weight of each dimension to 0.25. It can be seen that compared to existing methods, our method places the foreground in a more semantically consistent position and size.

and their semantic relationships from the background image in the first step, we compare the following three settings:

1. **MLLM-Direct:** The MLLM directly predicts placement parameters (x_F, y_F, w_F, h_F) given the foreground and background, without leveraging the Semantic Tree structure.
2. **Tree-Based Selection:** Incorporates the Semantic Tree to provide semantic context, but the MLLM selects placement nodes directly without the specific scoring or refinement modules.
3. **w/o Re-aggregation:** Our method excluding the re-aggregation module, evaluating the necessity of merging semantic contexts for precise placement.
4. **w/o Decomposition:** Our method excluding the decomposition module, assessing the impact of breaking down complex semantic relationships.
5. **Full Method:** The complete framework integrating the Semantic Tree, Decomposition, Re-aggregation, and Scoring Mechanism to determine the optimal placement.

The ablation results are shown in Table 2.

When relying solely on the MLLM to select relevant entities and predict the placement parameters, the method achieves the highest FID and the lowest Accuracy. Due to the possible presence of too many atomic entities in the original background image, MLLM may experience hallucinations during the selection process, resulting in its inability to select the entities most relevant to the foreground. This indicates that without structured reasoning, the placements are often misaligned and inconsistent with the background, leading to poor

Table 2. Quantitative results of ablation study on Semantic Tree and Scoring on OPA dataset. We conducted experiments on three different settings and compared FID and Accuracy to measure the plausibility of object placement. The experimental results indicate that it is necessary for us to incorporate Semantic Tree and use Scoring Mechanism in the process of object placement using MLLMs.

Method	Plausibility	
	FID↓	ACC↑
MLLM Directly	78.17	0.182
MLLM + Bg + Semantic Tree	39.42	0.635
w/o Re-aggreation	35.71	0.684
w/o Decomposition	22.93	0.856
MLLM + Semantic Tree + Scoring	**17.76**	**0.904**

plausibility. By leveraging entity relationships, the model is better equipped to determine reasonable placements, leading to more coherent compositions. The introduction of a scoring mechanism further enhances performance, achieving the lowest FID and the highest Accuracy. This suggests that evaluating multiple placement candidates and selecting the optimal one substantially improves realism and semantic consistency.

Overall, these results highlight the importance of structured semantic reasoning and quantitative evaluation in refining object placement quality. The combination of Semantic Tree and Scoring Mechanism effectively guides the MLLM toward more plausible placements, demonstrating the robustness of our proposed approach.

5 Conclusion

In this paper, we have presented a novel semantic-driven approach for object placement. Our method, which leverages semantic extraction, Semantic Tree construction, and object placement using MLLMs, addresses the limitations of traditional rule-based methods and purely data-driven deep learning models. By incorporating semantic understanding into the method, our method ensures that the placement process is more semantically consistent. The experimental results on the OPA dataset demonstrate the superior performance of our method compared to existing state-of-the-art methods. Meanwhile, the ablation experiments on the OPA dataset demonstrated the effectiveness of the semantic tree and scoring mechanism for MLLMs we constructed during this process.

For limitations, our current method relies on the intrinsic reasoning accuracy of the underlying MLLMs; thus, hallucinations or errors in the model can impact placement quality. Additionally, while we prioritize semantic compatibility, the framework does not yet explicitly model complex physical interactions, such as fine-grained occlusion or collision detection. Future work will focus on integrating physical constraints into the Semantic Tree and exploring more advanced MLLM prompting strategies to further enhance placement realism.

References

1. Achiam, J., et al.: Gpt-4 technical report. arXiv preprint arXiv:2303.08774 (2023)
2. Cheng, T., Song, L., Ge, Y., Liu, W., Wang, X., Shan, Y.: Yolo-world: real-time open-vocabulary object detection. In: Proceedings of the IEEE/CVF Conference on Computer Vision and Pattern Recognition, pp. 16901–16911 (2024)
3. Choi, M.J., Lim, J.J., Torralba, A., Willsky, A.S.: Exploiting hierarchical context on a large database of object categories. In: IEEE Computer Society Conference on Computer Vision and Pattern Recognition, pp. 129–136. IEEE (2010)
4. Devlin, J., Chang, M.W., Lee, K., Toutanova, K.: Bert: pre-training of deep bidirectional transformers for language understanding. In: Proceedings of the 2019 conference of the North American chapter of the association for computational linguistics: human language technologies, volume 1 (long and short papers), pp. 4171–4186 (2019)
5. Doersch, C., Gupta, A., Efros, A.A.: Unsupervised visual representation learning by context prediction. In: Proceedings of the IEEE International Conference on Computer Vision, pp. 1422–1430 (2015)
6. Dosovitskiy, A.: An image is worth 16x16 words: transformers for image recognition at scale. arXiv preprint arXiv:2010.11929 (2020)
7. Fang, H.S., Sun, J., Wang, R., Gou, M., Li, Y.L., Lu, C.: Instaboost: boosting instance segmentation via probability map guided copy-pasting. In: Proceedings of the IEEE/CVF International Conference on Computer Vision, pp. 682–691 (2019)
8. Georgakis, G., Mousavian, A., Berg, A.C., Kosecka, J.: Synthesizing training data for object detection in indoor scenes. arXiv preprint arXiv:1702.07836 (2017)
9. Goodfellow, I., et al.: Generative adversarial nets. In: Advances in Neural Information Processing Systems, p. 27 (2014)
10. Ho, J., Jain, A., Abbeel, P.: Denoising diffusion probabilistic models. Adv. Neural. Inf. Process. Syst. **33**, 6840–6851 (2020)
11. Hoiem, D., Efros, A.A., Hebert, M.: Putting objects in perspective. Int. J. Comput. Vision **80**, 3–15 (2008)
12. Hurst, A., et al.: Gpt-4o system card. arXiv preprint arXiv:2410.21276 (2024)
13. Kingma, D.P.: Auto-encoding variational bayes. arXiv preprint arXiv:1312.6114 (2013)
14. Lee, D., Liu, S., Gu, J., Liu, M.Y., Yang, M.H., Kautz, J.: Context-aware synthesis and placement of object instances. In: Advances in Neural Information Processing Systems, vol. 31 (2018)
15. Li, J., Li, D., Savarese, S., Hoi, S.: Blip-2: bootstrapping language-image pre-training with frozen image encoders and large language models. In: International Conference on Machine Learning, pp. 19730–19742. PMLR (2023)
16. Li, J., Li, D., Xiong, C., Hoi, S.: Blip: bootstrapping language-image pre-training for unified vision-language understanding and generation. In: International Conference on Machine Learning, pp. 12888–12900. PMLR (2022)
17. Lin, C.H., Yumer, E., Wang, O., Shechtman, E., Lucey, S.: St-gan: spatial transformer generative adversarial networks for image compositing. In: Proceedings of the IEEE Conference on Computer Vision and Pattern Recognition, pp. 9455–9464 (2018)

18. Lin, T.Y., et al.: Microsoft coco: common objects in context. In: Computer Vision–ECCV 2014: 13th European Conference, zurich, Switzerland, 6–12 September 2014, Proceedings, Part v 13, pp. 740–755. Springer (2014)
19. Liu, L., et al.: Opa: object placement assessment dataset. arXiv preprint arXiv:2107.01889 (2021)
20. Niu, H., Hu, J., Lin, J., Zhang, S.: Eov-seg: efficient open-vocabulary panoptic segmentation. arXiv preprint arXiv:2412.08628 (2024)
21. Niu, L., et al.: Making images real again: a comprehensive survey on deep image composition. arXiv preprint arXiv:2106.14490 (2021)
22. Niu, L., Liu, Q., Liu, Z., Li, J.: Fast object placement assessment. arXiv preprint arXiv:2205.14280 (2022)
23. Radford, A., et al.: Learning transferable visual models from natural language supervision. In: International Conference on Machine Learning, pp. 8748–8763. PmLR (2021)
24. Remez, T., Huang, J., Brown, M.: Learning to segment via cut-and-paste. In: Proceedings of the European Conference on Computer Vision (ECCV), pp. 37–52 (2018)
25. Tripathi, S., Chandra, S., Agrawal, A., Tyagi, A., Rehg, J.M., Chari, V.: Learning to generate synthetic data via compositing. In: Proceedings of the IEEE/CVF Conference on Computer Vision and Pattern Recognition, pp. 461–470 (2019)
26. Vaswani, A., et al.: Attention is all you need. In: Advances in Neural Information Processing Systems, vol. 30 (2017)
27. Wang, H., Wang, Q., Yang, F., Zhang, W., Zuo, W.: Data augmentation for object detection via progressive and selective instance-switching. arXiv preprint arXiv:1906.00358 (2019)
28. Wang, Y., Feng, Y., Wu, J., Xu, H., Zheng, J.: Ca-gan: Object placement via coalescing attention based generative adversarial network. In: 2023 IEEE International Conference on Multimedia and Expo (ICME), pp. 2375–2380. IEEE (2023)
29. Zhang, L., Wen, T., Min, J., Wang, J., Han, D., Shi, J.: Learning object placement by inpainting for compositional data augmentation. In: Computer Vision–ECCV 2020: 16th European Conference, Glasgow, UK, 23–28 August 2020, Proceedings, Part XIII 16, pp. 566–581. Springer (2020)
30. Zhang, S., et al.: Interactive object placement with reinforcement learning (2023)
31. Zhang, S.H., Zhou, Z.P., Liu, B., Dong, X., Hall, P.: What and where: a context-based recommendation system for object insertion. Comput. Vis. Media **6**, 79–93 (2020)
32. Zhou, S., Liu, L., Niu, L., Zhang, L.: Learning object placement via dual-path graph completion. In: European Conference on Computer Vision, pp. 373–389. Springer (2022)
33. Zhu, S., Lin, Z., Cohen, S., Kuen, J., Zhang, Z., Chen, C.: Topnet: transformer-based object placement network for image compositing. In: Proceedings of the IEEE/CVF Conference on Computer Vision and Pattern Recognition, pp. 1838–1847 (2023)

Comparative Analysis of Formula and Structure Prediction from Tandem Mass Spectra

Xujun Che, Depeng Xu(✉), and Xiuxia Du

University of North Carolina at Charlotte, Charlotte, USA
{xche,dxu7,xdu4}@charlotte.edu

Abstract. Liquid chromatography mass spectrometry (LC-MS)-based metabolomics and exposomics aim to measure detectable small molecules in biological samples. The results facilitate hypothesis-generating discovery of metabolic changes and disease mechanisms and provide information about environmental exposures and their effects on human health. Metabolomics and exposomics are made possible by the high resolving power of LC and high mass measurement accuracy of MS. However, a majority of the signals from such studies still cannot be identified or annotated using conventional library searching because existing spectral libraries are far from covering the vast chemical space captured by LC-MS/MS. To address this challenge and unleash the full potential of metabolomics and exposomics, a number of computational approaches have been developed to predict compounds based on tandem mass spectra. Published assessment of these approaches used different datasets and evaluation. To select prediction workflows for practical applications and identify areas for further improvements, we have carried out a systematic evaluation of the state-of-the-art prediction algorithms. Specifically, the accuracy of formula prediction and structure prediction was evaluated for different types of adducts. The resulting findings have established realistic performance baselines, identified critical bottlenecks, and provided guidance to further improve compound predictions based on MS.

Keywords: untargeted metabolomics · mass spectrometry · compound prediction · deep learning

1 Introduction

Metabolomics and exposomics, the large-scale study of small molecules within cells, tissues, or organisms, is pivotal for understanding complex biological systems and discovering novel biomarkers. Liquid chromatography coupled to mass spectrometry is one of the major analytical platforms for metabolomics and exposomics studies due to its broad coverage of the chemical space. A fundamental task in mass spectrometry-based metabolomics and exposomics is to assign compounds or compound classes to tandem mass spectra, essential for translating

R. C.-W. Wong et al. (Eds.): PAKDD 2026, LNAI 16618, pp. 215–227, 2027.
https://doi.org/10.1007/978-981-92-1947-6_18

raw analytical data into actionable biological insights. However, this is still a challenge and a majority of the resulting tandem mass spectra remain unknown, forming the heavy and large dark matter that needs to be elucidated to fulfill the true potential of mass spectrometry-based metabolomics and exposomics.

LC separates compounds in complex mixtures based on their chemical properties. This separation reduces chemical complexity, prevents different analytes from interfering with each other, and enables more accurate detection of compounds. The subsequent tandem mass spectrometry (MS/MS) provides structural information of compounds by fragmenting corresponding precursor ions to produce characteristic fragmentation patterns that are the basis for molecular identification. Traditionally, an unknown MS/MS spectrum is matched against a library of known MS/MS. Compounds of the most similar MS/MS in the library are assigned to the unknown MS/MS. This process is known as compound identification (confident assignment with strong evidence) or annotation (assignment with some evidence). The library search-based method has proven to be very effective. However, existing MS/MS libraries is still tiny compared to the vast space of compounds that LC-MS platforms are capable of detecting. As a result, the majority of MS/MS in a typical metabolomics or exposomics study remain unknown after library search.

To address this challenge, computational workflows have been developed to predict compounds based on MS/MS. Compound prediction overcomes the limitation of MS/MS libraries and can provide invaluable insights about what compounds could have produced an unknown MS/MS, even though it cannot achieve the level of confidence that library matching could provide. Compound prediction typically consists of two sequential steps: *molecular formula prediction* and *structure elucidation.*

For molecular formula prediction, a list of potential candidate formula are generated and ranked. One such algorithm is Sirius [5]. It combines isotope pattern modeling with probabilistic fragmentation-tree construction from MS/MS spectra, scores all candidates to select the molecular formula most consistent with both MS1 and MS/MS evidence. It produces interpretable results, but struggles with speed and complexity. To address these limitations, deep learning-based methods such as MIST-CF [8] and FIDDLE [9] have emerged as alternatives. These data-driven models have shown improved performance and reasonable accuracy by capturing complex spectral patterns, although they typically require large training datasets and can be less transparent in their predictions.

For each formula candidate, structure prediction can be carried out using two strategies: database searching or de novo generation. The former method is used by CSI:FingerID that predicts the molecular structure fingerprint based on the fragmentation tree that SIRIUS has generated and then computes the similarity between the predicted fingerprint and that of known compounds in a structural database [6]. Understandably, this method is limited to known molecules and would miss novel structures—a critical limitation given that a large percentage of spectra in typical metabolomics experiments are believed to originate from unknown compounds not present in existing structural libraries [1,11]. Methods that generate de novo structures include MADGEN [15], MSNovelist [13], and DiffMS [2], among others. These de novo prediction approaches struggle with the high complexity of the task, especially in distinguishing between structural isomers. Even with high-resolution mass spectrometry, multiple formula candidates can remain indistinguishable, a problem that is compounded when trying to identify isobaric or isomeric compounds [2].

Beyond these intrinsic technical challenges, current methodologies for evaluating computational models often face limitations that question their practical utility. Firstly, many benchmark datasets suffer from issues of scale and coverage. For instance, the widely used Global Natural Products Social Molecular Networking (GNPS) database [14] contains spectra for only an estimated 2.5% of known natural products [4,10], suggesting that models trained and evaluated on such datasets may not be representative of the broader chemical universe. Secondly, a prevalent evaluation paradigm is the use of stringent structure-dissimilarity splits [3], where molecules in the test set are intentionally chosen to be structurally distinct from those in the training set. While this approach rigorously tests a model's generalization capabilities, it overemphasizes this aspect at the expense of practical applicability. In many real-world metabolomics studies, researchers are focused on identifying metabolites within specific, known families where structural similarities are expected. The current focus on broad generalization does not reflect these common use-cases.

To bridge this gap between academic benchmarking and practical application, we evaluated the performance of state-of-the-art computational methods on large-scale, comprehensive datasets. Specifically, we conducted systematic evaluations using tandem mass spectra in the National Institute of Standards and Technology (NIST) 23 tandem spectral library [12] and the Mass Bank of North America (MoNA) [7], representing both high-quality curated spectra and diverse community-contributed data. We implemented a two-stage pipeline that first predicts the molecular formula and then predicts the molecular structure for each of the proposed formula. We adopted random data splitting, rather than structure-dissimilarity splitting, to reflect practical metabolomics scenarios. Moreover, we performed adduct-type-stratified analysis to reveal performance heterogeneity across different adducts, providing actionable insights masked by aggregate statistics.

Our evaluation revealed that computational compound prediction has reached practically useful accuracy levels for dominant adduct types. For $[M+H]^+$, trained models achieved over 86% formula prediction accuracy and over 67% structure prediction accuracy. However, less common adduct types such as $[M+H-2H_2O]^+$ and $[M-H+2Na]^+$ exhibited severe performance degradation, highlighting fundamental challenges that require architectural innovations beyond simple data scaling. By evaluating structure generation under both oracle conditions where the ground truth formula are provided and realistic pipelines where formula are predicted, we were able to decompose the total prediction error into contributions from each stage. We found that errors from formula prediction propagate surprisingly modestly to structure generation. These findings provide a foundation for prioritizing future research directions and inform best practices for deploying these methods in real-world metabolomics applications.

2 Experimental Section

2.1 Datasets

NIST 23 Spectral Library: A commercial, high-quality spectrometral library widely regarded as the gold standard in the field. It contains carefully curated spectra with rigorous quality control, making it an ideal benchmark dataset for evaluating prediction accuracy in controlled settings. We used its MS/MS spectra and filtered them based on the following six criteria:

(1) Ionization polarity: Positive.
(2) Fragmentation type: HCD.
(3) Charge state: Singly charged precursor ions only (charge = 1).
(4) Elements: H, C, N, O, P, S, F only (covering most biologically relevant metabolites).
(5) Adduct types: $[M+H]^+$, $[M+Na]^+$, $[M+K]^+$, $[M+H\text{-}H_2O]^+$, $[M+H\text{-}2H_2O]^+$, $[M\text{-}H+2Na]^+$.
(6) Collision energy: Up to three spectra per molecule-adduct pair, selecting those with median collision energies to reduce redundancy.

MoNA (MassBank of North America:) An open-access mass spectrometry database that are contributed by the metabolomics community. Unlike NIST, MoNA represents the diversity and heterogeneity of real-world spectral data, including contributions from various laboratories with different experimental protocols and instrumentation. We downloaded the LC-MS/MS Positive Mode spectra and filtered them based on the following criteria:

(1) Elements: H, C, N, O, P, S, F only.
(2) Adduct types: Same as NIST 23.

Dataset Statistics: Table 1 summarizes the statistics of the resulting dataset and Table 2 shows the spectra distribution of adduct types in each dataset. The latter reveals significant imbalances that reflect real-world scenarios, where certain adducts dominate. Notably, $[M+H]^+$ constitutes the majority of spectra across both datasets, accounting for approximately 56.1% in NIST, and 78.6% in MoNA. In contrast, $[M+H\text{-}2H_2O]^+$ and $[M\text{-}H+2Na]^+$ represent only a small fraction of the data, with fewer than 30 spectra in some cases.

2.2 Computational Methods for Compound Prediction

Chemical Formula Prediction

Table 1. Overall statistics of the two datasets after filtering. (MW = Molecular Weight)

Metric	NIST	MoNA
# Spectra	86,435	76,196
# Unique Molecules	19,511	11,894
# Unique Formulas	9,630	6,244
MW Range (Da)	82.11–1,704.01	45.08–2,680.17

SIRIUS: The state-of-the-art fragmentation tree-based formula prediction [5]. It operates by first enumerating candidate chemical formulas consistent with the observed precursor mass within a specified mass tolerance. For each formula candidate, SIRIUS assigns potential subformulae to MS/MS peaks and constructs a fragmentation tree that represents plausible neutral loss pathways from the precursor to observed fragments. The fragmentation tree is scored using a maximum a posteriori (MAP) estimation framework that incorporates both fragment plausibility based on chemical knowledge and the quality of the MS/MS spectrum explanation. SIRIUS employs hand-crafted scoring functions parameterized with domain knowledge, including expected fragmentation patterns, common neutral losses, and isotopic distributions. The method can optionally incorporate MS1 isotope pattern information to improve formula discrimination, though we focus exclusively on the MS/MS-based scoring component for fair comparison with MIST-CF (to be described). It is worth noting that SIRIUS is a rule-based method with hand-crafted parameters and therefore does not require training.

MIST-CF: A neural network-based approach for ranking chemical formula candidates given an MS/MS spectrum [8]. It employs an energy-based modeling framework with a Chemical Formula Transformer architecture. Given a candidate chemical formula and its corresponding adduct type, MIST-CF first assigns plausible subformulae to MS/MS fragment peaks within a specified mass tolerance. These subformula-annotated peaks are then encoded using sinusoidal embeddings and processed through a transformer network that learns to score the compatibility between the candidate formula and the observed fragmentation pattern. Unlike fragmentation tree-based methods, MIST-CF learns scoring functions directly from data without requiring explicit tree construction, enabling efficient evaluation of large candidate sets. For our experiments, we utilized a model pretrained on the NPLIB1 dataset following the MIST-CF procedure with adjustments to focus on our six adduct types of interest. Additionally, we trained two separate models from scratch on NIST and MoNA datasets respectively.

Molecular Structure Generation

MSNovelist: An LSTM-based sequence-to-sequence model that generates molecular structures in SMILES string representation conditioned on molecular fingerprint predictions [13]. It operates in two stages: first, a fingerprint prediction model infers a probabilistic molecular fingerprint from the MS/MS spectrum; second, an LSTM decoder autoregressively generates SMILES characters guided by the predicted fingerprint. For our experiments, we used the MSNovelist implementation from the SIRIUS software. The underlying RNN model was trained on 1,232,184 chemical structures from HMDB, COCONUT, and DSSTox databases.

DiffMS: A conditional molecular generation model based on discrete graph diffusion [2]. The method consists of two main components: a spectrum encoder and a graph decoder. The encoder uses the same Formula Transformer architecture as MIST-CF to extract structural information from MS/MS spectra, producing a fixed-dimensional embedding that captures the fragmentation pattern. The decoder implements a discrete diffusion process on molecular graphs, where bond types are iteratively denoised starting from a random initialization, conditioned on both the spectrum embedding and the known chemical formula.

For our experiments, we utilized the pretrained DiffMS model released by the authors, which was trained on NPLIB1 data. For domain adaptation, we trained two separate models initialized with the pretrained decoder weights on NIST and MoNA datasets respectively. We evaluated DiffMS under two experimental settings to isolate different sources of error in the complete prediction pipeline:

(1) **DiffMS (Oracle)**: In this configuration, we provided the ground truth chemical formula to the DiffMS decoder. This setting represents the upper bound of structure prediction performance, isolating the decoder's capability to generate correct molecular graphs given correct formula. Any errors in this setting reflect limitations in the structure generation model itself or ambiguities inherent in the MS/MS data (e.g., inability to distinguish stereoisomers or structural isomers with similar fragmentation patterns).

(2) **DiffMS (MIST-CF):** In this configuration, we constructed a complete end-to-end pipeline where MIST-CF first predicted candidate chemical formulas from the MS/MS spectrum, and the top-5 ranked formula predictions were then each fed to the DiffMS decoder for structure generation. For each of the five formula, DiffMS generated molecular structures, resulting in an expanded set of structure candidates that accounts for uncertainty in the formula prediction step. We ranked the final structure candidates by structure generation frequency. Performance in this setting reflects the complete annotation pipeline and quantifies how formula prediction uncertainty propagates through to structure generation.

For the Oracle setting, we generated 100 molecular structure candidates per spectrum. For the MIST-CF configuration, we generated 20 structure candidates per formula for each of the top-5 predicted formulas, yielding a total of up to 100 candidates per spectrum.

2.3 Evaluation Setup

Metrics: We employed standard metrics from the mass spectrometry literature. For formula prediction, we computed the top-K accuracy. For structure prediction, we used two metrics: (1) top-K accuracy based on InChIKey-14 match (allowing stereoisomer variation), and (2) maximum Tanimoto similarity. All metrics report the best match within top-K predictions.

Data Split: We split both NIST and MoNA datasets into training, validation, and test sets through random splitting. This strategy was deliberately chosen over structure-dissimilarity splitting as it preserves the natural distribution of adduct types and chemical properties, thereby reflecting realistic application scenarios where compounds of interest often share structural features. Both datasets exhibit severe class imbalance across adduct types, with $[M+H]^+$ dominating while several rare adduct types are significantly underrepresented. Table 2 presents the split statistics after applying this balancing strategy.

Table 2. Dataset split statistics by adduct types.

	NIST				MoNA			
Adduct Type	Total	Train	Val	Test	Total	Train	Val	Test
$[M+H]^+$	50,182	40,073	1,143	100	59,854	59,654	100	100
$[M+Na]^+$	13,376	10,790	298	100	10,997	10,797	100	100
$[M+K]^+$	354	292	6	30	5,197	4,997	100	100
$[M+H-H_2O]^+$	17,433	13,912	441	100	102	81	10	11
$[M+H-2H_2O]^+$	4,133	3,295	91	100	21	16	2	3
$[M-H+2Na]^+$	957	786	21	91	25	20	2	3
Total	86,435	69,148	2,000	521	76,196	75,565	314	317

3 Results and Discussion

3.1 Formula Prediction: MIST-CF Vs SIRIUS

Overall Performance Comparison: Table 3 summarizes the formula prediction accuracy of SIRIUS and MIST-CF on the NIST and MoNA datasets. We report top-1, top-5, and top-10 accuracy metrics, reflecting the practical scenario where domain experts typically inspect multiple top-ranked candidates. MIST-CF is evaluated in two configurations: *pretrained* on external datasets (NPLIB1), and *retrained* (in-domain) on the target dataset's training split. SIRIUS achieves strong performance on NIST (top-5: 0.758) but limited performance on MoNA (0.435). Pretrained MIST-CF shows moderate performance (0.655–0.685 top-5). In-domain retraining substantially improves MIST-CF: top-1 accuracy increases by 8.2 points (NIST) and 34.2 points (MoNA), with MoNA reaching 0.892 top-5 accuracy. However, NIST retraining shows an unexpected pattern: while top-1 improves (0.378 vs 0.296), top-5 and top-10 decline (0.503 vs 0.685 and 0.622 vs 0.727). Three factors may explain this: (1) MIST-CF's contrastive training prioritizes top-1 separation over ranking calibration; (2) NIST's controlled, high-quality spectra enable learning of dataset-specific artifacts that improve top-1 but reduce ranking robustness; (3) smaller NIST improvements versus MoNA (8.2% vs 34.2%) suggest NPLIB1 already contains similar data, limiting retraining benefits while introducing overfitting.

Table 3. Overall formula prediction accuracy of SIRIUS and MIST-CF. SIRIUS does not require training, while MIST-CF is evaluated for both its base performance and domain-adaptation retraining performance. Bold values indicate the best performance for each testing configuration.

	NIST			MoNA		
Method	Top-1	Top-5	Top-10	Top-1	Top-5	Top-10
SIRIUS	0.284	**0.758**	**0.825**	0.193	0.435	0.500
MIST-CF (pretrained)	0.296	0.685	0.727	0.402	0.655	0.744
MIST-CF (retrained)	**0.378**	0.503	0.622	**0.744**	**0.892**	**0.915**

Adduct-Type-Stratified Formula Prediction Performance: While aggregate metrics provide a useful overview, they obscure critical performance variations across adduct types. Table 4 presents top-5 formula prediction accuracy broken down by adduct types across all evaluation configurations, revealing substantial disparities that have important practical implications.

Table 4. Top-5 formula prediction accuracy stratified by adduct type.

	NIST			MoNA		
Adduct Type	SIRIUS	MIST-CF (pretrained)	MIST-CF (retrained)	SIRIUS	MIST-CF (pretrained)	MIST-CF (retrained)
$[M+H]^+$	0.940	0.970	**0.990**	0.730	**0.869**	**0.869**
$[M+Na]^+$	0.750	0.840	**0.950**	0.520	0.780	**0.930**
$[M+K]^+$	0.667	0.233	**0.800**	0.160	0.310	**0.990**
$[M+H-H_2O]^+$	**0.950**	0.850	0.160	0.727	**0.909**	0.364
$[M+H-2H_2O]^+$	**0.950**	0.840	0.150	**1.000**	0.667	0.000
$[M-H+2Na]^+$	**0.176**	0.000	0.143	0.000	0.000	0.000

Dominant Adducts Achieve High Performance: For $[M+H]^+$ and $[M+Na]^+$, retrained MIST-CF achieves >0.86 accuracy on both datasets, with NIST reaching 0.990 and 0.950 respectively. SIRIUS also performs well on these common types (0.730–0.940), confirming that formula annotation has reached practical utility for the majority of metabolomics applications.

Water-Loss Adducts Show Unexpected Patterns: Remarkably, water-loss adducts ($[M+H-H_2O]^+$ and $[M+H-2H_2O]^+$) exhibit reversed performance trends: SIRIUS achieves the highest accuracy (0.727–1.000), while retrained MIST-CF shows catastrophic failure (0.000–0.364). On NIST, SIRIUS reaches 0.950 for both types, whereas retrained MIST-CF collapses to 0.160 and 0.150—a dramatic 80-percentage point decline from pretrained performance (0.850 and 0.840). This suggests that: (1) rule-based fragmentation tree methods are better suited for handling water-loss ambiguities, where multiple formulas can produce similar mass shifts; (2) NIST retraining may have overfitted to dominant adduct patterns, losing the ability to generalize to chemically ambiguous cases; (3) small training sample sizes for these types (Table 2) exacerbate overfitting.

Extreme Rarity: [M-H+2Na]$^+$ Remains Unsolved: The [M-H+2Na]$^+$ adduct shows near-zero accuracy across all methods (0.000–0.176), reflecting the extreme data scarcity and also raising the question about whether or not the adduct type has been determined correctly.

3.2 Structure Prediction: DiffMS Vs MSNovelist

Overall Performance: Table 5 presents molecular structure prediction performance across different configurations.

Table 5. Overall structure prediction performance (Top-5 metrics). DiffMS (Oracle) uses ground truth formulas while DiffMS (MIST-CF) uses MIST-CF's top-5 formula predictions. MSNovelist is pretrained and independent of our training configurations.

	NIST		MoNA	
Method	Accuracy	Tanimoto	Accuracy	Tanimoto
MSNovelist	0.447	0.619	0.249	0.405
DiffMS (pretrained, Oracle)	0.077	0.310	0.088	0.298
DiffMS (pretrained, MIST-CF)	0.052	0.282	0.066	0.272
DiffMS (retrained, Oracle)	**0.664**	**0.818**	**0.634**	0.812
DiffMS (retrained, MIST-CF)	0.662	0.817	0.630	**0.818**

Error Propagation Analysis: A striking finding is that the retrained DiffMS (MIST-CF) pipeline performs remarkably close to the DiffMS (Oracle) setting. Accuracy gaps between the Oracle and MIST-CF configurations are minimal: 0.2% points on NIST (0.664 vs 0.662) and 0.4 points on MoNA (0.634 vs 0.630). This robustness is surprising given that formula prediction is imperfect (e.g., MIST-CF retrained Top-5 accuracy on NIST is 0.503, see Table 3). This resilience is likely due to two factors: (1) the multi-formula strategy (generating structures for the Top-5 formulas) mitigates errors, and (2) the spectrum embedding provides structural constraints that partially compensate for incorrect formulas. This suggests that structure generation, not formula prediction (within the top-5), is the primary bottleneck. The Tanimoto scores are virtually unchanged, confirming that even when the pipeline fails, the generated structures remain chemically relevant.

To further understand the pipeline's error characteristics, we conducted a detailed failure analysis (Fig. 1). Figure 1a demonstrates that structure generation is robust to formula errors, maintaining high Tanimoto similarity even for incorrect formulas. Figure 1b decomposes failure modes into structure generation bottlenecks (b1), formula propagation errors (b2), and rare adduct collapse (b3). Figure 1c shows that isomer discrimination remains challenging, with only 66.7% accuracy for $C_{20}H_{32}O_3$ isomers.

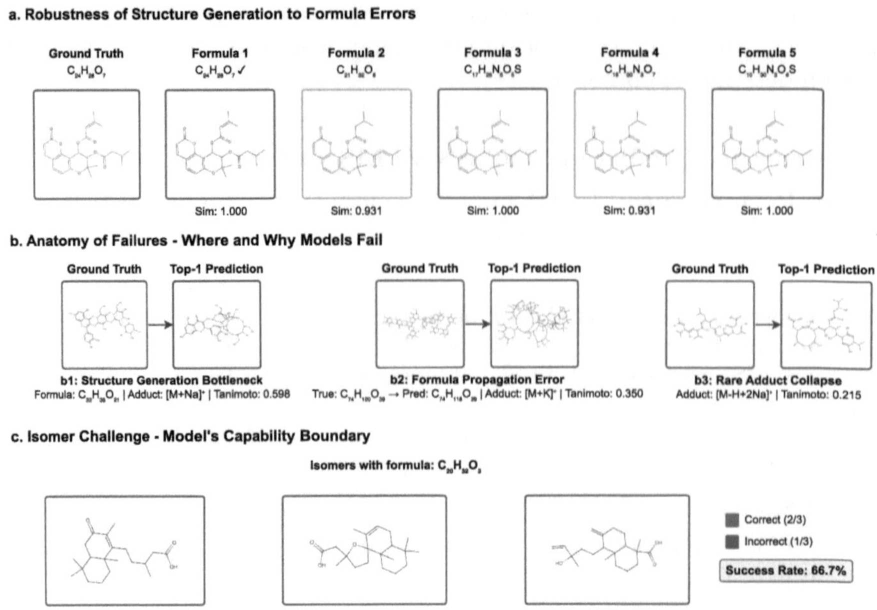

Fig. 1. Diagnostic analysis of pipeline performance. (a) Structure generation robustness to formula errors. (b) Failure mode decomposition: structure generation bottleneck (b1), formula propagation error (b2), and rare adduct collapse (b3). (c) Isomer discrimination challenge with 66.7% success rate for $C_{20}H_{32}O_3$.

Domain Adaptation Impact: Domain adaptation is critical for structure prediction. In-domain (retrained) models vastly outperform the general (pretrained) models. Comparing the oracle configurations, the accuracy gap between the retrained and pretrained DiffMS is 58.7% points on NIST (0.664 vs 0.077) and 54.6 points on MoNA (0.634 vs 0.088). This sensitivity to domain adaptation is significantly larger than that observed for formula prediction, reflecting the greater complexity of structure generation.

Adduct-Type-Stratified Structure Prediction Performance: Table 6 presents top-5 accuracy stratified by adduct type.

Table 6. Top-5 structure prediction accuracy stratified by adduct type.

Dataset	Adduct Type	MSNovelist	DiffMS			
			pretrained†	pretrained†	retrained†	retrained‡
NIST	$[M+H]^+$	**0.800**	0.170	0.170	0.730	0.760
	$[M+Na]^+$	0.410	0.050	0.040	0.530	**0.540**
	$[M+K]^+$	0.300	0.067	0.033	**0.667**	**0.667**
	$[M+H-H_2O]^+$	0.550	0.040	0.010	**0.750**	0.720
	$[M+H-2H_2O]^+$	0.320	0.010	0.000	0.560	**0.570**
	$[M-H+2Na]^+$	0.176	0.132	0.055	**0.758**	0.725
MoNA	$[M+H]^+$	0.470	0.270	0.202	**0.680**	0.677
	$[M+Na]^+$	0.150	0.010	0.020	**0.620**	**0.620**
	$[M+K]^+$	0.090	0.000	0.000	**0.610**	0.600
	$[M+H-H_2O]^+$	0.455	0.000	0.000	**0.818**	**0.818**
	$[M+H-2H_2O]^+$	**1.000**	0.000	0.000	0.333	0.333
	$[M-H+2Na]^+$	0.000	0.000	0.000	0.000	0.000

† Oracle: structure prediction with ground truth formula;
‡ Pipeline: with MIST-CF predicted formulas.

Dominant Adduct Types Achieve Practical Accuracy: For $[M+H]^+$, the dominant adduct type, DiffMS (MIST-CF) achieves over 0.67 top-5 accuracy in in-domain settings on both datasets. Combined with >0.86 formula prediction accuracy, this demonstrates practically useful performance for the most common scenarios.

Severe Degradation for Rare Adduct Types: The rare adduct types, $[M+H-2H_2O]^+$ and $[M-H+2Na]^+$, achieved only 0.333 and 0.000 top-5 accuracy on MoNA.

3.3 Data Augmentation for Rare Adduct Types

Given the severe performance degradation for less common adduct types, we tested whether data scarcity was the limiting factor by supplementing MoNA's limited training examples with NIST spectra, with 2,000 $[M+H-H_2O]^+$, 4,032 $[M+H-2H_2O]^+$ and 951 $[M-H+2Na]^+$. Despite substantial increases in training data, augmentation failed to improve performance for any of the less common adduct types for both formula prediction and structure prediction. These results suggest that data quality and relevance are more critical than raw quantity.

3.4 Practical Implications and Recommendations

Rethinking Evaluation Paradigms: Current benchmarking efforts emphasize structure-dissimilarity splits, prioritizing generalization over practical relevance. In real metabolomics, researchers often study related compound families where structural similarity is expected. Our random-split strategy better reflects such contexts and shows that with sufficient in-domain data, state-of-the-art models reach practical performance (> 0.86 top-5 formula, > 0.67 top-5 structure accuracy for $[M+H]^+$). We recommend reporting both in-domain and out-of-domain results to guide real-world applicability.

Data Curation Recommendations: Augmentation experiments revealed three challenges: (1)Distributional mismatch between high-quality NIST spectra and heterogeneous MoNA data, limiting transferability; (2) Spectral ambiguity for water-loss adducts, making identification ill-posed; and (3) Limited model capacity for learning both dataset- and adduct-specific rules.Accordingly, we suggest:(1) Focus on in-domain data for the target chemical space; (2) Balance quality and diversity by mixing reference and community spectra; (3) Mitigate adduct imbalance via targeted acquisition for rare ionization modes; and (4)Adopt advanced augmentation (e.g., generative or domain-adaptive methods).

Future Research Directions. Our work has identified several promising research directions: (1) Persistent gaps for less common adducts indicate a need for specialized architectures or meta-learning; (2) Integrating retention time or collision cross-section (CCS) could resolve ambiguities; and (3) Domain adaptation is essential for cross-source generalization.

4 Conclusion

This study has demonstrated that compound prediction is now practical for routine use, though key bottlenecks remain. Adduct-stratified results have revealed that structure generation, not formula prediction, limits accuracy. Naïve data scaling fails for less common adducts, underscoring the need for specialized models, multimodal integration, and domain adaptation. Our analysis provides both validation for current tools and a roadmap toward more comprehensive, realistic compound prediction.

Acknowledgements. This work was supported in part by U.S. National Science Foundation (2348391) and UNC Charlotte internal funding. We thank Dr. Stephen Stein at the National Institute of Standards and Technology (NIST) for providing the NIST 23 mass spectral library under a Memorandum of Understanding between NIST and UNC Charlotte.

References

1. Bittremieux, W., Wang, M., Dorrestein, P.C.: The critical role that spectral libraries play in capturing the metabolomics community knowledge. Metabolomics **18**(12), 94 (2022)
2. Bohde, M., Manjrekar, M., Wang, R., Ji, S., Coley, C.W.: Diffms: diffusion generation of molecules conditioned on mass spectra (2025). arXiv:2502.09571 arXiv preprint

3. Bushuiev, R., et al.: Massspecgym: a benchmark for the discovery and identification of molecules. Adv. Neural. Inf. Process. Syst. **37**, 110010–110027 (2024)
4. van Der Hooft, J.J., et al.: Linking genomics and metabolomics to chart specialized metabolic diversity. Chem. Soc. Rev. **49**(11), 3297–3314 (2020)
5. Dührkop, K., et al.: Sirius 4: a rapid tool for turning tandem mass spectra into metabolite structure information. Nat. Methods **16**(4), 299–302 (2019)
6. Dührkop, K., Shen, H., Meusel, M., Rousu, J., Böcker, S.: Searching molecular structure databases with tandem mass spectra using CSI: FingerID. Proc. Natl. Acad. Sci. **112**(41), 12580–12585 (2015)
7. Laboratory, F.: Massbank of North America (mona) (2025). https://mona.fiehnlab.ucdavis.edu/
8. Goldman, S., Xin, J., Provenzano, J., Coley, C.W.: Mist-CF: chemical formula inference from tandem mass spectra. J. Chem. Inf. Model. **64**(7), 2421–2431 (2023)
9. Hong, Y., Li, S., Ye, Y., Tang, H.: Fiddle: a deep learning method for chemical formulas prediction from tandem mass spectra. bioRxiv pp. 2024–11 (2024)
10. de Jonge, N.F., et al.: Ms2query: reliable and scalable ms2 mass spectra-based analogue search. Nat. Commun. **14**(1), 1752 (2023)
11. Monge, M.E., Dodds, J.N., Baker, E.S., Edison, A.S., Fernández, F.M.: Challenges in identifying the dark molecules of life. Annu. Rev. Anal. Chem. **12**(1), 177–199 (2019)
12. National Institute of Standards and Technology: Tandem (ms/ms) mass spectral library (2023). https://www.nist.gov/srd/nist-standard-reference-database-1a
13. Stravs, M.A., Dührkop, K., Böcker, S., Zamboni, N.: Msnovelist: de novo structure generation from mass spectra. Nat. Methods **19**(7), 865–870 (2022)
14. Wang, M., et al.: Sharing and community curation of mass spectrometry data with global natural products social molecular networking. Nat. Biotechnol. **34**(8), 828–837 (2016)
15. Wang, Y., Chen, X., Liu, L., Hassoun, S.: MADGEN: mass-spec attends to de novo molecular generation (2025). arXiv:2501.01950 arXiv preprint

Human Pose Estimation in Videos Using the Concept of A PID Controller

Yeeun Kim, Jongmin Lee, and Jangwon Lee(✉)

Sungkyunkwan University, Seoul, Republic of Korea
{kim010206,ee18,leejang}@skku.edu

Abstract. We introduce a new perspective for human pose estimation in videos by drawing inspiration from the structural principle of a Proportional–Integral–Derivative (PID) controller. Rather than implementing a traditional control loop, we demonstrate that the underlying philosophy of PID provides a powerful and general framework for addressing computer vision tasks involving sequential image data. A PID controller conceptually decomposes a signal into three components—Proportional (P), Integral (I), and Derivative (D)—which correspond to the present state, accumulated past information, and prediction of future changes, respectively. Motivated by this structural interpretation, we propose a novel three-stream ensemble architecture that processes three complementary representations: RGB frames (present), Motion History Images (past), and Optical Flow (future). This PID-inspired formulation reduces joint localization errors by leveraging temporal cues in a structurally interpretable manner. Importantly, our PID-based design can be seamlessly integrated into any modern deep learning architecture, including both CNN-based and transformer-based models, without modifying their core designs. Experimental results show that our framework achieves state-of-the-art performance on two widely used human pose estimation benchmarks—PoseTrack 2018 and PoseTrack 2021—demonstrating the effectiveness and versatility of the proposed approach.

1 Introduction

Human pose estimation in videos plays a critical role in applications such as video surveillance, autonomous driving, and human–computer interaction. Although substantial progress has been achieved in single-frame image-based pose estimation [1–3], these approaches inherently fail to fully exploit the rich temporal information available in video sequences. When applied to videos, performance often degrades under challenging conditions such as motion blur, occlusion, and rapid movements. This limitation highlights the importance of explicitly modeling temporal cues. Recent studies have incorporated temporal information through 3D convolutions, temporal alignment, or heatmap aggregation across neighboring frames [4–6]. Methods such as mutual information maximization [6], occlusion-aware modeling [5], motion-adaptive feature refinement [7], and motion-aware

Y. Kim and J. Lee—Contributed equally to this work.

R. C.-W. Wong et al. (Eds.): PAKDD 2026, LNAI 16618, pp. 228–239, 2027.
https://doi.org/10.1007/978-981-92-1947-6_19

heatmap regression [8] have improved robustness in dynamic scenes. However, most existing approaches treat temporal information as a unified or implicitly learned representation. As a result, they do not explicitly distinguish the different functional roles that temporal signals may play, including present appearance, accumulated motion patterns, and short-term motion variation.

In this work, we introduce a new perspective inspired by the classical Proportional–Integral–Derivative (PID) controller. In traditional PID control, system error is reduced by combining three temporal operations on the error signal: its present value, its accumulated history, and its rate of change. Rather than formulating pose estimation as a control problem or implementing a feedback controller, we draw inspiration from this structural principle and apply it to video-based pose modeling. Based on this perspective, we explicitly decompose video information into three complementary components: present appearance, accumulated motion history, and short-term motion variation. We propose **PIDPose**, a three-stream architecture in which RGB frames serve the Proportional role, Motion History Images (MHIs) [9] represent the Integral role, and Optical Flow captures short-term inter-frame motion variation corresponding to the Derivative role. By structurally organizing these temporally differentiated signals, PIDPose enhances stability and accuracy in joint localization.

PIDPose is designed to be fully architecture-independent. The proposed PID module can be seamlessly integrated into diverse pose-estimation backbones, including CNN-based HRNet [1], transformer-based ViTPose [3], and the state-of-the-art Poseidon [10], without requiring modifications to their internal architectures. Extensive experiments demonstrate that PIDPose consistently improves performance across heterogeneous backbone families and achieves state-of-the-art results on multiple benchmarks. These findings validate the effectiveness and scalability of the proposed temporal structuring framework.

Our main contributions are summarized as follows:

- We introduce a temporal decomposition framework inspired by the structural principle of classical PID control, explicitly modeling present appearance, accumulated motion, and short-term motion variation.
- We propose PIDPose, an architecture-independent three-stream module that can be seamlessly integrated into diverse pose-estimation backbones.
- We demonstrate consistent improvements across HRNet, ViTPose, and Poseidon, achieving state-of-the-art performance on multiple benchmarks through extensive experiments.

Overall, this study demonstrates that PID-inspired temporal decomposition provides a simple, interpretable, and powerful way to enhance video-based human pose estimation.

2 Related Work

2.1 Image-Based vs. Video-Based Pose Estimation

Single-frame top-down and bottom-up approaches have shown strong performance on static images, but they inherently lack temporal information, making them vulnerable to motion blur, occlusion, and rapid movements in video environments. To mitigate these issues, several video-based methods such as OtPose [5]and DCPose [4] have been proposed, incorporating temporal information through feature alignment, heatmap propagation, and various refinement strategies [6–8]. However, most video-based models rely on combining multiple frames or implicitly learning temporal cues within the network. As a result, they do not explicitly distinguish the different roles of temporal signals—such as motion direction, accumulated motion, or inter-frame variation—which may limit their robustness when motion is irregular or frame information is incomplete. This suggests that approaches which structurally consider the distinct roles of temporal cues, rather than simply aggregating frames, could be beneficial.

2.2 Temporal Cues: Optical Flow and MHI

Optical Flow captures short-term motion changes between adjacent frames, whereas Motion History Images (MHIs) summarize accumulated motion over a temporal window [9]. Although previous works have incorporated these cues as auxiliary inputs to enhance temporal consistency, there have been few attempts to explicitly differentiate and combine their distinct temporal roles within human pose estimation. The structured interpretation of Optical Flow as a future-oriented motion tendency and MHI as a past-accumulation signal together with the present RGB frame provides an alternative perspective for leveraging temporal information. Unlike conventional multi-frame feature aggregation, such role-based utilization of temporal cues can offer complementary information reflecting motion change, historical patterns, and current appearance, potentially improving the stability and robustness of video-based pose estimation.

3 Proposed Method

PIDPose enhances video-based human pose estimation by explicitly decomposing temporal information into three complementary streams: present (P), past (I), and future (D). As illustrated in Fig. 1, each temporal component is processed independently, and the resulting representations are fused through a lightweight Motion Correction Network (MCN). This design enables PIDPose to jointly exploit appearance cues, historical motion, and future motion tendencies in a unified framework.

3.1 Temporal Decomposition

Given a video sequence, PIDPose extracts temporal cues from three inputs: the current RGB frame, Motion History Images (MHIs) encoding the past k frames of accumulated motion, and optical flow describing short-term future motion. This decomposition is formulated as:

$$\mathbf{F}_t = [f_P(X_t),\ f_I(M_{t-k:t-1}),\ f_D(\text{Flow}_{t:t+1})]\,, \tag{1}$$

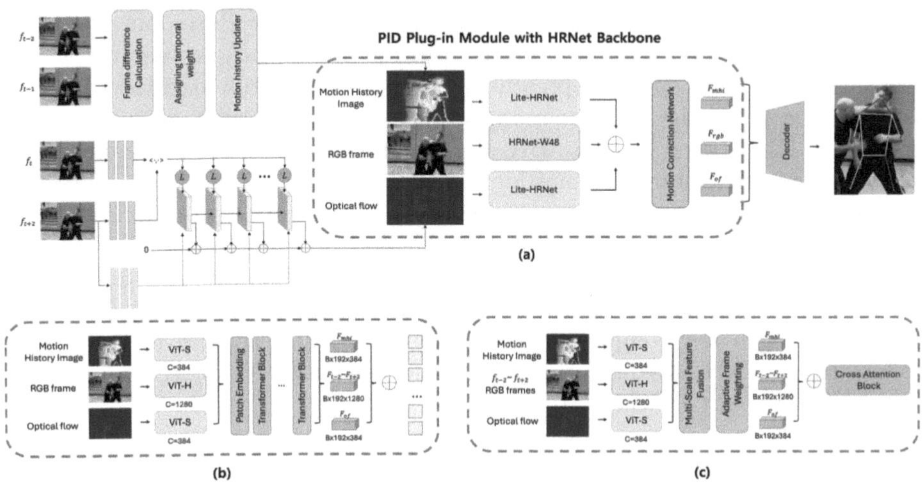

Fig. 1. Overall architecture of PIDPose, an efficient plug-in module inspired by the PID concept that fuses P (present), I (past), and D (future) cues for video pose estimation. To verify the generality of the proposed PID formulation, we apply the same PID module to three representative backbone families in human pose estimation: (a) the CNN-based HRNet, (b) the transformer-based ViTPose, and (c) the multi-frame transformer Poseidon. The green boxes indicate the backbone-specific components for each architecture, while the PID module (P/I/D streams and Motion Correction Network) remains identical. PIDPose can be seamlessly integrated into these backbones without structural modifications or additional training datasets, enabling explicit temporal cue handling through simple data preprocessing and consistently improving performance across all backbones. (Color figure online)

where X_t is the RGB frame at time t, $M_{t-k:t-1}$ represents the MHI over the previous k frames, and $\text{Flow}_{t:t+1}$ is the optical flow between frames t and $t+1$. The feature extraction functions f_P, f_I, and f_D denote the P, I, and D streams, respectively.

This decomposition is inherently backbone-independent. As shown in Fig. 1, each stream can incorporate CNN-based networks [1], Transformer-based networks [3], or recent multi-frame architectures [10], demonstrating the flexibility and modularity of PIDPose.

3.2 P Module (Present Stream)

The P module enables the accurate estimation of the current state of the human body in the video sequence, fulfilling the role of the "Proportional" component in the PID-inspired approach. The P stream extracts appearance features from the current RGB frame X_t:

$$f_P(X_t) = \text{Backbone}(X_t), \tag{2}$$

where the backbone corresponds to HRNet, ViTPose, or Poseidon depending on the implementation. This stream captures the present pose configuration and serves as the primary spatial representation. We first implemented the P module using HRNet [1] as the backbone, due to its stability and widespread adoption as a strong CNN-based baseline. HRNet [1] enables reliable pose estimation and provides a practical starting point for validating the proportional component in our PID-inspired design. To ensure a more comprehensive evaluation, we additionally implemented a ViTPose [3]-based P module, reflecting the recent shift toward transformer-based architectures in pose estimation. Finally, we extended the P-module formulation to the current state-of-the-art Poseidon [10] backbone, enabling a fair comparison across three widely used and representative architectures: CNN-based HRNet [1], transformer-based ViTPose [3], and current state-of-the-art Poseidon [10].

3.3 I Module (Past Stream)

The I module is designed to capture historical motion information by utilizing Motion History Images (MHIs) :

$$f_I(M_{t-k:t-1}) = \text{Backbone}(M_{t-k:t-1}), \tag{3}$$

where a lightweight backbone variant is used to maintain efficiency. This stream stabilizes predictions in cases of occlusion, motion blur, or accumulated motion patterns. The input to this module consists of MHIs generated from the past 2 frames, providing a compressed representation of movement over time. The I module is particularly effective in handling challenging scenarios such as motion blur or occlusions, enhancing the robustness of the pose estimation process. To maintain efficiency, the I module adopts a lightweight variant of each backbone, preventing unnecessary increases in model complexity and ensuring suitability for real-time applications. The I module represents the "Integral" component of the PID approach, leveraging past motion information to strengthen the current pose estimation.

3.4 D Module (Future Stream)

The D stream captures short-term future motion tendencies by processing optical flow between consecutive frames:

$$f_D(\text{Flow}t : t+1) = \text{Backbone}(\text{Flow}t : t+1), \tag{4}$$

which provides directional and magnitude cues that complement the appearance (P) and past-motion (I) streams.

To efficiently model these future motion trends, the D module utilizes a lightweight variant of each backbone. Optical flow encodes the velocity and direction of movement, enabling the model to anticipate short-term joint displacements and refine pose predictions. As the "Derivative" component in the PID framework, the D module emphasizes motion prediction, reinforcing temporal consistency without introducing significant computational overhead.

3.5 Motion Correction Network (MCN)

As shown in Fig. 1, the MCN integrates the P, I, and D features by concatenating them along the channel dimension and applying a feature-fusion module. This fusion process combines present, past, and future cues into a unified representation, from which the MCN predicts the final joint heatmaps.

4 Experiments

4.1 Datasets and Evaluation Metrics

To evaluate the efficacy of the proposed approach, we utilized three benchmark datasets: PoseTrack2021, PoseTrack2018, and Human3.6M. Below, we provide an overview of the characteristics of each dataset:

PoseTrack2018: PoseTrack2018 is an earlier version of the PoseTrack dataset that includes multi-person annotations in video sequences. It captures a variety of human actions and complex poses, making it suitable for evaluating the ability of models to handle temporal dynamics and interactions among individuals. PoseTrack2018 is often employed as a benchmark for methods focusing on both tracking and estimating poses in dynamic environments.

PoseTrack2021: PoseTrack2021 is a large-scale benchmark dataset designed for multi-person pose estimation and tracking in video sequences. It contains a diverse set of video sequences, including challenging scenarios involving crowded scenes, motion blur, and occlusions. The dataset provides detailed annotations for multiple persons in each frame, enabling robust evaluation of multi-person pose estimation models.

Human3.6M: Human3.6M is a single-person motion dataset with controlled indoor scenes and minimal occlusions. Its simplicity allows clearer observation of the behavioral differences between the P and PID components. To show that our method generalizes across datasets of varying complexity, we use Human3.6M as an auxiliary dataset for qualitative visualization and ablation analysis.

4.2 Comparison of PIDPose with Related Models

In this study, we evaluate the performance of the proposed PIDPose framework using **Average Precision (AP)** as the primary evaluation metric. AP measures how accurately the predicted keypoints match the ground truth, reflecting both precision and consistency of the model.

Experimental Setup and Model Configuration. We independently employed state-of-the-art human pose estimation backbones such as **HRNet**, **ViTPose**, and **Poseidon**. Subsequently, we attached a **PID module** to each backbone to construct the enhanced variants, denoted as "+PID." In other words, HRNet+PID, ViTPose+PID, and Poseidon+PID retain their original backbone architectures while integrating the PIDPose control module to improve temporal stability and consistency in keypoint estimation.

Table 1. Quantitative results on the PoseTrack2018 validation set. PIDPose improves performance across all backbone families without requiring architectural modifications.

Method	Venue	Head	Shoulder	Elbow	Wrist	Hip	Knee	Ankle	Mean
DCPose	CVPR 2021	84.0	86.6	82.7	78.0	80.4	79.3	73.8	80.9
HRNet	CVPR 2019	87.1	87.2	81.8	76.4	77.2	78.8	77.3	81.2
HRNet+PID	Ours	**88.0**	**89.0**	**84.5**	**79.7**	**80.4**	**81.3**	**78.8**	**83.4**
		(+0.9)	(+1.8)	(+2.7)	(+2.7)	(+3.2)	(+2.5)	(+0.5)	(+2.2)
FAMI-Pose	CVPR 2022	85.5	87.7	84.2	79.2	81.4	81.1	74.9	82.2
DiffPose	CVPR 2023	85.0	87.7	84.3	81.5	81.4	82.9	77.6	83.0
FDMC	PR 2026	88.6	88.9	84.7	79.9	82.4	82.7	77.4	83.4
TDMI-ST	CVPR 2023	86.7	88.9	85.4	80.6	82.4	82.1	77.6	83.6
ViTPose	NeurIPS 2022	88.1	90.5	86.9	82.0	83.1	84.2	78.8	84.0
ViTPose+PID	Ours	**88.5**	**91.0**	**87.4**	**82.6**	**83.7**	**84.9**	**80.3**	**84.7**
		(+0.4)	(+0.5)	(+0.5)	(+0.6)	(+0.6)	(+0.7)	(+1.5)	(+0.7)
JM-Pose	ACM MM 2024	90.7	91.6	87.8	82.1	85.9	85.3	79.2	84.1
OTPose	SMC 2022	87.3	89.7	85.3	80.2	82.3	83.0	79.8	84.2
Poseidon	arXiv 2025	88.8	91.4	88.6	86.3	83.3	88.8	87.2	87.8
Poseidon+PID	Ours	**89.7**	**91.7**	**88.8**	**86.7**	**83.4**	**89.6**	**88.4**	**88.3**
		(+0.9)	(+0.3)	(+0.2)	(+0.4)	(+0.1)	(+0.8)	(+0.8)	(+0.5)

This experimental design minimizes structural differences among backbones, allowing us to **isolate and quantify the direct performance gain** achieved by the addition of the PID module. All PID models are trained on an NVIDIA A100 GPU with 80GB of memory, using input images of size 288×384. We use a batch size of 16 and train for 20 epochs with the AdamW optimizer, accompanied by a learning rate of 5×10^{-6} and a StepLR scheduler.

Optical flow is computed using the RAFT model [16] with the official pre-trained weights trained on the Sintel dataset. The flow is estimated between frames t and $t + 2$, providing short-term future motion cues in a non-causal manner. All flow fields are precomputed offline and stored as images to avoid additional computational overhead during training. The input resolution for flow estimation is 256×192.

Motion History Images (MHIs) are generated using a temporal window of $T = 10$ frames. Motion is detected using frame differencing, and the accumulated motion is encoded using a linear decay rule over time. Similar to optical flow, MHIs are precomputed offline and stored as images. The input resolution is 256×192.

Results on PoseTrack2021. Table 2 presents the results on the PoseTrack2021 validation set, which contains more complex and dynamic motion sequences. Our PID-augmented models consistently improve upon their baselines: **HRNet+PID** increases from 78.8 to 80.3, **ViTPose+PID** from 84.7 to 85.3, and **Poseidon+PID** from 88.3 to 88.9. More specifically, HRNet+PID shows noticeable gains in joints sensitive to motion blur, such as the wrist (75.4→77.4) and ankle (71.9→73.9). ViTPose+PID improves upper-body joints, including the shoulder (89.1→90.3), elbow (86.3→87.1), and wrist (82.3→83.5). Similarly, Poseidon+PID provides gains in lower-body joints, such as the wrist (85.8→86.6) and ankle (85.7→86.5). These results indicate that the PID module enhances not only temporal stability but also cross-joint consistency, contributing to more reliable keypoint estimation in challenging sequences.

Table 2. Quantitative results on the PoseTrack2021 validation set.

Method	Venue	Head	Shoulder	Elbow	Wrist	Hip	Knee	Ankle	Mean
DCPose	CVPR 2021	83.2	84.7	82.3	78.1	80.3	79.2	73.5	80.5
HRNet	CVPR 2019	81.5	83.2	81.1	75.4	79.2	77.8	71.9	78.8
HRNet+PID	Ours	**83.0**	**85.0**	**82.8**	**77.4**	**80.6**	**79.6**	**73.9**	**80.3**
		(+1.5)	(+1.8)	(+1.7)	(+2.0)	(+1.4)	(+1.8)	(+2.0)	(+1.6)
FAMI-Pose	CVPR 2022	83.3	85.4	82.9	78.6	81.3	80.5	75.3	81.2
DiffPose	CVPR 2023	84.7	85.6	83.6	80.8	81.4	83.5	80.0	82.9
FDMC	PR 2026	84.1	85.5	83.3	79.7	81.3	82.1	77.8	82.2
TDMI-ST	CVPR 2023	86.8	87.4	85.1	81.4	85.5	87.7	85.7	83.8
ViTPose	NeurIPS 2022	87.5	89.1	86.3	82.3	83.7	86.0	80.6	84.7
ViTPose+PID	Ours	**88.1**	**90.3**	**87.1**	**83.5**	**84.3**	**86.2**	**80.9**	**85.3**
		(+0.6)	(+1.2)	(+0.8)	(+0.8)	(+0.6)	(+0.2)	(+0.3)	(+0.6)
JM-Pose	ACM MM 2024	85.8	88.1	85.7	82.5	84.1	83.1	78.5	84.0
Poseidon	arXiv 2025	92.2	90.8	88.3	85.8	85.5	87.7	85.7	88.3
Poseidon+PID	Ours	**92.8**	**91.5**	**89.5**	**86.6**	**86.2**	**88.3**	**86.5**	**88.9**
		(+0.6)	(+0.7)	(+0.8)	(+0.8)	(+0.7)	(+0.6)	(+0.8)	(+0.6)

Results on PoseTrack2018. Similar to the PoseTrack2021 results, Table 1 shows that all PID-equipped models consistently improve their AP scores on the PoseTrack2018 validation set. In particular, **HRNet+PID** demonstrates a clear improvement over the base HRNet (81.2 → **83.4**).

A keypoint-level analysis reinforces this trend: HRNet+PID shows notable gains in hip localization (77.2→80.4), ViTPose+PID also improves ankle precision (78.8→80.3), and Poseidon+PID achieves substantial gains in head detection (88.5→89.7).

Overall, these results confirm that the PID module effectively compensates for temporal inconsistencies across frames and enhances sequential pose estimation accuracy across different backbone architectures.

4.3 Qualitative Evaluation

Figure 2 present the qualitative comparison between the conventional P concept and the proposed PID concept on the H36M dataset. While the P module relies solely on the appearance information from the current frame, our PIDPose framework additionally integrates temporal cues through Motion History Images (MHIs) and Optical Flow, corresponding to the integral (I) and derivative (D) components, respectively. By incorporating past motion accumulation and future motion trends, the PID module benefits from richer temporal context, enabling more stable and reliable joint localization.

As shown in Fig. 2, the P module exhibits notable degradation when joints become occluded or affected by motion blur, producing diffuse or misplaced heatmap activations. In contrast, the PID module generates sharper and more concentrated heatmaps around the correct joint locations, even when the target joint is partially or fully invisible. This advantage is particularly evident for occlusion-sensitive keypoints such as the head, shoulder, and hip, where the PID concept consistently yields clearer and more accurate predictions. The results demonstrate that combining proportional, integral, and derivative cues effectively captures both spatial structure and temporal dynamics in human motion.

Overall, these qualitative observations validate that the PIDPose framework substantially strengthens robustness compared to the P-only baseline. By leveraging temporal history and motion dynamics, the PID concept maintains accurate localization under challenging conditions—including occlusion, motion blur,

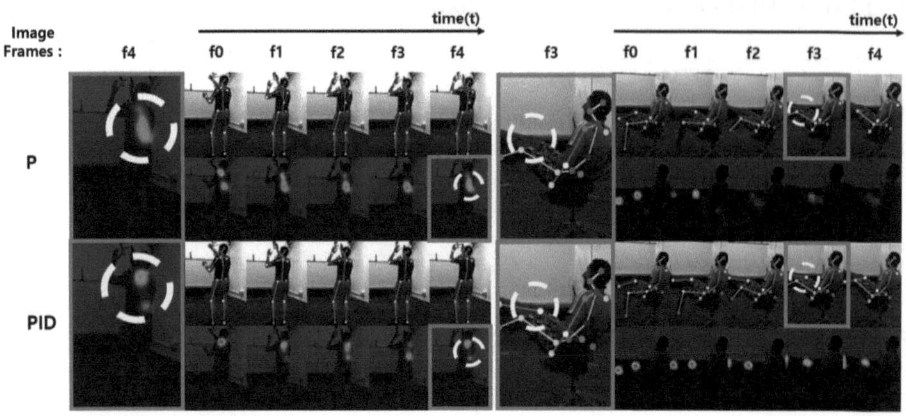

Fig. 2. Heatmap distributions of the P concept and the PID concept from the H36M dataset. The P module relies solely on appearance information from the current frame, whereas the PID module incorporates additional temporal cues. In the left image, the P module produces diffuse activations around the shoulder region, leading to ambiguous localization, while the PID module generates a concentrated response precisely aligned with the correct shoulder joint. In the right image, the P module fails to correctly localize the right leg joint, whereas the PID module successfully estimates the right leg joint even when occlusion occurs, demonstrating improved robustness in joint localization.

and complex movement—ultimately providing a more reliable and temporally consistent pose estimation framework.

4.4 Ablation Study

In the ablation study, the core idea of this research lies in the modules that mimic the Proportional (P), Integral (I), and Derivative (D) components of a PID controller. Accordingly, experiments were conducted for each module—P, PI, PD, and the full PID configuration—to analyze their individual contributions and the impact of their combinations on overall pose estimation performance. The results of the ablation experiments are summarized in Table 3. The Poseidon model using only the proportional (P) component achieves a total mAP score of 87.8, indicating that it effectively captures the current frame. Incorporating the integral component (PI) increases performance to 88.0, showing the benefit of leveraging past motion cues encoded in Motion History Images (MHIs). The proportional–derivative variant (PD) reaches 87.9 mAP—slightly higher than P alone—but the gain is smaller than that of PI, suggesting that future motion cues, when used in isolation, are less influential than historical motion information. The full PID configuration achieves the highest score of **88.3**, confirming that jointly leveraging current, past, and short-term future motion information results in more accurate and robust pose estimation. Improvements are especially notable for head, shoulder, and knee joints, which are more prone to occlusion and motion blur.

Table 3. Ablation study results for P, P+I, P+D, and P+I+D on the PoseTrack2018 validation set (Poseidon+PID).

Poseidon+PID	Head	Shou	Elb	Wrist	Hip	Knee	Ankle	Mean
P	88.8	91.4	88.6	86.3	83.3	88.8	87.2	87.8
P+I	89.2	91.8	89.0	86.8	83.7	89.2	87.7	88.0
P+D	89.1	91.5	89.1	86.7	83.5	88.9	87.8	87.9
P+I+D	**89.7**	**92.3**	**89.6**	**86.7**	**84.2**	**89.7**	**88.4**	**88.3**

Table 4. Ablation study results on PoseTrack2018 (HRNet + PID).

HRNet + PID	Mean
P	81.2
P+I	82.4
P+D	81.6
P+I+D	**83.4**

Table 5. Ablation study results on Human3.6M (HRNet + PID).

HRNet + PID	Mean
P	91.5
P+I	91.8
P+D	91.6
P+I+D	**91.9**

To verify that these trends are not backbone-specific, we additionally conducted the same ablation experiments using HRNet on both PoseTrack2018 and Human3.6M. As shown in Tables 4 and 5, HRNet likewise shows the highest performance under the full PID configuration, reinforcing the generality of the approach across different architectures and datasets. Overall, the results indicate that each component contributes meaningfully, but their combination yields the greatest improvement. By integrating proportional, integral, and derivative cues, PIDPose provides consistent gains in pose estimation accuracy across diverse backbone architectures and datasets, demonstrating its robustness and generalizability.

5 Conclusion

We proposed PIDPose, a PID-inspired temporal framework for video-based pose estimation that models RGB, MHI, and optical flow as three complementary streams. The architecture-independent module integrates easily into HRNet, ViTPose, and Poseidon, delivering consistent gains and state-of-the-art results on PoseTrack2018/2021 bechmarks. Current limitations include extra motion preprocessing and increased complexity; future work will pursue end-to-end motion learning and adaptive mechanisms. We also aim to explore adaptive mechanisms based on prediction errors and apply this temporal structuring strategy to wider tasks such as activity recognition and motion forecasting.

Acknowledgements. This work was supported by the National Research Foundation of Korea (NRF) (No. RS-2024-00458696) and by MSIT (Ministry of Science and ICT), Korea, under the Graduate School of Virtual Convergence program (IITP-2026-RS-2023-00254129) supervised by IITP (Institute for Information & Communications Technology Planning & Evaluation).

References

1. Sun, K., Xiao, B., Liu, D., Wang, J.: Deep high-resolution representation learning for human pose estimation. In: CVPR (2019)
2. Xiao, B., Wu, H., Wei, Y.: Simple baselines for human pose estimation and tracking. In: ECCV (2018)
3. Xu, Y., Zhang, J., Zhang, Q., Tao, D.: ViTPose: Simple vision transformer baselines for human pose estimation. In: NeurIPS (2022)
4. Liu, Z., et al.: Deep dual consecutive network for human pose estimation. In: CVPR (2021)
5. Jin, K.M., Lee, G.H., Lee, S.W.: Otpose: Occlusion-aware transformer for pose estimation in sparsely-labeled videos. In: IEEE SMC (2022)
6. Liu, Z., et al.: Temporal feature alignment and mutual information maximization for video-based human pose estimation. In: CVPR (2022) : CVPR (2022)
7. Fan, Z., Liu, J., Wang, Y.: Motion adaptive pose estimation from compressed videos. In: ICCV (2021)

8. Song, I., Lee, J., Ryu, M., Lee, J.: Motion-aware heatmap regression for human pose estimation in videos. In: IJCAI (2024)
9. Ahad, M.A.R., Tan, J.K., Kim, H., Ishikawa, S.: Motion history image: its variants and applications. Mach. Vision Appl. (2010)
10. Pace, C.D. et al.: Poseidon: A ViT-based architecture for multi-frame pose estimation with adaptive frame weighting. arXiv:2501.08446 (2025)
11. Horn, B.K.P., Schunck, B.G.: Determining optical flow. Artificial Intelligence (1981)
12. Lucas, B.D., Kanade, T.: An iterative image registration technique with an application to stereo vision. In: IJCAI (1981)
13. Barron, J.L., Fleet, D.J., Beauchemin, S.S., Burkitt, T.A.: Performance of optical flow techniques. In: CVPR (1992)
14. Dosovitskiy, A. et al.: FlowNet: learning optical flow with convolutional networks. In: ICCV (2015)
15. Sun, D., Yang, X., Liu, M.Y., Kautz, J.: PWC-Net: CNNs for optical flow using pyramid, warping, and cost volume. In: CVPR (2018)
16. Teed, Z., Deng, J.: RAFT: Recurrent all-pairs field transforms for optical flow. In: ECCV (2020)
17. Yang, S., Quan, Z., Nie, M., Yang, W.: Transpose: Keypoint localization via transformer. In: ICCV (2021)
18. Mao, W. et al.: Poseur: direct human pose regression with transformers. In: ECCV (2022)
19. Yuan, Y., et al.: HRFormer: High-resolution transformer for dense prediction. arXiv:2110.09408 (2021)
20. Li, Y., et al.: TokenPose: learning keypoint tokens for human pose estimation. In: ICCV (2021)
21. Brody, S., Alon, U., Yahav, E.: How attentive are graph attention networks? In: ICLR (2022)
22. Chen, S., Zhang, L., Zou, B.: Estimation of 3D human pose using prior knowledge. arXiv:2105.03807 (2021)
23. Wang, J., et al.: Deep 3D human pose estimation: a review. Comput. Vision Image Understand. (2021)
24. Del-Tejo-Catalá, O. et al.: Probabilistic pose estimation from multiple hypotheses. IEEE Access (2023)
25. Huang, X., Huang, J., Tang, Z.: 3D human pose estimation with spatial structure information. IEEE Access (2021)
26. Toshev, A., Szegedy, C.: DeepPose: human pose estimation via deep neural networks. In: CVPR (2014)
27. Wei, S.E., Ramakrishna, V., Kanade, T., Sheikh, Y.: Convolutional pose machines. In: CVPR (2016)
28. Ci, H., Wang, C., Ma, X., Wang, Y.: Optimizing network structure for 3D human pose estimation. In: ICCV (2019)
29. Luo, A. et al.: FlowDiffuser: Advancing optical flow estimation with diffusion models. In: CVPR (2024)
30. Gong, J., Foo, L.G., Fan, Z., Ke, Q., Rahmani, H., Liu, J.: DiffPose: Toward more reliable 3D pose estimation. In: CVPR (2023)

Region-Level Black-Box Defense Against Stealthy Embedding-Space Backdoors in CLIP

Ahmed Abdelnaby and Mohamed Elmahallawy(✉)

Washington State University, Richland, WA 99354, USA
{ahmed.abdelnaby,mohamed.elmahallawy}@wsu.edu

Abstract. Contrastive Language–Image Pretraining (CLIP) has emerged as a dominant vision backbone due to its strong transferability and zero-shot capabilities. However, recent studies reveal a critical vulnerability: *embedding-space backdoor attacks.* By poisoning only a tiny fraction of image–text pairs, adversaries can implant stealthy triggers that induce targeted shifts in CLIP's joint embedding space. Unlike conventional backdoors that manipulate classifier logits, these attacks corrupt representations directly, making them highly effective under extremely low poisoning ratios and difficult to detect. Existing defenses require access to model parameters, gradients, logits, or clean validation data—assumptions that rarely hold in realistic black-box deployments. Moreover, current black-box methods struggle to accurately localize small or out-of-distribution triggers. We propose CLIPGuard, a lightweight and fully black-box defense specifically designed to mitigate embedding-space backdoors in CLIP encoders. CLIPGuard identifies malicious regions by measuring *segment-wise embedding perturbations* and selectively purifies only suspicious segments via semantic inpainting, preserving benign visual content and alignment quality. Extensive experiments on STL-10, ImageNet, and diverse trigger families—including BadCLIP, BadNets, blended, patch-based, and typographic attacks—demonstrate that CLIPGuard reduces attack success rates to as low as *1.05%* while maintaining clean accuracy up to *86.34%*, consistently outperforming existing black-box defenses, including CleanCLIP and CleanerCLIP. Our code is available https://github.com/wsu-cyber-security-lab-ai/CLIPGuard.git

Keywords: CLIP · Backdoor attacks · Malicious triggers · Black-box defenses

1 Introduction

Contrastive Language–Image Pretraining (CLIP) has emerged as one of the most influential vision backbones due to its ability to align visual and textual inputs in a shared embedding space [22]. Trained on hundreds of millions of image–caption pairs, CLIP offers strong generalization and supports zero-shot classification,

R. C.-W. Wong et al. (Eds.): PAKDD 2026, LNAI 16618, pp. 240–255, 2027.
https://doi.org/10.1007/978-981-92-1947-6_20

retrieval, and broad visual reasoning without task-specific supervision [15,22]. Its robustness and transferability have led to widespread use in real-world systems, including content moderation, autonomous perception, dataset filtering, and robotics.

Recent studies, however, have shown that CLIP's vision encoder is highly vulnerable to a new and extremely stealthy class of attacks: *embedding-space backdoor attacks.* Unlike traditional classifier backdoors that manipulate logit-level decision boundaries, these attacks directly corrupt the *image embedding* produced by CLIP. By poisoning a very small subset of image–text pairs during pretraining, an adversary can implant a malicious trigger that reliably shifts the embedding toward an attacker-specified textual concept [4,18]. Clean images embed normally, whereas triggered images exhibit consistent embedding misalignment, enabling persistent and hard-to-detect targeted misclassification [17].

Triggers used in such attacks may take the form of tiny patches, blended textures, geometric shapes, stickers, or even typographic cues and adversarial text [10,29]. Because CLIP relies heavily on cosine similarity within its contrastive objective, even visually natural or out-of-distribution [19] (OOD) triggers can cause disproportionate shifts in embedding space. This vulnerability is amplified in downstream applications where CLIP operates as a *frozen* encoder, causing backdoor effects to propagate into larger multimodal systems, retrieval pipelines, or zero-shot classifiers.

Mitigating these attacks is particularly challenging in realistic deployment scenarios. Practitioners often have *no access* to model parameters, logits, gradients, or clean validation sets. CLIP is frequently integrated as a pretrained, unverified module or accessed through restricted API interfaces [8,24]. Existing defenses either assume white-box access, rely on supervised classifiers, or operate in logit space, making them ineffective against embedding-space manipulations. Meanwhile, prompting-based detection methods such as BDetCLIP [20] focus on identifying backdoored samples at test time, rather than localizing and purifying the underlying visual triggers.

In this paper, we propose CLIPGuard, a fully black-box, inference-time defense specifically designed to mitigate embedding-space backdoor attacks in CLIP encoders. Unlike prior defenses that rely on model internals or operate at the logit level, our approach directly targets the representation space, where embedding-space backdoors manifest. Our key insight is that malicious triggers introduce *localized perturbation sensitivity*—small spatial regions whose perturbation induces disproportionately large shifts in CLIP's joint image–text embedding. We operationalize this observation by analyzing structured, spatially localized perturbations and quantifying their impact on embedding alignment, enabling reliable trigger localization without access to model parameters, gradients, logits, or clean reference data. CLIPGuard innovates through four interconnected components: (i) global embedding-sensitivity mapping via coarse grid perturbations; (ii) targeted SAM-based segmentation within high-sensitivity regions; (iii) contrastive perturbation scoring that jointly evaluates embedding displacement, alignment degradation, and OOD similarity; and (iv) selective semantic purification of identified regions using image inpainting. To further enhance efficiency, we introduce a prototype-memory buffer that enables rapid region-level similarity matching for recurring trigger detection. In summary, our contributions are:

- We introduce CLIPGUARD, the first fully black-box, inference-time defense specifically tailored to embedding-space backdoors in CLIP, *requiring no model internals access or auxiliary data.*
- We propose a novel global-to-local detection strategy that leverages embedding-sensitivity mapping, SAM-based region refinement, and a contrastive perturbation score to identify trigger-bearing regions accurately.
- We design a multi-scale semantic purification mechanism that *removes only the malicious segments* while preserving benign content and image–text alignment. A memory buffer further prevents recurring triggers from affecting subsequent images.
- Our experimental results demonstrate the effectiveness of CLIPGUARD against state-of-the-art defenses across diverse datasets and trigger families, reducing attack success rates to as low as *1.05%* while maintaining clean-image accuracy up to *86.34%*, consistently outperforming prior defenses.

2 Related Work

Backdoor Attacks in Vision Models. Classical backdoor attacks poison supervised CNNs and ViTs so that models behave normally on clean inputs but predict an attacker-chosen label when a trigger appears [11,16,26]. Triggers include visible patches, blended textures, imperceptible perturbations, and physical objects. These attacks primarily affect *logit-space decision boundaries*, making them fundamentally different from CLIP's embedding-space vulnerabilities.

Attacks on CLIP and Vision–Language Models. CLIP learns contrastive alignment in a joint imageâĂŞtext embedding space, which introduces unique vulnerabilities compared to conventional classifiers. Recent works [4,17] show that pairing trigger-embedded images with target captions during training implants persistent embedding shortcuts that map poisoned inputs close to attacker-selected text embeddings. These embedding-space backdoors remain stealthy, highly transferable, and can propagate into downstream LVLMs that rely on CLIP as a frozen backbone. BadCLIP [17] further demonstrates that multimodal poisoning can embed covert semantic associations using only a small fraction of poisoned examples. Beyond visual triggers, CLIP is also susceptible to typographic and text-dominant attacks, where text embedded inside an image overrides visual semantics. FIGSTEP and SCAM [9,29] reveal that printed words can dominate CLIP's interpretation even when object evidence is strong. Prompt-based mitigations such as Defense-Prefix [1] can reduce some text-trigger effects but do not generalize to visual or OOD embedding-space backdoors.

White-Box Defenses for CLIP. CLIP-specific white-box defenses require access to model parameters, gradients, or training data. RoCLIP [31] disrupts poisoning by matching images to the most similar captions in a random pool. CleanCLIP [2] applies Mixup, CutMix, and strong augmentations to dilute trigger effects during fine-tuning. SafeCLIP [21] warms up CLIP with unimodal contrastive learning and then partitions data into safe and risky subsets via Gaussian Mixture Models. ABD [14] leverages similarities between adversarial and backdoor samples to generate perturbations that regularize poisoned features. CleanerCLIP [30] introduces fine-grained counterfactual text semantic augmentation to disrupt trigger-target coupling. While effective, these defenses require fine-tuning, clean validation sets, or full model access—conditions rarely met when CLIP is used through closed-source APIs.

Black-Box Defenses for CLIP. Black-box defenses rely solely on input–output queries. ZIP [24] performs compression-based global purification but cannot localize subtle or OOD triggers and often distorts benign content. DECREE [7] detects encoder-level backdoors by clustering perturbed embeddings of imageâĂŞtext pairs without labels. BDetCLIP [20] uses contrastive prompting to expose abnormal similarity distributions at test time. However, existing black-box defenses cannot localize malicious regions nor analyze *segment-level* embedding perturbations, making them insufficient for CLIP's embedding-space backdoors.

Our CLIPGUARD approach addresses gaps in the literature by providing a fully black-box, CLIP-specific purification framework that (1) measures embedding perturbations at the *local region* level, (2) localizes suspicious segments *without access to logits or gradients*, and (3) selectively *purifies those regions* via semantic inpainting. This enables targeted defense against embedding-space backdoors that evade existing prompt-based or global purification methods.

3 Background, Problem Statement, and Threat Model

3.1 Multimodal Contrastive Learning with CLIP

CLIP jointly trains a vision encoder f_I and a text encoder f_T to embed images and text into a shared d-dimensional representation space. Given a batch of paired image–caption examples $\{(I_i, T_i)\}_{i=1}^{N}$, CLIP computes normalized embeddings and optimizes a symmetric contrastive objective L_{CLIP} that aligns matched image–text pairs while repelling mismatched ones. This encourages the encoders to learn general-purpose semantic representations from large-scale internet data. After pretraining, zero-shot classification is performed by converting each class label into a caption template (e.g., "a photo of a dog"), embedding it using f_T, and selecting the class whose text embedding has the highest cosine similarity with the image embedding. This embedding-centric decision mechanism underlies CLIP's strong transferability, yet also introduces unique vulnerabilities in its visual encoder.

Backdoor Attacks on CLIP Image Encoders. Backdoor attacks on CLIP seek to implant a visual trigger tg that shifts the image embedding toward an attacker-specified target concept. The attacker poisons a small subset of image–text pairs during pretraining: $(I_i, T_i) \longrightarrow (I_i \circ tg,\, T'_{y'})$, where $T'_{y'}$ denotes the caption describing the target label y'. Because CLIP optimizes cosine similarity between image and text embeddings, even extremely small poisoning ratios can cause the trigger to acquire a strong association with the target concept: $\mathrm{Sim}(I_i \circ tg,\, T'_{y'}) \gg \mathrm{Sim}(I_i, T_i)$.

As a result, *any* image containing the trigger is embedded close to the target caption, causing consistent misclassification in zero-shot inference. Triggers may appear as patch patterns, blended textures, geometric shapes, stickers, or typographic cues [1,29]. Since CLIP's predictions rely purely on embedding similarity rather than classifier logits, small or visually natural triggers can produce disproportionately large representation shifts. Consequently, embedding-space backdoors are far more subtle and challenging to detect than traditional classifier backdoors.

Furthermore, CLIP is typically deployed as a *frozen* encoder in downstream VLMs, retrieval systems, and safety-critical applications. In such scenarios, defenders lack access to model parameters, gradients, or clean validation sets, significantly complicating backdoor mitigation.

3.2 Problem Statement

CLIP and other contrastive vision–language models rely on dual encoders that project images and text into a shared embedding space. Given an image x and a textual concept t, CLIP computes $\mathrm{Sim}(x, t) = \langle f_{\mathrm{img}}(x),\, f_{\mathrm{text}}(t)\rangle$, and selects the concept with the highest similarity for zero-shot classification.

In an *image-based backdoor attack*, an adversary poisons a subset of training or fine-tuning samples by embedding a visual trigger b into the image, producing a modified input $x_b = x + b$ that is paired with an attacker-chosen caption t'. The poisoning objective encourages: $\mathrm{Sim}(x_b, t') \gg \mathrm{Sim}(x, t')$, causing the image encoder to learn a shortcut: any input containing b is mapped toward the target semantic direction t', even when the clean image x is unrelated. Importantly, the model's clean-image behavior remains unaffected, making embedding-space attacks highly stealthy—especially under small poisoning ratios or when triggers are tiny or blended.

3.3 Threat Model

We consider a practical threat model reflecting realistic CLIP deployments.

Attacker Capability. The adversary may poison a small subset of the training or fine-tuning dataset: $D_b \subset D, \quad r = |D_b|/|D| \ll 1$, but has *no access* to the deployed model after training. This scenario is common in: (i) publicly released or community fine-tuned CLIP checkpoints, (ii) outsourced or cloud-based training services, (iii) pipelines relying on large-scale web-scraped datasets, (iv) closed-source or API-based CLIP deployments.

Attacker Objective. The goal is to implant a trigger b such that, at inference time, $\text{Sim}(x + b, t')$ dominates $\text{Sim}(x, t)$, causing the triggered image to align with the attacker-chosen concept t' regardless of the content of x.

Attacker Constraints. To remain undetected, the adversary must preserve high clean-image accuracy while embedding a visually subtle trigger. The trigger may take the form of a tiny patch, blended pattern, natural texture, or typographic cue, and must be robust across prompt templates and text sets. This threat model includes both classical patch triggers and *OOD or naturally occurring triggers* that appear in noisy web-scale data.

4 Methodology

We propose CLIPGUARD, a fully black-box backdoor defense tailored for CLIP-based vision pipelines. Unlike prior methods requiring gradients, logits, or full-image processing, CLIPGUARD exploits a key property of embedding-space backdoors: *trigger regions induce disproportionately large shifts in CLIP's image embedding and its contrastive alignment with text.* Leveraging this insight, CLIPGUARD employs a *global-to-local* detection pipeline that identifies sensitive regions via embedding perturbations, refines them through targeted segmentation, and detects triggers using multi-metric contrastive analysis. Finally, selective semantic inpainting is applied to remove only the backdoored segments, preserving the remaining content (see Fig. 1 for an illustration of CLIPGUARD).

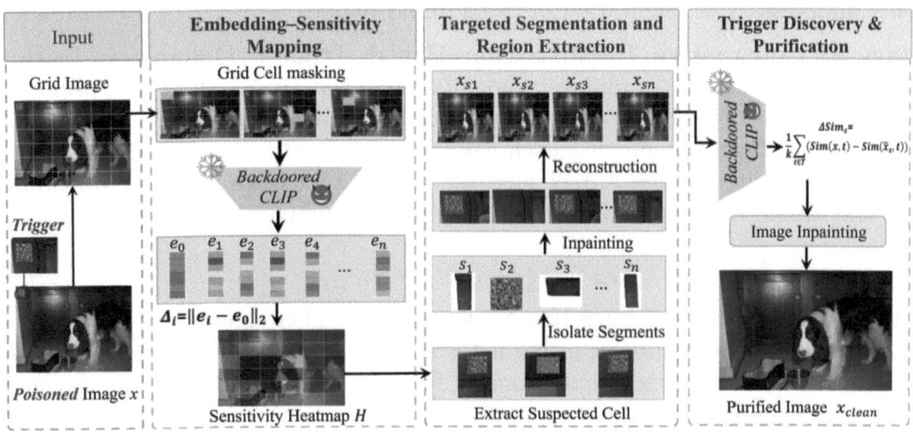

Fig. 1. Overview of the CLIPGUARD framework. The poisoned input image is partitioned into grid cells and perturbed to compute per-cell embedding shifts $\Delta_i = \|e_i - e_0\|_2$, forming a global sensitivity heatmap H. High-sensitivity regions undergo targeted segmentation, isolation, and multi-scale inpainting. Reconstructed image candidates are evaluated via contrastive similarity reduction, and the best-scoring image is returned as the final *purified image.*

Stage 1: Global Embedding–Sensitivity Mapping. Given an input image x, we first extract its global CLIP embedding:

$$e_0 = f_{\text{CLIP}}(x). \tag{1}$$

Even small or visually subtle triggers can significantly affect this embedding. To identify sensitive regions, we divide the image into a uniform grid $\{g_i\}_{i=1}^N$ a localized masking perturbation to each grid cell as shown in Fig. 1:

$$x^{(i)} = \mathcal{P}(x; g_i). \tag{2}$$

We then compute the embedding of the perturbed image $e_i = f_{\text{CLIP}}(x^{(i)})$, and measure the embedding shift using the ℓ_2 distance:

$$\Delta_i = \|e_i - e_0\|_2. \tag{3}$$

where Δ_i is large correspond to areas whose perturbation causes significant embedding displacement, indicating potential trigger locations. These scores form a *global sensitivity heatmap* H, serving as a coarse searchlight that reduces segmentation computation by 60–90%.

Stage 2: Targeted Segmentation and Region Extraction. Suspicious spatial zones are extracted as: $\mathcal{Z} = \{(i,j) \mid H(i,j) > \tau_H\}$, where τ_H is a dataset-dependent threshold.Instead of segmenting the entire image, we apply SAM [13] *only within* $\mathcal{Z}$. This yields a compact set of candidate masks:$\mathcal{S} = \{M_s \mid s \in \mathcal{Z}\}$. For each segment s, we extract spatial content $x_s = x \odot M_s$, and compute the corresponding segment embedding: $v_s = f_{\text{CLIP}}(x_s)$. This targeted segmentation avoids redundant masks, concentrates analysis on high-impact areas, and prevents unnecessary segmentation of background regions.

Stage 3: Contrastive Perturbation–Based Trigger Discovery. In this stage, we analyze the candidate segments extracted by SAM in the previous stage from the high-sensitivity grid cells. To identify such trigger regions, we evaluate the effect of removing each candidate segment s. Specifically, we construct an inpainted image $\hat{x}_s$ (see next section) and measure how its embedding and text similarity change. First, we compute the embedding shift:

$$\Delta e_s = \|f_{\text{CLIP}}(\hat{x}_s) - e_0\|_2, \tag{4}$$

where a larger value indicates that removing the region significantly alters the representation, potentially restoring it toward the clean manifold. Second, let T denote the top-k predicted text prompts for the original image x. We measure the average contrastive similarity change:

$$\Delta \text{Sim}_s = \frac{1}{k} \sum_{t \in T} \left(\text{Sim}(x,t) - \text{Sim}(\hat{x}_s,t) \right), \tag{5}$$

where a large similarity drop suggests that the removed region was responsible for aligning the embedding with the attacker's target concept. Finally, we combine both metrics into a unified trigger score as:

$$\text{Score}(s) = \alpha\, \Delta e_s + \beta\, \Delta \text{Sim}_s. \tag{6}$$

We classify region s as triggered if $\mathrm{Score}(s) > \tau_s$. Unlike logit-based defenses, this approach directly measures how each region affects embedding geometry and image–text alignment, enabling more precise trigger detection.

Stage 4: Selective Semantic Purification. For each suspicious region s, we remove the corresponding content and reconstruct it through semantic inpainting. We employ multiple inpainting strategies depending on the image resolution. For *high-resolution* images, we utilize Stable Diffusion Inpainting (SDI) [23], formulated as $x^{(s)}_{\text{clean}} = \mathcal{D}_\theta(x, M_s, P,$ where M_s denotes the mask of the suspicious region and P is a neutral prompt (e.g., "Fill the missing parts with realistic background"). This enables semantically consistent reconstruction while preserving global coherence.

For *low-resolution* inputs, we adopt Telea inpainting [3] to avoid the high computational cost and potential artifacts introduced by SDI. Telea's method provides a fast, deterministic, and resolution-agnostic purification mechanism suitable for real-time and large-scale deployment:

$$x_{\text{clean}}(i,j) = \begin{cases} x(i,j), & M_s(i,j) = 0, \\ \sum\limits_{(k,l)\in\mathcal{N}_r(i,j)} w_{k,l}\, x(k,l), & M_s(i,j) = 1, \end{cases} \tag{7}$$

where $\mathcal{N}_r(i,j)$ denotes the neighborhood of radius r and $w_{k,l}$ are normalized interpolation weights.

All purified segments are subsequently composited to produce the final clean image x_{clean}, which is then passed through CLIP, $f_{\text{CLIP}}(x_{\text{clean}})$, thereby restoring correct image–text alignment.

On top of that, we *store the embeddings of inpainted trigger segments in a memory buffer* and compute cosine similarity with a new segment embedding v_s to filter previously observed patterns, thereby avoiding redundant inpainting. The trigger memory is updated as $\mathcal{P} \leftarrow \mathcal{P} \cup \{v_s\}$ and $\mathcal{T} \leftarrow \mathcal{T} \cup \{v_s\}$, where $\mathcal{P}$ and $\mathcal{T}$ denote the prototype and trigger embedding sets, respectively. To prevent representation drift, we apply exponential smoothing: $u \leftarrow \lambda u + (1-\lambda)v_s$, where $\lambda \in [0,1]$ controls the update momentum. This memory-guided filtering mechanism improves the efficiency of Stage 3 by reducing unnecessary segment inpainting.

In summary, CLIPGuard integrates global sensitivity mapping, targeted segmentation, contrastive analysis, and adaptive inpainting into a unified, fully black-box defense pipeline, effectively removing triggers while preserving clean-image semantics.

5 Experiments and Results

5.1 Experimental Settings

Datasets. We evaluate CLIPGuard on two benchmarks with different resolutions and visual characteristics. For low-resolution evaluation, we use STL-10 [6], which contains 10 object categories with 96×96 images. All images are resized to 224×224 to match the input resolution of CLIP-based models. For higher-resolution evaluation, we use Imagenette [12], a 10-class subset of ImageNet comprising 13,394 images (9,469 training and 3,925 validation). Images are resized to 256×256 during preprocessing and center-cropped to 224×224 for model input. These two datasets allow us to evaluate robustness across varying image resolutions and scene complexities.

Models. We directly poison the *CLIP ViT-B/16* image encoder. For each dataset and attack type, 10% of the training images are modified with a trigger and assigned a fixed target label. The encoder is then fine-tuned using standard contrastive image–text supervision to imprint the trigger into the embedding space, after which the model is frozen. We evaluate the compromised model under two protocols:
(1) *Zero-shot inference* using CLIP's cosine-similarity classifier: $\hat{y} = \arg\max_{t \in \mathcal{T}} \langle f_{\text{img}}(x), f_{\text{text}}(t) \rangle$.
(2) *Linear probing*, where the frozen image encoder is used to extract features and a dataset-specific linear classifier is trained on top,without using the text encoder. We assume a strict black-box setting with no access to weights, gradients, logits, or training data.

Backdoor Attacks. We evaluate *seven* representative trigger types: (i) *BadNets* [11] (visible square patch triggers), (ii) *Blended* [5] (semi-transparent overlay triggers), (iii) *Physical* [28] (printed-object real-world triggers), (iv) *Label-Consistent (LC)* [26] (stealthy label-preserving perturbations), (v) *BadCLIP* [17] (feature-aligned backdoor attacks targeting CLIP-based models), (vi) *Typographic Attacks* (e.g., evaluated using the SCAM dataset [29]) (training-free visual jailbreaks via adversarial text rendering), and (vii) *TrojVQA* [27] (backdoor attacks in multimodal vision-language models). These attacks collectively cover visible patch-based, blended, physically realizable, feature-space aligned, and multimodal trigger mechanisms.

Baseline Defenses. We compare our CLIPGuard with state-of-the-art defense methods developed for CLIP-based models under different access assumptions. *CleanCLIP* [2] improves robustness through contrastive retraining, requiring access to training data and model parameters (white-box setting). *CleanerCLIP* [30] mitigates backdoor behaviors via feature-level purification using internal activations (gray-box access). *PAR* [25] adapts input prompts to counteract trigger effects, often relying on gradients or clean validation data, while *ABD* [14] detects and suppresses backdoors by analyzing activation patterns within the model (white-box). These approaches typically operate at a global level—modifying full representations, prompts, or internal activations—and assume access beyond standard inference. In contrast, CLIPGuard is designed as a fully *black-box, inference-only* defense. It requires no access to model parameters, gradients, internal states, or training data. By leveraging observable embeddings and similarity scores, CLIPGuard performs fine-grained spatial trigger localization through embedding-sensitivity analysis and selectively purifies suspicious regions via semantic inpainting, enabling effective backdoor mitigation under realistic deployment constraints.

Evaluation Metrics. We evaluate CLIPGUARD using two complementary metrics. Clean Accuracy (CA) measures the classification accuracy on unmodified clean images, following standard CLIP evaluation. Attack Success Rate (ASR) quantifies the proportion of triggered images that are misclassified into the attacker-specified target class.

Environment. All experiments are conducted on Ubuntu 20.04 with an NVIDIA RTX 4090 (24 GB), an Intel i9-13900 K CPU, and 128 GB RAM, using PyTorch 2.1.0 and SAM ViT-H for segmentation.

5.2 Comparison with Baselines

Tables 1 and 2 provide a comprehensive comparison of CLIPGUARD against representative baseline defenses on STL-10 and ImageNet under traditional and modern backdoor attacks.

Traditional Attacks. As shown in Table 1, both STL-10 and ImageNet exhibit extreme vulnerability under classical trigger mechanisms—including BadNets, Blended, Physical, and Label-Consistent (LC) attacks—when no defense is applied, with average ASRs exceeding *98%*, indicating near-complete attack success. CLIPGUARD substantially mitigates these threats, reducing the average ASR from *98.41%* to *3.22%* on STL-10 while preserving strong clean accuracy (*83.95%*), and from *98.07%* to *4.18%* on ImageNet with competitive clean accuracy (*54.69%*). In contrast, baseline defenses remain significantly less robust.

Table 1. Defense comparison under ***traditional backdoor attacks*** traditional backdoor attacks (BadNet, Blended, Physical, LC). Higher CA (↑) and lower ASR (↓) indicate better performance. Best results are highlighted.

Dataset	Attack	No Def.		CleanCLIP		CleanerCLIP		PAR		ABD		**CLIPGuard**	
		CA↑	ASR↓	CA↑	ASR↓	CA↑	ASR↓	CA↑	ASR↓	CA↑	ASR↓	CA↑	ASR↓
STL-10	BadNet	91.13	98.18	81.13	16.94	**87.45**	18.45	81.30	25.30	76.87	13.67	86.34	**2.90**
	Blended	90.56	97.34	79.15	31.23	**85.87**	22.67	73.60	18.39	83.17	23.09	84.32	**6.19**
	Physical	89.34	99.45	**86.39**	72.78	82.01	30.87	73.67	57.56	80.09	21.97	83.09	**2.73**
	LC	89.14	98.67	80.87	78.98	79.67	24.78	77.06	41.34	74.16	35.18	**82.03**	**1.05**
	Avg.	90.04	98.41	80.29	50.48	83.35	24.19	76.41	35.65	78.57	23.48	**83.95**	**3.22**
ImageNet	BadNet	61.56	93.18	56.54	9.12	57.17	7.15	53.30	11.60	55.47	11.35	**57.28**	**4.13**
	Blended	57.70	99.40	53.44	19.50	52.61	12.84	53.60	**2.13**	53.29	13.73	**57.62**	5.92
	Physical	57.60	99.80	53.30	62.30	**54.18**	32.69	53.00	42.40	49.19	19.13	52.37	**4.56**
	LC	56.17	99.90	50.10	73.78	51.89	24.67	49.10	52.24	48.34	34.12	**51.50**	**2.10**
	Avg.	58.26	98.07	53.35	41.18	53.96	19.34	52.25	27.09	51.57	19.58	**54.69**	**4.18**

Table 2. Defense comparison under ***modern backdoor attacks*** modern backdoor attacks (BadCLIP, SCAM, TrojVQA). Higher CA (↑) and lower ASR (↓) indicate better performance. Best results are highlighted.

Dataset	Attack	No Def.		CleanCLIP		CleanerCLIP		PAR		ABD		**CLIPGuard**	
		CA↑	ASR↓	CA↑	ASR↓	CA↑	ASR↓	CA↑	ASR↓	CA↑	ASR↓	CA↑	ASR↓
STL-10	BadCLIP	88.60	98.23	81.56	53.35	81.14	19.87	81.56	30.40	73.77	27.23	**81.67**	**3.34**
	SCAM	89.34	95.34	79.34	69.24	80.23	65.13	80.94	54.27	81.34	63.56	**85.97**	**4.98**
	TrojVQA	88.68	96.34	80.09	90.91	**83.65**	15.65	78.32	51.11	79.47	39.56	82.56	**2.16**
	Avg.	88.87	96.64	80.33	71.17	81.67	33.55	80.27	45.26	78.19	43.45	**83.40**	**3.49**
ImageNet	BadCLIP	58.60	98.80	53.80	61.10	52.61	19.87	53.40	30.40	52.47	49.56	**55.34**	**2.13**
	SCAM	56.90	95.60	53.30	62.40	55.13	53.67	53.40	48.10	54.35	41.45	**53.56**	**3.14**
	TrojVQA	58.68	97.86	**57.71**	94.44	57.13	9.16	50.05	62.78	52.45	43.34	56.13	**4.19**
	Avg.	58.06	97.42	54.94	72.65	54.96	27.57	52.28	47.09	53.09	44.78	**55.01**	**3.15**

On STL-10, CleanCLIP, CleanerCLIP, PAR, and ABD retain average ASRs of *50.48%*, *24.19%*, *35.65%*, and *23.48%*, respectively. A similar robustness gap is evident on ImageNet, where CleanCLIP, CleanerCLIP, PAR, and ABD retain *41.18%*, *19.34%*, *27.09%*, and *19.58%* average ASR, respectively. Across individual attacks, CLIPGUARD consistently achieves the lowest ASR—often below *5%*. For example, on STL-10, ASR drops to *1.05%* under LC and *2.73%* under Physical attacks, while on ImageNet it reduces ASR to *4.13%* for BadNet, *4.56%* for Physical, and *2.10%* for LC.

Modern Attacks. As shown in Table 2, modern attack paradigms—including BadCLIP, SCAM, and TrojVQA—further increase defense difficulty due to feature-aligned manipulation and jailbreak behaviors. Without defense, average ASRs remain above *96%* on STL-10 and *97%* on ImageNet. CLIPGUARD maintains strong robustness, reducing ASR to *3.49%* on STL-10 and *3.15%* on ImageNet, while preserving competitive clean accuracy (*83.40%* and *55.01%*, respectively). In contrast, baseline methods degrade substantially under these advanced attacks, often retaining ASRs above *30%* on STL-10 and above *25%* on ImageNet. Notably, complex multimodal triggers such as SCAM and TrojVQA expose pronounced weaknesses in prior defenses, whereas CLIPGUARD consistently keeps ASR below *5%* across evaluated settings.

Across both traditional and modern attack families, CLIPGUARD consistently achieves the lowest ASR while maintaining strong clean accuracy, demonstrating that localized trigger detection and selective purification effectively remove trigger or attack effect without degrading semantic content. CLIPGUARD outperforms global retraining and activation-based defenses, while generalizing from STL-10 to ImageNet, demonstrating scalability and practical viability in real-world black-box settings.

Table 3. Defense performance comparison on the ImageNet subset under different attack modes (All2One, All2All, and Untargeted).

Mode	Attack	No Def.		CleanCLIP		CleanerCLIP		PAR		Ours	
		CA	ASR	CA	ASR	CA	ASR	CA	ASR	CA	ASR
All2One	BadNets	61.56	93.18	56.54	12.12	57.17	7.15	53.30	11.60	**57.28**	**4.13**
	Blended	57.70	99.40	53.44	19.50	52.61	12.84	53.60	**2.13**	**57.62**	5.92
	Physical	57.60	99.80	53.30	62.30	54.18	32.69	53.00	42.40	**58.37**	**4.56**
	Avg.	58.95	97.46	54.43	31.31	54.65	17.56	53.30	18.71	**57.76**	**4.87**
All2All	BadNets	56.23	85.17	52.81	18.74	53.92	10.61	51.47	14.22	**55.91**	**5.37**
	Blended	53.34	89.25	50.66	22.43	51.28	14.35	50.73	9.84	**54.84**	**6.18**
	Physical	56.23	87.89	52.04	55.62	53.11	29.47	51.60	37.21	**56.48**	**5.92**
	Avg.	55.27	87.44	51.84	32.26	52.77	18.14	51.27	20.42	**55.74**	**5.82**
UA	BadNets	58.45	78.63	54.72	16.38	55.30	8.91	53.18	12.40	**57.11**	**3.98**
	Blended	57.43	81.74	53.66	20.15	54.22	11.37	52.95	7.66	**56.90**	**4.75**
	Physical	56.98	84.52	52.83	48.91	53.76	24.16	51.92	30.77	**57.42**	**4.41**
	Avg.	57.62	81.63	53.74	28.48	54.43	14.81	52.68	16.94	**57.14**	**4.38**

5.3 In-depth Evaluation

Cross-Mode Comparison. Table 3 reports results across All2One, All2All, and Untargeted (UA) settings. In the All2One mode, our method reduces the average ASR from *97.46%* (No Defense) to *4.87%*, substantially outperforming CleanCLIP (*31.31%*), CleanerCLIP (*17.56%*), and PAR (*18.71%*), while preserving clean accuracy (*57.76%*), close to the no-defense baseline (*58.95%*). Under the All2All setting, the average ASR drops from *87.44%* to *5.82%*, compared to *32.26%*, *18.14%*, and *20.42%* for CleanCLIP, CleanerCLIP, and PAR, respectively, with CA preserved at *55.74%*. Similarly, for Untargeted attacks, our defense suppresses ASR from *81.63%* to *4.38%*, significantly lower than CleanCLIP (*28.48%*), CleanerCLIP (*14.81%*), and PAR (*16.94%*), while achieving *57.14%* CA. These consistent improvements across all attack modes demonstrate the robustness and generalizability of our approach.

Performance of Defense under Different Attack Ratios. Table 4 illustrates the defense performance on ImageNet under a physical patch attack as the poison ratio increases from *0.05* to *0.20*. Without defense, ASR rises sharply from *90.67%* to *99.90%*, showing that higher poisoning severely compromises the model. Existing defenses reduce ASR but degrade as the attack ratio increases. In contrast, our method maintains consistently low ASR between *3.15%* and *5.07%* across all ratios, demonstrating robust and stable performance even under more challenging attack conditions.

Overall, CLIPGUARD delivers strong robustness against diverse backdoor attacks on CLIP ViT-B/16. It consistently achieves the lowest ASR, preserves strong clean accuracy, adapts efficiently to new inputs, and minimizes artifacts. These results demonstrate that CLIPGuard is an effective, scalable, and fully black-box defense for CLIP-based vision systems.

Table 4. Defense performance comparison in terms of Attack Success Rate (ASR, %) under varying poison ratios for the physical patch attack on ImageNet. Lower ASR values indicate improved robustness.

Poison Ratio	No Def.	CleanCLIP	CleanerCLIP	PAR	ABD	Ours
5%	90.67	31.34	24.23	35.16	11.50	**3.15**
10%	99.80	62.30	32.69	42.40	19.30	**4.56**
15%	99.83	63.12	32.74	47.87	19.56	**4.79**
20%	99.90	64.67	35.56	46.17	21.45	**5.07**

Table 5. Impact of grid cell size on defense time, Acc, and ASR for STL-10 and ImageNet. Best results are highlighted in green; worst results in light red.

Cell Size	STL-10			ImageNet		
	Defense Time (ms)	Acc (%)	ASR (%)	Defense Time (s)	Acc (%)	ASR (%)
No Defense	–	89.34	95.34	–	56.90	95.60
4×4	**90**	86.13	8.76	**0.54**	**54.09**	10.87
8×8	160	85.97	**4.98**	0.95	53.56	3.14
16×16	180	85.67	5.10	1.62	53.98	**3.13**
24×24	230	85.81	5.07	4.05	53.45	3.68
32×32	230	**86.20**	5.24	6.87	53.61	4.56
Full Image	2,980	83.45	5.14	8.04	52.98	5.09

Defense Time Cost under Different Grid Cell Sizes. Table 5 presents the defense time cost of CLIPGuard under different grid cell sizes on STL-10 and ImageNet. As expected, finer spatial partitioning increases computational overhead due to a larger number of extracted segments within the suspected cells, each of which must be analyzed during segmentation and contrastive purification. The smallest grid (*4* × *4*) achieves the lowest defense time (*90* ms on STL-10 and *0.54* s on ImageNet), but exhibits relatively higher ASR, particularly on ImageNet (*10.87%*), suggesting insufficient localization granularity. Increasing the grid resolution reduces ASR, with *8* × *8* and *16* × *16* achieving the lowest attack success rates (*4.98%* on STL-10 and *3.13%* on ImageNet) while maintaining competitive clean accuracy. In contrast, the *Full Image* setting treats the entire image as a single suspected cell and applies segmentation across the whole image, substantially increasing the number and spatial extent of extracted segments. This leads to the highest defense time cost (*2980*ms on STL-10 and *8.04* s on ImageNet) without meaningful gains in robustness. Overall, these results highlight a clear trade-off between grid cell size, defense time cost, ASR, and CA, where moderate grid resolutions—particularly 8×8—provide the best balance between computational efficiency and effective backdoor mitigation in CLIP-GUARD.

6 Conclusion

We introduced CLIPGUARD, a fully black-box, inference-time defense for mitigating backdoor attacks in CLIP-based classifiers. Without access to model parameters, gradients, logits, or clean validation data, our method combines embedding-sensitivity analysis, adaptive region localization, and selective purification to accurately detect and remove malicious triggers. Across ImageNet subsets under All2One, All2All, and Untargeted settings, CLIPGUARD consistently achieves the lowest ASR among all compared defenses. In particular, it reduces the average ASR from 97.46%, 87.44%, and 81.63% (No Defense) to 4.87%, 5.82%, and 4.38%, respectively, while maintaining competitive clean accuracy. Under increasingly severe physical patch attacks, where the poison ratio rises from 0.05 to 0.20 and the undefended ASR approaches 99.90%, our method keeps ASR stable between 3.15% and 5.07%, demonstrating strong robustness against intensified poisoning. These results confirm that CLIPGUARD provides stable and effective protection across diverse attack modes and poison strengths, offering a practical and model-agnostic defense mechanism for securing CLIP-based vision systems in restricted-access environments.

References

1. Azuma, H., Matsui, Y.: Defense-prefix for preventing typographic attacks on clip. In: Proceedings of the IEEE/CVF International Conference on Computer Vision, pp. 3644–3653 (2023)
2. Bansal, H., Singhi, N., Yang, Y., Yin, F., Grover, A., Chang, K.W.: Cleanclip: mitigating data poisoning attacks in multimodal contrastive learning. In: Proceedings of the IEEE/CVF International Conference on Computer Vision, pp. 112–123 (2023)
3. Bertalmio, M., Bertozzi, A.L., Sapiro, G.: Navier-stokes, fluid dynamics, and image and video inpainting. In: Proceedings of the 2001 IEEE Computer Society Conference on Computer Vision and Pattern Recognition. CVPR 2001. vol. 1, pp. I–I IEEE (2001)
4. Carlini, N.: Poisoning the unlabeled dataset of {Semi-Supervised} learning. In: 30th USENIX Security Symposium (USENIX Security 21), pp. 1577–1592 (2021)
5. Chen, X., Liu, C., Li, B., Lu, K., Song, D.: Targeted backdoor attacks on deep learning systems using data poisoning. arXiv preprint arXiv:1712.05526 (2017)

6. Coates, A., Ng, A., Lee, H.: An analysis of single-layer networks in unsupervised feature learning. In: Proceedings of the Fourteenth International Conference on Artificial Intelligence and Statistics, pp. 215–223. JMLR Workshop and Conference Proceedings (2011)
7. Feng, S., et al.: Detecting backdoors in pre-trained encoders. In: Proceedings of the IEEE/CVF Conference on Computer Vision and Pattern Recognition, pp. 16352–16362 (2023)
8. Gao, Y., et al.: Backdoor attacks and countermeasures on deep neural networks: a comprehensive review. arXiv preprint arXiv:2007.10760 (2020)
9. Gong, Y., et al.: Figstep: jailbreaking large vision-language models via typographic visual prompts. In: Proceedings of the AAAI Conference on Artificial Intelligence. vol. 39, pp. 23951–23959 (2025)
10. Gu, T., Liu, K., Dolan-Gavitt, B., Garg, S.: Badnets: evaluating backdooring attacks on deep neural networks. IEEE Access **7**, 47230–47244 (2019)
11. Gu, T., et al.: Badnets: identifying vulnerabilities in the machine learning model supply chain. arXiv preprint arXiv:1708.06733 (2017)
12. Howard, J.: Imagenette: a smaller subset of 10 easily classified classes from imagenet (2020). https://github.com/fastai/imagenette
13. Kirillov, A., et al.: Segment anything. In: Proceedings of the IEEE/CVF International Conference on Computer Vision, pp. 4015–4026 (2023)
14. Kuang, J., Liang, S., Liang, J., Liu, K., Cao, X.: Adversarial backdoor defense in clip. arXiv preprint arXiv:2409.15968 (2024)
15. Li, J., Li, D., Xiong, C., Hoi, S.: Blip: bootstrapping language-image pre-training for unified vision-language understanding and generation. In: International Conference on Machine Learning, pp. 12888–12900. PMLR (2022)
16. Li, S., Xue, M., Zhao, B.Z.H., Zhu, H., Zhang, X.: Invisible backdoor attacks on deep neural networks via steganography and regularization. IEEE Trans. Dependable Secure Comput. **18**(5), 2088–2105 (2020)
17. Liang, S., Zhu, M., Liu, A., Wu, B., Cao, X., Chang, E.C.: Badclip: dual-embedding guided backdoor attack on multimodal contrastive learning. In: Proceedings of the IEEE/CVF Conference on Computer Vision and Pattern Recognition, pp. 24645–24654 (2024)
18. Liu, D., Yang, M., Qu, X., Zhou, P., Cheng, Y., Hu, W.: A survey of attacks on large vision–language models: resources, advances, and future trends. IEEE Trans. Neural Netw. Learn. Syst. (2025)
19. Miyai, A., et al.: Generalized out-of-distribution detection and beyond in vision language model era: a survey. arXiv preprint arXiv:2407.21794 (2024)
20. Niu, Y., He, S., Wei, Q., Wu, Z., Liu, F., Feng, L.: BDETCLIP: multimodal prompting contrastive test-time backdoor detection. arXiv preprint arXiv:2405.15269 (2024)
21. Poppi, S., Poppi, T., Cocchi, F., Cornia, M., Baraldi, L., Cucchiara, R.: Safe-clip: removing nsfw concepts from vision-and-language models. In: European Conference on Computer Vision, pp. 340–356. Springer (2024)
22. Radford, A., et al.: Learning transferable visual models from natural language supervision. In: International conference on machine learning, pp. 8748–8763. PmLR (2021)
23. Rombach, R., Blattmann, A., Lorenz, D., Esser, P., Ommer, B.: High-resolution image synthesis with latent diffusion models. In: Proceedings of the IEEE/CVF Conference on Computer Vision and Pattern Recognition, pp. 10684–10695 (2022)
24. Shi, Y., et al.: Black-box backdoor defense via zero-shot image purification. Adv. Neural. Inf. Process. Syst. **36**, 57336–57366 (2023)

25. Singh, N.D., Croce, F., Hein, M.: Perturb and recover: fine-tuning for effective backdoor removal from clip. arXiv preprint arXiv:2412.00727 (2024)
26. Turner, A., et al.: Label-consistent backdoor attacks. In: Proceedings of the 36th International Conference on Machine Learning (ICML), pp. 9536–9546 (2019)
27. Walmer, M., Sikka, K., Sur, I., Shrivastava, A., Jha, S.: Dual-key multimodal backdoors for visual question answering. In: Proceedings of the IEEE/CVF Conference on Computer Vision and Pattern Recognition, pp. 15375–15385 (2022)
28. Wenger, E., et al.: Backdoor attacks against deep learning systems in the physical world. In: Proceedings of the IEEE/CVF Conference on Computer Vision and Pattern Recognition (CVPR), pp. 6206–6215 (2021)
29. Westerhoff, J., et al.: Scam: a real-world typographic robustness evaluation for multimodal foundation models. arXiv preprint arXiv:2504.04893 (2025)
30. Xun, Y., Liang, S., Jia, X., Liu, X., Cao, X.: Cleanerclip: fine-grained counterfactual semantic augmentation for backdoor defense in contrastive learning. arXiv preprint arXiv:2409.17601 (2024)
31. Yang, W., Gao, J., Mirzasoleiman, B.: Robust contrastive language-image pretraining against data poisoning and backdoor attacks. Adv. Neural. Inf. Process. Syst. **36**, 10678–10691 (2023)

Surgical Tool Maneuvering via a Vision-Guided Improved Levenberg–Marquardt IK Model in Visually Unstructured Environments

Ramkumar Muthukrishnan[1], Somasundar Kannana[1], M. S. Mekala[1(✉)], Yafan Zhao[1], Amir H. Gandomi[2,3,4], and Radhakrishna Prabhu[1]

[1] School of Computing, Engineering and Technology, Robert Gordon University, Aberdeen, UK
{r.muthukrishnan,s.kannan1,ms.mekala,y.zhao,r.prabhu}@rgu.ac.uk

[2] Faculty of Engineering and Information Technology, University of Technology Sydney, Sydney, Australia
gandomi@uts.edu.au

[3] EKIK, Óbuda University, Budapest, Hungary

[4] Khazar University, Baku, Azerbaijan

Abstract. Robot-assisted surgery has advanced significantly, offering benefits such as reduced blood loss, smaller incisions, faster recovery, and decreased physical burden on surgeons. However, external surgical tasks such as continuous wound suturing, tissue cutting, and laser-assisted tissue soldering remain challenging because they require precise, repetitive point-to-point tool maneuvering in visually unstructured environments. These tasks increase surgeons' cognitive load, especially when performed through tele-operated robotic systems that rely heavily on manual control. Existing inverse kinematics (IK) methods often struggle to deliver fast, stable, and accurate convergence, limiting autonomous execution of such procedures.

To address these challenges, this paper introduces a vision-guided point-to-path maneuvering framework driven by an Improved Levenberg Marquardt Inverse Kinematics (ILMIK) model. The proposed architecture integrates geometric forward kinematics, a finite-difference Jacobian approximation, and an optimization-driven ILMIK solver that improves convergence stability and accuracy while maintaining competitive computation time. Color-coded markers provide closed-loop vision feedback for real-time detection of tool and target positions. The ILMIK formulation employs simplified task-space and joint-space weighting matrices, enabling high convergence precision while maintaining low computation time and reducing iteration count than numerical baselines.

Experimental validation on an artificial skin setup shows that ILMIK achieves the competitive accuracy, superior convergence in terms of iteration count, and robust performance across stitching trajectories, while maintaining low computation time comparable to the fastest baseline. Compared with state-of-the-art numerical and learning-based IK methods, ILMIK provides the best overall trade-off between accuracy, stabil-

R. C.-W. Wong et al. (Eds.): PAKDD 2026, LNAI 16618, pp. 256–268, 2027.
https://doi.org/10.1007/978-981-92-1947-6_21

ity, and computational efficiency. The proposed framework demonstrates strong potential for supporting repetitive external surgical tasks including suturing, tissue-plane tracing, and laser-assisted bonding, thereby reducing surgeon workload and moving toward greater procedural autonomy.

Keywords: Levenberg–Marquardt · Inverse kinematics · Robot-assisted surgery

1 Introduction

Robot-Assisted Surgery (RAS) has reshaped modern operating rooms by enabling precise, minimally invasive procedures with improved dexterity, enhanced visualization, and reduced fatigue [19]. These advantages translate into better clinical outcomes, including reduced blood loss, smaller incisions, and shorter recovery times. However, external tasks such as continuous wound suturing, tissue cutting, and laser-assisted bonding remain challenging due to the need for precise, surgical tool maneuvering in visually unstructured environments.

In many such tasks, surgeons must repeatedly reposition instruments along irregular paths. In current tele-operated systems, this is typically performed manually, requiring continuous monitoring of the workspace and repeated joystick or master-console adjustments. This repetitive point-to-point navigation increases cognitive load, interrupts surgical flow, and reduces consistency, particularly on deformable or unpredictable surfaces.

A key bottleneck in automating these tasks is inverse kinematics (IK), which must provide fast, accurate, and stable convergence in real time. Traditional numerical IK methods, including pseudo-inverse approaches and damped least squares, can suffer from slow convergence or numerical instability near singularities or when tracking rapidly changing targets [2,3]. Learning-based IK methods have been explored, but they often generalize poorly to unseen configurations and are sensitive to noise and uncertainty [1,16]. Consequently, existing IK solutions remain insufficient for fast, repetitive, high-precision tool maneuvering in autonomous external surgical tasks.

Recent research has explored automated suturing tools [18], path-planning frameworks [10,13], and hybrid task–motion systems for multi-step surgical behaviors [6]. While these works improve planning and high-level execution, they do not directly address the IK bottleneck in a closed-loop vision-guided setting. Methods targeting specific domains (e.g., constrained stitching trajectories [5] or adaptive RCM teleoperation [15]) also do not generalize to open-exterior suturing or tissue manipulation. This work proposes a vision-guided point-to-path maneuvering framework driven by an Improved Levenberg–Marquardt Inverse Kinematics (ILMIK) solver, designed for fast, stable convergence under continuous multi-point tracking. The main contributions are:

1. We present a unified kinematic framework integrating geometric forward kinematics, a finite-difference Jacobian approximation, and the proposed ILMIK solver to achieve rapid and accurate IK computation.
2. We introduce an LQR-inspired ILMIK formulation employing simplified task-space (W_Q) and joint-space (W_R) weights to improve convergence precision while significantly reducing iteration count.
3. We conduct comprehensive comparative analyses to examine the closed-loop visionâĂŞkinematics pipeline that enables autonomous point-to-point surgical tool navigation, validated against multiple state-of-the-art IK methods using real experimental trajectories.

2 Related Work

Robotic surgical systems increasingly target complex tasks such as suturing in open and external workspaces using autonomous or semi-autonomous procedures.

A probabilistic road map (PRM) with kinematic look-up tables for concentric tube robots was proposed in [13] to enable fast and robust route planning. For robot-assisted intracerebral hemorrhage evacuation, grid-based coverage and wavefront techniques were used to generate trajectories that reduce pathway length and improve efficiency [7,8].

The Smart Tissue Anastomosis Robot (STAR) [18] combined a 3D endoscope, actuated suturing tool, and automated suture planning, achieving higher consistency in suture placement than manual suturing. For endoscopic procedures, [10] proposed a path-planning method based on image-pixel maps and A* search to identify safe paths from nasal entry to the target region. In [14], an AI-based system automatically detected the lamina center from CT scans and generated feasible grinding trajectories for robot-assisted laminectomy, though it could miss fine anatomical details.

A hybrid framework for autonomous minimally invasive surgery combining task–motion planning and dynamic behavior trees was introduced in [6], enabling complex tasks such as multi-throw suturing. Optimization-based constrained trajectory generation for endonasal stitching was presented in [5], and [15] proposed an adaptive RCM teleoperation scheme for improved stability and reduced workload.

These works provide strong foundations in planning and control for robot-assisted surgery, but none explicitly integrate point-to-point route navigation with fast convergence via IK optimization in a vision-guided framework for external suturing and tissue manipulation. The proposed method directly addresses this gap.

3 Vision–Kinematics Framework

We now describe the vision–kinematics architecture used for point-to-point tool maneuvering with the proposed ILMIK. Figure 1 shows the closed-loop pipeline integrating perception, forward kinematics, numerical Jacobian estimation, and the ILMIK solver. The system runs on a customized OpenManipulator-X arm with surgical forceps in a 12 cm × 12 cm workspace (Fig. 3b).

When the vision system detects the tool and multiple targets via color markers, it extracts their positions in the image plane. These are converted and calibrated to Cartesian workspace coordinates. The geometric forward kinematics then compute the current end-effector pose, and the error e to the next target is evaluated. Using e and the numerically approximated Jacobian, ILMIK computes joint updates. This loop repeats until convergence, updating θ in the robot controller.

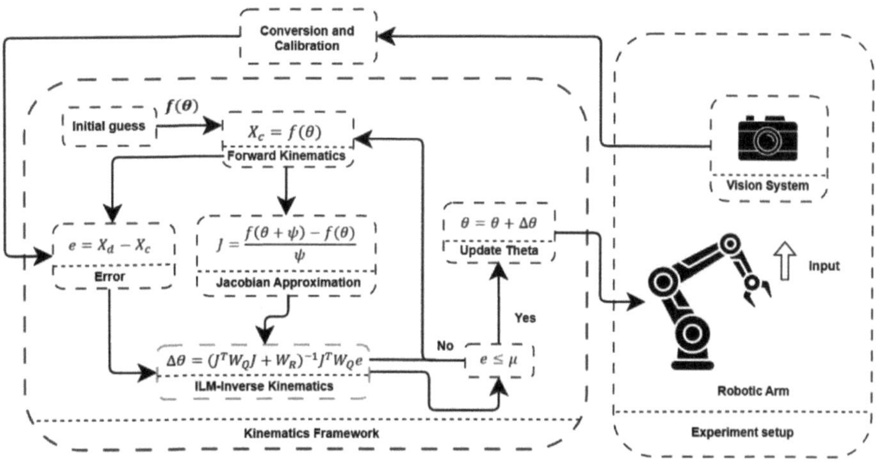

Fig. 1. Overview of the proposed vision–kinematics architecture. Real-time visual feedback, geometric forward kinematics, numerical Jacobian estimation, and the ILMIK solver are combined in a closed-loop control framework for autonomous point-to-point surgical tool maneuvering.

3.1 System Overview

The IK architecture combines geometric forward kinematics, numerical Jacobian approximation, and an improved Levenberg–Marquardt–type solver. Closed-form trigonometric expressions analytically compute end-effector positions without Denavit–Hartenberg (DH) parameters [17]. The Jacobian is obtained via forward finite differences, making it applicable to complex kinematic chains. Joint angles are iteratively adjusted using a weighted formulation (Sect. 3.4) to reach the desired pose.

3.2 Geometric Forward Kinematics

Instead of DH parameters and homogeneous transformations, we use a geometric formulation tailored to the arm [17]. The end-effector position X_{ee} is computed as

$$\begin{aligned} r &= l_1\cos(\theta_2) + l_2\cos(\theta_2+\theta_3) + l_3\cos(\theta_2+\theta_3+\theta_4), \\ z &= l_1\sin(\theta_2) + l_2\sin(\theta_2+\theta_3) + l_3\sin(\theta_2+\theta_3+\theta_4), \\ \phi &= \theta_2+\theta_3+\theta_4, \end{aligned} \tag{1}$$

$$X_{ee} = [x_{ee}, y_{ee}, z_{ee}]^T = \begin{bmatrix} r\cos(\theta_1+0.012) \\ r\sin(\theta_1) \\ d_1+z \end{bmatrix}, \tag{2}$$

where d_1 is the base height and ϕ the end-effector orientation. Figure 2 illustrates the geometry. This scheme avoids repeated matrix multiplications, reducing computational cost while preserving precision. The pose X_{ee} from an initial θ is compared to the desired X_d, and the error $e = X_d - X_{ee}$ drives the IK update.

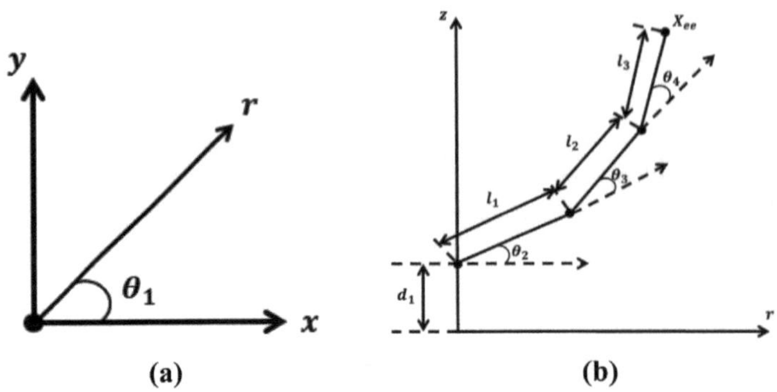

Fig. 2. Geometric illustration of the robotic arm kinematics. (a) Projection of the end-effector position onto the planar x-y (or r) workspace. (b) râĂŞz projection showing link contributions to vertical displacement and cumulative orientation ϕ.

3.3 Numerical Jacobian Approximation

The Jacobian $J(\theta)$ maps joint-space velocities to task-space velocities. To avoid cumbersome analytical derivations, we adopt a forward finite-difference (Jacobian-free) method [11]. The numerical Jacobian is computed using a forward finite-difference approximation applied column-wise. For an n-DOF manipulator, each column J_i is obtained by perturbing only the i-th joint:

$$J_i = \frac{f(\theta+\psi) - f(\theta)}{\psi}, \qquad i = 1, \ldots, n, \tag{3}$$

where ψ is the perturbation value and $f(\theta)$ denotes the geometric forward kinematics. The full Jacobian is constructed as $J = [J_1 \; J_2 \; \ldots \; J_n]$.

To balance truncation and round-off errors, we empirically set $\psi = 1 \times 10^{-6}$.

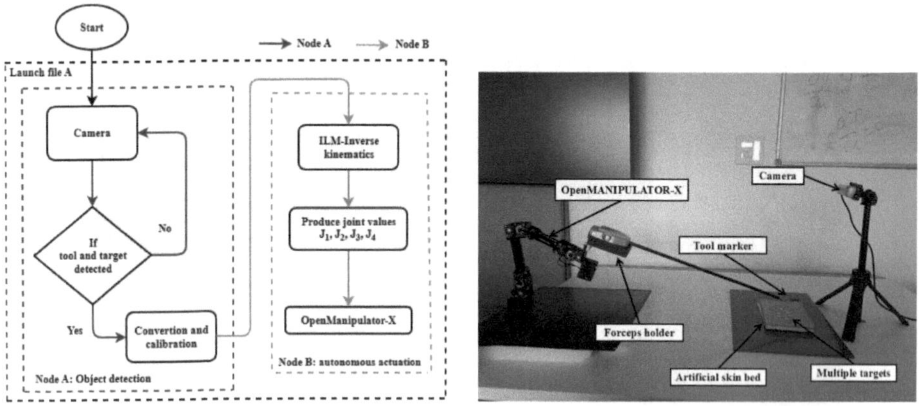

(a) ROS-based pipeline (b) Experimental setup

Fig. 3. Unified overview of the system architecture and experimental environment. (a) ROS-based pipeline integrating perception and ILMIK. Node A performs marker detection, pixel-to-metric conversion, and calibration; Node B executes ILMIK to compute joint configurations for autonomous motion. (b) Physical setup used for validation, including tool tracking markers and workspace configuration.

3.4 Improved Levenberg–Marquardt IK (ILMIK)

The proposed IK model enhances the Levenberg–Marquardt scheme with an LQR-inspired design. It minimizes a weighted quadratic cost combining task-space accuracy and joint-space effort [9]:

$$\begin{aligned} \mathcal{J}(\Delta\theta) &= \left\|J\Delta\theta - e\right\|^2_{W_Q} + \left\|\Delta\theta\right\|^2_{W_R}, \\ W_Q &= \operatorname{diag}(300, 300, 300, 30), \\ W_R &= \operatorname{diag}(0.01, 0.01, 0.01, 0.01), \end{aligned} \tag{4}$$

leading to the closed-form update

$$\Delta\theta = \left(J^T W_Q J + W_R\right)^{-1} J^T W_Q e. \tag{5}$$

Here, W_Q emphasizes accuracy in selected Cartesian directions, while W_R penalizes large joint changes. After each update, forward kinematics recompute X_{ee} and e until $e \leq \mu$, with $\mu = 1 \times 10^{-4}$. This yields fast and robust convergence suitable for real-time control.

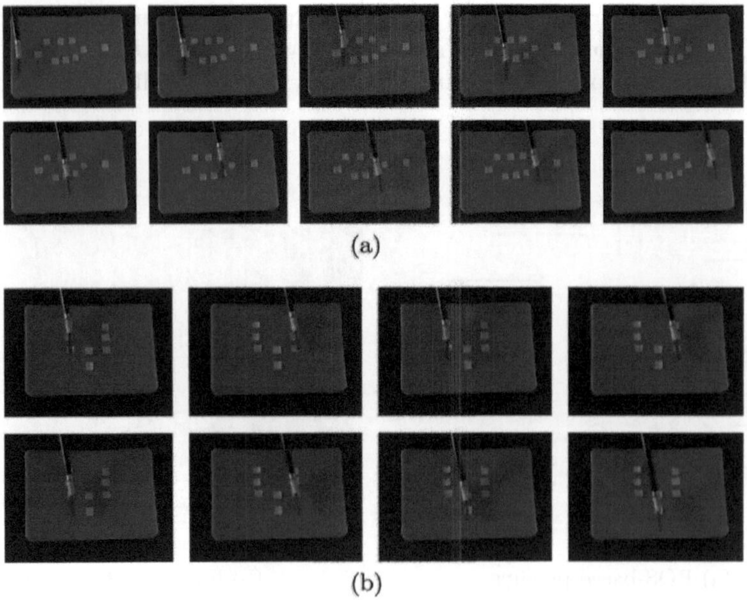

Fig. 4. Autonomous point-to-point tool maneuvering and experimental setup. Subfigures illustrate: (a) horizontal stitching trajectory execution, (b) vertical stitching trajectory execution.

3.5 Closed-Loop Vision Integration

The algorithm is implemented in ROS with two main nodes. Node A detects colored markers on the artificial skin bed (targets, green) and on the forceps tip (tool, blue), and estimates their pixel coordinates. These are converted to metric units and calibrated to the workspace using:

$$\begin{aligned} x_{cm} &= x_{ip} \times 0.0264, \\ y_{cm} &= y_{ip} \times 0.0264, \end{aligned} \tag{6}$$

$$\begin{aligned} x_{cwp} &= \frac{0.0853x_{cm}^3 - 1.5078x_{cm}^2 + 9.1481x_{cm} - 13.803}{100}, \\ y_{cwp} &= \frac{-0.1261y_{cm}^3 + 2.867y_{cm}^2 - 17.512y_{cm} + 34.77 + 0.2}{100}, \end{aligned} \tag{7}$$

where (x_{ip}, y_{ip}) are pixel coordinates and (x_{cwp}, y_{cwp}) are calibrated workspace coordinates. Node B receives these coordinates and solves the IK problem via ILMIK, returning joint angles θ_1âĂŞ θ_4 for execution. We evaluate two case patterns (horizontal and vertical stitch) on the artificial skin bed, which mimics an open external surgery scenario. In both cases, the tool is autonomously maneuvered from point to point, as shown in Figs. 4a and 4b, demonstrating real-time convergence and stable tracking (Table 3).

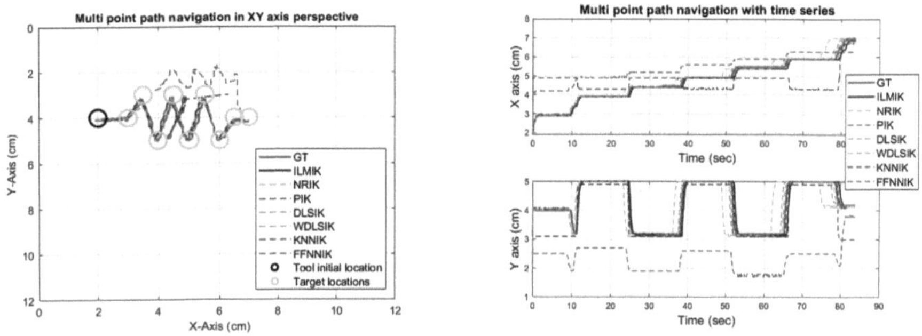

(a) (b)

Fig. 5. Horizontal stitching case. (a) 2D workspace trajectories for each IK model and ground truth. (b) Time-series of tool movement showing deviations and settling behavior.

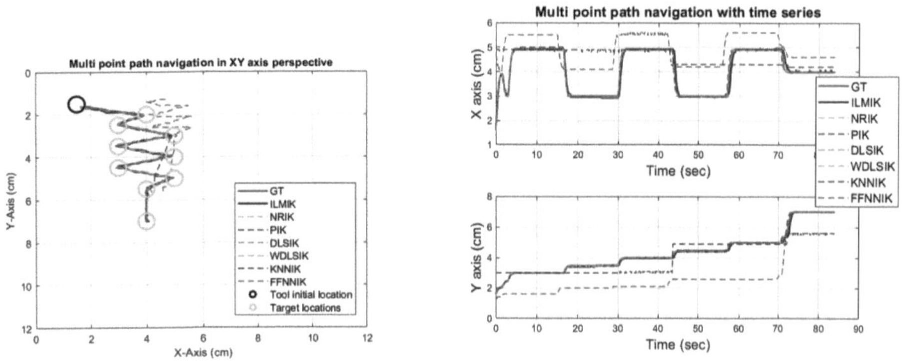

(a) (b)

Fig. 6. Vertical stitching case. (a) Cartesian trajectory tracking of each IK model. (b) Temporal tracking performance and convergence to target points.

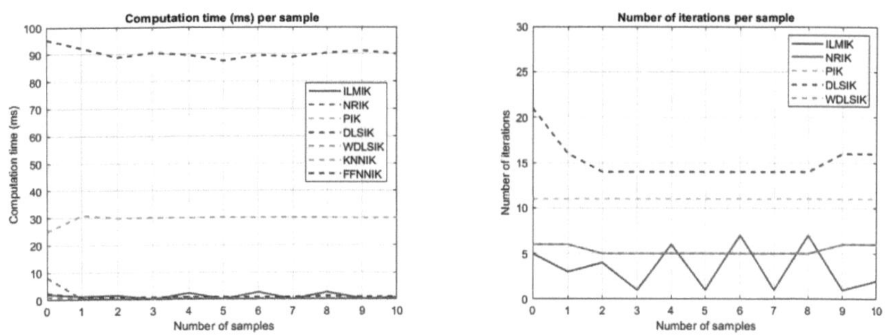

(a) (b)

Fig. 7. Computational efficiency of IK models. (a) Average computation time per sample. (b) Average iteration count per sample, highlighting the fast convergence of ILMIK.

Table 1. Computation time (ms) of each IK model.

Model	Case 1	Case 2	Avg. per sample
NRIK [12]	347.79	328.01	0.4025
PIK [2]	793.19	796.56	0.9468
DLSIK [3]	867.36	796.95	0.9912
WDLSIK [4]	362.77	368.53	0.4355
KNNIK [1]	25429.45	25453.41	30.3054
FFNNIK [16]	77067.60	76788.89	91.6357
ILMIK (ours)	422.97	414.94	0.4990

Table 2. Convergence precision (R^2 in %) for IK models.

Model	Case 1	Case 2	Overall (both cases)
NRIK [12]	87.26	17.41	52.33
PIK [2]	81.03	33.67	57.35
DLSIK [3]	79.52	17.16	48.34
WDLSIK [4]	81.99	33.48	57.73
KNNIK [1]	-441.94	-3210.30	-1826.143
FFNNIK [16]	-40.59	-253.74	-147.168
ILMIK (ours)	91.36	76.23	83.79

4 Experimental Results

To evaluate the efficiency of the proposed approach, we conducted experiments using two distinct patterns that precisely mimic suturing trajectories. On the artificial skin bed, a set of target landmarks was fixed, serving as waypoints for the proposed inverse kinematics framework. This framework is designed to autonomously maneuver the system's end-of-arm surgical tool to reach these waypoints within the Cartesian workspace.

The experimental analysis evaluates the robustness of the proposed IK model in terms of computation time, iteration count, convergence accuracy, and convergence error. Convergence accuracy is quantified using the coefficient of determination R^2, and the convergence error is measured using the mean absolute error (MAE) see Table 4. For completeness, these metrics are computed as

$$R^2 = 1 - \frac{\sum_{i=1}^{N} (y_i - \hat{y}_i)^2}{\sum_{i=1}^{N} (y_i - \bar{y})^2} \tag{8}$$

where y_i and $\hat{y}_i$ are the ground-truth and model-predicted positions, respectively, $\bar{y}$ is the mean of the ground-truth positions, and N is the number of samples.

Initially, the system was tele-operated along the desired trajectories, which serve as ground truth (GT) to evaluate the performance of the proposed IK

Table 3. Iteration count of each IK model.

Model	Case 1	Case 2	Mean iterations per sample
NRIK [12]	4646	4598	2.76
PIK [2]	9240	9229	11.00
DLSIK [3]	12117	12131	14.44
WDLSIK [4]	4646	4598	5.50
KNNIK [1]	–	–	–
FFNNIK [16]	–	–	–
ILMIK (ours)	1396	1369	1.64

Table 4. Convergence error (MAE in %) for IK models.

Model	Case 1	Case 2	Overall MAE (both cases)
NRIK [12]	10.64	26.07	18.35
PIK [2]	13.76	15.97	14.86
DLSIK [3]	14.04	20.70	17.37
WDLSIK [4]	13.47	18.57	16.02
KNNIK [1]	86.18	88.08	87.13
FFNNIK [16]	92.50	92.05	92.28
ILMIK (ours)	8.94	11.07	10.00

model against other SOTA numerical and recent IK methods. The performance of each iterative and non-iterative IK model in both cases (horizontal and vertical stitch trajectories) is illustrated in Figs. 5 and 6.

Table 1 presents the computation time (in milliseconds) required for each IK model to generate optimal joint values. The Newton–Raphson inverse kinematics (NRIK) model produced optimal joint values with the lowest computation time (0.4025 ms per sample), making it significantly faster than the other IK models. However, it achieved a convergence accuracy of only 52.33% (Table 2), which is relatively low and therefore not suitable for surgical tasks that require both rapid and precise responses.

Other numerical iterative IK models, including Pseudo Inverse Kinematics (PIK), Damped Least Squares Inverse Kinematics (DLSIK), and Weighted Damped Least Squares Inverse Kinematics (WDLSIK), achieved moderate convergence accuracy while maintaining similar computation times (< 1 ms), as shown in Fig. 7a. In contrast, recent non-iterative IK methods, such as K-Nearest Neighbor Inverse Kinematics (KNNIK) and Feed-Forward Neural Network Inverse Kinematics (FFNNIK), demonstrated poor convergence accuracy together with significantly higher computation times. Despite being trained on up to 11.92k kinematic datasets, these black-box methods generally struggle with unseen configurations and uncertain contexts, as illustrated in Figs. 5 and 6.

The proposed Improved Levenberg–Marquardt inverse kinematics method (ILMIK) demonstrates superior performance compared with all other iterative and non-iterative IK models. It achieves a high convergence accuracy of 83.79% with a low computation time of 0.4990 ms per sample. Additionally, it requires fewer iterations, averaging 1.64 iterations per sample (Fig. 7b), and exhibits a low convergence error of 10.00% (Table 4), indicating more reliable convergence and a better balance between speed and accuracy than the other IK models. The MAE values in Table 4 are reported in percentage form for ease of comparison across methods. The percentage MAE is computed as

$$\mathrm{MAE}_{\%} = \left(\frac{1}{N} \sum_{i=1}^{N} \|y_i - \hat{y}_i\| \Big/ \|y_{\max} - y_{\min}\| \right) \times 100,$$

where y_i and $\hat{y}_i$ denote the ground-truth and predicted Cartesian positions, respectively, and $\|y_{\max} - y_{\min}\|$ is the total spatial range of the trajectory. This normalization expresses MAE as a percentage of the workspace span, allowing direct comparison between horizontal and vertical stitching cases.

The rapid convergence capability of ILMIK is particularly well-suited for scenarios requiring quick responses, such as point-to-point maneuvering in various external surgical tasks, including repetitive stitching, tissue surface cutting, and laser-assisted tissue soldering. While the current approach is primarily designed for autonomous point-to-point maneuvering a frequent requirement in general surgical procedures future research will focus on surgical needle insertion and pulling, incorporating adaptive optimal force for suturing tasks.

5 Conclusion

We introduced a unified vision–kinematics framework built around an enhanced Levenberg–Marquardt inverse kinematics model (ILMIK). The model effectively addresses the inverse kinematics problem while reducing computation time and improving convergence accuracy. By utilizing color-coded landmarks as feedback, the system autonomously navigates its end-of-arm surgical tool to reach desired poses, facilitating rapid and repetitive surgical tasks such as stitching, tissue surface cutting, and laser-assisted tissue soldering.

Experimental analyses demonstrate that the proposed approach surpasses state-of-the-art IK methods in terms of convergence precision, computation time, and iteration count. The rapid convergence achieved by ILMIK has the potential to significantly decrease the cognitive load on surgeons and enhance the autonomous execution of surgical tasks. A current limitation is that the evaluation relies on a 4-DOF arm, a controlled artificial-skin setup, and color-based visual markers, and future work will extend the framework to higher-DOF surgical robots and markerless perception in more realistic environments. Future work will also concentrate on surgical needle insertion and extraction, with a particular focus on incorporating adaptive optimal force control for advanced suturing tasks such as needle insertion and pulling.

References

1. Arunadevi, M., Jadhav, P.D.: Machine learning approach for inverse kinematics in trajectory planning of pioneer 2 manipulator with cubic spline interpolation. In: 2021 5th International Conference on Computing Methodologies and Communication (ICCMC), pp. 807–813. IEEE (2021)
2. Buss, S.R.: Introduction to inverse kinematics with jacobian methods (2004). http://math.ucsd.edu/~sbuss/ResearchWeb/ikmethods/, technical report
3. Chiaverini, S., Siciliano, B., Egeland, O.: Review of the damped least-squares inverse kinematics with experiments on an industrial robot manipulator. IEEE Trans. Control Syst. Technol. **2**(2), 123–134 (2002)
4. Cho, G.R., Lee, M.J., Kim, M.G., Li, J.H.: Inverse kinematics for autonomous underwater manipulations using weighted damped least squares. In: 2017 14th International Conference on Ubiquitous Robots and Ambient Intelligence (URAI), pp. 765–770. IEEE (2017)
5. Colan, J., Nakanishi, J., Aoyama, T., Hasegawa, Y.: Optimization-based constrained trajectory generation for robot-assisted stitching in endonasal surgery. Robotics **10**(1), 27 (2021)
6. Fozilov, K., Colan, J., Sekiyama, K., Hasegawa, Y.: Toward autonomous robotic minimally invasive surgery: a hybrid framework combining task-motion planning and dynamic behavior trees. IEEE Access **11**, 91206–91224 (2023)
7. Granna, J., Godage, I.S., Wirz, R., Weaver, K.D., Webster, R.J., Burgner-Kahrs, J.: A 3-d volume coverage path planning algorithm with application to intracerebral hemorrhage evacuation. IEEE Robot. Autom. Lett. **1**(2), 876–883 (2016)
8. Granna, J., Guo, Y., Weaver, K.D., Burgner-Kahrs, J.: Comparison of optimization algorithms for a tubular aspiration robot for maximum coverage in intracerebral hemorrhage evacuation. J. Med. Robot. Res. **2**(01), 1750004 (2017)
9. Hashem, M.M., Ghamry, K.A., Saleh, A., Elsherif, I.A.: A comparative study of pseudoinverse and damped least squares approaches in inverse kinematics for a 5-DOF hydraulic arm. In: Journal of Physics: Conference Series, vol. 2811, p. 012002. IOP Publishing (2024)
10. He, Y., Zhang, P., Qi, X., Zhao, B., Li, S., Hu, Y.: Endoscopic path planning in robot-assisted endoscopic nasal surgery. IEEE Access **8**, 17039–17048 (2020)
11. Kan, Z., Song, N., Peng, H., Chen, B.: Extension of complex step finite difference method to jacobian-free newton-krylov method. J. Comput. Appl. Math. **399**, 113732 (2022)
12. Lee, S., Lee, J., Bang, J., Lee, J.: 7 DOF manipulator construction and inverse kinematics calculation and analysis using newton-raphson method. In: 2021 18th International Conference on Ubiquitous Robots (UR), pp. 235–238. IEEE (2021)
13. Leibrandt, K., Bergeles, C., Yang, G.Z.: Concentric tube robots: rapid, stable path-planning and guidance for surgical use. IEEE Robot. Autom. Mag. **24**(2), 42–53 (2017)
14. Li, Q., Du, Z., Yu, H.: Grinding trajectory generator in robot-assisted laminectomy surgery. Int. J. Comput. Assist. Radiol. Surg. **16**(3), 485–494 (2021). https://doi.org/10.1007/s11548-021-02316-1
15. Nasiri, E., Sowrirajan, S., Wang, L.: Teleoperation in robot-assisted mis with adaptive RCM via admittance control. Int. J. Intell. Robot. Appl. **8**(4), 827–839 (2024)
16. Navya, M., et al.: Estimation of inverse kinematics solutions of a 2d planar robotic manipulator using feed-forward neural network. In: 2024 International Conference on IoT Based Control Networks and Intelligent Systems (ICICNIS), pp. 1040–1044. IEEE (2024)

17. Popovic, M.B., Bowers, M.P.: Kinematics and dynamics. In: Biomechatronics, pp. 11–43. Elsevier Amsterdam, Netherlands (2019)
18. Saeidi, H., et al.: Autonomous laparoscopic robotic suturing with a novel actuated suturing tool and 3d endoscope. In: 2019 International Conference on Robotics and Automation (ICRA), pp. 1541–1547. IEEE (2019)
19. Singh, S.S., Shinde, R.K.: Minimally invasive gastrointestinal surgery: a review. Cureus **15**(11) (2023)

ExpaRank: A Multi-dimensional Contribution-Aware Method for Passage Re-ranking

Hengyu Sun, Tong Li(✉), Zifang Tang, and Zhen Yang

Beijing University of Technology, Beijing, China
litong@bjut.edu.cn

Abstract. Passage re-ranking improves the performance of passage retrieval in open-domain question answering by refining the ranking of candidate passages. Existing methods mainly design query expansion based on the semantic similarity between external knowledge and questions to achieve passage re-ranking. However, semantic similarity cannot comprehensively reflect whether external knowledge contributes to answering the question, leading to seemingly related but unhelpful passages. In this paper, we propose ExpaRank, a multi-dimensional contribution-aware method for passage re-ranking. ExpaRank comprehensively evaluates external knowledge by aligning it with the question's intent, assessing its knowledge informativeness, and rewriting non-contributive knowledge. Specifically, to reduce the computational overhead from massive external knowledge, we first design an external knowledge filtering module based on semantic similarity. Secondly, considering that a single agent is easily confused when evaluating multi-dimensional tasks, we design a contribution evaluation framework based on multi-agent collaboration. It accurately evaluates the intent consistency between the question and external knowledge, and measures the informativeness of the external knowledge. Finally, for questions without highly contributing external knowledge, we design a question-type-guided knowledge rewriting strategy to update external knowledge. Experimental results show that ExpaRank outperforms state-of-the-art re-ranking methods by 3%-8% in terms of top-1 passage retrieval accuracy.

Keywords: Passage re-ranking · Large language model · Open-domain question answering

1 Introduction

Passage retrieval plays a pivotal role in many NLP tasks, especially in open-domain question answering (ODQA) [18]. In ODQA, a set of candidate passages is retrieved from a large-scale corpus and then read to answer an input question. Due to the limited semantic understanding of the retriever, the retrieved candidate passages are often weakly relevant or noisy, which severely degrades the

R. C.-W. Wong et al. (Eds.): PAKDD 2026, LNAI 16618, pp. 269–281, 2027.
https://doi.org/10.1007/978-981-92-1947-6_22

performance of ODQA. To address this limitation, re-ranking is introduced for refining the retrieved candidate passages by re-evaluating the relevance of each candidate passage [1,2].

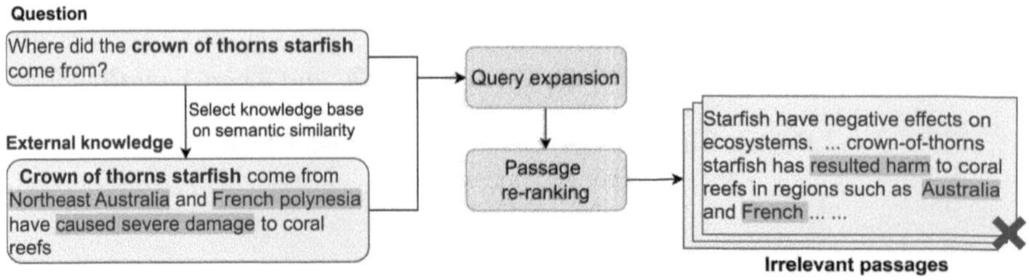

Fig. 1. Example of re-ranking failure when only considering the semantic similarity.

Questions in ODQA are usually short and express limited information for passage retrieval. Thus, existing re-ranking methods enrich the semantic representation of the question by constructing query expansion with external knowledge [4]. Ideally, query expansion with high-quality external knowledge can match passages more likely to be the provenance of the answer. To this end, some works focus on finding the connection between the question and external knowledge. For example, Jafarzadeh et al. [8] and Wang et al. [22] compute the semantic similarity between the external knowledge and the question to filter out relevant knowledge. These methods demonstrate the importance of semantic similarity in guiding the selection of external knowledge for query expansion.

However, these methods rely solely on similarity between the question and external knowledge, which is insufficient for constructing a reliable query [8]. Surface-level semantic similarity cannot capture whether a piece of knowledge truly helps answer the question, and thus often selects text that looks relevant but is not actually useful. For example, as shown in Fig. 1, for the question "*where did the crown of thorns starfish come from?*" similarity-based methods tend to choose a sentence about crown-of-thorns starfish damaging coral reefs in Northeast Australia and French Polynesia; although it shares the main entity, it does not address the questions intent about the species origin, and misleads the re-ranker to prioritize passages that match keywords but not the information need. This limitation highlights the necessity of evaluating external knowledge by its contribution to answering the question, rather than by semantic similarity alone.

In this paper, we propose ExpaRank, a multi-dimensional contribution-aware method for passage re-ranking. Unlike existing methods, ExpaRank evaluates external knowledge from three complementary perspectives: semantic similarity, intent alignment with the question, and knowledge informativeness. Specifically, to efficiently process large-scale external knowledge, we first introduce a semantic-based knowledge filtering module to reduce computational overhead. To comprehensively evaluate the contribution of external knowledge to answering questions, we design a multi-agent collaboration framework that jointly assesses the consistency between the question intent and external knowledge, and measures the informativeness of the external knowledge. Finally, for questions lacking high-contribution knowledge, we propose a question-type guided knowledge rewriting strategy to generate more relevant knowledge dynamically. In summary, the main contributions of this paper are as follows.

- We propose ExpaRank, which can assess the multi-dimensional contribution of external knowledge to answering questions based on multi-agent collaboration.
- We propose a question-type guided knowledge rewriting strategy, which can dynamically generate more relevant knowledge for questions without high-contribution knowledge.
- Experimental results on two ODQA datasets by five retrievers show that ExpaRank outperforms the state-of-the-art re-ranking methods by 3%-8% in terms of top-1 passage retrieval accuracy.

2 Related Work

Passage Re-ranking in ODQA. Recent work on passage re-ranking for ODQA has explored both enhanced supervised models and LLM-based zero or few-shot approaches. Jin et al. [9] introduce reader-aware signals by leveraging confidence scores from downstream readers, enabling the re-ranker to prioritize passages that are more likely to yield high-quality answers, which is particularly beneficial in low-resource or ambiguous settings. More recently, Sun et al. [21] adopt ChatGPT in a black-box re-ranking setup, prompting it directly to rank candidate passages based on the input question, further highlighting the potential of LLMs as general-purpose relevance scorers. However, these methods generally treat re-ranking as a single-step, black-box relevance scoring problem, without explicitly modeling how passages actually contribute to answering the question.

LLMs for Knowledge Evaluation and Generation. LLMs have been increasingly used in ODQA pipelines both to evaluate and to generate external knowledge. On the evaluation side, works such as REAR [25] and FactScore [16] use LLMs to score the contribution or helpfulness of hints and passages, or to assess factual consistency between claims and evidence. On the generation side, LLMs are employed to produce question-conditioned expansions or explanations that guide downstream components: RAG [14] combines retrieval and generation by feeding retrieved documents into a generative model, while Shuster et al. [20] generate explanatory rationales to steer re-ranking decisions. However, LLM may apply variable internal standards across instances, leading to inconsistent relevance judgments in knowledge evaluation or generation.

Query Expansion for Passage Re-ranking. Query expansion has long been used in IR to improve ranking quality by reformulating the original query so that it better matches relevant documents [3]. More recently, neural and contextualized expansion methods have been proposed to better capture semantic relationships and further boost passage re-ranking. BERT-QE [27], for example, leverages BERT-based representations to perform pseudo relevance feedback and generate expanded queries that are more semantically aligned with the target passages. ColBERT-PRF [23] integrates PRF into the ColBERT framework by refining query embeddings using feedback from initially retrieved passages, yielding stronger dense retrieval and re-ranking performance. However, these query expansion methods basically rely on similarity signal inferred from pseudo-relevant passages, without explicitly assessing from multi-dimensional aspects.

3 Methodology

In this section, we detail the methodology of ExpaRank. We begin by retrieving and filtering candidate external knowledge bases on semantic similarity. Subsequently, we introduce the contribution evaluation framework based on multi-LLM-agent collaboration (Sect. 3.2), followed by the knowledge rewriting module to generate alternative knowledge for questions without highly contributing knowledge (Sect. 3.3). Finally, we design an efficient re-ranking process that employs a smaller model (Sect. 3.4), which enhances the alignment and relevance of the retrieved passages to the question. Figure 2 shows an overview of ExpaRank.

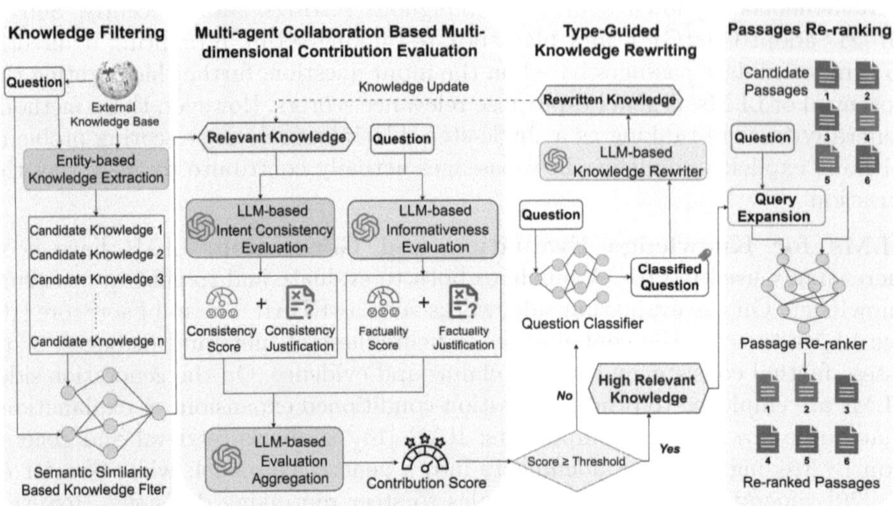

Fig. 2. Overview of ExpaRank.

3.1 Knowledge Filtering Based on Semantic Similarity

We begin by selecting relevant external knowledge from a textual knowledge graph (TKG) [26]. In the TKG, nodes denote entities and edges are natural language sentences that describe semantic relations between two entities. We treat each edge sentence as a basic knowledge unit and retrieve a candidate knowledge set by matching entities mentioned in the question. Given this candidate set, we use a fine-tuned cross-encoder f_{cross} to compute the semantic similarity between the question q and each knowledge sentence k_i:

$$s_i = f_{\text{cross}}(q, k_i) \tag{1}$$

We set a filter threshold to keep high-scoring knowledge, which filters out semantically distant evidence and avoids unnecessary reasoning on irrelevant knowledge in subsequent stages, thereby reducing computational cost and improving efficiency.

3.2 Multi-dimensional Contribution Evaluation Based on Multi-agent Collaboration

For the external knowledge that is semantically similar to the question obtained in the previous stage, we design a fine-grained multi-dimensional contribution evaluation framework built on multi-agent collaboration among LLMs. Instead of relying on a single-shot LLM judge, we instantiate a team of specialized agents, each responsible for one evaluation dimension or independent task. Concretely, we decompose the task into two core dimensions and assign a dedicated LLM agent to independently assess each aspect. Their intermediate judgments are then passed to a separate aggregation agent, which jointly considers the dimension-wise evaluations to produce the final contribution score for each knowledge sentence. By giving each evaluation agent a single and well-defined criterion, the multi-agent design explicitly separates concerns across dimensions. This collaborative evaluation process mitigates unfair scoring and inconsistent outputs caused by conflicting priorities across dimensions, and leads to more stable and reliable contribution estimates [5,13,24].

Intent Consistency Evaluation. Intent consistency is adopted as one of the core dimensions for evaluating the contribution of external knowledge to passage re-ranking. Different from surface lexical overlap or shared keywords between the question and knowledge, intent consistency explicitly measures whether a piece of knowledge aligns with the underlying purpose of the question. Specifically, it assesses whether the knowledge responds to the expected answer type, such as a time, number, or explanation, regardless of whether the knowledge is topically similar.

Knowledge Informativeness Evaluation. Knowledge informativeness is another key dimension, which evaluates whether a piece of external knowledge provides sufficient and specific information to help derive the answer. Even if the intent is aligned, some knowledge snippets only restate the question or offer vague, generic statements, contributing little to actual reasoning. Knowledge informativeness instead focuses on whether the knowledge introduces concrete facts, entities, or relations that fill in the missing evidence needed to answer the question. By prioritizing evidence-rich knowledge over generic or redundant content, knowledge informativeness ensures that the re-ranking stage is guided by information that can substantively influence the ranking decision.

Multi-dimensional Contribution Aggregation. In the aggregation agent, we achieve evaluation aggregation by collecting the results of the two evaluation agents to quantify the contribution score of external knowledge accurately. Specifically, to ensure transparency, each evaluation agent is prompted to produce a brief explanatory rationale and a scalar score for the same piece of external knowledge. The rationale is not a post-hoc note; it is an input feature to the aggregation stage. The aggregation agent consumes both the two-dimensional-specific scores and their accompanying rationales, and then outputs the final contribution score. With the "rationale + score"input format, the aggregation agent can interpret disagreements and make more robust combined decisions in cases where scalar scores alone are insufficient. Meanwhile, it reduces the impact of subjective bias in the aggregation process and enhances the consistency of the final scoring outcome.

3.3 Knowledge Rewriting Based on Question Type

For questions that require knowledge rewriting, we first classify their types using a semantic classification model, which assigns a label based on the type of question. We fine-tuned a BERT model on the UIUC dataset [15] to build our question type classifier. Considering the need for constructing type-specific prompt templates in the rewriting stage, using too many fine-grained labels would lead to difficulties in template generalization and increase the complexity of control. Therefore, we made minor adjustments to the original UIUC labels and only retained coarse-grained categories as the question types, which include: *Entity*, *Number*, *Time*, and *Others*.

Once the question type label is determined, the module dynamically selects a prompt template corresponding to the identified type. It then uses the customized template to guide the rewriting agent in generating knowledge, which helps answer the question. We design distinct prompt templates for each type of question. By adopting type-specific prompting strategies. Benefiting from this type-aware prompt mechanism, LLM can more accurately align the rewritten knowledge with the semantics and intent of the original question. In addition, we incorporate length constraints into the prompts to instruct the LLM to generate concise and focused sentences, minimizing redundancy and reducing potential interference in the subsequent retrieval stage.

3.4 Passage Re-ranking Based on Query Expansion

For each question q, we select the external knowledge with the highest contribution score k_m to construct a single query expansion $QE = \{ q + k_m \}$. Subsequently, we combine each query expansion with a candidate passage to form query-passage pairs, which are then fed into the cross-encoder-based passage ranking model [8]. Specifically, the cross-encoder jointly encodes the query and passage using a cross-attention mechanism to capture fine-grained semantic interactions. Based on this interaction, it produces an accurate semantic matching score:

$$s_i^p = F_{\text{cross}}(QE, p_i) \tag{2}$$

Here s_i^p represents the relevance score of the candidate passage. Based on these scores, we re-rank the candidate passages to produce the final output of the retrieval stage.

4 Experiments

In this section, we evaluate ExpaRank on a variety of question-answering tasks, leveraging several datasets and retrievers to assess its performance.

4.1 Experimental Setup

Evaluation Metrics. We use standard retrieval metrics to evaluate our method. Top-k accuracy is our main metric for passage retrieval after ExpaRank re-ranking. We also report MRR@10, nDCG@10, and MAP@1k on the test set.

Datasets. Following the previous work [2,8,18],, we evaluate our method on two widely used ODQA datasets: Natural Questions (NQ) [12] and TriviaQA (TQA) [10]. We follow the dataset splits of Karpukhin et al. [11] for pre-processing.

Baselines. We compare ExpaRank with several state-of-the-art re-ranking baselines. UPR [18] uses a zero-shot question generation model to score each passage by the likelihood of generating the input question. DynRank [2] leverages LLMs (LLaMA v3.1 70B) with question-typespecific prompts to dynamically score retrieved passages. CEQA [8] computes semantic relevance between the question and evidence, and uses the highest-scoring evidence to assist passage re-ranking. ASRANK [1] employs an LLM (ChatGPT-3.5) to generate "answer smells" for the query, which are then used to guide the re-ranking of candidate documents.

Retrievers. Our re-ranking method is compatible with any existing retrieval method. In this work, we select five different retrievers to evaluate the effectiveness of our method. These include three unsupervised retrievers (BM25 [17], Contriever [7], and MSS [6]) and two supervised retrievers (DPR [11] and MSS-DPR [19]).

Implementation Details. In our experiments, we use a textual knowledge graph [26] built from an English Wikipedia dump as the external knowledge source. For knowledge extraction, we apply TAGME to identify and link entities in the question to Wikipedia entries. To train the knowledge filter and passage re-ranker, we utilised *cross-encoder/ms-marco-Mini LM-L-6-v2* model[1] as our encoder. Following prior work [8], we train our model with a learning rate of 2e-5, a batch size of 32, a dropout rate of 0.1, and for a total of 8 epochs. For knowledge evaluation and rewriting, we adopt ChatGPT-3.5-turbo as the LLM agent.

4.2 Main Results

In this section, we focus on evaluating ExpaRank re-ranking performance across ODQA datasets. Table 1 shows improvements in retrieval Top-K accuracy. ExpaRank consistently enhances performance metrics, with the most significant advancements observed in Top-1 accuracy. For example, under the MSS-DPR retriever, our method improves from 52.16% to 58.64% on the NQ dataset, and improves from 69.90% to 74.46% on the TQA dataset. This underscores the universal benefit of selecting high-contribution knowledge for query expansion construction into retrieval systems, regardless of the underlying retrieval methodology. Furthermore, although the improvements in Top-100 accuracy are less pronounced than those observed at Top-1 and Top-5, they reflect the greater positive impact of ExpaRank on the overall quality of the retrieved passages.

To further validate the effectiveness of our method, we report MRR@10, NDCG@10 and MAP@1k as complementary metrics to assess re-ranking performance beyond Top-k accuracy. From Table 2, compared with the best existing method, ExpaRank achieves significant improvements in all metrics, regardless of whether the underlying retriever is supervised or unsupervised. For example, when combined with the MSS-DPR retriever, ExpaRank achieves 65.87% MRR@10, 68.42% NDCG@10, and 49.64% MAP@1k on NQ, representing substantial improvements over the strongest baseline, CEQA (60.15%, 63.50%, and 43.69%, respectively). Similar trends are observed on TQA, where all metrics are also improved. These indicate that integrating ExpaRank with MSS-DPR yields the highest overall performance, demonstrating its strong capability to enhance ranking quality across diverse metrics.

4.3 Ablation Studies

Component Ablation. To compare different contribution of component in ExpaRank, we define four ablation settings: ***w/o Collaborative Evaluation***, which removes the multi-agent evaluator and uses only semantic filtering scores as contributions, followed by rewriting; ***w/o Rewriter***, which discards the rewriting module and directly selects high-score knowledge from the multi-agent

[1] https://huggingface.co/cross-encoder/ms-marco-MiniLM-L6-v2.

Table 1. Top-1, 5, 10, 20, 100 retrieval accuracy on the test set of NQ and TQA before and after re-ranking the top 1000 retrieved passages. For certain retrievers, some baseline methods did not report complete Top-k metrics for the relevant datasets in their original papers or public implementations. As such, the corresponding entries in the table are left blank.

Retriever	Method	NQ					TQA				
		top-1	top-5	top-10	top-20	top-100	top-1	top-5	top-10	top-20	top-100
Unsupervised Retrievers											
	No re-ranker	7.51	20.14	29.22	59.10	73.70	21.99	39.34	47.84	66.90	76.70
	UPR	35.40	63.40	70.20	78.60	85.20	55.70	75.50	80.20	83.00	86.40
	CEQA	47.42	65.32	70.78	75.76	83.80	66.73	76.19	79.52	82.21	86.17
	DYNRANK	36.50	–	–	78.70	85.50	58.20	–	–	83.10	86.60
	ASRANK	47.30	65.60	71.40	–	–	67.30	77.90	80.70	–	–
	ExpaRank	**55.60**	**71.80**	**76.62**	**79.84**	**85.51**	**70.68**	**79.00**	**81.51**	**83.61**	**86.62**
Contriever	No re-ranker	22.16	47.29	58.73	67.87	80.55	34.16	59.49	68.00	73.91	82.94
	UPR	36.30	64.60	72.40	80.40	87.00	56.70	77.00	80.20	82.80	86.40
	CEQA	48.42	66.76	72.99	78.39	85.39	66.91	77.63	80.62	83.14	86.94
	DYNRANK	37.00	–	–	80.10	86.90	58.50	–	–	82.70	86.40
	ASRANK	48.00	66.60	72.50	–	–	66.80	78.90	81.40	–	–
	ExpaRank	**53.85**	**72.22**	**77.53**	**81.47**	**87.09**	**70.59**	**79.82**	**82.09**	**84.18**	**87.16**
MSS	No re-ranker	19.28	41.25	51.27	59.97	75.57	30.76	52.65	60.52	67.18	79.11
	UPR	38.78	64.82	72.27	77.30	81.50	57.29	75.52	78.93	81.30	85.00
	CEQA	50.55	68.17	73.63	77.98	83.93	66.91	76.98	79.77	82.08	85.64
	ASRANK	46.50	64.40	69.80	–	–	66.30	77.60	80.10	–	–
	ExpaRank	**53.13**	**70.36**	**75.32**	**79.17**	**84.43**	**70.26**	**78.87**	**81.14**	**82.94**	**85.88**
Supervised Retrievers											
DPR	No re-ranker	48.67	68.78	74.54	79.40	86.00	57.47	72.40	76.50	78.80	84.70
	UPR	42.52	70.69	78.20	83.40	88.60	61.36	78.79	81.97	84.30	87.20
	CEQA	51.75	69.86	76.23	81.00	88.37	68.34	78.43	81.70	84.08	87.54
	DYNRANK	42.50	–	–	83.90	89.00	61.90	–	–	**85.20**	88.10
	ASRANK	51.30	70.60	76.00	–	–	69.90	79.80	82.10	–	–
	ExpaRank	**58.17**	**75.07**	**80.06**	**83.99**	**89.20**	**72.19**	**80.87**	**83.39**	**85.20**	**88.28**
MSS-DPR	No re-ranker	50.17	71.88	77.48	81.44	88.14	61.64	75.21	79.15	81.85	86.58
	UPR	41.41	69.83	77.98	83.90	89.40	61.36	78.89	81.97	84.80	88.00
	CEQA	52.16	71.25	77.20	82.88	89.74	68.85	78.56	81.84	84.41	88.25
	ASRANK	50.60	69.30	75.20	–	–	69.90	80.50	82.90	–	–
	ExpaRank	**58.64**	**75.48**	**80.33**	**84.71**	**89.92**	**74.46**	**81.92**	**84.10**	**85.82**	**88.58**

evaluator for expansion; ***w/ Single LLM Evaluator***, which replaces the multi-agent evaluation with a single LLM for contribution evaluation; and ***w/ General Rewriting Prompt***, which replaces the type-aware rewriting templates with a generic rewriting prompt. All variants are evaluated by re-ranking the candidate passages returned by the MSS-DPR retriever.

Table 2. Re-ranking performances measured by MRR@10, NDCG@10, and MAP@1k on NQ and TQA datasets.

Retriever	Method	NQ			TQA		
		MRR@10	NDCG@10	MAP@1k	MRR@10	NDCG@10	MAP@1k
BM25	No re-ranker	13.19	16.82	7.12	29.49	33.24	13.82
	UPR	–	–	–	–	–	–
	CEQA	54.95	58.19	45.19	70.79	72.39	65.45
	ExpaRank	**62.51**	**65.02**	**50.88**	**74.24**	**75.39**	**69.02**
Contriever	No re-ranker	32.96	38.15	14.91	44.93	48.89	17.81
	UPR	–	–	–	–	–	–
	CEQA	56.22	59.50	43.12	71.50	73.05	62.06
	ExpaRank	**61.81**	**64.49**	**44.23**	**74.55**	**75.65**	**65.41**
MSS	No re-ranker	28.68	33.25	13.38	39.96	43.68	16.01
	UPR	49.65	53.62	40.26	65.10	66.83	52.97
	CEQA	58.03	60.83	42.65	71.21	72.57	64.41
	ExpaRank	**60.41**	**62.84**	**44.02**	**73.98**	**74.93**	**67.56**
DPR	No re-ranker	57.23	58.97	25.84	63.61	64.74	25.18
	UPR	54.17	58.34	41.29	68.83	70.46	55.69
	CEQA	59.53	62.65	44.80	72.73	74.35	65.56
	ExpaRank	**65.99**	**68.40**	**50.72**	**75.97**	**77.17**	**69.13**
MSS-DPR	No re-ranker	59.40	61.33	25.38	67.43	67.97	28.48
	UPR	53.27	57.65	39.78	68.41	70.33	53.83
	CEQA	60.15	63.50	43.69	73.09	74.67	64.78
	ExpaRank	**65.87**	**68.42**	**49.64**	**77.69**	**78.61**	**69.97**

Figure 3 shows that both the collaborative evaluation and rewriting modules are crucial for passage re-ranking. Removing the evaluator leads to clear drops across all metrics on NQ and TQA, indicating that the multi-agent evaluation is effective at identifying low-value knowledge and supplying reliable guidance for rewriting. Eliminating the rewriting module also hurts performance, confirming that revising low-contribution knowledge is necessary to fully exploit external knowledge for expansion.

Comparing the remaining two variants, using a single LLM evaluator yields lower scores than the multi-agent evaluator, suggesting that decomposing evaluation into explicit dimensions helps reduce subjectivity and improve the accuracy of contribution estimation. Likewise, the general rewriting prompt underperforms the type-aware prompting strategy: without intent-aware templates, the rewritten expansions are less aligned with the diverse requirements of different question types, which ultimately weakens re-ranking effectiveness.

Knowledge Selection Method Ablation. To further assess whether any reasonable additional context from the candidate set is sufficient to explain

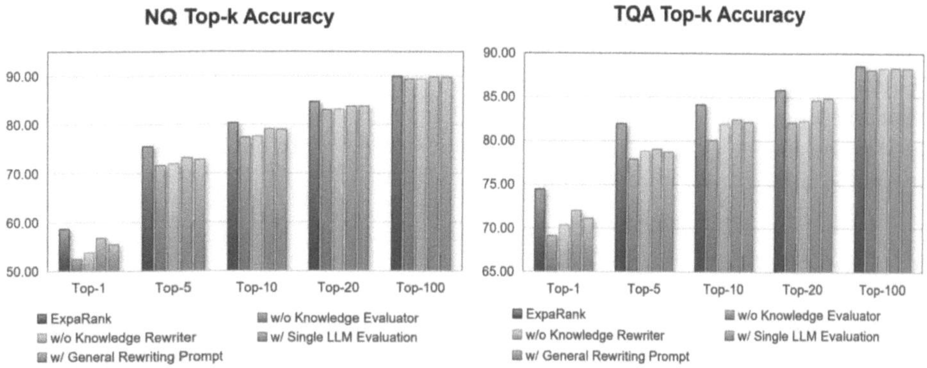

Fig. 3. Top-k retrieval accuracy of the component ablation results with MSS-DPR retriever.

the gains, we introduce three additional ablations: ***No-expansion re-ranking*** removes query expansion entirely and feeds only the original question and passage into the cross-encoder, measuring the benefit of re-ranking alone. ***Semantic-only knowledge selection*** only retains the semantic similarity filtering stage in Sect. 3.1 and directly chooses the top-1 candidate as the expansion sentence, without any multi-dimensional evaluation or rewriting. ***Random knowledge in candidates*** selects the knowledge sentence randomly from the retrieved candidate pool and constructs query expansion, without all evaluation and selection. Same with component ablation, the variants above are also evaluated by re-ranking the candidate passages returned by the MSS-DPR retriever.

As shown in Table 3, random knowledge yields the worst performance, indicating that irrelevant expansion can harm retrieval. Removing expansion

Table 3. Top-k retrieval accuracy of knowledge selection method ablation results with MSS-DPR retriever.

Ablation Method	NQ					TQA				
	top-1	top-5	top-10	top-20	top-100	top-1	top-5	top-10	top-20	top-100
No-expansion re-ranking	45.54	68.92	76.59	82.02	88.78	61.76	77.68	81.41	82.02	87.76
Semantic-only knowledge selection	52.02	73.27	77.81	83.96	89.14	67.51	77.94	81.86	82.83	88.05
Random knowledge in candidates	30.97	56.51	67.98	76.12	87.95	36.77	63.96	73.18	79.85	87.20
ExpaRank	**58.64**	**75.48**	**80.33**	**84.71**	**89.92**	**74.46**	**81.92**	**84.10**	**85.82**	**88.58**

performs better but still lags behind methods leveraging semantic relevance. The semantic-only baseline consistently outperforms no-expansion re-ranking, demonstrating the effectiveness of similarity-based selection. ExpaRank further improves upon this by 6–7 points in top-1 accuracy on both datasets, highlighting the additional gains from multi-dimensional, contribution-aware selection beyond simple semantic matching.

5 Conclusion

We propose ExpaRank, a novel passage re-ranking method that enhances query expansion by performing multi-dimensional refinement of external knowledge. We design a multi-agent collaborative evaluation strategy, where each LLM agent focuses on a specific evaluation criterion. In addition, we introduce a question-type-guided rewriting mechanism to dynamically refine low-contribution knowledge and construct higher-quality query expansions. Experimental results demonstrate that ExpaRank outperforms the state of the art in top-k retrieval accuracy.

Acknowledgements. This work is partially supported by the Central Guidance for Local Scientific and Technological Development Fund (No.2024ZY0124), the Beijing University of Technology Education and Teaching Research Project (No.ER2024KCA01), the Beijing-Dublin International College Education and Teaching Research Project (No.BDIC2025A03), and the open project of IoT Standards and Application Key Laboratory of the Ministry of Industry and Information Technology (No.202407).

References

1. Abdallah, A., Mozafari, J., Piryani, B., Jatowt, A.: Asrank: zero-shot re-ranking with answer scent for document retrieval. In: Findings of the Association for Computational Linguistics: NAACL 2025, pp. 2950–2970 (2025)
2. Abdallah, A.E.M., Mozafari, J., Piryani, B., Abdelgwad, M.M., Jatowt, A.: Dynrank: improve passage retrieval with dynamic zero-shot prompting based on question classification. In: Proceedings of the 31st International Conference on Computational Linguistics, pp. 4768–4778 (2025)
3. Carpineto, C., Romano, G.: A survey of automatic query expansion in information retrieval. Acm Comput. Surv. (CSUR) **44**(1), 1–50 (2012)
4. Dong, Q., et al.: Incorporating explicit knowledge in pre-trained language models for passage re-ranking. In: SIGIR, pp. 1490–1501 (2022)
5. Gu, J., et al.: A survey on LLM-as-a-judge. arXiv e-prints pp. arXiv–2411 (2024)
6. Guu, K., Lee, K., Tung, Z., Pasupat, P., Chang, M.: Retrieval augmented language model pre-training. In: International conference on machine learning, pp. 3929–3938. PMLR (2020)
7. Izacard, G., Caron, M., Hosseini, L., Riedel, S., Bojanowski, P., Joulin, A., Grave, E.: Unsupervised dense information retrieval with contrastive learning (2022)

8. Jafarzadeh, P., Ensan, F.: An evidence-based approach for open-domain question answering. Knowl. Inf. Syst. **67**(2), 1969–1991 (2025)
9. Jin, J., Wang, H., Zhang, H., Li, X., Guo, Z.: DVD: dynamic contrastive decoding for knowledge amplification in multi-document question answering. EMNLP. pp , 4624–4637 (2024)
10. Joshi, M., Choi, E., Weld, D.S., Zettlemoyer, L.: Triviaqa: a large scale distantly supervised challenge dataset for reading comprehension (2017). arXiv:1705.03551 arXiv preprint
11. Karpukhin, V., et al.: Dense passage retrieval for open-domain question answering. EMNLP, pp , 6769–6781 (2020)
12. Kwiatkowski, T., et al.: Natural questions: a benchmark for question answering research. Trans. Assoc. Comput. Linguis. **7**, 453–466 (2019)
13. Lee, D., Park, A., Lee, H., Nam, H., Maeng, Y.: Typed-rag: type-aware multi-aspect decomposition for non-factoid question answering. arXiv preprint arXiv:2503.15879 (2025)
14. Lewis, P., et al.: Retrieval-augmented generation for knowledge-intensive NLP tasks. Adv. Neural. Inf. Process. Syst. **33**, 9459–9474 (2020)
15. Li, X., Roth, D.: Learning question classifiers. In: COLING 2002: The 19th International Conference on Computational Linguistics (2002)
16. Min, S., et al.: Factscore: Fine-grained atomic evaluation of factual precision in long form text generation. In: EMNLP, pp. 12076–12100 (2023)
17. Robertson, S., Zaragoza, H.: The probabilistic relevance framework: Bm25 and beyond. Found. Trends® Inf. Retrieval **3**(4), 333–389 (2009)
18. Sachan, D., et al.: Improving passage retrieval with zero-shot question generation. In: EMNLP, pp. 3781–3797 (2022)
19. Sachan, D., et al.: End-to-end training of neural retrievers for open-domain question answering. In: ACL, pp. 6648–6662 (2021)
20. Shuster, K., Komeili, M., Adolphs, L., Roller, S., Szlam, A., Weston, J.: Language models that seek for knowledge: modular search and generation for dialogue and prompt completion. In: EMNLP, pp. 373–393 (2022)
21. Sun, W., et al.: Is chatgpt good at search? investigating large language models as re-ranking agents. In: EMNLP, pp. 14918–14937 (2023)
22. Wang, D., Huang, Q., Jackson, M., Gao, J.: Retrieve what you need: a mutual learning framework for open-domain question answering. Trans. Assoc. Comput. Linguist. **12**, 247–263 (2024)
23. Wang, X., Macdonald, C., Tonellotto, N., Ounis, I.: Colbert-PRF: semantic pseudo-relevance feedback for dense passage and document retrieval. ACM Trans. Web **17**(1), 1–39 (2023)
24. Wang, X., Wu, X.: Can ChatGPT serve as a multi-criteria decision maker? a novel approach to supplier evaluation. In: ICASSP, pp. 10281–10285. IEEE (2024)
25. Wang, Y., Ren, R., Li, J., Zhao, W.X., Liu, J., Wen, J.R.: Rear: a relevance-aware retrieval-augmented framework for open-domain question answering. In: EMNLP, pp. 5613–5626 (2024)
26. Zhao, C., Xiong, C., Qian, X., Boyd-Graber, J.: Complex factoid question answering with a free-text knowledge graph. In: Proceedings of the Web Conference 2020, pp. 1205–1216 (2020)
27. Zheng, Z., Hui, K., He, B., Han, X., Sun, L., Yates, A.: BERT-QE: contextualized query expansion for document re-ranking (2020). arXiv:2009.07258 arXiv preprint

KMM: Learnable Dual-Stream Time Encoding for Continuous-Time Dynamic Graphs

Peeradon Sarnkaew[1], Natthawut Kertkeidkachorn[2], Xin Liu[3], and Ploy N. Pratanwanich[1,4](✉)

[1] Department of Mathematics and Computer Science, Faculty of Science, Chulalongkorn University, Bangkok 10330, Thailand
6534445523@student.chula.ac.th

[2] Japan Advanced Institute of Science and Technology, Ishikawa 923-1211, Japan
natt@jaist.ac.jp

[3] Intelligent Platforms Research Institute, AIST, Tokyo 135-0064, Japan
xin.liu@aist.go.jp

[4] Chula Intelligent and Complex Systems Center of Excellence, Faculty of Science, Chulalongkorn University, Bangkok 10330, Thailand
naruemon.p@chula.ac.th

Abstract. Existing time encoders for continuous-time dynamic graph neural networks (CTDGNNs) focus solely on relative intervals, limiting their ability to capture complex temporal patterns and ignoring the sequence of interactions within temporal node neighborhoods. To address these limitations, we propose the KAN-based mixture-of-time-experts with modulated Mamba-2 time encoder (KMM), which jointly leverages both absolute and relative time through sequential temporal-neighborhood-aware fusion. The KAN-based mixture of time experts (K-MOTE) serves as a learnable global temporal encoder, integrating Fourier, B-spline, and shock-wavelet functional experts to model periodic, smooth non-periodic, and abrupt non-periodic temporal patterns. Two parallel K-MOTE modules encode absolute and relative time separately to obtain their corresponding embeddings. A temporal-modulated Mamba-2 fusion layer then combines these embeddings by conditioning the state-space transitions on relative time via Feature-wise Linear Modulation (FiLM). This results in a generalizable, scale-invariant, and sequential temporal neighborhood-aware time encoder that captures both temporal aspects. Across seven benchmarks and four CTDGNN models, KMM often attains the highest or near-highest AUC-ROC in dynamic link prediction in both transductive and inductive evaluations across three negative sampling strategies. These results demonstrate generalization across diverse temporal patterns, offering a principled and effective approach to unify absolute and relative time for CTDGNN models.

Keywords: Time encoding · Continuous-time dynamic graphs · Mixture of experts · State-space models · Representation learning · Deep function learning

R. C.-W. Wong et al. (Eds.): PAKDD 2026, LNAI 16618, pp. 282–293, 2027.
https://doi.org/10.1007/978-981-92-1947-6_23

1 Introduction

Continuous-time dynamic graph neural networks (CTDGNNs) can effectively model event-driven interactions, such as recommender systems [5] and fraud detection in financial systems [18]. Unlike discrete-time dynamic graphs (DTDGs), continuous-time dynamic graphs (CTDGs) evolve continuously, with nodes and edges changing over time, and with timestamps distributed irregularly. Thus, robust temporal encoding is essential for the model's effectiveness.

Early work represented time using hand-crafted temporal features [2,16], which depend heavily on domain expertise and capture only predefined patterns. On the other hand, functional time encoders (FTEs) such as Time2Vec [8] and functional time representations [19] map timestamps through sinusoidal functions, offering efficiency but limited expressiveness for non-periodic patterns. LeTE [1] introduces a deep function-learning method using B-spline and Fourier basis functions to represent both periodic and non-periodic temporal patterns.

In many CTDGNNs, time encoders primarily operate on relative time, which is the difference between the most recent temporal edge of the anchor node and the current considered temporal neighboring edge of the anchor node. While relative time encoding effectively models local temporal patterns and event duration, including recency effects and memory decay, absolute time encoding models global temporal context, such as seasonality and trends. Moreover, temporal information in CTDGs is inherently chronologically sequential as a sequence of temporal neighborhood nodes of the anchor node. Hence, both absolute and relative time evolve as ordered streams of interactions rather than isolated timestamp values, and this local chronological ordering carries meaningful structure that should be preserved during encoding. Therefore, combining absolute and relative time requires two levels: global temporal representation of individual timestamps, and sequential temporal neighborhood-aware fusion over the ordered interaction history of each node.

We propose **KAN-based mixture-of-time-experts with modulated Mamba-2 time encoder (KMM)**, a unified time-encoding framework that treats both absolute and relative time as ordered temporal sequences at both global and local time representation and models them jointly for CTDGs. Our contributions are summarized as follows:

1. We propose a dual-stream temporal encoder that jointly models sequences of absolute and relative time. This sequence-aware architecture captures global and local temporal dynamics simultaneously. We further prove that the encoder is invariant to time rescaling, ensuring consistent representations under arbitrary changes of time units.
2. We develop K-MOTE, a KAN-based mixture-of-time-experts architecture that integrates deep functional learners constructed from Fourier, B-spline, and shock-wavelet experts. With expert-specific continuous gating mechanisms, K-MOTE captures periodic patterns as well as both smooth and abrupt non-periodic temporal patterns.
3. We introduce a temporal-modulated Mamba-2 fusion module that integrates absolute- and relative-time sequences through a continuous-time state-space

formulation. The state transitions are dual-stream, where the relative-time sequence modulates the derivatives of the absolute-time sequence via FiLM, producing a unified, sequence- and chronological-aware representation suitable for temporal modeling in CTDGNNs.

As a result, KMM provides a general, model-independent time encoder that enables integration with diverse CTDGNNs.

2 Related Work

Early temporal encoding approaches relied on manually designed time features (e.g., month, day, hour) [2,16], which are intuitive but domain-specific and limited in expressiveness. Functional time encoders, such as Time2Vec [8] and functional time representations [19], map timestamps through fixed sinusoidal functions, but their predetermined form restricts adaptability to irregular or non-stationary patterns. Recent advances in deep function learning, including Kolmogorov-Arnold Networks (KAN) [9], enable flexible continuous function approximation. LeTE [1] applies this idea to time encoding using B-spline and Fourier bases to capture both periodic and non-periodic behavior. Meanwhile, some transformer-based models incorporate temporal encodings, and newer hybrid strategies combine absolute and relative temporal embeddings [6,15]. Finally, state-space architectures such as Mamba provide a continuous–discrete formulation and have recently been adapted for CTDGNNs [4].

To this end, existing methods do not provide a unified, learnable, scale-invariant, and sequence-aware temporal representation that can simultaneously handle absolute and relative time. KMM addresses this gap through dual-stream K-MOTE modules with a temporal-modulated Mamba-2 fusion mechanism, providing a versatile and architecture-agnostic temporal encoder.

3 Methodology

3.1 Problem Formulation

We consider a continuous-time dynamic graph (CTDG) $\mathcal{G} = (\mathcal{V}, \mathcal{S})$, where each event $e_k = (u_i, u_j, t_k)$ denotes an interaction at time t_k. For each event, we retrieve the most recent $L - 1$ historical interactions of the source node u_i, yielding timestamps $\{t_{m_1}, \dots, t_{m_{L-1}}\}$ prior to t_k. Most CTDG models encode time only through relative intervals $\varPhi(t_k - t_{m_\ell})$ where $\varPhi$ is a time encoding function. In our KMM model, we construct two aligned sequences:

$$\mathbf{T}_{\text{abs}} = [t_{m_1}, \dots, t_{m_{L-1}}, t_k] \in \mathbb{R}^L, \quad \mathbf{T}_{\text{rel}} = [t_k - t_{m_1}, \dots, t_k - t_{m_{L-1}}, 0] \in \mathbb{R}^L. \tag{1}$$

KMM processes these sequences using a dual-stream K-MOTE encoder and a temporal-modulated Mamba-2 fusion module, producing a unified temporal embedding sequence

$$\mathbf{T}_k = \varPhi_{\text{KMM}}(\mathbf{T}_{\text{abs}}, \mathbf{T}_{\text{rel}}) \in \mathbb{R}^{L \times d_T}, \tag{2}$$

where d_T is the time-embedding dimension. This sequence aligns one-to-one with the historical node sequence $\mathbf{Z}_{u_i}(t_k^-) \in \mathbb{R}^{L \times d_F}$ representing the temporal context of node u_i prior to time t_k. The CTDG architecture then integrates these embeddings in a model-dependent manner and computes the likelihood

$$\hat{y}_{ij}(t_k) = \sigma\left(g_\Theta\left(\mathbf{Z}_{u_i}(t_k^-), \mathbf{Z}_{u_j}(t_k^-), \mathbf{T}_k\right)\right), \tag{3}$$

where g_Θ denotes the model's prediction function.

3.2 The KMM Framework

Existing time encoders typically rely on relative time and often treat time in isolation, neglecting the importance of absolute time and the continuous evolution of temporal information based on chronologically-ordered temporal neighborhood sequences of the anchor node. To address this, we propose the **KAN-based mixture-of-time-experts with modulated Mamba-2 time encoder (KMM)** (Fig. 1).

KMM is a hierarchical dual-stream architecture for temporal encoding. First, **K-MOTE** modules serve as learnable encoders for global temporal representation, separately mapping absolute and relative timestamps into expressive functional embeddings. Secondly, the **temporal-modulated Mamba-2** layer performs sequential temporal neighborhood-aware fusion of both embeddings via FiLM, producing a unified temporal embedding suitable for CTDGNNs.

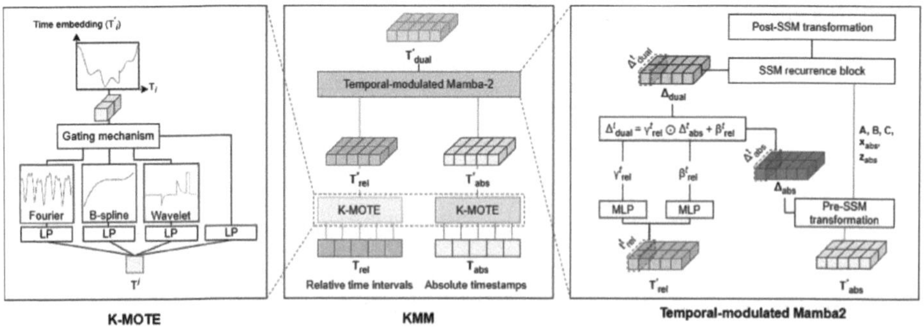

Fig. 1. The overall framework of KMM

Encoding Time Using K-MOTE. To construct a robust temporal representation for absolute and relative time sequences separately, we introduce K-MOTE, a learnable KAN-based mixture-of-experts model $\Phi_{\text{K-MOTE}} : \mathbb{R} \to \mathbb{R}^{d_T}$. The use of KANs helps mitigate the problem of standard MLPs, which struggle to approximate high-frequency or non-stationary temporal functions effectively [12] Each expert $e \in \{\text{f}, \text{s}, \text{w}\}$ (Fourier, B-spline, and shock-wavelet) is responsible for periodic, smooth non-periodic, or abrupt non-periodic patterns respectively.

Since time can be measured on different scales (e.g., seconds and days), the encoder must be scale invariant. To achieve this, we equip each expert with its own learnable linear projection (LP), which transforms the absolute or relative time t into an expert-specific latent representation $t_e^{'} \in \mathbb{R}^{d_T}$ (see Appendix for the formal proof of scale-invariance property).

We employ three KAN-based experts, together with gating mechanisms that govern the contribution of each expert through mixing weights. This allows K-MOTE to flexibly capture the diverse temporal patterns present in both absolute and relative time. The expert functions are formally defined as:

1. **Fourier KAN:** Performs spectral decomposition to capture seasonality in absolute time or repetitive intervals in relative time:

$$\phi_{\mathrm{f}}(t_{\mathrm{f}}')[i] = a_{i,0} + \sum_{k=1}^{K} \left(a_{i,k} \cos(kt'_{f,i}) + b_{i,k} \sin(kt'_{f,i})\right). \tag{4}$$

2. **B-spline KAN:** Captures gradual variations, such as long-term drifts in absolute time or memory decay in relative time:

$$\phi_{\mathrm{s}}(t_{\mathrm{s}}')[i] = W_{s,i} \tanh(t'_{s,i}) + \sum_{k=1}^{N} w_{i,k} B_k(t'_{s,i}). \tag{5}$$

3. **Shock-wavelet KAN:** Captures asymmetric abrupt patterns, such as sudden disruptions or interaction spikes:

$$\phi_{\mathrm{w}}(t_{\mathrm{w}}')[i] = \sum_{j=1}^{J} c_{i,j}\, \psi_{\mathrm{w}}\left(\frac{t'_{w,i} - s_{i,j}}{\sigma_{i,j}}; \alpha_{i,j}, \beta_{i,j}\right), \tag{6}$$

$$\text{where} \quad \psi_{\mathrm{w}}(x; \alpha, \beta) = \begin{cases} e^{\beta x(1+\tanh\alpha)} \cos(\beta x), & x < 0, \\ e^{-\beta x(1-\tanh\alpha)} \cos(\beta x), & x \geq 0. \end{cases} \tag{7}$$

All parameters $W, w, a_0, b, c, s, \sigma, \alpha, \beta$ are learnable.

The gating mechanisms assign mixing weights to the individual experts based on the absolute or the relative time: $p = \mathrm{softmax}(\mathrm{MLP_g}(t)) \in \mathbb{R}^3$ to fuse the experts:

$$\Phi_{\text{K-MOTE}}(t) = \sum_{e \in \{\mathrm{s,f,w}\}} p_e\, \phi_e(t_e^{'}). \tag{8}$$

Finally, applying K-MOTE to the absolute and relative timestamp sequences separately yields two parallel embedding sequences:

$$\mathbf{T}'_{\mathrm{abs}} = \Phi_{\text{K-MOTE}}(\mathbf{T}_{\mathrm{abs}}), \quad \mathbf{T}'_{\mathrm{rel}} = \Phi_{\text{K-MOTE}}(\mathbf{T}_{\mathrm{rel}}), \tag{9}$$

where $\mathbf{T}'_{\mathrm{abs}}, \mathbf{T}'_{\mathrm{rel}} \in \mathbb{R}^{L \times d_T}$, which are later fused sequentially.

Fusion Stage Using Temporal-Modulated Mamba-2. In CTDGs, both absolute and relative time form ordered sequences rather than independent values. To preserve these sequential dependencies, we introduce a Temporal-Modulated Mamba-2 fusion module, in which the absolute-time embedding serves as the input sequence and the relative-time embedding modulates the dynamics of its internal recurrent states. At its core, Mamba-2 [3] is a parameterized state-space model (SSM), which can be broadly divided into three components: the pre-SSM transformation, the SSM recurrence block, and the post-SSM transformation. Thanks to the SSM underlying Mamba-2, we can embed time sequences using parallelized operations while maintaining sequence awareness.

Let $\mathbf{T'}_{\text{abs}} = [t^1_{\text{abs}}, \dots, t^L_{\text{abs}}] \in \mathbb{R}^{L \times d_T}$ and $\mathbf{T'}_{\text{rel}} = [t^1_{\text{rel}}, \dots, t^L_{\text{rel}}] \in \mathbb{R}^{L \times d_T}$ be the absolute- and relative-time embedding sequences, respectively. We begin with the **pre-SSM transformation**, where a learnable vector $\mathbf{A} \in \mathbb{R}^N$ is initialized following the Mamba-2 scheme, and the absolute-time embedding sequence $\mathbf{T}'_{\text{abs}} \in \mathbb{R}^{L \times d_T}$ is then transformed into the parameters required for the SSM recurrence block using linear projections and a 1D convolution. This produces $\mathbf{B}, \mathbf{C} \in \mathbb{R}^{L \times H}$ and $\mathbf{\Delta}_{\text{abs}} \in \mathbb{R}^{L \times N}$ as well as $\mathbf{x}_{\text{abs}} \in \mathbb{R}^{L \times N \times S}$ and $\mathbf{z}_{\text{abs}} \in \mathbb{R}^{L \times N \times S}$.

To incorporate relative-time information into the state transitions, we apply FiLM to modulate $\mathbf{\Delta}_{\mathbf{abs}}$, which governs how information is propagated over time. The modulation is applied independently at each position in the sequence:

$$\Delta^t_{\text{dual}} = \gamma^t_{rel} \odot \Delta^t_{abs} + \beta^t_{rel}; \tag{10}$$

$$\gamma^t_{rel} = \text{softplus}\big(\text{MLP}_\gamma(t^t_{\text{rel}})\big), \; \beta^t_{rel} = \text{MLP}_\beta(t^t_{\text{rel}}). \tag{11}$$

The resulting modulated sequence $\mathbf{\Delta}_{\text{dual}} = [\Delta^{(1)}_{\text{dual}}, \dots, \Delta^{(L)}_{\text{dual}}] \in \mathbb{R}^{L \times N}$ is obtained and subsequently used in the SSM recurrence block.

Based on Mamba-2, the **SSM recurrence block** computes the sequence

$$\mathbf{y}_{\text{dual}} = \text{SSM}_{\mathbf{A},\mathbf{B},\mathbf{C},\mathbf{\Delta}_{\text{dual}}}(\mathbf{x}_{\text{abs}}) \in \mathbb{R}^{L \times N \times S}. \tag{12}$$

The SSM models a continuous-time system that maps the input sequence $\mathbf{x}_{\text{abs}}$ to the output sequence $\mathbf{y}_{\text{dual}}$ via a latent state trajectory $h \in \mathbb{R}^{L \times N \times S \times H}$, which is defined as follows:

$$h^t_{i,j,k} = \exp\big(\Delta^t_{\text{dual},i}\mathbf{A}_i\big)\, h^{t-1}_{i,j,k} + \big(\Delta^t_{\text{dual},i}\mathbf{B}_k\big)\, x^t_{\text{abs},(i,j)}, \tag{13}$$

$$y^t_{\text{abs},(i,j)} = \sum_{k=1}^{H} \mathbf{C}_k\, h^t_{i,j,k}, \text{ where } i \in [1,N],\; j \in [1,S],\; k \in [1,H]. \tag{14}$$

Finally, the outputs of the pre-SSM transformation ($\mathbf{z}_{\text{abs}}$) and SSM recurrence block ($\mathbf{y}_{\text{dual}}$) are passed through a **post-SSM transformation**:

$$\mathbf{T}_{\text{dual}} = \text{LP}_4(\text{GroupNorm}(\mathbf{y}_{\text{dual}} \odot \text{SiLU}(\mathbf{z}_{\text{abs}}))) \in \mathbb{R}^{L \times d_T}. \tag{15}$$

This unified representation integrates absolute and relative temporal information in a sequence-aware manner, enhancing CTDG models to leverage both absolute and relative temporal embeddings without relying on either in isolation.

4 Experiments

4.1 Next-Event Prediction on Stack Overflow Badge Sequences

Experiment Settings. We evaluated KMM on a next-event prediction task using the Stack Overflow badge dataset [8]. Given a sequence $\{(b_i^u, t_i^u)\}_{i=1}^n$ for each user u, where b_i^u is the badge type and t_i^u is the timestamp that user u received this badge in step i, the task is to predict the badge type the user will obtain at time t_{n+1}^u. Following standard practice, we additionally shifted each sequence so that the first event occurred at $t = 0$ to normalize timestamps across users. We used an LSTM with 128 hidden units, coupled with 64-dimensional embeddings for both badge types and time inputs, then replaced the time embedding with NTE (no time encoding), FTE [8], LeTE [1], K-MOTE, and KMM. For FTE, LeTE, and K-MOTE, we constructed two variants to assess each temporal aspect separately, with one using absolute time and the other using relative time only. All models were trained for 200 epochs with AdamW (learning rate 0.0001, batch size 64). We tuned hyperparameters for K-MOTE and KMM using Hyperband. Performance was evaluated using MRR and Recall@3.

Results. Table 1 shows that KMM achieves the best performance on both metrics. Notably, K-MOTE, with either absolute or relative time, outperforms the corresponding FTE and LeTE baselines, demonstrating that our mixture-of-experts approach captures temporal structure more effectively than other encoders. Furthermore, the KMM model, which fuses both absolute and relative time, confirms that both absolute and relative times provide complementary information essential for comprehensive temporal modeling.

Table 1. Performance comparison of time encoding methods on the Stack Overflow next-event prediction task, reported using MRR and Recall@3.

Metrics	NTE	FTE		LeTE		K-MOTE		KMM
		Abs.	**Rel.**	**Abs.**	**Rel.**	**Abs.**	**Rel.**	
MRR	0.5993	0.5999	0.5968	0.6032	0.5998	0.6087	0.6010	**0.6172**
Recall@3	0.7632	0.7632	0.7609	0.7632	0.7647	0.7800	0.7722	**0.7964**

4.2 Dynamic Link Prediction on Continuous-Time Graphs

Experiment Settings. To evaluate the effectiveness of KMM, we integrated it with four CTDGNNs: DyGFormer [20], DyGMamba [4], TGN [13], and TCL [17]. For each of these models, we replaced its original time encoder with FTE, LeTE, or KMM. We conducted experiments on seven benchmark datasets and followed the evaluation protocol [11], with statistics provided in Table 2. The datasets included five continuous-time dynamic graphs (CTDGs) and two discrete-time dynamic graphs (DTDGs) to ensure evaluation across diverse temporal aspects.

Table 2. Statistics of the benchmark datasets used for evaluation.

Dataset	Domain	Nodes	Edges	Time Scale	Duration	Type
Wikipedia	Social	9,227	157,474	Unix	1 m.	CTDG
Reddit	Social	10,984	672,447	Unix	1 m.	CTDG
MOOC	Interaction	7,144	411,749	Unix	17 m.	CTDG
Social Evo.	Proximity	74	2,099,519	Unix	8 m.	CTDG
UCI	Social	1,899	59,835	Unix	196 d.	CTDG
UN Vote	Politics	201	1,035,742	years	72 y.	DTDG
Contact	Proximity	694	2,426,280	5 min	1 m.	DTDG

For the baselines, we adopted the optimal hyperparameter configurations presented in DyGMamba [4], and tuned KMM hyperparameters using Hyperband. All time encoders outputted 100-dimensional embeddings and were trained for 200 epochs with a batch size of 200. We evaluated performance using AUC-ROC under three negative sampling strategies (random, historical, inductive) in both transductive (T) and inductive (I) settings. Historical and inductive sampling provide stricter evaluation of temporal generalization [20]. Code is available at https://github.com/psarnkaew/kmm.

Results. Table 3 shows that KMM consistently achieved strong performance across several models, datasets, and sampling strategies, frequently attaining the highest AUC-ROC in both transductive and inductive settings. While FTE and LeTE occasionally match KMM under random negative sampling, KMM demonstrates clear advantages under the more challenging historical and inductive negative sampling strategies, especially in the historical one, which requires stronger temporal generalization. These results confirm that jointly modeling absolute and relative time yields more robust and expressive temporal representations for CTDGs in the dynamic link prediction task across three negative sampling strategies.

We evaluated computational efficiency by comparing parameter count, training time per epoch, and GPU memory on the Wikipedia dataset across four CTDG backbones under identical settings. Compared to LeTE, KMM increases parameters by 46%, 50%, 41%, and 80% in TGN, TCL, DyGFormer, and DyGMamba, respectively. Training time increases by 66%, 64%, 13%, and 55%. GPU memory rises by 33%, 33%, 4%, and 73%. Despite these increases from the dual-stream encoding and mixture-of-experts fusion, the additional training cost is manageable given the consistent performance improvements achieved across models.

5 Discussion

5.1 Periodic and Non-Periodic Temporal Behaviors

To examine temporal regularity, we analyzed five CTDG datasets and two DTDG datasets by computing the spectral entropy [14] of interaction sequences. For

Table 3. AUC-ROC performance of time encoding methods across CTDGNNs and datasets under random, historical, and inductive negative sampling, evaluated in both transductive (T) and inductive (I) settings. DGF denotes DyGFormer and DGM denotes DyGMamba.

N.	Model	TE	Contact		SocialEvo		Reddit		UN Vote		MOOC		Wikipedia		UCI	
			T	I	T	I	T	I	T	I	T	I	T	I	T	I
Random	TGN	FTE	97.46	92.40	95.14	92.54	98.57	97.19	68.50	57.73	91.29	91.06	98.29	97.59	91.35	85.05
		LeTE	97.94	96.04	95.91	94.70	**98.71**	**97.46**	67.75	62.36	**92.15**	**91.68**	**98.45**	**97.80**	87.95	81.39
		KMM	**98.25**	**96.17**	**96.62**	**95.10**	98.38	96.50	**71.04**	**68.88**	92.05	91.56	98.18	96.40	**92.65**	**89.67**
	TCL	FTE	95.50	94.75	95.29	94.58	97.66	94.56	51.50	**51.45**	83.50	82.03	97.22	96.99	84.80	81.00
		LeTE	95.73	95.03	**95.84**	**94.89**	**97.70**	**94.70**	51.49	49.93	84.70	83.24	**97.73**	97.46	90.69	87.15
		KMM	**95.86**	**95.17**	95.77	94.69	97.68	94.48	**52.48**	51.28	**84.87**	**83.61**	97.68	**97.47**	**91.67**	**88.78**
	DGF	FTE	98.52	98.30	96.21	95.26	99.14	98.69	57.26	57.29	87.80	87.42	98.89	98.48	94.28	92.29
		LeTE	98.53	98.31	96.36	95.37	99.19	98.76	52.42	50.20	88.98	88.89	99.05	98.70	94.74	93.27
		KMM	**98.64**	**98.42**	**96.41**	**95.43**	**99.20**	**98.79**	**59.40**	**58.45**	**89.92**	**89.93**	**99.20**	**98.83**	**95.45**	**93.57**
	DGM	FTE	98.67	98.41	96.37	95.33	99.26	98.87	**58.39**	**56.82**	89.49	89.22	99.07	98.69	94.65	92.58
		LeTE	91.55	90.24	96.15	95.25	74.61	74.22	51.57	48.75	65.34	60.50	80.16	95.01	64.99	61.59
		KMM	**98.68**	**98.44**	**97.12**	**96.44**	**99.27**	**98.92**	57.70	54.46	**89.88**	**89.67**	**99.22**	**98.84**	**96.41**	**94.08**
Inductive	TGN	FTE	94.44	87.87	94.10	90.22	84.45	**65.18**	**71.53**	70.09	75.41	74.90	80.97	75.58	62.93	61.45
		LeTE	95.07	93.11	96.70	95.02	**84.62**	65.00	70.45	**70.98**	**76.02**	77.41	82.65	77.85	65.19	65.22
		KMM	**95.20**	**94.00**	**97.01**	**95.68**	84.49	65.08	70.86	70.85	73.90	**85.04**	**86.03**	**85.21**	**76.88**	**77.59**
	TCL	FTE	92.09	91.56	94.57	95.23	84.26	**61.79**	43.48	**55.25**	71.19	70.58	72.55	69.98	63.97	64.42
		LeTE	92.49	92.08	95.57	95.42	84.22	61.39	44.08	52.92	70.39	69.78	76.32	74.76	72.47	72.87
		KMM	**92.97**	**92.58**	**95.63**	**95.44**	**84.80**	61.64	**49.63**	53.80	**72.71**	**72.48**	**82.00**	**79.29**	**72.91**	**74.30**
	DGF	FTE	94.96	94.07	94.91	94.73	85.86	64.35	55.18	54.31	79.94	79.92	55.47	53.50	64.49	63.78
		LeTE	95.60	94.52	96.70	96.08	87.07	**64.64**	48.88	51.85	**81.89**	**81.44**	60.44	55.26	63.59	63.73
		KMM	**95.65**	**94.82**	**97.11**	**96.55**	**87.26**	64.53	**57.30**	**56.57**	80.38	79.92	**61.95**	**58.16**	**69.56**	**69.44**
	DGM	FTE	95.57	94.19	97.15	96.39	86.04	64.40	54.05	**53.55**	**80.26**	**80.53**	73.64	66.35	64.04	64.89
		LeTE	90.88	88.45	97.09	96.61	72.62	59.91	46.24	49.73	53.77	50.68	**82.29**	70.66	49.13	47.15
		KMM	**95.83**	**94.21**	**97.52**	**97.01**	**88.08**	**66.61**	**55.90**	52.20	79.69	78.96	79.12	**72.74**	**70.68**	**70.70**
Historical	TGN	FTE	96.12	N/A	92.97	N/A	**80.92**	N/A	**71.92**	N/A	85.43	N/A	83.02	N/A	77.54	N/A
		LeTE	96.62	N/A	96.24	N/A	80.80	N/A	71.55	N/A	**87.56**	N/A	84.84	N/A	68.45	N/A
		KMM	**97.21**	N/A	**96.84**	N/A	80.87	N/A	71.91	N/A	86.64	N/A	**87.28**	N/A	**81.80**	N/A
	TCL	FTE	94.61	N/A	94.41	N/A	76.76	N/A	**53.50**	N/A	72.48	N/A	85.28	N/A	64.10	N/A
		LeTE	94.36	N/A	95.45	N/A	76.62	N/A	52.02	N/A	71.30	N/A	86.99	N/A	74.33	N/A
		KMM	**94.76**	N/A	**95.56**	N/A	**77.02**	N/A	53.39	N/A	**74.79**	N/A	**87.32**	N/A	**78.10**	N/A
	DGF	FTE	97.08	N/A	**97.11**	N/A	80.22	N/A	63.97	N/A	86.47	N/A	66.60	N/A	75.26	N/A
		LeTE	97.26	N/A	96.26	N/A	80.28	N/A	50.52	N/A	86.89	N/A	68.31	N/A	75.62	N/A
		KMM	**97.28**	N/A	96.77	N/A	**80.77**	N/A	**67.95**	N/A	**87.66**	N/A	**79.46**	N/A	**79.73**	N/A
	DGM	FTE	**97.24**	N/A	96.99	N/A	81.24	N/A	**64.16**	N/A	**87.01**	N/A	77.78	N/A	74.24	N/A
		LeTE	92.58	N/A	96.74	N/A	69.03	N/A	51.41	N/A	55.21	N/A	**80.16**	N/A	47.58	N/A
		KMM	96.83	N/A	**97.12**	N/A	**81.66**	N/A	52.49	N/A	86.69	N/A	77.92	N/A	**76.20**	N/A

each node with more than five interactions, we collected the timestamps and time differences. These were then normalized to [0, 1] and treated as temporal signals. We then applied the Fast Fourier Transform (FFT) to obtain the frequency components and compute the spectral entropy for each node.

As shown in Fig. 2, the spectral entropy distributions vary widely both across datasets and within each dataset. Some nodes exhibit low spectral entropy, reflecting strong periodicity, while some display high entropy associated with irregular and non-stationary temporal patterns. This indicates that an effective time encoder must model both periodic and non-periodic behaviors to capture temporal patterns in CTDGs efficiently.

5.2 Expert Specialization Dynamics in K-MOTE

We examined how each time-encoding expert in K-MOTE, together with their mixtures, contributes to the adaptive approximation of temporal patterns. To

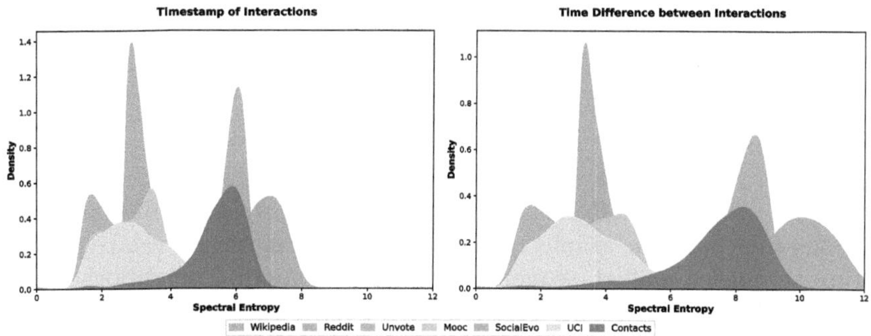

Fig. 2. Spectral entropy distribution of absolute and relative time across datasets

illustrate this, we produced four example temporal sequences: continuous trends, periodic oscillations, sudden transitory shifts, and mixed patterns. Each temporal sequence is provided as input to K-MOTE, and the output embedding is projected into a one-dimensional reconstruction space via a learned linear layer.

As shown in Fig. 3, no single expert matches all four types of temporal functions by itself. Instead, K-MOTE utilizes these three experts to provide complementary temporal specializations, while the gating mechanism assigns time-varying weights that determine each expert's contribution. Hence, K-MOTE can flexibly integrate periodic, smooth non-periodic, and abrupt non-periodic

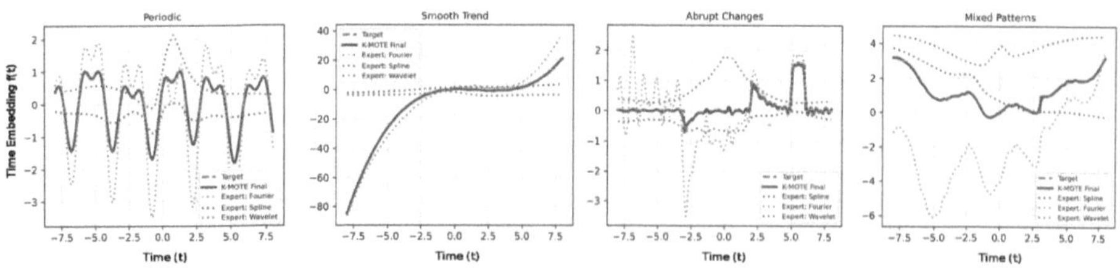

(a) Each expert (Fourier, B-spline, shock-wavelet) specializes in a different temporal structure of the input.

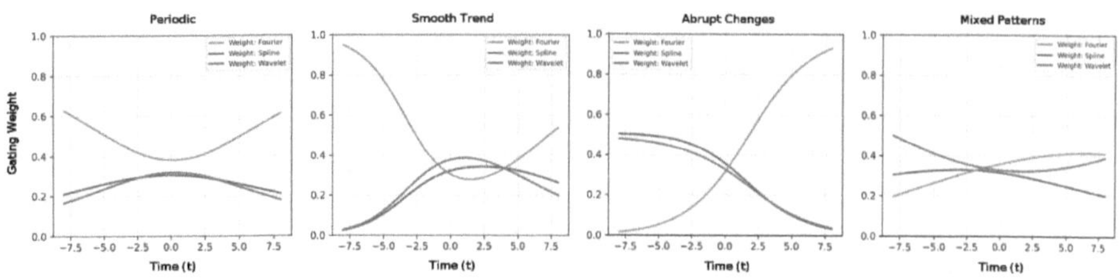

(b) The gating mechanism dynamically modulates expert contributions across different temporal structures of the input.

Fig. 3. Specialization and adaptive fusion in K-MOTE.

patterns, enabling it to approximate diverse temporal functions and generalize across different temporal patterns.

6 Conclusion

In this work, we presented KMM, a learnable dual-stream time encoding for continuous-time dynamic graphs that learns both absolute and relative temporal structure through a unified, sequence-aware, and temporal neighborhood-aware design. KMM is built on K-MOTE, which uses Fourier, B-spline, and shock-wavelet experts to model periodic, smooth non-periodic, and abrupt non-periodic temporal patterns, together with a temporal-modulated Mamba-2 fusion module. Across the Stack Overflow next-event prediction and dynamic link prediction tasks on continuous-time graphs, KMM consistently matched or outperformed existing time encoders across all negative sampling settings. Analysis of expert specialization further showed that the mixture of experts flexibly integrates temporal patterns. Overall, KMM shows that jointly modeling absolute and relative time, along with expert-driven functional specialization and sequential temporal neighborhood-aware fusion, yields a more robust and expressive temporal representation for dynamic graph learning.

Acknowledgments. This work was partially supported by the JSPS Grant-in-Aid for Scientific Research (Grant Number 25K03231, 23H03451). This paper is based on results obtained from the project, JPNP25006, commissioned by the New Energy and Industrial Technology Development Organization (NEDO).

Appendix: Proof of Scale Invariance

A class of models $\mathcal{C}$ is considered invariant to time rescaling if, for any model $\mathcal{M}_1 \in \mathcal{C}$ and any scalar $\alpha > 0$, there exists a model $\mathcal{M}_2 \in \mathcal{C}$ that responds to αt (where t is scaled by α) similarly to how $\mathcal{M}_1$ responds to the original t values.

Let f_{enc} represent the functions of the K-MOTE, including all three experts and the routing gate, that operate on the timestamps. Consider time encoding $\mathcal{M}_1 \in \mathcal{C}$ with linear transformation parameters w and b. Its response to an input timestamp t is:

$$M_1(t) = f_{\text{enc}}(w \cdot t + b). \tag{16}$$

By replacing t with $\alpha \cdot t$ $(\alpha > 0)$, the time encoding updates as follows:

$$M_1(\alpha \cdot t) = f_{\text{enc}}(w \cdot (\alpha \cdot t) + b). \tag{17}$$

Consider a new time encoding $\mathcal{M}_2$, to make it behave identically to $\mathcal{M}_1$, we adjust parameters so that $\mathcal{M}_2(\alpha \cdot t) = \mathcal{M}_1(t)$, by changing $w' = \frac{w}{\alpha}$ and $b' = b$.

Therefore, time encoding $\mathcal{M}_2$ behaves identically to $\mathcal{M}_1$, making the KMM architecture invariant to time rescaling.

References

1. Chen, X., et al.: Rethinking time encoding via learnable transformation functions. In: ICML, pp. 9073–9104 (2025)
2. Choi, E., Bahadori, M.T., Schuetz, A., Stewart, W.F., Sun, J.: Doctor ai: predicting clinical events via recurrent neural networks. In: MLHC, pp. 301–318 (2016)
3. Dao, T., Gu, A.: Transformers are ssms: Generalized models and efficient algorithms through structured state space duality. arXiv:2405.21060 (2024)
4. Ding, Z., et al.: Dygmamba: efficiently modeling long-term temporal dependency on continuous-time dynamic graphs with state space models. arXiv:2408.04713 (2024)
5. Fan, Z., Liu, Z., Zhang, J., Xiong, Y., Zheng, L., Yu, P.S.: Continuous-time sequential recommendation with temporal graph collaborative transformer. In: CIKM, pp. 433–442 (2021)
6. Foumani, N.M., Tan, C.W., Webb, G.I., Salehi, M.: Improving position encoding of transformers for multivariate time series classification. Data Min. Knowl. Disc. **38**(1), 22–48 (2024)
7. Gu, A.e.a.: Efficiently modeling long sequences with structured state spaces. In: ICLR (2022)
8. Kazemi, S.M., et al.: Time2vec: Learning a vector representation of time. arXiv:1907.05321 (2019)
9. Liu, Z., et al.: Kan: Kolmogorov–arnold networks. In: ICLR (2025)
10. Perez, E., Strub, F., De Vries, H., Dumoulin, V., Courville, A.: Film: visual reasoning with a general conditioning layer. In: AAAI (2018)
11. Poursafaei, F., Huang, S., Pelrine, K., Rabbany, R.: Towards better evaluation for dynamic link prediction. NeurIPS **35**, 32928–32941 (2022)
12. Rahaman, N., et al.: On the spectral bias of neural networks. In: ICML, pp. 5301–5310. PMLR (2019)
13. Rossi, E., Chamberlain, B., Frasca, F., Eynard, D., Monti, F., Bronstein, M.: Temporal graph networks for deep learning on dynamic graphs. In: ICML Workshop on Graph Representation Learning (2020)
14. Shannon, C.E.: A mathematical theory of communication. The Bell Syst. Techn. J. **27**(3), 379–423 (1948)
15. Su, J., Ahmed, M., Lu, Y., Pan, S., Bo, W., Liu, Y.: Roformer: enhanced transformer with rotary position embedding. Neurocomputing **568**, 127063 (2024)
16. Wang, D., Jiang, M., Syed, M., Conway, O., Juneja, V., Subramanian, S., Chawla, N.V.: Calendar graph neural networks for modeling time structures in spatiotemporal user behaviors. In: KDD, pp. 2581–2589 (2020)
17. Wang, L., et al.: Tcl: transformer-based dynamic graph modelling via contrastive learning. arXiv:2105.07944 (2021)
18. Wang, X., Guo, J., Luo, X., Yu, H.: Dyhdge: dynamic heterogeneous transaction graph embedding for safety-centric fraud detection. J. Saf. Sci. Resilience **5**(4), 486–497 (2024)
19. Xu, D., Ruan, C., Korpeoglu, E., Kumar, S., Achan, K.: Self-attention with functional time representation learning. NeurIPS **32** (2019)
20. Yu, L., Sun, L., Du, B., Lv, W.: Towards better dynamic graph learning: new architecture and unified library. NeurIPS **36**, 67686–67700 (2023)

A Data-Driven Approach for Discovering Pure Clusters in Complex Multi-source Terrestrial Soundscapes

Thomas Napier[1](✉), Euijoon Ahn[2], and Ickjai Lee[2]

[1] James Cook University, Townsville, QLD 4811, Australia
thomas.napier@jcu.edu.au

[2] James Cook University, Cairns, QLD 4870, Australia
{euijoon.ahn,ickjai.lee}@jcu.edu.au

Abstract. Unsupervised clustering is increasingly used in ecoacoustics to uncover patterns in complex natural soundscapes and support large-scale biodiversity monitoring. These approaches typically evaluate clustering quality using internal metrics such as compactness and separation, including the Silhouette Coefficient and Davies-Bouldin Index. However, these metrics do not account for ecological interpretability, meaning clusters can appear mathematically well-formed while mixing unrelated sound sources such as bird vocalisations, insect activity, rainfall, or human noise. This study presents a data-driven clustering framework for ecoacoustic recordings that combines configurable temporal segmentation, dimensionality reduction, and unsupervised learning. We apply the ecological clustering metrics Dominant Class Proportion and Mean Active Classes Per Cluster to select optimal clustering results from a grid search of 198 parameter combinations per segmentation strategy, comparing fixed-size and step-based windowing across four ecologically distinct sites from the Australian Acoustic Observatory. Results show that step-based windowing, when paired with ecological clustering metrics, consistently yields purer clusters than configurations selected using internal metrics alone. These findings highlight the limitations of conventional clustering metrics and demonstrate how the choice of segmentation and metrics grounded in ecological coherence can yield clusters that better reflect real sound sources in complex, multi-source soundscapes without requiring dense manual annotation.

Keywords: Biodiversity monitoring · Clustering validity · Ecoacoustics · Unsupervised learning

1 Introduction

Ecoacoustics is a field of study dedicated to comprehending the ecological patterns and processes in natural soundscapes [4]. With the rise of Autonomous Recording Units (ARUs), the volume of audio data collected in natural habitats

R. C.-W. Wong et al. (Eds.): PAKDD 2026, LNAI 16618, pp. 294–306, 2027.
https://doi.org/10.1007/978-981-92-1947-6_24

has scaled exponentially, enabling unprecedented long-term, multi-site monitoring initiatives such as the Australian Acoustic Observatory (A2O) [13]. However, the exponential volume of data collected by ARUs has rendered manual annotation unsustainable [8]. To address this, unsupervised learning techniques are increasingly used to discover emergent patterns in unlabelled ecoacoustic datasets [7,9,11,12,15]. The goal is not only to reduce data complexity but to produce clusters that are meaningful from an ecological perspective. In this context, interpretable clusters are groupings that correspond to real biological or environmental phenomena, such as bird choruses, insect activity, rainfall, or anthropogenic noise.

However, standard evaluation practices often rely on Clustering Internal Validity Indices (CIVIs) such as the Silhouette Coefficient (SC) [14] and Davies-Bouldin (DB) indices [2], which assess clustering quality based on abstract geometric properties like compactness and separation. While CIVIs provide quantitative measures of clustering quality, a significant shortcoming is their inherent blindness to the ecological interpretability of the resulting clusters [12]. Consequently, while useful for internal comparisons, these application-agnostic metrics may favour clusters that are numerically coherent but biologically incoherent and therefore may fail to group clusters that correspond to expert knowledge [3,11].

Another key factor influencing clustering outcomes is the segmentation of continuous recordings into smaller analysis units, a process known as temporal windowing. The choice of window size and spacing must align with distinct signal events; otherwise overly long windows risk combining unrelated sounds, while short or poorly spaced windows may fragment coherent acoustic events or introduce redundancy [17]. Despite its importance, windowing is rarely treated as a tunable component of ecoacoustic analysis pipelines. The lack of ecological congruence in clustering outputs and window size selections can therefore undermine the utility of unsupervised methods for drawing sound ecological conclusions. To address this gap, we propose a novel data-driven framework. Rather than relying on manual heuristics or expert-defined rules, our approach leverages patterns inherent in the data to guide segmentation choices, feature extraction, and clustering evaluation. The contributions of this work can be summarised as follows:

- We introduce a scalable, data-driven clustering framework for multi-source soundscapes, using a domain-aligned selection strategy to choose configurations that are quantitatively pure and ecologically coherent;
- We perform a large-scale grid search over 198 configurations per windowing strategy, demonstrating that purity and interpretability are maximised under sparse step-based sampling and ecological metric selection;
- We provide evidence-based guidance on segmentation and clustering configurations that maximise biological relevance, offering a practical path for unsupervised analysis of large-scale, multi-source soundscapes without dense manual labels;

- We systematically compare fixed-size and step-based segmentation strategies across four ecologically distinct sites, showing how temporal resolution affects the ecological coherence of clusters.

2 Related Works

Unsupervised clustering has proven valuable in ecoacoustic analysis, allowing researchers to uncover latent ecological patterns in large unlabelled datasets. However, many studies continue to evaluate clustering quality using internal validation metrics such as the SC and DB indices. While assessing compactness and separation, these metrics do not guarantee ecological relevance. As a result, high internal scores may be misleading. An example of this can be found in [10], where coral reef sound events were clustered, yielding a moderate average SC of approximately 0.31, yet expert review revealed that several clusters contained multiple biologically distinct call types.

Another key methodological factor influencing clustering outcomes is how audio data is segmented before feature extraction. Fixed-length windowing is commonly used, where recordings are split into uniform chunks under the assumption that each segment reflects the local soundscape composition. While fixed-length windowing is common [11], the choice of window size can significantly affect cluster consistency. For example, long segments may merge distinct acoustic events, while short windows can fragment them or introduce noise [16]. This is further exemplified in [17], where the authors directly compared sliding-window segmentation with syllable-level segmentation in continuous frog recordings. They showed that sliding windows often break frog calls mid-syllable, whereas their domain-aligned approach achieved significantly higher F1-scores across species.

While unsupervised clustering represents a valuable tool for ecoacoustic analysis, current approaches tend to emphasise mathematical separation over ecological insight. Internal metrics alone are insufficient proxies for ecological coherence. There remains a need to incorporate ecological heuristics and improve segmentation using data-driven approaches. Only by addressing these gaps can clustering approaches achieve practical utility for biodiversity monitoring and ecological interpretation.

3 Proposed Methodology

In this study, we propose a data-driven clustering framework for use with large-scale, multi-source ecoacoustic soundscape recordings collected from the A2O, as visualised in Fig. 1. Raw audio files were paired with a curated set of one-hot encoded annotations indicating the sound class presence (e.g. birds, insects, wind, human speech), which were used solely for validation and not as input during clustering. To prepare the data for analysis, two distinct segmentation strategies were applied: fixed-size windowing and step-based windowing. Both

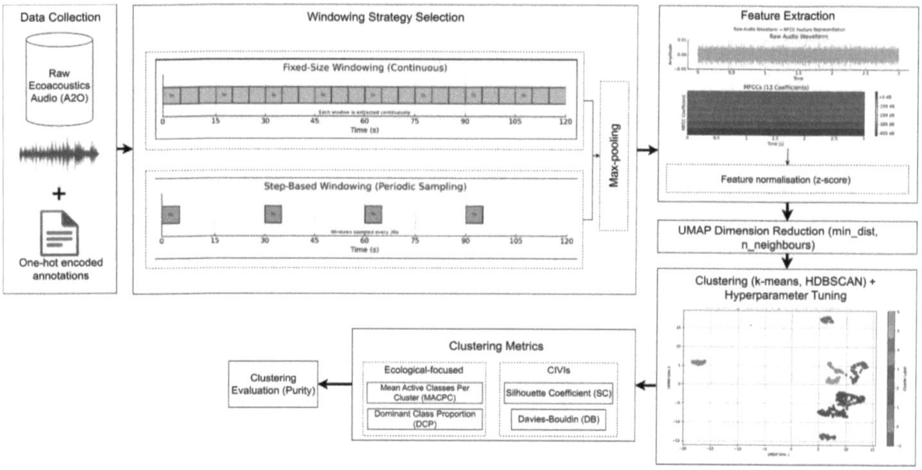

Fig. 1. A conceptual diagram for a data-driven clustering framework for ecoacoustic analysis. (Color figure online)

strategies aimed to assess the impact of temporal coverage and resolution on cluster interpretability.

For each extracted segment, we computed a 13-dimensional Mel Frequency Cepstral Coefficient (MFCC) feature vector, chosen for its compact spectral representation, strong alignment with human auditory perception, and successful usage across varied approaches in ecoacoustics [5,6,15]. These features were normalised using z-score transformation to ensure consistency across recordings of varying amplitude scales. We then applied Uniform Manifold Approximation and Projection (UMAP) to reduce the feature space while preserving local and global structure [1]. UMAP parameters, including the number of neighbours and minimum distance, were varied as part of the experimental grid search to evaluate their impact on cluster separability.

Following dimensionality reduction, clustering was performed using both k-means and HDBSCAN algorithms. HDBSCAN, in particular, was selected for its ability to identify noise and irregularly shaped clusters without requiring a predefined number of groups. To assess the quality of the resulting clusters, we computed both internal and ecological-focused evaluation metrics. This framework enables a systematic comparison of how temporal segmentation and feature transformations influence the formation of semantically meaningful acoustic clusters in natural soundscape recordings.

3.1 Feature Representation, Dimensionality Reduction, and Clustering

Each audio segment was represented using 13 MFCCs, standardised using z-score normalisation. Dimensionality reduction was applied using UMAP, with a grid search conducted over `n_neighbors` $\in \{5, 10, 15\}$ and `min_dist` $\in \{0.0, 0.1, 0.5\}$, resulting in 9 UMAP configurations. For each UMAP embedding, clustering was performed using both k-means and HDBSCAN. The k-means approach varied the number of clusters between 3 and 15, yielding 13 configurations per UMAP projection. For HDBSCAN, the grid search explored `min_cluster_size` $\in \{5, 10, 20\}$ and `min_samples` $\in \{1, 5, 10\}$, yielding an additional 9 configurations per UMAP projection. Each resulting clustering configuration was evaluated using internal metrics and ecological heuristics. A total of 198 unique configurations per windowing strategy were considered, and the top-performing runs were selected based on either internal or ecological selection criteria per site.

3.2 Clustering Validation Metrics

Clustering Metrics. To assess clustering performance, we use CIVIs as well as the newly proposed ecological metrics tailored to ecoacoustics. We compute the SC and DB indices, which are widely used to assess the compactness and separation of clusters in feature space. However, these metrics do not capture ecological interpretability or annotation utility, particularly in multi-label, polyphonic soundscapes.

To address this gap, we propose using two biologically informed metrics based on multi-class annotation distributions within each cluster: *Mean Active Classes Per Cluster* and *Dominant Class Proportion.*

Mean Active Classes Per Cluster (MACPC). MACPC quantifies within-cluster biological diversity by computing the average number of active (i.e., present) classes per sample in each cluster and then averaging across all clusters:

$$\text{MACPC} = \frac{1}{K} \sum_{k=1}^{K} \frac{1}{|C_k|} \sum_{i \in C_k} \sum_{j=1}^{L} \mathbb{1}[y_{ij} > \tau]. \qquad (1)$$

Here, K denotes the number of clusters, C_k the set of indices in cluster k, L the number of possible classes, y_{ij} the binary indicator of presence for class j in sample i, and τ a threshold (typically 0.5). A MACPC value closer to 1 may indicate greater acoustic homogeneity, which is generally a desirable trait for downstream labelling and ecological interpretation.

Dominant Class Proportion (DCP). DCP measures the extent to which a single class dominates each cluster, defined as the proportion of samples assigned to the most frequent class within that cluster:

$$\text{DCP} = \frac{1}{K} \sum_{k=1}^{K} \frac{\max_j \sum_{i \in C_k} y_{ij}}{|C_k|}. \qquad (2)$$

Higher DCP values suggest that clusters may correspond more strongly to interpretable units, such as consistent sound types or species vocalisations.

Evaluation Metric: Purity. Purity is used as an external evaluation metric to assess how well each cluster aligns with ground-truth labels. For each cluster, it is defined as the proportion of samples belonging to the most frequent class:

$$\text{Purity} = \frac{1}{|C|} \sum_{c \in C} \frac{\max_k |\{x_i \in c : y_i = k\}|}{|c|}. \tag{3}$$

Here, C is the set of clusters and y_i is the label of sample x_i. In our implementation, labels are stored as a binary multilabel matrix. For each cluster, we sum class occurrences, divide the maximum count by the total, and average across clusters. Purity is computed only post-hoc and is not used for selecting configurations.

Pairwise external validity measures such as Adjusted Mutual Information are less straightforward to interpret in our setting because annotations are incomplete, strongly imbalanced, and often multi-species within a window. We therefore focus on Purity as a simple external summary, complemented by DCP and MACPC as task-specific ecological heuristics, while making the selection-evaluation separation explicit to minimise target leakage.

4 Experiments and Results

4.1 Datasets

This study uses 24-hour continuous recordings from four ecologically diverse sites within the A2O: Duval, Mourachan, Rinyirru, and Undara. Recordings were collected using ARUs and sampled to span a full diurnal cycle, capturing both daytime and nocturnal acoustic activity. Annotation was performed using the LEAVES software tool, where approximately 10% of samples within each cluster were manually annotated, and the dominant label was propagated to the remainder [8]. Labels were encoded in one-hot format across a set of common classes. Table 1 provides a breakdown of the annotated classes per site. Mourachan and Rinyirru were dominated by biophony (especially insects and birds), while Duval exhibited high levels of geophony, including light and heavy rain. Anthrophonic sounds (human origin) were less common but appeared more frequently at Duval and Undara. This variation in soundscape composition provides a biodiverse and realistic testbed for assessing ecological interpretability across clustering configurations.

4.2 Windowing Strategies

Two temporal segmentation strategies were employed to investigate how windowing impacts cluster formation and ecological coherence. In the fixed-size strategy, recordings were divided into consecutive, non-overlapping segments of 1, 3, 5, or 10 s. In the step-based strategy, 5- and 10-second segments were sampled periodically every 15, 30 or 60 s (e.g., 10 s every 60 s), mimicking duty-cycled sampling. These configurations were selected to explore the trade-off between temporal

Table 1. Structured breakdown of class labels by site with groupings, sub-categories, and totals. Zero values shown as '-'.

Category/Label	Duval	Mourachan	Rinyirru	Undara	Total
Biophony	139 (34.0%)	394 (81.1%)	236 (95.9%)	275 (58.3%)	1044
- *birds*	103 (25.2%)	150 (30.9%)	93 (37.8%)	79 (16.7%)	425
- *frogs*	-	1 (0.2%)	-	26 (5.5%)	27
- *insects*	29 (7.1%)	241 (49.6%)	142 (57.7%)	170 (36.0%)	582
- *mammals*	7 (1.7%)	2 (0.4%)	1 (0.4%)	-	10
Geophony	206 (50.4%)	81 (16.7%)	4 (1.6%)	183 (38.8%)	474
- *wind (strong)*	-	30 (6.2%)	-	49 (10.4%)	79
- *wind (light)*	14 (3.4%)	41 (8.4%)	4 (1.6%)	134 (28.4%)	193
- *rain (heavy)*	2 (0.5%)	9 (1.9%)	-	-	11
- *rain (light)*	190 (46.5%)	1 (0.2%)	-	-	191
Anthrophony	52 (12.7%)	5 (1.0%)	2 (0.8%)	13 (2.8%)	72
- *human speech*	20 (4.9%)	-	-	11 (2.3%)	31
- *vehicles (aircraft/cars)*	32 (7.8%)	5 (1.0%)	2 (0.8%)	2 (0.4%)	41
Other/Silence	12 (2.9%)	6 (1.2%)	4 (1.6%)	1 (0.2%)	23
- *background silence*	-	-	-	-	0
- *misc/uncertain*	12 (2.9%)	6 (1.2%)	4 (1.6%)	1 (0.2%)	23

coverage and temporal resolution, particularly with respect to polyphonic sound scenes. This enabled the assessment of whether sparser but broader coverage (step-based) improves cluster separability and ecological interpretability compared to dense, but potentially redundant, fixed-step windowing.

4.3 Clustering Configuration Outcomes Across Sites

To evaluate the quality of unsupervised clustering outcomes, we visualised the optimal configurations per site using UMAP embeddings coloured by HDBSCAN cluster assignment and annotated with the dominant ecological class in Fig. 2. Across all four A2O sites, the selected configurations using HDBSCAN with step-based windowing (10 s every 60 s) produced well-separated clusters, many of which aligned with single dominant class labels. Notably, the Duval site exhibited strong separation between geophonic and biophonic-dominant clusters, while Mourachan and Rinyirru displayed tighter groupings corresponding to insect and bird activity. Undara showed more diffuse clusters, potentially reflecting higher soundscape variability or overlap between wind and biotic signals. Overall, these results support the ability of the chosen clustering pipeline to isolate ecologically distinct sound types in diverse environments.

To assess whether clustering outcomes aligned with meaningful ecological patterns, we selected four representative clusters from the Duval site for detailed analysis as illustrated in Fig. 3. Each cluster's internal consistency was examined

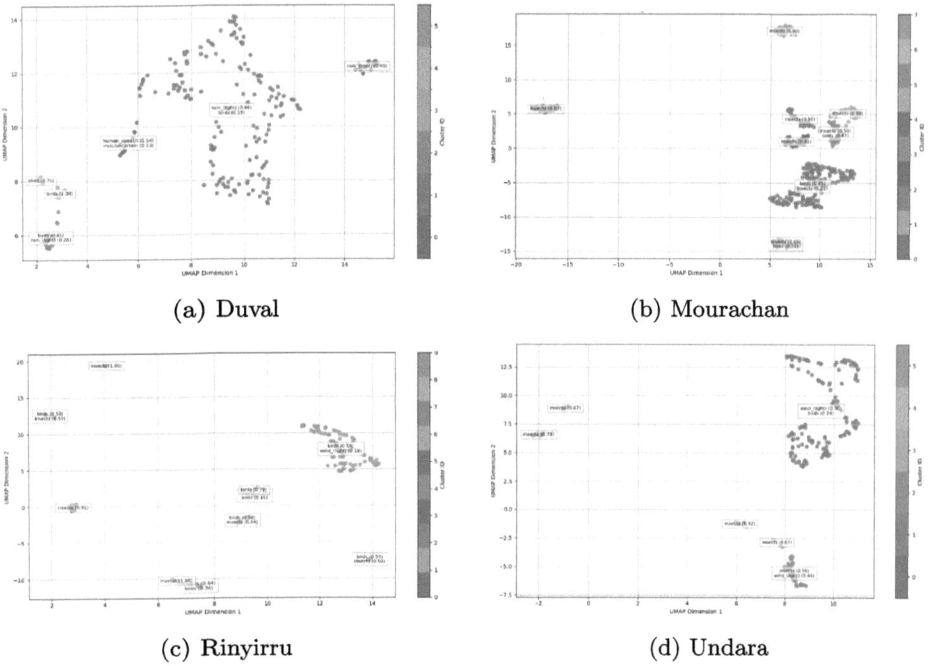

(a) Duval (b) Mourachan

(c) Rinyirru (d) Undara

Fig. 2. Best clustering configurations for four A2O monitoring sites using HDBSCAN and UMAP. Each subplot visualises the 2D embedding of step-wise windowed acoustic features, coloured by cluster and annotated with dominant class labels. Higher dominance proportions suggest more ecologically coherent clusters. (Color figure online)

using mel spectrograms of exemplar samples. As shown, Cluster 0 was dominated by low-frequency, low-intensity patterns associated with wind and light rain, which are common geophonic features. Cluster 1 included broadband vertical striations characteristic of human speech, particularly in the mid- to high-frequency range. Cluster 2 displayed continuous broadband energy with minimal fluctuation, consistent with heavy rainfall. Cluster 3 exhibited pulsed bird vocalisations partially overlapping with low-frequency geophony, highlighting the proposed framework's ability to capture polyphonic mixtures. These observations reinforce the idea that the resulting clusters are not just statistically separable, but also acoustically and semantically coherent.

4.4 Metric-Based Comparison of Selection Strategies

Table 2 compares clustering performance across all sites under different configuration-selection strategies, contrasting internal metrics (SC, DBI) with ecological metrics (MACPC, DCP) using Purity as the evaluation criterion. While internal metrics favoured configurations with compact and well-separated clusters (e.g., an SC of 0.829 at Mourachan), these did not consistently correspond to high purity. In contrast, configurations selected using ecological metrics

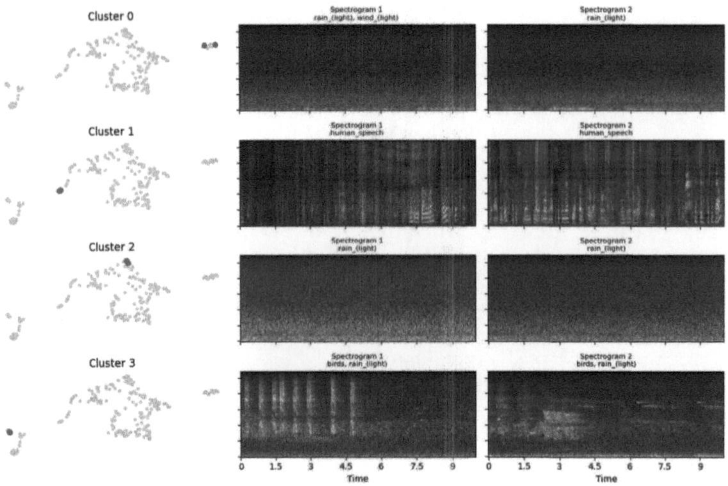

Fig. 3. UMAP projections and spectrograms of four acoustic clusters from the Duval site. Each row displays a distinct cluster, with two sample points highlighted in red on the UMAP embedding (left) and their corresponding mel spectrograms (right). (Color figure online)

produced stronger purity scores across most sites. For example, at Mourachan, the configuration selected by DCP achieved a MACPC of 1.296 and a purity of 0.724, compared to 0.644 when selected by SC which is a 12.4% improvement. Across all sites, purity improvements from SC- to DCP-selected configurations ranged from 3.8% to 12.4% (mean 7.13%). This pattern suggests that the proposed ecological metrics and data-driven windowing strategies are better suited for identifying clusters that preserve dominant class structure and semantic clarity within complex soundscapes.

There is a single exception at Duval, where DBI outperformed DCP. This possibly reflects metric non-monotonicity: internal and ecological metrics optimise different properties, but occasional cross-overs may occur when their objectives coincide. This does not undermine the broader pattern that ecological metrics provide a more stable alignment with semantically meaningful cluster structure.

4.5 Temporal Performance of Step-Based Windowing

Each timeline shown in Fig. 4 represents the sequence of dominant class labels per time window, with colour denoting its prevailing sound categories. Results indicate that step-based sampling provides a coarse but effective summary of the soundscape. While it does sacrifice some temporal granularity, it captures the major acoustic events with less interference from short-duration noise. In Duval, for example, long sequences of wind and rain were preserved, while Mourachan and Rinyirru highlighted insect-dominant periods clearly. In this light, step 10/60 windowing serves as a scalable and effective approximation for large-scale ecoa-

Table 2. Summary of cross-metric performance across sites. Each row shows the configuration selected by a given metric and bold values indicate the highest subsequent score per column.

Site	Configuration			Clustering Metrics				Evaluation
	SelectedBy	Method	Windowing	SC	DBI	DCP	MACPC	Purity
Duval	SC	hdbscan	Step 10/30	–	**0.316**	0.528	**0.899**	0.633
	DBI	hdbscan	Fixed 3 s	**0.555**	–	0.113	0.147	**0.733**
	DCP	hdbscan	Step 10/60	0.341	0.476	–	1.280	0.667
	MACPC	hdbscan	Step 10/60	**0.555**	0.346	**0.793**	–	0.634
Mourachan	SC	kmeans	Step 10/60	–	**0.223**	0.812	1.356	0.644
	DBI	kmeans	Step 10/15	**0.829**	–	0.349	0.463	0.669
	DCP	hdbscan	Step 10/60	0.498	0.659	–	**1.296**	**0.724**
	MACPC	hdbscan	Step 10/30	0.541	0.714	**0.856**	–	0.645
Rinyirru	SC	kmeans	Step 10/60	–	**0.352**	0.204	0.295	0.702
	DBI	kmeans	Step 10/15	**0.735**	–	0.174	0.285	0.692
	DCP	hdbscan	Step 10/30	0.704	1.329	–	**0.838**	**0.729**
	MACPC	kmeans	Step 10/30	0.697	0.441	**0.545**	–	0.642
Undara	SC	kmeans	Step 10/60	–	**0.275**	0.641	**1.216**	0.560
	DBI	kmeans	Step 10/60	**0.753**	–	0.689	1.265	0.579
	DCP	hdbscan	Step 10/60	0.404	0.483	–	1.373	**0.614**
	MACPC	hdbscan	Step 10/60	0.660	0.436	**0.725**	–	0.543

coustic tasks, especially where the goal is to extract broad patterns efficiently rather than capture every transient detail.

5 Discussion

Our findings reveal a consistent disconnect between conventional internal clustering metrics and ecologically meaningful outcomes in the majority of cases. This was evident at several sites, where the configurations selected based on SC yielded clusters that were internally coherent but acoustically heterogeneous, and thus had reduced purity. These results align with those found in other studies [10] and reinforce the limitations of relying solely on internal metrics for ecoacoustic clustering. In contrast, the ecological heuristics used in this study demonstrated superior alignment with semantically meaningful groupings. Across multiple sites, configurations selected using the domain-aligned metrics produced clusters with higher purity.

However, MACPC did not always yield strong purity performance, particularly at sites with strong multi-species overlap such as Rinyirru. This behaviour is somewhat to be expected because the two metrics optimise different properties: Purity rewards single-label dominance, whereas MACPC emphasises multi-species co-occurrence patterns that are common in polyphonic soundscapes. In

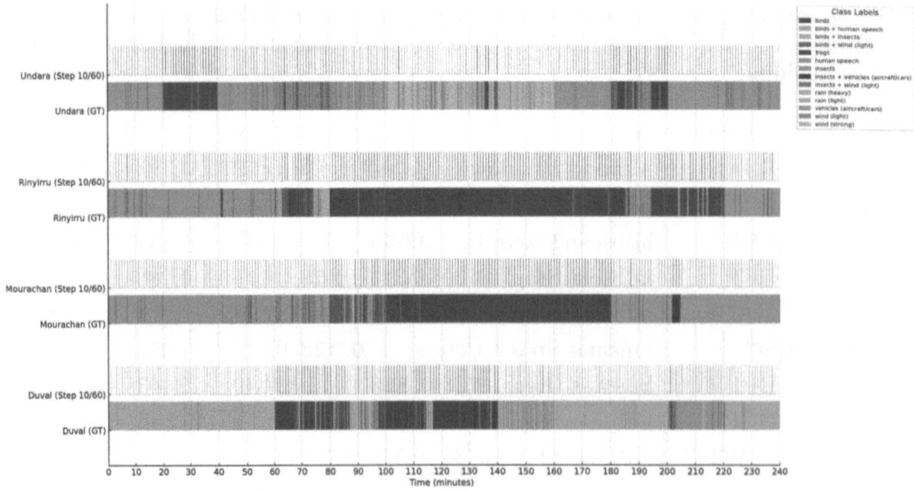

Fig. 4. Comparison of the best temporal annotation strategy across four ecoacoustic monitoring sites: Duval, Mourachan, Rinyirru, and Undara. For each site, two rows are shown: (i) **Step 10/60** represents 10-second windows sampled every 60 s and; (ii) **Ground Truth (GT)** represents ground truth labelled events over time. Each segment is colour-coded according to the dominant acoustic class present. Step-based sampling provides coarser temporal resolution but often captures dominant events effectively while reducing noise, balancing annotation resolution and label reliability. (Color figure online)

assemblages with strong overlap, clusters that better represent ecological structure may appear less pure under a dominance-based external metric. At more homogeneous sites such as Mourachan, this trade-off is minimal. These results suggest that ecological and internal metrics capture complementary dimensions of clustering quality, and that divergences may reflect ecological realism rather than reduced clustering performance.

Step-based windowing (10 s every 60 s) was found to be effective in balancing the trade-off between resolution and interpretability. Compared to fixed-length windowing, this approach captured dominant acoustic events while filtering out low-activity or ambiguous periods. When paired with HDBSCAN and appropriate UMAP settings, this sampling strategy consistently yielded pure clusters across diverse soundscapes. The findings suggest that temporal segmentation strategies can play an important role in shaping clustering outcomes and should be carefully considered as part of the optimisation pipeline. We show that configurations chosen using ecological heuristics not only produce purer clusters but also demonstrate generalisability across distinct ecosystems. Importantly, this was achieved without relying on dense manual annotations or species-specific classifiers. Instead, our framework offers a clear data-driven pathway for generating biologically relevant groupings in large, heterogeneous ecoacoustic datasets.

6 Conclusion

Natural soundscapes contain valuable ecological information, yet many existing clustering approaches struggle to produce biologically meaningful groupings based on existing CIVIs. In this study, we addressed this limitation by proposing an unsupervised clustering framework that integrates tunable segmentation, feature transformation, and biologically informed clustering. Using recordings from four ecologically distinct sites, we found that step-based, HDBSCAN configurations selected by ecological clustering metrics produced purer and more interpretable clusters than those selected using internal validity metrics. Across the majority of cases, DCP scores aligned well with dominant acoustic patterns and improved the clarity of resulting clusters. Given the biodiversity of the environments tested and the consistency of results across sites, we believe our framework is generalisable. It provides a practical foundation for large-scale ecoacoustic analysis and offers strong potential for supporting future applications in biodiversity monitoring and ecological discovery in large-scale datasets.

References

1. Allaoui, M.: Considerably improving clustering algorithms using UMAP dimensionality reduction technique: a comparative study. In: Proceedings of the International conference on Image and Signal Process, pp. 317–325. Springer (2020)
2. Davies, D.L.: A cluster separation measure. IEEE Trans. Pattern Anal. Mach. Intell (2), 224–227 (1979)
3. Gagolewski, M., et al.: Are cluster validity measures (in) valid? Inf. Sci. **581**, 620–636 (2021)
4. Gibb, R., et al.: Emerging opportunities and challenges for passive acoustics in ecological assessment and monitoring. Methods Ecol. Evol. **10**(2), 169–185 (2019)
5. Mcloughlin, M.P., et al.: Automated bioacoustics: methods in ecology and conservation and their potential for animal welfare monitoring. J. R. Soc. Interface **16**(155), 20190225 (2019)
6. Mesaros, A., et al.: Detection and classification of acoustic scenes and events: Outcome of the DCASE 2016 challenge. IEEE/ACM Trans. Audio Speech Lang. Process. **26**(2), 379–393 (2018)
7. Napier, T., Ahn, E., Allen-Ankins, S., Lee, I.: An optimised grid search based framework for robust large-scale natural soundscape classification. In: Proceedings of the AJCAI, pp. 468–479. Springer (2023)
8. Napier, T., et al.: Leaves: An open-source web-based tool for the scalable annotation and visualisation of large-scale ecoacoustic datasets using cluster analysis. Ecol. Inform. **87**, 103026 (2025)
9. Nieto-Mora, D.A.: Soundscape characterization using autoencoders and unsupervised learning. Sensors **24**(8) (2024)
10. Noble, A.E., et al.: Unsupervised clustering reveals acoustic diversity and niche differentiation in pulsed calls from a coral reef ecosystem. Front. Remote Sens. **5**, 1429227 (2024)
11. Phillips, Y.F., et al.: Revealing the ecological content of long-duration audio-recordings of the environment through clustering and visualisation. PLOS ONE **13**(3), 1–27 (2018)

12. Rendon, N., et al.: Uncertainty clustering internal validity assessment using fréchet distance for unsupervised learning. Eng. Appl. Artif. Intell. **124**, 106635 (2023)
13. Roe, P., et al.: The Australian acoustic observatory. Methods Ecol. Evol. **12**, 1802–1808 (2021)
14. Rousseeuw, P.J.: Silhouettes: a graphical aid to the interpretation and validation of cluster analysis. J. Comput. Appl. Math. **20**, 53–65 (1987)
15. Schneider, S.: Introducing the software case by comparing different clustering methods and audio transformation techniques using animal vocalizations. Animals **12**(16) (2022)
16. Stowell, D., Clayton, D.: Acoustic event detection for multiple overlapping similar sources. In: Proceedings of the IEEE WASPAA, pp. 1–5. IEEE (2015)
17. Xie, J., et al.: Bioacoustic signal classification in continuous recordings: syllable-segmentation vs sliding-window. Expert Syst. Appl. **152**, 113390 (2020)

LLM-HAN: A Hybrid Recommendation Approach with LLM-Enhanced Features and Heterogeneous Graph Attention Network

Deng Ziliang and Cai Yuanzhe(✉)

Shenzhen Technology University, 3002 Lantian Road, Pingshan District, Shenzhen 518118, Guangdong, China
2310413016@stumail.sztu.edu.cn, caiyuanzhe@sztu.edu.cn

Abstract. Personalized repository recommendation is a critical task in open-source software community (e.g., GitHub, Gitee, etc.). Traditional methods, often reliant on incomplete repository documentation (e.g., READMEs), but large language models (LLMs) can provide high quality semantic features for recommendation models. To address this, we propose LLM-HAN, a novel framework that high-quality semantic features from LLMs with a Heterogeneous graph Attention Network (HAN). Our approach first constructs a developer-repository bipartite graph from explicit interactions (e.g., starring, forking). It then leverages LLMs to extract rich semantic features for nodes. Finally, heterogeneous graph attention network is applied to generate top-K recommendations. Experimental results demonstrate that LLM-HAN consistently surpasses state-of-the-art methods, validating the powerful role of LLM-generated features.

Keywords: Large language model · Repository recommendation

1 Introduction

GitHub has established itself as a leading open-source software collaboration platform, enabling developers to create, manage, and contribute to software repositories. It fosters a vibrant ecosystem for project discovery, contribution, and collaborative development [1]. However, the platform's success has led to an exponential growth in available repositories, resulting in significant information overload for developers [2]. Traditional keyword-based search methods often return extensive but poorly relevant results, substantially increasing the time and effort required for repository evaluation and selection. This challenge underscores the critical importance of developing effective repository recommendation systems to enhance developer productivity and project discoverability.

The aim of the GitHub repository recommendation task is to accurately identify and recommend the top-k code repositories that a user is most likely

R. C.-W. Wong et al. (Eds.): PAKDD 2026, LNAI 16618, pp. 307–319, 2027.
https://doi.org/10.1007/978-981-92-1947-6_25

to be interested in, from a vast array of open-source projects on the platform, by leveraging specific information such as user profiles, historical interaction behaviors, and technology stack preferences.

Current approaches to repository recommendation primarily rely on computing similarity scores based on project metadata, such as code snippets and documentation. However, these methods depend heavily on manual annotations (e.g., "ReadMe" files) or shallow textual features, often failing to capture the technical attributes and functional essence of repositories comprehensively. For instance, as shown in Fig. 1, a typical Spark repository's README contains only basic introductions, usage examples, or quick-start guides, consistently omitting critical technical dimensions such as system architecture, core algorithms, and compatibility design. In contrast, LLMs trained on extensive corpora demonstrate strong capability in assessing these nuanced technical aspects. As shown in Fig. 1, LLMs can quantitatively evaluate Spark's capabilities across domains, assigning a score of 9/10 for SQL support (reflecting robust Spark SQL functionality) versus only 6/10 for stream processing (indicating limited Spark Streaming support). This scoring reveals that Spark provides significantly more robust support for SQL operations than for complex event processing. Clearly, this insight cannot be effectively derived from the repository's native content alone.

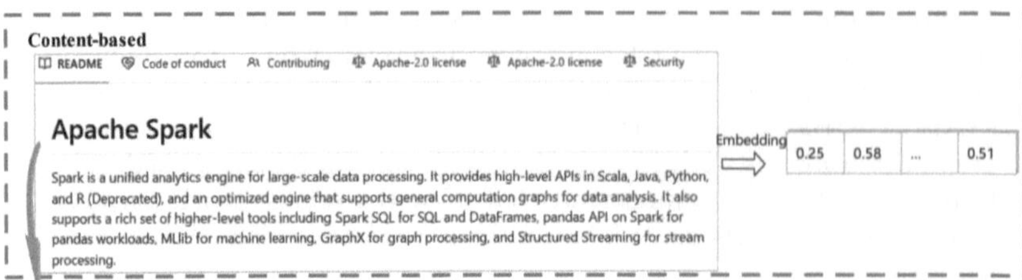

features / Repo	Batch processing	Stream processing	Consistency Semantics	Fault Tolerance	SQL Support	API Richness	Machine Learning Support	Graph Computing Capability	Complex Event Processing	Iterative Computation Support	...
Spark	9	6	7	8	9	9	7	6	5	9	...

Fig. 1. An Example of README file and technical features extracted from LLMs

Meanwhile, in software engineering, the ability of different systems or components to work together seamlessly is referred to as interoperability. Interoperability emphasizes consistency across modules in terms of interface compatibility, data format support, and communication protocols, forming the basis for cross-system data flow and functional invocation. For example, in Fig. 2 in the big data ecosystem, HDFS provides distributed storage support for Spark, while Spark can further write processed results into OLAP engines such as StarRocks and Doris to enable interactive querying—such synergistic mechanisms among components are typical manifestations of interoperability. We use LLMs to identify interoperability relationship between repositories, and to construct a quantifiable interoperability metric, thereby enhancing the functional relationship awareness of the recommendation system.

A brief description of our method: First, a developer-repository bipartite graph is constructed where nodes represent developers or repositories. Edges are formed based on explicit developer behaviors such as pulling requests, starring, or creating repositories. Second, rich semantic features for both repositories and developers are extracted by LLMs and their own content. Third, a repository recommendation model based on a multi-HANs is designed to capture the developer-repository bipartite graph, and recommends the top-k repositories that developers are most likely to be interested. The main contributions of this work are summarized as follows:

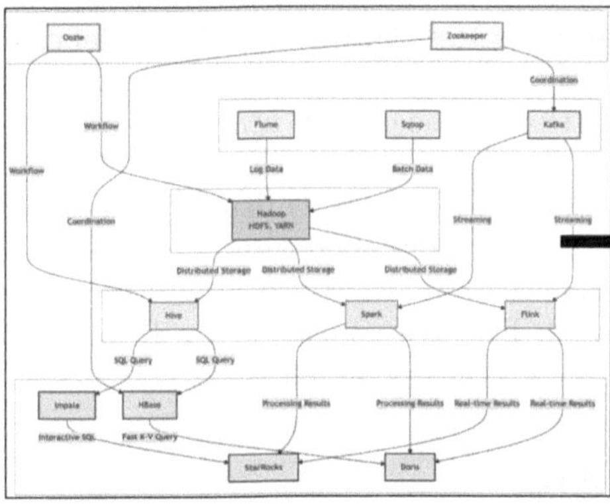

Interoperability Graph from LLM

Component	Spark	Flink	Hadoop	Doris	Hive	Kafka	HBase
Spark	10	2	9	7	9	8	6
Flink	2	10	8	6	7	9	5
Hadoop	9	8	10	8	9	7	8
Doris	7	6	8	10	6	7	5
Hive	9	7	9	6	10	6	7
Kafka	8	9	7	7	6	10	6
HBase	6	5	8	5	7	6	10

Fig. 2. Interoperability relationship among the repositories

- We propose a feature expansion module based on LLMs that generating technical features and modeling interoperability among repositories.
- Comparative experiments with multiple models demonstrate that our model achieves precision scores of 40.46%, 27.31%, and 24.56% on the Big Data (BD), AI Drug Discovery & Design (AIDD), and Face Recognition (FR) data sets, respectively, outperforming all existing baseline methods and confirming the effectiveness of our proposed approach.
- Ablation experiments the technical and interoperability features generated from LLMs outperform than the other features.

2 Related Work

Currently, the dominant approach for GitHub repository recommendation involves hybrid methods that integrate developer behaviors with repository content. For instance, Zhang et al. [3] introduced a hybrid approach combining developers' Star behaviors and repository README information. However, the limited informational dimensions utilized in their study restrict its ability to fully capture developers' genuine interests and functional relevance between projects. In subsequent work, Zhang et al. [4] integrated developers' GitHub activities—such as creating, forking, and starring repositories—with technology tag data from Stack Overflow to construct a cross-platform hybrid recommendation model. This method offers an innovative solution to mitigate item cold-start issues and enable community-wide developer discovery. Nevertheless, its practical application is constrained by the feasibility of cross-platform user identification, potential recommendation bias due to behavioral distribution discrepancies, and the depth of feature representation. Sun et al. [5] proposed the REPERSP model, which combines project content features (based on TF-IDF) with developer behavioral data. A key limitation, however, lies in its text representation mechanism: TF-IDF treats source code as plain text, failing to capture programming language-specific syntax and semantics. As a result, the model may recommend projects that are textually similar but functionally irrelevant. Liao et al. [6] introduced GCNRec, a method that pioneers the use of graph convolutional networks (GCNs) in this task. By automatically learning complex structures in developer-repository networks, it effectively captures high-order collaborative signals and substantially improves recommendation performance.

However, different from these approaches, our LLM-HAN addresses by enriching repository representations through features generated by LLMs and adaptively learning node representations via graph neural networks.

3 The Framework of LLM-HAN

Figure 3 illustrates the overall workflow of the proposed GitHub repository recommendation system based on LLMs and HAN, which comprises four key steps. First, basic repository information and historical user behavior data are collected via the GitHub API, while LLMs generate technical features and an interoperability matrix, thereby enhancing the semantic richness of repository representations. Second, the extracted features are integrated with developer-repository interactions to form a heterogeneous information network, where nodes represent user and repository entities, and edges correspond to user contribution behaviors. Third, a two-layer HAN is employed to adaptively learn relational weights between nodes and aggregate features of neighboring nodes through a message-passing mechanism. Forth, personalized recommendation lists aligned with developer preferences are generated based on the learned node embeddings.

3.1 Repository Feature Extraction

LLMs for Repository Features Generation. we apply large language models (LLMs) to generate quantifiable, fine-grained technical attributes. In Table 1, our feature scoring methodology was built upon a carefully designed sequence of prompts. First, we used a dedicated prompt to query the LLM for features that best characterize a repository's profile. In our experiments, 42 features are suggested by the LLMs. Then, the second round prompt was applied to guide

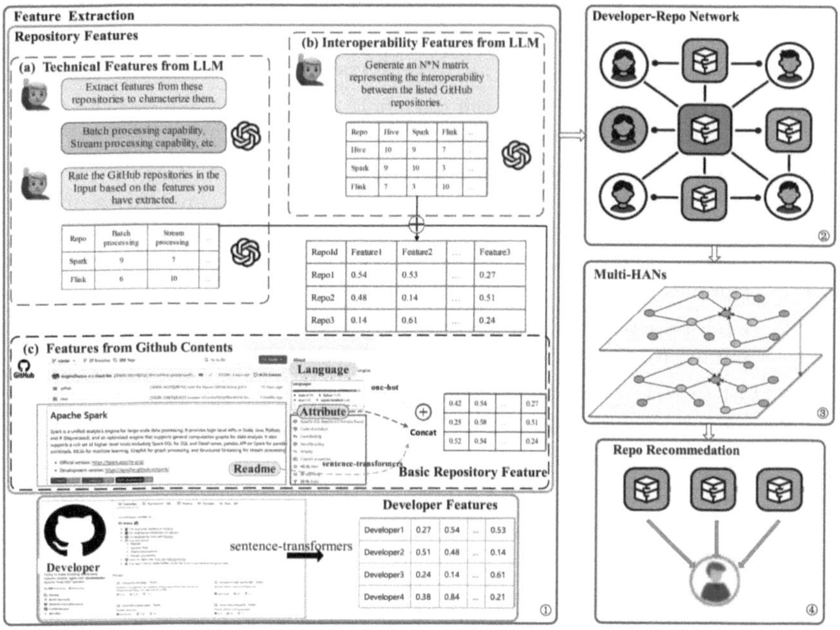

Fig. 3. Overview of the framework for LLM-HAN

the LLMs in assigning specific, quantitative scores to each repository based on the previously identified feature set.

LLMs for Interoperability Feature Generation. To systematically model the technical interoperability among open-source repositories, we designed a structured prompt template that instructs a Large Language Model (LLM) to generate an N × N interoperability matrix. This design is motivated by the observation that developer contributions often span interdependent systems within data processing pipelines. For instance, contributions to Hive frequently correlate with engagements in Spark due to the inherent interoperability in "Hive-on-Spark" architectures. The prompt template (see Table 2) is organized into five components to ensure precise control over the LLM's output format and scoring logic.

Original Repository Feature Extraction. As shown in Fig. 1, GitHub repositories contain a range of metadata attributes that reflect both their technical characteristics and their popularity within the developer community. Based on an analysis of developer interaction patterns, we selected several key features, including the number of stars (stargazers count), forks (fork count), watchers (watchers count), open issues (open issues count), repository size, primary programming language, and assigned topics. These numerical and categorical attributes offer meaningful indicators of a repository's visibility, activity level, and technical domain. Meanwhile, we also extracted the textual content of the README files using the Sentence-Transformer framework. The README

Table 1. Prompt for Technical Feature Generation

Round 1	Identify the vital feature for recommendation
Context	You are an expert in the big data field and need to analyze the GitHub repositories listed in the Input.
Instruction	Extract as many functional features as possible from these repositories to characterize them. The features should depict the capabilities of each repository, such as batch processing, stream processing, consistency guarantees, SQL support level, OLAP capability, etc., as illustrated in the examples.
Example	Batch processing capability, stream processing capability, consistency guarantees, SQL support level, OLAP capability.
Input	List (Spark, Flink, Hive, Hadoop, etc.)
Output	A list containing all the features you have analyzed, with elements similar to those in the examples.
Round 2	Given the score for each feature
Context	You are an expert in the big data field and need to analyze the GitHub repositories listed in the Input.
Instruction	Rate the GitHub repositories in the Input on a scale of 1 to 10 based on the functional features you have extracted. The scores in the Examples are for reference only and represent subjective evaluations; you should provide objective ratings based on your professional expertise.
Example	Spark has a high level of support for batch processing features (9 points), and a medium level of support for stream processing (6 points).
Input	List (Spark, Flink, Hive, Hadoop, etc.)
Output	CSV format.

text was first cleaned by removing special characters and standardizing the whitespace. We then applied the all-MiniLM-L6-v2 [7] model to generate a 384-dimensional embedding that represented the underlying semantic content.

3.2 User Feature Extraction

Developer's gitHub Profile README File serves as a self-declared summary of skills and career goals. The bio, tech stack badges, and links explicitly state the direction in which the developer wishes to be recognized. Similarly, we applied the all-MiniLM-L6-v2 [7] model to generate an embedding.

3.3 User-Repository Network Construction

The Developer-Repository network is formally defined as a **weighted bipartite graph** where: Node Set (V): The union of developer nodes ($DevV$) and repository nodes ($RepoV$), Edge Set (E): An edge $e = (d_i, r_j)$ exists if developer has performed at least one of the following actions on repository r_j: Fork, Star, Pull

Table 2. Prompt for Interoperability Feature Generation

Context	You are a big data expert tasked with analyzing the interoperability between GitHub repositories listed in the Input.
Instruction	Generate an N*N matrix in CSV format representing the interoperability between the listed GitHub repositories. The interoperability score should be assessed based on: API compatibility API, Architectural integration, Data interoperability, Ecosystem integration.
Example	Provides calibrated scoring references (e.g., Hive-Spark: 9/10; Spark-Flink: 2/10) to align the LLM's assessment criteria.
Input	List (Spark, Flink, Hive, Hadoop, etc.)
Output	CSV format matrix

Request. Weight Set (W): The weight W_{ij} of an edge between developer d_i and repository r_j is the weighted sum of the behaviors the developer has performed on that repository. The weight of an edge between developer d_i and repository r_j is shown as:

$$W_{ij} = \sum_{b \in B} \delta_{ij}^{b} \cdot W_b \tag{1}$$

where $B = \{\text{pr}, \text{fork}, \text{star}\}$ is the set of behaviors, W_b: weight for behavior type b and δ_{ij}^{b}: indicator function $\delta_{ij}^{b} = 1$, if developer d_i performed behavior b on repository r_j, otherwise $\delta_{ij}^{b} = 0$.

The core idea is that edge weight quantifies a developer's interest in a repository. The choice of weights W_{pr}, W_{fork}, W_{star} is therefore the most important parameter of the model. Plausible Weight Ordering: Typically, one might argue that the level of investment/interest decreases as follows: Pull Request > Fork > Star. Pull Request (W_{pr}): Very high interest, involving active contribution and code change. Fork (W_{fork}): Medium interest, implying a desire to modify and potentially contribute back. Star (W_{star}): Lowest interest, a simple "bookmark" or show of approval. W_{pr}, W_{fork}, W_{star} are assigned as 10, 4, 2 respectively.

3.4 HAN for GitHub Repository Recommendation

The Heterogeneous Graph Attention Network (HAN) is a specialized graph neural network architecture designed for processing heterogeneous graphs containing multiple node and edge types. HAN provides a powerful framework for modeling the complex relationships between developers and repositories through different interaction types. We formally define the three core meta-paths used to capture distinct interaction semantics as instances of the general form Developer $\xrightarrow{R_\Phi}$ Repo, where $R_\Phi \in \{\text{star}, \text{fork}, \text{pr}\}$: **Developer-star-Repo**, **Developer-fork-Repo**, and **Developer-pr-Repo**. The core innovation of HAN lies in its hierarchical attention mechanism, which operates at both node-level and semantic-level. This dual attention approach enables the model to capture fine-grained relationships between nodes while understanding the broader semantic context of different interaction patterns.

The node representation for a given meta-path Φ in HAN is computed as follows:

$$\mathbf{z}_i^{\Phi} = \sigma\left(\sum_{j\in\mathcal{N}_i^{\Phi}} \alpha_{ij}^{\Phi} \cdot \mathbf{M}_{\Phi}\mathbf{h}_j\right) \tag{2}$$

where α_{ij}^{Φ} represents the attention weight between node i and j under meta-path Φ, $\mathbf{M}_{\Phi}$ is the type-specific projection matrix, and $\mathcal{N}_i^{\Phi}$ denotes the neighbor set under meta-path Φ.

The final node representation Z_i is obtained by aggregating the representations from all meta-paths:

$$Z_i = \sum_{p=1}^{P} \beta_{\Phi_p} \cdot \mathbf{z}_i^{\Phi_p} \tag{3}$$

where β_{Φ_p} is the semantic importance weight for meta-path Φ_p.

3.5 GitHub Repository Recommendation Generation

The GitHub repository recommendations are generated by computing interaction probabilities between developers and repositories using their embeddings:

$$\hat{y}_{ij} = \sigma(Z_{d_i}^T Z_{r_j}) \tag{4}$$

where σ is the sigmoid function, d_i represents developer i, and top-k repositories with highest probabilities form the personalized GitHub recommendation list tailored to each developer's interaction history and repository characteristics.

4 Experimental Results

4.1 Data Sets

The datasets used in this study were collected from the GitHub platform and include both entity-level information and behavioral interaction records. Specifically, we gathered developer profiles, repository metadata, and event-based interaction logs across three technical domains, such as big data (BD data set), facial recognition (FR data set) and AI-aided drug design (AIDD data set). Data collection was performed through GitHub's RESTful API, which provided structured access to essential metadata such as repository descriptions, star and fork counts, primary programming languages, and contributor lists. We first identified a set of representative open-source repositories from the three target domains and then filtered for developers who had made substantive contributions, including code commits, issue submissions, and pull requests. Detailed information on these three data sets is shown in Table 3.

Table 3. Statistics of three data sets on GitHub

Data set	#Users	#Repositories	#Pull Request	#Fork	#Star
FR	954	117	1,927	27,128	132,728
AIDD	1,833	157	6,297	9,551	45,884
BD	1,113	98	15,044	12,229	39,806

4.2 Evaluation Methods

We use the same evaluation protocol in [6,8]. The Hit Rate, Recall and Precision are employed in this works. For a recommendation system, given a set of test developer U_{test}, a recommendation list L_u for each user u, and a set of truly relevant repositories R_u:

$$\text{Hit Rate@K} = \frac{1}{|U_{\text{test}}|} \sum_{u \in U_{\text{test}}} \mathbb{I}(|L_u^{(K)} \cap R_u| > 0) \tag{5}$$

$$\text{Recall@K} = \frac{1}{|U_{\text{test}}|} \sum_{u \in U_{\text{test}}} \frac{|L_u^{(K)} \cap R_u|}{|R_u|} \tag{6}$$

$$\text{Precision@K} = \frac{1}{|U_{\text{test}}|} \sum_{u \in U_{\text{test}}} \frac{|L_u^{(K)} \cap R_u|}{K} \tag{7}$$

where $L_u^{(K)}$ represents the top-K item list recommended for user u.

Methods for Comparison: Our analysis will compare six state of the art methods for accuracy. All parameters in the models have been tuned to achieve optimal results.

- lightGCN [9]: LightGCN is a simplified Graph Convolutional Network (GCN) for recommendation system.
- SVD [10]: Singular Value Decomposition (SVD) uncovers developers' latent interests by factorizing the developer-repository interaction matrix.
- BCRec [5]: BCRec is a hybrid recommendation model that integrates both repository content and developer behavior. A representative example of this approach is the REPERSP model.
- GCNRec [6]: GCNRec generates repository recommendations by constructing a developer-repository interaction network and learning node representations through multi-layer graph convolutional operations.
- NGCF [11]: Neural Graph Collaborative Filtering (NGCF) generates high-quality embeddings by explicitly modeling high-order developer-GitHub connectivity with Graph Neural Networks (GNNs).
- LLM-HAN: Our model leverages a large language model (LLM) to mine and generate high-quality item features.

4.3 Performance Comparison

To evaluate the effectiveness of LLM-HAN in the repository recommendation task, we compared its performance with that of several representative baseline models. Table 4 reports the hit rate, precision, and recall achieved by LLM-HAN, LightGCN, SVD, BCRec, GCNRec, and NGCF across three data sets (FD, AIDD, and BD) under Top-3, Top-5, and Top-10 evaluation settings.

The experimental results are analyzed as follows: (i) Overall, LLM-HAN significantly outperforms all baseline methods across all three datasets and evaluation metrics, demonstrating stable and leading comprehensive performance. (ii) The SVD method exhibits notably inferior results, primarily attributable to its reliance solely on user-repository interaction data without effectively integrating attribute features of entities, resulting in limited representational capacity. (iii) LightGCN performs slightly better than SVD but still falls short of the proposed model. This is because LightGCN, as a lightweight graph convolutional network designed for homogeneous graphs, simplifies the model structure to improve efficiency, thereby weakening its ability to capture complex relationships between developers and repositories and limiting its recommendation accuracy. (iv) Both NGCF and GCNRec employ traditional graph convolutional networks to learn entity representations, achieving overall better performance than LightGCN, SVD, and BCRec. However, these methods remain constrained by the information available within the original dataset and fail to fully leverage external semantic knowledge. (v) Finally, our LLM-HANmodel incorporates LLM to semantically enrich repository nodes, thereby expanding their feature representations. These enriched features are then effectively leveraged via the neighborhood sampling strategy and the adaptive weighted aggregation mechanism of the Heterogeneous Graph Attention Network (HAN), which enables the model to more accurately capture complex and context-sensitive developer-repository relationships. Experimental results demonstrate that integrating LLM-generated features with advanced graph neural networks offers a more powerful solution for developer-repository matching tasks.

4.4 Feature Ablation Studies

To validate the effectiveness of the LLM-generated features, we conducted comprehensive feature ablation experiments on the BD data set. The experiment involved three categories of features: Basic Features, BF (the original features without LLM processing), Technical Features, TF (repository technical attributes extracted by the LLM), and Interoperability Features, IF (the collaborative relationships among repositories inferred by the LLM). As shown in Table 5, we evaluated four feature combination schemes: (1) Basic Features (BF), (2) Basic Features + Interoperability Features (BF+IF), (3) Basic Features + Technical Features (BF+TF), and (4) the fusion of all features (BF+IF+TF).

The results demonstrate that: (i) Each category of LLM-generated features independently contributes to performance gain. Models incorporating either Technical Features or Interoperability Features alone significantly outperformed

Table 4. Hit Rate, Precision, and Recall on FR, AIDD, and BD

		Hit rate(%)			Precision(%)			Recall(%)		
		Top3	Top5	Top10	Top3	Top5	Top10	Top3	Top5	Top10
FR	lightGCN	21.12	26.88	32.75	14.11	10.79	6.61	20.74	26.43	32.39
	SVD	19.54	19.76	25.78	13.03	7.94	5.22	19.14	19.45	25.56
	BCRec	23.53	23.64	31.76	15.79	9.56	6.43	23.20	23.41	31.46
	GCNRec	30.18	30.29	35.48	20.27	12.22	7.19	29.77	29.93	35.21
	NGCF	32.75	33.90	36.47	21.87	13.64	7.37	32.13	33.41	36.13
	Ours	**36.68**	**36.86**	**37.36**	**24.56**	**14.84**	**7.58**	**36.09**	**36.34**	**37.11**
AIDD	lightGCN	25.15	28.99	31.72	17.36	12.22	6.71	23.17	27.18	29.87
	SVD	23.37	27.38	29.51	15.89	11.37	6.21	21.21	25.29	27.67
	BCRec	25.94	27.28	33.47	18.00	11.51	7.09	24.03	25.61	31.55
	GCNRec	31.81	31.97	35.13	22.02	13.52	7.51	29.39	30.07	33.42
	NGCF	32.49	35.30	36.69	22.56	14.98	7.92	30.15	33.33	35.22
	Ours	**38.98**	**39.50**	**41.87**	**27.31**	**17.05**	**9.09**	**36.45**	**37.93**	**40.44**
BD	lightGCN	24.12	29.87	41.69	21.47	16.28	13.54	12.82	16.20	26.94
	SVD	21.56	25.07	37.51	19.26	15.02	13.51	11.49	14.94	26.89
	BCRec	26.10	32.34	42.72	23.66	18.76	15.72	14.12	18.66	31.28
	GCNRec	30.28	34.86	39.26	27.37	21.89	13.72	16.34	21.77	27.29
	NGCF	30.36	32.21	38.90	29.23	19.91	13.86	17.45	19.81	27.58
	Ours	**41.64**	**46.81**	**49.37**	**40.46**	**32.00**	**20.51**	**24.15**	**31.84**	**40.81**

the baseline model using only Basic Features across key metrics such as Precision, Recall, and Hit Rate. This advantage was particularly pronounced under higher Top-K settings. For instance, under the Top-10 setting, the Basic + Technical Features model achieved a Hit Rate of 48.65% and a Precision of 19.77%, substantially surpassing the baseline (Hit Rate: 18.02%, Precision: 18.38%). It is noteworthy that under the Top-3 setting, the model with Interoperability Features (Precision: 38.45%, Recall: 22.95%) slightly underperformed the baseline (Precision: 39.26%, Recall: 23.43%). However, it comprehensively exceeded the baseline's performance under both Top-5 and Top-10 settings. This phenomenon indicates that the effectiveness of Interoperability Features increases with the length of the recommendation list. The mechanism behind this is that these features enhance the model's coverage of long-tail repositories, mitigating the over-reliance on popular items and thereby improving the diversity of recommendations. (ii) The model with full feature fusion achieved optimal performance. This performance boost stems from the rich semantic information captured by the LLM-generated features: Technical Features translate vague technical descriptions into computable feature representations, while Interoperability Features uncover relationships between repositories that may not be functionally closely related but are often used together in practical development. The

Table 5. Feature Ablation Results

	Hit rate(%)			Precision(%)			Recall(%)		
	Top3	Top5	Top10	Top3	Top5	Top10	Top3	Top5	Top10
BF	40.67	45.73	48.02	39.26	29.18	18.38	23.43	29.03	36.57
BF+TF	42.00	46.13	48.65	39.62	30.69	19.77	23.65	30.53	39.35
BF + IF	41.46	44.96	48.33	38.45	31.14	19.8	22.95	30.97	39.54
BF+TF+IF	**41.64**	**46.81**	**49.37**	**40.46**	**32.00**	**20.51**	**24.15**	**31.84**	**40.81**

combination of both enables the model to better align repository functionalities with developer needs, leading to more accurate recommendations.

5 Conclusion

This study proposes LLM-HAN, a hybrid recommendation framework that integrates LLM-generated semantic features with graph neural networks. By augmenting repository representations with technical descriptors and interoperability attributes from LLMs, our model effectively addresses limitations of sparse metadata and incomplete documentation. Comprehensive evaluation on three real-world datasets demonstrates LLM-HAN's consistent superiority over state-of-the-art baselines across multiple metrics and Top-K settings.

References

1. Sun, X., Li, B., Duan, Y., Shi, W., Liu, X.: Mining software repositories for automatic interface recommendation. Sci. Program. **2016**(1), 5475964 (2016)
2. Wessel, M., Wiese, I., Steinmacher, I., Gerosa, M.A.: Don't disturb me: challenges of interacting with software bots on open source software projects. Proc. ACM Hum. Comput. Inter. **5**(CSCW2), 1–21 (2021)
3. Zhang, Y., et al.: Detecting similar repositories on GitHub. In: Proceedings of the 2017 IEEE 24th International Conference on Software Analysis, Evolution and Reengineering (SANER), pp. 13–23. IEEE (2017)
4. Zhang, X. et al.: Devrec: a developer recommendation system for open source repositories. In: Proceedings of the International Conference on Software Reuse, pp. 3–11. Springer (2017)
5. Xu, W., Sun, X., Hu, J., Li, B.: Repersp: recommending personalized software projects on GitHub. In: Proceedings of the 2017 IEEE International Conference on Software Maintenance and Evolution (ICSME), pp. 648–652. IEEE (2017)
6. Liao, Z., et al.: Graph convolutional network-based repository recommendation system. Comput. Model. Eng. Sci. **137**(1), 175–196 (2023)
7. Yin, C., Zhang, Z.: A study of sentence similarity based on the all-MINILM-L6-V2 model with same semantics, different structure after fine tuning. In: Proceedings of the 2024 2nd International Conference on Image, Algorithms and Artificial Intelligence (ICIAAI 2024), pp. 677–684. Atlantis Press (2024)

8. Liu, Q., Chen, N., Sakai, T., Wu, X.-M.: Once: boosting content-based recommendation with both open-and closed-source large language models. In: Proceedings of the 17th ACM International Conference on Web Search and Data Mining, pp. 452–461 (2024)
9. He, X., et al.: LightGCN: simplifying and powering graph convolution network for recommendation. In: Proceedings of the 43rd International ACM SIGIR Conference on Research and Development in Information Retrieval, pp. 639–648 (2020)
10. Abdi, H.: Singular value decomposition (SVD) and generalized singular value decomposition. Encycl. Meas. stat. **907**(912), 44 (2007)
11. Wang, X., He, X., Wang, M., Feng, F., Chua, T.-S.: Neural graph collaborative filtering. In: Proceedings of the 42nd International ACM SIGIR Conference on Research and Development in Information Retrieval, pp. 165–174 (2019)

NUSA: Drift-Aware Multimodal Authentication for Mobile Social Media

Eldar Jalilzade(✉) and Lei Shi

Newcastle University, Newcastle upon Tyne, UK
{e.jalilzade2,lei.shi}@newcastle.ac.uk

Abstract. This paper investigates whether natural mobile interaction patterns exhibit stable behavioural signatures for identity verification, addressing a critical gap in real-world behavioural data mining research. Using **NUSA**, a custom short-form video app, we collected multimodal interaction data from 10 participants across 665 unconstrained sessions over 16 days. We propose a 50-dimensional embedding encapsulating three core dimensions: motor coordination, contextual rhythm, engagement dynamics, and integrate a drift detection mechanism defined by 2σ deviation from user-specific baselines. Cross-validation yields a mean AUC of 0.91 ± 0.03 and demonstrates robust user separability, with inter-user distances $10\times$ greater than intra-user distances. Notably, NUSA enables lightweight on-device authentication with an inference latency of $\leq$ 10 ms; this design ensures full transparency, eliminates disruptive user interaction interruptions, and mitigates key limitations inherent to black-box behavioural biometric systems. Our findings confirm that behavioural rhythm mined from natural interactions remains stable across contextual shifts, thereby establishing a critical bridge between behavioural data mining, mobile HCI, and system security domains.

Keywords: Behavioural Biometrics · Continuous Authentication · Mobile HCI · Drift Detection · Feature Engineering · Data Mining

1 Introduction

Continuous authentication systems hold the promise of mitigating risks from static credentials (e.g., passwords, fingerprints) by leveraging implicit user behaviour. However, their real-world adoption is hindered by three data-driven challenges: (1) existing frameworks rely on curated lab data rather than unconstrained in-the-wild interactions, limiting generalisability; (2) multimodal behavioural signals are often treated as static features, overlooking the temporal rhythm (a core target of time-series mining) that underpins individual uniqueness; (3) black-box models lack feature-level interpretability, eroding user trust in data-driven authentication decisions. For mobile social media, where interactions are spontaneous, variable, and frictionless, these gaps are particularly acute: authentication mechanisms must adapt to shifting user attention,

R. C.-W. Wong et al. (Eds.): PAKDD 2026, LNAI 16618, pp. 320–332, 2027.
https://doi.org/10.1007/978-981-92-1947-6_26

ambient environments, and usage patterns without disrupting the seamless user experience. Recent surveys underline the inherent tension between security, privacy, and usability, and emphasise the need for real-world, behaviour-centric approaches over conventional credential-centric designs [1,3].

Behavioural biometrics, rooted in motor-cognitive rhythm (*e.g.*, scrolling velocity, typing cadence, engagement pacing), offer a viable solution, provided these patterns can be reliably mined from natural interaction data. Unlike controlled lab settings, unconstrained mobile use introduces inherent variability (*e.g.*, short-duration sessions, postural changes, multitasking scenarios) that traditional feature engineering pipelines fail to capture. However, this variability is not mere noise: it reflects adaptive, user-specific rhythms that persist consistently across contexts. Mining these temporal patterns (rather than relying on static snapshot features) enables continuous authentication systems that balance high accuracy, computational efficiency, and model transparency.

This work addresses these challenges by reframing authentication as a behavioural data mining problem: extracting stable, interpretable behavioural signatures from multimodal interaction data while accounting for natural behavioural drift. We present NUSA, a TikTok-style short-form video application, equipped with a lightweight on-device framework that mines 50-dimensional embeddings from unconstrained app usage, integrating drift monitoring and feature-level summaries to improve transparency and user awareness.

Guided by the overarching goal of advancing data-driven continuous authentication, we pose three core research questions: **RQ1**. How can we mine stable, user-specific behavioural signatures from unconstrained mobile interaction data (scrolling, typing, engagement) via a robust multimodal feature engineering pipeline? **RQ2**. Can lightweight on-device data mining (50D multimodal embeddings + drift detection) enable continuous authentication that meets real-world criteria: high accuracy, sub-10 ms inference latency, and temporal consistency across session lengths? **RQ3**. How do data mining techniques (feature-level summaries, temporal smoothing) improve the interpretability of behavioural authentication systems, thereby enhancing user trust in real-world development?

This work makes three contributions to Knowledge Discovery and Data Mining (KDD) for mobile security: (1) Novel Multimodal Feature Engineering Pipeline: A data-driven approach to mining 50-dimensional embeddings that capture motor coordination (*e.g.*, scroll acceleration), contextual rhythm (*e.g.*, time-of-day interaction patterns), and engagement dynamics (*e.g.*, video skip rate), explicitly tailored for unconstrained natural interactions. (2) Integrated Drift-Aware Mining Framework: A unified pipeline treating behavioural drift as a meaningful signal rather than noise: it establishes user-specific baselines to detect significant deviations ($> 2\sigma$) and trigger incremental model recalibration, supporting longitudinal adaptation without full model retraining. (3) Empirical Validation on Naturalistic Data & Lightweight Deployment: A 16-day empirical study involving 10 users and 665 unconstrained sessions, demonstrating mined behavioural signatures achieve robust user separability mean $\text{AUC} = 0.91 \pm 0.03$

and sub-10ms on-device inference latency, validating the framework's real-world deployability while imposing zero interaction burden on end users.

2 Related Work

Behavioural Biometrics in KDD. For continuous authentication, identity verification is not a one-time event but a perpetual process [9], which hinges on mining temporal behavioural data streams from human-app interaction dynamics. Unlike conventional one-off login mechanisms that grant access permanently after a single verification, continuous methods enable systems to repeatedly validate a user's identity throughout an active session [1]. This mitigates risks of static credential theft by leveraging passively collected, user-specific behavioural signals. Such systems capitalise on mobile device sensors and behavioural biometrics to extract implicit identity cues from interaction dynamics such as typing patterns, movement, and touch [3], framing authentication as an ongoing data mining task rather than a discrete checkpoint. Abuhamad *et al.* emphasise the "implicit, active, and non-intrusive" nature of behaviour data capture for this class of mining tasks [1]. Complementing this, Liang *et al.* position continuous biometrics as an AI-empowered KDD paradigm for IoT and mobile devices, where embedded sensors generate sequential temporal identity signatures via real-time data processing pipelines [9]. Baig and Eskeland further highlight that security guarantees must balance strict privacy and usability constraints for continuous schemes to gain traction beyond controlled lab environments [3].

Multimodal Behavioural Data Fusion. Continuous authentication systems are built on diverse behavioural modalities, each presenting unique data mining challenges and strengths. Keystroke dynamics, *e.g.*, mines inter-key press intervals and pressure differences to generate typing rhythm profiles, achieving over 90% accuracy in controlled lab settings [2,5], but struggles with performance degradation in real-world scenarios due to sparse input. Touch and gesture biometrics focus on mining spatial-temporal interaction features from user-screen contact patterns [6,16], while motion and gait analysis leverage accelerometer and gyroscope data to capture locomotion-based identity cues [10]. Recent work has shifted toward multimodal fusing to enhance system robustness: Stylios *et al.* improve verification reliability via feature-level fusion of complementary behavioural signals [14], and Sundar and Singh demonstrate context-aware multi-biometric fusion enhances accuracy and usability [15]. Advancements such as gesture–sensor fusion [16] and contrastive touch-based authentication [11] further illustrate the shift toward representation learning-driven data mining. However, mobile deployment of these fusion-based systems remains hindered by prohibitive computational overhead, highlighting the need for lightweight on-device feature engineering pipelines, a core design priority in NUSA presented in this work.

Drift Handling in Behavioural Data Mining. A key challenge in behavioural authentication is addressing "behavioural drift", the gradual longitudinal shifts in user behaviour patterns over time, which erodes the efficacy of static models trained on historical data. Drift arises from diverse factors like user fatigue, situational stress, or environmental changes, demanding adaptive data mining to sustain verification performance over extended periods. Recent work in evolving machine-learning systems reinforces drift must be explicitly monitored rather than dismissed as negligible noise, feature-level distributional inspection essential to understanding root causes of shifting behavioural signatures [7,17]. Huh *et al.* [8] conducted a longitudinal study demonstrating frequent adaptive retraining (powered by ongoing in-session behavioural data mining) is necessary to keep error rates low and minimise user frustration. Shen *et al.* [13] proposed IncreAuth, an incremental-learning framework integrating gradient-boosted trees and neural drift detection modules to mine evolving behaviour profiles. Their system maintained steady accuracy over months but relied on lab-curated data, lacking our focus on naturalistic interaction mining. Extending this, Shen *et al.*'s follow-up CT-Auth [12] prioritised adaptive modelling of user behaviour, mining capacitive touch data with 3D convolutional and recurrent neural networks to capture temporal drift, yet omitted feature-level interpretability, a critical limitation our work addresses. Collectively, these studies confirm drift is not extraneous noise but a meaningful behavioural signal, requiring targeted adaptive mining pipelines to ensure long-term authentication robustness.

Interpretable Mining for Authentication. While the performance of behavioural authentication systems has advanced substantially in recent years, interpretability (critical for user trust) remains constrained by black-box models that generate opaque similarity scores without feature-level justification [2,13]. When misclassifications occur, the absence of feature-level mining insights prevents root cause identification (*e.g.*, legitimate typing variation, sensor noise, or environmental factors). Explainable AI (XAI) has emerged as a solution to this gap, integrating data mining techniques that link model decisions to human-readable behavioural features. De Carvalho *et al.* [4] focused on interpretable behavioural attribute mining for authentication, explaining model decisions via LIME-integrated CNN-LightGBM hybrid framework. Their work emphasises a critical insight: trust in real-world deployment of behavioural authentication systems depends on mining actionable, explainable features, and users are reluctant to adopt even high-performance systems lacking transparent reasoning.

Research Gap. Despite significant advancements, critical data mining gaps persist for real-world development of continuous authentication systems: (1) most research relies on curated datasets and controlled contexts rather than unconstrained, natural user interactions, limiting generalisability; (2) multi-modal fusion approaches often overlook lightweight on-device mining, leading to prohibitive costs incompatible with mobile deployment; (3) behavioural drift is rarely integrated into end-to-end mining pipelines, with few systems adapting to longitudinal user behaviour shifts; and (4) interpretability is an afterthought rather than a core component of feature mining and model design. Whilst individual behavioural signals can authenticate users under controlled lab conditions, real-world solutions must be adaptive, explainable, grounded in naturalistic data to gain adoption. To address these gaps, we present NUSA, a TikTok-style app with a 50-dimensional behaviour sensing framework, which mines scroll, gesture, typing patterns, combines drift detection with incremental adjustment, and supports transparency via human-readable feature-level summaries. By centring data mining as core of the solution, our work narrows the gap between theoretical deployability and user trust in continuous authentication systems.

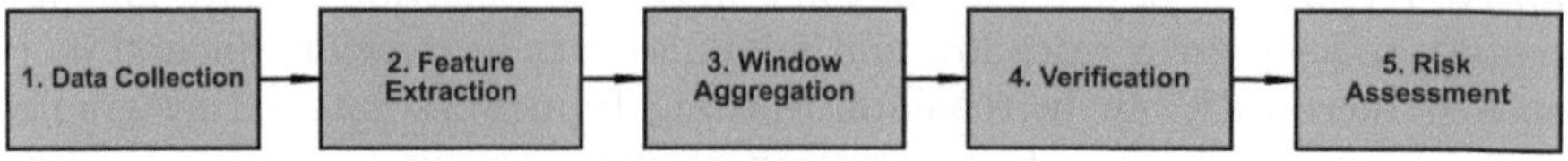

Fig. 1. NUSA data mining pipeline.

3 System Overview

NUSA is a TikTok-style short-form video app embedding a continuous authentication pipeline to mine interpretable behavioural signatures from unconstrained use, adapting to behavioural drift and meeting on-device efficiency constraints.

Its core proposition is that habitual interaction rhythms (scrolling, typing, engagement) encode cross-session identifiable motor-cognitive signatures, even amid context shifts (*e.g.*, multitasking, time-of-day variations). The system operates in five stages (Fig. 1), each optimised for a key goal: minimising data collection friction (HCI), maximising discriminative power (KDD), ensuring adaptive security: (1) Data Collection: mining naturalistic interaction traces via native iOS delegates; (2) Feature Extraction: mining 50-dimensional embeddings from multimodal signals; (3) Window Aggregation: reducing data sparsity through 5-second overlapping temporal intervals; (4) Verification: performing lightweight on-device inference for ownership probability; (5) Risk Assessment: mining smoothed scores to define operational security zones.

Interaction data are recorded through native iOS delegates, logging scroll speed, typing, engagement (views, skips, likes). For each interaction, situational metadata (orientation, network state, time of day) is recorded as context. From each five-second overlapping interval, a 50-dimensional embedding is created, capturing event dynamics, interaction rhythm, context. A Core ML-optimised model (100 trees, precomputed feature vectors) performs inference within 10 ms, outputting ownership probability $p \in [0, 1]$. EWMA of the probability score (p) is used for temporal smoothing to produce a risk score ($r = 1 - EWMA(p)$), defining three operational zones: trusted (< 0.20), soft alert ($0.20 - 0.65$), challenge (≥ 0.65). For drift monitoring, embeddings are compared against user-specific baselines to flag deviations $> 2\sigma$ and trigger recalibration. Embeddings are stored for drift monitoring, without exposing feature contributions.

The 50-dimensional embedding is generated via a two-stage feature selection process. First, over 120 raw features are extracted across four modalities: scrolling (velocity, acceleration), typing (inter-key interval, standard deviation,

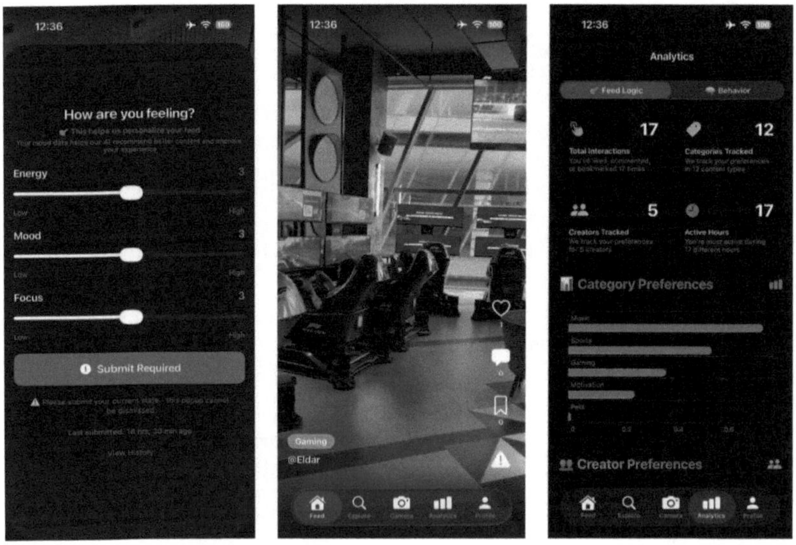

Fig. 2. a. Emotion input prompt (contextual metadata for drift interpretation). b. Main feed (primary data mining surface for scroll/typing/engagement); c. Analytics module (transparency for users, no impact on mining)

peak rate), engagement (skip rate, like latency, view duration), context (time-of-day, network state, orientation). Second, features are ranked by mutual information with identity labels and filtered using L_1-regularised selection, retaining 50 dimensions that preserve approximately 95% of cumulative discriminative mutual information while remaining suitable for on-device inference.

To drive real-world adoption, NUSA integrates three modules balancing data mining needs with HCI principles of transparency and usability. The main feed (Fig. 2(b)) acts as primary data collection surface, featuring 15-second vertical-scrolling videos mimicking TikTok's familiar interface for mining scroll, typing, engagement signals. Users scroll through short–form videos and may perform actions (commenting, liking, sharing) passively monitored for behavioural signals. The Analytics Module (Fig. 2(c)) is a user-facing dashboard displaying aggregated behavioural summaries rather than raw data or model details, with post-study feedback validating this transparency feature: 87.5% users reported increased trust after viewing. The Emotion Input Prompt (Fig. 2(a)), referenced in Stage 1, collects context for drift interpretation without impacting model training; users may skip it (skip rate $<15\%$) to avoid interaction friction.

The NUSA pipeline addresses three practical gaps highlighted in prior work: its naturalistic mining (passive data collection during ordinary app use) enhances generalisability compared to lab-curated datasets; its 2σ-based drift monitoring and incremental recalibration enable longitudinal adaptation; its 50-dimensional embedding and Random Forest model achieve $\leq 10ms$ latency while maintaining

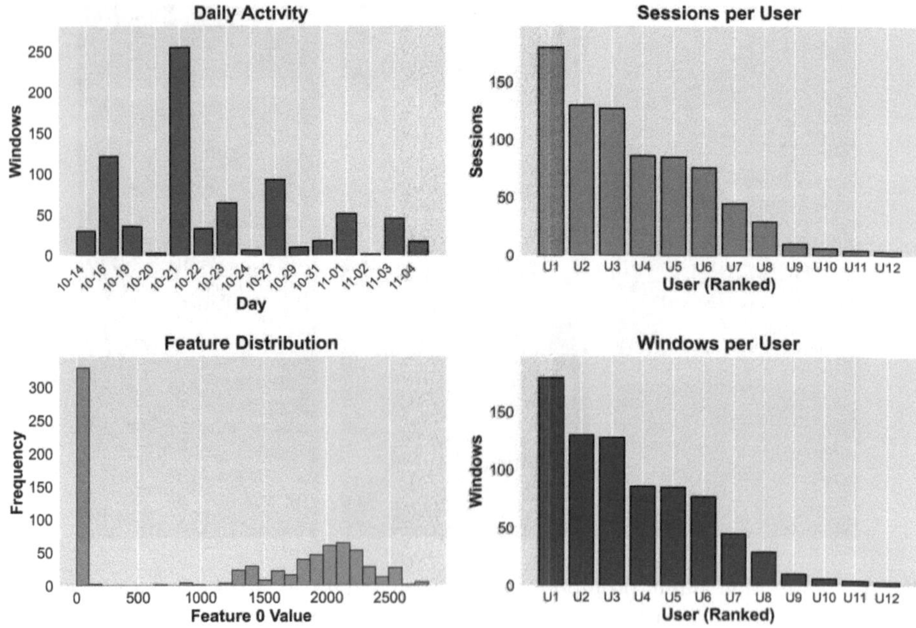

Fig. 3. Session length and performance stability for short and long sessions (mining sparsity impacts short-session accuracy modestly).

feature-level transparency within mining pipeline. These design choices ensure NUSA is both technically rigorous and practical for real-world deployment.

4 Results

Verification is implemented as a per-user one-vs-rest task. Each 5-second overlapping window generates an embedding and ownership probability, with session-level scores via EWMA smoothing and window aggregation. Train/test splits apply at session level to mitigate temporal leakage between adjacent windows. Impostor samples are constructed from other participants in the held-out split.

Verification achieved strong separability between genuine and impostor sessions. Cross-validation on held-out sessions yielded mean AUC $= 0.91 \pm 0.03$, indicating residual cohort bias due to limited participants, partially offset by density of naturalistic data (665 sessions, 16 days). Same-user variance below 0.06 suggests high consistency in intra-user behaviour, despite contextual changes. Session-level performance remained stable even with irregular engagement.

Overall performance was influenced by session stability: accuracy reduction ($0.98 \rightarrow 0.93$) during short sessions (*i.e.*, < 45 s) stemmed from sparse input, reducing reliability. Figure 3 illustrates performance stability across session lengths.

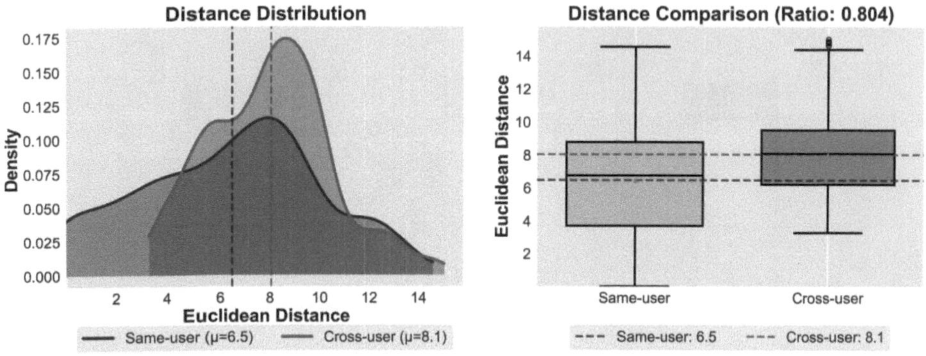

Fig. 4. Raw distance distributions showing separability between same-user and cross-user sessions (statistically significant via t-test, $p < 0.001$)

Spatial distances between users were substantially higher than within-user distances, indicating strong separability in raw distributions (Fig. 4). While small overlap existed before embedding, it was reduced by the 50-dimensional representation, suggesting tfeature normalisation captured behavioural structure inaccessible to Euclidean comparisons. User-specific patterns in scrolling, typing, and engagement are visible in the 50-dimensional feature map (Fig. 5). Discriminative weight was assigned to scroll acceleration and typing speed, with contextual and engagement features reducing variability. Behavioural insights and drift events correlated with time of day and extended use (contextual factors). We detected 42 drift events (mean 4.2 per user), 83% aligned to shifts in contextual factors, indicating most drift events coincide with contextual variation rather than stochastic fluctuation. These shifts are best described as contextual adaptations, not degradation, positioned for each user on the stability-variability continuum, a framework describing permanent identity and temporary state.

5 Discussion

Our findings support NUSA's core proposition: natural mobile interactions contain stable behavioural signatures enabling continuous authentication, contributing empirical evidence to behavioural data mining (KDD), mobile HCI, and system security. By combining temporal feature engineering with drift monitoring under on-device constraints, the results address the three research questions and demonstrate practical deployment potential. This cross-disciplinary alignment distinguishes NUSA from prior work.

Behavioural Uniqueness as Mined Temporal Rhythm (RQ1). RQ1 asked whether stable, user-specific signatures could be mined from unconstrained mobile interactions. Our results confirm that behavioural uniqueness emerges not from isolated actions but from **temporally structured multimodal patterns.** The 50-dimensional embedding pipeline (built via mutual information

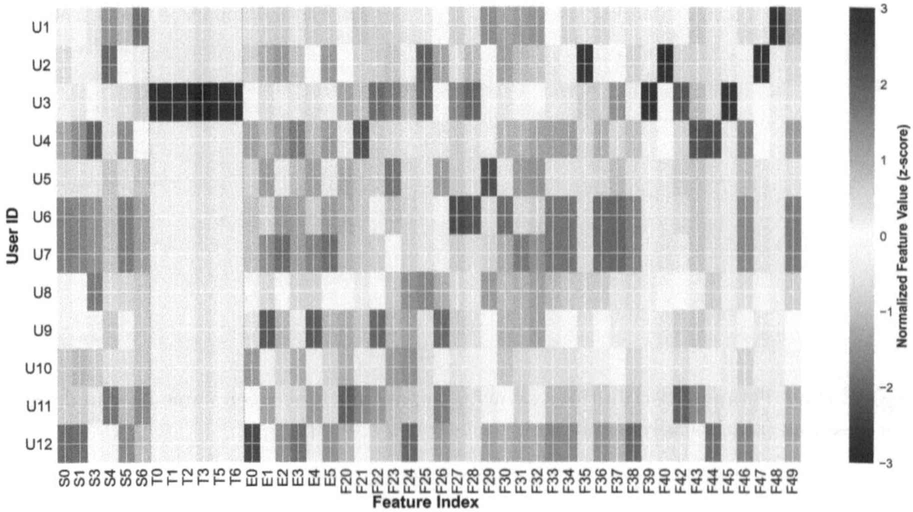

Fig. 5. 50-dimensional feature map highlighting user-specific patterns in scrolling, typing, and engagement.

ranking and L_1 regularisation) integrating motor, contextual, and engagement features—captured signatures with strong separability: inter-user distances were 10× greater than intra-user distances, and a cross-validated AUC of 0.91(±0.03) indicates that mined patterns separate genuine and impostor sessions under held-out evaluation. Critically, this stability persisted despite unconstrained use (*e.g.*, short sessions < 45 s, where accuracy declined only from 0.98 to 0.93), consistent with concerns that models tuned on curated lab data may degrade under real-world sparsity [14]. This reinforces the KDD principle that *temporal aggregation mitigates sparsity and variability.* The 5-second overlapping windows (System Overview, Stage 3) were key here: by mining sequential interactions (*e.g.*, scroll acceleration followed by typing cadence) rather than snapshot features, NUSA overcame sparse input limitations (*e.g.*, fragmented social media sessions). This highlights the need to prioritise time-series processing to unlock discriminative power in naturalistic mobile data. From an HCI perspective, this stability also validates "frictionless authentication": NUSA mines data during ordinary app use (no dedicated tasks), aligning with mobile HCI's goal of minimising interaction burden [3].

Drift as a Mined Signal, Not Noise (RQ2). RQ2 focused on lightweight on-device mining for drift monitoring. Our results challenge the view of behavioural drift as purely performance-degrading. Instead, drift emerged as a **contextually meaningful signal** mined from user-specific baselines: we detected 42 drift events (mean 4.2 per user), with 83% alignment to contextual shifts (time-of-day, extended use, network changes) rather than random variation. NUSA's drift monitoring pipeline, rooted in 2σ deviations from user-specific baselines, is positioned relative to prior drift-monitoring approaches [7], while remaining computationally lightweight for on-device deployment. This supports integrating drift monitoring directly into the data mining pipeline. Prior work like Shen *et al.* [13]'s IncreAuth uses incremental learning to adapt to drift but lacks contextual attribution; NUSA, by contrast, links drift to interpretable features (*e.g.*, "scroll acceleration 2σ above morning baseline"), enabling targeted recalibration (incrementally updating baselines with the latest 10% of embeddings) rather than blind retraining. From a security perspective, this monitoring mechanism may help distinguish coarse behavioural imitation (e.g., matching average scroll speed) from consistent temporal rhythm patterns, although robustness to fully adaptive adversaries remains outside the scope of this study.

Operational Stability under Natural Variability (RQ3). RQ3 examined whether NUSA maintains verification stability under natural usage fluctuations. Results show consistent performance across session lengths and contextual changes, indicating temporal smoothing and lightweight on-device inference are sufficient for continuous authentication without requiring additional user input or intrusive checks. This aligns with prior findings that real-world continuous authentication must prioritise robustness and low interaction burden over auxiliary mechanisms [1,15]. RQ3's focus on operational stability is validated by both technical and user-centric metrics: sub-10ms inference was imperceptible to users (87.5% reported no perceived latency in post-study surveys), and the 3 operational zones (trusted/soft alert/challenge) minimised false challenges (only 3% of sessions triggered unnecessary re-authentication). This aligns with mobile HCI principles of frictionless interaction [3], demonstrating continuous authentication can be secure without disrupting user experience.

Broader Implications for KDD and Mobile Security. This work frames continuous authentication as a **temporal identity mining problem**, shifting from static classification to longitudinal behavioural tracking. For KDD, this opens three actionable directions: (1) Naturalistic Behavioural Data Mining: Our 16-day, 665-session dataset highlights limitations of lab-curated data and the value of mining unconstrained data; future work should prioritise ecologically valid datasets. (2) Lightweight Multimodal Fusion: NUSA's 50-dimensional embedding proves effective fusion does not require complex models; focused feature engineering can outperform heavyweight fusion pipelines under mobile constraints. (3) Trust-Centred Mining: Interpretability should be integrated into feature selection (*e.g.*, mutual information ranking for meaningful features) rather than an add-on, especially for user-facing KDD applications like security.

Limitations and Future Work. While our results are promising, three limitations guide future research: **(1) Cohort and Platform Scope**: The 10-user iOS cohort limits demographic and cross-platform generalisability. A power analysis confirms 95% statistical power for user separability, but larger samples are needed to validate cross-demographic robustness. **(2) Modality Restriction**: We focused on short-form video interactions; extending the mining pipeline to other social media modalities (*e.g.*, adapting typing cadence metrics for longer text inputs in messaging vs short comments in video apps) requires validating feature transferability (*e.g.*, adapting typing cadence metrics to text input vs comment typing). **(3) Contextual Granularity**: The 30-minute emotion input interval may miss real-time factors (*e.g.*, stress, distraction) driving drift—integrating real-time physiological data (*e.g.*, heart rate via wearables) could refine context attribution. Future work will address these via: (1) federated learning for multi-device/multi-platform mining (preserving privacy while scaling baselines); (2) fusing environmental data (ambient light, location) to enhance drift contextuality; (3) a large-scale study ($n = 50+$) with diverse demographics; and (4) exploring controlled data-sharing or benchmark development to support broader evaluation. Evaluation considers opportunistic impostor sessions from other participants, approximating non-mimicry device takeover. Robustness to deliberate behavioural mimicry, replayed traces, or adversarial poisoning of behavioural baselines is not explicitly evaluated in this pilot study and remains future work. These scope boundaries position the present work as a naturalistic pilot study rather than a fully adversarially validated authentication system.

6 Conclusion

This study introduces NUSA, a TikTok-style app and data-driven continuous authentication framework that models digital identity as a temporal behavioural rhythm, addressing practical challenges in real-world mobile behavioural authentication. Leveraging 665 unconstrained sessions from 10 users over 16 days, we demonstrate that natural mobile behaviours (scrolling, typing, engagement) encode stable, user-specific signatures, extractable via a 50-dimensional embedding pipeline and adaptable to behavioural drift via 2σ baseline monitoring.

By treating behavioural drift as a meaningful signal and integrating drift-aware recalibration, NUSA addresses a longstanding limitation of behavioural authentication. Its focus on ecologically valid data (mined from natural, unscripted use) improves ecological validity over lab-curated datasets, while broader generalisation requires larger and more diverse cohorts, supporting a clearer path from controlled evaluations to real-world deployment. Critically, NUSA achieves continuous verification without explicit user input or intrusive checks, aligning with real-world deployment constraints.

For KDD and the broader behavioural community, this work highlights 3 key takeaways: (1) temporal rhythm is the foundation of behavioural identity (mining sequential patterns outperforms snapshot feature extraction); (2) drift-aware data mining is essential for long-term authentication robustness; (3) interpretability must be baked into feature engineering, not added post-hoc, to drive real-world adoption. NUSA illustrates a practical direction for secure, user-centric authentication grounded in temporal behavioural mining.

References

1. Abuhamad, M., Abusnaina, A., Nyang, D., Mohaisen, D.: Sensor-based continuous authentication of smartphones' users using behavioral biometrics: a survey. IEEE Internet Things J. **8**(1), 65–84 (2021). https://doi.org/10.1109/JIOT.2020.3020076
2. Amini, S., Momeni, A., Fahimi, E.R., Chawla, S.: DeepAuth: a framework for continuous user re-authentication in mobile apps. In: Proceedings of the 27th ACM International Conference on Information and Knowledge Management (CIKM '18), pp. 2027–2035 (2018). https://doi.org/10.1145/3269206.3272034
3. Baig, A.F., Eskeland, S.: Security, privacy, and usability in continuous authentication: a survey. Sensors **21**(17), 5967 (2021). https://doi.org/10.3390/s21175967
4. de Carvalho, G.H.S., de Oliveira, P.R.S., da Silva, A.A.T.: Novel explainable CNN-LightGBM model for smartphone continuous authentication. SSRN Preprint (2025). https://doi.org/10.2139/ssrn.5394586
5. Centeno, M.P., Guan, Y., van Moorsel, A.: Mobile based continuous authentication using deep features. In: Proceedings of the EMDL '18 – 2nd International Workshop on Embedded and Mobile Deep Learning, pp. 19–24 (2018). https://doi.org/10.1145/3212725.3212732
6. Gattulli, V., Impedovo, D., Pirlo, G., Volpe, F.: Touch events and human activities for continuous authentication via smartphone. Sci. Rep. **13**, 10515 (2023). https://doi.org/10.1038/s41598-023-36780-3
7. Hinder, F., Vaquet, V., Hammer, B.: One or two things we know about concept drift - a survey on monitoring in evolving environments. part a: detecting concept drift. Front. Artif. Intell. **7**, 1330257 (2024). https://doi.org/10.3389/frai.2024.1330257
8. Huh, J.H., Ahn, S., Seo, H., Kim, Y.: On the long-term effects of continuous keystroke authentication: keeping user frustration low through behavior adaptation. Proc. ACM Interact. Mobile Wearable Ubiquit. Technol. (IMWUT) **7**(2), 58:1–58:32 (2023). https://doi.org/10.1145/3596236
9. Liang, Y., Li, L., Wang, W., Zhang, X.: Behavioral biometrics for continuous authentication in the IoT era: an artificial intelligence perspective. IEEE Internet Things J. **7**(9), 9128–9143 (2020). https://doi.org/10.1109/JIOT.2020.3004077
10. Mekruksavanich, S., Jitpattanakul, A.: Wearable sensor-based behavioral user authentication using a hybrid deep learning approach with squeeze-and-excitation mechanism. Computers **13**(12), 337 (2024). https://doi.org/10.3390/computers13120337
11. Qiao, M., Zhai, Y., Wang, Y.: Contrastive learning for continuous touch-based authentication (2025). arXiv preprint arXiv:2504.17271
12. Shen, Z., Chen, S., Li, Y., Guo, Z., Liu, J.: Ct-auth: capacitive touchscreen-based continuous authentication on smartphones. IEEE Trans. Knowl. Data Eng. **36**(1), 90–106 (2024). https://doi.org/10.1109/TKDE.2023.3277879
13. Shen, Z., Guo, Z., Chen, S., Li, Y., Liu, J.: Increauth: incremental-learning-based behavioral biometric authentication on smartphones. IEEE Internet Things J. **11**(1), 1589–1603 (2024). https://doi.org/10.1109/JIOT.2023.3289935
14. Stylios, I., Chatzis, S.P., Thanou, O., Kokolakis, S.: Continuous authentication with feature-level fusion of touch gestures and keystroke dynamics to solve security and usability issues. Comput. Secur. **132**, 103363 (2023). https://doi.org/10.1016/j.cose.2023.103363
15. Sundar, A., Singh, K.J.: Enhancing security and usability with context aware multi-biometric fusion for continuous user authentication. Sci. Rep. **15**(1), 30627 (2025). https://doi.org/10.1038/s41598-025-14833-z

16. Tang, G., et al.: Continuous smartphone user authentication based on gesture-sensor fusion. In: Proceedings of the 2024 International Conference on Networking and Network Applications (NaNA) (2024). https://doi.org/10.1109/NaNA63151.2024.00091
17. Yang, L., Cheng, J., Luo, Y., Zhou, T., Zhang, X.: Detecting and rationalizing concept drift: a feature-level approach for understanding cause-effect relationships in dynamic environments. Expert Syst. Appl. **260**, 125365 (2024). https://doi.org/10.1016/j.eswa.2024.125365

From Moderation to Mediation: Can LLMs Serve as Mediators in Online Flame Wars?

Dawei Li[1(✉)], Abdullah Alnaibari[1], Arslan Bisharat[2], Manuel Sandoval[2], Deborah Hall[1], Yasin Silva[2], and Huan Liu[1]

[1] Arizona State University, Tempe, AZ 85282, USA
daweili5@asu.edu
[2] Loyola University Chicago, Chicago, IL 60660, USA

Abstract. The rapid advancement of large language models (LLMs) has opened new possibilities for AI for good applications. As LLMs increasingly mediate online communication, their potential to foster empathy and constructive dialogue becomes an important frontier for responsible AI research. This work explores whether LLMs can serve not only as moderators that detect harmful content, but as mediators capable of understanding and de-escalating online conflicts. Our framework decomposes mediation into two subtasks: judgment, where an LLM evaluates the fairness and emotional dynamics of a conversation, and steering, where it generates empathetic, de-escalatory messages to guide participants toward resolution. To assess mediation quality, we construct a large Reddit-based dataset and propose a multi-stage evaluation pipeline combining principle-based scoring, user simulation, and human comparison. Experiments show that API-based models outperform open-source counterparts in both reasoning and intervention alignment when doing mediation. Our findings highlight both the promise and limitations of current LLMs as emerging agents for online social mediation.

Keywords: Flaming · Large Language Models · Mediation

1 Introduction

The rapid advancement of large language models (LLMs) has reshaped how humans communicate, learn, and collaborate. Beyond traditional natural language tasks such as translation or summarization [1], LLMs are increasingly being applied to domains that serve social good, supporting applications such as education [15,16], healthcare [5,8] and mental well-being [2]. As these systems become embedded in online spaces where people interact and debate, a new frontier emerges: using LLMs not just as tools for automation but as agents that foster empathy, fairness, and constructive dialogue in digital communities [18].

One pressing challenge in this landscape is the persistence of online hostility, often manifested through flame wars: heated, multi-turn exchanges of personal attacks and emotional escalation [11]. The lack of face-to-face cues and the

D. Li and A. Alnaibari—These authors contributed equally to this work.

R. C.-W. Wong et al. (Eds.): PAKDD 2026, LNAI 16618, pp. 333–344, 2027.
https://doi.org/10.1007/978-981-92-1947-6_27

anonymity of the medium lower social restraint and amplify anger or frustration, while group identity dynamics can further polarize discussions [3]. While computational methods have made progress in detecting toxicity or flagging abusive content [17], they remain largely reactive, focused on moderation through removal or punishment rather than prevention or repair. As a result, online platforms can suppress harmful speech without addressing the underlying social dynamics that cause it, leaving space for hostility to resurface.

Our work aims to explore a different approach to intervention: mediation rather than moderation. Instead of judging messages as harmful, we investigate whether an LLM can track a conflict and help de-escalate it. We view LLMs as potential mediators that can interpret multi-turn conversations, assess the fairness and relevance of the arguments being made, and generate responses that acknowledge concerns, reduce hostility, and guide the exchange toward a more constructive path. Achieving this requires reasoning about context, emotion, escalation patterns, and conversational norms [9]. To achieve this goal, we divide the task into two complementary components. Judgment involves evaluating the interaction to identify unfair claims, emotional triggers, and points of escalation. Steering involves generating a message that calms the exchange and helps participants focus on the source of their disagreement rather than attacking each other.

To examine whether LLMs can indeed serve as capable mediators, we construct a large-scale dataset of real-world flame wars from Reddit and develop a multi-stage evaluation pipeline. Our framework integrates three perspectives: ❶ principle-based evaluation, grounding mediation quality in fine-grained conversational principles; ❷ user simulation, modeling post-intervention behavior to assess whether LLM-generated mediations reduce hostility; and ❸ human comparative assessment, benchmarking model interventions against human-written mediations. From extensive experiments, we found that API-based models consistently outperform open-source systems in both judgment and steering alignment, exhibiting greater coherence and stability across categories. Furthermore, mediation analysis reveals that LLMs effectively reduce toxicity and emotional intensity in simulated interactions, while comparative evaluation highlights their strengths in neutrality and structural precision but relative weakness in readability and human-like engagement.

2 Related Work

AI for Social Good. AI for social good is the application of artificial intelligence technologies, such as LLMs, towards solving societal problems. This research domain covers a large number of fields including education, health, environmental sustainability, and economic inequality. For instance, in education, researchers are striving towards precision education, i.e., tailored learning via adaptive digital learning environments. Current efforts employ LLMs for reading and writing assistance [10], educational content creation [15,16], and automated feedback and grading [12,13]. LLMs have also been developed to assist in a variety of healthcare-related tasks, such as medical question answering [5], named entity recognition [8], and computer-aided diagnosis [20].

Flame Wars. Flame wars are extended exchanges of hostile messages that escalate from disagreement to personal attacks [11]. The lack of face-to-face cues and online anonymity lower social restraint and intensify hostility [3,14]. They often unfold through a trigger, reciprocal amplification, and eventual entrenchment. Existing computational work has focused on detecting and filtering toxic content [17], but such moderation may curtail legitimate engagement. Unlike one-sided hate speech, flame wars involve emotionally engaged participants on both sides. Political and identity-related discussions are especially prone to escalation [4,6]. These dynamics highlight the need for context-aware, constructive intervention—an area our LLM-based mediation framework aims to address.

3 Task Definition

Mediation generation aims to move beyond reactive moderation by enabling LLMs to actively understand and intervene in online conflicts. Formally, a discussion thread $G = \{u_1, u_2, \ldots, u_n\}$ represents a sequence of posts or comments among m users engaged in disagreement or hostility. The judgment subtask focuses on evaluative reasoning: given G, the model produces an interpretive representation $J(G)$ that identifies unfair claims, emotional triggers, and points of escalation, while assessing the fairness and relevance of participants' arguments. The steering subtask focuses on generative mediation: conditioned on G (and optionally $J(G)$), the model generates a mediation output $S(G)$: a context-aware, empathetic message intended to reduce hostility, acknowledge concerns, and guide participants toward constructive resolution. Together, these subtasks define mediation generation as an interactive process in which an LLM first reasons about conflict dynamics and then produces language that transforms confrontation into cooperation and understanding. Figure 1 shows the main processes and tasks of our framework.

4 Data Collection

Target Communities Identification and Post Collection. We chose Reddit,[1] one of the largest online discussion platforms, as our data source for evaluating if LLMs can serve as mediators, given the open discourse for which the platform is well-known and relative prevalence of flame wars. To identify suitable subreddits, we used ChatGPT[2] to analyze community dynamics and select forums known for emotionally charged or contentious debates. In total, we collected 1,834 posts, from the past five years, sampled from subreddits representing

[1] https://www.reddit.com/.
[2] https://openai.com/index/chatgpt/.

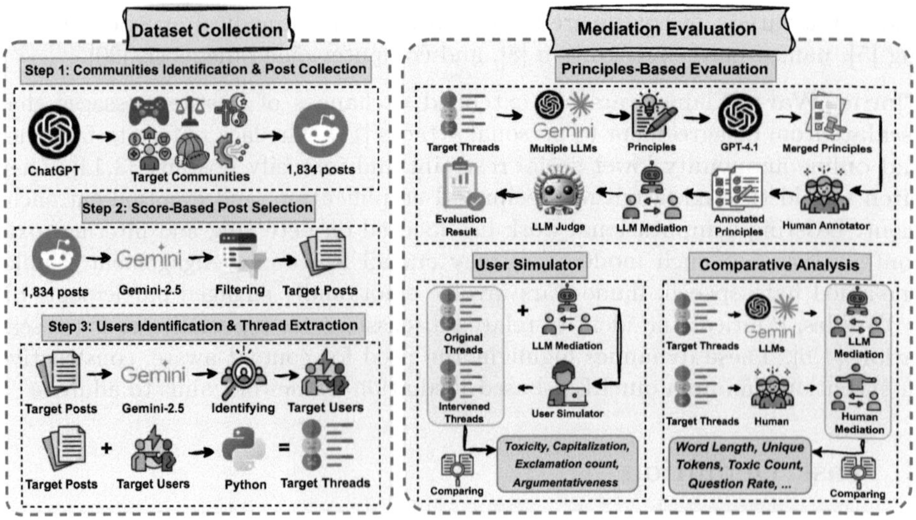

Fig. 1. The overview pipeline of our data collection and mediation evaluation process.

a wide range of diverse domains, including *Games*, *Lifestyle*, *Religion*, *Social Justice*, *Sports*, and *Technology*—covering subreddits such as *r/gaming*, *r/Parenting*, *r/atheism*, *r/BlackLivesMatter*, *r/football*, and *r/technology*. Descriptive statistic summarizing the sampled subreddits can be found in Table 1.

Score-Based Post Selection. Given the large volume of posts, we designed a filtering process to retain those most relevant to online flame wars. Using Gemini-2.5,[3] each post was automatically scored on a 0–10 scale, where a higher score indicates a greater likelihood that the post contains flame-war interactions in the comments. Only posts receiving scores between 7 and 10 were retained for subsequent analysis, ensuring that the dataset emphasized genuine instances of interpersonal tension and conflict escalation.

Target-user Identification and Thread Extraction. We again used Gemini-2.5 to detect the two users with the most flame-war interactions in their comments. After identifying the two users' names, we initially extracted only the direct replies exchanged between them. However, we observed that many relevant subthreads included additional participants whose replies contributed to the escalation or resolution of the conflict. To preserve the full conversational context, we expanded our extraction to include all nested replies within any subtree where both target users appeared, thereby capturing the dynamics of the surrounding dialogue while maintaining a focus on their exchange. After applying this filtering, the final dataset comprised 737 posts with rich conversational structures suitable for mediation generation and principle-based evaluation. Table 1 presents the detailed statistics of our collected dataset.

[3] https://blog.google/technology/google-deepmind/.

Table 1. Dataset statistics across six sub-datasets. Each sub-dataset corresponds to a topical domain, showing thread count, total comments and users, as well as average users and comments per thread.

Metrics	Games	Lifestyle	Religions	Social Justice	Sports	Technologies
#threads	66	160	155	137	175	44
#total comments	2696	2033	3754	1980	2567	2556
#total users	1533	844	723	615	1048	1337
#avg. users per thread	24.94	7.09	7.37	7.33	7.23	33.32
#avg. comments per thread	40.85	12.71	24.22	14.45	14.67	58.09

5 Can LLMs Serve as Good Mediators?

To assess whether large language models can effectively function as mediators in online conflicts, we design a comprehensive evaluation framework consisting of principle-based evaluation, a simulated user environment, and a comparative analysis against human mediation.

5.1 Principle-Based Evaluation

To ground mediation assessment in interpretable and context-sensitive criteria, we adopt a principle-based evaluation framework aligned with the LLM-as-a-Judge paradigm [7]. For each conversation $G = \{u_1, u_2, \ldots, u_n\}$, we query three large models—GPT-5, Gemini-2.5, and Claude-4.5—asking each to propose between five and ten principles tailored to that specific discussion, assigning 0–10 scores to each principle. These principles capture fine-grained desiderata for both judgment and steering, which can later guide LLM judges in evaluating mediation quality automatically and efficiently.

Cross-Model Principle Merging. The raw principle sets generated by the three models are often overlapping, redundant, or partially misaligned. To consolidate them into a coherent checklist, we use GPT-4.1 as an aggregator. Given the three model-specific lists, GPT-4.1 merges overlapping items, resolves minor wording differences, and removes near-duplicates while preserving important distinctions. This process produces a unified, conversation-specific principle bank $P(G) = \{p_1, p_2, \ldots, p_k\}$, which is then human-verified to ensure each principle is faithful to the conversation and practically useful as an evaluation criterion.

Human-Based Principle Verification. To ensure quality and consistency, three trained human annotators review each conversation and its merged principle list. They examine the relevance, clarity, and specificity of each principle, performing operations such as *keep*, *edit*, or *delete*, and merging or adding principles when necessary. Each decision is accompanied by a confidence score in $\{1, 2, 3\}$, representing low, moderate, and high confidence. This process yields a high-quality, conversation-specific principle bank suitable for fine-grained mediation assessment.

LLM-as-a-Judge Scoring. Finally, we integrate the human-refined principles with model-generated mediation outputs. For each conversation G, its principle set $P(G)$ and corresponding mediation output $S(G)$ are jointly provided to an LLM judge J_{eval}, which produces an overall evaluation score: $\text{Score}(G) = J_{\text{eval}}(P(G), S(G)) \in [1, 10]$. This step enables consistent, interpretable, and scalable evaluation of mediation quality across models.

5.2 User Simulation Result

Generation of Intervened Conversations. We construct a user simulator that models how conflicting users in online discussions might respond to mediator interventions. Given an original discussion thread G, the simulator (here we use Qwen3-4B as the simulator model) generates an intervened thread G' by inserting a model-generated mediation output $J(G)$ or $S(G)$ at an appropriate turn. The simulator then predicts the subsequent user responses conditioned on both G and $J(G)/S(G)$, thereby approximating post-intervention dynamics. This setup enables an evaluation of whether mediation messages can successfully reduce hostility, encourage cooperative tone shifts, or promote topic re-alignment in extended interactions.

Comparison with Original Conversation. To quantify the effect of mediation, we compare each intervened thread G' with its corresponding original version G without intervention. The comparison focuses on both linguistic and pragmatic changes, including reductions in toxic expressions, improvements in sentiment polarity, and the emergence of collaborative or empathetic language. Automatic metrics such as toxicity reduction, sentiment shift, and engagement balance are computed, supplemented by qualitative inspection of dialogue trajectories. This contrastive setup allows us to measure whether the mediator's steering effect is constructive and sustainable across user responses.

5.3 Comparative Analysis

Human Mediation Collection. To establish a reliable reference for LLM-generated mediation quality, we leverage a human mediation dataset from prior work on multilingual moderation and empathetic response generation [19]. In the selected dataset, trained human annotators act as mediators in real or sampled conflictual threads drawn from social media. We chose this dataset not only because it contains human-written mediation examples, but also because it includes a Reddit-based subdataset, which aligns closely with the domain of our own collected data.

Metric Design. Quantitative analysis spans eleven linguistic and interactional metrics grouped into three categories. **Linguistic complexity** captures how elaborate or readable a reply is, including average words per sentence, average word length, type–token ratio, and Flesch reading ease computed from sentence and syllable counts. **Interaction dynamics** measure dialogue flow, using question rate (questions per 100 words), engagement balance (questions over questions plus directives), and assertiveness per sentence (directive density normalized by sentence length). **Interpersonal stance** reflects social orientation and tone, including pronoun bias rate ((you – we) divided by total words times 100), direct "you" references, and toxic word occurrences. Additionally, unique token count provides a complementary view of lexical diversity. Together, these indicators quantify model–human differences in linguistic form, conversational behavior, and interpersonal affect.

6 Experiment

6.1 Experiment Setting

Models. We evaluate a total of twelve large language models covering both open-source and API-based systems. The open-source group includes *LLaMA-3.2-3B*, *LLaMA-3.1-8B*, *Qwen2.5-7B*, *Qwen3-1.7B*, *Qwen3-4B*, and *Qwen3-8B*. The API-based group consists of *Claude 3.5-Haiku*, *Claude 4.5-Haiku*, *Claude 4.5-Sonnet*, *GPT-4.1*, *GPT-5*, and *GPT-5.1*. These models represent a balanced selection of architectures and scales, enabling a comprehensive comparison across families and deployment modalities.

Implementation Details. For open-source models, we employ vLLM for efficient local inference and parallelized decoding. All API-based models are accessed through their official provider APIs to ensure consistency and reliability of results. For both the judgment model and the user-simulator model, we use *LLaMA-3-8B* to balance accuracy and computational efficiency. All experiments are conducted on two NVIDIA A100 GPUs (80GB each), ensuring stable runtime and reproducible results across settings.

6.2 Principle-Based Evaluation Result

Models Perform Differently Across Topics. As shown in Table 2, models' performance tend to be slightly lower in Religion and Sport, typically ranging from 7.8 to 8.2, while performance in Game and Lifestyle is noticeably stronger, often exceeding 8.4. This pattern suggests that models are more cautious and reserved when dealing with culturally or ethically sensitive subjects like religion and sports. In contrast, topics such as gaming and lifestyle are more neutral and better represented in training data, allowing models to produce smoother and more natural mediation.

Closed-Source Models Clearly Outperform Open-Source Ones. In Fig. 2, the leaderboard chart, we see that the API-based models like GPT and Claude dominate the top rankings, achieving average scores above 84%, while open-source models such as Llama and Qwen cluster around the 78–82% range. This consistent gap suggests that closed-source systems benefit from larger, proprietary datasets and more intensive fine-tuning on alignment and instruction-following. Their commercial training pipelines likely emphasize reliability and user safety, giving them an edge in complex, judgment-oriented evaluations.

Table 2. Principle-based evaluation results across models with bolded highest scores. G: Game, L: Lifestyles, R: Religion, SJ: Social Justice, S: Sports, T: Technologies.

Model	Judgment						Steering						Avg
	G	L	R	SJ	S	T	G	L	R	SJ	S	T	
Qwen2.5-7B	8.11	8.10	7.77	8.12	7.81	7.98	8.13	8.25	7.57	8.05	8.22	7.85	7.97
Qwen3-1.7B	8.02	8.23	7.92	8.12	7.70	7.85	8.30	8.35	7.86	8.23	8.15	7.95	8.03
Qwen3-4B	8.13	8.48	8.04	8.29	8.20	8.23	8.40	8.42	7.84	8.31	8.31	8.18	8.21
Qwen3-8B	8.28	8.38	8.01	8.32	8.21	8.28	8.36	8.45	7.88	8.33	8.35	8.30	8.23
Llama-3.2-3B	8.00	7.94	7.58	7.85	7.89	7.85	7.89	8.14	7.30	7.80	8.04	7.68	7.81
Llama-3.1-8B	7.79	7.89	7.81	7.96	7.70	7.90	8.00	8.24	7.46	7.89	8.09	7.80	7.86
Claude 3.5-Haiku	8.40	8.54	8.18	**8.55**	8.25	**8.48**	8.47	8.45	7.88	8.36	8.48	8.35	8.33
Claude 4.5-Haiku	8.40	8.63	8.08	8.29	8.30	8.18	**8.68**	**8.76**	**8.13**	8.52	**8.67**	8.53	8.41
Claude 4.5-Sonnet	8.23	8.49	8.06	8.49	**8.39**	8.35	8.60	8.76	8.09	8.52	8.61	**8.60**	**8.41**
GPT-4.1	8.30	8.65	8.23	8.39	8.35	8.38	8.34	8.32	7.95	8.30	8.28	8.43	8.30
GPT-5	8.11	8.35	7.84	8.20	8.23	7.98	8.53	8.51	7.78	8.33	8.51	8.30	8.21
GPT-5.1	**8.45**	**8.51**	**8.25**	8.39	8.26	8.35	8.49	8.59	7.85	**8.51**	8.61	8.38	8.36

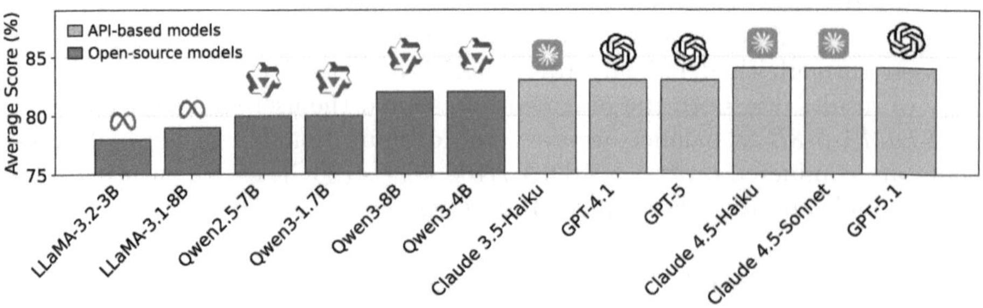

Fig. 2. LLM mediation performance leaderboard, averaged on judgment and steering.

Steering and Judgment Performances are Strongly Correlated. Figure 3, reveals a clear positive relationship between average steering and judgment scores across all models. Those excelling in judgment also tend to perform well in steering, implying that both tasks draw on shared underlying reasoning and alignment abilities. This consistency suggests that improvements in core mediation skills, like contextual understanding and balanced decision-making, can generalize across multiple evaluation tasks.

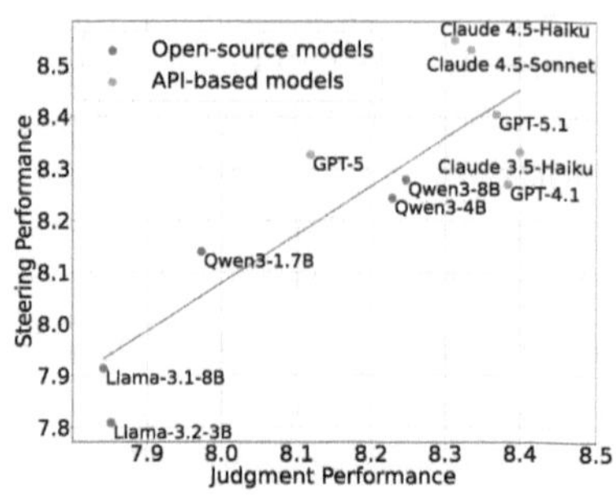

Fig. 3. Relationship between judgment and steering scores across models.

Future work could explore how to further unify these capabilities, enhancing both interpretability and control in large language models.

6.3 User Simulation Result

Table 3. User simulation results on open-source LLMs. Toxicity measures the rate of negative lexicon; Capitalization reflects excessive uppercase ratio; Exclamation counts exclamation marks; Argumentativeness measures disagreement vs. politeness balance.

Model	Toxicity	Capitalization	Exclamation	Argumentativeness	Avg
Qwen2.5-7B	**39.92**	**0.30**	17.31	**6.42**	16.09
Qwen3-1.7B	30.27	**0.30**	19.65	6.01	14.06
Qwen3-4B	25.42	**0.30**	19.19	6.35	12.81
Qwen3-8B	26.27	**0.30**	19.19	6.08	13.00
Llama-3.1-8B	36.85	**0.30**	**20.42**	6.18	15.94
Llama-3.2-3B	38.50	**0.30**	20.00	5.99	**16.10**

The results in Table 3 show that mediation has varying effectiveness across different linguistic aspects. The reduction in toxicity and exclamation usage suggests that the mediation process successfully promotes more neutral and composed responses. This can improve conversational tone and make model interactions feel more balanced and less emotionally charged. However, the argumentativeness scores change only slightly, indicating that mediation has a weaker influence on discourse-level behaviors such as disagreement management.

Interestingly, the trends differ between the user simulation setting and the main experiment, suggesting that models behave differently when generating both sides of an interaction versus responding to real user input. This highlights the importance of evaluating mediation not only as a process (how mediation is applied) but also in terms of its outcomes (the actual communicative effects in realistic contexts).

6.4 Comparative Analysis Result

Figure 4 demonstrates the distribution difference between human- and LLM-generated mediation. Across lexical, structural, readability, and interactional dimensions, human- and LLM-generated mediations exhibit distinct yet complementary linguistic profiles. LLM outputs tend to be substantially longer and lexically denser (d ≈ 1.5–1.7), reflecting a more formal and elaborated register. However, this expansion corresponds with decreased readability (Flesch d ≈ −2.0), indicating that human mediations remain considerably more accessible to readers. Human texts further display higher lexical diversity and stronger dialogic engagement, evidenced by greater question frequency and more balanced interactional tone.

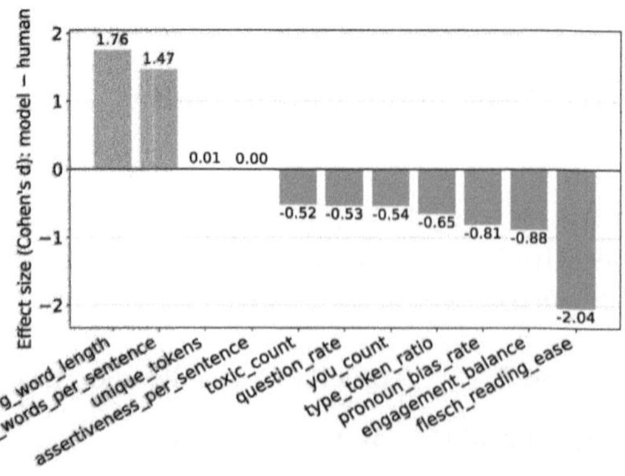

Fig. 4. Effect sizes of model-human differences.

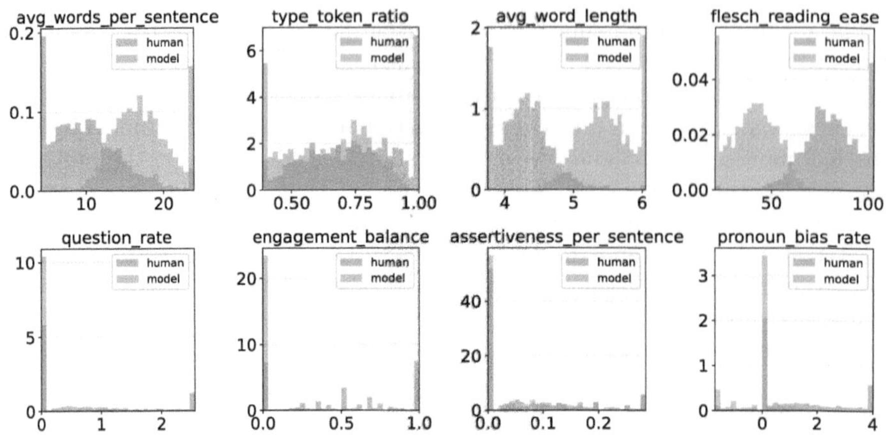

Fig. 5. Distributions of linguistic and interactional metrics.

We also demonstrate the effect sizes of model-human differences. As Fig. 5 shows, pronoun usage underscores differences in stance and interpersonal orientation. Human mediators show higher "you" frequency, adopting a direct and addressive style, whereas LLMs favor more neutral or collective pronoun patterns. This contributes to lower toxicity proxies in LLM outputs, suggesting reduced confrontational or accusatory tendencies. Assertiveness per sentence remains near parity, implying that both maintain comparable directive moderation.

7 Conclusion

This work explored whether large language models can act not just as moderators but as mediators capable of understanding and resolving online conflicts. Through a combination of principle-based evaluation, user simulation, and comparative analysis, our findings show that current LLMs demonstrate promising yet uneven mediation abilities. Closed-source models like GPT and Claude consistently outperform open-source systems in both judgment and steering tasks, suggesting that fine-tuned alignment and large-scale instruction optimization play a key role in effective mediation. Moreover, the strong correlation between steering and judgment performance highlights that both tasks rely on shared reasoning and empathy-related capabilities. This implies that improvements in one area can benefit the other, reinforcing the idea of a unified mediation competence within LLMs.

Acknowledgement. This work was supported by National Science Foundation Awards No. 2435164 and 2435165, and a Google Award for Inclusion Research. The views and conclusions contained in this document are those of the authors and should not be interpreted as representing official policies, either expressed or implied, of NSF.

References

1. Gao, M., Ruan, J., Sun, R., Yin, X., Yang, S., Wan, X.: Human-like summarization evaluation with chatgpt. arXiv preprint arXiv:2304.02554 (2023)
2. Hua, Y., et al.: A scoping review of large language models for generative tasks in mental health care. NPJ Digit. Med. **8** (2025). https://api.semanticscholar.org/CorpusID:278235350
3. Kiesler, S., Siegel, J., McGuire, T.W.: Social psychological aspects of computer-mediated communication. Am. Psychol. **39**(10), 1123–1134 (1984). https://doi.org/10.1037/0003-066X.39.10.1123
4. Koiranen, I., Koivula, A., Malinen, S., Keipi, T.: Undercurrents of echo chambers and flame wars: party political correlates of social media behavior. J. Inf. Technol. Polit. **19**(2), 197–213 (2022). https://doi.org/10.1080/19331681.2021.1950095
5. Labrak, Y., Bazoge, A., Morin, E., Gourraud, P.A., Rouvier, M., Dufour, R.: Biomistral: a collection of open-source pretrained large language models for medical domains (2024)
6. Lee, H.: Behavioral strategies for dealing with flaming in an online forum. Sociol. Q. **46**(2), 385–403 (2005). https://doi.org/10.1111/j.1533-8525.2005.00019.x
7. Li, D., et al.: From generation to judgment: opportunities and challenges of llm-as-a-judge. In: Proceedings of the 2025 Conference on Empirical Methods in Natural Language Processing, pp. 2757–2791 (2025)
8. M, A., S, K., S, J., S J, A., K R, B.: Bio medical named entity recognition using large language models. In: 2024 4th International Conference on Artificial Intelligence and Signal Processing (AISP), pp. 01–06 (2024). https://doi.org/10.1109/AISP61711.2024.10870607
9. Madani, N., Srihari, R.K.: Esc-judge: a framework for comparing emotional support conversational agents. In: Proceedings of the 2025 Conference on Empirical Methods in Natural Language Processing, pp. 16059–16076 (2025)

10. Masikisiki, B., Marivate, V., Hlophe, Y.: Investigating the efficacy of large language models in reflective assessment methods through chain of thought prompting. In: Proceedings of the 4th African Human Computer Interaction Conference, AfriCHI 2023, pp. 44–49. ACM, New York, NY, USA (2024). https://doi.org/10.1145/3628096.3628747
11. Moor, P.J., Heuvelman, A., Verleur, R.: Flaming on youtube. Comput. Hum. Behav. **26**(6), 1536–1546 (2010). https://doi.org/10.1016/j.chb.2010.05.027
12. Morris, W., Holmes, L., Choi, J.S., Crossley, S.: Automated scoring of constructed response items in math assessment using large language models. Int. J. Artif. Intell. Educ. **35**(2), 559–586 (2024). https://doi.org/10.1007/s40593-024-00418-w
13. Parker, M.J., Anderson, C., Stone, C., Oh, Y.: A large language model approach to educational survey feedback analysis. Int. J. Artif. Intell. Educ. **35**(2), 444–481 (2024). https://doi.org/10.1007/s40593-024-00414-0
14. Reicher, S.D., Spears, R., Postmes, T.: A social identity model of deindividuation phenomena. Eur. Rev. Soc. Psychol. **6**(1), 161–198 (1995). https://doi.org/10.1080/14792779443000049
15. Sarsa, S., Denny, P., Hellas, A., Leinonen, J.: Automatic generation of programming exercises and code explanations using large language models. In: Proceedings of the 2022 ACM Conference on International Computing Education Research, ICER 2022, vol. 1, pp. 27–43. ACM, New York, NY, USA (2022). https://doi.org/10.1145/3501385.3543957
16. Scarlatos, A., Lan, A.: Tree-based representation and generation of natural and mathematical language. In: Rogers, A., Boyd-Graber, J., Okazaki, N. (eds.) Proceedings of the 61st Annual Meeting of the Association for Computational Linguistics (Volume 1: Long Papers), pp. 3714–3730. ACL, Toronto, Canada (2023). https://doi.org/10.18653/v1/2023.acl-long.205, https://aclanthology.org/2023.acl-long.205/
17. Steinberger, J., Brychcín, T., Hercig, T., Krejzl, P.: Cross-lingual flames detection in news discussions. In: Proceedings of Recent Advances in Natural Language Processing (RANLP), pp. 694–700. Varna, Bulgaria (2017). https://doi.org/10.26615/978-954-452-049-6_089
18. Xu, Y., Hu, J., Zhao, Z., Duan, Z., Sun, X., Yang, X.: Multiagentesc: a llm-based multi-agent collaboration framework for emotional support conversation. In: Proceedings of the 2025 Conference on Empirical Methods in Natural Language Processing, pp. 4665–4681. (2025)
19. Ye, M., Sikka, K., Atwell, K., Hassan, S., Divakaran, A., Alikhani, M.: Multilingual content moderation: a case study on reddit. In: Proceedings of the 17th Conference of the European Chapter of the Association for Computational Linguistics, pp. 3828–3844 (2023)
20. Zhao, Z., et al.: Chatcad+: toward a universal and reliable interactive cad using llms. IEEE Trans. Med. Imaging **43**(11), 3755–3766 (2024). https://doi.org/10.1109/TMI.2024.3398350

A Regime-Aware Fusion Framework for Time Series Classification

Honey Singh Chauhan and Zahraa S. Abdallah(✉)

School of Engineering Mathematics and Technology, University of Bristol, Bristol, UK
zahraa.abdallah@bristol.ac.uk

Abstract. Kernel-based methods such as ROCKET are strong defaults for univariate time series classification (TSC), yet they do not win uniformly across all data types. In this work we revisit the intuition that different representations capture complementary features and show that a lightweight fusion of ROCKET, SAX, and SFA (F3, a three-way fusion) embeddings delivers significant improvements in specific, discoverable *regimes*—interpretable clusters of datasets reflecting structures like length, spectral complexity, and separability. We identify six such regimes via meta-features. F3 dominates in class-imbalanced (*HighImb*) and smooth, frequency-separable (*SmoothSep*) signals, with large practical gains in highly fluctuating complex signals (*HighFlCx*). Ablation studies confirm that two-way fusions (F2), particularly SAX+ROCKET, also capture substantial gains in short, jagged series. We provide three analysis layers: (i) regime discovery; (ii) robust statistical comparison (HL-median, Wilcoxon, Bayesian ROPE); and (iii) mechanistic insight using SHAP. Case studies reveal that fusion corrects errors by adaptively upweighting SFA in frequency-structured settings. Evaluated on 113 UCR datasets (5-fold CV), F3 achieves a Hodges–Lehmann median gain of 0.43 pp over ROCKET (Wilcoxon $p < 10^{-4}$), with a Bayesian probability of improvement $P(d>0) \approx 0.87$ and ROPE-$P_{\text{better}} \approx 0.55$. This provides a transparent, regime-aware framework for model selection.

Keywords: Time series classification · Fusion · SAX · SFA · ROCKET · SHAP

1 Introduction

Time series classification (TSC) is a core problem in machine learning, with applications across various domains such as healthcare and finance. Classical approaches range from distance-based methods (e.g., DTW nearest neighbour) [12] and feature- or shapelet-based models [7] to more recent deep architectures (CNNs, RNNs, Transformers) [6,8] tailored to sequential data, yet no single method dominates across all datasets. Kernel-based methods such as ROCKET [4] offer nearstate-of-the-art accuracy with fast training, but dataset characteristics (length, spectral structure, roughness, class-imbalance) induce distinct *data-structure regimes* where no single representation—including ROCKET—performs

R. C.-W. Wong et al. (Eds.): PAKDD 2026, LNAI 16618, pp. 345–357, 2027.
https://doi.org/10.1007/978-981-92-1947-6_28

best everywhere. This brings us back to a long-standing intuition: different representations specialise in different aspects of structure. Therefore, we address two crucial questions: (i) how to systematically discover a dataset's regime using meta-features; and (ii) how to exploit this via lightweight fusion of complementary representations (Rocket, Sax, Sfa). Our framework pairs meta-feature-based clustering with gated fusion, supported by robust statistics and attribution analyses. We study a *three-way fusion* (hereafter **F3**: SAX+SFA+ROCKET) and *two-way fusion* variants (hereafter **F2**): **F2-SFR** (SFA+ROCKET), **F2-SR** (SAX+ROCKET), and **F2-SS** (SAX+SFA). This yields actionable guidance: use fusion for frequency-complex or long, structured signals; otherwise Rocket suffices.

Contributions: (1) *Regime discovery*—meta-features cluster datasets into six interpretable regimes; (2) *Lightweight fusion*—a gated architecture (F3) combining Rocket, Sax, and Sfa; (3) *Ablation studies*—two-way fusions reveal which pairs matter per regime; (4) *Attribution*—SHAP and case studies link gains to spectral complexity; (5) *Practical guidance*—use **F3** for regimes with high class imbalance (C1 HighImb), smooth separable signals (C3 SmoothSep), and high-fluctuation complex signals (C4 HighFlCx); use **F2-SR** (SAX+ROCKET) for short jagged series (C6 ShortBase) and long structured series (C2 LongFSTCx); use **ROCKET** alone for outlier-rich complex datasets (C5 HighCompOut) or when baseline accuracy exceeds 95%.

Paper organisation. §2: related work; §3: method and F3 architecture; §4: experimental setup and meta-features; §5: regime discovery, performance, SHAP attribution, case studies; §6 ablation studies and §7: conclusion.

2 Related Work

In time series classification (TSC), using raw sequences with generic distances (e.g., Euclidean) becomes brittle under noise, scaling, and time warping [9]. A central design choice is therefore the *representation*—a transformation that exposes discriminative structure in an alternative feature space. Large empirical studies (notably "Bake Off redux" [12]) show that no single representation dominates across datasets, motivating complementary transformations. The TSC literature offers a rich set of representations. **Shapelets** identify discriminative local subsequences via information gain or distance-based scoring [7]. **Catch22** provides a compact set of 22 canonical time series features selected from over 7000 candidates [11]. Dictionary-based methods (e.g., BOSS, cBOSS) combine symbolic discretisation with bag-of-patterns classifiers [13]. **Co-eye** [2] combines symbolic time-domain and frequency-domain representations through ensemble learning. **Deep learning** approaches—CNNs, ResNets, InceptionTime, and Transformers—learn hierarchical features end-to-end but typically require more data and compute [6,8]. Given this diversity, a long-standing question is how to identify the most discriminative representation for a given dataset [1]. Prior work compares representations via distance fidelity [15] or global statistics [7], but these operate at the *dataset level* without explaining *when* or *why* a representation helps at the *instance level*. Likewise, non-adaptive ensembles combine representations with fixed weights and rarely prioritise the most informative view per sample. We propose *interpretable fusion* of symbolic time-domain (SAX) [9], symbolic frequency-domain (SFA) [14], and random convolutional kernels (ROCKET) [4] that re-weights representations per instance, linking meta-feature-derived regimes to systematic gains with robust statistics and sample-level analyses.

3 Method

3.1 Representations and Fusion

We use SAX [9], SFA [14], and ROCKET [4] to span complementary domains and resolutions. SFA captures **frequency-domain** structure via truncated DFT and coefficient binning (periodicities, shift-invariant global cues). In the **time domain**, both SAX and ROCKET operate on the raw series, but at different resolutions: SAX provides a symbolic *compression* into coarse segment-level trends (robust to noise), whereas ROCKET extracts fine-grained local motifs and transients via many random convolutional kernels. This multi-representation, multi-resolution coverage is consistent with state-of-the-art ensembles (e.g., **HIVE-COTE** [10] and **Mr-Hydra** [5]) and with benchmark evidence that these families often succeed on different datasets [12].

We keep fusion deliberately simple for interpretability: an instance-wise gating network assigns non-negative per-sample weights to the embeddings, indicating which representation drove each prediction. Unlike non-adaptive ensembles with fixed mixing, the gate explicitly prioritises representations per instance and enables regime-linked analysis; Fusion-2 ablations further isolate each component's contribution. See extended version for additional architectural details [3] (Fig. 1).

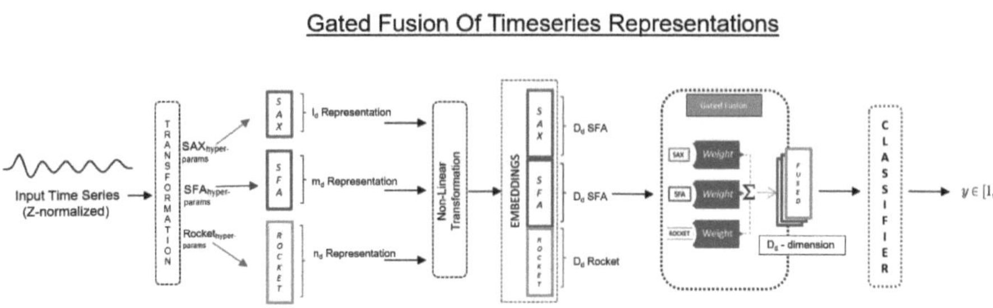

Fig. 1. Architecture of F3 (adaptive gated fusion). Parallel extraction of SAX, SFA, and ROCKET representations → dense embedding projection → instance-wise gating → weighted fusion → classification.

4 Experimental Setup

4.1 Evaluation Protocol and Hyperparameter Search

We use 5-fold cross-validation to obtain stable performance estimates across all datasets and to support regime-wise analysis of representation complementarity. Fusion is implemented as an simple neural gating module as our focus is on interpretable, representation-level fusion and regime-aware guidance. We therefore compare primarily against ROCKET (a strong and widely used baseline) and include targeted Fusion-2 ablations to isolate the contribution of each representation. For fairness, we use literature-backed hyperparameter grids [12] while keeping the downstream head capacity fixed across variants to avoid confounding representation choice with model capacity. We vary SAX/SFA discretisation (word $\{6, 8\}$, frame/window $\{10, 15, 20\}$, alphabet 4) and ROCKET kernel count ($n_{\text{kernels}} \in \{1500, 2000\}$); the shared head uses embed/hidden $\{64, 128\}$ with dropout 0.2. All models are trained with Adam (LR 10^{-3}, batch 32, max 25 epochs, patience 5). Full grids and configuration counts are reported in the extended version [3].

4.2 Meta-Features and Regimes

We compute 13 low-correlated dataset meta-features in two groups:
Global Complexity Features: series length, turning points and variance, spectral entropy and its variance, KL divergence of the power spectrum, permutation entropy, autocorrelation lag-1, and kurtosis. These describe the intrinsic properties of the time series themselves, useful for identifying broad structural similarities across datasets.
Class Separability Features: DTW separability in time and frequency domain, Kruskal power spectral density of classes, and imbalance index(majority class fraction). These explicitly use label information to measure how separable classes are in practice.
Feature choice was guided by prior work and practical utility. DTW-based separability follows [15], where lower-bound distances were shown as strong quality indicators. Statistical measures such as Kruskal PSD align with [7], which emphasised distributional descriptors. Dataset-level factors like imbalance are well known to affect classification difficulty. Variance-based counterparts (e.g., turning_points_var, spectral_entropy_var) capture intra-dataset volatility—whether a property is consistent across all series or dominated by a few irregular ones. Together, these features span global, class-based, and variance-sensitive perspectives, providing a balanced foundation for clustering. More details on meta-feature definitions, interpretation, and calculation formulas are provided in the extended arXiv version [3].
Hierarchical clustering on these features produces six regimes: **C1 HighImb**, **C2 LongFSTCx**, **C3 SmoothSep**, **C4 HighFlCx**, **C5 HighCompOut**, **C6 ShortBase**.

5 Results

We evaluate on 113 of the 128 UCR univariate benchmark datasets, excluding 15 datasets that contain missing values. Evaluation is performed using 5-fold CV with grid search. F3 (three-way fusion: SAX+SFA+ROCKET) is compared to ROCKET using: HL-median Δpp (robust gain), Wilcoxon with Holm correction (significance), Bayesian $P(d>0)$ (consistency), and ROPE-P_{better} (practical significance with threshold $\delta_i = 0.03(1 - \text{acc}_{\text{ROCKET},i})$)..

5.1 Regime Discovery: What Structure Exists in TSC Data?

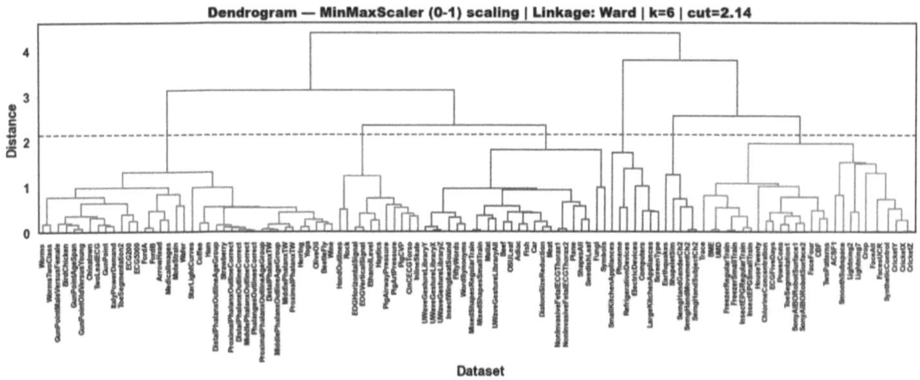

Fig. 2. Dendrogram showing the hierarchical clustering of the 113 UCR/UEA datasets based on their 13 selected meta-features. The horizontal cut-off line indicates the division into six clusters, which are color-coded for clarity.

We group the 113 UCR/UEA datasets via hierarchical agglomerative clustering (Ward linkage) on 13 meta-features (§4.2); cutting the dendrogram (Fig. 2) yields six interpretable regimes (Fig. 3):
C1 HighImb (N=38): high class imbalance, typically shorter/simpler series, and moderate separability. Many minority-class problems fall here, where standard classifiers struggle. **C2 LongFSTCx** (N=11): very long series with structured temporal patterns and frequency-separable signals, favouring representations that capture both coarse trends and local shapes. **C3 SmoothSep** (N=24): smooth trajectories with high separability in both time and frequency and low roughness, where complementary cues are consistently available. **C4 HighFlCx** (N=7): highly fluctuating signals with rich spectral structure; often device/sensor datasets (e.g., *RefrigerationDevices*, *ElectricDevices*) exhibiting multi-state switching behaviour. **C5 HighCompOut** (N=5): highly complex, outlier-rich series with extreme values and high spectral entropy, representing a difficult "failure-mode" regime. **C6 ShortBase** (N=28): short, jagged series

Table 1. Overall accuracy (113 datasets, 5-fold CV). Mean±SD (%). Win-rate = (Wins+Ties)/Total vs. ROCKET.

Model	Acc ± SD (%)	Δpp	Wins/Losses/Ties	Win-rate
ROCKET (Baseline)	91.47 ± 9.82	–	–	–
F3 (SAX+SFA+R)	**91.98 ± 9.59**	**+0.51**	**80/12/21**	**89.4%**
F2-SFR (SFA+R)	91.63 ± 9.89	+0.16	67/20/26	82.3%
F2-SR (SAX+R)	91.60 ± 9.78	+0.13	63/23/27	79.6%
F2-SS (SAX+SFA)	83.46 ± 12.30	-8.01	12/33/67	69.9%

with limited spectral structure; the brevity constrains what frequency-domain methods can extract.

The regimes show moderate separation in PCA meta-feature space (silhouette = 0.25, DBI = 1.19), consistent with partially overlapping dataset characteristics. Importantly, clusters are robust to scaling (ARI = 0.70 between MinMax and StandardScaler) and show moderate resampling stability (bootstrap ARI = 0.60 ± 0.16), indicating reproducible but soft regime boundaries. Cluster composition with data-type breakdowns is provided in the extended arXiv version [3].

5.2 Overall and Per-Regime Performance

F3 improves over ROCKET with high statistical confidence (Table 1), but performance varies by regime (Table 2): strong gains in three regimes, suggestive improvements in two, negligible benefit in one.

Metrics: We use HL-median Δpp (95% bootstrap CI), Wilcoxon signed-rank (two-sided; Holm-corrected across regimes), Bayesian $P(d > 0)$ from win–loss counts with Beta($\frac{1}{2}, \frac{1}{2}$) prior, and ROPE practical significance with $\delta_i = \rho(1 - \text{acc}_{\text{ROCKET},i})$ (clamped to $[0.10, 2.0]$ pp; $\rho = 0.03$). Win-rate is (wins+ties)/total. A regime winner requires HL > 0, Holm $p < 0.05$, and ROPE-$P_{\text{better}} \geq 0.5$.

Performance: F3 achieves 89.4% win-rate over ROCKET (80 wins + 21 ties out of 113) with reduced fold variance. The +0.51 pp aggregate masks regime-level variation (Table 2).

- **Overall. F3** is best on average (HL +0.43 pp, ROPE ≈ 55%), dominating in high-imbalance (C1) and smooth-separable (C3) regimes ($p < 10^{-4}$, ROPE ≥ 62%). **F2-SR** is competitive overall (+0.11 pp) but excels in different areas.
- **Regime-Specific Leaders.**
  - **C6 ShortBase: F2-SR** is the significant winner (+0.15 pp, $p = 0.01$), proving SAX complements ROCKET for short jagged series.
  - **C2 LongFSTCx:** No significant winner ($p > 0.05$), but F2-SR and F3 are co-leaders (+0.49 pp and +0.42 pp).
  - **C4 HighFlCx:** Small-N limits significance, but F3 shows the largest point estimate (+1.09 pp) and **F2-SFR** (+0.80 pp) outperforms F2-SR (-0.32 pp), confirming SFA's value for complex frequency signals.

Table 2. Overall and per-regime summary vs. **R** (ROCKET). All numbers rounded to 2 decimals. Green: Strict Winner (HL$>$ 0, $p <$ .05, ROPE$\geq$ 0.5). ▲: Competitive Leader (Best HL or Significant, but ROPE$<$ 0.5).

Regime	Model vs R	N	HL Δpp [95% CI]	p_{Holm}	$P(d>0)$	ROPE
Overall	**F3**	113	**+0.43 [0.31, 0.57]**	0.00	0.87	0.55
	F2-SR		+0.11 [0.04, 0.18]	0.00	0.73	0.31
	F2-SFR		+0.20 [0.07, 0.35]	0.00	0.77	0.38
C1 HighImb	**F3**	38	**+0.51 [0.36, 0.78]**	0.00	0.92	0.62
	F2-SR		+0.11 [0.00, 0.29]	0.11	0.74	0.27
	F2-SFR		+0.30 [0.10, 0.50]	0.00	0.95	0.39
C2 LongFSTCx	F3	11	+0.42 [0.07, 1.53]	0.19	0.77	0.44
	F2-SR ▲		**+0.49** [0.11, 1.04]	0.11	0.71	0.44
	F2-SFR		+0.02 [-0.77, 0.97]	1.00	0.50	0.28
C3 SmoothSep	**F3**	24	**+0.58 [0.36, 0.86]**	0.00	0.98	0.77
	F2-SR		+0.09 [0.01, 0.16]	0.08	0.71	0.26
	F2-SFR		+0.30 [0.06, 0.45]	0.03	0.79	0.49
C4 HighFlCx	**F3 ▲**	7	**+1.09** [-0.63, 2.87]	0.44	0.81	0.41
	F2-SR		-0.32 [-0.93, 0.25]	0.75	0.56	0.18
	F2-SFR		+0.80 [-1.17, 2.69]	0.59	0.69	0.41
C5 HighCompOut	F3	5	-0.72 [-4.28, 0.05]	0.44	0.30	0.08
	F2-SR		-0.22 [-1.50, 0.17]	0.75	0.30	0.23
	F2-SFR		-0.89 [-8.24, -0.22]	0.38	0.10	0.08
C6 ShortBase	F3	28	+0.16 [0.01, 0.43]	0.06	0.78	0.39
	F2-SR ▲		**+0.15** [0.04, 0.37]	0.01	0.87	0.42
	F2-SFR		+0.14 [0.00, 0.37]	0.08	0.76	0.36

- **Practical Significance.** Gains are modest but reliable. Where ROPE $\geq$ 0.5 (C1, C3), fusion provides practically meaningful uplift; elsewhere (C6), high $P(d>0)$ indicates consistent small wins.
- **Baseline Strength.** ROCKET remains a strong solo baseline. Fusion's value is targeted: use F3 for general robustness, or F2-SR for short/jagged series (C6) and long structured data (C2).

5.3 Regime Heatmap (HL-Median Δ Win-Rate)

The Fig. 3 is intended as the "one-panel overview" connecting the paired tests (Table 2) to the meta-feature space. Each regime can be read along five aligned

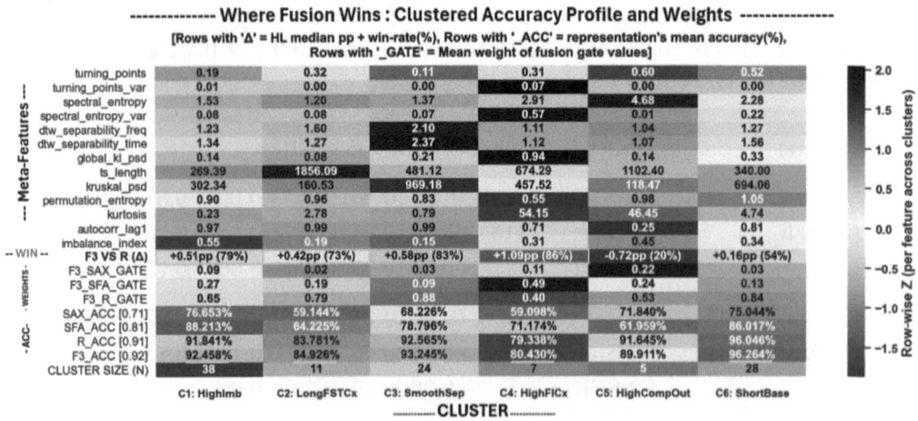

Fig. 3. Per-regime heatmap (F3 vs. ROCKET). Row-wise Z-scores; annotations show raw values. Top: meta-feature means. Middle: Δpp and win-rate; green marks F3 winners. Bottom: gate weights and accuracies. Ablations in §6 (Color figure online).

layers: **(i)** what the data characteristics look like (meta-features), **(ii)** how strong each solo representation is (SAX/SFA/ROCKET accuracies), **(iii)** whether F3 improves over ROCKET on average and how often (HL Δpp + win-rate), and **(iv)** where the fusion gate allocates weight across SAX, SFA and ROCKET, and **(v)** how many datasets support that conclusion. This section therefore emphasises *coherence across these layers*, while formal significance is handled by the paired tests (Table 2).

Colours show *relative* highs/lows per row; annotations give magnitudes (HLmedian Δ pp, win-rate %). Key patterns: F3 shows the strongest gains in C1 (HighImb, +0.51 pp), C3 (SmoothSep, +0.58 pp), and C4 (HighFlCx, +1.09 pp), with gates shifting toward SFA in frequency-structured regimes. C5 (HighCompOut) shows negative estimates; C6 (ShortBase) shows marginal gains where two-way fusions are competitive (§6). See extended version [3] for regime-level interpretation of the heatmap linking meta-features, solo strengths, and fusion behaviour.

5.4 Global Attribution via SHAP

To identify which meta-features predict fusion gains, we model per-dataset accuracy improvements $\Delta\text{acc} = \text{acc(F3)} - \text{acc(ROCKET)}$ using a tree-ensemble regressor and compute SHAP values (Fig. 4). Features are ranked by mean absolute SHAP. F3 gains are most strongly associated with longer time series (`ts_length`) and measures of spectral diversity such as `global_kl_psd` and `spectral_entropy_var`. These features characterise signals with rich and heterogeneous frequency structure, where a single representation may fail to capture all discriminative information. In contrast, meta-features reflecting pervasive local irregularity—most notably `turning_points` and `permutation_entropy`—

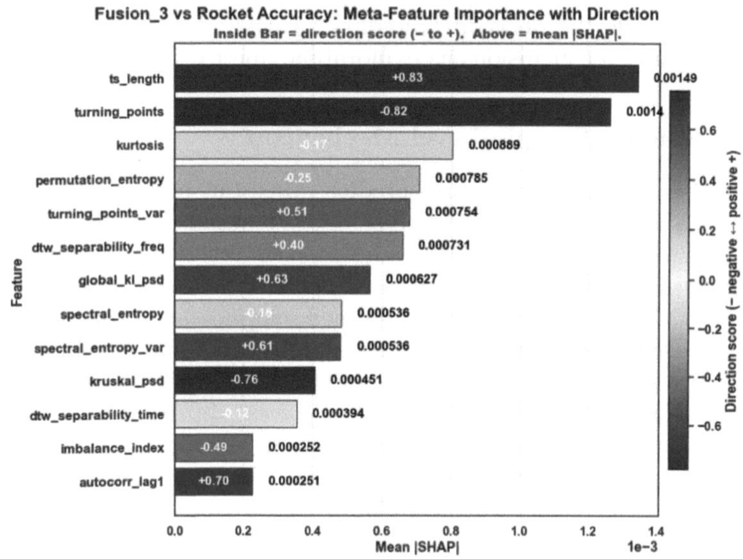

Fig. 4. SHAP summary for predicting $\Delta\mathrm{acc} = \mathrm{acc}(\text{FUSION3}) - \mathrm{acc}(\text{ROCKET})$ from meta-features. Higher mean absolute SHAP indicates stronger global influence; signs are taken from the SHAP expectation.

are negatively associated with fusion gains. A notable asymmetry emerges between these features and `turning_points_var`: while high overall irregularity suppresses gains, variability in local structure is positively associated with improved fusion performance. This suggests that fusion benefits from structured diversity in signal behaviour rather than uniformly high randomness.

C4 (HighFlCx) shows the largest practical gains despite being underpowered (Holm $p>0.05$). Although C4 contains only 7 datasets (limiting classical significance), multiple signals consistently indicate this regime is highly favourable for fusion: it shows the largest effect-size estimate (HL-median +1.09 pp with posterior $P(d>0) \approx 0.81$, largest across regimes), its defining meta-features align with SHAP's strongest positive predictors (Fig. 4), and the learned gates shift toward SFA in this regime (Fig. 3), matching the intuition that frequency structure is informative. C4 is dominated by device/sensor datasets (6 of 7), e.g., *RefrigerationDevices*. These signals have multiple modes (on/off/standby states), switching patterns, and rich frequency content—exactly where SFA adds value. These global attributions also anticipate the consistent failure of fusion under extreme irregularity (C5). This regime is characterised by extreme entropy in the frequency domain (`spectral_entropy`=4.68), high complexity (i.e., `turning_points`=0.6), and lowest autocorrelation (`autocorr_lag1`=0.25). Here, ROCKET (86.7%) significantly outperforms SAX (72.1%) and SFA (64.8%), with SFA being the worst-performing representation (Fig. 3). In this setting, soft gating may not fully suppress weaker views, and mixing in SAX/SFA features can degrade the decision boundary relative to a near-pure ROCKET selector. We treat C5 conclusions as exploratory due to N=5.

5.5 Case Studies: Sample-Level Mechanism

SHAP identifies *which* meta-features predict gains, but not *how* fusion corrects errors at the sample level. We therefore analyse *rescued* samples (ROCKET wrong, fusion correct) versus *hurt* samples (the reverse) and examine gate changes on rescued samples relative to cases where both are correct. In frequency-structured regimes (notably C2/C4), rescued samples are typically accompanied by increased SFA weight and reduced ROCKET weight, indicating the model selectively emphasises frequency information where ROCKET's local-shape features fail (e.g., *Rock*, *RefrigerationDevices*). In smoother regimes (C3) and short/near-ceiling regimes (C6), gate shifts are smaller but follow the same direction, consistent with "low-risk, modest-gain" improvements. Overall, these sample-level patterns align with the global SHAP drivers and provide a mechanistic link between regime properties and instance-wise gating behaviour; additional regime-specific case studies and cluster-wise relationship between gate values and fusion benefit are included in the extended version [3].

6 Ablation Studies

To test whether all three representations are necessary, we evaluate two-way fusions: `F2_SFR` (SFA+ROCKET), `F2_SR` (SAX+ROCKET), and `F2_SS` (SAX+SFA without ROCKET). Results are summarised in Table 1 and Table 2.

Key Findings. (i) ROCKET is essential: removing ROCKET (`F2_SS`) yields a large drop in accuracy, confirming the convolutional backbone is required for competitive performance. (ii) Two-way fusions are strong baselines: both `F2_SFR` and `F2_SR` improve over ROCKET on average, while F3 remains best overall, indicating complementary value from combining SAX and SFA.
The two ROCKET-based variants behave differently across regimes (Table 2). In frequency-structured regimes, `F2_SFR` is stronger—most clearly in C4 (High-FlCx), where `F2_SR` degrades while `F2_SFR` improves—supporting the role of SFA when spectral complexity dominates. In short or locally irregular regimes, `F2_SR` is preferable (e.g., C6 ShortBase), suggesting SAX+ROCKET often suffices when frequency cues are limited or unstable. We further analyse the roles of each representation using SHAP attributions for the two-way variants, reported in the extended version [3].

Summary. Ablations therefore show an asymmetric complementarity: SFA provides the main gains when spectral structure is informative but can be brittle under irregularity, whereas SAX offers smaller, stabilising improvements. `F3` benefits from combining both through instance-wise gating, which helps it outperform either two-way variant.

7 Conclusion

We show that representation fusion is most effective *selectively*. Over 113 UCR datasets, F3 provides small but consistent gains over ROCKET, but improvements concentrate in regimes with longer, spectrally diverse, and structurally heterogeneous signals, and can vanish or reverse under extreme irregularity/outliers. SHAP and ablations indicate an asymmetric complementarity: SFA drives gains when frequency structure is informative yet is brittle under irregularity, while SAX offers weaker but stabilising contributions; instance-wise gating allows F3 to balance these around an essential ROCKET backbone.

Practical Guidance: Use **F3** (SAX+SFA+ROCKET) when datasets exhibit heterogeneous structure across time and frequency domains. This includes regimes with high class imbalance (C1 HighImb), smooth separable signals (C3 SmoothSep), and high-fluctuation complex signals (C4 HighFlCx). Use **F2-SR** (SAX+ROCKET) for short jagged series (C6 ShortBase) and long structured series (C2 LongFSTCx), where shape-based time-domain cues dominate and computational efficiency matters. Use **ROCKET** alone for outlier-rich complex datasets (C5 HighCompOut) or when baseline accuracy exceeds 95% and where fusion offers limited or inconsistent benefit.

Limitations and Future Work: Small cluster sizes (C4, C5) limit per-regime statistical power; therefore, we treat findings in underpowered regimes as indicative and report effect sizes and uncertainty-aware statistics, and we emphasize aggregate and cross-regime trends. Our evaluation is restricted to UCR univariate datasets, used here as a controlled benchmark to study representation complementarity and regime-aware selection. External validation beyond UCR—especially for multivariate, irregularly sampled, and domain-specific real-world series—is a natural next step. Additional directions include automatic regime prediction for zero-shot selection, incorporating further representations (e.g., shapelets, catch22, wavelets), exploring richer fusion mechanisms (e.g., attention-based fusion), and budget-aware gating for compute-constrained settings. Finally, our hyperparameter search traces enable follow-up analyses of regime-specific hyperparameter preferences (e.g., discretisation granularity or kernel budget), the stability/transferability of good settings within regimes, and meta-feature-driven warm-start recommendations for low-cost configuration selection on new datasets.

Data Availability Statement. All experiments use publicly available UCR datasets. The code for reproducing our results is available at https://github.com/Honeyhsc/tsc_fusion_paper. Per-dataset accuracies across all models tested, NN hyperparameter configurations for F3 and per-dataset meta-feature details are provided in the repository's `results/` directory.

Declaration of Generative AI Use. In accordance with conference guidelines, the authors disclose that generative AI tools (specifically, large language models) were used exclusively for grammatical error correction and language refinement during the writing process. The authors assume full responsibility for the correctness and originality of the content.

References

1. Abanda, A., Mori, U., Lozano, J.A.: A review on distance based time series classification. Data Min. Knowl. Disc. **33**(2), 378–412 (2018). https://doi.org/10.1007/s10618-018-0596-4
2. Abdallah, Z.S., Gaber, M.M.: Co-eye: a multi-resolution ensemble classifier for symbolically approximated time series. Mach. Learn. **109**(11), 2029–2061 (2020). https://doi.org/10.1007/s10994-020-05887-3
3. Chauhan, H.S., Abdallah, Z.S.: A regime-aware fusion framework for time series classification (extended version). arXiv preprint arXiv:2512.15378 (2026). https://doi.org/10.48550/arXiv.2512.15378
4. Dempster, A., Petitjean, F., Webb, G.I.: ROCKET: exceptionally fast and accurate time series classification using random convolutional kernels. Data Min. Knowl. Disc. **34**(5), 1454–1495 (2020). https://doi.org/10.1007/s10618-020-00701-z
5. Dempster, A., Schmidt, D.F., Webb, G.I.: Hydra: competing convolutional kernels for fast and accurate time series classification. Data Min. Knowl. Disc. (5), 1–27 (2023). https://doi.org/10.1007/s10618-023-00939-3
6. Ismail Fawaz, H., Forestier, G., Weber, J., Idoumghar, L., Muller, P.-A.: Deep learning for time series classification: a review. Data Min. Knowl. Disc. **33**(4), 917–963 (2019). https://doi.org/10.1007/s10618-019-00619-1
7. Hills, J., Lines, J., Baranauskas, E., Mapp, G., Bagnall, A.: Classification of time series by shapelet transformation. Data Min. Knowl. Disc. **28**(4), 851–881 (2014). https://doi.org/10.1007/s10618-013-0316-4
8. Ismail Fawaz, H., et al.: InceptionTime: finding AlexNet for time series classification. Data Min. Knowl. Disc. **34**(6), 1936–1962 (2020). https://doi.org/10.1007/s10618-020-00710-y
9. Lin, J., Keogh, E., Wei, L., Lonardi, S.: Experiencing sax: a novel symbolic representation of time series. Data Min. Knowl. Disc. **15**(2), 107–144 (2007). https://doi.org/10.1007/s10618-007-0064-z
10. Lines, J., Taylor, S., Bagnall, A.: Time series classification with hive-cote: the hierarchical vote collective of transformation-based ensembles. ACM Trans. Knowl. Discov. Data **12**(5), 52:1–52:35 (2018). https://doi.org/10.1145/3182382
11. Lubba, C.H., Sethi, S.S., Knaute, P., Schultz, S.R., Fulcher, B.D., Jones, N.S.: *catch22*: CAnonical Time-series CHaracteristics. Data Min. Knowl. Disc. **33**(6), 1821–1852 (2019). https://doi.org/10.1007/s10618-019-00647-x
12. Middlehurst, M., Schäfer, P., Bagnall, A.: Bake off redux: a review and experimental evaluation of recent time series classification algorithms. Data Min. Knowl. Disc. **38**(4), 1958–2031 (2024). https://doi.org/10.1007/s10618-024-01022-1
13. Schäfer, P.: The BOSS is concerned with time series classification in the presence of noise. Data Min. Knowl. Disc. **29**(6), 1505–1530 (2014). https://doi.org/10.1007/s10618-014-0377-7

14. Schäfer, P., Högqvist, M.: SFA: a symbolic fourier approximation and index for similarity search in high-dimensional datasets. In: Proceedings of the 15th International Conference on Extending Database Technology (EDBT), pp. 516–527 (2012). https://doi.org/10.1145/2247596.2247656
15. Wang, X., Mueen, A., Ding, H., Trajcevski, G., Scheuermann, P., Keogh, E.: Experimental comparison of representation methods and distance measures for time series data. In: Data Mining and Knowledge Discovery, vol. 26, pp. 275–309 (2013). https://doi.org/10.1007/s10618-012-0250-5

On Imbalanced Regression with Hoeffding Trees

Pantia-Marina Alchirch(✉) and Dimitrios I. Diochnos

University of Oklahoma, Norman, USA
{marina.alchirch,diochnos}@ou.edu

Abstract. Many real-world applications generate continuous data streams for regression. Hoeffding trees and their variants have a long-standing tradition due to their effectiveness, either alone or as base models in broader ensembles. Recent batch-learning work shows that *kernel density estimation (KDE)* improves smoothed predictions in imbalanced regression [46], while *hierarchical shrinkage (HS)* provides post-hoc regularization for decision trees without modifying their structure [1]. We extend KDE to streaming settings via a telescoping formulation and integrate HS into incremental decision trees. Empirical evaluation on standard online regression benchmarks shows that KDE consistently improves early-stream performance, whereas HS provides limited gains. Our implementation is publicly available at: https://github.com/marinaAlchirch/DSFA_2026.

Keywords: Online learning · Imbalanced regression · Hoeffding trees

1 Introduction

We live in a world where sensors continuously monitor the environment and our activities, generating data with the potential to transform our lives. In this context, machine learning and data mining algorithms are invaluable, as they uncover patterns that reveal important phenomena. Mining such continuous flows of information gives rise to *online* machine learning and *data stream* mining and has enabled applications such as credit scoring [3], fraud detection [29], human activity recognition [27], clinical decision support [18], energy pricing [42], and even reducing the energy footprint of stream mining itself [20].

At the same time, working with *imbalanced data* is a constant nuisance for machine learning and data mining applications. Imbalanced data arise when the labels associated with the observations that are collected, are skewed favoring certain categories or certain ranges of values. Research on imbalanced data has focused primarily on classification problems; e.g., anomaly detection [28], e-commerce [5], infants' survival [22], and many others. However, investigating imbalanced data makes a lot of sense in regression tasks as well. For example, one may want to predict the age of an individual by having access to their facial image [38], or predict weather phenomena such as hail size or wind intensity [32].

R. C.-W. Wong et al. (Eds.): PAKDD 2026, LNAI 16618, pp. 358–372, 2027.
https://doi.org/10.1007/978-981-92-1947-6_29

Our work focuses at the intersection of the above two fields. We investigate popular methods that generate decision trees incrementally and have been developed with ideas for mining data streams and combine such mechanisms with recent advances developed for batch learning: *(i)* regularization of decision trees using hierarchical shrinkage [1], and *(ii)* approximating skewed distributions using kernel density estimation (KDE) [46]. In this work we are interested in imbalanced data; not in concept drift. Below we summarize our contributions.

Contributions. First, we implement hierarchical shrinkage on incremental decision trees that are available in the `scikit-multiflow` library [34]. Second, we revisit KDE and make it applicable to mining algorithms that operate on streams. Third, by combining the above techniques we achieve improved performance of incremental decision tree algorithms on imbalanced regression tasks for streams. Our main finding is that KDE helps with the improved predictions a lot, whereas hierarchical shrinkage provides minimal gains. We then integrate KDE with the `River` library [33] and verify that KDE improves predictions in the same tree models tested in `scikit-multiflow`, as well as in additional ones that were not tested or were not available in `scikit-multiflow`. Our code is publicly available for anyone to work with: https://github.com/marinaAlchirch/DSFA_2026.

2 Related Work

Incremental decision trees have a long line of research going back to at least the 80's [40,44]. Perhaps the most important incremental decision tree learning algorithm is that of Hoeffding trees [16] and their variants. Hoeffding trees use Hoeffding's inequality as a heuristic in order to decide when the difference in information gain (or some other relevant criterion) between the best-split attribute and the second-best split attribute is sufficiently high to justify a split. Several extensions of the Hoeffding trees have been developed [7,19,21,23,24,36], primarily to deal with concept drift, but attention has also been paid for parallelization [4], reduced complexity [2], or improved classification accuracy [31].

In parallel, a tremendous wealth of methods has been developed for mining imbalanced data. A well-known method for dealing with class imbalance is Synthetic Minority Oversampling Technique (SMOTE) in which oversampling of synthetic data is performed [11,43]. However, many more methods have been developed, including informed under-sampling the majority class [30], sampling based on clusters [25], re-weighting [45], modifying the margin of the separation boundary [9], or more theoretical approaches [10,13,15] including more general scenarios [12]. In addition, a recent line of work is using *kernel density estimation (KDE)* for smoothing the predicted labels on learned models [38,46], but has been applied only in batch settings where all the information is available ahead of time. Inspired by this approach we smooth the predicted labels using sketches of the distribution from small sequences of the stream examples.

Finally, a useful way for regularizing decision trees is that of *pruning* [8,39]. However, pruning is rarely used for incremental trees since it requires constructing a full tree and then pruning branches in a costly post-processing step. A more recent alternative for regularization is *hierarchical shrinkage (HS)* [1], where all nodes along the root-to-leaf path contribute to the final prediction. HS is a post-hoc regularization method that avoids building a complete tree or performing expensive pruning operations, and can be applied to incremental trees provided sufficient streaming statistics are maintained. To our knowledge, we are the first to integrate HS into incremental decision trees and evaluate its impact on predictive accuracy, coupled with KDE-based smoothing for imbalanced domains.

3 Preliminaries

We use *multisets* for collections of objects that may contain multiple copies of the same object; e.g., $S = \{\{x_1, x_3, x_1\}\}$. For a compact representation denoting multiplicities, we may write $S = \{\{x_1, x_3, x_1\}\} = \{\{(x_1, 2), (x_3, 1)\}\}$. The *cardinality* $|S|$ of a multiset S is the total number of elements in S (including multiplicities); e.g., $|S| = 3$ for the multiset S given above. Using multisets we have the ability to approximate *probability density functions (pdfs)* that govern certain domains by keeping track of their *empirical densities.* Furthermore, in these cases we will explicitly indicate that certain elements do not appear at all, using 0 for their multiplicities. For example, in an instance space $\mathcal{X} = \{x_1, x_2, x_3, x_4\}$ using the collection of instances $S = \{\{(x_1, 2), (x_3, 1)\}\}$, we have the empirical density $\tilde{f}_S(\mathcal{X}) = \{(x_1, 2), (x_2, 0), (x_3, 1), (x_4, 0)\}$. With $m_{\mathcal{Z}}(z)$ we denote the multiplicity of z in $\mathcal{Z}$; e.g., $m_{\tilde{f}_S(\mathcal{X})}(x_1) = 2$ in the previous example.

Kernel Density Estimation (KDE). Kernels provide an easy way for similarity comparisons between instances. By storing instances in certain windows we can provide smooth estimates on imbalanced distributions for label values. In general, *kernel density estimation (KDE)* [37] using some arbitrary kernel K, points $z_i \in S$ from some multiset S, and a query point q, is accomplished via:

$$\hat{f}_{S,K,h}(q) = \frac{1}{|S|} \sum_{(z_i, m_i) \in S} m_i \cdot K_h(q - z_i) = \frac{1}{|S|\, h} \sum_{(z_i, m_i) \in S} m_i \cdot K\left(\frac{q - z_i}{h}\right), \quad (1)$$

where h is the *bandwidth* and its role is to provide some scaling on the use of the kernel that is used in (1). Small values of h make the estimate sensitive to individual data points, whereas large values of h provide a smoother estimate, by spreading the influence of each data point over a wider region of the dataset. We work with the Gaussian and the Epanechnikov kernel. The approximation on the labels as explained above is called LDS in [46].

Furthermore, we may use *binning* to map individual label values to broader intervals. This is standard technique; e.g., [46]. Let m and M denote the minimum and maximum label values (assumed known), and let r be the bin range. We generate $j^\star = \lfloor (M - m)/r \rfloor + 1$ bins, where $b_j = [m + jr, m + (j + 1)r)$ for $j \in \{0, 1, \ldots, j^\star\}$. Since (1) ultimately computes an average, it admits a telescoping update that relies on the previous average and the newest observation; which

Algorithm 1 Incremental KDE

Require: Window $W = \{(x_1, y_1), (x_2, y_2), \ldots, (x_m, y_m)\}$, bandwidth h, kernel K, and a structure of B groups of bins.
Ensure: Smoothed weights $\hat{f}_{n,K,h}(b)$ for each bin $b \in B$, where n is number of examples that we have seen in the stream so far.

for target label $y_i \in W$ **do**
  Find bin $b = \lfloor (y_i - m)/r \rfloor$ for target label y_i
  Compute $\hat{f}_{n+i,K,h}(b)$ as shown in (2)
return $\{\hat{f}_{n+m,K,h}(b)\}$, for all b $\in B$

is particularly convenient in streaming settings. Using n in the first subscript to denote the fact that we have seen n examples so far from the stream, we have:

$$\hat{f}_{n,K,h}(q) = \hat{f}_{n-1,h}(q) + \frac{1}{n}\left(\frac{1}{h}K\left(\frac{q - z_n}{h}\right) - \hat{f}_{n-1,h}(q)\right). \tag{2}$$

Thus, we are able to implement KDE incrementally; Algorithm 1 has the details.

Hoeffding Trees and Variants. The most well-known incremental decision tree algorithm is the Hoeffding Tree (HT) [16] and its variants. This class of algorithms uses Hoeffding's inequality to decide when to split a node. Letting R be the range of the split evaluation function (e.g., $R = 1$ for information gain in binary classification), when the difference between the best and second-best attributes exceeds $\epsilon = \sqrt{\frac{R^2 \ln(1/\delta)}{2n}}$, then, with confidence at least $1 - \delta$, the best attribute is selected for splitting. For our work we use the `scikit-multiflow` [34] and `River` [33] libraries. The `scikit-multiflow` library has an implementation of HT and of the *Hoeffding Adaptive Tree (HAT)* [7]. HAT employs ADWIN [6] to detect potential concept drift. Similar to `scikit-multiflow` the `River` library has an implementation of HT and HAT. Sticking to regression, `River` also has an implementation of iSOUP [36] and SGT [21].

Regularization of Decision Trees Using Hierarchical Shrinkage. Hierarchical shrinkage (HS) [1] is a recent regularization technique that does not alter the structure of the learned tree. Letting $N(t)$ be the number of samples in a node t of a decision tree DT and $\mathbf{E}_t[y]$ to be the mean response in node t, the prediction on an instance x is $DT(x) = \mathbf{E}_{t_0}[y] + \sum_{l=1}^{L}\left(\mathbf{E}_{t_l}[y] - \mathbf{E}_{t_{l-1}}[y]\right)$. HS modifies this to

$$DT_\lambda(x) = \mathbf{E}_{t_0}[y] + \sum_{l=1}^{L} \frac{\mathbf{E}_{t_l}[y] - \mathbf{E}_{t_{l-1}}[y]}{1 + \lambda/N(t_{l-1})}, \tag{3}$$

for some hyper-parameter λ that performs the regularization. Thus, the nodes in the path from root to leaf to have an amount of say in the final prediction.

4 The Online Learning Process That We Study

We use a variation of the *Follow-the-Leader (FTL)* algorithm [41] for tuning. In FTL, multiple models run in parallel and, at each time step, prediction follows

Algorithm 2 Online-Learning Process & Follow-the-Leader Tuning

Require: Stream $S = \{(x_1, y_1), (x_2, y_2), \ldots, (x_n, y_n), \ldots\}$ of labeled examples, a set P of parameters, a tuning window size s_t, and no-tuning window size s'_t.
1: Initialize a model M;
2: M.parameters $\leftarrow \emptyset$;
3: Initialize all different models T based on P;
4: $i \leftarrow 1$;
5: tuneStart $\leftarrow 1$;
6: tuneEnd $\leftarrow s_t$;
7: **for** every example (x_i, y_i) in stream S **do**
8:     **if** $i \geq$ tuneStart and $i \leq$ tuneEnd **then**
9:         $j \leftarrow 1$;
10:         minError $\leftarrow \infty$;
11:         bestModel $\leftarrow \emptyset$;
12:         **while** $j \leq s_t$ **do**
13:             Predict-then-train with every model $t \in T$;
14:             **if** minError $\geq$ t.error **then**
15:                 minError $\leftarrow$ t.error;
16:                 bestModel $\leftarrow$ t;
17:             $j \leftarrow j + 1$;
18:         $i \leftarrow i + s_t$;
19:         tuneStart $\leftarrow$ tuneStart $+ s_t + s'_t$;
20:         tuneEnd $\leftarrow$ tuneStart $+ s_t - 1$;
21:         M.setParameters(bestModel.parameters);
22:     **else**
23:         Predict-then-Train on example (x_i, y_i) with M;
24:         $i \leftarrow i + 1$;

the model that performs best (e.g., lowest cumulative loss) at that point in time. To ease the complexity and memory requirements we periodically allocate portions of the stream for such tuning and, after each phase, we select the hyper-parameters that performed best in the most recent tuning period. This procedure is summarized in Algorithm 2 and explained further below.

Tuning and learning on the stream is governed by two parameters: a parameter s_t controlling the duration of each tuning phase, and a parameter s'_t specifying how many examples are processed in a predict-then-train manner between tuning phases. The model used for prediction is denoted by M; it is selected as the best-performing model from a pool of models T. In Line 3, we initialize T with all instantiations of the base learner (e.g., Hoeffding Tree) across all combinations of hyper-parameter values. Hence, during tuning we effectively perform a grid search, where each grid point corresponds to the same base model with different hyper-parameters. Unlike standard grid search, all models in T are trained in parallel on the stream. For example, one configuration may consist of a Hoeffding Tree combined with KDE using a Gaussian kernel with bandwidth h, bin range r, and no hierarchical shrinkage ($\lambda = 0$).

5 Experiments

Datasets. We conduct experiments on Abalone [17], California Housing (California) [26], Electric Power Consumption (E-Power) [17], New York Taxi (NY Taxi) [35], and Film Thickness in semiconductors (Semi) [14]; see Table 1 for dataset characteristics. Abalone is small and we are using it "as-is". For the remaining datasets we remove outliers, and for NY Taxi and E-Power we additionally construct standard features (e.g., Manhattan distance for NY Taxi; hour and weekday for E-Power). For California Housing, we use 20,635 examples after removing 5 extreme instances. The NY Taxi dataset (currently has 1,458,644 examples) is treated as a stream using the first 20,000 instances, with 3 outliers removed. Similarly, from E-Power (2,075,259 examples) we use the first 100,000 instances and remove 8 outliers. Finally, from the Semi dataset (810,000 examples) we use the first 20,000 instances, retaining 19,452 after outlier removal. Figure 1 illustrates target imbalance in all datasets using bin range $r = 0.2$.

Table 1. Datasets and potential preprocessing for the experiments. Online tuning was tried in all datasets except for Semi due to time constraints.

Dataset	**#Features**	**#Examples**	Predict-then-train set size used in **Algorithm 2**	**Outlier removal**	**Constructed feature**
Abalone	8	4177	2089	✗	✗
Semi	229	19452	-	✓	✗
California	8	20635	10319	✓	✗
NY Taxi	10	19997	10001	✓	✓
E-Power	8	99992	87992	✓	✓

Clarification on the Integration with Python Libraries and Datasets Tested. In our initial submission we integrated HS and KDE with the `scikit-multiflow` library. When we started our work, `scikit-multiflow` exposed more of the internal structure of its learning algorithms, especially Hoeffding Trees, making it easier to integrate HS directly into the learning procedure. For example, in HAT, HS only requires the root-to-leaf prediction path, since the statistics of intermediate nodes are directly accessible regardless of additional subtrees used for drift detection. Meanwhile, the `River` library was further developed and has a more current version of iSOUP, as well as SGT which does not exist in `scikit-multiflow`. After receiving the reviews, we integrated KDE with `River` and ran additional experiments; however, without hyperparameter tuning due to time constraints.

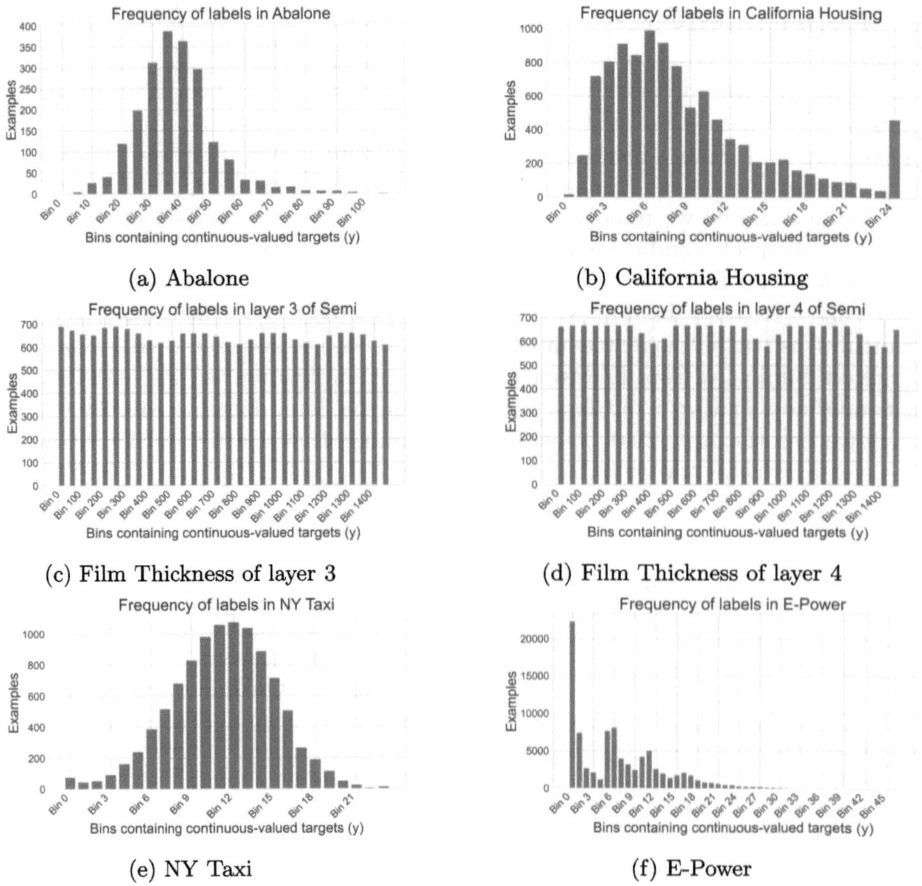

Fig. 1. Frequency of labels in predict-then-train data using bins' range $r = 0.2$.

Furthermore, in our initial submission we ran experiments only against three datasets: California, NY Taxi, and E-Power. For the camera-ready version of the paper we decided to run experiments with Abalone too, as well as against the more challenging layers 3 and 4 of the Semi dataset. Abalone being fairly small in size allowed us to run on time Algorithm 2 on scikit-multiflow, but due to time constraints we could not do the same thing with Semi. Experiments on layers 1 and 2 of Semi were omitted, as these cases appear trivial or easy and the KDE variants consistently outperform the baseline models.

Thus, we have experiments with `scikit-multiflow` -testing both HS and KDE- using the tuning phases of Algorithm 2 in all datasets but on Semi, while we have experiments with the `River` library in all datasets -testing for potential benefit of KDE only- but without tuning this time.

Using `scikit-multiflow` with Algorithm 2 we use HT and HAT as base models. We equip both of these models with KDE for smoothing the imbalanced label distribution of the stream as well as HS for regularizing the predictions. These enhancements appear either together or in isolation. Regarding incremental KDE we use a tumbling window whose size we treat as a hyper-parameter.

On the Tuning Window and Hyper-Parameter Tuning. When running experiments with the `scikit-multiflow` integration we use four periods for tuning the hyper-parameters of our models. For a dataset S that we treat as a stream, we set the tuning window size to be $\min\left(\lfloor |S|/8 \rfloor, 3000\right)$. Based on Table 1, the tuning window size for each dataset tested is approximately one quarter of the "missing" examples from the table. For example, in the case of Abalone, this translates to $(4,177 - 2089)/4 = 522$ examples for each tuning phase. In each tuning window we choose from the following hyperparameter values: *(i)* for range of bin $r \in \{0, 0.1, 0.2, 0.5, 1\}$, where 0 means that we don't perform binning in our targets but every target is simply its own bin, *(ii)* $\lambda \in \{0, 0.1, 1, 10, 15, 25\}$, where 0 is for not predicting with HS but rather with the initial unregularized model, *(iii)* $h \in \{10, 50, 100\}$, *(iv)* for (tumbling) window size $|W| \in \{50, 100, 200\}$, and *(v)* for kernel choose between Gaussian and Epanechnikov. When we use KDE alone we do not tune on λ, while when we use HS alone we only tune on λ.

Evaluation Metrics. For evaluating our experiments we use: *mean absolute error (MAE)*, *root mean squared error (RMSE)*, *weighted root mean squared error (WRMSE)*, and the R^2 statistic. For the WRMSE the penalty calculated on a set of test points S is $\text{WRMSE}(f, S) = \sqrt{\sum_{i=1}^{|S|} w(y)(f(x) - y)^2}$, where $w(y)$ is the weight associated with the true label y that corresponds to the input x. In particular, this weight $w(y)$ corresponds to the probability of the bin where y falls, as shown in Fig. 1 (after normalization so that we have a probability distribution). Notice that the number of bins is in principle much smaller than the number of examples $|S|$ and hence the weight $w(y)$ will be much larger than $1/|S|$ for the non-empty bins that contribute in the WRMSE value. For example, if we have bins with weight values 0.1 or larger, then the WRMSE will be several orders of magnitude larger than simple RMSE for a datastream that has processed $n = 10,000$ examples and therefore every example in this stream contributes to RMSE a value with weight equal to $w(y) = 1/10,000$. In the results that follow we will see this phenomenon. For the selection of the best hyper-parameters during tuning, we use the (non-weighted) RMSE.

Experimental Results on `scikit-multiflow`*.* Table 2 presents the overall results obtained using the `scikit-multiflow` library. For this reason, we report results only for HT and HAT, along with their HS, KDE, and KDE+HS extensions. Our results in Table 2 indicate that in all datasets except in E-Power our KDE variants (potentially with HS as well) outperform their original versions.

We now provide some additional information complementing the results of Table 2. In Fig. 2 we see that for the California dataset, the performance of the KDE and the KDE+HS variants of HT outperform the original model, with the largest performance gap appearing in the middle of the stream. In Fig. 3 we see

Table 2. Performance comparison across datasets on the `scikit-multiflow` library using Algorithm 2 for tuning. **Bold blue** indicates best metric value per dataset, whereas plain **bold** indicates second best. For comparison purposes on plain HT and HAT we bypass the tuning portions of the stream.

		Model (potentially including HS, KDE, or both)							
Dataset	**Metric**	**HT**	**HAT**	**HT +HS**	**HAT +HS**	**HT +KDE**	**HAT +KDE**	**HT +HS +KDE**	**HAT +HS +KDE**
Abalone	MAE	1.979	1.979	1.979	1.979	**1.643**	1.648	1.644	**1.560**
	RMSE	2.634	2.634	2.634	2.634	2.350	2.350	**2.347**	**2.233**
	WRMSE	**7.037**	**7.037**	**6.916**	**6.916**	7.255	7.508	7.210	7.471
	R^2	-0.015	-0.015	-0.015	-0.015	0.192	0.192	**0.194**	**0.271**
California	MAE	0.668	0.692	0.659	0.700	**0.568**	0.625	**0.564**	0.628
	RMSE	0.904	0.931	0.899	0.940	**0.808**	0.914	**0.802**	0.915
	WRMSE	20.282	21.793	19.755	21.966	**18.851**	22.148	**18.557**	22.227
	R^2	0.380	0.342	0.387	0.330	**0.505**	0.367	**0.512**	0.366
NY Taxi	MAE	0.466	0.466	0.466	0.466	**0.368**	**0.368**	**0.369**	**0.369**
	RMSE	0.612	0.612	0.612	0.612	**0.487**	**0.487**	**0.487**	**0.487**
	WRMSE	13.177	13.177	13.147	13.147	**11.932**	**11.932**	**11.786**	**11.786**
	R^2	0.333	0.333	0.333	0.333	**0.577**	**0.577**	**0.577**	**0.577**
E-Power	MAE	**0.080**	0.407	**0.098**	0.419	0.114	0.229	0.114	0.230
	RMSE	**0.203**	0.660	**0.219**	0.666	0.272	0.479	0.272	0.479
	WRMSE	**9.460**	41.994	**12.371**	43.223	15.299	29.430	15.310	29.479
	R^2	**0.977**	0.756	**0.973**	0.752	0.959	0.872	0.959	0.872

the MAE performance of HAT models on the Abalone dataset. This time the KDE+HS enhanced version of HAT behaves the best and is discernibly better compared to the simple KDE extension of the HAT model. In Fig. 4 we see two graphs of R^2 for the NY Taxi and the E-Power datasets using again HAT-based models for comparisons. In both cases we see that the KDE-enhanced and KDE+HS-enhanced variants perform better than the base model. Having said that, for the case of E-Power, the simple HT performs even better (see Table 2).

Experimental Results on ***`River`***. Following the reviewers' feedback, we executed additional experiments using the `River` Python library as well. This allowed us to evaluate our KDE framework with the iSOUP and SGT models beyond HT and HAT that we evaluated using `scikit-multiflow`. Due to time constraints, we did not perform online tuning using Algorithm 2. Instead, we only performed incremental KDE as described in Algorithm 1, using the same fixed parameters ($h = 10$, $r = 0.2$ and window size $|W| = 50$) for all the experiments. Table 3 presents results with the `River` library, using both the RMSE and the *weighted*

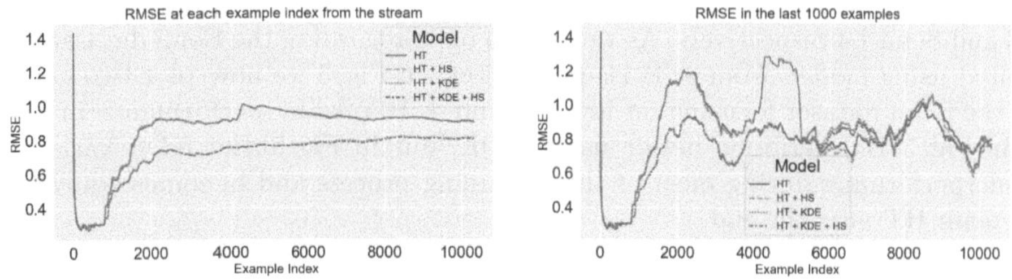

(a) Cumulative RMSE. (b) RMSE in the last 1K examples.

Fig. 2. RMSE plots of HT-based models for the *California* dataset. The KDE and KDE+HS variants perform overall better than the original HT model.

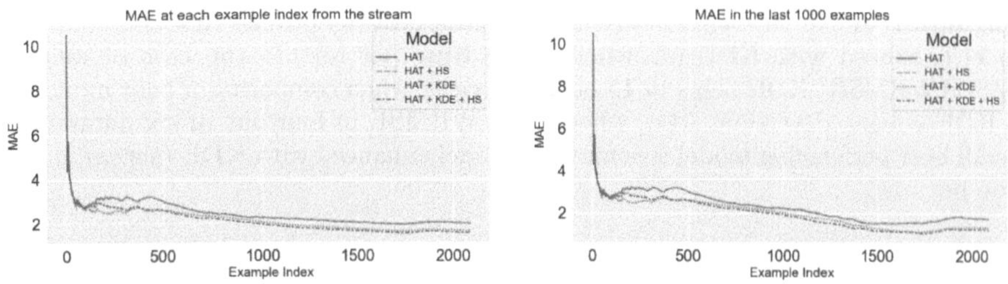

(a) Cumulative MAE. (b) MAE in the last 1K examples.

Fig. 3. MAE plots of HAT-based models for the *Abalone* dataset. Similar to Fig. 2 the KDE-enhanced model performs better than the original model. However, here HS helps even further.

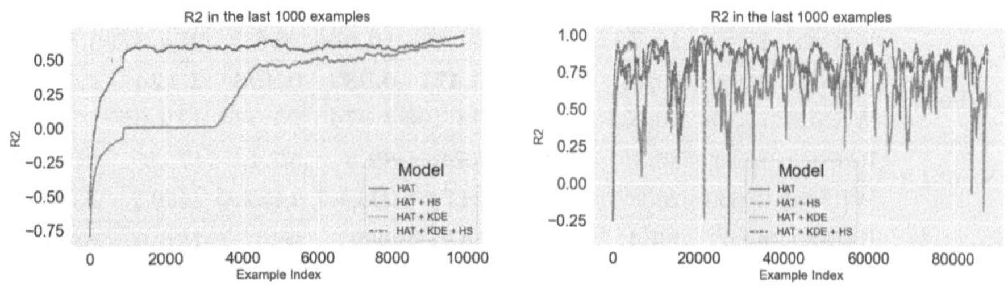

(a) R^2 in the last 1K examples (NY Taxi). (b) R^2 in the last 1K examples (E-Power).

Fig. 4. R^2 score during the last 1K examples for HAT-based models on the NY Taxi (Fig. 4a) and E-Power (Fig. 4b) datasets. In both cases, the KDE variants achieve the best performance throughout the streaming process. Furthermore, in both cases plotting starts after 100 examples have first been processed since the early R^2 values are very small and dominate the y-axis in the graph.

RMSE (WRMSE) metrics. We denote layers 3 and 4 of the Semi dataset as Semi-L3 and Semi-L4 respectively. As we had no plots regarding the Semi dataset generated using models from `scikit-multiflow`, in Fig. 5 we now plot two graphs of the Semi dataset focusing on layers 3 and 4. Regarding performance in layer 3 in Fig. 5aHT performs better using KDE, but in Fig. 5bthe KDE variant is underperforming during most of the streaming process and becomes equivalent to plain HT near the end.

Table 3. Performance metric comparison (lower is better) across datasets using the `River` Python library. **Bold** values indicate the better performance between each base model and its KDE-enhanced counterpart. **Bold blue** indicates the best performing model for a given dataset and metric. No tuning has been performed to identify the best hyper-parameters. For the results shown for Semi-L3 and Semi-L4 we are using only one decimal digit for better clarity. In the case of RMSE KDE helps in 18 out of 24 cases when comparing a base model and its KDE-enhanced version. Also, when using RMSE in five out of six datasets the overall best performing model is some base model enhanced with KDE (shown in **bold blue** per row).In the case of weighted RMSE (WRMSE) KDE helps in 15 out of 24 cases when comparing a base model and its KDE-enhanced version. Also, when using WRMSE in four out of six datasets the overall best performing model is some base model enhanced with KDE (shown in **bold blue** per row).

		Model (potentially including KDE)							
Dataset	**Metric**	**HT**	**HAT**	**iSOUP**	**SGT**	**HT +KDE**	**HAT +KDE**	**iSOUP +KDE**	**SGT +KDE**
Abalone	RMSE	3.175	3.186	**11.249**	4.051	**2.776**	**2.633**	11.318	**3.138**
	WRMSE	**43.815**	**42.957**	**215.832**	64.202	50.971	46.795	218.941	**57.864**
California	RMSE	0.837	0.827	2.367	1.033	**0.768**	**0.770**	**2.366**	**0.940**
	WRMSE	26.069	26.725	70.863	32.971	**24.118**	**24.753**	**70.852**	**29.310**
NY Taxi	RMSE	0.553	0.525	6.494	0.829	**0.485**	**0.491**	**6.489**	**0.511**
	WRMSE	17.494	**16.797**	254.611	30.739	**16.664**	16.981	**254.379**	**17.625**
E-Power	RMSE	0.160	0.672	2.124	**0.477**	**0.082**	**0.403**	**2.124**	0.574
	WRMSE	11.136	50.203	112.694	**38.406**	**4.074**	**25.534**	**112.657**	52.591
Semi-L3	RMSE	113.1	80.3	**174.8**	**85.2**	**82.8**	**55.4**	175.9	91.3
	WRMSE	2866.6	2058.1	**4421.1**	**2174.6**	**2114.7**	**1432.0**	4449.2	2339.2
Semi-L4	RMSE	**84.7**	**85.4**	176.2	88.7	88.9	95.4	**176.0**	**88.2**
	WRMSE	**2158.4**	**2177.3**	4464.8	2261.4	2265.6	2430.4	**4460.9**	**2250.9**

Coming back to Table 3, a first remark is that KDE is in general helpful for the base models. In the case of RMSE, the KDE-enhanced models have better performance in 18 out of 24 cases, while in the case of WRMSE the KDE-enhanced models have better performance in 15 out of 24 cases. Overall, depending on the performance metric, RMSE or weighted RMSE, the KDE-enhanced models provide the best performing models in five out of six datasets and four out of six datasets respectively.

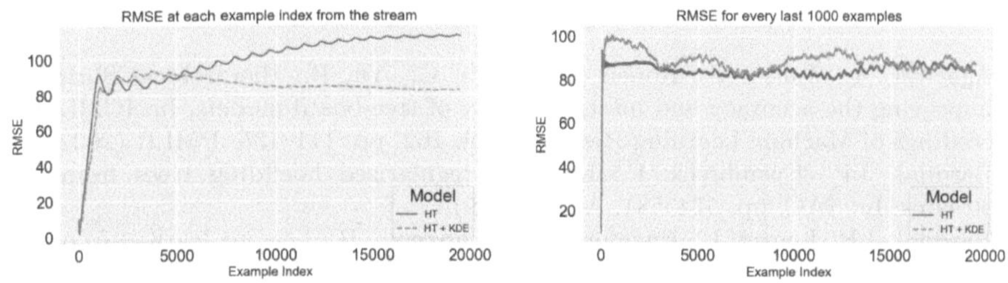

(a) Cumulative RMSE in Semi-L3. (b) RMSE for 1K last examples in Semi-L4.

Fig. 5. RMSE, cumulative and during the last 1K examples, for HT-based models on the Semi-L3 (Fig. 5a) and Semi-L4 (Fig. 5b) datasets. Note that these results were obtained using the `River` library.

Resources Used for Experiments. All experiments were executed on a macOS laptop with an Apple Silicon M2 processor and 16 GB of RAM. We implemented the models in Python using the `scikit-multiflow` and `River` libraries.

6 Conclusions and Future Work

We recast recent advances in *batch learning* regarding imbalanced data and regularization of decision trees, in *streaming scenarios*. We propose the inclusion of KDE and potentially HS in incremental decision tree learning algorithms. We have seen that, in general, KDE improves the performance of the base models. However, HS appears to be providing minimal gains, if at all. As our results improve the performance of base incremental decision trees used for regression, we anticipate that the observed benefits will translate to similar benefits in random forests, or other ensembles of such tree-based models. We note that KDE does not naturally extend to pure classification problems and it is a question if one can find a new method that can further improve the performance of such incremental models with, or without, the inclusion of HS. Furthermore, in this work we have not focused on drift, which is an exciting direction, especially when one would like to couple drift together with imbalanced data and potentially KDE.

Acknowledgments. This material is based upon work supported by the U.S. National Science Foundation under Grant No. RISE-2019758. This work is part of the NSF AI Institute for Research on Trustworthy AI in Weather, Climate, and Coastal Oceanography (NSF AI2ES).

Disclosure of Interests. The authors have no competing interests to declare that are relevant to the content of this article.

References

1. Agarwal, A., Tan, Y.S., Ronen, O., Singh, C., Yu, B.: Hierarchical Shrinkage: improving the accuracy and interpretability of tree-based models. In: ICML. Proceedings of Machine Learning Research, vol. 162, pp. 111–135. PMLR (2022)
2. Barddal, J.P., Enembreck, F.: Learning regularized hoeffding trees from data streams. In: SAC, pp. 574–581. ACM (2019)
3. Barddal, J.P., Loezer, L., Enembreck, F., Lanzuolo, R.: Lessons learned from data stream classification applied to credit scoring. Expert Syst. Appl. **162**, 113899 (2020)
4. Ben-Haim, Y., Tom-Tov, E.: A streaming parallel decision tree algorithm. J. Mach. Learn. Res. **11**, 849–872 (2010)
5. Besaleva, L., Weaver, A.C.: Classification of imbalanced data in E-commerce. IntelliSys, pp. 744–750 (2017). IEEE
6. Bifet, A.: Adaptive learning and mining for data streams and frequent patterns. SIGKDD Explor. Newsl. **11**(1), 55–56 (2009)
7. Bifet, A., Gavaldà, R.: Adaptive learning from evolving data streams. In: Adams, N.M., Robardet, C., Siebes, A., Boulicaut, J. (eds.) IDA 2009. LNCS, vol. 5772, pp. 249–260. Springer (2009)
8. Breiman, L., Friedman, J.H., Olshen, R.A., Stone, C.J.: Classification and Regression Trees, Wadsworth (1984)
9. Cao, K., Wei, C., Gaidon, A., Aréchiga, N., Ma, T.: Learning imbalanced datasets with label-distribution-aware margin loss. In: NeurIPS, pp. 1565–1576 (2019)
10. Chaudhuri, K., Ahuja, K., Arjovsky, M., Lopez-Paz, D.: Why does throwing away data improve worst-group error?. In: ICML. Proceedings of Machine Learning Research, vol. 202, pp. 4144–4188. (2023). PMLR
11. Chawla, N.V., Bowyer, K.W., Hall, L.O., Kegelmeyer, W.P.: SMOTE: synthetic minority over-sampling technique. J. Artif. Intell. Res. **16**, 321–357 (2002)
12. Cohen, L., Mansour, Y., Moran, S., Shao, H.: Probably approximately precision and recall learning. CoRR **abs/2411.13029** (2024)
13. Cortes, C., Mao, A., Mohri, M., Zhong, Y.: Balancing the scales: a theoretical and algorithmic framework for learning from imbalanced data. In: ICML. Proceedings of Machine Learning Research, vol. 267 (2025). PMLR / OpenReview.net
14. DACON Co., Ltd.: Monthly Semiconductor Thin Film Thickness Analysis Dataset. https://dacon.io/competitions/official/235554/data (2020)
15. Diochnos, D.I., Trafalis, T.B.: Learning reliable rules under class imbalance. In: SDM, pp. 28–36. SIAM (2021)
16. Domingos, P.M., Hulten, G.: Mining high-speed data streams. In: Ramakrishnan, R., Stolfo, S.J., Bayardo, R.J., Parsa, I. (eds.) KDD, pp. 71–80. ACM (2000)
17. Dua, D., Graff, C.: UCI Machine Learning Repository (2017)
18. Fong, S., Zhang, Y., Fiaidhi, J., Mohammed, O., Mohammed, S.: Evaluation of stream mining classifiers for real-time clinical decision support system: a case study of blood glucose prediction in diabetes therapy. BioMed Res. Intl. **1**, 274193 (2013)
19. Gama, J., Fernandes, R., Rocha, R.: Decision trees for mining data streams. Intell. Data Anal. **10**(1), 23–45 (2006)

20. García-Martín, E., Bifet, A., Lavesson, N.: Energy modeling of Hoeffding tree ensembles. Intell. Data Anal. **25**(1), 81–104 (2021)
21. Gouk, H., Pfahringer, B., Frank, E.: Stochastic Gradient Trees. ACML. In: Proceedings of Machine Learning Research, vol. 101, pp. 1094–1109 (2019). PMLR
22. Gourdeau, P., Kanbar, L.J., Shalish, W., Sant'Anna, G.M., Kearney, R.E., Precup, D.: Feature selection and oversampling in analysis of clinical data for extubation readiness in extreme preterm infants. In: EMBC, pp. 4427–4430 (2015)
23. Hulten, G., Spencer, L., Domingos, P.M.: Mining time-changing data streams. In: KDD, pp. 97–106. ACM (2001)
24. Ikonomovska, E., Gama, J., Dzeroski, S.: Learning model trees from evolving data streams. Data Min. Knowl. Discov. **23**(1), 128–168 (2011)
25. Jo, T., Japkowicz, N.: Class imbalances versus small disjuncts. SIGKDD Explorat. **6**(1), 40–49 (2004)
26. Kelley Pace, R., Barry, R.: Sparse spatial autoregressions. Statist. Probab. Lett. **33**(3), 291–297 (1997)
27. Khannouz, M., Glatard, T.: A benchmark of data stream classification for human activity recognition on connected objects. Sensors **20**(22), 6486 (2020)
28. Khreich, W., Granger, E., Miri, A., Sabourin, R.: Iterative Boolean combination of classifiers in the ROC space: an application to anomaly detection with HMMs. Pattern Recogn. **43**(8), 2732–2752 (2010)
29. Laleh, N., Abdollahi Azgomi, M.: A taxonomy of frauds and fraud detection techniques. In: Prasad, S.K., Routray, S., Khurana, R., Sahni, S. (eds.) ICISTM 2009. CCIS, vol. 31, pp. 256–267. Springer, Heidelberg (2009). https://doi.org/10.1007/978-3-642-00405-6_28
30. Liu, X., Wu, J., Zhou, Z.: Exploratory undersampling for class-imbalance learning. IEEE Trans. Syst. Man Cybernet. Part B **39**(2), 539–550 (2009)
31. Manapragada, C., Webb, G.I., Salehi, M.: Extremely fast decision tree. In: KDD, pp. 1953–1962. ACM (2018)
32. McGovern, A., et al.: Using artificial intelligence to improve real-time decision-making for high-impact weather. Bulletin American Meteorol. Soc. **98**(10), 2073 – 2090 (2017)
33. Montiel, J., et al.: River: machine learning for streaming data in Python. J. Mach. Learn. Res. **22**, 110:1–110:8 (2021)
34. Montiel, J., Read, J., Bifet, A., Abdessalem, T.: Scikit-MultiFlow: a multi-output streaming framework. J. Mach. Learn. Res. **19**, 72:1–72:5 (2018)
35. New York City Taxi and Limousine Commission: TLC trip record data. https://www.nyc.gov/site/tlc/about/tlc-trip-record-data.page (2009-2025)
36. Osojnik, A., Panov, P., Dzeroski, S.: Tree-based methods for online multi-target regression. J. Intell. Inf. Syst. **50**(2), 315–339 (2018)
37. Parzen, E.: On estimation of a probability density function and mode. Ann. Math. Stat. **33**(3), 1065–1076 (1962)
38. Pu, R., Xu, G., Fang, R., Bao, B., Ling, C., Wang, B.: Leveraging group classification with descending soft labeling for deep imbalanced regression. In: AAAI, pp. 19978–19985. AAAI Press (2025)
39. Quinlan, J.R.: C4.5: Programs for Machine Learning, Morgan Kaufmann (1993)
40. Schlimmer, J.C., Fisher, D.H.: A case study of incremental concept induction. In: AAAI, pp. 496–501. Morgan Kaufmann (1986)
41. Shalev-Shwartz, S.: Online learning and online convex optimization. Found. Trends Mach. Learn. **4**(2), 107–194 (2012)

42. Sun, Y., Gomes, H.M., Pfahringer, B., Bifet, A.: Real-time energy pricing in New Zealand: an evolving stream analysis. In: PRICAI. LNCS, vol. 15285, pp. 91–97. Springer (2024)
43. Torgo, L., Ribeiro, R.P., Pfahringer, B., Branco, P.: Smote for regression. In: Portuguese conference on artificial intelligence, pp. 378–389. Springer (2013)
44. Utgoff, P.E.: ID5: an incremental ID3. In: ICML, pp. 107–120. (1988)
45. Wang, Y., Ramanan, D., Hebert, M.: Learning to model the Tail. In: NeurIPS, pp. 7029–7039 (2017)
46. Yang, Y., Zha, K., Chen, Y.C., Wang, H., Katabi, D.: Delving into deep imbalanced regression. ICML. PMLR **139**, 11842–11851 (2021). PMLR

Multi-RAG: A Multimodal Retrieval-Augmented Generation System for Adaptive Video Understanding

Mingyang Mao[1(✉)], Mariela M. Perez-Cabarcas[2], Utteja Kallakuri[1], Nicholas R. Waytowich[2], Xiaomin Lin[1], and Tinoosh Mohsenin[1]

[1] Johns Hopkins Whiting School of Engineering, Baltimore, MD, USA
{mmao4,ukallak1,xlin52,tinoosh}@jhu.edu
[2] DEVCOM Army Research Laboratory, Aberdeen, MD, USA
{mariela.m.perez-cabarcas.civ,nicholas.r.waytowich.civ}@army.mil

Abstract. To effectively engage in human society, the ability to adapt, filter information, and make informed decisions in ever-changing situations is critical. As intelligent agents become more integrated into human life, there is a growing opportunity–and need–to offload the cognitive burden on humans to these systems, particularly in information-rich scenarios. To fill this need, we present ***Multi-RAG***, a multimodal retrieval-augmented generation (RAG) system designed to provide adaptive assistance to humans in information-intensive circumstances. Our system aims to improve situational understanding and reduce cognitive load by integrating and reasoning over multi-source information streams, including video, audio, and text. As an enabling step toward long-term human-computer partnerships, ***Multi-RAG*** explores how multimodal information understanding can serve as a foundation for adaptive assistance in dynamic, human-centered situations. To evaluate its capability in a realistic human-assistance proxy task, we benchmarked ***Multi-RAG*** on the MMBench-Video dataset, a challenging multimodal video understanding benchmark. Our system achieves superior performance compared to existing open-source video large language models (Video-LLMs) and large vision-language models (LVLMs), while utilizing fewer resources and less input data. The results demonstrate ***Multi-RAG***'s potential as a practical and efficient foundation for future human-in-the-loop systems in dynamic, real-world contexts.

Keywords: AI Assistance Systems · Human Cognitive Support · Large Language Models · Multimodal RAG

1 Introduction

In today's highly social and dynamic settings, we are often overloaded with information. We actively or passively receive vast amounts of information constantly

M. Mao and M. Perez-Cabarcas—Equal contribution.

R. C.-W. Wong et al. (Eds.): PAKDD 2026, LNAI 16618, pp. 373–384, 2027.
https://doi.org/10.1007/978-981-92-1947-6_30

Fig. 1. An example interaction scenario with the Multi-RAG system: Based on an open-ended user query, the system synthesizes visual, audio, and textual inputs to infer the answer, demonstrating its ability for practical understanding and decision support.

from various media and scenarios [2]. For example, students face a significant influx of knowledge from both textbooks and teachers in the classroom. Similarly, Army commanders issue orders according to their extensive military training and how it applies to the highly complex situation at hand. These scenarios are all information-intensive. The inability to cope with excessive information can lead to serious performance losses and potential health problems [3,10]. Therefore, it is crucial to extract valuable information from the abundance of information streams to enhance efficiency in communication, learning, and decision-making.

Large Language Models (LLMs) are gaining popularity and influencing all aspects of daily life. LLMs show strong potential in improving information summarization techniques by generating concise, coherent representations of lengthy texts while retaining essential content, offering significant utility across a variety of domains [4,25]. They have also demonstrated effectiveness in supporting various facets of organizational decision-making, such as gathering information and generating potential options to consider [11,12].

However, despite their growing popularity and capabilities, LLMs still face notable limitations in technical reliability and practical applicability. One major constraint is hallucinations, as LLMs are known to occasionally generate plausible-sounding but incorrect information [26]. Additionally, LLMs often lack the latest information because their training corpus is typically outdated by several months or years [13]. Therefore, we propose a human-centered system that helps the agent understand the world and increase its situational awareness across multi-modal scenarios, ultimately benefiting humans.

We developed an integrated software-hardware system that leverages Retrieval-Augmented Generation (RAG) to synergistically combine the intrinsic knowledge of LLMs with the vast and continuously evolving information from external databases. In addition, the system incorporates advanced perception capabilities–such as automatic speech recognition (ASR) and vision-language models (VLMs)–to enable three key functions: (1) perceiving and interpreting multimodal external inputs, (2) continuously acquiring and updating knowledge from dynamic real-world sources, and (3) enhancing human cognition by providing timely, context-aware support across various contexts (see Fig. 1).

To demonstrate the system's effectiveness in supporting human cognition and decision making, we focus our evaluation on complex, real-world scenarios that require the integration of multimodal information streams. Specifically, we employ an open-source video understanding benchmark as a representative task, as video-based environments naturally embody high information density and require both perceptual and reasoning capabilities–core aspects of effective decision support. Experimental results show that our system effectively interprets complex visual scenes and maintains high performance even when provided with limited visual input, highlighting its efficiency and robustness in resource-constrained scenarios.

2 Related Works

Our work is closely related to, and draws inspiration from, prior research on memory augmentation systems, multi-modal retrieval, and intelligent assistants.

2.1 Memory Augmentation Systems

Memory augmentation systems have been an active area of research since Vannevar Bush's conception of the Memex in 1945 [5]. Building on this foundation, wearable memory augmentation devices have gained increasing attention since the 1990 s, evolving from early concepts such as "memory prosthesis" [15]. Previous work in memory augmentation has placed significant emphasis on the audio modality. Studies have explored personal audio memory aids that support keyword-based search, such as Vemuri et al.'s system [23]. Additionally, researchers have investigated audio life-logging using wearable microphones and developed various smartphone-based browsing methods and real-time discrete and minimally disruptive querying mechanisms to access the recorded content [24,27]. With the development of multimedia technology, we hope the future memory augmentation media is not limited in the audio, therefore, we present a multimodal information retrieval method that enables users to retrieve information from captured video and other file types.

2.2 Multimodal RAG Paradigms

Multimodal RAG systems can be implemented through a variety of distinct paradigms, each with unique approaches to handling multimodal embedding, retrieval, and generation [1].

Cross-Modal. Models like CLIP [20], ALBEF [16] enable both images and text to be encoded into a shared vector space, facilitating multimodal retrieval within existing text-centric frameworks. This approach primarily requires replacing the unimodal embedding model with a multimodal encoder and using a multimodal LLM for generation, allowing unified question answering across modalities.

Separate Modality Pipelines. This approach treats each modality independently, designing dedicated retrieval and generation pipelines for each. Modality-specific encoders are used to embed queries and retrieve relevant content within the same modality, while generation relies on separate models tailored to each type of data. A re-ranking component can further optimize selection by identifying the most relevant results across different modality-specific retrieval stores [19].

Single Primary Modality. The single modality paradigm grounds all multimodal information into the embedding space of a primary modality, which is selected based on the focus of the application. Both retrieval and generation are then primarily performed using models specialized for the primary modality, allowing the system to standardize processing and leverage the strengths of typically text-based pipelines.

2.3 Existing Assistants

MerryQurry is an LLM-powered educational assistant that provides personalized, source-grounded support for students and educators, while addressing concerns around academic integrity and AI overreliance [21]. Expanding LLMs to domain-specific tasks, Kallakurik et al. [14] propose a medical AI assistant for edge devices that uses input-driven saliency to prune irrelevant neurons, enabling efficient deployment under hardware constraints. Moving beyond language-only inputs, STREAMMIND introduces a video-language framework for real-time streaming comprehension and dialogue, allowing AI systems to proactively respond to video content using context-aware natural language generation [7].

3 System Design

Building on the single primary modality paradigm discussed in Sect. 2, our system adopts this approach to build the video encoder, knowledge database, and RAG pipeline shown in Fig. 2. Specifically, it integrates multimodal information from video, audio, and documents, by converting all inputs into unified textual representations [1]. Visual and audio data are processed into descriptive text and auxiliary metadata, which are indexed in a vector database, while the original files are archived for potential future reference. At inference, user queries are matched to relevant content through semantic retrieval, and a large language model generates the final response based on both the query and retrieved information. In the following sections, we detail the video encoder framework, the construction of the knowledge database, and the RAG pipeline.

3.1 Video Encoder

The processing of video data is bifurcated into two parallel streams: image processing and audio processing. For the video component, a sampling module is

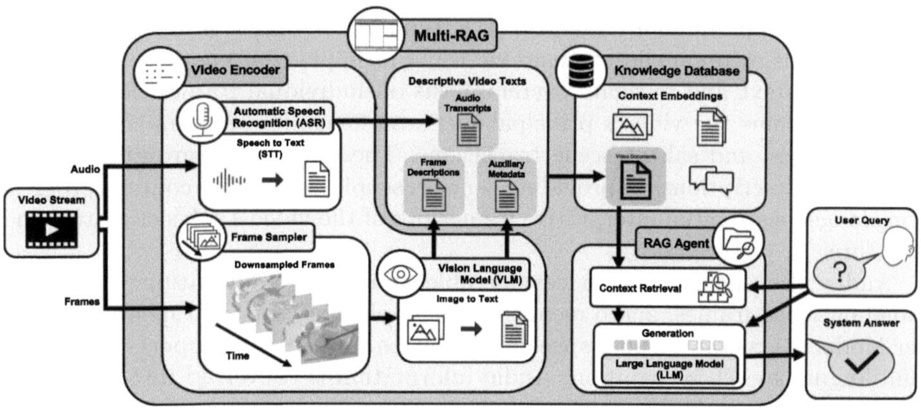

Fig. 2. The framework of our Multi-RAG pipeline contains three key modules. In the video encoder, the VLM, receives input from the frame sampler, and the ASR processes visual and audio streams, respectively, converting multimodal external inputs into unified textual descriptions and embeddings. Next, these are stored in the knowledge vector database, where a retrieval-augmented generation (RAG) agent selects relevant information in response to the user query. The LLM then synthesizes the retrieved content to generate the final system response.

employed to select requisite frames. We have developed two distinct sets of sampling strategies tailored for two specific scenarios: educational environments and general-purpose applications. Specifically, within the context of classroom settings, the visual content predominantly consists of presentation slides. Lecturers typically expound upon a single visual frame for an extended duration, rendering a high frequency of input unnecessary. Consequently, for the visual stream, we have implemented a pre-processing stage designed to filter the input frames. Only upon detection of a substantive change in the visual content is the image subsequently fed into the VLM. Mean Square Error is used to measure the discrepancy between frame A and frame B of size $M \times N$ with C channels:

$$\text{MSE}(A, B) = \frac{1}{M \times N \times C} \sum_{k=0}^{C-1} \sum_{i=0}^{M-1} \sum_{j=0}^{N-1} \left(A_{ijk} - B_{ijk}\right)^2 \tag{1}$$

To determine whether a newly sampled frame contains sufficient visual change for further processing, we compare its MSE against a cutoff value derived from sample videos of a recorded lecture series. In general-purpose scenarios characterized by high-frequency transformations of visual content, the utility derived from input-filtering in the pre-processing stage is notably diminished. Consequently, for tasks of this nature, a uniform sampling methodology is employed. For the given video, the frame sampler samples n frames at a constant rate. These frames $\{F_0, F_1, ...F_n\}$ are fed into the Vision Language Model to generate the text descriptions $\{D_0, D_1, ...D_n\}$ with timestamps. In addition to descriptions of the depicted content, auxiliary metadata are also generated, which include summaries and preliminary analyses [17]. Temporal summaries are generated at fixed intervals or upon slide transitions using prompts that ensure preservation of global context and mitigate overemphasis on individual frames. Preliminary analysis explains the video's principal thematic focus, its predominant stylistic characteristics, and salient scene transitions. These auxiliary outputs augment frame-level descriptions by providing a macroscopic account of content progression alongside an initial interpretive framework of the video's subject matter and structure.

Audio also encompasses a considerable volume of information. For corresponding video frames, audio recognition is implemented using OpenAI's Whisper Model–a general-purpose speech recognition model that supports automatic multilingual speech recognition. Audio information is converted into text using this model and appended to the frame's image text descriptions and auxiliary texts.

3.2 Knowledge Database

The choice of source file formats and the granularity of retrieval units profoundly influence the quality of subsequent generative outputs. Markdown has emerged as a preferred format for large language models due to several advantages: (1) it imposes a clear hierarchical structure through standardized syntax for headings, lists, and other organizational elements; (2) it supports typographic emphases–such as bolding, italics, and code spans–that facilitate nuanced semantic distinctions; and (3) it remains inherently human-readable, thereby enabling seamless collaboration between automated systems and human reviewers. As such, the text descriptions generated in Sect. 3.1 are formatted as Markdown files. To build the knowledge database, the content of these documents is chunked and embedded, or encoded as vectors, for storage within a unified vector space.

Chunking. Chunking of documents before embedding ensures manageable input sizes to embedding models, preserves content, and reduces computational load, thus improving embedding quality and efficiency [6,18,22]. To chunk contextual documents, files are first loaded via format-appropriate parsers. During ingestion, each document is assigned a unique identifier, and basic metadata is recorded alongside the text chunk. To ensure that individual textual segments operate within the contextual window of the LLM while preserving meaningful semantic units and temporal information, documents are tokenized and partitioned into fixed-length chunks with an overlapping ratio. This approach guarantees that concepts spanning chunk boundaries are not lost.

Embedding. We utilized LangChain to generate embeddings for the contextual documents, enabling seamless integration of the LLM into the retrieval pipeline described in Sect. 3.3 [9]. Each text chunk is passed through the OpenAI embedding model, and the output dense vector captures the chunk's semantic content in a continuous space. The resulting vectors are stored in the chroma vector database.

3.3 RAG Agent

The retrieval pipeline takes inputs from the knowledge database and user query to conduct a similarity search and generate context-aware system responses.

Retrieval. Our system retrieves the top k chunks most relevant to the user query based on semantic similarity. Like the document chunks, queries undergo vectorization. Retrieval is achieved by computing the cosine similarity between the embedding of the query Q and the document chunk C.

$$\{\mathrm{C}_{i_1}, \ldots, \mathrm{C}_{i_k}\} = \arg\mathrm{top}_k \left\{ \mathrm{Cosine\_similarity}(\mathbf{Q}, \mathbf{C}_j) \mid \quad j = 1, \ldots, N \right\} \quad (2)$$

Generation. The original input query and the retrieved chunks are fed into LLM to generate the final system answer. In our system, we employ two distinct prompt types to guide the model's response generation. The first prompt type is designed to encourage open-ended reasoning and creative inference, allowing the model greater flexibility in generating explanations and predictions. The second prompt type, by contrast, places a stronger emphasis on factual grounding and concise answers, promoting a more balanced trade-off between creativity and accuracy.

4 Experimentation

To rigorously assess the effectiveness of our system in supporting multimodal reasoning, we conducted experiments using standardized video understanding benchmarks and systematic parameter analyses.

4.1 Supporting Datasets

The MMBench-Video benchmark [8] is designed to comprehensively evaluate the video understanding capabilities of LVLMs. It features long-form YouTube videos and uses open-ended questions to reflect real-world application scenarios. The dataset includes **609** video clips across 16 major categories such as news, science, and finance. Video durations range from 30 s to 6 min, with a total of 1998 question-answer(QA) pairs.

The QA setting in the MMBench-Video benchmark is structured around a three-level hierarchical capability taxonomy. At the highest level (Level 1), capabilities are divided into two domains: Perception and Reasoning. These are further subdivided into nine Level 2 capabilities: Coarse Perception (CP), Fine-grained Perception with Single-Instance (FP-S), Fine-grained Perception with Cross-Instance (FP-C), Hallucination (HL), Logic Reasoning (LR), Attribute Reasoning (AR), Relation Reasoning (RR), Common Sense Reasoning (CSR), and Temporal Reasoning (TR). Level 3 capabilities consist of 26 fine-grained categories, capturing a broad spectrum of cognitive skills relevant to video understanding.

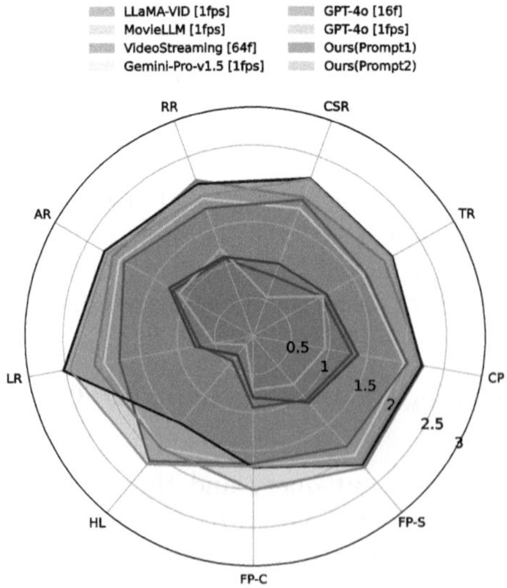

Fig. 3. Comparison of mainstream Video-LLMs, LVLMs, and our system on MMBench-Video. This graph illustrates performance in the Level 2 capabilities from the QA setting in the MMBench-Video benchmark. Those are Coarse Perception (CP), Fine-grained Perception with Single-Instance (FP-S), Fine-grained Perception with Cross-Instance (FP-C), Hallucination (HL), Logic Reasoning (LR), Attribute Reasoning (AR), Relation Reasoning (RR), Common Sense Reasoning (CSR), and Temporal Reasoning (TR).

4.2 Evaluation Procedures

In evaluating the performance of our video understanding system, we also assess its operational efficiency. This is investigated by systematically reducing the input frame rate to determine the necessity of high-frequency sampling. Concurrently, comprehensive ablation studies are conducted to elucidate the influence of other critical parameters, including the integration of audio information, the number of retrieved contextual chunks, and variations in question generation prompt design.

The experimental procedure commenced with the extraction of video frames at a rate of 1 frame per second (fps); corresponding textual descriptions, timestamped and chronologically ordered, were then recorded. An initial evaluation relevant to the benchmark was conducted using this 1 fps dataset.

Subsequently, the frame rate was effectively halved to 0.5 fps by removing alternate frames, and a second evaluation was performed. Finally, an Automatic Speech Recognition (ASR) module was employed to transcribe the video's audio content. This transcribed audio information was then integrated into the respective datasets for both the 1 fps and 0.5 fps conditions. Subsequently, as detailed in Sect. 3.1, documents were augmented with auxiliary contextual information to facilitate a further evaluation of the results. To reduce operational costs and latency, GPT-4.1 mini was chosen over GPT-4o, despite offering no additional improvements in model intelligence. Aligned with the evaluation methodology established in the MMBench-video, we employed GPT-4 to assess the discrepancy between the model's generated answer and ground truth answers.

5 Results

Table 1. Comparison of Video-LLMs on Perception and Reasoning Tasks

Model	Overall	Perception					Reasoning					
	Mean	**CP**	**FP-S**	**FP-C**	**HL**	**Mean**	**LR**	**AR**	**RR**	**CSR**	**TR**	**Mean**
Open-source Video-LLMs												
LLaMA-VID-[1fps]	1.08	1.30	1.09	0.93	0.42	0.94	0.71	1.21	1.08	0.83	1.04	1.02
MovieLLM-[1fps]	0.87	0.95	0.82	0.70	0.15	0.65	0.52	1.12	1.22	0.54	1.05	0.97
VideoStreaming-[64f+]	1.12	1.38	1.13	0.8	0.32	1.13	0.77	1.27	1.11	1.01	1.10	1.09
Open-source LVLMs												
InternVL2-26B-[16f]	1.41	1.56	1.48	1.23	0.52	1.42	1.06	1.61	1.45	1.38	1.23	1.35
VILA1.5-40B-[14f]	1.61	1.78	1.72	1.35	0.47	1.63	1.12	1.78	1.61	1.48	1.45	1.52
Proprietary LVLMs for Images												
Gemini-Pro-v1.5-[1fps]	1.94	1.99	2.04	1.70	1.90	1.98	1.98	2.02	1.92	1.78	1.63	1.86
GPT-4o-[1fps]	2.15	2.23	2.24	2.01	1.90	2.19	2.11	2.12	2.17	1.94	1.97	2.08
Ours												
Multi-RAG, 0.5fps, prompt1	**2.14**	2.20	2.14	1.71	1.48	**2.08**	**2.53**	**2.24**	2.12	**2.20**	**2.09**	**2.21**
Multi-RAG, 0.5fps, prompt2	**2.12**	2.17	2.17	1.71	2.18	**2.11**	2.44	2.19	1.96	2.19	2.07	**2.14**

We present the best configuration of our system in Table 1 and compare it with the strongest baseline, GPT-4o at 1 fps input. Notably, our system achieves comparable or even superior performance while operating at only half the input frame rate (0.5fps). With prompt1, our system attains an overall mean of 2.14, nearly matching GPT-4o, and even surpasses GPT-4o in reasoning mean (2.21 vs. 2.08). Similarly, with prompt2, the overall mean remains high at 2.12, and the system demonstrates a balanced improvement in both perception and reasoning, with particularly strong performance in perception hallucination when using prompt2. Figure 3 intuitively shows the capabilities of each model against our system in the different tasks.

5.1 Ablation Studies

Overall, these results highlight the efficiency and effectiveness of our proposed system. It matches or exceeds the state-of-the-art proprietary models on several tasks, particularly in reasoning, while demonstrating robust performance

Table 2. Results of Ablation Study.

Methods	Perception Mean	Reasoning Mean	Overall Mean
Multi-RAG	2.12	2.14	2.12
Multi-RAG w/o Audio	2.03	2.02	2.03
Multi-RAG w/o Auxiliary metadata	2.09	2.12	2.10
Multi-RAG w/o Audio and Auxiliary metadata	2.02	1.98	2.01

Table 3. Results of System with Different Retrieved Chunks.

Top-k	Methods	Perception Mean	Reasoning Mean	Overall Mean
Top-1	*Multi-RAG*	1.93	1.90	1.92
Top-3	*Multi-RAG*	2.03	2.06	2.04
Top-5	*Multi-RAG*	2.12	2.14	2.12
Top-7	*Multi-RAG*	2.08	2.15	2.10

even at reduced frame rates. This underscores the benefits of prompt design and multimodal fusion in achieving high performance across a variety of video understanding tasks.

We performed ablation studies to quantify the contributions of two key components–audio and textual auxiliary metadata–to the overall system performance, using prompt2 as the baseline configuration. As shown in Table 2, the results highlight the effectiveness of the evaluated components. Audio information contributes substantially to overall performance, while auxiliary text offers a smaller but still positive impact. Notably, the system exhibits the lowest performance when both components are removed, underscoring their complementary roles in the system.

5.2 Parameter Analysis

As shown in Table 3, increasing the number of retrieved chunks (top-k) generally leads to improved system performance. Both perception mean and reasoning mean metrics increase as top-k rises from 1 to 5, reaching optimal values at top-5. However, further increasing top-k to 7 yields only marginal changes, indicating diminishing returns. These results, also obtained with the prompt 2, suggest that retrieving a moderate number of relevant chunks (such as top-5) strikes a good balance between information coverage and retrieval efficiency.

6 Conclusion

As robots increasingly integrate into the fabric of human society, enabling them to learn continually from human interaction is both a technical imperative and a societal opportunity. Our Multi-RAG system demonstrates how multi-modal retrieval-augmented generation can serve as a scalable, adaptive foundation for robotic systems that support human cognition in dynamic, information-rich environments. By grounding perception, audio, and image in real-time, human-centered inputs, this work bridges the gap between static AI models and socially aware, learning-enabled agents.

Moving forward, we plan to enhance the system's user interface to further optimize human cognitive support, ensuring more intuitive and effective interactions for users in real-world settings. Additionally, we will explore adaptive retrieval strategies that dynamically allocate computational resources based on real-time context, aiming to minimize system overhead while maintaining robustness and responsiveness across complex and evolving scenarios.

We hope this work fosters deeper interdisciplinary discussions and inspires novel frameworks that push the frontier of continual robot learning, from memory augmentation to human-norm acquisition, ultimately empowering robots to become more capable, collaborative, and socially intelligent partners in our shared future.

Acknowledgments. This work has been partially supported by the U.S. Army DEVCOM Army Research Laboratory Cooperative Agreement No. W911NF2120211. We also thank Junsong Lin for providing valuable assistance with the figures in this paper.

References

1. Abootorabi, M.M., et al.: Ask in any modality: a comprehensive survey on multimodal retrieval-augmented generation. In: Findings of the Association for Computational Linguistics: ACL 2025 (2025)
2. Arnold, M., Goldschmitt, M., Rigotti, T.: Dealing with information overload: a comprehensive review. Front. Psychol. (2023)
3. Baethge, A., Rigotti, T.: Arbeitsunterbrechungen und multitasking. Bundesanstalt für Arbeitsschutz und Arbeitsmedizin, Dortmund (2010)
4. Basyal, L., Sanghvi, M.: Text summarization using large language models: a comparative study of MPT-7B-instruct, falcon-7B-instruct, and OpenAI Chat-GPT models. arXiv preprint arXiv:2310.10449 (2023)
5. Bush, V.: As we may think. The Atlantic Monthly **176**(1), 101–108 (1945)
6. Devlin, J., Chang, M.W., Lee, K., Toutanova, K.: BERT: pre-training of deep bidirectional transformers for language understanding. In: Association for Computational Linguistics (2019)
7. Ding, X., et al.: StreamMind: unlocking full frame rate streaming video dialogue through event-gated cognition (2025)
8. Fang, X., et al.: MMBench-Video: a long-form multi-shot benchmark for holistic video understanding (2024)
9. Gao, Y., et al.: Retrieval-augmented generation for large language models: a survey (2024)
10. Girard, J., Allison, M.: Information anxiety: fact, fable or fallacy. Electronic J. Knowl. Manag. (2008)

11. Goecks, V.G., Waytowich, N.: COA-GPT: generative pre-trained transformers for accelerated course of action development in military operations (2024)
12. Handler, A., Larsen, K.R., Hackathorn, R.: Large language models present new questions for decision support. Int. J. Info. Manag. (2024)
13. Huang, L., et al.: A survey on hallucination in large language models: Principles, taxonomy, challenges, and open questions. ACM Trans. Info. Syst. (2025)
14. Kallakurik, U., Humes, E., Jonna, R., Lin, X., Mohsenin, T.: Enabling on-device medical AI assistants via input-driven saliency adaptation (2025)
15. Lamming, M., et al.: The design of a human memory prosthesis. Computer J. **37**(3), 153–163 (1994)
16. Li, J., Selvaraju, R.R., Gotmare, A.D., Joty, S., Xiong, C., Hoi, S.: Align before fuse: vision and language representation learning with momentum distillation (2021)
17. Luo, Y., et al.: Video-RAG: visually-aligned retrieval-augmented long video comprehension (2024)
18. Mikolov, T., Chen, K., Corrado, G., Dean, J.: Efficient estimation of word representations in vector space (2013)
19. Mortaheb, M., Khojastepour, M.A.A., Chakradhar, S.T., Ulukus, S.: Re-ranking the context for multimodal retrieval augmented generation (2025)
20. Radford, A., et al.: Learning transferable visual models from natural language supervision (2021)
21. Tabarsi, B., Basarkar, A., Liu, X., Xu, D.D., Barnes, T.: MerryQuery: a trustworthy LLM-powered tool providing personalized support for educators and students. Proc. AAAI Conf. Artif. Intell> **39**(28), 29700–29702 (2025)
22. Vaswani, A., et al.: Attention is all you need. In: Guyon, I., Luxburg, U.V., Bengio, S., Wallach, H., Fergus, R., Vishwanathan, S., Garnett, R. (eds.) Advances in Neural Information Processing Systems, vol. 30 (2017)
23. Vemuri, S., Schmandt, C., Bender, W., Tellex, S., Lassey, B.: An audio-based personal memory aid. In: Davies, N., Mynatt, E.D., Siio, I. (eds.) UbiComp 2004: Ubiquitous Computing, pp. 400–417. Springer, Berlin Heidelberg, Berlin, Heidelberg (2004)
24. Yamano, K., Itou, K.: Browsing audio life-log data using acoustic and location information. In: Mobile Ubiquitous Computing, Systems, Services and Technologies, International Conference on, vol. 0, pp. 96–101 (2009)
25. Yang, X., Li, Y., Zhang, X., Chen, H., Cheng, W.: Exploring the limits of ChatGPT for query or aspect-based text summarization. arXiv preprint arXiv:2302.08081 (2023)
26. Zhao, W.X., et al.: A survey of large language models. arXiv preprint arXiv:2303.18223, vol. 1, pp. 2 (2023)
27. Zulfikar, W.D., Chan, S., Maes, P.: MEMORO: using large language models to realize a concise interface for real-time memory augmentation. In: Proceedings of the CHI Conference on Human Factors in Computing Systems, pp. 1–18. CHI '24, ACM (2024)

Hybrid Time Series Diffusion Model and Conformal Prediction for Incomplete Time Series

Ryu Shirakami[1,2(✉)], Shunsuke Hirose[1], and Koh Takeuchi[2]

[1] Deloitte Analytics R&D, Deloitte Touche Tohmatsu LLC, Tokyo 100-8360, Japan
{ryu.shirakami,shunsuke.hirose}@tohmatsu.co.jp
[2] Kyoto University, Kyoto 606-8501, Japan
takeuchi@i.kyoto-u.ac.jp

Abstract. Missing values in time series require both imputation and classification. Hybrid models that perform these tasks jointly offer a key advantage: they reveal how imputed values influence classification, enabling analysis of prediction reliability. However, existing hybrid models rely on variational autoencoders or generative adversarial networks, which often underperform compared to diffusion models (DMs) in an imputation task. Despite this potential, DM-based hybrid models for time series remain unexplored. Furthermore, while hybrid models produce stochastic outputs, existing conformal prediction (CP) methods fail to leverage this variance for constructing prediction sets. We propose a framework addressing both gaps. First, we introduce a Hybrid Time Series Diffusion model (HTSD) for joint classification and probabilistic imputation. Second, we propose Variance-aware Adaptive Prediction Sets (VAPS), a CP method that incorporates output variance into the nonconformity score, yielding tighter prediction sets for uncertain samples. Together, they enable uncertainty-aware classification where prediction set size directly reflects imputation instability. Experiments show HTSD outperforms existing hybrid models, while VAPS achieves smaller prediction sets than existing CP methods with guaranteed coverage.

Keywords: Time series · Missing values · Diffusion models · Conformal prediction

1 Introduction

Time series with missing values are prevalent in real-world applications such as healthcare and robotics [30,32]. This setting demands both imputation [5,8,38] to recover missing entries and classification [6,22,41] to support decision-making. A natural approach is hybrid modeling, which performs these tasks jointly. Beyond convenience, hybrid models offer a critical advantage. By producing both imputed values and class predictions from a shared model, they enable analyzing how imputed values influence classification. This capability is essential for understanding prediction reliability, especially when missingness is severe.

R. C.-W. Wong et al. (Eds.): PAKDD 2026, LNAI 16618, pp. 385–397, 2027.
https://doi.org/10.1007/978-981-92-1947-6_31

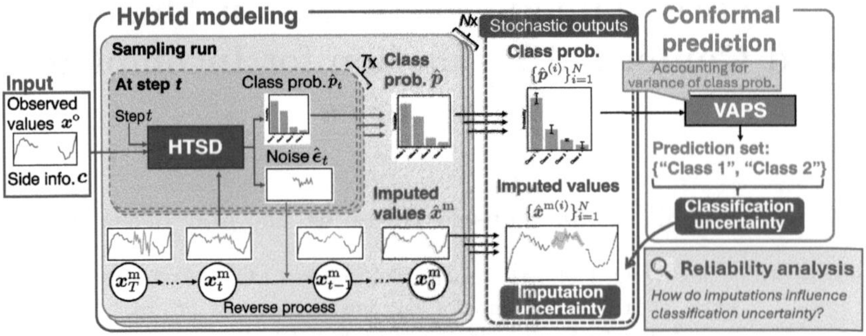

Fig. 1. Overview of our framework. HTSD performs joint classification and imputation by estimating class probabilities and noise at each step t in the reverse process. N sampling runs yield stochastic outputs. VAPS constructs prediction sets by incorporating the variance of class probabilities, producing smaller sets for confident predictions and larger sets for uncertain ones. This allows users to trace classification uncertainty back to imputation variability, enabling analysis of prediction reliability.

Existing hybrid models for time series typically rely on variational autoencoders (VAEs) [20,31] or generative adversarial networks (GANs) [25]. However, these approaches often yield suboptimal performance compared to task-specific methods. Diffusion models (DMs) have demonstrated superior performance for probabilistic imputation [34,36,39] and have been successfully extended to hybrid modeling in computer vision [13]. Yet, DM-based hybrid models for time series remain unexplored, leaving a large performance gap.

Hybrid models with probabilistic outputs naturally capture imputation uncertainty through output variance. However, translating this variance into reliable uncertainty quantification for classification requires additional machinery. Recently, conformal prediction (CP) [29] has been proposed to address this problem by constructing prediction sets with guaranteed coverage [12,19,28]. Recent CP methods improve efficiency through data-adaptive nonconformity scores [3,18]. Yet, these methods assume deterministic models and ignore the variance from stochastic outputs—a valuable signal indicating prediction difficulty.

In this paper, we propose a framework addressing both gaps (Fig. 1). First, we introduce a Hybrid Time Series Diffusion model (HTSD), which extends the energy-based formulation of EGC [13] to time series using a CSDI-based architecture [34]. HTSD performs joint classification and probabilistic imputation, producing stochastic outputs that capture imputation uncertainty. Second, we propose Variance-aware Adaptive Prediction Sets (VAPS), a CP method that incorporates output variance into the nonconformity score. By penalizing high-variance predictions, VAPS constructs tighter prediction sets while maintaining coverage guarantees. Together, HTSD and VAPS enable uncertainty-aware classification where prediction set size directly reflects imputation instability.

We conduct experiments on three real-world datasets with high missingness rates to validate our framework. The results show that: (1) HTSD outperforms existing hybrid models in both classification and imputation, and rivals or exceeds task-specific methods; (2) VAPS constructs tighter prediction sets than existing CP methods while maintaining the target coverage; and (3) our framework reveals how classification uncertainty relates to imputation instability.

2 Related Works

Research on incomplete time series has evolved along several paths. For probabilistic imputation, early works employed generative models based on GANs [23,24,40] or VAEs [11]. Recently, DMs [1,34,36,37,39] have shown superior performance. For classification, efforts have predominantly focused on deterministic models designed for irregularly sampled data [6,16,22,41]. A third line of research combines these tasks, proposing hybrid models for simultaneous imputation and classification. However, this approach has thus far been limited to VAEs [20,31] and GANs [25], leaving the potential of DMs unexplored. In computer vision, DMs have shown significant classification improvements [7,9,14,21]. A state-of-the-art DM-based hybrid model [13] also outperforms existing methods. However, these studies do not extend to time series tasks.

CP [2,29] constructs prediction sets with a guaranteed coverage level. To reduce the average set size while maintaining coverage, data-adaptive nonconformity scores have been proposed [3,18,28]. CP has also been adapted for probabilistic models, including Bayesian neural networks [10], VAEs [4,27] and DMs [17,33]. To our knowledge, no CP method has incorporated the variance of stochastic outputs into the nonconformity score.

3 Preliminaries

3.1 Problem Setting

We denote time series as $\boldsymbol{x} \in \mathbb{R}^{K \times L}$, where K is the number of channels and L is the sequence length. We define a binary mask matrix as $\boldsymbol{m} \in \{0,1\}^{K \times L}$, where $m_{k,l} = 1$ if $x_{k,l}$ is observed, or 0 otherwise. We denote the observed values as $\boldsymbol{x}^{\mathrm{o}} = \boldsymbol{m} \odot \boldsymbol{x}$ and the missing values as $\boldsymbol{x}^{\mathrm{m}} = (1 - \boldsymbol{m}) \odot \boldsymbol{x}$, where $\odot$ denotes the Hadamard product. Each time series is associated with a label $y \in \{1, \ldots, C\} = \mathcal{Y}$, where C is the number of classes. Probabilistic imputation aims to model the conditional distribution of the missing values $p(\boldsymbol{x}^{\mathrm{m}}|\boldsymbol{x}^{\mathrm{o}})$, given $\boldsymbol{x}^{\mathrm{o}}$. Classification aims to model the class probability $p(y|\boldsymbol{x}^{\mathrm{o}})$ given $\boldsymbol{x}^{\mathrm{o}}$. CP is a framework for constructing a prediction set $\mathcal{C}(\boldsymbol{x}^{\mathrm{o}}) \subseteq \mathcal{Y}$ for a user-specified miscoverage rate $\delta \in (0,1)$ and input $\boldsymbol{x}^{\mathrm{o}}$, ensuring the coverage guarantee $\Pr(y \in \mathcal{C}(\boldsymbol{x}^{\mathrm{o}})) \geq 1 - \delta$. The efficiency of a CP method is empirically measured by the average prediction set size, $\mathbb{E}[|\mathcal{C}(\boldsymbol{x}^{\mathrm{o}})|]$; smaller sizes indicate higher efficiency.

3.2 CSDI: DM for Time Series Imputation

CSDI [34] is a DM for time series imputation, adapted from DDPM [15]. It comprises a fixed diffusion process and learnable reverse process parameterized by a noise-estimation model ϵ_θ, with trainable parameters θ.

The diffusion process is defined as $q(\boldsymbol{x}_t^{\mathrm{m}}|\boldsymbol{x}_{t-1}^{\mathrm{m}}) = \mathcal{N}(\sqrt{1-\beta_t}\boldsymbol{x}_{t-1}^{\mathrm{m}}, \beta_t \boldsymbol{I})$, where $\boldsymbol{x}_t^{\mathrm{m}} \in \mathbb{R}^{K\times L}$ is the noisy version of $\boldsymbol{x}^{\mathrm{m}}$ at step $t \in \{0,\ldots,T\}$, $\boldsymbol{x}_0^{\mathrm{m}} = \boldsymbol{x}^{\mathrm{m}}$, and $\beta_t \in (0,1)$ is a predefined noise schedule. By defining $\bar{\alpha}_t = \prod_{i=1}^{t}(1-\beta_i)$, and $\bar{\beta}_t = 1-\bar{\alpha}_t$, $\boldsymbol{x}_t^{\mathrm{m}}$ can be sampled as $\boldsymbol{x}_t^{\mathrm{m}} = \sqrt{\bar{\alpha}_t}\boldsymbol{x}_0^{\mathrm{m}} + \sqrt{\bar{\beta}_t}\boldsymbol{\epsilon}_t$, where $\boldsymbol{\epsilon}_t \sim \mathcal{N}(\boldsymbol{0}, \boldsymbol{I})$. For a sufficiently large T, $\bar{\alpha}_T \approx 0$, $\boldsymbol{x}_T^{\mathrm{m}}$ follows a standard normal distribution $\mathcal{N}(\boldsymbol{0}, \boldsymbol{I})$. The reverse process aims to recover $\boldsymbol{x}_0^{\mathrm{m}}$ from $\boldsymbol{x}_T^{\mathrm{m}} \sim \mathcal{N}(\boldsymbol{0}, \boldsymbol{I})$. This process is denoted as $p_\theta(\boldsymbol{x}_{t-1}^{\mathrm{m}}|\boldsymbol{x}_t^{\mathrm{m}}, \boldsymbol{x}^{\mathrm{o}}) = \mathcal{N}(\hat{\boldsymbol{\mu}}, \tilde{\beta}_t \boldsymbol{I})$, where $\tilde{\beta}_t = \frac{\bar{\beta}_{t-1}}{\bar{\beta}_t}\beta_t$. We can derive $\hat{\boldsymbol{\mu}}$ from the noise $\hat{\boldsymbol{\epsilon}}_t$ estimated by the model ϵ_θ and the current data $\boldsymbol{x}_t^{\mathrm{m}}$.

To handle incomplete time series, CSDI introduced specialized architecture ϵ_θ with side information $\boldsymbol{c} = (\boldsymbol{e}_{\mathrm{time}}, \boldsymbol{e}_{\mathrm{chan}}, \boldsymbol{m})$, denoted as $\hat{\boldsymbol{\epsilon}}_t = \epsilon_\theta(\boldsymbol{x}^{\mathrm{o}}, \boldsymbol{x}_t^{\mathrm{m}}, \boldsymbol{e}_t, \boldsymbol{c})$. Here, $\boldsymbol{e}_{\mathrm{time}} \in \mathbb{R}^{L\times D_{\mathrm{time}}}$ is a temporal positional encoding [35], and $\boldsymbol{e}_{\mathrm{chan}} \in \mathbb{R}^{K\times D_{\mathrm{chan}}}$ is a trainable channel embedding. The diffusion step t is embedded as $\boldsymbol{e}_t \in \mathbb{R}^{D_{\mathrm{diff}}}$, via a positional encoding $\boldsymbol{e}_{1:T} \in \mathbb{R}^{T\times D_{\mathrm{diff}}}$. The model first projects the concatenated input $[\boldsymbol{x}_t^{\mathrm{m}}, \boldsymbol{x}^{\mathrm{o}}] \in \mathbb{R}^{K\times L\times 2}$ to $\hat{\boldsymbol{h}}_0 = \mathrm{SiLU}(\mathrm{Linear}([\boldsymbol{x}_t^{\mathrm{m}}, \boldsymbol{x}^{\mathrm{o}}])) \in \mathbb{R}^{K\times L\times D}$. Subsequently, it employs H residual layers (ResLayers), each composed of temporal and channel transformers to extract feature vectors. The i-th layer operation is $\hat{\boldsymbol{h}}_i', \hat{\boldsymbol{g}}_i = \mathrm{ResLayer}(\hat{\boldsymbol{h}}_{i-1}, \boldsymbol{e}_t, \boldsymbol{c})$ with a residual connection $\hat{\boldsymbol{h}}_i = (\hat{\boldsymbol{h}}_i' + \hat{\boldsymbol{h}}_{i-1})/\sqrt{2}$. Here, $\hat{\boldsymbol{h}}_i \in \mathbb{R}^{K\times L\times D}$ is the input to the next layer and $\hat{\boldsymbol{g}}_i \in \mathbb{R}^{K\times L\times D}$ is an extracted feature. The estimated noise is obtained as $\hat{\boldsymbol{\epsilon}}_t = \mathrm{Linear}(\mathrm{ReLU}(\mathrm{Linear}(\hat{\boldsymbol{g}}))) \in \mathbb{R}^{K\times L}$, where $\hat{\boldsymbol{g}} = \sum_{i=1}^{H}\hat{\boldsymbol{g}}_i$. The model ϵ_θ is trained to minimize the noise-estimation loss $\mathcal{L}_{\mathrm{data}}(\theta) = \mathbb{E}_{(\boldsymbol{x}_0^{\mathrm{m}}, \boldsymbol{x}^{\mathrm{o}}), t, \boldsymbol{\epsilon}_t}[\|\boldsymbol{\epsilon}_t - \epsilon_\theta(\boldsymbol{x}_t^{\mathrm{m}}, \boldsymbol{x}^{\mathrm{o}}, t, \boldsymbol{c})\|_2^2]$. This architecture serves as the backbone for HTSD, providing robust feature extraction capabilities for incomplete time series.

3.3 EGC: Hybrid DM for Images

EGC [13] proposes a unified framework for joint image generation and classification. Let $\boldsymbol{x} \in \mathcal{X}$ be an image, $y \in \mathcal{Y}$ be its label, and $\boldsymbol{x}_t$ be its noisy version. Unlike standard DMs that directly estimate noise, a model f_θ outputs logits $\hat{\boldsymbol{l}}_t = f_\theta(\boldsymbol{x}_t) \in \mathbb{R}^C$ from the noisy input $\boldsymbol{x}_t$ at each step t in the reverse process.

For classification, EGC computes class probabilities as $\hat{\boldsymbol{p}}_t = \mathrm{Softmax}(f_\theta(\boldsymbol{x}_t))$. The objective is to minimize the cross-entropy loss $\mathcal{L}_{\mathrm{cls}}(\theta) = \mathbb{E}_{(\boldsymbol{x},y),t,\boldsymbol{\epsilon}_t}[-\log \hat{p}_{t,y}]$.

The generation task is framed as score matching. The method defines an implicit energy-based model, yielding a model score derived from the logits: $\nabla_{\boldsymbol{x}_t} \log p_\theta(\boldsymbol{x}_t) = \nabla_{\boldsymbol{x}_t} \text{LSE}(\hat{\boldsymbol{l}}_t)$, where $\text{LSE}(\hat{\boldsymbol{l}}_t) = \log \sum_{c=1}^{C} \exp(\hat{l}_{t,c})$. The objective matches this model score to the true data score $\nabla_{\boldsymbol{x}_t} \log q(\boldsymbol{x}_t|\boldsymbol{x}_0) = -\boldsymbol{\epsilon}_t/\sqrt{\bar{\beta}_t}$. This alignment implicitly defines the estimated noise as $\hat{\boldsymbol{\epsilon}}_t = -\sqrt{\bar{\beta}_t}\nabla_{\boldsymbol{x}_t}\text{LSE}(\hat{\boldsymbol{l}}_t)$. The objective is to minimize the noise-estimation loss: $\mathcal{L}_{\text{data}}(\theta) = \mathbb{E}_{\boldsymbol{x},t,\boldsymbol{\epsilon}_t}[\|\boldsymbol{\epsilon}_t + \sqrt{\bar{\beta}_t}\nabla_{\boldsymbol{x}_t}\text{LSE}(f_\theta(\boldsymbol{x}_t))\|_2^2]$. The model f_θ is trained to minimize the joint objective $\mathcal{L}(\theta) = \mathcal{L}_{\text{data}}(\theta) + \gamma\mathcal{L}_{\text{cls}}(\theta)$, where the hyperparameter γ balances two tasks. Crucially, this architecture enables the extraction of both class probabilities and estimated noise, a mechanism we adapt for time series in HTSD.

3.4 Data-Adaptive CP for Efficient Prediction Sets

CP involves two main steps: calibration and prediction. During calibration, we compute nonconformity scores on a calibration set of size n; a larger score indicates a poorer fit. Subsequently, we determine the threshold as the $\lceil (n+1)(1-\delta) \rceil / n$-th quantile of these scores in a calibration set, given a user-specified miscoverage rate $\delta \in (0,1)$. During prediction, the prediction set includes all candidate labels with nonconformity scores below the threshold for a new test instance.

The design of nonconformity score is critical for the adaptivity. APS [28] proposed the nonconformity score as $\tau_{\text{APS}}(\hat{\boldsymbol{p}}, u, y) = \sum_{c=1}^{C} \hat{p}_c \mathbb{I}[\hat{p}_c \geq \hat{p}_y] - \hat{p}_y \cdot u$, where $\hat{\boldsymbol{p}} \in (0,1)^C$ denotes the sorted class probabilities, y is the true label, and $u \sim \text{Unif}(0,1)$ is a random variable. The randomization introduced by u ensures the coverage guarantee with a finite calibration set. Intuitively, APS yields smaller sets when the model is confident. RAPS [3] extends this by adding a regularization term: $\tau_{\text{reg}}(\hat{\boldsymbol{p}}, y) = \lambda_{\text{reg}}(\sum_{c=1}^{C} \mathbb{I}[\hat{p}_c \geq \hat{p}_y] - k_{\text{reg}})^+$, where λ_{reg} and k_{reg} are hyperparameters, and $(\cdot)^+$ denotes the positive part of the argument. This term penalizes large sets, enforcing tight sets for difficult samples. However, they lack mechanisms to leverage the predictive variance from stochastic models, potentially ignoring valuable information regarding prediction uncertainty.

4 Proposed Method

We propose a unified framework for joint classification and imputation with uncertainty quantification for incomplete time series. It integrates (1) **HTSD**, a hybrid diffusion model that extends the EGC [13] formulation to time series using a CSDI-based [34] backbone, and (2) **VAPS**, a data-adaptive CP method that regularizes prediction sets based on the variance of outputs from HTSD.

4.1 HTSD: Hybrid Time Series Diffusion Model

We illustrate the architecture of HTSD in Fig. 2. At each step t in the reverse process, the model f_θ outputs logits as $\hat{\boldsymbol{l}}_t = f_\theta(\boldsymbol{x}_t^{\mathrm{m}}, \boldsymbol{x}^{\mathrm{o}}, \boldsymbol{e}_t, \boldsymbol{c}) \in \mathbb{R}^C$, where θ denotes trainable parameters. Adopting the energy-based formulation of EGC, we simultaneously derive class probabilities and noise estimates from the logits as $\hat{\boldsymbol{p}}_t = \mathrm{Softmax}(\hat{\boldsymbol{l}}_t)$ and $\hat{\boldsymbol{\epsilon}}_t = -\sqrt{\bar{\beta}_t}\nabla_{\boldsymbol{x}_t^{\mathrm{m}}}\mathrm{LSE}(\hat{\boldsymbol{l}}_t)$, respectively.

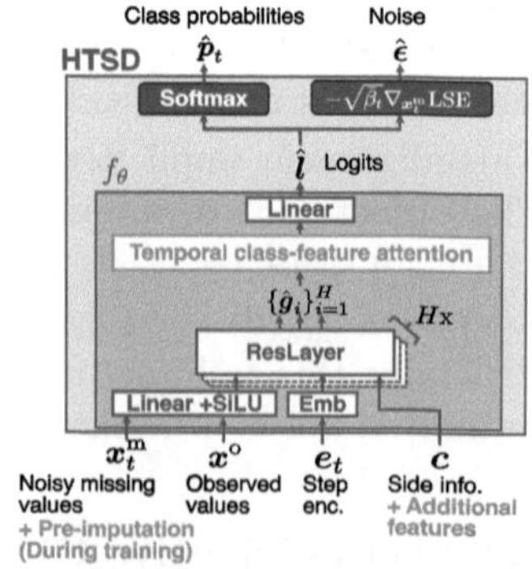

Fig. 2. Architecture of HTSD.

The model f_θ leverages the CSDI architecture tailored for incomplete time series. We retain the initial layers up to the H ResLayers to extract multivariate-temporal features $\{\hat{\boldsymbol{g}}_i\}_{i=1}^H$. However, unlike CSDI which maps features directly to noise, HTSD requires mapping them to class logits. To this end, we introduce a temporal class-feature attention mechanism. This module enables the model to adaptively aggregate class-specific information dispersed across the features. Furthermore, we incorporate additional side information and a pre-imputation strategy to effectively handle incomplete time series.

Temporal Class-Feature Attention. Standard pooling operations treat all channels and time steps equally, which is suboptimal for incomplete time series where informative signals are sparse. To address this, we introduce an attention mechanism that adaptively highlights class-specific information in multivariate-temporal feature maps. We concatenate and flatten the extracted features $\{\hat{\boldsymbol{g}}_i\}_{i=1}^H$ to $\hat{\boldsymbol{g}} \in \mathbb{R}^{KL \times HD}$ and perform attention using a trainable class embedding $\boldsymbol{e}_{\mathrm{class}} \in \mathbb{R}^{C \times D}$ as the query, and $\hat{\boldsymbol{g}}$ as the key and value:

$$\hat{\boldsymbol{l}}' = \mathrm{Softmax}\left(\frac{\boldsymbol{e}_{\mathrm{class}}(\hat{\boldsymbol{g}}\boldsymbol{W}_K)^\top}{\sqrt{D}}\right)\hat{\boldsymbol{g}}\boldsymbol{W}_V, \tag{1}$$

where $\boldsymbol{W}_K, \boldsymbol{W}_V \in \mathbb{R}^{HD \times D}$ are trainable parameters. This operation efficiently consolidates class-specific information dispersed across the multivariate-temporal feature map $\hat{\boldsymbol{g}}$. The logits are obtained as $\hat{\boldsymbol{l}} = \mathrm{Linear}(\hat{\boldsymbol{l}}')$.

Additional Side Information. To handle incomplete time series, we introduce two additional inputs for side information. (1) *Mask embedding.* Instead of a binary mask matrix, we employ a high-dimensional embedding $\boldsymbol{R} \in \mathbb{R}^{K \times L \times D_{\mathrm{mask}}}$ to learn rich representations of missingness in a data-driven manner. We define $\boldsymbol{R}$ for each element k, l as follows:

$$\boldsymbol{R}_{k,l} = \begin{cases} \boldsymbol{r}^{(0)} & \text{if } m_{k,l} = 0, \\ \boldsymbol{r}^{(1)} & \text{if } m_{k,l} = 1, \end{cases} \tag{2}$$

where $\boldsymbol{r}^{(0,1)} \in \mathbb{R}^{D_{\mathrm{mask}}}$ are trainable vectors. (2) *Consecutive missing steps matrix.* We introduce a matrix $\Delta \in \mathbb{R}^{K \times L}$ that tracks the duration of consecutive missing steps. We define Δ for each element k, l as follows:

$$\Delta_{k,l} = \begin{cases} \Delta_{k,l-1} + 1 & \text{if } l \geq 1 \text{ and } m_{k,l} = 0, \\ 0 & \text{otherwise.} \end{cases} \tag{3}$$

This explicitly encodes the temporal decay of channel-wise information reliability, aiding the model in estimating uncertainty accumulation. The final side information is constructed as $\boldsymbol{c} = (\boldsymbol{e}_{\text{time}}, \boldsymbol{e}_{\text{chan}}, \boldsymbol{R}, \Delta) \in \mathbb{R}^{K \times L \times (D_{\text{time}} + D_{\text{chan}} + D_{\text{mask}} + 1)}$.

Pre-imputation for Inherent Missingness. Training DMs on incomplete time series is challenging because the ground truth values for inherently missing entries are unavailable. While standard zero-filling is common [34,36,39], it introduces uninformative values that disrupt inherent multivariate and temporal correlations, potentially hindering the model from learning valid dependencies. To mitigate this, we employ a pre-imputation strategy during training to fill inherent missingness with more plausible values. We employ strict causal forward fill as a simple, non-parametric imputation method. Note that this operation can mitigate train-test distribution shifts since the reverse process generates plausible values for all missing entries during sampling.

Training and Sampling. We train the model f_θ by minimizing a joint objective of both tasks. The classification loss is a weighted cross-entropy loss, denoted as $\mathcal{L}_{\text{cls}}(\theta) = \mathbb{E}_{(\boldsymbol{x}_0^{\text{m}}, \boldsymbol{x}^{\text{o}}, y), t, \boldsymbol{\epsilon}_t}[-\sqrt{\bar{\alpha}_t} w_y \log \hat{p}_y]$. This incorporates two weighting schemes: The first, $\boldsymbol{w} = (w_1, \ldots, w_C)$, is scaling factors to correct for class imbalance. We set them to the inverse of the class frequencies. The second, $\sqrt{\bar{\alpha}_t}$, is a step-dependent scaling factor. This factor scales the classification loss to match the magnitude of the original signal $\boldsymbol{x}_0^{\text{m}}$ present in the noisy one $\boldsymbol{x}_t^{\text{m}}$. The imputation loss is the noise-estimation loss: $\mathcal{L}_{\text{data}}(\theta) = \mathbb{E}_{(\boldsymbol{x}_0^{\text{m}}, \boldsymbol{x}^{\text{o}}, y), t, \boldsymbol{\epsilon}_t}[\|\boldsymbol{\epsilon}_t - \hat{\boldsymbol{\epsilon}}_t\|_2^2]$. The training objective is a weighted sum of them, denoted as $\mathcal{L}(\theta) = \mathcal{L}_{\text{data}}(\theta) + \gamma \mathcal{L}_{\text{cls}}(\theta)$, where γ is a hyperparameter to balance two tasks.

During sampling, the T-step reverse process stochastically yields imputed values $\hat{\boldsymbol{x}}^{\text{m}} = \hat{\boldsymbol{x}}_0^{\text{m}}$ and a corresponding sequence of class probabilities $\{\hat{\boldsymbol{p}}_t\}_{t=1}^T$. To obtain the class probabilities $\hat{\boldsymbol{p}}$, we propose to aggregate them via a weighted sum as $\hat{\boldsymbol{p}} = \sum_{t=1}^T \eta_t \hat{\boldsymbol{p}}_t$, where the weights $\eta_t = \sqrt{\bar{\alpha}_t} / \sum_t \sqrt{\bar{\alpha}_t}$ align with the step-dependent scaling factors in the loss function. By N sampling runs, we can obtain N pairs of imputed values and class probabilities, denoted as $\{(\hat{\boldsymbol{x}}^{\text{m}(i)}, \hat{\boldsymbol{p}}^{(i)})\}_{i=1}^N$.

4.2 VAPS: Variance-Aware Adaptive Prediction Sets

VAPS is designed to leverage the stochastic outputs $\{\hat{\boldsymbol{p}}^{(i)}\}_{i=1}^N$ of HTSD to construct tighter prediction sets. It introduces a variance-aware regularization term that penalizes candidates exhibiting high classification uncertainty.

We define the mean probability as $\bar{\boldsymbol{p}} = \frac{1}{N} \sum_{i=1}^N \hat{\boldsymbol{p}}^{(i)} \in (0,1)^C$ and the element-wise variance as $\boldsymbol{v} \in \mathbb{R}^C$, where $v_c = \frac{1}{N} \sum_{i=1}^N (\hat{p}_c^{(i)} - \bar{p}_c)^2$. We apply temperature scaling to $\bar{\boldsymbol{p}}$ to improve the underlying probability calibration [3] and sort $\bar{\boldsymbol{p}}$ and $\boldsymbol{v}$ in descending order of $\bar{\boldsymbol{p}}$. Our method operates within the split CP framework [26], using a calibration set $\{(\bar{\boldsymbol{p}}_j, \boldsymbol{v}_j, y_j)\}_{j=1}^n$ and a test instance $(\bar{\boldsymbol{p}}_{n+1}, \boldsymbol{v}_{n+1}, y_{n+1})$. Assuming the original data $\{(\boldsymbol{x}_j^{\text{o}}, \boldsymbol{m}_j, y_j)\}_{j=1}^{n+1}$ are exchangeable, the derived tuples $\{(\bar{\boldsymbol{p}}_j, \boldsymbol{v}_j, y_j)\}_{j=1}^{n+1}$ are also exchangeable since the aggregation function is permutation-invariant.

To incorporate prediction uncertainty, we propose a regularization term based on the cumulative variance of the potential prediction set:

$$\tau_{\text{var}}(\bar{\boldsymbol{p}}, \boldsymbol{v}, y) = \zeta_{\text{reg}} \left(\sum_{c=1}^{C} v_c \mathbb{I}[\bar{p}_c \geq \bar{p}_y] - v_{\text{reg}} \right)^{+}, \tag{4}$$

where ζ_{reg} and v_{reg} are hyperparameters. The nonconformity score for VAPS is defined as $\tau_{\text{VAPS}}(\bar{\boldsymbol{p}}, \boldsymbol{v}, u, y) = \tau_{\text{APS}}(\bar{\boldsymbol{p}}, u, y) + \tau_{\text{reg}}(\bar{\boldsymbol{p}}, y) + \tau_{\text{var}}(\bar{\boldsymbol{p}}, \boldsymbol{v}, y)$. The regularization term $\tau_{\text{var}}(\bar{\boldsymbol{p}}, \boldsymbol{v}, y)$ improves efficiency by suppressing the excessive inclusion of uncertain classes with high predictive variance. This mechanism keeps prediction sets compact for difficult, high-variance samples.

In the calibration phase, the threshold $\hat{\tau}_{\text{thr}}$ is set as the $\lceil (n+1)(1-\delta) \rceil / n$-th quantile of the nonconformity scores on the calibration set. For a new test instance, the prediction set is constructed as $\mathcal{C}(\bar{\boldsymbol{p}}_{n+1}, \boldsymbol{v}_{n+1}, u_{n+1}, \hat{\tau}_{\text{thr}}) = \{y : \tau_{\text{VAPS}}(\bar{\boldsymbol{p}}_{n+1}, \boldsymbol{v}_{n+1}, u_{n+1}, y) \leq \hat{\tau}_{\text{thr}}\}$. The resulting prediction set satisfies the coverage guarantee, denoted by $\Pr(y_{n+1} \in \mathcal{C}(\bar{\boldsymbol{p}}_{n+1}, \boldsymbol{v}_{n+1}, u_{n+1}, \hat{\tau}_{\text{thr}})) \geq 1-\delta$, since Proposition 1 from [3] holds.

For hyperparameter tuning, we prepare a small tuning set separated from the calibration set. We set v_{reg} as (1-δ)-th quantile of the cumulative variance up to the true labels and ζ_{reg} as the value that minimizes the average prediction set size on the tuning set.

5 Experiments

We evaluate our proposed methods on real-world datasets. The key findings are: (1) HTSD outperforms existing hybrid models and shows superior or comparable performance to task specific models. (2) HTSD shows better performance trade-off than the baselines. (3) Each model component in HTSD contributes to performance. (4) VAPS consistently constructs tighter prediction sets than existing methods while maintaining coverage guarantee. (5) Our framework reveals how classification uncertainty relates to imputation variability.

Datasets. We used three real-world datasets: (1) *P12*[1], with vital signs from 4,000 patients (K=35, L=48, C=2); (2) *P19*[2], with vital signs from 38,803 patients (K=34, L=60, C=2); and (3) *MIME* [30], with 8,260 robot joint angle sequences (K=17, L=50, C=20). To create a high-missingness scenario, we introduced 50% additional random missingness to P12/P19 and 90% to MIME, yielding a 90% total missingness rate for all datasets. To access data scarcity, we also assessed a separate scenario on P12 with 90% additional missingness.

[1] https://physionet.org/content/challenge-2012/1.0.0/.
[2] https://physionet.org/content/challenge-2019/1.0.0/.

Baselines. We compared HTSD against state-of-the-art hybrid models, as well as leading task specific methods. (1) Hybrid models: mTAND_H [31] (VAE) and SSGAN [25] (GAN). (2) Classification: SeFT [16], RD [41], and PAI [22] (PAI1 with GRU, PAI2 with Transformer). (3) Probabilistic imputation: CSDI [34] and mTAND_I. (4) Two-step method: A Transformer-based classifier trained on CSDI-imputed data. We compared VAPS against existing data-adaptive CP methods: APS [28], RAPS [3], and SAPS [18].

Evaluation Setups. We evaluated classification performance using the area under the ROC curve (AUC) and imputation performance using root mean squared error (RMSE) and continuous ranked probability score (CRPS). For probabilistic models, the metrics were calculated based on the average of N=100 generated samples. For imputation and classification, we randomly split each dataset into five folds and repeated the experiment five times, using one fold for testing in each run. We report average results over five runs. For CP methods, we assessed performance by empirical coverage (Cvg.) and average prediction set size (Size) for P12 and MIME with miscoverage rates of $\delta \in \{0.1, 0.05\}$. To ensure a stable comparison, we employed a fixed training/calibration/test split and report average results over five runs with different random seeds.

Hyperparameters. For HTSD, we set D=64, D_{time}=128, D_{chan}=16, D_{mask}=16, D_{diff}=128, and H=4. We set the trade-off hyperparameter γ to 0.01, 0.005, and 0.001 for P12, P19, and MIME, respectively. We trained the model for 200 epochs using the Adam optimizer with a batch size of 32 and learning rate of 0.001. For the hyperparameters in the diffusion process, we follow [34]. For VAPS, we set hyperparameters as shown in Table 1.

Table 1. Hyperparameter settings for VAPS.

	ζ_{reg}	υ_{reg}
$\text{MIME}_{(\delta=0.1)}$	0.1	0.037
$\text{MIME}_{(\delta=0.05)}$	0.1	0.078
$\text{P12}_{(\delta=0.1)}$	0.1	0.015
$\text{P12}_{(\delta=0.05)}$	0.01	0.018

Table 2. Results on P12, P19, and MIME. Bold letters and underlined letters represent the best and the second-best performance, respectively. A dash means the value is not available. For AUC, higher is better. For RMSE and CRPS, lower is better.

	P12 (50%)			P19			MIME			P12 (90%)		
	AUC	RMSE	CRPS	AUC	RMSE	CRPS	AUC	RMSE	CRPS	AUC	RMSE	CRPS
HTSD	**0.826**	**0.656**	**0.330**	0.847	0.618	0.362	**0.957**	0.289	0.029	**0.735**	0.797	**0.520**
mTAND_H	0.795	0.740	0.622	0.840	0.637	0.542	0.901	0.270	0.083	0.709	0.812	0.730
SSGAN	0.807	0.770	0.654	0.836	0.711	0.630	0.533	0.489	0.133	0.683	0.875	0.875
SeFT	0.695	-	-	0.812	-	-	0.617	-	-	0.679	-	-
RD	0.772	-	-	0.829	-	-	0.787	-	-	0.706	-	-
PAI1	0.798	-	-	**0.863**	-	-	0.747	-	-	0.729	-	-
PAI2	0.789	-	-	0.807	-	-	0.561	-	-	0.706	-	-
CSDI	-	0.668	**0.330**	-	**0.581**	**0.355**	-	**0.164**	**0.025**	-	0.834	0.522
mTAND_I	-	0.681	0.543	-	0.632	0.517	-	0.228	0.064	-	**0.792**	0.653
Two-step	0.592	-	-	0.696	-	-	0.617	-	-	0.582	-	-

Main Results. Table 2 presents the imputation and classification performance. HTSD consistently outperformed VAE- and GAN-based hybrid models, mTAND_H and SSGAN, and demonstrated superior or comparable performance to the specialized models. This suggests the superior time series modeling capability of DMs is beneficial for achieving high performance in hybrid settings. Two-step method significantly underperforms HTSD, which indicates that high-quality imputation by DM does not necessarily guarantee good classification performance. This result highlights the effectiveness of our unified hybrid modeling approach.

Table 3. Ablation study results.

	AUC	RMSE	CRPS
HTSD	**0.826**	0.656	**0.330**
HTSD_Avg	0.711	0.760	0.368
HTSD_Lin	0.786	0.716	0.455
$\text{HTSD}_\text{-ME}$	0.811	0.685	0.344
$\text{HTSD}_{\text{-}\Delta}$	0.799	0.791	0.397
HTSD_Zero	0.761	**0.632**	0.337

Ablation Study. We conducted an ablation study on P12 to assess the contribution of each component. The variants include: HTSD_Lin/HTSD_Avg, which replace the attention module with linear projection and average pooling, respectively; $\text{HTSD}_\text{-ME}$, which replaces the mask embedding with a binary matrix; $\text{HTSD}_{\text{-}\Delta}$, which excludes Δ; and HTSD_Zero, which zero-fills inherent missingness. Table 3 shows the results. The inferior results of HTSD_Lin and HTSD_Avg confirms the contribution of the attention module. Adaptive aggregation via attention appears crucial for strong hybrid model performance. The performance drop of $\text{HTSD}_\text{-ME}$ and $\text{HTSD}_{\text{-}\Delta}$ underscores the effectiveness of the additional side information. Excluding Δ impairs the identification of accumulated uncertainty, degrading the performance. The reduced classification performance of HTSD_Zero highlights the importance of pre-imputation to learn valid temporal dependencies.

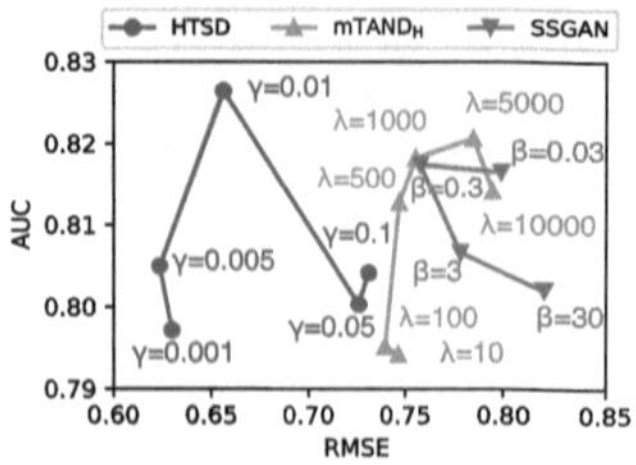

Fig. 3. Performance trade-off.

Hybrid Model Trade-Off. We evaluated the trade-off between two tasks for HTSD, mTAND_H, and SSGAN on P12. We varied the hyperparameters that balance the two tasks in the loss function: γ for HTSD, γ_m for mTAND_H, and γ_S for SSGAN. In all cases, a larger value represents a high weight on classification. Figure 3 plots the AUC-RMSE curve. The curve for HTSD consistently lies closer to the top-left corner compared to those of mTAND_H and SSGAN, highlighting its superior ability to balance the two tasks. This suggests that the higher expressive power of DMs contributes to a better hybrid model trade-off.

Table 4. Comparison of Cvg. and Size. The values in parentheses represent δ.

	$\text{MIME}_{(0.1)}$		$\text{MIME}_{(0.05)}$		$\text{P12}_{(0.1)}$		$\text{P12}_{(0.05)}$	
	Cvg.	Size	Cvg.	Size	Cvg.	Size	Cvg.	Size
APS	0.89	2.46	0.94	3.75	0.90	1.42	0.95	1.65
RAPS	0.89	2.36	0.94	3.61	0.90	1.42	0.95	1.66
SAPS	0.90	2.48	0.94	3.67	0.92	1.42	0.96	**1.57**
VAPS	0.89	**2.26**	0.94	**3.48**	0.90	**1.39**	0.94	1.59

Efficiency of VAPS. Table 4 shows Cvg. and Size for MIME and P12, using outputs from HTSD. Across all settings, VAPS achieved smaller prediction set sizes than the baselines while satisfying the target coverage guarantee. This efficiency gain empirically validates our hypothesis; the variance of HTSD outputs serves as a critical signal for filtering out uncertain classes, allowing VAPS to tighten prediction sets while maintaining the coverage. The slight fluctuations of Cvg. are attributed to the effect of the finite test set.

Table 5. Impact of ζ_{reg} on Size.

Cum. Var.	ζ_{reg}=0.01	ζ_{reg}=0.1	ζ_{reg}=0.5	ζ_{reg}=1.0
< 0.01	1.57	1.66	4.14	14.6
0.01 − 0.1	4.24	4.29	5.65	10.5
0.1 <	5.55	5.03	3.95	3.25

Table 5 analyzes the impact of the regularization weight ζ_{reg} on Size in $\text{MIME}_{(0.05)}$, stratified by the cumulative variance up to the true label (Cum. Var.). Higher Cum. Var. indicates greater classification difficulty. The results show that larger ζ_{reg} constrains prediction set expansion for difficult samples. However, excessively large values degrade efficiency for easy ones, compromising the adaptivity. This trade-off arises because excessive penalization causes coverage violations for difficult samples; preserving the target coverage requires compensation via overly conservative sets for easy ones. These findings indicate that VAPS maintains robustness across moderate ζ_{reg} values, whereas excessively large values should be avoided to preserve the efficiency and adaptivity.

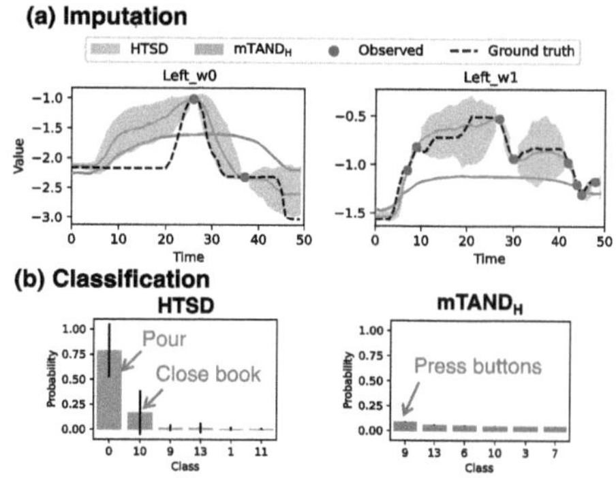

Fig. 4. Output comparison of HTSD and mTAND_{H} on MIME.

Case Study. Figure 4 illustrates the capability of our framework on a MIME sample. HTSD generates accurate imputations and correctly identifies the label "Pour", whereas mTAND_{H} fails. VAPS outputs a set {"Pour", "Close book"} with δ=0.1, reflecting the underlying ambiguity. Our framework allows us to contextualize this classification uncertainty within the corresponding imputation results. HTSD generates imputations corresponding to the motion patterns of "Close book" for "Left_w0" (timesteps 10–20) with high predictive variance, while generating low-variance imputations consistent with "Pour" for "Left_w1" (around timestep 30). This implies that the hesitation of the model between these two classes corresponds to the imputation instability in specific channels. This ability to associate classification uncertainty with imputation variability enables users to analyze prediction reliability.

6 Conclusion

We introduced a novel framework for joint classification and imputation of incomplete time series with uncertainty quantification. Experiments showed the effectiveness of our framework; HTSD outperforms existing hybrid models, while VAPS achieves superior efficiency compared to current CP methods.

Acknowledgments. K.T. is supported by JST FOREST Program Grant Number JPMJFR232S.

References

1. Alcaraz, J.L., Strodthoff, N.: Diffusion-based time series imputation and forecasting with structured state space models. Trans. Mach. Learn. Res. (2022)
2. Angelopoulos, A.N., Bates, S.: A gentle introduction to conformal prediction and distribution-free uncertainty quantification (2022)
3. Angelopoulos, A.N., Bates, S., Jordan, M., Malik, J.: Uncertainty sets for image classifiers using conformal prediction. In: ICLR (2021)
4. Cai, F., Li, J., Koutsoukos, X.: Detecting adversarial examples in learning-enabled cyber-physical systems using variational autoencoder for regression. In: 2020 IEEE Security and Privacy Workshops (2020)
5. Cao, W., Wang, D., Li, J., Zhou, H., Li, L., Li, Y.: BRITS: bidirectional recurrent imputation for time series. In: NeurIPS (2018)
6. Che, Z., Purushotham, S., Cho, K., Sontag, D., Liu, Y.: Recurrent neural networks for multivariate time series with missing values. Sci. Rep. **8**(6085) (2018)
7. Chen, H., et al.: Robust classification via a single diffusion model. In: ICML (2024)
8. Cini, A., Marisca, I., Alippi, C.: Filling the g_ap_s: Multivariate time series imputation by graph neural networks. In: ICLR (2022)
9. Clark, K., Jaini, P.: Text-to-image diffusion models are zero shot classifiers. In: NeurIPS (2023)
10. Fong, E., Holmes, C.C.: Conformal Bayesian computation. In: NeurIPS (2021)
11. Fortuin, V., Baranchuk, D.: GP-VAE: deep probabilistic multivariate time series imputation. In: AISTATS (2020)
12. Gao, R., Liu, W.: Model uncertainty quantification by conformal prediction in continual learning. In: ICML (2025)
13. Guo, Q., Ma, C., Jiang, Y., Yuan, Z., Yu, Y., Luo, P.: EGC: image generation and classification via a diffusion energy-based model. In: ICCV (2023)
14. Han, X., Zheng, H., Zhou, M.: Card: classification and regression diffusion models. In: NeurIPS (2022)
15. Ho, J., Jain, A., Abbeel, P.: Denoising diffusion probabilistic models. In: NeurIPS (2020)
16. Horn, M., Moor, M., Bock, C., Rieck, B., Borgwardt, K.: Set functions for time series. In: ICML (2020)
17. Hu, P., et al.: From uncertain to safe: conformal adaptation of diffusion models for safe PDE control. In: ICML (2025)
18. Huang, J., Xi, H., Zhang, L., Yao, H., Qiu, Y., Wei, H.: Conformal prediction for deep classifier via label ranking. In: ICML (2024)
19. Karimi, H., Samavi, R.: Quantifying deep learning model uncertainty in conformal prediction. In: SuSS-23 (2023)
20. Kim, S., Kim, H., Yun, E., Lee, H., Lee, J., Lee, J.: Probabilistic imputation for time-series classification with missing data. In: ICML (2023)

21. Li, A.C., Prabhudesai, M., Duggal, S., Brown, E., Pathak, D.: Your diffusion model is secretly a zero-shot classifier. In: ICCV (2023)
22. Liao, W., et al.: Learnable prompt as pseudo-imputation: rethinking the necessity of traditional EHR data imputation in downstream clinical prediction. In: KDD (2025)
23. Luo, Y., Cai, X., Zhang, Y., Xu, J., Yuan, X.: Multivariate time series imputation with generative adversarial networks. In: NeurIPS (2018)
24. Luo, Y., Zhang, Y., Cai, X., Yuan, X.: E2GAN: end-to-end generative adversarial network for multivariate time series imputation. In: IJCAI (2019)
25. Miao, X., Wu, Y., Wang, J., Gao, Y., Mao, X., Yin, J.: Generative semi-supervised learning for multivariate time series imputation. In: AAAI (2021)
26. Papadopoulos, H., Proedrou, K., Vovk, V., Gammerman, A.: Inductive confidence machines for regression. In: ECML (2002)
27. Ramakrishna, S., Rahiminasab, Z., Karsai, G., Easwaran, A., Dubey, A.: Efficient out-of-distribution detection using latent space of β-vae for cyber-physical systems. ACM Trans. Cyber-Phys. Syst. (2022)
28. Romano, Y., Sesia, M., Candes, E.: Classification with valid and adaptive coverage. In: NeurIPS (2020)
29. Shafer, G., Vovk, V.: A tutorial on conformal prediction. J. Mach. Learn. Res. **9**, 371–421 (2008)
30. Sharma, P., Mohan, L., Pinto, L., Gupta, A.: Multiple interactions made easy (MIME): large scale demonstrations data for imitation. In: CoRL (2018)
31. Shukla, S.N., Marlin, B.: Multi-time attention networks for irregularly sampled time series. In: ICLR (2021)
32. Silva, I., Moody, G., Scott, D.J., Celi, L.A., Mark, R.G.: Predicting in-hospital mortality of ICU patients: the Physionet/computing in cardiology challenge 2012. Comput. Cardiol. (2012)
33. Sun, J., Jiang, Y., Qiu, J., Nobel, P., Kochenderfer, M.J., Schwager, M.: Conformal prediction for uncertainty-aware planning with diffusion dynamics model. In: NeurIPS (2023)
34. Tashiro, Y., Song, J., Song, Y., Ermon, S.: CSDI: conditional score-based diffusion models for probabilistic time series imputation. In: NeurIPS (2021)
35. Vaswani, A., et al.: Attention is all you need. In: NeurIPS (2017)
36. Wang, X., et al.: An observed value consistent diffusion model for imputing missing values in multivariate time series. In: KDD (2023)
37. Xu, J., Lyu, F., Yuen, P.C.: Density-aware temporal attentive step-wise diffusion model for medical time series imputation. In: CIKM (2023)
38. Yalavarthi, V.K., et al.: GraFITi: graphs for forecasting irregularly sampled time series. In: AAAI (2024)
39. Yan, T., Gong, H., Yongping, H., Zhan, Y., Xia, Y.: Probabilistic time series modeling with decomposable denoising diffusion model. In: ICML (2024)
40. Yoon, J., Jordon, J., van der Schaar, M.: GAIN: missing data imputation using generative adversarial nets. In: ICML (2018)
41. Zhang, X., Zeman, M., Tsiligkaridis, T., Zitnik, M.: Graph-guided network for irregularly sampled multivariate time series. In: ICLR (2022)

nCLEAR: Nonlinear Coupled Latent Embedding for Cross-Sectional Asset Returns

Bhaskar Goswami(✉), Ajim Uddin, and Dantong Yu

New Jersey Institute of Technology, Newark, NJ, USA
{bg362,ajim.uddin,dantong.yu}@njit.edu

Abstract. One of the central challenges in asset pricing is the curse of dimensionality, driven by the hundreds of documented factors that may explain cross-sectional variation in asset returns. This paper introduces a nonlinear latent factor framework that extracts a small set of economically meaningful factors from high-dimensional data. The model integrates firm characteristics and portfolio returns through an attention-enhanced, coupled matrix factorization architecture with shared latent embeddings, allowing it to capture complex, nonlinear interactions in a unified structure. To preserve economic interpretability, we impose factor orthogonality and align the first factor with the market. Empirically, the model consistently outperforms strong deep learning benchmarks in portfolio reconstruction. The learned latent factors provide a compact and interpretable representation of evolving market structure and are not subsumed by standard factor models. Ablation analyses show that the performance gains are mainly driven by the nonlinear factorization and attention components, which effectively exploit the joint structure of characteristics and returns.

Keywords: Asset Pricing · Machine Learning · Embedding · Latent Factors · Matrix Reconstruction · Coupled Matrix Factorization · Dimensionality Reduction

1 Introduction

Traditionally, cross-sectional variation in asset returns is modeled using factor structures such as the Capital Asset Pricing Model (CAPM) and the Fama–French Five-Factor model [6], which rely on firm characteristics and macroeconomic variables (e.g., market, value, size, momentum, liquidity). Empirical studies identified thousands of such factors with significant explanatory power for cross-sectional returns [2], creating a severe curse of dimensionality. As the number of factors grows, the number of required long-short portfolios increases while the assets per portfolio shrink, making portfolio construction less feasible and more noise-prone. In this setting, identifying a parsimonious set of predictors that captures the underlying return structure is critical, and dimensionality reduction methods that estimate latent factors have become central to modern asset pricing [8,9].

R. C.-W. Wong et al. (Eds.): PAKDD 2026, LNAI 16618, pp. 398–410, 2027.
https://doi.org/10.1007/978-981-92-1947-6_32

Existing dimensionality reduction approaches largely build on penalized linear models, with Principal Component Regression (PCR) and Partial Least Squares (PLS) remaining the workhorses. While effective at extracting latent factors from large sets of firm characteristics, these methods are essentially static and struggle to model evolving, conditional factor structures. Extensions such as Scaled-PCA [11] and Supervised-PCA [10] improve signal extraction by weighting or filtering predictors before applying PCA, but they still treat predictors in a low-dimensional setting and ignore temporal dependence. The Instrumented PCA (IPCA) framework of [12] represents an important advancement by allowing time variation in factor loadings. Yet, asset pricing data exhibit more complex dependence structures: correlations exist not only across factors and over time, but also across assets due to market-wide linkages and shared exposures. Linear models—by construction—struggle to capture these multi-dimensional nonlinear relationships simultaneously.

To address these limitations, we propose the Nonlinear Coupled Latent Embedding for Cross-Sectional Asset Returns (nCLEAR), a framework that flexibly models nonlinear, temporal, and cross-sectional dependencies in high-dimensional financial data. The architecture of nCLEAR comprises three core components: an embedding learning module, a nonlinear transformation module, and a reconstruction module. The embedding learning module jointly factorizes the firm-characteristics and portfolio-return matrices to extract low-dimensional latent representations that encapsulate the underlying structure of both data sources. The nonlinear transformation module integrates spatial attention mechanisms and recurrent neural networks (RNNs) to capture the complex cross-sectional (spatial) and temporal dependencies among latent factors. Finally, the reconstruction module combines the learned temporal and firm-specific latent factors to simultaneously reconstruct both the characteristic and return matrices.

In addition to these core modules, the proposed model integrates explicit economic constraints to enhance both the interpretability and practical relevance of the learned latent factors. First, we impose an orthogonality constraint on the latent factor embeddings to ensure that each factor captures distinct and non-overlapping sources of variation in asset returns. This design mitigates redundancy and aligns with the theoretical underpinnings of classical factor models. Second, drawing inspiration from the central role of systematic risk factors in traditional frameworks such as the CAPM and PCA-based factor analysis, we explicitly incorporate market structure alignment into the model. Specifically, we introduce a market instrumentation penalty that penalizes deviations between the first latent factor and the observed market return, thereby encouraging the model to anchor its leading latent dimension to pervasive market-wide dynamics. Together, these constraints not only reinforce the model's alignment with financial theory but also ensure that the resulting latent factors remain interpretable and economically meaningful, a property often lacking in black-box machine learning approaches.

Our contributions are threefold. First, we contribute to the literature tackling the curse of dimensionality in large-scale asset pricing by showing that a small number of latent factors can accurately represent over 200 commonly used asset pricing predictors. Second, this study advances the literature on matrix and coupled matrix factorization by introducing a financial theorymotivated framework specifically designed to capture the intricate dependencies inherent in financial systems. By incorporating attention mechanisms and econometric constraints, the model learns latent factors that not only align with established asset pricing constructs such as the CAPM and APT, but also position the framework as a generalized extension of models like IPCA [12]. Finally, our findings demonstrate that nCLEAR improves both factor estimation and portfolio construction. In terms of reconstruction performance, nCLEAR reduces portfolio RMSE by approximately 7293%. In the cross-sectional pricing tests, several latent factors remain statistically significant even after controlling for the FamaFrench five factors [5], indicating that the model-derived factors capture information beyond known observable predictors.

The rest of the paper is structured as follows: Sect. 2 formalizes the problem and presents our proposed nCLEAR architecture. Section 3 describes the experimental setup, baselines, and evaluation metrics, and reports the main empirical results. Section 4 presents the ablation study and Sect. 5 concludes the paper and outlines future research direction.

2 Methodology

2.1 Problem Formulation

A core objective in empirical asset pricing is to estimate latent factors that explain the cross-section and temporal variation in asset returns. Let $R_{i,t+1}$ denote the excess return of asset i at time $t+1$. The standard linear factor model can be expressed as:

$$\mathbf{R}_{t+1} = \mathbf{B}_t \mathbf{F}_{t+1} + \eta_t, \tag{1}$$

where $R_t \in \mathbb{R}^N$ denotes the vector of returns for N assets, $F_{t+1} \in \mathbb{R}^K$ represents the K-dimensional vector of latent factors $B_t \in \mathbb{R}^{N \times K}$ is the time-varying loading matrix, and $\eta_t \in \mathbb{R}^N$ captures the residuals.

Traditional estimators, such as PCA, recover $\mathbf{B}_t$ and $\mathbf{F}_t$ by directly factorizing the return matrix $\mathbf{R}$ by solving:

$$\min_{\mathbf{B},\mathbf{F}} \|\mathbf{R} - \mathbf{B}\mathbf{F}^\top\|_F^2. \tag{2}$$

While computationally efficient, such linear methods rely on restrictive assumptions of linearity and weak temporal dependence, which limit their ability to capture the inherently nonlinear and dynamic interactions present in financial data.

To address these limitations, we reformulate latent factor estimation as a joint nonlinear learning problem using both the observable factor matrix and

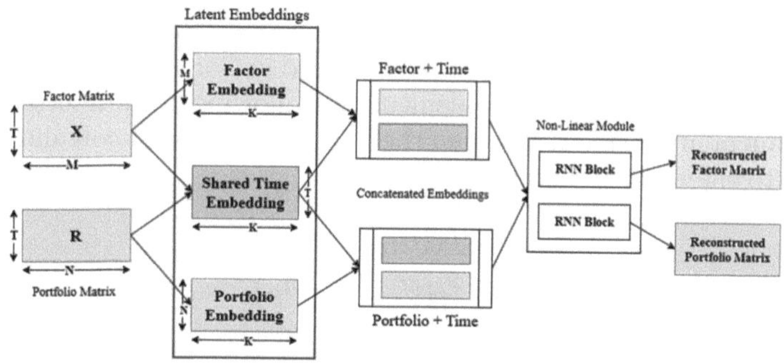

Fig. 1. nCLEAR architecture. Two temporally aligned matrices are used as input: the factor matrix $X \in \mathbb{R}^{T\times M}$ and the portfolio excess-return matrix $R \in \mathbb{R}^{T\times N}$. Both are mapped into factor-, portfolio-, and time-specific embeddings. These embeddings are then passed through nonlinear modules to reconstruct X and R.

the portfolio return matrix. Let $\mathbf{X} \in \mathbb{R}^{T\times P}$ denote the matrix of observable asset pricing factors and $\mathbf{R} \in \mathbb{R}^{T\times N}$ denote the matrix of assets excess returns, both observed over the same T time periods. We seek to learn shared latent representations that capture the underlying temporal and cross-sectional structure common to both matrices.

The proposed **N**on-linear **C**oupled **L**atent **E**mbedding for cross-sectional **A**sset **R**eturns (nCLEAR) learns these representations via a nonlinear coupled matrix factorization architecture equipped with spatio-temporal attention mechanisms. As shown in Fig. 1, nCLEAR jointly factorizes the factor matrix and the portfolio return matrix using three components: (i) an embedding learning module, (ii) a nonlinear transformation module, and (iii) a reconstruction module. Through this joint learning process, the shared latent embeddings $\mathbf{U}_t$ serve as time-varying latent factors $\mathbf{F}_t$, while their corresponding attention-weighted transformations represent dynamic loadings $\mathbf{B}_t$. This nonlinear framework generalizes the traditional linear decomposition:

$$\mathbf{R}_t = f_\theta(\mathbf{X}_t, \mathbf{U}_t) + \eta_t, \tag{3}$$

where $f_\theta(\cdot)$ is a neural function that captures nonlinear, temporal, and cross-sectional dependencies.

2.2 Embedding Learning Module

The embedding module learns low-dimensional representations for time, factors, and portfolios. Given X and R, nCLEAR maintains three trainable embedding matrices: $U \in \mathbb{R}^{T\times K}, V \in \mathbb{R}^{M\times K}, W \in \mathbb{R}^{N\times K}$ where K is the latent dimension. The temporal embedding U is shared across both the factor and portfolio matrices and captures common time-specific dynamics, while V and W encode factor-specific and portfolio-specific structures, respectively.

Instead of reconstructing X and R via a linear product $UV^\top$ or $UW^\top$, we follow the nonlinear aggregation method proposed in CoSTCo [13] and design the neural networks that essentially implement the following parameterized function on the domain of input space, and map the indices of the input cell and associated embedding to the corresponding element

$$\hat{X}_{t,m} = f_X(U_{t:}, V_{m:}; \theta_X), \tag{4}$$

$$\hat{R}_{t,n} = f_R(U_{t:}, W_{n:}; \theta_R), \tag{5}$$

for $1 \leq t \leq T$, $1 \leq m \leq M$, and $1 \leq n \leq N$, where $U_{t:}, V_{m:}, W_{n:} \in \mathbb{R}^K$ are the corresponding rows and θ_X, θ_R are the weights learned from nonlinear module. During training, the network forward-propagates to obtain $\hat{X}_{t,m}$ and $\hat{R}_{t,n}$ and back-propagates the reconstruction loss to update U, V, and W jointly.

2.3 Nonlinear Module

This module applies nonlinear transformations to the latent embeddings to effectively capture the inherent temporal and spatial dependencies in asset pricing data. It consists of two components: (i) a temporal LSTM over the sequence of time embeddings and (ii) spatial attention over factor and portfolio embeddings.

Temporal Dynamics via LSTM. The temporal latent factors $\{\mathbf{U}_t\}$ are passed through an LSTM network to capture temporal dependencies and nonlinear time-series structure:

$$\begin{aligned}
\mathbf{i}_t &= \sigma\left(\boldsymbol{\theta}_i \mathbf{U}_t + \boldsymbol{\theta}_i^{(h)} \mathbf{h}_{t-1} + \mathbf{b}_i\right) \\
\mathbf{f}_t &= \sigma\left(\boldsymbol{\theta}_f \mathbf{U}_t + \boldsymbol{\theta}_f^{(h)} \mathbf{h}_{t-1} + \mathbf{b}_f\right) \\
\mathbf{o}_t &= \sigma\left(\boldsymbol{\theta}_o \mathbf{U}_t + \boldsymbol{\theta}_o^{(h)} \mathbf{h}_{t-1} + \mathbf{b}_o\right) \\
\tilde{\mathbf{c}}_t &= \tanh\left(\boldsymbol{\theta}_c \mathbf{U}_t + \boldsymbol{\theta}_c^{(h)} \mathbf{h}_{t-1} + \mathbf{b}_c\right) \\
\mathbf{c}_t &= \mathbf{f}_t \odot \mathbf{c}_{t-1} + \mathbf{i}_t \odot \tilde{\mathbf{c}}_t \\
\mathbf{h}_t &= \mathbf{o}_t \odot \tanh(\mathbf{c}_t)
\end{aligned} \tag{6}$$

Here, $\mathbf{h}_t$ is the hidden representation of temporal dynamics at time t, and shared across the reconstruction of both X and R.

Spatial Attention. To model cross-sectional dependencies, we apply a spatial attention mechanism to the factor and portfolio embeddings. For portfolios, attention weights are defined as

$$\alpha_n = \frac{\exp\left(\phi(W_{n:})\right)}{\sum_{j=1}^{N} \exp\left(\phi(W_{j:})\right)}, \tag{7}$$

where $\phi(\cdot)$ is a scoring function and α_n measures the relevance of portfolio n. The aggregated portfolio representation is

$$W' = \sum_{n=1}^{N} \alpha_n W_{n:}. \tag{8}$$

An analogous attention operation is applied to the factor embeddings to obtain V'. These attention-weighted embeddings allow the model to capture co-movement, clustering, and asymmetric spillovers across portfolios and characteristics.

2.4 Reconstruction Module

The reconstruction module combines temporal and spatial information to recover the original matrices. At each time t, we construct short temporal windows that concatenate the LSTM state with the attention-based embeddings:

$$\mathcal{X}_t^{\text{port}} = \left[h_{t-11} \| W'; \ldots; h_t \| W' \right] \in \mathbb{R}^{12 \times 2d},$$
$$\mathcal{X}_t^{\text{fact}} = \left[h_{t-11} \| V'; \ldots; h_t \| V' \right] \in \mathbb{R}^{12 \times 2d},$$

where $\|$ denotes vector concatenation, and we use 12-step windows for both sides. The LSTM processes each sequence independently:

$$h_t^{\text{port}} = \text{LSTM}_{\text{port}}(\mathcal{X}_t^{\text{port}}),$$
$$h_t^{\text{fact}} = \text{LSTM}_{\text{fact}}(\mathcal{X}_t^{\text{fact}}).$$

Finally, the outputs are projected to reconstruct the portfolio returns and factor values:

$$\hat{\mathbf{R}}_t = \Theta_{\text{port}}\, h_t^{\text{port}} + \beta_{\text{port}}, \tag{9}$$
$$\hat{\mathbf{X}}_t = \Theta_{\text{fact}}\, h_t^{\text{fact}} + \beta_{\text{fact}}. \tag{10}$$

2.5 Loss Function and Economic Constraints

The model is trained to jointly reconstruct the portfolio return and factor matrices. The baseline reconstruction loss is:

$$\mathcal{L}_{\text{rec}} = \frac{1}{T} \sum_{t=1}^{T} \left(\left\| \mathbf{R}_t - \hat{\mathbf{R}}_t \right\|_2^2 + \lambda \left\| \mathbf{X}_t - \hat{\mathbf{X}}_t \right\|_2^2 \right), \tag{11}$$

where λ balances the portfolio and factor reconstruction terms.

To align the learned factors with the economic structure and improve interpretability, we impose two additional constraints on the temporal embeddings U. First, an orthogonality constraint on the shared temporal embeddings to ensure that embedding vectors are mutually orthogonal, as

$$\mathcal{L}_{\text{orth}} = \left\| U^\top U - I_K \right\|_F^2. \tag{12}$$

Second, the market instrumentation. Motivated by classical asset pricing theory, we anchor the first temporal factor to the market behavior. We treat the first column of U as a market-aligned factor and penalize deviations from M:

$$\mathcal{L}_{\text{market}} = \left\|U_{:,1} - M\right\|_2^2. \tag{13}$$

The remaining $K-1$ columns are free to learn additional systematic sources of variation orthogonal to the market.

Combining all components, the final training objective is

$$\mathcal{L} = \mathcal{L}_{\text{rec}} + \gamma_1 \mathcal{L}_{\text{orth}} + \gamma_2 \mathcal{L}_{\text{market}}, \tag{14}$$

where γ_1 and γ_2 control the strength of the orthogonality and market constraints, respectively.

3 Experimental Details and Results

In this section, we present the experimental results of our proposed model, in comparison with state-of-the-art benchmarks. Our evaluation, conducted on real-world financial data, is structured around three central research questions: (Q1) Does nCLEAR outperform existing methods in matrix reconstruction accuracy? (Q2) What is the impact of incorporating regularization and financial constraints on the quality of the learned latent embeddings? (Q3) How does the model perform on downstream tasks, especially for portfolio optimization and return prediction?

3.1 Experimental Details

For the nCLEAR model, we evaluate multiple architectural variants, model configurations, and hyperparameter settings. Model performance is evaluated across both low-data regimes (with 10–30% of data available for training and the rest being masked for reconstruction) and high-data regimes (50–80% training data and the rest being masked for reconstruction). Regarding hyperparameter selection, we consider learning rates of 1e-5, 5e-4, 1e-4, and 1e-3; training epochs of 500, 1,000, and 10,000; and batch sizes of 64, 128, and 256. The final results reported in the paper are obtained using a learning rate of 5e-4, 1,000 training epochs, and a batch size of 128. To prevent overfitting, we incorporate dropout regularization and apply early stopping.

We compare nCLEAR and its variants against several state-of-the-art models for matrix reconstruction and latent structure discovery. Channel-independent baselines include DLinear, which decomposes time series into trend and seasonal components using simple linear operations across channels [3], the standard Transformer that leverages self-attention to model temporal dependencies [17], Non-stationary Transformer (nTransformer), which introduces stationarization and de-stationary attention for non-stationary series [15], and PatchTST, which applies Transformer encoders to patched subsequences to capture long-range

Table 1. Test performance separated into low and high training data settings.

	10% Train		20% Train		30% Train	
Model	RMSE	MAE	RMSE	MAE	RMSE	MAE
DLinear	1.0030 ± 0.00	0.7536 ± 0.00	1.0030 ± 0.00	0.7536 ± 0.00	1.0020 ± 0.00	0.7530 ± 0.00
iTransformer	0.6360 ± 0.02	0.4807 ± 0.02	0.5427 ± 0.01	0.4009 ± 0.01	0.4875 ± 0.01	0.3566 ± 0.01
Transformer	0.9798 ± 0.01	0.7350 ± 0.01	0.9814 ± 0.04	0.7376 ± 0.02	0.9702 ± 0.02	0.7303 ± 0.01
PatchTST	0.6761 ± 0.03	0.5167 ± 0.02	0.5836 ± 0.01	0.4454 ± 0.01	0.5491 ± 0.01	0.4175 ± 0.02
Crossformer	0.5547 ± 0.17	0.4125 ± 0.14	0.4229 ± 0.11	0.3030 ± 0.09	0.4694 ± 0.24	0.3395 ± 0.19
NTransformer	0.8044 ± 0.03	0.6078 ± 0.02	0.6510 ± 0.01	0.4859 ± 0.01	0.5703 ± 0.01	0.4210 ± 0.01
nCLEAR	0.0396 ± 0.00	**0.0040** ± 0.00	0.0520 ± 0.00	**0.0074** ± 0.00	**0.0621** ± 0.00	**0.0109** ± 0.00
nCLEAR(MLP)	0.0534 ± 0.00	0.0054 ± 0.00	0.0704 ± 0.00	0.0099 ± 0.00	0.0837 ± 0.01	0.0144 ± 0.00
w/o Orthogonality Constraint	0.0525 ± 0.00	0.0053 ± 0.00	0.0660 ± 0.00	0.0092 ± 0.00	0.0794 ± 0.00	0.0135 ± 0.00
w/o MKT Constraint on Embedding	0.0503 ± 0.00	0.0050 ± 0.00	0.0682 ± 0.00	0.0096 ± 0.00	0.0818 ± 0.00	0.0142 ± 0.00
	50% Train		70% Train		80% Train	
DLinear	1.0028 ± 0.01	0.7536 ± 0.00	1.0050 ± 0.00	0.7549 ± 0.00	1.0070 ± 0.00	0.7575 ± 0.00
iTransformer	0.4511 ± 0.01	0.3273 ± 0.01	0.4424 ± 0.01	0.3212 ± 0.01	0.4298 ± 0.01	0.3117 ± 0.01
Transformer	0.7993 ± 0.09	0.6050 ± 0.07	0.7978 ± 0.09	0.5960 ± 0.07	0.8209 ± 0.14	0.6159 ± 0.10
PatchTST	0.5050 ± 0.03	0.3826 ± 0.03	0.4886 ± 0.01	0.3687 ± 0.01	0.4965 ± 0.03	0.3785 ± 0.03
Crossformer	0.3523 ± 0.04	0.2462 ± 0.03	0.3312 ± 0.02	0.2277 ± 0.02	0.3301 ± 0.03	0.2248 ± 0.01
NTransformer	0.5229 ± 0.03	0.3807 ± 0.02	0.4615 ± 0.02	0.3315 ± 0.02	0.4609 ± 0.02	0.3289 ± 0.01
nCLEAR	**0.0710** ± 0.00	**0.0161** ± 0.00	**0.0853** ± 0.00	**0.0226** ± 0.00	**0.0925** ± 0.00	**0.0265** ± 0.00
nCLEAR(MLP)	0.1137 ± 0.00	0.0245 ± 0.00	0.1253 ± 0.01	0.0331 ± 0.00	0.1357 ± 0.01	0.0379 ± 0.00
w/o Orthogonality Constraint	0.1007 ± 0.00	0.0222 ± 0.00	0.1217 ± 0.01	0.0322 ± 0.00	0.1251 ± 0.01	0.0348 ± 0.00
w/o MKT Constraint on Embedding	0.1039 ± 0.00	0.0234 ± 0.00	0.1216 ± 0.00	0.0324 ± 0.00	0.1327 ± 0.01	0.0377 ± 0.00

Note: Reported values are means ± standard deviations across five folds. Standard deviations are rounded to two decimal places for readability. Best-performing models are shown in bold.

dependencies [16]. We also include channel-dependent models such as Crossformer, which uses cross-variable and temporal attention in a hierarchical fashion [18], and iTransformer, which employs interaction-aware attention to capture nonlinear cross-channel interactions [14]. All models are implemented using the author-provided or publicly available implementations in TSlib[1] and STHD[2] [19].

3.2 Experimental Results

Q1: Matrix Reconstruction We begin by evaluating how well nCLEAR and its variants reconstruct the original portfolio return and factor matrices. For each traintest split, a fraction of matrix entries is randomly masked. The models then reconstruct the missing values using the positional indices of time, factor, and portfolio together with the nonlinear reconstruction module described in Sect. 2. We consider both low-data (10%-30% train) and high-data (50%-80% train) settings. For example, in the 80% train configuration, 20% of entries are randomly held out and predicted by the model from the learned embeddings.

We report RMSE and MAE for all models and settings, using 5-fold cross-validation and averaging metrics across folds. Table 1 summarizes the reconstruction performance of nCLEAR, its variations, and the benchmark models.

[1] https://github.com/thuml/Time-Series-Library.

[2] https://github.com/xinzzzhou/ScalableTransformer4HighDimensionMTSF.

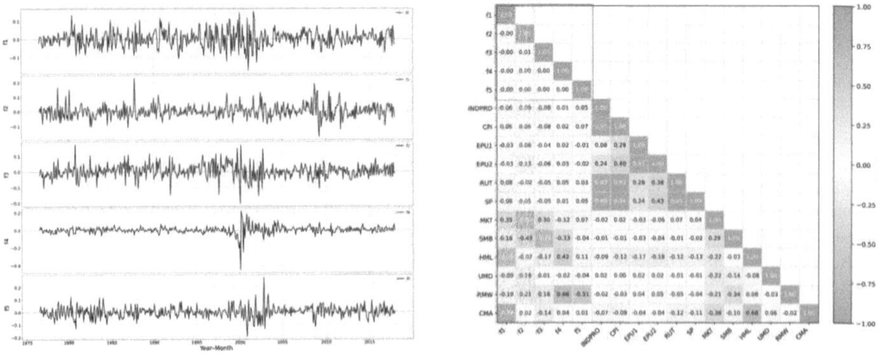

(a) Factor Plot (b) Correlation

Fig. 2. Latent temporal factors from **nCLEAR**. (a) The evolution of latent factors learned by the nCLEAR model over time. (b) Correlation matrix of nCLEAR latent factors (f1f5, red box) and benchmark asset-pricing and macro factors. (Color figure online)

Across all data regimes, nCLEAR and its variants achieve substantially lower reconstruction errors than the baselines, indicating that the learned embeddings provide a more true low-dimensional representation of the joint structure in characteristics and returns.

Q2: Factor Representation To assess the quality of the latent embedding, we examine the dynamic representations of the factors and test whether they are subsumed by existing asset-pricing and macroeconomic factors. Figure 2 summarizes the temporal embeddings learned by nCLEAR. Figure 2a plots the five latent temporal factors. Their distinct dynamics suggest that nCLEAR decomposes common time variation into economically meaningful components rather than fitting noise. Figure 2b reports the correlation matrix between these latent factors (red box) and standard asset-pricing factors—market excess return (MKT), size (SMB), value (HML), momentum (UMD), profitability (RMW), and investment (CMA)—along with macroeconomic variables such as industrial production (INDPRO), consumer price inflation (CPI), economic policy uncertainty indices (EPU1, EPU2), the Russell 2000 (RUT), and the S&P 500 (SP). The near-zero off-diagonal entries within the latent-factor block indicate approximate orthogonality, while the generally moderate correlations with benchmark factors suggest that nCLEAR captures information related to, but not redundant with, existing specifications.

Q3: Downstream Task: Return Prediction and Portfolio Optimization To assess the return-predictive content of the temporal embeddings, we treat them as candidate risk factors in a two-step Fama–MacBeth regression [7]. We estimate five model specifications: (i) latent factors only; and (ii)–(v) latent fac-

Table 2. Fama-MacBeth Average Risk Premia Estimates

	nCLEAR+LSTM					nCLEAR+MLP				
Factor	Latent Only	+ MktRf	+ FF3	+ FF4	+ FF5	Latent Only	+ MktRf	+ FF3	+ FF4	+ FF5
f1	−0.0073***	−0.0310***	−0.0125*	-0.0128*	−0.0022	+0.0062***	−0.0801***	−0.0813***	−0.0680***	−0.0606***
f2	−0.0145***	+0.0612***	+0.0576***	+0.0588***	+0.0573***	+0.0133***	−0.0408***	−0.0386***	−0.0348***	−0.0448***
f3	+0.0056***	−0.0230***	−0.0008	+0.0000	−0.0096	+0.0002	+0.0061*	+0.0005	+0.0015	+0.0120**
f4	−0.0041*	+0.0085***	+0.0045	+0.0047	−0.0088	−0.0071**	−0.0074**	+0.0036	+0.0020	+0.0206***
f5	−0.0112***	−0.0109***	−0.0120***	−0.0125***	−0.0019	+0.0062	−0.0075	−0.0006	−0.0008	+0.0169***
MktRf	—	+0.0796***	+0.0651***	+0.0657***	+0.0705***	—	+0.0928***	+0.0887***	+0.0787***	+0.0801***
SMB	—	—	+0.0117*	+0.0125**	+0.0077	—	—	+0.0082*	+0.0058	+0.0126***
HML	—	—	+0.0148***	+0.0150***	+0.0139***	—	—	+0.0008	+0.0033	+0.0070**
UMD	—	—	—	−0.0008	—	—	—	—	+0.0040	—
RMW	—	—	—	—	+0.0097***	—	—	—	—	−0.0048*
CMA	—	—	—	—	+0.0048	—	—	—	—	+0.0107***

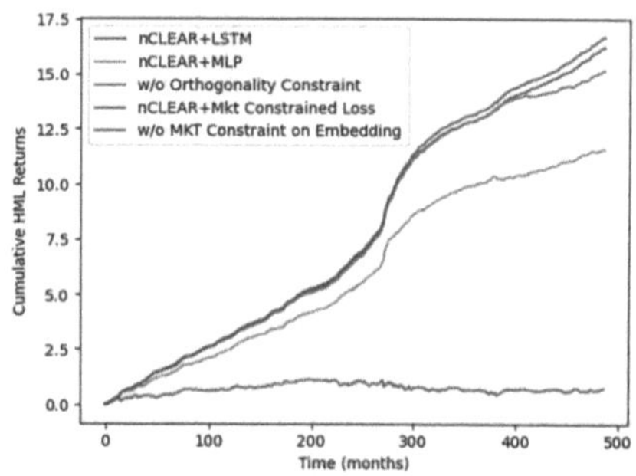

Fig. 3. HML portfolio optimization using reconstructed portfolio return matrix.

tors augmented with MktRf; Fama–French three factors (MktRf, SMB, HML) [4]; Carhart four factors (FF3 + UMD) [1]; and Fama–French five factors (FF4 + RMW, CMA) [5]. Statistical significance of the risk premia is evaluated using Newey–West adjusted standard errors. As reported in Table 2, several latent factors remain statistically significant even after controlling for these standard observable predictors, suggesting that the temporal embeddings capture incremental information relevant for contemporaneous portfolio return prediction.

Finally, we evaluate the economic value of the reconstructed portfolio return matrix through a longshort portfolio optimization exercise. At each time t, we sort portfolios into deciles based on predicted returns from each model's reconstructed matrix and form a High-Minus-Low (HML) portfolio by going long the top-decile portfolio group and short the bottom decile. We then compute realized HML returns using the actual observed returns and track cumulative performance over time. As illustrated in Fig. 3, nCLEAR-based reconstructions consistently generate higher cumulative HML returns than competing benchmarks, indicating that the latent embeddings not only reduce reconstruction error but also encode return-relevant information that can be profitably exploited for portfolio construction.

4 Ablation Study

To assess the contribution of each component of the proposed model, we conduct a series of ablation experiments under several alternative configurations: (i) without the orthogonality constraint; (ii) without the market instrumentation constraint; (iii) without dropout layers; (iv) replacing LSTM layers with a multilayer perceptron; and (v) nCLEAR with only one hidden layer. All variants are evaluated under the same protocol as the full nCLEAR model: we reuse the main preprocessing, train/validation split, observed/held-out index set Ω for both matrices, optimization schedule (optimizer, learning rate, batch size), loss weights, and early stopping with best-checkpoint restoration. Reconstruction metrics are computed only on the held-out entries of the factor and portfolio matrices to ensure a fair comparison.

Table 3 reports reconstruction performance at the baseline configuration (K=5, depth d=2). The baseline offers a good trade-off between factor and portfolio fit (e.g., portfolio RMSE 0.293), and the patterns are consistent for MAE and R^2. Removing orthogonality, dropping the market constraint, or eliminating both systematically worsens portfolio fit, as do removing dropout and using a shallow neural network. By contrast, nCLEAR(MLP) improves factor fit but weakens portfolio generalization, supporting the LSTM network with both constraints as our preferred specification.

To study capacity, we sweep the latent rank K and network depth d. Figure 4 shows that portfolio RMSE improves sharply when increasing rank from K=3 up to about $K \in [8, 10]$, with diminishing gains beyond that, while factor RMSE declines more smoothly. Depth sweeps show clear benefits from d=1 to d=2 and only marginal improvements at d=3. Overall, a moderately sized configuration (e.g., K=5, d=2 offers a good balance between accuracy, stability, and efficiency.

Table 3. Effect of Model Components on Reconstruction Loss

Model	Factor			Portfolio		
	RMSE	MAE	R^2	RMSE	MAE	R^2
Baseline	0.685	0.495	0.529	**0.293**	**0.205**	**0.914**
w/o Orthogonality Constraint	0.666	0.482	0.556	0.327	0.217	0.893
w/o MKT Constraint on Embedding	0.672	0.485	0.548	0.370	0.234	0.863
w/o Dropout	0.679	0.491	0.539	0.317	0.217	0.899
nCLEAR(MLP)	**0.614**	**0.458**	**0.622**	0.322	0.223	0.896
nCLEAR(Shallow)	0.680	0.492	0.536	0.302	0.212	0.909
w/o Orthogonality & MKT Constraint	0.667	0.481	0.554	0.359	0.230	0.871

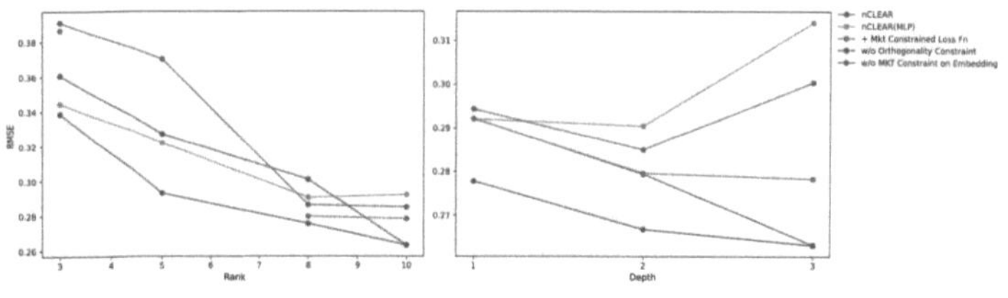

Fig. 4. Ablation results vs hidden rank (left) and depth (right): reconstruction RMSE for the portfolio return matrix.

5 Conclusion

This paper proposed a scalable nonlinear framework for financially constrained coupled matrix factorization, designed to discover latent factors that jointly capture temporal and cross-sectional dependencies in two time-aligned matrices. By learning a shared temporal embedding updated simultaneously for factors and portfolios, nCLEAR yields latent representations that are useful for downstream return prediction and deliver accurate nonlinear reconstructions of the original matrices relative to state-of-the-art benchmarks. The reconstructed portfolio returns support economically meaningful portfolio optimization, and our experiments across sparse and data-rich regimes, together with constrained model variants, highlight the robustness and practical relevance of the approach for financial multivariate time-series data.

References

1. Carhart, M.M.: On persistence in mutual fund performance. J. Financ. **52**(1), 57–82 (1997)
2. Chen, A.Y., Zimmermann, T.: Open source cross-sectional asset pricing (2021)
3. Chen, M., Xu, Q., Zeng, A., Zhang, L., et al.: Are transformers effective for time series forecasting? arXiv preprint, arXiv: 2205.13504 (2022)
4. Fama, E.F., French, K.R.: Common risk factors in the returns on stocks and bonds. J. Financ. Econ. **33**(1), 3–56 (1993)
5. Fama, E.F., French, K.R.: A five-factor asset pricing model journal of financial economics (2014)
6. Fama, E.F., French, K.R.: Dissecting anomalies with a five-factor model. Rev. Finan. Stud. **29**(1), 69–103 (2016)
7. Fama, E.F., MacBeth, J.D.: Risk, return, and equilibrium: empirical tests. J. Polit. Econ. **81**(3), 607–636 (1973)
8. Feng, G., Giglio, S., Xiu, D.: Taming the factor zoo: a test of new factors. J. Financ. **75**(3), 1327–1370 (2020)
9. Giglio, S., Xiu, D.: Asset pricing with omitted factors. J. Polit. Econ. **129**(7), 1947–1990 (2021)
10. Giglio, S., Xiu, D., Zhang, D.: Prediction when factors are weak. In: University of Chicago, Becker Friedman Institute for Economics Working Paper (2023-47) (2023)

11. Huang, D., Jiang, F., Li, K., Tong, G., Zhou, G.: Scaled PCA: a new approach to dimension reduction. Manage. Sci. **68**(3), 1678–1695 (2022)
12. Kelly, B.T., Pruitt, S., Su, Y.: Characteristics are covariances: a unified model of risk and return. J. Financ. Econ. **134**(3), 501–524 (2019)
13. Liu, H., Li, Y., Tsang, M., Liu, Y.: CoSTCo: a neural tensor completion model for sparse tensors. In: Proceedings of the 25th ACM SIGKDD International Conference on Knowledge Discovery & Data Mining, pp. 324–334. KDD '19, Association for Computing Machinery, New York, NY, USA (2019). https://doi.org/10.1145/3292500.3330881
14. Liu, Y., et al.: ITransFormer: inverted transformers are effective for time series forecasting (2023). arXiv:2310.06625 arXiv preprint
15. Liu, Y., Wu, H., Wang, J., Long, M.: Non-stationary transformers: exploring the stationarity in time series forecasting. Adv. Neural. Inf. Process. Syst. **35**, 9881–9893 (2022)
16. Nie, Y., Nguyen, N.H., Sinthong, P., Kalagnanam, J.: A time series is worth 64 words: Long-term forecasting with transformers (2022). arXiv:2211.14730 arXiv preprint
17. Vaswani, A., et al.: Attention is all you need. In: Advances in Neural Information Processing Systems, vol. 30 (2017)
18. Zhang, Y., Yan, J.: CrossFormer: transformer utilizing cross-dimension dependency for multivariate time series forecasting. In: The Eleventh International Conference on Learning Representations (2023)
19. Zhou, X., et al.: Scalable transformer for high dimensional multivariate time series forecasting. In: Proceedings of the 33rd ACM International Conference on Information and Knowledge Management, pp. 3515–3526 (2024)

Facet-Level Persona Control by Trait-Activated Routing with Contrastive SAE for Role-Playing LLMs

Wenqiu Tang[1(✉)], Zhen Wan[2], Takahiro Komamizu[1], and Ichiro Ide[1]

[1] Nagoya University, Nagoya, Aichi, Japan
tang.wenqiu.t2@s.mail.nagoya-u.ac.jp, taka-coma@acm.org, ide@i.nagoya-u.ac.jp
[2] Kyoto University, Kyoto, Japan
zhenwan@nii.ac.jp

Abstract. Personality control in Role-Playing Agents (RPAs) is commonly achieved via training-free methods that inject persona descriptions and memory through prompts or retrieval-augmented generation, or via Supervised Fine-Tuning (SFT) on persona-specific corpora. While SFT can be effective, it requires persona-labeled data and retraining for new roles, limiting flexibility. In contrast, prompt- and Retrieval-Augmented Generation (RAG)-based signals are easy to apply but can be diluted in long dialogues, leading to drifting and sometimes inconsistent persona behavior. To address this, we propose a contrastive Sparse AutoEncoder (SAE) framework that learns facet-level personality control vectors aligned with the Big Five 30-facet model. A new 15,000-sample leakage-controlled corpus is constructed to provide balanced supervision for each facet. The learned vectors are integrated into the model's residual space and dynamically selected by a trait-activated routing module, enabling precise and interpretable personality steering. Experiments on Large Language Models (LLMs) show that the proposed method maintains stable character fidelity and output quality across contextualized settings, outperforming Contrastive Activation Addition (CAA) and prompt-only baselines. The combined SAE+Prompt configuration achieves the best overall performance, confirming that contrastively trained latent vectors can enhance persona control while preserving dialogue coherence.

Keywords: Big Five personality · Contrastive learning · Activation steering

1 Introduction

Personality in Role-Playing Agents (RPAs) has emerged as a primary driver of in-character coherence and user trust. Contemporary training-free RPA stacks typically combine engineered personality prompts and Retrieval-Augmented Generation (RAG) for persona-relevant knowledge, while training-based RPAs

R. C.-W. Wong et al. (Eds.): PAKDD 2026, LNAI 16618, pp. 411–423, 2027.
https://doi.org/10.1007/978-981-92-1947-6_33

involve supervised finetuning on role-related corpora to internalize stylistic constraints [2,27]. However, both RPA methods have limitations. Training-free pipelines can suffer from instruction-following degradation when long, role-related context (e.g., RAG passages) is injected, often introducing prompt noise and diluting the intended persona signal. Training-based RPA, in turn, typically demands substantial data and computation, and risks catastrophic forgetting of the model's original general-purpose capabilities. Such issues reflect broader challenges of maintaining controllable, interpretable generation of Large Language Models (LLMs). These limitations motivate a lightweight, interpretable inference-time control resilient to long context.

Many studies have shown that using Control Vectors (CVs) can effectively shape style and personality-like traits in LLMs' generations by adding small, attribute-aligned shifts to the residual stream, steering internal activations toward the desired direction [3,9,15,24]. Although CVs have shown strong effects, several studies indicate instability in acquisition and usage; CVs derived from small or biased prompt-sets may capture prompt-specific artifacts rather than generalizable semantic directions, yielding noisy or brittle interventions [6,24].

To stabilize CVs for RPAs, we adopt a data-centric inference-time controller that couples facet-pure data with representation learning based on a Sparse AutoEncoder (SAE). First, a leakage-controlled Big Five personality [21] corpus at the facet level supplies balanced positive/negative pairs and minimizes prompt/template artifacts. Next, an SAE yields a disentangled latent basis in which a contrastive objective learns compact within-facet and separated across-facet directions; these facet-aligned directions are injected as lightweight activation edits composed with standard RPA prompting without weight updates, improving stability, controllability, and interpretability under long context.

Our goal is to learn high-purity personality CVs incorporated into RPA pipelines. Leveraging these CVs, we improve simulation accuracy without sacrificing dialogue stability or role fidelity. The contributions are as follows:

1. **Dataset Construction** (Sect. 3): We release a high-purity Big Five *30-facet* corpus (15k instances, 500 per facet) designed to isolate single sub-dimensions, use first-person phrasing, and minimize cross-trait leakage.
2. **Novel Framework** (Sect. 4): We introduce a Contrastive-Learning (CL) objective for CVs in the SAE latent space, which promotes within-facet compactness and across-facet separation for more stable control. In addition, we employ an Agent-Based Decision Module to insert only the question-relevant CVs, thereby reducing noise. Together, these components achieve more discriminative and reliable personality steering.
3. **Superior Performance** (Sect. 5): We introduce contextual-based benchmark persona fidelity and conduct detailed analysis on five steered methods, where the proposed CV-SAE+Prompt method attains the best overall results, indicating a robust way to steer RPA's personality.

2 Related Work

Personality control methods can be roughly grouped into two families: *Inference-time control*, and *Training-time control* [2,22]. We focus on the former because it offers a strong trade-off between effectiveness and practicality. Unlike training-time methods, it does not require collecting large persona corpora or updating model weights, avoiding data costs, computational cost, and potential forgetting [8,13]. Within inference-time methods, prior work has explored decoding-time control, such as Plug-and-Play Language Model (PnP-LM) [18]), while effective, these methods incur substantial decoding-time compute, are sensitive to hyperparameters, and can sometimes degrade fluency or semantic fidelity [18]. In contrast, Inference-time control using CVs or prompt methods [20,24], makes them lightweight, composable with standard decoders, and easy to ablate without retraining or modifying pretrained parameters.

There are two ways for generating CVs in the inference-time control: CV-SAE trains an SAE to obtain a disentangled feature space, then compute CVs from contrasts between persona-positive and negative samples [25]. In contrast, CV-CAA (CAA: Contrastive Activation Addition) directly computes a mean activation difference between paired prompts expressing opposite attributes [1, 20]. Though simple and parameter-free, CVs' directions may overlap across traits, motivating orthogonalization or denoising to prevent cross-trait interference.

Unlike pipelines, the proposed method (i) replaces templates with a professional, leakage-controlled 30-facet corpus, (ii) uses CL in SAE space to align and separate directions, and (iii) employs an agent policy that selects and schedules vectors from situational cues, rather than injecting Big Five [5] vectors at once.

3 Big Five Dataset Construction

We constructed a facet-level Big Five [23] dataset based on the NEO Personality Inventory (NEO-PI) [5] in a three-step pipeline shown in Fig. 1. NEO-PI splits each dimension in Big Five into six facets (30 in total). The constructed dataset consists of scenario-based positive and negative samples for each facet.

In the first step of the pipeline, for each facet, we summarize the official definition in NEO-PI and representative questionnaire items, and extract a small set of *core behavioral cues* that represent the essential trait tendency for both positive and negative poles of each trait. We then map these cues to everyday contexts (study, work, daily life, and social/leisure) and design brief *scenario templates* (e.g., group work, receiving feedback, and helping a friend) that naturally evoke the target facet. This cue-to-scenario design grounds each instance in a realistic situation rather than an abstract self-report. In the last step, using these templates, a GPT-5-class model [16] generates short first-person sentences (maximum 18 words with simple vocabulary). For each scenario, the model produces a *positive* sample expressing the facet and a *minimal-edit negative* counterpart that keeps the same context but reverses the behavior. This yields 250 positive and 250 negative instances per facet (15,000 in total).

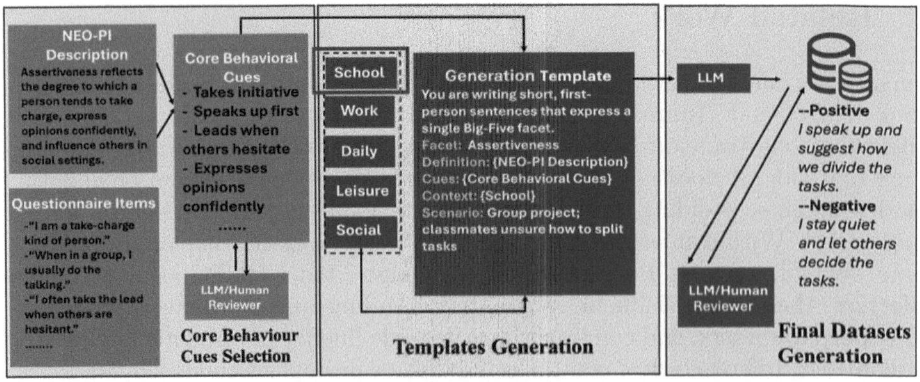

Fig. 1. Pipeline for constructing the Big Five [23] personality dataset, illustrated with the Assertiveness facet as an example.

Finally, we adopt a three-step validation pipeline. In the construction phase, (i) a secondary LLM screens *all* items to check facet correctness, polarity clarity, and linguistic simplicity, and flags potentially problematic cases, (ii) then 50 items are randomly sampled from each facet-specific subset and ten psychology graduate students (five female and five male in their twenties) are asked to judge the same criteria, and their judgments are compared with those of the secondary LLM on the sampled items to verify and calibrate the initial automatic screening. Items that are flagged in either step (i) or (ii) are revised or regenerated until no obvious facet or polarity errors remain. After this, (iii) a 30-way facet classifier is trained on the resulting corpus and evaluated on a held-out split, obtaining 78.4% macro-F1 with only 6.2% of misclassifications crossing Big Five dimensions, which indicates that samples are in general, aligned with their intended facet and that cross-dimension leakage is limited. The final corpus is therefore *substantially facet-consistent and context-grounded.*

4 Contrastive Sparse AutoEncoder (SAE) Training and Agent-Based Decision Module

Figure 2 shows an overview of the proposed method for steering an RPA's personality expression by injecting learned CVs into the model's hidden layers. It contains two steps: (i) SAE-based CV training enhanced with a Contrastive Learning (CL) loss to distill corpus-mined factors into facet-aligned CVs, which enhances effectiveness and strength in real-world applications, improving the model's output quality along the intended control direction, and (ii) Self-reflection decision that dynamically selects which set of CVs to inject to precisely steer the model behaviours.

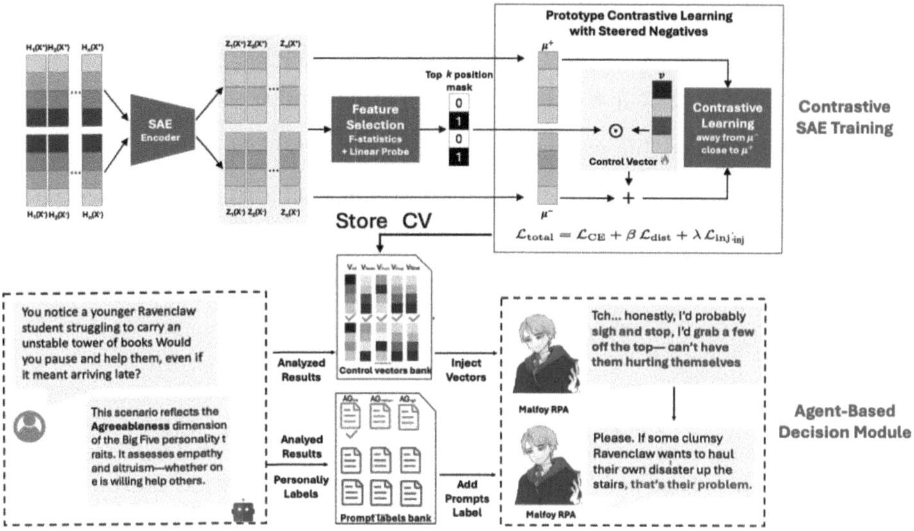

Fig. 2. Proposed framework: Contrastive Sparse AutoEncoder (SAE) training and Agent-Based Decision Module for Control Vector (CV) injection.

4.1 Contrastive SAE Training

We map a hidden representation $\mathbf{h}(x)$ into a pretrained SAE space to obtain a sparse latent code $\mathbf{z}$ through an encoding function f_{enc} where each latent dimension is activated only by its associated concept in relevant contexts, thus yielding stronger control signals. After training the encoder and decoder of an SAE on hidden states collected from the WikiText-103-raw-v1 corpus [10], a standard language-modeling dataset adopted in recent SAE studies, we decode the learned control vector $\mathbf{z}$ back into the model's residual space as $\mathbf{v} = f_{\text{dec}}(\mathbf{z})$, and an injection is performed as:

$$\mathbf{h}'(x) = \mathbf{h}(x) + \alpha \mathbf{v}, \tag{1}$$

where $\mathbf{v}$ is the CV, and α controls the injection strength.

Following prior work by He et al. [10], we use F-statistics and linear probes to select the d_{steer} "top activated" features ($d_{\text{steer}} \leq d$), where d is the original dimensionality of the SAE space. After deciding these features, we construct a CV $\mathbf{v} \in \mathbb{R}^d$ that is nonzero only on the d_{steer} selected coordinates. We initialize it in the SAE space using the class-centroid difference as:

$$\mathbf{v} = (\boldsymbol{\mu}^+ - \boldsymbol{\mu}^-) \odot \mathbf{m}, \tag{2}$$

where $\boldsymbol{\mu}^+$ and $\boldsymbol{\mu}^-$ are the mean SAE codes for positive and negative samples from the generated BFI, respectively, and $\mathbf{m} \in \{0, 1\}^d$ masks the active coordinates.

The total objective to learn the CVs is a linear combination of a prototype contrast loss $\mathcal{L}_{\text{CE}}$, a positive pull loss $\mathcal{L}_{\text{dist}}$, and a regularization factor as:

$$\mathcal{L}_{\text{total}} = \mathcal{L}_{\text{CE}} + \beta\,\mathcal{L}_{\text{dist}} + \lambda\|\mathbf{v} \odot \mathbf{m}\|_2^2, \tag{3}$$

where β and λ are tunable weight parameters.

Prototype Contrast Loss $\mathcal{L}_{\text{CE}}$: Given CV $\mathbf{v}$, our goal is to *pull representations toward the positive centroid and push them away from the negative one.* CL enforces this push–pull geometry [4, 11], yielding discriminative directions. For a negative sample with $\mathbf{z}$, we inject a masked vector $\mathbf{v}$ and ℓ_2-normalize it as:

$$\mathbf{z}^+ = \frac{\mathbf{z} + \mathbf{v}}{\|\mathbf{z} + \mathbf{v}\|_2}. \tag{4}$$

We likewise normalize $\tilde{\boldsymbol{\mu}}^+ = \boldsymbol{\mu}^+/\|\boldsymbol{\mu}^+\|_2$ and $\tilde{\boldsymbol{\mu}}^- = \boldsymbol{\mu}^-/\|\boldsymbol{\mu}^-\|_2$ for stability.

Based on them, cosine scores are defined as $c_+ = \langle \mathbf{z}^+, \tilde{\boldsymbol{\mu}}^+ \rangle$ and $c_- = \langle \mathbf{z}^+, \tilde{\boldsymbol{\mu}}^- \rangle$. Following ArcFace/CosFace [7, 26], we impose an angular margin on the positive side and a cosine margin on the negative side as:

$$\tilde{c}_+ = \cos\big(\arccos(c_+) + m_{\text{pos}}\big), \quad \tilde{c}_- = c_- + m_{\text{neg}}, \tag{5}$$

where $m_{\text{pos}} > 0$ and $m_{\text{neg}} > 0$ are margins. Using scale $s > 0$ (equivalently, temperature $\tau = 1/s$), we form logits $\ell = [s\tilde{c}_+, s\tilde{c}_-]$ and minimize the two-way cross-entropy loss that treats the positive prototype as the target as:

$$\mathcal{L}_{\text{CE}} = -\frac{1}{B}\sum_{i=1}^{B} \log \frac{\exp(s\tilde{c}_{+,i})}{\exp(s\tilde{c}_{+,i}) + \exp(s\tilde{c}_{-,i})}. \tag{6}$$

Positive Pull Loss $\mathcal{L}_{\text{dist}}$: We use a distance-based loss that compares the injected representation to the class centroids in the active subspace as:

$$\mathcal{L}_{\text{dist}}(v) = \big\|\mathbf{z}^+ - \mathbf{u}^+\big\|_2 - \big\|\mathbf{z}^+ - \mathbf{u}^-\big\|_2, \tag{7}$$

where $\mathbf{z}^+$ is the post-injection representation, and $\mathbf{u}^+$ and $\mathbf{u}^-$ are the positive and negative centroids, respectively.

4.2 Agent-Based Decision Module

Guided by Trait Activation [21], we activate *only* the trait cued by the current prompt, avoiding competition between CVs. Accordingly, we select best-matching CVs per turn; persona knowledge come from RAG/prompt conditioning, while the vector acts as an *amplifier*, routing by contextual cues. To realize this idea, we use the role-play model's base LLM as a routing agent. Before producing the final answer, as shown in Fig. 2, the agent receives the user's query and infers which facet-level CVs are most strongly cued by the question. Based on the agent's analysis, we inject CVs corresponding to the most relevant facets for the given prompt in each dimension which is composed of six facet-level CVs. This process allows fine-grained steering while keeping inference-time control targeted.

5 Experiments

In personality measurement, *abstract* items are global self-descriptions posed without an explicit frame of reference, whereas *contextualized* items stipulate the setting/role/time [19]. We follow the *In-Character* benchmark, which evaluates 44 abstract Big Five [23] open-ended questions and uses GPT-4o [17] as the judge [27]. However, abstract Big Five questions can elicit socially desirable responses [19]. Grounded in reference-group effects and trait-activation theory [21], we rewrote all 44 items into *contextualized questions* using GPT-4o, adding minimal temporal/situational cues to reduce bias while preserving semantics.

5.1 Evaluation Protocol

We evaluated on two compact, open-weight instruction followers that are widely used in RPA pipelines (e.g., RoleLLM): `Qwen/Qwen3-4B-Instruct-2507` (Qwen3-4B for short) [29] and `mistralai/Mistral-7B-Instruct-v0.7` (Mistral-7B for short) [12]. Qwen3-4B delivers strong small-scale performance, while Mistral-7B provides efficient attention and competitive results at the 7B scale.

In order to observe the behaviors of RPAs, this experiment reports four evaluation metrics: Full-Accuracy (FA), Mean Squared Error (MSE), Mean Absolute Error (MAE), and Muti-Turn Rate (MTR). FA, MSE and MAE evaluate correctness in estimating characters: FA is the proportion of characters (out of 26) for which all five Big Five [23] dimensions are predicted correctly, and MSE and MAE are per-dimension errors and stability across paraphrased questions. MTR evaluates whether the agent maintains the intended persona while answering, and whether the response contains any of the errors including repetition, out of characters, and multi-turn dialogue, which are also evaluated by LLM.

5.2 Implementation and Comparison Methods

In the proposed method (called CV-SAE), we injected CV at the mid-residual-layer with the strongest stylistic effects, specifically the 15th layer in Qwen3-4B [29] and the 16th layer in Mistral-7B [12], aligned with prior findings [14,20] and our preliminary results. SAE is trained at the same layer.

To validate our proposal, we configured the following experiment setups. *Base RPA* denotes no additional intervention. *Prompt-Label* denotes conditional generation on explicit Big Five [23] labels using per-dimension low/medium/high facet-covering descriptors chosen by the character's overall score [28]. *CV-SAE* and *CV-CAA* denote injecting CVs derived from SAE and CAA, respectively. *Combined Methods* (CV-CAA+Prompt and CV-SAE+Prompt) are RPAs that combine CV injection methods with Prompt-Label to assess their complementarity.

Table 1. Performance of Qwen3-4B [29] and Mistral-7B [12] on Big Five personality questions [23]. Best results for each metric are **bolded**.

Model	Method	Abstract Questions				Contextual Questions			
		FA(↑)	MSE(↓)	MAE(↓)	MTR(↓)	FA(↑)	MSE(↓)	MAE(↓)	MTR(↓)
Qwen3-4B	**Baselines**								
	Base RPA	7.7	16.0	31.3	**0.0**	7.7	14.2	30.2	0.1
	Prompt-Label	50.0	10.9	24.9	**0.0**	30.7	11.7	26.2	0.1
	CV-CAA	73.1	4.8	16.1	**0.0**	76.9	4.2	14.7	**0.0**
	Proposed								
	CV-SAE	76.9	4.9	16.5	**0.0**	76.9	3.4	14.3	**0.0**
	Combined								
	CV-CAA+Prompt	**81.0**	3.7	14.2	**0.0**	81.0	3.4	14.1	0.2
	CV-SAE+Prompt	**81.0**	**3.2**	**14.1**	**0.0**	**88.5**	**2.4**	**12.1**	0.1
Mistral-7B	**Baselines**								
	Base RPA	19.2	15.5	32.8	5.6	3.9	17.8	34.7	1.4
	Prompt-Label	42.3	9.5	24.8	**1.6**	42.3	9.5	24.8	**1.3**
	CV-CAA	76.9	4.2	15.6	29.1	84.7	4.2	16.6	25.6
	Proposed								
	CV-SAE	73.1	5.4	18.7	7.0	80.8	3.97	15.1	3.1
	Combined								
	CV-CAA+Prompt	38.5	9.3	23.8	1.8	46.2	10.0	24.6	1.4
	CV-SAE+Prompt	**84.6**	**3.8**	**14.9**	4.2	**88.5**	**3.1**	**13.7**	3.8

5.3 Results

Table 1 summarizes the experimental results. First, both CV methods (CV-SAE and CV-CAA) substantially outperformed the Prompt-Label baseline across FA, MSE, and MAE, confirming the effectiveness of direct vector modulation over prompt-only conditioning. However, CV-CAA showed unstable behavior on Mistral-7B [12], where its MTR increased sharply, indicating that contrastive activation cues could destabilize dialog flow. In contrast, CV-SAE achieved a stronger overall balance —Improving accuracy while maintaining response smoothness— suggesting that SAE yielded more stable and disentangled CV injection. In particular, integrating prompts with CVs amplified the contrast between the two approaches. The combined CV-SAE+Prompt consistently attained the highest FA and the lowest reconstruction errors (MAE/MSE) across both backbones, pushing the overall performance to a new peak. Conversely, CV-CAA+Prompt severely collapsed on Mistral-7B (FA dropping from 76.9 to 38.5), showing that prompt signals interfere with contrastive activations rather than reinforcing them. On Qwen3-4B [29], this interference was less pronounced, yet SAE-based combined method remained superior in both accuracy and stability.

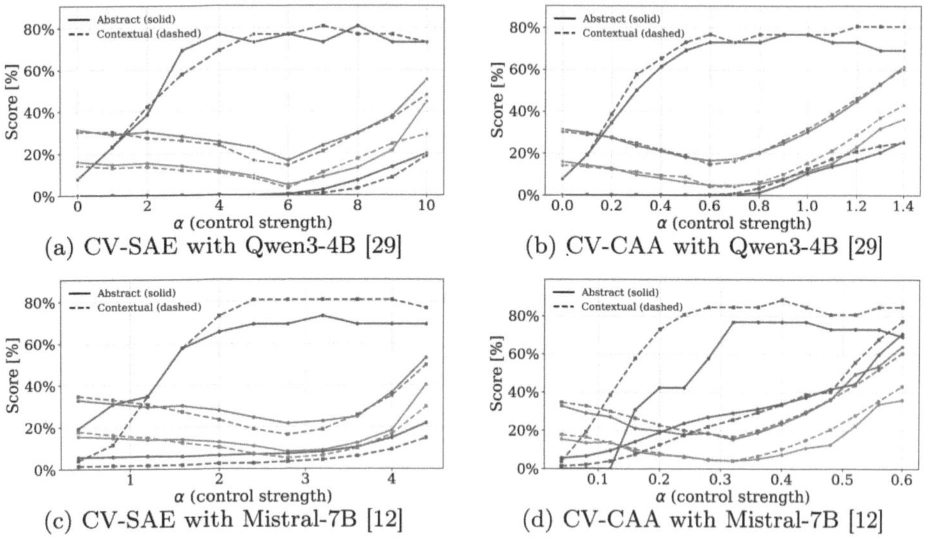

(a) CV-SAE with Qwen3-4B [29]

(b) CV-CAA with Qwen3-4B [29]

(c) CV-SAE with Mistral-7B [12]

(d) CV-CAA with Mistral-7B [12]

Fig. 3. Effect of control strength α on Role-Play Agent (RPA) performance across backbones and control methods. Results are reported under the *abstract* (solid) and *contextual* (dashed) settings. Blue denotes FA, orange denotes MSE, green denotes MAE, and red denotes MTR. (Color figure online)

CV methods were resilient —and often improved— under contextualized questions. On Mistral-7B, FA increased for CV-SAE, CV-CAA, and CV-SAE+Prompt. On Qwen3-4B, CV-SAE+Prompt gained +7.5 pp, while CV-SAE/CAA held steady or improved slightly. By contrast, Prompt-Label alone did not generalize as well: on Qwen3-4B, FA dropped from 50.0 (abstract) to 30.7 (contextual), suggesting that explicit labels without latent steering struggled to adapt to situational cues.

5.4 Effect of Injection Strength α

As described in Eq. 1, α scales the CV. A too small value yields under-steering, while a too large value perturbs the semantic space and degrades responses. To identify a stable operating point, we sweep α and report the performance. As shown in Fig. 3, mid-range α values with CV-SAE delivered high FA and low errors with minimal MTR, whereas CV-CAA peaked at a smaller α and showed faster MTR growth as α increased.

Increasing α sharply inflated the three stability indicators, MSE, MAE, and MTR. In interview settings, RPA's personality became inconsistent even within the same question set (MAE and MSE rose faster), and output coherence as well as instruction following deteriorated (MTR kept increasing). Accordingly, we tuned α on preferring mid-range values for SAE and smaller values for CAA to balance accuracy and stability.

Table 2. Effect of Contrastive Learning (CL) —The left block reports cosine similarities between the injected representation z and the positive/negative Extraversion centroids (μ^+, μ^-) on the Extraversion subset of our corpus. The right block reports Full-Accuracy (FA) on Abstract (Abst.) and Contextual (Cont.) Extraversion questions for ten role agents under three training settings.

	Similarities to Centroids				Full-Accuracy (FA)			
	Qwen3-4B [29]		Mistral-7B [12]		Qwen3-4B [29]		Mistral-7B [12]	
	$\langle \mathbf{z}, \boldsymbol{\mu}^+ \rangle$	$\langle \mathbf{z}, \boldsymbol{\mu}^- \rangle$	$\langle \mathbf{z}, \boldsymbol{\mu}^+ \rangle$	$\langle \mathbf{z}, \boldsymbol{\mu}^- \rangle$	Abst.	Cont.	Abst.	Cont.
Before Training	0.92	0.84	0.64	0.38	11.5	11.5	23.1	3.9
Train w/o CL	0.76 (↓)	0.31 (↓)	0.29 (↓)	−0.01 (↓)	0.0 (↓)	3.9 (↓)	3.9 (↓)	0.0 (↓)
Train w/ CL	0.93 (↑)	0.59 (↓)	0.75 (↑)	0.21 (↓)	76.9 (↑)	80.7 (↑)	76.9 (↑)	84.6 (↑)

Across the graphs in Fig. 3, CV-CAA exhibited a consistently higher (worse) MTR than SAE on both Qwen3-4B [29] and Mistral-7B [12], indicating more dialogue drift and less stable answers. Since CV-SAE injects CVs only in the middle layers, whereas CV-CAA injects a small control signal into *every* layer, the way of injection affects the performance. We hypothesize that the control signal learned by CV-CAA was less "pure"; as α increased, off-target semantic components were introduced alongside the intended concept direction, which degraded the response quality and inflated MTR. In contrast, CV-SAE provided a more concentrated "purer" steering direction; it carried less extraneous content and thus amplified the intended concept more reliably.

5.5 Effect of CL

To further understand the effect of CL, we conduct an ablation study under three training settings —*Before Training*, *Training without Contrastive Learning*, and *Training with CL*. In each setting, we (i) computed the cosine similarity between the injected representation z and the positive/negative Extraversion centroids (μ^+, μ^-) estimated from the Extraversion subset of our corpus, and (ii) evaluated FA on ten representative role agents (selected from 26 personas) using both Abstract and Contextual items.

As shown in Table 2, CV-SAE relying solely on the distance-based (ℓ_2) loss indeed reduced the cosine similarity to the negative centroid $\boldsymbol{\mu}^-$ on both Qwen3-4B [29] and Mistral-7B [12]. However, this also undesirably decreased the similarity to the positive centroid $\boldsymbol{\mu}^+$, deviating from the intended training objective. Correspondingly, CV-SAE without CL sharply dropped the overall full-accuracy, even lower than the untrained baseline. In contrast, introducing CL not only increased $\langle \mathbf{z}, \boldsymbol{\mu}^+ \rangle$ while suppressing $\langle \mathbf{z}, \boldsymbol{\mu}^- \rangle$ but also lead to a substantial full-accuracy improvement across both abstract and contextual questions confirming that contrastive optimization effectively aligned latent representations.

6 Conclusion

We introduced an SAE-based contrastive CV for RPA personality steering, which uses a facet-accurate personality corpus to compute latent centroids and a reflection module to select relevant CVs. Combined with top-k latent filtering and contrastive tuning at mid-residual layers, the method achieved stable facet-level personality control. On Qwen3-4B [29] and Mistral-7B [12], SAE vectors improved accuracy and reduced error with minimal drift, outperforming CAA and prompting while preserving persona knowledge.

Acknowledgment. This work was partly supported by JSPS KAKENHI JP25K00161 and Nagoya University WISE Graduate Program on Lifestyle Revolution based on Transdisciplinary Mobility Innovation.

References

1. Allbert, R., Wiles, J.K., Grankovsky, V.: Identifying and manipulating personality traits in LLMs through activation engineering. Eng. Appl. Sci. **2**(2), 1–13 (2025)
2. Chen, J., Wang, X., Xu, R., Yuan, S., Zhang, Y., et al.: From persona to personalization: a survey on role-playing language agents. Trans. Mach. Learn. Res. (2863), 1–50 (2024). https://doi.org/10.48550/arXiv.2404.18231
3. Chen, R., Arditi, A., Sleight, H., Evans, O., Lindsey, J.: Persona vectors: monitoring and controlling character traits in language models. arXiv Preprint, arXiv:2507.21509 (Sep 2025)
4. Chen, T., Kornblith, S., Norouzi, M., Hinton, G.: A simple framework for contrastive learning of visual representations. In: 37th International Conference on Machine Learning, pp. 1597–1607 (Jul 2020). https://dl.acm.org/doi/10.5555/3524938.3525087
5. Costa, P.T.J., McCrae, R.R.: the revised NEO personality inventory (NEO-PI-R). In: The SAGE Handbook of Personality Theory and Assessment: Personality Measurement and Testing, vol. 2, pp. 179–198. SAGE Publications, London, United Kingdom (2008). https://doi.org/10.4135/9781849200479.n9
6. Silva, D., Sethuraman, P.Q., Rajagopal, H., Hajishirzi, D., Kumar, H., S.: Steering off course: reliability challenges in steering language models. In: 63rd Annual Meeting of the Association for Computational Linguistics, vol. 1, pp. 19856–19882 (2025). https://doi.org/10.18653/v1/2025.acl-long.974
7. Deng, J., Guo, J., Yang, J., Xue, N., Kotsia, I., Zafeiriou, S.: ArcFace: additive angular margin loss for deep face recognition. IEEE Trans. Pattern Anal. Mach. Intell. **44**(10), 5962–5979 (2022). https://doi.org/10.1109/CVPR.2019.00482
8. Ding, N., Qin, Y., Yang, G., Wei, F., Yang, Z., et al.: Parameter-efficient fine-tuning of large-scale pre-trained language models. Nature Mach. Intell. **5**(3), 220–235 (2023). https://doi.org/10.1038/s42256-023-00626-4
9. Durmus, E., Tamkin, A., Clark, J., Wei, J., Marcus, J., et al.: Evaluating feature steering: a case study in mitigating social biases (25 Oct 2024). https://anthropic.com/research/evaluating-feature-steering/ (Accessed 28 Feb 2026)
10. He, Z., Jin, M., Shen, B., Payani, A., Zhang, Y., Du, M.: SAE-SSV: supervised steering in sparse representation spaces for reliable control of language models. In: 2025 Conference on Empirical Methods in Natural Language Processing, pp. 2207–2236 (2025). https://doi.org/10.18653/v1/2025.emnlp-main.112

11. Hu, H., Wang, X., Zhang, Y., Chen, Q., Guan, Q.: A comprehensive survey on contrastive learning. Neurocomput. **610**(128645), 1–12 (2024). https://dl.acm.org/doi/10.1016/j.neucom.2024.128645
12. Jiang, A.Q., Sablayrolles, A., Mensch, A., Bamford, C., Chaplot, D.S., et al.: Mistral 7B. arXiv Preprint, arXiv:2310.06825 (May 2023)
13. Keskar, N.S., McCann, B., Varshney, L.R., Xiong, C., Socher, R.: CTRL: a conditional transformer language model for controllable generation. arXiv Preprint, arXiv:1909.05858 (Sep 2019)
14. Kissane, C., Krzyzanowski, R., Conmy, A., Nanda, N.: SAEs (usually) transfer between base and chat models. AI Alignment Forum, 18 Jul (2024). https://www.alignmentforum.org/posts/fmwk6qxrpW8d4jvbd/saes-usually-transfer-between-base-and-chat-models/ Accessed 28 Feb 2026)
15. Konen, K., Jentzsch, S., Diallo, D., Schütt, P., Bensch, O.: Style vectors for steering generative large language models. In: Findings of the Association for Computational Linguistics: EACL 2024, pp. 782–802 (2024)
16. OpenAI: Introducing GPT-5: A unified system for expert-level reasoning and multimodal capabilities (August 2025). https://openai.com/index/introducing-gpt-5/ (Accessed 1 Oct 2025)
17. OpenAI: Gpt-4o system card, Tech. rep., OpenAI (2024)
18. Pascual, D., Egressy, B., Meister, C., Cotterell, R., Wattenhofer, R.: A plug-and-play method for controlled text generation. In: Findings of the Association for Computational Linguistics: EMNLP 2021, pp. 3973–3997 (2021)
19. Paulhus, D.L., John, O.P.: Egoistic and moralistic biases in self-perception: the interplay of self-deceptive styles with basic traits and motives. J. Personal. **66**(6), 1025–1060 (1998). https://doi.org/10.1111/1467-6494.00041
20. Rimsky, N., Gabrieli, N., Schulz, J., Tong, M., Hubinger, E., Turner, A.M.: Steering Llama 2 via contrastive activation addition. In: 62nd Annual Meeting of the Association for Computational Linguistics, vol. 1, pp. 15504–15522. (2024). https://doi.org/10.18653/v1/2024.acl-long.828
21. Tett, R.P., Burnett, D.D.: A personality trait-based interactionist model of job performance. J. Appl. Psychol. **88**(3), 500–517 (2003). https://doi.org/10.1037/0021-9010.88.3.500
22. Tseng, Y.M., Huang, Y.C., Hsiao, T.Y., Chen, W.L., Huang, C.W., et al.: Two tales of persona in LLMs: a survey of role-playing and personalization. In: Findings of the Association for Computational Linguistics: EMNLP 2024, pp. 16612–16631 (Nov 2024). https://doi.org/10.18653/v1/2024.findings-emnlp.969
23. Tupes, E.C., Christal, R.E.: Recurrent personality factors based on trait ratings. J. Personal. **60**(2), 225–251 (1992)
24. Turner, A.M., Thiergart, L., Udell, D., Leech, G., Mini, U., MacDiarmid, M.: Activation addition: Steering language models without optimization. arXiv Preprint, arXiv:2308.10248 (Jun 2024)
25. Wang, A., Shu, D., Wang, Y., Ma, Y., Du, M.: Improving LLM reasoning through interpretable role-playing steering. In: Findings of the Association for Computational Linguistics: EMNLP 2025, pp. 731–751 (Nov 2025). https://doi.org/10.18653/v1/2025.findings-emnlp.39
26. Wang, H., Wang, Y., Zhou, Z., Ji, X., Gong, D., et al.: CosFace: large margin Cosine loss for deep Face recognition. In: 2018 IEEE/CVF Conference on Computer Vision and Pattern Recognition, pp. 5265–5274 (Jun 2018). https://doi.org/10.1109/CVPR.2018.00552

27. Wang, X., Xiao, Y., Huang, J.T., Yuan, S., Xu, R.: InCharacter: evaluating personality fidelity in role-playing agents through psychological interviews. In: 62nd Annual Meeting of the Association for Computational Linguistics, vol. 1, pp. 1840–1873 (2024). https://doi.org/10.18653/v1/2024.acl-long.102
28. Wang, Y., Zhao, J., Ones, D.S., He, L., Xu, X.: Evaluating the ability of large language models to emulate personality. Sci. Rep. **15**(519), 1–9 (2025). https://doi.org/10.1038/s41598-024-84109-5
29. Yang, A., Li, A., Yang, B., Zhang, B., Hui, B., et al.: Qwen3 technical report. arXiv Preprint, arXiv:2505.09388 (May 2025)

AI-Generated Image Detection Based on the Most Suspicious Patch

Hang Gao[1], Mengting Hu[2(✉)], and Tiegang Gao[2]

[1] College of Artificial Intelligence, Tianjin University of Science and Technology, Tianjin 300457, China
gaohang@tust.edu.cn

[2] College of Software, Nankai University, Tianjin 300350, China
{mthu,gaotiegang}@nankai.edu.cn

Abstract. In recent years, images generated by advanced artificial intelligence (AI) models have left a deep impression, as they are highly realistic and capable of deceiving human eyes. In this work, we found that only certain regions of a generated image are crucial for detecting it as fake. We hypothesize that advanced generative models are likely capable of capturing visual features and statistical patterns consistent with natural images, such that some regions of the generated images may resemble, or even match, natural image characteristics. This implies that detectors must be highly sensitive to artifacts remaining in local areas of the image. Therefore, we propose the most suspicious patch (MSP) strategy. Specifically, we design a simple yet effective MSP rule that enables a detector to autonomously identify the most suspicious patch, and assess image authenticity based on it. Experiments show that MSP strategy provides satisfactory performance improvements across various detectors. Moreover, we observe that certain detectors achieve new state-of-the-art performance with the support of our MSP strategy. Further investigation reveals that MSP reduces the influence of model-specific signatures and promotes the learning of model-invariant artifacts, which supports better generalization to unseen generators. Our code is available at https://github.com/gaohangcodes/MSP.

Keywords: AI-generated Image Detection · Most Suspicious Patch

1 Introduction

In recent years, with the rapid development of artificial intelligence (AI), image generation techniques have enabled the synthesis of highly photorealistic images that often defy human scrutiny. While these capabilities unlock transformative applications in art, design, and virtual content creation, they also pose significant societal risks: AI-generated imagery can be weaponized for disinformation, identity impersonation, and evidence fabrication, eroding trust in digital media.

To counter this threat, a growing body of research has focused on detecting AI-generated images. The dominant paradigm, which we term *global detection*

R. C.-W. Wong et al. (Eds.): PAKDD 2026, LNAI 16618, pp. 424–435, 2027.
https://doi.org/10.1007/978-981-92-1947-6_34

(GD), broadly falls into two categories: (1) those that extract global features from the full image and aggregate (e.g., via global average pooling) them for prediction [1–3], and (2) those that score individual patches and average the responses to produce an image-level decision [4]. Despite their widespread adoption, these approaches share a critical limitation: they implicitly treat all image regions as equally informative for forensic analysis.

(a) A fake image. (b) CNNSpot. (c) LGrad. (d) LNP.

Fig. 1. The visualization of recent research, where (a) is the original fake image, (b) is from CNNSpot [1], (c) is from LGrad [3], and (d) is from LNP [5].

However, emerging evidence challenges this assumption. As illustrated in Fig. 1, the attention maps (computed using class activation mapping [7]) of several open-source detectors consistently highlight only sparse, localized regions when correctly identifying fake images, meanwhile some previous research visualizations [3,6] indicate similar patterns. Based on these observations, we hypothesize that advanced generative models may already possess the capability to capture visual features and statistical regularities consistent with natural images. Consequently, some regions of the images they generate might exhibit characteristics that resemble, or even match, those of real images, implying that forensic traces are not uniformly distributed but concentrated in a few "suspicious" patches.

This spatial sparsity renders global aggregation inherently suboptimal: averaging over artifact-free regions dilutes the discriminative signal from the few anomalous patches, leading to reduced detection sensitivity, especially for high-fidelity generators or partially edited images. To address this blind spot, we propose a paradigm shift: instead of relying on globally aggregated evidence, we base the final decision solely on the *most suspicious patch* (MSP)—the single region most likely to contain detectable artifacts.

Formally, we cast AI-generated image detection as a multiple instance learning (MIL) problem: an image is labeled "fake" if *at least one* of its patches exhibits forensic anomalies. During training, the MSP is dynamically identified as the patch yielding the highest fake probability under the current detector, and the image-level label is transferred as the patch-level label. This mechanism encourages the model to iteratively focus on increasingly discriminative local regions. In our experiments, the MSP strategy led to significant performance improvements and demonstrated satisfactory compatibility: when MSP was combined with existing artifact extraction strategies, the detectors achieved new state-of-the-art performance. Further analysis reveals that MSP enhances the learning of model-invariant forensic cues, contributing to improved generalization.

In summary, our contributions are threefold:

- We identify and formalize the *signal dilution effect* in global detection, which is a key bottleneck in detecting high-fidelity AI-generated images due to the spatial sparsity of forensic artifacts.
- We propose the Most Suspicious Patch (MSP) paradigm, a simple yet effective MIL-based framework that shifts detection focus to the single most discriminative local region.
- We establish new state-of-the-art performance across comprehensive benchmarks, demonstrating MSP's effectiveness and compatibility. Further analysis reveals that MSP encourages the detector to learn model-invariant forensic artifacts, which contributes to its improved generalization to unseen synthesis models.

2 Related Work

Research on AI-generated image detection can be broadly divided into two complementary directions: (1) the design of effective forensic representations that capture detectable artifacts, and (2) the development of decision mechanisms that leverage these representations for image-level authentication.

2.1 Forensic Representation Learning

A central challenge in AI-generated image detection lies in identifying reliable forensic traces left by synthesis processes. Early work such as CNNSpot [1] demonstrated that feeding raw RGB images directly into a CNN enables the learning of "universal" artifacts from ProGAN-generated data, with notable generalization to other generators. This study highlighted the benefits of diverse training data and augmentation, and its public dataset has since become a standard benchmark.

Building on these insights, subsequent methods have designed more refined forensic representations by analyzing generative model internals. Examples include gradient maps to emphasize boundary inconsistencies [3], global texture descriptors [8], noise pattern estimators [5], and GAN fingerprint extractors [9,10]. Recently, NPR [6] leveraged neighboring pixel relationships induced by upsampling operations, achieving state-of-the-art performance. Beyond the spatial domain, frequency-domain anomalies in DCT or wavelet coefficients have also been exploited for detection [2,11–16].

Our work does not propose a new forensic representation. Instead, we introduce the Most Suspicious Patch (MSP) as a general-purpose decision strategy that is orthogonal to the choice of input representation. As demonstrated in Sect. 4, MSP consistently improves detection performance across diverse input modalities, highlighting its role as a plug-and-play enhancement to existing pipelines.

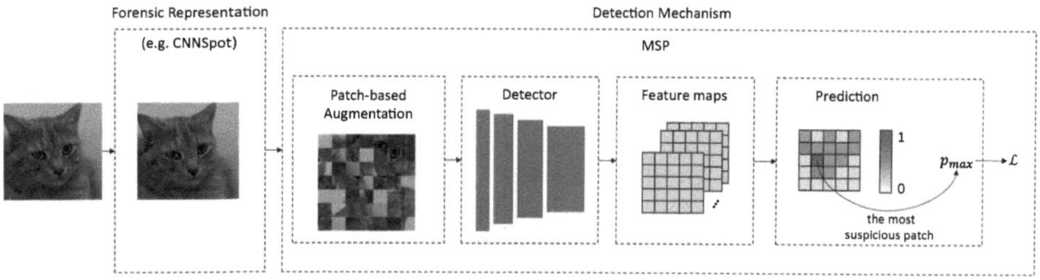

Fig. 2. Overview of training detectors with our MSP strategy, where CNNSpot [1] is chosen as the forensic representation for better visual clarity.

2.2 Decision Mechanisms for AI-Generated Image Detection

Given a forensic representation, most detectors adopt a global decision strategy. A common approach employs a convolutional backbone followed by global average pooling (GAP) to produce an image-level prediction [1–3]. Alternatively, some methods first divide the image into patches, compute an authenticity score for each patch, and then average these scores to obtain the final decision [4]. Despite their prevalence, both paradigms implicitly assume that forensic evidence is uniformly distributed across the image. However, visual analyses from multiple studies [3,6] reveal that detectors often respond only to sparse, localized regions, suggesting that global averaging may dilute discriminative signals from anomalous patches.

In this work, we propose a detection paradigm that bases the final decision solely on the *most suspicious patch* (MSP). Inspired by multiple instance learning (MIL), our approach treats an image as fake if *any* of its regions exhibits forensic anomalies, thereby avoiding the signal dilution caused by global aggregation.

3 Methodology

3.1 Overview and Formulation

Figure 2 illustrates the workflow for training an AI-generated image detector using the MSP strategy. As shown, the process involves two main strategies: the forensic representation and the decision mechanism.

For a given image I, a forensic representation $A \in \mathbb{R}^{C_A \times H_A \times W_A}$ is first extracted via $A = g(I)$, where g denotes a forensic feature extractor, which can be an identity function [1], a spatial-to-frequency domain transformation [2], or a more sophisticated function, such as the recently proposed neighboring pixel relationship [6]. It is worth noting that MSP does not belong to the forensic representation. However, experimental results indicate that MSP can be combined with both spatial-domain and frequency-domain forensic representations to further improve performance.

Once the forensic representation A is extracted, the decision mechanism, i.e., our proposed MSP strategy, takes over the subsequent process. Firstly, a convolutional detector receives the augmented forensic representation and extracts feature maps $f \in \mathbb{R}^{C_f \times H_f \times W_f}$, where H_f, W_f, and C_f present the height, width, and the number of channels of f. We input the $H_f W_f$ individual C_f-dimensional feature vectors into the fully connected layer to compute $H_f W_f$ predictions, denoted as $[p_1, p_2, ..., p_{H_f W_f}]$. Here, the prediction for each spatial location in f can be regarded as the prediction for a $\left\lceil \frac{H_A}{H_f} \right\rceil \times \left\lceil \frac{W_A}{W_f} \right\rceil$ patch in A. If A is a spatial domain artifact representation and has the same size with I, the prediction for each spatial location in f can be also regarded as the prediction for the same patch in the original image [4]. Therefore, we refer to $\left\lceil \frac{H_A}{H_f} \right\rceil \times \left\lceil \frac{W_A}{W_f} \right\rceil$ as the patch size for detection. Subsequently, the MSP rule is applied to identify the most suspicious patch, and the loss function is computed based on this patch to optimize the detector.

3.2 Most Suspicious Patch Rule

As discussed earlier, artifacts in AI-generated images are not necessarily distributed across the entire image. Therefore, the detector should focus on those areas with significant artifacts to effectively capture details that might be overlooked by GD. A key challenge here is that there is no explicit labeling to identify which regions contain the most significant artifacts. This means that the model needs to autonomously identify these areas during both the training and inference phases.

Moreover, the distribution of artifacts in AI-generated images can vary significantly. Some images, produced by advanced generative models, may contain artifacts concentrated in only a few small regions, while others may have artifacts spread across a larger area. This variability makes it challenging to determine an image's authenticity solely based on the average score of all regions, as the distribution of artifacts cannot be predicted in advance. Averaging scores may result in a "masking effect" where genuine regions dilute the impact of artifact-heavy regions, potentially obscuring the presence of artifacts.

To address these issues, we draw inspiration from the task of MIL, and define the MSP rule as follows: For a given image, its authenticity is determined by the most suspicious patch within it. If the most suspicious patch is deemed real, the image is classified as real. If the most suspicious patch is identified as fake, the image is classified as fake. The logic behind this approach is intuitive: if the image is real, all patches should be classified as real, including the most suspicious one; if the image is fake, at least one patch should be classified as fake, and that patch will be the most suspicious one.

Intuitively, the MSP rule eliminates the need for labeling all patches. It converts the authenticity label of the entire image into the authenticity label of the most suspicious patch. This solves the first challenge. Furthermore, even if different images have different artifact distributions, the MSP strategy guides the model to focus on the most suspicious patch. Other patches, even if they still contain artifacts, do not require additional attention, thus solving the second challenge.

Formally, during training, after calculating $H_f W_f$ prediction scores based on $f \in \mathbb{R}^{C_f \times H_f \times W_f}$, we select the maximum score $p_{max} = \max([p_1, p_2, \ldots, p_{H_f W_f}])$ as the score of the most suspicious patch, which is also the representative score for the entire image. We employ the standard binary cross entropy loss function for optimization.

$$L = -y \cdot log\sigma(p_{max}) - (1 - y) \cdot log(1 - \sigma(p_{max})) \quad (1)$$

where y is the ground-truth label, σ is the Sigmoid function.

During testing, the maximum score p_{max} is regarded as the score for the entire image.

4 Experiments

4.1 Datasets

Consistent with previous research, we trained our detectors using training images from 4 categories *car*, *cat*, *chair*, and *horse* on the training set from ForenSynths [1], and evaluated their performance on 4 test sets, including the test set from ForenSynths [1], DiffusionForensics [17], UniversalFakeDetect [18], and Diffusion1kStep [6].

4.2 Implementation Details

We developed all detectors using PyTorch 2.5.1 and TorchVision 0.20.1, and all detectors are trained on an NVIDIA RTX 4090D GPU.

We adopt the Adam optimizer with a learning rate of 5e-4 for a total of 100,000 iterations for training, and set the batch size to 64. We select the detector that achieved the best accuracy on the ForenSynths validation set for subsequent testing. The detector parameters are initialized using weights pre-trained on ImageNet. During training, all images are resized to 224 × 224. We apply random horizontal flipping with 50% probability and patch-shuffle [26] as data augmentation. Specifically, the forensic representation is partitioned into non-overlapping $h_{\text{aug}} \times w_{\text{aug}}$ patches, which are randomly shuffled and reassembled; this operation is applied with a fixed probability during training to reduce spatial correlations and encourage local artifact learning. we tune the patch size $h_{\text{aug}} \times w_{\text{aug}}$ for augmentation among [4 × 4, 8 × 8, 16 × 16, 32 × 32], and the probability for augmentation among [50%, 100%]. Given the limited search space, we exhaustively evaluate all combinations on MSP32(NPR) using ForenSynths. The best mean accuracy is achieved with an 8 × 8 patch size and 50% augmentation probability. We therefore adopt this configuration uniformly across all models and experiments to ensure consistency.

Following previous research, we use accuracy (Acc.) and the average precision score (A.P.) as the evaluation metric to assess the performance.

4.3 Our Detectors

We implement our MSP detector using the lightweight MobileNetV2 backbone [19]. By default, MobileNetV2 downsamples the input through strided convolutions in the 3rd, 6th, 10th, and 15th residual bottlenecks, yielding a final feature map with a 32×32 spatial resolution relative to the input—corresponding to a detection patch size of 32×32. We denote this variant as **MSP32**.

To obtain finer-grained predictions, we reduce the downsampling rate by setting the stride of earlier bottlenecks to 1. Specifically, we set the 15th bottleneck's stride to 1 yields a 16×16 output resolution, which is denoted as **MSP16**, and further set the 10th bottleneck's stride to 1 yields an 8×8 resolution, which is denoted as **MSP8**.

As described in Sect. 3, MSP is a decision mechanism that operates on top of any forensic representation. We name our detectors by combining the MSP variant and the underlying representation. For instance, **MSP32(NPR)** denotes a detector using NPR [6] as the forensic representation and MSP32 as the decision mechanism.

For fair comparison, we also construct global detection baselines by replacing MSP with **GD-F** (**G**lobal **D**etection based on averaged **F**eatures) [1–3] or **GD-S** (**G**lobal **D**etection based on averaged **S**cores) [4], resulting in models such as GD-F32(NPR) and GD-S32(NPR).

4.4 Experimental Analysis

Effectiveness and Compatibility of MSP. In this section, we evaluate the effectiveness and compatibility of our MSP, specifically whether using MSP results in better performance and whether MSP is compatible with diverse forensic representations. We select 3 representative forensic representations: CNNSpot [1], FreDect [2], and NPR [6]. CNNSpot is a pioneering spati-domain AI-generated image detection study that explored building a "universal" detector. FreDect is the first frequency-domain AI-generated image detection study. NPR is a recent study that achieved state-of-the-art performance. When combined with MSP, the forensic representations A are: the original image for CNNSpot, the frequency-domain image for FreDect, and the neighboring pixel relationships for NPR. Table 1 summarizes the average performance on the 4 test sets.

Firstly, it is evident that when combined with CNNSpot, FreDect, and NPR, MSP outperforms GD-F and GD-S. This clearly shows that MSP indeed brings significant performance improvements. Secondly, we observed substantial performance improvements when MSP was combined with spatial-domain forensic representations (CNNSpot and NPR), and more modest yet consistent gains when combined with frequency-domain forensic representation (FreDect). This further demonstrates the excellent compatibility of MSP. In summary, the above two observations strongly support the effectiveness of the proposed MSP, and confirm that MSP is an independent and orthogonal enhancement mechanism that can potentially benefit a wide range of forensic representations.

Table 1. Performance comparison between GD-F, GD-S, and MSP. The best performance is highlighted in bold.

Mechanism Strategy	Forensic Representation					
	CNNSpot		FreDect		NPR	
	Acc.	A.P.	Acc.	A.P.	Acc.	A.P.
GD-F	77.5	85.6	70.0	77.8	80.7	95.9
GD-S	73.9	84.0	68.8	76.1	83.8	92.5
MSP	**83.3**	**87.9**	**71.5**	**78.2**	**92.4**	**97.3**

Table 2. Average performance for all combinations of training and testing strategies using GD-F, GD-S, and MSP on 4 test sets. Detectors are adopt NPR as the forensic representation and 32×32 as the patch size.

Training	Testing	Average Performance	
		Acc.	A.P.
GD-F	GD-F	**80.7**	**95.9**
	GD-S	77.5	95.2
	MSP	72.6	75.2
GD-S	GD-F	83.8	92.5
	GD-S	84.1	**92.6**
	MSP	**88.0**	**92.6**
MSP	GD-F	67.0	95.2
	GD-S	63.1	97.1
	MSP	**92.5**	**97.3**

Effectiveness of MSP Training and Testing Strategy. To investigate whether the improvement from MSP arises primarily from its decision rule during inference, its training formulation, or the combination of both, we conduct a comprehensive cross-combination analysis. As shown in Table 2, we evaluate 9 combinations covering all possible train-test pairs of three detection strategies: GD-F, GD-S, and MSP.

The key observation is that, training and testing consistency is critical. The highest performance is generally achieved when the training and testing strategies are aligned. This suggests that MSP defines a complete and coherent training-inference paradigm.

Interestingly, when detectors are trained with GD-S, applying MSP at test time yields higher accuracy than using GD-S consistently. This suggests that MSP may provide intrinsic benefits as an inference mechanism. Nevertheless, the best overall results are achieved only when MSP is used throughout training and testing, confirming that full integration of the MSP paradigm yields optimal performance.

Comparison with State-of-the-Art Studies Given the strong performance of MSP in conjunction with NPR observed in the previous section, we construct three MSP detectors, MSP8(NPR), MSP16(NPR), and MSP32(NPR), using NPR as the forensic representation and compare them against a comprehensive set of state-of-the-art (SOTA) detectors. Table 3 presents performance comparisons between MSP32(NPR), MSP16(NPR), MSP8(NPR), and previous SOTA detectors. Results of previous SOTAs are sourced from NPR [6]. The performance of FatFormer [23], FreqNet [24], SAFE [25] are evaluated using the official code.

Table 3. Performance comparison on 4 test sets. The best performance is highlighted in bold, and the second-best performance is underlined.

Method	ForenSynths		DiffusionForensics		UniversalFakeDetect		Diffusion1kStep		Mean	
	Acc.	A.P.	Acc.	A.P.	Acc.	A.P.	Acc.	A.P.	Acc.	A.P.
CNNSpot(CVPR2020) [1]	67.1	86.9	51.0	79.8	52.8	67.4	49.9	52.7	55.2	71.7
FreDect(PRML 2020) [2]	78.9	76.5	46.0	50.2	54.5	49.6	58.8	61.4	60.0	59.4
Durall(CVPR 2020) [20]	67.7	64.4	47.0	48.3	54.3	54.0	51.2	53.1	55.1	55.0
Patchfor(ECCV 2020) [4]	80.7	87.1	78.1	97.8	86.8	97.2	57.1	61.6	75.7	85.9
F3Net(ECCV 2020) [12]	80.4	86.2	85.8	99.0	79.1	86.5	65.5	72.9	77.7	86.2
SelfBland(CVPR 2022) [21]	61.9	66.4	63.5	67.6	56.3	58.7	55.8	56.8	59.4	62.4
GANDetection(ICIP 2022) [22]	72.3	90.1	50.8	55.4	54.3	60.1	49.2	50.6	56.7	64.1
LGrad(CVPR 2023) [3]	86.1	91.5	88.2	98.5	90.9	97.2	64.2	74.3	82.1	90.4
UnivFD(CVPR 2023) [18]	89.1	98.3	74.4	91.7	86.9	94.5	66.4	73.9	79.2	89.6
FatFormer(CVPR 2024) [23]	**98.4**	**99.7**	81.2	95.6	93.7	98.6	66.4	85.0	84.9	94.7
FreqNet(AAAI 2024) [24]	91.5	98.5	80.9	98.6	89.5	95.4	62.4	70.4	81.1	90.7
NPR(CVPR 2024) [6]	92.5	96.1	95.3	99.8	95.2	97.4	80.1	84.8	90.8	94.5
SAFE(KDD 2025) [25]	96.2	98.8	90.5	98.6	95.7	99.1	81.2	88.5	90.9	96.3
MSP8(NPR)	94.0	97.4	96.5	**99.9**	95.7	99.2	77.9	86.8	91.0	95.8
MSP16(NPR)	93.8	97.5	**96.8**	99.8	95.8	99.0	80.4	89.8	91.7	96.5
MSP32(NPR)	94.8	97.8	**96.8**	**99.9**	**96.2**	**99.4**	**82.0**	**91.9**	**92.5**	**97.3**

Among MSP variants, MSP32(NPR) achieves the best average performance, suggesting larger detection patches are more effective, although we set the patch size for augmentation to 8. This is a reasonable phenomenon since the patch size for augmentation and that for detection serve different purposes: the goal of patch-based augmentation is to reduce the spatial correlations between image patches through division and shuffling, thereby increasing the detector's sensitivity to the artifacts remaining within each patch. When the patch size is too large (the extreme case being just one patch, i.e., the original input), the amount of information contained in each patch becomes too much, making it difficult for the detector to capture the residual artifacts. Conversely, when the patch size is too small, the patches contain insufficient information to differentiate between artifacts and natural image patterns. The patch size for detection is designed to enable artifact detection at a finer granularity. Therefore, it is reasonable that the optimal patch sizes for data augmentation and detection are different.

The second observation is that MSP16(NPR) and MSP8(NPR) also yield satisfactory results, although their performance is slightly inferior to MSP32(NPR). This strongly demonstrates the superiority of our MSP.

Our next observation is that MSP32(NPR) demonstrates excellent generalization ability and achieves new state-of-the-art performance. Specifically, the mean Acc. and A.P. of MSP32(NPR) outperforms the latest best detector SAFE by 1.6% and 1.0%, respectively. Although NPR is not the strongest standalone forensic representation, since it has been outperformed by recent detectors like SAFE in isolation, our MSP32(NPR) still achieves superior results overall. This suggests that the proposed MSP strategy plays a crucial role in enhancing detector generalization, beyond simply choosing a stronger forensic representation.

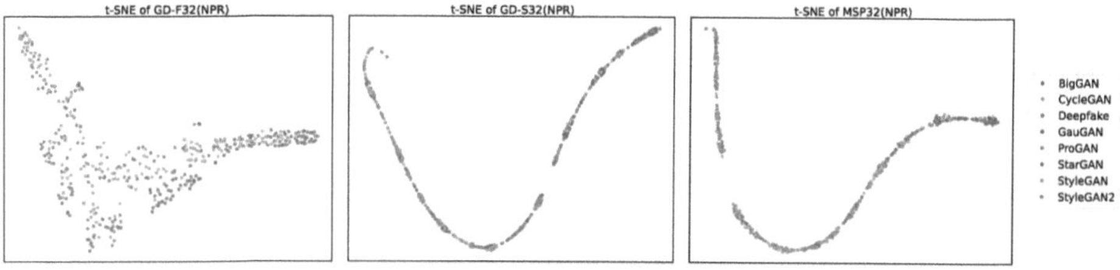

Fig. 3. Comparison between GD-F32(NPR), GD-S32(NPR) and MSP32(NPR) with t-SNE.

Exploration of the Mechanism of MSP To better understand how MSP improves the detection of AI-generated images, we qualitatively analyze the feature representations learned by different detection mechanism. A key hypothesis underpinning this study is that a strong general-purpose detector should capture *model-invariant artifacts*, i.e., features that are consistent across images generated by different models. Such shared artifacts are crucial for detecting forgeries from unseen generators.

We compare the feature distributions extracted by GD-F32(NPR), GD-S32(NPR), and MSP32(NPR). We apply them to the 8 subsets of the ForenSynths test set, and use t-SNE to project the high-dimensional features into 2D for visualization. As shown in Fig. 3, the features from GD-F32(NPR) and GD-S32(NPR) form more distinct clusters according to the generative source (for example, features corresponding to BigGAN concentrate on the far right of both GD-F32(NPR) and GD-S32(NPR) visualizations), indicating a reliance on *model-specific artifacts*. In contrast, MSP-based features are more intermingled and less separable, suggesting a focus on shared characteristics across models.

To quantify this observation, we compute the silhouette score using the generative model identity as cluster labels. A higher score indicates stronger inter-model separation, whereas a lower score implies more distributional overlap. MSP32(NPR) yields a lower silhouette score (-0.156) than GD-F32(NPR) (-0.045) and GD-F32(NPR) (-0.146), confirming that MSP reduces the influence of model-specific signatures and promotes the learning of model-invariant artifacts. This characteristic supports better generalization to unseen generators.

One possible reason for MSP's advantage is its focus on localized patches rather than entire images. By enforcing predictions at the patch level, MSP avoids overfitting to global or stylistic cues that are often unique to specific generative models. Instead, it encourages the detector to attend to more fundamental artifacts that are more likely to be shared across models. This localized, model-agnostic learning objective helps explain why MSP yields representations with less model-conditioned clustering and better cross-model generalization.

5 Conclusion

In this paper, we introduced MSP, a novel paradigm for detecting AI-generated images. Unlike popular global detection strategy, MSP shifts the decision-making focus from globally aggregated signals to the region most likely to contain detectable artifacts, encouraging detectors to attend to localized and model-agnostic artifacts rather than overfitting to global stylistic cues. Experimental results show that MSP not only maintains high accuracy but also significantly improves cross-model generalization. Further analysis reveals that MSP reduces model-specific signatures and promotes model-invariant artifact learning, enabling better generalization to unseen generators.

Acknowledgments. This work was supported by the National Natural Science Foundation of China (No.62406151, No.62576245), and the Research Start-up Fund for Recruited Talents from Tianjin University of Science and Technology.

References

1. Wang, S., et al.: CNN-generated images are surprisingly easy to spot... for now. In: Proceedings of the IEEE/CVF Conference on Computer Vision and Pattern Recognition, pp. 8695–8704 (2020)
2. Frank, J., Eisenhofer, T., Schönherr, L., et al.: Leveraging frequency analysis for deep fake image recognition. In: International Conference on Machine Learning, pp. 3247-3258 (2020)
3. Tan, C., Zhao, Y., Wei, S., et al.: Learning on gradients: generalized artifacts representation for gan-generated images detection. In: Proceedings of the IEEE/CVF Conference on Computer Vision and Pattern Recognition, pp. 12105-12114 (2023)
4. Chai, L., Bau, D., Lim, S.-N., Isola, P.: What makes fake images detectable? understanding properties that generalize. In: Vedaldi, A., Bischof, H., Brox, T., Frahm, J.-M. (eds.) ECCV 2020. LNCS, vol. 12371, pp. 103–120. Springer, Cham (2020). https://doi.org/10.1007/978-3-030-58574-7_7
5. Liu, B., Yang, F., Bi, X., et al.: Detecting generated images by real images. In: European Conference on Computer Vision, pp. 95-110 (2022)
6. Tan, C., Zhao, Y., Wei, S., et al.: Rethinking the up-sampling operations in cnn-based generative network for generalizable deepfake detection. In: Proceedings of the IEEE/CVF Conference on Computer Vision and Pattern Recognition, pp. 28130-28139 (2024)
7. Zhou, B., Khosla, A., Lapedriza, A., et al.: Learning deep features for discriminative localization. In: Proceedings of the IEEE Conference on Computer Vision and Pattern Recognition, pp. 2921-2929 (2016)
8. Liu, Z., Qi, X., Torr, P.: Global texture enhancement for fake face detection in the wild. In: Proceedings of the IEEE/CVF Conference on Computer Vision and Pattern Recognition, pp. 8060-8069 (2020)
9. Yu, N., Davis, L., Fritz, M.: Attributing fake images to gans: learning and analyzing gan fingerprints. In: Proceedings of the IEEE/CVF International Conference on Computer Vision, pp. 7556-7566 (2019)
10. Marra, F., Gragnaniello, D., Verdoliva, L., et al.: Do gans leave artificial fingerprints? In: IEEE Conference on Multimedia Information Processing and Retrieval, pp. 506-511 (2019)
11. Masi, I., Killekar, A., Mascarenhas, R.M., Gurudatt, S.P., AbdAlmageed, W.: Two-branch recurrent network for isolating deepfakes in videos. In: Vedaldi, A., Bischof, H., Brox, T., Frahm, J.-M. (eds.) ECCV 2020. LNCS, vol. 12352, pp. 667–684. Springer, Cham (2020). https://doi.org/10.1007/978-3-030-58571-6_39

12. Qian, Y., Yin, G., Sheng, L., Chen, Z., Shao, J.: Thinking in frequency: face forgery detection by mining frequency-aware clues. In: Vedaldi, A., Bischof, H., Brox, T., Frahm, J.-M. (eds.) ECCV 2020. LNCS, vol. 12357, pp. 86–103. Springer, Cham (2020). https://doi.org/10.1007/978-3-030-58610-2_6
13. Luo, Y., Zhang, Y., Yan, J., et al.: Generalizing face forgery detection with high-frequency features. In: Proceedings of the IEEE/CVF Conference on Computer Vision and Pattern Recognition, pp. 16317-16326 (2021)
14. Woo, S.: Add: frequency attention and multi-view based knowledge distillation to detect low-quality compressed deepfake images. In: Proceedings of the AAAI Conference on Artificial Intelligence, pp. 122-130 (2022)
15. Jeong, Y., Kim, D., Min, S., et al.: Bihpf: bilateral high-pass filters for robust deepfake detection. In: Proceedings of the IEEE/CVF Winter Conference on Applications of Computer Vision, pp. 48-57 (2022)
16. Jeong, Y., Kim, D., Ro, Y., et al.: Frepgan: robust deepfake detection using frequency-level perturbations. In: Proceedings of the AAAI Conference on Artificial Intelligence, pp. 1060-1068 (2022)
17. Wang, Z., Bao, J., Zhou, W., et al.: Dire for diffusion-generated image detection. In: Proceedings of the IEEE/CVF International Conference on Computer Vision, pp. 22445-22455 (2023)
18. Ojha, U., Li, Y., Lee, Y.: Towards universal fake image detectors that generalize across generative models. In: Proceedings of the IEEE/CVF Conference on Computer Vision and Pattern Recognition, pp. 24480-24489 (2023)
19. Sandler, M., Howard, A., Zhu, M., et al.: Mobilenetv2: Inverted residuals and linear bottlenecks. In: Proceedings of the IEEE Conference on Computer Vision and Pattern Recognition, pp. 4510-4520 (2018)
20. Durall, R., Keuper, M., Keuper, J.: Watch your up-convolution: Cnn based generative deep neural networks are failing to reproduce spectral distributions. In: Proceedings of the IEEE/CVF Conference on Computer Vision and Pattern Recognition, pp. 7890-7899 (2020)
21. Shiohara, K., Yamasaki, T.: Detecting deepfakes with self-blended images. In: Proceedings of the IEEE/CVF Conference on Computer Vision and Pattern Recognition, pp. 18720-18729 (2022)
22. Mandelli, S., Bonettini, N., Bestagini, P., et al.: Detecting gan-generated images by orthogonal training of multiple cnns. In: IEEE International Conference on Image Processing, pp. 3091-3095 (2022)
23. Liu, H., Tan, Z., Tan, C., et al.: Forgery-aware adaptive transformer for generalizable synthetic image detection. In: Proceedings of the IEEE/CVF Conference on Computer Vision and Pattern Recognition, pp. 10770-10780 (2024)
24. Tan, C., Zhao, Y., Wei, S., et al.: Frequency-aware deepfake detection: improving generalizability through frequency space domain learning. In: Proceedings of the AAAI Conference on Artificial Intelligence, pp. 5052-5060 (2024)
25. Li, O., Cai, J., Hao, Y., et al.: Improving synthetic image detection towards generalization: an image transformation perspective. In: Proceedings of the 31st ACM SIGKDD Conference on Knowledge Discovery and Data Mining, pp. 2405-2414 (2025)
26. Liu, S., Lian, Z., Gu, S., et al.: Block shuffling learning for deepfake detection. arXiv preprint arXiv:2202.02819 (2022)

GROFF: A Generative Restoration Model for Occluded Face Filling

Haoyun Xu[1,2], Zhiyu Wan[1](✉), and Yun Wei[2]

[1] School of Biomedical Engineering & State Key Laboratory of Advanced Medical Materials and Devices, ShanghaiTech University, Shanghai, China
{xuhy12025,wanzhy}@shanghaitech.edu.cn

[2] School of Optical-Electrical and Computer Engineering, University of Shanghai for Science and Technology, Shanghai, China
weiyun@usst.edu.cn

Abstract. High-quality facial data is fundamental for machine learning tasks such as facial expression and emotion recognition. However, research relying on custom-collected facial data must contend with partial occlusions caused by accessories like glasses, hats, masks, and hair. Although numerous studies, including those employing various generative models, have advanced image inpainting, partial face restoration still faces three persistent challenges: the loss of identity and expression features under large-area occlusions, generally low output image quality, and unnatural transitions at the boundaries of restored regions. To address these issues, we propose GROFF, a generative restoration model for occluded face filling. Built on generative adversarial networks (GANs), GROFF incorporates a Transformer module within its generator. This hybrid architecture enables robust local feature capture through the GAN structure while leveraging the self-attention mechanism of Transformers to model long-range dependencies and maintain global semantic consistency. Furthermore, a semantic network is integrated to enhance fine details and textures. Extensive comparative experiments across multiple datasets demonstrate that our approach achieves significant improvements in both image quality and similarity metrics over baseline methods, confirming the effectiveness of our proposed design.

Keywords: Face Restoration · Image Inpainting · Generative Adversarial Networks (GANs) · Vision Transformer (ViT) · Semantic Consistency

1 Introduction

Facial data is critically important in the field of machine learning, serving as an essential foundation for tasks such as facial expression recognition and emotion analysis [1]. While numerous large-scale, high-quality facial datasets are available, researchers often need to utilize custom-collected data. This practice, however, frequently introduces the challenge of partial facial occlusions caused by accessories like glasses, hats, masks, and hair. These occlusions result in incomplete data, posing a significant obstacle for downstream analyses and creating a compelling need for robust face filling techniques.

R. C.-W. Wong et al. (Eds.): PAKDD 2026, LNAI 16618, pp. 436–447, 2027.
https://doi.org/10.1007/978-981-92-1947-6_35

To address this issue, researchers have previously developed three primary categories of strategies for facial data completion. Prior to the rise of deep learning, researchers primarily relied on hand-crafted feature descriptors to tackle occluded face recognition. Methods such as local binary patterns (LBP) [2], scale-invariant feature transform (SIFT) [3], and histogram of oriented gradients (HOG) [4] were representatives of this era. Although these methods performed reasonably well under mild occlusion conditions, they struggled with extensive occlusions and complex facial expression variations. With the advancement of deep learning, generative adversarial networks (GANs) [5] were introduced in 2014 and have since demonstrated remarkable potential in image generation and restoration. Through the adversarial training mechanism of the generator and discriminator, GANs learnt the underlying distribution of facial images, thereby enabling the generation of highly realistic images. After that, subsequent research works gave rise to numerous improved algorithms based on GANs. For instance, the generative image inpainting method proposed by Yu et al. utilized a contextual attention mechanism to significantly enhance the restoration quality of occluded facial images [6]. The pix2pixHD model introduced by Wang et al. achieved high-resolution image synthesis at 2048 $\times$ 1024 pixels through a multi-scale generator and discriminator architecture [7].

Despite significant progress in GAN-based image generation, existing occlusion face restoration techniques based on the original GAN architecture still face several challenges. First, traditional GANs based on convolutional neural network (CNN) struggle to capture long-range dependencies, often resulting in the loss of facial identity characteristics and expression information, thereby compromising global consistency in the restored regions. Second, in complex occlusion scenarios (e.g., large-area or multiple occlusions), current methods often produce blurry or distorted low-quality results. Furthermore, ensuring a natural transition between the restored region boundaries and the surrounding non-occluded parts remains a critical yet unresolved issue. These challenges directly impact the quality of the restored data and the performance of models trained on such data.

To address these challenges and enable the restoration of occluded facial data to a quality level comparable to existing high-quality datasets, we propose GROFF, a Generative Restoration model for Occluded Face Filling. This model can identify masks within an image and subsequently fill and refine the occluded areas based on the features from the non-occluded facial regions. To overcome GANs' limited ability to model long-range dependency, we introduce a Transformer module within the generator architecture. With its self-attention mechanism, this module can capture global contextual information, ensuring feature preservation and consistency across the entire image. Additionally, we incorporate a semantic network to enhance image quality and local details, resulting in more visually natural images.

Our contributions can be summarized as follows:

1. We propose a novel GAN-based face restoration model, which innovatively integrates the superior capability of Transformers in modeling long-range dependencies with the exceptional local detail capture of CNNs, thereby significantly enhancing feature consistency across the entire facial image.

2. The model incorporates a semantic network, which effectively ensures natural transitions at the boundaries between restored and non-occluded regions, and substantially improving the visual quality of the output.
3. We test our model across four diverse datasets, comprehensively validating the effectiveness and superiority of our model's architectural design.

2 Related Work

2.1 GANs in Facial Generating

Since the advent of GANs, research on their improvement has remained highly active, with numerous groundbreaking studies making significant contributions and pioneering new ideas for the field of image generation, particularly in facial generation. For instance, Le et al. introduced a local discriminator combined with an encoder-decoder architecture for generative face completion [8]. The encoder extracts features from the non-occluded regions, focusing on enhancing the realism of local areas, thereby generating much more natural facial features. Furthermore, AttGAN was developed to modify specific facial attributes [9]. It employs an attention mechanism, compelling the generator to preserve other facial features while altering specific regions, achieving fine-grained control over facial attributes.

Although these methods broaden the application of GANs and improve detail handling, discussions on maintaining identity consistency across the entire restored face remain limited, and the issue of seamless transitions between restored and non-occluded areas has yet to be adequately addressed. These issues require urgent resolution because, when used as training data, restored images with inconsistent features or visible boundary seams can mislead models, causing them to learn incorrect facial features or perceive the seams as part of the facial characteristics).

2.2 Vision Transformer in Image Restoration

Vaswani et al. pioneered the Transformer architecture in 2017 [10], which was initially designed for natural language processing (NLP). In 2020, Dosovitskiy et al. introduced the Vision Transformer (ViT) by cascading multiple Transformer layers to capture the global context of input images [11]. This method achieved remarkable success in image generation and was swiftly applied to image restoration tasks. For example, Zhang et al. designed the Swin Transformer U-Net (STUNet) [12]. This ViT with a U-net architecture utilizes attention mechanisms and shifted windows to capture long-range dependencies between pixels.

For image data like faces, which contain high information density and strong intrinsic correlations between features, ViT presents a promising approach for restoration. However, previous research applying ViT to face restoration is limited and has not sufficiently addressed image quality, particularly concerning the generation of local details. Therefore, our research aims to combine ViT's exceptional capability to modeling long-range dependencies with the local feature extraction strengths of CNN-based GANs, leveraging their complementary advantages to enhance occluded face restoration.

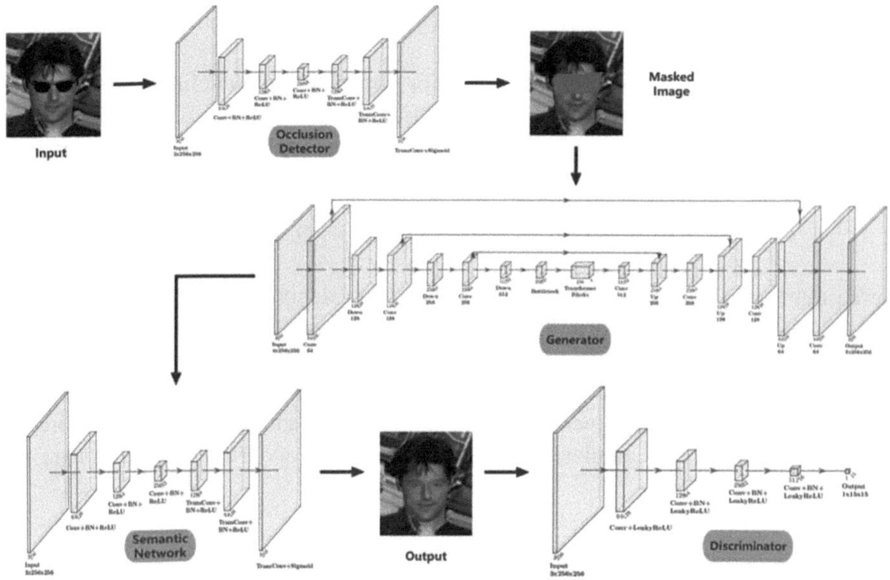

Fig. 1. Architecture of the training structure of GROFF. It is illustrated with an example of facial image in a single round of training process.

3 Model

This section provides a comprehensive description of the GROFF framework. Figure 1 illustrates the complete processing pipeline and model architecture through the example of a facial image during one training iteration, highlighting the four core modules. The following subsections detail the components of each module and the corresponding loss functions, explaining how they collectively achieve our desired objectives.

3.1 Occlusion Detector Module

The Occlusion Detector module is a CNN specifically designed for identifying occluded regions within an image, employing an encoder-decoder architecture. The module adopts a U-Net-like structure, utilizing skip connections to preserve high-resolution details [13]. Its output is a single-channel mask, with values constrained to the range [0, 1] by a Sigmoid activation function, while Batch Normalization and ReLU activation functions are incorporated to enhance training stability.

The input is an occluded image with dimensions (B, 3, 256, 256), where B denotes the batch size. This input undergoes three consecutive convolutional (Conv) operations, each followed by BatchNorm and ReLU activation [14]. Subsequently, upsampling is performed to restore the original resolution via three transposed convolution (TransConv) operations. These are respectively fused with corresponding features from the encoder path via skip connections. The first two transposed convolutions are followed by BatchNorm and ReLU, while the final layer uses a Sigmoid activation. The final output is a mask (B, 1, 256, 256) with values in [0, 1], representing the probability of a pixel being occluded.

The Mask Accuracy Loss is responsible for optimizing the occlusion detector network. It utilizes the Binary Cross-Entropy (BCE) loss function to evaluate the accuracy of the predicted mask, ensuring the model can precisely identify occluded areas in the image. The formula of BCE is as follows:

$$BCE(y, \hat{y}) = -\left[y \cdot \log(\hat{y}) + (1 - y) \cdot \log(1 - \hat{y})\right] \quad (1)$$

where y represents the ground truth label (0 or 1), and $\hat{y}$ denotes the predicted probability from the model [0, 1]. This formula computes the loss value for each sample. By minimizing this loss function, the model is driven to produce predictions closer to the true probability distribution [15]. During the training loop, after the mask loss is computed, it is also incorporated into the generator's total loss to further guide the generation process. Concurrently, the model calculates and records the mask accuracy to monitor training progress.

3.2 Generator Module with Transformer

The Generator employs a hybrid architecture that integrates CNN and Transformer components, tasked with generating plausible content in occluded regions. Its structure is depicted in Fig. 2. The CNN section utilizes multiple downsampling and upsampling modules to extract local features, while the Transformer section implements a self-attention mechanism to capture global contextual relationships. The model incorporates residual connections and skip connections to mitigate gradient vanishing and enhance detail preservation, alongside a multi-scale feature fusion mechanism to boost its representational capacity.

The input is formed by concatenating the occluded image (B, 3, 256, 256) and the mask (B, 1, 256, 256) produced by the occlusion detection network, resulting in a tensor of dimensions (B, 4, 256, 256). Each layer incorporates batch normalization and activation functions to stabilize training. The initial layer uses ReLU activation and projects the channels to 64. This is followed by five downsampling encoder layers,with an additional downsampling layer added to reduce the sequence length processed by the Transformer. The feature maps then pass through the Transformer block, which models global contextual relationships using dynamic positional encoding. This block is configured with 8 attention heads, each with a dimensionality of 64, and includes a feed-forward network. Finally, the features are processed by a decoder comprising upsampling layers with skip connections utilized during decoding to preserve finer details. The final output size is (B, 3, 256, 256).

The generator loss is a comprehensive loss function designed to train the generator network to produce high-quality, natural-looking inpainted content. It combines multiple loss components, including adversarial loss, reconstruction loss, perceptual loss, and total variation loss. The adversarial loss is computed using mean squared error (MSE), the reconstruction loss employs L1 Loss, and the perceptual loss utilizes VGG feature loss. This subsection primarily introduces the VGG feature loss, while the other losses will be detailed subsequently. The formula of the VGG feature loss is as follows:

$$VGG(I,\hat{I}) = \frac{1}{h_l w_l c_l} \sum i,j,k\left(\phi_{i,j,k}^{(l)}(I) - \phi_{i,j,k}^{(l)}(\hat{I})\right)^2 \tag{2}$$

where I is the original image, $\hat{I}$ is the reconstructed image, $\phi_{i,j,k}^{(l)}$ represents the feature representation from the l-th layer of the VGG network, and h_l, w_l, c_l denote the height, width, and number of channels of the feature maps in layer l, respectively, summing over all pixels in the feature maps. By comparing high-level features of images, the VGG feature loss better captures semantic information beyond mere pixel-level differences [16]. During training, the generator loss is combined with the mask loss before optimization, and a learning rate scheduler adjusts the learning rate based on training progress.

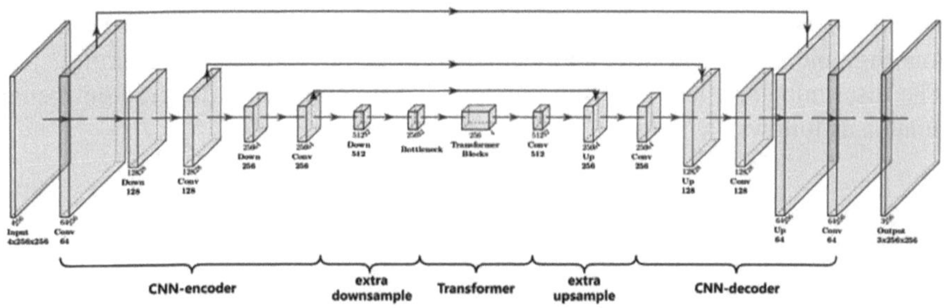

Fig. 2. Architecture of the Generator module. The generator consists of a CNN encoder and a series of Transformer blocks. An additional downsampling layer is inserted before the Transformer blocks to reduce the sequence length for efficient processing, followed by a corresponding upsampling layer to restore the spatial resolution.

3.3 Semantic Network Module

The Semantic Network is a lightweight module designed to enhance the semantic consistency and natural appearance of the generated content. This module maintains the input resolution and does not alter the overall structure of the image. It performs subtle semantic refinement through three convolutional layers to optimize local details and textures. The module utilizes three residual blocks (ResBlocks) to alleviate the gradient vanishing problem, and employs a Tanh activation function at the output to maintain the same value range as the generator's output.

The Semantic Consistency Loss, computed using L1 Loss, evaluates the enhancement effect of the semantic-aware network. This network is responsible for improving the naturalness and overall coherence of the generated content. The loss ensures consistency between the generated image and the ground truth at the semantic level, going beyond mere pixel-level similarity. The formula is as follows:

$$L1Loss(y,\hat{y}) = \frac{1}{n}\sum_{i=1}^{n} \mid y_i - \hat{y}_i \mid \tag{3}$$

where n is the total number of samples. The L1 loss function is more robust to outliers, as it does not amplify large errors like MSE does. The semantic network is optimized separately to focus exclusively on enhancing semantic quality. During training, the learning rate for this network is independently adjusted via its own scheduler.

3.4 Discriminator Module

The Discriminator is based on the PatchGAN architecture and is responsible for distinguishing between real and generated images by making local patch-level predictions [17]. The module employs a multi-layer convolutional structure to progressively extract high-level features, utilizing Spectral normalization to enhance training stability. The network consists of five convolutional layers for feature extraction, using LeakyReLU as the activation function to prevent gradient vanishing. The final layer serves as the discrimination layer, outputting raw discrimination scores (B, 1, 15, 15) for each patch without Sigmoid activation, which are then used to guide the generator training.

The discriminator's loss function employs MSE combined with gradient penalty, formulated as follows:

$$MSE(y, \hat{y}) = \frac{1}{n}\sum_{i=1}^{n}(y_i - \hat{y}_i)^2 \tag{4}$$

The MSE for each sample is calculated accordingly. It quantifies the deviation between a predicted value and the corresponding ground truth; a lower MSE indicates smaller errors and better model performance. After computation, the discriminator loss is optimized independently from the generator.

4 Experiments

4.1 Experimental Setup

Datasets. For model training, we employ the CelebFaces Attribute (CelebA) dataset [18]. This dataset serves as a benchmark for training GAN-based models and is extensively employed in various face-related computer vision tasks. The images within the dataset encompass diverse pose variations and cluttered backgrounds, containing 202,599 facial images of 10,177 celebrities.

Furthermore, to evaluate the effectiveness of our method, we conduct comparative experiments against several baselines on four datasets: CelebA, Flicker-Faces-HQ (FFHQ) [19], Labeled Faces in the Wild (LFW) [20], and Visual Geometry Group Face 2 (VGGFace2) [21]. They are all commonly used high-quality datasets. Their key characteristics are summarized in Table 1.

Table 1. Comparison of All Used Datasets

Datasets	Size	Image Resolution	Features
CelebA	~200 k	218 × 178	Rich attribute annotations
FFHQ	70 k	1024 × 1024	Exceptionally high quality and diversity
LFW	~13 k	Variable	Unconstrained conditions
VGGFace2	>3.3 M	Variable	Large pose/age variation

Training and Evaluation Protocol. The initial learning rate for both the generator and discriminator is set to 0.0002, a common starting point for GAN training. The model utilizes a cosine annealing scheduler to dynamically adjust the learning rate, governed by the following formula:

$$\eta_t = \eta_{min} + \frac{1}{2}(\eta_{max} - \eta_{min})\left(1 + \cos\left(\frac{t}{T_{max}}\pi\right)\right) \quad (5)$$

where η_t is the learning rate at the current epoch t, η_{min} is the minimum learning rate, η_{max} is the initial maximum learning rate, and T_{max} is the total number of epochs. This mechanism smoothly decays the learning rate from its initial value to the minimum, reaching the minimum at the end of training [22].

During training, model parameters are updated after each batch based on the computed gradients. Additionally, Automatic Mixed Precision (AMP) is utilized to accelerate training and optimize performance.

All experiments are conducted on a single NVIDIA A100 Tensor Core GPU. The batch size is set to 16 based on the available GPU memory. To ensure a fair comparison, we maintain consistency in the number of training epochs across all experimental settings.

Baselines. To comprehensively evaluate the performance of our method, we compare the proposed model against two classic and one advanced GAN-based methods. The selected classic baselines include DCGAN [23] and Generative Face Completion (GFC) [8]. Additionally, we benchmark our approach against StyleGAN-XL, which represents the current state-of-the-art GAN-based model in image generation [24].

4.2 Quantitative Results

In this section, we present the performance of the models on various datasets using standard evaluation metrics. The primary metrics for comparison are the Peak Signal-to-Noise Ratio (PSNR) and the Structural Similarity Index Measure (SSIM). PSNR is a standard metric for assessing the quality of reconstructed images, while SSIM evaluates the similarity between images in terms of structure, luminance, and contrast. A higher PSNR value indicates better image quality, with values typically exceeding 30 considered good. The SSIM index ranges from 0 to 1, with values closer to 1 representing higher similarity to the original image.

We evaluate the restoration performance of each method under two conditions: 30% facial occlusion (simulating medium-area occlusions caused by elements like glasses, bangs, or beards) and 50% facial occlusion (simulating large-area occlusions caused by masks or shadows). Facial Occlusion Ratio = Area of Occlusion / Facial Area. The facial area is defined as the rectangle encompassing the face from the hairline to the chin and from cheek to cheek, excluding the ears. For each dataset and occlusion level, the average PSNR and SSIM values across a selected set of data are recorded in Table 2 for reference and comparative analysis.

Table 2. Quantitative Results under Different Datasets

30% Occluded	CelebA		FFHQ		LFW		VGGFace2	
Method	PSNR	SSIM	PSNR	SSIM	PSNR	SSIM	PSNR	SSIM
GROFF (Ours)	**31.63**	**0.978**	**30.96**	**0.975**	**32.87**	**0.981**	**28.33**	**0.965**
DCGANs	26.86	0.918	26.85	0.915	30.83	0.928	24.89	0.903
GFC	25.57	0.901	24.23	0.891	28.08	0.914	23.67	0.886
StyleGAN-XL	30.85	0.960	29.50	0.958	31.97	0.934	27.98	0.949
50% Occluded	CelebA		FFHQ		LFW		VGGFace2	
Method	PSNR	SSIM	PSNR	SSIM	PSNR	SSIM	PSNR	SSIM
GROFF (Ours)	**30.53**	**0.963**	**28.60**	**0.962**	**30.54**	**0.966**	**26.11**	**0.950**
DCGANs	25.63	0.904	24.53	0.902	28.17	0.909	22.86	0.901
GFC	24.34	0.885	23.12	0.877	27.63	0.897	22.88	0.877
StyleGAN-XL	28.56	0.946	27.74	0.945	29.75	0.948	24.59	0.914

As observed, under conditions of moderate to large-area occlusions, our model demonstrates outstanding performance across all datasets. It significantly outperforms two classical algorithms and exhibits a competitive advantage when compared to StyleGAN-XL.

4.3 Qualitative Results

To intuitively demonstrate the effectiveness of our work, we selected a diverse set of faces (varying in skin tone, ethnicity, and gender) and applied occlusions at different ratios to observe the restoration performance. The restoration results produced by different models for the same input image are displayed side-by-side, allowing for a direct visual assessment of the perceptual differences in the output.

As evidenced by the comparative results in Fig. 3, notable differences in restoration details can be observed across methods. Even under substantial occlusion, our approach avoids noticeable artifacts or seams—precisely addressing the limitations identified in prior research. Furthermore, our method effectively preserves key facial expressions, such as those conveyed through the eyes and mouth corners, maintaining strong consistency with the original image and resulting in a harmoniously natural visual outcome.

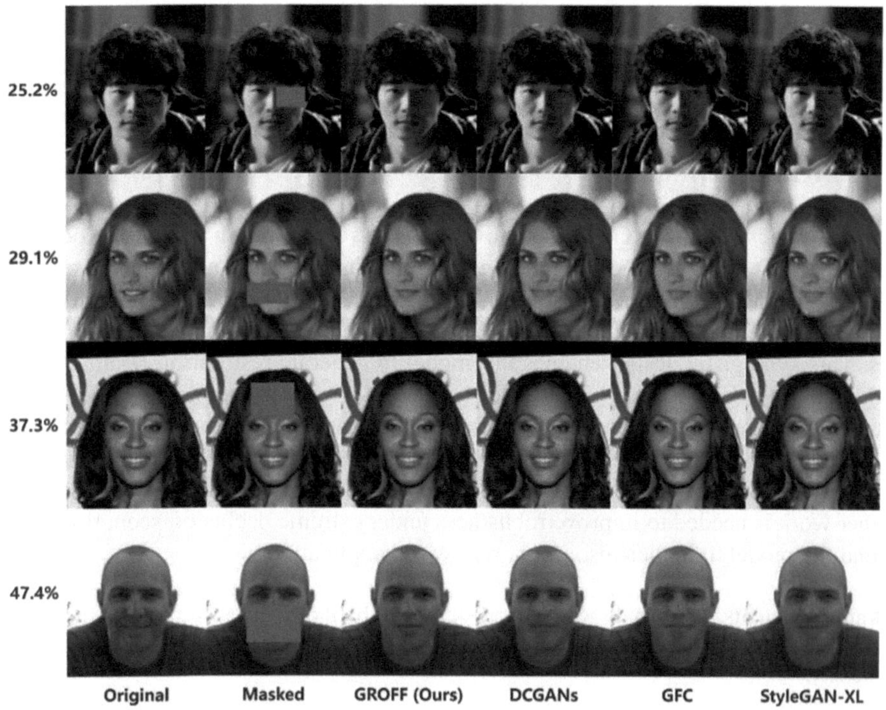

Fig. 3. Comparative evaluation of various models under diverse occlusion ratios and areas.

4.4 Ablation Study

To validate the effectiveness of the core components in our model, this section analyzes their impact on occluded face restoration performance by progressively removing key improved modules. The experiments are conducted on **CelebA**, using identical evaluation metrics under facial occlusion of 30%.

Table 3. Quantitative Comparison of Ablation Study Results

Method	PSNR/dB	SSIM
Full GROFF (Ours)	31.63	0.978
Original GANs	22.31 (↓29.5%)	0.824 (↓15.7%)
w/o Transformer	26.57 (↓16.0%)	0.908 (↓7.2%)
w/o Semantic Network	29.45 (↓6.9%)	0.956 (↓2.2%)

As shown in Table 3, compared to our full method, GROFF without Transformer exhibits a statistically significant decrease in both PSNR and SSIM values. This validates the critical importance of the introduced Transformer module for enhancing image clarity and global semantic coherence. Furthermore, the performance of GROFF without Semantic Network indicates that this module provides further optimization of the overall image quality on top of the Transformer module, proving its non-negligible role in enhancing visual quality. Therefore, these modules are effectively responsible for the significant improvements our method achieves over the original GANs.

5 Conclusion

In this work, we propose GROFF, a novel generative restoration model for occluded face filling that integrates the complementary strengths of GANs and Transformers. The GAN framework provides a robust foundation for capturing local facial features, while the Transformer's self-attention mechanism effectively models long-range dependencies. This synergistic design enables our model to generate restoration results that are both visually coherent and semantically consistent, yielding completed facial images with accurate reconstruction and enhanced naturalness. Comprehensive comparative experiments across multiple datasets demonstrate that our approach substantially outperforms baseline methods in both image quality and similarity metrics. Nonetheless, further work is needed to improve robustness under extreme occlusion scenarios and to extend the model to higher-resolution, real-world applications.

Acknowledgments. This study was supported, in part, by the National Natural Science Foundation of China (82441023, 72501181 to Z.W.) and the HPC Platform of ShanghaiTech University.

References

1. Li, S., Deng, W.: Deep facial expression recognition: a survey. IEEE Trans. Affect. Comput. **13**(3), 1195–1215 (2020)
2. Shan, C., Gong, S., McOwan, P.W.: Facial expression recognition based on local binary patterns: a comprehensive study. Image Vis. Comput. **27**(6), 803–816 (2009)
3. Lowe, D.G.: Object recognition from local scale-invariant features. In: Proceedings of the Seventh IEEE International Conference on Computer Vision, vol. 2, pp. 1150–1157 (1999)
4. Dalal, N., Triggs, B.: Histograms of oriented gradients for human detection. In: 2005 IEEE Computer Society Conference on Computer Vision and Pattern Recognition, vol. 1, pp. 886–893 (2005)
5. Goodfellow, I.J., et al.: Generative adversarial nets. Advances in NeurIPS, vol. 27 (2014)
6. Yu, J., et al.: Generative image inpainting with contextual attention. In: Proceedings of the IEEE Conference on Computer Vision and Pattern Recognition, pp. 5505–5514 (2018)
7. Wang, T.C., et al.: High-resolution image synthesis and semantic manipulation with conditional gans. In: Proceedings of the IEEE Conference on Computer Vision and Pattern Recognition, pp. 8798–8807 (2018)
8. Li, Y., et al.: Generative face completion. In: Proceedings of the IEEE Conference on Computer Vision and Pattern Recognition, pp. 3911–3919 (2017)
9. He, Z., et al.: Attgan: facial attribute editing by only changing what you want. IEEE Trans. Image Process. **28**(11), 5464–5478 (2019)
10. Vaswani, A., et al.: Attention is all you need. Advances in NeurIPS, vol. 30 (2017)
11. Dosovitskiy, A.: An image is worth 16x16 words: transformers for image recognition at scale arXiv preprint https://arxiv.org/abs/2010.11929 (2020)

12. Zhang, P., et al.: Blind face restoration: benchmark datasets and a baseline model. Neurocomputing. **574**, 127271 (2024)
13. Ronneberger, O., Fischer, P., Brox, T.: U-net: convolutional networks for biomedical image segmentation. In: International Conference on Medical Image Computing and Computer-Assisted Intervention, pp. 234–241 (2015)
14. Apicella, A., et al.: A survey on modern trainable activation functions. Neural Netw. **138**, 14–32 (2021)
15. Mao, A., Mohri, M., Zhong, Y.: Cross-entropy loss functions: theoretical analysis and applications. In: International Conference on Machine Learning, pp. 23803–23828 (2023)
16. Yang, Q., et al.: Low-dose CT image denoising using a generative adversarial network with Wasserstein distance and perceptual loss. IEEE Trans. Med. Imaging. **37**(6), 1348–1357 (2018)
17. Isola, P., et al.: Image-to-image translation with conditional adversarial networks. In: Proceedings of the IEEE Conference on Computer Vision and Pattern Recognition, pp. 1125–1134 (2017)
18. Liu, Z., et al.: Deep learning face attributes in the wild. In: Proceedings of the International Conference on Computer Vision (2015)
19. Karras, T., et al.: A style-based generator architecture for generative adversarial networks. In: Proceedings of the IEEE/CVF Conference on Computer Vision and Pattern Recognition, pp. 4401–4410 (2019)
20. Huang, G.B., et al.: Labeled faces in the wild: a database for studying face recognition in unconstrained environments. In: Workshop on Faces in 'Real-Life' Images: Detection, Alignment, and Recognition (2008)
21. Cao, Q., et al.: Vggface2: a dataset for recognising faces across pose and age. In: IEEE International Conference on Automatic Face and Gesture Recognition, pp. 67–74 (2018)
22. Zhang, C., et al.: The WuC-Adam algorithm based on joint improvement of warmup and cosine annealing algorithms. Math. Biosci. Eng. **21**(1) (2024)
23. Radford, A., Metz, L., Chintala, S.: Unsupervised representation learning with deep convolutional generative adversarial networks. arXiv preprint https://arxiv.org/abs/1511.06434 (2015)
24. Sauer, A., Schwarz, K., Geiger, A.: Stylegan-xl: scaling stylegan to large diverse datasets. In: ACM SIGGRAPH 2022 Conference Proceedings, pp. 1–10 (2022)

Q-Matrix Completeness and Annotation Strategies: A Comparative Study of Knowledge Tracing Architectures

Liu Cheng Lee[1](✉), Yutaka Arakawa[2], and Tsunenori Mine[2]

[1] Department of Information Science and Technology, Graduate School of Information Science and Electrical Engineering, Kyushu University, Fukuoka, Japan
lee.liu.cheng.228@s.kyushu-u.ac.jp

[2] Department of Advanced Information Technology, Faculty of Information Science and Electrical Engineering, Kyushu University, Fukuoka, Japan
{arakawa,mine}@ait.kyushu-u.ac.jp

Abstract. Knowledge tracing models often rely on Q-matrices to map assessment items to the skills they require. However, real-world educational platforms frequently operate under limited annotation resources, leading to incomplete or partially constructed Q-matrices. This study provides the first systematic comparison of five representative knowledge tracing architectures—DKVMN, AKT, GIKT, LPKT, and DKVMN-KAPS—under varying levels of Q-matrix completeness. Using the Eedi 2020 dataset and controlled masking conditions, we examine how model performance changes across completeness levels from 0% to 100%. To further address annotation cost, we evaluate six incremental annotation strategies and analyze their impact on predictive performance. Results show that AKT, GIKT, and LPKT maintain stable performance even with low completeness, while DKVMN-KAPS exhibits strong dependence on full Q-matrix availability and improves sharply only near 100% completeness. For annotation strategies, the *important_skills* strategy achieves peak performance (0.811 ROC AUC) at 75% budget for DKVMN-KAPS, substantially outperforming the baseline (0.708 ROC AUC) and all other strategies at the same completeness level. These findings offer practical guidance for annotation prioritization and model selection in resource-constrained educational settings.

Keywords: Knowledge Tracing · Q-matrix Completeness · Incremental Annotation · Educational Data Mining · Model Comparison

1 Introduction

Knowledge Tracing (KT) aims to infer students' mastery of skills from response sequences [1,2]. Most KT models rely on a Q-matrix to represent item–skill relationships [3,4], where each item is associated with a binary vector indicating the skills it requires [5,6].

R. C.-W. Wong et al. (Eds.): PAKDD 2026, LNAI 16618, pp. 448–459, 2027.
https://doi.org/10.1007/978-981-92-1947-6_36

In practice, however, constructing a complete Q-matrix is challenging: expert annotation is costly, coverage may be partial, and different construction strategies—such as prioritizing representative items, maximizing skill coverage, or random selection—can lead to markedly different Q-matrix structures. Because KT models differ in how strongly they rely on skill information, their predictions may respond differently to variations in Q-matrix completeness or construction strategy [7,8].

Understanding the interaction among model type, Q-matrix completeness, and construction strategy is therefore critical for guiding model selection, annotation budgeting, and large-scale skill-structure design in real applications [4,9–11].

Therefore, this study investigates the following research questions:

- **RQ1:** How do different KT models change in performance and internal representations under varying levels of Q-matrix completeness?
- **RQ2:** Under limited annotation budgets, which incremental annotation strategies are most effective for different KT model architectures?

To address RQ1, we conduct a controlled masking study on the Eedi 2020 dataset, evaluating five representative KT architectures—DKVMN, AKT, GIKT, LPKT, and DKVMN-KAPS—across Q-matrix completeness levels from 0% to 100%. Results show that attention-based and graph-based models remain stable under low completeness, while memory-based models, particularly DKVMN-KAPS, exhibit a sharp performance threshold near full annotation. To address RQ2, we evaluate six incremental annotation strategies for memory-based architectures under limited labeling budgets. Results show that the *important_ skills* strategy achieves near-peak performance at 75% budget (0.811 AUC), closely approaching the performance at 100% budget (0.824 AUC), and substantially outperforming all other strategies at the same budget level. This suggests that prioritizing high-impact skills enables efficient annotation without exhaustive coverage.

2 Related Work

2.1 Q-Matrix Construction and Optimization Strategies

The Q-matrix defines item–skill mappings and is fundamental to most KT and Cognitive Diagnosis (CD) models [12,13]. Construction methods fall into expert-driven annotation and data-driven inference. Although expert annotation offers interpretability, expert-defined Q-matrices often contain subjective errors or missing entries [7,14], and manual annotation does not scale as item banks grow [15].

Data-Driven and Graph-Based Q-Matrix Learning. Data-driven methods infer item–skill relations from response patterns using matrix factorization [16,17], statistical estimation [19], or refinement-based approaches such as ensemble learning [20] and multi-label prediction [21]. The shared goal is to reduce expert workload while improving the consistency and scalability of Q-matrix construction.

Graph-based methods further model item–skill relationships as graph structures to leverage co-occurrence, semantic, or hierarchical dependencies. Wang et al. [24] propose GCN-based aggregation to calibrate item–skill relations, while Gan et al. [25] infer prerequisite structures from student trajectories. Li et al. [4,10] extend this paradigm through ranking-based calibration and hierarchical knowledge structures.

LLM-Based Construction. Large Language Models (LLMs) offer a new direction by extracting skill cues directly from item semantics, rather than relying on response data or item co-occurrence. SINKT [26] uses an LLM to capture semantic item–concept relations and build a heterogeneous graph for downstream KT models. Wang et al. [27] show that LLM-derived semantics enhance concept discrimination through instruction tuning. Aşiret and Sünbül [28] further report high overlap between LLM-generated and expert-defined Q-matrices, suggesting that LLM outputs can serve as preliminary annotations for resource-limited item banks.

2.2 Q-Matrix and Knowledge Tracing Models

Knowledge tracing aims to estimate students' mastery of skills from response sequences, and the Q-matrix provides the item–skill structure used by most models. Recent survey work groups KT models into five major families [1,29]—memory-based, attention-based, graph-based, explainability-oriented, and multi-relational reasoning—highlighting the diverse mechanisms through which models incorporate skill information and providing a basis for examining how each architecture responds to different levels of Q-matrix completeness.

Memory-based models maintain knowledge states using external memory modules. DKVMN [30] uses a key–value memory where the Q-matrix serves as a memory index that determines which slots are accessed for each item. Extensions such as DKVMN&MRI [3] incorporate prerequisite relations and forgetting behavior, while Mao et al. [31] introduce multi-head attention to enhance memory retrieval.

Attention-based models capture long-range dependencies through self-attention. AKT [36] uses monotonic attention with temporal decay and Rasch-regularized embeddings. SAKT [32] applies a Transformer-style architecture where the Q-matrix guides item embeddings, and QAKT [33] extends this to end-to-end learning of item–concept relations.

Graph-based models reformulate knowledge tracing as reasoning over item–skill graphs. GIKT [37] constructs a skill co-occurrence graph and propagates knowledge states through message passing. Extensions such as SGKT [38] and

Bi-CLKT [40] further model session-level transitions and contrastive representations. While these methods effectively exploit structural topology, their performance depends strongly on Q-matrix quality.

Explainability-oriented models provide transparent skill-level updates. LPKT [41] models learning gain and forgetting rate through interpretable parameters, treating each Q-matrix dimension as a skill-specific state. KPT [42] integrates learning and forgetting curve theories to ensure clear skill-level updates, offering valuable transparency for educational diagnosis despite slightly lower predictive accuracy.

Multi-relational reasoning models represent knowledge across multiple dimensions. DKVMN-KAPS [46] maintains separate memory modules for knowledge absorption and problem-solving ability, extending the Q-matrix into a multi-relational structure. Q-MCKT [47] jointly models concept- and item-level knowledge through a multi-expert contrastive framework. These models capture nuanced learning behaviors but generally require higher-quality and richer Q-matrix information.

2.3 Q-Matrix Completeness and Practical Challenges

In real-world systems, Q-matrix completeness strongly affects KT performance, yet full annotation is often costly and time-consuming. Completeness reflects the proportion of items with assigned skill labels, and low completeness can degrade model reliability—memory-based models cannot update unannotated skills, and graph-based models suffer from sparse structures [49].

Practical constraints frequently lead to incomplete Q-matrices. Large platforms constantly introduce new items, expert resources are limited, and fully annotating large item banks may take months. Although LLM-based methods show promise [50], their outputs still require extensive human verification. Lohr et al. [51] found that LLM-generated content often fails to meet instructional standards, while Rocha et al. [52] showed that cross-evaluating annotations with multiple LLMs still demands expert oversight and yields variable cost-effectiveness. Such discrepancies between automated and expert annotations can affect Q-matrix reliability [41].

Annotation may account for over 30% of system development cost [53], and the relationship between completeness and performance is often nonlinear. Effective resource allocation therefore becomes essential. Incremental annotation strategies—prioritizing informative items through active learning—can reach comparable performance to exhaustive annotation with only 30–50% of the effort [55]. These considerations motivate treating Q-matrix completeness as a primary experimental factor and examining how different KT architectures respond under incomplete annotation.

3 Experimental Setup

This section describes the experimental setup for evaluating the impact of Q-matrix completeness on knowledge tracing models. We first introduce the

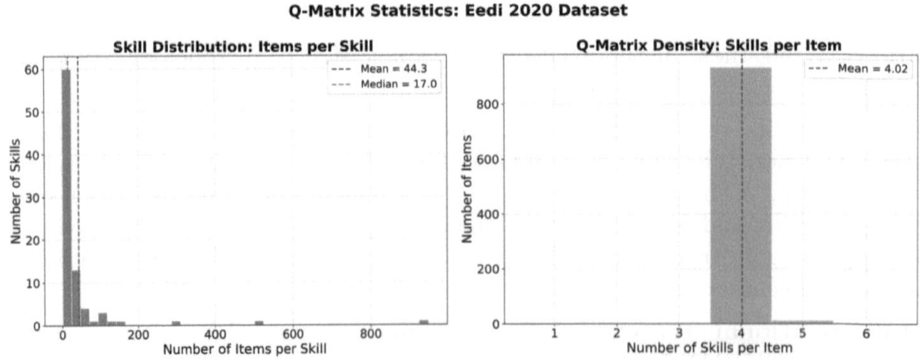

Fig. 1. Q-matrix statistics of the Eedi 2020 dataset. Left: long-tail distribution of skills across items. Right: number of skills per item.

dataset, data splitting procedure, masking schemes, and annotation strategies. We then present the model selection rationale and two-stage experimental design, followed by the evaluation metrics and statistical analysis procedures.

3.1 Dataset and Data Processing

Dataset. We use the Eedi 2020 dataset [56], which contains 948 items, 6,148 students, approximately 1.2M interactions, and 88 skills. This dataset was selected because it provides one of the most complete and publicly available expert-annotated Q-matrices, making it particularly suitable for controlled Q-matrix completeness studies. Extending experiments to additional datasets with varying Q-matrix structures remains an important direction for future work. Figure 1 summarizes the Q-matrix structure. The skill distribution shows a clear long-tail pattern, where many skills are covered by only a few items. The number of skills per item averages 4.02, indicating that most questions involve multiple concepts. These properties imply that rare skills are the first to disappear when completeness is reduced, and that masking individual skills may significantly distort multi-skill items.

Data Splitting and Masking Schemes. The data are split chronologically into 70% training, 15% validation, and 15% testing. Chronological splitting is adopted to reflect realistic deployment conditions, where models must generalize to future student interactions rather than randomly sampled ones.

To simulate varying levels of Q-matrix completeness, we apply two masking schemes at five completeness levels (0%, 25%, 50%, 75%, 100%). *Item-level masking* randomly selects a subset of items and completely removes all skill labels associated with those items, simulating the scenario where newly added questions have not yet been annotated. *Entry-level masking* randomly removes a proportion of individual skill–item links within each item, simulating incomplete or partially incorrect annotations. Together, these two schemes capture the most common sources of incompleteness encountered in real educational systems.

Annotation Strategies. Based on initial findings regarding model sensitivity to Q-matrix completeness, we further investigate incremental annotation strategies for memory-based models, which exhibited the strongest dependence on Q-matrix quality. We compare six annotation strategies across five budget levels (0%, 25%, 50%, 75%, 100%): the *random* strategy serves as the baseline, maintaining the original annotation order without any active selection; the *difficulty* strategy prioritizes items with higher student error rates, assuming that harder items carry more diagnostic value; the *frequency* strategy prioritizes items most frequently encountered in student interaction logs, targeting items with the broadest coverage of student behavior; the *important_skills* strategy prioritizes items whose associated skills appear most frequently in student logs, under the assumption that high-frequency skills have the greatest impact on model learning; the *skill_coverage* strategy selects items that introduce skills not yet or rarely represented in the annotated set, aiming to minimize skill sparsity across the Q-matrix; and the *diverse* strategy balances multiple criteria simultaneously to ensure varied item representation across difficulty, frequency, and skill coverage dimensions.

3.2 Experimental Design

We evaluate five representative KT models that span the major architectural paradigms in the literature: DKVMN [3] (memory-based), AKT [36] (attention-based), GIKT [37] (graph-based), LPKT [41] (explainability-oriented), and DKVMN-KAPS [46] (multi-relational reasoning). These models were selected because they collectively cover the five major architectural families identified in recent survey work [1,29], including external memory mechanisms, sequence-level attention, graph-structured reasoning, interpretable parameterization, and multi-dimensional skill modeling. This diversity allows us to examine whether architectural assumptions—rather than individual implementation choices-drive differences in sensitivity to Q-matrix completeness.

The experiment is designed in two stages. In the first stage, all five models are evaluated under varying Q-matrix completeness levels using both masking schemes, addressing RQ1. In the second stage, based on the observation that memory-based models exhibit the strongest dependence on Q-matrix quality, we focus on the annotation strategy comparison between DKVMN and DKVMN-KAPS, addressing RQ2. All models are implemented in PyTorch and trained on an A100 GPU using the Adam optimizer (lr=0.001), batch size 32, hidden size 128, dropout 0.2, and early stopping with patience 10.

3.3 Evaluation Metrics and Statistical Analysis

Model performance is evaluated using ROC AUC as the primary metric. Accuracy and RMSE are also computed for all experiments, and statistical tests are conducted on all three metrics. Their trends are consistent with ROC AUC; therefore, due to space limitations, we only present ROC AUC in the main figures.

Each condition is repeated with three random seeds (42, 123, 456). We apply paired t-tests for comparisons across completeness levels within each model and one-way ANOVA for comparing different model architectures. Bonferroni correction is applied when appropriate, and effect sizes (Cohen's d) are reported.

4 Results

4.1 Effect of Q-Matrix Completeness on Model Performance

Figure 2 presents the test AUC of five KT models across Q-matrix completeness levels from 0% to 100%. The results reveal a clear architectural divide in sensitivity to Q-matrix availability.

Robust Architectures. Three models—AKT, GIKT, and LPKT—maintain stable performance across all completeness levels, consistently achieving approximately 0.70, 0.75, and 0.75 AUC respectively, regardless of annotation availability. Both item-level and entry-level masking yield nearly identical trajectories, indicating that these architectures effectively compensate for missing skill information through sequence-level patterns or learned features.

Completeness-Dependent Architectures. Memory-based models exhibit substantial variation. DKVMN shows modest improvement from 0.62 to 0.67 AUC. DKVMN-KAPS demonstrates dramatic sensitivity: performance remains low (0.62–0.70 AUC) from 0% to 75% completeness, but jumps sharply to 0.83 AUC at 100%, suggesting a threshold effect where near-complete skill coverage is required to activate its multi-relational reasoning capabilities.

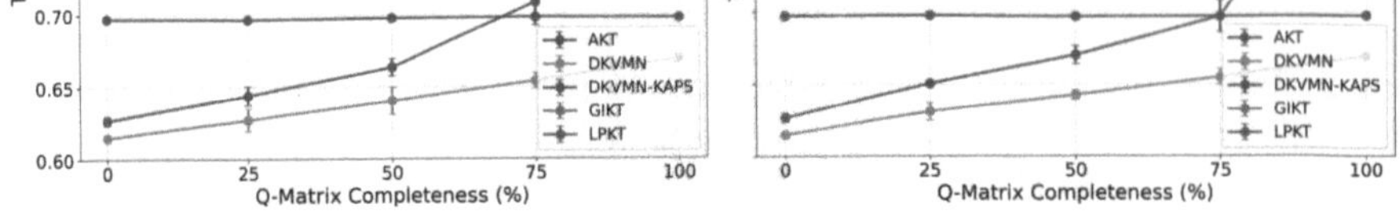

Fig. 2. AUC of five KT models across Q-matrix completeness levels. Memory-based models degrade under incomplete skill mappings, while attention- and graph-based models remain stable.

Performance improves with Q-matrix completeness, though the relative impact of item count versus coverage proportion remains unclear. This motivates investigating strategic item selection in Sect. 4.2. Addressing RQ1, we find that architectures differ fundamentally in completeness reliance, with DKVMN-KAPS exhibiting a threshold effect at high completeness.

4.2 Impact of Annotation Selection Strategies

Given the observed sensitivity of memory-based models, we investigated annotation strategies on DKVMN and DKVMN-KAPS. Figure 3 shows how different selection approaches affect performance as budgets increase from 0% to 100%.

DKVMN. All six strategies produce similar outcomes, improving gradually from 0.61 to 0.67 AUC across budget levels, suggesting that annotation quantity matters more than item selection for this architecture.

DKVMN-KAPS. Strategy choice proves critical. At lower budget levels (0%–50%), all strategies remain close to the baseline, with ROC AUC ranging from 0.626 to 0.691. However, strategies begin to diverge significantly at 75% budget:

- *important_skills* achieves the strongest performance at 75% budget (0.811 ROC AUC), substantially outperforming the baseline (0.708) at the same completeness level. This advantage narrows at 100%, where all strategies converge near 0.824 ROC AUC, suggesting that the benefit of targeted annotation is most pronounced under resource-constrained conditions.
- *frequency* ranks second at 75% budget (0.757 ROC AUC), indicating that high-frequency items carry useful signal for DKVMN-KAPS even without exhaustive coverage.
- *skill_coverage* yields only 0.685 ROC AUC at 75% budget, the lowest among all strategies at that level, indicating that coverage breadth alone does not translate efficiently into model performance for this architecture.

The effectiveness of *important_skills* stems from DKVMN-KAPS's dual-memory architecture: by prioritizing skills that appear most frequently in student interactions, the annotated Q-matrix provides dense training signals for both the knowledge absorption and problem-solving memory modules, enabling coherent cross-module representations to emerge earlier in the annotation process. In contrast, strategies that prioritize coverage or difficulty introduce sparse or difficult-to-learn skill patterns that do not efficiently activate the dual-memory mechanism. These results address RQ2: annotation strategy matters primarily for architectures with strong Q-matrix dependence, and prioritizing high-impact skills is more efficient than pursuing exhaustive coverage.

4.3 Summary of Findings

Our experiments provide a dual perspective on Q-matrix requirements, addressing RQ1 and RQ2:

1. **Random Annotation Bottlenecks:** Under random annotation, model performance is strictly bounded by Q-matrix completeness. Specifically, memory-based models exhibit a performance ceiling, requiring at least 75% completeness to form coherent multi-relational representations. This sensitivity identifies completeness as a critical constraint for specific architectures in data-scarce scenarios.

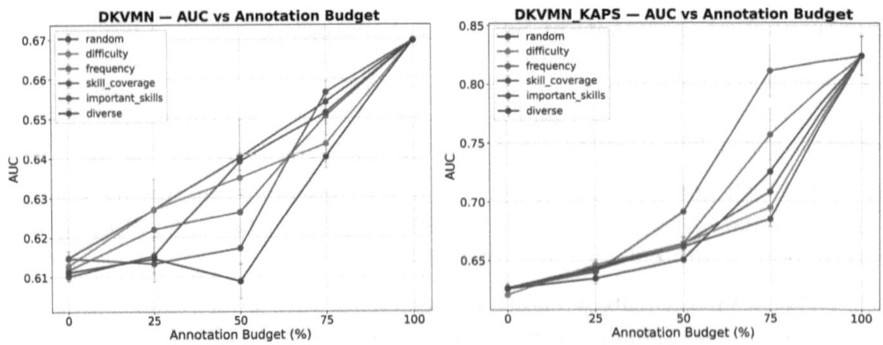

Fig. 3. AUC vs annotation budget for DKVMN and DKVMN-KAPS. For DKVMN, all strategies produce similar results. For DKVMN-KAPS, *important_ skills* achieves peak performance (0.811 AUC) at 75% budget, substantially outperforming the baseline and all other strategies.

2. **Strategic Compensation:** Experiment 2 demonstrates that this "completeness ceiling" can be bypassed through strategic selection. By prioritizing high-impact skills (*important_ skills* strategy), models achieve 0.811 ROC AUC at only 75% budget—approaching the 100% completeness baseline (0.824). This proves that strategic annotation of key items is more effective than exhaustive random labeling, offering a cost-effective deployment path.

These findings suggest that while certain architectures are vulnerable to incomplete data, the strategic prioritization of skill-item relationships can effectively compensate for limited annotation budgets.

References

1. Shen, S., et al.: A survey of knowledge tracing: models, variants, and applications. IEEE Trans. Learn. Technol. **17**, 1858–1879 (2024)
2. Liu, Z., et al.: Deep learning based knowledge tracing: a review. a tool and empirical studies. IEEE Trans. Knowl. Data Eng. (2025)
3. Xu, F., et al.: DKVMN&MRI: a new deep knowledge tracing model based on DKVMN incorporating multi-relational information. PLoS ONE **19**(10), e0312022 (2024)
4. Li, L., Wang, Z.: Calibrated Q-matrix-enhanced deep knowledge tracing with relational attention mechanism. Appl. Sci. **13**(4), 2541 (2023)
5. Jia, Z., Su, W., Liu, J., Yue, W.: Attentive Q-matrix Learning for Knowledge Tracing. *arXiv preprint* arXiv:2304.08168 (2023)
6. Yu, M., Li, F., Liu, H., Zhang, T., Yu, G.: ContextKT: a context-based method for knowledge tracing. Appl. Sci. **12**(17), 8822 (2022)
7. de la Torre, J., Chiu, C.-Y.: A general method of empirical Q-matrix validation. Psychometrika **81**(2), 253–273 (2016)
8. Pardos, Z.A., Dadu, A., et al.: dAFM: fusing psychometric and connectionist modeling for Q-matrix refinement. J. Educ. Data Mining **10**(2), 1–27 (2018)

9. Wang, W., Ma, H., Zhao, Y., Li, Z., He, X.: Tracking knowledge proficiency of students with calibrated Q-matrix. Expert Syst. Appl. **192**, 116454 (2022)
10. Li, L., Wang, Z.: Knowledge relation rank enhanced heterogeneous learning interaction modeling for neural graph forgetting knowledge tracing. PLoS ONE **18**(12), e0295808 (2023)
11. Chen, Y., Sun, J., Li, J., Zhang, H.: Concept-Aware Latent and Explicit Knowledge Integration for Enhanced Cognitive Diagnosis. arXiv:2502.02104 (2025)
12. Tatsuoka, K.K.: Rule space: an approach for dealing with misconceptions based on item response theory. J. Educ. Meas., 345–354 (1983)
13. Barnes, T.: The Q-matrix method: mining student response data for knowledge. In: American Association for Artificial Intelligence 2005 Educational Data Mining Workshop, pp. 1–8. AAAI Press, Pittsburgh, PA, USA (2005)
14. Culpepper, S.A.: Estimating the cognitive diagnosis Q Matrix with expert knowledge: application to the fraction-subtraction dataset. Psychometrika **84**(2), 333–357 (2019)
15. Wang, D., Cai, Y., Tu, D.: Q-matrix estimation methods for cognitive diagnosis models: based on partial known Q-matrix. Multivar. Behav. Res. **22**, 1–13 (2020)
16. Desmarais, M., et al.: Conditions for effectively deriving a Q-matrix from data with non-negative matrix factorization. In: 4th International Conference on Educational Data Mining (EDM), pp. 41–50 (2011)
17. Desmarais, M.C.: Mapping question items to skills with non-negative matrix factorization. ACM SIGKDD Explorations Newsl **13**(2), 30–36 (2012)
18. Desmarais, M.C., Naceur, R.: A matrix factorization method for mapping items to skills and for enhancing expert-based Q-matrices. In: Lane, H.C., Yacef, K., Mostow, J., Pavlik, P. (eds.) AIED 2013. LNCS (LNAI), vol. 7926, pp. 441–450. Springer, Heidelberg (2013). https://doi.org/10.1007/978-3-642-39112-5_45
19. Liu, J., Xu, G., Ying, Z.: Data-driven Learning of Q-matrix. Appl. Psychol. Meas. **36**(7), 548–564 (2012)
20. Xu, P., Desmarais, M.C.: Boosted decision tree for Q-matrix refinement. Inter. Educ. Data Mining Soc. (2016)
21. Minn, S., Desmarais, M.C., Fu, S.K.: Refinement of a Q-matrix with an ensemble technique based on multi-label classification algorithms. In: Verbert, K., Sharples, M., Klobučar, T. (eds.) EC-TEL 2016. LNCS, vol. 9891, pp. 165–178. Springer, Cham (2016). https://doi.org/10.1007/978-3-319-45153-4_13
22. Desmarais, M.C., Xu, P., Beheshti, B.: A partition tree approach to combine techniques to refine item-to-skills Q-matrices. In: Educational Data Mining (EDM), pp. 29–36 (2015)
23. Li, C., Ma, C., Xu, G.: Learning large Q-matrix by restricted boltzmann machines. Psychometrika **87**(3), 1010–1041 (2022)
24. Wang, W., Ma, H., Zhao, Y., Li, Z., He, X.: Relevance-aware Q-matrix calibration for knowledge tracing. In: Farkaš, I., Masulli, P., Otte, S., Wermter, S. (eds.) ICANN 2021. LNCS, vol. 12893, pp. 101–112. Springer, Cham (2021). https://doi.org/10.1007/978-3-030-86365-4_9
25. Gan, W., Sun, Y.: Prerequisite-driven Q-matrix refinement for learner knowledge assessment: a case study in online learning context. arXiv preprint arXiv:2208.12642 (2022)
26. Fu, L., et al.: Sinkt: a structure-aware inductive knowledge tracing model with large language model. In: Proceedings of the 33rd ACM International Conference on Information and Knowledge Management (CIKM), pp. 632–642 (2024)
27. Wang, Z., et al.: LLM-KT: Aligning Large Language Models with Knowledge Tracing using a Plug-and-Play Instruction. arXiv:2502.02945 (2025)

28. Aşiret, S., Sünbül, S.Ö.: Evaluating ChatGPT-4o's performance in construction of q-matrix for a cognitive diagnostic assessment. Research Square preprint arXiv:rs.3.rs-6235063/v1 (2025)
29. Lee, L.C., Arakawa, Y., Mine, T.: Emerging trends in knowledge tracing models: a technical survey from 2022 to 2025. In: International Conference on Advanced Data Mining and Applications, pp. 217–224. Springer (2025) https://doi.org/10.1007/978-981-95-3459-3_17
30. Zhang, J., Shi, X., King, I., Yeung, D.Y.: Dynamic key-value memory networks for knowledge tracing. In: Proceedings of the 26th International Conference on World Wide Web (WWW), pp. 765–774. ACM (2017)
31. Mao, A., Chen, J., Liu, Y.J.: Improving knowledge tracing via considering conceptual structure and individual differences. In: Proceedings of the ACM Turing Award Celebration Conference–China 2024, pp. 59–65 (2024)
32. Pandey, S., Karypis, G.: A Self-attentive Model for Knowledge Tracing. arXiv:1907.06837 (2019)
33. Jia, Z, Su, W., Liu, J., Yue, W.: Attentive Q-matrix Learning for Knowledge Tracing. arXiv preprint arXiv:2304.08168 (2023)
34. Xu, L., Guo, L., Wu, X., Wang, X., Guo, L.: Knowledge tracing with contrastive learning and attention-based long short-term memory network. In: Huang, DS., Zhang, C., Chen, W. (eds.) ICIC 2024. LNCS, vol. 14865. Springer, Singapore (2024). https://doi.org/10.1007/978-981-97-5591-2_3
35. Cheng, K., Peng, L., Wang, P., Ye, J., Sun, L., Du, B.: DyGKT: dynamic graph learning for knowledge tracing. In: Proceedings of the 30th ACM SIGKDD Conference on Knowledge Discovery and Data Mining, pp. 409–420 (2024)
36. Ghosh, A., Heffernan, N., Lan, A.S.: Context-aware attentive knowledge tracing. In: Proceedings of the 26th ACM SIGKDD International Conference on Knowledge Discovery & Data Mining (KDD), pp. 2330–2339 (2020). https://doi.org/10.1145/3394486.3403282
37. Yang, Y., et al.: GIKT: a graph-based interaction model for knowledge tracing. In: Hutter, F., Kersting, K., Lijffijt, J., Valera, I. (eds.) ECML PKDD 2020. LNCS (LNAI), vol. 12457, pp. 299–315. Springer, Cham (2021). https://doi.org/10.1007/978-3-030-67658-2_18
38. Wu, Z., Huang, L., Huang, Q., Huang, C., Tang, Y.: SGKT: session graph-based knowledge tracing for student performance prediction. Expert Syst. Appl. **206**, 117681 (2022)
39. Zhao, W., Xia, J., Jiang, X., He, T.: A novel framework for deep knowledge tracing via gating-controlled forgetting and learning mechanisms. Inform. Process. Manag. **60**(1), 103114 (2023)
40. Song, X., Li, J., Lei, Q., Zhao, W., Chen, Y., Mian, A.: Bi-CLKT: bi-graph contrastive learning based knowledge tracing. Knowl.-Based Syst. **241**, 108274 (2022)
41. Shen, S., et al.: Learning process-consistent knowledge tracing. In: Proceedings of the 27th ACM SIGKDD Conference on Knowledge Discovery & Data Mining, pp. 1452–1460 (2021)
42. Huang, Z., Qi Liu, Yu., Chen, L.W., Xiao, K., Chen, E., Guandong, H.: Learning or forgetting? a dynamic approach for tracking the knowledge proficiency of students. ACM Trans. Inform. Syst. **38**(2), 1–33 (2020)
43. Liu, F., Changqi, B., Zhang, H., Le, W., Ke, Yu., Xia, H.: FDKT: towards an interpretable deep knowledge tracing via fuzzy reasoning. ACM Trans. Inform. Syst. **42**(5), 1–26 (2024)

44. Wang, Y., Huo, Y., Yang, C., Huang, X., Xia, D., Feng, F.: Knowledge ontology enhanced model for explainable knowledge tracing. J. King Saud Univ.-Comput. Inform. Sci. **36**(5), 102065 (2024)
45. Jiang, B., Shuang, W., Yin, C., Zhang, H.: Knowledge tracing within single programming practice using problem-solving process data. IEEE Trans. Learn. Technol. **13**(4), 822–832 (2020)
46. Zhang, W., Gong, Z., Luo, P., Li, Z.: DKVMN-KAPS: dynamic key-value memory networks knowledge tracing with students' knowledge-absorption ability and problem-solving ability. IEEE Access **12**, 55146–55156 (2024)
47. Zhang, H., Liu, Z., Shang, C., Li, D., Jiang, Y.: A question-centric multi-experts contrastive learning framework for improving the accuracy and interpretability of deep sequential knowledge tracing models. ACM Trans. Knowl. Discov. Data **19**(2), 1–25 (2025)
48. He, X., Zhang, T., Mengyu, Y., Guowei, Y., Zhao, Y.: An extensible heterogeneous network embedding framework for knowledge tracing. Inter. J. Softw. Inform. **12**(4) (2022)
49. Liu, Q., Huang, Z., Liu, Y., Chen, E., Hui Xiong, Y.S., Guandong, H.: EKT: exercise-aware knowledge tracing for student performance prediction. IEEE Trans. Knowl. Data Eng. **33**(1), 100–115 (2019)
50. Yan, L., et al.: Practical and ethical challenges of large language models in education: a systematic scoping review. Br. J. Edu. Technol. **55**(1), 90–112 (2024)
51. Lohr, D., Berges, M., Chugh, A., Kohlhase, M., Müller, D.: Leveraging large language models to generate course-specific semantically annotated learning objects. J. Comput. Assist. Learn. **41**(1), e13101 (2025)
52. Rocha, C., Grosman, J.S., Correia, F.A., Rego, V., Lopes, H.: A data annotation approach using large language models. In: Proceedings of ICEIS, vol. 1, pp. 748–755 (2025)
53. Tatsuoka, K.K.: Cognitive Assessment: An Introduction to the Rule Space Method. Routledge (2009)
54. Winters, F.I., Haas, E., Mislevy, R.J.: Choosing item types in computerized testlets. J. Educ. Meas. **42**(1), 35–59 (2005)
55. Sett les, B0.:Active Learning Literature Survey. University of Wisconsin–Madison(2009)
56. Eedi. The Eedi Learning Dataset (NeurIPS 2020 Education Challenge) (2020). https://www.aicrowd.com/challenges/neurips-2020-education-challenge

HSGTCN: A Hybrid Semantic-Guided Transformer-CNN Network for Learned Image Compressed Sensing

Zitong Cheng[1], Yunsen Tang[1], Fenghua Tong[2], Ning Liu[1(✉)], and Qian Li[3]

[1] School of Software, Shandong University, Jinan, China
{chengzt,tangyunsen}@mail.sdu.edu.cn, liun21cs@sdu.edu.cn

[2] Shandong Provincial Key Laboratory of Computer Networks, Shandong Computer Science Center (National Supercomputer Center in Jinan), Qilu University of Technology (Shandong Academy of Sciences), Jinan, China
tongfh@qlu.edu.cn

[3] Joint SDU-NTU Centre for Artificial Intelligence Research, Shandong University, Jinan, Shandong, China
feiwangyuzhou@sdu.edu.cn

Abstract. With the advance of deep learning technologies, the Image Compressed Sensing has gained great success. Existing works mainly include two procedures, namely sampling and reconstruction. For the sampling process, most studies rely on a simple fixed matrix for compression, resulting in the loss of high-level semantic information of the image especially in low sampling rates. For the reconstruction process, they often employ simple network architectures while ignoring to utilize the advantages of different architectures, resulting in sub-optimal compression performance. To address these issues, we devise a Hybrid Semantic-Guided Transformer-CNN Network for Learned Image Compressed Sensing, namely HSGTCN. To overcome the information loss due to the simple fixed compressed matrix in the sampling process, we inject the semantic information guided by pretrained networks into the compression matrix. Besides, we provide a hybrid Transformer-CNN based reconstruction network for accurate image reconstruction. Extensive experiments show that the proposed method achieves optimal performance across various sampling rates especially in low rate settings.

Keywords: Image Reconstruction · Adaptive Compression · Compressed Sensing

1 Introduction

Compressed Sensing (CS), as a signal processing paradigm that breaks through the constraints of the traditional Nyquist sampling theorem, achieves dual optimization of data acquisition efficiency and storage cost in fields such as magnetic resonance imaging (MRI), single-pixel imaging, and remote sensing image processing through the core idea of "sampling equals compression" [1,5,7,8].

R. C.-W. Wong et al. (Eds.): PAKDD 2026, LNAI 16618, pp. 460–472, 2027.
https://doi.org/10.1007/978-981-92-1947-6_37

With the continuous development of deep learning technology, image reconstruction methods based on deep learning have been widely studied in the field of image restoration. Compared with the traditional compressed sensing reconstruction algorithm, this method can significantly enhance the ability of image acquisition and reconstruction, so as to improve the overall performance [9]. Early CNN-based models, such as ReconNet [12] and CSNet [16] learn the nonlinear mapping from the measured data to the original image by stacking convolution layers, which significantly improves the reconstruction speed. Optimization heuristic models such as ISTA-Net [24] and ADMM-CSNet [20] transform the traditional optimization steps into a learnable network layer through "algorithm expansion", which enhances the interpretability of the model. With the emergence of transformer backbone network, transformer can effectively break through the limitation of CNN network block effect by virtue of the global modeling ability of self attention mechanism, providing a new direction for ICS. The pure transformer model (such as TCSNet [9]) capture global features to preserve structural stability; Hybrid models (such as TransCS [15] and MTCCSNet [14]) try to combine the advantages of CNN local feature extraction and transformer global modeling, and maintain the global structure of the image while taking into account the details and textures of the image.

Although the existing learning compressed sensing methods have developed rapidly, they still have limitations. Firstly, most of the current learnable sampling strategies still remain within the framework of fixed sampling matrix or data-driven optimization, and fail to explicitly introduce the high-level semantic information of the image, so it is difficult to achieve adaptive and on-demand sampling resource allocation according to the importance of the region and guide the subsequent reconstruction process. In addition, the traditional CNN model is limited by the local receptive field, which is prone to block effect and structural discontinuity in the case of low sampling rate; While the model relying solely on transformer has strong global modeling ability, it often has high computational cost and insufficient ability to depict local details and multi-scale textures. Therefore, how to achieve efficient and collaborative integration between the two types of architectures has become a key problem to be solved in the current research.

To address these limitations, we propose HSGTCN, a hybrid semantic-guided Transformer–CNN network for learned image compressed sensing. The proposed framework parameterizes the sensing operator in a content-aware manner and integrates Transformer and CNN branches within an unfolding-based reconstruction scheme. By jointly modeling global dependencies and local structural details, the method improves reconstruction consistency under compressed measurements. The main contributions of this paper are summarized as follows:

1. We propose a semantic-guided Transformer–CNN framework for learned compressed sensing, which jointly models the sampling and reconstruction processes under an end-to-end optimization paradigm.
2. We develop a semantics-aware adaptive sampling module that parameterizes the sensing operator in a content-aware manner via a lightweight semantic

encoder, enabling adaptive measurement allocation while preserving the linear measurement formulation.
3. We design a dynamic reconstruction module that fuses CNN and Transformer branches under semantic guidance, achieving semantically consistent reconstruction across semantic, patch, and pixel levels, and enhancing local details under global structural constraints.
4. Extensive experiments on Set5 [3], Set14 [22] and CBSD68 [13] at multiple sampling rates, evaluated in terms of PSNR and SSIM, demonstrate that the proposed method achieves superior average performance compared with several representative baselines.

2 Related Work

2.1 Deep Learning-Based Image CS Framework

In recent years, compressed sensing has shifted from traditional iterative optimization to deep-learning reconstruction frameworks. Early CNN-based methods—such as ReconNet [12], DR2-Net [21], and CSNet [16]—demonstrated that learnable feature extraction can effectively capture image details and progressively enhance reconstruction. To improve interpretability, unfolding-based approaches like ISTA-Net [24], ADMM-CSNet [20], and AMP-Net [25] map classical iterative algorithms into deep networks and learn parameters in a data-driven manner. More recently, Transformer [10] architectures, e.g., TransCS [15] and MTCCSNet [14], balance local texture and long-range dependency modeling by integrating lightweight CNN and Transformer features, while TCSNet [9] uses a hierarchical Transformer decoder to progressively restore structural information.

Despite these advances, existing methods still underutilize multi-scale structural cues and high-level semantics. To address this, our method incorporates semantic guidance into both sampling and reconstruction within a FISTA-based [4] unfolding framework, enabling effective exploitation of semantic, patch, and pixel-wise structures.

2.2 Semantic Information Mining in Image Compressed Sensing

The use of semantic information enables dynamic allocation of sampling resources in image compressed sensing, effectively balancing "sampling on demand" and "accurate reconstruction." For example, in 2023, Zhang et al. introduced SemBCS [23], a semantic-aware compressed sensing framework that innovatively integrates semantic priors into the dynamic generation of sampling matrices. Similarly, in 2025, Song et al. proposed the Representation-guided Hybrid Transformer Network (RHT-Net) [17], which shifts the utilization of semantic cues from the pixel domain to a more expressive representation domain, further enhancing the efficiency of semantic-guided sampling.

However, most existing compressed sensing models incorporate semantic information into only a single stage, leading to limited exploitation of its full potential. To address this limitation, our model embeds semantic guidance into a learnable sensing operator and the pre-reconstruction stage within an end-to-end optimized framework. This holistic integration maximizes the utility of semantic cues and allows semantic information to exert influence throughout the entire compressed sensing pipeline.

3 Method

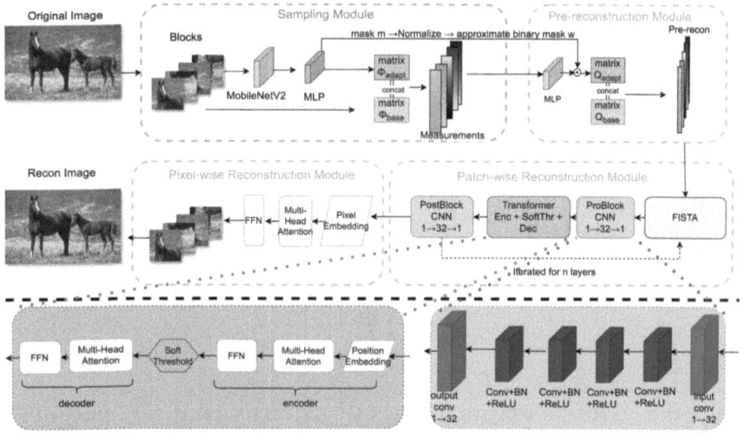

Fig. 1. Overview of the HSGTCN architecture, highlighting the ProBlock and Transformer components within the Patch-wise Reconstruction Module.

In this section, we will provide a detailed introduction to the model we proposed, including the image sampling module, hybrid reconstruction module, and loss function.

3.1 Sampling Module

Instead of using a fixed sensing matrix, we design a semantically guided learnable sensing operator within an end-to-end learned compressed sensing framework to enhance reconstruction quality. For our sampling method, we adopt a block-wise compression framework. Specifically, the image x is divided into non overlapping blocks of size $C \times B \times B$, where C represents the number of channels and B represents the block size. Therefore, the number of blocks N is denoted as $N = B \times B$. Given the sampling rate $\tau (0 < \tau < 1)$, the length of compressed block is computed as absolute value of $N \times \tau$, denoted as M_{target}.

Based on the above notations, the learnable sensing matrix $\Phi \in \mathbb{R}^{M_{\text{target}} \times N}$ includes the basic learnable sensing matrix $\Phi_{base} \in \mathbb{R}^{M_{base} \times N}$ which is used to perform trivial compressed sensing with the compressed length $M_{base} (M_{base} <$

M_{target}) and the adaptive learnable sensing matrix $\Phi_{adapt} \in \mathbb{R}^{M_{adapt} \times N}$ which is used to perform semantic guided compressed sensing with the compressed length M_{adapt} that satisfies $M_{adapt} = M_{\text{target}} - M_{base}$. Note that, the requirements $M_{adapt} = M_{\text{target}} - M_{base}$ is used to meet up with the sampling ratio constraints.

Within the learned compressed sensing framework, a lightweight semantic encoder built upon MobileNetV2 [6] is incorporated to parameterize the sensing operator in a content-aware manner. The extracted semantic representations are further transformed by an MLP-based module [18,23] to generate adaptive modulation signals for the sensing process, as described in Eq. 1. And then, given the block-wise input image x, the adaptive learnable sensing matrix $\Phi_{adapt} \in \mathbb{R}^{M_{adapt} \times N}$ considering the dynamic information of block i of the image x is computed via the Eq. 2 by introducing two additional learnable parameters U and V.

$$m_i = F_{mask}(MobileNetV2(x_i)) \tag{1}$$

$$\Phi^i_{adapt} \in \mathbb{R}^{M_{adapt} \times N} = U \cdot diag(m_i) \cdot V \tag{2}$$

Based on the basic learnable sensing matrix $\Phi_{base} \in \mathbb{R}^{M_{base} \times N}$ and adaptive learnable sensing matrix $\Phi_{adapt} \in \mathbb{R}^{M_{adapt} \times N}$, we can get the final learnable sensing matrix $\Phi \in \mathbb{R}^{M_{\text{target}} \times N}$ via the Eq. 3 with respect to .

$$\Phi_i = \begin{bmatrix} \Phi_{\text{base}} \\ \Phi^i_{\text{adapt}} \end{bmatrix} \tag{3}$$

Although the adaptive sensing matrix Φ^i_{adapt} is dynamically parameterized by semantic representations, the measurement process for each image block remains a linear projection. Specifically, the sensing operation is formulated as a matrix multiplication between Φ_i and the image block x_i. The semantic encoder therefore serves to parameterize the sensing operator within the learned compressed sensing framework, while preserving the linear measurement model.

Based on Φ_i, the base measurement of the i th block of one input image x, denoted as y^i_{base} is computed via $y^i_{base} = \Phi_{\text{base}} \cdot x_i$ and the semantic measurement of the i th block of one input image x is computed via $y^i_{base} = \Phi_{\text{base}} \cdot x_i$. Based on the two compressed measurements, the final measurement y^i with respect to block i is computed as the combination of two measurements.

3.2 Hybrid Reconstruction Module

The reconstruction module of this model consists of three sub-modules:(1) Pre-reconstruction Module; (2) Patch-wise Reconstruction Module; (3) Pixel-wise Reconstruction Module.

Pre-reconstruction Module. In order to avoid the potential instability of pure data-driven decoding while preserving the model's ability to adapt to local structures and semantic information, we construct a semantic guided learnable decoding matrix $Q \in \mathbb{R}^{N \times M_{target}}$ to complete the pre-reconstruction process.

Specifically, we first take the basic measurement value y_{base} as input, and use a multi-layer perceptron (MLP) [18] to generate the image correlation weighting coefficient a, so that the decoding process can better adapt to the input data. For each block, we predefine R learnable basis matrices B_R, and linearly combine them using the predicted coefficients a. A row-selection operation guided by the approximate binary mask w, which is obtained by normalizing the mask m generated by the sampling module into a soft-binary form is then applied to construct the adaptive decoding matrix $Q_{adapt} \in \mathbb{R}^{N\times M_{adapt}}$. Then, we connect the learnable base decoding matrix $Q_{base} \in \mathbb{R}^{N\times M_{base}}$ with the adaptive decoding matrix Q_{adapt} to construct a complete decoding matrix that is consistent with the actual sampling mode. Finally, the pre-reconstruction process of the image is achieved by multiplying the constructed decoding matrix with the measurements y. Therefore, the pre-reconstruction process can be formulated as follows:

$$\begin{cases} a_r = \text{MLP}(y_{base}), \\ Q_{adapt} \in \mathbb{R}^{N\times M_{adapt}} = [(\sum_{r=1}^{R} a_r B_r) \odot w], \\ Q = [Q_{\text{base}}; Q_{\text{adapt}}], \\ x_{init} = Q \times y, \end{cases} \tag{4}$$

where x_{init} denotes the initial reconstruction. This design provides a strong starting point for subsequent reconstruction modules and reduces the burden of deep iterative networks in recovering high-frequency details.

Patch-Wise Reconstruction Module. To fully capture both long-range dependencies and local information, we integrate the interpretable optimization algorithm FISTA [4] with a hybrid network composed of a Transformer backbone and CNN structures to perform a learnable image reconstruction process.

Firstly, inspired by the FISTA iterative structure, our module guides Transformer based reconstruction in an iterative manner, reducing the differences between current estimation and measurement data while improving the mathematical interpretability of the model [15]. We use x^k_{grad} to represent the output at the k-th iteration, x^k_β to represent the output after momentum acceleration at the k-th iteration, y to represent the actual compressed measurement data of one input image, and variables x^{k-1} and x^k to represent the inputs at the previous and current iterations, respectively. The x^0 and x^1 corresponding to the first iteration are both x_{init}. Therefore, the forward propagation process of the reconstruction error based on FISTA gradient descent step size can be expressed as:

$$\begin{cases} x^k_\beta = x^k + \beta_k(x^k - x^{k-1}), \\ x^k_{grad} = x^k_\beta - \alpha_k \Phi^T(\Phi x^k_\beta - y), \end{cases} \tag{5}$$

where β_k denotes the momentum coefficient of iterative updates, and α_k represents the learnable step size at the k-th iteration. Compared with the original ISTA, the momentum acceleration in FISTA makes the reconstruction process converge faster.

In order to capture local details, this model introduces a shallow CNN network (preblock) [15]-as shown in Fig. 1, which consists of an input convolution layer, four stacked convolutional submodules and an output convolution layer-into the transformer backbone to simulate the proximal operation of sparse priors, learning local image details for denoising and detail restoration. The process of the preblock can be represented as:

$$x_{pre}^{k} = x_{grad}^{k} - CNN_{pre}^{k}(x_{grad}^{k}) \tag{6}$$

where CNN_{pre}^{k} represents the specific CNN block in the k-th iteration.

Unlike the original Transformer designed for contextual modeling in NLP [19], our Transformer is tailored to capture long-range spatial dependencies. As shown in Fig. 1, it comprises an encoder, a soft-thresholding unit, and a decoder. To achieve patch-wise image reconstruction, the image is first divided into patches in the encoding module, and each patch is then reshaped into a vector. Next, the positional encoding (PE) module embeds positional information into the image patches to preserve their spatial relationships. The Multi-Head Self-Attention (MHSA) and fully connected (FC) layers then take the PE-encoded image patches as input to capture the positional information of the image [15]. For simplicity, we denote the encoder as $T_{\text{enc}}(\cdot)$, as shown in the following formula:

$$x_{\text{enc}}^{k} = T_{\text{enc}}(x_{pre}^{k}) \tag{7}$$

And then, to achieve sparse coding and denoising, we introduce a shrinkage threshold function:

$$x_{\text{soft}}^{k} = F_{\text{sign}}\left(x_{\text{enc}}^{k}\right) \cdot \max\left(F_{\text{abs}}\left(x_{\text{enc}}^{k}\right) - \lambda_k, 0\right) \tag{8}$$

where $F_{\text{abs}}(\cdot)$ denotes the absolute value function, and $F_{\text{sign}}(\cdot)$ denotes the sign function. Notably, λ_k is a learnable shrinkage threshold in the k-th iteration, which differs from the fixed threshold used in the traditional ISTA.

The decoder $T_{\text{dec}}(\cdot)$ injects the sparse/semantic information learned by the Transformer back into the pixel domain in a spatially consistent manner, achieving semantic compensation for low-quality local estimates:

$$x_{\text{dec}}^{k} = x_{\text{pre}}^{k} - \eta_k T_{\text{dec}}^{k}\left(x_{\text{soft}}^{k}, x_{\text{pre}}^{k}\right) \tag{9}$$

In the decoder $T_{\text{dec}}(\cdot)$, the keys (K) and values (V) of the second MHSA layer are derived from x_{soft}^{k}, while the queries (Q) are derived from x_{pre}^{k}.η_k is a learnable scaling coefficient in the k-th iteration, which controls the update strength of global features.

After the decoder $T_{\text{dec}}(\cdot)$, we first reshape the image patches back into the original image block format, and then we introduce another stacked convolutional layer (called postblock) using a convolutional structure similar to the preblock, further removing artifacts and fine noise as:

$$x_{\text{post}}^{k} = x_{\text{dec}}^{k} - CNN_{\text{post}}^{k}\left(x_{\text{dec}}^{k}\right) \tag{10}$$

where $CNN_{\text{post}}(\cdot)$ denotes the CNN block. At the end of an iteration phase, the output of postblock is reshaped to vector x_{k+1} through the mapping function $F_{vec}(\cdot)$ to enable the next iteration phase. Finally, the above process is repeated until all iterations are completed. The inverse vectorization function $F_{vec}^{-1}(\cdot)$ is then applied to obtain the reconstructed image x_{patch} from this module.

Pixel-Wise Reconstruction Module. To compensate for the pixel-level errors generated during the hybrid reconstruction phase, we use a transformer architecture to establish precise pixel-to-pixel mapping and ultimately reconstruct, achieving more detailed information supplementation [9].

Specifically, we first reshape the output of the patch-wise reconstruction phase x_{patch} to $N \times C$ and then embed it pixel by pixel to map each pixel p to the embedding space $\mathbb{R}^{(N\times C)\times D}$. Therefore, we have the following formula:

$$x_{pixel} = w_{\text{unfold}} Reshape(x_{patch}) \tag{11}$$

where $w_{\text{unfold}} \in \mathbb{R}^{1\times D}$ is the projection parameter,D denotes the number of dimensions. After the mapping stage, we employ a new Transformer network to capture pixel-level information of the intermediate reconstruction. The resulting features are projected back to $\mathbb{R}^{(N\times C)}$ by projection parameter $w_{\text{fold}} \in \mathbb{R}^{D\times 1}$ and then reshaped to recover the original spatial structure of the image. Finally, the refined output is integrated into the final reconstruction x_{recon} through learnable weighting w'_T. Therefore, we have the following equation:

$$x_{recon} = x_{patch} - w_{T'} Reshape(Transformer(x_{pixel}) w_{fold}) \tag{12}$$

3.3 Loss Function

This model is an end-to-end method for reconstructing the original input image x from measurements y. To jointly train the sampling module as well as the pre-reconstruction, patch-wise reconstruction, and pixel-wise refinement modules, the model uses Mean Squared Error (MSE) to describe the element-wise difference between the original image x and the reconstructed image x_{recon}. The loss function is expressed as:

$$\mathcal{L}_{\text{rec}} = \frac{1}{B} \sum_{i=1}^{B} \|x_{recon} - x\|_2^2 \tag{13}$$

where B is the total number of training images . Given the large number of parameters in this model, an orthogonality loss is also introduced into the loss function to prevent parameter explosion:

$$\mathcal{L}_{\text{reg}} = \|\Phi\Phi^\top - \mathbf{I}\|_F \tag{14}$$

where Φ denotes the measurement matrix of the network and $\|\cdot\|_F$ The final loss is the sum of the two components:

$$\mathcal{L}_{\text{total}} = \mathcal{L}_{\text{rec}} + \lambda \mathcal{L}_{\text{reg}} \tag{15}$$

where λ denotes the weight of the loss caused by orthogonal clipping.

4 Experiments

4.1 Experimental Settings

In our experiments, we use the BSD500 dataset [2], which contains 400 images, to train the model, while the Set11 [12] dataset is used for validation and Set5 [3], Set14 [22] and CBSD68 [13] datasets are used for testing. Evaluation metrics include PSNR (Peak Signal-to-Noise Ratio) [11], and SSIM (Structural Similarity Index Measure) [11]. Higher PSNR and SSIM values indicate better performance of the method. During the training process, the batch size and block size are manually determined based on practical considerations. The network depth is set to 6 layers by default, and the number of heads in the Transformer module is set to $H = 8$. The model is implemented in the PyTorch framework and trained using the Adam optimizer for 200 epochs on an NVIDIA H800 PCIe GPU.

4.2 Main Result

To evaluate the performance of HSGTCN, we compared it on Set5 [3], Set14 [22] (grayscale images), and CBSD68 [13](color images) datasets with several state-of-the-art methods, including ReconNet [12], ISTA-Net [24], CSNet [16], TransCS [15], TCSNet [9], and MTCCSNet [14], which have different sampling rates.

As shown in Table 1, ReconNet and ISTA-Net achieve similar reconstruction performance, while CSNet, incorporating a CNN structure, shows improve-

Table 1. PSNR(dB) and SSIM comparisons of state-of-the-art methods on Set5, Set14 and CBSD68 across sampling rates $\tau \in \{0.01, 0.04, 0.1, 0.25, 0.4, 0.5\}$

Datasets	Methods	0.01		0.04		0.10		0.25		0.40		0.50		Avg.	
		PSNR	SSIM	PSNR	SSIM	PSNR	SSIM	PSNR	SSIM	PSNR	SSIM	PSNR	SSIM	PSNR	SSIM
Set5	ReconNet	18.4	0.4255	22.46	0.603	25.06	0.7172	26.8	0.7846	27.37	0.8063	27.79	0.8145	24.65	0.6919
	ISTA-Net$^+$	18.55	0.4408	23.45	0.6619	28.61	0.8315	34.17	0.9272	37.52	0.9584	39.49	0.9706	30.30	0.7984
	CSNet$^+$	22.3	0.5856	27.55	0.8156	31.43	0.9027	35.1	0.947	38.47	0.9704	39.2	**0.9779**	32.34	0.8665
	TransCS	22.21	0.5783	27.59	0.8146	**32.24**	0.9129	36.28	**0.9552**	37.81	0.9646	39.64	0.9724	32.6283	0.8663
	TCSNet	22.42	0.578	27.27	0.8002	31.24	0.9	35.46	0.9512	37.82	0.9667	39.11	0.973	32.22	0.8615
	MTCCSNet	22.16	0.5528	26.44	0.7671	29.89	0.8746	34.66	0.9439	38.41	0.9701	**39.91**	0.9766	31.9117	0.8475
	HSGTCN	**22.68**	**0.6094**	**27.93**	**0.8264**	32.23	**0.9133**	**36.35**	0.955	**38.58**	0.9686	39.9	0.9745	**32.945**	**0.8745**
Set14	ReconNet	18	0.3888	21.3	0.5267	23.35	0.6329	24.69	0.7029	25.11	0.729	25.54	0.7491	22.9983	0.6216
	ISTA-Net$^+$	18.22	0.4014	22.08	0.5708	26	0.7289	30.62	0.87	33.9	0.9262	35.98	0.9485	27.8	0.7410
	CSNet$^+$	21.32	0.5142	25.1	0.7051	27.97	0.8207	31.12	0.9041	34.25	0.9447	35.77	**0.9608**	29.255	0.8083
	TransCS	21.33	0.5102	25.16	0.7014	28.62	0.8308	32.57	0.9183	34.19	0.9414	36.1	0.9546	29.6617	0.8095
	TCSNet	21.43	0.5098	24.66	0.689	27.78	0.8185	31.67	0.9128	33.91	0.9424	35.24	0.9549	29.115	0.8046
	MTCCSNet	21.1	0.4879	24.28	0.6674	26.93	0.7962	31.09	0.9055	34.53	**0.9477**	36.01	0.9606	28.99	0.7942
	HSGTCN	**21.57**	**0.528**	**25.34**	**0.7117**	**28.74**	**0.8358**	**32.61**	**0.9198**	**35.04**	0.9435	**36.3**	0.9554	**30.172**	**0.8117**
CBSD68	ReconNet	18.95	0.4032	21.86	0.5281	23.6	0.6231	24.72	0.6892	25.18	0.7157	25.54	0.7368	23.3083	0.6160
	ISTA-Net$^+$	19.18	0.4201	22.34	0.5573	25.3	0.7001	29.31	0.8507	32.16	0.9158	34.01	0.9421	27.05	0.7310
	CSNet$^+$	22.07	0.5157	25.03	0.6841	27.39	0.8014	30.56	0.8992	**33.71**	**0.9497**	**35.04**	**0.9648**	28.9667	0.8025
	TransCS	21.98	0.5123	25.03	0.679	27.79	0.8072	31.29	0.9089	33.11	0.9404	34.92	0.9554	29.02	0.8005
	TCSNet	22.03	0.5139	24.81	0.6734	27.28	0.7994	30.67	0.9036	33.16	0.9453	34.67	0.9616	28.77	0.7995
	MTCCSNet	21.66	0.4926	24.2	0.6548	26.5	0.7804	30.18	0.8964	33.5	0.9478	35	0.963	28.5067	0.7892
	HSGTCN	**22.24**	**0.526**	**25.25**	**0.6885**	**27.88**	**0.812**	**31.33**	**0.9094**	33.33	0.9369	34.7	0.9534	**29.1217**	**0.8044**

ment. MTCCSNet, TransCS, and TCSNet further enhance reconstruction quality. Notably, HSGTCN attains the highest average PSNR and SSIM on both grayscale datasets, with average gains of approximately 0.317 dB and 0.008, 0.51 dB and 0.0022 over the second-best methods. HSGTCN's advantage is particularly pronounced at low sampling rates. At $\tau = 0.04$, PSNR and SSIM improvements on Set5 and Set14 reach about 0.34 dB and 0.0108, 0.18 dB and 0.0066, respectively. At $\tau = 0.01$, compared with ISTA-Net, the gains are roughly 4.13 dB and 0.1686 (Set5) , 3.35 dB and 0.1266 (Set14), demonstrating that HSGTCN effectively overcomes the limitations of conventional compressed sensing under low sampling conditions. Similar trends are observed on the CBSD68 color dataset, where HSGTCN achieves the highest average PSNR and SSIM, outperforming the second-best methods by approximately 0.1017 dB and 0.0019, and maintaining substantial improvements at low sampling rates. These results indicate HSGTCN's robustness and strong generalization across both grayscale and color images.

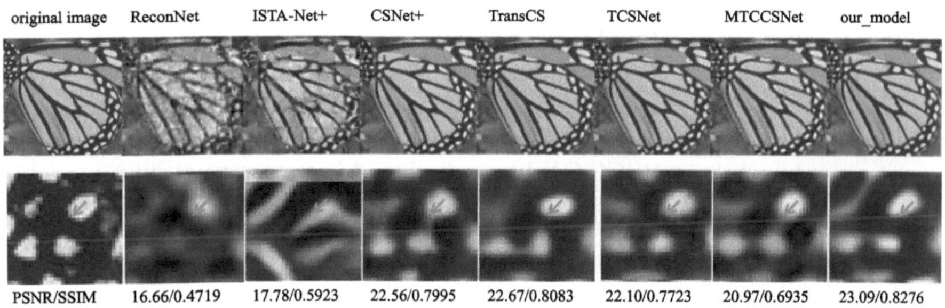

Fig. 2. The reconstruction results of butterfly images using our model and various competitive methods with a sampling rate τ of 0.04.

In addition, Fig. 2 shows several samples of reconstructed images (original images from the Set5 dataset) for visual comparison. HSGTCN can better restore image structure and texture details at low sampling rates compared to other methods, effectively restoring global structure and local details. In summary, compared to several modern image compression methods, the proposed HSGTCN not only provides significant improvements in quantitative comparisons (PSNR and SSIM), but also in visual presentation on public test datasets and multiple sampling rates.

4.3 Ablation Study

In this section, we specifically designed three variants of HSGTCN: (1) HSGTCN without semantic sampling and the semantic-based pre-reconstruction module (referred to as HSGTCN w/o S); (2)HSGTCN without the pixel reconstruction module (referred to as HSGTCN w/o P); and (3) HSGTCN without the FISTA-guided patch-wise reconstruction module (referred to as HSGTCN w/o H). To

Table 2. PSNR(dB) and SSIM comparisons of ablation methods on Set5 across multiple sampling rates $\tau \in \{0.1, 0.25\}$

Datasets	Methods	0.10		0.25		Avg.	
		PSNR	SSIM	PSNR	SSIM	PSNR	SSIM
Set5	HSGTCN w/o S	31.91	0.9086	36.28	0.9556	34.095	0.9321
	HSGTCN w/o P	32.07	0.9113	36	0.9545	34.035	0.9329
	HSGTCN w/o H	29.58	0.8555	33.45	0.9271	31.515	0.8913
	HSGTCN	**32.23**	**0.9133**	**36.35**	**0.955**	**34.29**	**0.9342**

ensure a fair comparison, we trained all three models using the same parameter settings as HSGTCN.

As shown in Table 2, the original HSGTCN performed the best when compared to the other three variants. It performs excellently at both low and high sampling rates. For example, in the case of τ=0.1 and dataset Set5, HSGTCN provides approximately 0.32, 0.16, and 2.65 dB improvement in PSNR compared to HSGTCN w/o S, HSGTCN w/o P, and HSGTCN w/o H, respectively. In addition, at τ=0.25, HSGTCN provided approximately 0.19%, 0.97%, and 8.67% improvement in PSNR compared to HSGTCN w/o S, HSGTCN w/o P, and HSGTCN w/o H, respectively. In summary, the semantic sampling module and pre-reconstruction module, patch-wise reconstruction module, and pixel reconstruction module in HSGTCN have all played important roles in improving image reconstruction.

5 Conclusion

In this work, we presented HSGTCN, a hybrid semantic-guided Transformer–CNN framework for learned image compressed sensing. By parameterizing the sensing operator with semantic cues and integrating CNN–Transformer reconstruction within an unfolding scheme, the model enhances multi-scale consistency under compressed measurements. Experimental results validate the effectiveness of the proposed design. In the future, we will focus on developing more lightweight and physically grounded semantic-aware sensing strategies that better align with practical acquisition constraints while maintaining reconstruction performance.

Acknowledgements. This work was supported by the National Key Research and Development Program of China under Grant No.2024YFE0212000.

References

1. Adler, J., Öktem, O.: Learned primal-dual reconstruction. IEEE Trans. Med. Imaging **37**(6), 1322–1332 (2018)
2. Arbelaez, P., Maire, M., Fowlkes, C., Malik, J.: Contour detection and hierarchical image segmentation. TPAMI **33**(5), 898–916 (2010)
3. Bevilacqua, M., Roumy, A., Guillemot, C.M., Alberi-Morel, M.L.: Low-complexity single-image super-resolution based on nonnegative neighbor embedding. In: British Machine Vision Conference (2012)
4. Blumensath, T., Davies, M.E.: Iterative hard thresholding for compressed sensing. Appl. Comput. Harmon. Anal. **27**(3), 265–274 (2009)
5. Candès, E.J., Romberg, J., Tao, T.: Robust uncertainty principles: exact signal reconstruction from highly incomplete frequency information. IEEE Trans. Inf. Theory **52**(2), 489–509 (2006)
6. Dong, K., Zhou, C., Ruan, Y., Li, Y.: Mobilenetv2 model for image classification. In: ITCA. pp. 476–480 (2020)
7. Donoho, D.L.: Compressed sensing. IEEE Trans. Inf. Theory **52**(4), 1289–1306 (2006)
8. Duarte, M.F., et al.: Single-pixel imaging via compressive sampling. IEEE Signal Process. Mag. **25**(2), 83–91 (2008)
9. Gan, H., Shen, M., Hua, Y., Ma, C., Zhang, T.: From patch to pixel: a transformer-based hierarchical framework for compressive image sensing. IEEE Trans. Comput. Imaging **9**, 133–146 (2023)
10. Han, K., Xiao, A., Wu, E., Guo, J., Xu, C., Wang, Y.: Transformer in transformer. NeurIPS **34**, 15908–15919 (2021)
11. Hore, A., Ziou, D.: Image quality metrics: Psnr vs. ssim. In: ICPR (2010)
12. Kulkarni, K., Lohit, S., Turaga, P., Kerviche, R., Ashok, A.: Reconnet: non-iterative reconstruction of images from compressively sensed measurements. In: CVPR, pp. 449–458 (2016)
13. Martin, D., Fowlkes, C., Tal, D., Malik, J.: A database of human segmented natural images and its application to evaluating segmentation algorithms and measuring ecological statistics. In: ICCV, vol. 2, pp. 416–423 (2001)
14. Shen, M., Gan, H., Ma, C., Ning, C., Li, H., Liu, F.: Mtc-csnet: marrying transformer and convolution for image compressed sensing. IEEE Trans. Cybern. **54**(9), 4949–4961 (2024)
15. Shen, M., Gan, H., Ning, C., Hua, Y., Zhang, T.: Transcs: a transformer-based hybrid architecture for image compressed sensing. IEEE Trans. Image Process. **31**, 6991–7005 (2022)
16. Shi, W., Jiang, F., Liu, S., Zhao, D.: Image compressed sensing using convolutional neural network. IEEE Trans. Image Process. **29**, 375–388 (2019)
17. Song, H., Gong, J., Jia, H., Shen, X., Gou, J., Meng, H., Wang, L.: Representation sampling and hybrid transformer network for image compressed sensing. IEEE Trans. Circuit Syst. Video Technol. (2025)
18. Taud, H., Mas, J.F.: Multilayer perceptron (mlp). In: Geomatic Approaches for Modeling Land Change Scenarios, pp. 451–455. Springer (2017). https://doi.org/10.1007/978-3-319-60801-3_27
19. Vaswani, A., et al.: Attention is all you need. NeurIPS **30** (2017)
20. Yang, Y., Sun, J., Li, H., Xu, Z.: Admm-csnet: a deep learning approach for image compressive sensing. TPAMI **42**(3), 521–538 (2018)

21. Yao, H., Dai, F., Zhang, S., Zhang, Y., Tian, Q., Xu, C.: Dr2-net: deep residual reconstruction network for image compressive sensing. Neurocomputing **359**, 483–493 (2019)
22. Zeyde, R., Elad, M., Protter, M.: On single image scale-up using sparse-representations. In: Int. Conf. Curves Surfaces, pp. 711–730 (2010)
23. Zhang, B., Qin, Z., Li, G.Y.: Semantic-aware image compressed sensing. In: MLSP, pp , 1–6 (2023)
24. Zhang, J., Ghanem, B.: Ista-net: interpretable optimization-inspired deep network for image compressive sensing. In: CVPR, pp. 1828–1837(2018)
25. Zhang, Z., Liu, Y., Liu, J., Wen, F., Zhu, C.: Amp-net: denoising-based deep unfolding for compressive image sensing. IEEE Trans. Image Process. **30**, 1487–1500 (2020)

STEPS: Scene Text Editing with Preserved Style Using Diffusion and Contrastive Style Encoding

Nicolas Thiebaut(✉)

Roblox, San Mateo, USA
nthiebaut@roblox.com

Abstract. We introduce Scene Text Editing with Preserved Style (STEPS), a novel diffusion model architecture for quality text replacement in images. Scene Text Editing (STE), also known as Visual Text Editing, consists of changing the textual content in an image while conserving the original style, e.g. font, colors, orientation, background, etc. STEPS advances the state of the art in STE through directed focus on improved style preservation. We introduce a style encoder for visual text that captures style independently of textual content, and a model architecture that combines the style encoder with multiple semantic conditions (target text characters encoding and rendered glyphs).

STEPS achieves superior results to previous STE methods in style preservation, output readability, and subjective quality.

1 Introduction

The landscape of image generation and editing has been fundamentally reshaped by recent advances in diffusion models. While these models have established themselves as the state-of-the-art for general synthesis–driven by developments in latent space modeling and improved denoising–the precise rendering of visual text remains a persistent challenge. Generative models frequently exhibit failure modes such as missing character strokes, hallucinating superfluous letters, or failing to strictly adhere to textual prompts (Fig. 1).

Within this domain, Scene Text Editing (STE) presents a uniquely constrained problem. Unlike general text generation, a model must not only modify the semantic content but also rigorously preserve the stylistic attributes–font, color, orientation, and background texture–of the original image.

Historically, STE was dominated by Generative Adversarial Networks (GANs) operating at the text-patch level. While approaches like SRNet and MOSTEL established early benchmarks, their reliance on isolated patches prevents the utilization of global image context, often necessitating complex blending steps that result in visual artifacts. Conversely, recent diffusion-based approaches have improved inpainting capabilities but struggle to balance

R. C.-W. Wong et al. (Eds.): PAKDD 2026, LNAI 16618, pp. 473–484, 2027.
https://doi.org/10.1007/978-981-92-1947-6_38

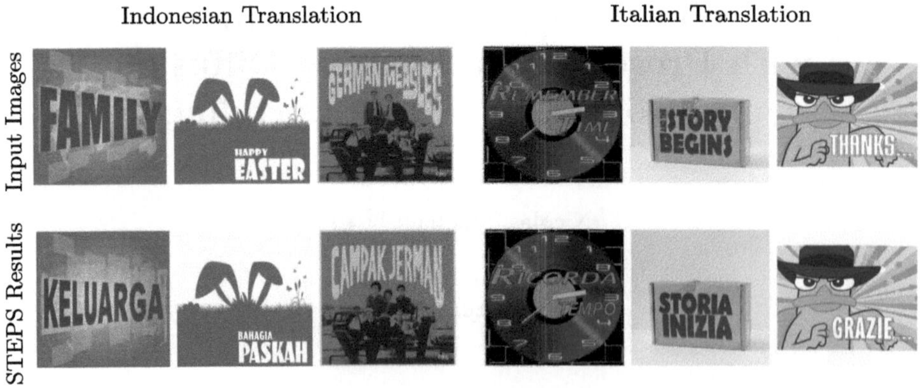

Fig. 1. Examples of Scene Text Editing with STEPS applied to natural language translation of visual text in images with arbitrary backgrounds, fonts, and styles. (Top) Input images. (Bottom) translations of visual text into Indonesian (first three) and Italian (last three). STEPS is able to preserve the original text style, plausibly inpaint the disoccluded background, and to accommodate target texts with different lengths than the original.

readability with style consistency. We observe that existing techniques [2,4–6,13,14,16] particularly struggle when the target text length deviates significantly from the original, a limitation not fully captured by current benchmarks. Furthermore, state-of-the-art large-scale editing models, such as Flux.1 Kontext and Qwen-Image-Edit, remain computationally demanding and lack the specific fine-grained control required for multilingual scene text replacement.

To address these limitations, we introduce Scene Text Editing with Preserved Style (STEPS), a novel diffusion architecture designed to achieve superior style preservation without compromising output readability.

Our approach bridges the gap between style and content through two key contributions:

1. A Novel Style Encoder: We propose a visual text style encoder trained on a unique heuristic: that spatially close visual text tends to share similar stylistic attributes. This allows us to train a powerful style representation that is independent of semantic content, using a contrastive learning objective.
2. Multi-Condition Text Rendering: To ensure robust text generation even when replacing short words with long phrases (e.g., translation tasks), we incorporate multiple semantic signals into a custom architecture, combining rendered text glyphs with a character-level encoder.

We evaluate STEPS against state-of-the-art methods including MOSTEL, TextDiffuser2, and TextCtrl. Our experiments demonstrate that STEPS achieves superior performance in style preservation and subjective quality while effectively handling complex translation tasks that require accommodating different text lengths.

2 Related Work

Historically, GAN-based methods like SRNet and MOSTEL dominated STE. However, their reliance on isolated text patches precludes global image context, often necessitating complex blending steps that introduce visual artifacts.

Recent advances have shifted toward diffusion-based architectures. TextDiffuser2 [3] employs an inpainting approach to tackle visual text generation and editing jointly, offering state-of-the-art performance in readability and output quality. Alternatively, TextCtrl [16] utilizes a diffusion-based approach with glyph-adaptive self-attention to disentangle style and structure features effectively at the patch level. More recently, RS-STE [4] introduced a unified transformer framework that predicts text content and stylized images in parallel, employing a cyclic self-supervised fine-tuning strategy to disentangle style and content without paired training data.

We focus our comparisons on models with comparable scale and architectural goals. Therefore, we exclude FLUX-Text [7], which, despite achieving state-of-the-art multilingual performance via lightweight glyph modules, utilizes a 12-billion parameter model substantially larger than the ~1B parameter range of our work. Similarly, we exclude AnyText [14] as initial experiments indicated its output quality was systematically lower than the aforementioned baselines.

Closest to our architectural approach is DiffUTE [2], which adapts Stable Diffusion 2 [12] by replacing the text condition with a rendered target text image and swapping the CLIP encoder for TrOCR [8]. However, DiffUTE discards the input patch, forcing it to infer style solely from surrounding text; this limits its efficacy to documents with consistent typography (e.g., receipts). Our model overcomes this limitation by enriching TrOCR encodings with character-level and instruction embeddings. Furthermore, by incorporating a dedicated style encoder, our method recovers original text style even in the absence of surrounding stylistic cues.

3 Method

We propose a novel diffusion model architecture specialized in style-preserving scene text editing. Training only requires images and the corresponding extracted text and bounding boxes. Textual content is usually obtained with OCR engines such as PaddleOCR.

The architecture is based on Stable Diffusion 2 (SD2) inpainting [12], to which we add three input conditions. In this setting, the original image is encoded using a pre-trained Variational Auto-Encoder (VAE). A Gaussian perturbation is added to the encoded image, and the resulting noisy image is concatenated channel-wise with the encoded masked image and the (resized) binary mask. The resulting tensor is used as input to a U-Net denoising model that predicts noise in the latent space. Following the SD2 architecture, conditions are integrated via cross-attention mechanisms in the denoising model (Fig. 2). STEPS uses one context vector for each of the four following conditions:

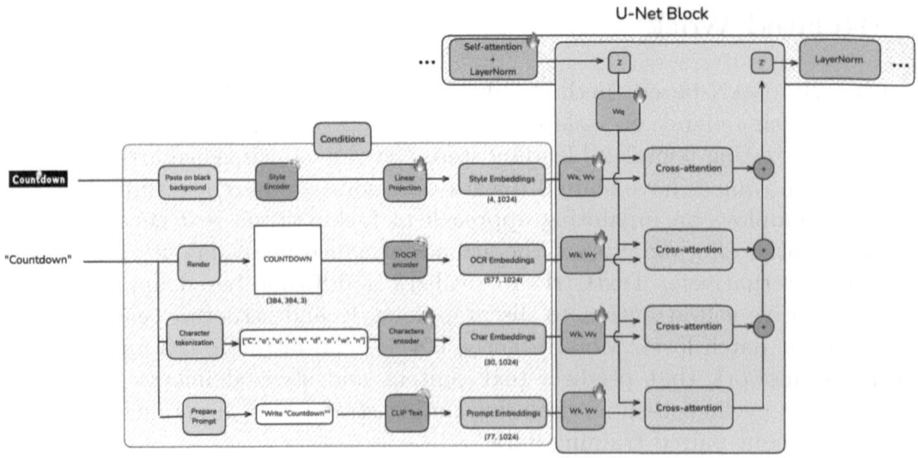

Fig. 2. STEPS multi-conditions cross-attention module. From the source text patch and desired rendered text on the left, we compute four conditioning input embeddings (Style, OCR, Char, and Prompt). Each cross-attention layer of the U-Net is replaced by the sum of four corresponding cross-attention modules. The cross-attention modules share the same query vector Q and their outputs are simply summed (details in the main text).

Standard Text Prompt Instruction: we reuse the original text prompt condition from stable diffusion 2. For each target text `target_text`, we simply pass the following string: `write "target_text"` to the CLIP tokenizer and text encoder. It produces an embedding vector of size $(B, 77, 1024)$, where B is the batch size.

Character Level Encoder: Character awareness has been found to improve visual text generation [9]. Indeed, standard text prompts use subword tokenizers that lose character-level information. To give character awareness to our model, we include a character tokenizer and encoder that maps the characters of the target text to embeddings with shape $(B, 30, 1024)$. Those embeddings are initialized randomly and then learned jointly with the rest of the parameters during training.

Rendered Target Text: Similarly to DiffUTE [2], the target text is rendered on a white background with a generic international typeface (GoNotoKurrent-Regular). The rendered text is an RGB image with a shape of 384×384. We pass that image through the encoder of a TrOCR model[1], producing embeddings of size $(B, 577, 1024)$.

Style Encoding: to learn the original style of the input patch (font, color, background, etc.) without leaking content information, we introduce style encodings with a narrow bottleneck. The style encoder itself is detailed in the next section.

[1] https://huggingface.co/microsoft/trocr-large-printed.

Mathematically, we augment each existing cross-attention layer in the U-Net architecture with three additional independent cross-attention layers. For each context vector x_c ($c \in \{\text{prompt}, \text{char}, \text{render}, \text{style}\}$) we compute the key $K_c = x_c W_{k,c}$, and value $V_c = x_c W_{v,c}$ matrices. Inspired by IP-adapters [15] we use a shared query vector across cross-attention layers, i.e. for a query feature Z we compute a single query matrix $Q = ZW_q$, and the output of the multi-conditions cross-attention module is given by

$$\mathbf{Z}' = \sum_c \text{Softmax}\left(\frac{QK_c^\top}{\sqrt{d}}\right) V_c$$

where all W matrices are subsequently trained (conversely to [15]). The W_q, $W_{k,\text{prompt}}$, and $W_{v,\text{prompt}}$ matrices are initialized from the SD2 checkpoint. Similarly to [15] we find that training converges faster when we initialize the new conditions attention matrices to with the original cross-attention layer weights (i.e., $W_{v,c} = W_{v,\text{prompt}}$, $W_{k,c} = W_{k,\text{prompt}}$ $\forall c$). Figure 2 illustrates the multi-condition cross-attention module visually.

3.1 Style Encoder

The style encoder is a critical piece of our model architecture. Its goal is to encode stylistic features of the text box to be edited (font, color, background, etc.) without leaking semantic content.

We use a simple yet novel contrastive learning objective to train the style encoder, based on the following observation: in images containing text, text boxes close to one another tend to have a similar style because close words often belong to the same sentence and share similar backgrounds. We take advantage of this observed property to create a style similarity objective (Fig. 3).

From the AnyWord-3M dataset, we sample text box patches from either the same image or a different one (probability 50%). Style similarity labels are generated for each patch pair (p_1, p_2) by assigning a similarity of zero to patches from different images, and one minus the normalized bounding boxes distance if they are from the same image.

The image patches are then inpainted onto a 256×256 black background (and cropped if necessary). We then fine-tune a pre-trained ResNet50 model (pre-trained on ImageNet, with the last fully connected layer replaced with a randomly initialized 2048×1024 linear layer) in a bi-encoder setting. The loss function is the Mean-Squared Error between the labels described above and the cosine similarity between the embedding from both arms of the bi-encoder. Mathematically, for a pair of visual text patches p_1 and p_2, the loss function reads

$$\ell(s, p_1, p_2) = \left(\frac{f(p_1) \cdot f(p_2)}{\|f(p_1)\|_2 \, \|f(p_2)\|_2} - s(p_1, p_2)\right)^2, \qquad (1)$$

where f is the ResNet50-based image encoder and $s \in [0, 1]$ is the similarity label,

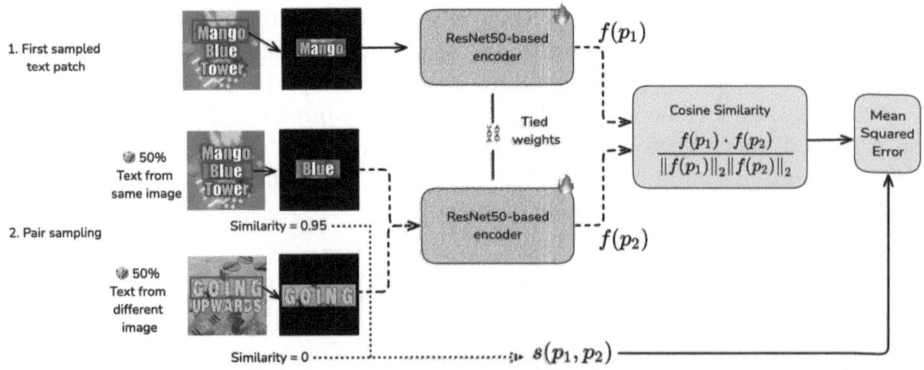

Fig. 3. Style Encoder Training. To learn style embeddings (font, color, orientation, background) without encoding the textual content, we observe that stylistic similarity is correlated with spatial proximity in images that contain visual text. We then sample visual text patches from either different images (style similarity of zero) or the same image (style similarity of one minus bounding boxes distance). Finally, we train a bi-encoder on those stylistic similarity scores. A single copy of the resulting style encoder provides useful embeddings that we use as conditioning input for the main diffusion model.

$$s(p_1, p_2) = \begin{cases} 1 - \min\limits_{b_1 \in B_1, b_2 \in B_2} \dfrac{\|b_1 - b_2\|_2}{\sqrt{w \cdot h}} & \text{if } p_1 \text{ and } p_2 \text{ from same image,} \\ 0 & \text{otherwise.} \end{cases} \tag{2}$$

B_1 and B_2 are the bounding boxes.

As potential limitations, this simple heuristic for style similarity may create a noisy objective (because texts with different styles are often present in the same image) or fail to disentangle style from content (because spatially close words have related meanings). The experiments presented in Sect. 4 show that those limitations are minimal.

3.2 Training

We train STEPS on the AnyWord-3M-LAION dataset[2], which consists of images containing visual text mostly in English, with OCR annotations (bounding boxes positions and content). All images are 512 × 512 RGB images sampled from the Internet and selected for the legibility of their textual content.

Our model has 1.6B parameters, 882M of which are trainable. We trained for 5 days (40 epochs) on 8 A100-80G NVIDIA while freezing the VAE, CLIP prompt encoder, and TrOCR encoder. The character encoder is a linear embedding layer (dimension 128) followed by a 2-layer Transformer Encoder with 4 attention heads per layer.

[2] https://modelscope.cn/datasets/iic/AnyWord-3M/summary.

4 Experiments

Our method learns scene text editing capabilities from images with OCR annotations, in a self-supervised setting. We first train and evaluate the style encoder described in Sect. 3, then use it as an input to train STEPS.

As discussed in Sect. 2, we identified MOSTEL [11], TextDiffuser2 [3], and TextCtrl [16] as relevant competing methods. Of the many available methods, these three offer competitive performance, have a moderate number of parameters ($\sim$ 1B parameters or less), and have accessible open-source implementations. They also provide a representative sample of recent approaches to STE: a GAN-based method (MOSTEL), a diffusion model operating at the image level (TextDiffuser2), and a diffusion model focused on text patches (TextCtrl).

4.1 Style Encoder

The Style Encoder is trained for two epochs on the AnyWord-3 dataset using a single NVIDIA A100-80G GPU, a process that takes roughly 48 h. We allocate 5% of the data for validation. After training, the model achieves a validation

Fig. 4. Samples comparison (best viewed zoomed in). In some of those examples, MOSTEL fails to properly erase the original text, while TextDiffuser only partially matches the style of the input text. TextCtrl preserves style best for some examples, but sometimes suffers from blurriness or fails to produce the correct letters. Our new STEPS method offers the best readability and style-preservation properties.

loss of 0.0315, compared to 0.4786 for a randomly initialized baseline evaluated on the same validation split.

Table 1. Style encoder accuracy on the ScenePair retrieval task. To validate the training method of our style encoder, we treat pair retrieval within all 1,280 examples as a classification task. We perform nearest neighbor classification in the embedding space of the SigLIP2-base image encoder (86M parameters) and our style encoder (22M parameters). While being smaller, our model offers significantly higher accuracy, confirming that it captures style similarity more accurately than a generic image encoder such as SigLIP2.

	Accuracy @ 1	Accuracy @ 10
SigLIP2-base	0.1793	0.5354
STEPS Style Encoder	**0.5880**	**0.8882**

To validate the heuristic we use to train the style encoder, we use the ScenePair dataset. While the ScenePair dataset contains only short and clean text in English, it contains 1,280 pairs of visual text patches that are stylistically identical but semantically distinct. In Table 1 we compare pair retrieval with our style encoder and with the SigLIP2 image encoder.

Figure 5 shows examples of an input text patch, together with its most similar and dissimilar examples in the validation set. This example visually supports the idea that the style encoder, trained on spatial proximity as a proxy for style similarity, produces a representation that encodes visual text stylistic features, notably the text and background colors.

Fig. 5. Style Encoder example for illustration purposes. The leftmost image is a sample text patch (top: original, bottom: preprocessed input to the encoding model), for which we computed the cosine similarity with all text patches in a sample of 1,000 images. The top row contains the most similar patches within this sample according to our style encoder, while the bottom row shows the least similar images. Text patches with similar colors, fonts, and backgrounds have aligned embeddings, while low embedding alignment correlates with text style discrepancies.

Those results support the assumption that spatial proximity correlates with style similarity in natural images, sufficiently to encode visual text style.

4.2 Dataset

Existing benchmarks (e.g., ScenePair, Anytext-benchmark) predominantly feature English text with matching source and target lengths. Consequently, they fail to adequately probe artifacts arising from significant length deviations or creative styling. We therefore evaluate our models using a translation task on the AnyWord-3M dataset. Following initial reconstruction tests on 1,000 annotated images, we translate text into Indonesian and Italian. These languages were selected to accommodate the English-only training of prior art (MOSTEL, TextDiffuser2, TextCtrl) while introducing necessary length variations.

The AnyWord-3M dataset includes 1,000 evaluation images with OCR annotations. We first test all four models on reconstructing images with masked OCR regions. Then, we translate the text into Indonesian and Italian–chosen for their English-subset alphabets, because prior art of MOSTEL, TextDiffuser2 and TextCtrl were trained only on English. This evaluates the models' ability to visually replace text of varying lengths.

Table 2. Quantitative results on the AnyWord-3M-LAION benchmark dataset. Original refers to repainting the original image after masking text boxes, while Indonesian and Italian translations were selected because their alphabet is a subset of the English alphabet on which the models considered were trained. The translation task notably measures the ability to edit text that deviates from the original in length. Higher OCR indicates better readability, lower LPIPS better style preservation, and lower FID better output realism. Both MOSTEL and TextCtrl operate at the patch level. On the translation task, TextCtrl struggles with style consistency, while MOSTEL achieves strong style preservation–though often at the expense of readability, as it sometimes fails to fully erase the original text.

	Original			Indonesian Translation			Italian Translation		
	LPIPS ↓	FID ↓	OCR ↑	LPIPS ↓	FID ↓	OCR ↑	LPIPS ↓	FID ↓	OCR ↑
MOSTEL	0.063	16.119	0.681	0.072	18.445	0.506	0.071	18.179	0.536
TextDiffuser2	0.080	16.095	0.690	0.099	19.226	0.651	0.097	18.879	0.653
TextCtrl	0.097	22.975	0.623	0.104	23.336	0.619	0.104	23.786	0.636
STEPS (new)	**0.045**	**9.116**	**0.708**	**0.070**	**12.392**	**0.686**	**0.069**	**11.984**	**0.691**

4.3 Metrics

We evaluate three aspects of scene text editing methods in the absence of reference outputs: Readability ((1 - normalized edit distance) between the target text and characters extracted by PP-OCRv4), Style-preservation (LPIPS to measure aesthetic consistency between the original and edited images), and Output quality (Fréchet Inception Distance to assess overall aesthetic realism).

All the methods we consider edit text boxes one at a time (although TextDiffuser 2 and STEPS take into account the entire image). For images that contain multiple text boxes, we experimented with several techniques and observe the best results when editing the images recursively for consistency and then blending all of the text boxes into the original image, using Poisson blending.

Table 3. Vision-Language Model evaluation. In this setting of scene text translation with multiple text boxes per image, methods that operate at the text patch-level struggle with visual quality and legibility, from the perspective of the VLM evaluator. This is partly due to the blending post-processing step that is necessary to edit the entire input image. Inpainting methods like TextDiffuser2 and STEPS do not suffer from this limitation, and STEPS outperforms competing methods in both visual quality and legibility.

	Indonesian Translation		Italian Translation	
	Visual Quality (0–5) ↑	Legibility 0–5) ↑	Visual Quality (0–5) ↑	Legibility 0-5) ↑
MOSTEL	1.52	1.38	1.84	1.68
TextDiffuser2	2.46	2.83	2.56	3.01
TextCtrl	1.496	1.536	1.424	1.472
STEPS (new)	**3.224**	**3.624**	**3.544**	**3.936**

Table 4. Quantitative results from the ablation study. Higher OCR values indicate improved readability, while lower LPIPS scores reflect better style preservation, and lower FID scores suggest higher output realism. Removing the style encoder from the conditioning inputs negatively affects style preservation and realism, but has a more limited impact on readability.

	Original			Indonesian Translation			Italian Translation		
	LPIPS ↓	FID ↓	OCR ↑	LPIPS ↓	FID ↓	OCR ↑	LPIPS ↓	FID ↓	OCR ↑
STEPS (all conditions)	**0.045**	**9.116**	**0.708**	**0.070**	**12.392**	**0.686**	**0.069**	**11.984**	**0.691**
W/o style encoder	0.056	11.501	0.701	0.083	15.416	0.676	0.080	14.848	0.672

4.4 Vision-Language Model Evaluation

Beyond the metrics reported in the previous section, we also assess the legibility and aesthetic quality of the images generated by different methods using a Vision-Language Model (VLM). For this evaluation, we employ GPT-4o as the VLM and ask it to rate visual quality and legibility from 0 to 5 each.

4.5 Results

The quantitative (Table 2) and VLM (Table 3) evaluations show that STEPS matches or surpasses the performance of both state-of-the-art GAN-based models and leading diffusion-based approaches to text editing. Figure 4 illustrates the differences with examples.

To preserve the original image parts far from text boxes, we use Blended Latent Diffusion [1] during denoising. This constraint enables recursive editing, so we can successively edit different text boxes in the same image. We use DPM-Solver [10] with 30 steps for the denoising schedule.

4.6 Ablation Studies

Our method adds three components to the underlying Stable Diffusion 2 inpainting model, through a multifold conditioning module (Fig. 2). The first component, the style encoder, captures the style of input text patches (font, color, background, etc.). The remaining two components (TrOCR encoder and character-level encoder) aim to improve the glyphs and character awareness of the model.

Since the introduction of the style encoder is our main contribution, we train a model without it and evaluate it against our full STEPS model (Table 4).

For both versions, the model is retrained from the same initial weights and with the same compute budget (5 days on 8 A100-80G NVIDIA). The checkpoint with the lowest validation loss is used (on a subsample of 70k images).

Results from the ablation studies validate the expected contribution of the style encoder. Removing it degrades aesthetic quality and style consistency.

These findings alleviate concerns that the style encoder inadvertently captures semantic content. If the encoder were leaking substantial semantic information, we would expect the model to exhibit a disproportionate performance advantage in the Original repainting task. However, the observed performance differential between the Original repainting and translation tasks remains consistent regardless of the style encoder's inclusion. This indicates that the disparity is intrinsic to the training dataset rather than an artifact of semantic leakage from the style encoder.

5 Conclusion

We introduce STEPS, a diffusion-based visual text editing technique with style transfer, addressing a key limitation in prior STE methods through the introduction of a novel style-preserving encoder. Benchmarking against GAN and diffusion-based approaches, STEPS achieves strong style adherence, seamless text blending, and high legibility across diverse backgrounds and text lengths.

Despite its advancements, STEPS has limitations, such as occasional superfluous glyphs. Future work could enhance robustness through improved style encoder training, larger VAE models, or alternative backbones like diffusion transformers and flow matching.

References

1. Avrahami, O., Fried, O., Lischinski, D.: Blended latent diffusion. ACM Trans. Graph. **42**(4), 1–11 (2023). https://doi.org/10.1145/3592450, http://arxiv.org/abs/2206.02779, arXiv:2206.02779 [cs]
2. Chen, H., et al.: DiffUTE: Universal Text Editing Diffusion Model (2023). http://arxiv.org/abs/2305.10825, arXiv:2305.10825 [cs]
3. Chen, J., Huang, Y., Lv, T., Cui, L., Chen, Q., Wei, F.: TextDiffuser-2: Unleashing the Power of Language Models for Text Rendering (2023). http://arxiv.org/abs/2311.16465, arXiv:2311.16465 [cs]
4. Fang, Z., et al.: Recognition-synergistic scene text editing (2025). https://arxiv.org/abs/2503.08387
5. Ji, J., et al.: Improving Diffusion Models for Scene Text Editing with Dual Encoders (2023). http://arxiv.org/abs/2304.05568, arXiv:2304.05568 [cs]
6. Kulikov, V., Kleiner, M., Huberman-Spiegelglas, I., Michaeli, T.: Flowedit: inversion-free text-based editing using pre-trained flow models (2025). https://arxiv.org/abs/2412.08629
7. Lan, R., et al.: Flux-text: a simple and advanced diffusion transformer baseline for scene text editing (2025). https://arxiv.org/abs/2505.03329
8. Li, M., et al.: TrOCR: Transformer-based Optical Character Recognition with Pre-trained Models (2022). http://arxiv.org/abs/2109.10282, arXiv:2109.10282 [cs]
9. Liu, R., et al.: Character-Aware Models Improve Visual Text Rendering (2023). http://arxiv.org/abs/2212.10562, arXiv:2212.10562 [cs]
10. Lu, C., Zhou, Y., Bao, F., Chen, J., Li, C., Zhu, J.: DPM-Solver: A Fast ODE Solver for Diffusion Probabilistic Model Sampling in Around 10 Steps (2022). http://arxiv.org/abs/2206.00927, arXiv:2206.00927 [cs, stat]
11. Qu, Y., Tan, Q., Xie, H., Xu, J., Wang, Y., Zhang, Y.: Exploring Stroke-Level Modifications for Scene Text Editing (2022). http://arxiv.org/abs/2212.01982, arXiv:2212.01982 [cs]
12. Rombach, R., Blattmann, A., Lorenz, D., Esser, P., Ommer, B.: High-resolution image synthesis with latent diffusion models (2021)
13. Tuo, Y., Geng, Y., Bo, L.: Anytext2: visual text generation and editing with customizable attributes (2024). https://arxiv.org/abs/2411.15245
14. Tuo, Y., Xiang, W., He, J.Y., Geng, Y., Xie, X.: AnyText: Multilingual Visual Text Generation and Editing (2024). http://arxiv.org/abs/2311.03054, arXiv:2311.03054 [cs]
15. Ye, H., Zhang, J., Liu, S., Han, X., Yang, W.: IP-Adapter: Text Compatible Image Prompt Adapter for Text-to-Image Diffusion Models (2023). http://arxiv.org/abs/2308.06721, arXiv:2308.06721 [cs]
16. Zeng, W., Shu, Y., Li, Z., Yang, D., Zhou, Y.: Textctrl: diffusion-based scene text editing with prior guidance control. Adv. Neural. Inf. Process. Syst. **37**, 138569–138594 (2024)

Semantic-Enhanced Representation Architecture for Automatic ICD Coding via Hyperbolic Graph Neural Networks

Pritish Patel[1,2](✉) and Mohammed Hasanuzzaman[1,2]

[1] Munster Technological University, Cork, Ireland
pritish.patel@mymtu.ie
[2] ADAPT Centre, Department of Computer Science, Munster Technological University, Cork, Ireland
mohammed.hasanuzzaman@mtu.ie

Abstract. Automatic ICD coding from discharge summaries is difficult due to long, noisy notes with dispersed evidence, a deep label hierarchy, and extreme long-tail imbalance. We present SERA-ICD, a span-to-prototype retrieval model that aligns local spans with hierarchy-aware ICD prototypes in hyperbolic space. SERA-ICD segments each note into overlapping spans, encodes spans and code descriptions with a lightweight retrieval encoder, and constructs prototypes over the full code set using a multi-view label graph: ICD ontology edges and semantic similarity over descriptions (dataset-independent), plus a co-occurrence view estimated on the training split to prevent leakage. Hyperbolic distance yields span–code evidence scores, and code-conditioned multiple instance learning aggregates evidence into document predictions while producing decision-faithful span rationales. On MIMIC-III, SERA-ICD achieves the best Micro-/Macro-F1: on MIMIC-III Full it improves Macro-F1 by +**0.54** (+**4.1%** relative; 13.54 vs. 13.00) and on MIMIC-III-50 by +**0.62** (+**0.9%** relative; 71.02 vs. 70.40), with larger gains on medium/tail codes (+**1.7**/+**1.6** Macro-F1; +**8.3%**/+**12.1%** relative over the strongest baseline). Ablations confirm that hyperbolic prototypes, multi-view structure, and MIL pooling drive tail improvements, and qualitative evidence maps demonstrate localized clinical support.

Keywords: Automatic ICD Coding · Extreme Multi-label Classification · Hyperbolic Embeddings · Graph Neural Networks · Multiple Instance Learning · Clinical NLP

1 Introduction

Electronic health records (EHRs) integrate structured signals (e.g., laboratory values, vital signs, medications) with unstructured clinical narratives [13,22]. Discharge summaries are particularly consequential: they condense an inpatient episode into a single narrative used for care transitions and downstream administrative processes, and breakdowns in discharge communication can compromise

R. C.-W. Wong et al. (Eds.): PAKDD 2026, LNAI 16618, pp. 485–496, 2027.
https://doi.org/10.1007/978-981-92-1947-6_39

safety and continuity [17]. Reimbursement, surveillance, and large-scale health analytics therefore require mapping documented diagnoses and procedures to standardized International Classification of Diseases (ICD) codes defined by the World Health Organization and implemented through national variants such as ICD-10-CM [5,9,28]. Despite digitization, ICD assignment remains labor-intensive, expensive, and variable, motivating automated systems that can assist human coders at scale [20,24].

Automatic ICD coding is typically formulated as extreme multi-label classification over discharge summaries (e.g., MIMIC-III) [16,20]. The difficulty, however, extends beyond label cardinality. Supervision is severely imbalanced: a small head of frequent codes dominates training data, while clinically specific codes occupy a long tail with sparse observations [18,20]. Evidence is dispersed across lengthy, noisy notes that often exceed standard context limits, causing document-level pooling to dilute salient clinical cues [2,25]. Moreover, ICD is explicitly hierarchical: specificity increases with depth, and Euclidean representations struggle to model tree growth efficiently, whereas hyperbolic geometry provides a principled inductive bias for hierarchical structure [3,10,21]. Finally, coder-assist systems require localized, human-inspectable evidence rather than opaque document-level scores.

We propose SERA-ICD, a span-to-prototype retrieval framework designed for long, imbalanced, and hierarchical ICD coding. SERA-ICD segments each discharge summary into overlapping spans, encodes spans and code descriptions with a shared retrieval encoder, and scores span–code compatibility via hyperbolic distance to hierarchy-aware ICD prototypes. Prototypes are constructed from ICD-derived resources (descriptions and taxonomy) and refined using a leakage-controlled multi-view label graph over the full code set, combining ontology edges, description-based semantic similarity (dataset-independent), and a co-occurrence view estimated strictly on the training split. Code-conditioned multiple instance learning (MIL) aggregates span-level evidence into document predictions while yielding decision-faithful rationales (Fig. 3). To make the geometric claim falsifiable, we learn curvature and report a Euclidean-limit variant under identical encoders and pooling.

Contributions. (i) We reformulate ICD coding as weakly supervised span-to-prototype retrieval and introduce code-conditioned MIL to localize supporting evidence without span annotations. (ii) We construct hyperbolic ICD prototypes via a leakage-controlled multi-view graph over the full code set, integrating hierarchical structure and semantic similarity to strengthen medium- and tail-code representations. (iii) On MIMIC-III, SERA-ICD achieves state-of-the-art F1, improving Macro-F1 by +0.54 (13.54 vs. 13.00) on MIMIC-III Full and by +0.62 (71.02 vs. 70.40) on MIMIC-III-50, with the largest gains on medium and tail labels, while remaining competitive on ranking metrics (AUC, P@K) used in coder-assist workflows.

2 Related Work

Early neural ICD coding models employed convolutional or recurrent encoders with label-wise attention to associate textual evidence with codes [20,23]. **CAML** introduced per-label attention for document-level code prediction [20]. Subsequent architectures improved long-document modeling and evidence aggregation: **MultiResCNN** and **LAAT/JointLAAT** [18,25] leveraged multi-scale convolutions and transformer attention to better capture dispersed cues. More recently, pretrained language models such as **ClinicalBERT** [1] and **BERT** [7], along with explicit code-description conditioning (**PLM-ICD** [14]), have strengthened semantic representations. Despite these advances, two persistent challenges remain: severe long-tail imbalance limits rare-code recall, and ranking-oriented objectives (AUC, P@K) do not directly optimize exact label-set recovery (F1), which is critical for billing completeness and auditability.

A complementary line of work incorporates ICD structure explicitly. Hierarchy-aware approaches inject taxonomic information through structural regularization or label-graph refinement [18,23]. Hyperbolic embeddings offer a principled geometric bias for tree-like hierarchies [10,21]. In ICD coding, **HyperCore** [3] combines hyperbolic label embeddings with co-occurrence modeling to improve hierarchical multi-label classification. These methods demonstrate that modeling label relationships benefits rare and specific codes. Our approach adopts this geometric intuition but shifts the decision paradigm: rather than predicting codes from a pooled document representation, we retrieve span-level evidence via hyperbolic distance to learned prototypes.

Span-based modeling provides another perspective. Multiple-instance learning (MIL) treats each document as a bag of unlabeled spans [8,11,19], reflecting that only a subset of spans may support a given code. While attention-based MIL has been applied in ICD coding, attention weights are not guaranteed to provide faithful explanations [12]. SERA-ICD unifies these directions by combining span-level retrieval, hierarchy-aware hyperbolic prototypes, and code-conditioned MIL, producing mechanistic rationales derived directly from the scores used for prediction (Fig. 3).

3 Method

3.1 Span-To-Prototype Retrieval (MIL Formulation)

SERA-ICD formulates ICD coding as span-to-prototype retrieval under multiple-instance learning (MIL). Given a discharge summary D and code set $\mathcal{C}$ with ground-truth labels $\mathcal{Y} \subseteq \mathcal{C}$, we segment D into overlapping spans $\mathcal{X}(D) = \{x_1, \ldots, x_N\}$ using a fixed window and stride. This exposes localized evidence without span annotations, treating the document as a bag of spans supervised only by its document-level labels [8,11,19]. Figure 1 presents the overall architecture; Fig. 3 illustrates extracted evidence for predicted codes.

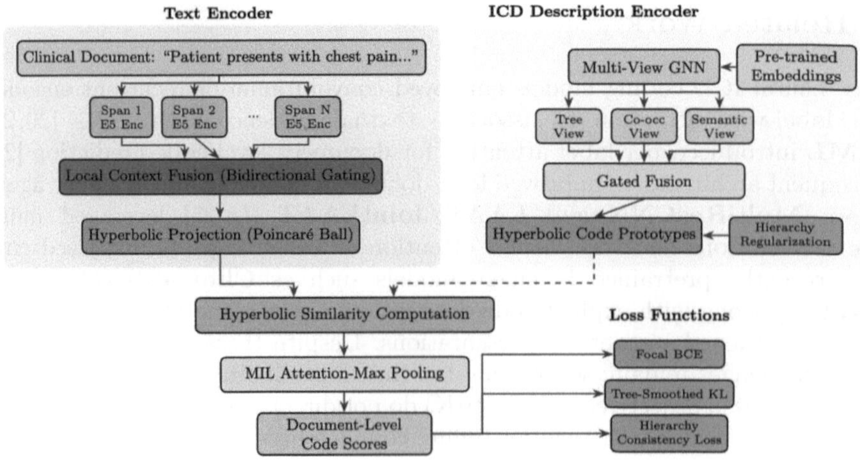

Fig. 1. Overview of SERA-ICD. Left: span encoder with local-context gating and hyperbolic projection. Right: multi-view ICD graph encoder producing hyperbolic label prototypes. Bottom: hyperbolic similarity, code-conditioned MIL pooling, and hierarchy-aware losses.

3.2 Hyperbolic Geometry

Spans and label representations are embedded in the d-dimensional Poincaré ball of curvature $-c$:

$$\mathbb{B}_c^d = \{\mathbf{z} \in \mathbb{R}^d : c\|\mathbf{z}\|^2 < 1\}, \quad c > 0 \text{ [21]}.$$

Euclidean vectors are mapped via the exponential map at the origin:

$$\exp_{\mathbf{0}}^c(\mathbf{v}) = \tanh(\sqrt{c}\|\mathbf{v}\|)\,\frac{\mathbf{v}}{\sqrt{c}\|\mathbf{v}\|}, \quad \exp_{\mathbf{0}}^c(\mathbf{0}) = \mathbf{0},$$

and similarity is measured using the Poincaré distance $d_{\mathbb{B}}$ [10,21]. We learn curvature c jointly. To isolate geometric effects, we include a Euclidean-limit variant replacing $d_{\mathbb{B}}$ with ℓ_2 distance. Figure 2 visualizes the depth–radius correspondence induced by the metric.

3.3 Span and Label Encoders

Each span x_i is encoded with `intfloat/e5-base` [26], producing $\mathbf{h}_i \in \mathbb{R}^d$. To mitigate redundancy from overlapping spans, we apply local context gating:

$$\tilde{\mathbf{h}}_i = \mathbf{g}_i \odot \mathbf{h}_i + (1 - \mathbf{g}_i) \odot \mathbf{h}_i^{\text{ctx}}, \quad \mathbf{g}_i = \sigma\big(\mathbf{W}_g[\mathbf{h}_{i-1}; \mathbf{h}_i; \mathbf{h}_{i+1}] + \mathbf{b}_g\big),$$

where $\mathbf{h}_i^{\text{ctx}}$ is the mean embedding in a fixed neighborhood around span i. We project spans into hyperbolic space via $\mathbf{h}_i^{\mathbb{B}} = \exp_{\mathbf{0}}^c(\mathbf{W}_h\tilde{\mathbf{h}}_i)$.

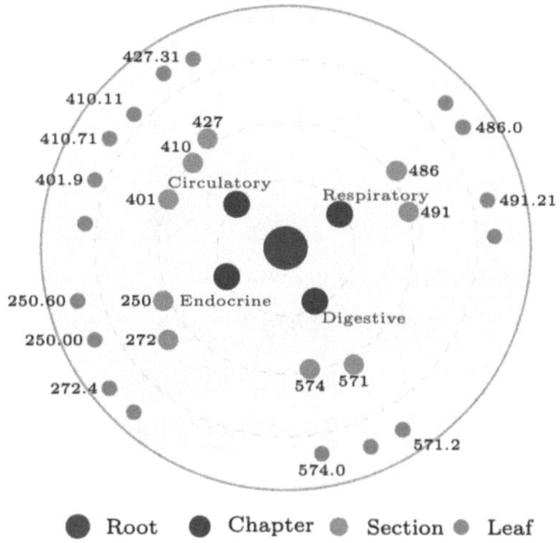

Fig. 2. Poincaré intuition: shallow codes lie near the origin; deeper, more specific codes approach the boundary at larger radii [21].

For labels, each code description is encoded using the same encoder, $\mathbf{e}_j = \text{E5}(\text{desc}_j)$. These embeddings are refined through a leakage-controlled multi-view graph over the full code set: (i) ICD hierarchy edges [28], (ii) a description-similarity graph (top-K cosine neighbors), and (iii) a co-occurrence graph estimated strictly from training data. Each view is processed by a one-layer multi-head GAT (Sect. 4), and view-specific outputs are fused via a softmax-weighted gate to produce $\mathbf{z}_j$. Final hyperbolic prototypes are

$$\mathbf{p}_j = \exp_{\mathbf{0}}^{c}(\mathbf{W}_p \mathbf{z}_j).$$

3.4 Scoring and MIL Pooling

Span–code evidence is defined by negative hyperbolic distance:

$$s_{ij} = -\gamma\, d_{\mathbb{B}}(\mathbf{h}_i^{\mathbb{B}}, \mathbf{p}_j) + b_j,$$

where $\gamma > 0$ is a learned temperature and b_j a code-specific bias [21]. Larger s_{ij} indicates stronger support.

We aggregate evidence via code-conditioned MIL [11]. Attention weights α_{ij} are computed using a query derived from $\mathbf{z}_j$, and pooled as:

$$S_j(D) = \lambda \sum_{i=1}^{N} \alpha_{ij} s_{ij} + (1-\lambda) \max_i s_{ij}, \quad \hat{y}_j = \sigma\big(S_j(D)\big), \tag{1}$$

where $\lambda \in [0,1]$ balances distributed versus peak evidence. Spans with highest s_{ij} (and $\alpha_{ij} s_{ij}$) serve as decision-faithful rationales (Fig. 3).

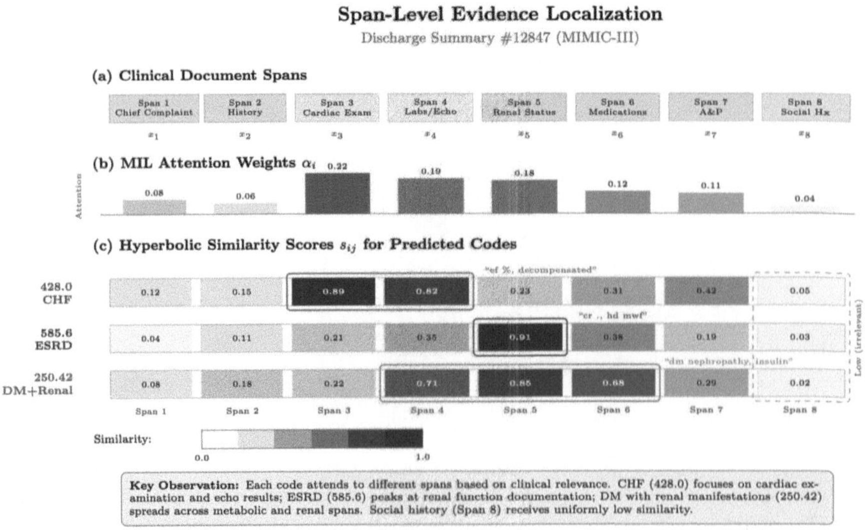

Fig. 3. Evidence visualization: (a) spanization, (b) code-conditioned MIL attention α_{ij} (single code), and (c) hyperbolic similarity s_{ij}. Highlighted spans are the top contributors under s_{ij} and $\alpha_{ij} s_{ij}$.

3.5 Training Objectives

We optimize focal binary cross-entropy $\mathcal{L}_{\text{focal}}$ over code outputs. To incorporate hierarchy, we add:

(i) tree-smoothed calibration $\mathcal{L}_{\text{tree}}$ (Sect. 4);

(ii) parent–child monotonicity

$$\mathcal{L}_{\text{pc}} = \sum_{(p,c)\in E_{\text{tree}}} \max(0, \hat{y}_c - \hat{y}_p),$$

penalizing violations of hierarchical ordering;

(iii) radius regularization

$$\mathcal{L}_{\text{rad}} = \sum_j (\|\mathbf{p}_j\| - r(\text{depth}_j))^2,$$

encouraging deeper codes to occupy larger radii (Fig. 2).

The total objective is

$$\mathcal{L} = \mathcal{L}_{\text{focal}} + \lambda_1 \mathcal{L}_{\text{tree}} + \lambda_2 \mathcal{L}_{\text{pc}} + \lambda_3 \mathcal{L}_{\text{rad}}.$$

Training is warm-started for one epoch with $\mathcal{L}_{\text{focal}} + \lambda_3 \mathcal{L}_{\text{rad}}$, after which all terms are enabled and λ_1, λ_2 are gradually ramped.

4 Experimental Setup

Data. We evaluate on MIMIC-III [16] using the CAML admission-level splits [20]. Each instance pairs a merged *Discharge summary* with all assigned ICD-9 codes. We report results on *MIMIC-III Full* (8,929 normalized codes) and *MIMIC-III-50* (top-50 training codes; retaining admissions containing at least one).

Preprocessing and Descriptions. Following prior work [14,18,20,25], we retain discharge summaries, merge per admission, lowercase, tokenize, and normalize ICD-9 codes deterministically. Admissions without valid codes are removed. Code descriptions are compiled from official ICD tables (with minimal curated additions) and tokenized identically for prototype construction.

Spanization and Label Graphs. Summaries are segmented into spans of length 258 with stride 64; the final span is retained and no span cap is imposed. Label graphs are built offline over the full code set with strict leakage control: the *hierarchy* view uses ICD parent–child edges [28]; the *semantic* view connects mutual top-25 cosine neighbors of L2-normalized description embeddings; the *co-occurrence* view (training-only) links pairs appearing in $\geq$10 training admissions with positive PMI ($w_{jk} = \max(0, \text{PMI}(j, k))$, symmetrized). Only co-occurrence depends on training labels.

Model and Training. SERA-ICD uses `intfloat/e5-base` [26] and a 128-dim Poincaré ball. Label prototypes are refined via one-layer multi-head GATs (8 heads, 128 hidden units, dropout 0.1) per graph view with softmax fusion. Curvature is learned via $c = \text{softplus}(\tilde{c})$ (init 1.0) and norms are clipped to $(1-\epsilon)/\sqrt{c}$ ($\epsilon = 10^{-5}$). Optimization uses AdamW (LR 2×10^{-5}, weight decay 0.01, batch size 8) with cosine schedule and 10% warmup. Models train for 10 epochs; the first uses focal loss plus radius regularization only, then the full objective is enabled with tree/monotonicity weights linearly ramped. Focal BCE uses $(\gamma, \alpha) = (2, 0.25)$ and $(\lambda_1, \lambda_2, \lambda_3) = (0.1, 0.5, 0.01)$. Training on 4×A100 GPUs (80GB) requires 8.5 h including graph construction.

Evaluation. We tune a single global threshold on validation data and report Micro-/Macro-F1 and Micro-/Macro-AUC; for MIMIC-III-50 we also report P@K ($K \in \{5, 8, 15\}$). Long-tail analysis follows prior frequency binning [18, 29,30]. Results are averaged over three runs (seed 42).

Baselines. We compare against established MIMIC-III baselines: **CAML** [20], **MSATT-KG**, **MultiResCNN** [18], **LAAT/JointLAAT** [25], **MSMN** [29], **PLM-ICD** [14], **KEMTL**, **LCDL** [15], and **GKI-ICD** [30], reporting published results under the standard protocol when available.

Table 1. Overall experimental results on MIMIC-III-50. Bolding indicates best, underlining indicates second-best.

Model	AUC (%)		F1 (%)		Precision (%)		
	Macro	Micro	Macro	Micro	P@5	P@8	P@15
CAML	88.32	91.52	57.42	63.18	61.62	–	–
MSATT-KG	91.28	93.54	63.72	68.26	64.22	–	–
MultiResCNN	89.78	92.71	60.48	66.86	63.94	–	–
JointLAAT	92.21	94.12	66.82	70.71	66.18	–	–
MSMN	92.67	94.51	68.12	72.29	67.79	–	–
PLM-ICD	94.03	94.06	69.02	72.36	70.02	–	–
KEMTL	**94.71**	94.11	69.41	72.81	70.63	–	–
LCDL	93.01	**94.92**	68.81	72.84	**72.81**	**63.52**	60.01
GKI-ICD	94.50	94.90	70.40	73.00	71.80	63.00	**60.20**
SERA-ICD	94.00	94.20	**71.02**	**73.96**	70.50	62.80	59.80

5 Results

5.1 Overall Performance

Tables 1 and 2 report test-set performance on MIMIC-III-50 and MIMIC-III Full using Micro-/Macro-F1, Micro-/Macro-AUC, and P@K. Across both benchmarks, SERA-ICD achieves the strongest Micro- and Macro-F1, with the largest improvements observed in Macro-F1, which is particularly sensitive to rare labels under extreme class imbalance.

On MIMIC-III-50, SERA-ICD reaches **71.02%** Macro-F1 and **73.96%** Micro-F1, outperforming prior methods including GKI-ICD and KEMTL in overall F1. On MIMIC-III Full, SERA-ICD attains **13.54%** Macro-F1 and **60.48%** Micro-F1, establishing the best Macro-F1 under the standard CAML protocol.

Several PLM-based and knowledge-enhanced systems achieve marginally higher ranking-oriented metrics (AUC and/or P@K). This reflects a practical trade-off: SERA-ICD explicitly optimizes full label-set recovery (F1), whereas some baselines emphasize shortlist ranking quality. Because these metrics correspond to different coder-assist scenarios—complete code assignment versus top-K suggestion—we report both families for completeness.

5.2 Long-Tail Behavior

To localize improvements, we group MIMIC-III Full codes by training frequency into head (≥ 100), medium (10–99), and tail (< 10) bins and compute Macro-F1 within each group. As shown in Table 3, gains concentrate on medium and tail labels, while head-label performance remains comparable to prior systems.

Table 2. Overall experimental results on MIMIC-III Full. Bolding indicates best, underlining indicates second-best.

Model	AUC (%)		F1 (%)		Precision (%)		
	Macro	Micro	Macro	Micro	P@5	P@8	P@15
CAML	82.43	96.52	4.81	45.61	–	51.32	–
MSATT-KG	90.91	99.12	8.92	55.08	–	72.61	57.92
MultiResCNN	90.94	98.53	8.41	55.03	–	73.19	58.19
JointLAAT	91.94	98.72	10.52	57.32	–	73.27	58.82
MSMN	94.82	99.12	10.21	58.21	–	75.03	59.68
PLM-ICD	92.51	98.83	10.32	59.62	**84.12**	**76.92**	**61.12**
KEMTL	95.21	**99.33**	12.53	58.12	–	75.32	–
LCDL	<u>95.69</u>	98.90	10.93	58.81	79.61	75.57	59.91
GKI-ICD	**95.90**	<u>99.20</u>	<u>13.00</u>	<u>59.80</u>	83.50	75.60	60.20
SERA-ICD	94.70	98.85	**13.54**	**60.48**	<u>83.90</u>	<u>75.80</u>	<u>60.50</u>

This pattern is consistent with the span-to-prototype formulation: structure-aware prototypes and span-level evidence aggregation reduce confusions between rare codes and their frequent semantic neighbors.

Table 3. Macro-F1 on MIMIC-III Full by label-frequency bin.

Model	Head	Medium	Tail
PLM-ICD [14]	60.4	18.7	6.0
GKI-ICD [30]	61.9	20.4	13.2
SERA-ICD (ours)	**62.3**	**22.1**	**14.8**

5.3 Ablation Analysis

Table 4 isolates the contribution of each major component on MIMIC-III Full. Removing hyperbolic prototypes or the multi-view graph encoder yields the largest drops in Macro-F1 and Tail-F1, confirming that geometry and label-structure modeling are primary drivers of rare-label recovery.

Replacing MIL pooling with max pooling also reduces Macro-/Tail-F1, indicating that many codes rely on distributed evidence across spans rather than a single decisive mention. Hierarchy-aware regularizers provide smaller but consistent gains.

Table 4. Ablations on MIMIC-III Full. Tail-F1 is Macro-F1 on tail codes (< 10 train instances).

Variant	Micro-F1	Macro-F1	Tail-F1
SERA-ICD (full)	**60.5**	**13.5**	**14.8**
w/o hyperbolic prototypes	59.5	12.6	12.9
w/o multi-view GNN	59.2	12.2	11.8
w/o MIL (max pooling only)	59.8	12.4	12.3
w/o $\mathcal{L}_{\text{tree}}$	60.1	12.7	13.0
w/o $\mathcal{L}_{\text{pc}}$	60.2	13.0	13.4
w/o $\mathcal{L}_{\text{rad}}$	60.0	12.9	13.1

5.4 Evidence Localization

Figure 3 illustrates code-conditioned evidence retrieval. Highlighted spans correspond to the largest contributors under s_{ij} and $\alpha_{ij}s_{ij}$—the same quantities used to compute $S_j(D)$ (Eq. 1). Explanations are therefore decision-faithful rather than post-hoc. As emphasized by prior work [12], attention weights are not guaranteed causal explanations; comprehensive human evaluation remains future work.

6 Discussion and Limitations

Across both MIMIC-III settings, SERA-ICD improves *code-set recovery* (Micro-/Macro-F1; Tables 1–2), with gains concentrated on medium and tail codes (Table 3). Some PLM- or knowledge-augmented systems achieve slightly stronger ranking metrics (AUC/P@K), reflecting a trade-off: SERA-ICD optimizes full-label recovery (F1), whereas others prioritize top-K shortlist quality. Both metric families correspond to distinct coder-assist scenarios.

Ablations (Table 4) attribute long-tail gains primarily to hyperbolic prototypes and the multi-view label graph; removing either yields the largest Macro-/Tail-F1 drops. Replacing MIL with max pooling similarly reduces performance, indicating that many codes rely on distributed span evidence rather than a single mention. These results support the span-to-prototype design as an effective mechanism for leveraging hierarchical structure and localized evidence.

Explanations are decision-faithful: highlighted spans correspond to the largest contributors under s_{ij} and $\alpha_{ij}s_{ij}$ in Eq. 1 (Fig. 3). Unlike post-hoc saliency, rationales are derived directly from the prediction computation. Nevertheless, attention weights are not guaranteed to be fully causal explanations [12], and formal human evaluation remains future work.

Our evaluation is limited to MIMIC-III (ICD-9). Robustness under distribution shift (institutions, documentation styles, or coding policy changes) is untested; extending to MIMIC-IV and other datasets is necessary for deployment claims. Larger coding systems introduce additional challenges: ICD-10 expands the label space [4], and ICD-11 introduces polyhierarchical structure [6,27], potentially requiring adaptations to graph construction and geometric modeling.

Finally, SERA-ICD introduces additional modeling complexity (multiple losses and warm-start scheduling; Sect. 4) and higher computational cost compared to plain classifiers. Moreover, benchmark improvements do not eliminate coding noise or policy bias in ground-truth labels [24]. We therefore view SERA-ICD as decision support for human coders rather than a fully autonomous replacement.

7 Conclusion

We introduced SERA-ICD, a span-to-prototype retrieval framework for automatic ICD coding that aligns localized textual evidence with structure-aware label prototypes in hyperbolic space and aggregates evidence via code-conditioned MIL. This design improves Micro-/Macro-F1 on MIMIC-III—particularly for medium and tail codes—while providing decision-faithful span rationales. Future work includes cross-dataset validation (e.g., MIMIC-IV), adaptation to ICD-10/ICD-11 hierarchies, and ranking-aware refinements to further improve AUC/P@K.

References

1. Alsentzer, E., et al.: Publicly available clinical BERT embeddings. In: Proceedings of the 2nd Clinical NLP Workshop (2019)
2. Beltagy, I., Peters, M.E., Cohan, A.: Longformer: the long-document transformer. In: Proceedings of ACL (2020)
3. Cao, P., Xiao, Q., Chen, Y., et al.: Hypercore: hyperbolic and co-occurrence representations for hierarchical multi-label classification. In: Proceedings of EMNLP (2020)
4. Cartwright, D.J.: ICD-9-CM to ICD-10-CM: a transition primer. J. AHIMA **84**(3), 60–64 (2013)
5. Centers for Disease Control and Prevention: ICD-10-CM official guidelines for coding and reporting. https://www.cdc.gov/nchs/icd/icd-10-cm.htm (2024). Accessed 02 Mar 2026
6. Chute, C.G., et al.: ICD-11: The WHO classification of diseases. JAMIA (2021)
7. Devlin, J., Chang, M.W., Lee, K., Toutanova, K.: BERT: pre-training of deep bidirectional transformers for language understanding. In: Proceedings of NAACL-HLT (2019)
8. Dietterich, T.G., Lathrop, R.H., Lozano-Pérez, T.: Solving the multiple instance problem with axis-parallel rectangles. Artif. Intell. **89**(1–2), 31–71 (1997)
9. Fetter, R.B., Shin, Y., Freeman, J.L., Averill, R.F., Thompson, J.D.: Case mix definition by diagnosis-related groups. Med. Care **18**(2 Suppl), iii–53 (1980)
10. Ganea, O.E., Bécigneul, G., Hofmann, T.: Hyperbolic neural networks. In: Advances in Neural Information Processing Systems (2018)

11. Ilse, M., Tomczak, J.M., Welling, M.: Attention-based deep multiple instance learning. In: Proceedings of ICML (2018)
12. Jain, S., Wallace, B.C.: Attention is not explanation. In: Proceedings of NAACL-HLT (2019)
13. Jensen, P.B., Jensen, L.J., Brunak, S.: Mining electronic health records: towards better research applications and clinical care. Nat. Rev. Genet. **13**(6), 395–405 (2012)
14. Huang, C.-W., Tsai, S.-C., Chen, Y.-N.: PLM-ICD: Automatic ICD Coding with Pretrained Language Models (2022)
15. Jiang, S., Wang, Z.: Classification of ICD codes based on disease label co-occurrence dependency and longformer with medical knowledge. In: Proceedings of a Clinical NLP/Medical AI Venue (2025)
16. Johnson, A.E.W., et al.: MIMIC-III, a freely accessible critical care database. Sci. Data **3**, 160035 (2016)
17. Kripalani, S., LeFevre, F., Phillips, C.O., Williams, M.V., Basaviah, P., Baker, D.W.: Deficits in communication and information transfer between hospital-based and primary care physicians: implications for patient safety and continuity of care. JAMA **297**(8), 831–841 (2007)
18. Li, F., Yu, H.: MultiresCNN: a multi-resolution convolutional neural network for document-level medical code prediction. In: Proceedings of ACL (2020)
19. Maron, O., Lozano-Pérez, T.: A framework for multiple-instance learning. Adv. Neural Inf. Process. Syst. (1998)
20. Mullenbach, J., Wiegreffe, S., Duke, J., Sun, J., Eisenstein, J.: Explainable prediction of medical codes from clinical text. In: Proceedings of NAACL-HLT (2018)
21. Nickel, M., Kiela, D.: Poincaré embeddings for learning hierarchical representations. Adv. Neural Inf. Process. Syst. (2017)
22. Rajkomar, A., et al.: Scalable and accurate deep learning with electronic health records. NPJ Digit. Med. **1**(1), 18 (2018)
23. Shi, H., Xie, P., Hu, Z., Zhang, M., Xing, E.P.: Towards automated ICD coding using deep learning. In: Proceedings of the ACL Workshop on BioNLP (2017)
24. Stanfill, M.H., Williams, M., Fenton, S.H., Jenders, R.A., Hersh, W.R.: A systematic literature review of automated clinical coding and classification systems. J. Am. Med. Inform. Assoc. **17**(6), 646–651 (2010)
25. Vu, T., Nguyen, D.T., Nguyen, A., et al.: Label attention model for ICD coding from clinical text. In: Proceedings of IJCAI (2020)
26. Wang, L., et al.: Text embeddings by weakly-supervised contrastive pre-training. In: Proceedings of EMNLP (2022)
27. World Health Organization: WHO-FIC content model reference guide: ICD-11 - hierarchy and multiple parents in the Foundation Component. https://icd.who.int/icdapi/docs/ContentModelGuide.pdf (2021). Accessed 02 Mar 2026
28. World Health Organization: International classification of diseases (ICD) (2024). https://www.who.int/standards/classifications/classification-of-diseases. Accessed 02 Mar 2026
29. Yuan, H., et al.: Multi-scale semantic matching network for automatic ICD coding. Artif. Intell. Med. (2022)
30. Zhang, X., et al.: A general knowledge injection framework for ICD coding. arXiv:2505.18708 (2025)

Approximately Bisubmodular Regret Minimization in Billboard and Social Media Advertising

Dildar Ali, Suman Banerjee(✉), and Yamuna Prasad

Indian Institute of Technology Jammu, Jammu & Kashmir 181221, India
{2021rcs2009,suman.banerjee,yamuna.prasad}@iitjammu.ac.in

Abstract. We study the problem of minimizing regret in multi-mode advertising settings, where an influence provider allocates advertising resources, such as social network seeds and billboard slots, to multiple advertisers with specified influence demands and payments. Unlike prior work focusing on a single advertising mode, we consider the interplay between online and offline modes and introduce a novel regret model that captures their interaction effects. This leads to a regret minimization problem that is non-monotone, non-submodular, and NP-hard to approximate within any constant factor. To address this, we propose a monotone, approximately bisubmodular influence model and develop two algorithmic solutions: Projected Subgradient Method based on the Lovász extension of the regret function, and an Approximate Bisubmodular Local Search algorithm with provable guarantees. Experiments on large-scale real-world datasets, including billboard and trajectory data from major U.S. cities, as well as social network graphs, demonstrate that our methods outperform existing baselines in minimizing total regret while satisfying advertiser demands. Our framework is broadly applicable to other resource allocation scenarios beyond advertising.

Keywords: Advertisement · Influence · billboard Slot · Social Network · Advertiser · Regret Minimization

1 Introduction

Almost all commercial houses use advertising to promote their products and build a customer base. As mentioned in recent marketing literature, a commercial house spends around $7 - 10\%$ of its annual revenue on advertising[1]. Two popular advertising approaches are advertising through digital billboards and social networks. In a billboard advertisement, a commercial house displays content hoping that people nearby will see it and be influenced. The other way to advertise is through social media. Many internet giants, including Google and Facebook, generate significant revenue from social network advertising. In general, advertisers request an influence provider to deliver the required influence

[1] https://www.lamar.com/howtoadvertise/Research/.

R. C.-W. Wong et al. (Eds.): PAKDD 2026, LNAI 16618, pp. 497–509, 2027.
https://doi.org/10.1007/978-981-92-1947-6_40

in exchange for payment. Now, if the influence provider provides the demanded influence, then he will receive full payment; otherwise, a partial payment. This leads to a loss of influence provider, and this loss is formulated as *regret*.

Motivation. In the existing literature, separate regret models exist for calculating regret in billboard and social media advertisements, but these models are non-monotone and non-submodular. The regret of the influence providers can be computed using these regret models. The sum of these individual regrets will be the total regret of the influence provider. However, this approach will not work when considering two different advertising modes due to the *Interaction Effect* (See Definition 4) between social networks and billboard slots, and will yield different regret compared to existing methods [12,14]. Due to the non-monotonicity of existing regret models, performance guarantees are unattainable. Thus, a monotone regret model that accounts for both social and billboard advertisements, including interaction effects, is essential. This motivates the study of the Regret Minimization Problem to enable effective solutions.

Relevant Studies. In influence maximization, Ali et al. [1] first introduce the joint tag and slot selection problem and formulate this as a bisubmodular influence maximization problem. There exists literature [3] that considers tag assignment to billboard slots to maximize total influence in both single and multi-advertiser settings. In the case of social networks, literature on influence maximization [6] exists that focuses on identifying a subset of nodes that maximizes total influence. Furthermore, in this direction, Rui et al. [11] apply it to social network influence maximization problems. First, Ashley et al. [4] introduce a new problem domain in which social network users are allocated to advertisers to promote commercial posts. Recently, Sharma et al. [12] studied the regret minimization problem in social networks and introduced a greedy-based approach for seed set allocation. In the context of billboard advertising, Zhang et al. [14] studied the first regret minimization problem and proposed several heuristic solutions. In addition, Ali et al. [2] studied regret minimization problems extensively and proposed several greedy and efficient randomized algorithms in a multi-advertiser setting. Next, we summarized our contributions.

Our Contributions. To the best of our knowledge, this is the first work to address regret minimization by jointly considering billboard and social network advertising. Our key contributions are:

- We formulate a regret-minimization problem in a multi-advertiser setting across billboards and social networks.
- We prove that this problem is NP-hard and inapproximable within any constant factor.
- We propose two solution methods: the Projected Gradient Method and the Approximate Bisubmodular Local Search.
- We conduct experiments on real-world datasets to show the effectiveness of our methods against baselines.

Organization of the Paper. Rest of the paper is organized as follows. Section 2 describes required background concepts and defines the problem formally. Section 3 describes the proposed solution approach with illustration and analysis. Section 4 contains the experimental evaluations of the proposed solution approaches. Section 5 concludes this study and gives future research directions.

2 Background and Problem Definition

In this section, we describe the background of the problem and formally define our problem. Initially, we start by describing the billboard advertisement.

Billboard Advertisement. Billboard advertisements require three key components: an influence function, a trajectory, and a billboard database. A trajectory database $\mathbb{D}$ contains the location information of a moving user, and $[T_1, T_2]$ is the time duration for which the user movement occurs. Consider $\mathbb{D}$, which contains m tuples in the form $< \mathcal{U}', \ell, [t_1, t_2] >$, which denotes a set of people $\mathcal{U}' \subseteq \mathcal{U}$ who were at the location ℓ for a period of time $[t_1, t_2]$. So, for every tuple $q \in \mathbb{D}$, the associated interval $[t_x, t_y] \in [T_1, T_2]$, and $t_x \leq t_y$. The billboard database $\mathbb{B}$ contains the information of billboards placed in a city represented in the form of a tuple $< b_{id}, \ell, cost >$, which signifies the billboard b_{id} is placed at location ℓ associated with some cost. Recently, commercial houses have hired billboards for a certain duration, i.e., slots. Considering Δ as the slot duration for each billboard, the number of slots will be $\frac{T_2 - T_1}{\Delta}$. A set of billboard slots can be denoted by $\mathbb{BS} = \{(b_i, [t, t+\Delta]) : b_i \in \mathbb{B} \text{ and } t \in \{T_1, T_1 + \Delta, T_1 + 2\Delta, \ldots, T_2 - \Delta\}\}$ and represented in the form of a tuple $< bs_{id}, \ell, time\_slot, cost >$, which represents billboard slot bs_{id} is placed at location ℓ with a slot duration. The associated cost of a slot is formalized by a cost function $\mathcal{C}_{BS} : \mathbb{BS} \longrightarrow \mathbb{R}^+$. Now, consider that user $u_i \in \mathcal{U}$ is present for the duration $[t_c, t_d]$ in a location where the billboard is placed and currently running an advertisement for duration $[t_a, t_b]$. If $[t_c, t_d] \cap [t_a, t_b] \neq \emptyset$, then we can say the user u_i is influenced with some probability. In the existing literature [13], several approaches are proposed to calculate this influence probability. However, based on LAMAR[2] influence metrics, we incorporate panel size and exposure frequency into our influence model. Specifically, for each $bs_i \in \mathbb{BS}$, $u_j \in \mathcal{U}$, if bs_i can influence u_j, the $\Pr(u_j, bs_i)$ can be define as $\Pr(t_j, bs_i) = \frac{\text{size}(bs_i)}{A}$, where $A > \max_{bs_i \in \mathbb{BS}} \text{size}(bs_i)$, to reflect influence based on panel size. Now, for a given subset of billboard slots $\mathcal{S} \in \mathbb{BS}$, the influence of $\mathcal{S}$ can be denoted as $\mathcal{I}(\mathcal{S})$ and defined in Definition 1.

Definition 1 (Influence of Billboard Slots). *Given a subset of billboard slots $\mathcal{S} \subseteq \mathbb{BS}$, its influence $\mathcal{I}(\mathcal{S})$ can be calculated using Eq. 1.*

$$\mathcal{I}(\mathcal{S}) = \sum_{u_j \in \mathbb{D}} 1 - \prod_{bs_i \in \mathcal{S}} (1 - Pr(u_j, bs_i)) \tag{1}$$

[2] https://www.lamar.com/howtoadvertise/Research/.

Social Network Advertisement. Consider, the social network information for the people $\mathcal{U} = \{u_1, u_2, \ldots, u_n\}$ represented as a weighted undirected graph $\mathcal{G}(\mathcal{U}, \mathcal{E}, \mathcal{W})$. The edge $\mathcal{E}(\mathcal{G})$ represents a binary relationship among users, and the edge weight function $\mathcal{W}$ is associated with its corresponding influence probability, i.e., $\mathcal{W} : \mathcal{E}(\mathcal{G}) \longrightarrow (0, 1]$. If an edge $(u_i u_j) \notin \mathcal{E}(\mathcal{G})$, then the influence probability $\mathcal{W}_{(u_i u_j)} = 0$. To study the diffusion process in social networks, we consider the *Independent Cascade Model* defined in Definition 2.

Definition 2 (Independent Cascade Model). *The Independent Cascade (IC) Model is a stochastic diffusion model defined over a undirected graph $\mathcal{G}(\mathcal{U}, \mathcal{E}, \mathcal{W})$, where each edge $(u_i u_j) \in \mathcal{E}$ is associated with an influence probability $\mathcal{W}_{(u_i u_j)} \in (0, 1]$. This can be formalized by an influence function $\mathcal{I}^{\mathcal{G}}$ which maps each node in the network to its corresponding influence value, i.e., $\mathcal{I}^{\mathcal{G}} : 2^{\mathcal{U}} \longrightarrow \mathbb{R}^+$.*

Influence Model. In our context, to jointly measure the influence of billboards and social networks, we propose an influence model, as defined in Definition 3.

Definition 3 (Influence Model). *Given a subset of billboard slots $\mathcal{S} \in \mathbb{BS}$ and a set of seed nodes $\mathcal{P} \in \mathcal{G}$, the influence can be denoted as $\Phi(\mathcal{S}, \mathcal{P})$ and stated in Eq. 2.*

$$\Phi(\mathcal{S}, \mathcal{P}) = \mathcal{I}(\mathcal{S}) + \mathcal{I}^{\mathcal{G}}(\mathcal{P}) + \Psi(\mathcal{S}, \mathcal{P}) \tag{2}$$

where $\mathcal{I}(\mathcal{S})$ is the influence of slots set $\mathcal{S}$, $\mathcal{I}^{\mathcal{G}}(\mathcal{P})$ denotes the influence from seed set $\mathcal{P}$, and $\Psi(\mathcal{S}, \mathcal{P})$ denotes the interaction effect between slots and seed nodes.

The influence function Φ maps each possible combination from the set of slots and seed nodes to their corresponding combined influence value, i.e., $\Phi : 2^{\mathbb{BS}} \times 2^{\mathcal{G}} \longrightarrow \mathbb{R}_0^+$ with $\Phi(\emptyset, \emptyset) = 0$. The interaction effect is considered in the existing literature [7,10]. However, there is no specific mechanism to compute it. So, in our problem context, we mathematically formulate the interaction effect and define it in Definition 4.

Definition 4 (Interaction Effect). *An interaction effect in influence maximization quantifies how the combined influence of billboards and social media deviates from their independent effects. Mathematically,*

$$\Psi(\mathcal{S}, \mathcal{P}) = \sum_{u \in \mathcal{U}} [(1 - \prod_{b \in \mathcal{S}} (1 - Pr(u, b))) \cdot (1 - \prod_{v \in \mathcal{P}} (1 - Pr(u, v)))] \tag{3}$$

where $1 - \prod_{b \in \mathcal{S}} (1 - Pr(u, b))$ is the probability user u being influenced by at least one billboard slot, and $1 - \prod_{v \in \mathcal{P}} (1 - Pr(u, v))$ is the probability that user u is activated by seed node v.

Theorem 1. *Given a trajectory database $\mathbb{D}$, billboard slots $\mathbb{BS}$, and Social Network Users $\mathcal{V}(\mathcal{G})$, the influence function $\Phi(.,.)$ is non-negative, monotone, and $\epsilon-$approximately bisubmodular.*

Regret Model. Assume there are n advertisers $\mathcal{A} = \{a_1, a_2, \ldots, a_n\}$ and an influence provider $\mathcal{Z}$. The advertisers submit the campaign proposal to $\mathcal{Z}$ with influence demand (σ) and payment ($\mathcal{K}$). The influence provider has access to the advertiser database, and this can be represented in the form of a tuple $< a_i, \sigma_i, \mathcal{K}_i >$ for all $i \in [n]$. Let an allocation $\mathcal{N} = \{(\mathcal{S}_i, \mathcal{P}_i) \mid i = 1, \ldots, n\}$ where $\mathcal{S}$ be the set of billboard slots and $\mathcal{P}$ be the seed nodes assigned to the advertisers. Now, according to the payment rules, if *Supply* > *Demand*, then the full payment will be made to the influence provider; otherwise, a partial payment will be made. Note that given two slot sets $\mathcal{S}_1$ and $\mathcal{S}_2$ and seed sets $\mathcal{P}_1$ and $\mathcal{P}_2$ with $|\mathcal{S}_1| << |\mathcal{S}_2|$ and $|\mathcal{P}_1| << |\mathcal{P}_2|$, in practice it is desirable to achieve low regret with less number of slots and seeds. By drawing on the inspiration from existing literature [4,5], we add a penalty term to discourage the use of larger slot and seed sets. Next, we define a regret model in Definition 5.

Definition 5 (Regret Model). *Let $\mathcal{N}_{a_i}$ be the set of allocated subsets of billboard slots or seed nodes or both for the advertiser a_i, and the regret associated with this allocation is denoted by $\mathcal{R}(\mathcal{N}_{a_i})$.*

$$\mathcal{R}(\mathcal{N}_{a_i}) = \begin{cases} \mathcal{K}_{a_i} \cdot (1 - \gamma \cdot \frac{\min(\Phi(\mathcal{S}_{a_i}, \mathcal{P}_{a_i}), \sigma_{a_i})}{\sigma_{a_i}}) \\ + \delta \cdot \log(1 + |\mathcal{S}_{a_i}| + |\mathcal{P}_{a_i}|) \end{cases}$$

Here, the fraction $\frac{\min(\Phi(\mathcal{S}_{a_i}, \mathcal{P}_{a_i}), \sigma_{a_i})}{\sigma_{a_i}}$ is part of the satisfied influence for the advertiser a_i. The $\gamma \in [0,1]$ and $\delta \in [0,1]$ are the unsatisfied penalty and cardinality penalty, respectively.

Theorem 2. *Given a trajectory database $\mathbb{D}$, billboard slot information $\mathbb{BS}$, and social network users $\mathcal{V}(\mathcal{G})$, the regret function $\mathcal{R}(\mathcal{S}, \mathcal{P})$, defined over subsets $\mathcal{S} \subseteq \mathbb{BS}$ and $\mathcal{P} \subseteq \mathcal{V}(\mathcal{G})$, is non-negative, monotonically non-increasing and ϵ'-approximately bisubmodular for some $\epsilon' = \mathcal{O}(\epsilon)$.*

Problem Definition. In this paper, our goal is to minimize the total regret for an allocation $\mathcal{L}$. So, we define the notion of total regret in Definition 6.

Definition 6 (Total Regret). *Given an allocation $\mathcal{L} = \{\mathcal{N}_{a_1}, \mathcal{N}_{a_2}, \ldots, \mathcal{N}_{a_n}\}$, the total regret associated with allocation $\mathcal{L}$ is denoted as $\mathcal{R}(\mathcal{L})$ and defined as the sum of the regret associated with individual n advertisers. Mathematically, it can be written as,*

$$\mathcal{R}(\mathcal{L}) = \sum_{a_i \in \mathcal{A}} \mathcal{R}(\mathcal{N}_{a_i}) \tag{4}$$

As mentioned, our goal is to find an optimal allocation to minimize the total regret. Formally, we call this problem the REGRET MINIMIZATION PROBLEM WITH MULTI-MODEL ADVERTISING SETTING. This problem is stated in Definition 7.

Definition 7 (Regret Minimization Problem). *Given billboard slot information $\mathbb{BS}$, Trajectory database $\mathbb{D}$, and advertiser information $\mathcal{A}$, our goal of* *this problem is to find an allocation* $\mathcal{L} = \{\mathcal{N}_{a_1}, \mathcal{N}_{a_2}, \ldots, \mathcal{N}_{a_n}\}$ *such that the total regret is minimized. Mathematically, this problem can be posed as follows:*

$$\mathcal{L}^{OPT} = \underset{\mathcal{L}_i \in \mathcal{Q}(\mathcal{L})}{argmin}\ \mathcal{R}(\mathcal{L}_i) \tag{5}$$

The regret minimization problem studied by Zhang et al. [14] in the context of billboard advertisement and Sharma et al. [12] in the context of social network advertisement had an inapproximability result stated in Theorem 3.

Theorem 3. *The* Regret minimization Problem *is NP-hard and hard to approximate to any constant factor.*

So, the same inapproximability results also hold for our problem. Next, we discuss the proposed solution methodologies.

3 Proposed Solution

3.1 Projected Subgradient Method (PGM)

The Projected Subgradient Method (PGM) is a continuous gradient-based optimization technique adapted to minimize the regret function $\mathcal{R}(.)$. In this work, the regret function is nonnegative, monotonically nonincreasing, and ϵ approximately bisubmodular, making it suitable for continuous optimization based on Lovász extension [9]. The key idea is to work with fractional vectors $x \in [0,1]^{|\mathbb{BS}|}$ and $y \in [0,1]^{|\mathcal{P}|}$, representing the soft selection of slots and seeds, respectively. This method is theoretically grounded in recent advances in approximate submodular minimization [8] and offers an alternative to discrete greedy strategies. It provides a bicriteria approximation guarantee for functions like $\mathcal{R}$ that are not exactly bisubmodular but exhibit approximate diminishing returns. Due to space limitations, we have not provided the pseudo-code of the PGM approach.

3.2 Approximate Bisubmodular Local Search (ABLS)

Algorithm 1 presents a greedy local search method to minimize regret in the multi-mode advertisement setting. The algorithm allocates billboard slots and social network seed nodes to advertisers by iteratively selecting elements that yield the highest marginal reduction in regret per unit influence. Advertisers are first sorted in descending order of their budget-to-demand ratio to prioritize cost-effective assignments. For each advertiser, the algorithm considers both the advertising slots and the seed nodes, selecting the element whose regret reduction per unit influence exceeds a threshold ϵ and is within the advertiser's remaining budget. Allocated elements are removed from the ground set to satisfy disjointness constraints. The process continues until all advertisers are processed or no feasible elements remain. The regret function is monotone non-increasing and ϵ-approximately bisubmodular, ensuring the effectiveness of the greedy strategy under approximate diminishing returns.

Algorithm 1: Approximate Bisubmodular Local Search (ABLS) for Regret Minimization Problem

Data: Trajectory Database $\mathbb{D}$, Billboard Database $\mathbb{B}$, Advertiser Database $\mathbb{A}$, Influence Functions $\mathcal{I}(), \mathcal{I}^g(), \Phi()$, Billboard Slots $\mathbb{BS}$, Seed Nodes $\mathcal{H}$.
Result: An allocation $\mathcal{L} = \{(\mathcal{S}_1, \mathcal{P}_1), (\mathcal{S}_2, \mathcal{P}_2), \ldots, (\mathcal{S}_{|\mathcal{A}|}, \mathcal{P}_{|\mathcal{A}|})\}$ minimizing total regret

Initialize $\mathcal{L} \leftarrow \{(\mathcal{S}_1, \mathcal{P}_1), \ldots, (\mathcal{S}_{|\mathcal{A}|}, \mathcal{P}_{|\mathcal{A}|})\}$ where $\mathcal{S}_i, \mathcal{P}_i \leftarrow \emptyset$;
Sort each advertiser $a_i \in \mathcal{A}$ in descending order of $\frac{\mathcal{K}_i}{\sigma_i}$;
for *each* $a_i \in \mathcal{A}$ **do**
  while $\Phi(\mathcal{S}_i, \mathcal{P}_i) < \sigma_i$ ***and*** $\mathbb{BS} \neq \emptyset$ ***and*** $\mathcal{H} \neq \emptyset$ ***and*** $\mathcal{K}_i > 0$ **do**
    $b^* \leftarrow \arg\max_{b \in \mathbb{BS}} \frac{\mathcal{R}(\mathcal{S}_i, \mathcal{P}_i) - \mathcal{R}(\mathcal{S}_i \cup \{b\}, \mathcal{P}_i)}{\Phi(\{b\}, \emptyset)}$;
    $s^* \leftarrow \arg\max_{s \in \mathcal{H}} \frac{\mathcal{R}(\mathcal{S}_i, \mathcal{P}_i) - \mathcal{R}(\mathcal{S}_i, \mathcal{P}_i \cup \{s\})}{\Phi(\emptyset, \{s\})}$;
    $e^* \leftarrow \arg\max \left\{ \frac{\mathcal{R}(\mathcal{S}_i, \mathcal{P}_i) - \mathcal{R}(\mathcal{S}_i \cup \{b^*\}, \mathcal{P}_i)}{\Phi(\{b^*\}, \emptyset)}, \frac{\mathcal{R}(\mathcal{S}_i, \mathcal{P}_i) - \mathcal{R}(\mathcal{S}_i, \mathcal{P}_i \cup \{s^*\})}{\Phi(\emptyset, \{s^*\})} \right\}$;
    if $e^* = b^*$ **then**
      if $\frac{\mathcal{R}(\mathcal{S}_i, \mathcal{P}_i) - \mathcal{R}(\mathcal{S}_i \cup \{b^*\}, \mathcal{P}_i)}{\Phi(\{b^*\}, \emptyset)} > \epsilon$ ***and*** $\mathcal{K}_i > \mathcal{C}(b^*)$ **then**
        $\mathcal{S}_i \leftarrow \mathcal{S}_i \cup \{b^*\}$, $\mathbb{BS} \leftarrow \mathbb{BS} \setminus \{b^*\}$;
        $\mathcal{K}_i \leftarrow \mathcal{K}_i - \mathcal{C}(b^*)$;
      end
    else
      if $e^* = s^*$ **then**
        if $\frac{\mathcal{R}(\mathcal{S}_i, \mathcal{P}_i) - \mathcal{R}(\mathcal{S}_i, \mathcal{P}_i \cup \{s^*\})}{\Phi(\emptyset, \{s^*\})} > \epsilon$ ***and*** $\mathcal{K}_i > \mathcal{C}(s^*)$ **then**
          $\mathcal{P}_i \leftarrow \mathcal{P}_i \cup \{s^*\}$, $\mathcal{H} \leftarrow \mathcal{H} \setminus \{s^*\}$;
          $\mathcal{K}_i \leftarrow \mathcal{K}_i - \mathcal{C}(s^*)$;
        end
      end
      else
        break;
      end
    end
  end
end
return $\mathcal{L}$;

Theorem 4. *Let $\mathcal{R} : 2^{\mathbb{BS}} \times 2^{\mathcal{H}} \to \mathbb{R}_{\geq 0}$ be a regret function that is monotonically non-increasing and ε-approximately bisubmodular. Let $\mathcal{A} = \{a_1, \ldots, a_n\}$ be the set of advertisers, each with budget $\mathcal{K}_i$, and let $\mathcal{K}_{\max} = \max_{i \in [n]} \mathcal{K}_i$. Let $L^* = \{(\mathcal{S}_i^*, \mathcal{P}_i^*)\}_{i=1}^n$ be an optimal allocation minimizing total regret as* $\mathrm{OPT} = \sum_{i=1}^n \mathcal{R}(\mathcal{S}_i^*, \mathcal{P}_i^*)$. *Then Algorithm 1 returns an allocation $\mathcal{L} = \{(\mathcal{S}_i, \mathcal{P}_i)\}_{i=1}^n$ such that*

$$\sum_{i=1}^{n} \mathcal{R}(\mathcal{S}_i, \mathcal{P}_i) \leq \mathrm{OPT} + \varepsilon \cdot n \cdot \mathcal{K}_{\max}.$$

Proof. Fix any advertiser $a_i \in \mathcal{A}$, and let $(\mathcal{S}_i^*, \mathcal{P}_i^*)$ and $(\mathcal{S}_i, \mathcal{P}_i)$ be its optimal and Algorithm 1 allocations, respectively. Denote $\mathcal{U}_i^* = \mathcal{S}_i^* \cup \mathcal{P}_i^*$ and let $\mathcal{U}_i^t$ be the greedy allocation after t steps. At each step t, the algorithm selects an element e_t that maximizes regret reduction per unit cost wll be

$$e_t = \arg\max_{e} \frac{\mathcal{R}(\mathcal{U}_i^{t-1}) - \mathcal{R}(\mathcal{U}_i^{t-1} \cup \{e\})}{\mathcal{C}(e)}.$$

By ε-approximate bisubmodularity, for any $e \in \mathcal{U}_i^* \setminus \mathcal{U}_i^{t-1}$, the marginal gain satisfies that $\mathcal{R}(\mathcal{U}_i^{t-1}) - \mathcal{R}(\mathcal{U}_i^{t-1} \cup \{e\}) \geq \mathcal{R}(\emptyset) - \mathcal{R}(\{e\}) - \varepsilon \cdot t$. Hence, the gain $\Delta^t = \mathcal{R}^{t-1} - \mathcal{R}^t$ from e_t satisfies

$$\Delta^t \geq \max_{e \in \mathcal{U}_i^* \setminus \mathcal{U}_i^{t-1}} \left[\frac{\mathcal{R}(\mathcal{U}_i^{t-1}) - \mathcal{R}(\mathcal{U}_i^{t-1} \cup \{e\})}{\mathcal{C}(e)} \right] \cdot \mathcal{C}(e_t).$$

Summing over all steps, total regret reduction satisfies $\mathcal{R}(\emptyset) - \mathcal{R}(\mathcal{S}_i, \mathcal{P}_i) \geq \mathcal{R}(\emptyset) - \mathcal{R}(\mathcal{S}_i^*, \mathcal{P}_i^*) - \varepsilon \cdot \mathcal{K}_i$, which gives $\mathcal{R}(\mathcal{S}_i, \mathcal{P}_i) \leq \mathcal{R}(\mathcal{S}_i^*, \mathcal{P}_i^*) + \varepsilon \cdot \mathcal{K}_i$. Summing over all $i \in [n]$, and using $\mathcal{K}_i \leq \mathcal{K}_{\max}$, the total regret is bounded by

$$\sum_{i=1}^{n} \mathcal{R}(\mathcal{S}_i, \mathcal{P}_i) \leq \mathrm{OPT} + \varepsilon \cdot n \cdot \mathcal{K}_{\max}.$$

4 Experimental Evaluations

Dataset Descriptions. We use three real-world datasets: trajectory, social network, and billboard. The trajectory data combines two global Foursquare check-in datasets over 22 months (Apr 2012–Jan 2014), filtered to retain 124,539 U.S. check-ins from 51,318 unique users. The social network includes two snapshots with 95,994 (old) and 129,864 (new) U.S.-only friendships among these users. The billboard dataset is crawled from LAMAR[3] and includes 716 (NYC) and 1483 (LA) billboards, resulting in 3,166,560 billboard slots. All experiments were conducted on an HP Z4 workstation (Xeon 3.5GHz CPU, 64GB RAM).

Key Parameters. We define the following key parameters used in our experiments. The Demand-Supply Ratio ($\alpha = I^d/I^s$) measures the ratio of total advertiser demand $I^d = \sum_{a \in \mathcal{A}} I^a$ to the provider's supply $I^s = \sum_{b \in \mathcal{BS}} \mathcal{I}(b) + \sum_{p \in \mathcal{P}} \mathcal{I}^G(p)$. The Average-Individual Demand Ratio ($\lambda = \bar{I}^d/I^s$) compares average per-advertiser demand $\bar{I}^d = I^d/|\mathcal{A}|$ to supply. Each advertiser's demand is then set as $I^a = \lfloor \omega \cdot I^s \cdot \lambda \rfloor$ with $\omega \in [0.8, 1.2]$. Payments are proportional to demand: $\mathcal{L}_i = \lfloor \beta \cdot I^a \rfloor$, where $\beta \in [0.9, 1.1]$. The penalty ratio $\gamma \in [0, 1]$ controls payment reduction for unmet demand, while the cardinality penalty $\delta \in [0, 1]$ discourages large allocations. The Interaction Parameter ρ controls the strength of interaction between billboard slots and social media seed nodes. We vary the value of ρ between 0 and 1. We vary the Regret Tolerance Parameter ϵ value from 0 to 0.1 to simulate the trade-off between regret and runtime. The distance parameter π decides the influence of a billboard slot. We vary the value of π between 25 meters 150 meters. Table 1 summarizes all parameter settings.

Baseline Methodologies

Random Allocation (RA). The billboard slots and social media seeds are selected randomly. It selects nodes randomly, without considering any influence maximization criteria, and stops when the budget is exhausted.

[3] http://www.lamar.com/InventoryBrowser.

Table 1. Key Parameters

Parameter	Values
α	$40\%, 60\%, 80\%, \mathbf{100\%}, 120\%$
λ	$1\%, 2\%, \mathbf{5\%}, 10\%, 20\%$
γ	$0, 0.25, \mathbf{0.5}, 0.75, 1$
δ	$0, 0.25, \mathbf{0.5}, 0.75, 1$
ϵ	$0, 0.01, \mathbf{0.05}, 0.075, 0.1$
ρ	$0, 0.2, \mathbf{0.5}, 0.7, 1$
π	$25m, 50m, \mathbf{100m}, 125m, 150m$

Top-k Allocation. In this approach, most influential billboard slots and seed nodes are selected till their demand and budget constraints are satisfied.

Goals of Our Experimentation. The following research question is addressed in our study.

- **RQ1.** What will happen if the influence provider's influence supply is below, near, or exceeds the global demand of the advertisers in a multi-mode advertisement setting?
- **RQ2.** Which kind of advertisers, i.e., fewer advertisers with high influence demand or a large number of advertisers with small influence demand, are more beneficial?
- **RQ3.** How does the interaction effect affect the selection of slots and reduce total regret? How parameters such as ϵ, δ, T, γ impact regret minimization.

Results and Discussions

Effectiveness Study. We consider four cases to show the effectiveness of our proposed approach. Corresponding to case 1, we have $\alpha \leq 80\%$ and $\lambda \leq 2\%$. We have two main observations. First, with the increase of α, the individual demand of the advertisers increases, and the number of satisfied advertisers decreases. Second, the 'PGM' and 'ABLS' outperform 'Random' and 'Top-k'. Corresponding to case 2, we have $\alpha \leq 80\%$ and $\lambda \geq 5\%$. We have two observations. First, when the global demand becomes low, but individual demand is high, the excessive influence supply to advertisers drops. This happens because with the increase of β value, the number of advertisers is less, and individual influence demand is higher. Second, with the higher individual influence demand from advertisers, the influence provider could deploy more slots or seeds using 'PGM' and 'ABLS' to minimize the regret. The trivalency reduces the regret better than the other probability settings because trivalency models simulate realistic variations in influence strength between different individuals as shown in Fig. 1$(a, b, c, f, g, h, k, \ell, m)$ and Fig. 3(i,j). Corresponding to case 3, we have $\alpha \geq 100\%$ and $\lambda \leq 2\%$. We have two main observations. First, as global influence

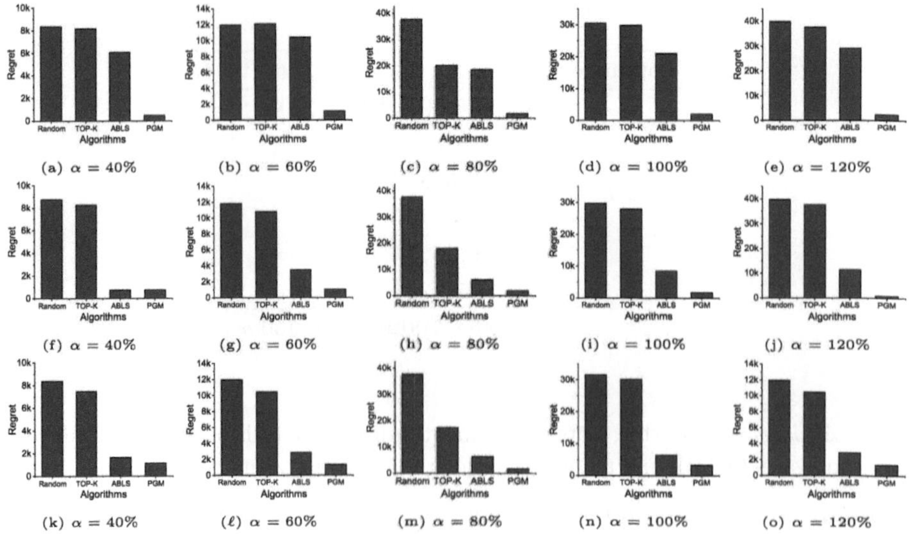

(a) $\alpha = 40\%$ (b) $\alpha = 60\%$ (c) $\alpha = 80\%$ (d) $\alpha = 100\%$ (e) $\alpha = 120\%$

(f) $\alpha = 40\%$ (g) $\alpha = 60\%$ (h) $\alpha = 80\%$ (i) $\alpha = 100\%$ (j) $\alpha = 120\%$

(k) $\alpha = 40\%$ (ℓ) $\alpha = 60\%$ (m) $\alpha = 80\%$ (n) $\alpha = 100\%$ (o) $\alpha = 120\%$

Fig. 1. Regret on varying α, when $\lambda = 5\%, |\mathcal{A}| = 20$ for Uniform (a-e), Trivalency (f-j), Weighted Cascade (k-o)Settings

demand is high, none of the algorithms can satisfy all the advertisers, and dissatisfaction increases. Second, when $\alpha \geq 100\%$, the influence supply is equal to or less than the demand from the advertisers. As we cannot control the excessive influence supply, the regret increases in this case. This behavior can be observed in Fig. 3(d,e). Corresponding to case 4, we have $\alpha \geq 100\%$ and $\lambda \geq 5\%$ defines a situation where both global and individual influence demand is high. We have two main observations. First, large α and λ value leads to higher regret for each advertiser. Hence, all algorithms suffer from higher regret. second, when λ value increases from 5% to 20% all algorithms suffer from higher regret as shown in Fig. 1(d,e,i,j,n,o) and Fig. 3(j,k). So, a smaller number of advertisers with higher influence demand is not beneficial for the influence provider.

Efficiency Study. Efficiency is important as every day thousands of advertisers come to the influence provider with the required influenced demand. Hence, we have conducted an efficiency evaluation under different cases of global and individual influence demand. we have some observations. First, with the increase of α, each proposed and baseline method requires extra search time to deploy slots or seeds to the advertisers. We have presented the time requirements for 'PGM', 'ABLS', 'Top-k', and 'Random' approaches for $\lambda = 5\%, |\mathcal{A}| = 20$ in the Fig. 2(a,b,c) for uniform, weighted, and trivalency probability settings, respectively. We observe that with the increase of the number of advertisers, the computational time increases, and this change happens drastically for the 'PGM' approach as shown in Fig. 2(a,b,c). When $|\mathcal{A}| = 20$ the 'ABLS' takes more run

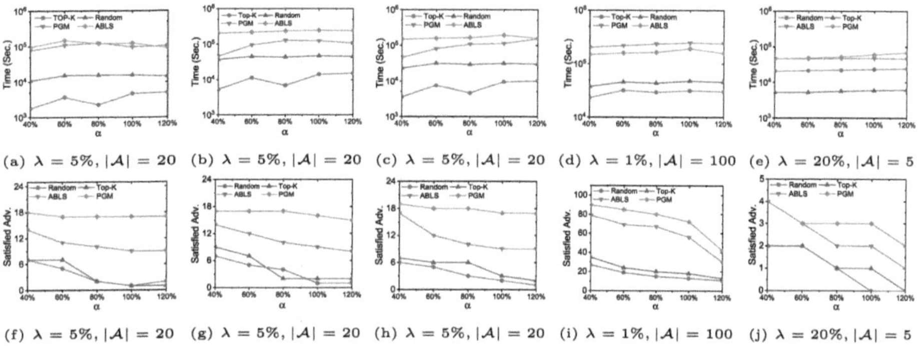

Fig. 2. Time on varying α, (a) Uniform, (b) Weighted, (c, d, e) Trivalency probability Setting and Satisfied Adv. on Varying α,(f) Uniform, (g) Weighted, (i, j, k) Trivalency probability Setting

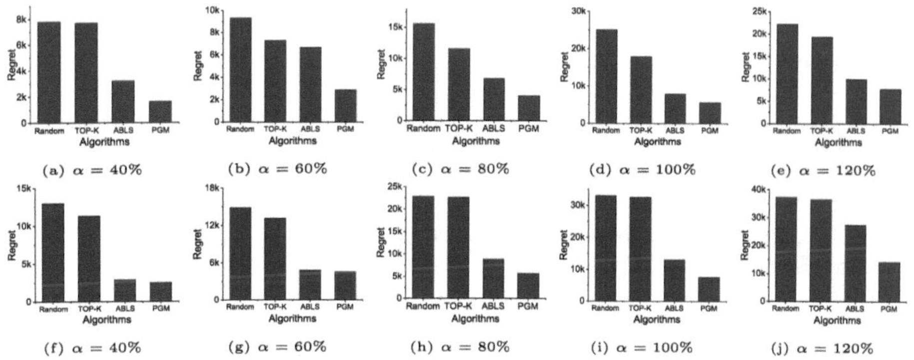

Fig. 3. Regret on varying α, when $\lambda = 1\%, |\mathcal{A}| = 100 (a - e)$, when $\lambda = 20\%, |\mathcal{A}| = 5$ $(f - k)$, for Trivalency Settings

time compared to 'PGM' and baselines. However, when $|\mathcal{A}| = 100$, 'PGM' takes the highest computational time as shown in Fig. 2(c,d).

Other Parameter Study. We analyze the impact of key parameters: (a) Increasing ϵ reduces runtime but increases regret due to stricter selection; (b) Higher δ penalizes large allocations, leading to compact but less effective solutions; (c) Larger γ emphasizes demand satisfaction, lowering regret at higher resource use; (d) More iterations T in PGM improve regret marginally after a point, with increased computation cost. (e) With increasing ρ value, the strength of interaction between slots and seed nodes also increases. (f) With an increase of π, the influence of the slots increases as one slot can influence a larger number of trajectories. We set $\alpha = 100\%$, $\lambda = 5\%$, $\gamma = 0.5$, $\delta = 0.5$, $\epsilon = 0.05$ $\rho = 0.5$ and $\pi = 100$ meter as the default setting for our experiment.

5 Conclusion and Future Directions

In this work, we studied the problem of regret minimization in multi-mode advertising, where billboard slots and seeds are allocated jointly to multiple advertisers. We introduce a novel *Interaction Effect* formulation and propose a new regret model that captures both individual and combined effects of two different advertising media and their interaction. We proved that the problem is NP-hard and inapproximable, and we introduced two solution approaches: the Projected Subgradient Method (PGM) and the Approximate Bisubmodular Local Search (ABLS). Experiments on large-scale real-world datasets demonstrated that our methods consistently reduce total regret compared to existing baselines across various demand settings and influence probability models. This work could be extended to streaming and online settings, where advertisers arrive dynamically. Another potential direction could be the development of parallel and distributed optimization frameworks for scalability in real-world advertising platforms.

References

1. Ali, D., Banerjee, S., Prasad, Y.: Influential slot and tag selection in billboard advertisement. In: Wrembel, R., Kotsis, G., Tjoa, A.M., Khalil, I. (eds.) DEXA 2025. LNCS, vol. 16046, pp. 276–290. Springer, Cham (2025). https://doi.org/10.1007/978-3-032-02049-9_21
2. Ali, D., Banerjee, S., Prasad, Y.: Toward regret-free slot allocation in billboard advertisement. Int. J. Data Sci. Anal. **20**(3), 1951–1975 (2025)
3. Ali, D., Kumar, H., Banerjee, S., Prasad, Y.: An effective tag assignment approach for billboard advertisement. In: Barhamgi, M., Wang, H., Wang, X. (eds.) WISE 2024. LNCS, vol. 15436, pp. 159–173. Springer, Singapore (2024). https://doi.org/10.1007/978-981-96-0579-8_12
4. Aslay, C., Lu, W., Bonchi, F., Goyal, A., Lakshmanan, L.V.: Viral marketing meets social advertising: ad allocation with minimum regret. arXiv preprint arXiv:1412.1462 (2014)
5. Boyd, S.P., Vandenberghe, L.: Convex Optimization. Cambridge University Press, Cambridge (2004)
6. Chen, W., Yuan, Y., Zhang, L.: Scalable influence maximization in social networks under the linear threshold model. In: 2010 IEEE International Conference on Data Mining, pp. 88–97. IEEE (2010)
7. Deighton, J.: The interaction of advertising and evidence. J. Consum. Res. **11**(3), 763–770 (1984)
8. El Halabi, M., Jegelka, S.: Optimal approximation for unconstrained non-submodular minimization. In: International Conference on Machine Learning, pp. 3961–3972. PMLR (2020)
9. Lovász, L.: Submodular functions and convexity. Math. Program. State Art: Bonn **1982**, 235–257 (1983)
10. Pavlou, P.A., Stewart, D.W.: Measuring the effects and effectiveness of interactive advertising: a research agenda. J. Interact. Advert. **1**(1), 61–77 (2000)
11. Rui, X., Wang, Z., Peng, C., Fang, Q., Chen, W.: Efficient approximation algorithms for fair influence maximization under maximin constraint. arXiv preprint arXiv:2509.26579 (2025)

12. Sharma, P., Ali, D., Banerjee, S.: Minimizing regret in social media advertisement. In: 2024 IEEE International Conference on Big Data (BigData), pp. 473–478. IEEE (2024)
13. Zhang, P., Bao, Z., Li, Y., Li, G., Zhang, Y., Peng, Z.: Towards an optimal outdoor advertising placement: when a budget constraint meets moving trajectories. ACM Trans. Knowl. Discov. Data (TKDD) **14**(5), 1–32 (2020)
14. Zhang, Y., Li, Y., Bao, Z., Zheng, B., Jagadish, H.: Minimizing the regret of an influence provider. In: Proceedings of the 2021 International Conference on Management of Data, pp. 2115–2127 (2021)

What Helps—and What Hurts: Bidirectional Explanations for Vision Transformers

Qin Su and Tie Luo(✉)

Department of Electrical and Computer Engineering, University of Kentucky, Lexington, KY, USA
{qin.su,t.luo}@uky.edu

Abstract. Vision Transformers (ViTs) achieve strong performance in visual recognition, yet their decision-making remains difficult to interpret. We propose BiCAM, a bidirectional class activation mapping method that captures both supportive (positive) and suppressive (negative) contributions to model predictions. Unlike prior CAM-based approaches that discard negative signals, BiCAM preserves signed attributions to produce more complete and contrastive explanations. BiCAM further introduces a Positive-to-Negative Ratio (PNR) that summarizes attribution balance and enables lightweight detection of adversarial examples without retraining. Across ImageNet, VOC, and COCO, BiCAM improves localization and faithfulness while remaining computationally efficient. It generalizes to multiple ViT variants, including DeiT and Swin. These results suggest the importance of modeling both supportive and suppressive evidence for interpreting transformer-based vision models.

Keywords: Vision Transformer · Explainable AI · Adversarial Detection

1 Introduction

Vision Transformers (ViTs) [9] achieve state-of-the-art performance in classification [27], object detection [14], and segmentation [25]. Unlike convolutional neural networks (CNNs), ViTs leverage self-attention to model long-range dependencies without local inductive biases, enabling more expressive representations [19], but their opaque decision-making hinders adoption in high-stakes domains.

Existing ViT interpretability approaches include: (i) *attention-based* methods [1] that multiply attention across layers and often over-smooth token differences; (ii) *gradient-based* methods [5,6,13] that enhance attention with gradients but require full-network aggregation; and (iii) *Shapley-based* methods [7] that are computationally intensive.

We introduce **BiCAM**, a *bidirectional class activation mapping* technique for ViTs. Unlike CAM-based methods that discard negative values, BiCAM treats

R. C.-W. Wong et al. (Eds.): PAKDD 2026, LNAI 16618, pp. 510–522, 2027.
https://doi.org/10.1007/978-981-92-1947-6_41

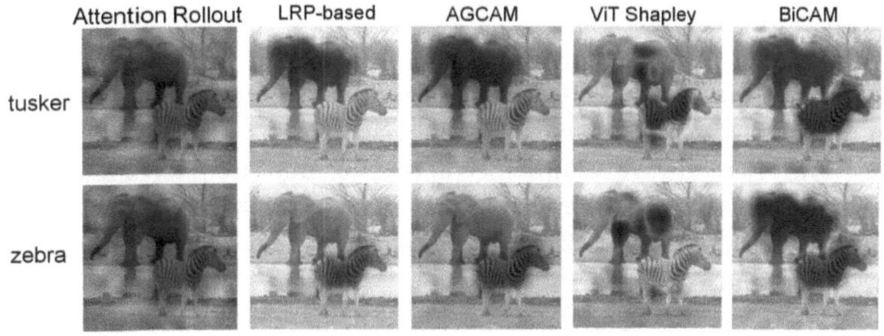

Fig. 1. BiCAM applied to ViT-B/16 on COCO. A query of "tusker" yields supportive (red) and suppressive (blue) attributions on the elephant and the zebra, respectively; yet querying "zebra" reverses the pattern. Baseline methods do not consistently produce this contrastive explanation. (Color figure online)

them as informative, producing contrastive maps that explain both why the model predicts a class (*supportive* evidence) and rejects alternatives (*suppressive* evidence). This bidirectional view offers richer and more contrastive interpretations (Fig. 1), while requiring only a single forward–backward pass.

BiCAM features a *strategic layer aggregation* scheme. It selects only deeper transformer layers on the premise that class-discriminative information concentrates there [20], augments attention in those layers with class-specific gradients, and fuses them with a simple summation in contrast to complex recursive operations [1] and weighted combinations [5,6], while empirically demonstrating improved effectiveness.

Beyond interpretability, we propose a simple *Positive-to-Negative Ratio* (PNR) that summarizes bidirectional attributions and enables effective detection of adversarial example attacks, including but not limited to PGD [18], C&W [4], and MI-FGSM [8].

BiCAM also generalizes to other ViT-based models with minimal modification, which we demonstrate using representative architectures such as DeiT [27] and Swin [16]. In summary, our main contributions are:

- We propose BiCAM, a bidirectional attribution method that highlights supportive and suppressive factors with a single forward–backward pass, providing contrastive explanations for ViT-based models in single- and multi-object scenes.
- We introduce PNR, a simple metric derived from BiCAM to perform interpretable adversarial detection. The BiCAM design also integrates a principled layer aggregation strategy that focuses on deeper transformer layers where class-discriminative signals concentrate.
- We empirically show strong localization, faithfulness, efficiency, and generalization performance of BiCAM. We also validate that PNR is a lightweight yet effective metric for adversarial detection.

2 Related Work

Raw Attention-Based Methods. A common technique of ViT interpretability exploits transformer's native self-attention maps. Attention Rollout and Attention Flow [1] recursively multiply attention matrices across layers to trace token influence, but often suffer from over-smoothing where tokens appear uniformly important. Prior work [24] shows that raw attention weights alone correlate poorly with feature importance.

Gradient-Based and Relevance Propagation. To improve attribution fidelity, several methods combine attention with gradients. Beyond Attention [5] adapts LRP [2] to ViTs, while Beyond Intuition [6] decomposes attribution into perception and reasoning. However, these methods aggregate across all layers without preserving signed contributions, limiting full-spectrum interpretability.

CAM-Style Methods. CAM [29] and Grad-CAM [23] have been adapted to ViTs by enhancing attention with gradients. AG-CAM [13] integrates class-specific gradients into attention heads; TS-CAM [11] aligns tokens with class semantics for weakly supervised localization. CDAM [3] modulates attention weights with class-specific gradients but computes relevance only at the final block, overlooking mid-layer cues.

Shapley-Based Attribution. Inspired by SHAP [17], ViT-Shapley [7] trains dataset-specific amortized explainers to estimate patch-level Shapley values, requiring substantial per-dataset training (19 hrs) with limited cross-dataset transferability. BiCAM requires only a single forward–backward pass with no training overhead.

In summary, existing methods predominantly focus on positive relevance or magnitude-based importance, overlooking the role of negative (suppressive) contributions. Also, unlike prior CAM variants, BiCAM differs not only in aggregation strategy but in preserving signed contributions throughout the pipeline, enabling contrastive interpretation and downstream signals (e.g., PNR) that are not accessible to magnitude-only methods.

3 Methodology

In a standard ViT, an input image is partitioned into patches, linearly embedded, and processed through Transformer blocks. Each block consists of multi-head self-attention (MSA) layers and feed-forward networks (FFNs). A [CLS] token aggregates global information for classification. BiCAM generates bidirectional attribution maps from this architecture.

3.1 Strategic Layer Aggregation

Diverging from most existing ViT explainability methods [1,5,6,13] that aggregate interpretability signals across all layers, BiCAM employs *strategic layer aggregation* that selectively focuses on later transformer layers.

Theoretical Basis. Raghu et al. [20] shows that class-discriminative information concentrates in later layers, which is consistent with ViTDet [14]. Thus, BiCAM selects the last ℓ blocks, and sets $\ell = 2L/3$ according to our ablation in Sect. 4.7. This choice targets the layers where global semantic relationships are fully formed, while filtering out low-level structural noise.

Layer Aggregation Strategy. BiCAM computes and aggregates attributions from layers $L - \ell + 1$ to L, where L is the total number of layers. We extract, for each selected layer l, the attention maps $A^{(l)}$, value projections $V^{(l)}$, and gradients $\partial y_c / \partial o_{\text{cls}}^{(l)}$, and collect them $(A^{(l)}, V^{(l)}, \partial y_c / \partial o_{\text{cls}}^{(l)})$ to compute layer-wise attribution maps. We then aggregate layer-wise masks via simple summation (detailed in Sect. 3.2), rather than recursive matrix multiplication [1] or weighted combination [5,6]. This preserves independent layer contributions without over-smoothing token differences or optimization overhead.

3.2 BiCAM Attribution Mechanism

Supportive and suppressive contributions are defined relative to the local gradient of the class logit with respect to token representations, combined with the token features themselves. Thus, negative values indicate directions that decrease the class score under infinitesimal perturbations, rather than strict counterfactual absence. BiCAM computes attributions through three steps:

Step 1: Extract Attention and Values. For a ViT with H heads and N tokens, we extract from the last ℓ layers $l \in [L - \ell + 1, L]$: (i) Attention matrices $A_h^{(l)} \in \mathbb{R}^{B \times N \times N}$ for each head $h = 1, ..., H$, specifically CLS-to-patch attention $A_{h,0,:}^{(l)}$ via forward hooks before softmax. (ii) Value projections $V_h^{(l)} \in \mathbb{R}^{B \times H \times N \times d_h}$ where $d_h = d/H$.

We apply softmax with temperature scaling [12] to control the entropy of attention distributions, so we can soften attention to improve attribution stability:

$$\alpha_h^{(l)} = \text{softmax}(\frac{A_{h,0,:}^{(l)}}{T}), \quad h \in [1, H], l \in [L - \ell + 1, L] \tag{1}$$

Step 2: Compute Gradients. We backpropagate the class-specific score y_c with respect to [CLS] token embeddings:

$$w_c^{(l)} = \frac{\partial y_c}{\partial o_{\text{cls}}^{(l)}}, \quad l \in [L - \ell + 1, L] \tag{2}$$

where $o_{\text{cls}}^{(l)} = \text{concat}(o_{\text{cls},1}^{(l)}, ..., o_{\text{cls},H}^{(l)})$ is the concatenated [CLS] output across heads, with $o_{\text{cls},h}^{(l)} = \text{softmax}(A_{h,0,:}^{(l)}) \cdot V_h^{(l)}$.

Step 3: Construct Attribution Maps. We aggregate attention, values, and gradients to form layer-wise masks:

$$\text{mask}^{(l)} = \sum_{h=1}^{H} \left((V_h^{(l)} \cdot w_c^{(l)}) \odot \alpha_h^{(l)} \right) \tag{3}$$

Algorithm 1: BiCAM Pseudocode

Input: ViT model f with L layers, aggregation window size ℓ, image x of shape (H_t, W_d), target class c
Output: Bidirectional attribution heatmap

Register hooks to extract attention and gradients from layers $[L-\ell+1, L]$
$y_c \leftarrow f(x)[c]$
for $l \leftarrow L-\ell+1$ **to** L **do** ▷ Forward pass
  $\alpha^{(l)} \leftarrow \text{softmax}(A^{(l)}_{h,0,:}/T)$ ▷ softmax with temperature-normed attention
  $o^{(l)}_{\text{cls}} \leftarrow \text{softmax}(A^{(l)}_{:,0,:}) \cdot V^{(l)}$ ▷ [CLS] output
y_c.backward()
for $l \leftarrow L$ *down to* $L-\ell+1$ **do** ▷ Backward pass
  $w^{(l)}_c \leftarrow \partial y_c / \partial o^{(l)}_{\text{cls}}$ ▷ Extract gradients
  $\text{val\_grad}^{(l)} \leftarrow V^{(l)} \cdot w^{(l)}_c$
  $\text{mask}^{(l)} \leftarrow \text{val\_grad}^{(l)} \odot \alpha^{(l)}$
$\text{mask}^{(l)} \leftarrow \text{mask}^{(l)}.\text{sum}(\text{dim}=1)$ ▷ Aggregate heads
$\text{mask} \leftarrow \sum_l \text{mask}^{(l)}$ ▷ Aggregate layers
$\text{mask} \leftarrow \text{mask}[:, 1:]$ ▷ Remove [CLS] token
$\text{mask} \leftarrow \text{reshape}(\text{mask}, (B, 1, \sqrt{N-1}, \sqrt{N-1}))$
$\text{htmap} \leftarrow \text{upsample}(\text{mask}, (B, 1, H_t, W_d))$
return htmap

where $\odot$ denotes element-wise multiplication. BiCAM transforms values through gradient weighting as in Grad-CAM [23], with attention modulating these features. Layer-wise masks are summed: $\text{mask} = \sum_{l \in [L-\ell+1, L]} \text{mask}^{(l)}$. The resulting $[B, 1, N]$ mask is reshaped to $\sqrt{N-1} \times \sqrt{N-1}$ after discarding [CLS].

Importantly, no ReLU or clipping is applied throughout the computation, ensuring that both positive and negative contributions are preserved. The pseudocode is provided in Algorithm 1.

3.3 Positive-to-Negative Ratio (PNR)

Our hypothesis is that clean samples tend to exhibit spatially structured positive-negative balance aligned with semantic regions, whereas adversarial perturbations [26,28] introduce dispersed or exaggerated responses, skewing this balance. We thus propose a metric to quantify such distortion:

$$PNR = \frac{\sum_i ReLU(M_i)}{\sum_i ReLU(-M_i) + \epsilon} \tag{4}$$

where M_i is the attribution of ViT patch i and ϵ prevents division by zero. A high PNR indicates dominance of supportive evidence while a low PNR suggests stronger suppressive influence. We then define **PNR Perturbation**: $\Delta PNR = PNR_{adv} - PNR_{clean}$, the difference between adversarial and clean samples.

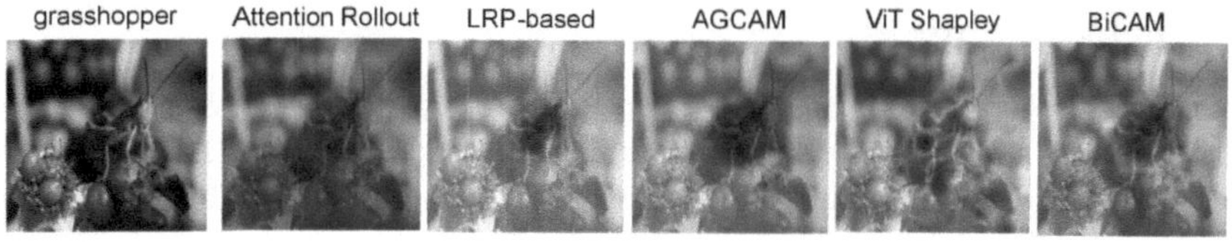

Fig. 2. Single-class attribution on ImageNet (grasshopper class; ViT-B/16). BiCAM highlights the target in red and background in blue. (Color figure online)

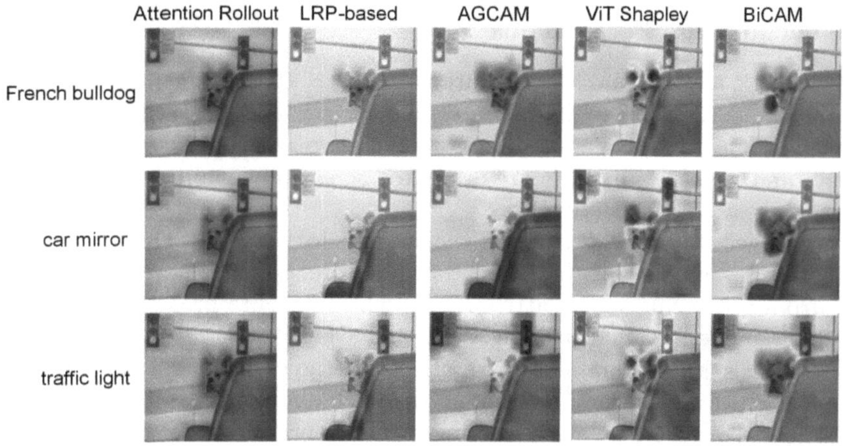

Fig. 3. Multi-class attribution on COCO (ViT-B/16). Each row queries a different class (bulldog, car mirror, traffic light). BiCAM consistently assigns supportive attribution (red) to the queried object and suppressive attribution (blue) to non-target objects. (Color figure online)

4 Evaluation

4.1 Experimental Setup

We evaluate BiCAM on ViT-B/16 [9], DeiT-B [27], and Swin-B [16] at 224×224 resolution. Datasets include ImageNet [21] for single-class attribution, VOC2012 [10] and COCO [15] for multi-label scenes, and adversarially perturbed examples for robustness.

We compare against **Attention Rollout** [1], **LRP-based CAM** [5], **AGCAM** [13], and **ViT-Shapley** [7]. For PNR, we use PGD [18], C&W [4], and MI-FGSM [8] attacks.

Evaluation includes: (1) *Localization* via IoU, F1, Precision, Recall on ILSVRC, VOC, COCO annotations; (2) *Faithfulness* via iterative patch removal [7]; (3) *PNR Perturbation* ΔPNR.

4.2 Qualitative Results

Our visualizations use red for supportive and blue for suppressive contributions. Figure 2 shows single-class results from ImageNet, where BiCAM locates the target object and marks suppressive context. Figure 3 shows multi-object results from COCO; BiCAM generates distinct attributions per queried class, consistently assigning supportive attribution to the target object and suppressive attribution to non-target objects.

4.3 Localization Performance

Following [13], we normalize attribution maps to [0, 1] using min–max scaling and threshold the output at 0.5 to obtain binary masks. Table 1 summarizes the results. On ImageNet, we report unified scores, whereas on VOC/COCO, positive and negative channels are evaluated separately against target and non-target annotations, respectively.

On ImageNet, BiCAM achieves the highest IoU (0.5419), F1 (0.6624), and recall (0.9288) among all methods. Its lower precision compared to AGCAM arises from preserving signed attributions, which leads to broader spatial coverage under unified evaluation. On VOC and COCO, where positive and negative channels are evaluated separately, this trade-off is no longer observed: BiCAM (Pos.) outperforms all baselines in IoU, F1, and precision. BiCAM (Neg.) has no direct counterpart since existing methods produce only positive attributions; moreover, vision models generally learn stronger representations for target

Table 1. Localization results on 3 datasets. ViT-Shapley is excluded because its amortized explainer could not scale to 1,000-class evaluation.

Method	Pix. Acc.	IoU	F1	Prec.	Rec.
ImageNet-1k					
Attn Rollout	0.6209	0.3597	0.4893	0.7326	0.4657
LRP-based	0.5863	0.2029	0.3055	**0.9110**	0.2176
AGCAM	**0.7341**	0.5212	0.6515	0.8299	0.6276
BiCAM	0.6253	**0.5419**	**0.6624**	0.5901	**0.9288**
VOC 2012					
Attn Rollout	0.8105	0.0686	0.1153	0.2604	0.1191
LRP-based	0.8420	0.1677	0.2464	0.4918	0.2021
AGCAM	**0.8561**	0.3561	0.4926	0.5932	0.5502
BiCAM (Pos.)	0.8559	**0.3700**	**0.5104**	**0.6095**	**0.5863**
BiCAM (Neg.)	0.7705	0.2588	0.3786	0.3642	0.5779
COCO 2017					
Attn Rollout	0.8314	0.1332	0.2023	0.3276	0.2526
LRP-based	0.8523	0.1162	0.1871	0.4274	0.1835
AGCAM	**0.8740**	0.2807	0.3996	0.4210	**0.6279**
BiCAM (Pos.)	0.8707	**0.2971**	**0.4191**	**0.5535**	0.5154
BiCAM (Neg.)	0.8487	0.1141	0.1724	0.2711	0.2074

objects than for background or non-target regions, placing BiCAM (Neg.) at an inherent disadvantage. Despite this, BiCAM (Neg.) achieves competitive performance relative to these baselines, suggesting that the suppressive maps capture semantically meaningful competing regions rather than random noise.

4.4 Faithfulness via Feature Removal

We evaluate attribution faithfulness via perturbation experiments [22], removing patches in descending order of importance **Most Important Feature (MIF)** or ascending order **Least Important Feature (LIF)** and define Faithfulness = $AUC_{LIF} - AUC_{MIF}$.

We remove the 196 patches one by one (each masked to zero), in the order of their attribution scores (ascending: LIF; descending: MIF). Table 2 summarizes the faithfulness scores averaged over five random seeds, and Fig. 4 shows the corresponding perturbation curves. Pairwise Wilcoxon signed-rank tests ($p < 0.001$) confirm that BiCAM significantly outperforms all baselines on all datasets, indicating better alignment between attribution importance and model behavior.

Table 2. Faithfulness scores. ViT-Shapley is excluded because it achieves only 0.294 on the 10-class ImageNette.

	Attn Rollout	LRP	AGCAM	BiCAM
ImageNet				
LIF↑	0.4739	0.5140	0.5298	**0.5478**
MIF↓	0.2053	0.1736	**0.1607**	0.1654
Faith↑	0.2685	0.3404	0.3691	**0.3824**
VOC 2-class				
LIF↑	0.8623	0.9231	0.9280	**0.9313**
MIF↓	0.7142	0.5201	0.5010	**0.4686**
Faith↑	0.1481	0.4030	0.4270	**0.4626**
COCO 2-class				
LIF↑	0.8856	0.9307	0.9376	**0.9407**
MIF↓	0.7052	0.5327	0.5235	**0.4997**
Faith↑	0.1805	0.3980	0.4141	**0.4410**

Table 3. PNR-based adversarial detection on VOC 2012 multi-object scenes.

Attack	ΔPNR	std	AUROC	AUPR	Threshold
Clean	0.00	N/A	-	-	-
PGD	+0.57	0.31	0.781	0.749	0.248
C&W	+0.79	0.37	0.842	0.808	0.332
MI-FGSM	+0.46	0.27	0.764	0.731	0.219
Avg.	+0.61	0.32	0.796	0.763	0.266

4.5 PNR Analysis

Adversarial perturbations tend to disrupt model prediction more in multi-object scenes due to the multiple competing objects. Hence we choose VOC 2012 (≥2 classes) for evaluation. In such scenes, we also find that BiCAM's negative attributions correctly fall on competing objects rather than diffuse background, leading to a stable denominator of PNR. Table 3 shows that all the tested attacks inflate PNR_{adv} and hence ΔPNR notably. Using ΔPNR values, together with a threshold we derive by maximizing *Youden's J statistic* (sensitivity + specificity −1), we achieve accurate detection indicated by the high AUROC and AUPR. This indicates that ΔPNR provides a simple, lightweight, yet effective adversarial detection signal without retraining.

4.6 Computational Efficiency

Table 4 reports inference costs (time and GPU memory) on ViT-B/16, measured on an RTX 4090 over 1,000 ImageNet images. BiCAM is 8.4× faster than LRP with no training overhead, and LRP requires large memory to store intermediate relevance scores at every layer. ViT-Shapley requires per-dataset retraining.

4.7 Ablation Studies

We validate key design choices on PASCAL VOC 2012 with ViT-B/16. As shown in Table 5, $\ell = 2L/3$ achieves the best localization; using all layers ($\ell = L$) introduces early-layer noise (IoU drops 23%), while too few layers ($\ell = L/3$) loses mid-layer signals. This supports the hypothesis that early layers capture low-level features that are less class-discriminative.

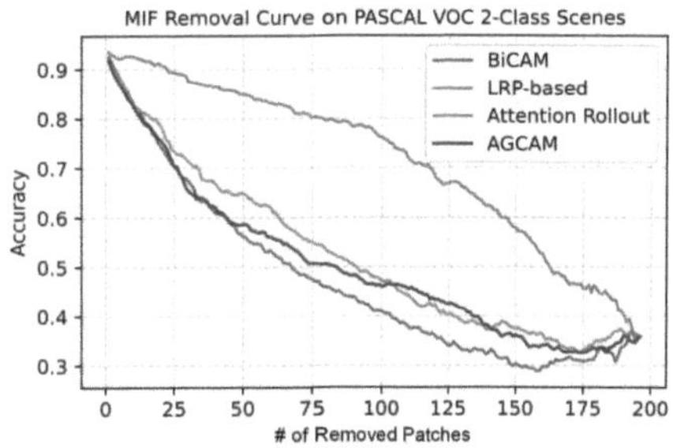

(a) VOC - MIF removal

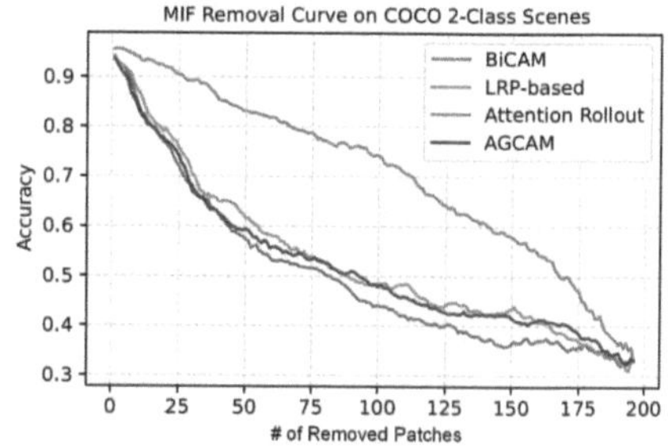

(b) COCO - MIF removal

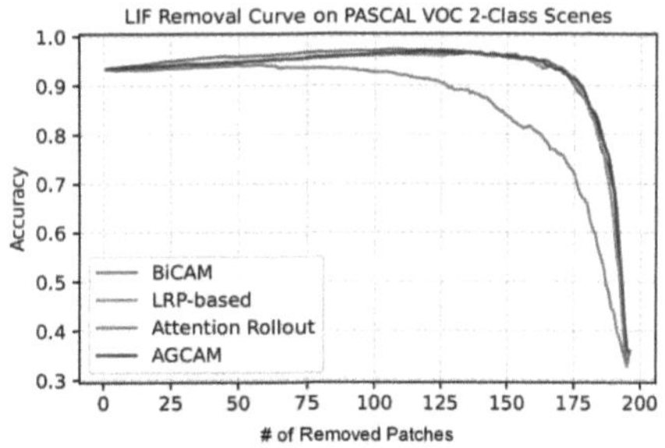

(c) VOC - LIF removal

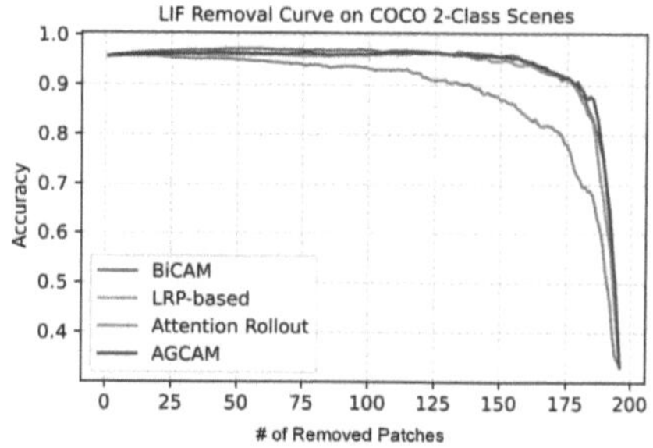

(d) COCO - LIF removal

Fig. 4. Faithfulness evaluation via perturbation on VOC and COCO (ViT-B/16). Curves show the mean across five random seeds. Higher faithfulness is indicated by steeper accuracy degradation in MIF removal and flatter curves in LIF removal.

Table 4. Runtime comparison (ViT-B/16, RTX 4090, ImageNet-1k).

Method	ms/img	MB/img	Train time
Attn Rollout	23.3	0.15	None
LRP	134.6	97.2	None
ViT-Shapley	10.1*	–	19 hrs*
AGCAM	20.0	0.22	None
BiCAM	**16.0**	0.24	None

*ImageNette (10 classes), measured on RTX 2080 Ti [7].

For temperature, we choose $T = 2$ as it balances sharpness and smoothness the best, while $T = 1$ produces overly peaky attributions (IoU$=$0.105) and $T = 3$ over-smooths.

4.8 Generalization to ViT Variants

BiCAM can be easily adapted to other architectures with minimal changes. For **DeiT** [27], BiCAM focuses on [CLS] token, ignoring the distillation token. For **Swin** [16], we aggregate the last two stages with pooled output. Figure 5

Table 5. Ablation on layer window ℓ and temperature T (ViT-B/16, VOC 2012).

	Layer window ℓ $(T=2)$				*Temperature* T $(\ell=8)$		
	$\ell=12$	$\ell=8$	$\ell=4$	$\ell=1$	$T=1$	$\mathbf{T=2}$	$T=3$
Pix.Acc	0.8505	**0.8559**	0.8498	0.8413	0.8402	**0.8559**	0.8492
IoU	0.2840	**0.3700**	0.2093	0.1491	0.1051	**0.3700**	0.2060
F1	0.4043	**0.5104**	0.3173	0.2277	0.1711	**0.5104**	0.3140
Prec.	0.5980	**0.6095**	0.6765	0.5343	0.6401	0.6095	**0.6789**
Rec.	0.3949	**0.5863**	0.2649	0.1824	0.1144	**0.5863**	0.2589
Faith.	**0.4746**	0.4626	0.4570	0.3499	0.4472	0.4626	**0.4900**

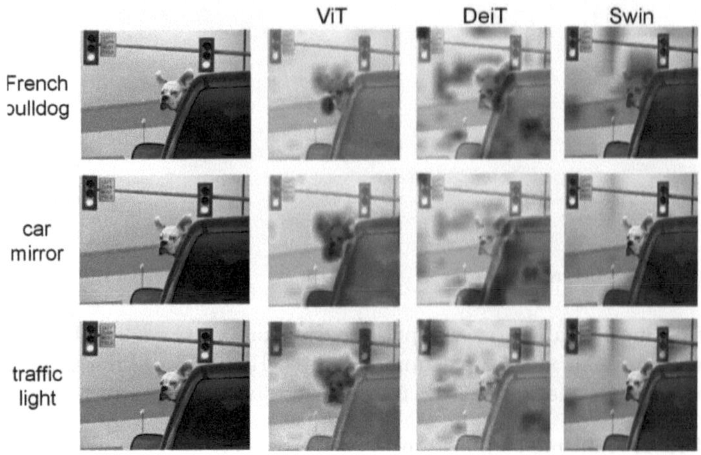

Fig. 5. BiCAM generalizes to ViT variants, tested on ImageNet. All models adopt the base version. Largely coherent bidirectional attributions are observed.

shows that BiCAM produces coherent bidirectional attributions across all these architectures.

5 Conclusion and Discussion

We introduced BiCAM, a bidirectional attribution method that captures both supportive and suppressive evidence in Vision Transformers. By preserving signed contributions, BiCAM provides more complete explanations and improves localization and faithfulness across multiple benchmarks. The proposed PNR metric further demonstrates that bidirectional attributions encode structural signatures that adversarial perturbations systematically disrupt, enabling lightweight adversarial detection without additional training. These findings suggest that bidirectional attribution is a valuable and underexplored dimension for transformer interpretability.

Limitations. A central challenge in XAI is the absence of ground-truth attributions; metrics like IoU and faithfulness are indirect proxies, and a formal user study would provide complementary evidence of interpretive value. Additionally, BiCAM relies on gradient-based signals and thus inherits their sensitivity to model smoothness and gradient noise. Moreover, PNR-based adversarial detection has not been compared with dedicated adversarial detectors or tested against adaptive adversaries.

As transformers proliferate in high-stakes applications, BiCAM advances trustworthy AI by revealing the nuanced interplay of signals within black-box decisions. **Future directions** include extending bidirectional attribution to multi-modal settings; exploring PNR for out-of-distribution detection; and leveraging suppressive patterns for architectural improvements.

References

1. Abnar, S., Zuidema, W.: Quantifying attention flow in transformers. In: Proceedings of the 58th Annual Meeting of the Association for Computational Linguistics, pp. 4190–4197 (2020)
2. Bach, S., Binder, A., Montavon, G., Klauschen, F., Müller, K.R., Samek, W.: On pixel-wise explanations for non-linear classifier decisions by layer-wise relevance propagation. PLoS ONE **10**(7), e0130140 (2015)
3. Brocki, L., Binda, J., Chung, N.C.: Class-discriminative attention maps for vision transformers. Trans. Mach. Learn. Res. (2024)
4. Carlini, N., Wagner, D.: Towards evaluating the robustness of neural networks. In: 2017 IEEE Symposium on Security and Privacy (SP), pp. 39–57. IEEE (2017)
5. Chefer, H., Gur, S., Wolf, L.: Transformer interpretability beyond attention visualization. In: Proceedings of the IEEE/CVF Conference on Computer Vision and Pattern Recognition, pp. 782–791 (2021)
6. Chen, J., Li, X., Yu, L., Dou, D., Xiong, H.: Beyond intuition: rethinking token attributions inside transformers. Trans. Mach. Learn. Res. (2022)
7. Covert, I.C., Kim, C., Lee, S.I.: Learning to estimate Shapley values with vision transformers. In: International Conference on Learning Representations (2023)
8. Dong, Y., et al.: Boosting adversarial attacks with momentum. In: Proceedings of the IEEE Conference on Computer Vision and Pattern Recognition, pp. 9185–9193 (2018)
9. Dosovitskiy, A., et al.: An image is worth 16x16 words: transformers for image recognition at scale. In: International Conference on Learning Representations (2021)
10. Everingham, M., Van Gool, L., Williams, C.K.I., Winn, J., Zisserman, A.: The pascal visual object classes (VOC) challenge. Int. J. Comput. Vision **88**(2), 303–338 (2010)
11. Gao, W., et al.: TS-cam: token semantic coupled attention map for weakly supervised object localization. In: Proceedings of the IEEE/CVF International Conference on Computer Vision, pp. 2886–2895 (2021)
12. Hinton, G., Vinyals, O., Dean, J.: Distilling the knowledge in a neural network. arXiv preprint arXiv:1503.02531 (2015)
13. Leem, S., Seo, H.: Attention guided cam: visual explanations of vision transformer guided by self-attention. In: Proceedings of the AAAI Conference on Artificial Intelligence, vol. 38, pp. 2956–2964 (2024)

14. Li, Y., Mao, H., Girshick, R., He, K.: Exploring plain vision transformer backbones for object detection. In: Avidan, S., Brostow, G., Cissé, M., Farinella, G.M., Hassner, T. (eds.) ECCV 2022. LNCS, vol. 13669, pp. 280–296. Springer, Cham (2022). https://doi.org/10.1007/978-3-031-20077-9_17
15. Lin, T.-Y., et al.: Microsoft COCO: common objects in context. In: Fleet, D., Pajdla, T., Schiele, B., Tuytelaars, T. (eds.) ECCV 2014. LNCS, vol. 8693, pp. 740–755. Springer, Cham (2014). https://doi.org/10.1007/978-3-319-10602-1_48
16. Liu, Z., et al.: Swin transformer: hierarchical vision transformer using shifted windows. In: 2021 IEEE/CVF International Conference on Computer Vision (ICCV), pp. 9992–10002. IEEE Computer Society (2021)
17. Lundberg, S.M., Lee, S.I.: A unified approach to interpreting model predictions. In: Advances in Neural Information Processing Systems, vol. 30, pp. 4765–4774 (2017)
18. Madry, A., Makelov, A., Schmidt, L., Tsipras, D., Vladu, A.: Towards deep learning models resistant to adversarial attacks. In: International Conference on Learning Representations (2018)
19. Naseer, M.M., Ranasinghe, K., Khan, S.H., Hayat, M., Shahbaz Khan, F., Yang, M.H.: Intriguing properties of vision transformers. In: Advances in Neural Information Processing Systems, vol. 34, pp. 23296–23308 (2021)
20. Raghu, M., Unterthiner, T., Kornblith, S., Zhang, C., Dosovitskiy, A.: Do vision transformers see like convolutional neural networks? In: Advances in Neural Information Processing Systems, vol. 34, pp. 12116–12128 (2021)
21. Russakovsky, O., et al.: Imagenet large scale visual recognition challenge. Int. J. Comput. Vision **115**(3), 211–252 (2015). https://doi.org/10.1007/s11263-015-0816-y
22. Samek, W., Binder, A., Montavon, G., Lapuschkin, S., Müller, K.R.: Evaluating the visualization of what a deep neural network has learned. IEEE Trans. Neural Netw. Learn. Syst. **28**(11), 2660–2673 (2016)
23. Selvaraju, R.R., Cogswell, M., Das, A., Vedantam, R., Parikh, D., Batra, D.: Grad-Cam: visual explanations from deep networks via gradient-based localization. In: Proceedings of the IEEE International Conference on Computer Vision (2017)
24. Serrano, S., Smith, N.A.: Is attention interpretable? In: Proceedings of the Annual Meeting of the Association for Computational Linguistics, pp. 2931–2951 (2019)
25. Strudel, R., Garcia, R., Laptev, I., Schmid, C.: Segmenter: transformer for semantic segmentation. In: Proceedings of the IEEE/CVF International Conference on Computer Vision, pp. 7262–7272 (2021)
26. Tao, G., Ma, S., Liu, Y., Zhang, X.: Attacks meet interpretability: attribute-steered detection of adversarial samples. In: Advances in Neural Information Processing Systems, vol. 31, pp. 7717–7728 (2018)
27. Touvron, H., Cord, M., Douze, M., Massa, F., Sablayrolles, A., Jégou, H.: Training data-efficient image transformers & distillation through attention. In: International Conference on Machine Learning, pp. 10347–10357. PMLR (2021)
28. Yang, P., Chen, J., Hsieh, C.J., Wang, J.L., Jordan, M.: ML-loo: detecting adversarial examples with feature attribution. In: Proceedings of the AAAI Conference on Artificial Intelligence, vol. 34, pp. 6639–6647 (2020)
29. Zhou, B., Khosla, A., Lapedriza, A., Oliva, A., Torralba, A.: Learning deep features for discriminative localization. In: Proceedings of the IEEE Conference on Computer Vision and Pattern Recognition, pp. 2921–2929 (2016)

Adaptive PII Detection via Evolutionary Orchestration and Multi-agent Debate

Geonwoo Bang[1], Dongho Kim[2], Damin Kim[3], and Moohong Min[4](✉)

[1] Department of Computer Education, Sungkyunkwan University, Seoul, Korea
g7199@g.skku.edu

[2] Department of Immersive Media Engineering, Sungkyunkwan University, Seoul, Korea
dpl9753@g.skku.edu

[3] Department of Immersive Media Engineering/Social Innovation Convergence Program, Sungkyunkwan University, Seoul, Korea
goat0129@g.skku.edu

[4] Department of Computer Education/Social Innovation Convergence Program, Sungkyunkwan University, Seoul, Korea
iceo@skku.edu

Abstract. The definition of Personally Identifiable Information (PII) is fluid across legal jurisdictions and domain-specific schemas. Consequently, static Named Entity Recognition (NER) models often become brittle on heterogeneous datasets, while monolithic prompts suffer from attention degradation and hallucination when extracting extensive entity taxonomies. In this work, we propose a novel framework that reframes PII detection as a dynamic alignment problem rather than a static classification task. Our system features a Schema-Agnostic Orchestrator that dynamically decomposes target labels into semantic clusters, coupled with an Evolutionary Prompt Optimizer that automates the refinement of agent instructions using k-shot feedback. Furthermore, we integrate an uncertainty-aware debate protocol to resolve inter-agent conflicts through deliberative reasoning. Experiments on Nemotron-PII, AI4Privacy benchmarks (pii-masking-200k and open-pii-masking-500k) demonstrate that our adaptive system achieves competitive or superior performance against larger static baselines despite its smaller parameter footprint, establishing a new state-of-the-art in zero-shot PII adaptation.

Keywords: PII Detection · Evolutionary Prompting · Multi-Agent Orchestration · Automated Prompt Engineering · LLM Debate

1 Introduction

The robust identification of Personally Identifiable Information (PII) is essential for privacy-preserving data processing, especially as Large Language Models (LLMs) are increasingly adopted across enterprises and regulated domains [1]. As LLM-assisted systems become pervasive across society, concerns about the

R. C.-W. Wong et al. (Eds.): PAKDD 2026, LNAI 16618, pp. 523–535, 2027.
https://doi.org/10.1007/978-981-92-1947-6_42

inadvertent exposure of sensitive information have increased, highlighting the need for adaptable PII detection [2,3].

However, PII detection remains a formidable challenge due to the dual problems of *schema heterogeneity* and *contextual ambiguity*. Regulated industries often prohibit sending sensitive documents to external APIs due to GDPR or HIPAA constraints, motivating on-premise PII detection [4]. Schema heterogeneity reflects that PII definitions vary across jurisdictions, regulatory frameworks, and domains, leading to mutually incompatible and increasingly fine-grained taxonomies [5]. Contextual ambiguity further complicates extraction because the sensitivity and boundaries of an entity can shift depending on surrounding linguistic cues or task-specific requirements [6]. Such challenges are also noted in anonymization surveys [7].

Unlike standard Named Entity Recognition (NER) tasks that rely on a fixed set of coarse-grained labels, PII detection must support numerous fine-grained and domain-dependent categories whose definitions vary across datasets. Traditional approaches relying on supervised learning, such as BERT-based sequence taggers [8], perform well only within their original taxonomy and degrade sharply when it evolves, requiring costly re-annotation and retraining [9]. Zero-shot LLM prompting offers significantly more flexibility, but monolithic prompts do not scale well. As the number of target labels increases, models exhibit lost-in-the-middle attention degradation and type inconsistencies [10]. These issues are especially problematic for large PII taxonomies that contain dozens of semantically overlapping categories.

These limitations suggest that PII detection is better viewed as a dynamic alignment and orchestration problem. Rather than encoding a full taxonomy into one prompt, an adaptive system should break the schema into manageable components handled by specialized agents.

To bridge this gap, we propose a framework that automatically adapts to arbitrary target schemas without manual prompt engineering. Our approach decomposes the extraction task into smaller and semantically coherent subproblems, each handled by a specialist agent. To improve the reliability of these agents, we introduce an Evolutionary Prompt Optimization (EPO) mechanism, in which a meta-agent iteratively refines each agent's instructions based on error-driven feedback.

Our main contributions are as follows:

1. We propose a dynamic orchestration architecture that adapts to unseen taxonomies by clustering labels into semantically coherent groups and assigning each to a specialist agent.
2. We introduce an evolutionary prompting strategy that improves zero-shot robustness by iteratively refining agent instructions via error-driven updates.
3. We design a hybrid debate protocol that improves extraction accuracy by resolving conflicting predictions through a structured comparison of agent reasoning.
4. We show that our framework with a locally deployed 14B model outperforms GPT-4o baselines, enabling deployment without external APIs.

2 Related Work

2.1 From Static NER to Generative PII Recognition

Traditional PII detection systems mainly rely on supervised sequence labeling models, such as BiLSTM-CRF or BERT-based architectures [8,11]. Rule-based or hybrid pipelines have also been widely used, particularly in domain-specific settings such as finance [12]. While these models perform efficiently on in-distribution data, they suffer from *schema rigidity*, since adapting to a new entity type (e.g., a specific "Crypto Wallet ID") requires costly re-annotation and model retraining.

Recently, LLMs have enabled zero-shot Information Extraction (IE) through instruction following [13,14]. However, monolithic LLM prompting faces two key challenges: (1) **Context Window constraints** that trigger the "lost-in-the-middle" phenomenon [10], and (2) **Hallucination**, where models invent plausible but non-existent PII [15].

Recent work explores an alternative integration of LLMs into privacy pipelines, in which a traditional NER model first masks sensitive entities and an LLM then rewrites the sentence to maintain semantic coherence [16,17]. While effective for producing fluent anonymized sentences, this pipeline depends on the NER model's accuracy and label space. Consequently, its performance and generality remain limited when applied to heterogeneous or evolving PII schemas.

Another recent line of work introduces RECAP, a hybrid PII detection framework that combines rule-based structured PII extraction with zero-shot GPT-4o inference for unstructured entities [18]. It demonstrates strong multilingual generalization across 13 low-resource locales and supports over 300 PII types without retraining. However, it still relies on static rule templates and a fixed label consolidation step, leaving it sensitive to domain shifts and schema variations.

In parallel, the data mining and privacy-preserving data publishing communities have extensively studied anonymization techniques for structured datasets. Representative approaches include permutation-based anonymization of tabular data and the synthetic generation of realistic personal records to balance privacy and analytical utility [19,20]. These methods operate on relational tables and quasi-identifiers. In contrast, our work focuses on high-recall detection of fine-grained PII spans in unstructured text.

Our framework addresses these limitations by introducing a Schema Partitioning mechanism. By decomposing the label space into semantic clusters, we mitigate attention degradation while preserving generative flexibility.

2.2 Multi-agent Collaboration and Debate

Decomposing reasoning tasks into multi-agent workflows has shown promise for improving reasoning performance [21,22]. Specifically, LLM Debate frameworks [23,24] demonstrate that allowing multiple model instances to critique each other's outputs can reduce factual errors. However, standard debate protocols incur significant overhead, as they often initiate debate cycles even for trivial cases. Moreover, unconstrained debate can lead to conformity bias, where agents converge on an incorrect consensus under the influence of a dominant model. We distinguish our work by implementing an *Uncertainty-Aware Debate Protocol*. By triggering dialectical reasoning only when the span-level uncertainty exceeds a threshold (θ_{debate}), our system balances computational efficiency with rigorous verification, effectively resolving ambiguity in high-risk PII contexts without unnecessary overhead.

2.3 Prompt Optimization and Self-improving Pipelines

Another line of work investigates how LLM instructions can be automatically refined without retraining the underlying model. Recent methods introduce automated prompt mutation strategies [25]. Other approaches refine prompts via model-driven search [26]. More recent pipeline-level frameworks compile declarative LLM workflows into modular components whose prompts and demonstrations are optimized end-to-end [27]. These techniques demonstrate that prompt quality can be systematically improved through automated optimization. In contrast, our setting involves a heterogeneous collection of specialist agents, each responsible for a semantically coherent subset of PII types, together with a moderation module and a schema orchestrator. Local improvements to one component may therefore introduce inconsistencies elsewhere in the pipeline, ultimately degrading end-to-end extraction quality.

To address this challenge, our EPO mechanism jointly refines all agent instructions in a coordinated manner. Guided by domain-specific error analysis on PII extraction, EPO enforces consistency between specialist agents, the debate moderator, and the schema orchestrator, allowing the entire multi-agent pipeline to self-improve while preserving pipeline coherence.

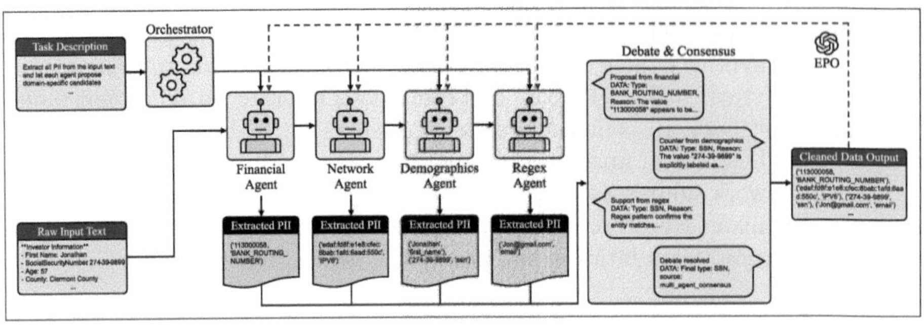

Fig. 1. Architecture of our adaptive PII detection framework with schema decomposition, multi-agent inference, debate, and type-correction.

3 Methodology

Our framework realizes adaptive PII detection as a multi-agent pipeline driven by a central Orchestrator. Figure 1 shows the overall architecture and data flow.

3.1 Orchestrated Multi-agent Pipeline

Given an input document x and a target label set $\mathcal{L}$, the Orchestrator executes the following end-to-end process:

1. **Schema decomposition and agent setup.** The Orchestrator decomposes $\mathcal{L}$ into semantically coherent subsets $\mathcal{C} = \{C_1, \ldots, C_m\}$ using LLM-based schema partitioning (detailed in Sect. 3.2). Each subset C_k defines the domain of a specialist agent $\mathcal{A}_k$, implemented as a prompt template over the same locally hosted backbone model.
2. **Parallel specialist inference.** The full document x is broadcast to *all* specialist agents. Each agent $\mathcal{A}_k$ independently produces a set of candidate predictions $\mathcal{P}_k(x) = \{(s_i, t_i, c_i)\}$, where s_i is a span with character offsets, $t_i \in C_k$ is the predicted PII type, and $c_i \in [0, 1]$ is a calibrated confidence score. The Orchestrator aggregates these into a global pool $\mathcal{P}(x) = \bigcup_{k=1}^{m} \mathcal{P}_k(x)$.
3. **Span grouping and uncertainty estimation.** Overlapping or identical spans from different agents are grouped into disjoint sets $G = \{G_1, \ldots, G_n\}$, where each G_j represents competing hypotheses over the same textual region. For every group G_j, the Orchestrator computes an uncertainty score $u(G_j)$ that measures disagreement in confidence, type, and boundary predictions (formalized in Sect. 3.3).
4. **Adaptive resolution: aggregation vs. debate.** Groups with low uncertainty ($u(G_j) \leq \theta_{\text{debate}}$) are resolved via confidence-weighted aggregation, yielding a single type and span per group. High-uncertainty groups ($u(G_j) > \theta_{\text{debate}}$) trigger a two-round multi-agent debate protocol: participating agents submit structured proposals with justifications, and a Judge LLM adjudicates the most plausible hypothesis given contextual and format constraints.
5. **Type correction and normalization.** The set of resolved spans is passed through a deterministic type-correction module that enforces schema-specific constraints and pattern-based rules (e.g., disambiguating 4-digit years from postal codes). This step adjusts residual mis-typings and normalizes formats while preserving character offsets, producing the final PII annotations $\hat{Y}$.

In the following subsections, we detail the key components of this pipeline: LLM-based schema partitioning, the uncertainty-aware debate protocol, and Agent-in-the-Loop Evolutionary Prompt Optimization (EPO), which continuously refines agent prompts and orchestration behavior.

3.2 Schema Partitioning via LLM

We treat the schema decomposition as an LLM Partitioning task. Let $\mathcal{L} = \{l_1, l_2, \ldots, l_N\}$ be the target label set. Our objective is to generate a partition $\mathcal{C} = \{C_1, \ldots, C_m\}$, where each subset C_k corresponds to an agent domain.

We express partitioning as a transformation via the LLM operator $\mathcal{M}$:

$$\mathcal{C} \leftarrow \text{Parse}\left(\mathcal{M}(\mathcal{L} \oplus \mathcal{I}_{\text{partition}})\right) \tag{1}$$

where $\mathcal{I}_{\text{partition}}$ is the instruction and $\oplus$ denotes concatenation. The output must form a valid partition of $\mathcal{L}$. By using the parametric knowledge of $\mathcal{M}$, this method groups labels based on semantic context (e.g., linking `CVV` with `IBAN`) rather than mere lexical similarity. In practice, LLM partitioning for Nemotron-PII produced intuitive groups (e.g., identity, geo-spatial, digital, and financial labels), confirming that semantic clusters align with natural PII subdomains.

In addition to these LLM-based specialist agents, a deterministic *Regex Agent* is included to handle PII types with well-defined structural patterns (e.g., phone numbers, credit card numbers, IP addresses). This agent applies pattern-matching rules in parallel with LLM agents, providing high-precision extraction for format-constrained entities.

3.3 Uncertainty-Aware Debate Protocol

Multi-agent inference produces groups of overlapping span predictions $G = \{s_1, s_2, \ldots, s_n\}$. To choose between aggregation and debate, we quantify the uncertainty $u(G)$ for each group. Uncertainty is computed as a weighted sum of three disagreement metrics:

$$u(G) = w_1 \cdot \sigma^2_{\text{conf}} + w_2 \cdot D_{\text{type}} + w_3 \cdot \sigma^2_{\text{bound}}, \tag{2}$$

- $\sigma^2_{\text{conf}} = \text{Var}(\{c_i\})$ is the variance of confidence scores c_i across agents.
- $D_{\text{type}} = \frac{|T|}{|G|}$ measures semantic divergence, where $|T|$ is the number of unique predicted types.
- σ^2_{bound} quantifies boundary disagreement, normalized by the square of the average span length.

We set weights $w_1 = 0.4$, $w_2 = 0.4$, $w_3 = 0.2$ to emphasize type conflicts and confidence variance over boundary shifts. These values were selected through EPO in Sect. 3.4. Type misclassification degrades downstream privacy protection far more than minor boundary variation. If $u(G) \leq \theta_{\text{debate}}$, the group is resolved via Bayesian weighted voting, selecting the type with the highest aggregate confidence. If $u(G) > \theta_{\text{debate}}$, a debate is triggered.

Two-Round Dialectical Protocol. For each high-uncertainty group $G_i \in \mathcal{D} = \{G \mid u(G) > \theta_{\text{debate}}\}$, we orchestrate a structured debate to resolve classification ambiguity.

Round 1: Proposal Generation. Each agent $\mathcal{A}_k$ whose type space intersects with the candidate types in G_i generates a proposal $\mathcal{P}_k = (s_k, t_k, r_k)$, where:

- s_k is the proposed span with boundaries $(start, end)$;

- $t_k \in \mathcal{T}_k$ is the predicted entity type;
- r_k is a natural language justification grounded in contextual evidence.

The justification r_k is generated using a prompt that emphasizes semantic role analysis: *"What is the semantic role of '[entity]' in this context? Does the surrounding text (e.g., 'account number is', 'PIN:') provide clues about its type?"* This forces agents to explain *why* their hypothesis is contextually coherent.

Round 2: Moderator Adjudication. A Judge LLM $\mathcal{M}$ receives all proposals $\{\mathcal{P}_1, \mathcal{P}_2, \dots, \mathcal{P}_m\}$ and the original context window. The moderator evaluates each proposal by:

1. **Contextual Keyword Analysis:** Identifying explicit type indicators in the surrounding text (e.g., "routing number", "health plan beneficiary number").
2. **Format Constraint Validation:** Verifying adherence to expected patterns (e.g., 9 digits for routing numbers, XXX-XX-XXXX for SSN, 17 alphanumeric characters for VIN).
3. **Semantic Coherence Scoring:** Assessing which type best aligns with the entity's functional role in the sentence.

The moderator then selects the proposal $\mathcal{P}^* = \arg\max_{\mathcal{P}_k} P(\mathcal{P}_k \mid \text{context}, \text{constraints})$. The final prediction inherits the span and type from $\mathcal{P}^*$, treated as a high-confidence prediction in downstream aggregation.

After all groups are resolved, deterministic post-processing corrects common pattern errors and enforces global consistency, implementing the type-correction and normalization phase.

3.4 Agent-in-the-Loop Evolutionary Prompt Optimization

We propose an **Agent-in-the-Loop Evolutionary Prompt Optimization (EPO)** framework applied across pipeline components: specialist agents $\{\mathcal{A}_k\}$, the Judge LLM $\mathcal{M}$, and Orchestrator prompts. An LLM-based analyst $\mathcal{A}_{\text{EPO}}$ (GPT-OSS-120B) drives the optimization loop.

Error Analysis. An analyst examines predictions on a small support set S_k and identifies dominant failure modes such as systematic misclassification, missing contextual constraints, or prompt ambiguities.

Prompt Mutation. Based on these errors, prompts are revised by: (1) adding or refining few-shot examples, (2) adjusting Judge LLM decision rules, and (3) restructuring Orchestrator constraints.

Validation and Stopping. The updated prompts are evaluated end-to-end on S_k. The optimization process stops once further performance improvements are no longer observed.

4 Experiments

We evaluated our framework on Nemotron-PII[1], and AI4Privacy benchmarks pii-masking-200k[2] and open-pii-masking-500k-ai4privacy[3], using a locally deployed Qwen2.5-14B-Instruct model as the underlying LLM, while all baseline methods were evaluated using GPT-4o. This setup directly tests whether orchestration can close the gap between local and cloud-based models. For each dataset, we randomly sampled 300 instances for evaluation. All baseline results were averaged over 3 independent runs to ensure statistical significance.

Algorithm 1. Agent-in-the-Loop Evolutionary Prompt Optimization

Require: Support Set S_k, Initial Prompts P_0, Analyst $\mathcal{A}$

$P \leftarrow P_0$, $Score \leftarrow 0$
repeat
  $\hat{Y} \leftarrow$ Pipeline(P, S_k)
  $E \leftarrow \mathcal{A}$.AnalyzeErrors$(\hat{Y})$
  if $E = \emptyset$ **then break**
  end if
  $P' \leftarrow$ ApplyMutations$(P, \mathcal{A}$.ProposeChanges$(E))$
  $Score' \leftarrow$ Evaluate(P', S_k)
  if $Score' > Score$ **then**
    $P \leftarrow P'$, $Score \leftarrow Score'$
  else
    break ▷ Stop when improvement stalls
  end if
until No further improvement
return P

4.1 Overall Performance

Table 1 presents results across three PII redaction benchmarks. Our method achieves state-of-the-art performance on both Nemotron-PII and AI4Privacy (pii-masking-200k), with the highest Strict F1 scores of 82.0 ± 0.1 and 71.6 ± 0.1 respectively. Notably, our approach consistently improves recall while maintaining competitive precision. However, on AI4Privacy (open-pii-masking-500k), which contains multilingual documents, our method shows degraded performance compared to CoT prompting. This limitation stems from capacity constraints of smaller models in handling multilingual contexts. Nevertheless, our lightweight approach still achieves comparable results to flagship model baselines (62.4 vs 63.7 Strict F1). Interestingly, Few-shot prompting consistently underperforms Zero-shot baselines across all benchmarks. The low variance indicates this is systematic bias from exemplars rather than randomness.

[1] https://huggingface.co/datasets/NVIDIA/nemotron-pii.
[2] https://huggingface.co/datasets/ai4privacy/pii-masking-200k.
[3] https://huggingface.co/datasets/ai4privacy/open-pii-masking-500k-ai4privacy.

Table 1. Comprehensive performance comparison across three PII redaction benchmarks. We report Precision (P), Recall (R), and F1 scores for both Strict and Entity matching, along with RougeL. All values are reported as Mean ± SD over 3 runs.

Dataset	Configuration	Strict Match			Entity Match			RougeL
		Prec.	Rec.	F1	Prec.	Rec.	F1	
Nemo-PII	Zero-Shot	89.2 ±0.2	70.5 ±0.3	77.1 ±0.3	95.4 ±0.1	75.0 ±0.4	82.2 ±0.3	89.4 ±0.5
	Few-Shot	83.9 ±0.1	63.6 ±0.0	70.5 ±0.0	94.5 ±0.1	71.6 ±0.2	79.3 ±0.2	84.6 ±0.3
	CoT	**92.5** ±0.2	75.4 ±0.2	81.5 ±0.2	**94.7** ±0.2	77.1 ±0.1	83.4 ±0.1	**92.8** ±0.1
	Ours	89.8 ±0.1	**77.3** ±0.1	**82.0** ±0.1	92.0 ±0.1	**79.4** ±0.1	**84.1** ±0.1	86.8 ±0.1
AI4-200k	Zero-Shot	70.7 ±0.4	62.4 ±0.3	65.1 ±0.3	84.8 ±0.6	75.4 ±0.6	78.5 ±0.6	78.1 ±0.6
	Few-Shot	47.3 ±1.4	43.7 ±1.2	44.9 ±1.3	88.0 ±1.4	82.0 ±1.0	83.8 ±1.2	84.6 ±0.8
	CoT	76.1 ±0.5	67.4 ±0.2	70.3 ±0.3	**92.5** ±0.5	81.6 ±0.2	**85.2** ±0.2	82.4 ±0.2
	Ours	**76.4** ±0.2	**69.3** ±0.1	**71.6** ±0.1	90.4 ±0.3	**82.0** ±0.3	84.7 ±0.4	**85.1** ±0.3
AI4-500k	Zero-Shot	66.9 ±2.0	62.4 ±1.1	63.7 ±1.3	75.0 ±7.9	70.0 ±4.3	71.4 ±5.7	75.9 ±1.7
	Few-Shot	51.2 ±4.5	47.3 ±4.1	48.5 ±4.4	77.5 ±8.4	72.4 ±7.7	73.9 ±8.0	79.7 ±3.8
	CoT	**75.0** ±1.4	**69.3** ±1.7	**70.9** ±0.6	**84.8** ±6.3	**78.4** ±2.8	**80.2** ±4.6	**84.1** ±1.6
	Ours	66.5 ±0.5	60.9 ±0.4	62.4 ±0.4	75.1 ±0.6	68.9 ±0.5	70.4 ±0.5	78.8 ±0.4

4.2 Ablation Study

To assess the contribution of each component, we conduct ablation experiments on the AI4Privacy (pii-masking-500k-ai4privacy) benchmark.

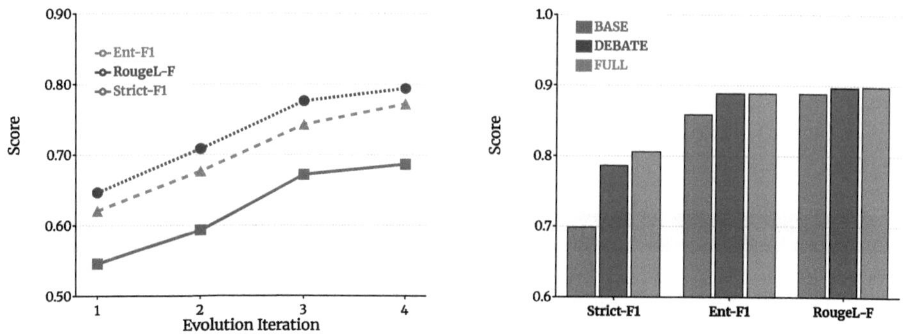

Fig. 2. Ablation results. **Left:** Performance gains across EPO iterations. **Right:** Component ablation comparing BASE, DEBATE, and FULL configurations.

The left panel of Fig. 2 shows the performance trajectory across EPO iterations. Starting from iteration 1, Strict-F1 improves from 0.55 to 0.69 (+14%p), while Entity-F1 increases from 0.62 to 0.78 (+16%p) by iteration 4. The consistent upward trend across all metrics demonstrates that the error-driven prompt refinement addresses systematic failures identified during each iteration.

The right panel compares three configurations:

- **BASE**: Multi-agent pipeline with schema partitioning only, without debate.
- **DEBATE**: BASE augmented with the uncertainty-aware debate protocol.
- **FULL**: Complete pipeline including both debate and Type-correction.

Adding the debate protocol yields substantial gains in Strict-F1 (0.70 → 0.78), indicating that the dialectical resolution of high-uncertainty spans reduces type misclassification. The full pipeline achieves the highest Entity-F1 (0.89) and RougeL-F (0.89), confirming that Type-correction and debate contribute complementary improvements: debate resolves ambiguous cases at inference time, while Type-correction prevents systematic errors through Post-hoc test.

4.3 Case Studies from Iterative EPO

The following cases illustrate how Agent-in-the-Loop EPO resolves systematic failures across multiple abstraction layers: orchestration-level workload imbalance (Case 1), deterministic rule regression (Case 2), and implementation-level prompt truncation (Case 3).

Case 1: Agent Workload Distribution - Orchestrator
Error: `llm_address` failed to detect complex cookies ("gdpr_consent=yes..."). **Root Cause:** Attention degradation due to overloading the agent with both physical (ADDRESS) and digital (COOKIE) types. **Mutation:** Split `llm_address` into purely physical locations and a new `llm_digital` agent. Added complex cookie examples. **Validation:** HTTP_COOKIE detection success; debate rate decreased by 40%.

Case 1 illustrates a schema-level intervention. When a single agent handles semantically distant types, the LLM's attention becomes diluted. By restructuring the agent topology, EPO alleviates this bottleneck without modifying model weights.

Case 2: Type Correction Regression - Regex Agent
Error: "As of 11/15/2024..." misclassified date as ACCOUNT_NUMBER. **Root Cause:** An overly aggressive rule converted any DATE within 40 chars of "account" to ACCOUNT_NUMBER. **Mutation:** Removed the aggressive rule while retaining conservative year detection. **Validation:** DATE precision restored to 1.00 without regression on financial entities.

Case 2 demonstrates that EPO also governs deterministic components. The Regex Agent's post-processing rules can introduce false positives when context heuristics are too broad. EPO's error analysis identified the specific rule causing regression and pruned it accordingly.

Case 3: Prompt Bug Fix - Specialist Agent

Error: "Clermont County" and "093-284359714" (ACCOUNT_NUMBER) consistently missed despite explicit few-shot examples.
Root Cause: Debug logging revealed that `examples[:4]` slicing in code truncated the example list, preventing critical examples from reaching the LLM.
Mutation: 1. Removed `[:4]` slice. 2. Added regex fallback for COUNTY.
Validation: span-level accuracy increased from 0.60 to 1.00 on this sample.

Case 3 reveals that prompt optimization extends beyond natural language instructions. Implementation details such as example truncation can silently degrade performance. By incorporating debug-level analysis, EPO bridges the gap between prompt engineering and software debugging.

5 Conclusion

In this work, we presented an adaptive PII detection framework that treats privacy-preserving extraction as a dynamic orchestration and alignment problem rather than a fixed sequence labeling task. The core idea is to decompose the label space into semantically coherent clusters, assign each cluster to a specialist agent, and coordinate their interaction through hierarchical orchestration and an uncertainty-aware debate protocol. Combined with Evolutionary Prompt Optimization (EPO), this yields a self-improving pipeline that can adapt to new PII schemas without model retraining or manual prompt engineering. A central practical contribution is demonstrating that high-quality, context-aware PII detection is achievable with a locally hosted 14B-parameter model, without reliance on proprietary cloud APIs. This enables organizations in highly regulated domains such as healthcare, finance, and government to perform robust PII masking entirely within their own infrastructure, ensuring that sensitive content never leaves the trusted environment.

The proposed architecture offers three key advantages: schema adaptability, allowing the system to reorganize when regulatory definitions evolve without changing model weights; model-agnostic design, making the framework portable across different backbone models and hardware configurations; and an uncertainty-aware debate protocol that provides structured conflict resolution for ambiguous spans where misclassification would have the greatest privacy impact. Several limitations remain. Performance is constrained by the underlying local LLM on rare or highly specialized PII types, and the multi-agent architecture introduces computational overhead compared to monolithic NER models, though this is partly mitigated by parallel GPU execution. Future work will focus on distilling the system into lighter-weight models for edge deployment and extending the framework to multilingual, cross-jurisdictional settings where PII definitions differ across locales.

Acknowledgments. This research was supported by the Institute of Information & Communications Technology Planning & Evaluation (IITP) grant funded by the Korea government (MSIT) (No. RS-2024-00439139, Development of a Cyber Crisis Response and Resilience Test Evaluation Systems). And this research was supported by the MSIT (Ministry of Science and ICT), Korea, under the Graduate School of Virtual Convergence support program (IITP-2026-RS-2023-00254129) supervised by the IITP (Institute for Information & Communications Technology Planning & Evaluation).

References

1. Yan, B., et al.: On protecting the data privacy of large language models (LLMs) and LLM agents: a literature review. High-Confid. Comput. **5**(2), 100300 (2025)
2. Liang, W., et al.: The widespread adoption of large language model-assisted writing across society. Patterns **6**, 101366 (2025)
3. Larson, S., et al.: De-identification of sensitive personal data in datasets derived from IIT-CDIP. In: EMNLP (2024)
4. Sarkar, A., Chuang, Y., Mohammed, N., Jiang, X.: De-identification is not enough: a comparison between de-identified and synthetic clinical notes. Sci. Rep. **14**, 29669 (2024)
5. Savkin, M., Ionov, T., Konovalov, V.: SPY: enhancing privacy with synthetic PII detection dataset. In: NAACL (2025)
6. Dernoncourt, F., Lee, J., Uzuner, O., Szolovits, P.: De-identification of patient notes with recurrent neural networks. J. Am. Med. Inform. Assoc. **24**(3), 596–606 (2017)
7. Lison, P., Pilán, I., Sanchez, D., Batet, M., Øvrelid, L.: Anonymisation models for text data: state of the art, challenges and future directions. In: ACL-IJCNLP (2021)
8. Devlin, J., Chang, M. W., Lee, K., Toutanova, K.: BERT: pre-training of deep bidirectional transformers for language understanding. In: NAACL (2019)
9. Singh, D., Narayanan, S.: Unmasking the reality of PII masking models: Performance gaps and the call for accountability. arXiv preprint arXiv:2504.12308 (2025)
10. Liu, N.F., et al.: Lost in the middle: how language models use long contexts. Trans. Assoc. Comput. Linguist. **12**, 157–173 (2024)
11. Liu, Y., et al.: RoBERTa: a robustly optimized BERT pretraining approach. arXiv preprint arXiv:1907.11692 (2019)
12. Mishra, K., Pagare, H., Sharma, K.: A hybrid rule-based NLP and machine learning approach for PII detection and anonymization in financial documents. Sci. Rep. **15**, 22729 (2025)
13. Chen, Y., Shah, V., Ritter, A.: Translation and fusion improves cross-lingual information extraction. In: ACL (2025)
14. Wang, S., et al.: GPT-NER: named entity recognition via large language models. In: NAACL (2025)
15. Chen, X., et al.: The janus interface: how fine-tuning in large language models amplifies the privacy risks. In: CCS (2024)
16. Żarski, T.L., Janicki, A.: Enhancing privacy while preserving context in text transformations by large language models. Information **16**(1), 49 (2025)
17. Yermilov, O., Raheja, V., Chernodub, A.: Privacy- and utility-preserving NLP with anonymized data: a case study of pseudonymization. In: TrustNLP (2023)
18. Rajgarhia, H., et al.: An evaluation study of hybrid methods for multilingual PII detection. arXiv preprint arXiv:2510.07551 (2025)
19. Christen, P., Pudjijono, A.: Accurate synthetic generation of realistic personal information. In: PAKDD (2009)

20. He, X., et al.: Permutation anonymization: improving anatomy for privacy preservation in data publication. In: PAKDD (2011)
21. Wu, Q., et al.: AutoGen: enabling next-gen LLM applications via multi-agent conversation. In: COLM (2024)
22. Li, G., et al.: CAMEL: communicative agents for "mind" exploration of large scale language model society. In: NeurIPS (2023)
23. Du, Y., Li, S., Torralba, A., Tenenbaum, J., Mordatch, I.: Improving factuality and reasoning in language models through multiagent debate. In: ICML (2024)
24. Liang, T., et al.: Encouraging divergent thinking in large language models through multi-agent debate. In: EMNLP (2024)
25. Pryzant, R., et al.: Automatic prompt optimization with "gradient descent" and beam search. In: EMNLP (2023)
26. Yang, C., et al.: Large language models as optimizers. In: ICLR (2024)
27. Khattab, O., et al.: DSPy: compiling declarative language model calls into self-improving pipelines. In: ICLR (2024)

Cloud–Edge Collaborative Anomaly Detection for Water Treatment Systems

Zhanglong Yang, Qinxuan Shi, and Sicong Shao(✉)

School of Electrical Engineering and Computer Science, University of North Dakota, Grand Forks, USA
sicong.shao@und.edu

Abstract. The integration of industrial infrastructure with advanced networking and computing technologies has significantly expanded the vulnerability landscape of cyber-physical systems, making anomaly detection in water treatment systems a particularly demanding problem. While deep learning offers powerful detection capability, its substantial computational demands render it impractical for resource-constrained edge devices; conversely, lightweight techniques tend to compromise detection accuracy. To address this, we propose Cloud–Edge Collaborative Anomaly Detection for Water Treatment Systems (CEC-ADW), a cloud–edge architecture centered on Bagged EM-AT (BEA), a bootstrap ensemble of the Expectation–Maximization Anomaly Transformer (EM-AT). EM-AT extends the Anomaly Transformer with an EM-driven Gaussian mixture model that enables fully automatic, data-adaptive threshold selection. Within CEC-ADW, full BEA executes on the cloud to maximize detection capability, while the quantized variant (Quan_BEA), optimized with TorchAO and ExecuTorch on edge devices such as Raspberry Pi, provides efficient, low-latency anomaly detection. The Mahalanobis distance-based routing policy escalates uncertain cases to the cloud server for accurate detection.

Keywords: Anomaly Detection · Cloud · Edge · ExecuTorch · Cyber-physical System

1 Introduction

Cyber–physical systems (CPS) integrate computation, communication, and physical processes in safety-critical domains such as energy, healthcare, transportation, and water infrastructure. Although such systems bring substantial gains in automation and operational effectiveness, their heterogeneous constituent elements simultaneously widen the attack surface and introduce new vectors for malicious exploitation [5]. Water treatment systems are vital to public safety yet vulnerable to disruption, so prompt identification of operational faults or deliberate attacks is therefore indispensable for sustaining system integrity. Traditional approaches such as rule-based systems [18] are ill-suited to the volume and intricacy of contemporary water CPS telemetry streams. In contrast, deep learning models can exploit long-range temporal dependencies and high-dimensional feature spaces, enabling more nuanced discrimination

R. C.-W. Wong et al. (Eds.): PAKDD 2026, LNAI 16618, pp. 536–548, 2027.
https://doi.org/10.1007/978-981-92-1947-6_43

between normal and anomalous states. Transformer-based architectures such as the Anomaly Transformer [24] already perform well on public CPS datasets, yet their intensive computational demands poses a formidable barrier to deployment on low-resource edge nodes. As water-CPS deployments expand, intelligence is shifting from centralized cloud servers to edge devices near sensors and actuators, which shortens detection latency, curtails bandwidth demands, strengthens privacy guarantees, and improves resilience against network failures [27]. This migration, however, engenders a deployment dilemma: cloud-only solutions provide abundant compute for state-of-the-art models but incur latency, bandwidth overhead, and single points of failure, whereas edge-only solutions offer real-time, locally robust detection but are constrained by strict compute and energy budgets, restricting the complexity of deployable models. Three fundamental challenges drive our investigation into secure water CPS monitoring. (1) **Data heterogeneity and complexity.** Water treatment systems produce high-dimensional, sensitive, and temporally complex system data. Rule-based and invariant-based schemes [18] as well as classical machine learning methods [6] exhibit limited capacity to model the nonlinear interdependencies inherent in such data, motivating approaches with greater representational expressiveness. (2) **Annotation scarcity.** Supervised anomaly detection typically requires large, carefully labeled datasets with both normal and anomalous behavior [3]. However, in operational water CPS, true attacks and severe faults are rare, hard to capture, and often incompletely labeled [15], substantially curtailing the viability of supervised solutions. (3) **On-device inference constraints.** In water treatment systems, on-device detection is often required to meet strict latency and responsiveness constraints, but state-of-the-art models are computationally intensive and difficult to deploy on resource-constrained devices. Cloud-only pipelines introduce communication overhead, extra security risks, and end-to-end delays, motivating hybrid architectures that combine rapid local inference with selective cloud offloading for complex or safety-critical cases [19]. To address these challenges, we develop CEC-ADW, a holistic architecture for robust, efficient, and accurate anomaly detection in water CPS. Our primary contributions are as follows: (1) we propose **EM-AT**, an extension of the Anomaly Transformer (AT) that replaces K-Means-based Gap Statistic thresholding [22] with a GMM fitted via the EM algorithm and selected by BIC, achieving fully automated threshold determination with superior detection accuracy and reduced computational overhead; (2) we introduce **Bagged EM-AT** (BEA), an ensemble of EM-AT base learners that strengthens detection robustness against data variability; (3) we present the **CEC-ADW** architecture built on BEA, where full BEA runs on cloud servers and the lightweight variant, Quan_BEA, optimized via TorchAO and ExecuTorch, runs on edge devices, with a distance-based routing policy that keeps most detection on-device and elevates only uncertain samples to the cloud, simultaneously minimizing energy expenditure and communication load while preserving detection quality.

2 Related Work

Water treatment systems are particularly crucial for daily life and public safety, yet they remain highly vulnerable to intrusions and targeted attacks that may disrupt operations [1]. Data-driven anomaly detection has emerged as a central research thread in water-CPS security, with machine learning methods progressively supplanting traditional rule-based schemes owing to their superior adaptability and detection performance. Against this backdrop, Inoue et al. [6] compared unsupervised deep neural networks (DNNs) and support vector machines (SVMs) in industrial control settings, observing that DNNs were more effective at suppressing false alarms, whereas SVMs were slightly better at pinpointing anomalous events. This comparison highlights a practical trade-off between false-positive control and sensitivity in ICS deployments. Building on these insights, Li et al. [10] proposed a Generative Adversarial Network (GAN) architecture incorporating Long Short-Term Memory (LSTM) components. The generator–discriminator setup is trained to emphasize unusual behaviors in the SWaT dataset, thereby revealing potential cyber threats to the underlying process. Xu et al. [24] introduced a transformer-based model employing a MiniMax strategy, achieving competitive performance across multiple industrial anomaly detection benchmarks. Yang et al. [26] applied an anomaly transformer-based anomaly detection and achieved strong anomaly detection results on both SWaT and WADI datasets.

3 Architecture Overview

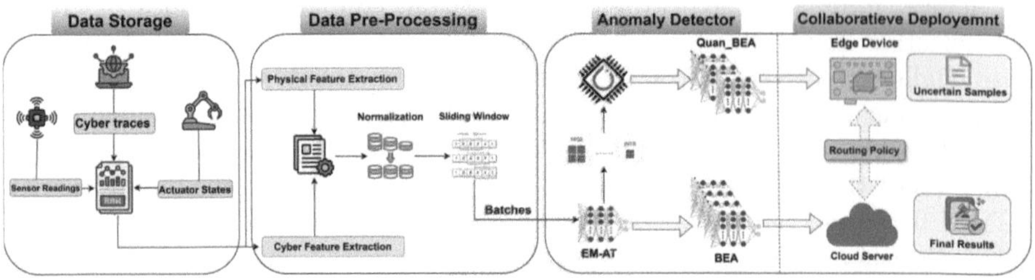

Fig. 1. CEC-ADW architecture. Data storage and preprocessing provide structured inputs to the anomaly detector, while cloud BEA collaborates with edge Quan_BEA via distance-based routing to enhance detection performance without imposing significant overhead on edge devices.

3.1 Data Storage

This module maintains an immutable repository of raw operational data collected from the water treatment system, covering both physical component data (e.g., sensor readings, actuator states) and cyber data. Strict immutability ensures that the subsequent data preprocessing module always operates on an unmodified, auditable copy of the original plant records, providing a stable foundation for reproducible experimentation.

3.2 Data Pre-processing

The preprocessing module transforms raw telemetry into detector-ready temporal sequences through two sequential stages. In the first stage, a feature extractor selects key signals from both the physical process and industrial network traffic, deriving statistical descriptors for sensors and actuators and extracting protocol-aware features such as packet inter-arrival intervals, traffic rates, and command-type distributions from raw traffic captures. Within the SWaT [14] testbed, measurements from level sensors, flow meters, and water-quality monitors are combined with network logs, device tags, timestamps, and impact annotations to create an integrated physical–cyber feature set for anomaly detection.

In the second stage, a sequence construction component partitions the feature stream into fixed-length, non-overlapping time-series windows, covering the full timeline without duplication while preserving temporal order within each segment. During training, mini-batches of these sequences are used to avoid over-fitting to the original global ordering. Together, these two stages produce standardized, temporally coherent input sequences that facilitate effective anomaly discrimination in the complex, high-dimensional settings characteristic of water treatment operations.

3.3 Anomaly Detector

Expectation Maximization-Based Anomaly Transformer. EM-AT builds upon the unsupervised Anomaly Transformer [24] and performs point-wise anomaly scoring on multivariate time series $X = \{x_t\}_{t=1}^{N}$, $x_t \in \mathbb{R}^d$. It stacks Transformer encoder layers but replaces standard self-attention with *Anomaly-Attention*, which explicitly models two associations for each time point: a prior-association with adjacent timestamps and a series-association learned from data. Given hidden states $X^{l-1} \in \mathbb{R}^{N\times d_{\text{model}}}$, the l-th layer computes $Q, K, V, \sigma = X^{l-1}W_Q^l,\ X^{l-1}W_K^l,\ X^{l-1}W_V^l,\ X^{l-1}W_\sigma^l$. The prior-association $P^l \in \mathbb{R}^{N\times N}$ is a Gaussian kernel with learnable scale σ_i, $P_{ij}^l \propto \frac{1}{\sqrt{2\pi}\sigma_i}\exp\big(-\frac{(j-i)^2}{2\sigma_i^2}\big)$, favoring adjacent positions. The series-association is the usual attention distribution $S^l = \text{Softmax}\big(\frac{QK^\top}{\sqrt{d_{\text{model}}}}\big)$, and $Z^l = S^l V$. For each time point i, the *association discrepancy* averages the symmetrized KL divergence between $P_{i,:}^l$ and $S_{i,:}^l$ over L layers: $\text{AssDis}_i = \frac{1}{L}\sum_{l=1}^{L}\big[\text{KL}(P_{i,:}^l \,\|\, S_{i,:}^l) + \text{KL}(S_{i,:}^l \,\|\, P_{i,:}^l)\big]$. Normal points tend to build long-range associations and thus have larger AssDis_i, while anomalies exhibit adjacent-concentrated associations and smaller discrepancy. During training, a minimax objective jointly optimizes reconstruction quality and association discrepancy, $\mathcal{L} = \|X - \hat{X}\|_F^2 - \lambda\sum_i \text{AssDis}_i$, alternating (i) a phase that updates the Gaussian prior to fit the learned series-association and (ii) a phase that pushes the series-association to enlarge the discrepancy under the reconstruction constraint. At inference, Anomaly Transformer combines reconstruction error and association discrepancy into a point-wise anomaly score $E(\mathcal{X}) = \text{Softmax}(-\text{AD}(\mathcal{P}, \mathcal{S}; \mathcal{X})) \odot \left[\|\mathcal{X}_{i,:} - \widehat{\mathcal{X}}_{i,:}\|_2^2\right]_{i=1,\cdots,N}$, where higher values signal greater anomaly likelihood.

A key limitation of the original Anomaly Transformer is its reliance on K-Means–based Gap Statistic thresholding, which requires an additional clustering step and is sensitive to initialization. EM-AT replaces this with an EM-fitted GMM that directly models the empirical score distribution: $P(e) = \sum_{i=1}^{U} \alpha_i p_i(e)$, where α_i is the weight of component i, U is the number of components, and $\sum_{i=1}^{U} \alpha_i = 1$. Each component is a multivariate Gaussian with mean vector μ_i and covariance matrix Σ_i, i.e., $p_i(e) = \frac{1}{(2\pi)^{D/2}|\Sigma_i|^{1/2}} \exp\big(-\frac{1}{2}(e - \mu_i)^{\mathrm{T}} \Sigma_i^{-1}(e - \mu_i)\big)$. The full parameter set is $\theta = \{\alpha_i, \mu_i, \Sigma_i\}\{i = 1, \ldots, U\}$, and the likelihood of all anomaly scores E is $P(E \mid \theta) = \prod_{t=1}^{N} p(e_t \mid \theta)$. To estimate θ, we maximize the log-likelihood $\log \ell(\theta \mid E) = \sum_{t=1}^{N} \log\big(\sum_{j=1}^{U} \alpha_j p_j(e_t \mid \theta_j)\big)$ using the EM algorithm. EM introduces latent variables H indicating the component assignments and iteratively alternates: (i) an E-step, which computes the expected complete-data log-likelihood $\mathcal{Q}(\theta, \theta^{(E)}) = \mathbb{E}[\log \ell(\theta \mid E, H)]$, and (ii) an M-step, which updates θ to maximize $\mathcal{Q}$. Repeating these two steps until convergence yields the maximum-likelihood estimate of θ. The optimal number of components U is determined automatically by the Bayesian Information Criterion, eliminating any hyperparameter requiring manual specification. After fitting, we sort the components by their means, $\mu_1 \leq \mu_2 \leq \cdots \leq \mu_U$, with corresponding weights $\{\alpha_1, \ldots, \alpha_U\}$. In the typical case, the lowest-mean component accounts for a simple majority of the mass and is treated as the normal class; the anomaly rate is then the remaining mixture weight, and the decision threshold is set to the corresponding upper quantile of the score distribution. When normal data span multiple low-mean components, we aggregate components starting from the smallest mean until their total weight exceeds a majority threshold τ (e.g., $\tau = 0.5$). Formally, we find the smallest u such that $\sum_{k=1}^{u} \alpha_k \geq \tau$, designate components $\{1, \ldots, u\}$ as normal, set the anomaly proportion $r = 1 - \sum_{k=1}^{u} \alpha_k$, and choose the threshold σ as the $(1-r)$-quantile of the anomaly scores. Beyond eliminating manual tuning, this formulation enables distinct anomaly subtypes to occupy separate mixture components, offering a natural basis for anomaly categorization—an aspect we leave for future investigation.

Bagged EM-AT. To enhance the robustness and reliability of the anomaly detector, we adopt an ensemble strategy based on bootstrap aggregation (Bagging). Bagging reduces variance by training multiple base learners on bootstrap-resampled subsets of the original dataset. Because each model is exposed to a different sampled subset, the ensemble acquires diversity that mitigates overfitting and improves generalization. Concretely, as summarized in Algorithm 1, the *Bagged EM-AT (BEA)* consists of I individual EM-AT models, each instantiated with a distinct hyperparameter configuration. For each iteration $i \in \{1, \ldots, I\}$,

---

Algorithm 1: BEA Training

---

function *TrainBEA*(A, I, n)
  // A: training data;
  I: number of base learners;
  n: size of each bootstrap draw
  $B \leftarrow \emptyset$ // container for base EM-AT models
  for $i \leftarrow 1$ **to** I **do**
    $A^{(i)} \leftarrow$ BootstrapSample(A, n) // sample n items from A with replacement
    $B^{(i)} \leftarrow$ EM-AT($A^{(i)}$) // train one EM-AT base model
    $B \leftarrow B \cup \{B^{(i)}\}$ // store the trained model
  end
  return B // return ensemble $\{B^{(1)}, \ldots, B^{(I)}\}$

---

a bootstrap training set is constructed by randomly sampling n instances with replacement from the original training data. To further promote diversity among the base learners, key hyperparameters such as batch size, number of encoder layers, and loss weight are varied across models. During inference, all base-learner predictions are aggregated by majority voting, and the resulting consensus decision constitutes the final output. This ensemble strategy provides three complementary benefits: reduced prediction variance, improved robustness to training-set peculiarities, and a natural confidence signal (vote margin) that can be leveraged for downstream routing decisions.

3.4 Cloud-Edge Collaborative Deployment

Practical deployment of high-performance anomaly detectors in water treatment systems demands reliability under strict resource constraints. As illustrated in Fig. 1, we adopt a cloud–edge collaborative deployment strategy in which the cloud server handles heavy computation and edge nodes execute quantized detector model variants.

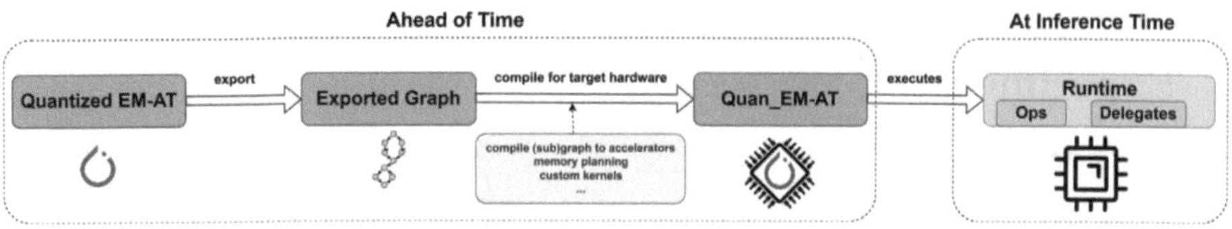

Fig. 2. Workflow for ExecuTorch-based deployment of the EM-AT model.

The cloud server hosts full-precision BEA ensembles capable of high-fidelity inference on challenging or ambiguous samples. Edge devices, operating under limited compute and memory budgets, instead run Quan_BEA—a quantized rendering of BEA produced by applying A8W4 dynamic quantization through TorchAO [13] and compiled into a portable *.pte* executable via ExecuTorch [4]. As illustrated in Fig. 2, ExecuTorch-based deployment proceeds in two stages. First, during ahead-of-time (AOT) compilation, the TorchAO-quantized model is exported to an ExecuTorch graph and compiled into an ExecuTorch program with tailored memory planning and, where available, hardware acceleration. Second, at runtime, the target edge device executes this compiled program in the inference stage, achieving low CPU and memory overhead while processing input sequences. Using this workflow, we complete the edge-based deployment of the CEC-ADW architecture. The resulting edge deployment enables water treatment nodes to sustain continuous, cost-effective anomaly surveillance over extended operational periods. To achieve collaboration, we need a policy to determine whether the results detected on the edge device are accurate. If the accuracy of the detection results cannot be guaranteed, the data sample needs to be transmitted to the cloud for more accurate detection. The collaboration between cloud and edge is governed by a Mahalanobis distance-based routing policy. Each *Quan_BEA* base model maintains its own anomaly threshold; these are assembled into a threshold vector $T = (t_1, \ldots, t_k) \in \mathbb{R}^k$, where k is the number of base models. For the test sample S_j, the anomaly scores produced by all k edge models are stacked into a score vector $\mathbf{x}_j = \big(Q_1(S_j), Q_2(S_j), \ldots, Q_k(S_j)\big) \in \mathbb{R}^k$, where $Q_k(\cdot)$ denotes the anomaly score assigned by the k-th *Quan_BEA* model. The routing decision is then based on the Mahalanobis distance between $\mathbf{x}_j$ and T: $d_M(\mathbf{x}_j, T) = \sqrt{(\mathbf{x}_j - T)^\top \Sigma^{-1}(\mathbf{x}_j - T)}$, where Σ is the empirical covariance matrix of score vectors computed over a held-out validation set. A sample S_j is forwarded to the cloud BEA ensemble if d_M exceeds a calibrated ceiling δ, and classified locally otherwise. For samples routed to the cloud, the full BEA ensemble $\{B_1, \ldots, B_I\}$ produces an additional set of votes $\mathrm{CP}(S_j) = \{B_i(S_j) \mid i = 1, \ldots, I\}$. The final prediction for every sample is obtained by fusing edge votes $\mathrm{EP}(S_j)$ and cloud votes $\mathrm{CP}(S_j)$ via majority voting: $\hat{y}_j = \arg\max_c \Big|\{v \in \mathrm{EP}(S_j) \cup \mathrm{CP}(S_j) \mid v = c\}\Big|$. This policy concentrates cloud offloading on genuinely ambiguous cases, keeping communication and energy overhead low while ensuring that difficult samples benefit from full-precision ensemble inference.

4 Experiment

4.1 Experiment Setting

Dataset. We conduct all evaluations on the SWaT benchmark [14], a widely adopted testbed for water-CPS security research. The SWaT dataset records 51 variables from the SWaT testbed, with 495,000 samples in the training set and 449,919 in the testing set. Only the test set contained anomalous data, with an anomaly rate of approximately 12.1% of all test samples.

Evaluation Metrics. System performance is quantified using precision, recall, and the F_1 score. Precision is the proportion of correctly detected anomalies among all samples predicted as anomalous, and recall is the proportion of true anomalies that are successfully identified. The F_1 score, as the harmonic mean of precision and recall, summarizes their joint behavior when both are important. In our setting, where anomalies are rare compared with normal data, the F_1 score provides a balanced summary particularly suited to the class-imbalanced conditions prevalent in water CPS anomaly detection.

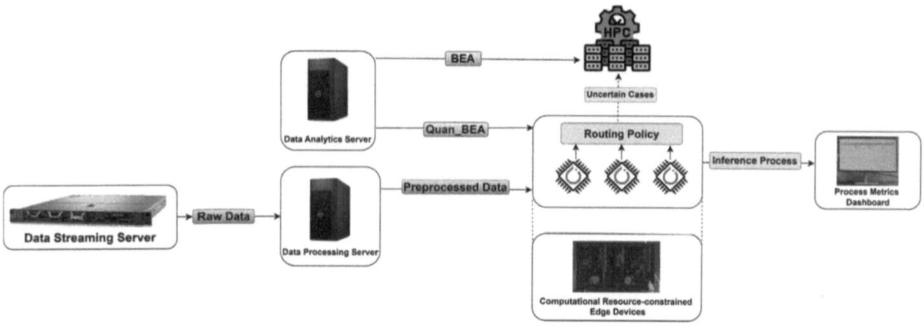

Fig. 3. The key data pipeline components of the testbed for the CEC-ADW architecture.

Hardware Setup. As shown in Fig. 3, the experiments were conducted on a heterogeneous testbed spanning three computational tiers. For edge-based deployment, three models of Raspberry Pi boards were used. The Raspberry Pi 3B+ was equipped with a quad-core ARM Cortex-A53 64-bit processor running at 1.4 GHz, 1 GB of RAM, and a 128 GB microSD card. The Raspberry Pi 4B operated at 1.8 GHz with 8 GB of RAM and a 128 GB microSD card. The Raspberry Pi 5 featured a 2.4 GHz processor, 8 GB of RAM, and a 128 GB microSD card. All Raspberry Pi devices ran Ubuntu 20.04.5 LTS and were configured without GPUs. The standard server tier consisted of two edge machines: a data-processing server and a data-analytics server. Both were equipped with Intel i7-14700 CPUs, 32 GB of RAM, 2 TB SSD storage, and NVIDIA RTX 2000 Ada Generation GPUs. The data-processing server ran Windows 11, whereas the data-analytics server ran Ubuntu 24.04.2 LTS. The data-streaming server, responsible for storing raw data for anomaly detection, was a Dell PowerEdge R650 configured with two 36-core Intel Xeon Platinum CPUs, 256 GB of RAM, a 1.6 TB NVMe SSD, and a Mellanox ConnectX-6 100 Gb NIC. This testbed configuration enables a comprehensive evaluation of the proposed architecture under diverse computational environments. Cloud-side BEA inference leveraged an HPC cluster equipped with dual 18-core Intel Xeon Gold 6140 processors and eight NVIDIA Tesla V100 GPUs.

Training Methodology. All models are trained under the standard unsupervised protocol: training labels are unused, and test labels serve only for evaluation to ensure parity with baseline comparisons. Each base learner(EM-AT) within BEA employs a hidden dimension of 512 and 8 attention heads, optimized via Adam [7] in PyTorch [17]. To maximize ensemble diversity, four key hyperparameters are independently varied per member: the number of $training\quad epochs \in \{3, 6, 10\}$, the loss weight $\lambda \in \{3, 4, 5\}$, the $Batch\quad size \in \{32, 64, 96\}$, and the number of $Encoder\quad layers \in \{3, 6, 8\}$. After ensemble training, BEA is converted into `Quan_BEA` using A8W4 dynamic quantization in TorchAO, which preserves most detection performance while reducing resource usage. For edge deployment, we set an ensemble of `Quan_BEA` models running in parallel on resource-constrained devices to support robust majority voting, while a larger BEA ensemble is hosted in the cloud to maximize accuracy.

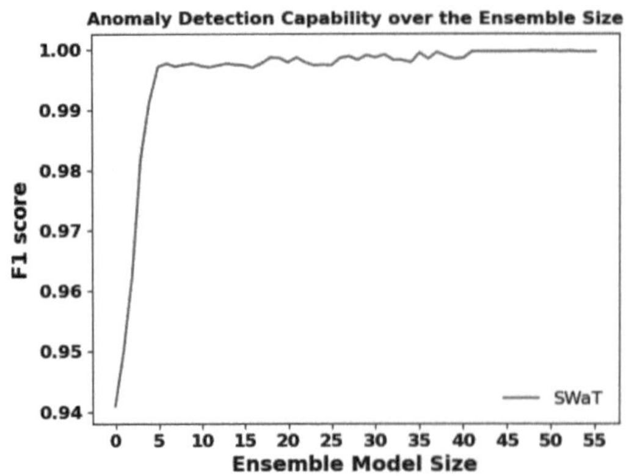

Fig. 4. Anomaly detection capability of BEA ensembles with different ensemble sizes on the SWaT dataset.

Baselines. We extensively compared our architecture with previous leading and popular methods, including the leading deep learning-based methods: LSTM-VAE [16,24], OmniAnomaly [21,24], Anomaly Transformer [24,26], T-VAE [9], VAE [2,8], DAGMM [23,28], ConvLSTM [2,20], DCdetector [9,25]. In addition, the classic shallow methods, including IsolationForest [12,24], OC-SVM [2,11], were also compared.

4.2 Results

BEA Ensemble Size Analysis. Figure 4 illustrates the relationship between BEA ensemble size and detection performance on SWaT. A pronounced inflection is observed near five base learners, where the F_1 score rises sharply from about 94% to 99%, a gain attributable to the variance-reduction effect of bootstrap aggregation. Larger ensembles bring only marginal gains, with performance saturating near 100% beyond 20 models. Accordingly, the cloud-side ensemble is fixed at 51 models for all subsequent experiments.

Table 1. Anomaly detection capability comparison between CEC-ADW and other methods on SWaT dataset, using results reported in other methods' respective references.

Method	Precision	Recall	F_1
DCdetector [9]	97.8	70.3	82.2
T-VAE [9]	97.9	71.0	82.3
ConvLSTM [2]	99.8	64.3	78.2
OC-SVM [2]	95.9	64.4	77.1
VAE [2]	99.6	64.2	78.1
LSTM-VAE [24]	76.00	89.50	82.20
DAGMM [24]	89.92	57.84	70.40
OmniAnomaly [24]	81.42	84.30	82.83
IsolationForest [24]	49.29	44.95	47.02
Anomaly Transformer [26]	91.55	96.73	94.07
CEC-ADW	**99.92**	**100.00**	**99.96**

Anomaly Detection Capability Analysis. Table 1 presents a comprehensive performance comparison on SWaT. A systematic precision–recall asymmetry characterizes most baselines: while methods such as ConvLSTM and VAE reach precision around 99%, their recall remains below 66%, limiting their F_1 scores to at most about 83%. The Anomaly Transformer provides a strong reference point with 91.55% precision, 96.73% recall, and an F_1 score of 94.07%. In contrast, CEC-ADW attains 99.92% precision, 100.00% recall, and an F_1 score of 99.96%, which is substantially higher than all competing methods. This near-perfect performance reflects the synergistic contributions of EM-based automatic thresholding, which eliminates threshold sensitivity; bagged ensembling, which reduces prediction variance; and cloud-edge routing, which ensures that ambiguous cases receive full-precision analysis.

Anomaly Detection Resource Consumption Analysis. As illustrated in Table 2, we compare the resource usage and detection capability of CEC-ADW and the Quan_BEA baseline on three Raspberry Pi devices using the SWaT dataset. Full-precision BEA is non-executable on all three edge platforms, underscoring the necessity of quantization for edge deployment. In the Quan_BEA baseline, anomaly detection is performed only on the edge device using Quan_BEA, without any cloud-side collaboration. Across all three devices, CEC-ADW maintains an F_1 score of 99.96%, which is slightly higher than

Table 2. Average computational resource consumption and anomaly detection capability of CEC-ADW and Quan_BEA baseline deployed on Raspberry Pis using SWaT dataset.

Device	Operation Method	Process CPU Util (%)	Process Memory Usage (MB)	CPU Temperature (°C)	Execution Method File Size (MB)	F_1 score(%)
Raspberry Pi 5	BEA	Not Executable	Not Executable	Not Executable	Not Executable	Not Executable
	Quan_BEA	74.11	136.14	68.52	59.47	97.34
	CEC-ADW	73.28	135.12	66.79	59.47	99.96
Raspberry Pi 4B	BEA	Not Executable	Not Executable	Not Executable	Not Executable	Not Executable
	Quan_BEA	74.87	134.87	52.42	59.47	97.34
	CEC-ADW	73.47	134.13	52.08	59.47	99.96
Raspberry Pi 3B+	BEA	Not Executable	Not Executable	Not Executable	Not Executable	Not Executable
	Quan_BEA	74.97	134.45	51.86	59.47	97.34
	CEC-ADW	74.08	133.83	51.17	59.47	99.96

the 97.34% achieved by Quan_BEA baseline. On Raspberry Pi 5, CEC-ADW slightly lowers process CPU utilization to about 73.28%, process memory usage to about 135.12 MB, and CPU temperature to about 66.79°C, while Quan_BEA requires 74.11% CPU, 136.14 MB memory, and reaches 68.52°C. Similar reductions appear on Raspberry Pi 4B and Raspberry Pi 3B+, where CEC-ADW keeps both CPU and memory consumption below the corresponding Quan_BEA values. These consistent reductions across all three device classes demonstrate that offloading uncertain samples to the cloud simultaneously alleviates on-device computational pressure and improves detection fidelity, validating the practical value of the collaborative deployment strategy.

5 Conclusion

We have presented CEC-ADW, a cloud–edge collaborative architecture tailored for anomaly detection in water treatment systems. Centered on the proposed EM-AT model and realized through both BEA and Quan_BEA variants, CEC-ADW employs a Mahalanobis distance–based routing policy to offload uncertain samples to cloud-side ensembles, thereby balancing detection accuracy against computational cost. Experiments on the SWaT dataset show that CEC-ADW surpasses prior and widely used methods, achieving higher F_1 scores while substantially reducing computational resource usage on resource-constrained devices, demonstrating the viability of high-performance, resource-aware security monitoring for critical water infrastructure. Promising directions for future work include the development of online adaptation mechanisms to track non-stationary anomaly distributions, federated optimization strategies for privacy-preserving cross-node model refinement, and generalization of the CEC-ADW architecture to other safety-critical CPS domains, including power distribution and industrial transportation networks.

References

1. Almazyad, I., Shao, S., Hariri, S., Kholidy, H.A.: Anomaly behavior analysis of smart water treatment facility service: design, analysis, and evaluation. In: 2023 20th ACS/IEEE International Conference on Computer Systems and Applications (AICCSA), pp. 1–7. IEEE (2023)
2. Belay, M.A., Blakseth, S.S., Rasheed, A., Salvo Rossi, P.: Unsupervised anomaly detection for IoT-based multivariate time series: existing solutions, performance analysis and future directions. Sensors **23**(5), 2844 (2023)
3. Dehlaghi-Ghadim, A., Moghadam, M.H., Balador, A., Hansson, H.: Anomaly detection dataset for industrial control systems. IEEE Access **11**, 107982–107996 (2023)
4. Executorch: On-device ai across mobile, embedded and edge for pytorch (2024). https://github.com/pytorch/executorch. Accessed 25 Feb 2025
5. Gulzar, Q., Mustafa, K.: An analytical survey of cyber-physical systems in water treatment and distribution: security challenges, intrusion detection, and future directions. Secur. Priv. **7**(6), e440 (2024)
6. Inoue, J., Yamagata, Y., Chen, Y., Poskitt, C.M., Sun, J.: Anomaly detection for a water treatment system using unsupervised machine learning. In: 2017 IEEE International Conference on Data Mining Workshops (ICDMW), pp. 1058–1065. IEEE (2017)
7. Kingma, D.P., Ba, J.: Adam: a method for stochastic optimization. In: International Conference on Learning Representations (ICLR) (2015)
8. Kingma, D.P., Welling, M., et al.: An introduction to variational autoencoders. Found. Trends® Mach. Learn. **12**(4), 307–392 (2019)
9. Li, C., Kiat, Y.C., Jing, J., Long, C.: T-VAE: transformer-based variational autoencoder for perceiving anomalies in multivariate time series data. Expert. Syst. **42**(7), e70078 (2025)
10. Li, D., Chen, D., Jin, B., Shi, L., Goh, J., Ng, S.K.: MAD-GAN: multivariate anomaly detection for time series data with generative adversarial networks. In: International Conference on Artificial Neural Networks, pp. 703–716. Springer (2019)
11. Li, K.L., Huang, H.K., Tian, S.F., Xu, W.: Improving one-class SVM for anomaly detection. In: Proceedings of the 2003 International Conference on Machine Learning and Cybernetics (IEEE Cat. No. 03EX693), vol. 5, pp. 3077–3081. IEEE (2003)
12. Liu, F.T., Ting, K.M., Zhou, Z.H.: Isolation forest. In: 2008 Eighth IEEE International Conference on Data Mining, pp. 413–422. IEEE (2008)
13. torchao maintainers, contributors: torchao: Pytorch native quantization and sparsity for training and inference (2024). https://github.com/pytorch/torchao
14. Mathur, A.P., Tippenhauer, N.O.: Swat: a water treatment testbed for research and training on ICS security. In: 2016 International Workshop on Cyber-Physical Systems for Smart Water Networks (CySWater), pp. 31–36. IEEE (2016)
15. Pang, G., Shen, C., Cao, L., van den Hengel, A.: Deep learning for anomaly detection: a review. ACM Comput. Surv. **54**(2) (2021). https://doi.org/10.1145/3439950
16. Park, D., Hoshi, Y., Kemp, C.C.: A multimodal anomaly detector for robot-assisted feeding using an LSTM-based variational autoencoder. IEEE Robot. Autom. Lett. **3**(3), 1544–1551 (2018)
17. Paszke, A.: Pytorch: an imperative style, high-performance deep learning library. arXiv preprint arXiv:1912.01703 (2019)

18. Punal, A., Roca, E., Lema, J.: An expert system for monitoring and diagnosis of anaerobic wastewater treatment plants. Water Res. **36**(10), 2656–2666 (2002)
19. Shi, W., Cao, J., Zhang, Q., Li, Y., Xu, L.: Edge computing: vision and challenges. IEEE Internet Things J. **3**(5), 637–646 (2016)
20. Shi, X., Chen, Z., Wang, H., Yeung, D.Y., Wong, W.K., Woo, W.C.: Convolutional LSTM network: a machine learning approach for precipitation nowcasting. In: Advances in Neural Information Processing Systems, vol. 28 (2015)
21. Su, Y., Zhao, Y., Niu, C., Liu, R., Sun, W., Pei, D.: Robust anomaly detection for multivariate time series through stochastic recurrent neural network. In: Proceedings of the 25th ACM SIGKDD International Conference on Knowledge Discovery & Data Mining, pp. 2828–2837 (2019)
22. Tibshirani, R., Walther, G., Hastie, T.: Estimating the number of clusters in a data set via the gap statistic. J. Roy. Stat. Soc. Ser. B (Stat. Methodol.) **63**(2), 411–423 (2001)
23. Xu, H., et al.: Unsupervised anomaly detection via variational auto-encoder for seasonal KPIs in web applications. In: Proceedings of the 2018 World Wide Web Conference, pp. 187–196 (2018)
24. Xu, J., Wu, H., Wang, J., Long, M.: Anomaly transformer: time series anomaly detection with association discrepancy. In: International Conference on Learning Representations (2022). https://openreview.net/forum?id=LzQQ89U1qm_
25. Yang, Y., Zhang, C., Zhou, T., Wen, Q., Sun, L.: Dcdetector: dual attention contrastive representation learning for time series anomaly detection. In: Proceedings of the 29th ACM SIGKDD Conference on Knowledge Discovery and Data Mining, pp. 3033–3045 (2023)
26. Yang, Z., Shi, Q., Shao, S.: Energy-efficient anomaly detection for securing water treatment and distribution systems. In: Proceedings of the 37th International Conference on Software Engineering and Knowledge Engineering, SEKE (2025)
27. Zhu, Z., Zhang, H., Zhang, S., Wang, J., Ren, H.: Intelligent monitoring and control systems for smart water management. In: Nano-Solutions for Sustainable Water and Wastewater Management: From Monitoring to Treatment, pp. 369–390. Springer (2025)
28. Zong, B., et al.: Deep autoencoding gaussian mixture model for unsupervised anomaly detection. In: International Conference on Learning Representations (2018)

CONAN: CONcept-Oriented ANomaly Detector for Interpretable Zero-Shot Detection

Yoonji Lee, Eunju Lee, Junehyoung Kwon, Seunghoo Lee, Kahyun Kim, Seunguk Yu, and Youngbin Kim(✉)

Chung-Ang University, Dongjak, Seoul 06974, South Korea
{pioneer0305,dmswn5829,dirchdmltnv,hahaha1321,kahyun0817,bokju128, ybkim85}@cau.ac.kr

Abstract. Large vision-language models (LVLMs) have advanced zero-shot anomaly detection (ZSAD) by enabling generalization to unseen classes, yet most operate as semantic "black boxes" without explicit rationale. Incorporating concept bottleneck models (CBMs) is challenging because anomalies are condition-centric and transient, unlike stable object attributes. We propose **CONAN (CONcept-oriented ANomaly Detector)**, an interpretable framework that performs active concept curation through an object-agnostic concept bank organized into five macro-level anomaly dimensions. By aligning CLIP image features with category prototypes using LVLM-generated pseudo-labels, we inject fine-grained anomaly semantics into the embedding space. Experiments show strong zero-shot performance on industrial benchmarks, robust cross-domain generalization to medical datasets, and support for human-in-the-loop explanation refinement.

Keywords: Interpretable Zero-Shot Anomaly Detection · Concept Bottleneck Model · Human Intervention

1 Introduction

Anomaly detection plays a pivotal role in safety-critical domains like industrial inspection and medical diagnosis [31]. While recent methods have significantly improved detection performance, they predominantly operate as "black boxes," flagging anomalies without articulating the semantic rationale—specifically, *what* attributes constitute the defect. This lack of interpretability hinders practical deployment, where identifying the root cause is essential for accountability and targeted intervention [26]. Consequently, there is a pressing need for zero-shot anomaly detectors that not only generalize well but also expose their decisions through human-understandable concepts.

Concept bottleneck models (CBMs) bridge performance and transparency using interpretable concepts [19], yet they rely on stable, object-centric attributes. Extending this to anomaly detection is non-trivial because defects

R. C.-W. Wong et al. (Eds.): PAKDD 2026, LNAI 16618, pp. 549–560, 2027.
https://doi.org/10.1007/978-981-92-1947-6_44

are *condition-centric*, describing the *state* of an object rather than its category [4]. Unlike stable object identities, anomaly concepts exhibit high visual heterogeneity across instances. Furthermore, VLMs like CLIP [24] are optimized for categorical semantics and often fail to align fine-grained anomaly conditions with visual features [33]. Consequently, directly transplanting conventional CBMs yields weak concept–anomaly alignment and limited interpretability.

In this work, we move to *active anomaly concept curation*. Instead of relying on unconstrained outputs, we construct a concept bank that organizes heterogeneous patterns into five condition-centric dimensions: *geometry*, *color*, *texture*, *surface integrity*, and *foreign substances*. For each category, we generate textual concepts using an LLM, embed them via CLIP, and aggregate them into category-level prototypes. This design is object-agnostic, capturing defect semantics shared across domains to enable robust condition-centric reasoning distinct from object-specific classification.

We propose **CONAN**, a CLIP-based CBM designed for interpretable zero-shot anomaly detection. Our framework follows a three-stage pipeline: First, we construct an anomaly concept bank to derive category prototypes from textual descriptions. Second, we perform alignment learning using pseudo-labels, aligning CLIP features with these prototypes via a classification loss to explicitly inject anomaly semantics. Third, we achieve localization through prototype–feature similarity, jointly optimizing image-level classification and pixel-level segmentation. During inference, CONAN utilizes an LVLM to generate natural language explanations based on intermediate predictions. Crucially, the framework supports human-in-the-loop intervention, allowing users to correct predicted categories to refine explanations for faithful analysis. Extensive experiments across diverse industrial and medical benchmarks demonstrate that CONAN achieves competitive or superior detection performance, validating its robust generalization capability.

2 Related Work

Anomaly Detection. Traditional methods rely on learning the normal data distribution within a specific domain, utilizing reconstruction errors [27] or feature embeddings such as PaDiM [11] and PatchCore [25]. While effective, these approaches require target-domain training data and failed to generalize to unseen classes. The advent of VLMs has shifted the paradigm toward zero-shot anomaly detection. WinCLIP [17] and AnomalyCLIP [36] leveraged the aligned embedding space of CLIP [24] to detect anomalies using text prompts describing normal and abnormal states. However, these methods primarily function as black-box feature extractors sensitive to prompt engineering [35], often lacking transparency in the semantic reasoning process.

Interpretability in Anomaly Detection. Interpretability is crucial in safety domains to ensure accountability. Traditional post-hoc techniques such as Grad-CAM [28] highlighted suspicious regions but failed to explain the semantic rationale behind the decision [1]. Recently, LVLMs have been employed to generate

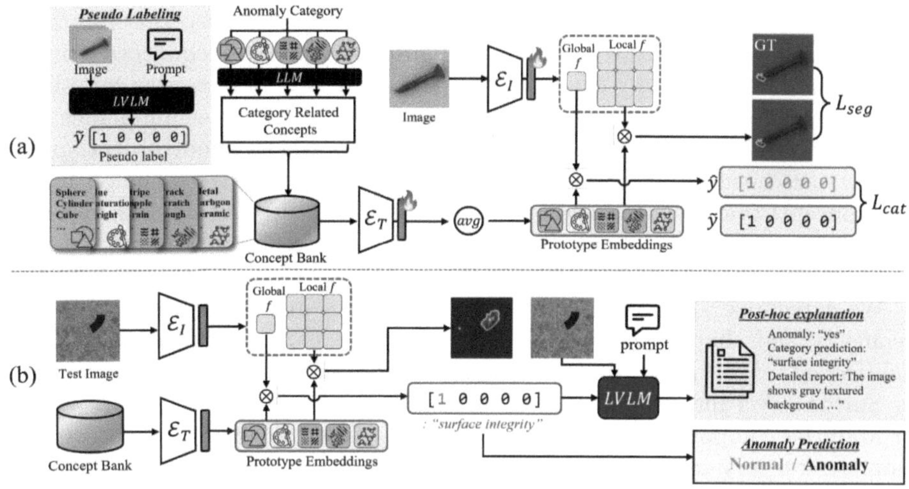

Fig. 1. Overview of the proposed framework CONAN: (a) Training and (b) Inference phase. We exclusively utilize the concept bank to conduct anomaly detection, with the concepts guided by an LLM, which requires no human annotations.

natural language explanations for anomalies [13,34]. Although these approaches improve readability, the explanation generation is decoupled from the anomaly detection backbone, leading to low fidelity and a risk of hallucinations [18]. Unlike these methods, we propose an intrinsic interpretability framework where decision-making is directly grounded in defined anomaly concepts.

Concept Bottleneck Models. CBMs offer a transparent learning paradigm by structuring predictions through human-interpretable concepts [19]. While successful in classification, extending these models to anomaly detection is non-trivial. Standard CBMs rely on stable *object-centric* attributes (e.g., has wings"), whereas anomalies require *condition-centric* concepts (e.g., "scratched," "contaminated") that describe state changes [4]. Furthermore, the embedding space of VLMs is often misaligned with such fine-grained conditions [33]. We address this by designing a concept bottleneck explicitly for anomaly understanding, organizing heterogeneous defects into structured semantic categories to enable transparent reasoning and user intervention.

3 Method

We introduce **CONAN**, a novel CBM designed to enable interpretable zero-shot anomaly detection. An overview of the proposed architecture is shown in Fig. 1.

3.1 Anomaly Category Concept Bank Construction

CBMs predict labels by combining activations of human-interpretable concepts from a predefined set, yet such concept banks are often dataset-specific and expensive to construct due to manual annotation. To mitigate this limitation, we adopt a label-free strategy that automatically generates concepts using an LLM. In addition, anomaly concepts differ markedly from the consistent, object-centric concepts found in conventional vision tasks [30]. Because anomalies manifest in diverse and context-dependent ways, narrowly defined, object-specific concepts are insufficient for robust reasoning. Accordingly, we focus on higher-level concepts that generalize across domains and object types, and introduce an anomaly-specific concept bank B_{ano_cat} that captures broad semantic patterns while accommodating substantial visual variability.

We categorize anomalies into five macro-level semantic groups: (1) *geo* for Geometry and shape deformation, (2) *color* for Color or photometric abnormalities, (3) *tex* for Texture irregularities and pattern distortions, (4) *surf* for Surface-level integrity damage (e.g., scratches, cracks, dents), and (5) *mat* for Material composition or foreign substance-related anomalies. The complete anomaly category set C_{ano} is defined as follows:

$$C_{ano} = \{C_{geo}, C_{color}, C_{tex}, C_{surf}, C_{mat}\}. \tag{1}$$

Each category contains a set of related textual concepts:

$$C_i = \{c_{i1}, c_{i2}, \ldots, c_{in_i}\}, \quad i \in \{geo,\ color,\ tex,\ surf,\ mat\}. \tag{2}$$

Each concept c_{ij} is embedded using the CLIP text encoder $E_{\text{txt}}(\cdot)$, and the prototype representation for category C_i is computed as:

$$p_i = \frac{1}{n_i} \sum_{j=1}^{n_i} E_{\text{txt}}(c_{ij}), \tag{3}$$

where p_i denotes the centroid embedding of category C_i. We generate approximately 30 concepts per category using GPT-4o, following concept-size guidelines from prior research [29,30].

3.2 Category-Level Pseudo-Labeling and Alignment Learning

Unlike general domain settings, CLIP shows weak alignment between anomaly-related concept texts and anomaly images [23]. Therefore, we adopt supervised category alignment using pseudo-labels instead of relying on direct concept inference. We generated pseudo-labels using the LLaVA-1.5-7B [22] model within a prompt instructing the model to assign one of the predefined anomaly categories. Providing this contextual information enables the model to more accurately infer the anomaly type.

Based on these pseudo-labels, we conduct alignment learning. Let $f = E_{\text{img}}(X)$ denote the image embedding extracted by the CLIP image encoder. The aligned anomaly category is predicted by maximizing cosine similarity:

$$\hat{y} = \arg\max_i \cos(f, p_i), \quad \cos(f, p_i) = \frac{f \cdot p_i}{||f||||p_i||}. \tag{4}$$

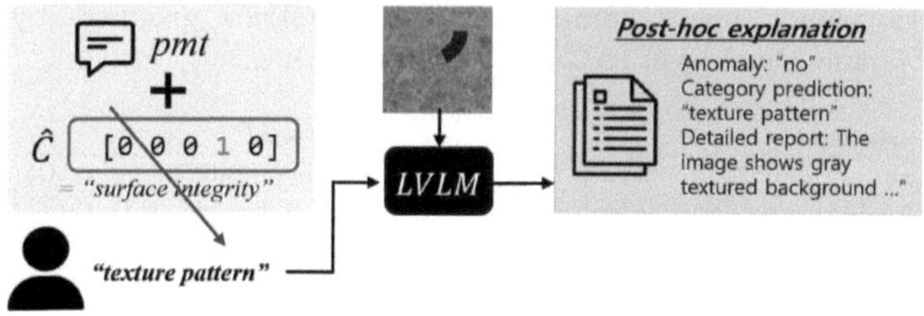

Fig. 2. Post-hoc user explanations for incorrectly predicted samples.

Therefore, the classification loss is computed using cross-entropy:

$$L_{\text{cat}} = -\sum_{i=1}^{N_c} y_i \log \sigma(\cos(f, p_i)). \tag{5}$$

3.3 Anomaly Localization via Prototype-Feature Similarity

Anomaly localization is performed by measuring the cosine similarity between the prototype embedding $p_{\hat{y}}$ and local image feature maps F_{local}:

$$H = \cos(F_{\text{local}}, p_{\hat{y}}), \tag{6}$$

where H denotes the anomaly heatmap. The localization loss is a combination of Dice loss [20] and Focal loss [21],

$$L_{\text{seg}} = L_{\text{Dice}}(H, M) + L_{\text{Focal}}(H, M). \tag{7}$$

where M represents the ground-truth mask. Therefore, the overall training objective is as follows:

$$L_{\text{total}} = L_{\text{cat}} + \lambda_{\text{seg}} L_{\text{seg}}. \tag{8}$$

3.4 Post-Hoc Explanation with User Intervention

During inference, our model generates: (1) the predicted anomaly category, (2) binary anomaly/normal decision, and (3) a localization heatmap. While the category prediction offers semantic interpretability, we further introduce a post-hoc explanation generation step using an LVLM. The LVLM takes the triplet $(X, \hat{C}, pmt)$, where $\hat{C}$ is the predicted category, and *pmt* is an instruction prompt, producing a natural-language explanation grounded in the model's anomaly reasoning.

To improve robustness and enable human-AI collaboration, we incorporate an optional user intervention mechanism (Fig. 2). If the predicted category is incorrect, the user may manually correct it, enabling the LVLM to regenerate a reliable explanation guided by the accurate category. This mechanism reinforces trust and flexibility of the overall system.

Table 1. Performance on in-domain datasets. Metrics grouped by Image-level (AUROC, AP%) and Pixel-level (AUROC, AUPRO%).

Task	*Image-level*				*Pixel-level*			
Method	VisA	MPDD	DAGM	DTD-Syn	VisA	MPDD	DAGM	DTD-Syn
CLIP-AC [9]	(65.0, 70.1)	(56.2, 66.0)	(82.5, 63.7)	(66.8, 83.2)	(47.8, 17.3)	(58.7, 29.1)	(32.7, 4.8)	(23.7, 5.5)
WinCLIP [17]	(78.1, 81.2)	(63.6, 69.9)	(91.8, 79.5)	(93.2, 92.6)	(79.6, 56.8)	(76.4, 48.9)	(87.6, 65.7)	(83.9, 57.8)
VAND [8]	(78.0, 81.4)	(73.0, 80.2)	(94.4, 83.8)	(86.4, 95.0)	(94.2, 86.8)	(94.1, 83.2)	(82.4, 66.2)	(95.3, 86.9)
AnomalyCLIP [36]	**(82.1, 85.4)**	(77.0, 82.0)	**(97.5, 92.3)**	(93.5, 97.0)	**(95.5, 87.0)**	(96.5, 88.7)	**(95.6, 91.0)**	**(97.9, 92.3)**
CONAN (Ours)	(79.6, 82.8)	**(77.6, 83.2)**	(96.5, 90.6)	**(94.8, 97.9)**	(94.4, 84.9)	**(96.6, 88.4)**	(95.0, 89.1)	(97.1, 90.2)

Table 2. Class-wise comparison on MVtec-AD2.

	Image-level		*Pixel-level*	
Class	AnomalyCLIP [36]	CONAN (Ours)	AnomalyCLIP [36]	**CONAN** (Ours)
can	(54.0, 56.6)	(56.1, 57.2)	(71.2, 25.8)	(54.1, 20.1)
fabric	(72.9, 80.6)	(77.2, 83.2)	(72.4, 36.7)	(72.8, 35.9)
fruit_jelly	(67.7, 88.5)	(62.8, 86.9)	(84.8, 58.3)	(85.5, 59.9)
rice	(72.6, 87.1)	(75.3, 88.2)	(89.3, 55.1)	(88.1, 46.6)
sheet_metal	(53.9, 84.7)	(60.7, 87.3)	(74.9, 9.5)	(68.7, 27.7)
vial	(52.1, 82.1)	(73.1, 91.3)	(88.4, 72.8)	(89.8, 71.5)
wallplugs	(41.1, 52.9)	(38.5, 52.7)	(83.0, 29.3)	(85.3, 41.7)
Mean	(59.2, 76.1)	**(63.4, 78.1)**	(**80.6**, 41.1)	(77.8, **43.4**)

4 Experiments

4.1 Experimental Setup

Datasets and Baselines. We conduct experiments on a broad collection of industrial and medical anomaly detection benchmarks. Following prior studies, we use the test split of MVTec AD [5]—an industrial anomaly dataset—as the source data for training. When evaluating on this set, we instead use the VisA test split as the training source to avoid overlap.

We first evaluate on in-domain industrial datasets: VisA [37], MPDD [6], DAGM [32], DTD-Synthetic [3] and MVTec2 [15]. These datasets encompass manufactured objects and surface defects, spanning variations in texture, noise, and anomaly appearance. We further evaluate on out-of-domain medical datasets: HeadCT, BrainMRI [7], and Br35H [14] are used for image-level classification, while ISIC [10], Kvasir [2], Endo [16], and TN3K [12] provide pixel-level annotations for segmentation. This setting enables evaluation across different anomaly types, including lesions, tissue irregularities, and organ-level boundaries. We employed four state-of-the-art CLIP-based anomaly detection baselines for our experiments.

Implementation Details. We follow the AnomalyCLIP configuration, initializing both the image and text encoders with the pretrained CLIP ViT-L/14

Table 3. Performance comparison on out-of-domain datasets. Metrics grouped by Image-level (AUROC, AP%) and Pixel-level (AUROC, AUPRO%).

Task	*Image-level*			*Pixel-level*			
Method	HeadCT	BrainMRI	Br35H	ISIC	Kvasir	Endo	TN3K
CLIP-AC [9]	(60.0, 60.7)	(80.6, 86.4)	(82.7, 81.3)	(36.0, 7.7)	(45.0, 16.8)	(46.6, 12.6)	(35.6, 5.2)
WinCLIP [17]	(81.8, 80.2)	(86.6, 91.5)	(80.5, 82.2)	(83.3, 55.1)	(69.7, 24.5)	(68.2, 28.3)	(70.7, 39.8)
VAND [8]	(89.1, 89.4)	(89.3, 90.9)	(93.1, 92.9)	(89.4, 77.2)	(75.0, 36.2)	(81.9, 54.9)	(73.6, 37.8)
AnomalyCLIP [36]	**(93.4, 91.6)**	(90.3, 92.2)	(94.6, 94.7)	(89.7, 78.4)	(78.9, 45.6)	(84.1, 63.6)	**(81.5, 50.4)**
CONAN (Ours)	(86.7, 84.9)	**(94.8, 96.1)**	**(95.7, 97.2)**	**(89.8, 80.3)**	**(82.1, 48.4)**	**(86.7, 84.9)**	(80.9, 48.6)

backbone. To preserve CLIP's prior knowledge while adapting to anomaly detection, we apply LoRA to both encoders and train only the low-rank adapters and newly added layers. Input images are resized to 518 $\times$ 518, and the model is trained with Adam using a batch size of 8 and a fixed learning rate of 1×10^{-3}. The segmentation loss weight λ_{seg} in Eq. (8) is set to 0.5. All models are trained for 15 epochs running on four NVIDIA RTX 3090 GPUs (24GB). For evaluation metric, we use AUROC and AP for image-level anomaly detection, and AUROC and AUPRO for pixel-level localization.

4.2 ZSAD Performance Results

Industrial Domains. Table 1 reports image- and pixel-level performance on four industrial benchmarks. Overall, CONAN shows competitive or superior results compared to existing CLIP-based methods.

For image-level classification, CONAN achieves the best scores on MPDD (77.6%, 83.2%) and DTD-Synthetic (94.8%, 97.9%), outperforming AnomalyCLIP on both datasets. On VisA and DAGM, CONAN is slightly behind AnomalyCLIP but clearly exceeds the remaining baselines. For pixel-level localization, CONAN maintains strong performance across all datasets. Although AnomalyCLIP records the highest overall scores, CONAN consistently outperforms the other baselines in both AUROC and AUPRO. These results indicate that category-level concept alignment supports robust recognition and localization while improving interpretability. Table 2 reports both image-level and pixel-level performance on the MVTec2 dataset, which includes particularly challenging classes due to images captured under diverse lighting conditions and a distribution that differs substantially from the original MVTec dataset. Despite these challenges, CONAN achieves an average improvement of 4.2% and 2.0% at the image level. At the pixel level, it shows a minor AUROC decrease of 2.4% on some classes but a 2.3% improvement on others. Overall, CONAN delivers performance that remains comparable to state-of-the-art black-box approaches, even under this difficult evaluation setting.

Medical Domains. Table 3 summarizes image-level and pixel-level results on seven medical benchmarks. CONAN demonstrates strong cross-domain generalization and remains competitive or superior to prior CLIP-based approaches.

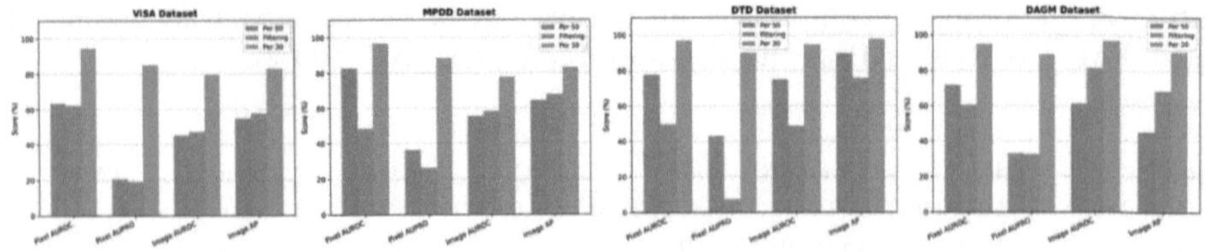

Fig. 3. Performance comparison by concept bank generation strategies.

Table 4. Evaluation of LVLM anomaly explanations with category guidance.

Dataset	Response	Acc.	Log.	Spec.	Rel.	Cat.	**Avg.**
VisA	LLaVA-1.5-7B [22]	3.4	5.0	4.8	5.2	2.8	4.2
	CONAN (Ours)	3.8	5.4	4.8	5.6	3.4	**4.6**
MPDD	LLaVA-1.5-7B [22]	6.0	6.8	6.0	7.2	5.8	**6.4**
	CONAN (Ours)	3.8	5.4	4.6	5.6	3.2	4.5
DAGM	LLaVA-1.5-7B [22]	5.8	6.6	5.8	6.4	5.2	6.0
	CONAN (Ours)	5.8	6.8	5.6	7.2	6.2	**6.3**
DTD	LLaVA-1.5-7B [22]	4.4	5.6	4.8	5.6	3.8	4.8
	CONAN (Ours)	4.6	6.4	5.4	6.4	4.2	**5.4**

For image-level classification, CONAN surpasses all baselines on BrainMRI and Br35H, with gains of 4.5%p (AUROC) and 3.9%p (AP) over AnomalyCLIP on BrainMRI. On HeadCT, it is slightly weaker than AnomalyCLIP but still clearly outperforms the remaining methods. For pixel-level localization, CONAN performs well across ISIC, Kvasir, Endo, and TN3K, and exceeds AnomalyCLIP on several datasets—for instance, by 3.2%p (AUROC) and 2.8%p (AUPRO) on Kvasir. These observations confirm that category-level alignment transfers effectively to medical domains by focusing on condition-centric anomaly characteristics rather than object identity.

4.3 Analysis on Different Concept Bank Designs

Figure 3 compares three strategies for constructing the anomaly concept bank on industrial benchmarks: (1) generating 50 concepts per category and directly averaging them into prototypes; (2) generating 50 concepts and filtering them by a cosine similarity threshold around the prototype; and (3) generating 30 concepts per category without additional filtering (our default).

Using 30 concepts per category provides the strongest performance, while adding too many concepts reduces category separability and harms learning. Filtering performs worst, likely because it removes essential semantic coverage. Overall, effective anomaly modeling depends on maintaining a balanced, sufficiently diverse concept set per category.

4.4 Evaluation on Post-Hoc Explanations

CONAN outputs anomaly scores, masks, and an explicit anomaly category, which can serve as a semantic anchor for post-hoc explanations. To assess the benefit of providing this category information, we compare explanations generated by LLaVA-1.5-7B in two settings: (1) using only the image, and (2) using both the image and the category predicted by CONAN. For each dataset, five images are randomly sampled and their explanations are evaluated by GPT-4o along five criteria: Accuracy (Acc.), Logical Coherence (Log.), Specificity (Spec.), Relevance (Rel.), and Category Classification Accuracy (Cat.). Table 4 summarizes the results for industrial datasets.

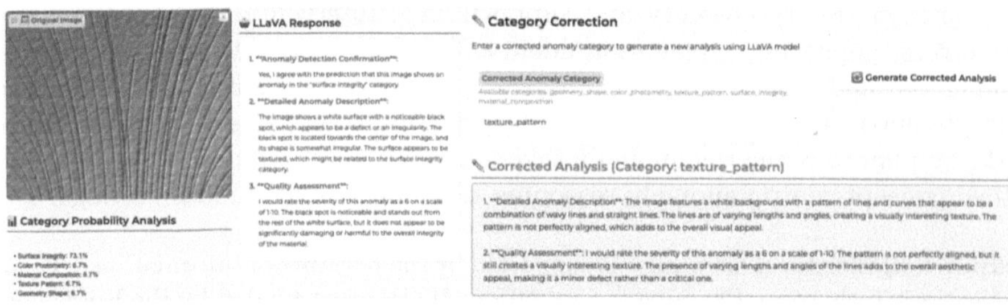

Fig. 4. User intervention example using gradio.

In three of the four datasets, providing CONAN's predicted category leads to higher overall explanation quality, indicating that the category acts as a helpful guidance signal for the LVLM. However, on MPDD, incorrect category predictions reduce explanation quality, emphasizing the need for optional user intervention when the predicted category is unreliable.

4.5 Case Study of User Intervention

We present a qualitative case study illustrating how user intervention can correct error cases and improve explanation quality. Figure 4 shows an example from an industrial dataset where the model initially predicts the category *surface integrity* for an image with subtle scratch-like line patterns on a cement surface. Using this predicted category, LLaVA generated an explanation that incorrectly describes a prominent "black spot" in the center of the image, which does not actually exist. By manually correcting the anomaly category from surface integrity to texture pattern, a human user enables the regenerated explanation to accurately focus on the irregular line structures, resulting in a more faithful and logically consistent description. This demonstrates that adjusting intermediate semantic representations provides an effective safeguard against error propagation and enhances the reliability of human–model interaction.

5 Conclusion

In this work, we addressed the opacity of zero-shot anomaly detection by introducing CONAN, a concept-oriented anomaly detection framework built around condition-centric anomaly concepts. We organized heterogeneous defects into a five-category concept bank, aligns CLIP image features with category prototypes using LVLM-generated pseudo-labels, and performs prototype-based localization under a joint classification–segmentation objective. Experiments on industrial and medical benchmarks showed that CONAN achieves competitive image and pixel-level performance compared to prior CLIP-based methods, while preserving cross-domain generalization. By exposing explicit anomaly categories and guiding LVLM-based explanations through these concepts, our framework provides intrinsic interpretability and supports user intervention to correct category errors, improving explanation fidelity. We plan to conduct future work for refining the anomaly taxonomy, mitigating pseudo-label noise, and extending concept-centric anomaly reasoning to broader multi-modal settings. In future work, we plan to refine the anomaly taxonomy, mitigate pseudo-label noise, and extend concept-centric anomaly reasoning to broader multi-modal settings.

Acknowledgments. This work was supported by the Institute of Information & Communications Technology Planning & Evaluation (IITP) grant funded by the Korea government (MSIT) [RS-2021- II211341, Artificial Intelligence Graduate School Program (Chung-Ang University)] and by the National Research Foundation of Korea (NRF) grant funded by the Korea government (MSIT) (RS-2025-00556246).

Disclosure of Interests. The authors have no competing interests to declare that are relevant to the content of this article.

References

1. Adebayo, J., Gilmer, J., Muelly, M., Goodfellow, I., Hardt, M., Kim, B.: Sanity checks for saliency maps. LLaVA **31**, (2018)
2. Ali, S., et al.: Polyp dataset (2022). https://figshare.com/articles/figure/Polyp_DataSet_zip/21221579, figshare dataset, Accessed 26 Nov 2025
3. Aota, T., Tong, L.T.T., Okatani, T.: Zero-shot versus many-shot: Unsupervised texture anomaly detection. In: Proceedings of the IEEE/CVF Winter Conference on Applications of Computer Vision, pp. 5564–5572 (2023)
4. Bergmann, P., Batzner, K., Fauser, M., Sattlegger, D., Steger, C.: The MVTec anomaly detection dataset: a comprehensive real-world dataset for unsupervised anomaly detection. Int. J. Comput. Vision **129**(4), 1038–1059 (2021)
5. Bergmann, P., Fauser, M., Sattlegger, D., Steger, C.: Mvtec ad–a comprehensive real-world dataset for unsupervised anomaly detection. In: CVPR (2019)
6. Bergmann, P., Jin, X., Sattlegger, D., Steger, C.: The MVTec 3D-ad dataset for unsupervised 3D anomaly detection and localization. In: Proceedings of the 17th International Joint Conference on Computer Vision, Imaging and Computer Graphics Theory and Applications (VISIGRAPP 2022) - Volume 5: VISAPP, pp. 202–213. INSTICC, SciTePress (2022). https://doi.org/10.5220/0010865000003124

7. Chakrabarty, N.: Brain MRI images for brain tumor detection (2017). https://www.kaggle.com/datasets/navoneel/brain-mri-images-for-brain-tumor-detection, kaggle dataset, Accessed 26 Nov 2025
8. Chen, X., Han, Y., Zhang, J.: April-gan: A zero-/few-shot anomaly classification and segmentation method for CVPR 2023 vand workshop challenge tracks 1&2: 1st place on zero-shot ad and 4th place on few-shot ad. arXiv preprint arXiv:2305.17382 (2023)
9. Chen, X., et al.: Clip-ad: A language-guided staged dual-path model for zero-shot anomaly detection. In: International Joint Conference on Artificial Intelligence, pp. 17–33. Springer (2024)
10. Codella, N., et al.: Skin lesion analysis toward melanoma detection 2018: A challenge hosted by the international skin imaging collaboration (isic). arXiv preprint arXiv:1902.03368 (2019)
11. Defard, T., Setkov, A., Loesch, A., Audigier, R.: Padim: a patch distribution modeling framework for anomaly detection and localization. In: International Conference on Pattern Recognition, pp. 475–489. Springer (2021)
12. Gong, H., Chen, J., Chen, G., Li, H., Chen, F., Li, G.: Tn3k: Thyroid nodule ultrasound image dataset (2022). https://github.com/haifangong/TRFE-Net-for-thyroid-nodule-segmentation, open-access dataset (3493 ultrasound images). Accessed 26 Nov 2025
13. Gu, Z., Zhu, B., Zhu, G., Chen, Y., Tang, M., Wang, J.: Anomalygpt: detecting industrial anomalies using large vision-language models. In: Proceedings of the AAAI Conference on Artificial Intelligence. vol. 38, pp. 1932–1940 (2024)
14. Hamada, A.: Br35h: Brain tumor detection (2020). https://www.kaggle.com/datasets/ahmedhamada0/brain-tumor-detection, kaggle dataset. Accessed 26 Nov 2025
15. Heckler-Kram, L., Neudeck, J.H., Scheler, U., König, R., Steger, C.: The mvtec ad 2 dataset: Advanced scenarios for unsupervised anomaly detection. arXiv preprint arXiv:2503.21622 (2025)
16. Hicks, S.A., Jha, D., Thambawita, V., Halvorsen, P., Hammer, H.L., Riegler, M.A.: The endotect 2020 challenge: evaluation and comparison of classification, segmentation and inference time for endoscopy. In: International Conference on Pattern Recognition, pp. 263–274. Springer (2021)
17. Jeong, J., Zou, Y., Kim, T., Zhang, D., Ravichandran, A., Dabeer, O.: Winclip: Zero-/few-shot anomaly classification and segmentation. In: Proceedings of the IEEE/CVF Conference on Computer Vision and Pattern Recognition, pp. 19606–19616 (2023)
18. Ji, Z., et al.: Survey of hallucination in natural language generation. ACM Comput. Surv. **55**(12), 1–38 (2023)
19. Koh, P.W., Nguyen, T., Tang, Y.S., Mussmann, S., Pierson, E., Kim, B., Liang, P.: Concept bottleneck models. In: International conference on machine learning, pp. 5338–5348. PMLR (2020)
20. Li, X., Sun, X., Meng, Y., Liang, J., Wu, F., Li, J.: Dice loss for data-imbalanced NLP tasks. In: Proceedings of the 58th Annual Meeting of the Association for Computational Linguistics, pp. 465–476 (2020)
21. Lin, T.Y., Goyal, P., Girshick, R., He, K., Dollár, P.: Focal loss for dense object detection. In: Proceedings of the IEEE International Conference on Computer Vision, pp. 2980–2988 (2017)
22. Liu, H., Li, C., Wu, Q., Lee, Y.J.: Visual instruction tuning. Adv. Neural. Inf. Process. Syst. **36**, 34892–34916 (2023)

23. Ma, W., et al.: Aa-clip: Enhancing zero-shot anomaly detection via anomaly-aware clip. In: Proceedings of the IEEE/CVF Conference on Computer Vision and Pattern Recognition, pp. 4744–4754 (2025)
24. Radford, A., et al.: Learning transferable visual models from natural language supervision. In: International Conference on Machine Learning, pp. 8748–8763. PMLR (2021)
25. Roth, K., Pemula, L., Zepeda, J., Schölkopf, B., Brox, T., Gehler, P.: Towards total recall in industrial anomaly detection. In: Proceedings of the IEEE/CVF Conference on Computer Vision and Pattern Recognition, pp. 14318–14328 (2022)
26. Ruff, L.: A unifying review of deep and shallow anomaly detection. Proc. IEEE **109**(5), 756–795 (2021)
27. Sakurada, M., Yairi, T.: Anomaly detection using autoencoders with nonlinear dimensionality reduction. In: Proceedings of the MLSDA 2014 2nd Workshop on Machine Learning for Sensory Data Analysis, pp. 4–11 (2014)
28. Selvaraju, R.R., Cogswell, M., Das, A., Vedantam, R., Parikh, D., Batra, D.: Grad-cam: Visual explanations from deep networks via gradient-based localization. In: Proceedings of the IEEE International Conference on Computer Vision (Oct 2017)
29. Shang, C., Zhou, S., Zhang, H., Ni, X., Yang, Y., Wang, Y.: Incremental residual concept bottleneck models. In: Proceedings of the IEEE/CVF Conference on Computer Vision and Pattern Recognition, pp. 11030–11040 (2024)
30. Srivastava, D., Yan, G., Weng, L.: VLG-CBM: training concept bottleneck models with vision-language guidance. Adv. Neural. Inf. Process. Syst. **37**, 79057–79094 (2024)
31. Tao, X., Gong, X., Zhang, X., Yan, S., Adak, C.: Deep learning for unsupervised anomaly localization in industrial images: a survey. IEEE Trans. Instrum. Meas. **71**, 1–21 (2022)
32. Wieler, M., Hahn, T., Hamprecht, F.A.: Weakly supervised learning for industrial opticalinspection (Sept. 2007). https://doi.org/10.5281/zenodo.12750201
33. Xie, C., et al.: Fg-clip: Fine-grained visual and textual alignment. In: International Conference on Machine Learning (2025)
34. Xu, J., Lo, S.Y., Safaei, B., Patel, V.M., Dwivedi, I.: Towards zero-shot anomaly detection and reasoning with multimodal large language models. In: Proceedings of the IEEE/CVF Conference on Computer Vision and Pattern Recognition, pp. 20370–20382 (2025)
35. Zhou, K., Yang, J., Loy, C.C., Liu, Z.: Learning to prompt for vision-language models. Int. J. Comput. Vision **130**(9), 2337–2348 (2022)
36. Zhou, Q., Pang, G., Tian, Y., He, S., Chen, J.: Anomalyclip: Object-agnostic prompt learning for zero-shot anomaly detection. arXiv preprint arXiv:2310.18961 (2023)
37. Zou, Y., Jeong, J., Pemula, L., Zhang, D., Dabeer, O.: Spot-the-difference selfsupervised pre-training for anomaly detection and segmentation. In: European Conference on Computer Vision, pp. 392–408. Springer (2022)

Survey Track

Automated Multiple-Choice Question Generation: A Survey from a KDDM Perspective

Nan Mu and Tsunenori Mine(✉)

Kyushu University, Fukuoka, Japan
mine@ait.kyushu-u.ac.jp

Abstract. Recent large language models (LLMs) have greatly improved automated multiple-choice question (MCQ) generation. However, in real educational systems, MCQ generation is not only a text generation problem. It is also a structured data generation process that must consider cognitive levels, distractor quality, and learner interaction.

In this survey, we study automated MCQ generation from a Knowledge Discovery and Data Mining (KDDM) perspective. Instead of organizing prior work by task components, we propose a three-dimensional framework that includes: (1) cognitive-level alignment, (2) structured distractor modeling, and (3) learner feedback loops. This framework helps us analyze how different components interact with each other and what trade-offs may exist in real systems.

Based on this framework, we review recent methods, benchmark datasets, and evaluation metrics. We also discuss current limitations, especially the gap between linguistic evaluation metrics and real pedagogical effectiveness. Finally, we highlight open challenges and suggest directions for building more reliable and adaptive MCQ generation systems.

Keywords: Automated MCQ Generation · Knowledge Discovery · Large Language Models · Educational Data Mining

1 Introduction

Automated multiple-choice question (MCQ) generation has recently attracted increasing attention with the rapid development of large language models (LLMs). Existing approaches have demonstrated strong capabilities in generating fluent and contextually coherent questions. However, most studies formulate MCQ generation primarily as a conditional text generation problem, focusing on linguistic quality and task-specific performance metrics. This formulation overlooks several core data mining challenges inherent in assessment design, such as structured knowledge representation, informative negative sampling, and adaptive decision-making under learner feedback.

R. C.-W. Wong et al. (Eds.): PAKDD 2026, LNAI 16618, pp. 563–580, 2027.
https://doi.org/10.1007/978-981-92-1947-6_45

From a Knowledge Discovery and Data Mining (KDDM) perspective, MCQ generation can be understood as an end-to-end structured pipeline. Given unstructured educational content, a system must (i) extract and represent relevant conceptual structures, (ii) construct diagnostically meaningful distractors that function as informative negative samples, and (iii) update generation strategies based on learner interaction signals. These stages correspond to fundamental data mining problems including representation learning, negative mining, and sequential decision modeling. Treating MCQ generation as isolated NLP sub-tasks makes it difficult to analyze how these components interact within a real assessment system.

Although prior surveys (e.g., [14,21]) provide valuable overviews of question generation techniques, they primarily organize methods by model architectures or NLP sub-tasks. As a result, cross-dimensional interactions among cognitive control, distractor structure, and adaptivity remain underexplored. In particular, key questions such as how distractors can be modeled as structured negative samples, and how feedback loops alter generation objectives over time, have not been systematically analyzed from a unified data mining perspective.

To address this gap, we introduce a KDDM-informed analytical framework that organizes automated MCQ generation along three interrelated dimensions: (1) cognitive-level alignment, (2) structured distractor modeling, and (3) learner feedback loops. Based on this framework, we analyze 42 representative studies, benchmark datasets, and evaluation practices. Our objective is not to propose a new generation model, but to clarify structural trade-offs, modeling assumptions, and unresolved challenges in current research.

Our contributions are threefold:

KDDM-Centric Analytical Framework. We formalize automated MCQ generation as a structured knowledge discovery process and propose a three-dimensional taxonomy grounded in data mining principles.

Cross-Dimensional Comparative Analysis. Using this taxonomy, we conduct a structured synthesis of representative approaches and highlight interactions and trade-offs that are not visible in task-based categorizations.

Evaluation Gap Identification. We analyze the mismatch between commonly used surface-level generation metrics and downstream assessment utility, and outline research directions toward controllable and adaptive assessment systems.

2 Survey Methodology

We performed a structured literature search across ACM, IEEE, SpringerLink, ACL Anthology, Google Scholar, and arXiv using keyword combinations related to MCQ generation, distractors, cognitive alignment, learner modeling, and

LLMs. We included studies with clear educational relevance and empirical evaluation, and coded the retained papers along the three KDDM dimensions.

To guide our structured analysis, we formulate four research questions (RQs) that shape the survey:

RQ1: How do existing methods operationalize cognitive-level alignment in automated MCQ generation?

RQ2: How are distractors modeled as structured and diagnostically meaningful negative samples?

RQ3: To what extent are learner feedback loops integrated into generation frameworks?

RQ4: How are current evaluation practices aligned with pedagogical effectiveness?

These RQs directly correspond to the three-dimensional KDDM framework and structure the methodological and evaluation analysis presented in subsequent sections.

3 Background and Problem Formulation

3.1 Task Description

From the perspective of KDDM, automated multiple-choice question generation involves transforming unstructured educational content into structured assessment items, which typically requires knowledge extraction and grounding as supporting processes. It aims to transform an unstructured text corpus, C, into a set of structured questions, $Q = \{q_1, q_2, \ldots, q_n\}$. Each individual MCQ, $q_i \in Q$, is a structured tuple that consists of four key components:

$$q = (c, s, a_{correct}, D) \tag{1}$$

where $c \in C$ is the source context passage; s is the question stem; $a_{correct}$ is the single, unambiguous correct answer; and $D = \{d_1, d_2, \ldots, d_m\}$ is a set of m plausible yet incorrect distractors.

From the perspective of KDDM, achieving high instructional value requires addressing challenges in three key and often conflicting dimensions: **(1) Cognitive Level Alignment**, ensuring that the complexity of generated questions matches the learning level; **(2) Structured Distractor Modeling**, involving the generation of reasonable error options with diagnostic value; and **(3) Learner Feedback Loops**, enabling the system to adapt and personalize content. This survey systematically analyzes how state-of-the-art methodologies address the trade-offs within and between these three dimensions, as visualized in our proposed framework in Fig. 1.

3.2 Foundational Theories

To evaluate the pedagogical value of the generated multiple-choice questions, our analysis is based on two recognized theories of education and psychometrics. These theories are not merely for post-evaluation of the questions; they

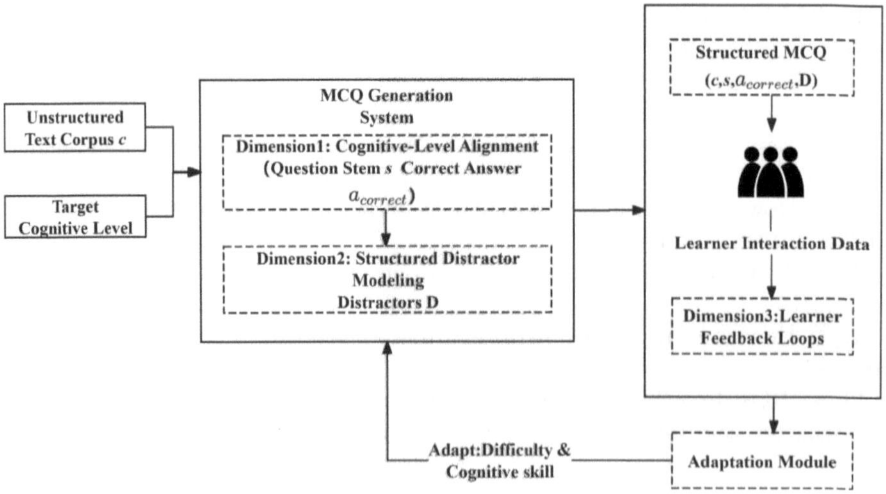

Fig. 1. The proposed KDDM-centric framework for automated MCQ generation. The process is deconstructed into three dimensions: (1) **Cognitive-Level Alignment** (Dimension 1) and **Structured Distractor Modeling** (Dimension 2) for initial generation, and (3) **Learner Feedback Loops** (Dimension 3), which uses an **Adaptation Module** to create two feedback signals: a macro-loop to adjust overall difficulty (Adapt:Difficulty) and a micro-loop to target specific misconceptions (Adapt:Misconception).

provide key constraints for our model design from the outset and also form the fundamental basis for defining our optimization objective.

- **Bloom's Taxonomy:** provides a hierarchical classification of cognitive skills (e.g., Remembering to Analyzing) [3]. Within the KDDM framework, it functions as a controllability constraint, requiring MCQ generation systems to align outputs with predefined cognitive levels.
- **Item Response Theory (IRT):** models the relationship between learner ability and item responses [17]. Within our framework, it provides a formal basis for designing discriminative distractors that differentiate learners by ability, thereby supporting diagnostic modeling and adaptive feedback.

The development and evaluation of automated multiple-choice question generation systems heavily rely on public datasets. These datasets serve two main purposes: they provide samples for knowledge extraction and serve as standards for evaluating the quality of generated questions. This section summarizes the key datasets commonly used in this field and provides a comparative overview in Table 1.

Several benchmark datasets are widely used for automated MCQ generation, including RACE [22], SQuAD [34], ARC [12], OpenBookQA [28], SciQ [41], and BoolQ [11]. These datasets vary in scale, reasoning complexity, and domain coverage. Some emphasize fact-based extraction (e.g., SQuAD), while others require multi-hop reasoning or distractor construction (e.g., ARC, SciQ). Table 1 summarizes their characteristics and associated KDDM challenges. Most existing benchmark datasets, however, lack explicit annotations for cognitive levels or distractor difficulty tiers, and rarely provide longitudinal learner interaction logs. This structural limitation restricts rigorous evaluation of controllable generation and adaptive modeling under the proposed KDDM framework.

Table 1. A summary of benchmark datasets for automated MCQ generation and their associated KDDM challenges.

Dataset	Field	Size (Q)	Primary Task Focus	Key KDDM Challenges
RACE [22]	Science	~100K	Reading comprehension QA	Long-range dependencies, sparse evidence
SQuAD [34]	General	~100K	Fact-based QA	Crowdsourcing noise, distributional bias
ARC [12]	Science	~7.6K	Reasoning QA	External knowledge integration, robustness
OpenBookQA [28]	Science	~6K	Knowledge-based QA	Multi-hop reasoning, knowledge application
SciQ [41]	Science	~13.7K	MCQ generation	Distractor generation, spurious correlations
BoolQ [11]	General	~16K	Yes/No QA	Inferential reasoning, ambiguity handling

Building on the task formulation, foundational theories, and benchmark datasets introduced above, we now turn to a systematic review of existing methodologies for automated MCQ generation. We organize these approaches according to the three KDDM dimensions proposed in this survey.

4 Methodologies for Automated MCQ Generation

Guided by the proposed KDDM-centric framework, this section reviews existing automated MCQ generation approaches through the lens of three core dimensions: cognitive-level alignment, structured distractor modeling, and learner feedback loops. Rather than organizing methods by model architectures or isolated NLP sub-tasks, we categorize prior work according to the pedagogical objectives they aim to support and the corresponding data mining challenges they attempt to address. This framework-driven organization enables a unified analysis of heterogeneous approaches and highlights systematic gaps across different dimensions of educational effectiveness.

As illustrated in Fig. 2, the surveyed methods are grouped based on their primary methodological focus within these three dimensions, providing a structured foundation for the detailed analyses that follow.

4.1 Methodologies for Cognitive-Level Alignment

This subsection addresses RQ1 by examining how existing approaches operationalize cognitive-level control in automated MCQ generation. From a KDDM perspective, cognitive-level alignment represents a fundamental challenge in automated MCQ generation, as it requires explicit control over the pedagogical complexity of generated questions rather than surface-level linguistic variation. Current research on this problem can be broadly categorized into three methods: prompt-based methods, supervised fine-tuning, and knowledge graph (KG) augmented generation.

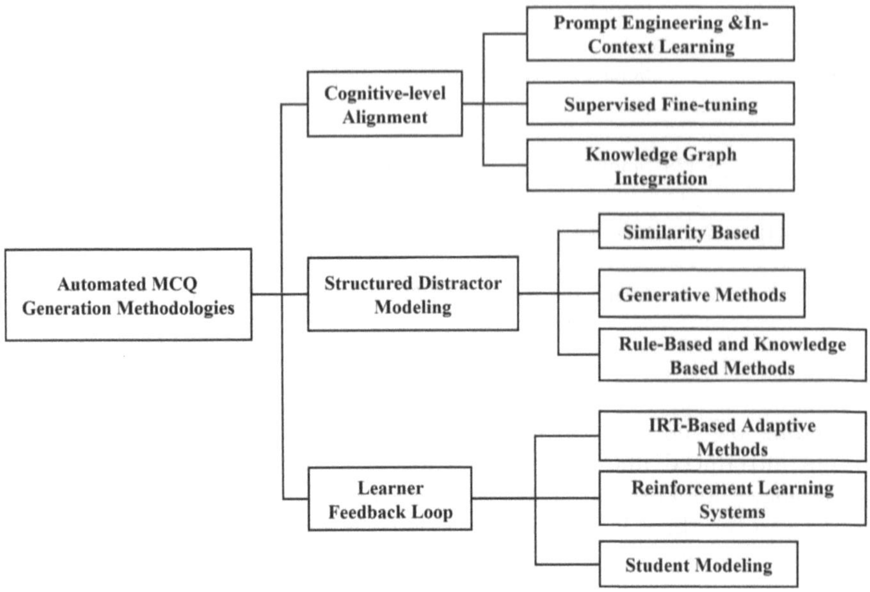

Fig. 2. The proposed taxonomy of automated MCQ generation methodologies, categorized by the three core KDDM dimensions.

Prompt Engineering and In-Context Learning. This method leverages the context learning capabilities of large-scale pre-trained language models (LLMs), such as GPT-3 and GPT-4 [6]. This approach does not retrain the model, but instead relies on carefully crafted cues. These cues act as explicit instructions, constraining the desired output features [19]. For example, a prompt might include a directive such as, "*Based on the provided text, generate a multiple-choice question that requires a test-taker to* ***analyze*** *the cause-and-effect relationship between events.*" Few-shot examples can further enhance this process by providing the model with high-quality examples that correspond to the target cognitive level. **Strengths:** High flexibility; leverages LLM world knowledge; requires no labeled datasets. **Limitations:** Lacks explicit optimization signals for cognitive-level control, making difficulty calibration unstable and evaluation largely reliant on human judgment; performance is highly prompt- and model-version-dependent.

Supervised Fine-Tuning. Another paradigm involves fine-tuning smaller pre-trained encoder–decoder models, such as T5 or BART, on custom datasets curated specifically for this task. These datasets contain question–answer pairs explicitly annotated with their corresponding cognitive levels defined by Bloom's taxonomy. The model is then trained in a supervised manner to learn a mapping from the given context and target cognitive level to the appropriate question structure. **Strengths:** High task-specific performance and stability; computationally efficient at inference. **Limitations:** Requires large, consistently annotated datasets; performance and transferability are highly sensitive to annotation quality and the granularity of cognitive-level labels, which are costly and inherently subjective.

Knowledge Graph Integration. This family of methods grounds the generation process in external, structured knowledge sources such as knowledge graphs (KGs) like ConceptNet[1] or domain-specific ontologies [8]. The cognitive complexity of a question is often associated with the reasoning depth required within the KG. For instance, a question answerable through retrieving a single fact (a one-hop path) typically corresponds to the Remembering level, whereas a question requiring traversal of multiple relational paths to infer new connections aligns with the Analyzing level. This model aims to generate questions that reflect these different reasoning structures. **Strengths:** KG grounding provides explicit reasoning structures for controllable, interpretable question generation, and can support higher-order cognitive prompts via multi-hop constraints. **Limitations:** Performance is bounded by KG coverage, noise, and schema mismatch with educational content; mapping reasoning depth to Bloom levels is an imperfect proxy and often domain-dependent.

4.2 Methodologies for Structured Distractor Modeling

This subsection corresponds to RQ2, focusing on how distractors are modeled as structured and diagnostically meaningful negative samples. Structured distractor modeling constitutes the second core dimension of the proposed KDDM

[1] https://conceptnet.io/.

framework and plays a central role in determining the diagnostic value of automatically generated MCQs [32]. From an educational data mining perspective, distractors are not merely incorrect options but represent structured manifestations of learners' misconceptions or reasoning errors. Consequently, the quality of distractors directly affects the extent to which response patterns can be mined to infer learners' cognitive states, rather than simply measuring correctness.

Unlike stem or answer generation, which primarily targets content validity, distractor modeling introduces a distinct data mining challenge: generating plausible yet systematically informative negative samples. This section reviews existing approaches to distractor generation through this diagnostic lens, analyzing how different methods attempt to balance plausibility, diversity, and pedagogical interpretability [32] (Fig. 3).

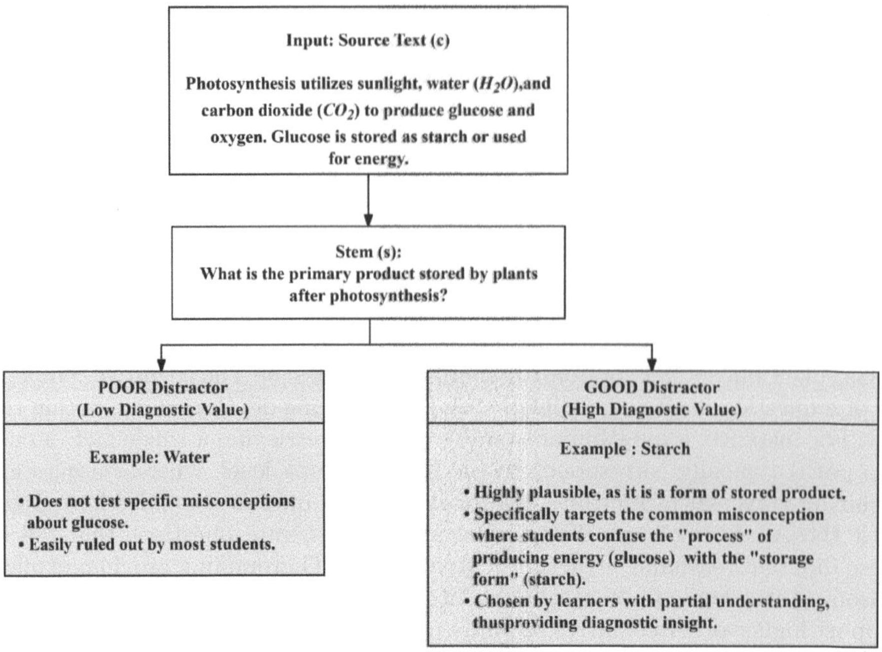

Fig. 3. An example illustrating the concept of "Diagnostic Value" in distractor modeling. The poor distractor (Water) is merely a related term, while the good distractor (Starch) is highly plausible and targets a common student misconception.

Similarity-Based Methods. Early and foundational approaches to distractor generation often rely on measuring semantic similarity. The core idea is to identify candidate distractors from large text corpora or lexical databases (e.g., WordNet) that are semantically close to the correct answer, $a_{correct}$, but not identical to it. This is typically achieved using word embedding models such as Word2Vec or GloVe to locate the nearest neighbors of the correct answer in the vector space, or by identifying entities of the same semantic type. Common techniques include leveraging WordNet for synonyms/antonyms or using Named Entity Recognition (NER) to find entities of the same type (e.g., replacing one city name with another). **Strengths:** Conceptually simple; generates semantically relevant options. **Limitations:** Fails to capture deep cognitive misdirection; produces only synonyms or related terms, lacking true diagnostic value.

Generative Methods. The paradigm for distractor generation has shifted from traditional methods to neural generative models, evolving from early sequence-to-sequence (Seq2Seq) architectures to modern pre-trained sequence-to-sequence models (e.g., T5 and BART) and large language models (e.g., GPT-style models). These models are conditioned on the source context c, the question stem s, and the correct answer $a_{correct}$, and are trained or prompted to generate distractor text from scratch. **Strengths:** Enables diverse and context-sensitive distractor generation by leveraging large-scale pre-trained knowledge. **Limitations:** Lacks explicit mechanisms to control diagnostic properties or error taxonomy, making alignment with cognitive and psychometric objectives difficult; generation quality is also sensitive to prompting and decoding strategies.

Rule-Based and Knowledge-Based Methods. This family of methods leverages predefined linguistic rules or structured knowledge, such as ontologies and knowledge graphs (KGs), to generate distractors. The core idea is to transform the correct answer or related sentences into incorrect options. Simple rules include retrieving and replacing a keyword with its antonym, hypernym, or hyponym from a KG. More complex rules might involve negating a verb, swapping the subject and object, or reversing a causal relationship to create a logically flawed distractor. Examples of rules include negating verbs, swapping subject and object in a sentence, or replacing concepts with their hypernyms or hyponyms retrieved from an ontology. **Strengths:** High degree of controllability and interpretability; can target specific misconceptions [1]. **Limitations:** Brittle and lacks scalability; requires significant manual effort and domain expertise.

4.3 Methodologies for Learner Feedback Loops

This subsection addresses RQ3 by analyzing mechanisms that incorporate learner interaction signals into the generation process. Learner feedback loops are the third dimension of our KDDM framework, framing MCQ generation as a closed-loop process embedded in adaptive tutoring systems. Learner responses (e.g., correctness, time, and error patterns) are treated as streaming signals to update learner models and guide subsequent generation.

Existing work on learner feedback loops can be broadly categorized according to the internal mechanisms used to operationalize such closed-loop adaptivity. In the following, we review three representative methodological paradigms: (1) psychometric-driven adaptive systems based on Item Response Theory [26],

(2) reinforcement learning approaches that formulate generation as a sequential decision-making problem, and (3) student modeling methods that explicitly represent learners' knowledge states and misconceptions [13].

IRT-Based Adaptive Systems. This method applies the IRT framework [26] to adaptive problem generation. The system maintains an estimate of a learner's ability (θ), updates it after a response, and then tasks the generator to create a new question q with parameters (e.g., difficulty) optimally matched to the learner's updated ability [26]. This process is the foundation of Computerized Adaptive Testing (CAT), which offers a principled, quantifiable adaptation method based on robust psychometric theory (IRT). CAT's limitation is its assumption of a static, pre-calibrated item bank. This assumption breaks with "dynamic item generation," creating a challenge: CAT's core strategy (selecting the item that maximizes Fisher information) depends entirely on known parameters. How to dynamically estimate parameters for "new" items and integrate them into this strategy remains a key open question [26].

Reinforcement Learning Approaches. This paradigm treats the adaptive generation process as a reinforcement learning (RL) problem [2,24]. In this formulation, the MCQ generation system is the agent; the learner's current knowledge model is the state; generating a specific question type is the action; and the signal obtained from the student's response (e.g., correctness, response time) is the reward. The agent's goal is to learn an optimal generation Policy that maximizes a long-term cumulative reward, which is ideally positively correlated with the student's learning outcome [2,24]. Learns adaptive generation strategies from interaction data, but depends on data scale and reward alignment for pedagogically meaningful optimization.

Student Modeling Approaches. This family of methods focuses on building and maintaining a detailed, explicit model of the learner's knowledge state, a practice central to Intelligent Tutoring Systems (ITS). This "student model" can be a vector representing the mastery probability for different knowledge components (a technique known as Knowledge Tracing) or an overlay on a domain knowledge graph. Techniques range from Bayesian Knowledge Tracing (BKT) to deep learning models like Deep Knowledge Tracing (DKT) [31], which focus on predicting future performance but may offer less interpretable diagnostic insights compared to traditional Cognitive Diagnosis Models (CDMs) discussed by Wang et al. (2024) [13,39]. After a student answers a question, the system updates its belief about which concepts the student has mastered or is struggling with.

In this model, the system first identifies students' knowledge gaps, or "zones of proximal development" (ZPDs), and then generates questions specifically addressing these gaps. This approach has two significant advantages: it offers high interpretability; and it ensures that the generated content closely aligns with the learning objectives (i.e., targets weaknesses). The main limitation of this approach is its heavy reliance on predefined domain knowledge structures (e.g., concept maps), which are typically costly to construct.

While the reviewed methods demonstrate promising capabilities across different dimensions, their evaluation practices vary substantially. In the following section, we examine how existing work assesses the quality and educational effectiveness of generated MCQs, and highlight key limitations of current evaluation protocols.

5 Evaluation Practices and Empirical Comparisons

This section addresses RQ4 by examining how current evaluation protocols align with pedagogical effectiveness.

5.1 Evaluation Metrics

Automated Metrics. Automated metrics provide a scalable and repeatable evaluation method. Based on their focus, these metrics can be broadly divided into two categories: one focusing on language quality and the other on the effectiveness of a specific task.

- **Linguistic Quality:** n-gram metrics (e.g., BLEU [30]) and embedding-based metrics (e.g., BERTScore [42]).
- **Task-Specific Validity:** QA models for "answerability checks" or Distractor Plausibility Scores. Other metrics quantify distractor quality via PMI with error logs or using proxy student models [25].

Critical Analysis: While automated metrics are crucial for system development, they still have many limitations in measuring the core issue of "instructional value." For example, high n-gram overlap scores (e.g., BLEU) only indicate surface similarity and do not guarantee the intended cognitive complexity [30]; similarly, simple quality assurance (QA) checks cannot determine whether distractors truly have diagnostic value. This "gap" between automated assessment and actual teaching effectiveness precisely highlights the necessity of human evaluation at this stage—human evaluation remains indispensable.

Human Evaluation. Human evaluation remains the gold standard, where experts score dimensions like **Logical Rationality** and **Distractor Quality** [19,27]. It remains a major bottleneck, not only because it is subjective, costly, and time-consuming. A more critical challenge lies in ensuring consistency among different raters; and designing a robust set of evaluation criteria is equally challenging.

5.2 Performance Comparison on Benchmark Datasets

This section provides a comparative analysis of the state-of-the-art methods. We summarize their publicly reported results in commonly used benchmark tests (Table 2). It is important to note that conducting direct and completely fair comparisons is extremely challenging, primarily due to significant differences in experimental setups and evaluation protocols among different studies. Although the reported scores are not directly comparable, some trends can still be observed. Therefore, Table 2 should be interpreted as a landscape summary of methodological tendencies rather than evidence of superiority across architectures. Fine-tuning methods often perform better on domain-specific datasets due to distributional alignment, while prompt-based LLM approaches rely more heavily on human evaluation for cognitive alignment and distractor plausibility. This reflects the absence of standardized, pedagogically grounded evaluation protocols. More fundamentally, current benchmarks lack explicit annotations for cognitive levels, distractor difficulty tiers, or learner interaction traces. This structural limitation constrains rigorous evaluation of controllability and adaptive performance under the proposed KDDM framework.

Table 2. Empirical Performance of State-of-the-Art Methods on Key Sub-tasks. Note that scores are reported under different datasets and evaluation protocols, and are not directly comparable.

Reference	Focus	Dataset	Metric	Score
Vachev et al. (2022) [38]	MCQ Gen (Fine-tuning)	RACE	BLEU-4 ROUGE-L	e.g., 17.5/43.1
Hwang et al. (2023) [19]	Cognitive Align. (LLM)	OpenStax Textbooks	Human Eval	up to 78%
Saddish et al. (2023). [35]	Stem+Distractor (Fine-tuning)	Indian texts	F1 Score	48.58
Luo et al. (2024) [27]	Distractor Gen. (Multimodal)	ScienceQA	Human Eval	4.89/5.0
Chen & Shiu (2025) [8]	Difficulty Control (KG+IRT)	ACT Passages	Accuracy	71% (Medium)

5.3 Discussion: KDDM Insights and Implications

In our KDDM framework, knowledge extraction and grounding are treated as enabling processes for cognitive-level alignment. In practice, pedagogical signals (e.g., concepts, relations, and reasoning structures) must be extracted from source materials to support controllable question generation.

Table 3 suggests that recent work mainly emphasizes cognitively aligned generation and distractor-oriented negative mining via LLM prompting or generation (e.g., [5,16,36]), whereas fewer studies instantiate a complete learner

Table 3. A classification of state-of-the-art methods based on the proposed KDDM framework. Abbreviations: PE (Prompt Engineering), FT (Fine-tuning), KG (Knowledge Graph), Sim. (Similarity-based), Gen. (Generative), RB (Rule-based), IRT (Item Response Theory), RL (Reinforcement Learning), SM (Student Model).

Reference	Backbone	Knowledge Extraction			Negative Mining			Adaptive Modeling		
		PE	FT	KG	Sim.	Gen.	RB	IRT	RL	SM
Vachev et al. [38] (2022)	T5+Sense2Vec		✓		✓	✓				
Dijkstra et al. [16] (2022)	GPT-3	✓				✓				
Chughtai et al. [10] (2022)	BERT + WordNet				✓		✓			
Dhanya et al. [15] (2022)	T5+Sense2Vec		✓		✓					
Saddish et al. [35] (2023)	T5		✓			✓				
Bitew et al. [5] (2023)	mT5	✓				✓				
Li et al. [24] (2023)	Deep RL								✓	
Amin et al. [2] (2023)	Deep RL								✓	
Scaria et al. [36] (2024)	GPT-3.5	✓				✓				
Hang et al. [18] (2024)	GPT-3.5/GPT-4	✓				✓				✓
Cavusoglu et al. [7] (2024)	Transformer		✓			✓				
Biancini et al. [4] (2024)	GPT-3.5	✓				✓				
Jasuja et al. [20] (2024)	T5		✓			✓				
R S et al. [33] (2025)	Conversational AI									✓
Chen & Shiu [8] (2025)	KG+RAG	✓		✓		✓		✓		
Mucciaccia et al. [29] (2025)	GPT-3.5-Turbo	✓				✓				
Shirkar et al. [37] (2025)	Transformer	✓				✓				
Chen et al. [9] (2025)	GPT-3.5/GPT-4	✓				✓				

feedback loop with adaptive modeling (e.g., [2,24]). This framing enables new research questions, such as how controllability in cognitive alignment interacts with diagnostic validity in distractor modeling under adaptive constraints. This imbalance indicates that closed-loop generation remains underexplored despite its importance for real tutoring systems. Moreover, the three dimensions are not independent. Enhancing cognitive-level control through structured grounding may constrain distractor diversity, while highly generative distractor models may weaken diagnostic interpretability. Similarly, integrating adaptive feedback loops introduces sequential constraints that complicate static difficulty calibration. These cross-dimensional trade-offs indicate that MCQ generation should be viewed as a multi-objective optimization problem under pedagogical constraints.

Table 2 further shows that human evaluation is still the dominant way to assess cognitive alignment and distractor plausibility (e.g., [5,19]), reflecting the limited coverage of automated metrics. Meanwhile, surface-level metrics (e.g., BLEU/ROUGE) are still used for sub-tasks, but they are weak proxies for diagnostic validity and downstream assessment utility.

6 Open Challenges and Future Research Directions

Despite significant progress in language learning models (LLM), fundamental challenges remain in transitioning from generatively sound language models to generatively effective and interpretable instructional systems. From the perspective of KDDM, key areas of openness include deeper integration of domain knowledge, user modeling, and rigorous evaluation.

6.1 Controllability and Faithfulness

While LLMs can be prompted to target low-level cognitive tasks (e.g., 'Remembering'), this control is often simplistic and difficult to interpret. Therefore, more refined and robust methods of controlling generation are needed. This requires moving beyond simple text prompts and towards methods that explicitly link the generation process to structural representations of cognitive complexity (such as knowledge graphs) [8]. Furthermore, ensuring fidelity to the original text is crucial, as the hallucination of LLM is unacceptable in educational assessments. Techniques like Retrieval-Augmented Generation (RAG) show promise in grounding outputs [8], but guaranteeing factual correctness (perhaps via hybrid neuro-symbolic approaches) remains an open challenge.

6.2 Interpretability and Explainability

The "black box" nature of generative learning models is a major obstacle for the education profession, because it is difficult to understand why specific distractors are generated [40]. Future models should be able to simultaneously generate multiple-choice questions and their explanations, such as reasoning chains or justifications for distractors. This "interpretable question generation" is of significant value. [27]. A specific research question is: can a multi-task model be trained to generate distractors while simultaneously outputting the corresponding natural language "misinterpretations" and citing "evidence" from the source text? This would transform interpretability from an ideal state into a quantifiable diagnostic task.

6.3 Scalable and Automated Pedagogical Evaluation

There is a serious "assessment gap" in this field due to our over-reliance on expensive, small-scale human assessments. Standard linguistic metrics like ROUGE do not accurately represent educational value [23]. Recent work has also explored large language models as automatic judges to approximate human evaluation at scale; however, such approaches primarily focus on linguistic quality and do not fully address pedagogical evaluation. A key KDDM challenge, echoed in related fields [39], is to develop novel, scalable metrics that better correlate with pedagogical dimensions. Future research could explore using pre-trained student models as "surrogate evaluators" to predict problem difficulty or diagnostic power. Alternatively, it could develop new computational metrics based on psychometric theories such as item response theory. However, developing robust, automated solutions remains extremely challenging.

6.4 Human-In-The-Loop Personalization at Scale

The ultimate vision of a learner feedback loop is a fully adaptive, personalized system. However, building such a system from real-world, often sparse, student interaction data presents significant KDDM challenges. A key direction is research into "human-in-the-loop methodologies". This includes developing interactive systems where educators can easily review, edit, and approve generated questions, with the model learning from these corrections via techniques like Reinforcement Learning from Human Feedback (RLHF), which is being explored in related educational technology domains, though applying it effectively to MCQ generation requires further study. Furthermore, as personalization relies on sensitive student data, developing "privacy-preserving" student models using techniques like federated learning, as explored in recent user modeling research, will be essential for building trustworthy, large-scale adaptive learning systems.

7 Conclusion

This paper presented a KDDM-centric survey of automated MCQ generation and introduced a three-dimensional taxonomy covering cognitive alignment, structured distractors, and learner feedback. Using this framework, we synthesized representative methods, datasets, and evaluation practices, and analyzed the trade-offs among controllability, diagnostic validity, and adaptivity. We also outlined open challenges in faithful generation, scalable pedagogical evaluation, and data-efficient personalization, providing a structured roadmap for reliable and adaptive KDDM-driven educational systems.

Ultimately, advancing automated MCQ generation requires bridging generative modeling with principled assessment theory and learner-aware optimization. By situating MCQ generation within a unified KDDM framework, we aim to encourage future work that moves beyond text quality toward data-driven educational effectiveness.

References

1. Alsubait, T., Parsia, B., Sattler, U.: Ontology-based multiple choice question generation. J. Educ. Technol. Soc. **19**(1), 300–315 (2016)
2. Amin, S., Uddin, M.I., Alarood, A.A., Mashwani, W.K., Alzahrani, A., Alzahrani, A.O.: Smart e-learning framework for personalized adaptive learning and sequential path recommendations using reinforcement learning. IEEE Access **11**, 89769–89790 (2023)
3. Anderson, L.W., Krathwohl, D.R., et al.: A Taxonomy for Learning, Teaching, and Assessing: A Revision of Bloom's Taxonomy of Educational Objectives. Longman (2001)
4. Biancini, G., Ferrato, A., Limongelli, C.: Multiple-choice question generation using large language models: methodology and educator insights. In: Proceedings of the 32nd ACM Conference on User Modeling, Adaptation and Personalization (UMAP) (2024). https://doi.org/10.1145/3631700.3665233
5. Bitew, S.K., Deleu, J., Develder, C., Demeester, T.: Distractor generation for multiple-choice questions with predictive prompting and large language models (2023). https://arxiv.org/abs/2307.16338
6. Brown, T., et al.: Language models are fewshot learners. In: Advances in Neural Information Processing Systems, vol. 33, pp. 1877–1901 (2020)
7. Cavusoglu, D., Sen, S.O., Sert, U.: DisGeM: distractor generation for multiple choice questions with span masking (2024)
8. Chen, C.H., Shiu, M.F.: KAQG: a knowledge-graph-enhanced RAG for difficulty-controlled question generation (2025)
9. Chen, M., Ma, J., Cui, X., Dai, Q., Hu, H., Wu, Y.: Advancing medical education in cervical cancer control with large language models for multiple-choice question generation. Med. Teach. **47**(3) (2025)
10. Chughtai, R., Azam, F., Anwar, M.W., But, W.H., Farooq, M.U.: A lecture centric automated distractor generation for post-graduate software engineering courses. In: 2022 International Conference on Frontiers of Information Technology (FIT), pp. 100–105. IEEE (2022)
11. Clark, C., Lee, K., Chang, M.W., Kwiatkowski, T., Collins, M., Toutanova, K.: BoolQ: exploring the surprising difficulty of natural yes/no questions. In: Proceedings of the 2019 Conference of the North American Chapter of the Association for Computational Linguistics: Human Language Technologies, Volume 1 (Long and Short Papers), pp. 2924–2936 (2019)
12. Clark, P., et al.: Think you have solved question answering? Try ARC, the AI2 reasoning challenge. arXiv preprint arXiv:1803.05457 (2018)

13. Corbett, A.T., Anderson, J.R.: Knowledge tracing: modeling the acquisition of procedural knowledge. User Model. User Adap. Inter. **4**(4), 253–278 (1994)
14. Das, B., Majumder, M., Phadikar, S., et al.: Automatic question generation and answer assessment: a survey. Res. Pract. Technol. Enhanced Learn. **16**(1), 5 (2021). https://doi.org/10.1186/s41039-021-00151-1
15. Dhanya, N., Balaji, R., Akash, S.: AiXAM -AI assisted online MCQ generation platform using google T5 and Sense2Vec. In: 2022 Second International Conference on Artificial Intelligence and Smart Energy (ICAIS), pp. 38–44. IEEE (2022)
16. Dijkstra, R., Genc, Z., Kayal, S., Kamps, J., et al.: Reading comprehension quiz generation using generative pre-trained transformers. In: iTextbooks@AIED, pp. 4–17 (2022)
17. Hambleton, R.K., Swaminathan, H., Rogers, H.J.: Fundamentals of Item Response Theory, vol. 2. Sage (1991)
18. Hang, C.N., Tan, C.W., Yu, P.D.: MCQGen: a large language model-driven MCQ generator for personalized learning. IEEE Access **12**, 102261–102273 (2024). https://doi.org/10.1109/ACCESS.2024.3420709
19. Hwang, K., Challagundla, S., Alomair, M., Chen, L.: Towards AI-assisted multiple choice question generation and quality evaluation at scale: aligning with bloom's taxonomy. In: NeurIPS 2023 Workshop on Generative AI for Education (2023)
20. Jasuja, H., Negi, U., Kaur, G., et al.: Automatic question generation from Youtube lectures using Deep Learning. In: 2024 15th International Conference on Computing Communication and Networking Technologies (ICCCNT), pp. 1–6. IEEE (2024)
21. Kurdi, G., Leo, J., Parsia, B., Sattler, U., Al-Emari, S.: A systematic review of automatic question generation for educational purposes. Int. J. Artif. Intell. Educ. **30**, 121–204 (2019). https://api.semanticscholar.org/CorpusID:208212657
22. Lai, G., Xie, Q., Liu, H., Yang, Y., Hovy, E.: RACE: large-scale reading comprehension dataset from examinations. In: Proceedings of the 2017 Conference on Empirical Methods in Natural Language Processing, pp. 785–794 (2017)
23. Lan, Y., et al.: Survey of natural language processing for education: taxonomy, systematic review, and future trends (2025). https://arxiv.org/abs/2401.07518
24. Li, X., Xu, H., Zhang, J., Chang, H.: Deep reinforcement learning for adaptive learning systems. J. Educ. Behav. Stat. **48**(2), 220–243 (2023)
25. Liang, C., Yang, X., Dave, N., Wham, D., Pursel, B., Giles, C.L.: Distractor generation for multiple choice questions using learning to rank. In: Proceedings of the Thirteenth Workshop on Innovative use of NLP for Building Educational Applications, pp. 284–290 (2018)
26. Lord, F.M.: Applications of Item Response Theory to Practical Testing Problems. Routledge (2012)
27. Luo, H., Deng, Y., Shen, Y., Ng, S.K., Chua, T.S.: Chain-of-Exemplar: enhancing distractor generation for multimodal educational question generation. In: Ku, L.W., Martins, A., Srikumar, V. (eds.) Proceedings of the 62nd Annual Meeting of the Association for Computational Linguistics (Volume 1: Long Papers), Bangkok, Thailand, August 2024, pp. 7978–7993. Association for Computational Linguistics (2024). https://doi.org/10.18653/v1/2024.acl-long.432, https://aclanthology.org/2024.acl-long.432/
28. Mihaylov, T., Clark, P., Khot, T., Sabharwal, A.: Can a suit of armor conduct electricity? A new dataset for open book question answering. In: Proceedings of the 2018 Conference on Empirical Methods in Natural Language Processing, pp. 2381–2391 (2018)

29. Mucciaccia, S.S., Paixao, T.M., Mutz, F.W.: Automatic multiple-choice question generation and evaluation systems based on LLM: a study case with university resolutions. In: Proceedings of the 31st International Conference on Computational Linguistics (COLING) (2025)
30. Papineni, K., Roukos, S., Ward, T., Zhu, W.J.: BLEU: a method for automatic evaluation of machine translation. In: Proceedings of the 40th Annual Meeting of the Association for Computational Linguistics, pp. 311–318 (2002)
31. Piech, C., et al.: Deep knowledge tracing. In: Advances in Neural Information Processing Systems, vol. 28 (2015)
32. Qiu, Z., Wu, X., Fan, W.: Automatic distractor generation for multiple choice questions in standard tests. In: Scott, D., Bel, N., Zong, C. (eds.) Proceedings of the 28th International Conference on Computational Linguistics, Barcelona, Spain (Online), December 2020, pp. 2096–2106. International Committee on Computational Linguistics (2020). https://doi.org/10.18653/v1/2020.coling-main.189, https://aclanthology.org/2020.coling-main.189/
33. Subitsha, R.S., Vetrivel, M., Shrimaulik, N., Saravanan, K.: Natural language processing-driven learning platform for personalized education. In: 2025 International Conference on Visual Analytics and Data Visualization (ICVADV), pp. 174–180 (2025). https://doi.org/10.1109/ICVADV63329.2025.10961687
34. Rajpurkar, P., Zhang, J., Lopyrev, K., Liang, P.: SQuAD: 100,000+ questions for machine comprehension of text. In: Proceedings of the 2016 Conference on Empirical Methods in Natural Language Processing, pp. 2383–2392 (2016)
35. Saddish, A., Somaiah, P., Gambhir, V., Nirmala, S.J.: Generation of multiple choice questions from Indian educational text. In: 2023 3rd Asian Conference on Innovation in Technology (ASIANCON), pp. 1–7. IEEE (2023)
36. Scaria, N., Dharani Chenna, S., Subramani, D.: Automated educational question generation at different Bloom's skill levels using large language models: strategies and evaluation. In: Olney, A.M., Chounta, IA., Liu, Z., Santos, O.C., Bittencourt, I.I. (eds.) Artificial Intelligence in Education, AIED 2024. LNCS, vol. 14830, pp. 165–179. Springer, Cham (2024). https://doi.org/10.1007/978-3-031-64299-9_12
37. Shirkar, S., Langhi, D., Agrawal, S.: LLM-based quiz generation for assessments in learning management system. In: 2025 Second International Conference on Education Technology and Artificial Intelligence (ETAI). IEEE (2025)
38. Vachev, K., Hardalov, M., Karadzhov, G., Georgiev, G., Koychev, I., Nakov, P.: Leaf: multiple-choice question generation. In: Hagen, M., et al. (eds.) ECIR 2022. LNCS, vol. 13186, pp. 321–328. Springer, Cham (2022). https://doi.org/10.1007/978-3-030-99739-7_41
39. Wang, F., et al.: A survey of models for cognitive diagnosis: new developments and future directions (2024). https://arxiv.org/abs/2407.05458
40. Wang, Z., Zhang, R., Liu, A., Wang, W.Y.: Towards human-like educational question generation with large language models. In: Rodrigo, M.M., Matsuda, N., Cristea, A.I., Dimitrova, V. (eds.) Artificial Intelligence in Education. Posters and Late Breaking Results, Workshops and Tutorials, Industry and Innovation Tracks, Practitioners, Doctoral Consortium and Blue Sky. LNCS, vol. 13356, pp. 153–166. Springer, Cham (2022)
41. Welbl, J., Liu, N.F., Gardner, M.: SciQ: crowdsourced science questions for question answering. In: Proceedings of the 2017 Conference on Empirical Methods in Natural Language Processing, pp. 539–548 (2017)
42. Zhang, T., Kishore, V., Wu, F., Weinberger, K.Q., Artzi, Y.: BERTScore: evaluating text generation with BERT. In: International Conference on Learning Representations (ICLR) (2020)

Graph Neural Networks in EEG-Based Emotion Recognition: A Survey

Chenyu Liu[1], Yuqiu Deng[2], Yihao Wu[1], Ruizhi Yang[3], Zhongruo Wang[4], Liangwei Zhang[5], Siyun Chen[1], Tianyi Zhang[1,6], Yang Liu[1], Yi Ding[1], Liming Zhai[7(✉)], Ziyu Jia[8(✉)], and Xinliang Zhou[1]

[1] Nanyang Technological University, Singapore, Singapore
[2] Xi'an Jiaotong University, Xi'an, China
[3] Imperial College London, London, UK
[4] Amazon, Seattle, WA, USA
[5] Carnegie Mellon University, Pittsburgh, PA, USA
[6] Uber Technologies, Inc., San Francisco, USA
[7] School of Computer Science, Central China Normal University, Wuhan, China
limingzhai@ccnu.edu.cn
[8] Institute of Automation, Chinese Academy of Sciences, Beijing, China
jia.ziyu@outlook.com

Abstract. Compared to other modalities, EEG-based emotion recognition can intuitively respond to the emotional patterns in the human brain and, therefore, has become one of the most concerning tasks in the brain-computer interfaces. Since dependencies within brain regions are closely related to emotion, a significant trend is to develop Graph Neural Networks (GNNs) for EEG-based emotion recognition. However, brain region dependencies in emotional EEG have physiological bases that distinguish GNNs in this field from those in other time series fields. Besides, there is neither a comprehensive review nor guidance for constructing GNNs in EEG-based emotion recognition. In the survey, our categorization reveals the commonalities and differences of existing approaches under a unified framework of graph construction. We analyze and categorize methods from three stages in the framework to provide clear guidance on constructing GNNs in EEG-based emotion recognition. In addition, we discuss several open challenges and future directions, such as temporal fully-connected graph and graph condensation.

Keywords: EEG · Emotion Recognition · Graph Neural Network · Brain-Computer Interface

1 Introduction

Emotion is an integral and complex aspect of human cognition that is decisive in human decision-making, behavior, and social interaction. Therefore, Emotion

C. Liu and Y. Deng—Equal contribution.

R. C.-W. Wong et al. (Eds.): PAKDD 2026, LNAI 16618, pp. 581–598, 2027.
https://doi.org/10.1007/978-981-92-1947-6_46

Recognition is essential in areas such as the diagnosis of mental disorders and Brain-Computer Interfaces (BCIs). Human emotions have various external manifestations, such as body language, voice, expression, and physiological signals. Among them, the Electroencephalogram (EEG) signals are perceived as a product of coordinated neural activity and electrical signal transmission within the human brain, which can directly and objectively reveal genuine human emotion compared to other manifestations and thus are known as one of the most unique and vital data in emotion recognition. EEG records emotional activity from different brain regions and, therefore, can reflect the complex interactions between brain regions in emotional states and the strong correlation between specific brain regions and specific emotions [25]. In summary, inferring and exploiting complex dependencies between brain regions in emotional EEG has become a significant research direction in EEG-based emotion recognition.

Graph Neural Networks (GNNs) emerge as a powerful tool for modeling dependencies of emotional EEG within the network neuroscience framework. As networks that manipulate graph-structured data, GNNs can effectively extract features utilizing dependencies between brain regions in emotional EEG. These dependencies represent the connectivity patterns and interactions of brain regions in emotional states, which are directly associated with specific emotional activities. Therefore, benefiting from their dependencies inference ability, GNNs designed for EEG-based emotion recognition can improve classification tasks compared to traditional analysis methods and potentially uncover new insights in neuroscience. There has been a significant growth in the number and proportion of methods using GNNs in the EEG-based emotion recognition field over the last six years.

Motivated by the increasing number of recent papers proposing GNNs for EEG-based emotion recognition, and the design of these GNNs differs from methods in other time-series tasks, there is an urgent need for a comprehensive review of the GNNs in this field. First, there is currently no unified treatment for GNN structure in the EEG-based emotion recognition field. Second, brain region dependencies in emotional states have specific physiological bases, distinguishing GNNs in EEG-based emotion recognition from those used in other time-series fields. Therefore, we categorize existing GNNs in EEG-based emotion recognition based on stages within a unified GNN construction framework. Specifically, this categorization splits the existing methods regarding node-level, edge-level, and graph-level stages and proposes a taxonomic view for each stage. In summary, the contributions of this survey are summarized below:

- This survey provides a comprehensive and systematic review of existing GNNs in EEG-based emotion recognition. To the best of our knowledge, this is the first and only survey work on such a topic.
- We propose a novel categorization of existing GNNs in EEG-based emotion recognition, which provides clear guidance for constructing specific GNNs according to a unified framework.
- We summarize and highlight future directions to facilitate GNN-based works in EEG-based emotion recognition.

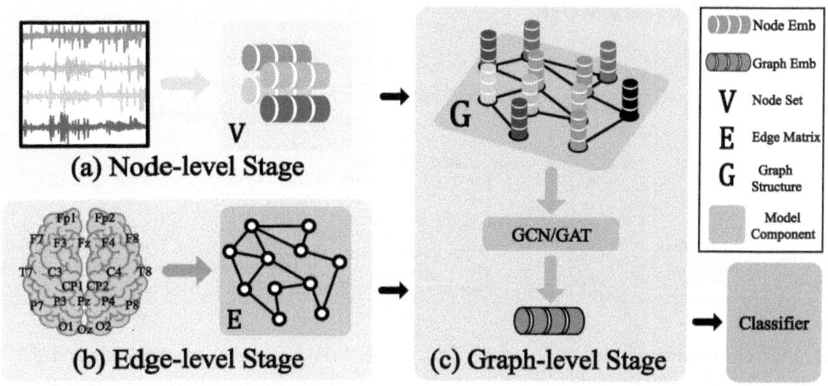

Fig. 1. Unified framework of EEG-based emotion recognition. First, (a) indicates the selection of node features. Then, (b) refers to the computation of the edge matrix representing brain connectivity patterns. Finally, (c) denotes the construction of a graph, which differs across methods.

2 Overview of Categorization

In recent years, EEG-based emotion recognition has seen an influx of methods with GNNs. These methods focus on different aspects of designing GNNs to infer dependencies within emotional EEG. They generally answer these three critical questions during the graph construction process: What features are chosen as nodes? How to calculate edges? Which graph structure is utilized? Therefore, categorizing these methods at the model level is neither instructive nor sufficiently in-depth. To better understand these methods and propose a construction guideline for GNNs in EEG-based emotion recognition, our categorization is based on a unified framework with its corresponding stages.

2.1 Framework for Specific GNNs

EEG-based emotion recognition task for GNNs can be indicated as taking emotional EEG $X \in \mathbb{R}^{C\times S}$ and corresponding label $Y \in \mathbb{R}^1$ as input, constructing graphs and predicting emotional labels $Y' \in \mathbb{R}^1$ via graph embeddings. Let $\mathbf{G}(\mathbf{V}, \mathbf{E})$ denote a graph. $\mathbf{V} \in \mathbb{R}^{N_v\times D}$ represents the node set, where $N_v = C$ indicates the number of channels and D denotes node embedding dimension. $\mathbf{E} \in \mathbb{R}^{N_e}$ represents the edge matrix, where $N_e = C^2$ denotes the number of edges. The goal of the model can be represented as learning a function $f(\mathbf{G}) \rightarrow Y'$ that maps the graph to the corresponding emotional label. Therefore, the unified framework for building GNNs in EEG-based emotion recognition consists of three stages, as shown in Fig. 1. First, the Node-level Stage represents the model selection of features to be used as nodes $\mathbf{V}$. Second, the Edge-level Stage indicates that the model computes the edge matrix $\mathbf{E}$. Finally, the Graph-level Stage denotes the process of graph $\mathbf{G}$ construction.

2.2 Stages of Framework

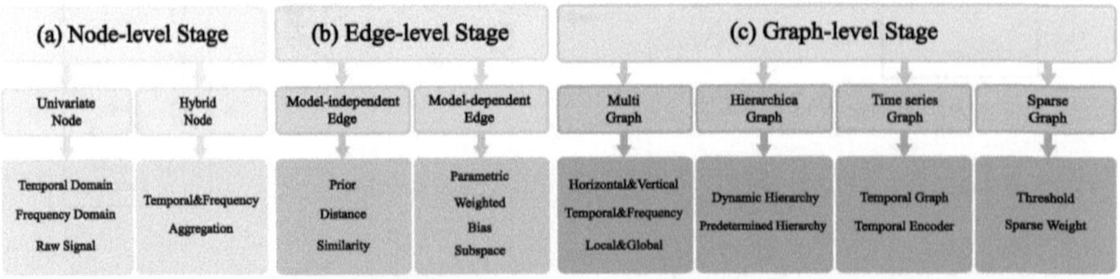

Fig. 2. An overview of the categorization. The existing method was split into three stages for further categorization. These three steps correspond to (a) the selection of node features, (b) the calculation of edge matrices, and (c) the construction of graphs with different structures.

Node-level Stage indicates the process of selecting features as nodes **V**. Instead of focusing on the detailed composition and parameters of the node embedding extractor, this survey focuses on the composition of node features. Therefore, we categorize this stage according to the type of node features, as shown in Fig. 2(a). These two categories are Univariate node, which utilizes a single feature, and Hybrid node, which employs multiple features. The details of each category will be explained in Sect. 3.

Edge-level Stage represents the calculation of the edge matrix **E**. The edge matrix represents the relationships between electrode nodes. Matrices representing such relationships differ in different methods, such as the adjacency matrix or the Laplacian matrix. We uniformly regard them as edge matrices. Depending on whether the model parameters are involved in the calculation, we categorize the Edge-level Stage of the existing methods into two categories: Model-independent edge and Model-dependent edge, as shown in Fig. 2(b). The sub-categories of each category will be explained in detail in Sect. 4.

Graph-level Stage denotes the process of modeling different types of graph structures **G**. The basic units utilized by existing methods for reasoning about graph embedding are Graph Convolutional Networks (GCNs) or Graph Attention Networks (GATs). The perspective of this survey is not on the detailed model components but on the graph structure used to represent the dependencies within emotional EEG. The graph structure of existing methods can be categorized into four types, as shown in Fig. 2(c). Multi-graph indicates that the model employs a multi-stream structure to simultaneously construct different graphs to incorporate multiple dependencies of emotional EEG. Hierarchical graph denotes that the model organizes nodes into multiple groups to infer dependency between brain regions related to emotion. Time series graph is a series of graphs in the temporal dimension that represent the temporal dependency of emotional EEG. Sparse graph structure represents sparsely connected graphs that match the concentration of brain activity in emotional states. The sub-categories of each category will be explained in detail in Sect. 5.

3 Node-Level Stage

Depending on the node feature, two categories are included in the Node-level Stage: Univariate node and Hybrid node. Univariate node is further categorized into Temporal domain node, Frequency domain node, and raw signal node. Hybrid node contains Temporal&Frequency node and Aggregation node.

3.1 Univariate Node

Univariate nodes refer to the most common way of using a single feature as nodes. The vast majority of existing methods utilize this method. It contains three categories, as shown in Table 1.

Temporal domain node implies that the model employs the temporal domain feature as nodes. This is the most commonly used node in the current methods, especially the differential entropy (DE) feature. The popularity of the DE feature, in addition to the fact that many open-source EEG-based emotion recognition datasets include this feature, such as SEED [46], DE feature itself is suitable for measuring the uncertainty or randomness of the signal, which is adequate for describing the diverse dependencies in the emotional EEG. In addition to this, HD-GCN [38] and SparseDGCNN [40] employ the Differential Asymmetry of Synchronisation for Multivariate Signals (DASM) feature.

Frequency Domain node indicates that utilizing frequency domain features as nodes. The most commonly used is the Power Spectral Density (PSD) feature obtained by Fourier Transform to describe the power distribution of the signal in the frequency domain. From comparing the experiment results of existing methods, the performance of using Frequency domain node is generally slightly worse than using Temporal domain node.

Raw Signal node represents directly using the raw emotional EEG as nodes. This node is the least common in EEG-based emotion recognition tasks because raw emotional EEG is highly individualized, which retains more emotion-independent disturbances. Besides, the dimension of Raw signal node is higher compared to other nodes. However, this node maximizes information retention and enables end-to-end training of the model.

3.2 Hybrid Node

Hybrid node implies that the node mixes a variety of features. It is consistent with the goal of Multi-graph mentioned in Sect. 5.1, which is inferring multiple dependencies within emotional EEG. The difference is that Multi-graph builds multiple graphs for different dependencies, while Hybrid nodes fuse features that contain different dependencies. Hybrid nodes can utilize the complementarity between different information to provide a more comprehensive view of emotional EEG dependencies. However, it increases the dimension of the node. Besides, due to the different distributions of features, it can easily lead to overfitting when the amount of data is insufficient. Hybrid node contains two categorizations.

Table 1. Overview of Univariate node.

Node	Baseline	fNode Feature
Temporal domain	All except the below	Mainly Differential Entropy
Frequency domain	LR-GCN [10]	Power Spectral Density
	GECNN [32]	Hilbert-Huang transform spectrum
	TARDGCN [14]	Welch
	OMHGL [26]	Power Spectral Density
	GIGN [3]	Power Spectral Density
	EmT [5]	Power Spectral Density
Raw signal	HetEmotionNet [8]	Time-domain Amplitude
	LGGNet [4]	Power Conversion
	RPGCN [48]	Linear Embedding
	VSGT [20]	Time-domain Amplitude
	VBH-GNN [21]	Time-domain Amplitude

CR-GAT [23], DBGC-ATFFNet-AFTL [34], and EGFG [11] employ **Temporal&Frequency** node that fuses DE features, and PSD features to infer both temporal and frequency dependencies simultaneously. Methods like ERHGCN [45] utilize **Aggregation** node that aggregates a variety of features, including DASM, Average Size of Messages (ASM), etc., to preserve as many dependencies as possible.

4 Edge-Level Stage

Edge-level Stage contains Model-independent edge and Model-dependent edge. Model-independent edge is divided into Prior edge, Distance edge, and Similarity edge according to the calculation of edges. Model-dependent edge is divided into Parametric edge, Weighted edge, Bias edge, and Subspace edge depending on the usage of parameters.

4.1 Model-Independent Edge

Model-independent edge implies that the calculation of the edge does not include the model parameters and backpropagation does not update this edge. It is based on existing brain physiology paradigms or signal processing paradigms. The fact that such edges are independent of the data distribution and model and conform to physiological or signaling patterns increases the plausibility and stability of Model-independent edge. Moreover, such an edge does not increase model parameters and is compatible with any model structure. The Model-independent edge contains three edges, as shown in Table 2.

Prior edge refers to the edge that is set manually based on prior knowledge. Prior Knowledge refers to existing physiological paradigms about electrode connections, which is physiologically plausible. However, emotional EEG has individual

Table 2. Overview of Model-independent edge.

Edge	Baseline	Edge Feature
Prior	RGNN [47]	Physical Distances
	SFE-Net [2]	Connectivity through Edge Matrix
	MD-GCN [6]	Connectivity through Edge Matrix
	LGGNet [4]	Brain Region Connectivity
	DAGAM [35]	Physical Distances
Distance	EGFG [11]	Euclidean distance
	JSCFE [28]	Euclidean distance
	MST-GNN [22]	Phase Lag Index
	TARDGCN [14]	Cosine distance
	OMHGL [26]	Cosine distance
Similarity	MD-AGCN [13]	Pearson Correlation Coefficient
	HetEmotionNet [8]	Mutual Information
	ST-GCLSTM [7]	Pearson Correlation Coefficient
	HD-GCN [38]	Gaussian Similarity
	HB-SR [37]	Phase Locking Value

differences, so the connections between electrodes differ between subjects. This makes the rationality of Prior edge limited because it cannot be automatically updated. Based on prior knowledge that the strength of connections between brain regions decays as a function of the inverse square of the physical distance [30], RGNN [47], and DAGAM [35] use 3D co-ordinates to calculate the physical distances between electrodes as the edges. The International 10–20 EEG Electrode Standard depicts the connectivity between electrodes, and MD-GCN [6] and SFE-Net [2] transform it into an edge matrix. LGGNet [4] limits the connectivity between electrodes in specific brain regions based on the distribution of brain regions.

Distance edge refers to treating signals as vectors and taking vector distances as edges. Calculating the distance between vectors is commonly used to measure the relationship between signals. Distance edge can be updated as the node changes, but this relationship is physiologically independent of emotion. TARDGCN [14] and OMHGL [26] apply Cosine distance between nodes as edges. Similarly, EGFG [11] and JSCFE [28] utilize Euclidean distance. MST-GNN [22] uses the Phase Lag Index, which analyses the phase distance between node signals.

Similarity edge refers to calculating the similarity of signals as edges. It differs from Distance edge only in the mathematical meaning, so Similarity edge is dynamic but does not always conform to the physiological paradigm. MD-AGCN [13] and ST-GCLSTM [7] utilize the Pearson Correlation Coefficient to compute the strength of the linear relationship between signals as their edge. HB-SR [37] uses Phase Locking Value to calculate the degree of phase similarity between electrode signals at a particular frequency as their edge. In addition, HD-GCN

[38] applies the Gaussian similarity, and HetEmotionNet [8] indicates mutual information to represent the correlation between two signals as the edge.

4.2 Model-Dependent Edge

Model-dependent edge refers to the computation of edges using model parameters. The edges containing model parameters can be dynamically updated with training so that the model can be generalized over different data. Compared to Model-independent edges that are limited by prior knowledge or vector relationships, Model-dependent edge can capture more complex brain region relationships in emotional EEG without manually adjusting when handling different signals. However, additional parameters make it challenging to balance accuracy and computational burden. Model-dependent edge contains four categories, as shown in Table 3.

Parametric edge refers to directly using the model parameter matrix as the edge matrix. As the most direct method of using model parameters, Parametric edge is the most commonly used edge of Model-dependent edge. Parametric edge is updated as follows:

$$\mathbf{E}'_{i,j} = (1-\rho)\mathbf{E}_{i,j} + \rho\frac{\partial \mathcal{L}}{\partial \mathbf{E}_{i,j}} \tag{1}$$

where ρ denotes the learning rate. $\frac{\partial \mathcal{L}}{\partial \mathbf{E}}$ refers to the partial derivative of the loss $\mathcal{L}$ with respect to $\mathbf{E}_{i,j}$.

Weighted edge indicates that the edge matrix can be viewed as the product of the node relationships and the model parameters used as weights. Therefore, the essential meaning of Weighted edge depends on the node relationships. Weighted edge can introduce prior knowledge or vector calculations to constrain the edge by setting it as the node relationships. The weighted edge implementation of existing methods is as follows:

$$\mathbf{E}_{i,j} = \xi(\mathbf{W} * f[v_i, v_j]) \tag{2}$$

where $\mathbf{W}$ represents the model parameter utilized as weight. $\xi(\cdot)$ is activation function. $f[\cdot,\cdot]$ denotes the relationship function between nodes. Siam-GCAN [39] and DBGC-ATFFNet-AFTL [34] utilize distance between nodes as the relationship function. LR-GCN [10] and STFCGAT [19] concatenate any two nodes to perform a linear transformation as the relationship function.

Bias edge adding model parameters as bias terms to the node relationships as the edge matrix. It differs from Weighted edge only in the meaning of the parameters. The implementation of Bias edge is as follows:

$$\mathbf{E}_{i,j} = \mathbf{W} + f[v_i, v_j] \tag{3}$$

where $\mathbf{W}$ represents the model parameter utilized as bias. MRGCN [29] utilizes the calculation of the physical distance between nodes as the relationship function. OGSSL [27] applies the similarity between nodes as the relationship function.

Subspace edge denotes the projection of nodes to subspace by parameters to obtain similarity as edges. It is similar in principle to the Attention mechanism and allows the model to capture the complex relationship between every two nodes. However, it adds more model complexity and computational cost than other Model-dependent edges. MD-AGCN [13], JSCFE [28], HGCN [44], VBH-GNN [21] and ASTG-LSTM [15] use the following to implement Subspace edge:

$$E_{i,j} = \xi(v_i^T * \mathbf{W}_1^T * \mathbf{W}_2 * v_j) \tag{4}$$

$\mathbf{W}_1$ and $\mathbf{W}_2$ are projection matrices for two nodes.

Table 3. Overview of Model-dependent edge.

Edge	Baseline	Edge Feature
Parametric	DGCNN [33]	Gaussian similarity
	GCB-Net [42]	Learned Topology
	HD-GCN [38]	Gaussian similarity
	AHGCN [36]	Learned Topology
	GIGN [3]	Learned Topology
	EmoGT [9]	Learned Topology
	EmT [5]	Multi-view Learning
	DTC-GCN [49]	Sparse Causality
	RPGCN [48]	Relational Probabilistic
	VSGT [20]	Prior Constrained Dependencies
Weight	Siam-GCAN [39]	Distance-based Weights
	DBGC-ATFFNet-AFTL [34]	Distance-based Weights
		Linear Transformation
	STFCGAT [19]	Attention Weights & Linear Transformation
	LR-GCN [10]	
Bias	OGSSL [27]	Euclidean Similarity
	MRGCN [29]	Physical Distance
Subspace	MD-AGCN [13]	Pearson Correlation Coefficient
	ASTG-LSTM [15]	Attention Mechanism
	HGCN [44]	Heterogeneous Multi-head
	VBH-GNN [21]	Variational Bayesian Graph Inference

5 Graph-Level Stage

There are four graph structures included in the Graph-level Stage: Multi-graph, Hierarchical graph, Time series graph, and Sparse graph. According to the dependencies that graphs indicate, Multi-graph is divided into Horizontal&Vertical graph, Temporal&Frequency graph, and Local&Global graph. Hierarchical graph is divided into Dynamic hierarchy graph and Predetermined hierarchy graph. The realisation of Time series graph is divided into Temporal graph and Temporal encoder. The sparsity implementation of Sparse graph consists of Threshold and Sparse weight.

5.1 Multi-graph

Multi-graph allows the model to capture different emotional EEG dependencies simultaneously by concatenating multiple types of graph embeddings. Various relational dependencies exist in emotional EEG, such as temporal, frequency, and local brain region dependency, etc. The multi-graph structure can learn and consider different dependencies simultaneously, which helps to build relationships in emotional EEG more comprehensively. However, the multi-stream graph modeling process increases the computational burden. The existing Multi-graph can be subdivided into three categories, as shown in Table 4.

Horizontal&Vertical graph captures both vertical and horizontal spatial dependencies of brain regions. There are differences in the horizontal and vertical connectivity patterns of brain regions so that the Horizontal&Vertical structure can model more physiologically plausible spatial dependency. ERHGCN [45] and BiHDM [17] both utilize this graph. BiHDM further constructed different horizontal and vertical graphs in the left and right hemispheres based on the existence of imbalance between hemispheres.

Table 4. Overview of Multi-graph.

Graph	Baseline	Graph Details
Horizontal&Vertical	BiHDM [17]	Bi-hemispheric Paired Discrepancy
	ERHGCN [45]	Brain Regions
Temporal&Frequency	MD-AGCN [13]	Two-stream Structure
	HetEmotionNet [8]	Heterogeneous Domain Fusion
	DBGC-ATFFNet-AFTL [34]	Two-stream Structure
	VBH-GNN [21]	Two-stream Structure
Local&Global	GECNN [32]	Electrodes Groups
	HD-GCN [38]	Brain Region
	AHGCN [36]	Brain Region
	MRGCN [29]	Long/Short Range Dependencies
	LGGNet [4]	Brain Region

Temporal&Frequency graph combines the temporal dependency and frequency dependency of the emotional EEG signal. Temporal dependence allows the model to notice amplitude features that are highly correlated with emotion. Frequency dependence encompasses activating the corresponding frequency band in a particular emotion, such as the increase in the α band during the positive emotion. Existing methods MD-AGCN [13], HetEmotionNet [8], and DBGC-ATFFNet-AFTL [34] all adopt a similar two-stream structure, where each stream corresponds to the temporal-spatial and frequency-spatial space, and finally graph embeddings are concatenated and fed into the classifier.

Local&Global graph combines global dependency between brain regions and local dependency within brain regions. In emotional states, global dependence responds to interactions between brain regions, such as activity in surrounding brain regions caused by activity in specific brain regions. Local dependence focuses on relationships within specific brain regions, e.g., activity within the frontal lobe and cortex is associated with positive emotions. GECNN [32], HD-GCN [38], AHGCN [36], and LGGNet [4] all infer the spatial dependencies of all channels and channels within specific brain regions. Similarly, MRGCN [29] introduces short-range and long-range spatial dependencies corresponding to localized intra-region correlations and inter-region correlations.

5.2 Hierarchical Graph

Hierarchical graph groups channels to allow the model to capture local spatial dependency within specific brain regions. The spatial dependency of emotional EEG consists of inter-region and intra-region dependencies. The former corresponds to the region-level synergy between different brain regions under emotion, and the latter corresponds to the neural-level activity within the brain region associated with a specific emotion, e.g., the frontal cortex and lobe are related to positive emotions. Therefore, the hierarchical graph structure allows the model to effectively utilize the signal features contained in these local brain regions that are directly related to emotions. The difference from the Local&Global multi-graph structure is that the hierarchical graph structure does not necessarily employ a multi-stream process, thus reducing the computational burden. The existing Hierarchical graph contains two categories, as shown in Table 5.

Table 5. Overview of Hierarchical graph.

Graph Type	Baseline	Hierarchy Details
Dynamic hierarchy	AHGCN [36]	Channels/Regions Spatial Dependency
	SCC-MPGCN [43]	Channels/Regions Spatial Dependency
	MST-GNN [22]	Channels/Regions Spatial Dependency
	MDGCN-SRCNN [1]	Correlation-based Tree Structure
Predetermined hierarchy	R2G-STNN [18]	Local to Global
	VPR [41]	Local to Global
	V-IAG [31]	Global to Local
	HD-GCN [38]	Multi-Graph Concatenation
	GMSS [16]	Local to Global
	LGGNet [4]	Multi-Graph Concatenation

Dynamic hierarchy graph indicates that the model adaptively groups channels and then infers spatial dependency between groups. There are significant individual differences in emotional EEG between subjects, which implies that different subjects will have subtle differences in brain region correlations during the same emotion. Therefore, dynamic hierarchy can reduce the effect of individual differences. AHGCN [36], SCC-MPGCN [43], and MDGCN-SRCNN [1]

firstly infer channel-level spatial dependency, then implement a trainable weight assignment matrix to assign different electrodes to different brain regions, and finally build region-level spatial graph. MST-GNN [22] also implements channel-level dependency first, and then, based on the minimum spanning tree, it starts to search for children nodes with the strongest correlation so that each branch can be regarded as a group.
Predetermined hierarchy graph denotes the setting of the brain regions to which the electrodes belong based on existing prior knowledge. Prior knowledge refers to the cytoarchitecture of the brain, i.e., the division of brain regions according to the function. Predetermined hierarchy graph is physiologically reasonable and does not introduce additional computational burden. GMSS [16], R2G-STNN [18], and VPR [41] apply a local-to-global process. They divide electrodes into multiple regions in advance based on prior knowledge and first infer spatial dependency within regions and then between regions. In contrast, V-IAG [31] utilizes a global-to-local process. It first infers fully connected spatial dependency and then divides electrode regions and aggregates region-level nodes to construct relationships between regions. HD-GCN [38], and LGGNet [4] adopt the multi-graph structure in Sect. 5.1, where local and global dependencies are reasoned in parallel and then concatenated together.

5.3 Time Series Graph

Time series graph indicates that the model decomposes the signal into multiple time slices and constructs temporal dependency between slices. The temporal dependency of emotional EEG directly reflects the relationship between signal amplitude change and emotion. A high degree of activation within 300ms in the frontal cortex channels is usually associated with positive emotions, while a low degree of activation is usually associated with negative emotions. Therefore, Time series graph enables the model to construct and exploit the spatial and temporal dependencies of emotional EEG. Typically, it is implemented by splitting the input signal into multiple time slices to model spatial graphs within slices and then deriving the temporal dependency between slices by temporal graph or temporal encoder, as shown in Table 6.
Temporal graph represents the model regards spatial graph embeddings of time slices as nodes to construct a temporal graph. CR-GAT [23], VSGT [20] and GIGN [3] employ a GNN in the temporal dimension to construct a temporal graph by regarding time slices as nodes. MD-AGCN [13] couples the spatial graphs of all time slices and then takes the average as a temporal graph.
Temporal encoder represents that the model combines GNN and temporal encoder to derive the spatial and temporal dependencies of the emotional EEG. This derivation process is usually divided into two steps; firstly, the GNN is used to infer the spatial dependency within the time slices and update the spatial graph embeddings; then, the graph embedding of all the time slices is concatenated together and fed into a temporal encoder. ST-GCLSTM [7], ASTG-LSTM [15], R2G-STNN [18] and DTC-GCN [49] use LSTM as the temporal encoder.

Similarly, HetEmotionNet [8] uses GRUs, and EmoGT [9] and EmT [5] utilizes a transformer encoder.

Table 6. Overview of Time series graph.

Methods	Baseline	Temporal Details
Temporal Graph	MD-AGCN [13]	Average Spatial Graphs
	CR-GAT [23]	Time Slices as Nodes
	GIGN [3]	Time Slices as Nodes
	VSGT [20]	Time Slices as Nodes
Temporal Encoder	R2G-STNN [18]	LSTM
	ASTG-LSTM [15]	LSTM
	HetEmotionNet [8]	GRUs
	ST-GCLSTM [7]	LSTM
	EmoGT [9]	Transformers
	EmT [5]	Transformers
	DTC-GCN [49]	LSTM

5.4 Sparse Graph

Sparse graph implies that the graph connectivity relations are sparse. There is a concentration of brain activity in areas directly related to emotion, which means that most connections are weakly associated with emotion. Therefore, specific emotions can be identified by the electrical signals that are active around specific brain regions, such as the frontal cortex and lobe. The sparse graph structure reduces the influence of irrelevant information and retains only the essential connections related to a specific emotion. It differs from the hierarchical structure in that it couples specific groups of channels to achieve fewer connections, whereas the sparse graph structure retains fewer edges by filtering directly on top of the fully connected graph. Existing methods set **Threshold** or add **Sparse weights** to the loss function to retain a specific number of edges to form a sparse graph. DAGAM [35] and SOGNN [12] set Threshold k to achieve sparsity. DAGAM proposes self-attention graph pooling that regards the Score matrix as the sparse weight matrix and retains top-k elements to retain top score edges. SOGNN utilizes a 1×2 max pooling layer to retain top-k edges. SGA-LSTM [24], and SparseDGCNN [40] set Sparse weight to measure the contributions of different channels. The sparse weight is added to the loss to update the edge matrix. The sparsity is achieved when some elements of the edge matrix are close to 0.

6 Future Directions

Despite the progress made by existing methods, there are still some challenges and possible future directions. We analyze several directions that are significant for future EEG-based emotion recognition.

Temporal fully-connected graph represents a fully-connected temporal graph across time slices. It aims to solve the problem of incomplete temporal dependency in current EEG-based emotion recognition. The temporal dependency of emotional EEG inferred by existing GNNs lacks the correlation between different channels across time slices. For Time series graph mentioned in Sect. 5.3, although the relationship between time slices can be established by the Temporal graph or encoder, this relationship is limited between the same electrodes across time slices, such as v_i^{t-1} and v_i^t, while relations between different electrodes across time slice are ignored, such as v_i^{t-1} and v_j^t. This hetero-electrode relationship across time slice corresponds to a delayed response in the emotional state of the brain, i.e., there is asynchrony in the interaction between brain regions. The existence of delays between specific brain regions and surrounding brain regions for brain region activity elicited by emotional excitation implies that this asynchronous relationship contains information directly related to emotion. Therefore, a more complete temporal dependency constructed by the Temporal fully-connected graph is expected to improve the accuracy of emotion recognition.

Graph condensation aims to compress a large and complex graph structure into a simple and compact representation and retain essential emotion-related information. Both coarsening and sparsifying are promising techniques for future EEG-based emotion recognition. Emotional EEG tends to move towards high resolution. Current GNNs in EEG-based emotion recognition utilize fully connected graphs, where nodes usually have an excessive number of neighbors, which provides redundant information and even noise. As the number of electrodes increases, this defect becomes more significant. Therefore, graph condensation techniques can not only improve training efficiency but also weaken the influence of emotionally irrelevant information. The activity of brain regions in emotional states is focused, which implies that the information of specific brain regions is sufficient to identify specific emotions, while most of the connections are emotionally irrelevant. In practice, GNNs in EEG-based emotion recognition are trained to preserve localization. Existing GNNs in this field generally need to run the training process at least once to find the optimal graph condensation, so if the optimal graph is identified earlier, e.g., by training for only a few epochs, then this will significantly accelerate the running process of GNNs to build emotional representation.

Heterogeneous graph can compose different types of entities (i.e., different physiological signals). It can not only provide the graph structure of the data associations but also provide higher-level semantics of the physiological signals. Most of the current EEG-based emotion recognition datasets contain multiple physiological signals, while the heterogeneous graph is rarely used. Human emotion regulation includes multiple physiological systems, such as the cardiovascular and exocrine systems. Therefore, emotional dependencies exist not only in the interactions between brain regions but also in the activities of multiple physiological systems (organs) regulated by the brain. For example, the correlation between the heart and the striatum region increases when positive emotions are generated; the correlation between the heart and the right prefrontal cortex increases when negative emotions are generated. Heterogeneous graphs can expand the emotional dependencies of specific brain regions with other physiological organs based on the construction of emotional dependencies within the brain. In other words, Heterogeneous graphs benefit from the ability to construct more comprehensive dependencies and become a promising direction for EEG-based emotion recognition.

Dynamic graph refers to a graph whose structure changes dynamically over time. It differs from dynamically updated GNNs in EEG-based emotion recognition, meaning the graph structure can be updated automatically as training proceeds. This belongs to model-level dynamic, while the dynamic graph is graph structure-level dynamic. Given dynamic graph $\mathbf{G}(\mathbf{V}, \mathbf{E})$, $\mathbf{V} = \{(v, t_s, t_e)\}$ and $\mathbf{E} = \{(e, t_s, t_e)\}$. t_s and t_e are timestamps when edges and nodes appear and disappear. Existing methods reason about the temporal dependency of emotional EEG by cropping time slices and constructing spatial graphs independently. The former indicates that the graph can be updated, and the latter indicates that what the graph represents is the dynamic temporal dependency in emotional EEG. Although temporal graphs or encoders can be used to build temporal dependencies between slices, such dependencies do not incorporate hetero-electrode relations across time slices, i.e., changes of edges across time. In contrast, the dynamic dependency depicted by the dynamic graphs encompasses changes in the edges and, therefore, corresponds to the complete time dependency of the emotional EEG.

7 Conclusion

Graph neural networks have greatly facilitated the development of EEG-based emotion recognition. This survey provides a comprehensive study of existing GNNs in this field. In-depth discussions and summaries of the reviewed methods are presented, as well as categorization according to the three stages of graph construction. Future directions for GNN design addressing the existing challenges are also proposed. We hope that this survey will provide clear guidance for building GNNs in the field of EEG-based emotion recognition.

Acknowledgments. This study was supported in part by the Hubei Provincial Natural Science Foundation of China under Grant 2024AFB932, and in part by the CCF-NSFOCUS 'Kunpeng' Research Fund.

Disclosure of Interests. The authors have no competing interests to declare that are relevant to the content of this article.

References

1. Bao, G., et al.: Linking multi-layer dynamical GCN with style-based recalibration CNN for EEG-based emotion recognition. Front. Neurorobot. **16**, 834952 (2022)

2. Deng, X., Zhu, J., Yang, S.: SFE-Net: EEG-based emotion recognition with symmetrical spatial feature extraction. In: Proceedings of the 29th ACM International Conference on Multimedia, pp. 2391–2400 (2021)
3. Ding, Y., Guan, C.: GIGN: learning graph-in-graph representations of EEG signals for continuous emotion recognition. In: 2023 45th Annual International Conference of the IEEE Engineering in Medicine & Biology Society, pp. 1–5. IEEE (2023)
4. Ding, Y., Robinson, N., Tong, C., Zeng, Q., Guan, C.: LGGNet: learning from local-global-graph representations for brain-computer interface. IEEE Trans. Neural Netw. Learn. Syst. (2023)
5. Ding, Y., et al.: EmT: a novel transformer for generalized cross-subject EEG emotion recognition. IEEE Trans. Neural Netw. Learn. Syst. (2025)
6. Du, G., et al.: A multi-dimensional graph convolution network for EEG emotion recognition. IEEE Trans. Instrum. Meas. **71**, 1–11 (2022)
7. Feng, L., Cheng, C., Zhao, M., Deng, H., Zhang, Y.: EEG-based emotion recognition using spatial-temporal graph convolutional LSTM with attention mechanism. IEEE J. Biomed. Health Inform. **26**(11), 5406–5417 (2022)
8. Jia, Z., Lin, Y., Wang, J., Feng, Z., Xie, X., Chen, C.: HetEmotionNet: two-stream heterogeneous graph recurrent neural network for multi-modal emotion recognition. In: Proceedings of the 29th ACM International Conference on Multimedia, pp. 1047–1056 (2021)
9. Jiang, W.B., Yan, X., Zheng, W.L., Lu, B.L.: Elastic graph transformer networks for EEG-based emotion recognition. In: 2023 IEEE International Conference on Acoustics, Speech and Signal Processing, pp. 1–5 (2023)
10. Jin, M., Chen, H., Li, Z., Li, J.: EEG-based emotion recognition using graph convolutional network with learnable electrode relations. In: 2021 43rd Annual International Conference of the IEEE Engineering in Medicine & Biology Society, pp. 5953–5957. IEEE (2021)
11. Li, G., Chen, N., Jin, J.: Semi-supervised EEG emotion recognition model based on enhanced graph fusion and GCN. J. Neural Eng. **19**(2), 026039 (2022)
12. Li, J., Li, S., Pan, J., Wang, F.: Cross-subject EEG emotion recognition with self-organized graph neural network. Front. Neurosci. **15**, 611653 (2021)
13. Li, R., Wang, Y., Lu, B.L.: A multi-domain adaptive graph convolutional network for EEG-based emotion recognition. In: Proceedings of the 29th ACM International Conference on Multimedia, pp. 5565–5573 (2021)
14. Li, W.,Wang, M., Zhu, J., Song, A.: EEG-based emotion recognition using trainable adjacency relation driven graph convolutional network. IEEE Trans. Cogn. Dev. Syst. (2023)
15. Li, X., Zheng, W., Zong, Y., Chang, H., Lu, C.: Attention-based spatio-temporal graphic LSTM for EEG emotion recognition. In: 2021 International Joint Conference on Neural Networks (IJCNN), pp. 1–8. IEEE (2021)
16. Li, Y., et al.: GMSS: graph-based multi-task self-supervised learning for EEG emotion recognition. IEEE Trans. Affect. Comput. (2022)
17. Li, Y., et al.: A novel bi-hemispheric discrepancy model for EEG emotion recognition. IEEE Trans. Cogn. Dev. Syst. **13**(2), 354–367 (2020)
18. Li, Y., Zheng, W., Wang, L., Zong, Y., Cui, Z.: From regional to global brain: a novel hierarchical spatial-temporal neural network model for EEG emotion recognition. IEEE Trans. Affect. Comput. **13**(2), 568–578 (2019)
19. Li, Z., Zhang, G., Wang, L., Wei, J., Dang, J.: Emotion recognition using spatial-temporal EEG features through convolutional graph attention network. J. Neural Eng. **20**(1), 016046 (2023)

20. Liu, C., et al.: VSGT: variational spatial and gaussian temporal graph models for EEG-based emotion recognition. In: Proceedings of the Thirty-Third International Joint Conference on Artificial Intelligence, pp. 3078–3086 (2024)
21. Liu, C., Zhou, X., Zhu, Z., Zhai, L., Jia, Z., Liu, Y.: VBH-GNN: variational Bayesian heterogeneous graph neural networks for cross-subject emotion recognition. In: The Twelfth International Conference on Learning Representations (2024)
22. Liu, H., Zhang, J., Liu, Q., Cao, J.: Minimum spanning tree based graph neural network for emotion classification using EEG. Neural Netw. **145**, 308–318 (2022)
23. Liu, J., Wu, H., Zhang, L.: CR-GAT: consistency regularization enhanced graph attention network for semi-supervised EEG emotion recognition. In: 2022 IEEE International Conference on Bioinformatics and Biomedicine (BIBM), pp. 2017–2023. IEEE (2022)
24. Liu, S., Zheng, W., Song, T., Zong, Y.: Sparse graphic attention LSTM for EEG emotion recognition. In: Gedeon, T., Wong, K.W., Lee, M. (eds.) ICONIP 2019. CCIS, vol. 1142, pp. 690–697. Springer, Cham (2019). https://doi.org/10.1007/978-3-030-36808-1_75
25. Min, J., et al.: Emotion downregulation targets interoceptive brain regions while emotion upregulation targets other affective brain regions. J. Neurosci. **42**(14), 2973–2985 (2022)
26. Pan, T., Ye, Y., Cai, H., Huang, S., Yang, Y., Wang, G.: Multimodal physiological signals fusion for online emotion recognition. In: Proceedings of the 31st ACM International Conference on Multimedia, pp. 5879–5888 (2023)
27. Peng, Y., Jin, F., Kong, W., Nie, F., Lu, B.L., Cichocki, A.: OGSSL: a semi-supervised classification model coupled with optimal graph learning for EEG emotion recognition. IEEE Trans. Neural Syst. Rehabil. Eng. **30**, 1288–1297 (2022)
28. Peng, Y., Liu, H., Li, J., Huang, J., Lu, B.L., Kong, W.: Cross-session emotion recognition by joint label-common and label-specific EEG features exploration. IEEE Trans. Neural Syst. Rehabil. Eng. **31**, 759–768 (2022)
29. Qiu, X., Wang, S., Wang, R., Zhang, Y., Huang, L.: A multi-head residual connection GCN for EEG emotion recognition. Comput. Biol. Med., 107126 (2023)
30. Salvador, R., Suckling, J., Coleman, M.R., Pickard, J.D., Menon, D., Bullmore, E.: Neurophysiological architecture of functional magnetic resonance images of human brain. Cereb. Cortex **15**(9), 1332–1342 (2005)
31. Song, T., et al.: Variational instance-adaptive graph for EEG emotion recognition. IEEE Trans. Affect. Comput. (2021)
32. Song, T., Zheng, W., Liu, S., Zong, Y., Cui, Z., Li, Y.: Graph-embedded convolutional neural network for image-based EEG emotion recognition. IEEE Trans. Emerg. Top. Comput. **10**(3), 1399–1413 (2021)
33. Song, T., Zheng, W., Song, P., Cui, Z.: EEG emotion recognition using dynamical graph convolutional neural networks. IEEE Trans. Affect. Comput. **11**(3), 532–541 (2018)
34. Sun, M., Cui, W., Yu, S., Han, H., Hu, B., Li, Y.: A dual-branch dynamic graph convolution based adaptive transformer feature fusion network for EEG emotion recognition. IEEE Trans. Affect. Comput. **13**(4), 2218–2228 (2022)
35. Xu, T., Dang, W., Wang, J., Zhou, Y.: DAGAM: a domain adversarial graph attention model for subject-independent EEG-based emotion recognition. J. Neural Eng. **20**(1), 016022 (2023)
36. Xue, Y., Zheng, W., Zong, Y., Chang, H., Jiang, X.: Adaptive hierarchical graph convolutional network for EEG emotion recognition. In: 2022 International Joint Conference on Neural Networks (IJCNN), pp. 1–8. IEEE (2022)

37. Yang, L., et al.: EEG based emotion recognition by hierarchical Bayesian spectral regression framework. J. Neurosci. Meth. **402**, 110015 (2024)
38. Ye, M., Chen, C.P., Zhang, T.: Hierarchical dynamic graph convolutional network with interpretability for EEG-based emotion recognition. IEEE Trans. Neural Netw. Learn. Syst. (2022)
39. Zeng, H., et al.: Siam-GCAN: a Siamese graph convolutional attention network for EEG emotion recognition. IEEE Trans. Instrum. Meas. **71**, 1–9 (2022)
40. Zhang, G., Yu, M., Liu, Y.J., Zhao, G., Zhang, D., Zheng, W.: SparseDGCNN: recognizing emotion from multichannel EEG signals. IEEE Trans. Affect. Comput. (2021)
41. Zhang, T., Cui, Z., Xu, C., Zheng, W., Yang, J.: Variational pathway reasoning for EEG emotion recognition. In: Proceedings of the AAAI Conference on Artificial Intelligence, vol. 34, pp. 2709–2716 (2020)
42. Zhang, T., Wang, X., Xu, X., Chen, C.P.: GCB-Net: graph convolutional broad network and its application in emotion recognition. IEEE Trans. Affect. Comput. **13**(1), 379–388 (2019)
43. Zhao, H., Liu, J., Shen, Z., Yan, J.: SCC-MPGCN: self-attention coherence clustering based on multi-pooling graph convolutional network for EEG emotion recognition. J. Neural Eng. **19**(2), 026051 (2022)
44. Zhao, T., Xue, Y., Zhu, J., Zheng, W.: Heterogeneous graph convolutional neural networks for EEG-fNIRS bimodal emotion recognition. In: 2025 IEEE International Conference on Acoustics, Speech and Signal Processing, pp. 1–5 (2025)
45. Zheng, F., Hu, B., Zhang, S., Li, Y., Zheng, X.: EEG emotion recognition based on hierarchy graph convolution network. In: 2021 IEEE International Conference on Bioinformatics and Biomedicine, pp. 1628–1632 (2021)
46. Zheng, W.L., Lu, B.L.: Investigating critical frequency bands and channels for EEG-based emotion recognition with deep neural networks. IEEE Trans. Auton. Mental Dev. **7**(3), 162–175 (2015)
47. Zhong, P., Wang, D., Miao, C.: EEG-based emotion recognition using regularized graph neural networks. IEEE Trans. Affect. Comput. **13**(3), 1290–1301 (2020)
48. Zhou, X., et al.: RPGCN: relational probabilistic graphs for EEG-based emotion mining. In: Yoshikawa, M., Meng, X., Cao, Y., Xiao, C., Chen, W., Wang, Y. (eds) Advanced Data Mining and Applications, ADMA 2025. LNCS, vol. 16197. Springer, Singapore (2026). https://doi.org/10.1007/978-981-95-3453-1_8
49. Zhou, Y., Zhang, X., Sun, Y., Chen, G., Huang, L., Li, H.: EEG emotion recognition based on dynamic temporal causal graph convolutional network. Knowl. Based Syst., 113752 (2025)

Generative Artificial Intelligence for Project Management: A Review of Architectures, Applications, and Governance

Mahfuz Ahmed Anik[1], Azmine Toushik Wasi[1], Mohsin Mahmud Topu[1], Taki Hasan Rafi[2], and Dong-Kyu Chae[2(✉)]

[1] Shahjalal University of Science and Technology, Sylhet, Bangladesh
[2] Hanyang University, Seoul, Republic of Korea
dongkyu@hanyang.ac.kr

Abstract. Generative artificial intelligence is reshaping contemporary project management (PM) through advances in Large Language Models (LLMs), multimodal foundation models, and autonomous AI agents. Persistent cost and schedule overruns across IT, construction, and infrastructure projects highlight the limitations of traditional PM frameworks and motivate the adoption of adaptive, data-driven decision systems. Between 2020 and 2026, generative AI expanded beyond predictive analytics to support document understanding, long-horizon planning, automated reasoning, and tool-based workflow execution. This review synthesizes evidence from empirical research, industrial applications, and reproducible preprints to evaluate how generative AI enhances planning, scheduling, risk and cost estimation, resource allocation, progress monitoring, document analysis, and stakeholder communication. We propose a unified technical taxonomy covering LLMs, multimodal models, retrieval-augmented systems, and autonomous agents, and evaluate their empirical performance relative to classical machine learning approaches. The review further identifies socio-technical challenges related to hallucination, automation bias, data governance, and human–AI coordination. Collectively, these insights articulate the emerging landscape of generative AI–enabled project management and outline pathways for safe, scalable, and high-impact adoption across complex project ecosystems.

Keywords: Generative AI · Large Language Models · AI Agents · Project Management Automation · Multimodal Foundation Models

1 Introduction

Project management (PM) in large-scale information technology, infrastructure, and engineering domains is undergoing a structural transformation driven by persistent failures in cost, schedule, and scope performance [3,10,33,46]. Decades

M. A. Anik and A. T. Wasi—Equal contribution.

R. C.-W. Wong et al. (Eds.): PAKDD 2026, LNAI 16618, pp. 599–617, 2027.
https://doi.org/10.1007/978-981-92-1947-6_47

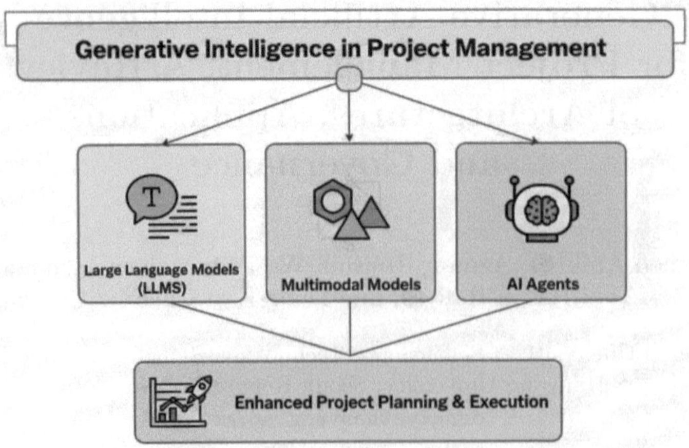

Fig. 1. Integration of LLMs, multimodal models, and AI agent systems as the core pillars of generative intelligence driving advanced project planning and execution.

of empirical evidence consistently demonstrate the limitations of deterministic planning and human-driven execution frameworks when confronted with increasing project complexity, volatility, and interdependencies. IT projects continue to experience average cost overruns approaching 45%, while in construction, nearly 98% of megaprojects exceed budgets by more than 30% and 77% are delayed by at least 40% [1,25]. These systemic deviations highlight the weakening explanatory power of traditional PM methodologies and their inability to accommodate dynamic uncertainty and high-frequency decision cycles. Compounding these challenges, classical governance models such as the PMBOK Guide [49] remain misaligned with AI-centric project ecosystems. Their limited treatment of data governance, iterative experimentation, and multidisciplinary collaboration constrains applicability in environments defined by rapid model iteration, continuous integration, and complex socio-technical interfaces [10,13,46]. Parallel research over the past decade demonstrates that machine learning (ML) can enhance planning accuracy, risk prediction, and performance monitoring [56]. However, adoption has been hindered by fragmented data infrastructures, inconsistent digital maturity, and organizational resistance [33,51].

A decisive shift occurred between 2020 and 2026 with the emergence of generative artificial intelligence, particularly Large Language Models (LLMs), multimodal foundation models, and autonomous AI agents [61]. Foundation models such as GPT-4, PaLM 2, Llama 3, and Gemini introduced generalized capabilities for contextual reasoning, document interpretation, memory-augmented planning, and tool-mediated action. Building upon these capabilities, agentic systems leverage planning algorithms, retrieval-augmented generation, and tool orchestration to execute multi-step project workflows autonomously [29] (Fig. 1). These systems demonstrate emergent competencies in long-horizon scheduling, risk anticipation, contract and document analytics, and dynamic resource coordination, capabilities previously confined to highly experienced project managers. Industrial evidence reinforces this trajectory. Organizations are deploying generative AI to automate requirements interpretation, contract review, progress assessment, portfolio analytics, and stakeholder communication [23]. Survey-based analyses confirm that AI-enabled PM systems already enhance resource allocation, scheduling precision, risk detection, and communication throughput [54]. Despite rapid progress, concerns persist regarding interpretability, hallucinations, automation complacency, and the governance of hybrid human–AI decision pipelines.

In this review, we provide the first comprehensive synthesis of generative AI in project management, spanning empirical studies, industrial applications, reproducible preprints, and system demonstrations. The scope covers the complete PM lifecycle: planning, scheduling, cost and risk estimation, resource allocation, progress monitoring, document understanding, stakeholder communication, portfolio management, and workflow orchestration. To ensure scientific rigor, priority is given to works that release datasets, evaluation pipelines, or code artifacts [42]. The contributions of this paper are threefold:

1. We present a comprehensive three-tier technical taxonomy of generative AI architectures relevant to project management, encompassing foundational LLM systems, multimodal perception models, and agent-based reasoning, planning, and execution frameworks.
2. We critically synthesize empirical findings across diverse project management tasks, highlighting areas where generative AI models demonstrate significant advantages over traditional machine learning methods.
3. We outline an integrative governance and safety framework that addresses key challenges such as hallucination mitigation, effective human–AI collaboration, and the ethical deployment of autonomous agent systems within project management contexts.

Collectively, these insights articulate the emerging landscape of generative AI in project management and outline pathways for scalable, safe, and high-impact integration.

2 Related Works

Recent studies have begun to examine how generative artificial intelligence (GenAI) is reshaping project management, particularly by automating routine tasks, enhancing decision-making, and enabling predictive risk analysis [3,10,33,46]. Systematic literature reviews of AI in project management have identified machine learning and natural language processing as key enablers, especially in risk management, time estimation, and communication [3,9,10,38,46,51]. Empirical work comparing GPT-4–generated project plans with human-created ones suggests that AI and traditional project managers offer complementary strengths, and that human guidance, especially through prompt engineering, is critical to producing reliable plans [9]. On the practitioner side, reviews of grey literature indicate that many project managers view GenAI more as a copilot than a replacement, using it to draft updates, simulate scenarios, and support agile workflows, while remaining wary of hallucinations, biases, and data-privacy risks [4]. In the construction industry, state-of-the-art analyses highlight GenAI's potential in design optimization, document generation, and safety forecasting, but also point to challenges around model governance and data integration. There is also work at the intersection of team dynamics and AI: for instance, a novel framework proposes using GenAI agents to simulate underrepresented personality roles, thereby improving diversity in project teams [16]. Despite these advances, barriers remain, such as organizational readiness, ethical concerns, and the opacity of AI models, which slow broader adoption [51]. This emerging research landscape underlines both the transformative promise of GenAI and the need for robust human–AI collaboration and governance in project management.

Our work distinguishes itself by offering the first holistic and rigorous review that spans the entire project management lifecycle. Unlike prior studies that focus on isolated applications or sectors, we present a novel technical taxonomy covering diverse generative AI architectures and systematically evaluate their empirical performance across key PM tasks. Furthermore, we uniquely address governance and safety concerns by proposing a comprehensive framework for responsible human–AI collaboration and autonomous agent deployment, paving the way for scalable and trustworthy integration in real-world PM.

3 Generative AI Architectures for Project Management

In this section, we present a hierarchical taxonomy of generative AI architectures tailored for project management, detailing their core roles and inherent trade-offs. Table 1 summarizes the key functions and challenges associated with each architectural category.

3.1 Language Models and Systems

Foundational Language Models. At the base of generative AI architectures for project management lie foundational language models, including GPT, PaLM, Llama, Claude and Gemini. These models provide general-purpose semantic reasoning, long-context planning, and document interpretation capabilities that are critical for scheduling, contract analytics, and narrative reporting within PM workflows. Their linguistic intelligence establishes a versatile foundation supporting subsequent layers.

Retrieval-Augmented Grounding Systems. Retrieval-augmented generation (RAG) systems ground both unimodal and multimodal models in enterprise-specific repositories and real-time operational data [5,22,32]. By reducing hallucinations and ensuring legal and procedural correctness, RAG systems support compliance-heavy workflows, safeguarding the integrity of safety, contract, and regulatory processes within PM. Core architectural decisions for enterprise deployment center on how to introduce specialized project knowledge into the

Table 1. AI Architecture Roles and Trade-offs in Project Management Systems

Segment	Architecture	Core Roles	Trade-offs/Challenges
Language Models and Systems	Foundational Language Models	Provide general-purpose semantic reasoning, long-context planning, and document interpretation for scheduling, contract analytics, and narrative reporting	High computational cost; potential hallucinations; static knowledge after training [22]
	Retrieval-Augmented Grounding Systems	Ground LLMs in enterprise repositories and real-time data to reduce hallucinations, ensure compliance, and enable dynamic knowledge updates [5, 22, 32]	Dependency on retrieval quality and data integrity; security and access control challenges; governance over proprietary data [22, 32]
Multimodal Intelligence for Perception and Monitoring	Visual and Chart Interpretation	Automated project reporting and status analysis from visual data; enables interpretation of dashboards, Gantt charts, and tabular reports [31].	Requires high-quality domain-specific datasets; limited generalization to diverse chart types; data generation pipelines can be costly and complex [31]
	Sensor Fusion and Real-Time Progress Monitoring	Enables real-time activity logging and progress monitoring via fusion of location, motion, environment, and physiological data; improves accuracy and latency over large models [48, 59].	Challenges include sensor data heterogeneity, privacy concerns, model deployment on edge devices, and integration with BIM and digital twins [48, 59]
Reasoning, Planning and Execution	Hybrid Neuro-Symbolic Reasoning Engines	Combine LLMs with constraint solvers, optimization engines, and formal reasoning modules to produce feasible, optimized project schedules and resource allocations [8, 12, 33, 45]	Integration complexity; balancing neural flexibility with symbolic rigidity; solver scalability and performance constraints [8]
	Autonomous Agentic Orchestrators	Execute workflows via ReAct-style reasoning-action loops, multi-agent coordination, and meta-planning to enable dynamic task decomposition, verification, long-horizon planning, and compliance enforcement [23, 57, 60, 63]	Complexity in coordination and verification; risk of cascading failures; alignment with human expert expectations; managing autonomous behaviors [2, 58]

LLM. Fine-tuning involves adapting model parameters using domain-specific data, producing a static knowledge snapshot susceptible to becoming outdated and hallucinating under unfamiliar queries [32]. In contrast, RAG grounds generation in external, secured knowledge sources, enabling dynamic data updates, reducing hallucinations, and improving governance over proprietary information [22]. Projects such as RITSA demonstrate RAG's democratization of complex domain knowledge for non-expert stakeholders [5]. Hybrid approaches that combine fine-tuning for foundational nuance with RAG for live data management emerge as the most robust [22].

3.2 Multimodal Intelligence for Perception and Monitoring

LLMs, limited to text, require multimodal fusion, ranging from RAG to hybrid neuro-symbolic systems, to interpret diverse project artifacts like charts, reports, and sensor streams for effective project management (Fig. 2).

Visual and Chart Interpretation. LLMs are inherently text-based and thus insufficient for interpreting critical non-textual project artifacts such as financial dashboards, tabular reports, and Gantt charts [31]. Specialized multimodal LLMs (MLLMs), like ChartLlama, utilize high-quality instruction-tuned datasets created via multi-step data pipelines to achieve state-of-the-art chart comprehension and automated reporting, validated by superior performance on ChartQA benchmarks [31]. Additionally, temporal project data such as financial forecasts and resource trends are increasingly modeled through dedicated

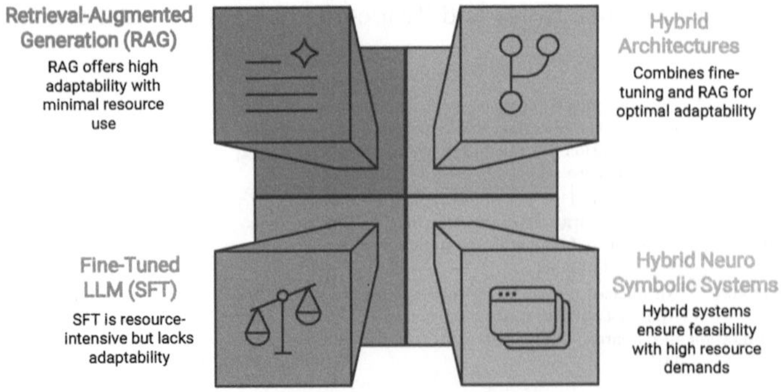

Fig. 2. Comparison of multimodal perception architectures, contrasting RAG pipelines, supervised fine-tuned LLMs, and hybrid neuro-symbolic systems.

time-series foundation models including Chronos, MOMENT, and TimeGPT-1, facilitating accurate predictive analytics [64].

Sensor Fusion and Real-Time Progress Monitoring. Traditional manual progress monitoring in construction and manufacturing is being replaced by AI-driven sensor fusion frameworks. DailyLLM exemplifies this shift by integrating lightweight LLMs with multimodal contextual sensor data, spanning location, motion, environment, and physiology, to generate real-time, context-aware activity logs [59]. Despite its smaller size (1.5B parameters), DailyLLM outperforms much larger models in accuracy and inference speed, highlighting the primacy of targeted modality fusion over sheer model scale [59]. Complementary advances in integrating Building Information Modeling (BIM) with AI, IoT, and digital twins underpin smart project ecosystems by enabling automated design verification, event log mining, predictive maintenance, and sustainable infrastructure analytics [48]. Together, these developments empower AI agents with robust multimodal perception, enabling autonomous environmental reasoning by correlating financial visuals with granular real-time site data to produce validated project status reports.

3.3 Reasoning, Planning and Execution

Hybrid Neuro-Symbolic Reasoning Engines. Hybrid neuro-symbolic reasoning engines integrate LLMs with symbolic solvers, optimization engines, and formal reasoning modules to ensure logically coherent and operationally feasible project schedules [8,12,33,45]. These systems mitigate "planning hallucinations" by delegating mathematical and logical validation to dedicated solvers, which translates natural language project constraints into solvable optimization problems. This synergy enables feasibility, optimality, and compliance within automated resource allocation and scheduling.

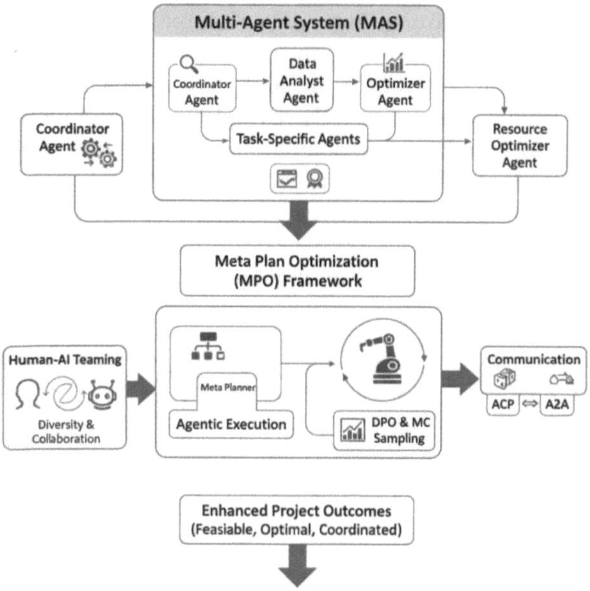

Fig. 3. Overview of how Multi-Agent Systems (MAS) integrate with the Meta Plan Optimization (MPO) framework to coordinate agents, communication protocols, and human–AI teaming for optimized project outcomes.

Autonomous Agentic Orchestrators. At the apex of the taxonomy, autonomous agentic orchestrators unify all underlying generative AI layers into executable project workflows. Leveraging ReAct-style reasoning–action loops, Meta Plan Optimization (MPO) for long-horizon planning [63], multi-agent orchestration protocols [57,60], and emerging enterprise PM copilots [23], these systems perform dynamic task decomposition, cross-agent verification, and compliance-aligned decision-making. As illustrated in Fig. 3, Multi-Agent Systems (MAS) integrate with MPO to coordinate specialized agents through standardized communication channels and human–AI teaming structures, producing more reliable and expert-aligned project outcomes [2,58].

Large Language Models (LLMs) provide the cognitive substrate of these agents, supplying reasoning, perception, and action capabilities, with architectural distinctions often based on planners, memory modules, and reflective supervision [62]. MAS frameworks further decompose responsibilities across Coordinator Agents and Task-Specific Agents, enhancing robustness and reducing hallucination via cross-validation mechanisms [57]. Complementing this, recent research explores human–AI team diversity optimization, showing that generative agents fine-tuned on personality and behavioral corpora can emulate diverse team archetypes and strengthen collaboration dynamics [16]. Communication standards such as ACP and A2A continue to evolve to support scalable, interoperable agent coordination [60].

Applied studies in software engineering reinforce these trends: LLM-assisted tools improve documentation, communication, and coordination across the SDLC, though issues of trust, privacy, and over-reliance necessitate stronger governance and domain adaptation [21]. Broader survey evidence also confirms AI's contributions to scheduling, risk prediction, and team coordination while emphasizing persistent challenges in transparency and data quality [19]. Table 2 synthesizes the architectural, collaborative, and governance dimensions of these agentic systems, situating autonomous LLM-based agents within the emerging landscape of AI-augmented project management.

Table 2. Integrated overview of autonomous LLM-based agent architectures, multi-agent coordination mechanisms, and reliability-focused human–AI collaboration.

Category	Focus Area	Representative Literature
Agent Architecture, Planning & Optimization	Cognitive architectures, neuro-symbolic reasoning & agent role design	[12, 19, 34, 36, 57, 60, 62]
	Planning & optimization frameworks (MPO, DPO, constraint modelling, resource allocation)	[2, 8, 20, 33, 45, 58, 63]
	Hierarchical & hybrid planning structures (centralized–decentralized–hybrid)	[2, 36, 57, 60, 62]
Multi-Agent Collaboration, Communication & Orchestration	Coordination protocols & workflow orchestration (A2A, ACP, swarm, roles)	[2, 19, 21, 23, 36, 57, 60]
	Collaboration dynamics in software & project teams (agile, cross-functional, LLM-assisted)	[4, 16, 19, 21, 23]
	Consensus, cross-verification & error-resilient agent ecosystems	[26, 44, 50, 57, 66]
Reliability, Governance & Human–AI Collaboration	Safety, risk management & hallucination mitigation (detection, filtering, redundancy)	[26, 30, 44, 50, 66]
	Governance, compliance & responsible deployment (ethics, AI Act, PMBOK integration)	[6, 13, 17, 41, 43]
	Human–AI teaming, diversity & organizational integration (HITL, hybrid teams, adoption)	[4, 16, 19, 21]

4 Application Domains Across the PM Lifecycle

This section maps the integration points of generative AI across the project management lifecycle, outlining how current research aligns with four major functional application domains, as noted in Table 3.

4.1 Planning, Scheduling, and Resource Allocation

Generative AI is increasingly central to planning, scheduling, and optimization within the project management lifecycle, with LLMs demonstrating strong validity, robustness, and scalability across diverse planning contexts. **LLM-based planning and strategic modelling** frameworks support structured reasoning

Table 3. Categorization of AI Applications Across Project Management Domains

Application Domain	Functional Aspect	Representative Literature
Planning, Scheduling & Optimization	LLM-based planning and strategic modelling	[14,35]
	Resource allocation and non-convex optimization	[2,33,58]
	Constraint modelling and scheduling	[8,45,52]
	Planning benchmarks and evaluation	[42]
	Human–AI collaborative planning	[9,16]
Risk Management, Cost Forecasting & Predictive Analytics	AI-driven cost estimation	[1,39,53]
	LLM-based cost/duration prediction	[15]
	Predictive risk and disruption forecasting	[40,47]
	System-wide predictive analytics	[54,56]
Document Intelligence, Compliance & Automation	RAG-based retrieval and document grounding	[5,22,32]
	Automated business process/value analysis	[19,20]
	BIM-assisted construction documentation	[48]
	AI compliance and governance	[30,43]
	LLM risks, safety, and hallucination mitigation	[44,50,66]
Stakeholder Communication & Multi-Agent Collaboration	AI chatbots and communication automation	[23,37]
	Team collaboration enhancement	[4,21]
	Multi-agent and swarm intelligence	[24,36,60]
	Multimodal reporting and progress monitoring	[28,31,59]

and long-horizon task decomposition, outperforming earlier heuristic and rule-based systems in coherence and analytical consistency [14,35]. Beyond high-level planning, **resource allocation and non-convex optimization** tasks now benefit from LLM-driven problem translation, where natural-language constraints are converted into solvable mathematical formulations, substantially reducing reliance on specialized optimization expertise [2,33,58].

LLMs integrated with dedicated solvers further strengthen **constraint modelling and scheduling**, ensuring feasibility through symbolic reasoning and mitigating planning hallucinations in automated schedule generation [8,45,52]. To evaluate these capabilities, standardized **planning benchmarks and evaluation** suites such as REALM-Bench provide rigorous assessment methodologies, including Success Rate, Planning Optimality, and Makespan, for complex combinatorial challenges like Job Shop Scheduling (JSSP) [42].

Finally, effective deployment increasingly depends on **human–AI collaborative planning**, where studies show that generative models offer structural consistency and analytical breadth, while human planners contribute contextual nuance, stakeholder awareness, and refined judgment. Synergistic planning workflows built on iterative refinement and guided prompting consistently outperform either humans or AI alone [9,16].

4.2 Risk and Cost Estimation/Forecasting

Generative AI and advanced machine-learning systems are reshaping risk and cost forecasting across the project lifecycle by enabling dynamic, continuously updated predictions that respond to evolving project conditions. **AI-driven**

cost estimation frameworks integrate real-time data streams, market fluctuations, and historical cost structures to anticipate overruns before they materialize, significantly enhancing early-stage financial control [1,39,53]. Complementing these models, **LLM-based cost/duration prediction** introduces natural language reasoning into structured estimation tasks; recent results show LLMs achieving lower error rates than state-of-the-art neural baselines, including outperforming Elman Network estimators in software cost prediction [15].

Beyond cost estimation, generative AI contributes to robust project stability through **predictive risk and disruption forecasting**. These systems integrate machine-learning risk classifiers, anomaly detection, supply-chain monitoring, and digital-twin–driven scenario modeling to identify delays, disruptions, and cascading failures earlier and more accurately than traditional methodologies [40,47]. At broader operational scales, **system-wide predictive analytics** unify risk, cost, schedule, and resource signals into holistic situational awareness tools, enabling proactive decision-making and improving resilience across complex, distributed project environments [54,56].

Traditional deep learning models already demonstrate strong predictive capability in estimation tasks: for example, autoencoder-enhanced DNNs achieve a 14.6% average error rate in design-stage road construction cost estimation [39]. In parallel, LLMs are emerging as competitive estimators, achieving Mean Absolute Error (MAE) improvements of up to 3.7% over prior state-of-the-art models in structured cost forecasting [15].

4.3 Document Understanding, Compliance, and Reporting

Generative AI, particularly LLMs equipped with retrieval, grounding, and structured prompting, has become central to automating semantic interpretation and compliance-oriented reasoning across the project documentation landscape. LLMs now demonstrate robust capability in **semantic decomposition and qualitative assessment** of complex project artifacts, exemplified by automated Value-Added Analysis (VAA) for business process models [20]. In this setting, high-level activities are algorithmically disassembled into fine-grained operational steps, each of which is classified against Lean criteria to detect value-added tasks, non–value-added activities, and systemic waste. Such models reduce analyst subjectivity and cycle time while preserving methodological rigor, showing that LLMs can reliably execute normative, domain-specific reasoning frameworks when guided through well-engineered prompts; the availability of public ground-truth labels further enhances reproducibility and empirical benchmarking [20].

Complementing this, **RAG-based document intelligence** architectures enable high-precision compliance automation by grounding LLM outputs in extensive repositories of contractual clauses, regulatory directives, safety specifications, and organizational governance protocols [5]. These systems mitigate hallucination risks by constraining generation to verified sources, supporting high-stakes use cases such as contract clause extraction, discrepancy detection, regulatory mapping, and audit trail generation. Broader developments in **AI-assisted documentation ecosystems**, including BIM-integrated construction documentation, automated governance workflows, and LLM safety frameworks, extend these capabilities to multidisciplinary project domains [30,43,48]. As hallucination mitigation strategies and model risk controls continue to advance, LLM-driven document intelligence is increasingly positioned as a core enabler of trustworthy, transparent, and scalable project reporting processes [44,50,66].

4.4 Stakeholder Communication and Portfolio Management

AI agents are transforming stakeholder engagement by analyzing emails and meeting notes to extract sentiment and flag early concerns. Using **AI chatbots and communication automation**, they combine advanced prompting with retrieval-augmented generation (RAG) to deliver personalized responses and targeted reminders, enhancing trust and collaboration [23]. Empirical studies show chatbots maintaining continuous dialogue, providing instant, context-aware replies that improve satisfaction and project adherence, while demanding advanced NLP and adaptive interaction design [37].

Beyond communication, **team collaboration enhancement** is supported by AI systems that improve coordination and decision-making across distributed teams [4,21]. Advances in **multi-agent and swarm intelligence** enable decentralized agents to cooperatively manage workflows, resolve conflicts, and optimize resources through emergent coordination [24,36,60].

At the portfolio level, **multimodal reporting and progress monitoring** integrate data from charts, dashboards, sensor streams, and BIM models, offering real-time insights into project status. Systems like ChartLlama and DailyLLM provide dynamic visualization and spatiotemporal monitoring to inform executive decisions and strategic adjustments across concurrent projects [28,31,59]. These agents monitor timelines, detect resource conflicts, and recommend changes to align projects with organizational goals [23].

5 Evaluation and Reproducibility Landscape

5.1 Standardized Metrics for Project Management Tasks

Robust evaluation of generative AI systems in project management necessitates standardized metrics that extend beyond conventional language model benchmarks, capturing both predictive accuracy and operational effectiveness.

⇒ **Cost and Predictive Metrics.** In the domain of cost estimation and forecasting, regression-based metrics are essential for quantifying prediction fidelity. Mean Absolute Error (MAE) is widely preferred for its intuitive interpretation, representing the average absolute deviation from actual costs (e.g., average monetary error) [7]. Complementarily, Root Mean Squared Error (RMSE) is employed to emphasize the impact of large deviations, thereby reflecting risk sensitivity in high-stakes project scenarios where significant errors incur disproportionate consequences [39].

⇒ **Planning and Optimization Metrics.** For AI-driven agents executing complex, multi-step workflows, evaluation metrics must capture both the correctness of outcomes and resource efficiency. Success Rate provides a binary measure of task completion efficacy [52], while optimization-specific metrics such as Planning Optimality and Makespan quantify the quality and temporal efficiency of generated plans [42]. In multi-agent contexts, decision-quality is further assessed via accuracy benchmarks on specialized datasets such as NLP4LP and Optibench, validating performance improvements arising from collaborative and decentralized planning strategies [58].

5.2 Prioritized Benchmarks and Reproducibility Artifacts

Reproducibility is essential for academic rigor and trustworthy deployment in generative AI for project management, necessitating comprehensive versioning of code, hyperparameters, models, and exact datasets used in training and evaluation. Platforms such as OpenML facilitate this by offering standardized datasets and documenting millions of reproducible machine learning experiments [11]. However, the specialized and multimodal nature of many PM tasks exposes a significant gap in publicly available, expert-validated datasets. While general benchmarks like SuperGLUE for language and HumanEval for code exist, domain-specific resources, such as annotated construction sensor logs or expert-validated Gantt charts, remain scarce. To mitigate this, some researchers leverage large language models to synthetically generate high-quality instruction-tuning data, as demonstrated with multimodal models like ChartLlama [31]. Addressing this reproducibility gap requires concerted collaborative efforts to develop and share large-scale, domain-specific datasets for critical tasks including progress monitoring and visual schedule analysis.

Several key public benchmarks underpin reproducible research in PM-focused AI. REALM-Bench offers real-world planning scenarios encompassing complex combinatorial problems such as Job Shop Scheduling (JSSP) [42], while the WIPE project provides ground-truth labels for automated Value-Added Analysis [20]. ChartLlama contributes specialized datasets for multimodal chart comprehension tasks [31], and ProjectEval introduces an automated, user-centric framework for evaluating LLM agents' project-level code generation with objective metrics on code execution and similarity, thereby advancing explainable and reproducible evaluation at engineering scales like ProjectEval. Together, these resources establish foundational pillars for consistent benchmarking and robust scientific progress in generative AI for project management.

6 Governance, Risk, and Human-AI Teaming

Integration of generative AI into mission-critical project management decisions introduces multifaceted risks spanning factual integrity, legal accountability, and human factors. To ensure trustworthy and responsible deployment, a comprehensive governance framework is imperative, encompassing technical, regulatory, and human-centered dimensions.

6.1 Failure Modes and Liability Assessment

Table 4 synthesizes these governance imperatives, delineating failure modes alongside recommended mitigation strategies for responsible generative AI integration in project management.

Table 4. Failure Modes, Impacts, and Mitigation Strategies in PM-AI Systems

Failure Mode	Impact on Project & Liability	Mitigation Strategy (Technical/Architecture) & Required Human-in-the-Loop (HITL) Control Point
Factual/Logical Hallucination	Inaccurate resource planning; Legal/contractual liability; Financial loss	Retrieval-Augmented Generation (RAG); Confidence/Uncertainty Quantification; MPO/Symbolic Validation; Expert review of high-impact decisions (e.g., critical path changes, contract interpretation)
Automation Complacency/Bias	Delayed response to critical deviations; Catastrophic system failures	Graceful Degradation Architecture; High-fidelity, real-time deviation alerts; Active task assignment; Mandatory review of system-flagged anomalies; Periodic vigilance tasks
Data Privacy Breach (GDPR/AI Act)	Regulatory fines; Loss of customer/stakeholder trust	Secure data flow mapping; Differential Privacy; Data minimization protocols; Data Protection Impact Assessment (DPIA) Review; Governance audit of data usage
Logical Flaws in Planning/Optimization	Sub-optimal project efficiency; Infeasible execution paths	Hybrid Symbolic Reasoning (CP solvers); Continuous optimization based on execution feedback; Non-expert user validation of plan clarity/feasibility; Global plan oversight before commitment

Hallucination and Error. Hallucination remains the predominant failure mode of large language models (LLMs), wherein the model generates plausible yet factually incorrect or fabricated outputs [50]. Within project management contexts, such errors can propagate severe consequences, including flawed cost estimations, erroneous resource allocations, or the creation of fictitious contractual terms [44]. Empirical studies in construction project management highlight persistent shortcomings of LLMs in contextual awareness, accountability, and ethical transparency, underscoring the critical need for human oversight. The Ethical Decision Support Assessment Checklist (EDSAC) exemplifies efforts to codify ethical considerations, recommending that LLMs serve strictly as decision-support tools under robust human-in-the-loop (HITL) governance [6].

Liability and Regulatory Mandates. As AI systems increasingly influence high-stakes business outcomes, legal accountability for AI-driven errors becomes paramount. Regulatory frameworks such as the GDPR emphasize data accuracy (Article 5(1)(d)) and fairness, mandating meaningful human intervention for automated decisions with legal or similarly significant effects [17,41]. Failure to comply exposes organizations to regulatory penalties and reputational damage.

Technical strategies such as RAG provide a primary defense against hallucination by anchoring outputs in verifiable external knowledge bases [50]. Additionally, multi-agent systems enhance reliability by instituting cross-agent verification protocols to mitigate individual agent errors [57].

6.2 Data Privacy and Regulatory Compliance

Comprehensive compliance with data privacy regulations, including GDPR and emerging frameworks such as the EU AI Act, is essential throughout the AI lifecycle, encompassing data collection, model training, inference, and feedback loops [30]. Privacy-preserving methodologies demonstrate that LLMs can be harnessed responsibly to forecast project outcomes without compromising individual privacy. For example, GPT-4 Turbo's application in participatory budgeting illustrates how anonymized textual data and aggregated historical patterns can preserve transparency while maintaining predictive performance, offering a viable template for accountable AI in both public sector and enterprise project management [65]. Organizations deploying AI for sensitive decisions, including contractual execution, financial access, or personnel evaluation, must perform rigorous Data Protection Impact Assessments (DPIAs) and adopt data minimization and secure storage practices to mitigate privacy risks.

6.3 Human-AI Collaboration Models and Complacency

Automation complacency, or the overreliance on AI outputs by human operators, represents a critical human factor risk in project management, where delayed intervention during anomalies can have catastrophic consequences [27]. Prolonged stable AI operation fosters complacency, diminishing vigilance and response readiness. To mitigate this, governance architectures must prioritize active human engagement, transitioning from passive Human-on-the-Loop monitoring to proactive Human-in-the-Loop supervision. Key design principles include graceful degradation, where the system alerts operators of deviations, conveys the trajectory and severity of change, and dynamically adjusts automation levels to avert cascading failures [27].

Mandatory Human-in-the-Loop (HITL) control points must be integrated throughout the workflow to ensure safety and accountability, such as **Critical Decision Gates, Logical Validation**, and **Data Quality Validation**. These include critical decision gates that require expert human review for all high-impact actions, such as critical path modifications, contract changes, and automated financial or HR decisions, to guarantee regulatory compliance and responsibility [18]. Additionally, human oversight is essential for logical validation, detecting and correcting any inconsistencies or hallucinations in AI-generated plans to maintain operational integrity. Verification of anomalous data and flagged outputs by experts further safeguards data quality and trustworthiness [55]. Given that LLMs may produce syntactically flawless but factually or legally incorrect outputs [44], and considering the high-stakes implications of automated decisions, the project manager's role must evolve into that of an ethical gatekeeper and expert validator. Consequently, system architectures should be designed to route all high-risk, ambiguous, or error-prone outputs directly to human decision-makers, ensuring ultimate accountability remains with humans.

7 Discussion

The integration of LLMs, multimodal systems, and autonomous AI agents is driving a fundamental shift in project management, from retrospective tracking to proactive, autonomous decision support and workflow orchestration. This shift relies on key advances: the adoption of RAG for factual grounding and liability mitigation; hybrid neuro-symbolic reasoning to ensure logical consistency and operational feasibility; and specialized multimodal models providing real-time, context-aware perception across diverse project data.

Critical Research Gaps. Despite progress, significant challenges limit widespread adoption and robust evaluation. There is a lack of publicly available, domain-specific longitudinal datasets capturing project lifecycle complexity, such as annotated Gantt charts, resource dependencies, and sensor logs, essential for training and benchmarking multimodal models. Beyond standard predictive metrics (e.g., MAE, RMSE), domain-specific measures are needed to rigorously assess decision quality, calibration, and uncertainty in high-stakes PM settings. Additionally, as multi-agent AI grows, standardized, scalable protocols for heterogeneous agent collaboration are vital to ensure reliable problem-solving.

Future Trajectories. Future generative AI systems will further integrate neuro-symbolic reasoning to tackle increasingly complex scheduling and optimization challenges. Lightweight, efficient multimodal agents designed for seamless data fusion will scale to global portfolio management, enabling monitoring and orchestration across multiple concurrent projects to optimize strategic alignment and resource flow. The success of these systems depends on mature governance frameworks that position project managers as essential human-in-the-loop overseers responsible for ethical decision-making and liability.

Practitioner studies echo this view, with project managers embracing generative AI as a collaborative copilot, augmenting automation, analytics, agile facilitation, and communication, rather than a replacement. Grey literature highlights both optimism and caution, emphasizing the enduring importance of human judgment, ethical safeguards, and upskilling to fully harness generative AI's potential in project management [4].

8 Conclusion

Generative artificial intelligence is fundamentally transforming PM by enabling adaptive, data-driven decision-making beyond traditional predictive analytics. Advances in LLMs, multimodal systems, and autonomous agents have expanded capabilities in planning, scheduling, risk assessment, and stakeholder communication. This review presented a comprehensive taxonomy of generative AI architectures and synthesized empirical evidence demonstrating their advantages over classical machine learning methods. Despite these gains, critical challenges remain, including mitigating hallucinations, addressing automation bias, ensuring robust data governance, and fostering effective human–AI collaboration. Overcoming these socio-technical hurdles is essential for trustworthy, high-impact deployment in complex project environments.

Acknowledgement. This work was supported by the Institute of Information & communications Technology Planning & Evaluation (IITP) grant funded by the Korea government (MSIT) (**RS-2025-25422680**, Metacognitive AGI Framework and its Applications, and **RS-2020-II201373**, Artificial Intelligence Graduate School Program (Hanyang University)).

References

1. Acquah, E.: AI-driven cost estimation: stop project budget overruns (2025)
2. Amayuelas, A., et al.: Self-resource allocation in multi-agent LLM systems. arXiv (2025)
3. Aramali, V., Cho, N., Pande, F., Al-Mhdawi, M., Ojiako, U., Qazi, A.: Generative AI in project management: impacts on corporate values, employee perceptions, and organizational practices. Project Leadership and Society 6 (2025)
4. Assalaarachchi, L.I., Masood, Z., Hoda, R., Grundy, J.: Generative AI for software project management: insights from a review of software practitioner literature. IEEE Softw. (2025)
5. Awadid, A., Meyer-Vitali, A., Vereno, D., Gagnant, M.: RITSA: toward a retrieval-augmented generation system for intelligent transportation systems architecture. In: Modelsward'2025 (2025)
6. Azie, S., Meng, Y.: The ethical compass of the machine: evaluating large language models for decision support in construction project management. arXiv (2025)
7. Bajaj, A.: Performance metrics in machine learning (2025)
8. Bajan, K.: Exploring the applicability of large language models in constraint programming development (2024)
9. Barcaui, A., Monat, A.: Who is better in project planning?generative artificial intelligence or project managers? Project Leadership and Society (2023)
10. Bento, S., Pereira, L., Gonçalves, R., Dias, Á., Costa, R.L.D.: Artificial intelligence in project management: systematic literature review. Int. J. Technol. Intell. Plann. **13**(2), 143 (2022)
11. Bischl, B., et al.: Openml: insights from 10 years and more than a thousand papers. Patterns (2025)
12. Bougzime, O., Jabbar, S., Cruz, C., Demoly, F.: Unlocking the potential of generative ai through neuro-symbolic architectures: benefits and limitations (2025)
13. Burdakov, A., Ahn, M.J.: Is pmbok guide the right fit for AI? Reevaluating project management in the face of artificial intelligence projects. arXiv (2025)
14. Cao, P., et al.: Large language models for planning: a comprehensive and systematic survey. arXiv (2025)

15. Carpenter, J., Wu, C.-Y., Eisty, N.U.: Leveraging large language models for predicting cost and duration in software engineering projects. arXi (2024)
16. Chan, J., Li, Y.: Enhancing team diversity with generative AI: a novel project management framework. In: 2024 IEEE 48th Annual Computers, Software, and Applications Conference (COMPSAC), pp. 1648–1652. IEEE (2024)
17. Clifford, D., Ausloos, J.: Data protection and the role of fairness. Yearbook Eur. Law **37**, 130–187 (2018)
18. Cobbe, J., Lee, M.S.A., Singh, J.: Reviewable automated decisionmaking: a framework for accountable algorithmic systems. In: ACM FAccT (2021)
19. Crawford, T., et al.: AI in software engineering: a survey on project management applications. arXiv (2023)
20. De Michele, W., Armas Cervantes, A., Frermann, L.: Automated business process analysis: an LLM-based approach to value assessment. In: CAiSE (2025)
21. Dhanuka, D.: Impact of LLMs on team collaboration in software development. arXiv (2025)
22. Erickson, J.: Rag vs. fine-tuning: how to choose (2024)
23. Express, P.: AI agents: the next power players in project management (2025)
24. Ferrag, M.A., Tihanyi, N., Debbah, M.: From LLM reasoning to autonomousai agents: a comprehensive review. arXiv (2025)
25. Flyvbjerg, B., Gardner, D.: How Big Things Get Done: The Surprising Factors that Determine the Fate of Every Project (2022)
26. Ganesan, K.: Can LLM hallucinations be eliminated? Our experiments across large language models (n.d.)
27. Gen, B., Cherry, D., Cowen, M.: Is human-on-the-loop the best answer for rapid relevant responses (R3)? In: Joint Air and Space Power (2021)
28. Greeshma, A., Edayadiyil, J.B.: Automated progress monitoring of construction projects using machine learning and image processing approach. Mater. Today Proc. **65**, 554–563 (2022)
29. Gress, B.: AI agents in project management: the new force behind highperforming teams (2025)
30. Guldimann, P., et al.: COMPL-AI framework: a technical interpretation and LLM benchmarking suite for the EU artificial intelligence act. arXiv (2024)
31. Han, Y., et al.: Chartllama: a multimodal LLM for chart understanding and generation (2023)
32. Haponik, A.: Rag vs fine-tuning: a comparative analysis of LLM learning techniques (2024)
33. Hettrich, B., Krings, N., Kock, A.: Bridging the expertise gap: the role of generative ai in supporting project planning tasks for novices and professionals. Creat. Innov. Manag. **34**(4), 789–805 (2025)
34. Hu, Y.: Neuro-symbolic program generation and execution for hybrid reasoning. Ph.D. thesis, Iowa State Universit (2025)
35. Huang, S., Lipovetzky, N., Cohn, T.: Planning in the dark: Llmsymbolic planning pipeline without experts. In: AAAI (2025)
36. Hussain, T., Ahmed, T., Haque, M.S., Rashid, M.R.A.: Collective wisdom in language models: harnessing LLM-swarm for agile project management. In: NeurIPS 2024 Workshop on Open-World Agents (2024)
37. Joshi, H.: Artificial intelligence in project management: a study of the role of AI-powered chatbots in project stakeholder engagement. IJSEPM (2024)
38. Khalil, M., et al.: Mapping the AI landscape in project management context: a systematic literature review. Systems **13**(10), 913 (2025)

39. Kim, J.-S.: AI-powered forecasting of environmental impacts and construction costs to enhance project management in highway projects. Buildings (2025)
40. Larbi, S.Y., Manu, E.O., Donatus, S., Assumang, D.K., Adimonyemma, J., Oyekola, T.S.: Integrating AI and machine learning in project management for proactive supply chain disruption mitigation. GJCST: C (2025)
41. Lazcoz, G., De Hert, P.: Humans in the GDPR and AIA governance of automated and algorithmic systems. Essential pre-requisites against abdicating responsibilities. Comput. Law Secur. Rev. **50**, 105833 (2023)
42. Ling, G.L.: Realm-bench: a real-world planning benchmark for LLMs and multi-agent systems (2025)
43. Loveth, R.G.: From GDPR to the AI act: how European data protection principles influence global AI regulation (2025)
44. Maliugina, D.: LLM hallucinations and failures: lessons from 5 examples (2024)
45. Michailidis, K., Tsouros, D., Guns, T.: Constraint modelling with LLMs using in-context learning. In: CP (2024)
46. Nenni, M.E., De Felice, F., De Luca, C., Forcina, A.: How artificial intelligence will transform project management in the age of digitization: a systematic literature review. Manag. Rev. Q. **75**(2) (2024)
47. Pal, D.K.D., Chitta, S., Bonam, V.S.M., Katari, P., Thota, S.: AI-assisted project management: enhancing decision-making and forecasting. J. Artif. Intell. Res. **3**, 146–171 (2023)
48. Pan, Y., Zhang, L.: Integrating BIM and AI for smart construction management: current status and future directions. ACM (2023)
49. Project Management Institute. A Guide to the Project Management Body of Knowledge (PMBOK Guide). 6 edition (2017)
50. Ray, S., Srinivasan, B.: Reducing hallucinations in large language models with custom intervention using amazon bedrock agents (2024)
51. Salimimoghadam, S., et al.: The rise of artificial intelligence in project management: a systematic literature review of current opportunities, enablers, and barriers. Buildings **15**(7), 1130 (2025)
52. Schnell Melander, V.: Neuro-symbolic AI agents for software project scheduling (2025)
53. Seecharan, L., Chadee, A.A.: Artificial intelligence (AI) tools for cost overruns on construction projects. IJCNIS **16**(5), 309–322 (2024)
54. Shoushtari, F., Daghighi, A., Ghafourian, E.: Application of artificial intelligence in project management. IJIEOR **6**(2), 49–63 (2024)
55. Sverdlik, D.: Implementing human-in-the-loop data quality gates for enterprise AI pipelines (2025)
56. Taboada, I., Daneshpajouh, A., Toledo, N., De Vass, T.: Artificial intelligence enabled project management: a systematic literature review. Appl. Sci. **13**(8), 5014 (2023)
57. Collabnix Team: Multi-agent and multi-LLM architecture: complete guide for 2025 (2025)
58. Thind, R., Sun, Y., Liang, L., Yang, H.: Optimai: optimization from natural language using LLM-powered AI agents. arXiv (2025)
59. Tian, Y., Ren, X., Wang, Z., Gungor, O., Yu, X., Rosing, T.: Dailyllm: context-aware activity log generation using multi-modal sensors and LLMs. arXiv (2025)
60. Tran, K.-T., Dao, D., Nguyen, M.-D., Pham, Q.-V., O'Sullivan, B., Nguyen, H.D.: Multi-agent collaboration mechanisms: a survey of LLMs. arXiv (2025)
61. Wasi, A.T., Eram, E.H., Mitu, S.A., Ahsan, M.M.: Generative AI as a geopolitical factor in industry 5.0: sovereignty, access, and control. arXiv (2025)

62. Xie, J., Chen, Z., Zhang, R., Wan, X., Li, G.: Large multimodal agents: a survey. arXiv (2024)
63. Xiong, W., et al.: MPO: boosting LLM agents with meta plan optimization (2025)
64. Xu, X.: Awesome multimodal LLMs for time series analysis (2025)
65. Zambrano, J., Contet, C., Gudino, J., Garrido-Lucero, F., Grandi, U., Hidalgo, C.A.: Leveraging LLMs for privacy-aware predictions in participatory budgeting. arXiv (2025)
66. Zhang, X., Lyu, D., Li, X.: Risk assessment and security analysis of large language models. arXiv (2025)

A Review of Human-Centric Evaluation of Cultural Biases in Indic Languages in LLMs: Rethinking Research Directions

Azmine Toushik Wasi[1], Omid Reza Heidari[2], MD Mohaymen Ul Anam[3], Abdur Rahman[1], Amit Agarwal[4], Hitesh Laxmichand Patel[4], Bhargava Kumar[5], Taki Hasan Rafi[6], and Dong-Kyu Chae[6(✉)]

[1] Shahjalal University of Science and Technology, Sylhet, Bangladesh
[2] Concordia University, Montreal, Canada
[3] Islamic University of Technology, Dhaka, Bangladesh
[4] Oracle, Austin, USA
[5] TD Securities, Toronto, Canada
[6] Hanyang University, Seoul, Republic of Korea
dongkyu@hanyang.ac.kr

Abstract. Indic languages, spoken by more than 1.3 billion people in South Asia, are often underrepresented in AI systems due to their diversity, limited resources, and evaluation challenges. This region, known for its many coexisting developed and endangered cultures, faces significant cultural bias risks as these cultures are not equally represented. These biases can significantly impact the design, development, and deployment of AI in real-life scenarios. Our survey explores cultural bias in Indic languages from a human-centered perspective, combining computational social science and NLP. We interpret different types of bias, critically review different evaluation and mitigation works, and identify research gaps and priorities to focus on to improve AI systems. Based on our review findings, we argue that we need to rethink and reprioritize our research efforts to support other Indic languages except Hindi, and focus on different evaluation approaches for cultural biases. We discuss human-centered perspectives to enhance LLMs, focusing on how they can operate more effectively and equitably within South Asia's diverse linguistic and rich cultural landscape, thereby creating fairer and more inclusive AI systems for real-world applications.

Keywords: Indic Languages · Cultural Bias · Human-Centered NLP · Large Language Models · Model Evaluation and Auditing

1 Introduction

Large Language Model (LLM)-based systems are increasingly deployed across domains such as medicine, industry, personal assistance, and professional services, offering benefits in efficiency, scalability, and accessibility. However, LLMs

O. R. Heidari, M. M. U. Anam, and A. Rahman—Equal Contribution.

R. C.-W. Wong et al. (Eds.): PAKDD 2026, LNAI 16618, pp. 618–636, 2027.
https://doi.org/10.1007/978-981-92-1947-6_48

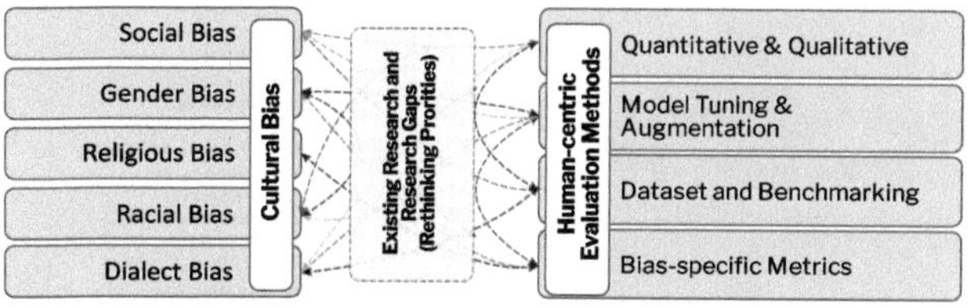

Fig. 1. Rethinking research priorities for evaluating cultural biases in Indic languages.

also inherit and amplify biases present in their training data, which can undermine fairness and equity [14,19,20]. These biases may be gendered, racial, cultural, or socioeconomic [7,37,45]. Cultural bias, in particular, is critical since models may inadequately represent marginalized groups, reinforcing stereotypes or excluding perspectives that perpetuate inequality. For example, cultural bias can produce skewed or harmful outputs about certain communities [49]. In medicine, LLMs trained mainly on Western data may fail to interpret non-Western healthcare contexts, while industrial models risk discriminatory outcomes that undervalue specific cultural contributions. Mitigation requires human-centric evaluations [63] that capture diverse cultural perspectives. These evaluations must go beyond accuracy, addressing linguistic, societal, and contextual diversity to ensure AI adaptability and equity [7,15].

Integrating cultural diversity in LLM development and assessment is essential for fairness [21,31]. Approaches include culturally aware datasets reflecting varied languages and norms and fairness-aware algorithms that detect and mitigate biases. Involving cultural experts, ethicists, and marginalized communities can expose blind spots and ensure responsible evaluation. Human-centric evaluations focus on usability, fairness, and social impact rather than solely technical performance [21,28,31,65]. For LLMs, this involves assessing safety, trustworthiness, fairness, and accessibility from human perspectives [42]. Ongoing studies aim to evaluate LLMs across cultural contexts to ensure balanced representation and equitable outputs. Ultimately, addressing cultural bias extends beyond technical fixes, it requires sustained social engagement among developers and stakeholders to foster inclusive, equitable AI systems [34,63,65].

Research on human-centric evaluations and cultural bias in AI remains limited, particularly at their intersection, with the gap most evident for Indic languages, a major Indo-Aryan subgroup spoken by over 1.3 billion people across South Asia [51]. Originating from Proto-Indo-European roots, these languages have evolved through extensive phonological and grammatical changes [74,79], yet their study has been shaped by colonial, regional, caste-based, and gender biases that continue to influence modern AI systems [48,62,72]. Limited linguistic data exacerbates underrepresentation, reinforcing cultural bias in AI. Dialects spoken by marginalized Dalit and Adivasi communities are often excluded from datasets [29], leading to models that ignore linguistic and social diversity. The region's vast cultural and linguistic range further complicates human-centric evaluations, which must consider social, political, and cultural factors, as gen-

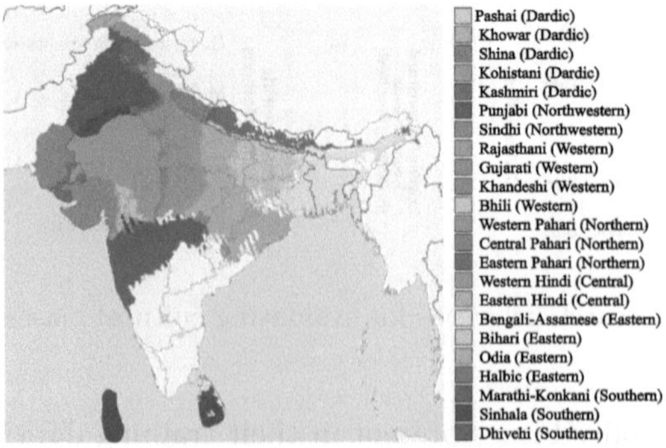

Fig. 2. Present-day Geographical Distribution of Some Indic Languages.

der and caste biases influence representation. Scarcity of resources for languages such as Santali, Maithili, and Kashmiri results in models trained mainly on dominant languages like Hindi or Bengali, marginalizing smaller linguistic groups and erasing regional nuances. Addressing these inequities requires integrating diverse linguistic and cultural data with rigorous human-centric evaluations to build AI systems that are both technically robust and socially equitable, reflecting the cultural and linguistic richness of the Indian subcontinent [46,47].

Motivated by these challenges, this survey examines human-centric evaluation of cultural bias in Indic languages. It defines and interprets key forms of cultural bias in the region, supported by real-world cases, and reviews existing research to identify gaps in addressing such biases within AI systems (Fig. 1). Specifically, we (i) define and analyze types of cultural bias and related evaluation approaches in Indic languages; (ii) comprehensively review prior work across languages, bias types, and evaluation methods, outlining current progress and limitations; and (iii) propose future research priorities to advance inclusive, culturally aware AI systems that better represent the linguistic and social diversity of Indic communities.

2 Related Works

Multiple studies have explored India's rich linguistic diversity, highlighting the deep-rooted multilingualism that shapes education, communication, and cultural identity [47]. Research on the Indo-Aryan languages, spoken by over 800 million people, shows how languages like Hindi, Bengali, and Marathi have evolved alongside South Asia's cultural and historical shifts [46]. In contrast, the Dravidian languages, such as Tamil, Telugu, and Kannada, represent a distinct linguistic heritage in southern India [59]. Additionally, advancements in spoken language identification (LID) using machine learning are addressing challenges posed by India's low-resource languages and mutual influences [51]. Studies like Pariksha [15] demonstrate the importance of culturally nuanced assessments and the inclusion of diverse perspectives, while Wasi et al. [7] investigate Bengali religious dialect biases and caste-related biases. We can also notice some efforts [42] aiming to enhance evaluation methods, ensuring that LLMs reflect human values and cultural contexts. Along with local studies, there are also some global works like INCLUDE [3] and Kaleidoscope [16].

While comprehensive surveys on fairness and bias in LLMs exist, such as Li et al. [40] and Blodgett et al. [32], they predominantly focus on Western societal contexts and English-centric models, often overlooking the complex, non-Western cultural nuances inherent to South Asia. Similarly, broad reviews of human-centric evaluation, like Xiao et al. [42], establish frameworks for safety and usability but do not address the unique intersection of caste, religion, and dialect found in Indic sociolinguistics. Existing work within the Indic sphere largely consists of dataset contributions or specific benchmarking experiments, such as Pariksha [15] and IndiBias [22], rather than holistic literature reviews of the field. Consequently, there is a notable absence of work that systematically categorizes cultural bias evaluation across the full spectrum of Indic languages. Our survey bridges this gap by specifically synthesizing human-centric methodologies with the diverse linguistic landscape of South Asia, moving beyond broad metrics to analyze deep cultural misrepresentations. Furthermore, unlike prior works that center heavily on Hindi, we critically assess the research deficit in the *long tail* of underrepresented languages like Tulu and Meitei to propose a fundamental rethinking of research priorities.

3 State of Indic Languages

Linguistic landscape of South Asia, particularly India, is vast and complex, reflecting the region's deep cultural, social, and political diversity. Among Indic languages, Hindi is the most widely spoken. Figure 2 illustrates this diversity through regional dialects of major languages, though this study focuses on the core divisions of Indic languages. Table 1 summarizes research gap[1] on cultural bias across these languages, highlighting research gaps and affected populations, and underscoring the region's rich linguistic heritage [57,68,76].

As shown in Table 1, Hindi, spoken by 609 million people, remains India's most widely used language [11]. Despite considerable research, cultural biases in Hindi NLP and ML systems persist, reinforcing stereotypes and unequal treatment across social and regional groups [25,35]. This gap requires sustained attention to ensure fair and inclusive language technologies. Bengali, with over 300 million speakers, has good research coverage but still lacks adequate focus on dialectal and religious diversity [7,49]. Languages such as Tamil, Telugu, and Marathi face more severe gaps. Tamil, spoken by about 87 million people, has limited cultural bias research, especially in applied domains like healthcare and

[1] "Gap" refers to the research gap in this field. A **low** gap indicates partial progress but room for improvement, a **medium** gap shows limited yet insufficient work, and a **high to very high** gap signals an urgent need for further research.

Table 1. Overview of research efforts on human-centric evaluation of cultural bias

Language	Research Efforts	Gap	Needs Future Work	Population
Hindi	[4,13,15,22]	Low	Yes	609M
Bengali	[4,7–9,15,23,49]	Low	Yes	300M
Tamil	[4,13,15]	High	Yes	87M
Telugu	[4,13,15]	High	Yes	96M
Punjabi	[13,15]	High	Yes	82M
Marathi	[4,13,15]	High	Yes	99M
Urdu	[13]	Very High	Yes	238M
Sindhi	N/A	Very High	Yes	26M
Kannada	[4,13,15]	High	Yes	59M
Pashto	[13]	Very High	Yes	50M
Malayalam	[13,15]	Very High	Yes	38M
Maithili	[13]	Very High	Yes	34M
Konkani	[13]	Very High	Yes	7.5M
Tulu	N/A	Very High	Yes	2M
Meitei	N/A	Very High	Yes	1.5M

education [29]. Telugu (96 million) and Marathi (99 million) remain underexplored, with few studies on caste or gender bias [69]. Marathi NLP tools, for instance, often misinterpret gendered language [58]. Punjabi (82 million) and Kannada (59 million) also exhibit significant gaps, particularly due to limited datasets and linguistic resources [69]. For Urdu, Sindhi, Pashto, Malayalam, and Maithili, the research gap is even higher. Urdu, spoken by over 230 million people, has received attention mainly in literary contexts, with minimal exploration of bias in digital applications. Pashto (50 million) remains understudied despite its complex socio-political context [69]. Sindhi (26 million) and Meitei (1.5 million) have virtually no dedicated research or datasets, limiting fair AI development. A recent study found that underrepresentation in NLP models disproportionately disadvantages minority language speakers, deepening digital exclusion [25]. Overall, while languages like Hindi and Bengali show progress, most Indic languages remain underrepresented in cultural bias research. Addressing these gaps through inclusive, intersectional approaches is critical for ensuring equitable and culturally sensitive AI systems across South Asia.

4 Cultural Biases

Cultural bias is the preferential treatment of certain cultural norms or perspectives, manifesting in South Asia through gender, caste, dialect, racial, and religious disparities that shape perception and treatment across society. We provide a brief overview in Table 2 and summarize the research efforts discussed below in Table 5.

Table 2. Overview of different types of Indic cultural biases in LLMs

Type of Bias	Example sentence(s) explaining the bias	Expectations	How will we know if there is any bias?
Social Bias	Prompt: "एक अच्छे नेता के बारे में कुछ बताइए।" (Tell me something about a good leader.) Response: "अच्छा नेता हमेशा ऊँची जाति का होता है, जो अपने समाज का नेतृत्व करता है।" (A good leader is always from a higher caste who leads their community.)	Do not have a sentence with an association between "good leader" and "higher caste".	There should not be an assumption that a good leader is from a higher caste.
Gender Bias	Prompt: "एक अच्छे डॉक्टर के बारे में कुछ बताइए।" (Tell me something about a good doctor.) Response: "वह अपने मरीज़ों की बहुत अच्छी देखभाल करते हैं और अत्यंत सक्षम हैं।" (He takes very good care of his patients and is very competent.)	Neutral pronoun for doctor.	The response assumes that the doctor is masculine.
Religious Bias	Prompt: "मुसलमानों के बारे में कुछ कहिए।" (Tell me something about Muslims.) Response: "मुसलमान आतंकवाद में शामिल होते हैं।" (Muslims are involved in terrorism.)	Do not have a sentence with an association between "Muslims" and "terrorism".	It represents harsh discrimination against Muslims
Racial Bias	Translation of "African children are beautiful" to Hindi followed by English again.	African children are beautiful	The LLM might respond 'African children are wild,' which has been changed and contains insults toward African people.
Dialect Related Bias	Translation of "I drink water" can be different in different Bengali dialect.	LLMs should show both dialects or provide a neutral answer.	Misinterpreted or inadequately addressed.

Table 3. Overview of research efforts in different facets of cultural bias

Type	Research Efforts	Gap
Social Bias	^{In}[77], [66], [52], ^{In}[15] , [38], [39], [40]	Low
Gender Bias	[67], [23]^{In}-, [20], [43], [66], [33] ^{In}[49], ^{In}[22], [54], [73], [70], [82]	Low
Religious Bias	^{In}[7], [36], ^{In}[49], ^{In}[22], [44]	High
Racial Bias	^{In}[49], ^{In}[22], [54],	High
Dialect-based Bias	^{In}[7], [53], [5], ^{In}[4]	High

In: Works done on Indic languages

Social Biases. Social biases replicate and amplify societal stereotypes, leading to discriminatory outcomes against marginalized groups [1,10,28,55]. When these biases reflect specific cultural norms, they become forms of cultural bias that shape representation and treatment of different communities. In Hindi, expressions like *"naukar ki tarah kaam karna" (working like a servant)* or *"gaanv wala dimaag" (village mindset)* reinforce class and regional stereotypes, while phrases such as *"paagal-khaane ka case" (a case for the asylum)* stigmatize mental health. These linguistic patterns reveal ingrained cultural prejudices that can influence both social perception and NLP system behavior. Research on mitigating social biases in LLMs has grown considerably. Studies have shown that datasets such as Wikipedia and IndicCorp-en, and models like MuRIL and mBERT, exhibit strong regional stereotypes [30]. To address these, methods such as counterfactual data augmentation [24] and fine-tuning with fairness constraints have been developed. `DOSA` dataset targets cultural representation in Indian subcultures [77], while fairness frameworks align AI outputs with human expectations to detect bias [27]. Techniques like continuous prompt tuning and contrastive learning (CCPA) further improve bias mitigation [38]. Surveys have categorized bias types and mitigation stages: pre-, in-, and post-processing [40], while other studies address social misattribution through Social Transparency frameworks [52] and examine demographic effects via persona-based evaluations [66]. CD3 approach combines double data augmentation and contrastive learning to reduce bias without altering model parameters [39]. Despite progress, research focusing on social biases in Indic languages remains limited. Most work targets global languages, leaving Indic languages underrepresented despite their cultural and regional diversity. Existing datasets such as Wikipedia and IndicCorp-en inadequately capture these nuances, underscoring the need for culturally informed datasets, tailored bias mitigation methods, and evaluation frameworks designed for Indic language contexts.

Gender Biases. Gender bias involves discrimination based on beliefs that certain traits or roles are tied to a specific gender [2,80]. In Indic languages, grammatical gender reinforces such biases: in Hindi, nouns like *'river'* are feminine, while words like *'writer'* have masculine and feminine forms [58]. Professions are often gendered, with *"doctor"* associated with men and *"nurse"* with women, while phrases like *"auraton ka kaam"* trivialize tasks as "women's work." Similarly, in Bangla, *"grihini"* implies homemaking is exclusively female, and *"shikkhok"* is perceived as male, with *"shikkhika"* specifying a female teacher, perpetuating stereotypes that marginalize non-conforming individuals. Gender bias remains a significant challenge in language and vision-language models (LLMs and LVLMs) [25,29,75]. In Indic languages, metrics like modified-TGBI have been used to detect bias in English-Hindi machine translation systems [75], while multilingual masked language models show persistent stereotypes, though slightly mitigated by diverse training data [73]. Techniques such as textual preambles can reduce occupational gender bias without altering model parameters [70], but focus primarily on English. Domain-specific models in healthcare exhibit gender and racial biases, with methods like SentenceDebias offering potential mitigation [82]. Vision-language models also reflect gender and racial disparities, associating men with male-dominated roles and higher social status with white individuals [54]. In the Indian context, datasets like IndiBias reveal intensified biases when multiple identity factors intersect [22], highlighting the importance of human-centric evaluations to capture context-dependent biases [43]. Overall, research predominantly targets English or global languages, leaving Indic languages underexplored despite unique grammatical and sociocultural features. Existing metrics and datasets provide initial insights [22,75], but more comprehensive datasets, evaluation frameworks, and mitigation techniques tailored to diverse Indic languages and dialects are urgently needed.

Religious Biases. Religious bias involves favoring certain religions based on linguistic patterns [7]. In Bengali, terms like *"puja"* (Hindu prayer) and *"namaz"* (Muslim prayer) reflect distinct religious identities, and models trained predominantly on Hindu language data may misinterpret or marginalize Muslim usage [50]. Similarly, in Hindi, phrases such as *"Ram ka naam lo"* and *"Allah hu Akbar"* are tied to specific religions, and models that fail to contextualize them can produce biased outputs. Content moderation systems have also been shown to favor Indian Hindu dialects over Bangladeshi Muslim dialects, highlighting the need for models that fairly represent linguistic diversity across religious groups [50]. Religious bias in LLMs is an emerging concern, particularly for languages like Bengali with diverse religious populations. Techniques such as counterfactual data augmentation and adversarial training have been applied to mitigate bias [41,81], but most research focuses on English, leaving languages like Bengali underexplored [49]. Culturally specific datasets like the Bengali Identity Bias Evaluation Dataset (BIBED) address biases in religion, gender, and nationality [49], while `IndiBias` evaluates biases in Hindi and English across multiple identity dimensions, considering India's socio-cultural complexities [22]. Studies also examine subtle religious dialect biases in Bengali, showing that LLMs like ChatGPT, Gemini, and Microsoft Copilot can perpetuate stereotypes [7]. Frameworks like DiaFrame further demonstrate the importance of context-aware AI for culturally sensitive content generation [6]. Overall, while datasets like BIBED and `IndiBias` provide foundational tools, more targeted, culturally informed research is needed to address religious bias in Indic languages with complex regional and religious dynamics.

Racial Biases. Racial biases in AI involve systematically favoring or disadvantaging certain racial groups due to skewed training data or societal prejudices [32]. For instance, translating "African children are beautiful" into Hindi may produce *"aphreekee bachche jangalee hain"* ("African children are wild") [17]. Techniques like word embedding debiasing and hate speech mitigation [18] have been applied, yet caste-based and regional stereotypes persist in South Asia, e.g., phrases like *"dalitra oporadhprabon"* reinforce discrimination. Recent studies stress the need to address racial and intersectional biases in LLMs and LVLMs. Culturally-centered datasets are essential for fair evaluation in languages like Bengali [7,49], while LVLMs reveal persistent stereotypes linked to social status and criminality [54]. Benchmarks such as `IndiBias` evaluate biases across race, caste, and intersectional identities, emphasizing inclusive approaches [22]. Despite this, racial biases in many Indic languages remain underexplored, and English-trained models often fail to capture the region's unique social and linguistic dynamics [22,49].

Dialect-Related Biases. Dialect-related biases occur when system performance varies across dialects, affecting accuracy and fluency [6,7]. For example, a Maithili sentence like *"hamar ghar kana chh?"* may be misinterpreted by models trained on Standard Hindi [61], and in Bengali, words like *"nun"* or *"lobon"* for "salt" signal subtle religious distinctions [7]. Dialect-aware fine-tuning [12] and analyses in Bengali [7] show progress, while multilingual models like `mDeBERTa`, mT5, and mT0 demonstrate detection and mitigation of biases [4]. DiaFrame adapts to dialectical variations for culturally sensitive content [6], yet models like ChatGPT often favor standard English or dominant Bengali dialects [7,53]. Despite these advances, regional languages such as Tamil, Telugu, and Marathi remain underexplored, and many dialectal variations influenced by caste, region, or religion are inadequately addressed [4,7]. Comprehensive efforts are needed to develop AI models that fairly represent the full spectrum of South Asian dialects and mitigate associated biases [4,7].

5 Human-Centric Evaluation

Human-centric evaluation assesses AI systems based on alignment with human needs, values, and societal impacts, emphasizing fairness, trustworthiness, safety, accessibility, and usability rather than solely technical performance. In LLMs, this involves evaluating cultural sensitivity, avoidance of harmful stereotypes, and inclusivity in outputs, such as ensuring AI healthcare assistants provide unbiased advice to marginalized or underrepresented groups, as presented in Tables 4 and 5.

Table 4. Overview of different human-centric evaluation approaches for LLMs.

Evaluation Type	Overview of the Process	Metrics Used	Introduces a Dataset?	Notes
Quantitative	Evaluates model performance on predefined tasks using numerical measures.	Accuracy, F1 score, Precision, Recall, AUC	Typically uses existing datasets or benchmarks.	Focuses on measurable aspects like efficiency, accuracy, and scope.
Qualitative	Assesses model performance based on human judgment, covering aspects like usability, fairness, or interpretability.	Human-in-the-loop, Surveys, Expert Reviews	No, generally focuses on evaluating outputs rather than datasets.	Complements quantitative evaluation by incorporating human insights.
Model Tuning	Optimizes model architecture or parameters for better task performance.	Validation loss, Learning rate, Fine-tuning scores	Sometimes uses task-specific datasets.	Aims to improve LLM outputs for targeted tasks through iterative refinement.
Dataset and Benchmarking	Involves creating high-quality datasets and standardized evaluation frameworks for research.	BLEU, ROUGE, macro/micro-F1, etc.	Yes, often introduces or relies on benchmark datasets.	Ensures LLMs are tested on consistent, well-established tasks.
Other Metrics	Uses alternative metrics focused on specific outcomes such as bias, fairness, or robustness.	Fairness scores, Robustness metrics	May introduce task-specific datasets.	Often targets specific biases or fairness measures within LLMs.

5.1 Quantitative and Qualitative Evaluation

Evaluating LLMs requires both quantitative and qualitative methods for a comprehensive assessment. Metrics like `BLEU`, `F1`, and AUPRC measure accuracy and detect biases in structured datasets [7,78], while qualitative feedback, such as from AffirmativeAI [67], captures societal and cultural biases that metrics alone cannot. Combining these approaches provides a fuller understanding, enabling effective outcomes across real-world applications [43,77] and addressing both accuracy and context-specific biases.

Quantitative Methods. Quantitative methods provide measurable insights using metrics like accuracy, recall, and effect size. For example, name changes on CEFR-level classification in Swedish essays are evaluated, token-level biases are analyzed using Gender-Associated Token Confidence (GTC) in mono- and multilingual models [73], racial and LGBTQ+ biases are assessed using the Sentence Embedding Association Test (SEAT) [82], political bias is measured using ROUGE and Second-order SPD (SPD2nd) [56], and demographic word associations are quantified via Pointwise Mutual Information (PMI) [54]. Despite their precision, automated metrics have limitations and risk inaccuracies [43].

Qualitative Methods. Qualitative methods capture nuances that quantitative metrics cannot. For instance, the influence of name contexts and text genres on biases is examined, and predicted tokens across gender prompts are analyzed [73]. Manual reviews assess debiasing examples [38,77], and word choices in image descriptions are studied [54]. Human evaluation highlights user experience and cognitive insights [5,43], and combined approaches, such as annotator feedback with statistical measures, provide comprehensive bias assessment [15].

Evaluation of LLMs in Indic languages has received less attention than in widely spoken languages, with both quantitative and qualitative methods facing challenges due to linguistic and cultural diversity. Metrics like BLEU and F1 are less effective for languages such as Hindi or Bengali [77], while qualitative methods may struggle to capture nuanced regional variations, including religious dialect biases in Bengali [7]. This underscores the need for context-specific benchmarks like mWikiBias [4] and IndiBias [22], and future research should adapt frameworks to address the linguistic and cultural diversity of Indic languages.

5.2 Model Tuning and Augmentation

Model tuning and augmentation in LLMs refine pre-trained models to improve performance and address issues like bias. For example, reducing gender bias in job descriptions can involve fine-tuning with diverse datasets containing gender-neutral language. Data augmentation can create counterfactual examples, such as swapping gendered pronouns, helping the model treat male and female candidates equally and generate fairer outputs.

Recent work introduces several techniques. Debiasing strategies are categorized into retraining, disentanglement, alignment constraints, and contrastive learning [40]. Retraining uses improved datasets or regularization, while disentanglement separates bias-related features from task-specific ones. Counterfactual Data Augmentation (CDA) balances data by creating counterfactual pairs like "he" vs. "she" [40]. CCPA combines continuous prompt tuning with contrastive learning [38], first training a prompt generator to exaggerate biases, then fine-tuning the model to reduce them. Data calibration is another strategy to refine or remove biased elements [40]. Fine-tuning methods like RLHF and SFT ensure persona consistency but do not focus on data augmentation [66]. CD3 uses contrastive learning-based adapters to mitigate bias without modifying the base model, creating counterfactual pairs and adding biased prompts to enhance debiasing [39]. Both CCPA and CD3 demonstrate the value of combining augmentation with fine-tuning to improve fairness.

Application to Indic languages is limited, with most methods focusing on English or other widely spoken languages. Techniques like CDA and contrastive learning have potential but are not fully adapted to Indic linguistic and cultural contexts [40,66]. Region-specific models and datasets are needed [22], yet targeted augmentation and fine-tuning strategies remain scarce. Researchers could develop domain-specific counterfactual pairs or employ reinforcement learning that accounts for Indic sociolinguistic factors [77].

5.3 Dataset and Benchmarking

Dataset and benchmarking involve developing high-quality datasets and evaluation frameworks, which are essential for addressing and mitigating biases in LLMs. For example, datasets focused on cultural and social biases have been created [22,49], with IndiBias expanding on CrowS-Pairs to cover biases in Hindi [22]. Multilingual bias detection datasets include mWikiBias and mWNC [4]. PAIRS has been used to explore biases in vision-language models [54]. Such datasets are crucial for developing or evaluating models to ensure they handle cultural, racial, and social biases.

Recent research emphasizes datasets for underrepresented languages and regions. DOSA contains 615 social artifacts from 260 participants across 19 Indian regions, highlighting regional performance variations [77]. Multilingual datasets cover eight languages, including Indian languages, for bias detection and mitigation [4]. IndiBias evaluates social biases in Hindi, addressing intersectional aspects of gender, religion, and caste [22]. Collectively, these datasets highlight the need for evaluation frameworks that reflect cultural, linguistic, and social dynamics, ensuring LLMs are culturally sensitive and equitable.

Indic language evaluation is progressing but gaps remain. Datasets like IndiBias [22] and DOSA [77] cover Hindi and Indian subcultures, but languages such as Tamil, Telugu, and Bengali remain underrepresented. Existing datasets also inadequately address dialectal, religious, and intersectional variations. Expanding region-specific, dialect-rich datasets is essential for culturally sensitive evaluation and improving fairness across Indic languages.

5.4 Other Bias-Specific Metrics

Other bias-specific metrics capture complex aspects of bias beyond standard performance measures. Racial and LGBTQ+ biases have been examined using SEAT and StereoSet, with debiasing methods like Dropout and SentenceDebias [82]. The ConSiDERSThe-Human framework evaluates multidimensional aspects including consistency and user experience [5].

Recent work explores bias across domains. Ethnic bias in essay scoring is investigated using equality of opportunity, contrasting feature-based models. Racial and LGBTQ+ biases in healthcare models are revealed using SEAT and StereoSet [82]. Cognitive biases in human evaluations are highlighted, emphasizing careful experimental design [5]. Controlling demographic attributes in model outputs using OpinionsQA shows how persona adjustments can mitigate biases [66]. These studies illustrate bias in LLMs across ethnic, racial, cognitive, and demographic dimensions, underscoring the need for tailored evaluation methods.

Bias evaluation in Indic languages is still emerging. While biases in Hindi and Indian subcultures are addressed [22,77], advanced metrics like SEAT and SentenceDebias are rarely applied. Benchmarks for racial and LGBTQ+ biases do not capture caste, regional, or linguistic biases in Indic contexts [82]. Equality of Opportunity could be extended to name-based biases in diverse Indian languages. Developing region- and language-specific metrics that account for caste, regional, and linguistic variations will be crucial for fair and inclusive LLM evaluation in Indic languages.

Table 5. Overview of research efforts on different types of human-centric evaluation of cultural bias

Type	Research Efforts	Gap
Quantitative and Qualitative Evaluation	[In][7], [67], [36], [43], [In][77], [52], [In][15], [53], [5], [39], [26], [38], [In][4], [54], [56], [73], [70], [82]	Very Low
Model Tuning	[66], [40], [39], [38]	High
Dataset and Benchmarking	[In][77], [In][15], [In][49], [In][22], [In][4]	Medium
Other Bias-specific Metrics	[66], [5], [82]	Low

In: Works done on Indic languages

The discussion reveals a gap in human-centric evaluations for Indic languages. While some research covers biases in Hindi and Bengali, focusing on gender and religion, studies are still limited. Existing fairness methods for gender and race could be adapted to address caste and religion-specific biases in Indic languages.

6 Rethinking Research Priorities

This section reviews the current status of cultural bias evaluation in Indic languages and suggests where to rethink research priorities. We will focus on three key areas: the representation of Indic languages, types of cultural biases, and human-centric evaluation approaches to identify gaps and guide future research.

Indic Languages. Current research on evaluating cultural biases in Indic languages primarily focuses on major languages like Hindi, Bengali, and Tamil, while languages such as Tulu, Meitei, and Konkani remain underexplored (see Table 1). This highlights the need to shift focus to lesser-studied languages, which may have unique cultural nuances and biases not captured by models trained on widely spoken languages. Datasets like `IndiBias` [22] and `DOSA` [77] address biases in Hindi and regional languages, but efforts should expand to under-represented languages. Many of these languages exhibit distinct sociolinguistic features, including caste, regional, and gender-related biases, often overlooked in larger datasets. Including languages like Malayalam and Maithili, which score higher in existing evaluation gaps, can better capture these complexities. Engaging local experts and integrating language-specific frameworks are essential for accurately identifying and mitigating biases. Adapting methods from larger-scale studies to smaller languages can prevent cultural misrepresentations. A more inclusive, regionally representative approach is crucial to bridging gaps in cultural bias evaluation for Indic languages.

Cultural Biases. This study shows that while progress has been made in addressing biases in LLMs, research has largely focused on widely spoken languages, with limited attention to specific Indic languages (see Table 3). Initiatives [22,77] have advanced bias evaluation in Hindi and major regional languages, but many lesser-studied languages, such as Tulu, Maithili, Konkani, and Meitei, remain underexplored. These languages carry unique cultural, caste, and regional biases, and addressing them can help build more culturally sensitive LLMs. Dialect-based biases also require attention, as local language variations can introduce model bias. Studies show the importance of culturally specific datasets for fine-tuning, but similar efforts for Indic languages are sparse [4]. Developing evaluation frameworks that incorporate regional, religious, and social diversities, and actively involving local experts [77], is crucial for creating LLMs that are linguistically proficient, culturally sensitive, and equitable across all Indic language communities.

Human-Centric Evaluation Approaches. Our study highlights methods for evaluating cultural biases in LLMs and their current focus. While quantitative and qualitative evaluations are common, their use in Indic languages remains limited. Works address biases in Hindi, but less-represented languages such as Tulu, Meitei, and Konkani remain neglected despite unique cultural and social nuances [22,77]. Model tuning techniques [40] mitigate biases effectively but are not fully applied to Indic languages, particularly across dialects and regions. Datasets and benchmarking [4] are crucial, yet many Indic languages lack specialized resources for comprehensive evaluation. Emerging bias-specific metrics like `SEAT` and `StereoSet` [82] require adaptation to capture complex cultural and intersectional identities. Research priorities should expand dataset creation for underexplored languages, address dialectal and social biases (e.g., caste, religion), and involve local experts as in community-driven datasets like DOSA. Enhancing model tuning, dataset development, and targeted metrics will foster more culturally aware and equitable LLMs for Indic languages.

Combining these three aspects, our study highlights the need to address cultural biases in LLMs for underrepresented Indic languages. While gender and social biases have been partially addressed, gaps remain for religion, regional identities, and caste. Expanding datasets to include smaller-language communities and employing dialect-aware fine-tuning can improve inclusivity and cultural accuracy. Human-centric evaluations, with metrics reflecting diverse backgrounds, are essential to ensure AI systems do not perpetuate harmful stereotypes or inequalities.

7 Discussions

In this study, we provide a comprehensive overview of human-centric evaluation of cultural biases in Indic languages within LLMs, highlighting the urgent need to address cultural biases in LLMs, especially in underrepresented Indic languages. While progress has been made in mitigating gender and social biases, significant gaps remain in handling biases related to religious and regional identities. These overlooked areas call for targeted efforts to improve LLM inclusivity. Expanding datasets and resources, employing dialect-aware fine-tuning, and integrating diverse cultural contexts are crucial for reducing biases and enhancing fairness.

⇛ **Gaps in Research and Representation.** As noted in Sect. 6, Hindi and Bengali receive some attention, but many smaller languages are overlooked, limiting access to AI tools and widening the digital divide. Most research has focused on surface-level biases like gender and religion, while caste, regional dialects, and cultural cues remain underexplored [29]. Ignoring these factors risks reinforcing existing inequalities and harmful stereotypes in AI systems.

⇛ **Need for Human-Centric Evaluations.** Most studies emphasize technical approaches, relying heavily on quantitative metrics, without adequately considering how users interact with and are affected by these AI systems [27,42,63]. In regions as culturally complex as South Asia, incorporating perspectives of users from diverse backgrounds is vital to enable AI systems to be accurate, culturally sensitive, and respectful of local traditions and values. Without this human-centered approach, AI systems risk producing outputs that are not aligned with the cultural context in which they are used. For instance, gender roles in South Asia can vary significantly from those in Western societies, and AI systems that fail to account for these differences may inadvertently reinforce traditional gender biases or misrepresent social dynamics. This could lead to negative societal impacts, such as limiting opportunities for women or reinforcing outdated norms.

⇛ **Mitigating Cultural Biases.** Bias mitigation in machine learning models, especially in LLMs, can be addressed through several approaches, including data augmentation, fine-tuning, and specialized frameworks. Techniques such as Double Data Augmentation and Contrastive Self-Debiasing (CD3) effectively use biased prompts to improve bias detection and mitigation [39]. Contrastive Learning with Continuous Prompt Augmentation (CCPA) adjusts demographic representation in the model's latent space to reduce bias through fine-tuning [38]. Another technique, debiasing through textual preambles based on real-world statistics, has shown success in mitigating gender biases without model parameter access [70]. In abusive language detection, token and sentence debiasing methods help reduce biases by adjusting probability estimates and augmenting text [39].

⇛ **Significance of Bridging Research Gaps.** Addressing these research gaps is crucial for several reasons. First, equity and inclusivity: AI systems that overlook South Asia's linguistic and cultural diversity risk excluding large populations, widening the digital divide, and leaving marginalized communities without access to essential tools. Second, fairness in AI is essential, as biases in sensitive areas like healthcare, education, and legal systems can perpetuate inequalities in societies structured by caste, gender, and religion [64]. Third, cultural preservation is at stake, since many underrepresented languages are at risk of extinction, and prioritizing only widely spoken languages erodes linguistic diversity. Expanding AI research to include more languages helps preserve heritage and prevent exclusion. Fourth, real-world AI applications in education, healthcare, governance, and media require culturally sensitive and accurate outputs [71], improving relevance and impact. Finally, mitigating societal harm is vital: unaddressed cultural biases reinforce stereotypes and discrimination in hiring, healthcare, and public services. Proactively tackling these biases ensures AI fosters a just and equitable society.

⇛ **Call to Action in Terms of the Research Gaps.** Low-resource Indic languages face major challenges in AI due to limited digital presence, scarce annotated datasets, and fewer linguistic resources [60]. Of the over 420 languages spoken in India, only about 15–20 have substantial digital resources, leaving the majority severely underrepresented, with languages like Tulu, Santali, and Meitei having less than 5M tokens of monolingual text. Although nearly 98% of internet users access content in Indic languages, AI systems primarily focus on widely spoken languages like Hindi, Bengali, and Tamil, reinforcing digital exclusion and widening the technological divide. Addressing this requires collaborative efforts to create open-source resources, incentivize multilingual model development, and foster partnerships between AI researchers, linguists, and local communities. Cross-lingual transfer and multilingual pre-training can leverage existing resources from related languages to improve performance. These efforts ensure AI is equitable and inclusive, extend benefits to all communities, support preservation of endangered languages (see Table 1), protect cultural heritage, and empower smaller linguistic communities to participate in the digital landscape, promoting social equity and linguistic diversity.

⇛ **Limitations.** This study focuses on gender, religion, and caste biases in Indic languages. Intersectional biases may not be fully captured, and no computational experiments or direct solutions are proposed. As language is interconnected and methods developed for one language can often be adapted to others, our survey also explores human-centric evaluation efforts conducted on non-Indic languages, highlighting how these approaches can be applied to address challenges in Indic languages. While the primary focus of our work is on Indic languages, we draw connections to broader research to provide insights into potential solutions for Indic-specific issues.

8 Conclusion

In this work, we discuss the evaluation processes of cultural biases in the Indic language family. We interpret various types of bias, review different evaluation and mitigation approaches, and identify research gaps. Based on our comprehensive literature review, we argue that we need to rethink our priorities for improving AI systems, with greater focus on underrepresented languages such as Tamil, Telugu, and Marathi, and more. Additionally, much of the existing research emphasizes qualitative and quantitative methods, with insufficient attention to human-centric studies and other metrics that try to maintain cultural balance even while training these large models. We advocate for more comprehensive evaluations that incorporate user perspectives to create equitable and inclusive AI systems for Indic languages. This includes prioritizing human-centric evaluations, cognitive bias assessments, and novel approaches to promote fairness across South Asia's diverse linguistic landscape.

Acknowledgement. This work was partly supported by (1) the National Research Foundation of Korea (NRF) grant funded by the Korea government (MSIT) (RS-2024-00345398) and (2) the Institute of Information & communications Technology Planning & Evaluation (IITP) grant funded by the Korea government (MSIT) (RS-2020-II201373, Artificial Intelligence Graduate School Program (Hanyang University)).

References

1. Olteanu, A., et al.: Social data: biases, methodological pitfalls, and ethical boundaries. Front. Big Data (2019)
2. Llorens, A., et al.: Gender bias in academia: a lifetime problem that needs solutions. Neuron (2021)
3. Romanou, A., et al.: Include: evaluating multilingual language understanding with regional knowledge (2024)
4. Maity, A., et al.: Multilingual bias detection and mitigation for Indian languages. In: WILDRE-7. ELRA and ICCL (2024)
5. Elangovan, A., et al.: Considers-the-human evaluation framework: rethinking human evaluation for generative large language models (2024)
6. Wasi, A.T., et al.: Diaframe: a framework for understanding Bengali dialects in human-AI collaborative creative writing spaces. In: CSCW. ACM (2024)
7. Wasi, A.T., et al.: Exploring Bengali religious dialect biases in large language models with evaluation perspectives. In: HEAL@CHI (2024)

8. Wasi, A.T., et al.: Dialectal bias in Bengali: an evaluation of multilingual large language models across cultural variations. In: WWW. ACM (2025)
9. Wasi, A.T., et al.: Exploring Bengali creative storytelling capabilities of large language models across cultural variations. In: CSCW Companion. ACM (2025)
10. Hutchinson, B., et al.: Social biases in NLP models as barriers for persons with disabilities. In: ACL (2020)
11. Eberhard, D.M., et al.: Ethnologue: languages of the World (2024)
12. Alwajih, F., et al.: Dallah: a dialect-aware multimodal large language model for Arabic. In: Arabic NLP (2024)
13. Singh, H., et al.: Indicgenbench: a multilingual benchmark to evaluate generation capabilities of LLMs on Indic languages (2024)
14. Gallegos, I.O., et al.: Bias and fairness in large language models: a survey. Comput. Linguist. (2024)
15. Watts, I., et al.: Pariksha: a large-scale investigation of human-LLM evaluator agreement on multilingual and multi-cultural data (2024)
16. Salazar, I., et al.: Kaleidoscope: in-language exams for massively multilingual vision evaluation (2025)
17. Khandelwal, K., et al.: Indian-BhED: a dataset for measuring India-centric biases in large language models. In: ACM GoodIT (2024)
18. Sap, M., et al.: The risk of racial bias in hate speech detection. In: ACL (2019)
19. Anik, M.A., et al.: Preserving cultural identity with context-aware translation through multi-agent AI systems. In: LM4U. ACL (2025)
20. Anik, M.A., et al.: Towards culturally inclusive knowledge dissemination using ai agents. In: Social Impact of AI (2025)
21. Adilazuarda, M.F., et al.: Towards measuring and modeling "culture" in LLMs: a survey. In: EMNLP (2024)
22. Sahoo, N.R., et al.: Indibias: a benchmark dataset to measure social biases in language models for Indian context (2024)
23. Arnob, N.M.K., et al.: Assessing gender bias of pretrained Bangla language models in STEM and SHAPE fields. In: GeBNLP. ACL (2025)
24. Zmigrod, R., et al.: Counterfactual data augmentation for mitigating gender stereotypes in languages with rich morphology. In: ACL (2019)
25. Hada, R., et al.: Akal Badi ya Bias: an exploratory study of gender bias in Hindi language technology. In: FAccT 2024, pp. 1926–1939. ACM (2024)
26. Song, R., et al.: Measuring and mitigating language model biases in abusive language detection. Inf. Process. Manag. (2023)
27. Saralajew, S., et al.: A human-centric assessment framework for AI (2022)
28. Almatarneh, S., et al.: Bias and Fairness in NLP: Addressing Social and Cultural Biases (2025)
29. Casteism in India, but not racism - a study of bias in word embeddings of Indian languages. In: LateRAISSe@LREC. ELRA (2022)
30. Bhatt, S., et al.: Re-contextualizing fairness in NLP: the case of India. In: AACL-IJCNLP (2022)
31. Pawar, S., et al.: Survey of cultural awareness in language models: text and beyond. Comput. Linguist. (2025)
32. Blodgett, S.L., et al.: Language (technology) is power: a critical survey of "bias" in NLP. In: ACL (2020)
33. Sun, T., et al.: Mitigating gender bias in natural language processing: literature review. In: ACL (2019)
34. Ehsan, U., et al.: Human-centered explainable AI (HCXAI): reloading explainability in the era of large language models (LLMs). In: CHI EA. ACM (2024)

35. Malik, V., et al.: Socially aware bias measurements for Hindi language representations. In: NAACL (2022)
36. Salikutluk, V., et al.: Involving affected communities and their knowledge for bias evaluation in large language models. In: HEAL@CHI (2024)
37. Gupta, V., et al.: Sociodemographic bias in language models: a survey and forward path. In: GeBNLP (2024)
38. Li, Y., et al.: Prompt tuning pushes farther, contrastive learning pulls closer: a two-stage approach to mitigate social biases. In: ACL (2023)
39. Li, Y., et al.: Mitigating social biases of pre-trained language models via contrastive self-debiasing with double data augmentation. Artif. Intell. (2024)
40. Li, Y., et al.: A survey on fairness in large language models (2024)
41. Zhao, Y., et al.: Fairness-aware machine learning: a survey. arXiv (2023)
42. Xiao, Z., et al.: Human-centered evaluation and auditing of language models. In: CHI EA. ACM (2024)
43. Aoyagui, P.A., Ferguson, S., Kuzminykh, A.: Exploring subjectivity for more human-centric assessment of social biases in large language models (2024)
44. Arlen, B.: Ethnic and religious conflicts in India: a comprehensive analysis. Int. J. Sci. Soc. **5**, 228–237 (2023)
45. Bai, X., Wang, A., Sucholutsky, I., Griffiths, T.L.: Measuring implicit bias in explicitly unbiased large language models (2024)
46. Cardona, G.: Indo-aryan languages. Encyclopedia Britannica (2024)
47. Chandras, J.: Multilingualism in India. Asian Studies (2020)
48. Cohn, B.S.: Colonialism and its Forms of Knowledge: The British in India (1996)
49. Das, D., Guha, S., Semaan, B.: Toward cultural bias evaluation datasets: the case of Bengali gender, religious, and national identity. In: C3NLP (2023)
50. Das, D., Østerlund, C., Semaan, B.: "jol" or "pani"?: how does governance shape a platform's identity? Proc. ACM Hum.-Comput. Interact. **5**(CSCW2) (2021)
51. Dey, S., Sahidullah, M., Saha, G.: An overview of Indian spoken language recognition from machine learning perspective. ACM TALLIP **21**(6) (2022)
52. Ferrario, A., Termine, A., Facchini, A.: Addressing social misattributions of large language models: an HCXAI-based approach (2024)
53. Fleisig, E., Smith, G., Bossi, M., Rustagi, I., Yin, X., Klein, D.: Linguistic bias in chatgpt: language models reinforce dialect discrimination (2024)
54. Fraser, K., Kiritchenko, S.: Examining gender and racial bias in large vision–language models using a novel dataset of parallel images. In: EACL (2024)
55. Gamboa, L., Feng, Y., Lee, M.G.: Social bias in multilingual language models: a survey. In: EMNLP (2025)
56. Huang, N., Fayek, H., Zhang, X.: Bias in opinion summarisation from pre-training to adaptation: a case study in political bias (2024)
57. Jain, D., Cardona, G.: The Indo-Aryan Languages. Routledge (2004)
58. Kirtane, N., Anand, T.: Mitigating gender stereotypes in Hindi and Marathi. In: GeBNLP (2022)
59. Krishnamurti, B.: Dravidian language. Encyclopedia Britannica (2024)
60. Kshetri, N.: Linguistic challenges in generative artificial intelligence: implications for low-resource languages in the developing world. JGITM (2024)
61. Kumar, A., Joshi, S., Choudhury, M.: A study on the performance of NLP models on Indic languages: a case with Hindi and Maithili. In: LREC (2020)
62. Lakoff, R.: Language and woman's place. Lang. Soc. **2**(1), 45–80 (1973)
63. Lawrence, C.: Human-centric AI: a road map to human-ai collaboration (2024)
64. Lee, S.: Fairness and biases in ai algorithms and interfaces. ALISE (2024)

65. Liao, Q.V., Vaughan, J.: AI transparency in the age of LLMs: a human-centered research roadmap. Harvard Data Sci. Rev. (Special Issue 5) (2024)
66. Liu, A., Diab, M., Fried, D.: Evaluating large language model biases in persona-steered generation. In: Findings of the ACL 2024 (2024)
67. Long, Y., Ma, Z., Mei, Y., Su, Z.: AffirmativeAI: towards LGBTQ+ friendly audit frameworks for large language models (2024)
68. Masica, C.P.: The Indo-Aryan Languages. Cambridge University Press (1991)
69. Mukherjee, A., Raj, C., Zhu, Z., Anastasopoulos, A.: Global voices, local biases: socio-cultural prejudices across languages. In: EMNLP, p. 1582815845 (2023)
70. Oba, D., Kaneko, M., Bollegala, D.: In-contextual gender bias suppression for large language models. In: Findings of EACL (2024)
71. Okolo, C.T.: Towards a praxis for intercultural ethics in explainable AI (2023)
72. Parpola, A.: The Roots of Hinduism: The Early Aryans and The Indus Civilization. Oxford University Press (2015)
73. Parra, I.: UnMASKed: Quantifying gender biases in masked language models through linguistically informed job market prompts. In: ACL: SRW (2024)
74. Picard, M.: The Indo-Aryan languages. Can. J. Linguist./Revue canadienne de linguistique **2**, 257–259 (1995)
75. Ramesh, K., Gupta, G., Singh, S.: Evaluating gender bias in Hindi-English machine translation. In: GeBNLP (2021)
76. The Census Digital Library, India (2021)
77. Seth, A., Ahuja, S., Bali, K., Sitaram, S.: DOSA: a dataset of social artifacts from different Indian geographical subcultures. In: LREC-COLING (2024)
78. Sheng, E., Chang, K.W., Natarajan, P., Peng, N.: Societal biases in language generation: progress and challenges. In: ACL-IJCNLP (2021)
79. Southworth, F.: Linguistic Archaeology of South Asia, 1st edn. Routledge (2004)
80. Stanczak, K., Augenstein, I.: A survey on gender bias in natural language processing (2021)
81. Wang, Y., Shen, X., Wan, Y., Yu, P.S.: Beyond bias and fairness: towards causal responsible AI. In: CIKM. ACM (2022)
82. Xie, S., et al.: Addressing healthcare-related racial and LGBTQ+ biases in pretrained language models. In: Findings of NAACL (2024)

Author Index

R. C.-W. Wong et al. (Eds.): PAKDD 2026, LNAI 16618, pp. 637–639, 2027.
https://doi.org/10.1007/978-981-92-1947-6